The Mind's Machine
FOUNDATIONS OF BRAIN AND BEHAVIOR

Additional Features

- An **interactive Brain Explorer** offers a 3D look at the brain anatomy discussed in each chapter.
- **Activities**, which help you learn key structures and important processes.
- **"A Step Further"** topics, which expand on material in the textbook.
- **Flashcards** for each chapter offer a convenient way to learn the many new terms introduced in the textbook.
- A **complete glossary** for quick access to definitions.

QR Codes

Using your smartphone or tablet, scan the QR codes that appear throughout the textbook (or type in the Web address shown) to instantly access animations and videos on the Companion Website. (QR code reader app required. These are available for free from your device's app store.)

To see a video, go to

mindsmachine.com/10.1
Narcolepsy

Video 10.1: Narcolepsy

Textbook Reference: Introduction: When Sleep Gets Out of Control
Courtesy of Muhammad Daud

Videos

Videos present real-world examples of some key concepts and conditions.

---

chapter **10** **Biological Rhythms and Sleep**

When Sleep Gets Out of Control

Starting college always brings its share of new experiences and adjustments, but "Barry" knew something was wrong freshman year when he seemed to be sleepy all the time (S. Smith, 1997). Barry napped so often that his friends called him the hibernating bear. Of course, college can be exhausting, and many students seek refuge in long snooze sessions. But one day while Barry was camping with his pals, an even odder thing happened: "I laughed really hard, and I kind of fell on my knees … After that, about every week I'd have two or three episodes where if I'd laugh … my arm would fall down or my muscles in my face would get weak. Or if I was running around playing catch and someone said something, I would get weak in the knees. And there was a time there that my friends kinda used it as a joke. If they're going to throw me the ball and they didn't want me to catch it, they'd tell me a joke and I'd fall down and miss it."

It was as if any big surge in emotion in Barry might trigger a sudden paralysis lasting anywhere from a few seconds to a few minutes, affecting either a body part or his whole body. Sex became something of a challenge because sometimes during foreplay, Barry's body would just collapse. "Luckily, you're probably laying down, so it's not that big a deal. But it just puts a damper on the whole thing."

What was happening to Barry? By the end of this chapter, we'll know a lot more about sleep and what went wrong in Barry's brain to cause these problems.

To see a video, go to

mindsmachine.com/10.1
Narcolepsy

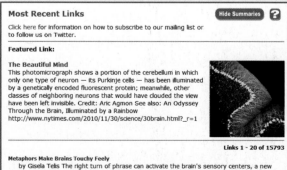

Most Recent Links

Click here for information on how to subscribe to our mailing list or to follow us on Twitter.

Featured Link:

The Beautiful Mind
This photomicrograph shows a portion of the cerebellum in which only one type of neuron — its Purkinje cells — has been illuminated by a genetically encoded fluorescent protein; meanwhile, other classes of neighboring neurons that would have clouded the view have been left invisible. Credit: Aric Agmon See also: An Odyssey Through the Brain, Illuminated by a Rainbow
http://www.nytimes.com/2010/11/30/science/30brain.html?_r=1

Links 1 - 20 of 15793

Metaphors Make Brains Touchy Feely
by Gisela Telis The right turn of phrase can activate the brain's sensory centers, a new study suggests. Researchers have found that textural metaphors—phrases such as "soft-hearted"—turn on a part of the brain that's important to the sense of touch. The result may help resolve a long-standing controversy over how the brain understands metaphors and may offer scientists a new way to study how different brain regions communicate. Scientists have disagreed for decades about how the brain processes metaphors, those figures of speech that liken one thing to another without using "like" or "as." One camp claims that when we hear a metaphor—a friend tells us she's had a rough day—we understand the expression only because we've heard it so many times.

BIOLOGICAL PSYCHOLOGY NewsLink
mindsmachine.com/news

This invaluable online resource helps you make connections between the science of biological psychology and your daily life, and keeps you apprised of the latest developments in the field. The site is updated 3–4 times a week, so it includes up-to-the-minute information, and contains thousands of news stories organized both by keyword and by textbook chapter.

Follow on Twitter (@biopsychology) and find us on Facebook (Biopsychology).

COMPANION WEBSITE RESOURCES (mindsmachine.com)

The Mind's Machine Companion Website includes animations, videos, and activities for each chapter (listed below), as well as an interactive version of each chapter's visual summary. Animations and videos are referenced with QR codes on the textbook pages indicated below.

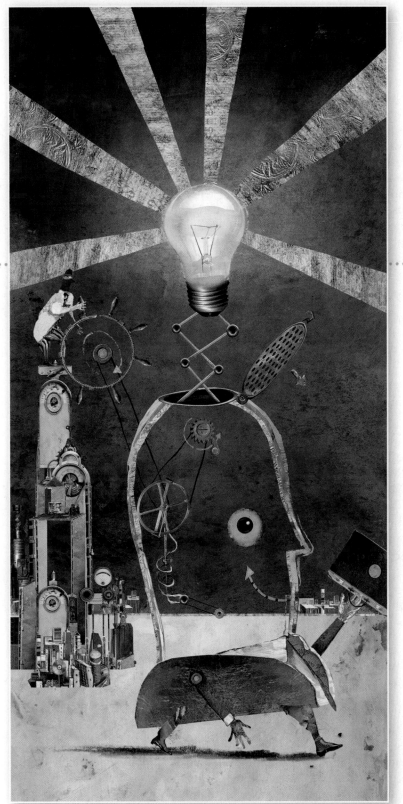

The Mind's Machine

FOUNDATIONS OF BRAIN AND BEHAVIOR

Neil V. Watson
Simon Fraser University

S. Marc Breedlove
Michigan State University

Sinauer Associates, Inc. Publishers
Sunderland, Massachusetts, USA

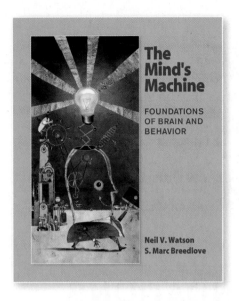

About the Cover and Chapter Opener Images

Bruno Mallart is one of the most talented European artists, his work having appeared in some of the world's premier publications: The New York Times, The Wall Street Journal, and the New Scientist, to name a few. A freelance illustrator since 1986, Mallart first worked for several children's book publishers and advertising agencies, using a classical realistic watercolor and ink style. Some years later he began working in a more imaginative way, inventing a mix of drawing, painting, and collage. His work speaks of a surrealistic and absurd world and engages the viewer's imagination and sense of fun. Despite the recurring use of the brain in his art, Mallart's background is not scientific—though his parents were both neurobiologists. He uses the brain as a symbol for abstract concepts such as intelligence, thinking, feeling, ideas, and knowledge. Attracted to all that is mechanical, Mallart's art frequently includes machine parts such as gears and wheels that imply movement and rhythm. These features together, in their abstract representation, beautifully illustrate the topics discussed in *The Mind's Machine*. To see more of Bruno Mallart's art, please go to his website: www.brunomallart.com.

The Mind's Machine: Foundations of Brain and Behavior
Copyright © 2012 by Sinauer Associates, Inc. All rights reserved.
This book may not be reproduced in whole or in part without permission.
Address inquiries and orders to
Sinauer Associates, Inc.
23 Plumtree Road
Sunderland, MA 01375 U.S.A.
Fax: 413-549-1118
E-mail: publish@sinauer.com
Internet: www.sinauer.com

Library of Congress Cataloging-in-Publication Data
Watson, Neil V. (Neil Verne), 1962-
  The mind's machine: foundations of brain and behavior / Neil V. Watson, S. Marc Breedlove.
     p. cm.
  Includes bibliographical references and index.
  ISBN 978-0-87893-933-6
1. Brain--Textbooks. 2. Brain--Physiology--Textbooks. 3. Human behavior--Physiological aspects--Textbooks. 4. Psychobiology--Textbooks. 5. Neurophysiology--Textbooks. 6. Neuropsychology--Textbooks. I. Breedlove, S. Marc. II. Title.
  QP376.W26 2012
  612.8'2--dc23   2012000922

Printed in U.S.A.

5 4 3 2

N. V. W.

*For my parents, Kathleen and Dennis.
Thank you for a lifetime of love
and encouragement.*

S. M. B.

For Joe

Brief Contents

Table of Contents

chapter 5 The Sensorimotor System 106

chapter 6 Hearing, Balance, Taste, and Smell 140

chapter 7 Vision: From Eye to Brain 168

chapter 8 Hormones and Sex 202

chapter 9 Homeostasis: Active Regulation of the Internal Environment 248

chapter 10 Biological Rhythms and Sleep 270

chapter 11 Emotions, Aggression, and Stress 300

chapter 12 Psychopathology: The Biology of Behavioral Disorders 326

chapter **13** Memory, Learning, and Development 354

chapter 14 Attention and Consciousness 394

chapter 15 Language and Our Divided Brain 422

Preface

Everywhere you turn these days, you run into stories about new discoveries in the brain. It's hard to browse the internet, open a newspaper, or flip through a magazine without encountering amazing images of brain activity, or new insights into the evolution, development, functioning or malfunctioning of the nervous system. The main reason for all this coverage is that the subject matter is intrinsically fascinating; who has not pondered their own consciousness, marveled at their many sensory experiences, or wondered how a small and lumpy organ can process so much information? But another reason neuroscience is in the news so frequently is simply that it has become one of the most active branches of science. The pace of discoveries about brain and behavior has increased at an exponential rate over the last few decades.

Every new edition of one of our books requires a major overhaul because so much is happening all the time. (We're not complaining, but boy, do we read a lot of reports and articles!) In fact, by far the hardest part of our job as authors lies in deciding which discoveries to include and which to (reluctantly) leave out. Our website (www.biopsychology.com/news) boasts a collection of over 15,000 news stories, all drawn from the mainstream media. You can follow updates on the website, or via email, Facebook (www.facebook.com/biopsychology) or Twitter (www.twitter.com/biopsychology).

So, we are sampling from an almost boundless scientific smorgasbord, but we have to watch our weight. Our goal for *The Mind's Machine* is to introduce you to the *basics* of behavioral neuroscience in a way that focuses on the foundational topics in the field—with a liberal sprinkling of the newest and most fascinating discoveries—and leaves you with an appetite for more. Whether you are beginning a program of study centered on the brain and behavior, or are just adding some breadth to your education, you will find that behavioral neuroscience now permeates all aspects of modern psychology, along with related life sciences like physiology, biology, and the health sciences. But that's not all. The tools and techniques of behavioral neuroscience are also propelling important new research activity in many nontraditional areas, such as economics, the performing arts, anthropology, sociology, computer science, and engineering. Researchers are beginning to probe mental processes that

seemed impenetrable only a decade or two ago: the neural bases of decision making, love and attachment, memory and learning, consciousness, and much of what we call the mind. A few examples of formerly mysterious questions that are being answered with cutting-edge research include:

- Do prenatal events influence the probability that a child will develop a heterosexual or homosexual orientation?
- Does the brain make new neurons throughout life, in numbers large enough to make a functional difference?
- Can we improve memory performance with some drugs, and use other drugs to erase unwanted, traumatic memories?
- What happens in the brain as we develop trust in another person?
- Does strong liking for sweet foods involve the same brain mechanisms as addiction to drugs?
- How can we share so many genes with chimpanzees and other primates, and yet be so different from them?
- How can recent discoveries about the neural control of appetite help us to curb the obesity epidemic?
- Does a gene that predisposes for Alzheimer's disease in old age actually improve cognitive functioning earlier in life?

Understanding the research probing these sorts of questions requires some familiarity with the physiology of behavior and experience. Our aim in *The Mind's Machine* is to provide a foundation that places these and other important problems in a unified scientific context.

We've found that students enrolled in our courses have diverse academic backgrounds and personal interests. In this book, we've tried to avoid making too many assumptions about our readers, and have focused on providing both behavioral and biological perspectives on major topics. If you've had some high-school level biology you should have no trouble with most of the material in the book.

For those readers who have more experience in science—or who want more detail—we have peppered the chapters with embedded links to more advanced material located on our website. These links, called A Step Further, are just one of several novel features we have included to aid your learning. Throughout the book you will find QR codes (small square bar codes) that will link your smartphone to animated versions of many figures, video clips, and more. (You'll need to download an app to read the codes; a variety of free or inexpensive codereaders are available for the major smartphones like iPhone, Android, and Blackberry.) Or you may use your computer to go to the web address provided below every QR code.

Each chapter also features a segment called Researchers at Work, which illustrates the nuts and bolts of experimentation through real-world examples. Every few pages, you will find a feature called How's it Going?, with self-test questions that will help you to gauge your progress. And every chapter ends with a Visual Summary, an innovative combination of the main points and figures from the chapter, that you can download for later study. We encourage you to explore the website for the book (mindsmachine.com), which contains a free comprehensive electronic study guide. This website is a powerful companion to the textbook that enhances the learning experience with a variety of multimedia resources.

The chapter lineup in *The Mind's Machine* encompasses several major themes. In the opening chapters, we trace the origins of behavioral neuroscience and introduce you to the structure of the brain, both as seen by the naked eye and as revealed by the microscope. We discuss how the cells of the brain use electrical signals to process information, and how they transmit that information to other cells within larger circuits. Along the way we'll look at the ways in which drugs affect nerve cells in order to change behavior, as well as some of the remarkable technology that lets us study the activity of the conscious brain as it perceives and thinks.

In the middle part of the book we look at the neural systems that underlie fundamental capabilities like feeling, moving, seeing, smelling, hearing and so on. We'll also consider biological and behavioral aspects of "mission-critical" functions such as feeding, sleeping, and sexual behavior. And we'll look at how the endocrine system acts as an interface between the brain and the rest of the body, as well as the reverse—ways in which the environment and behavior alter hormones and thus alter brain activity.

In the latter part of the book we turn to some of the high-level emotional and cognitive processes that color our lives and define us as individuals. We'll survey the systems that allow us to learn and remember information and skills, and the brain systems dedicated to language and spatial processing. Research on processes of attention has made great progress in recent years, and we'll also consider consciousness and decision-making from a neuroscientific perspective. Finally, we'll review some of the consequences of brain dysfunction, ranging from psychopathology to behavioral manifestations of brain damage, and some of the innovative strategies being developed to counter these problems.

As you make your way through the book, you'll learn that one of the outstanding features of the brain is its ability to remodel. Every new experience, every piece of information that you learn, every skill that you master, causes changes in the brain that can alter your future behavior. The changes may involve physical alterations in the connections between cells, or in the chemicals they use to communicate, or even the addition of whole new cells and circuits. It's a property that we neuroscientists refer to as "plasticity." And it's something that we aim to exploit—if we've done our job properly, *The Mind's Machine* should cause lots of changes in *your* brain. We hope you enjoy the process.

Neil V. Watson   S. Marc Breedlove

mindsmachine.com/watson   mindsmachine.com/breedlove

We welcome feedback on any aspect of The Mind's Machine.
Simply drop us a line at mindsmachine@sinauer.com.

Acknowledgments

This book bears the strong imprint of our late colleagues and coauthors Arnold Leiman (1932–2000) and Mark Rosenzweig (1922–2009). Arnie and Mark prepared the earliest editions of our more advanced text, *Biological Psychology*, and many illustrations and concepts in *The Mind's Machine* originated in their minds' machines.

In writing this book we benefited from the help of many highly skilled people. These include members of the staff of Sinauer Associates: Syd Carroll, Editor; Kathaleen Emerson and Chelsea Holabird, Production Editors; Christopher Small, Production Manager; Jefferson Johnson, Production Specialist; Jason Dirks, Media and Supplements Editor, and Suzanne Carter, Production Editor for Media and Supplements. Copy Editor Stephanie Hiebert skillfully edited the text, and Photo Researcher David McIntyre sought out many of the photographs. Mike Demaray, Craig Durant, and colleagues at Dragonfly Media Group transformed our rough sketches and wish list into the handsome and dynamic art program of this text.

Our greatest source of inspiration (and critical feedback) has undoubtedly been the thousands of students to whom we have had the privilege of introducing the mysteries and delights of behavioral neuroscience, over the course of the last couple of decades. We have benefited from wisdom generously contributed by a legion of academic colleagues, whose advice and critical reviews have enormously improved our books. In particular we are grateful to: Duane Albrecht, Anne E. Powell Anderson, Michael Antle, Benoit Bacon, Scott Baron, Mark S. Blumberg, Eliot A. Brenowitz, Chris Brill, Peter C. Brunjes, Rebecca D. Burwell, Catherine P. Cramer, Brian Derrick, Karen De Valois, Russell De Valois, Tiffany Donaldson, Loretta M. Flanagan-Cato, Francis W. Flynn, John D. E. Gabrieli, Jack Gallant, Kimberley P. Good, Diane C. Gooding, Janet M. Gray, James Gross, Ervin Hafter, Mary E. Harrington, Wendy Heller, Mark Hollins, Richard Ivry, Lucia Jacobs, Janice Juraska, Dacher Keltner, Raymond E. Kesner, Keith R. Kluender, Leah A. Krubitzer, Joseph E. LeDoux, Michael A. Leon, Simon LeVay, Stephen G. Lomber, Donna Maney, Stephen A. Maren, Joe L. Martinez, Jr., John J. McDonald, Robert J. McDonald, James L. McGaugh, Robert L. Meisel, Ralph E. Mistlberger, Jeffrey S. Mogil, Randy J. Nelson, Chris Newland, Miguel Nicolelis, Lee Osterhout, James Pfaus, Helene S. Porte, George V. Rebec, Scott R. Robinson, David A. Rosenbaum, Martin F. Sarter, Jeffrey D. Schall, Stan Schein, Frederick Seil, Dale R. Sengelaub, Matthew Shapiro, Arthur Shimamura, Rae Silver, Cheryl L. Sisk, Laura Smale, Robert L. Spencer, Steven K. Sutton, Harald K. Taukulis, Franco J. Vaccarino, David R. Vago, Cyma Van Petten, Charles J. Vierck, Robert Wickesberg, Christoph Wiedenmayer, Walter Wilczynski, S. Mark Williams, Richard D. Wright, Mark C. Zrull, and Irving Zucker.

A dedicated group of proofreaders pored over the text under severe time constraints; thanks to Evan Caldbick, Amrit Chauhan, Mario Ferrari, James Marchand, Kade Markson, Maria Watson, and Samuele Zilioli for catching errors we repeatedly missed. The following external reviewers read and critiqued the draft chapters of *The Mind's Machine*; their contributions and corrections really honed the final product. Any errors that remain are thus entirely our fault.

John Agnew, *University of Colorado*

William Boggan, *College of Charleston*

Aryn Bush, *University of South Florida Polytechnic*

Betty Deckard, *California State University, Long Beach*

Rena Durr, *Christian Brothers University*

Thomas Fischer, *Wayne State University*

Julia Fisher, *Coker College*

Lauren Fowler, *Weber State University*

Michael Foy, *Loyola Marymount University*

Kara Gabriel, *Central Washington University*

Gary Greenberg, *University of Illinois, Chicago*

Ron Harris, *Marymount College*

Christian Hart, *Texas Woman's University*

Chris Hayashi, *Southwestern College*

Dave Holtzman, *State University of New York, Geneseo*

Rick Howe, *College of the Canyons*

Mike Kisley, *University of Colorado, Colorado Springs*

Diane Lee, *California State University, Long Beach*

Robert Lennartz, *Sierra College*

Jeannie Loeb, *University of North Carolina, Chapel Hill*

Jeffrey Love, *Pennsylvania State University*

Daniel Montoya, *Sierra College*

Michelle Niculescu, *Lebanon Valley College*

Linda Perrotti, *The University of Texas, Arlington*

Eleni Pinnow, *University of Wisconsin, Superior*

Thomas Ritz, *Southern Methodist University*

Lawrence Ryan, *Oregon State University*

Victor Shamas, *University of Arizona*

Rachel Shoup, *California State University, East Bay*

Jeffrey Stowell, *Eastern Illinois University*

Jessica Thompson, *Wayne State University*

Sandra Trafalis, *San Jose State University*

Lucy J. Troup, *Colorado State University*

Meg Upchurch, *Transylvania University*

Finally, we would like to thank all our colleagues whose ideas and discoveries make behavioral neuroscience so much fun.

Media and Supplements
to accompany
The Mind's Machine: Foundations of Brain and Behavior

eBook (ISBN 978-0-87893-877-3)
www.coursesmart.com

The Mind's Machine is available as an eBook via CourseSmart, at a substantial discount off the price of the printed textbook. The CourseSmart eBook reproduces the look of the printed book exactly, and includes convenient tools for searching the text, highlighting, and note-taking. The eBook is viewable in any Web browser, and via free apps for iPhone/iPad, Android, and Kindle Fire.

For the Student
Companion Website
mindsmachine.com

The Mind's Machine Companion Website contains a wide range of study and review resources to help students master the material presented in the textbook and to engage them in the subject. Access to the site is free and requires no passcode. Tightly integrated with the text, with content corresponding to every major heading in the book, this online resource greatly enhances the learning experience. Key resources are linked throughout the textbook via QR codes (as well as standard Web addresses), making access to animations and videos easy from any smartphone, tablet, or computer. (Instructor registration is required in order for students to access the online quizzes.)

The Companion Website includes:

- Chapter outlines
- Extensive study questions
- Animations, videos, and activities
- Online versions of the visual summaries
- Online quizzes (multiple choice and essay)
- Flashcards and key terms
- "A Step Further," additional coverage of selected topics
- Complete glossary

Biological Psychology NewsLink
mindsmachine.com/news

This invaluable online resource helps students make connections between the science of biological psychology and their daily lives, and keeps them apprised of the latest developments in the field. The site includes links to thousands of news stories, all organized both by keyword and by textbook chapter. The site is updated 3–4 times per week. Follow on Twitter (@biopsychology) and find us on Facebook (facebook.com/biopsychology).

For the Instructor
Instructor's Resource Library

The Mind's Machine Instructor's Resource Library includes a variety of resources to aid in planning the course, development of lectures, and assessment of students.

The Instructor's Resource Library includes:

- Figures & Tables: All of the line-art illustrations, photos, and tables from the textbook are provided as both high-resolution and low-resolution JPEGs, all optimized for use in presentation software (such as PowerPoint)
- PowerPoint Resources: Three different types of PowerPoint presentations are provided for each chapter of the textbook:
  - All figures, photos, and tables
  - A complete lecture outline, including selected figures
  - Animations and videos
- Animations: These detailed animations help enliven lectures and illustrate dynamic processes
- Videos: A collection of video segments that illustrate interesting concepts and phenomena
- Instructor's Manual and Test Bank in Word format
- Computerized Test Bank: The entire Test Bank is provided in Diploma format (software included), making it easy to quickly assemble exams using any combination of publisher-provided and custom questions. Includes the Companion Website quiz questions.

Instructor's Manual & Test Bank

(Included on the Instructor's Resource Library)

David R. Vago, Harvard Medical School

The Mind's Machine Instructor's Manual & Test Bank includes useful resources for planning the course and lectures, and creating quizzes and exams. For each chapter of the textbook, the Instructor's Manual & Test Bank includes the following:

- Chapter overview
- Complete chapter outline
- Key concepts
- Detailed lecture outlines
- Additional references for lecture/course development
- Comprehensive test questions, including multiple choice, fill-in-the-blank, essay, matching, definition, and paragraph development questions. The Companion Website quiz questions are also included.

Online Quizzing

The Companion Website includes online quizzes that can be assigned by instructors or used as self-review exercises by students. Quizzes can be customized with any combination of the publisher-provided questions and an instructor's own questions, and can be assigned as desired. Results of the quizzes are stored in the online gradebook. (Instructors must register in order for their students to be able to access the online quizzes.)

Course Management System Support

Using the Computerized Test Bank provided in the Instructor's Resource Library, instructors can easily create and export quizzes and exams (or the entire test bank) for integration into their course management system, such as WebCT, Blackboard, Angel, and Moodle.

The Mind's Machine
FOUNDATIONS OF BRAIN AND BEHAVIOR

chapter 1

An Introduction to Brain and Behavior

Nature and Nurture: Building the Mind's Machine

We humans have a long history of using contemporary technology as a metaphor for the mysterious workings of the brain. Scholars in antiquity, influenced by inventions such as aqueducts, plumbing, and ornamental fountains, proposed that the shunting of liquid "spirits" within the body produced behavior. Later thinkers emphasized the possible importance of wires, switches, and relays. Today it is commonplace to see the brain described as a computer, with "hardware" and "software." Perhaps tomorrow's neuroscientists will describe the brain in terms of holograms, quantum devices, or a technology that has yet to be imagined.

Modern research aims to describe the complicated machine within each of our heads, but we also want to know how the operation of the brain produces the *mind*—the perceptions, emotions, thoughts, self-awareness, and other cognitive processes that govern our behavior. During the twentieth century, a lot of ink was spilled over the "nature-nurture" controversy, with scholars arguing passionately about the extent to which mental characteristics and abilities are the result of learning experiences versus innate, "hardwired" genetic programs.

The two perspectives have often been presented as mutually incompatible alternatives, but thanks to more-powerful techniques, we have come to realize that there is nothing controversial about nature versus nurture: they are two sides of the same coin. Consider the case of rat pups who have inattentive mothers. As adults, the formerly neglected pups show elevated stress hormone responses to stressors that have little effect on rats that were not neglected as pups (T. Y. Zhang and Meaney, 2010). How does this lasting reactivity develop—through experience or as a result of innate biological factors? Both, it turns out. As we'll see later in this chapter, and throughout the book, the mind and its machine are shaped by a precise combination of genes and experience, inextricably tied together.

To see a video, go to

mindsmachine.com/1.1
Nature and Nurture

There are now 7 billion of us, and while we can debate whether to fear or celebrate that number, there is no doubt that each of our 7 billion brains will at times contemplate its own existence and meaning. How does the operation of a three-pound organ generate our sense of self, express our unique personalities, record information, and guide our actions? Evolution has shaped our bodies and brains so that we closely resemble one another, yet our brains remain malleable throughout life, continually remolded by our environments and interactions with other people. So, through a remarkable intersection of genetic heritage and environmental influences, 7 billion unique individuals have been formed, and we literally change each other's minds on a daily basis.

Our goal in this book is to introduce you to some of the many ways in which the structures and actions of the brain produce mind and behavior, and also the reverse: some of the many ways in which experiences change the brain. We hope to kindle in you the same interest and excitement that we experienced as students (and still feel today) when reading and thinking about the biology of behavior. Let's start by considering the aims and scope of the science called *biological psychology*.

Figure 1.1   How Biological Psychology Relates to Other Fields

What's in a Name?

The general field of **neuroscience**—the scientific study of the nervous system—is divided into many subdisciplines because the topic is so vast. In fact, however, the first scholars to study the relationships between brain and behavior called themselves philosophers, because it was philosophy that established the foundations of scientific discovery and methods for creating new knowledge. Philosophers had long been concerned with biology, and with the origins of human behavior, so **biological psychology**, the field that relates behavior to bodily processes, naturally evolved from those beginnings. The names *behavioral neuroscience*, *brain and behavior*, and *physiological psychology* are all synonyms for *biological psychology*, but whichever name is used, the main goal of this field is to understand the brain structures and functions that respond to experiences and generate behavior.

Scholars with dramatically varied backgrounds—psychologists, biologists, physiologists, engineers, neurologists, psychiatrists, and many others—together make up the field of biological psychology. It is a field that spans both academia and industry, with focus that ranges from pure research on basic processes to entirely applied work in which findings are directly translated into goods and services (Hitt, 2007). The diverse branches of science that overlap with biological psychology are mapped in **Figure 1.1**.

The Science of Brain and Behavior Spans Past, Present, and Future

An early textbook famously opened with the observation that, as a science, "psychology has a long past but only a short history" (Ebbinghaus, 1908). That's certainly an apt description of biological psychology. The modern era of biological psychology—characterized by objective experimentation and use of the scientific method to test hypotheses—has a formal history of only 100 years or so. But curiosity about the genesis of behavior reaches much further into the past, shaped by religious ideas, folk knowledge, and ancient observations about the biology of humans and nonhuman animals. Only comparatively recently have scholars even recognized the central role of the brain in controlling behavior!

The role of the brain was uncertain to scholars in antiquity

The elaborate preparation of tombs and careful mummification of important people in ancient Egypt (especially about 1500–1000 BCE) reflected the belief that the dead would enter an afterlife that entailed both struggle and—for the adequately equipped individual—great reward. So, in addition to embalming the body with special salts and oils, the usual practice was to preserve four important organs in alabaster jars in the tomb: liver, lungs, stomach, and intestines. The heart, being especially esteemed, was preserved in its place within the body. The brain, however, was plucked out and unceremoniously discarded; apparently it was considered to be of no particular value in the afterlife.

There is no mention of the brain anywhere in the Bible (either Old Testament or New Testament), but the heart is mentioned hundreds of times, along with several references each to the liver, the stomach, and the bowels as the seats of passion, courage, and pity, respectively. Aristotle (about 350 BCE), the most prominent scientist of ancient Greece, likewise considered mental capacities to be properties of the heart. When we call people *kindhearted*, *openhearted*, *fainthearted*, *hardhearted*, or *heartless*, and when we speak of learning *by heart*, we are using language echoing this ancient notion. Aristotle thought the brain was little more than a cooling system for hot blood from the heart. But Aristotle's near contemporary, the great Greek physician Hippocrates (about 400 BCE), already suspected that Aristotle's view was—ahem—wrongheaded, and instead ascribed emotion, perception, and thought to the functioning of the brain.

To see the brain in 3D, go to

mindsmachine.com/1.2
Brain Explorer

Brain Removal Kit It seems the ancient Egyptians had little regard for the brain. During the mummification process, embalmers used specialized tools, like these examples in the British Museum, to first break up the small bones behind the nose and then extract the brain through the opening. Unlike other major organs, the brain was discarded, and the cranium was stuffed with linen or straw. (Photograph by Neil Watson.)

neuroscience The scientific study of the nervous system.

biological psychology Also called *behavioral neuroscience*, *brain and behavior*, and *physiological psychology*. The study of the biological bases of psychological processes and behavior.

A Brain on the Ceiling of the Sistine Chapel? Between 1508 and 1512, Michelangelo painted the Sistine Chapel in the Vatican. In one panel of Michelangelo's masterpiece, God is depicted reaching out to bestow the gift of life upon humanity, through Adam. But neuroscientists have noted that the oddly shaped drapery behind God, and the arrangement of his attendants, closely resembles part of a human brain (Meshberger, 1990); compare with the sagittal view in Figure 2.16. A keen student of anatomy, Michelangelo probably knew perfectly well what a dissected human brain looks like. So, was Michelangelo having some fun, making a subtle commentary about the origins of human behavior? We probably will never know. But we can all agree that our uniquely human qualities—language, reason, emotion, and the rest—are products of the brain.

By the second century ACE, this brain-centered view of mental processes had become more entrenched, appearing in the writings of the Greco-Roman physician Galen (the "Father of Medicine"). Galen's experiences in treating head injuries of gladiators lead him to propose that behavior results from the movement of "animal spirits" from the brain through nerves to the peripheral body, but his understanding of the relevant anatomy was poor. Not until much later were techniques developed for making highly detailed anatomical studies of the fine structure of the brain.

Skillfully applying newly developed innovations in drawing technique, Renaissance painter and scientist Leonardo da Vinci (1452–1519) produced exquisite neuroanatomical illustrations of nerves and brain structures (**Figure 1.2**). Religious dogma dominated Renaissance science—just ask Galileo—with the result that scientific writing from that era often presents the brain as a mysterious and intricate gift from God. But perhaps some thinkers of the day secretly held a more secular view of neuroscience; for example, it has been observed that the depiction of God on the ceiling of the Sistine Chapel, painted by Michelangelo (1475–1564), bears a striking resemblance to a midline view of the human brain (Meshberger, 1990).

(a)

In an early sketch, Leonardo simply copied old drawings that bore little resemblance to the actual structure of the brain, showing the fluid-filled ventricles as a balloon connected to the eye.

(b)

Leonardo's later drawings, made from direct observations, were much more anatomically correct.

Figure 1.2   Leonardo da Vinci's Changing View of the Brain

Figure 1.3 **An Early Account of Reflexes**

Nevertheless, reconciling religious notions of the soul with increasingly mechanistic views of the brain and body became a major scholarly preoccupation. Among his many contributions to math and science, René Descartes (1596–1650) tried to explain how the control of behavior might resemble the workings of a machine, proposing the concept of spinal reflexes and a neural pathway for them (**Figure 1.3**). But Descartes also argued (perhaps in order to deflect criticism), that free will and moral choice could not arise from a mere machine. So Descartes asserted that humans, at least, had a nonmaterial soul as well as a material body, and that the soul governed behavior through a point of contact (possibly the pineal gland) in the brain. This notion of **dualism** spread widely and left other philosophers with the task of determining how a nonmaterial soul could exert influence over a material body and brain. Today, biological psychologists reject dualism and insist that all the workings of the mind can also, in theory, be understood as purely physical processes in the material world, specifically in the brain.

Thanks in large part to systematic studies of the relation between various disorders and damage to regions of the human brain that were conducted by the English physician Thomas Willis (1621–1675), the notion that the brain coordinates and controls behavior eventually became widely accepted (Zimmer, 2004). A quasi-scientific fad of the early 1800s called **phrenology** (**Figure 1.4a**) capitalized on the emerging idea that specific behaviors, feelings, and personality traits were controlled by discrete regions of the brain. Although phrenology was wrong in several fundamental ways—for example,

René Descartes suggested that intense heat on the toe causes nervous activity to flow up the nerve to the brain, from which it is "reflected" back down to the leg muscles, causing them to contract and withdraw the foot. This mode of action—reflection—gave rise to the concept and word *reflex*.

dualism The notion, promoted by René Descartes, that the mind has an immaterial aspect that is distinct from the material body and brain.

phrenology The belief that bumps on the skull reflect enlargements of brain regions responsible for certain behavioral faculties.

(a)

Nineteenth-century phrenologists associated arbitrary "faculties" with bumps on the skull, using maps like this to infer an individual's talents, personality, and temperament.

(b)

Today, technology reveals that the whole brain is active most of the time, so this map simply reflects the *peaks* of brain activation during various behaviors.

Figure 1.4 **Old and New Phrenology** (Part *b* after Nichols and Newsome, 1999.)

(a)

Whether a bigger brain indicates greater intelligence is an old question. Investigators in the nineteenth century measured the volumes of skulls of various groups and estimated intelligence on the basis of people's occupations, teachers' guesstimates, and other doubtful criteria.

(b)

IQ tests improved the objectivity of intelligence measurement. When carefully controlled, MRI studies like this one do find a correlation between brain size and IQ scores (Andreasen et al., 1993), and IQ seems to correlate better with the volume of the front of the brain than the back (Colom et al., 2009). So it seems that bigger is better, but the correlations are of only modest size, meaning that other factors must also contribute to IQ scores (Stanovich, 2009).

Figure 1.5   Does Size Matter?   (Part *a* from the Bettmann Archive; *b* courtesy of Nancy Andreasen.)

phrenologists believed they could "read" a person's character by feeling the bumps on that person's head—the field helped establish the concept of **localization of function**, which asserts that different brain regions specialize in specific behaviors.

Later researchers found that damage to specific regions of the brain causes predictable impairments in people; for example, Paul Broca (1824–1880) noted that damage to a particular region of the left side of the brain reliably causes problems with speech production. Neuroscientists today accept that the localization of function within the brain is more or less true. Although the whole brain is active most of the time, when we are performing particular tasks, certain brain regions become *even more* activated, and different tasks activate different brain regions. So modern functional maps of the human brain track the locations where these *peaks* of activation occur (**Figure 1.4b**). A parallel concern has been the importance of brain size to intellectual function. After a couple of centuries of study, the evidence indicates that the overall size of your brain matters, but not as much as you might expect (**Figure 1.5**).

In 1890, William James's book *Principles of Psychology* signaled the beginnings of a modern approach to biological psychology. In James's work, psychological ideas such as consciousness and other aspects of human experience came to be seen as properties of the nervous system. A true biological psychology began to emerge from this approach.

Advances in experimental methodology propel modern biological psychology

By the beginning of the twentieth century, researchers were applying newly developed tools to study mental processes that had previously seemed unknowable. Rapid progress was made in developing techniques for measuring learning and memory in humans and animals, and Russian physiologist Ivan P. Pavlov (1849–1936) made his landmark discoveries of classical conditioning in animals—Nobel Prize–winning work that influences scientists to this day.

This rapid progress prompted a parallel interest in understanding the neural basis of learning, marked by one of the first true biological psychology research programs: the "search for the engram" by Karl Lashley (1890–1958). Although he would not accomplish his goal of linking a specific brain region to the formation of a specific long-term memory (an "engram"), Lashley gave us the idea (now well established) that memory is not localized to only one region of the brain.

localization of function   The concept that different brain regions specialize in specific behaviors.

One of Lashley's students, Donald O. Hebb (1904–1985), had a particularly profound impact on biological psychology. Hebb showed that cognitive processing could be accomplished by networks of active neurons, molded by repeated activation patterns into functional circuits. His hypothesis about how neurons strengthen their connections as a consequence of experiences led to the idea of the *Hebbian synapse,* a type of plastic (changeable) connection between neurons that remains a hot topic in neuroscience, as discussed in Chapter 13.

Present-day biological psychologists may draw on several different theoretical perspectives. Here are some of the major ones:

1. *Systematic description of behavior.* Until we describe what we want to study, we cannot accomplish much. Depending on our goals, we may describe behavior in terms of detailed acts or processes, or in terms of results or functions. To be useful for scientific study, a description must be precise and reveal the essential features of the behavior, using accurately defined terms and units.

2. *The evolution of brain and behavior.* Darwin's theory of evolution through natural selection is central to all modern biology and psychology. Biological psychologists employ evolutionary theory in two ways: by evaluating *similarities* among species due to shared ancestry, and by looking for species-specific *differences* in behavior and biology that have evolved as adaptations to different environments (**Box 1.1**). We will discuss many examples of both perspectives in this book.

3. *Life-span development of the brain and behavior.* **Ontogeny** is the process by which an individual changes in the course of its lifetime—that is, grows up and grows old. Observing the way a particular behavior changes during ontogeny may give us clues to its functions and mechanisms. For example, we know that learning ability in monkeys increases over several years of development. Therefore, we can speculate that prolonged maturation of brain circuits is required for complex learning tasks. Studying the development of reproductive capacity and of differences in behavior between the sexes, along with changes in body structures and processes, enables us to throw light on body mechanisms underlying sex behaviors.

4. *The biological mechanisms of behavior.* To learn about the mechanisms of an individual's behavior, we study how his or her present body works, separate from evolutionary or developmental concerns. To understand the underlying mechanisms of behavior, we must regard the organism (with all due respect) as a "machine," made up of billions of nerve cells, or **neurons**. In a sense, the mechanistic questions are the "how" questions of biological psychology, in contrast to the "why" questions that derive from the evolutionary and developmental perspectives. So in the case of learning and memory, for example, we might try to understand how a sequence of electrical and biochemical processes allows us to store information in our brains, and how a different process retrieves it.

The future of biological psychology is in interdisciplinary discovery and knowledge translation

There is reason to hope that some of the fundamental discoveries of biological psychology will be translated into a greater understanding of brain disorders, and the development of effective treatments. At least one person in five around the world currently suffers from a neurological or psychiatric illness. These disorders vary in severity, from illnesses that cause significant but manageable changes in the quality of everyday life, to devastating conditions that cause complete disability. **Figure 1.6** illustrates the estimated numbers of U.S. residents afflicted by some of the main neurological and psychiatric disorders. The toll of these disorders is enormous: the cost for treatment of dementia (severely disordered thinking) alone exceeds the costs of treating cancer and heart disease combined.

As the quest to understand and relieve these diseases gathers speed, some of the historical distinction between clinical and laboratory approaches has begun to fade

ontogeny   The process by which an individual changes in the course of its lifetime—that is, grows up and grows old.

neuron   Also called *nerve cell.* The basic unit of the nervous system.

(*a*) Prevalence of neurological disorders

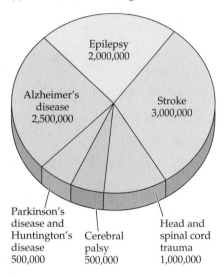

Epilepsy
2,000,000

Alzheimer's
disease
2,500,000

Stroke
3,000,000

Parkinson's
disease and
Huntington's
disease
500,000

Cerebral
palsy
500,000

Head and
spinal cord
trauma
1,000,000

(*b*) Prevalance of psychiatric disorders

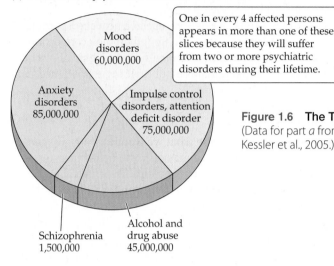

Mood
disorders
60,000,000

Anxiety
disorders
85,000,000

Impulse control
disorders, attention
deficit disorder
75,000,000

One in every 4 affected persons appears in more than one of these slices because they will suffer from two or more psychiatric disorders during their lifetime.

Schizophrenia
1,500,000

Alcohol and
drug abuse
45,000,000

Figure 1.6 The Toll of Brain Disorders (Data for part *a* from Hirtz et al., 2007; for *b*, from Kessler et al., 2005.)

neural plasticity or neuroplasticity The ability of the nervous system to change in response to experience or the environment.

adult neurogenesis The creation of new neurons in the brain of an adult.

away. For example, when clinicians encounter a pair of twins, one of whom has schizophrenia while the other seems healthy, the discovery of structural differences in their brains (**Figure 1.7**) immediately raises questions for laboratory scientists: Did the structural differences arise before the symptoms of schizophrenia, or the other way around? Were the brain differences present at birth or did they arise during puberty? Does medication that reduces symptoms affect brain structure? (We'll consider schizophrenia again in Chapter 12.)

The dawning of the twenty-first century has brought an explosion in new research areas and perspectives in biological psychology. In addition to the rapid progress that is occurring in the more established topic areas of biological psychology, which we survey in this book, some emerging research areas are attracting intense interest. In the paragraphs that follow, we'll take a brief look at a handful of these.

NEUROPLASTICITY When you think about it, the only explanation for our ability to learn skills and form memories is that the brain physically changes in some way to encode and store that information. In this book we'll see many examples of how behavior and experiences alter the physical brain—a phenomenon called **neural plasticity** (from the Greek *plassein*, "to mold or form") or **neuroplasticity**—but much remains to be discovered about mechanisms of neuroplasticity.

We know that experiences can alter the size of brain regions and interconnections between neurons, and cellular changes have been discovered that *could* be mechanisms for storing memories; scientists are actively testing that idea. We also know that certain experiences and physiological states can modify the rate at which new neurons are born in the adult brain, but again, the functional significance of this **adult neurogenesis** (see Chapter 13) remains to be determined. Perhaps nothing distinguishes biological psychology from other neurosciences more clearly than a fascination with neuroplasticity and the role of experience.

(*a*)

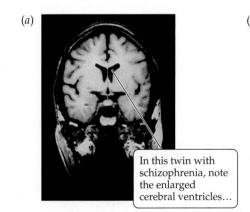

In this twin with schizophrenia, note the enlarged cerebral ventricles…

(*b*)

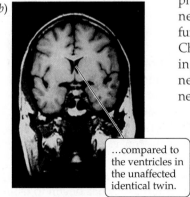

…compared to the ventricles in the unaffected identical twin.

Figure 1.7 Identical Twins but Nonidentical Brains and Behavior (Images courtesy of E. Fuller Torrey.)

BOX 1.1 We Are All Alike, and We Are All Different

Each person has some characteristics shared by…

all animals…

All animals use DNA to store genetic information.

all vertebrates…

All vertebrates have a backbone and spinal cord.

all mammals…

All mammals suckle their young.

all primates…

All primates have a relatively large, complex brain, and a hand with an opposable thumb.

all humans (people)…

All humans use symbolic language to communicate with each other.

some people…

Some people like to eat beets (no one knows why).

no other person.

No two people, even identical twins, are alike in each and every way, as individual experiences leave their unique stamp on every brain.

How do similarities and differences among people and animals fit into biological psychology? Each person is in some ways like all other people, in some ways like some other people, and in some ways like no other person. As the figure shows, we can extend this observation to the much broader range of animal life. In some ways each person is like all other animals (e.g., needing to ingest complex organic nutrients), in some ways like all other vertebrates (e.g., having a spinal column), in some ways like all other mammals (e.g., nursing our young), and in some ways like all other primates (e.g., having a relatively large, complex brain and a hand with an opposable thumb). The electrical messages used by nerve cells (see Chapter 3) are essentially the same in a jellyfish, a cockroach, and a human being, and many species employ identical hormones. Species share these **conserved** characteristics because the features first arose in a shared ancestor. But

mere similarity of a feature between species does not guarantee that the feature came from a common ancestral species. Our eyes resemble those of octopuses, but certain key differences reveal that their eyes and our eyes evolved separately.

Whether knowledge gained about a process in another species applies to humans depends on whether we are like that species in regard to that process. The fundamental research on the mechanisms of inheritance in the bacterium *Escherichia coli* proved so widely applicable that some molecular biologists proclaimed, "What is true of *E. coli* is true of the elephant." To a remarkable extent that statement is true, but there are also some important differences in the genetic mechanisms of *E. coli* and mammals.

With respect to each biological property, researchers must determine how animals are identical and how they are different. When we seek animal models for studying human behavior or biological processes, we must ask the following question: Does the proposed animal model really have some things in common with the process at work in humans? We will see many cases in which it does.

Even within the same species, however, individuals differ from one another: cat from cat, blue jay from blue jay, and person from person. Biological psychology seeks to understand individual differences as well as similarities. Therefore, the way in which each person is able to process information and store the memories of these experiences is another part of our story.

SOCIAL NEUROSCIENCE   Because of neuroplasticity, even simple interactions with other people can remodel our brains. Indeed, the whole point of coming to a lecture hall is to have the instructor use words and figures to alter your brain so that you can retrieve that information in the future (in other words, she is teaching you something). Most aspects of our social behavior are learned—from the language we speak to the clothes we wear and the kinds of foods we eat, as well as our identity in belonging to larger groups (clubs, teams, schools, nationalities, and so on).

Social neuroscience is an emerging discipline that uses the tools of neuroscience to discover how biological and social factors continually interact and affect each other as behavior unfolds. For example, the amount of testosterone in a male's circulation affects his dominance behavior and aggression, expressed in social settings ranging from friendly games to overt physical aggression (see Chapter 11). But the *outcome* of those contests can cause changes in relative testosterone levels—winners show more testosterone, and losers have less—so testosterone concentration in the blood at any particular moment is determined (in part) by the male's recent history of dominant-submissive social experience. The modified testosterone level, in turn, helps determine the male's dominance and aggression in the future.

EVOLUTIONARY PSYCHOLOGY   Zoologists have long viewed animal behaviors as adaptations that evolved to solve specific ecological pressures, such as the need to find food and avoid predators. More recently, speculations about how natural selection might have shaped our own behavior, including specific cognitive abilities, have given rise to a lively and controversial field called **evolutionary psychology** (Barkow et al., 1992; Buss, 2000). For example, it has been argued (G. F. Miller, 2000) that sexual selection was crucial for evolution of the human brain. If early ancestors of modern humans had come to favor mates who sang, made jokes, or produced artistic works, an "arms race" might have ensued as the ever more discriminating brains of one sex demanded ever more impressive performances from the brains of the other sex. Did humor, song, and art originate from the drive to be sexy? And does sexual selection account for the large size of the human brain?

Although evolutionary psychology excels at generating intriguing hypothetical accounts of the evolution of behaviors, the challenge for the future is to come up with ways to test and potentially disprove these hypotheses. Because they have no access to the ancestral environments in which cognitive systems evolved, evolutionary psychologists must often rely on correlations and surveys, rather than true experiments.

EPIGENETICS   Nearly all of the cells in your body have a complete copy of your *genome* (that is, a copy of all your genes), but each cell *uses* only a small subset of those genes at any one time. **Epigenetics** is a young field focusing on factors that have a lasting effect on patterns of **gene expression**—the turning on or off of specific genes—without changing the structure of the genes themselves. In some cases the acquired alteration in gene expression is passed down through generations, despite the absence of genetic modifications.

At the beginning of the chapter, we briefly discussed rats that show heightened stress reactivity throughout their lives if neglected by their mothers while they are pups, and we asked whether this phenomenon was more attributable to "nature" or to "nurture." The answer is: neither. Or perhaps both. It is an epigenetic phenomenon, in which the maternal neglect causes lasting inactivation of a gene (a process called *methylation*) in the brain that's involved in stress hormone signals. Reduced expression of that gene causes the pups to be hyperresponsive to stress for the rest of their lives. So, early experience produced a permanent change in the genes of the neglected rats that altered their behavior in adulthood—nurture *and* nature.

A similar mechanism may apply to humans, because this same gene is also more likely to be methylated in the postmortem brains of suicide victims than of controls, *but only if the victim was subjected to childhood abuse* (McGowan et al., 2009). So, methylation of the

social neuroscience A field of study that uses the tools of neuroscience to discover the biological bases of social behavior, and the effects of social circumstances on brain activity.

evolutionary psychology A field of study devoted to asking how natural selection has shaped behavior in humans and other animals.

epigenetics The study of factors that affect gene expression without making any changes in the nucleotide sequence of the genes themselves.

gene expression The turning on or off of specific genes.

"How Beautifully Blue the Sky?" We would all agree that this sky is the color we call "blue." But in Chapter 14 we'll ask whether everyone who sees that sky has the same experience of the color.

gene in abused children may make them more susceptible to stress, and ultimately suicidal, as adults—a powerful demonstration of epigenetic influences on behavior. (For additional examples of social influences on the structure of the brain, see **A Step Further 1.1**, on the website.)

NEUROECONOMICS A growing number of neuroscience labs are focusing on how we decide what to do. Involving perspectives ranging from philosophy to social psychology to traditional experimental psychology and economics, **neuroeconomics** exploits new brain-imaging technologies that identify brain regions activated under differing decision-making circumstances, such as playing games, managing resources, and other traditional economic models. Naturally, this research has some shorter-term benefits relating to product marketing—what makes us want to buy something? But researchers also hope that, over the longer term, we will develop a more complete understanding of the massive brain networks that are active while we choose among various alternatives and decide what to do next, and of the ways in which we perceive and express our free will (as well as if, indeed, we actually *have* free will!).

Early indications are that we possess at least two major neuroeconomic brain systems: one that assesses the relative value of the choices available, and one that sifts through the evaluated choices in order to make a conscious decision (Kable and Glimcher, 2009). There is good reason to expect exciting new discoveries about how these neural systems interact with other cognitive systems to produce our conscious feeling of self.

THE FINAL FRONTIER: CONSCIOUSNESS Ultimately, many of the traditional and emerging topics in biological psychology converge on the problem of **consciousness**: the personal, private awareness of our emotions, intentions, thoughts, and movements, and of the sensations that impinge upon us. How is it possible that you are aware of the words on this page, the room you're occupying, the goals you have in life? Scientists have laid some of the groundwork for conceptualizing consciousness as a property of the brain, and for establishing it as an area of scientific inquiry (Zeman, 2002), but the devil is in the details. Later in the book we will consider experiments that demonstrate properties of consciousness, such as the role of arousal systems of the brain, and the neural timing of our conscious perception of our inner life. Some of these experiments lead us to interesting—possibly disturbing—conclusions that our consciousness may track the operation of our brains much less accurately than we perceive (as discussed in Chapter 14).

However consciousness is brought about, any satisfying understanding would be able, for example, to explain why a certain pattern of activity in your brain causes you to experience the sensation of blue when looking at the sky, and a really good theory would tell us how we could cause you to experience the sky as yellow, just by changing your brain activity for you (not, of course, by simply wearing colored goggles, but rather through a change in the deeper *conscious* experience of the world around you). However, we are nowhere near understanding consciousness this clearly. We generally have no idea what the actual *inner experience* of a human or animal is—only what an individual's behavior tells us about it. So even if you tell me that the sky is blue to you, I can't tell whether blue *feels* the same in your mind as it does in mine. Until we can get a more complete grasp of these complex issues of brain and behavior, we are in no position to know whether complicated machines like computers are, or might one day be, conscious.

neuroeconomics The study of brain mechanisms at work during economic decision making.

consciousness The state of awareness of one's own existence, thoughts, emotions, and experiences.

How's it going?*

1. Define *biological psychology*. Name some fields that are closely allied to biological psychology.

2. What do we mean when we say that biological psychology has a long past but only a short history? Review the prehistory of biological psychology, and the gradual process of elimination that linked the brain and behavior.

3. Discuss the concept of localization of function.

4. Describe the four major theoretical perspectives employed by modern-day biological psychologists that we discussed in the chapter: behavioral description, evolution, development, and biological mechanisms.

5. Comment on the prevalence of psychiatric and neurological disorders in contemporary society, and discuss their economic and emotional impact.

6. Where is biological psychology headed? Discuss some of the probable hot topics for future biological psychologists.

*Near the end of each section of text, we stop to ask you some questions so you can assess how well you've absorbed the main points. These questions are intended as a self-check, so if you're having problems answering them, you may find it helpful to review the preceding section.

Careful Research Design Is Critical for Progress in Brain Research

somatic intervention   An approach to finding relations between body variables and behavioral variables that involves manipulating body structure or function and looking for resultant changes in behavior.

independent variable   The factor that is manipulated by an experimenter.

dependent variable   The factor that an experimenter measures to monitor a change in response to changes in an independent variable.

Because it is both fantastically complex and somewhat inaccessible, the brain poses special challenges when it comes to the formulation of research questions and the design of experiments to answer those questions. For example, it is difficult to physically manipulate the structure and activity of the brain with pinpoint accuracy, so technological advances have been responsible for the modern explosion in neuroscience research. And because we can't ethically manipulate the brains of human subjects (other than through transient and noninvasive means), we often must rely on alternatives such as purely observational research, research in which behavioral means are used to alter brain activity, or research in which we study neural function in lab animals in order to gain insights about our own nervous systems.

Three kinds of studies probe brain-behavior relationships

Biological psychologists use three general types of studies for research on the biological bases of behavior. In an experiment employing **somatic intervention** (**Figure 1.8a**), we alter a structure or function of the brain or body to see how this alteration changes behavior. In this sort of experiment, the physical alteration is an **independent variable** (a general term used to describe the manipulated aspect of any experiment), and the behavioral effect is the **dependent variable** (a general term used to describe the measured consequence of an experimental manipulation). Some examples of somatic intervention experiments include (1) administering a hormone to some animals, but not others, and comparing the later sexual behavior of both groups; (2) electrically stimulating a specific brain region and measuring alterations in movement; and (3) destroying a specific region in the brain and observing subsequent changes in sleep patterns. In each case,

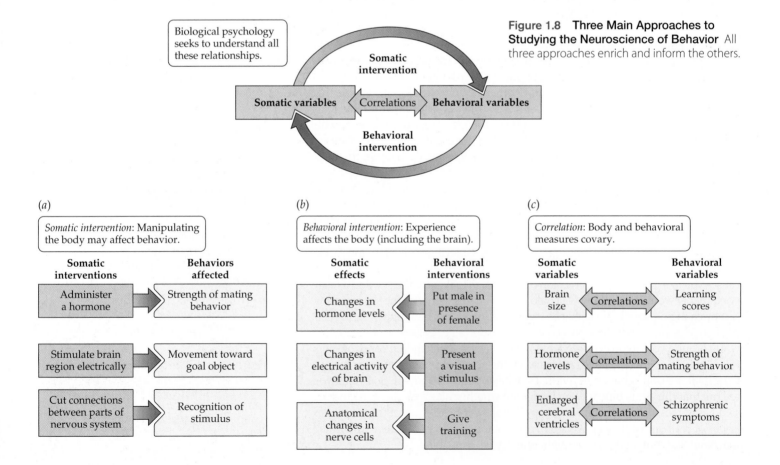

Figure 1.8   Three Main Approaches to Studying the Neuroscience of Behavior All three approaches enrich and inform the others.

the behavioral measurements follow the bodily intervention; furthermore, in each case the behavioral measurements are compared to a **control group**. In a **within-subjects experiment**, the control group is simply the same individuals, tested before the somatic intervention occurred. In a **between-subjects experiment**, the experimental subjects are compared with a different group of individuals who have been treated identically in every way except that they haven't received the somatic intervention.

The approach opposite to somatic intervention is **behavioral intervention** (**Figure 1.8b**). In this approach the scientist alters or controls the behavior of an organism and looks for resulting changes in body structure or function. Here, behavior is the independent variable, and change in the body is the dependent variable. A few examples include (1) allowing adults of the opposite sex to interact, and measuring subsequent changes in sex hormones; (2) having a person perform a cognitive task while in a brain scanner, and measuring changes in activity in specific regions of the brain; and (3) training an animal to fear a previously neutral stimulus, and observing electrical changes in the brain that may encode the newly learned association. As with somatic intervention, these experimental approaches may employ either within-groups or between-groups designs.

The third type of study is **correlation** (**Figure 1.8c**), in which the researcher quantifies the co-occurrence of a behavior and a somatic change. If one of the two always goes up when the other goes down (and vice versa), it is called a **negative correlation**. If both always increase together, or always decrease together, it is called a **positive correlation**. A few examples of correlational studies include observing the extent to which high IQ is associated with brain size, or noting that increases in a certain hormone are accompanied by increases in aggressive behavior. Note that although this type of study can reveal that the measured variables are associated in some way, it says nothing about **causality**; we can't conclude, for example, whether the hormones cause the aggression, or whether the aggression causes the increase in hormones. The benefit of correlational research is that it can tell researchers which things are linked, thus helping us to develop hypotheses that can be tested experimentally using behavioral and somatic interventions.

As Figure 1.8 illustrates, biological psychology research is guided by the understanding that relations between brain and body are reciprocal: each affects the other in an ongoing cycle of bodily and behavioral interactions. We will see examples of this reciprocal relationship throughout the book.

Biological psychologists use several levels of analysis

Another consideration in designed experiments is the level of complexity at which to work. Even the most complex behavior could, in theory, be understood at the level of cellular activity or even lower, at the level of biochemistry and molecular interactions. This idea, that we can understand complex systems by dissecting their simpler constituent parts, is known as **reductionism**. But we wouldn't get very far if we set out to explain, say, the use of grammar, in terms of chemical reactions; the behavior is so complex that an explanation at the molecular level would involve a vast amount of data. So instead, the reductionist approach aims to identify **levels of analysis** that are *just simple enough* that they allow us to make rapid progress on the more complex phenomenon under study. Finding explanations for behavior often requires several levels of biological analysis, ranging from social interactions, to brain systems, to circuits and single nerve cells and their even simpler, molecular constituents.

Naturally, in all fields different problems are carried to different levels of analysis, and fruitful work is often being done simultaneously by different workers at several levels (**Figure 1.9**). For example, in their research on visual perception, some cognitive psychologists carefully analyze behavior. They try to determine how the eyes move while looking at a visual pattern, or how the contrast among parts of the pattern determines its visibility. Meanwhile, other biological psychologists study the differences in visual abilities among species and try to determine the adaptive significance of these

control group A group of research subjects that are identical to an experimental (or test) group in every way except that they do not receive the experimental treatment or manipulation. The experimental group is then compared to the control group to assess the effect of the treatment.

within-subjects experiment An experiment in which the same set of subjects is compared before and after an experimental manipulation. The subjects thus serve as their own controls.

between-subjects experiment An experiment in which a group of experimental subjects is compared with a control group of individuals who have been treated identically in every way except that they haven't received the experimental manipulation.

behavioral intervention An approach to finding relations between body variables and behavioral variables that involves intervening in the behavior of an organism and looking for resultant changes in body structure or function.

correlation The covariation of two measures.

negative correlation A covariation of two measures in which one of the two usually goes up when the other goes down (and vice versa).

positive correlation A covariation of two measures in which they both usually increase together, or always decrease together.

causality The relation of cause and effect, such that we can conclude that an experimental manipulation has specifically caused an observed result.

reductionism The scientific strategy of breaking a system down into increasingly smaller parts in order to understand it.

levels of analysis The scope of experimental approaches. A scientist may try to understand behavior by monitoring molecules, nerve cells, brain regions, or social environments, or using some combination of these levels of analysis.

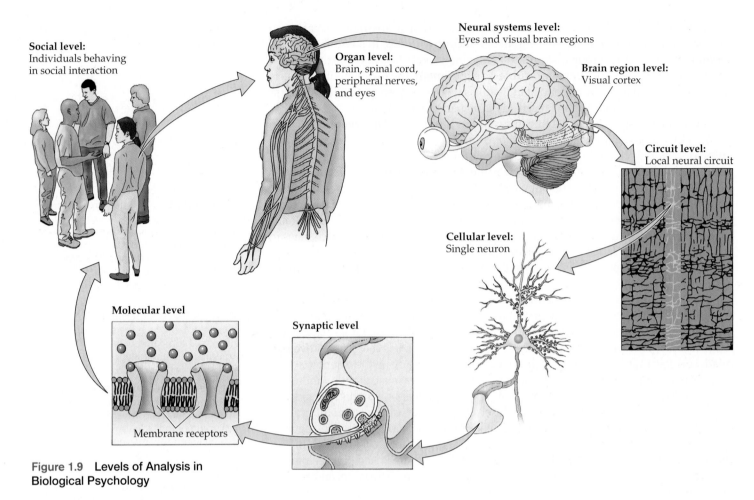

Social level:
Individuals behaving
in social interaction

Organ level:
Brain, spinal cord,
peripheral nerves,
and eyes

Neural systems level:
Eyes and visual brain regions

Brain region level:
Visual cortex

Circuit level:
Local neural circuit

Cellular level:
Single neuron

Molecular level

Membrane receptors

Synaptic level

Figure 1.9 Levels of Analysis in
Biological Psychology

differences. For example, how is the presence (or absence) of color vision related to the life of a species? At the same time, other investigators trace out brain structures and networks involved in different visual tasks. Still other scientists try to understand the electrical and chemical events that occur in the brain during vision.

Animal research is crucial for life sciences research, including biological psychology

Because we will draw on animal research throughout this book, we should comment on some of the ethical issues of experimentation on animals. Human beings' involvement and concern with other species predates recorded history. Early humans had to study animal behavior and physiology in order to escape some species and hunt others. To study biological bases of behavior inevitably requires research on animals of other species, as well as on human beings. Psychology students usually underestimate the contributions of animal research to psychology because the most widely used introductory psychology textbooks often present major findings from animal research as if they were obtained with human subjects (Domjan and Purdy, 1995).

A vocal minority of people believe that research with animals, even if it does lead to lasting benefits, is unethical. Others, like Peter Singer in his influential book *Animal Liberation* (1975), argue that animal research is acceptable only when it produces immediate and measurable benefits. The problem with this perspective is that we have no way of predicting which experiments will lead to a breakthrough. The whole point of studying the unknown is that it is *unknown*; there is a long history of chance observation, based on the steady accumulation of basic knowledge, leading to unexpected benefits.

Of course, researchers have an obligation to minimize the discomfort of their animal subjects, and ironically enough, animal research has provided us with drugs and techniques that make most research painless for lab animals, while also leading to improved veterinary care for our animal companions (Sunstein and Nussbaum, 2004). Researchers are also subject to continual ethical oversight, and they are bound by animal protection legislation. They also adhere to nationally mandated animal care policies, formally adopted by virtually all university administrations, that emphasize the use of as few animals as possible without jeopardizing research integrity, and the use of the simplest species that can answer the questions under study.

As human beings with the full range of emotions and empathetic feelings toward animals, we all wish there was an alternative to the use of animals in research. But if we want to understand how the nervous system works, we have to actually study it, in detail. The life sciences would slow to a crawl without the basic knowledge that we derive from studying animals.

Looking Forward: A Glimpse inside the Mind's Machine

Our mission in this book is to acquaint you with the broad topic of biological psychology, from historical underpinnings to cutting-edge investigations of the most complex aspects of our intellect. Along the way, we are going to touch on some of the most interesting questions in modern neuroscience, including these:

- How does the nervous system capture, process, and represent information about the environment? For example, sometimes brain damage causes a person to lose the ability to identify other people's faces; what does that tell us about how the brain recognizes faces?

- How does sexual orientation develop? Some brain regions are different in heterosexual versus homosexual men; what do those differences tell us about the development of human sexual orientation?

- What brain sites and activities underlie feelings and emotional expression? Are particular parts of the brain active in romantic love, for example (**Figure 1.10a**)?

- Some people suffer damage to the brain and afterward seem alarmingly unconcerned about dangerous situations and unable to judge the emotions of other people. What parts of the brain are damaged to cause such changes?

- How does the brain manage to change during learning, and how are memories retrieved?

How's it going?

1. What are the three general forms of research studies in biological psychology? What is the issue of "causality"? How do the three research perspectives inform and shape one another?

2. Define *independent variable*, *dependent variable*, *control group*, *within-subjects experiment*, and *between-subjects experiment*.

3. What is the general principle behind reductionism? How does this influence the level of analysis at which a researcher works. And for that matter, what is meant by "level of analysis"?

4. Consider both sides of the debate over animal research, weighing the pros and cons of the "for" and "against" positions. How do you think animal use should be regulated?

(a) The parts of the brain highlighted here become especially active when a person thinks about his or her romantic partner.

(b) Different brain regions are activated when people perform four different language tasks.

Figure 1.10 **"Tell Me, Where Is Fancy Bred?"** (Images from Bartels and Zeki, 2000, and courtesy of Marcus Raichle.)

Hearing words

Seeing words

Reading words

Generating words

A Bright Idea The symbolic lightbulb coming on over someone's head, representing a sudden insight or idea, is an especially apt metaphor for the functioning of the brain, given the lightbulb's rapid action and ability to penetrate the gloom (both literal and metaphorical). This particular lightbulb, in a fire station in Livermore, California, is the world's longest-burning bulb (you can check in on it, live, at http://www.centennialbulb.org/cam. htm). It has been continually lit for more than 110 years—since the dawn of the scientific discipline of biological psychology.

• Why are different brain regions active during different language tasks (**Figure 1.10b**)?

The relationship between the brain and behavior is, on the one hand, very mysterious because it is difficult to understand how a physical device, the brain, could be responsible for our subjective experiences of fear, love, and awe. Perhaps it is the "everyday miracle" aspect of the topic that has generated so much folk wisdom—and unfounded mythology—about the brain. For example, the oft-repeated claim that we normally use only 10% of the brain is total nonsense; brain scans show that the entire brain is active most of the time while we go about normal daily activities. There are lots of other examples of commonplace beliefs about the brain. We've compiled a few of these in **Table 1.1**; no doubt you can think of others—some of which are unfounded, interspersed with others that are true but may sound improbable.

Of course, it wasn't long ago that the idea of making light from electricity seemed far-fetched too. With each passing year, technological developments and the progress of thousands of neuroscientists in labs around the world provide a clearer view of what is happening when a lightbulb goes on in the mind and someone has a clever idea. Our hope for this book is that it will turn on a few lightbulbs for you too.

TABLE 1.1 Neuromythology: Facts or Fables?

Some human nerve cells are more than 3 feet long.	True
Nerve impulses travel at the speed of light.	False
More people die each year from the use of legal drugs than illegal drugs.	True
Our bodies make chemicals that are similar in structure to heroin and marijuana	True
Testosterone is made only by males, and estrogen is made only by females.	False
Once our brains are developed, we can never grow new nerve cells.	False
Some people are incapable of feeling pain.	True
Different parts of the tongue are specialized to recognize certain tastes.	False
Dogs are color-blind.	False
Each side of the brain controls the muscles on the opposite side of the body.	True
There are no anatomical differences between men's and women's brains.	False
Some people are "born gay."	Uncertain
During sleep the brain is relatively inactive.	Not always
Sleepwalkers are acting out dreams.	False
Prolonged sleep deprivation will make you temporarily crazy.	False
Some animals can have half their brain asleep and the other half awake.	True
The left side of the face is more emotionally expressive than the right side.	True
All cultural groups recognize the same facial expressions for various emotions.	Uncertain
Scientists are not sure why antidepressant drugs work.	True
Some people are incapable of producing any new memories.	True
Each memory is stored in its own brain cells.	False (probably)
A stimulating environment can change the structure of an animal's brain.	True
We can take in a whole visual scene in just a single glance.	False
My brain decides what I will do next, before my conscious self is aware of the decision.	Uncertain
People are "right-brained" or "left-brained."	False
A child can have half of the brain removed and still develop normal intelligence.	True

Recommended Reading

Blackmore, S. (2011). *Consciousness: An Introduction* (2nd ed.). New York, NY: Oxford University Press.

Carter, R., Aldridge, S., Page, M., and Parker, S. (2009). *The Human Brain Book.* London, England: Dorling Kindersley.

Decety, J., and Cacioppo, J. T. (2011). *The Oxford Handbook of Social Neuroscience.* New York, NY: Oxford University Press.

Doidge, N. (2007). *The Brain That Changes Itself.* New York, NY: Penguin.

Finger, S. (2001). *Origins of Neuroscience.* New York, NY: Oxford University Press.

Gallagher, S. (2006). *How the Body Shapes the Mind.* New York, NY: Oxford University Press.

Koch, C. (2012). *Consciousness: Confessions of a Romantic Reductionist.* Cambridge, MA: MIT Press.

Mandler, G. (2007). *A History of Modern Experimental Psychology: From James and Wundt to Cognitive Science.* Cambridge, MA: MIT Press, 2007.

CHAPTER **1** VISUAL SUMMARY

You should be able to relate each summary to the adjacent illustration, including structures and processes. If you need to review, go to the figures indicated and read the accompanying text.

mindsmachine.com/vs1

1 **Biological psychology** is a branch of **neuroscience** that focuses on the biological bases of behavior. It is closely related to many other neuroscience disciplines. Review **Figure 1.1, Animation 1.2**

2 Although humans have wondered about the control of behavior for thousands of years, only comparatively recently has a mechanistic view of the brain taken hold. Review **Figure 1.3**

3 The concept of **localization of function**, which originated in **phrenology**—despite obvious flaws with the phrenologists' methodology—was an important milestone for biological psychology. Today we know that the part of the brain that shows a *peak* of activity varies in a predictable way depending on what task we're doing. Review **Figure 1.4**

4 Localization of cognitive functions remains a major focus of biological psychology. With modern imaging technology and a more carefully validated understanding of cognitive abilities, a detailed view of the organization of the brain is emerging. Review **Figure 1.4**

6 Although genes can have a major impact on brain function, it is clear that experience physically alters the brain, and that genetically identical people will not necessarily suffer from the same brain disorders. Review **Figure 1.7**

5 The prevalence of neurological and psychiatric disorders exacts a very high emotional and economic toll. Review **Figure 1.6**

7 Biological psychologists balance three general research perspectives—**correlation, somatic intervention,** and **behavioral intervention**—in designing their research. Review **Figure 1.8**

8 Research in biological psychology is conducted at **levels of analysis** ranging from molecular events to the functioning of the entire brain and complex social situations. Review **Figure 1.9**

Go to **mindsmachine.com** for study questions, quizzes, flashcards, and other resources.

2

Cells and Structures:
The Anatomy of the Nervous System

Peering into Simon's Mind

Simon had been complaining about feeling a bit odd all day; he thought perhaps he was coming down with a bug. But when he collapsed unconscious to the floor of the lunchroom at his office and began twitching and jerking, showing the classic signs of a seizure, it was clear that he had a much bigger problem than the flu. By the time Simon arrived at the hospital, the seizure had stopped, and although he was confused and slow to respond to commands, he didn't seem to be in distress. But Simon was in his thirties and had never had a seizure before, or any other illness. In the emergency room, Simon smiled at Dr. Higgs, the attending neurologist, and offered to shake her hand. Alarmed by what she observed, Dr. Higgs ordered an emergency brain scan: Simon could offer only half a smile, because only the left side of his face was working, and he was unable to grip Dr. Higgs's hand at all.

Although we now know quite a bit about the organization of basic functions, the brain's control of complex cognition remains mostly a tantalizing mystery. However, the advent of sophisticated brain-imaging technology has infused new vigor into the search for answers to fundamental questions about brain organization: Does each brain region control a specific behavior? Conversely, can every behavior be linked to a particular brain region? Or do some regions act as general-purpose processors? Is everybody's brain organized in the same way? Can an understanding of brain organization offer clues to what's happening to Simon?

To see a video, go to

mindsmachine.com/2.1
Inside the Brain

Almost everything about you—your thoughts, feelings, and behavior, however serious or silly—is the product of the functioning of the three pounds of tissue inside your head, the most complicated object in the known universe. In this chapter we'll have a look at the structure of the brain from several different perspectives: the brain's cellular composition, its major anatomical divisions, and its appearance in computerized brain imaging. In later chapters we will build on this information as we learn how cells within the brain communicate through electrical (see Chapter 3) and chemical (see Chapter 4) signals.

The Nervous System Is Composed of Cells

neuron or nerve cell   The basic unit of the nervous system, each composed of receptive extensions called dendrites, an integrating cell body, a conducting axon, and a transmitting axon terminal.

glial cells   Also called *glia*. Nonneuronal brain cells that provide structural, nutritional, and other types of support to the brain.

synapse   The cellular location at which information is transmitted from a neuron to another cell.

To see the brain in 3D, go to

mindsmachine.com/2.2
Brain Explorer

All of your organs and muscles are in communication with the nervous system, which, like all other living tissue, is made up of cells. The most important of these are the **neurons** (**nerve cells**), arranged into the neural circuits that underlie the simplest and the most complex of behaviors. Each neuron receives inputs from many other neurons, integrates those inputs, and then distributes the processed information to other neurons. Your brain uses 100–150 billion of these tiny little information-processing units to handle vast amounts of information with apparent ease. There appears to be a similarly huge number of **glial cells** (sometimes called *glia*) in the human brain, providing a variety of support functions and also participating in information processing. Because neurons are larger and produce readily measured electrical signals, we know much more about them than about glial cells.

An important early controversy in neuroscience concerned the functional independence of individual neurons: Was each neuron a discrete component? Or were the cells of the nervous system fused together into larger functional units, like continuous circuits? Using then newly developed techniques for labeling the fine details of individual neurons, the celebrated Spanish anatomist Santiago Ramón y Cajal (1852–1934) was able to show that although neurons come very close together, they are not quite *continuous* with one another. Instead, Ramón y Cajal and his contemporaries showed (1) that the neurons and other cells of the brain are structurally, metabolically, and functionally independent; and (2) that information is transmitted from neuron to neuron across tiny gaps, later named **synapses**—a notion that came to be known as the *neuron doctrine*.

It has been estimated that the brain has 10^{15} synapses. This is a remarkably large number: if you gathered that many grains of sand, each a millimeter in diameter, they would fill a cube with each side longer than an American football field. These vast networks of connections are responsible for all of humanity's achievements.

The neuron has four principal divisions

Like any other cell, a neuron contains DNA inside a cell nucleus, as well as a wide assortment of organelles that are used to produce energy and proteins for cellular activities. But the neuron also has some unique and highly specialized features that allow it to collect signals from multiple sources, integrate these signals, and distribute the processed information to other cells. These information-processing features, illustrated in **Figure 2.1**, can be viewed as belonging to four functional zones:

Nineteenth-Century Drawings of Neurons   Santiago Ramón y Cajal perfected methods for visualizing the detailed structure of individual neurons. Ramón y Cajal and his collaborators proposed that neurons are discrete cells that communicate via tiny contacts, which were later named *synapses*.

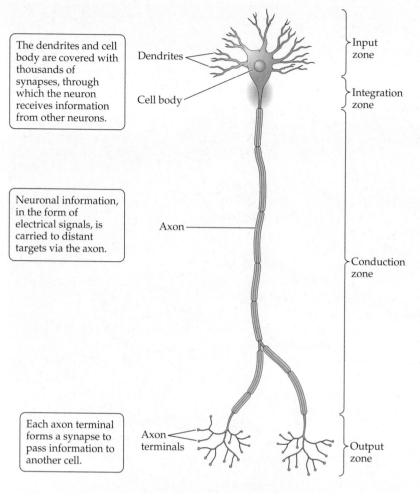

The dendrites and cell body are covered with thousands of synapses, through which the neuron receives information from other neurons.

Neuronal information, in the form of electrical signals, is carried to distant targets via the axon.

Each axon terminal forms a synapse to pass information to another cell.

Dendrites

Cell body

Axon

Axon terminals

Input zone

Integration zone

Conduction zone

Output zone

Figure 2.1 The Major Parts of the Neuron

1. **Input zone**. At cellular extensions called **dendrites** (from the Greek *dendron*, "tree"), neurons receive information from other neurons. Dendrites may be elaborately branched, to accommodate synapses from many other neurons.

2. **Integration zone**. In addition to receiving additional synaptic inputs, the neuron's **cell body** (or **soma**, plural *somata*) integrates (combines) the information that has been received to determine whether to send a signal of its own.

3. **Conduction zone**. A single extension, the **axon** (or **nerve fiber**), conducts the cell's output information, in the form of electrical impulses, away from the cell body.

4. **Output zone**. Specialized swellings at the ends of the axon, called the **axon terminals** (or *synaptic boutons*), transmit the cell's signals across synapses to other cells.

There are hundreds of different forms of neurons, their shapes reflecting the functions that they are specialized to perform. For example, **motoneurons** (also called *motor neurons*) are large and have long axons reaching out to synapse on muscles, causing muscular contractions. As the name implies, **sensory neurons** are specialized to gather sensory information, and they have very diverse shapes, depending on whether they detect light or sound or touch and so on. Most of the neurons in the brain are **interneurons**, analyzing information gathered from one set of neurons and communicating with others. The axons of interneurons may measure only a few micrometers (μm; one micrometer is a millionth of a meter), while motoneurons and sensory neurons may have axons a meter or more long, conveying information to and from the most distant parts of the body. In general, larger neurons tend to have more-complex inputs and outputs, cover greater distances, and/or convey information more rapidly than smaller neurons. The relative sizes of some of the neural structures that we will be discussing throughout the book are illustrated in **Figure 2.2**.

input zone The part of a neuron that receives information, from other neurons or from specialized sensory structures.

dendrite An extension of the cell body that receives information from other neurons.

integration zone The part of a neuron that initiates nerve electrical activity.

cell body or soma The region of a neuron that is defined by the presence of the cell nucleus.

conduction zone The part of a neuron over which the nerve's electrical signal may be actively propagated.

axon Also called *nerve fiber*. A single extension from the nerve cell that carries action potentials from the cell body toward the axon terminals.

output zone The part of a neuron at which the cell sends information to another cell.

axon terminal Also called *synaptic bouton*. The end of an axon or axon collateral, which forms a synapse on a neuron or other target cell.

motoneuron Also called *motor neuron*. A neuron that transmits neural messages, to muscles (or glands).

sensory neuron A nerve cell that is directly affected by changes in the environment, such as light, odor, or touch.

interneuron A nerve cell that is neither a sensory neuron nor a motoneuron; interneurons receive input from and send output to other neurons.

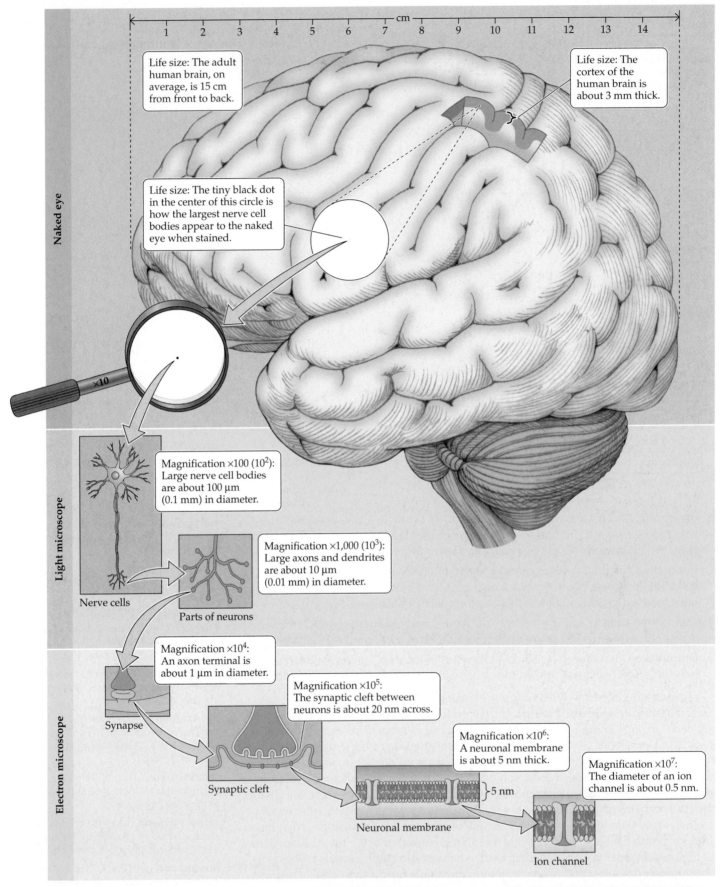

Naked eye

cm
1 2 3 4 5 6 7 8 9 10 11 12 13 14

Life size: The adult human brain, on average, is 15 cm from front to back.

Life size: The cortex of the human brain is about 3 mm thick.

Life size: The tiny black dot in the center of this circle is how the largest nerve cell bodies appear to the naked eye when stained.

×10

Light microscope

Magnification ×100 (10^2): Large nerve cell bodies are about 100 μm (0.1 mm) in diameter.

Nerve cells

Parts of neurons

Magnification ×1,000 (10^3): Large axons and dendrites are about 10 μm (0.01 mm) in diameter.

Electron microscope

Magnification ×10^4: An axon terminal is about 1 μm in diameter.

Synapse

Magnification ×10^5: The synaptic cleft between neurons is about 20 nm across.

Synaptic cleft

Magnification ×10^6: A neuronal membrane is about 5 nm thick.

5 nm

Neuronal membrane

Magnification ×10^7: The diameter of an ion channel is about 0.5 nm.

Ion channel

Figure 2.2   Sizes of Some Neural Structures and the Units of Measure and Magnification Used in Studying Them

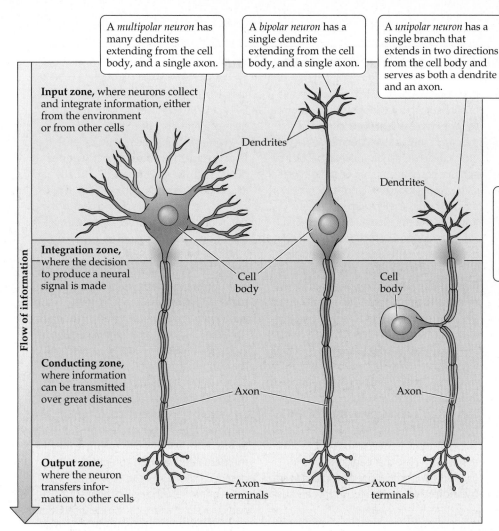

A *multipolar neuron* has many dendrites extending from the cell body, and a single axon.

A *bipolar neuron* has a single dendrite extending from the cell body, and a single axon.

A *unipolar neuron* has a single branch that extends in two directions from the cell body and serves as both a dendrite and an axon.

Figure 2.3   Neurons Are Classified into Three Principal Types

Input zone, where neurons collect and integrate information, either from the environment or from other cells

Dendrites

Dendrites

All neurons have the same four functional zones—*input, integration, conduction,* and *output*—although they are organized in different ways.

Flow of information

Integration zone, where the decision to produce a neural signal is made

Cell body

Cell body

Conducting zone, where information can be transmitted over great distances

Axon

Axon

Output zone, where the neuron transfers information to other cells

Axon terminals

Axon terminals

multipolar neuron   A nerve cell that has many dendrites and a single axon.

bipolar neuron   A nerve cell that has a single dendrite at one end and a single axon at the other end.

unipolar neuron   Also called *monopolar neuron*. A nerve cell with a single branch that leaves the cell body and then extends in two directions; one end is the input zone, and the other end is the output zone.

presynaptic   Referring to the region of a synapse that releases neurotransmitter.

In addition to size, anatomists classify neurons according to three general shapes, each specialized for a particular kind of information processing (**Figure 2.3**):

1. **Multipolar neurons** have many dendrites and a single axon. They are the most common type of neuron.

2. **Bipolar neurons** have a single dendrite at one end of the cell and a single axon at the other end. Bipolar neurons are especially common in sensory systems, such as vision.

3. **Unipolar neurons** (also called monopolar) have a single extension (or process), usually thought of as an axon, that branches in two directions after leaving the cell body. One end is the input zone with branches like dendrites; the other, the output zone. Unipolar neurons transmit touch information from the body into the spinal cord.

In all three types of neurons, the dendrites are the input zone. In multipolar and bipolar cells, the cell body also receives synapses, so it is also part of the input zone. Some of the techniques used to visualize neurons are discussed in **Box 2.1**.

Information is received through synapses

A neuron's dendrites reflect the complexity of the inputs that are received. Some simple neurons have just a couple short dendritic branches, while others have huge and complex dendritic trees covered in many thousands of synaptic contacts from other neurons. At each synapse, information

5 cm

Mammalian Brain Sizes Vary 100,000-Fold   Shown here, in ascending order of brain size: common shrew, sugar glider, platypus, chimpanzee, human, bottlenose dolphin, and elephant. (From www.brainmuseum.org.)

BOX 2.1 Visualizing the Cellular Structure of the Brain

In the mid-1800s, dyes used to color fabrics provided a breakthrough in anatomical studies. Preserved nerve cells treated with these dyes suddenly become vivid, and hidden parts become evident. Different dyes have special affinities for different parts of the cell, such as membranes, the cell body, or the sheaths surrounding axons.

Two traditional cell stains allow detailed study of the size and shape of neurons. **Golgi stains** fill the whole cell, including details such as dendritic spines (Figure A). For reasons that remain a mystery, this technique stains only a small number of cells, each of which stands out in dramatic contrast to adjacent unstained cells, so Golgi staining is useful for identifying the type and shape of cells in a region. In contrast, **Nissl stains** outline *all* cell bodies because the dyes are attracted to RNA distributed within the cell (Figure B). Nissl stains allow us to measure cell body size and the density of cells in particular regions.

In a procedure known as **autoradiography**, cells are manipulated into taking photographs of themselves. For example, in order to identify the parts of the brain that are affected by a newly discovered drug, experimenters might bathe thin sections of brain tissue in a solution with a radioactively labeled form of the drug. Time is allowed for the radioactive drug to reach its target, and then the brain sections are rinsed and placed on slides covered with photographic emulsion. Radioactivity emitted by the labeled drug in the tissue "exposes" the emulsion—like light striking film—producing a collection of fine, dark grains wherever the drug has accumulated.

Another method for labeling cells that have an attribute in common—termed **immunocytochemistry** (**ICC**)—capitalizes on the affinity of antibodies for specific proteins. Brain slices are exposed to antibodies that are selective for a particular protein of interest (it is possible to make antibodies for almost any protein). After allowing time for the antibodies to attach to molecules of the target protein, unattached antibodies are rinsed off and chemical treatments make the antibodies visible. The process reveals only those cells that were making that particular protein (Figure C). A related procedure, called *in situ hybridization*, goes a step further and, using radioactively labeled lengths of nucleic acid (RNA or DNA), identifies neurons in which a gene of interest has been turned on.

When neurons become more active, they tend to express **immediate early genes** (**IEGs**), such as *c-fos*. By using ICC to label the IEG product, researchers can identify brain regions that were active during particular behaviors being performed by the animal shortly before it was sacrificed (Figure D).

Some research questions are most concerned with connections between brain regions, so methods for labeling axon pathways have also been developed. The old way to do this was simply to damage neurons of interest and then look for their degenerating axons. Newer procedures accomplish the same goal via injection of radioactively labeled amino acids into a collection of cell bodies. These radioactive molecules are taken up by the cell, incorporated into proteins, and transported to the tips of the axons (a process termed *anterograde labeling*), where they are then visualized through autoradiography, described above.

Alternatively, the cells of origin of a particular set of axons can be identified using a tract tracer such as **horseradish peroxidase** (**HRP**), an enzyme found in the roots of horseradish. HRP is taken up into the axon at the terminals and transported back to the cell body, where it is readily visualized (a process known as *retrograde labeling*) (Figure E). All along the way, visible reaction products are formed—akin to footprints along a pathway. (Figure A courtesy of Timothy DeVoogd; C from Daniele and MacDermott, 2009; D from Sunn et al., 2002; E courtesy of Dale Sengelaub.)

(A) Golgi stain

(B) Nissl stain

(C) Immunocytochemistry

(D) Expression of *c-fos* in activated cells

(E) HRP-filled motoneuron

is transmitted from the axon terminal of a **presynaptic** neuron to the **postsynaptic** neuron (**Figure 2.4a**). A synapse is typically composed of the following elements (**Figure 2.4b**):

1. The specialized **presynaptic membrane** on the axon terminal of the presynaptic neuron
2. The specialized **postsynaptic membrane** on the dendrite or cell body of the postsynaptic neuron
3. A **synaptic cleft**, the gap of about 20–40 nanometers (nm; one nanometer is a billionth of a meter) that separates the presynaptic and postsynaptic membranes

Within the presynaptic axon terminals are tiny spheres called **synaptic vesicles** containing molecules of **neurotransmitter**, the special chemical with which a presynaptic neuron communicates with postsynaptic cells. The presynaptic neuron signals the postsynaptic cell by fusing many synaptic vesicles to the presynaptic membrane, releasing

postsynaptic   Referring to the region of a synapse that receives and responds to neurotransmitter.

presynaptic membrane   The specialized membrane on the axon terminal of a nerve cell that transmits information by releasing neurotransmitter.

postsynaptic membrane   The specialized membrane on the surface of a nerve cell that receives information by responding to neurotransmitter from a presynaptic neuron.

synaptic cleft   The space between the presynaptic and postsynaptic neurons at a synapse.

synaptic vesicle   A small, spherical structure that contains molecules of neurotransmitter.

neurotransmitter   Also called *synaptic transmitter*, *chemical transmitter*, or simply *transmitter*. The chemical released from the presynaptic axon terminal that serves as the basis of communication between neurons.

(a) Axon terminals typically form synapses on the cell body or dendrites of a postsynaptic neuron.

Presynaptic neuron

Postsynaptic neuron

Axon hillock

On dendrites, synapses may form on dendritic spines or on the dendrite's shaft.

Dendritic spines

(b)

Flow of information

Presynaptic terminal (bouton)

Mitochondrion

Synaptic vesicles

Presynaptic membrane

Synaptic cleft

Neurotransmitter molecules

Postsynaptic membrane

Dendritic spine

Information flows through a synapse from the presynaptic membrane across a gap called the *synaptic cleft* to the postsynaptic membrane.

(c) This electron micrograph shows a synapse with some structures color coded.

Figure 2.4   Synapses

their contents into the synaptic cleft (see Figure 2.4b). After crossing the cleft, the released neurotransmitter interacts with matching **neurotransmitter receptors**, special protein molecules that stud the postsynaptic membrane. These receptors capture and react to molecules of the neurotransmitter, altering the level of excitation of the postsynaptic neuron and making the neuron more or less likely to release neurotransmitter from its own axon terminals.

The configuration of synapses on a neuron's dendrites and cell body is constantly changing: in response to new patterns of synaptic activity and the formation of new neural circuits, synapses come and go, and dendrites change their shape. We use the general term **neural plasticity** to refer to this capacity for continual remodeling of the connections between neurons. We will take a much more detailed look at neurotransmission in Chapters 3 and 4.

The axon is specialized for integrating and transmitting information

Most neurons feature a distinctive cone-shaped hump on the cell body, called the **axon hillock** ("little hill"), from which the neuron's axon projects. The hillock has unique properties that allow it to gather and integrate incoming information from the synapses on the dendrites and cell body, and convert those inputs into a code of electrical impulses that we'll describe in detail in Chapter 3. These electrical signals race down the axon toward the targets that the neuron is said to **innervate**.

The axon itself is a narrow tube that may divide into branches near the end, called **axon collaterals**. Various important substances, such as enzymes and structural proteins, are conveyed inside the axon from the cell body, where they are produced, to the axon terminals, where they are used. This **axonal transport** works in both directions, also carrying used materials back to the cell body for recycling. So the axon has two quite different functions: the rapid transmission of electrical signals along the membrane, and the much slower transportation of substances *within* the axon, to and from the axon terminals.

Glial cells protect and assist neurons

As the name *glial cell* suggests (the Greek *glia* means "glue"), early neuroscientists thought of glial cells as mostly filler, holding the nervous system together. But we now know that glial cells are much more important than that. Glial cells directly affect neuronal functioning by providing neurons with raw materials, chemical signals, and specialized structural components. These diverse functions are accomplished by four basic classes of glial cells (**Figure 2.5**).

Two of the four types of glia—**oligodendrocytes** and **Schwann cells**—wrap around axons to provide **myelin**, a fatty insulating substance. The myelin sheaths give the axon the appearance of a string of slender beads. Between adjacent beads, small uninsulated patches of axonal membrane, called **nodes of Ranvier**, remain exposed (**Figure 2.5a**). Within the brain and spinal cord, myelination is provided by the oligodendrocytes, each cell typically supplying myelin beads to several nearby axons (also illustrated in Figure 2.5a). In the rest of the body, it is Schwann cells that do the ensheathing, with each Schwann cell wrapping itself around an axon to provide a single bead of myelin. But whether it is provided by oligodendrocytes or by Schwann cells, myelination has the same result: a large increase in the speed with which electrical signals pass down the axon, jumping from one node to the next. So it's not surprising that anything that interferes with the myelin sheath, such as the demyelinating disease **multiple sclerosis**, can have catastrophic consequences for the individual, just as losing the outer insulation from a computer cable can cause short circuits and the loss of vital information.

The other two types of glial cells—astrocytes and microglial cells—perform more diverse functions in the brain. **Astrocytes** (from the Greek *astron*, "star") weave around and between neurons with tentacle-like extensions (**Figure 2.5b**). Some astrocytes stretch between neurons and fine blood vessels, controlling local blood flow to increase the amount of blood reaching more-active brain regions (Schummers et al., 2008).

neurotransmitter receptor   Also called simply *receptor*. A protein that captures and reacts to molecules of a neurotransmitter or hormone.

neural plasticity   Also called *neuroplasticity*. The ability of the nervous system to change in response to experience or the environment.

axon hillock   The cone-shaped area on the cell body from which the axon originates.

innervate   To provide neural input to.

axon collateral   A branch of an axon.

axonal transport   The transportation of materials from the neuronal cell body to distant regions in the dendrites and axons, and from the axon terminals back to the cell body.

oligodendrocyte   A type of glial cell that forms myelin in the central nervous system.

Schwann cell   A type of glial cell that forms myelin in the peripheral nervous system.

myelin   The fatty insulation around an axon, formed by glial cells. This sheath improves the speed at which nerve impulses are conducted.

node of Ranvier   A gap between successive segments of the myelin sheath where the axon membrane is exposed.

multiple sclerosis   Literally, "many scars"; a disorder characterized by the widespread degeneration of myelin.

astrocyte   A star-shaped glial cell with numerous processes (extensions) that run in all directions.

(a)

Extensions of *oligodendrocytes* form myelin wrapping (blue) on axons (yellow).

Oligodendrocytes

Nodes of Ranvier

Myelin   Axon

The myelin sheath around a myelinated axon has many layers.

(b)

Star-shaped *astrocytes* detect neural activity and regulate adjacent capillaries to control blood flow, supplying neurons with more energy when they are active.

Capillary

Astrocyte

(c)

Microglia

Activated *microglial cells* surround and break down any debris that forms, especially after damage to the brain.

Microglia engulf and destroy debris

Figure 2.5   Glial Cells (Micrograph *a* [*left*] courtesy of Mark Ellisman and the National Center for Microscopy and Imaging Research; [*right*] from Peters et al., 1991.)

Astrocytes also secrete chemicals that modulate neural activity and the formation of synapses (R. D. Fields and Stevens-Graham, 2002; Mauch et al., 2001; Zonta et al., 2003), as well as helping to form the tough outer membranes that swaddle the brain. In contrast, **microglial cells** (or *microglia*) are tiny and mobile (**Figure 2.5c**); their primary job appears to be to contain and clean up sites of injury (Davalos et al., 2005).

Although glial cells perform many beneficial functions, they can also cause problems. For one thing, because they continue to divide in adulthood (unlike neurons), glial cells can give rise to deadly brain tumors. In addition, some glial cells, especially astrocytes, respond to brain injury by changing size—that is, by swelling. This **edema** damages neurons and is responsible for many symptoms of brain injuries.

Neurons and glial cells form information-processing circuits

Supported and influenced by glial cells, and sharing information through synapses, neurons form groups that process information. In Chapter 3 we will turn to the incredible processes by which the basic units of information—electrical signals—are formed, modified, and transmitted by neurons. For complicated high-level processes, these cell assemblies may involve vast numbers of cells and synaptic contacts, combined together in circuits and structures that are visible to the naked eye as the major anatomical components of the nervous system. These major divisions are our next topic.

The Nervous System Extends throughout the Body

In this section we'll describe the **gross neuroanatomy** of the nervous system—the components that are visible to the unaided eye (in this context *gross* means "large," not

How's it going?

1. What are the four "zones" common to all neurons, and what are their functions?

2. Compare and contrast axonal signal transmission and axonal transport.

3. Describe the main components of the synapse. What are some of the specialized structures found on each side of the synapse?

4. What are the names and general functions of the four types of glial cells?

5. What special properties does myelin have?

microglial cells   Also called *microglia*. Extremely small glial cells that remove cellular debris from injured or dead cells.

edema   The swelling of tissue, especially in the brain, in response to injury.

gross neuroanatomy   Anatomical features of the nervous system that are apparent to the naked eye.

(a)

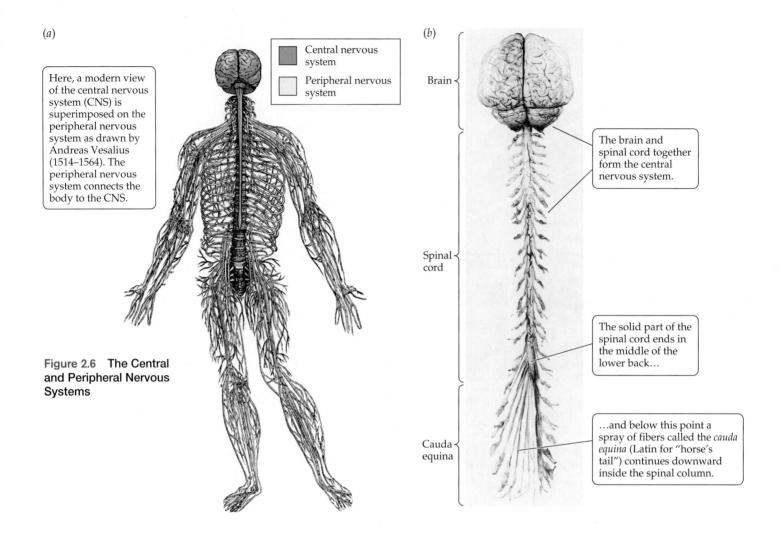

Here, a modern view of the central nervous system (CNS) is superimposed on the peripheral nervous system as drawn by Andreas Vesalius (1514–1564). The peripheral nervous system connects the body to the CNS.

| | Central nervous system |
| | Peripheral nervous system |

Figure 2.6   The Central and Peripheral Nervous Systems

(b)

Brain

The brain and spinal cord together form the central nervous system.

Spinal cord

The solid part of the spinal cord ends in the middle of the lower back…

Cauda equina

…and below this point a spray of fibers called the *cauda equina* (Latin for "horse's tail") continues downward inside the spinal column.

central nervous system (CNS)   The portion of the nervous system that includes the brain and the spinal cord.

peripheral nervous system   The portion of the nervous system that includes all the nerves and neurons outside the brain and spinal cord.

nerve   A collection of axons bundled together outside of the central nervous system.

motor nerve   A nerve that transmits information from the central nervous system to the muscles and glands.

sensory nerve   A nerve that conveys information from the body to the central nervous system.

cranial nerve   A nerve that is connected directly to the brain.

spinal nerve   Also called *somatic nerve*. A nerve that emerges from the spinal cord.

autonomic nervous system   The part of the peripheral nervous system that supplies neural connections to glands and to smooth muscles of internal organs.

"yucky"). The gross view of the entire human nervous system presented in **Figure 2.6** reveals the basic division between the **central nervous system** (**CNS**; consisting of the brain and spinal cord) and the **peripheral nervous system** (everything else).

The peripheral nervous system has three components

The peripheral nervous system consists of **nerves**—collections of axons bundled together—that extend throughout the body. Some nerves, called **motor nerves**, transmit information from the spinal cord and brain to the muscles and glands; others, called **sensory nerves**, convey information from the body to the CNS. The various nerves of the body are divided into three distinct systems:

1. The **cranial nerves**, which are connected directly to the brain
2. The **spinal nerves**, which are connected at regular intervals to the spinal cord
3. The **autonomic nervous system**, which consists of the nerves that connect to the viscera (internal organs)

THE CRANIAL NERVES   There are 12 pairs of cranial nerves—one left-sided and one right-sided nerve in each pair—that arise from the brain and innervate the head and neck directly, without ever joining the spinal cord. As you can see in **Figure 2.7**, some of these nerves are exclusively sensory: the olfactory (I) nerves serve the sense of smell, the optic (II) nerves carry visual information from the eyes, and the vestibulocochlear (VIII) nerves convey auditory and balance information. Five pairs of nerves are exclusively

Figure 2.7   The Cranial Nerves

I **Olfactory** Smell

II **Optic** Vision

III **Oculomotor**
IV **Trochlear**
VI **Abducens**
Muscles that move the eyes

Sensory

Motor

V **Trigeminal** Face, sinuses, teeth

Jaw muscles

XII **Hypoglossal** Tongue muscles

XI **Spinal accessory** Neck muscles

VII **Facial** Tongue, soft palate

Facial muscles, salivary glands, tear glands

X **Vagus** Information from internal organs

Internal organs

IX **Glossopharyngeal** Taste and other mouth sensations

Throat muscles

VIII **Vestibulocochlear** Hearing and balance

motor pathways from the brain: the oculomotor (III), trochlear (IV), and abducens (VI) nerves innervate muscles to move the eye; the spinal accessory (XI) nerves control neck muscles; and the hypoglossal (XII) nerves control the tongue.

The remaining cranial nerves have both sensory *and* motor functions. The trigeminal (V) nerves, for example, transmit facial sensation through some axons but control the chewing muscles through other axons. The facial (VII) nerves control facial muscles and receive taste sensation, and the glossopharyngeal (IX) nerves receive sensation from the throat and control the muscles there. The vagus (X) nerve extends far from the head, running to the heart, liver, and intestines. Its long, convoluted route is the reason for its name, which is Latin for "wandering."

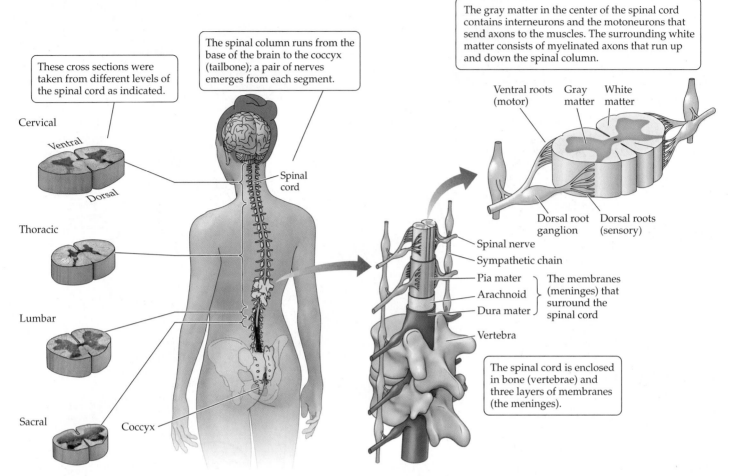

These cross sections were taken from different levels of the spinal cord as indicated.

The spinal column runs from the base of the brain to the coccyx (tailbone); a pair of nerves emerges from each segment.

The gray matter in the center of the spinal cord contains interneurons and the motoneurons that send axons to the muscles. The surrounding white matter consists of myelinated axons that run up and down the spinal column.

Cervical

Ventral

Dorsal

Thoracic

Lumbar

Sacral

Spinal cord

Coccyx

Ventral roots (motor)   Gray matter   White matter

Dorsal root ganglion   Dorsal roots (sensory)

Spinal nerve
Sympathetic chain
Pia mater
Arachnoid   The membranes (meninges) that surround the spinal cord
Dura mater
Vertebra

The spinal cord is enclosed in bone (vertebrae) and three layers of membranes (the meninges).

Figure 2.8 The Spinal Cord and Spinal Nerves

cervical Referring to the topmost 8 segments of the spinal cord, in the neck region.

thoracic Referring to the 12 spinal segments below the cervical (neck) portion of the spinal cord, corresponding to the chest.

lumbar Referring to the 5 spinal segments that make up the upper part of the lower back.

sacral Referring to the 5 spinal segments that make up the lower part of the lower back.

coccygeal Referring to the lowest spinal vertebra (the *coccyx*, also known as the *tailbone*).

sympathetic nervous system The division of the autonomic nervous system that arises from the thoracic and lumbar spinal cord. This division prepares the body for immediate action.

THE SPINAL NERVES   An additional 31 pairs of nerves—again, one member of each pair serves each side of the body—emerge from the spinal cord through regularly spaced openings along both sides of the backbone (**Figure 2.8**). Each nerve is made up of a group of motor fibers, projecting from the ventral (front) spinal cord to the organs and muscles, and a group of sensory fibers that enter the dorsal (rear) part of the spinal cord. Spinal nerves are named according to the segments of the spinal cord to which they are connected. There are 8 **cervical** (neck), 12 **thoracic** (trunk), 5 **lumbar** (lower back), 5 **sacral** (pelvic), and 1 **coccygeal** (bottom) spinal segments. The name of each spinal nerve reflects the position of the spinal cord segment to which it is connected; for example, the nerve connected to the twelfth thoracic segment is called *T12*, the nerve connected to the seventh cervical segment is *C7*, and so on. After leaving the spinal cord, axons from the spinal nerves spread out in the body and may join with axons from different spinal nerves to form the various peripheral nerves.

THE AUTONOMIC NERVOUS SYSTEM   Although it is "autonomous" in the sense that we don't have very much conscious, voluntary control over its actions, the autonomic nervous system is the brain's main system for controlling the organs of the body. These control functions are divided into two major divisions—the *sympathetic* and *parasympathetic* nervous systems—that act more or less in opposition (**Figure 2.9**).

Axons of the **sympathetic nervous system** exit from the middle parts of the spinal cord, travel a short distance, and then innervate the *sympathetic ganglia* (small clusters of neurons found outside the CNS), which run in two chains up the spinal cord, one on each side (Figure 2.9, left). Axons from the sympathetic ganglia then course throughout the body, innervating all the major organ systems. In general, sympathetic innervation prepares the body for immediate action: blood pressure increases, the pupils of the

Figure 2.9   The Autonomic Nervous System

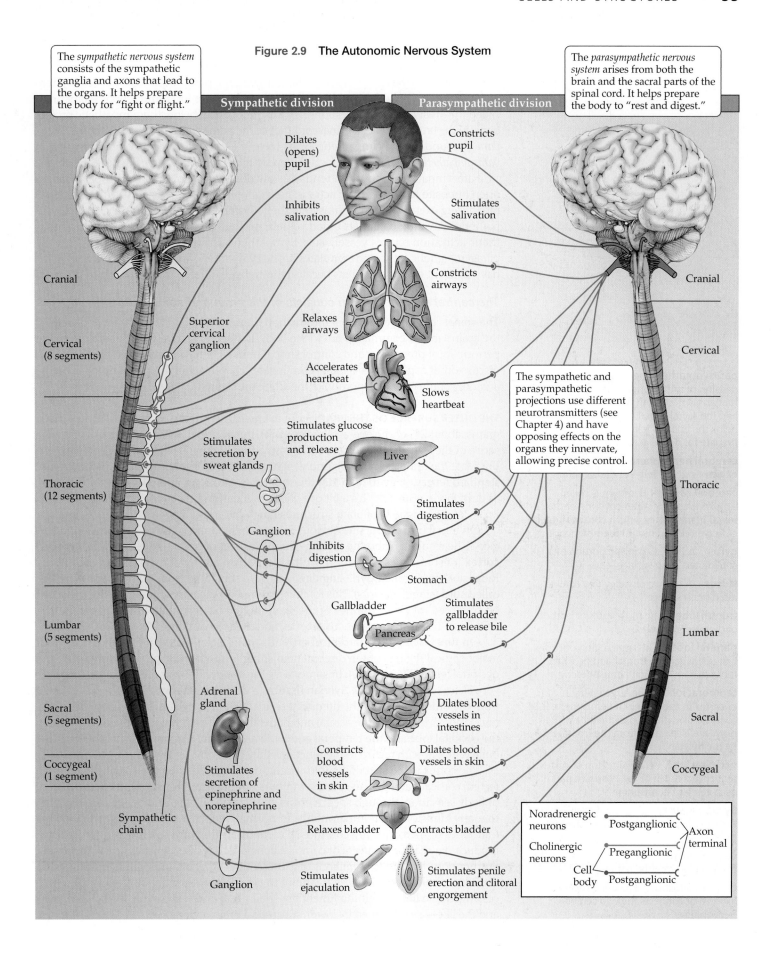

The *sympathetic nervous system* consists of the sympathetic ganglia and axons that lead to the organs. It helps prepare the body for "fight or flight."

The *parasympathetic nervous system* arises from both the brain and the sacral parts of the spinal cord. It helps prepare the body to "rest and digest."

Sympathetic division

Parasympathetic division

Dilates (opens) pupil

Constricts pupil

Inhibits salivation

Stimulates salivation

Cranial

Cranial

Superior cervical ganglion

Cervical (8 segments)

Cervical

Constricts airways

Relaxes airways

Accelerates heartbeat

Slows heartbeat

The sympathetic and parasympathetic projections use different neurotransmitters (see Chapter 4) and have opposing effects on the organs they innervate, allowing precise control.

Stimulates glucose production and release

Stimulates secretion by sweat glands

Liver

Thoracic (12 segments)

Thoracic

Stimulates digestion

Ganglion

Inhibits digestion

Stomach

Gallbladder

Stimulates gallbladder to release bile

Pancreas

Lumbar (5 segments)

Lumbar

Adrenal gland

Dilates blood vessels in intestines

Sacral (5 segments)

Dilates blood vessels in skin

Sacral

Constricts blood vessels in skin

Stimulates secretion of epinephrine and norepinephrine

Coccygeal (1 segment)

Coccygeal

Sympathetic chain

Relaxes bladder

Contracts bladder

Ganglion

Stimulates ejaculation

Stimulates penile erection and clitoral engorgement

Noradrenergic neurons

Cholinergic neurons

Postganglionic

Preganglionic

Cell body

Postganglionic

Axon terminal

eyes widen, and the heart quickens. This set of reactions is sometimes called simply the "fight or flight" response.

In contrast to the effects of sympathetic activity, the **parasympathetic nervous system** generally helps the body to relax, recuperate, and prepare for future action—sometimes called the "rest and digest" response. Arising above and below the sympathetic projections, in the brain and sacral spinal cord (hence the name *parasympathetic*, from the Greek *para*, "around"), parasympathetic axons travel a longer distance before terminating in *parasympathetic ganglia*, usually located close to the organs they serve (Figure 2.9, right).

Parasympathetic activation tends to slow down activity, producing effects that are often opposite to sympathetic actions. For example, sympathetic nerves increase heart rate during exercise and the parasympathetic system slows the heart during rest. Sympathetic activation constricts blood vessels, raising blood pressure, while parasympathetic activation relaxes vessel walls. Sympathetic activation inhibits digestion, while parasympathetic activation stimulates it. The sympathetic and parasympathetic systems have different effects on organs because they release different neurotransmitters.

The central nervous system consists of the brain and spinal cord

The spinal cord funnels sensory information from the body up to the brain and conveys the brain's motor commands out to the body. The spinal cord also contains circuits that perform local processing and control simple units of behavior, such as reflexes. We will discuss other aspects of the spinal cord in later chapters, but for now let's focus on the anatomy of the executive portion of the CNS: the brain.

THE OUTER SURFACE OF THE BRAIN   On average, the human brain weighs only 1,400 grams, about 2% of the average body weight. Put your two fists together and you get a sense of the size of the two **cerebral hemispheres**—smaller than most people expect. But what the brain lacks in size and weight it makes up for in intricacy. Anatomists use standard terminology to help identify structures, locations, and directions in the brain, as described in **Box 2.2**. (It's a bit of a chore, but learning the anatomical lingo now will make later discussions of brain structures much easier to follow.)

On initial inspection, one obvious feature of the brain is its lumpy, convoluted surface—the result of elaborate folding of a thick sheet of brain tissue called the **cerebral cortex** (or sometimes just *cortex*), which is made up mostly of neurons and their fibers. Ridges of tissue, called **gyri** (singular *gyrus*), are separated from each other by crevices called **sulci** (singular *sulcus*). This folding enormously increases the surface area that can be crammed into the confines of the skull; think of a crumpled ball of paper. In fact, about two-thirds of the cerebral cortex is hidden in the depths of these folds.

On functional and anatomical grounds, neuroscientists distinguish among four major cortical regions of the cerebral hemispheres: the **frontal**, **parietal**, **temporal**, and **occipital lobes** (**Figure 2.10**). In some cases the boundaries between adjacent lobes are very clear; for example, the **Sylvian fissure** (a deep sulcus) divides the temporal lobe from the other regions of the hemisphere. Likewise, the **central sulcus** provides a distinct landmark dividing the frontal and parietal lobes. The physical boundaries between the occipital lobe and the temporal and parietal lobes are less obvious, but the lobes are quite different with regard to the functions they perform.

The cortex is the seat of complex cognition. Depending on the specific regions affected, cortical damage can cause symptoms ranging from impairments of movement or body sensation, through speech errors, memory problems, and personality changes, to many kinds of visual impairments. In normal people with undamaged brains, the four lobes of the cortex are continually communicating and collaborating in order to produce the seamless control of complex behavior that distinguishes us as individuals. Furthermore, hundreds of millions of axons connect the left and right hemispheres via the **corpus callosum**, allowing the brain to act as a single entity during complex processing. Some life-sustaining functions—heart rate and respiration, reflexes, balance, and the like—are governed by lower, subcortical brain regions.

parasympathetic nervous system   The division of the autonomic nervous system that arises from both the cranial nerves and the sacral spinal cord. This division helps the body to relax, recuperate, and prepare for future action.

cerebral hemisphere   One of the two halves—right or left—of the forebrain.

cerebral cortex   Sometimes called simply *cortex*. The outer covering of the cerebral hemispheres, which consists largely of nerve cell bodies and their branches.

gyrus   A ridged or raised portion of a convoluted brain surface.

sulcus   A crevice or valley of a convoluted brain surface.

frontal lobe   The most anterior portion of the cerebral cortex.

parietal lobe   The large region of cortex lying between the frontal and occipital lobes in each cerebral hemisphere.

temporal lobe   The large lateral region of cortex in each cerebral hemisphere. It is continuous with the parietal lobe posteriorly and separated from the frontal lobe by the Sylvian fissure.

occipital lobe   A large region of cortex that covers much of the posterior part of each cerebral hemisphere.

Sylvian fissure   Also called *lateral sulcus*. A deep fissure that demarcates the temporal lobe.

central sulcus   A fissure that divides the frontal lobe from the parietal lobe.

corpus callosum   The main band of axons that connects the two cerebral hemispheres.

BOX 2.2 Three Customary Orientations for Viewing the Brain and Body

Because the nervous system is a three-dimensional structure, two-dimensional illustrations and diagrams cannot represent it completely. The brain is usually cut in one of three main planes to obtain a two-dimensional section from this three-dimensional object. Although it takes time and practice to master the lingo, it is useful to know the terminology that applies to these sections, as illustrated in the figure.

The plane that bisects the body into right and left halves is called the **sagittal plane**. The plane that divides the body into a front (anterior) and a back (posterior) part is called by several names: **coronal plane**, *frontal plane*, or *transverse plane*. The third main plane, which divides the brain into upper and lower parts, is called the **horizontal plane**.

In addition, several directional terms are used. **Medial** means "toward the middle" and is contrasted with **lateral**, "toward the side." Relative to one location, a second location is **ipsilateral** if it is on the same side of the body and **contralateral** if on the opposite side of the body. These terms are all relative, as are the terms **superior** ("above") and **inferior** ("below"); for example, the eye is lateral to the nose but medial to the ear, and the mouth is inferior to the nose but superior to the chin.

The head end is referred to as **anterior** or **rostral**, and the tail end is described as **posterior** or **caudal** (from the Latin *cauda*, "tail"). **Proximal** means "near the center," and **distal** means "toward the periphery" or "toward the end of a limb." We call an axon, tract, or nerve **afferent** if it carries information into a region that we're interested in, and **efferent** if it carries information away from the region of interest (a handy way to remember

this is that **e**fferents **e**xit but **a**fferents **a**rrive, relative to the region of interest).

Dorsal means "toward or at the back," and **ventral** means "toward or at the belly." In four-legged animals, such as cats or rats, *dorsal* refers to both the back of the body and the top of the head and brain. For consistency in comparing brains among species, this term is also used to refer to the top of the brain of a human or of a chimpanzee, even though in such two-legged animals the top of the brain is not at the back of the body. Similarly, *ventral* is understood to designate the bottom of the brain of a two-legged as well as of a four-legged animal. (Photographs courtesy of S. Mark Williams and Dale Purves, Duke University Medical Center.)

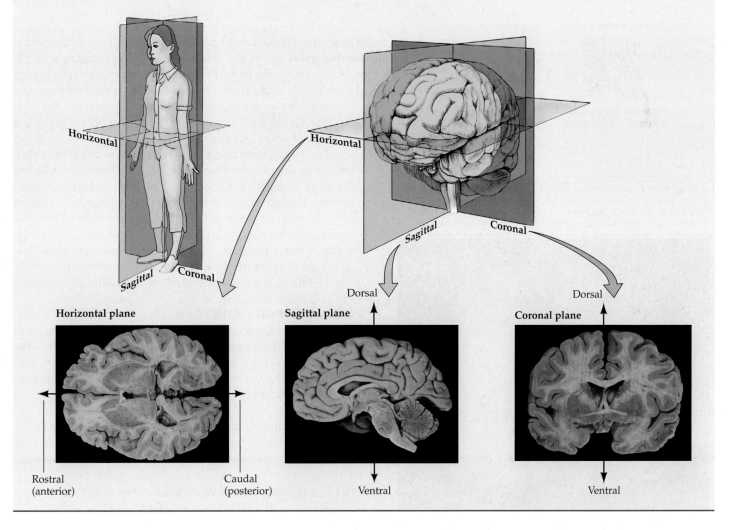

Horizontal plane

Rostral (anterior) — Caudal (posterior)

Sagittal plane

Dorsal — Ventral

Coronal plane

Dorsal — Ventral

postcentral gyrus The strip of parietal cortex, just behind the central sulcus, that receives somatosensory information from the entire body.

precentral gyrus The strip of frontal cortex, just in front of the central sulcus, that is crucial for motor control.

gray matter Areas of the brain that are dominated by cell bodies and are devoid of myelin. Gray matter mostly receives and processes information.

white matter A lighter-colored layer of tissue, consisting mostly of myelin-sheathed axons, that lies underneath the gray matter of the cortex. White matter mostly transmits information.

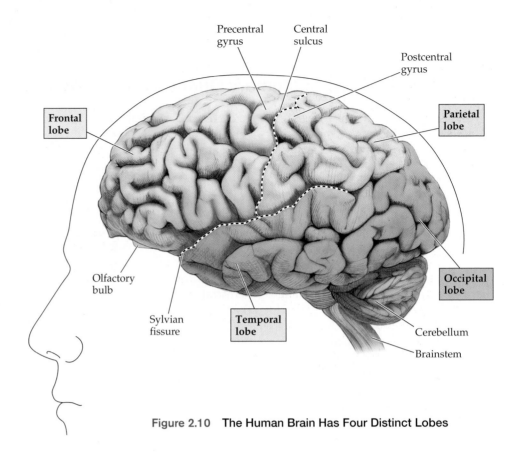

Figure 2.10 The Human Brain Has Four Distinct Lobes

To see a video, go to

mindsmachine.com/2.3
Brain Development

The sense of touch is mediated by a strip of parietal cortex just behind the central sulcus called the **postcentral gyrus** (see Figure 2.10). In front of the central sulcus, the **precentral gyrus** of the frontal lobe is crucial for motor control, organized like a map of the body (Penfield and Rasmussen, 1950). The occipital lobes are crucial for vision, and the temporal lobes receive auditory inputs and help in memory formation. But each lobe of the brain also performs a wide variety of other high-level functions. These will be major topics in later chapters.

Most people have heard brain tissue referred to as **gray matter**. When you cut into a brain, you see some regions (including the outer layers of the cortex) that have a darker grayish shade because they are made up of cell bodies and dendrites (**Figure 2.11**). In contrast, the underlying **white matter** gets its snowy appearance from the whitish fatty myelin that insulates the axons of many neurons. So, a somewhat oversimplified view is that gray matter mostly receives and processes information, while white matter mostly transmits information.

SUBDIVISIONS WITHIN THE BRAIN It can be difficult to understand some of the anatomical distinctions applied to the adult human brain. For example, the part of the brain closest to the *back* of the head is anatomically identified as part of the *fore-brain*. Why? The key to understanding this confusing terminology is to consider how the gross anatomy of the brain develops early in life.

In a very young embryo of any vertebrate, the CNS looks like a tube. The walls of this **neural tube** are made of cells, and the

The lighter-colored interior is *white matter*, packed with the fatty myelin that surrounds axons sending information in and out of the cortex.

Gray matter consists of cell bodies that form the outer layers of the cortex and nuclei within the brain.

Figure 2.11 Gray Matter, White Matter (Photograph courtesy of S. Mark Williams and Dale Purves, Duke University Medical Center.)

Figure 2.12   Divisions of the Human Nervous System in the Embryo and the Adult

interior is filled with fluid. A few weeks after conception, the human neural tube begins to show three separate swellings at the head end (**Figure 2.12a**): the **forebrain**, the **midbrain**, and the **hindbrain**. By about 50 days, the fetal forebrain features two clear subdivisions. At the very front is the **telencephalon** (the Greek term *encephalon* means "brain"), which will become the cerebral hemispheres (consisting of cortex plus some deeper structures). The other part of the forebrain is the **diencephalon**, which will go on to become the thalamus and the hypothalamus.

Similarly, the hindbrain further develops into several large structures: the cerebellum, pons, and medulla. The term **brainstem** usually refers to the midbrain, pons, and medulla combined. **Figures 2.12b, c** show the positions of these structures and their relative sizes in the adult human brain. Even when the brain achieves its adult form, it is still a fluid-filled tube, but a tube of very complicated shape.

The main sections of the brain can be subdivided in turn. We can work our way from the largest, most general divisions of the nervous system on the left of the schematic in Figure 2.12b to more-specific ones on the right.

Within and between the major brain regions are collections of neurons called **nuclei** (singular *nucleus*) and bundles of axons called **tracts**. Recall that outside the CNS,

neural tube   An embryonic structure with subdivisions that correspond to the future forebrain, midbrain, and hindbrain.

forebrain   The frontal division of the neural tube, containing the cerebral hemispheres, the thalamus, and the hypothalamus.

midbrain   The middle division of the brain.

hindbrain   The rear division of the brain, which, in the mature vertebrate, contains the cerebellum, pons, and medulla.

telencephalon   The anterior part of the fetal forebrain, which will become the cerebral hemispheres in the adult brain.

diencephalon   The posterior part of the fetal forebrain, which will become the thalamus and hypothalamus in the adult brain.

brainstem   The region of the brain that consists of the midbrain, the pons, and the medulla.

nucleus   Here, a collection of neuronal cell bodies within the central nervous system (e.g., the caudate nucleus).

tract   A bundle of axons found within the central nervous system.

How's it going?

1. Name and briefly describe the three main parts of the peripheral nervous system. What general function does each part perform?

2. Briefly sketch and describe the anatomical organization of the cranial nerves. How many nerves are there? Now do the same for the spinal nerves.

3. Give some examples of how each division of the autonomic nervous system affects organs of the body.

4. Why does the cortex look so lumpy on the outside?

5. What is special about the pre- and postcentral gyri?

6. Review the fetal development of the brain, and the three major divisions of the brain that arise from the earlier fetal form of the nervous system.

pyramidal cell A type of large nerve cell that has a roughly pyramid-shaped cell body and is found in the cerebral cortex.

cortical column One of the vertical columns that constitute the basic organization of the cerebral cortex.

The six layers of cortex can be distinguished with stains that reveal all cell bodies…

…or with stains that reveal a few neurons in their entirety.

One pyramidal neuron

100 µm   100 µm

Figure 2.13 Layers of the Cerebral Cortex

collections of neurons are called *ganglia*, and bundles of axons are called *nerves*. Unfortunately, the same word *nucleus* can mean either "a collection of neurons in the CNS" or "the spherical DNA-containing organelle within a single cell." You must rely on the context to understand which meaning is intended. Because brain tracts and nuclei are the same in different individuals, and often the same in different species, they have names too (many, many names).

You are probably more interested in the functions of all these parts of the brain than in their names but, as we noted earlier, each region serves more than one function, and our knowledge of the functional organization of the brain is continually being updated with new research findings. So, keeping that caveat in mind, let's briefly survey the functions of specific brain structures, leaving the detailed discussion for later chapters.

The Brain Is Described in Terms of Both Structure and Function

Vertebrates are *bilaterally symmetrical*: our bodies have mirror-image left and right sides. The brain is no exception, and almost all the structures of the brain also come in twos. One important principle of the vertebrate brain is that each side of the brain controls the opposite (or *contralateral*; see Box 2.2) side of the body: the right side of the brain controls and receives sensory information from the left side of the body, while the left side of the brain monitors and controls the right side of the body. In Chapter 15 we'll learn about how the two cerebral hemispheres interact, but for now let's review the various components of the brain and their functions.

The cerebral cortex performs complex cognitive processing

Neuroscientists are only just beginning to understand how the structures and functions of the cerebral cortex accomplish the feats of human cognition. If the human cortex were unfolded, it would occupy an area of about 2,000 square centimeters (315 square inches)—more than 3 times the area of this book's cover. How are all those millions of cells arranged?

Cortical neurons make up six distinct layers, as shown in **Figure 2.13**. Each cortical layer has a unique appearance because it consists of either a band of similar neurons, or a particular pattern of dendrites or axons. For example, the outermost layer, layer I, is distinct because it has few cell bodies; and layers V and VI stand out because of their many neurons with large cell bodies. The most prominent kind of neuron in the cerebral cortex—the **pyramidal cell**—usually has its pyramid-shaped cell body in layer III or V.

In some regions of the cerebral cortex, neurons are organized into regular columns, perpendicular to the layers, that seem to serve as information-processing units (Horton and Adams, 2005). These **cortical columns** extend through the entire thickness of the cortex, from the white matter to the surface. Within each column, most of the synaptic interconnections of neurons are vertical, although there are some horizontal connections as well (Mountcastle, 1979).

Important nuclei are hidden beneath the cerebral cortex

Buried within the cerebral hemispheres are several large gray matter structures, richly connected to each other and to other brain regions, and contributing to a wide variety of behaviors.

One prominent cluster—the **basal ganglia**, consisting primarily of the **caudate nucleus**, the **putamen**, and the **globus pallidus** (**Figure 2.14a**)—plays a critical role in the control of movement, which we will discuss in Chapter 5.

Overlapping and curled around the basal ganglia, the **limbic system** is a loosely defined, widespread network of structures (identified in **Figure 2.14b**) that are involved in emotion and learning. The **amygdala** consists of several subdivisions with quite diverse functions, including emotional regulation (see Chapter 11) and the perception of odor (see Chapter 6). The **hippocampus** and **fornix** are important for learning and memory (discussed in Chapter 13). Other components of the limbic system include a strip of cortex in each hemisphere called the **cingulate gyrus**, which is implicated in many cognitive functions, including the direction of attention (see Chapter 14); and the **olfactory bulb**, which is involved in the sense of smell. Limbic structures near the base of the brain, especially the hypothalamus, help to govern highly motivated behaviors like sex and aggression, and to regulate the hormonal systems of the body.

Toward the medial (middle) and basal (bottom) aspects of the forebrain are found the **thalamus** and the **hypothalamus** (the latter means simply "under thalamus"). You can see the thalamus in **Figure 2.15**, and both the hypothalamus and thalamus in Figures 2.14b and 2.16a. The thalamus is the brain's traffic cop, directing virtually all incoming sensory information to the appropriate regions of the cortex for further processing, and receiving instructions back from the cortex to control which sensory information is transmitted. The small but mighty hypothalamus has a much different role: it is packed with discrete nuclei involved in many vital functions, such as hunger, thirst, temperature regulation, sex, and many more. Furthermore, because the hypothalamus also controls the pituitary gland, it serves as the brain's main interface with the hormonal systems of the body. We'll encounter the hypothalamus again in several later chapters.

The midbrain has sensory and motor systems

Compared to the forebrain and hindbrain, the midbrain doesn't encompass a lot of tissue, but that doesn't mean its components are unimportant. The most prominent features of the midbrain are two pairs of bumps on the dorsal surface—one pair in

basal ganglia A group of forebrain nuclei, including the caudate nucleus, globus pallidus, and putamen, found deep within the cerebral hemispheres.

caudate nucleus One of the basal ganglia; it has a long extension or tail.

putamen One of the basal ganglia.

globus pallidus One of the basal ganglia.

limbic system A loosely defined, widespread group of brain nuclei that innervate each other to form a network.

amygdala A group of nuclei in the medial anterior part of the temporal lobe.

hippocampus A medial temporal lobe structure that is important for learning and memory.

fornix A fiber tract that extends from the hippocampus to the mammillary body.

cingulate gyrus A strip of cortex, found in the frontal and parietal midline, that is part of the limbic system and is implicated in many cognitive functions.

olfactory bulb An anterior projection of the brain that terminates in the upper nasal passages and, through small openings in the skull, provides receptors for smell.

thalamus The brain regions that surround the third ventricle.

hypothalamus Part of the diencephalon, lying ventral to the thalamus.

Figure 2.14 Two Important Brain Systems

(*a*) Lateral view showing planes of section

Figure 2.15 **Inside the Brain** (Photographs courtesy of S. Mark Williams and Dale Purves, Duke University Medical Center.)

(*b*) Horizontal section

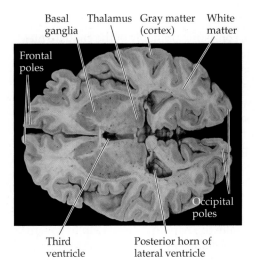

Basal ganglia   Thalamus   Gray matter (cortex)   White matter

Frontal poles

Third ventricle

Posterior horn of lateral ventricle

Occipital poles

(*c*) Coronal (transverse) section

Basal ganglia

Corpus callosum   Caudate nucleus   Putamen

Lateral ventricle   Amygdala   Temporal lobe

How's it going?

1. How are the cells of the cerebral cortex organized?

2. Name the major components of the basal ganglia and the limbic system. What behaviors especially rely on these systems?

3. What functions are served by the thalamus and hypothalamus?

4. Name and describe the general functions of the major components of the midbrain and hindbrain.

---

superior colliculi   Paired gray matter structures of the dorsal midbrain that process visual information.

inferior colliculi   Paired gray matter structures of the dorsal midbrain that process auditory information.

tectum   The dorsal portion of the midbrain consisting of the inferior and superior colliculi.

substantia nigra   A brainstem structure that innervates the basal ganglia and is the source of all dopaminergic projections.

reticular formation   An extensive region of the brainstem (extending from the medulla through the thalamus) that is involved in sleep and arousal.

cerebellum   A structure located at the back of the brain, dorsal to the pons, that is involved in the central regulation of movement.

pons   The portion of the brainstem that connects the midbrain to the medulla.

---

each hemisphere. The more rostral bumps are the **superior colliculi** (singular *colliculus*), and the caudal bumps are the **inferior colliculi** (see **Figure 2.16a**); taken together, the colliculi are referred to as the **tectum** (from the Latin for "roof," because it's atop the midbrain). The superior colliculi process visual information; the inferior colliculi process information about sound.

Two other important midbrain structures that we will discuss later in the book are the substantia nigra and the reticular formation (see Figures 2.14a and 2.16a). The **substantia nigra** is in many ways a part of the basal ganglia, and loss of its neurons (which normally release the neurotransmitter *dopamine* within the forebrain) leads to Parkinson's disease, discussed in Chapter 5. The **reticular formation** (*reticular* means "netlike") is a loose collection of neurons stretching right down into the medulla; reticular neurons are important in a variety of behaviors, including sleep and arousal (see Chapter 10).

The brainstem controls vital body functions

The midsagittal and basal views of the brain in **Figure 2.16** show the hemispheres of the **cerebellum**, which is tucked up under the posterior cortex and attached to the dorsal brainstem. Like the cerebral cortex, the cerebellum is highly convoluted, but it is made up of a simpler three-layered tissue instead of the six layers found in the cortex. The cerebellum has long been known to be crucial for motor coordination and control, but we now know that it also participates in certain aspects of cognition, including learning. The adjacent **pons** (see Figure 2.16) contains important motor control and sensory nuclei, and it is the point of origin for several cranial nerves.

The **medulla** marks the transition from the brain to the spinal cord. In addition to conveying all of the major motor and sensory fibers to and from the body, the medulla contains nuclei that drive such essential processes as respiration and heart rate, which is why brainstem injuries are so often lethal. And like other parts of the brainstem, the medulla gives rise to several cranial nerves.

Specialized Support Systems Protect and Nourish the Brain

The brain is relatively soft and easily damaged. It also needs a steady and substantial supply of fuel in order to maintain normal functioning, and thus keep us alive. Fortunately, the brain is equipped with systems that protect and cushion the brain, and that provide a continual source of energy, nutrients, and important chemicals.

The brain floats within layers of membranes

Within the bony skull and vertebrae, the brain and spinal cord are swaddled by three protective membranes called **meninges** (see Figure 2.8). Between a tough outer sheet

Figure 2.16   Midline and Basal Structures of the Brain

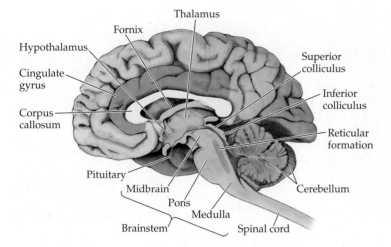

The four lobes of the cerebral cortex are color coded here as in Figure 2.10. In addition, the cingulate gyrus and brainstem are shaded red and yellow, respectively.

(a) Midsagittal (midline) view

Thalamus
Fornix
Hypothalamus
Cingulate gyrus
Corpus callosum
Superior colliculus
Inferior colliculus
Reticular formation
Pituitary
Midbrain
Pons
Medulla
Brainstem
Spinal cord
Cerebellum

(b) Basal view

Midbrain and brainstem structures are especially evident in this view.

Temporal lobe
Olfactory bulb
Medulla
Spinal cord
Frontal lobe
Pituitary
Pons
Cerebellum

called the **dura mater** (in Latin, literally "tough mother") and the delicate **pia mater** ("tender mother") that adheres tightly to the surface of the brain, a webby substance called the **arachnoid** ("spiderweb-like") suspends the brain in a bath of **cerebrospinal fluid** (**CSF**). The brain essentially floats in this watery liquid, protected from moderate impacts by the CSF's shock-absorbing action. However, the meninges can become inflamed by infections, and because the inflammation ends up squeezing the brain, the resultant **meningitis** is a medical emergency. Sometimes the meninges form into quite large tumors; these **meningiomas** are considered to be benign, because they do not invade the brain tissue, but in an enclosed space like the cranium, any mass that takes up space is far from harmless.

The brain relies on two fluids for survival

We've already seen one way that CSF is important to the brain: it acts as a shock absorber. But CSF is also a source of important materials, such as nutrients and signaling chemicals. Inside the brain is a series of chambers—the **ventricular system**—filled with CSF (**Figure 2.17**). Each hemisphere of the brain contains a **lateral ventricle** extending into all four lobes of the hemisphere. The lateral ventricles are lined with a specialized membrane called the **choroid plexus**, which produces CSF by filtering blood. CSF flows from the lateral ventricles into the **third ventricle** (located in the midline) and continues down a narrow passage to the **fourth ventricle**, which lies between the cerebellum and the pons. Just below the cerebellum, three small openings allow CSF to exit the ventricular system and circulate over the outer surface of the brain and spinal cord. CSF is absorbed back into the circulatory system through large veins beneath the top of the skull.

The second crucial fluid for the brain is, of course, blood. Without a continual supply of a high volume of oxygen- and nutrient-rich blood, the tissue of the brain would swiftly die. That's because brain tissue is unusually needy: it accounts for only 2% of the average human body but consumes more than 20% of the body's energy. So the brain is critically dependent on a set of large blood vessels. You can learn more about the brain's elaborate vascular system in **A Step Further 2.1**, on the website.

The general term **stroke** applies to a situation in which a clot, a narrowing, or a rupture interrupts the supply of blood to a discrete brain region,

medulla   The posterior part of the hindbrain, continuous with the spinal cord.

meninges   The three protective membranes—dura mater, pia mater, and arachnoid—that surround the brain and spinal cord.

dura mater   The outermost of the three meninges that surround the brain and spinal cord.

pia mater   The innermost of the three meninges that surround the brain and spinal cord.

arachnoid   The thin covering (one of the three meninges) of the brain that lies between the dura mater and the pia mater.

cerebrospinal fluid (CSF)   The fluid that fills the cerebral ventricles.

meningitis   An acute inflammation of the meninges, usually caused by a viral or bacterial infection.

meningioma   A noninvasive tumor of the meninges.

ventricular system   A system of fluid-filled cavities inside the brain.

lateral ventricle   A complexly shaped lateral portion of the ventricular system within each hemisphere of the brain.

choroid plexus   A specialized membrane lining the ventricles that produces cerebrospinal fluid by filtering blood.

third ventricle   The midline ventricle that conducts cerebrospinal fluid from the lateral ventricles to the fourth ventricle.

fourth ventricle   The passageway within the pons that receives cerebrospinal fluid from the third ventricle and releases it to surround the brain and spinal cord.

stroke   Damage to a region of brain tissue that results from the blockage or rupture of vessels that supply blood to that region.

(*a*) Cerebral ventricles of the brain

The positions of the cerebral ventricles are shown here within an adult brain.

(*b*) A closer view

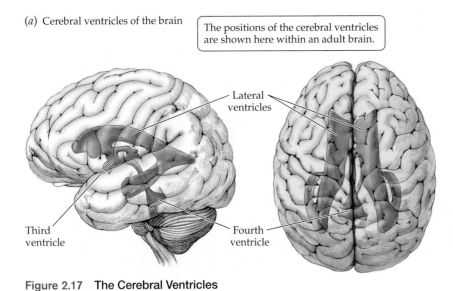

Lateral ventricle

Frontal horn

Temporal horn

Occipital horn

Lateral ventricles

Third ventricle

Choroid plexus

Cerebral aqueduct

Fourth ventricle

CSF

CSF

Cerebrospinal fluid (CSF) is made by the choroid plexus in the lateral ventricles…

…and exits from the fourth ventricle to surround the brain and spinal cord.

Third ventricle

Fourth ventricle

Figure 2.17   The Cerebral Ventricles

How's it going?

1. Name the three meninges, and describe how they're organized. Identify one special characteristic of each.
2. What is CSF? What function does it serve, where does it come from, and where does it go?
3. Describe the ventricular system of the brain.
4. What are the cardinal symptoms of stroke?

blood-brain barrier   The mechanisms that make the movement of substances from blood vessels into brain cells more difficult than exchanges in other body organs, thus affording the brain greater protection from exposure to some substances found in the blood.

computerized axial tomography (CAT or CT)   A noninvasive technique for examining brain structure through computer analysis of X-ray absorption at several positions around the head.

causing the affected region to stop functioning or die. Although the exact effects of stroke depend on the region of the brain that is affected, the five most common warning signs are sudden numbness or weakness, altered vision, dizziness, severe headache, and confusion or difficulty speaking. Effective treatments are available to help restore blood flow and minimize the long-term effects of a stroke, but only if the victim is treated immediately.

Fine vessels and capillaries branching off from the main arteries deliver nutrients and other substances to brain cells and remove waste products. In contrast to capillaries in the rest of the body, capillaries in the brain are highly resistant to the passage of large molecules across their walls and into neighboring neurons. This **blood-brain barrier** probably evolved to help protect the brain from infections and blood-borne toxins, but it also makes the delivery of drugs to the brain more difficult.

Brain-Imaging Techniques Reveal the Structure and Function of the Human Brain

Although techniques for diagnosing medical conditions have been around for decades—X-raying the head and its blood vessels, for example—more recent technological developments have allowed researchers to study the brains of healthy humans too. Some of these techniques are used primarily to identify brain structure; others focus more on tracking changes in brain *activity* as behavior occurs.

CT uses X-rays to reveal brain structure

In **computerized axial tomography** (**CAT** or **CT**), X-ray energy is used to generate images. In a CT scanner, an X-ray source is moved by steps in an arc around the head. At each point, detectors on the opposite side of the head measure the amount of X-ray radiation that is absorbed; this value is proportional to the density of the tissue through which the X-rays passed. When this process is repeated from many angles and the results are mathematically combined, an anatomical map of the brain based on tissue density can be generated by computer (**Figure 2.18a**). CT scans are medium-resolution images, useful for visualizing problems such as strokes, tumors, or cortical shrinkage.

a *Computerized tomography* (CT) helps us spot problems such as strokes or tumors, like the one evident here.

b *Magnetic resonance imaging* (MRI) shows great detail, enabling us to see fine structure and recognize subtle changes in the brain.

c *Functional MRI* (fMRI) detects small changes in brain metabolism. Changes in brain activity associated with visual or auditory stimuli are highlighted in this example.

Anterior 3-D view

Lateral 3-D view of right hemisphere

d *Positron emission tomography* (PET) provides a portrait of the brain's activity. Here, PET shows that metabolic activity is diminished in the brain of a person with Alzheimer's disease.

Normal (horizontal view)

Patient with Alzheimer's disease

e This patient is entering an MRI scanner.

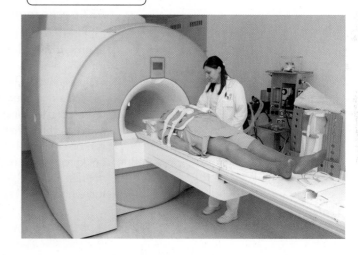

Figure 2.18 Visualizing the Living Human Brain (Images in part *c* courtesy of Semir Zeki.)

Simon, whom we met at the beginning of the chapter, had developed a type of tumor called a *meningioma* that was pressing on and deforming the motor cortex on the left side of his brain. The pressure caused abnormal firing—a *seizure*—that spread to adjacent areas, resulting in unconsciousness. The tumor subsequently impaired the functioning of regions of the motor cortex controlling the muscles of Simon's right arm and the right side of his face, producing his alarming symptoms. Fortunately, his emergency CT scan was able to pinpoint the meningioma within Simon's skull, and later that evening a surgeon removed the tumor in pieces without damaging nearby tissue. Simon experienced immediate improvement and has been healthy ever since.

MRI maps density to deduce brain structure with high detail

Magnetic resonance imaging (**MRI**) provides higher-resolution images than CT, and because MRI uses magnetic fields and radio waves instead of X-rays, MRI also has fewer damaging effects than CT. To make an MRI image of the brain, the person's head is first placed in an extremely powerful magnet that causes all the protons in the brain's tissues to line up in parallel, instead of in their usual random orientations (protons are

To see an animation, go to

mindsmachine.com/2.4
Visualizing the Living Human Brain

magnetic resonance imaging (MRI)
A noninvasive technique for examining brain structure that uses magnetic energy to generate images that reveal some structural details in the living brain.

How's it going?

1. Compare and contrast the main methods for producing still images of the structure of the brain. What do you think are some of the advantages and disadvantages of each method?

2. Compare and contrast the main functional imaging technologies used for visualizing the activity of brain regions. What do you think are some of the advantages and disadvantages of each method?

3. Describe the process that neuroscientists can use to isolate brain activity associated with a specific behavior, as visualized by functional imaging techniques.

found in the nuclei of atoms, especially water in the case of body tissues). Next, the protons are knocked over by a powerful pulse of radio waves. When this pulse is turned off, the protons relax back to their original configuration, emitting radio waves as they go. Detectors surrounding the head measure those radio waves, which differ for tissues of varying densities. This density-based information is then used by a computer to create a detailed cross-sectional view of the brain (**Figure 2.18b**) (Elster and Burdette, 2001). Thanks to their higher resolution, MRI images can reveal subtle changes in the brain, such as the local loss of myelin that is characteristic of multiple sclerosis.

Functional MRI uses local changes in metabolism to identify active brain regions

Functional MRI, which generates images of the brain's activity rather than details of its structure, has revolutionized cognitive neuroscience. Offering both reasonable speed (temporal resolution) and excellent sharpness (spatial resolution), fMRI uses rapidly oscillating magnetic fields to detect small changes in brain metabolism, particularly moment-to-moment oxygen use and blood flow in the most active regions of the brain. As with PET, scientists can use fMRI data to create difference images of the specific activity of different parts of the brain while people engage in various experimental tasks. The detailed activity maps provided by fMRI reveal how networks of brain structures collaborate on complex cognitive processes (**Figure 2.18c**).

PET tracks radioactive substances to produce images of brain activity

Like fMRI, **positron emission tomography** (**PET**) provides a means to visualize the brain's *activity* during behavioral tasks. Short-lived radioactive chemicals are injected into the bloodstream, and radiation detectors encircling the head map the destination of these chemicals in the brain. A particularly effective strategy is to inject a radioactively labeled sugar, glucose, while the subject is engaged in a cognitive task of interest to the researcher. Because the radioactive glucose is selectively taken up and used by the most active parts of the brain, a moment-to-moment color-coded portrait of brain activity can be created (**Figure 2.18d**) (P. E. Roland, 1993). Although PET can't match the detailed resolution of fMRI, it tends to be faster and thus better able to track quick changes in brain activity. Next we'll discuss how precise experimental methods allow researchers to identify brain regions that contribute to specific functions.

RESEARCHERS AT WORK

Subtractive analysis isolates specific brain activity

The advent of modern brain imaging has provided dramatic pictures showing the particular brain regions that are activated during specific cognitive processes; there are many such images in this book. But if you do a PET scan of a normal person, you find that almost all of the brain is active at any given moment (showing that the idea that "we use only 10% of our brain" is nonsense). How do researchers obtain these highly specific images of brain activity?

In order to associate specific brain regions with particular cognitive operations, researchers developed a sort of algebraic technique, in which activity during one behavioral condition is subtracted from activity during a different condition. So, for example, the data from a control PET scan made while a subject was gazing at a blank wall might be subtracted from a PET scan collected while the subject studied a complex visual stimulus. Averaged over enough trials, the specific regions that are almost always active during the processing task become apparent, even though, on casual inspection, a single experimental scan might not look much different from a single control scan (**Figure 2.19**).

functional MRI (fMRI)   Magnetic resonance imaging that detects changes in blood flow and therefore identifies regions of the brain that are particularly active during a given task.

positron emission tomography (PET) A technique for examining brain function that combines tomography with injections of radioactive substances used by the brain.

Figure 2.19   Isolating Specific Brain Activity

Hypothesis

Brain regions engaged in a specific behavior can be isolated by algebraic means, subtracting resting scans from scans during activity.

Test

Subjects are scanned twice—once while looking at a blank screen, and once while looking at test stimuli. The control scan is then subtracted from the test scan.

Visual stimulus   Control

Resulting brain activity   Difference image

Difference images from several subjects are added together and averaged…

…to arrive at a "mean difference image" that shows the most active brain areas across subjects in an experiment.

Mean difference image

Result

By repeating the process and averaging the results across multiple subjects, a stable "difference image" showing activation of just a few brain regions is formed.

Conclusion

The activated brain regions in the difference image—in this case, in the occipital cortex—are selectively involved in the particular cognitive processing required by the stimulus.

transcranial magnetic stimulation (TMS)   A noninvasive technique for examining brain function that applies strong magnetic fields to stimulate cortical neurons, in order to identify discrete areas of the brain that are particularly active during specific behaviors.

magnetoencephalography (MEG)   A passive and noninvasive technique for examining brain function that measures the tiny magnetic fields produced by active neurons, in order to identify regions of the brain that are particularly active during a given task.

Magnetism can be used to study brain activity

It is a simple matter to pass magnetic fields into the brain. However, it is technically more challenging to project magnetic fields in a highly focused and precise manner. In **transcranial magnetic stimulation (TMS)** (**Figure 2.20**), focal magnetic currents are used to briefly stimulate the cortex of alert subjects directly, without any lasting physical alterations or surgery (Y. Noguchi et al., 2003). TMS allows experimenters to activate a discrete area of the brain while simultaneously tracking any resulting changes in behavior.

Not only can magnets stimulate neurons, but neurons also act as tiny electromagnets themselves! In **magnetoencephalography (MEG)**, a large array of ultrasensitive detectors measures the minuscule magnetic fields produced by the electrical activity of cortical neurons. This information is used to construct real-time maps of brain activity during

Electromagnetic coil

Pulsed magnetic field

Stimulated cortical region

In *transcranial magnetic stimulation* (TMS), magnetic fields induced by electromagnetic coils stimulate neurons of the underlying cortical surface.

Figure 2.20   Transcranial Magnetic Stimulation

Face

Object

Anterior   Right

Left   Posterior

Magnetoencephalography (MEG) measures the minuscule magnetic fields given off by ensembles of cortical cells during specific behavioral functions. Here, MEG maps brain activity associated with viewing faces...

...versus viewing nonface objects.

Figure 2.21 Animal Magnetism (MEG images courtesy of Drs. Mario Liotti and Anthony Herdman, Simon Fraser University.)

ongoing cognitive processing (**Figure 2.21**). Because the temporal resolution of MEG responds quickly to moment-by-moment changes in brain activity, it is excellent for studying rapidly shifting patterns of brain activity in cortical circuits (F. H. Lin et al., 2004).

It is important to keep in mind that although functional brain images seem unambiguous and easy to label, they are subject to a variety of procedural and experimental limitations (Racine et al., 2005). In particular, they are not actual images of the brain, but rather computer-generated composites based on measurements of blood flow and other physiological signals, reflecting the metabolism and electrical activity of neurons. The nature of these neural signals is the topic of the next chapter.

Recommended Reading

Blumenfeld, H. (2010). *Neuroanatomy through Clinical Cases* (2nd ed.). Sunderland, MA: Sinauer.

Cabeza, R., and Kingstone, A. (2006). *Handbook of Functional Neuroimaging of Cognition* (2nd ed.). Cambridge, MA: MIT Press.

Huettel, S. A., Song, A. W., and McCarthy, G. (2009). *Functional Magnetic Resonance Imaging* (2nd ed.). Sunderland, MA: Sinauer.

Schoonover, C. (2010). *Portraits of the Mind: Visualizing the Brain from Antiquity to the 21st Century.* New York, NY: Abrams.

CHAPTER **2** VISUAL SUMMARY

mindsmachine.com/vs2

You should be able to relate each summary to the adjacent illustration, including structures and processes. If you need to review, go to the figures indicated and read the accompanying text.

1 Neurons (nerve cells) are the basic units of the nervous system. The typical neuron has four main parts: (1) **dendrites**, which receive information; (2) the **cell body (soma)**, which integrates the information; (3) an **axon**, which carries impulses from the neuron; and (4) **axon terminals**, which transmit the neuron's signals to other cells. Review **Figure 2.1, Animation 2.2**

2 Neurons take numerous forms but almost universally feature an **input zone**, an **integration zone**, a **conduction zone**, and an **output zone**. Thus each neuron gathers, analyzes, and transmits information. Review **Figure 2.3, Box 2.1, Activity 2.1**

3 Neurons make functional contacts with other neurons, or with muscles or glands, at specialized junctions called **synapses**. Synapses may be made onto dendritic spines, which exhibit **neural plasticity**, changing shape in response to experience. At most synapses a chemical **neurotransmitter** released from the **presynaptic membrane** diffuses across the **synaptic cleft** and binds to special **neurotransmitter receptor** molecules in the **postsynaptic membrane**. Review **Figure 2.4**

4 At the gross anatomical level (that is, to the naked eye), the nervous system of vertebrates is divided into **central nervous system** (**CNS**—the brain and spinal cord) and **peripheral nervous system**. The **cranial nerves**, which make up one part of the peripheral nervous system, arise from the brain to directly take in information or send out commands to the body, mostly the head and neck. Otherwise the brain uses the spinal cord and other parts of the peripheral nervous system to gather information and transmit commands. Review **Figures 2.6** and **2.7, Activity 2.2**

5 Another part of the peripheral nervous system consists of the 31 pairs of **spinal nerves**, spaced through the **cervical, thoracic, lumbar, sacral,** and **coccygeal** segments of the spinal cord. Review **Figure 2.8, Activity 2.3**

6 The third part of the peripheral nervous system—the **autonomic nervous system**—consists of the **sympathetic nervous system** (which tends to ready the body for immediate action) and the **parasympathetic nervous system** (which tends to have an effect opposite to that of the sympathetic system). We cannot consciously control autonomic activity. Review **Figure 2.9, Activity 2.4**

7 The human brain is dominated by the **cerebral hemispheres**, which include the **frontal, parietal, temporal,** and **occipital lobes**. The outermost parts of the cerebral hemispheres are known as **cerebral cortex**, or simply *cortex*. Review **Figure 2.10, Activity 2.5**

8 The major divisions of the brain are established during fetal development. These include the **forebrain** (cortex and embedded structures), the **thalamus** and **hypothalamus** (together called the **diencephalon**), and the **brainstem** components (**midbrain, pons,** and **medulla**), as well as the **cerebellum** atop the pons. Review **Figure 2.12, Box 2.2, Video 2.3, Activity 2.6**

9 The cerebral cortex is an extensive sheet of folded tissue. The six-layered cerebral cortex is responsible for higher-order functions such as vision, language, and memory. Review **Figure 2.13**

10 Important subcortical systems include the **basal ganglia**, which regulate movement; the **limbic system**, which controls emotional behaviors; and the **cerebellum**, which aids motor control. Review **Figure 2.14, Activities 2.7–2.10**

11 Modern brain-imaging technology provides us with a variety of ways to visualize the living brain. Structural imaging technologies like **computerized axial tomography** (**CT** or **CAT**) and **magnetic resonance imaging** (**MRI**) provide high-resolution images of the structure of the brain. Functional imaging technologies, such as **positron emission tomography** (**PET**), **functional MRI** (**fMRI**), and **magnetoencephalography** (**MEG**), provide maps of brain activity during behavior. Review **Figures 2.18** and **2.19, Animation 2.4**

12 The brain and spinal cord, surrounded and protected by the three **meninges** (**dura mater, pia mater,** and **arachnoid**), float in **cerebrospinal fluid** (**CSF**), which is produced in the **lateral ventricles** and exits the ventricles to surround the brain. Review **Figure 2.17, Activity 2.11**

CSF

13 Algebraic operations on scans under different experimental conditions can help pinpoint peaks of activity during various mental activities in functional brain imaging like PET and fMRI. Review **Figure 2.19**

Resulting brain activity   Difference image

Go to **mindsmachine.com** for study questions, quizzes, flashcards, and other resources.

chapter 3

Neurophysiology:
The Generation, Transmission, and Integration of Neural Signals

Stimulating Conversation

Perhaps the most dramatic demonstration in the history of neuroscience occurred on the day Yale Professor José Delgado strolled into an arena in Spain to face an enraged bull that had been bred and trained to attack humans. Armed only with a remote control, Delgado watched the massive bull paw the earth, lower its head, and charge right at him. Just before the bull reached him, Delgado pressed a button on the remote control that caused a wire, called an *electrode*, in the bull's brain to deliver a tiny trickle of electricity. The bull stopped cold. When Delgado pushed another button, electrically stimulating another part of the bull's brain, the animal turned to the right and calmly trotted away. Repeated stimulations rendered the bull docile for several minutes. Other animals responded differently to brain stimulation, depending on the brain region targeted. One bull produced a single "moo" for every button press—a hundred times in a row.

Delgado also used a remote control to electrically stimulate electrodes in the brains of people, in an attempt to pinpoint the cause of a neurological disorder. Depending on which part of the brain was stimulated, patients might suddenly become anxious or angry (Delgado, 1969). Maybe the creepiest response elicited by brain stimulation was in women who suddenly became romantically interested in the man interviewing them. Yet as soon as the electrical stimulation of their brains stopped, the women returned to their usual reserved behavior.

Why does a tiny bit of electrical stimulation in the brain produce such dramatic changes in mood and behavior? The reason is that neurons normally use electrical signals to sum up vast amounts of information. When Delgado injected electrical current into the brain, he was triggering those normal electrical signals in a very abnormal way, with sometimes dramatic results. To understand how even a tiny electrical charge to the brain can so dramatically affect the mind, we need to understand how electrical signaling works in the brain.

To see a video, go to

mindsmachine.com/3.1
Electrical Stimulation of the Brain

Neurophysiology is the study of life processes within neurons, which are specialized to use electrical signals for communication. Each neuron uses electrical processes to sum up vast amounts of information, and then uses chemical signals to pass information to other neurons. In this chapter we'll study the *electrical* processes at work *within* a neuron; in the next chapter we'll look at the *chemical* signals that pass *between* neurons. We'll see that brain function is an alternating series of electrical signals within neurons, and chemical signals between neurons.

Hold it Right There!   Dr. José Delgado stops a bull in the middle of a charge, using the remote control in his hand.

For example, a doctor may use a small rubber mallet to strike just below your knee and watch your leg kick upward in what is known as the *knee jerk reflex*. Simple as it appears, a lot happens during this test. First, sensory neurons in the muscle detect the hammer tap and send a rapid electrical signal along their axons to your spinal cord. That rapid electrical signal along the axon from knee to spinal cord is an *action potential*, which is a major topic in this chapter. When the action potential reaches the axon terminals, it releases a chemical, called a *neurotransmitter*, to stimulate spinal motoneurons. In response to the neurotransmitter, the motoneurons send action potentials down their own axons to release yet another neurotransmitter onto muscles. In response to that neurotransmitter, the muscles contract, kicking your foot into the air. Problems in electrical or chemical signaling in this circuit might cause the kick to be stronger or weaker, faster or slower, than it should be.

So this "simple" behavior involves several rounds of signaling: first electrical (along sensory neuron axons), then chemical (sensory neurons to motoneurons), then electrical again (along motoneuron axons), and finally chemical again (motoneurons to muscle). This is the classic pattern of neural function: information flows *within* a neuron via electrical signals (action potentials) and passes *between* neurons through chemical signals (neurotransmitters). This sequence also reflects the organization of this chapter. First we explain how neurons produce action potentials and send them along their axons. Then we describe how the action potential causes axon terminals to release neurotransmitter into the synapse. Next we discuss how the neurotransmitter affects the electrical state of the neuron on the other side of the synapse. And we conclude the chapter by discussing how electrical probing of the brain revealed that the brain's surface reflects a map of the body. All this will prepare us for the next chapter, where we will learn more details about the chemical signals between neurons.

neurophysiology   The study of the life processes of neurons.

polarized   Exhibiting a difference in electrical charge between the inside and outside of the cell.

ion   An atom or molecule that has acquired an electrical charge by gaining or losing one or more electrons.

anion   A negatively charged ion, such as a protein or a chloride ion.

cation   A positively charged ion, such as a potassium or sodium ion.

intracellular fluid   Also called *cytoplasm*. The watery solution found within cells.

extracellular fluid   The fluid in the spaces between cells (interstitial fluid) and in the vascular system.

cell membrane   The lipid bilayer that ensheathes a cell.

Electrical Signals Are the Vocabulary of the Nervous System

All living cells are more negative on the inside than on the outside, so we say they are **polarized**, meaning there is a difference in electrical charge between the inside and outside of the cell. Long ago, nerve cells began to exploit this electrical property to keep track of information, which works in much the same way in the neurons of animals as different as human beings and jellyfish. These neural signals underlie all our thoughts and actions, from composing music or solving a mathematical problem to feeling an itch on the skin and swatting a mosquito. To understand this system, we'll first review the physical forces at work and then discuss some details of why nerve cells are electrically polarized, how neuronal polarity is influenced by other cells, and how a change of polarity in one part of a neuron can spread throughout the cell.

A balance of electrochemical forces produces the resting potential of neurons

Let's start by considering a neuron at rest, neither perturbed by other neurons nor producing its own signals. Of the many **ions** (electrically charged molecules) that a neuron contains, a majority are **anions** (negatively charged ions), especially large protein anions that cannot exit the cell; the rest are **cations** (positively charged ions—it may help you to remember that the letter "t," which occurs in the word "cation," is shaped a bit like a plus sign "+"). All of these ions are dissolved in the **intracellular fluid** inside the cell and the **extracellular fluid** surrounding the **cell membrane**.

To see the brain in 3D, go to

mindsmachine.com/3.2
Brain Explorer

Reference electrode

Recording electrode

Amplifier

Outside axon

+ + + + + + + + + + + + + + +

Inside axon

+ + + + + + + + + + + + + +

There is zero potential difference when the two electrodes are in the bath…

Outside axon

+ + + + + + + + + + + + + + +

Inside axon

+ + + + + + + + + + + + + +

…but when the electrode enters the axon, it records a negative potential (the inside of the axon is more negative than the outside).

Time →

Microelectrode enters cell

Time →

Figure 3.1 Measuring the Resting Potential

microelectrode An especially small electrode used to record electrical potentials in living cells.

resting potential A difference in electrical potential across the membrane of a nerve cell during an inactive period.

millivolt (mV) A thousandth of a volt.

ion channel A pore in the cell membrane that permits the passage of certain ions through the membrane when the channels are open.

potassium ion (K⁺) A potassium atom that carries a positive charge because it has lost one electron.

If we insert a fine **microelectrode** into the interior of a neuron and compare it to the extracellular fluid (as in **Figure 3.1**), we find that the neuron is more negative on the inside than on the outside. Specifically, a neuron at rest exhibits a characteristic **resting potential** (an electrical difference across the membrane) of about –50 to –80 thousandths of a volt, or **millivolts (mV)** (the negative sign indicates that the cell's interior is more negative than the outside). To understand how this negative membrane potential comes about, we have to consider some special properties of the cell membrane, as well as two forces that drive ions across it.

Cell membranes consist of layers of fatty molecules studded with many sorts of specialized proteins. One important type of membrane-spanning protein is the **ion channel**, a tubelike pore that allows ions of a specific type to pass through the membrane (**Figure 3.2**). As we'll see later, some types of ion channels are *gated*: they can open and close rapidly in response to various influences. But some ion channels stay open all the time, and the cell membrane of a neuron contains many such channels that selectively allow only **potassium ions (K⁺)** to cross the membrane. Because it is studded with these

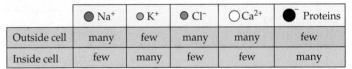

	Na⁺	K⁺	Cl⁻	Ca²⁺	Proteins
Outside cell	many	few	many	many	few
Inside cell	few	many	few	few	many

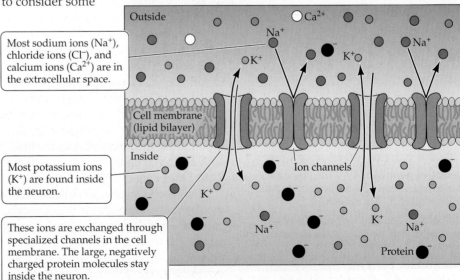

Most sodium ions (Na⁺), chloride ions (Cl⁻), and calcium ions (Ca²⁺) are in the extracellular space.

Cell membrane (lipid bilayer)

Most potassium ions (K⁺) are found inside the neuron.

Ion channels

These ions are exchanged through specialized channels in the cell membrane. The large, negatively charged protein molecules stay inside the neuron.

Figure 3.2 The Distribution of Ions Inside and Outside of a Neuron

(a) Diffusion   Figure 3.3   Ionic Forces Underlying Electrical Signaling in Neurons

Particles move from areas of high concentration to areas of low concentration. That is, they move down their concentration gradient.

(b) Diffusion through semipermeable membranes

Cell membranes permit some substances to pass through, but not others.

(c) Electrostatic forces

Like charges repel each other.

Opposite charges are attracted to each other.

K^+ channels, we say that the cell membrane of a neuron exhibits **selective permeability**, allowing some things to pass through, but not others. The membrane allows K^+ ions, but not other types of ions, to enter or exit the cell fairly freely.

The resting potential of the neuron reflects a balancing act between two opposing forces that drive K^+ ions in and out of the neuron. The first of these is **diffusion** (**Figure 3.3a**), which is the force that causes molecules of a substance to spread from regions of high concentration to regions of low concentration. For example, when placed in a glass of water, the molecules in a drop of food coloring will tend to spread from the drop out into the rest of the glass, where they are less concentrated. So we say that molecules tend to move down their concentration gradient until they are evenly distributed. If a selectively permeable membrane divides the fluid, particles that can pass through the membrane, such as K^+, will diffuse across until they are equally concentrated on both sides (**Figure 3.3b**). Other ions, unable to cross the membrane, will remain concentrated on one side.

The second force at work is **electrostatic pressure** (**Figure 3.3c**), which arises from the distribution of electrical charges rather than the distribution of molecules. Charged particles exert electrical force on one another: like charges repel, and opposite charges attract. Positively charged cations like K^+ are thus attracted to the negatively charged interior of the cell; and conversely, anions are repelled by the cell interior and so tend to exit to the extracellular fluid.

Now let's consider the situation across a neuron's cell membrane. Much of the energy consumed by a neuron goes into operating specialized membrane proteins called

selective permeability   The property of a membrane that allows some substances to pass through, but not others.

diffusion   The spontaneous spread of molecules until a uniform concentration is achieved.

electrostatic pressure   The propensity of charged molecules or ions to move, via diffusion, toward areas with the opposite charge.

sodium-potassium pumps that pump three **sodium ions** (Na⁺) out of the cell for every two K⁺ ions pumped in (**Figure 3.4a**). This action results in a buildup of K⁺ ions inside the cell (and Na⁺ outside the cell), but as we explained earlier, the membrane is selectively permeable to K⁺ ions (but not Na⁺ ions). Therefore, K⁺ ions can leave the interior, moving down their concentration gradient and causing a net buildup of negative charges inside the cell (**Figure 3.4b**). As negative charge builds up inside the cell, it begins to exert electrostatic pressure to pull positively charged K⁺ ions back inside. Eventually the opposing forces exerted by the K⁺ concentration gradient and by electrostatic pressure reach the **equilibrium potential**, the electrical charge that exactly balances the concentration gradient: any further movement of K⁺ ions into the cell (drawn by electrostatic pressure) is matched by the flow of K⁺ ions out of the cell (moving down the concentration gradient). This point corresponds to the cell's resting potential of about –60 mV (values may range between –50 and –80 mV), as **Figure 3.4c** depicts.

The actions of the sodium-potassium pump and the diffusion of K⁺ ions result in the distribution of ions inside and outside neurons that is illustrated in the table at the top

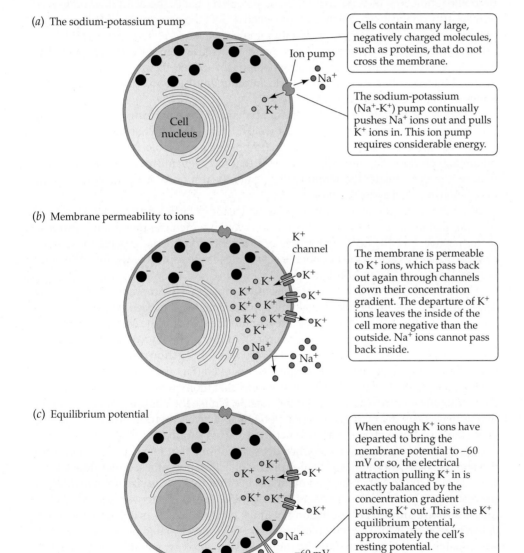

To see an animation, go to

mindsmachine.com/3.3
The Resting Membrane Potential

Figure 3.4 The Ionic Basis of the Resting Potential

sodium-potassium pump The energetically expensive mechanism that pushes sodium ions out of a cell, and potassium ions in.

sodium ion (Na⁺) A sodium atom that carries a positive charge because it has lost one electron.

equilibrium potential The point at which the movement of ions across the cell membrane is balanced, as the electrostatic pressure pulling ions in one direction is offset by the diffusion force pushing them in the opposite direction.

How's it going?

1. What two physical forces determine a neuron's resting potential?

2. What does it mean if K⁺ ions are at equilibrium? How does that state relate to a neuron's resting potential?

3. What does the sodium-potassium pump do, and how does its action relate to the resting potential?

To see an animation, go to

mindsmachine.com/3.4
The Action Potential

---

axon hillock   The cone-shaped area on the cell body from which the axon originates.

hyperpolarization   An increase in membrane potential (the interior of the neuron becomes even more negative).

depolarization   A decrease in membrane potential (the interior of the neuron becomes less negative).

local potential   An electrical potential that is initiated by stimulation at a specific site, which is a graded response that spreads passively across the cell membrane, decreasing in strength with time and distance.

threshold   The stimulus intensity that is just adequate to trigger an action potential at the axon hillock.

action potential   Also called *spike*. A rapid reversal of the membrane potential that momentarily makes the inside of the membrane positive with respect to the outside.

all-or-none property   The fact that the size (amplitude) of the action potential is independent of the size of the stimulus.

afterpotential   The positive or negative change in membrane potential that may follow an action potential.

---

of Figure 3.2. Notice the high *intra*cellular concentration of K⁺ and the high *extra*cellular concentration of Na⁺.

The resting potential of a neuron provides a baseline level of polarization found in all cells. But unlike most other cells, neurons routinely undergo a brief but radical *change* in polarization, sending an electrical signal from one end of the neuron to the other, as we'll discuss next.

A threshold amount of depolarization triggers an action potential

Action potentials are very brief but large changes in neuronal polarization that arise initially at the **axon hillock** (the specialized membrane located where the axon emerges from the cell body; see Figure 2.4a) and then move rapidly down the axon. The information that a neuron sends to other cells is encoded in patterns of these action potentials, so we need to understand their properties—where they come from, how they race down the axon, and how they send information across synapses to other cells. Let's turn first to the creation of the action potential.

Two concepts are central to understanding how action potentials are triggered. **Hyperpolarization** is an increase in membrane potential (that is, the neuron becomes *even more negative* on the inside, relative to the outside). So if the neuron already has a resting potential of, say, −60 mV, hyperpolarization makes it even *farther from zero*, maybe −70 mV. **Depolarization** is the reverse, referring to a decrease in membrane potential. The depolarization of a neuron from a resting potential of −60 mV to, say, −50 mV makes the inside of the neuron more like the outside. In other words, depolarization of a neuron brings its membrane potential *closer to zero*.

Figure 3.5a illustrates an apparatus for applying hyperpolarizing and depolarizing stimuli to a neuron, via electrodes. (Later we'll talk about how synapses produce similar hyperpolarizations and depolarizations.) Applying a *hyperpolarizing* stimulus to the membrane produces an immediate response that passively mirrors the stimulus pulse (**Figure 3.5b**). The greater the stimulus, the greater the response; so the neuron's change in potential is called a *graded response*.

If we measured the membrane response at locations farther and farther away from the stimulus location, we would see another way in which the membrane response seems passive. Like the ripples spreading from a pebble dropped in a pond, these graded **local potentials** across the membrane get smaller as they spread away from the point of stimulation (see Figure 3.5b, bottom).

Up to a point, the application of *depolarizing* pulses to the membrane follows the same pattern as for hyperpolarizing stimuli, producing local, graded responses. However, the situation changes suddenly if the stimulus depolarizes the cell to −40 mV or so (the exact value varies slightly among neurons). At this point, known as the **threshold**, a sudden and brief (0.5- to 2.0-millisecond) response—the **action potential**, sometimes referred to as a *spike* because of its shape—is provoked (**Figure 3.5c**). An action potential is a rapid reversal of the membrane potential that momentarily makes the inside of the membrane *positive* with respect to the outside. Unlike the passive graded potentials that we have been discussing, the action potential is actively reproduced (or *propagated*) down the axon, through mechanisms that we'll discuss shortly.

Applying strong stimuli to produce depolarizations that far exceed the neuron's threshold reveals another important property of action potentials: larger depolarizations do not produce larger action potentials. In other words, the size (or *amplitude*) of the action potential is independent of stimulus size. This characteristic is referred to as the **all-or-none property** of the action potential: either it fires at its full amplitude, or it doesn't fire at all. It turns out that information is encoded by changes in the *number* of action potentials rather than in their amplitude. With stronger stimuli, *more* action potentials are produced, but the size of each action potential remains the same.

A closer look at the form of the action potential shows that the return to baseline membrane potential is not simple. Many axons exhibit electrical oscillations immediately following the spike; these changes are called **afterpotentials** (see Figure 3.5c),

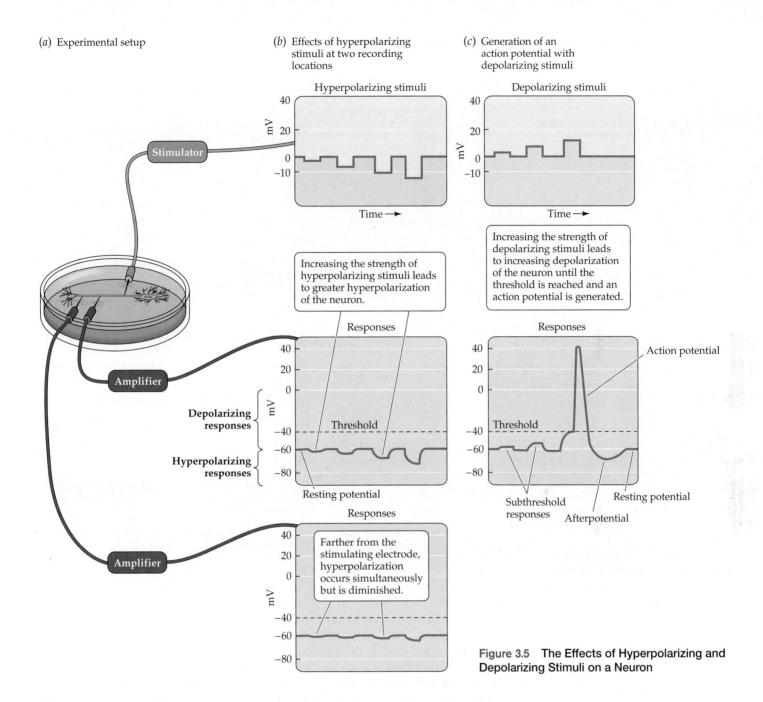

(*a*) Experimental setup

(*b*) Effects of hyperpolarizing stimuli at two recording locations

Hyperpolarizing stimuli

Time →

Increasing the strength of hyperpolarizing stimuli leads to greater hyperpolarization of the neuron.

Responses

Depolarizing responses

Hyperpolarizing responses

Threshold

Resting potential

Responses

Farther from the stimulating electrode, hyperpolarization occurs simultaneously but is diminished.

(*c*) Generation of an action potential with depolarizing stimuli

Depolarizing stimuli

Time →

Increasing the strength of depolarizing stimuli leads to increasing depolarization of the neuron until the threshold is reached and an action potential is generated.

Responses

Action potential

Threshold

Subthreshold responses

Afterpotential

Resting potential

Figure 3.5   The Effects of Hyperpolarizing and Depolarizing Stimuli on a Neuron

and they are also related to the movement of ions in and out of the cell, which we take up next.

Ionic mechanisms underlie the action potential

What events explain the action potential? The action potential is created by the sudden movement of sodium ions (Na$^+$) into the cell (Hodgkin and Katz, 1949). At its peak, the action potential approaches the equilibrium potential for Na$^+$: about +40 mV. At this point, the concentration gradient pushing Na$^+$ ions *into* the cell is exactly balanced by the positive charge pushing them *out*. The action potential thus involves a rapid shift in membrane properties, switching suddenly from the potassium-dependent resting state to a primarily sodium-dependent active state, and then swiftly returning to the resting state. This shift is accomplished through the actions of a very special kind of ion channel: the **voltage-gated Na$^+$ channel**. Like other ion channels, this channel is a tubular,

voltage-gated Na$^+$ channel   A Na$^+$-selective channel that opens or closes in response to changes in the voltage of the local membrane potential; it mediates the action potential.

Refractory period

Absolute | Relative

Sufficient depolarization of the axon results in an action potential.

Positive polarization

The membrane potential at any given time depends on how many and which channels are open.

Threshold

Afterpotential

Resting potential

Return to resting potential

Open K⁺ channel | Closed Na⁺ channel

Closed K⁺ channel

Inactivated Na⁺ channels | Open K⁺ channel

1 Open K⁺ channels create the resting potential.

2 Any depolarizing force will bring the membrane potential closer to threshold.

3 At threshold, voltage-gated Na⁺ channels open, causing a rapid change of polarity—the action potential.

4 Na⁺ channels are inactivated; gated K⁺ channels open, repolarizing and even hyperpolarizing the cell (afterpotential).

5 All gated channels close. The cell returns to its resting potential.

Figure 3.6 Mediation of the Action Potential by Voltage-Gated Sodium Channels

membrane-spanning protein, but its central Na⁺-selective pore is *gated*. The gate is ordinarily closed, but when the cell membrane becomes depolarized to threshold levels, the channel's shape changes, opening the "gate" to allow Na⁺ ions through.

Consider what happens when a patch of axonal membrane depolarizes (**Figure 3.6**). As long as the depolarization is below threshold, Na⁺ channels remain closed. But when the depolarization reaches threshold, a few Na⁺ channels open at first, allowing a few ions to start entering the neuron. The positive charges of those ions depolarize the membrane even further, opening still more Na⁺ channels. Thus, the process accelerates until the barriers are removed and Na⁺ ions rush in.

The voltage-gated Na⁺ channels stay open for a little less than a millisecond, and then they automatically close again. By this time, the membrane potential has shot up to about +40 mV. Positive charges inside the nerve cell start to push K⁺ ions out, aided by the opening of additional voltage-gated K⁺ channels that let lots of K⁺ ions rush out quickly, restoring the resting potential.

Applying very strong stimuli reveals another important property of axonal membranes. As we bombard the axon with ever-stronger stimuli, an upper limit to the frequency of action potentials becomes apparent at about 1,200 spikes per second. (Many neurons have even slower maximum rates of response.) Similarly, applying pairs of stimuli that are spaced closer and closer together reveals a related phenomenon: beyond a certain point, only the first stimulus is able to elicit an action potential. The axonal membrane is said to be **refractory** (unresponsive) to the second stimulus.

Refractoriness has two phases: During the **absolute refractory phase**, a brief period immediately following the production of an action potential, no amount of stimulation can induce another action potential, because the voltage-gated Na^+ channels can't respond (in Figure 3.6, see the brackets above the graph, as well as step 3). The absolute phase is followed by a period of reduced sensitivity, the **relative refractory phase**, during which only strong stimulation, well beyond threshold, can produce another action potential. The neuron is *relatively* refractory because K^+ ions are still flowing out, so the cell is temporarily hyperpolarized after firing an action potential (see Figure 3.6, step 4). The overall duration of the refractory phase is what determines a neuron's maximal rate of firing.

You might wonder whether the repeated inrush of Na^+ ions would allow them to build up, affecting the cell's resting potential. In fact, relatively few Na^+ ions need to enter to change the membrane potential, and the K^+ ions quickly restore the resting potential. In the long run, the sodium-potassium pump enforces the concentrations of ions that maintain the resting potential.

This tiny protein molecule, the voltage-gated Na^+ channel, is really quite a complicated machine. It monitors the axon's polarity, and at threshold the channel changes its shape to open the pore, shutting down again just a millisecond later. The channel then "remembers" that it was recently open and refuses to open again for a short time. These properties of the voltage-gated Na^+ channel are responsible for the characteristics of the action potential.

In general, the transmission of action potentials is limited to axons. Cell bodies and dendrites usually have few voltage-gated Na^+ channels, so they do not conduct action potentials. The ion channels on the cell body and dendrites are stimulated chemically at synapses, as we'll discuss later in this chapter. Because the axon has many such channels, once an action potential starts at the axon hillock, it regenerates itself down the length of the axon, as we discuss next.

Action potentials are actively propagated along the axon

Now that we've explored how voltage-gated channels underlie action potentials, we can turn to the question of how action potentials spread down the axon—another function for which voltage-gated channels are crucial. Consider an experimental setup like the one pictured in **Figure 3.7**: recording electrodes are positioned along the length of the axon, allowing us to record an action potential at various points on the axon. Recordings like this show that an action potential begun at the axon hillock spreads in a sort of chain reaction down the length of the axon.

How does the action potential travel? It is important to understand that the action potential is *regenerated* along the length of the axon. Remember, the action potential is a spike of depolarizing electrical activity (with a peak of about +40 mV), so it strongly depolarizes the next adjacent axon segment. Because this adjacent axon segment is similarly covered with voltage-gated Na^+ channels, the depolarization immediately creates a new action potential, which in turn depolarizes the *next* patch of membrane, which generates yet another action potential, and so on all down the length of the axon. An analogy is the spread of fire along a row of closely spaced match heads in a matchbook. When one match is lit, its heat is enough to ignite the next match and so on along the row. Voltage-gated Na^+ channels open when the axon is depolarized to threshold. In turn, the influx of Na^+ ions—the movement of positive charges into the axon—depolarizes the adjacent segment of axonal membrane and therefore opens new gates for the movement of Na^+ ions.

The axon normally conducts action potentials in only one direction—from the axon hillock toward the axon terminals—because, as it progresses along the axon, the action

How's it going?

1. What does it mean if a neuron is depolarized or hyperpolarized, and which action brings the cell closer to threshold?

2. Describe how the polarity of a neuron changes during the phases of an action potential.

3. How does the flow of ions account for that sequence of changes in electrical potential?

4. What mechanisms underlie the two phases of the refractory period?

To see an animation, go to

mindsmachine.com/3.5
Conduction along Unmyelinated
vs. Myelinated Axons

refractory Temporarily unresponsive or inactivated.

absolute refractory phase A brief period of complete insensitivity to stimuli.

relative refractory phase A period of reduced sensitivity during which only strong stimulation produces an action potential.

Figure 3.7 Propagation of the Action Potential

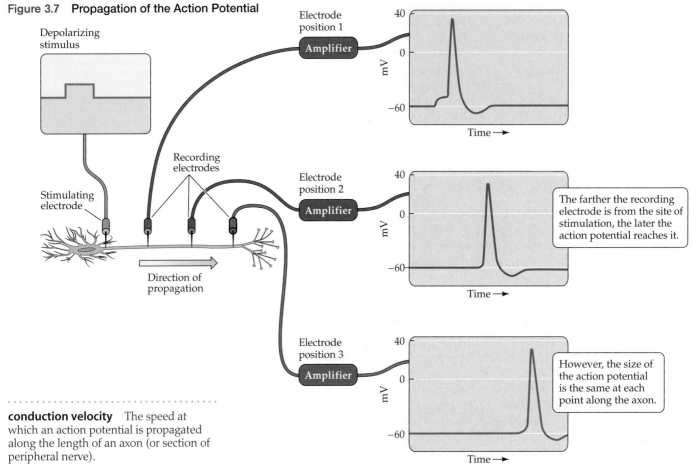

Depolarizing stimulus

Stimulating electrode

Recording electrodes

Direction of propagation

Electrode position 1

Amplifier

Electrode position 2

Amplifier

Electrode position 3

Amplifier

The farther the recording electrode is from the site of stimulation, the later the action potential reaches it.

However, the size of the action potential is the same at each point along the axon.

conduction velocity The speed at which an action potential is propagated along the length of an axon (or section of peripheral nerve).

myelin The fatty insulation around an axon, formed by glial cells. This sheath boosts the speed at which nerve impulses are conducted.

node of Ranvier A gap between successive segments of the myelin sheath where the axon membrane is exposed.

saltatory conduction The form of conduction that is characteristic of myelinated axons, in which the action potential jumps from one node of Ranvier to the next.

multiple sclerosis Literally, "many scars"; a disorder characterized by the widespread degeneration of myelin.

How's it going?

1. How is the action potential propagated along the axon?
2. What factor causes saltatory conduction, and why does it speed propagation of the action potential?
3. Why do action potentials move only *away* from the cell body?

potential leaves in its wake a stretch of refractory membrane (**Figure 3.8a**). The action potential does not spread from the axon hillock back over the cell body and dendrites, because the membrane there has very few voltage-gated Na⁺ channels, so they cannot produce an action potential.

If we record the speed of action potentials along axons that differ in diameter, we see that **conduction velocity** varies with the diameter of the axon. Larger axons allow the depolarization to spread faster through the interior. In mammals, the conduction velocity in large fibers may be as fast as 150 meters per second. (We will discuss axon diameter and conduction velocity again in Chapter 5.) Although not as fast as the speed of light (as was once believed), neural conduction can nevertheless be very fast: over 300 miles per hour. This relatively high rate of conduction ensures rapid sensory and motor processing.

The highest conduction velocities require more than just large axons. **Myelin** sheathing also greatly speeds conduction. As we described in Chapter 2, the myelin sheath is provided by glial cells. This sheath surrounding the axon is interrupted by **nodes of Ranvier**, small gaps spaced about every millimeter along the axon (see Figure 2.5a). Because the myelin insulation resists the flow of ions across the membrane, the action potential "jumps" from node to node. This process is called **saltatory conduction** (from the Latin *saltare*, "to jump") (**Figure 3.8b**). The evolution of rapid saltatory conduction in vertebrates has given them a major behavioral advantage over the invertebrates, whose axons are unmyelinated and thus slower in conduction. **Multiple sclerosis** results when the body makes antibodies that attack myelin, interfering with action potential conduction, which can have devastating and highly variable effects on brain function.

Many of the characteristics of action potentials have been whimsically likened to the action of a toilet as **Box 3.1** explores.

(*a*) Continuous conduction of action potential along unmyelinated axon (10 m/s)

Na+ entry locally depolarizes axon…

…which sufficiently depolarizes the adjacent region of the axon to open more of the voltage-gated Na+ channels, re-creating the action potential there.

The process continues down the length of the axon.

(*b*) Rapid saltatory conduction along myelinated axon (150 m/s)

Na+ channels open, generating an action potential.

Myelin prevents K+ leakage out, channeling the depolarization down the axon interior.

Depolarization spreads within the axon very rapidly, like electricity through a wire.

The depolarized Na+ channels open, re-creating the action potential at the new node…

… which continues from node to node as fast as 150 m/s, up to 15 times faster than in unmyelinated axons.

Figure 3.8 **Conduction along Unmyelinated versus Myelinated Axons**

BOX 3.1 Action Potentials Act, in Many Ways, like a Flushing Toilet

It might help you to remember basic facts about action potentials if you consider how much they resemble a flushing toilet. For example, if you gently push the lever on a toilet, nothing much happens. As you gradually increase the force you apply to the lever, you will eventually find the threshold—the amount of force that is just enough to trigger a flush (step 1 of the figure). Likewise, the neuron has a *threshold*—the amount of depolarization that is just enough to trigger an action potential at the start of an axon (see Figure 3.5). Once you're past the threshold, it doesn't matter how hard you pushed the toilet lever; the flush will always be the same. Similarly, once the neuron is pushed past threshold, the action potential will be the same. This is the *all-or-nothing* property of action potentials (step 2).

After a toilet has flushed, it takes a while (about a minute) before it can flush again (step 3). Likewise, after a neuron fires, it takes a while (about a millisecond) before it can fire again. This is the neuron's *refractory period*. Why do neurons have a refractory period for action potentials? The reason, if you remember, is that the voltage-gated sodium channels always slam shut for a while after they've opened, no matter what the membrane potential is. Until that time is up, the sodium channels won't open again. If the situation is urgent, we can flush our toilet about 60 times per hour or fire our neurons about 1,000 times per second. (If things are *really* urgent, we might do both.)

Also notice that when a properly working toilet flushes, the water always goes in the same direction (no one wants a toilet that sometimes flushes backward!)

(step 4). Likewise, the neuron's action potential goes *in only one direction down the axon*, from the end attached to the cell body to the axon terminals.

Of course, neurons are different from toilets in many ways. The outflow of a toilet goes only to the single sewer line leaving a house (step 5), but an action potential may flow down many axon branches, to communicate with hundreds of other neurons.

Voltage-gated sodium channels on the axon branches ensure that the action potential is just as large in each branch, so it's not diminished by spreading out among branches. A toilet has only one lever, but each neuron has hundreds or thousands of synapses, and by producing different sorts of local, graded potentials, some synapses make the neuron more likely to reach threshold, while others make it less likely.

1 Just as the toilet lever must be pushed hard enough to trigger a flush, the axon hillock must be depolarized enough to open voltage-gated sodium (Na⁺) channels to trigger an action potential.

2 Pushing the lever harder will not produce a bigger flush, and the axon hillock that has been depolarized past threshold will produce the same-sized action potential. In both cases, there is an all-or-none response.

3 After a flush, the toilet cannot flush again until the tank has refilled. After an action potential, the axon hillock cannot start a new action potential until the voltage-gated Na⁺ channels have recovered.

4 Once a flush is triggered, it always goes in the same direction (you hope). Likewise, the action potential starts at the axon hillock and always travels down to the axon terminals.

5 While the toilet flush goes to a single destination (the sewer), an axon sends an action potential down many branches, and it will be just the same in every branch, as the action potential is regenerated all along the way.

---

neurotransmitter or transmitter Also called simply *synaptic transmitter* or *chemical transmitter*. The chemical released from the presynaptic axon terminal that serves as the basis of communication between neurons.

presynaptic Referring to the region of a synapse that releases neurotransmitter.

postsynaptic Referring to the region of a synapse that receives and responds to neurotransmitter.

Synapses cause local changes in the postsynaptic membrane potential

At the beginning of the chapter, we told you that when the action potential reaches the end of an axon, it causes the axon to release a chemical, called a **neurotransmitter** (or **transmitter**) into the synapse. We will discuss the many different types of transmitters in detail in Chapter 4. For now, what you need to know is that when an axon releases neurotransmitter molecules into a synapse, they briefly alter the membrane potential of the other cell. Because information is moving from the axon to the target cell on the other side of the synapse, we say the axon is from the **presynaptic** cell, and the target neuron on the other side of the synapse is the **postsynaptic** cell.

Figure 3.9   Recording Postsynaptic Potentials

In this schematic model, when an excitatory presynaptic neuron (red) fires, it produces a normal action potential and causes depolarization (EPSP) in the postsynaptic neuron (yellow).

When an inhibitory presynaptic neuron (blue) fires, it also produces a normal action potential, but it causes hyperpolarization (IPSP) in the postsynaptic neuron (yellow).

The brief changes in the membrane potential of the postsynaptic cell in response to neurotransmitter are called, naturally enough, **postsynaptic potentials**. A given neuron, receiving synapses from hundreds of other cells, is subject to hundreds or thousands of postsynaptic potentials. When added together, this massive array of local potentials determines whether the neuron's membrane potential will reach threshold and therefore trigger an action potential. Eventually it was found that the nervous system employs electrical synapses too (see **A Step Further 3.1**, on the website), but the vast majority of synapses use neurotransmitters to produce postsynaptic potentials.

We can study postsynaptic potentials with a setup like that shown in **Figure 3.9**. This setup allows us to compare the effects of activity of excitatory versus inhibitory synapses on the local membrane potential of a postsynaptic cell. The responses of the presynaptic and postsynaptic cells are shown on the same graphs in Figure 3.9 for easy comparison of their timing. It is important to remember that excitatory and inhibitory neurons get their names from their *actions on postsynaptic neurons*, not from their effects on behavior.

Stimulation of the excitatory presynaptic neuron (red in Figure 3.9) causes it to produce an all-or-none action potential that spreads to the end of the axon, releasing transmitter. After a brief delay, the postsynaptic cell (yellow) displays a small local depolarization, as Na^+ channels open to let the positive ions in. This postsynaptic membrane depolarization is known as an **excitatory postsynaptic potential** (**EPSP**) because it pushes the postsynaptic cell a little closer to the threshold for an action potential.

Generally, the combined effect of many excitatory synapses is needed to elicit an action potential in a postsynaptic neuron. The delay between arrival of the action potential at the axon terminal and the beginning of the EPSP in the target cell is about half a millisecond. This **synaptic delay** reflects the time needed for the neurotransmitter to be released, diffuse across the synaptic cleft, and affect the postsynaptic cell, as we'll discuss later.

The action potential of the *inhibitory* presynaptic neuron (blue in Figure 3.9) looks exactly like that of the excitatory presynaptic neuron; all neurons use the same kind of action

postsynaptic potential   A local potential that is initiated by stimulation at a synapse, which can vary in amplitude, and spreads passively across the cell membrane, decreasing in strength with time and distance.

excitatory postsynaptic potential (**EPSP**)   A depolarizing potential in the postsynaptic neuron that is caused by excitatory presynaptic potentials. EPSPs increase the probability that the postsynaptic neuron will fire an action potential.

synaptic delay   The brief delay between the arrival of an action potential at the axon terminal and the creation of a postsynaptic potential.

TABLE 3.1 Comparing Axons and Dendrites

	Property			
	Size	**Number per neuron**	**Information flow**	**Voltage changes**
Axon	Thin, uniform	One (but may have branches)	Away from neuron	All-or-none
Dendrite	Thick, variable	Many	Into neuron	Graded variable

potential, as Figure 3.9 shows. But the effect on the *post*synaptic side is quite different. When the inhibitory presynaptic neuron is activated, the postsynaptic membrane potential becomes even more negative, or hyperpolarized. This hyperpolarization moves the cell membrane potential away from threshold—it *decreases* the probability that the neuron will fire an action potential—so it is called an **inhibitory postsynaptic potential** (**IPSP**).

Usually IPSPs result from the opening of channels that permit **chloride ions** (**Cl⁻**) to enter the cell. Because Cl⁻ ions are much more concentrated outside the cell than inside (see Figure 3.2), they rush into the cell, making its membrane potential more negative. What determines whether a synapse excites or inhibits the postsynaptic cell? One factor is the particular neurotransmitter released by the presynaptic cell. Some transmitters generate an EPSP in the postsynaptic cells; others generate an IPSP. So in the end, whether a neuron fires an action potential at any given moment is decided by the balance between the number of excitatory and the number of inhibitory signals that it is receiving, and it receives many signals of both types at all times.

Now that you know more about the parts of neurons and how they communicate, we can summarize the differences between axons (which send information via action potentials) and dendrites (which receive information from synapses), as we do in **Table 3.1**.

Spatial summation and temporal summation integrate synaptic inputs

Synaptic transmission is an impressive process, but complex behavior requires more than the simple arrival of signals across synapses. Neurons must also be able to integrate the messages they receive. In other words, they perform *information processing*—by using a sort of neural algebra, in which each nerve cell adds and subtracts the many inputs it receives from other neurons. As we'll see next, this is possible because of the characteristics of synaptic inputs, the way in which the neuron integrates the postsynaptic potentials, and the trigger mechanism that determines whether a neuron will fire an action potential.

We've seen that postsynaptic potentials are caused by transmitter chemicals that can be either depolarizing (excitatory) or hyperpolarizing (inhibitory). From their points of origin on the dendrites and cell body, these graded EPSPs and IPSPs spread passively over the postsynaptic neuron, decreasing in strength over time and distance. Whether the postsynaptic neuron will fire depends on whether a depolarization exceeding threshold reaches the axon hillock, the trigger zone for action potentials. If many EPSPs are received, the neuron may reach threshold and fire. But if both EPSPs and IPSPs arrive at the axon hillock, they partially cancel each other. Thus, the net effect is the *difference* between the two: the neuron subtracts the IPSPs from the EPSPs. Simple arithmetic, right?

When summed, EPSPs and IPSPs do tend to cancel each other out. But because postsynaptic potentials spread passively and dissipate as they cross the cell membrane, the resulting sum is also influenced by *distance*. For example, simultaneous EPSPs from two synapses close to the hillock will produce a larger sum there than will two EPSPs from farther away. The summation of potentials originating from different physical locations across the cell body is called **spatial summation**. Only if the overall sum of *all* the potentials—both EPSPs and IPSPs—is sufficient to depolarize the cell to threshold at the axon hillock is an action potential triggered (**Figure 3.10a**). Usually it takes excitatory messages from many presynaptic neurons to cause a postsynaptic neuron to fire an action potential.

To see an animation, go to

mindsmachine.com/3.6
Spatial Summation

·····

inhibitory postsynaptic potential (IPSP)
A hyperpolarizing potential in the postsynaptic neuron that is caused by inhibitory connections. IPSPs decrease the probability that the postsynaptic neuron will fire an action potential.

chloride ion (Cl⁻)   A chlorine atom that carries a negative charge because it has gained one electron.

spatial summation   The summation of postsynaptic potentials that reach the axon hillock from different locations across the cell body. If this summation reaches threshold, an action potential is triggered.

Figure 3.10 Spatial versus Temporal Summation

(a) Spatial summation

If three EPSPs arrive at three different parts of the dendrite, that may be enough to push the postsynaptic cell to threshold, triggering an action potential. Any IPSPs that might arrive (not shown) would counteract the EPSPs.

(b) Temporal summation

Even a single synapse may push the postsynaptic cell to threshold if many action potentials arrive in quick succession; providing overlapping EPSPs.

Postsynaptic effects that are not absolutely simultaneous can also be summed, because the postsynaptic potentials last a few milliseconds before fading away. The closer they are in time, the greater is the overlap and the more complete is the summation, which in this case is called **temporal summation**. Temporal summation is easily understood if you imagine a neuron with only one input. If EPSPs arrive one right after the other, they sum and the postsynaptic cell eventually reaches threshold and produces an action potential (**Figure 3.10b**). But these graded potentials fade quickly, so if too much time passes between successive EPSPs, they will never sum and no action potentials will be triggered. **Table 3.2** summarizes the many properties of action potentials, EPSPs, and IPSPs, noting the similarities and differences among the three kinds of neural potentials.

It should now be clear that, although action potentials are all-or-none phenomena, the postsynaptic effect they produce is graded in size and determined by the processing

temporal summation The summation of postsynaptic potentials that reach the axon hillock at different times. The closer in time the potentials occur, the more complete the summation is.

TABLE 3.2 Characteristics of Electrical Signals of Nerve Cells

Type of signal	Signaling role	Typical duration (ms)	Amplitude	Character	Mode of propagation	Ion channel opening	Channel sensitive to:
Action potential	Conduction along a neuron	1–2	Overshooting, 100 mV	All-or-none, digital	Actively propagated, regenerative	First Na+, then K+, in different channels	Voltage (depolarization)
Excitatory postsynaptic potential (EPSP)	Transmission between neurons	10–100	Depolarizing, from less than 1 to more than 20 mV	Graded, analog	Local, passive spread	Na+–K+	Chemical (neurotransmitter)
Inhibitory postsynaptic potential (IPSP)	Transmission between neurons	10–100	Hyperpolarizing, from less than 1 to about 15 mV	Graded, analog	Local, passive spread	Cl−–K+	Chemical (neurotransmitter)

How's it going?

1. What are EPSPs and IPSPs?
2. Compare and contrast spatial summation versus temporal summation.
3. Discuss the electrical properties of a neuron that allow it to process information.
4. Where does information enter a neuron, and how does a neuron send information to other cells?

To see an animation, go to

mindsmachine.com/3.7
Synaptic Transmission

synaptic vesicle A small, spherical structure that contains molecules of neurotransmitter.

synaptic cleft The space between the presynaptic and postsynaptic neurons at a synapse. This gap measures about 20–40 nm.

calcium ion (Ca^{2+}) A calcium atom that carries a double positive charge because it has lost two electrons.

---

of many inputs occurring close together in time. The membrane potential at the axon hillock thus reflects the moment-to-moment integration of all the neuron's inputs, which the hillock encodes into action potentials.

Dendrites add to the story of neuronal integration. A vast number of synaptic inputs, arrayed across the dendrites and cell body, can induce postsynaptic potentials. So dendrites expand the receptive surface of the neuron and increase the amount of input the neuron can handle. All other things being equal, the farther out on a dendrite a potential occurs, the less effect it should have at the axon hillock, because the potential decreases in size as it passively spreads. When the potential arises at a dendritic *spine* (see Figure 2.4), its effect is even smaller because it has to spread down the shaft of the spine. Thus, information arriving at various parts of the neuron is *weighted*, in terms of the distance to the axon hillock and the path resistance along the way.

Synaptic Transmission Requires a Sequence of Events

The following overview summarizes the events that take place during chemical synaptic transmission, which are illustrated in **Figure 3.11**:

1. The action potential arrives at the presynaptic axon terminal.
2. Voltage-gated calcium channels in the membrane of the axon terminal open, and *calcium ions* (*Ca^{2+}*) enter the axon terminal.
3. Ca^{2+} causes *synaptic vesicles* filled with neurotransmitter to fuse with the presynaptic membrane and rupture, releasing the transmitter molecules into the *synaptic cleft*.
4. Some transmitter molecules bind to special *receptor molecules* in the postsynaptic membrane, leading—directly or indirectly—to the opening of ion channels in the postsynaptic membrane. The resulting flow of ions creates a local EPSP or IPSP in the postsynaptic neuron.
5. The IPSPs and EPSPs in the postsynaptic cell spread toward the axon hillock. (If the sum of all the EPSPs and IPSPs ultimately depolarizes the hillock enough to reach threshold, an action potential will arise.)
6. Synaptic transmission is rapidly stopped, so the message is brief and accurately reflects the activity of the presynaptic cell.
7. Synaptic transmitter may also activate *presynaptic receptors*, resulting in a decrease in transmitter release.

Let's look at each step in this process in a little more detail.

Action potentials cause the release of transmitter molecules into the synaptic cleft

When an action potential reaches a presynaptic terminal, it causes hundreds of **synaptic vesicles** near the presynaptic membrane to fuse with the membrane and discharge their contents—molecules of neurotransmitter—into the **synaptic cleft** (the space between the presynaptic and postsynaptic membranes). The key event in this process is an influx of **calcium ions (Ca^{2+})**, rather than K^+ or Na^+, into the axon terminal. These ions enter through voltage-gated Ca^{2+} channels opening in response to the arrival of an action potential. Synaptic delay is caused by the time needed for Ca^{2+} to enter the terminal, for the transmitter to diffuse across the synaptic cleft, and for transmitter molecules to interact with their receptors.

The presynaptic terminal normally produces and stores enough transmitter to ensure that it is ready for activity. Intense activity of the neuron reduces the number of available vesicles, but soon more vesicles are produced to replace those that were discharged. Neurons differ in their ability to keep pace with a rapid rate of incoming action potentials. Furthermore, the rate of making the transmitter is regulated by enzymes that are manufactured in the neuronal cell body and transported actively down the axons to the terminals.

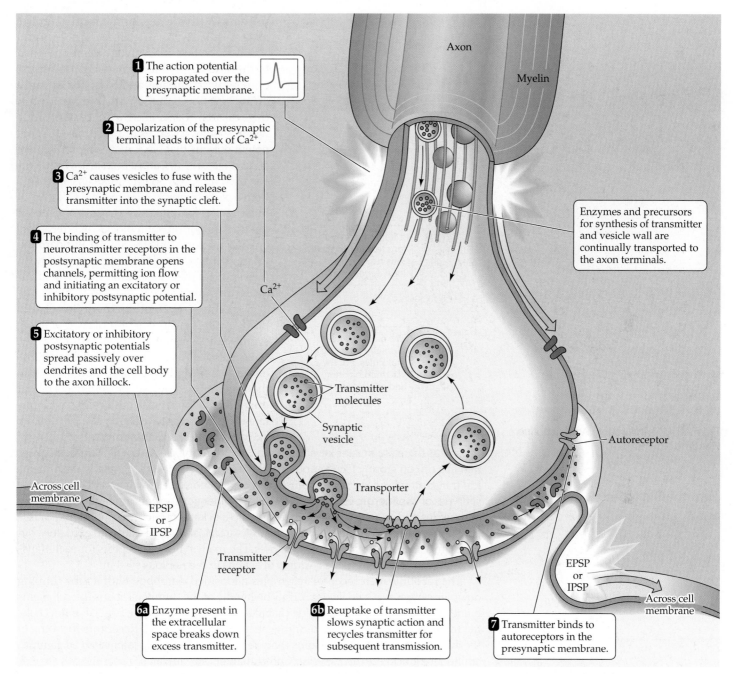

1 The action potential is propagated over the presynaptic membrane.

2 Depolarization of the presynaptic terminal leads to influx of Ca²⁺.

3 Ca²⁺ causes vesicles to fuse with the presynaptic membrane and release transmitter into the synaptic cleft.

4 The binding of transmitter to neurotransmitter receptors in the postsynaptic membrane opens channels, permitting ion flow and initiating an excitatory or inhibitory postsynaptic potential.

5 Excitatory or inhibitory postsynaptic potentials spread passively over dendrites and the cell body to the axon hillock.

Enzymes and precursors for synthesis of transmitter and vesicle wall are continually transported to the axon terminals.

Axon

Myelin

Ca^{2+}

Transmitter molecules

Synaptic vesicle

Autoreceptor

Across cell membrane

EPSP or IPSP

Transporter

Transmitter receptor

EPSP or IPSP

Across cell membrane

6a Enzyme present in the extracellular space breaks down excess transmitter.

6b Reuptake of transmitter slows synaptic action and recycles transmitter for subsequent transmission.

7 Transmitter binds to autoreceptors in the presynaptic membrane.

Figure 3.11 Steps in Transmission at a Chemical Synapse

Receptor molecules recognize transmitters

The action of a key in a lock is a good analogy for the action of a transmitter on a receptor protein. Just as a particular key can open a door, a molecule of the correct shape, called a **ligand** (see Chapter 4), can fit into a receptor protein and activate or block it. So, for example, at synapses where the transmitter is **acetylcholine** (**ACh**), the ACh fits into *ligand-binding sites* in **neurotransmitter receptor** molecules located in the postsynaptic membrane (**Figure 3.12**).

The nature of the postsynaptic receptors at a synapse determines the action of the transmitter (see Chapter 4). For example, ACh can function as either an inhibitory or an excitatory neurotransmitter, at different synapses. At excitatory synapses, binding of ACh opens channels for Na⁺ and K⁺ ions. At inhibitory synapses, ACh opens channels that allow chloride ions (Cl⁻) to enter, thereby hyperpolarizing the

ligand A substance that binds to receptor molecules, such as a neurotransmitter or drug that binds postsynaptic receptors.

acetylcholine (ACh) A neurotransmitter that is produced and released by parasympathetic postganglionic neurons, by motoneurons, and by neurons throughout the brain.

neurotransmitter receptor Also called *receptor*. A protein that captures and reacts to molecules of a neurotransmitter or hormone.

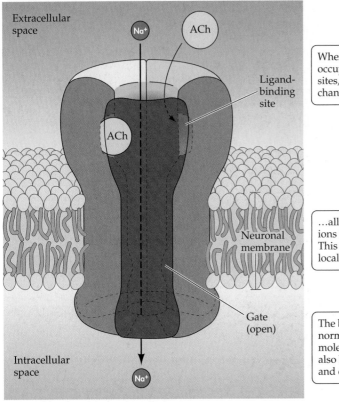

When ACh molecules occupy both binding sites, the sodium channel opens…

Ligand-binding site

…allowing sodium ions to enter the cell. This results in a local depolarization.

Gate (open)

The binding sites normally bind ACh molecules, but they also bind nicotine and other drugs.

Figure 3.12 A Nicotinic Acetylcholine Receptor

curare A neurotoxin that causes paralysis by blocking acetylcholine receptors in muscle.

bungarotoxin A neurotoxin, isolated from the venom of the banded krait, that selectively blocks acetylcholine receptors.

agonist A molecule, usually a drug, that binds a receptor molecule and initiates a response like that of another molecule, usually a neurotransmitter.

antagonist A molecule, usually a drug, that interferes with or prevents the action of a neurotransmitter.

cholinergic Referring to cells that use acetylcholine as their synaptic transmitter.

membrane (that is, making it more negative and so less likely to create an action potential).

The lock-and-key analogy is strengthened by the observation that various chemicals can fit onto receptor proteins and block the entrance of the key. Some of the preparations used in this research sound like the ingredients for a witches' brew. As an example, consider some potent poisons that block ACh receptors: curare and bungarotoxin. **Curare** is an arrowhead poison used by native South Americans. Extracted from a plant, it greatly increases the efficiency of hunting: if the hunter hits any part of the prey, the arrow's poison soon blocks ACh receptors on muscles, paralyzing the animal. **Bungarotoxin**, another blocker of ACh receptors, is found in the venom of the banded krait (*Bungarus multicinctus*), a snake native to India and China.

The chemical nicotine, found in tobacco products, mimics the action of ACh at some synapses, increasing alertness and heart rate. Molecules such as nicotine that act like a transmitter at a receptor are called **agonists** (from the Greek *agon*, "contest" or "struggle") of that transmitter. Conversely, molecules that interfere with or prevent the action of a transmitter, like curare, are called **antagonists**.

Just as there are master keys that fit many different locks, there are submaster keys that fit a certain group of locks, and keys that fit only a single lock. Similarly, each chemical transmitter binds to several different receptor molecules. ACh acts on at least four subtypes of **cholinergic** receptors. Nicotinic cholinergic receptors are found at synapses on muscles and in autonomic ganglia; it is the blockade of these receptors that causes paralysis brought on by curare and bungarotoxin. Most nicotinic sites are excitatory, but there are also inhibitory nicotinic synapses. The many types of receptors for each transmitter have evolved to enable a variety of actions in the nervous system.

The nicotinic ACh receptor resembles a lopsided dumbbell with a tube running down its central axis (see Figure 3.12). The handle of the dumbbell spans the cell membrane, with two sites on the outside that fit ACh molecules (Karlin, 2002). For the channel to open, both of the ACh-binding sites must be occupied. Receptors for some of the synaptic transmitter molecules that we will be considering later, such as gamma-aminobutyric acid (GABA), glycine, and glutamate, are similar.

The coordination of different transmitter systems of the brain is incredibly complex. Each subtype of neurotransmitter receptor has a unique pattern of distribution within the brain. Different receptor systems become active at different times in fetal life. The number of any given type of receptor remains plastic in adulthood: not only are there seasonal variations, but many kinds of receptors show a regular daily variation of 50% or more in number, affecting the sensitivity of cells to that variety of transmitter. Similarly, the numbers of some receptors have been found to vary with the use of drugs. We'll learn more about these properties of neurotransmitter receptors in Chapter 4.

The action of synaptic transmitters is stopped rapidly

When a chemical transmitter such as ACh is released into the synaptic cleft, its postsynaptic action is not only prompt but usually very brief as well. It is important that each activation of the synapse be brief in order to maximize how much information can be transmitted. Think of it this way: the worst doorbell in the world is one that, when the button is pushed, rings forever. Such a doorbell would be able to transmit only one piece of information, and only once. But a doorbell that could ring as fast as a thousand times per minute would be able to send a lot of information—Morse code maybe. Likewise, a synapse can signal over a thousand times per second, potentially sending a lot of information (but not by Morse code).

Two processes bring transmitter effects to a prompt halt:

1. *Degradation.* Transmitter molecules can be rapidly broken down and thus inactivated by special enzymes—a process known as **degradation** (step 6a in Figure 3.11). For example, the enzyme that inactivates ACh is **acetylcholinesterase (AChE)**. AChE breaks down ACh very rapidly into products that are recycled (at least in part) to make more ACh in the axon terminal.

2. *Reuptake.* Alternatively, transmitter molecules may be swiftly cleared from the synaptic cleft by being absorbed back into the axon terminal that released them—a process known as **reuptake** (step 6b in Figure 3.11). Norepinephrine, dopamine, and serotonin are examples of transmitters whose activity is terminated mainly by reuptake. In these cases, special receptors for the transmitter, called **transporters**, are located on the presynaptic axon terminal and bring the transmitter back inside. Once taken up into the presynaptic terminal, transmitter molecules may be repackaged into newly formed synaptic vesicles to await re-release, conserving the resources that would be needed to make new transmitter molecules. Malfunction of reuptake mechanisms is suspected to cause some kinds of mental illness, such as depression (see Chapter 12).

Neural circuits underlie reflexes

For simplicity, so far we have focused on the classic, directed **axo-dendritic synapses** (from axon to dendrite) and **axo-somatic synapses** (from axon to cell body, or soma). But many nonclassic forms of chemical synapses exist in the nervous system. As the name implies, **axo-axonic synapses** form on axons, often near the axon terminal, allowing the presynaptic neuron to strongly facilitate or inhibit the activity of the postsynaptic axon. Similarly, neurons may form **dendro-dendritic** contacts, allowing coordination of their activities (**Figure 3.13**).

degradation The chemical breakdown of a neurotransmitter into inactive metabolites.

acetylcholinesterase (AChE) An enzyme that inactivates the transmitter acetylcholine.

reuptake The process by which released synaptic transmitter molecules are taken up and reused by the presynaptic neuron, thus stopping synaptic activity.

transporter A specialized receptor in the presynaptic membrane that recognizes transmitter molecules and returns them to the presynaptic neuron for reuse.

axo-dendritic synapse A synapse at which a presynaptic axon terminal synapses onto a dendrite of the postsynaptic neuron, either via a dendritic spine or directly onto the dendrite itself.

axo-somatic synapse A synapse at which a presynaptic axon terminal synapses onto the cell body (soma) of the postsynaptic neuron.

axo-axonic synapse A synapse at which a presynaptic axon terminal synapses onto the axon terminal of another neuron.

dendro-dendritic synapse A synapse at which a synaptic connection forms between the dendrites of two neurons.

Figure 3.13 Different Types of Synaptic Connections

(a) Axo-dendritic   (b) Axo-somatic   (c) Axo-axonic   (d) Dendro-dendritic

Soma

Dendrite

Axon

Most synapses are formed by an axon stimulating a dendrite, but axons also sometimes synapse on cell bodies or even other axons…

…and in some instances, specialized dendrites synapse on other dendrites.

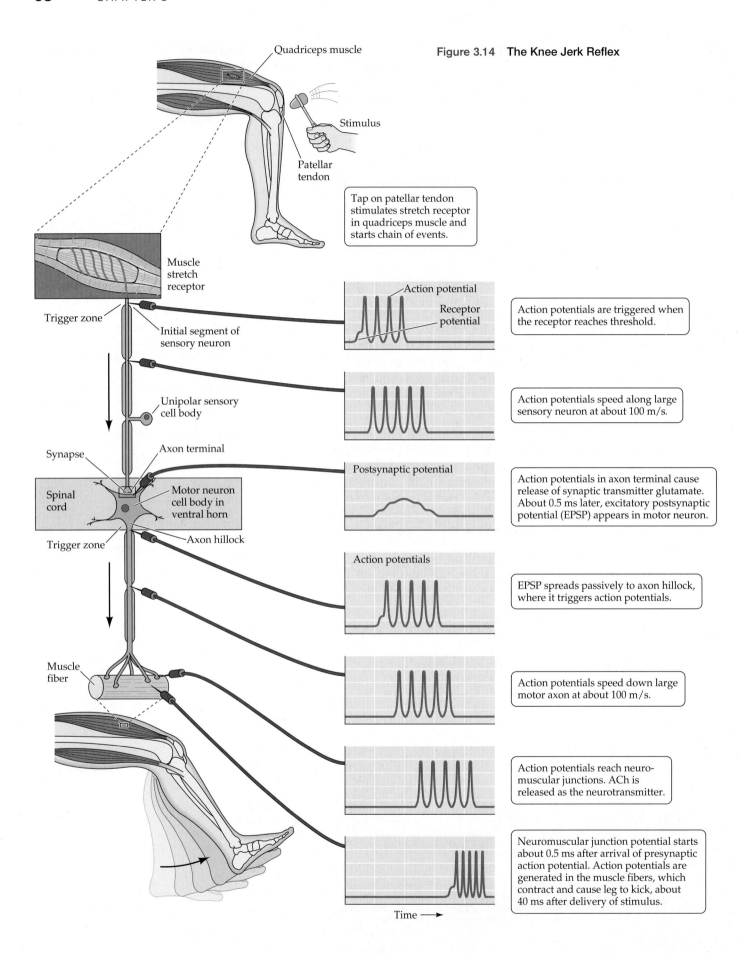

Quadriceps muscle

Stimulus

Patellar tendon

Figure 3.14   The Knee Jerk Reflex

Tap on patellar tendon stimulates stretch receptor in quadriceps muscle and starts chain of events.

Muscle stretch receptor

Trigger zone

Initial segment of sensory neuron

Action potential

Receptor potential

Action potentials are triggered when the receptor reaches threshold.

Unipolar sensory cell body

Action potentials speed along large sensory neuron at about 100 m/s.

Synapse

Axon terminal

Spinal cord

Motor neuron cell body in ventral horn

Postsynaptic potential

Action potentials in axon terminal cause release of synaptic transmitter glutamate. About 0.5 ms later, excitatory postsynaptic potential (EPSP) appears in motor neuron.

Trigger zone

Axon hillock

Action potentials

EPSP spreads passively to axon hillock, where it triggers action potentials.

Muscle fiber

Action potentials speed down large motor axon at about 100 m/s.

Action potentials reach neuro-muscular junctions. ACh is released as the neurotransmitter.

Neuromuscular junction potential starts about 0.5 ms after arrival of presynaptic action potential. Action potentials are generated in the muscle fibers, which contract and cause leg to kick, about 40 ms after delivery of stimulus.

Time ⟶

Now that we know more about the electrical signaling that takes place *within* each neuron and the neurotransmitter signaling that goes on *between* neurons, we can revisit the **knee jerk reflex** that we discussed at the start of the chapter (**Figure 3.14**). Note that this reflex is extremely fast: only about 40 milliseconds elapse between the hammer tap and the start of the kick. Several factors account for this speed: (1) both the sensory and the motor axons involved are myelinated and of large diameter, so they conduct rapidly; (2) the sensory cells synapse directly on the motor neurons; and (3) both the central synapse and the neuromuscular junction are fast synapses. We discuss other aspects of neural circuits in **A Step Further 3.2**, on the website.

We offered this reflex at the start of the chapter as an example of all neural processing—electrical signaling within each neuron alternating with chemical signaling between neurons. The next chapter will explain how drugs can interfere with the chemical signaling between neurons. For the final part of this chapter, let's see how scientists exploit the electrical signaling within neurons to learn more about brain function.

Gross Electrical Activity of the Human Brain

The electrical activity of millions of cells working together combines to produce electrical potentials large enough that we can detect them at the surface of the scalp, using large electrodes either on the scalp or within the brain. Recordings of these spontaneous brain potentials (or *brain waves*), called **electroencephalograms** (**EEGs**) (**Figure 3.15a**), can provide useful information about the activity of brain regions during behavioral processes. As we will see in Chapter 10, EEG recordings can distinguish whether a person is asleep or awake. In many countries, EEG activity determines whether someone is legally dead.

Event-related potentials (**ERPs**) are EEG responses to a single stimulus, such as a flash of light or a loud sound. Typically, many ERP responses to the same stimulus are averaged to obtain a reliable estimate of brain activity (**Figure 3.15b**). ERPs have very distinctive characteristics of wave shape and *latency* (time delay) that reflect the type of stimulus, the state of the subject, and the site of recording (Luck, 2005). ERPs can also be used to detect hearing problems in babies, evident as reduced or absent auditory ERPs in response to sounds. In Chapter 14 we'll learn how ERPs are used to study subtler psychological processes, such as attention.

EEG recordings can also provide vital information for diagnosing seizure disorders, as we discuss next.

Electrical storms in the brain can cause seizures

Since the dawn of civilization, people have been fascinated with **epilepsy**, a disorder that, in its most dramatic form, is accompanied by **seizures**, when the person suddenly loses consciousness, with muscles tensed, and then falls to the ground as the body rhythmically convulses for seconds to minutes. These seizures have spawned a lot of speculation about the cause—from demons to gods. Worldwide, about 30 million people suffer from epilepsy, but today we know it is a disorder of electrical potentials in the brain.

In the normal, active brain, electrical activity tends to be desynchronized; that is, different brain regions carry on their functions more or less independently. In contrast, during a seizure there is widespread synchronization of electrical activity: broad stretches of the brain start firing in simultaneous waves, which are evident in the EEGs as an abnormal "spike-and-wave" pattern of brain activity. Many abnormalities of the brain, such as trauma, injury, or metabolic problems, can predispose brain tissue to produce such synchronized activity, which, once begun in one brain region, may readily spread to others.

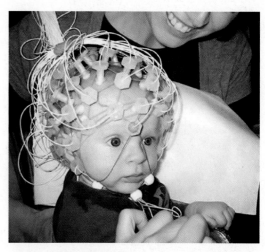

Did You Hear That? If this infant's hearing is normal, presentation of sounds should evoke an ERP from auditory centers in the infant's brain. (Courtesy of Brett Martin, Jen Gerometta, and Christine Rota-Donahue.)

knee jerk reflex A variant of the stretch reflex in which stretching of the tendon beneath the knee leads to an upward kick of the leg.

electroencephalogram (EEG) A recording of gross electrical activity of the brain via large electrodes placed on the scalp.

event-related potential (ERP) Also called *evoked potential*. Averaged EEG recordings measuring brain responses to repeated presentations of a stimulus. Components of the ERP tend to be reliable because the background noise of the cortex has been averaged out.

epilepsy A brain disorder marked by major, sudden changes in the electrophysiological state of the brain that are referred to as seizures.

seizure An epileptic episode.

(a) Multichannel EEG recording

Electrode array for EEG recording.

Each electrode can be assigned a letter on a map of the scalp.

Left hemisphere

AC
CG
GK
KO
DH
HL
LO

Right hemisphere

BF
FJ
JN
NP
EI
IM

Typical EEG recordings showing potential measured between various points on the scalp.

200 μV

1 s

(b) Event-related potentials (average of many stimulus presentations)

Negative

Gross scalp potential

N_1

CNV

P_2

N_1

I II III IV V VI P_0

N_0 N_a N_b

P_a P_1

N_2

P_2

P_3

0

−1000   −500   0   10   100 ms

Warning signal

Auditory stimulus

Following stimulus presentation, a fixed sequence of processing-related potentials is generated.

Early components (labeled I–VI) are associated with brainstem activity…

…followed by large-amplitude negative- and positive-voltage events (labeled N_0–N_2 and P_0–P_3) associated with cognitive processing in the cortex.

Figure 3.15   Gross Potentials of the Human Nervous System

grand mal seizure   A type of generalized epileptic seizure in which nerve cells fire in high-frequency bursts, usually accompanied by involuntary rhythmic contractions of the body.

petit mal seizure   Also called *absence attack*. A seizure that is characterized by a spike-and-wave EEG and often involves a loss of awareness and inability to recall events surrounding the seizure.

complex partial seizure   In epilepsy, a type of seizure that doesn't involve the entire brain, and therefore can cause a wide variety of symptoms.

aura   In epilepsy, the unusual sensations or premonition that may precede the beginning of a seizure.

There are several major categories of seizure disorders. The dramatic seizures we mentioned earlier, with loss of consciousness and rhythmic convulsions, are called **grand mal seizures** and are accompanied by abnormal EEG activity all over the brain (**Figure 3.16a**). In the more subtle **petit mal seizures**, the characteristic spike-and-wave EEG activity is evident for 5–15 seconds at a time (**Figure 3.16b**), sometimes occurring many times per day. The person is unaware of the environment during these periods, and later cannot recall events that occurred during the episode. Behaviorally, people experiencing petit mal seizures show no unusual muscle activity; they just stop what they're doing and stare into space.

Complex partial seizures do not involve the entire brain and thus can produce a wide variety of symptoms, often preceded by an unusual sensation, or **aura**. In one example, a woman felt an unusual sensation in the abdomen, a sense of foreboding, and tingling in both hands before the seizure spread. At the height of the episode, she was unresponsive and rocked her body back

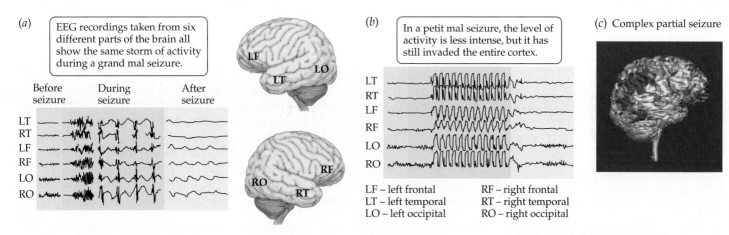

(a) EEG recordings taken from six different parts of the brain all show the same storm of activity during a grand mal seizure.

Before seizure	During seizure	After seizure

LT
RT
LF
RF
LO
RO

LF

LT

LO

RF

RO

RT

(b) In a petit mal seizure, the level of activity is less intense, but it has still invaded the entire cortex.

LT
RT
LF
RF
LO
RO

LF – left frontal   RF – right frontal
LT – left temporal   RT – right temporal
LO – left occipital   RO – right occipital

(c) Complex partial seizure

Figure 3.16   Seizure Disorders

and forth while speaking nonsensically, twisting her left arm, and looking toward the right. Of course, her seemingly random set of behavioral symptoms actually reflected the functions of the particular brain regions affected by the seizure (**Figure 3.16c**); other seizure patients would produce a completely different set of behaviors. In some individuals, complex partial seizures may be provoked by stimuli, like loud noises or flashing lights, and may produce strikingly abnormal behavior.

Many seizure disorders can be effectively controlled with the aid of antiepileptic drugs. Although these drugs have a wide variety of neural targets, they tend to selectively reduce the excitability of neurons (Rogawski and Löscher, 2004). But some cases of epilepsy do not respond to medication, and if the seizures are severe, or happen very often, they may be life-threatening. Individuals suffering from such severe epilepsy may resort to the drastic step of having parts of their brain removed, as we'll see next.

RESEARCHERS AT WORK

Surgical probing of the brain revealed a map of the body

Usually the electrical activity causing seizures begins in one part of the brain and then spreads to others. So in the twentieth century, neurosurgeons began taking dramatic measures to help people with severe epilepsy that did not respond to medication: surgical removal of the part of the brain where the seizures begin. The trick, of course, is to remove the part of the brain where the seizures begin, and *only* that part. Otherwise the patient might take the risks of surgery and still suffer from seizures, or might suffer impairment of a vital function, like verbal or memory skills, if healthy tissue is removed. One way to locate the origin of the seizures is to compare EEG readings from different places on the skull (see Figure 3.16). But this approach gives only a rough idea of where the seizures begin, and it is problematic because the recording must be made when a seizure is actually taking place.

To improve the success rate of such surgeries, neurosurgeon Wilder Penfield developed a procedure that, 80 years later, is still compelling (Foerster and Penfield, 1930). Using only local anesthesia to deaden the pain of cutting the scalp and opening up the skull, Penfield had patients remain awake and alert as he exposed their brain. Then he used electrodes to provide a tiny electrical stimulation to the surface of the cortex, asking the patient to report the results. One strategy for people whose epileptic seizures were preceded by an aura was to try to find the point where stimulation recreated the aura.

In one famous case of a woman whose seizures were preceded by the smell of burnt toast, Penfield was able to find a spot where stimulation caused her to smell

A Notable Actor with Epilepsy   Actor Hugo Weaving reports taking medication to control his epilepsy.

burnt toast and, presuming that region was the origin of the seizures, surgically removed it. (The brain itself has no pain receptors, so cutting the cortex didn't hurt.) Using this refined technique, Penfield was able to cure about half of his patients, and seizures were reduced in another 25%. José Delgado's stimulation of patients' brains, which we discussed at the start of the chapter, also sought the origin of seizures. Delgado altered the technique by implanting several electrodes temporarily, so the patient could walk around while doctors used a remote control to probe brain regions and observe the results. In Chapters 5 and 12 we'll learn that today electrodes are sometimes implanted in the brain as a treatment for other disorders.

In his pioneering work, Penfield did more than help his patients. He also made major discoveries about the organization of the human cortex (**Figure 3.17**). By

---

Figure 3.17   Mapping the Human Brain

Hypothesis

Sensory information from the body arrives in an organized fashion in the cortex.

Experiment

Electrically stimulate the surface of the cortex in alert patients, carefully recording the patient's experience with stimulation at each site. Compare these maps in various patients.

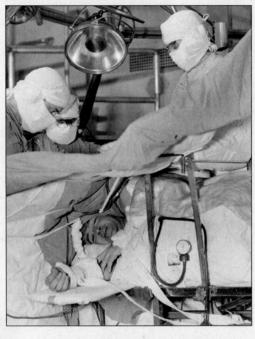

Result

Each side of the brain receives sensory information from the opposite side of the body, organized along the postcentral gyrus of the parietal lobe. Across the central sulcus, in the precentral gyrus, cortical regions control movement of that same part of the body, so that sensory and motor regions are aligned.

Conclusion

The maps of sensory cortex and motor cortex are remarkably consistent from one person to another.

carefully recording the effects of stimulating different regions of the brain, he found that stimulation of occipital cortex often caused the patient to "see" flashes of light. Stimulating another region might cause the person's thumb to tingle, while stimulation elsewhere might cause the patient's leg to move. Through these studies, Penfield confirmed that each side of the cortex receives information from, and sends commands to, the opposite side of the body. He found that stimulating the postcentral gyrus of the parietal cortex caused patients to experience sensations on various parts of the body in a way that was consistent from one person to another (see Figure 5.10). Just across the central sulcus from each site, in the precentral gyrus, stimulations caused that same part of the body to move (see Figure 5.23). These "maps" of how the various parts of the body are laid out on the cortex (Jasper and Penfield, 1954) have been reproduced in countless textbooks, providing the basis of the *homunculus*, the "little man" drawn on the surface of the cortex to depict Penfield's maps, as we discuss further in Chapter 5.

These groundbreaking observations taught us that brain function is organized in a map that reproduces body parts. We also learned that the map is distorted in the sense that parts of the body that are especially sensitive to touch, such as the lips or fingers, are monitored by a relatively large area of cortex compared to, say, the back of the legs.

Penfield's studies also stimulated a rich store of speculation about the relationship between the workings of the brain and the mind. In a small minority of patients, electrical stimulation in some sites would sometimes elicit a memory of, for example, sitting on the porch step and hearing a relative's voice, or hearing a snatch of music. As we saw at the start of this chapter, other researchers would find that electrical stimulation of the brain could make people think they loved their examiner, or could make an angry, murderous bull peaceful and calm. In another case, electrical stimulation of one part of her brain caused a young woman to find whatever was happening around her to be humorous (Fried et al., 1998).

These startling observations—showing that electrical stimulation of the brain triggers mental processes—remain a cornerstone of neuroscience, and a tantalizing demonstration that our mind is a result of physical processes at work in the machine we call the brain.

The Little Man   In drawings like this of a homunculus, the size of various body parts reflect how much representation each has in motor and sensory cortex.

How's it going?

1. What are EEGs and ERPs? How have these techniques been useful?

2. What are the two main categories of epileptic seizures, and what are the main characteristics of each type?

3. Describe Penfield's surgical procedure and what it revealed about organization of the brain.

Recommended Reading

Kandel, E. R., Schwartz, J. H., and Jessell, T. M. (2000). *Principles of Neural Science* (4th ed.). New York, NY: McGraw-Hill.

LeDoux, J. (2002). *Synaptic Self: How Our Brains Become Who We Are.* New York, NY: Viking.

Luck, S. J. (2005). *An Introduction to the Event-Related Potential Technique.* Cambridge, MA: MIT Press.

Nicholls, J. G., Martin, A. R., Fuchs, P. A., Brown, D. A., Diamond, M. E., and Weisblat, D. A. (2012). *From Neuron to Brain* (5th ed.). Sunderland, MA: Sinauer.

Purves, D., Augustine, G. J., Fitzpatrick, D., Hall, W. C., et al. (2012). *Neuroscience* (5th ed.). Sunderland, MA: Sinauer.

Valenstein, E. S. (2005). *The War of the Soups and the Sparks: The Discovery of Neurotransmitters and the Dispute over How Neurons Communicate.* New York, NY: Columbia University Press.

mindsmachine.com/vs3

You should be able to relate each summary to the adjacent illustration, including structures and processes. If you need to review, go to the figures indicated and read the accompanying text.

1 Chemical signals transmit information *between* neurons; electrical signals transmit information *within* a neuron. Neurons exhibit a small electrical potential across the cell membrane; neural signals are changes in this **resting potential**. Review **Figure 3.1, Animation 3.2**

2 Different concentrations of **ions** inside and outside the neuron—especially **potassium ions (K⁺)**, to which the resting membrane is **selectively permeable**—account for the **resting potential**. At the K⁺ **equilibrium potential**, the **electrostatic pressure** pulling K⁺ ions into the neuron is balanced by the concentration gradient pushing them out; at this point, the membrane potential is about −60 mV, the resting potential. Review **Figures 3.2–3.4, Activity 3.1, Animation 3.3**

3 Reducing the resting potential (**depolarization**) of axons until it reaches a **threshold** value opens **voltage-gated sodium (Na⁺) channels**, making the membrane completely permeable to Na⁺. The **sodium ions (Na⁺)** rush in, and the axon becomes briefly more positive inside than outside. This event is called an **action potential**. Review **Figure 3.5, Animation 3.4**

4 Following the action potential, the resting potential is quickly restored by the influx of K⁺ ions. The **sodium-potassium pumps** maintain the resting potential in the long run, counteracting the influx of Na⁺ ions during action potentials. Review **Figure 3.6**

5 The action potential strongly depolarizes the adjacent patch of axonal membrane, causing it to generate its own action potential. In this manner, the action potential is recreated and propagated down the axon. **Saltatory conduction** of the action potential along the **nodes of Ranvier** between **myelin** sheaths speeds propagation down the axon. Review **Figures 3.7** and **3.8, Box 3.1, Animation 3.5**

6 Like all other **local potentials**, **postsynaptic potentials** spread very rapidly but are not regenerated, so they diminish as they spread passively along dendrites and the cell body. **Excitatory postsynaptic potentials (EPSPs)** are depolarizing (they decrease the resting potential) and *increase* the likelihood that the neuron will fire an action potential. **Inhibitory postsynaptic potentials (IPSPs)** are **hyperpolarizing** (they make the cell more polarized), *decreasing* the likelihood that the neuron will fire. Review **Figure 3.9**

7 Neurons process information by integrating (summing algebraically) the postsynaptic potentials through both **spatial summation** (summing potentials from different locations) and **temporal summation** (summing potentials across time). Review **Figure 3.10, Animation 3.6**

8 Action potentials are initiated at the **axon hillock** when the excess of EPSPs over IPSPs reaches threshold. During the action potential, the neuron cannot be excited by a second stimulus; it is **absolutely refractory**. For a few milliseconds afterward, the hyperpolarized neuron is **relatively refractory**, requiring a stronger stimulation than usual in order to fire. Review **Figure 3.6**

9 Synaptic transmission occurs when a chemical neurotransmitter diffuses across the **synaptic cleft** and binds to **neurotransmitter receptors** in the postsynaptic membrane. Review **Figures 3.11** and **3.12, Animation 3.7**

10 Summing electrical activity over millions of nerve cells as detected by electrodes on the scalp, **electroencephalograms (EEGs)** can reveal rapid changes in brain function—for example, in response to a brief, controlled stimulus that evokes an **event-related potential (ERP)**. They can also reveal the highly synchronized electrical outbursts of a **seizure** in people with **epilepsy**. Review **Figures 3.15–3.17**

Go to **mindsmachine.com** for study questions, quizzes, flashcards, and other resources.

4 The Chemistry of Behavior:
Neurotransmitters and Neuropharmacology

A Dream of Soups and Sparks

As the twentieth century began, scientists knew that neurons were important for brain function, but there was a big controversy about how neurons communicated. What happened at those newly discovered synapses between one neuron and another? Did sparks of electricity pass from cell to cell? Or was some unknown chemical substance involved? Some scientists, nicknamed "sparks," favored the idea that electrical signals crossed synapses; other scientists, nicknamed "soups," thought neurons released a chemical that flowed across synapses. No one knew how to distinguish between these two possibilities.

Otto Loewi was so consumed with the question of neural communication that he even dreamed about it. One night he awoke suddenly, remembering a dream in which one experiment could provide a definitive answer to whether the "soups" or the "sparks" were right. He made a few notes and went back to sleep, only to discover the next day that he couldn't make any sense of the previous night's scribblings. So when he had the same dream again the following night, he got up and went straight to the lab to do the experiment while it was still fresh in his mind. The result was a discovery that would revolutionize the study of the brain.

To see a video, go to

mindsmachine.com/4.1
Synaptic Transmission

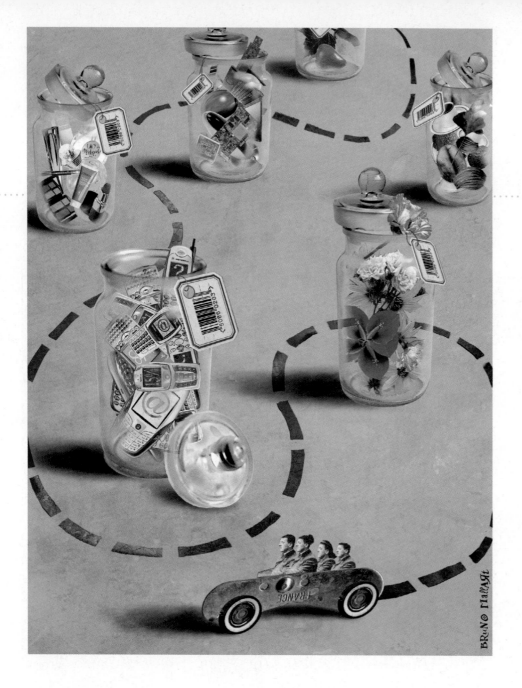

Throughout the ages, people have used **exogenous** substances (substances from external sources) to try to change the functioning of their bodies and brains. Our ancestors sipped, swallowed, and smoked their way to euphoria, calmness, pain relief, and hallucination. They discovered deadly poisons in frogs, miraculous antibiotics in mold, powerful painkillers in poppies, and all the rest of a vast catalog of helpful and harmful substances. By studying the physiological actions of these substances, modern scientists have been able to unlock many mysteries of brain function.

exogenous Arising from outside the body.

endogenous Produced inside the body.

The preceding chapters showed us that the brain is an electrochemical system. Today we know that each neuron processes information through *electrical* responses from many synapses, and then releases a *chemical* to pass that information to the next cell. Specifically, a presynaptic neuron releases an **endogenous** substance (a substance from an internal source), a chemical called a *neurotransmitter*. The neurotransmitter then communicates with the postsynaptic cell. As you might have guessed, most drugs that affect behavior do so by altering this chemical communication process at millions, or even billions, of synapses.

Let's start the chapter by reviewing synaptic transmission. Then we'll dig deeper into the chemical anatomy of the brain, looking at the major families of neurotransmitters,

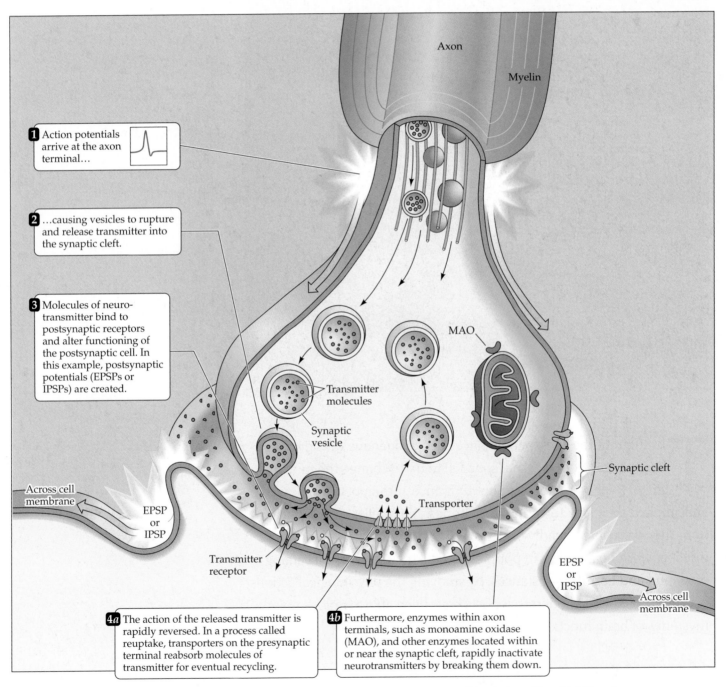

Axon

Myelin

1 Action potentials arrive at the axon terminal…

2 …causing vesicles to rupture and release transmitter into the synaptic cleft.

3 Molecules of neurotransmitter bind to postsynaptic receptors and alter functioning of the postsynaptic cell. In this example, postsynaptic potentials (EPSPs or IPSPs) are created.

MAO

Transmitter molecules

Synaptic vesicle

Synaptic cleft

Across cell membrane

EPSP or IPSP

Transporter

Transmitter receptor

EPSP or IPSP

Across cell membrane

4a The action of the released transmitter is rapidly reversed. In a process called reuptake, transporters on the presynaptic terminal reabsorb molecules of transmitter for eventual recycling.

4b Furthermore, enzymes within axon terminals, such as monoamine oxidase (MAO), and other enzymes located within or near the synaptic cleft, rapidly inactivate neurotransmitters by breaking them down.

Figure 4.1   Synapses Convert Electrical Signals into Chemical Signals

especially how each exerts its distinctive influence over unique networks in the brain. This survey will set the stage for discussing how drugs and toxins alter brain function and thereby modify behavior. We'll wrap up the chapter with a discussion of substance abuse and dependency.

Electrical Signals Are Turned into Chemical Signals at Synapses

As we learned in the previous chapter, electrical signals called *action potentials* move down axons until they reach the *axon terminal*, which forms the **presynaptic** side of a **synapse**. **Figure 4.1** recaps the events at a typical synapse. When action potentials reach the terminal, they cause vesicles to fuse with the membrane, spilling their contents into the synaptic cleft—a process known as **exocytosis**. Molecules of **neurotransmitter** (also called just *transmitter*) leave the vesicles and cross the synaptic cleft to bind to **neurotransmitter receptors** (or just *receptors*) that span the membrane of the **postsynaptic** cell, which is receiving the chemical signal.

The binding of neurotransmitter molecules to receptors can affect the postsynaptic cell in several different ways, which we'll discuss shortly. Eventually the neurotransmitter molecules are either (1) broken down by enzymes into simpler chemicals (because this action also occurs inside the terminal), or (2) brought back into the presynaptic terminal in a process called **reuptake**. Reuptake of transmitters relies on special proteins called **transporters**, complex structures that bind molecules of transmitter and then, using electrical energy derived from the movement of ions across the cell membrane, conduct the transmitter molecules back inside the presynaptic terminal. Once inside, the transmitter can be broken down or repackaged in vesicles for reuse.

Let's look at what happens when the neurotransmitter binds to the postsynaptic receptors.

Receptor proteins recognize transmitters and their mimics

Neurotransmitter receptors are very picky about the substances that they will respond to. For this reason, the action of transmitters on receptors is often likened to a key opening a lock. However, in Chapter 3 we saw that even though receptors vary enormously in the chemical "keys" they respond to, and can produce many different specific responses, there are two basic kinds of neurotransmitter receptors, which respond in two different ways.

Some receptors are just fancy ion channels; when bound by transmitter molecules, these **ionotropic receptors** quickly change their shape to open or close their ion channel (**Figure 4.2**). The opening of the channel allows more (or less) of the channel's favorite ion to flow into or out of the postsynaptic neuron, thus changing the local membrane potential. If that change in the postsynaptic membrane potential is a depolarization, bringing the cell closer to its threshold, then it will be more likely to produce an action potential. In that case we say the synapse had

presynaptic   Located on the "transmitting" side of a synapse.

synapse   The location at which information flows between a presynaptic neuron and a postsynaptic neuron, often through the conversion of electrical activity in the presynaptic neuron into a secretion of chemical neurotransmitter that alters the functioning of the postsynaptic neuron.

exocytosis   A cellular process that results in the release of a substance into the extracellular space.

neurotransmitter   Also called simply *transmitter*. A signaling chemical, released by a presynaptic neuron, that diffuses across the synaptic cleft to alter the functioning of the postsynaptic neuron.

neurotransmitter receptor   Also called simply *receptor*. A specialized protein that is embedded in the cell membrane, allowing it to selectively sense and react to molecules of the corresponding neurotransmitter.

postsynaptic   Located on the "receiving" side of a synapse.

reuptake   The reabsorption of molecules of neurotransmitter by the neurons that released them, thereby ending the signaling activity of the transmitter molecules.

transporter   A specialized membrane component that returns transmitter molecules to the presynaptic neuron for reuse.

ionotropic receptor   Also called *ligand-gated ion channel*. A receptor protein containing an ion channel that opens when the receptor is bound by an agonist.

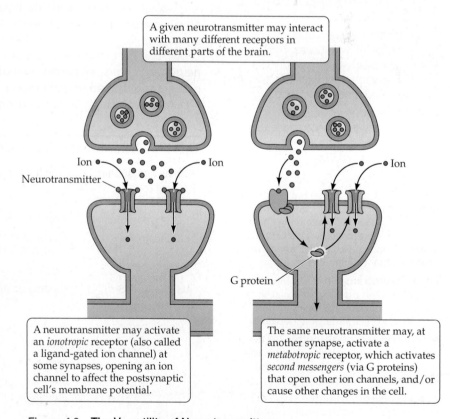

A given neurotransmitter may interact with many different receptors in different parts of the brain.

Ion

Neurotransmitter

Ion

Ion

G protein

A neurotransmitter may activate an *ionotropic* receptor (also called a ligand-gated ion channel) at some synapses, opening an ion channel to affect the postsynaptic cell's membrane potential.

The same neurotransmitter may, at another synapse, activate a *metabotropic* receptor, which activates *second messengers* (via G proteins) that open other ion channels, and/or cause other changes in the cell.

Figure 4.2   The Versatility of Neurotransmitters

To see the brain in 3D, go to

mindsmachine.com/4.2
Brain Explorer

How's it going?

1. Distinguish between endogenous and exogenous substances, and give a few examples of each.

2. Review the sequence of events that occurs when an action potential arrives at the axon terminal and causes a release of neurotransmitter. Use the following terms in your answer: *exocytosis, receptors, ionotropic, metabotropic, reuptake.*

3. Identify the criteria that are used to establish whether a substance in the brain can be considered a neurotransmitter. Briefly discuss why each one is important.

4. Name and briefly describe each of the major categories of neurotransmitters.

metabotropic receptor A receptor protein that does not contain ion channels but may, when activated, use a G protein system to open nearby ion channels or to produce other cellular effects.

amine neurotransmitter A neurotransmitter based on modifications of a single amino acid nucleus. Examples include acetylcholine, serotonin, and dopamine.

amino acid neurotransmitter A neurotransmitter that is itself an amino acid. Examples include GABA, glycine, and glutamate.

peptide neurotransmitter Also called *neuropeptide*. A neurotransmitter consisting of a short chain of amino acids.

an excitatory effect. If ions passing through the ionotropic receptor hyperpolarize the postsynaptic cell, then it will be less likely to produce an action potential, and we say the synapse was inhibitory.

But not all receptors work by opening an ion channel. Receptors belonging to the other major category—the **metabotropic receptors**—don't contain ion channels. Instead, they link across the cell membrane to complicated chemical machinery inside the postsynaptic neuron (see Figure 4.2). When activated, metabotropic receptors alter the inner workings of the postsynaptic cell, using a system of *second messengers* to cause changes in excitability or other, slower but larger-scale responses. For example, the metabotropic receptor may kick off a chain of chemical reactions that will affect *gene expression* (the use of genes to produce proteins). The change in gene expression could include, for example, the production of more receptors!

Together, the two major categories of transmitter receptors allow not only for rapid responses where timing is crucial, but also for more complex, integrative, slower behaviors such as emotional responses, social behavior, and so on.

Many neurotransmitters have been identified

Over the years, neuroscientists have agreed on some basic principles for deciding whether a brain chemical qualifies as a classical neurotransmitter. We can conclude that a candidate substance is a transmitter if

- It can be synthesized by presynaptic neurons and stored in axon terminals.

- It is released when action potentials reach the terminals.

- It is recognized by specific receptors located on the postsynaptic membrane.

- It causes changes in the postsynaptic cell.

- Blocking its release interferes with the ability of the presynaptic cell to affect the postsynaptic cell.

According to these criteria, the brain contains many different neurotransmitters. **Table 4.1** summarizes the major categories of transmitters that we will consider in the next portion of this chapter. The family of **amine neurotransmitters** includes some of the best-known classical transmitters, such as acetylcholine, dopamine, and serotonin. **Amino acid neurotransmitters** and **peptide neurotransmitters** (or *neuropeptides*), as their names suggest, are based on single amino acid molecules or on short chains of amino acids (called *peptides*), respectively. Each year the list of probable neurotransmitters grows, and the

TABLE 4.1 Some Synaptic Transmitters and Families of Transmitters

Family and subfamily	Transmitter(s)
AMINES	
Quaternary amines	Acetylcholine (ACh)
Monoamines	*Catecholamines*: Norepinephrine (NE), epinephrine (adrenaline), dopamine (DA)
	Indoleamines: Serotonin (5-hydroxytryptamine [5-HT]), melatonin
AMINO ACIDS	Gamma-aminobutyric acid (GABA), glutamate, glycine, histamine
NEUROPEPTIDES	
Opioid peptides	*Enkephalins*: Met-enkephalin, leu-enkephalin
	Endorphins: Beta-endorphin
	Dynorphins: Dynorphin A
Other neuropeptides	Oxytocin, substance P, cholecystokinin (CCK), vasopressin, neuropeptide Y (NPY), hypothalamic-releasing hormones
GASES	Nitric oxide, carbon monoxide

search for new transmitters has occasionally yielded surprises like the **gas neurotransmitters**, soluble gases that diffuse between neurons to alter ongoing processes (and defy several of the criteria for transmitters that we just listed!). Considering the rate at which these substances are being discovered and characterized, it would not be surprising if there turned out to be several hundred different neurotransmitters at work in synapses throughout the central nervous system. But for now, let's content ourselves with a look at a few of the best-known neurotransmitter systems in the brain. We'll see that each neurotransmitter is distributed in a unique pattern across brain regions.

RESEARCHERS AT WORK

The first transmitter to be discovered was acetylcholine

Our chapter began with the classic story of Otto Loewi's dream of an experiment that would reveal the first neurotransmitter. After forgetting the details of the dream the first night, Loewi was quick to get out of bed when the dream returned the following night. He went straight to the lab to conduct the experiment depicted in **Figure 4.3**.

Figure 4.3 "Soups" versus "Sparks": The First Neurotransmitter

Question

Do neurons release a chemical to communicate with other cells, or is the communication based on electrical signals?

Experiment

Stimulate the vagus nerve to slow the heart. Collect fluid from around the slowed heart and apply the fluid to a second heart.

Result

The second heart also slowed.

Conclusion

The vagus nerve uses a chemical neurotransmitter, not a direct electrical connection, to communicate to cells of the heart and cause it to slow down.

Otto Loewi Following the Nazi annexation of Austria in 1938, Loewi, then a professor at the University of Graz, was forced to flee to the United States, where he remained for the rest of his life. He was photographed in the summer of 1955 by his associate, Dr. Morris Rockstein, at the Woods Hole Marine Biological Laboratory. (Photograph courtesy of Dr. Edward D. Rockstein.)

gas neurotransmitter A neurotransmitter that is a soluble gas. Examples include nitric oxide and carbon monoxide.

Loewi's first step was to electrically stimulate the vagus nerve in a frog, which he knew would cause its heart to slow down. The question was, why did the heart slow down? Had the electricity flowed from the vagus nerve to the heart as the "sparks" believed? Or were the "soups" right, and the nerve had released a chemical to slow the heart?

Loewi's critical, dream-inspired experiment was to collect the fluid that surrounded the slowing heart. Then he applied that fluid to the heart of another frog. If the first heart had been slowed by electrical signals from the vagus, then the fluid should have no effect on the second heart. But if electrical stimulation of the vagus had caused it to release a chemical, then the fluid from the first heart should slow the beating of the second. In fact, the fluid did cause the second heart to slow its rate, providing Loewi with evidence for chemical neurotransmission (and a nice shiny Nobel Prize, in 1936). That neurotransmitter was later chemically identified as **acetylcholine** (**ACh** for short). The "soups" were vindicated.

Neurotransmitter Systems Form a Complex Array in the Brain

It is possible to stain brain tissue in such a way that only the neurons making a particular neurotransmitter end up being labeled (see Box 2.1). Studies of brain sections stained in this way have shown that transmitters are found in complex networks of neurons that extend throughout the brain. In **Figure 4.4**, this complicated anatomy is depicted for some of the major amine transmitters. The point to remember is that each of these amine neurotransmitters is carried by a different set of axons, and those axons project to different brain regions. Each "flavor" of neurotransmitter is talking to a distinct set of brain targets, and there may be overlap as two different transmitters arrive at the same target. How those targets respond depends on which neurotransmitter is being released, and which kind of receptors for that transmitter the target neurons possess. Despite its appearance, Figure 4.4 is a simplification; there are many more transmitters at work than the few we have shown here, and they are arranged in much more complicated networks.

Four amine neurotransmitters project throughout the brain

Some of the most thoroughly studied transmitters are amines; they have been implicated in many categories of behavior and pathology. Because they are involved in a wide range of disorders—Parkinson's disease, schizophrenia, Alzheimer's disease, and depression, to name just a few—amine neurotransmitter mechanisms are a major target for drug development. Here we look at four important amine transmitters: acetylcholine, dopamine, serotonin, and norepinephrine. (To learn more about the neuronal synthesis of neurotransmitters, see **A Step Further 4.1**, on the website.)

ACETYLCHOLINE We now know that acetylcholine (ACh) plays a major role in transmission in the forebrain. Many **cholinergic** (ACh-containing) neurons are found in nuclei within the **basal forebrain**. These cholinergic cells project widely in the brain, to sites such as the cerebral cortex, amygdala, and hippocampus (see Figure 4.4). Widespread loss of cholinergic neurons is associated with Alzheimer's disease, and experimental disruption of cholinergic pathways in rats interferes with learning and memory.

DOPAMINE Of the 100 billion or so neurons in the human brain, only about a million contain **dopamine** (**DA**), but they are critically important for many aspects of behavior. Figure 4.4 shows the path of the major **dopaminergic** projections. One of these projections, called the *mesostriatal pathway*, originates in and around the **substantia nigra** of the midbrain. From there, axons project to parts of the basal ganglia. There aren't all that many neurons in the system—hundreds of thousands—but keep in

acetylcholine (ACh) A neurotransmitter found in the autonomic nervous system, motor systems, and throughout the brain.

cholinergic Referring to cells that use acetylcholine as their synaptic transmitter.

basal forebrain A region, ventral to the basal ganglia, that is the major source of acetylcholine in the brain.

dopamine (DA) A monoamine transmitter found in the midbrain—especially the substantia nigra—and in the basal forebrain.

dopaminergic Referring to cells that use dopamine as their synaptic transmitter.

substantia nigra A brainstem structure that innervates the basal ganglia and is the source of all dopaminergic projections.

To see an animation of this figure, go to

mindsmachine.com/4.3
Neurotransmitter Pathways

In this midline view, the brain nuclei containing cell bodies of neurons that release four of the major transmitters are shown in different colors, as are the projections of their axons. Although the projections may overlap, each neurotransmitter projects to a distinct set of brain targets.

Cholinergic

Basal forebrain

Dopaminergic

Mesolimbocortical pathway: ventral tegmental area (VTA) to nucleus accumbens and cortex

Mesostriatal pathway: substantia nigra to basal ganglia

Noradrenergic

Locus coeruleus to forebrain

Serotonergic

Midbrain raphe nuclei to forebrain; brainstem raphe nuclei to spinal cord.

Figure 4.4 Neurotransmitter Pathways in the Brain

mind that a single axon can divide to supply thousands of synapses. Those synapses play a crucial role in motor control. When people lose a significant number of mesostriatal dopaminergic neurons, from either exposure to poisons or just old age, they develop the profound movement problems of Parkinson's disease (described in Chapter 5), including tremors.

Another dopaminergic projection, called the *mesolimbocortical pathway*, also originates in the midbrain, in a region called the **ventral tegmental area** (**VTA**) (see Figure 4.4). From there, the pathway projects to various locations in the limbic system (see Chapter 2) and cortex. The mesolimbocortical system appears to be especially important for the perception of reward; it's probably where feelings of pleasure arise. Thus, it makes sense that the mesolimbocortical dopamine system is important for learning that is shaped by *positive reinforcement* (which is just a fancy term for "reward"; see Chapter 13). Abnormalities in the mesolimbocortical pathway are associated with some of the symptoms of schizophrenia, as we discuss in Chapter 12. This pathway also seems to be important for addictive behaviors, as we discuss at the end of this chapter.

SEROTONIN Dopaminergic neurons may be scarce, but there are even fewer **serotonergic** neurons in the human brain—just 200,000 or so. Nevertheless, wide expanses of the

ventral tegmental area (VTA) A portion of the midbrain that projects dopaminergic fibers to the nucleus accumbens.

serotonergic Referring to cells that use serotonin as their synaptic transmitter.

brain are innervated by serotonergic fibers, originating from neurons sprinkled along the midline of the midbrain and brainstem in the **raphe nuclei** (*raphe* is pronounced "ra-FAY") (see Figure 4.4).

Serotonin (or **5-HT**, short for its chemical name, 5-hydroxytryptamine) participates in the control of all sorts of behaviors: mood, vision, sexual behavior, anxiety, sleep, and many other functions. As we'll see a little later, drugs that either directly mimic serotonin or, like Prozac, cause serotonin to accumulate, are often effective for relieving depression and anxiety. The precise behavioral actions of serotonergic drugs depend on which of the many 5-HT receptor subtypes are affected (see Table 4.2) (Gorzalka et al., 1990; Miczek et al., 2002).

NOREPINEPHRINE   As Figure 4.4 shows, many of the brain's **noradrenergic** neurons (we use this term because **norepinephrine [NE]** is also known as *noradrenaline*) have their cell bodies in two regions of the brainstem and midbrain: the **locus coeruleus** ("blue spot") and the **lateral tegmental area**. Noradrenergic axons from these regions project broadly throughout the cerebrum, including the cerebral cortex, limbic system, and thalamic nuclei. They participate in the control of behaviors ranging from alertness to mood to sexual behavior (and many more).

Some amino acids act as neurotransmitters

The most common transmitters in the brain are amino acids, and of these, the two most studied are the excitatory transmitter **glutamate** and the inhibitory transmitter **gamma-aminobutyric acid** (**GABA**). Both have wide-ranging effects at synapses throughout the central nervous system, and from an evolutionary perspective they are among the most ancient transmitter substances.

Glutamate interacts with several subtypes of receptors (see Table 4.2), but one subtype in particular, called the NMDA receptor, has been singled out for special attention by researchers. As we discuss in Chapter 13 (and on the website in **A Step Further 4.2**), NMDA receptors have unique characteristics that suggest they play a central role in memory formation.

Among the subtypes of receptors for GABA, the GABA$_A$ receptors have received decades of special scrutiny, because of their relationship to anxiety relief. GABA$_A$ receptors are ionotropic; when activated they allow more Cl$^-$ ions to flow into the postsynaptic cell, thus inhibiting that cell's activity. Drugs that mimic this action of GABA$_A$ tend to be effective calming agents because they produce a widespread decrease in neural activity. Drugs called *benzodiazepines*—examples include Valium (diazepam) and Ativan (lorazepam)—are widely used to reduce anxiety, as well as to aid muscle relaxation, sleep induction, and the like.

Many peptides function as neurotransmitters

Among the many peptides that serve as neurotransmitters are several that we'll discuss in later chapters:

- **Opioid peptides** are endogenous peptides that mimic well-known exogenous opiate drugs such as opium (after which opioids and opiates are named), morphine, and codeine. Four principal endogenous opioids are met-enkephalin, leu-enkephalin, beta-endorphin, and dynorphin A. Like morphine, these peptides act in the brain to reduce our perception of pain.

- Many peptides originally found in peripheral organs like the gut (which explains some of their names) are also made by neurons in the spinal cord and brain. In the brain, these peptides may act as synaptic transmitters, and they are often co-localized with classical transmitters. Examples include substance P, cholecystokinin (CCK), neurotensin, neuropeptide Y (NPY), vasoactive intestinal polypeptide (VIP), and others.

- A variety of peptide hormones, such as oxytocin and vasopressin, are products of the hypothalamus and pituitary. Peptides are involved in an astonishing range of func-

---

raphe nuclei   A string of nuclei in the midline of the midbrain and brainstem that contain most of the serotonergic neurons of the brain.

serotonin (5-HT)   A synaptic transmitter that is produced in the raphe nuclei and is active in structures throughout the cerebral hemispheres.

noradrenergic   Referring to cells using norepinephrine (noradrenaline) as a transmitter.

norepinephrine (NE)   Also called *noradrenaline*. A neurotransmitter that is produced and released by sympathetic postganglionic neurons to accelerate organ activity. It is also produced in the brainstem and found in projections throughout the brain.

locus coeruleus   A small nucleus in the brainstem whose neurons produce norepinephrine and modulate large areas of the forebrain.

lateral tegmental area   A brainstem region that provides some of the norepinephrine-containing projections of the brain.

glutamate   An amino acid transmitter, the most common excitatory transmitter.

gamma-aminobutyric acid (GABA)   A widely distributed amino acid transmitter, and the main inhibitory transmitter in the mammalian nervous system.

opioid peptide   A type of endogenous peptide that mimics the effects of morphine in binding to opioid receptors and producing marked analgesia and reward.

tions; vasopressin, for one example, was first known for its role in urine production, but it also contributes to such high-level processes as memory and pair-bonding!

Some neurotransmitters are gases

Neurons sometimes use certain gas molecules to communicate information; the best studied of these is nitric oxide (not to be confused with "laughing gas," which is nit*rous* oxide). Carbon monoxide also serves as a transmitter in some cells. Although we call them *gas neurotransmitters*, these substances are different from traditional neurotransmitters in at least three important ways:

1. Gas transmitters are produced outside axon terminals, especially in the dendrites, and are not held in vesicles; the substance simply diffuses out of the neuron as it is produced.

2. No receptors in the membrane of the target cell are involved. Instead, the gas transmitter diffuses into the target cell to trigger second messengers inside.

3. Most important, these gases can function as **retrograde transmitters**: by diffusing from the postsynaptic neuron back to the presynaptic neuron, the gas transmitter conveys information that is used to physically change the synapse. This process may be crucial for memory formation (see Chapter 13).

Drugs Fit Like Keys into Molecular Locks

Any substance that binds to a receptor is termed a **ligand**. The natural ligands for receptors are molecules of neurotransmitters, of course. But as you may have guessed, many (but not all) drugs that affect the brain are also receptor ligands.

In everyday English, we use the term *drug* in different ways. One common meaning is "a medicine used in the treatment of a disease" (as in *prescription drug* or *over-the-counter drug*). Quite a different meaning of *drug*, but also a common one, is "a psychoactive agent," especially an addictive one—that is, a drug of abuse. The common element of these meanings is a substance that, taken in relatively small amounts, has clear effects on experience, mood, emotion, activity, and/or health.

When the neurotransmitter (the endogenous ligand) binds a receptor, it activates a change in the receptor, such as opening an ion channel (**Figure 4.5a**). When

How's it going?

1. Describe how the first neurotransmitter was discovered. Why do you think we selected this discovery for this chapter's "Researchers at Work" feature?

2. Name and describe the anatomical organization of the four major "classical" amine neurotransmitters. What are some of the functions in which each transmitter has been implicated?

3. What are the main excitatory and inhibitory amino acid transmitters of the brain, and what importance do they have?

4. What is a peptide? Where do peptides come from—give a few examples—and what are some functions they perform?

5. Discuss the ways in which the gas transmitters resemble and differ from traditional amine transmitters.

retrograde transmitter   A neurotransmitter that diffuses from the postsynaptic neuron back to the presynaptic neuron.

ligand   A substance that binds to receptor molecules, such as a neurotransmitter or drug that binds postsynaptic receptors.

(a)

Transmitter
Open

(b)

Drug
Open

(c)

Antagonist
Closed

Unbound receptor. In this example, it is normally closed.

An endogenous ligand is a naturally occurring molecule, such as a transmitter, that binds to the receptor. An endogenous ligand usually activates its receptor and is therefore classified as an *agonist*.

An exogenous ligand (that is, a drug or toxin) that resembles the endogenous ligand and is capable of binding to the receptor and activating it is also classified as a *receptor agonist*.

Some substances bind to receptors but do not activate them. Instead, they simply block agonists from binding to the receptors. These are classified as *antagonists*.

To see an animation of this figure, go to

mindsmachine.com/4.4
Agonists and Antagonists

Figure 4.5   The Agonistic and Antagonistic Actions of Drugs

agonist   A molecule, usually a drug, that binds a receptor molecule and initiates a response like that of another molecule, usually a neurotransmitter.

antagonist   A molecule, usually a drug, that interferes with or prevents the action of a neurotransmitter.

an exogenous ligand, such as a drug molecule, binds the receptor, it may partially or completely activate the receptor; substances that have this kind of action are called **agonists** (**Figure 4.5b**). So agonist drugs are substances that mimic the effects of the normal transmitter for that receptor. Other ligands, called receptor **antagonists**, bind to the receptor but do *not* activate it. Antagonists therefore effectively block the receptor from being activated by the receptor's normal neurotransmitter (**Figure 4.5c**). For that reason, drugs with this action are sometimes called receptor *blockers*.

Some drugs—caffeine, opium, nicotine, and cocaine are just a few examples—originally evolved in plants, often as a defense against being eaten. Other modern drugs, are synthetic (human-made) and tuned to affect specific transmitter systems. For example, benzodiazepine antianxiety drugs, like Ativan, alter GABA neurotransmission; classic antischizophrenics like haloperidol (trade name Haldol) target dopamine receptors; selective serotonin reuptake inhibitors, like Prozac, are antidepressants. So to understand how drugs work, we must perform analysis at many levels—from molecules to anatomical systems to behavioral effects and experiences.

In Chapter 3 we explained that a given neurotransmitter interacts with a variety of different *subtypes* of receptors. To give you a sense of just how diverse the list of transmitter receptor subtypes can be, we've compiled the subtypes for a few transmitters in **Table 4.2**. For example, there are more than a dozen different subtypes of serotonin receptors. Some are inhibitory, some excitatory, some ionotropic, some metabotropic; in fact, the only thing they all really share is that they are normally stimulated by serotonin. They even differ in their anatomical distribution within the brain. This division of transmitter

---

TABLE 4.2 The Bewildering Multiplicity of Transmitter Receptor Subtypes

Transmitter	Known receptor subtypes	Function
Acetylcholine (ACh)	Muscarinic receptors (metabotropic) Nicotinic receptors (ionotropic)	Both are involved in cholinergic transmission in the cortex. Nicotinic receptors are crucial for muscle contraction.
Dopamine (DA)	D_1 through D_5 receptors (all are metabotropic) D_6 and D_7 are probable	Found throughout the forebrain Involved in complex behaviors, including motor function, reward, higher cognition
Norepinephrine (NE)	α_1, α_2, β_1, and β_2 receptors (all are metabotropic)	Multiple effects in visceral organs; important part of sympathetic nervous system and "fight or flight" responses In the brain, NE transmission provides an alerting and arousing function.
Serotonin	5-HT_1 receptor family (5 members) 5-HT_2 receptor family (3 members) 5-HT_3 through 5-HT_7 receptors All but one subtype (5-HT_3) are metabotropic	Different subtypes differ in their distribution in the brain. May be involved in mood, sleep, and higher cognition 5-HT_3 receptors are particularly involved in nausea.
Gamma-aminobutyric acid (GABA)	$GABA_A$ (ionotropic) $GABA_B$ (metabotropic)	$GABA_A$ receptors are inhibitory in many brain regions, reducing excitability and preventing seizure activity. $GABA_B$ receptors are also inhibitory, by a different mechanism.
Glutamate	AMPA, kainate, and NMDA receptors (ionotropic) mGluR's (**m**etabotropic **glu**tamate **r**eceptors)	Glutamate is the most abundant of all neurotransmitters, and the most important excitatory transmitter. Glutamate receptors are crucial for excitatory signals, and NMDA receptors are especially implicated in learning and memory.
Miscellaneous peptides	Many specific receptors for peptides such as opiates (delta, kappa, and mu receptors), cholecystokinin (CCK), neurotensin, neuropeptide (NPY), and dozens more (metabotropic)	Peptide transmitters have many different functions, depending on their anatomical localization. Some important examples include the control of feeding, sexual behaviors, and social functions.

receptors into multiple subtypes presents us with an opportunity because, although the natural transmitter will act on *all* its receptor subtypes, we humans can craftily design drugs that single out just one or a few receptor subtypes. Selectively activating or blocking specific subtypes of receptors can produce diverse effects, some of which are beneficial. For example, treating someone with large doses of the neurotransmitter serotonin would necessarily activate *all* of her different subtypes of serotonin receptors, producing a confusing welter of different effects. But drugs that selectively block 5-HT$_3$ receptors while ignoring other subtypes of serotonin receptors produce a powerful and specific anti-nausea effect that brings relief to people undergoing cancer chemotherapy.

The effects of a drug depend on its dose

The tuning of drug molecules to receptor subtypes is not absolutely specific. In reality, a particular drug will generally bind strongly to one kind of receptor, more weakly to a few other types, and not at all to many others. This chemical attraction is known as **binding affinity** (or simply **affinity**). At low doses, when relatively few drug molecules are in circulation, drugs will preferentially bind to their highest-affinity receptors. At higher doses, enough molecules of the drug are available that they can bind to both the highest-affinity receptors and lower-affinity receptors. Once it is bound to a receptor, the drug has a certain propensity to *activate* the receptor; this propensity is referred to as its **efficacy** (or **intrinsic activity**). As you might guess, agonists have high efficacy, and antagonists have low or no efficacy (see Figure 4.5). So it is a combination of affinity and efficacy—where it binds and what it does—that determines the overall action of a drug. For example, the classic antischizophrenia drugs tend to have high affinity and low efficacy at the D$_2$ subtype of dopamine receptors; in other words, they are D$_2$ blockers. It's a topic we'll revisit later in this chapter and in Chapter 12.

Administering larger doses of a drug ultimately increases the proportion of receptors that are bound and affected by the drug. Within certain limits, this increase in receptor binding also increases the response to the drug; in other words, greater doses tend to produce greater effects. When plotted as a graph, the relationship between drug doses and observed effects is called a **dose-response curve** (**DRC**), typically taking the shape shown in **Figure 4.6a**. Careful analysis of DRCs reveals many aspects of a drug's

binding affinity or affinity The propensity of molecules of a drug (or other ligand) to bind to receptors.

efficacy or intrinsic activity The extent to which a drug activates a response when it binds to a receptor.

dose-response curve (DRC) A formal graph of a drug's effects (on the *y*-axis) versus the dose given (on the *x*-axis).

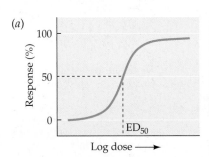

The basic dose-response curve (DRC) plots increasing drug doses (usually on a logarithmic scale) against increasing strength of the response being studied. The dose at which the drug shows half of its maximal effect is termed the *effective dose 50%* (*ED$_{50}$*).

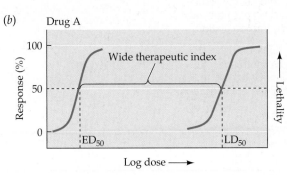

The *therapeutic index* is the separation between the effective doses of a drug and the toxic doses. Comparing the ED$_{50}$ with the dose at which 50% of the animals die (*lethal dose 50%, or LD$_{50}$*), reveals a greater difference for drug A (blue) than for drug B (yellow), so A is the safer drug. Someone using drug B has a much greater risk of accidentally taking a toxic, even fatal, dose than does someone using drug A.

Figure 4.6 The Dose-Response Curve

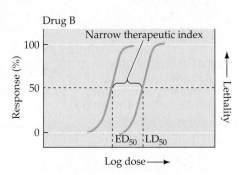

bioavailable   Referring to a substance, usually a drug, that is present in the body in a form that is able to interact with physiological mechanisms.

biotransformation   The process in which enzymes convert a drug into a metabolite that is itself active, possibly in ways that are substantially different from the actions of the original substance.

blood-brain barrier   The mechanisms that make the movement of substances from blood vessels into brain cells more difficult than exchanges in other body organs, thus affording the brain greater protection from exposure to some substances found in the blood.

activity, such as useful and safe dose ranges (**Figure 4.6b**), and it is one of the main tools for understanding the functional relationships between drugs and their targets.

Drug doses are administered in many different ways

Drug molecules aren't magic bullets; they don't somehow know where to go to find particular receptor molecules. Instead, drug molecules just spread widely throughout the body, binding to their favorite receptors when they happen to encounter them. This binding triggers a chain of cellular events, but it is usually temporary, and when the drug (or transmitter) breaks away from the receptor, the receptor resumes its unbound shape and functioning.

The amount of a drug that gets to the brain, and how fast it gets there, depends in part on the drug's *route of administration*. Some routes, such as smoking or intravenous injection, rapidly ramp up the amount of drug that is **bioavailable** (free to act on the target tissue, and thus not in use elsewhere or in the process of being eliminated). With other routes, such as swallowing, the concentration of drug builds up more slowly over longer periods of time. The duration of a drug effect also depends on how the drug is metabolized and excreted from the body—via the kidneys, liver, lungs, or other routes. In some cases, the metabolites of drugs are themselves active; this **biotransformation** of drugs can produce substances with beneficial or harmful actions.

Humans have devised an ingenious variety of techniques for introducing substances into the body; these are summarized in **Table 4.3**. In Chapter 2 we discussed the **blood-brain barrier**: the tight junctions between the cells making up blood vessels within the central nervous system, which inhibit the movement of larger molecules out of the bloodstream and into the brain. This barrier poses a major challenge for neuropharmacology because many drugs that might be clinically useful are too large to pass the blood-brain barrier to enter the brain. To a limited extent this problem can be circumvented by administering the drugs directly into the brain, but that is a drastic step.

TABLE 4.3 The Relationship between Routes of Administration and Effects of Drugs

Route of administration	Examples and mechanisms	Typical speed of effects
INGESTION Tablets and capsules Syrups Infusions and teas Suppositories	Many sorts of drugs and remedies; depends on absorption by the gut, which is somewhat slower than most other routes.	Slow to moderate
INHALATION Smoking Nasal absorption Inhaled powders and sprays	Nicotine, cocaine, organic solvents such as airplane glue and gasoline, and other drugs of abuse; also used for a variety of prescription drugs and hormone treatments. Inhalation methods take advantage of the rich vascularization of the nose and lungs to convey drugs directly into the bloodstream.	Moderate to fast
PERIPHERAL INJECTION Subcutaneous Intramuscular Intraperitoneal (abdominal) Intravenous	Many drugs; subcutaneous (under the skin) injections tend to have the slowest effects because they must diffuse into nearby tissue in order to reach the bloodstream; intravenous injections have very rapid effects because the drug is placed directly into circulation.	Moderate to fast
CENTRAL INJECTION Intracerebroventricular (into ventricular system) Intrathecal (into the cerebrospinal fluid of the spine) Epidural (under the dura mater) Intracerebral (directly into a brain region)	Central methods involve injection directly into the central nervous system; used in order to circumvent the blood-brain barrier, to rule out peripheral effects, or to directly affect a discrete brain location.	Fast to very fast

Alternatively, some drugs can take advantage of active transport systems that normally move nutrients out of the bloodstream and into the brain.

Repeated treatments can reduce the effectiveness of drugs

Our bodies are well equipped to maintain a constant internal environment, optimized for cellular activities. Many body systems may change to counteract challenges such as drug treatments. For example, once the body has been exposed to a drug, it may change to counteract the drug's effects. This response is called **drug tolerance** (or just *tolerance*), in which a drug's effectiveness diminishes over repeated treatments. Consequently, more and more drug is needed to cause the same effect.

Drug tolerance can develop in several different ways. Some drugs provoke **metabolic tolerance**, in which the body (especially metabolic organs like the liver) becomes more effective at eliminating the drug before it can have an effect. Sometimes the target tissue itself may change its sensitivity to the drug—a phenomenon called **functional tolerance**. Often the cause of functional tolerance is that the target cell changes how many receptors it has on its surface. If the target neuron has fewer receptors, then more drug molecules will be needed to have the same effect as before. So, for example, after repeated doses of an *agonist* drug, neurons may **down-regulate** their receptors (decrease the number of available receptors to which the drug can bind), thereby countering the drug effect. If the drug is an *antagonist*, target neurons may instead **up-regulate** (increase the number of receptors).

Tolerance to a particular drug often generalizes to other drugs of the same chemical class; this effect is termed **cross-tolerance**. For example, people who have developed tolerance to heroin tend to exhibit a degree of tolerance to all the other drugs in the opiate category, including codeine, morphine, and methadone. This is because all those drugs act on the same general class of receptors.

Drugs Affect Each Stage of Neural Conduction and Synaptic Transmission

As the saying goes, it takes two to tango. Synaptic transmission involves a complicated choreography of the two participating neurons, and drugs that affect the brain and behavior may act on either side of the synapse. Let's consider these two sites of action in turn.

Some drugs alter presynaptic processes

One of the ways that a drug may change synaptic transmission is by altering the presynaptic neuron, changing the system that converts an electrical signal (an action potential) into a chemical signal (secretion of neurotransmitter). As **Figure 4.7** illustrates, the most common presynaptic drug effects can be grouped into three main categories: effects on transmitter *production*, effects on transmitter *release*, and effects on transmitter *clearance*.

TRANSMITTER PRODUCTION   In order for the presynaptic neuron to produce neurotransmitter, a steady supply of raw materials and enzymes must arrive at the axon terminals and carry out the needed reactions. Drugs are available that alter this process in various ways (**Figure 4.7a**). For example, drugs may block synthesis enzymes, causing a depletion of transmitter. Alternatively, drugs that block axonal transport prevent raw materials from reaching the axon terminals in the first place, which could also cause the presynaptic terminal to run out of neurotransmitter. In either case, the presynaptic terminal would release less transmitter, which would have less of an effect on behavior. A third class of drug (e.g., reserpine) doesn't prevent the *production* of transmitter but instead interferes with the cell's ability to *store* the transmitter in synaptic vesicles for later release. The effect on behavior may be complicated, depending on how much transmitter is able to reach the postsynaptic cell.

How's it going?

1. Briefly explain agonist and antagonist actions of a ligand, with respect to effects on receptors.

2. What are receptor subtypes? What is their significance for drug development?

3. Briefly explain how dose-response curves are calculated, and why they are useful to pharmacologists. Distinguish between a drug's binding affinity and its efficacy.

4. Provide a review of the different ways in which drugs can be administered, in particular noting some considerations that are taken into account when deciding on a route of drug administration. How does repeated exposure to a drug alter its effects? (*Hint:* Use the words *tolerance* and *regulate* in your answer.)

drug tolerance   Also called simply *tolerance*. A condition in which, with repeated exposure to a drug, an individual becomes less responsive to a constant dose.

metabolic tolerance   The form of drug tolerance that arises when repeated exposure to the drug causes the metabolic machinery of the body to become more efficient at clearing the drug.

functional tolerance   The form of drug tolerance that arises when repeated exposure to the drug causes receptors to be up-regulated or down-regulated.

down-regulation   A compensatory decrease in receptor availability at the synapses of a neuron.

up-regulation   A compensatory increase in receptor availability at the synapses of a neuron.

cross-tolerance   A condition in which the development of tolerance for one drug causes an individual to develop tolerance for another drug.

a Effects on Transmitter Production

1 **Inhibition of transmitter synthesis**
Para-chlorophenylalanine inhibits tryptophan hydroxylase, preventing synthesis of serotonin from its metabolic precursor.

2 **Blockade of axonal transport**
Colchicine impairs maintenance of microtubules and blocks axonal transport.

3 **Interference with the storage of transmitters**
Reserpine blocks the packaging of transmitter molecules within vesicles, thereby allowing the transmitter to be broken down by enzymes.

b Effects on Transmitter Release

4 **Prevention of synaptic transmission**
Tetrodotoxin, found in puffer fish, blocks voltage-gated Na$^+$ channels and prevents nerve conduction.

5 **Alteration of synaptic transmitter release**
Calcium channel blockers (e.g., verapamil) inhibit release of transmitters. Amphetamine stimulates release of catecholamine transmitters. Black widow spider venom causes overrelease, and thus depletion, of ACh.

6 **Modulation of transmitter release by presynaptic receptors**
Caffeine competes with adenosine for presynaptic receptors, thus preventing its inhibitory effects.

c Effects on Transmitter Clearance

7 **Inactivation of transmitter reuptake**
Cocaine and amphetamine inhibit reuptake mechanisms, thus prolonging synaptic activity. Certain antidepressants inhibit serotonin reuptake.

8 **Blockade of transmitter degradation**
Some drugs (e.g., monoamine oxidase inhibitors) inhibit enzymes that normally break down neurotransmitter molecules in the axon terminal or in the synaptic cleft. As a result, transmitter remains active longer and to greater effect.

Figure 4.7   Drug Effects on Presynaptic Mechanisms For each of the eight general postsynaptic drug effects named here, we provide an example of drugs or toxins that has that type of action.

autoreceptor A receptor for a synaptic transmitter that is located in the presynaptic membrane and tells the axon terminal how much transmitter has been released.

TRANSMITTER RELEASE   As we saw in Chapter 3, transmitter is released when action potentials arrive at the axon terminal and trigger an inflow of calcium ions. But a number of drugs and toxins can block those action potentials from ever arriving. For example, compounds that block sodium channels (like the toxin that make puffer fish a dangerous delicacy, called *tetrodotoxin*), prevent axons from firing action potentials, shutting down synaptic transmission with deadly results. And drugs called *calcium channel blockers* do exactly as their name suggests, blocking the calcium influx that normally drives the release of transmitter into the synapse (**Figure 4.7b**). The active ingredient in Botox—botulinum toxin—specifically blocks ACh release from axon terminals near the injection site. The resulting local paralysis of underlying muscles reduces wrinkling of the overlying skin, but may also interfere with the ability to produce normal facial expressions.

A different way to alter transmitter release is to modify the systems that the cell normally uses to monitor and regulate its own transmitter release. For example, presynaptic neurons often use **autoreceptors** to monitor how much transmitter they have released; it's a kind of feedback system. Drugs that stimulate these receptors provide a false feedback signal, prompting the presynaptic cell to release less transmitter. Drugs that instead *block* autoreceptors prevent the presynaptic neuron from receiving its normal feedback, tricking the cell into releasing more transmitter than usual.

TRANSMITTER CLEARANCE   After action potentials have arrived at the axon terminals and prompted a release of transmitter substance, the transmitter is rapidly cleared from the synapse by several processes. Obviously, getting rid of the used transmitter is an important step, because until it is gone, new releases of transmitter from the presynaptic side won't be able to have much extra effect. However, researchers think that under certain circumstances, neurons may be *too* good at clearing the used transmitter, and that a significant lack of transmitter in certain synapses may contribute to disorders such as depression. As we'll see shortly, some important psychiatric drugs, called *reuptake inhibitors*, work by blocking the presynaptic system that normally reabsorbs transmitter molecules after their release; this blocking action allows transmitter molecules to accumulate in the synaptic cleft and have a bigger effect on the postsynaptic cell. Other drugs achieve a similar result by blocking the enzymes that normally break up molecules of neurotransmitter into inactive metabolites, again allowing the transmitter to accumulate, having a greater effect on the postsynaptic cell (**Figure 4.7c**).

Some drugs alter postsynaptic processes

An alternate way for drugs to change synaptic transmission is by altering the postsynaptic systems that respond to the released neurotransmitter. This change may be accomplished either by direct actions on the transmitter receptors of the postsynaptic membrane, or by tinkering with other cellular processes within the postsynaptic cell, as illustrated in **Figure 4.8**.

TRANSMITTER RECEPTOR–SELECTIVE DRUGS   As we discussed earlier in the chapter, selective receptor antagonists bind directly to postsynaptic receptors and block them from being activated by their neurotransmitter (**Figure 4.8a**). The results may be immediate and dramatic. Curare, for example, blocks the nicotinic ACh receptors found on muscles, resulting in immediate paralysis of all skeletal muscles, including those used for breathing (which is why curare is an effective arrow poison).

Selective receptor *agonists* bind to specific receptors and activate them, mimicking the natural neurotransmitter at those receptors. These drugs are often very potent, with effects that vary depending on the particular types of receptors activated. LSD is an

Botox: How Much Is Too Much?

Figure 4.8   Drug Effects on Postsynaptic Mechanisms

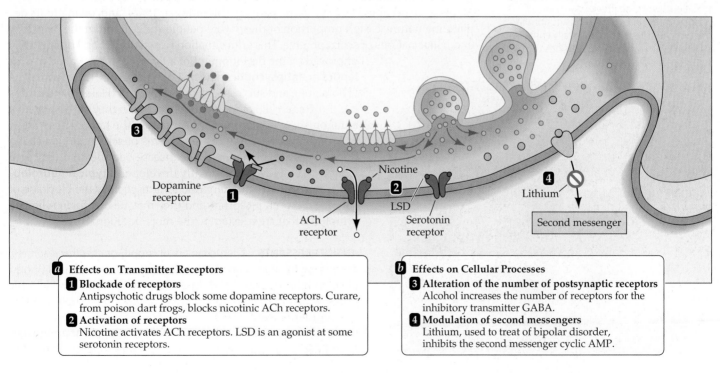

a **Effects on Transmitter Receptors**
1 Blockade of receptors
Antipsychotic drugs block some dopamine receptors. Curare, from poison dart frogs, blocks nicotinic ACh receptors.
2 Activation of receptors
Nicotine activates ACh receptors. LSD is an agonist at some serotonin receptors.

b **Effects on Cellular Processes**
3 Alteration of the number of postsynaptic receptors
Alcohol increases the number of receptors for the inhibitory transmitter GABA.
4 Modulation of second messengers
Lithium, used to treat of bipolar disorder, inhibits the second messenger cyclic AMP.

neuroleptics or antipsychotics Any of a class of antipsychotic drugs that alleviate symptoms of schizophrenia, typically by blocking dopamine receptors.

atypical neuroleptic An antipsychotic drug that has actions other than or in addition to the dopamine D_2 receptor antagonism that characterizes the typical neuroleptics.

antidepressant A drug that relieves the symptoms of depression.

monoamine oxidase (MAO) An enzyme that breaks down monoamine transmitters, thereby inactivating them.

example, producing bizarre visual experiences through strong stimulation of a serotonin receptor subtype found in visual cortex.

PROCESSES INSIDE POSTSYNAPTIC NEURONS When they bind to their matching receptors on postsynaptic membranes, neurotransmitters can stimulate a variety of changes within the postsynaptic cell, such as the activation of second messengers, the activation of genes, and the production of various proteins. These intracellular processes present additional targets for drug action (**Figure 4.8b**). For example, some drugs induce the postsynaptic cell to produce more receptors, thus changing the sensitivity of the synapse. Other drugs cause a decrease in receptor density. Some drugs, like lithium chloride, directly alter second-messenger systems, with widespread effects in the brain. Future research will probably focus on drugs to selectively activate, alter, or block targeted genes within the DNA of neurons. These *genomic* effects could produce profound long-term changes in the structure and function of neurons.

Drugs That Affect the Brain Can Be Divided into Functional Classes

Classifying drugs on the basis of their cellular actions is useful for understanding the physiology of drug effects, but many people are more concerned with the behavioral and therapeutic aspects of these compounds. In the sections that follow, we will briefly review some of the major categories of psychoactive drugs, based on how they affect behavior.

Psychoactive drugs relieve severe symptoms

Mental disorders have bedeviled people throughout history. No doubt many ancient beliefs about miraculous visions, possession, sorcery, and so on had their origins in the symptoms of severe mental disturbances (the topic of Chapter 12). Sadly, because of the lack of effective treatments and the strong stigma attached to mental disorders, the tendency was to separate the afflicted from the rest of society, locking them away in dismal institutions. But during the mid–twentieth century the development of potent drug therapies revolutionized psychiatry.

The Neuroleptic Revolution The introduction of antischizophrenia drugs, or *neuroleptics*, relieved the suffering of millions of patients who had previously required hospitalization in psychiatric institutions like this one. Neuroleptics dramatically curb the striking hallucinations and delusions that are symptomatic of schizophrenia.

ANTISCHIZOPHRENICS Prior to 1950, almost half of all hospital beds in the United States were occupied by psychiatric patients (Menninger, 1948), and, owing to its debilitating nature, a high proportion of these were people suffering from the delusions and hallucinations of schizophrenia. This grim situation was suddenly and dramatically improved by the development of a family of drugs called **neuroleptics** or **antipsychotics**. The first of these drugs, chlorpromazine (Thorazine), and successors like haloperidol (Haldol) and loxapine (Loxitane), all share one crucial feature: they act as selective antagonists of dopamine D_2 receptors in the brain. These drugs are so good at relieving the symptoms of schizophrenia that a dopaminergic explanation of the disease became dominant (see Chapter 12). However, recently developed **atypical neuroleptics** feature nondopaminergic actions, especially the blockade of certain serotonin receptors, and they may be helpful in relieving symptoms that are resistant to the more traditional drugs.

ANTIDEPRESSANTS Disturbances of mood, or *affective disorders*, are among the most common of all psychiatric complaints (World Health Organization, 2001). In contrast to the antischizophrenic drugs, which reduce synaptic activity by blocking receptors, effective **antidepressant** drugs act to *increase* synaptic transmission. Some of the earliest antidepressants were the **monoamine oxidase (MAO)** inhibitors, which, as their name suggests, block the enzyme responsible for breaking down monoamine transmitters like dopamine, serotonin, and norepinephrine. This action allows transmitter molecules to accumulate in the synapses (see Figure 4.7, step 8), with an associated improvement in mood. Later generations of antidepressants also increase synaptic transmitter availability, but they focus on specific transmitters: the **tricyclic antidepressants** block the reuptake of serotonin and norepinephrine, while more recently developed drugs like fluoxetine (Prozac) and citalopram (Celexa) are called **selective serotonin reuptake inhibitors** (**SSRIs**) because they act specifically at serotonergic synapses.

ANXIOLYTICS Severe anxiety, in the form of panic attacks, phobias (specific irrational fears), and generalized anxiety, can spiral out of control and become disabling; many millions of people suffer from anxiety disorders (see Chapter 12). Anything that reduces or *depresses* the excitability of neurons tends to counter these states, which explains some of the historical popularity of **depressants** like alcohol and opium. Unfortunately, these substances are burdened with strong potential for intoxication and addiction, so they are not suitable for therapeutic use. **Barbiturate** drugs were originally developed to reduce anxiety, promote sleep, and avoid epileptic seizures. They are still used for those purposes, but they are also addictive and easily overdosed, often fatally.

Nowadays, the safest and most specific **anxiolytics** (antianxiety drugs) are the **benzodiazepines**, and they are among the most heavily prescribed of all drugs. Members of this class of drug, like diazepam (trade name Valium) and lorazepam (Ativan), bind to specific sites on GABA$_A$ receptors and enhance the activity of GABA (Walters et al., 2000). Because GABA$_A$ receptors are inhibitory, benzodiazepines help GABA to produce larger inhibitory postsynaptic potentials than would be caused by GABA alone. The net effect is a reduction in the excitability of neurons. The hunt for new antianxiety agents—both exogenous and endogenous—is an area of intense research efforts. Hormones that interact with GABA receptors, and new drugs that subtly alter serotonergic neurotransmission, are examples of these novel anxiolytics.

OPIATES **Opium**, extracted from poppy flower seedpods, has been used by humans since at least the Stone Age. **Morphine**, the major active substance in opium, is a very effective **analgesic** (painkiller) that has brought relief from severe pain to many millions of people (see Chapter 5). Unfortunately, morphine also has a strong potential for addiction, as does its close relative **heroin** (diacetylmorphine), because it produces powerful feelings of euphoria when injected intravenously.

Opiates like morphine, heroin, and codeine bind to specific receptors— **opioid receptors**—that are concentrated in various regions of the brain. The profusion of opioid receptors in an area called the **periaqueductal gray** (**Figure 4.9**) is especially important, because it is here that opiates exert their painkilling effects (see Chapter 5).

As we mentioned earlier in the chapter, we now know that the brain makes its own morphinelike compounds, called **endogenous opioids**. Researchers have identified three major families of these potent peptides: the **enkephalins**, from the Greek *en*, "in," and *kephale*, "head" (Hughes et al., 1975); the **endorphins**, a contraction of *endogenous morphine*; and the **dynorphins**, short for *dynamic endorphins*, in recognition of their potency and speed of action (see Table

The Source of Opium and Morphine The opium poppy has a distinctive flower and seedpod. The bitter flavor and brain actions of opium may provide the poppy plant a defense against being eaten.

tricyclic antidepressant An antidepressant that acts by increasing the synaptic accumulation of serotonin and norepinephrine.

selective serotonin reuptake inhibitor (SSRI) A drug that blocks the reuptake of transmitter at serotonergic synapses.

depressant A drug that reduces the excitability of neurons.

barbiturate An early anxiolytic drug and sleep aid that has depressant activity in the nervous system.

anxiolytic A drug that is used to combat anxiety.

benzodiazepine Any of a class of antianxiety drug that are agonists of GABA$_A$ receptors in the central nervous system. One example is diazepam (Valium).

opium An extract of the seedpod juice of the opium poppy, *Papaver somniferum*. Drugs based on opium are potent painkillers.

morphine An opiate compound derived from the poppy flower.

analgesic Having painkilling properties.

heroin Diacetylmorphine; an artificially modified, very potent form of morphine.

opioid receptor A receptor that responds to endogenous opioids and/or exogenous opiates.

periaqueductal gray The neuronal body–rich region of the midbrain surrounding the cerebral aqueduct that connects the third and fourth ventricles; it is involved in pain perception.

endogenous opioid Any of a class of opium-like peptide transmitters that have been called the body's own narcotics. The three kinds are enkephalins, endorphins, and dynorphins.

enkephalin One of the three kinds of endogenous opioids.

endorphin One of the three kinds of endogenous opioids.

dynorphin One of the three kinds of endogenous opioids.

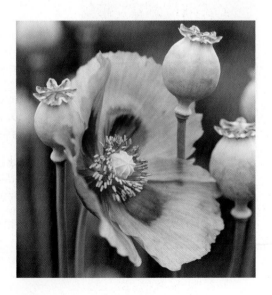

tobacco A highly addictive North American plant whose leaves (usually dried and smoked) are a major source of nicotine.

nicotine A compound found in plants, including tobacco, that acts as an agonist on a large class of cholinergic receptors.

stimulant A drug that enhances the excitability of neurons.

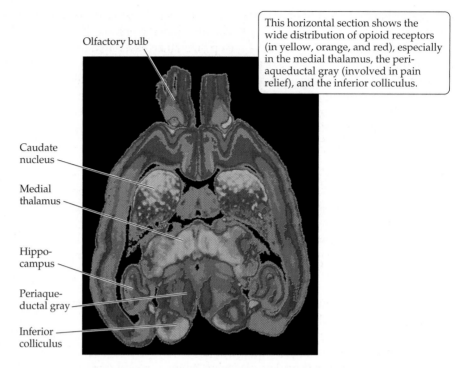

Olfactory bulb

This horizontal section shows the wide distribution of opioid receptors (in yellow, orange, and red), especially in the medial thalamus, the periaqueductal gray (involved in pain relief), and the inferior colliculus.

Caudate nucleus

Medial thalamus

Hippocampus

Periaqueductal gray

Inferior colliculus

Figure 4.9 The Distribution of Opioid Receptors in the Rat Brain (Courtesy of Miles Herkenham, National Institute of Mental Health.)

4.1). There are also three main kinds of opioid receptors—delta (δ), kappa (κ), and mu (μ)—all of which are metabotropic receptors (see Table 4.2). Powerful drugs that block opioid receptors—naloxone (Narcan) is an example—can rapidly reverse the effects of opiates and rescue people from overdose. Opiate antagonists also block the rewarding aspects of drugs like heroin, so they can be helpful for treating addiction, as we discuss at the end of this chapter.

Psychoactive drugs alter consciousness

Whether to experience pleasurable sensations, to artificially increase vigor and wakefulness, or simply to satisfy curiosity, people have a long history of chemically altering their perceptions of themselves and the world. Unfortunately, the habitual use of drugs to alter consciousness is often costly to the user and to society. Governments attempt to minimize these costs by controlling (or preventing) the production and distribution of designated drugs, but the division of drugs into licit and illicit categories is largely a matter of historical accident. Some classes of drugs—the opiates, for example—span both categories, being both useful medicines and harmful drugs of abuse. And some substances, like tobacco, are legal only because they have been cultivated for centuries and are backed by powerful economic interests. In terms of illness, death, lost productivity, and sheer human misery, some of the legal drugs may be the worst offenders.

Smoking Kills The many active components of cigarette smoke cause a variety of serious diseases.

TOBACCO Tobacco is native to the Americas, where European explorers first encountered smoking; these explorers brought tobacco back to Europe with them. Tobacco use became much more widespread following technological innovations that made it easier to smoke, in the form of cigarettes (W. Bennett, 1983). Exposed to the large surface of the lungs, the **nicotine** from cigarettes enters the blood and brain much more rapidly than does nicotine from other tobacco products. Nicotine acts as a **stimulant**, increasing heart rate, blood pressure, digestive action, and alertness. In the short run, these effects make tobacco use pleasurable. But these alterations of body function, quite apart from the effects of tobacco tar on the lungs, make prolonged tobacco use very unhealthful.

The *nicotinic* ACh receptors didn't get their name by coincidence; it is through these receptors that the nicotine from tobacco exerts its effects in the body. Nicotinic receptors drive the contraction of skeletal muscles, and the activation of various visceral organs, but they are also found in high concentrations in the brain, including the cortex. This is one way in which nicotine enhances some aspects of cognitive performance. Nicotine also stimulates the ventral tegmental area (VTA) to exert its rewarding/addicting effects (Maskos et al., 2005). (We will discuss the VTA in more detail when we discuss positive reward models later in the chapter.)

ALCOHOL   The most widely consumed depressant drug, **alcohol**, is easily produced by the fermentation of fruit or grains. Taken in moderation, alcohol is harmless or even beneficial to the health of adults; for example, consumption of one drink or so per day is associated with reduced risk of cardiovascular and Alzheimer's diseases, and with improved control of blood sugar levels (Leroi et al., 2002; Mukamal et al., 2003). *Excessive* alcohol consumption, however, is very damaging and linked to more than 60 disease processes.

Alcohol has a biphasic effect on the nervous system: at first it acts as a stimulant, and then it has a more prolonged depressant phase. (Remember, the word *depressant* relates to a depression or inhibition of *neural activity*, not an effect on mood.) Alcohol acts via GABA receptors to enhance postsynaptic inhibition, similar to the anxiety-reducing benzodiazepines we discussed earlier, resulting in the social disinhibition, poor motor control, and sensory disturbances that we call drunkenness.

Chronic abuse of alcohol damages or destroys nerve cells in many regions of the brain. Alcohol abuse by expectant mothers can cause grievous permanent damage to the developing fetus, termed **fetal alcohol syndrome**, which is characterized by facial deformities and stunted brain growth, sometimes including the absence of the corpus callosum that normally connects the two hemispheres of the brain (**Figure 4.10**). In adults, the frontal lobes are especially affected by chronic alcohol use (Kril et al., 1997). However, some of the anatomical changes associated with chronic alcoholism may be

(*a*) Normal infant   Corpus callosum   (*b*) Infant with fetal alcohol syndrome

Compared to MRI images of a normal infant's brain…

…the MRI of an infant affected by fetal alcohol syndrome—caused by heavy consumption of alcohol by the mother during pregnancy—shows extensive abnormality, including reduced gray matter, complete absence of the corpus callosum, abnormal organization of the brain, and characteristic deformities of the head and face.

Figure 4.10   Abnormal Brain Development in Fetal Alcohol Syndrome

alcohol   A neuroactive compound (primarily the ethyl alcohol found in various beverages) that first stimulates and then depresses neural activity, with varied behavioral consequences.

fetal alcohol syndrome   A disorder, including intellectual disability and characteristic facial abnormalities, that affects children exposed to too much alcohol (through maternal ingestion) during fetal development.

marijuana   A dried preparation of the *Cannabis sativa* plant, usually smoked to obtain THC.

delta-9-tetrahydrocannabinol (THC)   The major active ingredient in marijuana.

endocannabinoid   An endogenous ligand of cannabinoid receptors; thus, an analog of marijuana that is produced by the brain.

anandamide   An endogenous substance that binds the cannabinoid receptor molecule.

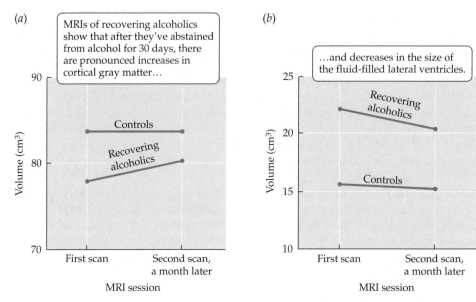

Figure 4.11   **The Effects of Alcohol on the Brain**   (After Pfefferbaum et al., 1995.)

reversible with abstinence. In humans suffering from alcoholism, MRI studies show an increase in the volume of cortical gray matter and an associated reduction in ventricular volume within weeks of giving up alcohol (**Figure 4.11**) (Pfefferbaum et al., 1995).

Even in the absence of clear-cut alcoholism, periodic overconsumption of alcohol—*bingeing*—may cause brain damage. After only 4 days of bingeing on alcohol, rats exhibit neural degeneration in several areas of the brain. Alcohol bingeing also significantly reduces the rate of *neurogenesis*—the formation of new neurons—in the adult hippocampus (Nixon and Crews, 2002).

MARIJUANA   Smoking **marijuana** or related preparations, such as hashish, brings a rush of dozens of active ingredients, chief among which is the compound **delta-9-tetrahydrocannabinol** (**THC**) (Gaoni and Mechoulam, 1964). Although it may also produce mild hallucinogenic effects, marijuana use usually produces relaxation and alters mood, as you would expect with a depressant. However, occasionally the drug causes stimulation and paranoia instead. In addition to harming the lungs, heavy use of marijuana can be addicting and has been associated with schizophrenia (Murray et al., 2007), although whether marijuana use causes schizophrenia, or schizophrenia causes marijuana use, remains in dispute.

As with opiates and benzodiazepines, researchers found that the brain contains specific cannabinoid receptors that mediate the effects of compounds like THC. Cannabinoid receptors are found in the substantia nigra, the hippocampus, the cerebellar cortex, and the cerebral cortex (**Figure 4.12**) (Devane et al., 1988). Later research revealed that the brain makes several THC-like endogenous ligands for these receptors. The most studied of these **endocannabinoids** is **anandamide** (from the Sanskrit *ananda*, "bliss") (Devane et al., 1992), which produces some of the most familiar symptoms of marijuana use: hunger, poor memory, and reduced sensitivity to pain (Marsicano et al., 2003). The study of endocannabinoids will aid the search for drugs that share the beneficial effects of marijuana: relieving pain, lowering blood pressure, combating nausea, lowering eye pressure in glaucoma, and so on. The documented use of cannabis for medicinal purposes spans over 6,000 years, but treatment with "medical marijuana" remains illegal in most jurisdictions.

An Indoor Marijuana Farm   Although growing the marijuana plant (*Cannabis sativa*) is widely prohibited, it is believed to be the largest cash crop in several U.S. states, parts of Canada, and other locations around the globe. Growers have developed sophisticated hydroponic techniques for growing highly potent strains of cannabis in indoor "grow ops" like this one.

STIMULANTS   Proper functioning of the nervous system involves a fine balance between excitatory and inhibitory influences. Stimulants are drugs that tip the balance

Figure 4.12   The Distribution of Cannabinoid Receptors in the Rat Brain (Courtesy of Miles Herkenham, National Institute of Mental Health.)

Substantia nigra   Globus pallidus   Hippocampus

Areas with high concentrations of cannabinoid receptors are indicated by yellow, orange, and red in this horizontal section.

Cerebellum

toward the excitatory side; they therefore have an alerting, activating effect. Some stimulants act directly by increasing excitatory synaptic potentials. Others act by blocking normal inhibitory processes. For example, *adenosine receptors* are found on presynaptic terminals and normally reduce transmitter release. **Caffeine** blocks these adenosine receptors, resulting in more transmitter release and, consequently, increased brain activity.

Some stimulants have a much more powerful effect than caffeine or tobacco, and they are among the most addictive drugs. Leaves of the South American coca shrub—either chewed or brewed as a tea—increase endurance, alleviate hunger, and promote a sense of well-being without causing many problems. But processing and concentrating an extract from this plant produces a much more potent and dangerous compound: **cocaine**. Although cocaine was initially used as a food additive (e.g., in *Coca*-Cola) and as a local anesthetic, people soon discovered that the rapid hit of cocaine resulting from snorting or smoking it (see Table 4.3) has a stimulant effect that is powerful and pleasurable. Unfortunately, it is also highly addictive. Furthermore, heavy cocaine use raises the risk of serious side effects like stroke, psychosis, loss of gray matter, and severe mood disturbances (Franklin et al., 2002; Holman et al., 1993). Cocaine acts by blocking the reuptake of monoamine transmitters from synapses. This action causes monoamines to accumulate in synapses throughout much of the brain (**Figure 4.13**), therefore boosting their effects.

The synthetic stimulant **amphetamine** (and its relatives, like *methamphetamine*, or "meth") has a mode of action that superficially resembles that of cocaine, inducing an accumulation of the synaptic monoamine transmitters norepinephrine and dopamine. However, the mechanics of amphetamine's actions, involving two steps, are quite different from those of cocaine. First, amphetamine acts within axon terminals to cause a larger-than-normal release of neurotransmitter when the synapse is activated. Second, amphetamine then interferes with the metabolic breakdown of the released transmitter. The result is that monoaminergic synapses become unnaturally potent, having strong effects on behavior.

Over the short term, amphetamine causes increased vigor and stamina, wakefulness, decreased appetite, and feelings of euphoria. For these reasons, amphetamine

caffeine   A stimulant compound found in coffee, cacao, and other plants.

cocaine   A drug of abuse, derived from the coca plant, that acts by enhancing catecholamine neurotransmission.

amphetamine   A molecule that resembles the structure of the catecholamine transmitters and enhances their activity.

In this coronal image, brain regions with high degrees of cocaine binding are shown in orange and yellow. Cocaine acts in these areas to cause an accumulation of monoamine transmitters.

Caudate

Putamen

Cortex

Amygdala

Figure 4.13   Cocaine Action in the Monkey Brain (Courtesy of Bertha K. Madras.)

Faces of Meth   These before and after photos, taken only two and a half years apart, are a stark testament to the heavy toll that accompanies chronic methamphetamine abuse. (Mugshots courtesy of the Multnomah County Sheriff's Office and the Faces of Meth™ program.)

has historically been used in military applications and other settings where intense sustained effort is required. However, the quality of the work being performed may suffer, and the costs of amphetamine use soon outweigh the benefits. Addiction and tolerance to amphetamine and methamphetamine develop rapidly, requiring ever-larger doses that lead to sleeplessness, severe weight loss, and general deterioration of mental and physical condition.

Prolonged use of amphetamine or methamphetamine may lead to symptoms that closely resemble those of schizophrenia: compulsive, agitated behavior and irrational suspiciousness. In their pursuit of more drug, users may neglect their diet and basic hygiene, aging rapidly. Users also experience a variety of peripheral effects, like high blood pressure, tremor, dizziness, sweating, rapid breathing, and nausea. And worst of all, people who chronically abuse amphetamine often display symptoms of brain damage—such as memory and attention deficits, psychosis, and symptoms of Parkinson's disease—long after they quit using the drug (Ernst et al., 2000). As we'll discuss a little later in the chapter, increased activation of the mesolimbocortical dopaminergic reward system of the brain appears to be crucial for the rewarding aspects of drug use.

hallucinogen   A drug that alters sensory perception and produces peculiar experiences.

LSD   Also called *acid*. Lysergic acid diethylamide, a hallucinogenic drug.

MDMA   Also called *Ecstasy*. 3,4-Methylenedioxymethamphetamine, a drug of abuse.

HALLUCINOGENS   Humans have long prized **hallucinogens**, substances that produce powerful sensory alterations, often believing the resultant experiences to have deep spiritual or psychological meaning. Dozens of such hallucinogens are found in nature—psilocybin and muscarine (from "magic" mushrooms), mescaline (from the peyote plant), and bufotenine (from toads) are a few examples. But the term *hallucinogen* is really a misnomer because, whereas a hallucination is a novel perception that takes place in the absence of sensory stimulation (hearing voices, or seeing something that isn't there), the drugs in this category mostly alter or distort *existing* perceptions (mainly visual in nature). Users may see fantastic images, often with intense colors (**Figure 4.14**), but often they are aware that these strangely altered perceptions are not real events.

Hallucinogenic agents are diverse in their neural actions. Whereas muscarine affects the ACh system, mescaline acts via noradrenergic and serotonergic systems. The Mexican herb *salvia* is unusual among hallucinogens because it acts on the opioid kappa receptor. But research with LSD and related drugs suggests that perhaps the most important shared neural action of hallucinogens is the stimulation of serotonin receptors. Discovered by Albert Hofmann in the 1940s, **LSD** (lysergic acid diethylamide, or more simply *acid*) structurally resembles serotonin. Even in tiny doses, LSD strongly activates serotonin 5-HT$_{2A}$ receptors that are found in especially heavy concentrations in the visual cortex. Other hallucinogens, such as mescaline and psilocybin, share this action. In addition to its impressive effects on visual perception, LSD produces mood changes and feelings of creativity that have led to resurgent interest in the possible application of hallucinogens to treat various psychiatric disorders, including depression and obsessive-compulsive disorder (Moreno et al., 2006).

Like LSD, the hallucinogenic amphetamine derivative **MDMA** (3,4-methylenedioxymethamphetamine, or *Ecstasy*) stimulates visual cortical 5-HT$_{2A}$ receptors, but it also changes the levels of dopamine and certain hormones, such as prolactin. Exactly how these activities account for the subjective effects of MDMA—positive emotions, empathy, euphoria, a sense of well-being, and colorful visual phenomena—remains uncertain.

The Father of LSD   Albert Hofmann discovered LSD by accidentally taking some in 1943, and he devoted the rest of his career studying it. A prohibited drug in most jurisdictions, LSD is sometimes distributed on colorful blotter paper. This example, picturing Hofmann and the LSD molecule, is made up of 1,036 individual doses, or "hits."

These images are portraits produced by a professional artist just after taking LSD (leftmost drawing) and then at three successive time points as the drug took effect. The model for all four drawings is the same man (the researcher, in fact).

Figure 4.14 Changes in Visual Perception after Taking LSD

20 minutes   Time   3 hours

The major hallucinogens seem to have low addiction potential, and LSD has relatively few negative side effects (although some users report long-lasting visual changes). However, long-term Ecstasy use may cause damage to serotonergic neurons (**Figure 4.15**), problems with mood and memory performance (Sumnall and Cole, 2005; Wareing et al., 2000), and long-lasting changes in patterns of brain activation, even at low doses (de Win et al., 2008).

Drugs categorized as **dissociatives** differ from the major hallucinogens in that they produce feelings of depersonalization and detachment from reality, rather than primary sensory alterations. *Phencyclidine* (*PCP*, or *angel dust*) and *ketamine* (*Special K*) are examples of drugs with this action; both are antagonists at NMDA-type glutamate receptors. Regular use causes a variety of undesirable effects, including symptoms that resemble psychosis, as well as possible lasting degenerative changes in the brain.

Serotonin axons in the dorsal cortex of a control squirrel monkey…

…and a squirrel monkey treated with a single dose of MDMA (Ecstasy) 18 months earlier.

Figure 4.15 **Long-Term Effects of a Single Dose of Ecstasy on the Monkey Brain** (Fischer et al., 1995; photo courtesy of George Ricaurte.)

How's it going?

1. Compare and contrast the three major categories of presynaptic effects of psychoactive drugs. Give examples of each kind of action. (*Hint*: The words *production*, *release*, and *clearance* will be important for your discussion.)

2. Compare and contrast the three major categories of *post*synaptic effects of psychoactive drugs. Give examples of each kind of action, distinguishing between actions at receptors versus actions within the postsynaptic neuron.

3. At least four general categories of psychoactive drugs are used to relieve disorders. Describe these categories, and give some examples of each class of drugs. Be sure to discuss the mode of action of the drugs you cite.

4. Identify and discuss the major categories of drugs that people use to alter their consciousness. In what ways are the major categories similar, and in what ways do they differ? Aside from their addictive potential, what are some of the worst threats to health that these compounds present?

dissociative A type of drug that produces a dreamlike state in which consciousness is partly separated from sensory inputs.

Drug Abuse Is Pervasive

Substance abuse and addiction have become a social problem that afflicts many millions of people and disrupts the lives of their families, friends, and associates. Just one example reveals the extent of the problem: in the United States each year, more men and women die of smoking-related lung cancer than of colon, breast, and prostate cancers *combined*. In addition to the personal impact of so much illness and early death, there are dire social costs: huge expenses for medical and social services; millions of hours lost in the workplace; elevated rates of crime associated with illicit drugs; and scores of children who are damaged by their parents' substance abuse behavior, in the uterine environment as well as in the childhood home. Males are much more likely than females to abuse drugs and have their lives disrupted by drug use. It is unclear whether this sex difference is related to biological differences between the sexes, or to differences in social influences on males versus females.

In the discussion that follows, we will look at some of the most prevalent perspectives on drug addiction: what it is, where it comes from, how it can be treated. Some of these models stem from social forces, others are more deeply rooted in scientific observations and theories. But for any model of drug abuse, the challenge is to come up with a single account that can explain the addicting power of substances as diverse as, for example, cocaine (a stimulant), heroin (an analgesic and euphoriant), and alcohol (largely sedative). We will focus primarily on addiction to cocaine, the opiate drugs (such as morphine and heroin), nicotine, and alcohol because these substances have been studied the most thoroughly. According to the 2010 National Survey of Drug Use and Health, some 22.1 million people in the United States alone suffer from substance-related disorders (Substance Abuse and Mental Health Services Administration, 2011). Worldwide, the number is probably in the hundreds of millions. Some terminology specific to substance dependence (addiction) and substance abuse is clarified in **Box 4.1**.

Several perspectives help us understand drug abuse

Any comprehensive model of drug abuse has to answer several difficult questions: What social and environmental factors cause someone to start abusing a substance? What factors cause the person to continue abusing? What physiological mechanisms make a substance rewarding? What is addiction, physiologically and behaviorally, and why is it so hard to quit? Four major models attempt to answer at least some of these questions:

1. The *moral model* takes the perspective that addiction results from weakness of character and a lack of self-control. Proponents may apply exhortation, peer pressure, and/or religious intervention in order to curb abusive practices, but usually with limited success. The temperance movement of the 1800s did seem to reduce alcohol consumption, but there is little evidence that more modern moral campaigns (such as "Just Say NO" and Project D.A.R.E.) have had much effect on rates of drug addiction.

2. The *disease model* takes the view that the person who abuses drugs requires medical treatment rather than moral exhortation or punishment. The problem is that substance abuse is not like any other disease we know about. We usually reserve the term *disease* for cases involving a physical abnormality, and no such condition has been found in the case of drug addiction (although some people are genetically more susceptible to addiction than others). Nevertheless, this model continues to appeal to many, and much research is focused on looking for pathological states that create addiction after initial exposure to a drug.

3. The *physical dependence model* argues that people keep taking drugs in order to avoid unpleasant **withdrawal symptoms**. The specific withdrawal symptoms depend on the drug, but they are often the opposite of the effects produced by the drug itself. For example, withdrawal from morphine causes irritability, a racing heart, and waves of goose bumps (that's where the term *cold turkey* comes from—the skin looks like

"The Needle and the Damage Done" Addiction has a powerful grip, inducing people to go to sometimes extreme lengths to obtain larger and more frequent doses.

withdrawal symptom   An uncomfortable symptom that arises when a person stops taking a drug that he or she has used frequently, especially at high doses.

BOX 4.1 The Terminology of Substance-Related Disorders

For definitions of mental disorders, psychiatrists, psychologists, and neuroscientists rely on the *Diagnostic and Statistical Manual of Mental Disorders* (fourth edition, text revised), known as the *DSM-IV-TR* (American Psychiatric Association, 2000). The DSM-IV-TR provides descriptions of a spectrum of substance-related disorders. Within this category, **dependence** (commonly called *addiction*) is a more severe disorder than **substance abuse**. Males are 3 times more likely than females to be diagnosed, at some point in life, with substance abuse or dependence (see the figure).

The essential feature of *dependence* on psychoactive substances (e.g., alcohol, tobacco, cocaine, marijuana) is "a cluster of cognitive, behavioral, and physiological symptoms indicating that the individual continues use of the substance despite significant substance-related problems." To be diagnosed as dependent, a person must meet at least three of seven criteria relating to patterns of consumption, craving, expenditure of time and energy in serving the addiction, and impact on other aspects of the person's life. Furthermore, once dependence has been diagnosed, it is placed on a scale ranging from mild to moderate to severe, depending on how many of the seven criteria have been met.

When the minimum criteria for dependence have not been met but maladaptive patterns of substance use have persisted at least a month or have occurred repeatedly, the diagnosis is *substance abuse*. The following situations are examples in which a diagnosis of substance abuse is appropriate:

- A student has substance-related absences, suspensions, or expulsion from school.
- A person is repeatedly intoxicated with alcohol in situations that are hazardous—for example, when driving a car, operating machinery, or engaging in risky recreational activities such as swimming or rock climbing.
- A person has recurrent substance-related legal problems—for example, arrests for disorderly conduct, assault and battery, or driving under the influence.

(A) Alcohol

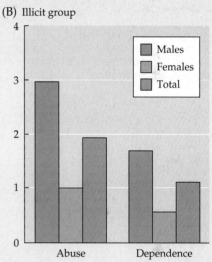

(B) Illicit group

Typical proportions of adults who at some point in their life receive a DSM-IV-TR diagnosis of (A) alcohol or (B) illicit drug abuse and/or dependence.

---

the skin of a plucked turkey). And of course, the opposite of the euphoria caused by many drugs is **dysphoria**: strongly negative feelings that can be relieved only by administration of the withdrawn drug. So the model does a good job of explaining why addicts will go great lengths to obtain their addicted drug, but it has an important shortcoming: the model is mute as to how the addiction becomes established in the first place. Why do some people, but not all, start to abuse a drug before physical dependence (tolerance) has developed? And how is it that some people can become addicted to some drugs even in the absence of clear physical withdrawal symptoms? For example, cocaine withdrawal is not accompanied by the shaking and vomiting that are seen during heroin withdrawal, yet cocaine seems to be at least as addictive as heroin.

4. The *positive reward model* proposes that people get started with drug abuse, and become addicted, because the abused drug provides powerful reinforcement. Using an apparatus that allows animals to administer drugs to themselves (**Figure 4.16**), researchers have collected plenty of evidence in support of this view. Laboratory animals will quickly learn to press a lever repeatedly in order to receive a small dose of an addictive drug like cocaine or morphine (McKim, 1991; T. Thompson and Schuster, 1964). We can infer that the more lever presses animals will perform for a single dose, or the smaller the dose that will support the lever-pressing behavior,

dysphoria Unpleasant feelings; the opposite of euphoria.

A syringe pump is controlled by a computer, delivering a small dose of drug after a certain number of lever presses.

Computerized syringe pump controller

A drug's rewarding properties and addictive potential are reflected in the number of lever presses performed to receive a dose. Lab animals will press the lever thousands of times to receive a single small dose of highly addictive compounds like cocaine and methamphetamine.

Figure 4.16   Experimental Setup for Drug Self-Administration

the more rewarding and addictive the drug must be. For example, it turns out that animals will happily self-administer doses of morphine that are so low that no signs of physical dependence ever develop (Schuster, 1970). Animals will also furiously press a lever to self-administer tiny doses of cocaine and other stimulants (Koob, 1995; Pickens and Thompson, 1968; Tanda et al., 2000). In fact, cocaine supports some of the highest rates of lever pressing ever recorded.

Experiments using drug self-administration suggest that, by itself, the physical dependence model is inadequate to explain drug addiction, although physical dependence and tolerance may contribute to drug hunger. The more comprehensive view of drug self-administration interprets it as a behavior controlled by a powerful pattern of positive and negative rewards (a variant of operant conditioning theory; see Chapter 13), without the need to implicate a disease process.

Many addictive drugs cause the release of dopamine in the **nucleus accumbens**, just as occurs with more conventional rewards, such as food, sex, and gambling (D'Ardenne et al., 2008; Di Chiara et al., 1999; Reuter et al., 2005). As we mentioned previously, dopamine released from axons originating in the ventral tegmental area (VTA), part of the mesolimbocortical dopaminergic pathway illustrated in Figure 4.3, has been widely implicated in the perception of reward (**Figure 4.17**). If the dopaminergic pathway from the VTA to the nucleus accumbens serves as a reward system for a wide variety of experiences, then the addictive power of drugs may come from their artificial stimulation of this pathway. When the drug hijacks this system, providing unnaturally powerful reinforcement, the user learns to associate the drug-taking behavior with that pleasure and begins seeking out drugs more and more until life's other pleasures fade into the background. If natural activities like conversation, food, and even sex no longer provide appreciable reward, addicts may seek drugs as the only source of pleasure available to them.

Intriguingly, people suffering damage to a brain region tucked within the frontal cortex, called the **insula** (Latin for "island"), are reportedly able to effortlessly quit smoking (Naqvi et al., 2007), indicating that this brain region is also involved in addiction. The reciprocal connections between the VTA and the insula (Oades and Halliday, 1987) suggest that these two regions may normally interact to mediate addiction, although this association remains to be established.

Not everyone who uses an addictive drug becomes addicted. For example, very, very few hospitalized patients treated with opiates for pain relief go on to abuse opiates after leaving the hospital (Brownlee and Schrof, 1997). However, prescription painkillers are highly effective at activating the dopamine reward system, so the use of these drugs outside of medical contexts carries a high risk of addiction. The individual and environmental factors that account for differential susceptibility are the subject of active investigation (Glantz and Pickens, 1992; Karch, 2006). Some of the major risk factors include biological factors (being male; heritable tendencies to addiction), poor family life, personality factors (poor emotional control), and environmental factors (living in a neighborhood with high rates of addiction). Simply returning to a neighborhood where drugs were previously used can trigger drug craving in an addict (Ciccocioppo et al., 2004).

Drug use, abuse, and dependence can be prevented or treated in multiple ways

Given the health and social costs of substance abuse, there is a pressing need for effective treatment programs. Many people who become dependent are able to overcome their addiction without outside help: more than 90% of ex-smokers and about half of those who recover from alcoholism appear to have quit on their own (S. Cohen et al., 1989; Institute

nucleus accumbens   A region of the forebrain that receives dopaminergic innervation from the ventral tegmental area.

insula   A region of cortex lying below the surface, within the lateral sulcus, of the frontal, temporal, and parietal lobes.

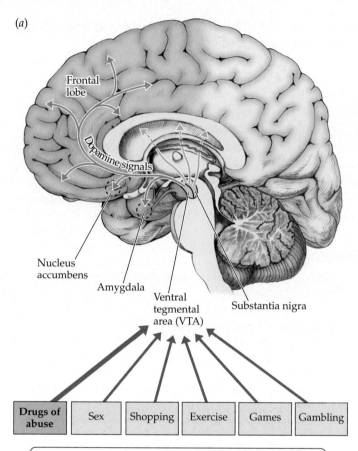

(a)

A variety of pleasurable activities, like the ones suggested here, probably activate the dopaminergic pathway that produces rewarding sensations. Drugs of abuse powerfully activate this system and may eclipse other sources of pleasure.

(b)

In the microdialysis technique, an implanted probe samples the chemical environment of the nucleus accumbens in awake, behaving animals.

Some of the dopamine released in the nucleus accumbens crosses the dialysis membrane and can be detected in the fluid flowing out.

(c)

Microdialysis reveals that dopamine release in the nucleus accumbens rises sharply during self-administration of cocaine.

Figure 4.17   A Neural Pathway Implicated in Drug Abuse (After Pettit and Justice, 1991.)

of Medicine, 1990), while others gain great benefit from counseling or social interventions such as 12-step programs. For those who require medical intervention, several categories of medication are available, including the following:

- *Drugs for detoxification.* For example, benzodiazepines and other sedatives help reduce withdrawal symptoms during the early drug-free period.

- *Agonist or partial agonist analogs of the addictive drug.* Analogs partially activate the same mechanisms that the addictive drug activates, to help wean the individual. For example, the opioid receptor agonist methadone reduces heroin appetite and lessens withdrawal symptoms; similarly, nicotine patches provide reduced doses of the addictive compound, without the other harmful components of cigarette smoke.

- *Antagonists to the addictive drug.* Specific antagonists block the effects of an abused drug (e.g., the opiate antagonist naloxone [Narcan] blocks heroin's actions), but they also may produce harsh withdrawal symptoms.

- *Medications that alter drug metabolism.* Patients on disulfiram (trade name Antabuse) accumulate acetaldehyde, a toxic metabolite of alcohol that can make them ill, counteracting the rewarding aspects of alcohol.

- *Reward-blocking medications.* Researchers are looking at ways to block the positive reward associated with drugs of abuse, primarily by using dopamine receptor blockers to reduce the activity of the mesolimbocortical dopamine reward system that we discussed earlier. One problem with this approach is the tendency of treatments to produce a generalized loss of pleasurable feelings.

- *Anticraving medications.* These medications reduce the appetite for the abused substance; for example, naltrexone (trade name ReVia) blocks the rewarding aspects of consuming alcohol or other abused substances in some people, and acamprosate (trade name Campral) eases alcohol-associated withdrawal symptoms.

- *Immunization.* Vaccines against such drugs as cocaine, heroin, and nicotine have been developed and are being tested (Maurer and Bachmann, 2007). Here the strategy is to prompt the individual's immune system to produce antibodies that remove the targeted drugs from circulation before they ever reach the brain.

No single approach appears to be uniformly effective, and rates of relapse remain high. Research breakthroughs are therefore badly needed.

Recommended Reading

Cooper, J. R., Bloom, F. E., and Roth, R. H. (2002). *The Biochemical Basis of Neuropharmacology* (8th ed.). New York, NY: Oxford University Press.

Grilly, D. M. (2005). *Drugs and Human Behavior* (5th ed.). Boston, MA: Allyn & Bacon.

Julien, R. J. (2007). *A Primer of Drug Action* (11th ed.). New York, NY: Worth.

Karch, S. B. (2006). *Drug Abuse Handbook* (2nd ed.). Boca Raton, FL: CRC Press.

Meyer, J. S., and Quenzer, L. F. (2005). *Psychopharmacology: Drugs, the Brain, and Behavior.* Sunderland, MA: Sinauer.

Schatzberg, A. F., and Nemeroff, C. B. (Eds.). (2004). *Textbook of Psychopharmacology.* Arlington, VA: American Psychiatric Publishing.

Thombs, D. L. (2006). *Introduction to Addictive Behaviors* (3rd ed.). New York, NY: Guilford Press.

CHAPTER 4 VISUAL SUMMARY

mindsmachine.com/vs4

You should be able to relate each summary to the adjacent illustration, including structures and processes. If you need to review, go to the figures indicated and read the accompanying text.

1 The function of the classical **synapse** is to communicate information from a **presynaptic** neuron to a **postsynaptic** cell. It does so by converting an electrical signal—the action potential—into secretion of a **neurotransmitter** that crosses to the postsynaptic cell and alters that cell's functioning. Review **Figure 4.1, Animation 4.2**

2 Neurotransmitters exert their effects via **neurotransmitter receptors**; these are also the site of action for many psychoactive drugs. Most transmitters have several different subtypes of receptors, which may be individually targeted by drugs. A given neurotransmitter may normally bind several different subtypes of receptors. Review **Figure 4.2, Table 4.2**

3 The major categories of neurotransmitters are **amine**, **amino acid**, **peptide**, and soluble **gas neurotransmitters**. Neurotransmitter systems form complex, overlapping patterns of projections throughout the brain. Review **Figures 4.3** and **4.4, Table 4.1, Animation 4.3, Activity 4.1**

4 Drugs classified as **agonists** activate transmitter pathways, and **antagonists** block transmitter pathways. Repeated exposure to drugs may cause a compensatory decrease (**down-regulation**) or increase (**up-regulation**) in the number of receptors. Changes in receptor density are one mechanism of **drug tolerance**. Review **Figure 4.5, Animation 4.4**

5 The **dose-response curve (DRC)** quantifies the relationship between doses of a drug and its physiological effects, and it can be used to deduce characteristics such as drug potency and safety. Review **Figure 4.6**

6 Psychoactive drugs have three main presynaptic actions: some drugs alter transmitter synthesis, others alter transmitter release, and some block the clearance of transmitter after it has been released. Review **Figure 4.7**

7 Many psychoactive drugs have postsynaptic effects, especially activation or blockade of postsynaptic receptors. Other drugs affect metabolic processes within the postsynaptic neuron, such as alterations in second-messenger systems, or changes in the production of crucial proteins (like transmitter receptors). Most antipsychotic medications block postsynaptic **dopamine (DA)** receptors, but some also block **serotonin (5-HT)** receptors. Review **Figure 4.8**

8 Opiates such as **morphine** are potent painkillers; the brain also makes its own **endogenous opioids** with a variety of effects. Opiates act on specific **opioid receptors**, especially in a major pain pathway that includes the **periaqueductal gray**. Review **Figure 4.9**

9 **Alcohol** acts on **gamma-aminobutyric acid (GABA)** receptors to produce some of its effects. In moderation, alcohol has beneficial effects; but in higher doses it is very harmful, damaging neurons in many areas of the brain. Review **Figures 4.10** and **4.11**

10 The active ingredient in marijuana—**delta-9-tetrahydro-cannabinol**, or **THC**—acts on cannabinoid receptors to produce its effects. An **endocannabinoid**, **anandamide**, serves as a **retrograde transmitter** at some synapses. Review **Figure 4.12**

11 Some stimulants, such as **nicotine**, imitate an excitatory synaptic transmitter. Others, such as **amphetamine**, cause the release of excitatory synaptic transmitters and block the reuptake of transmitters. Cocaine causes the release of transmitters, especially dopamine, in wide regions of the brain. Review **Figure 4.13**

12 Some drugs are called **hallucinogens** because they alter sensory perception and produce peculiar experiences. Although hallucinogens vary in their actions, many share activity at serotonin receptors in the visual cortex, perhaps explaining their effects on visual perception. Review **Figures 4.14** and **4.15**

13 **Substance abuse** and **dependence** (*addiction*) are being studied intensively, and several explanatory models have been proposed. The positive reward model, based on the observation that animals will work very hard to self-administer highly addictive drugs, has received the most support from research. Review **Figure 4.16, Box 4.1**

14 A dopamine-based neural pathway from the **ventral tegmental area** to the **nucleus accumbens** appears to be a system for experiencing pleasure and reward. Researchers believe that this reward system plays an important role in the formation of addictions. Some experimental treatments for addiction involve blocking the reward signal from drugs. Review **Figure 4.17**

Go to **mindsmachine.com** for study questions, quizzes, flashcards, and other resources.

What You See Is What You Get

Ian Waterman had a perfectly ordinary life until he caught a viral infection at age 19. For reasons no one understands, the infection targeted a very specific set of nerves sending information from his body to his brain. Ian can still feel pain or deep pressure, as well as warm and cool surfaces on his skin, but he has no sensation of light touch below his neck. What's more, although Ian can still move all of his muscles, he receives no information about muscle activity or body position (Cole, 1995). You might think this deficiency wouldn't cause any problem, because you've probably never thought much about your "body sense"; it's not even one of the five senses that people talk about, is it?

In fact, however, the loss of this information was devastating. Ian couldn't walk across a room without falling down, and he couldn't walk up or down stairs. The few other people suffering a loss like this have spent the rest of their lives in wheelchairs. But Ian was a young and determined person, so he started teaching himself how to walk using another source of feedback about his body: his vision. Now, as long as the lights are on, Ian can carefully watch his moving body to judge which motor commands to send out to keep walking. If the lights go out, however, he collapses; and he has learned that in that circumstance he just has to lie where he is until the lights come on again. He has so finely honed this ability to guide movements with vision that if asked to point repeatedly to the same location in the air, he does so more accurately than control subjects do. Still, it's a mental drain to have to watch and attend constantly to his body just to do everyday tasks.

Today Ian has a good job and an active, independent life, but he is always vigilant. Lying in bed, he has to be very careful to remain calm, tethering his limbs with the covers to prevent them from flailing about. And the lights are always on at Ian's house.

To see a video, go to

mindsmachine.com/5.1
Sensory Systems

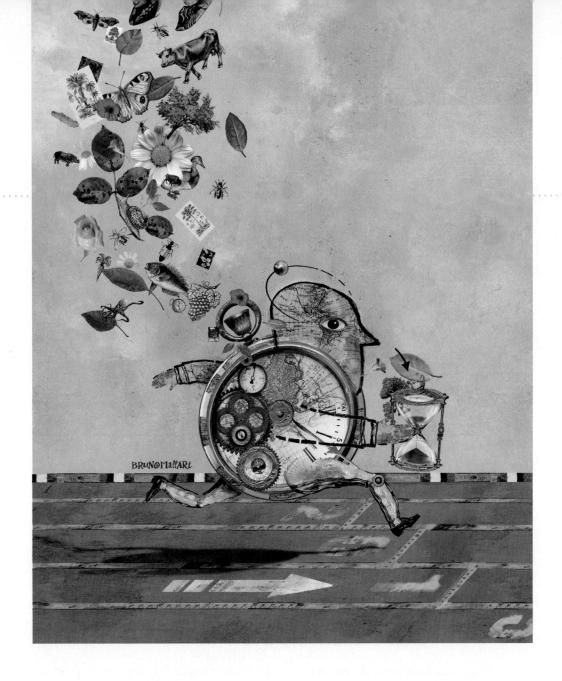

Every species, including our own, is surrounded by forms of environmental energy that may signal life-or-death events. Molecules in the air are sensed as odors—of food, or mates, or smoke. Vibrations traveling through air are perceived as sounds, ranging from infant cries to the roar of a predator (or a waterfall). Light particles reflected from surfaces present a visual representation of the world. And because species differ in the environmental features they must sense for survival, evolution has endowed each species with its own unique set of capabilities. Bats are specially equipped to detect their own ultrasonic cries, which we humans are unable to hear. Some snakes have infrared-sensing organs in their faces that allow them to "see" heat sources in the dark. **Table 5.1** documents the impressive array of sensory modalities that animals may possess.

TABLE 5.1 Classification of Sensory Systems

System type	Modality	Sensed stimuli
Mechanical	Touch	Contact with or deformation of body surface
	Hearing	Sound vibrations in air or water
	Vestibular	Head movement and orientation
	Joint	Position and movement
	Muscle	Tension
Photic	Vision	Photons, from light sources or reflected from surface
Thermal	Cold	Decrease in skin temperature
	Warmth	Increase in skin temperature
Chemical	Smell	Odorant chemicals in air
	Taste	Substances in contact with the tongue or other taste receptor
	Common chemical	Changes in CO_2, pH, osmotic pressure
	Vomeronasal	Pheromones in air or water
Electrical	Electroreception	Differences in density of electrical currents
Magnetic	Magnetoreception	Magnetic fields

Sensory systems rely on specialized receptor cells to detect specific energies, as well as brain systems that receive input from these receptors. We open this chapter by considering some basic principles of sensory processing, using the sense of touch to illustrate some of the major concepts. In the second part of the chapter, we take a closer look at an unpleasant but crucial sense: pain. And in the third and final part of the chapter we turn our attention to the integration of sensory inputs and motor control mechanisms: the streamlined system that allows us to interact with our environment.

PART I Sensory Processing and the Somatosensory System

All animals have sensory organs containing **receptor cells** that sense some forms of energy—called **stimuli**—but not others. So in a way, receptor cells act as filters, ignoring the environmental background and converting the key stimuli into the language of the nervous system: electrical signals. Information from sensory receptors floods the brain in an unending barrage of action potentials traveling along millions of axons, and our brains must make sense of it all. Of course, different kinds of energy—light, sound, touch, and so on—need different sensory organs to convert them into neural activity, just as taking a photograph requires a camera, not a microphone. There is tremendous diversity in sensory organs across the animal kingdom; for example, the eye is just one type of sensory organ, yet it is found in a dazzling array of sizes, shapes, and forms reflecting the varying survival needs of different animals (**Figure 5.1**). Likewise, the specific auditory abilities of species reflect their unique ecological pressures (**Figure 5.2**).

Although the end product of sensory receptors—action potentials—is the same for all the different sensory modalities, the brain recognizes the modalities as separate and distinct because the action potentials for each sense are carried in separate nerve tracts. This is the concept of **labeled lines**: particular neurons that are, right from the outset, labeled for distinctive sensory experiences. Action potentials in one line signal a sound, activity in another line signals a smell, and activity in other lines signals touch. And there are labeled lines within general sensory categories too; for example, we can

To see the brain in 3D, go to

mindsmachine.com/5.2
Brain Explorer

receptor cell   A specialized cell that responds to a particular energy or substance in the internal or external environment, and converts this energy into a change in the electrical potential across its membrane.

stimulus   A physical event that triggers a sensory response.

labeled lines   The concept that each nerve input to the brain reports only a particular type of information.

Figure 5.1 **The Variety of Eyes** The range of sensitivity of the eyes varies from species to species, reflecting the species' particular lifestyle. (*a*) This scanning electron micrograph shows the compound eye of a blackfly (*Simulium damnosum*). (*b*) The panther chameleon can move its two eyes independently. (*c*) The eyes of the Philippine tarsier are specialized for nighttime foraging. (*d*) The eyes of the American bald eagle are particularly sharp, to aid hunting from great distances.

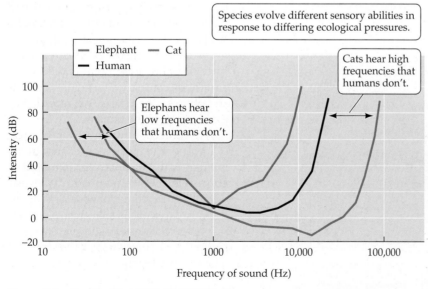

Figure 5.2 **Do You Hear What I Hear?**

Figure 5.3   Labeled Lines

Within the sense of touch, each type of receptor (stretch, vibration, pain, touch) has a distinct pathway to the brain, so different qualities of skin stimulation can be communicated to distinct places in the brain.

Pain   Touch

Vibration   Stretch

generator potential   A local change in the resting potential of a receptor cell that mediates between the impact of stimuli and the initiation of action potentials.

sensory transduction   The process in which a receptor cell converts the energy in a stimulus into a change in the electrical potential across its membrane.

Pacinian corpuscle or lamellated corpuscle   A skin receptor cell type that detects vibration and pressure.

distinguish different types of touch because our skin contains a variety of receptors and uses some lines to signal light touch, others to signal vibration, and yet other lines to signal stretching of the skin (**Figure 5.3**).

Receptor Cells Convert Sensory Signals into Electrical Activity

The structure of a receptor cell determines the particular kind of energy or chemical to which it will respond. And although a wide variety of cellular mechanisms are used to detect different stimuli, the outcome is always the same: an electrical change in the receptor, called a **generator potential**, that resembles the excitatory postsynaptic potentials we discussed in Chapter 3. Converting the signal in this way—from environmental stimuli into action potentials that our brain can understand—is called **sensory transduction**.

Our skin contains a rich array of receptors (**Figure 5.4**) that transduce different forms of energy to provide our sense of touch. But touch is not just touch. Careful studies of skin sensations reveal qualitatively different sensory experiences: pressure, vibration, tickle, "pins and needles," and more-complex dimensions, such as smoothness or wetness—all recorded by the receptors in the skin.

A skin receptor that provides a clear example of the process of sensory transduction is the **Pacinian** (or **lamellated**) **corpuscle** (Loewenstein, 1971), a tiny onionlike structure embedded in the innermost layer of the skin that selectively responds to vibration and pressure (see Figure 5.4). Acting as a filter, the corpuscle allows only vibrations of more than about

Hair

Free nerve endings (pain, temperature)

Merkel's disc (touch)

Meissner's corpuscle (touch)

Hair follicle receptor (touch)

Epidermis

Dermis

Hypodermis

Pacinian (or lamellated) corpuscle (vibration and pressure)

Ruffini corpuscle (stretch)

Figure 5.4   Receptors in Skin

Action potentials are recorded from individual somatosensory neurons of the cortex while different locations of the skin are touched. Each neuron has a receptive field on the skin with a concentric center-surround organization; in this case, touch in the center of the receptive field increases the firing rate of the corresponding cortical neuron and touch in the surround inhibits firing.

Figure 5.6   Identifying Somatosensory Receptive Fields

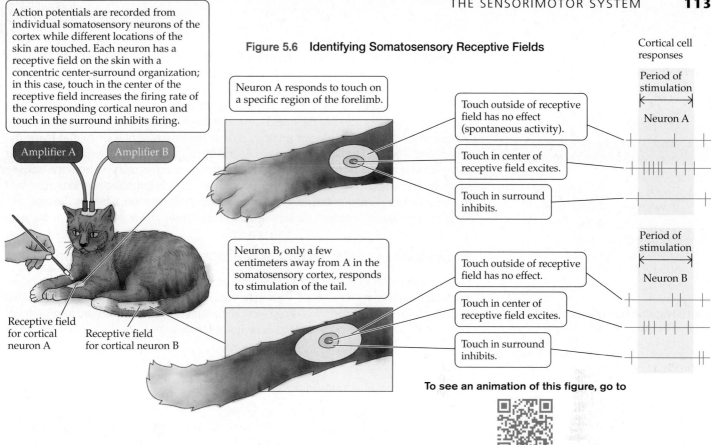

Cortical cell responses

Period of stimulation

Neuron A responds to touch on a specific region of the forelimb.

Touch outside of receptive field has no effect (spontaneous activity).

Touch in center of receptive field excites.

Touch in surround inhibits.

Neuron A

Amplifier A   Amplifier B

Receptive field for cortical neuron A

Receptive field for cortical neuron B

Neuron B, only a few centimeters away from A in the somatosensory cortex, responds to stimulation of the tail.

Touch outside of receptive field has no effect.

Touch in center of receptive field excites.

Touch in surround inhibits.

Period of stimulation

Neuron B

To see an animation of this figure, go to

mindsmachine.com/5.3
Somatosensory Receptive Fields

Receptors may show adaptation to unchanging stimuli

Adaptation is the progressive decrease in a receptor's response to sustained stimulation. This process allows us to ignore unimportant events. By not noticing the touch of our clothes on our skin, the sound of ticking clocks, and other stimuli that are unchanging or in the environmental background, our sensory systems avoid overload and can remain vigilant for critical events (**Figure 5.7**). Neuroscientists distinguish between **phasic receptors**, which display this sort of adaptation; and **tonic receptors**, which show little or no adaptation and thus can signal the duration of a stimulus. (As each of us knows all too well, pain sensors are often tonic receptors, maintaining a high level of activity to help us avoid further injury.)

The process of adaptation illustrates the principle we stated earlier: that sensory systems often shift *away from accurate portrayal* of the external world. In some mechanical receptors, such as the Pacinian corpuscle described earlier, adaptation develops from the elasticity of the receptor cell itself. When the corpuscle (which is a separate, accessory structure) is removed, the uncovered sensory nerve fiber does not adapt, but continues discharging action potentials in response to a constant stimulus.

Sometimes we need receptors to be quiet

We've already noted that survival depends more on sensitivity to important *changes* than on exact reporting of stimuli. To maintain such sensitivity

adaptation   The progressive loss of receptor sensitivity as stimulation is maintained.

phasic receptor   A receptor in which the frequency of action potentials drops rapidly as stimulation is maintained.

tonic receptor   A receptor in which the frequency of action potentials declines slowly or not at all as stimulation is maintained.

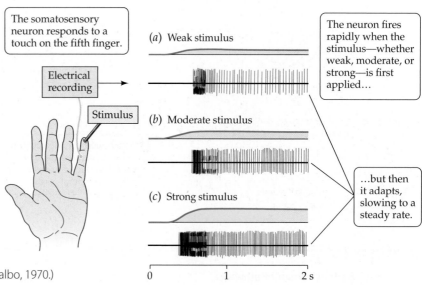

The somatosensory neuron responds to a touch on the fifth finger.

Electrical recording

Stimulus

(a) Weak stimulus

(b) Moderate stimulus

(c) Strong stimulus

The neuron fires rapidly when the stimulus—whether weak, moderate, or strong—is first applied…

…but then it adapts, slowing to a steady rate.

0   1   2 s

Figure 5.7   Sensory Adaptation (After Knibestol and Valbo, 1970.)

How's it going?

1. In general terms, explain how a sensory event is encoded in action potentials in sensory fibers.
2. What is range fractionation? How is it important for sensory processes?
3. Describe receptive fields, and how scientists detect them.
4. Name and briefly describe a couple of processes that change a sensory neuron's response to stimuli over time.

central modulation of sensory information The process in which higher brain centers, such as the cortex and thalamus, suppress some sources of sensory information and amplify others.

means that unneeded or unimportant sensory activity must be suppressed. As we just discussed, adaptation is one way in which sensory activity is controlled, and our bodies are equipped with two additional suppression systems.

One way to suppress sensory activity is simply to physically prevent the stimuli from reaching the sensors. Closing the eyelids provides this function in the visual system; in the auditory system, tiny middle-ear muscles reduce the intensity of sounds that reach the inner ear. A second kind of suppression of sensory inputs is entirely neural in nature. In many sensory and pain pathways, reciprocal neural connections descend from the brain to synapse on lower sensory levels, where they can then actively inhibit activity in the ascending sensory axons. This **central modulation of sensory information**, whereby the brain actively controls the information it receives, is a feature of many sensory and pain pathways.

Successive Levels of the CNS Process Sensory Information

Sensory information travels from the sensory surface to the highest levels of the brain, and each sensory system—such as touch, vision, or hearing—has its own distinctive pathway from the periphery to successively higher levels of the spinal cord and/or brain. For example, the somatosensory touch receptors that we've been discussing send their

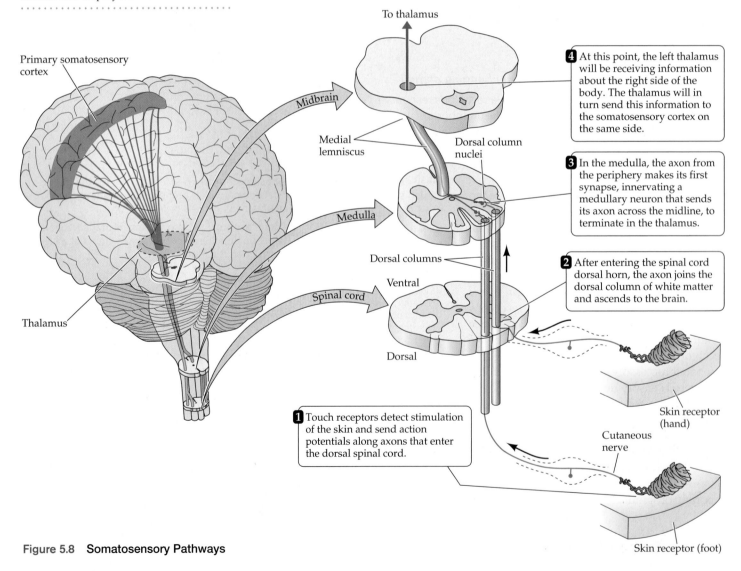

Figure 5.8 Somatosensory Pathways

axons—eventually bundled into sensory nerves—from the skin to the dorsal (rear) part of the spinal cord. On entering the cord, the somatosensory projections ascend as part of the spinal cord's **dorsal column system**, a large wedge of white matter in the dorsal spinal cord (**Figure 5.8**). These axons go all the way up to the brainstem, where they synapse onto neurons that project across the midline to the opposite side and then go to the thalamus. From there, the incoming sensory information is directed to cortex. At all levels, the inputs are organized according to a somatosensory map in which the body surface is divided into discrete bands. Each of these bands, called a **dermatome** (from the Greek *derma*, "skin," and *tome*, "part" or "segment") is the strip of skin that is innervated by a particular spinal nerve. This maplike organization of sensory inputs is a feature of several sensory systems, including touch, vision, and hearing.

Each station in a sensory pathway accomplishes a basic aspect of information processing. For example, painful stimulation of the finger leads to reflexive withdrawal of the hand, which is mediated by spinal circuits. At the brainstem level, other circuits turn the head toward the source of pain. Eventually, sensory pathways reach the cerebral cortex, where the most complex aspects of sensory processing take place, perhaps consciously identifying the source of the pain (darn, another sliver!) and planning a response (where did I leave those tweezers?). For most senses, information reaches the **thalamus** before being relayed to the cortex (**Figure 5.9**). Information about each sensory modality is sent to a separate division of the thalamus. One way for the brain to suppress particular stimuli is for the cortex to direct the thalamus to emphasize some sensory information and suppress other information.

Sensory cortex is highly organized

Researchers have identified a region designated as **primary sensory cortex** for each sensory modality—primary somatosensory cortex, primary auditory cortex, and so on—that is generally the initial destination of sensory inputs to the cortex. However, other cortical regions may receive and process the same information, often in collaboration

dorsal column system   A somatosensory system that delivers most touch stimuli via the dorsal columns of spinal white matter to the brain.

dermatome   A strip of skin innervated by a particular spinal nerve.

thalamus   The brain regions at the top of the brainstem that trade information with the cortex.

primary sensory cortex   For a given sensory modality, the region of cortex that receives most of the information about that modality from the thalamus or, in the case of olfaction, directly from the secondary sensory neurons.

Figure 5.9   **Levels of Sensory Processing**

nonprimary sensory cortex Also called *secondary sensory cortex*. For a given sensory modality, the cortical regions receiving direct projections from primary sensory cortex for that modality.

primary somatosensory cortex or somatosensory 1 (S1) The gyrus just posterior to the central sulcus where sensory receptors on the body surface are mapped. Primary cortex for receiving touch and pain information, in the parietal lobe.

polymodal neuron A neuron upon which information from different sensory systems converges.

synesthesia A condition in which stimuli in one modality evoke the involuntary experience of an additional sensation in another modality.

with the primary sensory cortex; sensibly enough (pardon the pun), we call these regions **nonprimary sensory cortex** (see Figure 5.9). Each cortical sensory region processes different aspects of our perceptual experiences.

Primary somatosensory cortex of each hemisphere—known as **somatosensory 1** or **S1**—is located in the postcentral gyrus, the long hump of tissue that lies just posterior to the central sulcus dividing the parietal lobe from the frontal lobe (**Figure 5.10a**). S1 receives touch information from the opposite side of the body. The cells in S1 are arranged as a map of the body (**Figure 5.10b**), but it is a very unusual map: it is distorted so that the size of each region on the map is proportional to the density of sensory receptors found in that region of the skin. Parts of the body where we are especially sensitive to touch (like the hand and fingers) have a large representation in S1 compared to less sensitive areas (like the shoulder). This proportional mapping is illustrated in the strange-looking character in **Figure 5.10c**, called a *sensory homunculus*, in whom the size of each body part reflects the proportion of S1 devoted to that part. We discuss other aspects of cortical organization in **A Step Further 5.1**, on the website.

Sensory brain regions influence one another and change over time

Often the use of one sensory system influences perception from another sensory system. For example, humans detect a visual signal more accurately if it is accompanied by a sound from the same part of space (McDonald et al., 2000).

Many sensory areas in the brain—so-called *association areas*—process a mixture of inputs from different modalities. Some "visual" cells, for instance, also respond to auditory or touch stimuli. The convergence of information from different sensory systems on these **polymodal neurons** allows different sensory systems to interact (B. E. Stein and Stanford, 2008). And for a few people, a stimulus in one sensory modality may evoke an additional perception in another sensory modality, as when seeing a number evokes a color, or music literally becomes a matter of taste, where each note has both a sound and a flavor (Beeli et al., 2005). This condition is known as **synesthesia**. For more information and an example of synesthesia, see **A Step Further 5.2**, on the website.

At one time, most researchers thought that sensory regions of cortex were fixed early in life. Now, however, we know that cortical maps are highly plastic, changing considerably as a result of experience (Blake et al., 2006). For example, professional musicians who play stringed instruments have expanded cortical representations of their left fingers, presumably because they use these fingers to depress the strings for precisely the right note (Elbert et al., 1995; Münte et al., 2002). Brain imaging also reveals cortical reorganization in people who lose a hand in adulthood (**Figure 5.11**). One man received a transplanted

Figure 5.10 Representation of the Body Surface in Somatosensory Cortex

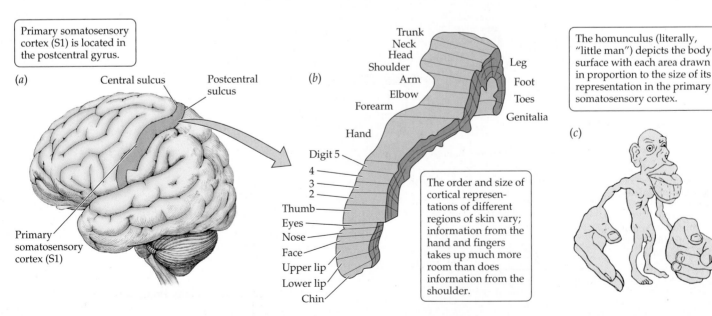

(a) Central sulcus | Postcentral sulcus

Primary somatosensory cortex (S1) is located in the postcentral gyrus.

Primary somatosensory cortex (S1)

(b) Trunk / Neck / Head / Shoulder / Arm / Elbow / Forearm / Hand / Digit 5 / 4 / 3 / 2 / Thumb / Eyes / Nose / Face / Upper lip / Lower lip / Chin

Leg / Foot / Toes / Genitalia

The order and size of cortical representations of different regions of skin vary; information from the hand and fingers takes up much more room than does information from the shoulder.

The homunculus (literally, "little man") depicts the body surface with each area drawn in proportion to the size of its representation in the primary somatosensory cortex.

(c)

(a)

Normally, the hand region of S1 lies between the regions representing the upper arm and the face.

Face
Hand
Arm
Central sulcus

(b)

After the loss of one hand, the cortical regions representing the upper arm and face expand, taking over the cortical region previously representing the missing hand. The lack of sensory input from the lost hand allows those cortical neurons to become innervated by neighboring cortical neurons.

Region formerly stimulated by receptors in the hand now responds to touch on face or arm.

Figure 5.11 **Plasticity in Somatosensory Cortex** (After T. T. Yang et al., 1994.)

hand (from an accident victim) 35 years after losing his own. Despite the length of time that had passed, his brain reorganized in just a few months to receive sensation from the hand in the appropriate part of S1 (Frey et al., 2008).

Some changes in cortical maps occur after weeks or months of use or disuse; they may arise from the production of new synapses and dendrites (Florence et al., 1998; Hickmott and Steen, 2005) or from the loss of others. As described on the website in **A Step Further 5.3**, we must actively manipulate objects in order for the somatosensory cortex to perceive them.

PART II Pain: The Body's Emergency Signaling System

One important aspect of body sensation is at best a mixed blessing. The International Association for the Study of Pain defines **pain** as "an unpleasant sensory and emotional experience associated with actual or potential tissue damage, or described in terms of such damage." Pain forcefully guides our behavior in several ways that minimize the risk to our bodies (Dennis and Melzack, 1983). Immediate, short-lasting pain causes us to withdraw from the source, often reflexively, thus preventing further damage. Longer-lasting pain encourages behaviors, such as sleep, inactivity, grooming, feeding, and drinking, that promote recuperation. And the pain-related social communication—grimacing, groaning, shrieking, and the rest of the miserable lineup—provides a warning to kin, and elicits caregiving behaviors from them, including grooming, defending, and feeding.

Human Pain Varies in Several Dimensions

Learning, experience, emotion, and culture all affect our perception of pain in striking ways, and these factors may strongly influence people's descriptions of pain, ranging from an apparent absence of pain in badly injured soldiers and athletes, to the anguish of a child with a paper cut. A widely used quantitative measure of pain perception—the *McGill Pain Questionnaire* (Melzack, 1984)—asks subjects to select words that tap three different dimensions of pain:

1. The *sensory-discriminative* dimension (e.g., throbbing, gnawing, shooting)
2. The *motivational-affective* (emotional) dimension (e.g., tiring, sickening, fearful)
3. An overall *cognitive* evaluative dimension (e.g., no pain, mild, excruciating)

How's it going?

1. Name the main somatosensory pathway to the brain, describe its organization, and name its main components.
2. Where is the main somatosensory cortex located? How is it organized?
3. Discuss interactions between sensory modalities—for example, effects of auditory inputs on visual perception.

pain The discomfort normally associated with tissue damage.

THE HUMAN PINCUSHION WHO INCURS CONSTANT
RISKS OF BLOOD POISONING.

Doesn't That Hurt? Although it might seem like a blessing, people with *congenital insensitivity to pain*, like the "Human Pincushion" pictured here (Dearborn, 1932), tend to die young as a consequence of repeated body injuries. Pain is an important adaptation that provides us with constant guidance to protect our bodies (Hirsch et al., 1995). (Photograph by Culver Pictures, Inc.)

Researchers found that subjects use different constellations of descriptors in various forms of pain: tooth pain is described differently from arthritic pain, which in turn is described differently from menstrual pain. This more detailed analysis provides better information for the diagnosis and treatment of painful problems.

A Discrete Pain Pathway Projects from Body to Brain

Most tissues of the body (but not all) contain receptors specialized for detecting painful stimuli. These receptors are particularly well studied in the skin; in this section we discuss some features of these receptors, along with the peripheral and CNS pathways that mediate pain.

Peripheral receptors get the initial message

When tissue is injured, the affected cells release chemicals that activate nearby pain receptors (called **nociceptors**) on free nerve endings, as well as causing inflammation (**Figure 5.12**). Many different substances in injured tissue—serotonin, histamine, and various enzymes and peptides, to name just a few—can stimulate these nociceptors. Different nociceptors respond to various stimuli, such as pain and/or changes in temperature.

Studies of *capsaicin*, the chemical that makes chili peppers spicy hot, helped reveal the receptor that signals sudden increases in temperature (this action is the reason spicy food seems to *burn*) (Caterina et al., 1997). This receptor, with the not-so-spicy name *transient receptor potential vanilloid type 1* (*TRPV1*; or just *vanilloid receptor 1*), belongs to a larger family of proteins called transient receptor potential (TRP) ion channels. Mice lacking the gene for TRPV1 still respond to mechanosensory pain, but not to mild heat or capsaicin (Caterina et al., 2000).

TRPV1's normal job is to report a rise in temperature to warn us of danger, so chili peppers cleverly evolved capsaicin to ward off mammalian predators, by falsely signaling burning heat. A related receptor, **transient receptor potential 2** (**TRP2**), detects even higher temperatures than does TRPV1, but it does *not* respond to capsaicin. TRP2

nociceptor A receptor that responds to stimuli (e.g., pain or changes in temperature) that produce tissue damage or pose the threat of damage.

transient receptor potential 2 (TRP2) A receptor, found in some free nerve endings, that opens its channel in response to rising temperatures.

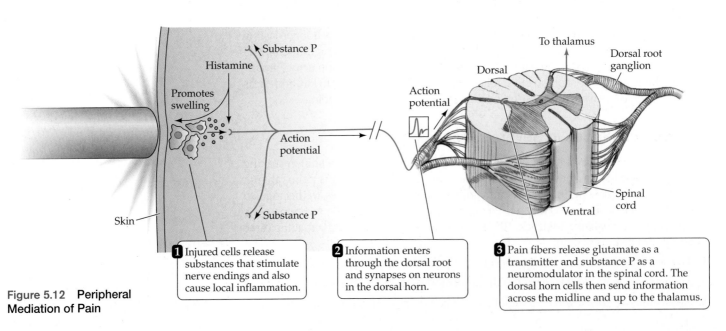

① Injured cells release substances that stimulate nerve endings and also cause local inflammation.

② Information enters through the dorsal root and synapses on neurons in the dorsal horn.

③ Pain fibers release glutamate as a transmitter and substance P as a neuromodulator in the spinal cord. The dorsal horn cells then send information across the midline and up to the thalamus.

Figure 5.12 Peripheral Mediation of Pain

receptors are found on **A delta (Aδ) fibers**, which are large-diameter, myelinated axons. Because of the relatively large axon diameter and myelination, action potentials in these fibers reach the spinal cord very quickly. In contrast, the nerve fibers that possess TRPV1 receptors consist of thin, unmyelinated fibers called **C fibers**. So, when you burn your hand on that hot pan, the initial sharp pain you feel is conducted by the fat A delta fibers activated by their TRP2 receptors, and the long-lasting dull ache that follows arises from slower C fibers and their TRPV1 receptors. Other members of the TRP family of receptors detect coolness, and constituents of spices like oregano, cloves, garlic, and wasabi (Bautista et al., 2007; Jordt et al., 2004; Salazar et al., 2008), but their relation to pain receptors remains a delicious mystery (sorry).

Identification of the nociceptor that detects *physical* damage is tricky because so many different chemicals are released by damaged tissue. Which one is the key signal? Through careful study of the family of a Pakistani boy who died in tragic circumstances—performing dangerous pranks because he could feel no pain—scientists isolated a mutation in a gene (called *SCN9A*) that appears to be responsible for pain insensitivity in other members of the boy's family. The gene encodes a sodium channel expressed in many free nerve endings (Cox et al., 2006). Researchers are hopeful that this sodium channel is the sought-after specific pain receptor protein, because that would provide a new target for developing high-potency pain medication.

Special neural pathways carry pain information to the brain

Nerve fibers carrying information about pain and temperature send their axons to enter the dorsal horns of the spinal cord, where they synapse onto spinal neurons that project across the midline to the opposite side and then up toward the thalamus of the brain (via several brainstem sites), forming the **anterolateral**, or **spinothalamic**, **system** (**Figure 5.13**). This projection is distinct from the somatosensory system that we discussed earlier (the dorsal column

A delta (Aδ) fiber A moderately large, myelinated, and therefore fast-conducting, axon, usually transmitting pain information.

C fiber A small, unmyelinated axon that conducts pain information slowly and adapts slowly.

anterolateral system or spinothalamic system A somatosensory system that carries most of the pain information from the body to the brain.

Pain sensation travels from its origin to the brain via the spinothalamic system, crossing the midline in the spinal cord.

5 Cingulate cortex is especially activated by pain information.

4 Pain information is distributed to many thalamic and cortical areas.

3 Pain information is provided to various brainstem sites, which control pain-related behavior such as vocalization.

2 Axons of dorsal horn neurons cross the midline and ascend the spinal cord in the anterolateral quadrant.

1 Pain information is carried by rapidly conducting myelinated A delta fibers and slowly conducting unmyelinated C fibers.

Somatosensory cortex (S1)

Thalamic nuclei

Forebrain

Midbrain

Pons

Medulla

Spinal cord

Periaqueductal gray

Anterolateral or spinothalamic system

Aδ and C fibers

Figure 5.13 Ascending Pain Pathways in the CNS

Figure 5.14   Using a Visual Illusion to Relieve Phantom Limb Pain (After Ramachandran and Rogers-Ramachandran, 2000.)

The mirror seems to show that both limbs are intact. The subject is asked to command *both* hands to move in symmetry, and observe them.

The illusion of controlling the missing hand relieves the phantom sensation that the missing hand is painfully clenched shut.

How's it going?

1. Define *pain*. Why should it be viewed as a positive adaptation?

2. Provide a general explanation of the way pain receptors work. How do pain receptors differ from touch receptors?

3. Name and distinguish between the two types of pain fibers that carry pain information from the periphery to the spinal cord.

4. Sketch the pain pathways from the periphery to the cortex.

substance P   A peptide transmitter that is involved in pain transmission.

neuropathic pain   Pain that persists long after the injury that started it has healed. It is caused by damage to peripheral nerves and is often difficult to treat.

cingulate cortex   Also called *cingulum*. A region of medial cerebral cortex that lies dorsal to the corpus callosum.

analgesia   Absence of or reduction in pain.

endorphin   One of three kinds of endogenous opioids.

system; see Figure 5.8), but like that system, each hemisphere receives its inputs from the contralateral side of the body. Within the spinal cord, the arriving pain fibers release the excitatory transmitter glutamate along with a peptide, **substance P**, that selectively boosts pain signals and remodels pain pathway neurons (Mantyh et al., 1997). Mice lacking substance P cannot feel intense pain, but they still feel mild pain (Cao et al., 1998; De Felipe et al., 1998).

Sometimes pain persists long after the injury that started it has healed. This **neuropathic pain** is a disagreeable example of neural plasticity, where neurons continue to directly signal pain, and indeed *amplify* the pain signal, in the absence of any tissue damage (Woolf and Salter, 2000). In one example of neuropathic pain called *phantom limb pain*, patients experience great pain that seems to come from a limb that was previously amputated. It is notoriously difficult to treat. One approach that has met with some success involves using a mirror to trick the brain into believing it is controlling the missing limb (**Figure 5.14**) (Ramachandran and Rogers-Ramachandran, 2000); apparently, visual feedback (even if false) allows the brain to recalibrate the pain signal.

Pain information is eventually integrated in the **cingulate cortex**. The extent of activation in the cingulate (as well as in somatosensory cortex) correlates with how much discomfort different people report in response to the same mildly painful stimulus (Coghill et al., 2003). Different subregions of the cingulate cortex seem to mediate emotional versus sensory aspects of pain (Vogt, 2005); one part of the cingulate becomes active even when we just empathize with a loved one experiencing pain (T. Singer et al., 2004).

Pain Control Can Be Difficult

Throughout history, suffering humans have sought remedies to reduce their experience of pain. It's not easy; even cutting nerves may provide only temporary relief, until the pain system finds a way to restore its signal to the brain. A dominant model of pain transmission, called the *gate control theory*, hypothesizes that spinal "gates"—modulation sites at which pain can be facilitated or blocked—control the signal that gets through to the brain (Melzack and Wall, 1965). If this theory is right, effective pain relief may depend on finding ways to keep the gates closed, cutting off the pain signal. Popular strategies for **analgesia** (absence of pain; from the Greek *an-*, "not," and *algesis*, "feeling of pain") fall into four general categories, which we'll discuss next.

Analgesic drugs are highly effective

The opiates (opium-related drugs, like morphine) have been known for centuries to relieve pain sensations. Along with the endogenous opioids (which are brain-derived painkillers such as the **endorphins**), opiate drugs bind to specific receptors in the brain to reduce pain (see Chapter 4). Researchers have found that this action is especially pronounced in the brainstem region called the periaqueductal gray (see Figure 5.13); one possibility is that the brainstem system activates the pain gating mechanism of the spinal cord via descending projections, thereby blocking the transmission of pain signals. Similar benefits can be obtained by (carefully!) injecting opiates directly into the spinal cord; this is called an *epidural* or *intrathecal* injection (Landau and Levy, 1993).

Although people sometimes do become addicted to painkillers, that is usually not true of people who are using them to treat severe pain; in fact, the danger of addiction

Placebos Affect Opioid Systems in the Brain Volunteers were subjected to a painful procedure and given a placebo for the pain. Some subjects seemed to respond to the placebo, but others did not. This difference image pinpoints brain regions that were more activated in responders than in nonresponders. These regions are rich in receptors for endogenous opioids (D. J. Scott et al., 2008). (From Wager et al., 2007; courtesy of Jon-Kar Zubieta.)

from the use of morphine to relieve surgical pain has been vastly exaggerated (Melzack, 1990) and is estimated to be no more than 0.04% (Brownlee and Schrof, 1997). A greater concern seems to be the undertreatment of severe pain, which can lead to the development of chronic pain.

Of course, there are other painkilling drugs, but none are as effective as the opiates. Over-the-counter medications like aspirin and acetaminophen (Tylenol) act via nonopiate mechanisms (especially the cyclooxygenase enzymes called COX-1 and COX-2) to reduce pain and inflammation. Marijuana reduces pain by stimulating endogenous cannabinoid receptors (CB_1 receptors) in the spinal cord and in the brain (Agarwal et al., 2007; Pernía-Andrade et al., 2009).

Electrical stimulation can sometimes relieve pain

In **transcutaneous electrical nerve stimulation** (**TENS**), mild electrical stimulation is applied to nerves around the injury sites to relieve pain. The exact mechanism of this pain relief is not clear, but one possibility is that TENS closes the spinal "gate" for pain that Melzack and Wall (1965) described. Recall, for example, the last time you stubbed your toe. In addition to expelling a string of expletives, you may have vigorously rubbed the injured area, bringing a little relief. TENS is a more efficient way of stimulating those adjacent nerves, and it may bring dramatic relief lasting for hours. We know that TENS acts at least in part by releasing endogenous opioids, because administration of **naloxone**, an opioid antagonist, partially blocks this analgesic action.

Placebos effectively control pain in some people, but not all

In some people, simply believing that they are receiving a proven treatment can effectively relieve pain. In a striking example of this **placebo effect**, subjects who had just had their wisdom teeth extracted were given morphine or a placebo (J. D. Levine et al., 1978). Fully a third of patients receiving the placebo experienced pain relief. But when the placebo was coadministered with a drug that blocks opioid receptors (naloxone), the subjects did not experience the benefits of the placebo effect. This latter finding strongly implies that placebos work by activating the brain's endogenous opioid system. In fact, functional brain imaging indicates that opioids and placebos activate the same brain regions (Petrovic et al., 2002). For reasons unknown, some people consistently experience relief from placebos while others do not.

Activation of endogenous opioids relieves pain

Although the ancient pain-relieving technique **acupuncture** (**Figure 5.15**) remains very popular, only a minority of people using acupuncture achieve lasting relief from chronic pain. In those people for whom acupuncture is effective, a release of endorphins may be an important part of the process, since treatment with naloxone blocks acupuncture's effectiveness (N. M. Tang et al., 1997). Acupuncture thus resembles placebos in this regard. Although many rules govern needle placement in acupuncture, systematic research indicates that the placement of the needles actually has little to do with its effects on pain (Linde et al., 2009). The *expectation* that the needles will relieve pain appears to be the important factor, presumably inducing a release of endogenous opioids.

Likewise, stressful life events can produce significant analgesia; for example, tales abound of gravely wounded soldiers who feel no pain for some time after their injuries occur. Research in animals indicates that stress activates both an opioid-dependent form of analgesia, which can be blocked by naloxone, and another, non-opioid

transcutaneous electrical nerve stimulation (TENS) The delivery of electrical pulses through electrodes attached to the skin, which excite nerves that supply the region to which pain is referred. TENS can relieve the pain in some instances.

naloxone A potent antagonist of opiates that is often administered to people who have taken drug overdoses. It binds to receptors for endogenous opioids.

placebo effect Relief of a symptom, such as pain, that results following a treatment that is known to be ineffective or inert.

acupuncture The insertion of needles at designated points on the skin to alleviate pain or neurological malfunction.

Figure 5.15 Acupuncture for Controlling Pain In some cases, acupuncture controls pain. Opioid antagonists block this analgesia, indicating that acupuncture, like placebos, activates endogenous opioids.

TABLE 5.2 Types of Pain Relief

Type	Mechanism
PSYCHOGENIC	
Placebo	May activate endorphin-mediated pain control system
Hypnosis	Alters brain's perception of pain
Stress	Both opioid and non-opioid mechanisms
Cognitive (learning, coping strategies)	May activate endorphin-mediated pain control system
PHARMACOLOGICAL	
Opiates	Bind to opioid receptors in periaqueductal gray and spinal cord
Spinal block	Drugs block pain signals in spinal cord
Anti-inflammatory drugs	Block chemical inflammatory signals at the site of injury (see Figure 5.12)
Cannabinoids	Act in spinal cord and on nociceptor endings
STIMULATION	
TENS/mechanical	Tactile or electrical stimulation of large fibers blocks or alters pain signal to brain
Acupuncture	Activation of endogenous opioids and/or placebo-like effect; possible modulating effect on activity of peripheral pain pathways
Central gray	Electrical stimulation activates endorphin-mediated paincontrol systems, blocking pain signal in spinal cord
SURGICAL	
Cut peripheral nerve cord	
Rhizotomy (cutting dorsal root)	Create physical break in pain pathway
Cord hemisection	
Frontal lobotomy	Disrupts affective response to pain

How's it going?

1. What is the most effective pharmacological method of pain control? How and where do these drugs work in the brain?

2. How is TENS thought to work to control pain?

3. Compare and contrast placebos and acupuncture for pain. Discuss the possibility that they the act on the same neural system.

analgesia system that has not yet been characterized (but may rely on endocannabinoids) (A. G. Hohmann et al., 2005).

Pain relief remains a major challenge for neuroscience research. Chronic pain can have dramatic effects on the brain: for example, the prefrontal cortex in people with chronic back pain shrinks much faster than normal, as if the patients are rapidly aging (Apkarian et al., 2004). The wide range of pain relief strategies (summarized in **Table 5.2**), some of which reflect desperation in the face of great anguish, testifies to the elusive nature of pain. As we learn more about how the brain controls pain, we can hope for better, safer analgesics in the future.

PART III Movement and the Motor System

Our apparently effortless adult motor abilities—such as reaching out and picking up an object, walking across the room, sipping a cup of coffee—require complex muscular systems with constant feedback from the body. Ian, whom we met at the beginning of the chapter, knows this all too well. Our survey of motor control starts with a discussion of a theoretical framework for studying motor behavior, followed by a tour of the anatomy and pathology of movement.

Behavior Requires Movements That Are Precisely Programmed and Monitored

movement   A single relocation of a body part, usually resulting from a brief muscle contraction; less complex than an act.

When you think about it, *all* behavior must involve **movements**—contractions of muscles that provide our sole means of interacting with the world around us (with only rare, technological exception, as we'll see later). Centuries of research focused on the organization of motor behavior as both an engineering problem (how is movement programmed?) and a physiological system (how is movement produced?). Early discoveries suggested that **reflexes**—simple, unvarying, and unlearned responses to sensory stimuli such as touch, pressure, and pain—might be the basic units of behavior. It was thought that more-complex behaviors, or **acts**, such as getting dressed, walking, or speaking a sentence, might result from simply connecting together different reflexes, the sensation from one reflex triggering the next.

The flaws of this perspective soon became apparent: for most acts we have a *plan* in which several units (arm movements, leg movements, speech sounds) are placed in a larger pattern (the intended complete act), and they are not always produced in the same (or even the correct) order. So, researchers realized that acts require a **motor plan** (or *motor program*), a complex set of commands to muscles that is established *before* an act occurs. Feedback from movements informs and fine-tunes the motor program as the execution is unfolding, but the basic sequence of movements is planned. Examples of behaviors that exhibit this kind of internal plan range from highly skilled acts, such as piano playing, to the simple escape behaviors of animals such as crayfish.

Researchers can track the simple movements that make up an act by recording the electrical activity of muscles as they contract—a technique called **electromyography** (**EMG**)—and the moment-to-moment positions of the body. The EMG recordings in **Figure 5.16** show that a person pulling a lever will adjust his legs just before moving his arm—another example of motor planning. Motor plans resemble engineering concepts that are applied to the operation of machines. In designing machines, engineers commonly have two goals: (1) accuracy, to prevent or minimize error; and (2) speed, to complete a task quickly and efficiently. Improvements in one goal usually come at some cost to the other goal; in other words there is a trade-off between speed and accuracy, and this trade-off is also apparent in motor planning by the nervous system.

reflex   A simple, highly stereotyped, and unlearned response to a particular stimulus (e.g., an eye blink in response to a puff of air).

act   Complex behavior, as distinct from a simple movement.

motor plan   Also called *motor program*. A plan for a series of muscular contractions, established in the nervous system prior to its execution.

electromyography (EMG)   The electrical recording of muscle activity.

Biceps activity

Gastrocnemius (calf muscle) activity

When asked to pull up on the lever, the subject first adjusts his legs to steady himself—an example of a simple motor plan.

Figure 5.16   Electromyography (After Purves et al., 2001.)

Figure 5.17 A Closed-Loop System

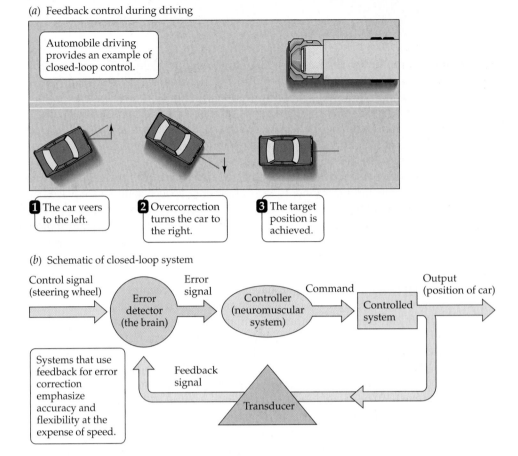

(a) Feedback control during driving

Automobile driving provides an example of closed-loop control.

1 The car veers to the left.

2 Overcorrection turns the car to the right.

3 The target position is achieved.

(b) Schematic of closed-loop system

Control signal (steering wheel) → Error detector (the brain) → Error signal → Controller (neuromuscular system) → Command → Controlled system → Output (position of car)

Systems that use feedback for error correction emphasize accuracy and flexibility at the expense of speed.

Feedback signal ← Transducer

closed-loop motor control A control mechanism that provides a flow of information from whatever is being controlled to the device that controls it.

open-loop motor control A control mechanism in which feedback from the output of the system is not provided to the input control.

ballistic Referring to a rapid muscular movement that is generally fully preprogrammed and thus not susceptible to error correction during execution.

How's it going?

1. Distinguish among reflexes, movements, and acts.
2. Discuss the importance of sensory feedback for the control of movements. How are speed and accuracy related, in the context of movement control?
3. What is a ballistic movement?
4. Identify the six major levels of the motor control hierarchy.

Closed-loop motor control maximizes *accuracy*: feedback information is obtained through sensory monitoring of the movement as it is being performed, and it is used for error correction while the movement is being made (**Figure 5.17**). Some examples include precise tool use, grasping an object, or learning to play a tune. In contrast, **open-loop motor control** maximizes *speed*; no feedback information affects the execution of the movement, and the activity is considered to be preprogrammed, or **ballistic**. Most of our movements represent a blending of these two control systems: preprogrammed sequences of movements (open-loop) that are fine-tuned by sensory feedback (closed-loop). With practice we may learn a behavior so thoroughly that we require little or no feedback. Piano playing is an example of such a behavior: we could learn to do it with our eyes shut—but that would never be a good way to drive a car!

The neuromuscular system consists of the muscles of the body plus a collection of brain mechanisms and nerves that prepare and execute motor plans and obtain feedback information from the sensory system for use in error correction. The system is organized according to a distinct hierarchy:

1. The *skeletal system* and the muscles attached to it determine which movements are possible.
2. The *spinal cord* controls skeletal muscles in response to motor commands from the brain or, in the case of simple reflexes, in direct response to sensory inputs.
3. The *brainstem* integrates motor commands from higher levels of the brain and transmits them to the spinal cord. It also relays sensory information about the body from the spinal cord to the forebrain.
4. Some of the main commands for action are initiated in the *primary motor cortex*.
5. Areas adjacent to the primary motor cortex, *nonprimary motor cortex*, provide an additional source of motor commands, acting indirectly via primary motor cortex and through direct connections to lower levels of the motor hierarchy. At the very top of the movement hierarchy is the prefrontal cortex, which is crucial to the conscious formulation of behavioral plans.

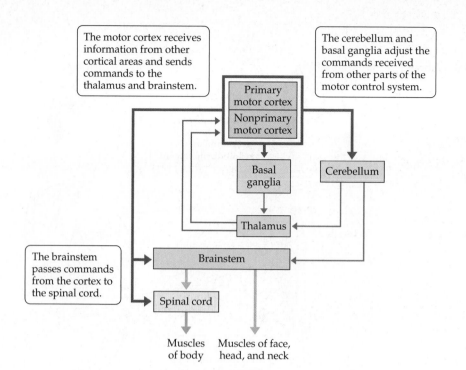

The motor cortex receives information from other cortical areas and sends commands to the thalamus and brainstem.

The cerebellum and basal ganglia adjust the commands received from other parts of the motor control system.

Figure 5.18 **The Hierarchy of Movement Control**

The brainstem passes commands from the cortex to the spinal cord.

6. Other brain regions—the *cerebellum* and *basal ganglia*, via the *thalamus*—modulate the activities of the other parts of the control system.

Through the remainder of the chapter we'll look in turn at each element of this hierarchy, as outlined in **Figure 5.18**, in a bit more detail.

A Complex Neural System Controls Muscles to Create Behavior

So much processing power is devoted to movement that the range of possible behaviors and their speed of execution can be astonishing. One of the primary factors in determining the range of movements of a species is the type and arrangement of its muscles around joints, so we begin there and then work our way up through the central nervous system.

Muscles and the skeleton work together to move the body

Our skeleton, like those of other species with bones, is articulated with joints that vary in their planes of movement—ranging from "universal" joints, like the hip or shoulder, to joints that act more like hinges and move mostly in one direction, such as the elbow or knee. Around a joint, different muscles are arranged in a reciprocal fashion, connected to the bone by *tendons*, such that when one muscle group contracts, it stretches the other group; that is, the muscles are **antagonists**. Some groups of muscles, called **synergists**, may work together to move a limb in one direction. A simple example of muscle action around a joint is shown in **Figure 5.19**. The movement of a limb is determined by the degree and rate of contraction in some muscles and relaxation in others, or we can lock a limb in position by contracting opposing muscles simultaneously.

The muscles that we use for movement of the skeleton are called **skeletal muscles**. Because they have a striped appearance on microscopic examination, due to overlapping layers of contractile proteins called *myosin* and *actin*, skeletal muscles are said to be made of **striate muscle**. (*Smooth muscle*, which has a different appearance and is found in visceral organs and blood vessels, is not generally involved in voluntary behavior, so we will not concern ourselves with it here.) Contraction of the muscle increases the overlap of the actin and myosin filaments within *muscle fibers*, and as they slide past each other the muscle shortens. Most muscles consist of a specific mixture

antagonist A muscle that counteracts the effect of another muscle.

synergist A muscle that acts together with another muscle.

skeletal muscle A muscle that is used for movement of the skeleton, typically under our conscious control.

striate muscle A type of muscle that has a striped appearance; it is generally under voluntary control.

Figure 5.19   The Arrangement of Muscles around the Elbow

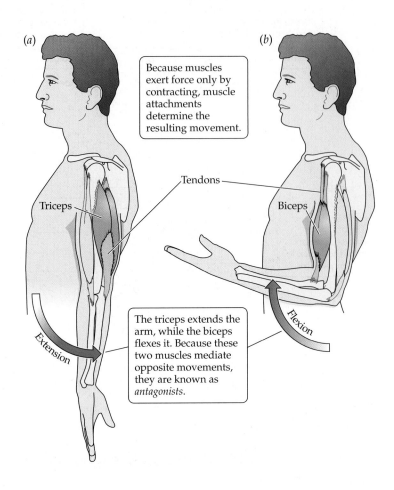

(a)   (b)

Because muscles exert force only by contracting, muscle attachments determine the resulting movement.

Tendons

Triceps

Biceps

Extension

Flexion

The triceps extends the arm, while the biceps flexes it. Because these two muscles mediate opposite movements, they are known as *antagonists*.

of two types of fibers: *slow-twitch fibers* that contract with relatively low intensity but fatigue slowly, and *fast-twitch fibers* that contract strongly but fatigue quickly.

Muscles contract because **motoneurons** of the spinal cord and brainstem (see Figures 2.7 and 2.8) send action potentials along their axons and axon collaterals to terminate at specialized synapses, called **neuromuscular junctions**, that are found on muscle fibers (**Figure 5.20**). The production of an action potential by a motoneuron triggers a release of the neurotransmitter **acetylcholine** (**ACh**) at all of the motoneuron's axon terminals. The motoneuron, together with all of the muscle fibers it innervates, is known as a *motor unit* (see Figure 5.20); the fibers respond to the release of ACh by triggering the molecular events that cause actin and myosin to produce contraction.

Some large motor units—motoneurons innervating thigh muscle, for example—may involve hundreds or thousands of muscle fibers. But muscles that require more precise control—muscles of the face, for example—tend to have much smaller motor units, with each motoneuron controlling only a few muscle fibers. Many people experience "jumping nerves" in the eyelids when they're fatigued (from studying biological psychology, maybe). This tiny but incredibly annoying twitch, called a *fasciculation*, is actually a misfiring facial motor unit. A fasciculation in the thigh, in contrast, produces a twitch the size of a pencil.

Within the spinal cord, motoneurons tend to have large cell bodies and very widespread dendritic fields because they receive and integrate inputs from so many different sources—incoming sensory inputs, as well as descending signals from the brain—that form thousands of synapses onto the motoneurons. Virtually all motoneuron axons are myelinated (Kaar and Fraher, 1985), so the action potentials that result from the integration process quickly reach their target muscles. In a somewhat dramatic turn of phrase, neuroscientists refer to motoneurons as the **final common pathway**: the sole route through which the spinal cord and brain can control our many muscles.

motoneuron   Also called *motor neuron*. A neuron that transmits neural messages to muscles (or glands).

neuromuscular junction   The region where the motoneuron terminal and the adjoining muscle fiber meet; the point where the nerve transmits its message to the muscle fiber.

acetylcholine (ACh)   A neurotransmitter that is produced and released by parasympathetic postganglionic neurons, by motoneurons, and by neurons throughout the brain.

final common pathway   The motoneurons of the spinal cord, so called because they receive and integrate all motor signals from the brain and then direct movement accordingly.

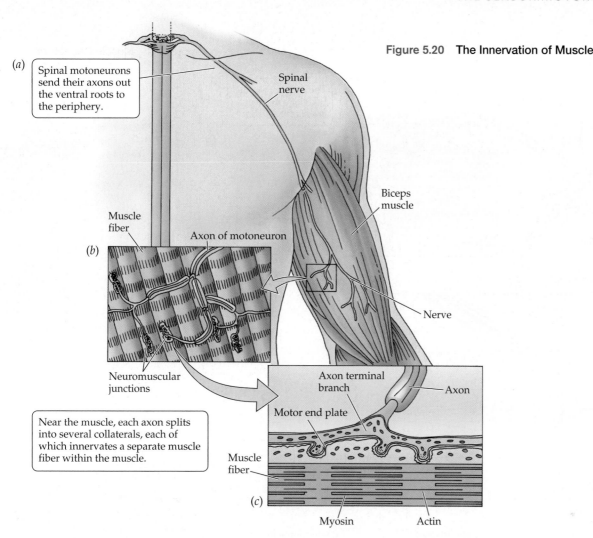

(a)

Spinal motoneurons send their axons out the ventral roots to the periphery.

Spinal nerve

Biceps muscle

Muscle fiber

Axon of motoneuron

(b)

Nerve

Neuromuscular junctions

Near the muscle, each axon splits into several collaterals, each of which innervates a separate muscle fiber within the muscle.

Axon terminal branch

Axon

Motor end plate

Muscle fiber

(c)

Myosin   Actin

Figure 5.20   The Innervation of Muscle

Sensory feedback from muscles, tendons, and joints governs movement

To produce rapid coordinated movements of the body, the brain and spinal cord continually monitor the state of the muscles, the positions of the limbs, and the instructions being issued by the motor centers. This collection of information about body movements and positions is called **proprioception** (from the Latin *proprius*, "own," and *recipere*, "to receive"). Ian, whom we met at the start of this chapter, was attacked by a virus that selectively killed proprioceptive axons; his predicament illustrates how important this "sixth sense" is for movement. Let's consider the two special proprioceptors—muscle spindles and Golgi tendon organs—that monitor muscle length and muscle tension.

The **muscle spindle** is basically a capsule, buried within the other fibers of the muscle, that contains a special kind of muscle fiber called an **intrafusal fiber** (from the Latin *intra*, "within," and *fusus*, "spindle") (**Figure 5.21a, c**). When a muscle is stretched—imagine someone handing you a heavy book, causing your arm to bend downward and stretching the biceps muscle—sensory endings within the spindle fiber become excited and trigger action potentials in afferent sensory nerves. This proprioceptive signal informs the spinal cord and brain about the extent and rate of change in the stretch of the muscle, and therefore about the load being imposed (**Figure 5.21d**). Interestingly, a special motoneuron controls the length of the intrafusal fiber, adjusting it according to the movements being planned by the brain—in a sense, calibrating the muscle spindle to the *expected* limb position.

While muscle spindles respond primarily to *stretch*, the other proprioceptive receptors for muscle—**Golgi tendon organs**—are especially sensitive to muscle *tension*. Loads that are strong enough to stretch the tough tendon are sensed by the nerve endings of

proprioception Body sense; information about the position and movement of the body that is sent to the brain.

muscle spindle A muscle receptor that lies parallel to a muscle and sends impulses to the central nervous system when the muscle is stretched.

intrafusal fiber Any of the small muscle fibers that lie within each muscle spindle.

Golgi tendon organ Any of the receptors within tendons that send impulses to the central nervous system when a muscle contracts.

(a)

Golgi tendon organ

Muscle spindle

(b) Innervation of a Golgi tendon organ

Muscle fiber

The receptors in the body of a muscle are *muscle spindles*.

The receptors in tendons are *Golgi tendon organs*.

Figure 5.21 Muscle Receptors

(c) Innervation of a muscle spindle

Motor fiber

Sensory fibers

Motor fiber

Sensory fiber

Intrafusal muscle fiber

Muscle fiber

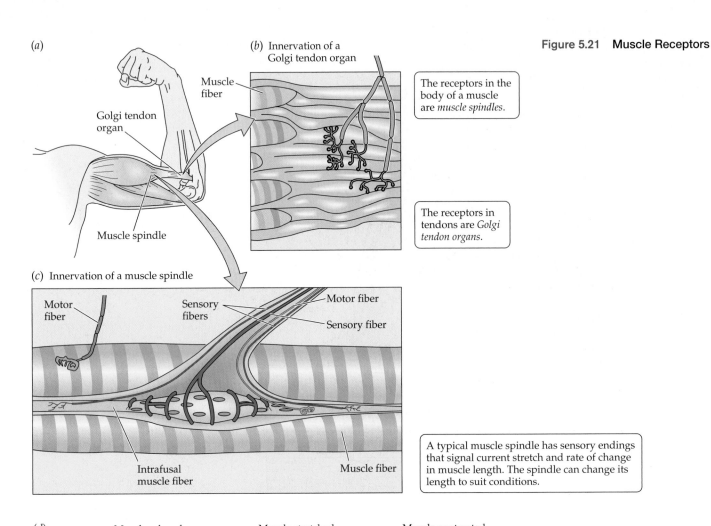

A typical muscle spindle has sensory endings that signal current stretch and rate of change in muscle length. The spindle can change its length to suit conditions.

(d)

Muscle relaxed

Muscle fibers

Muscle spindle

Intrafusal muscle fiber

Golgi tendon organ

Low level of excitation of both receptors

Muscle stretched

Both receptors excited

Muscle contracted

Tendon organ excited; spindle not excited

Spindle activity

Golgi tendon organ activity

Stretch

Shorten

Muscle length

When a load is imposed on the muscle, muscle receptors are excited as shown here.

the Golgi tendon organ that weave through the tendon (**Figure 5.21b**). It takes a pretty strong load to stretch a tendon to this degree, so it makes sense that the primary function of Golgi tendon organs is to monitor the force of muscle contractions, providing a second source of sensory information about the muscles. This arrangement makes the tendon organs useful in another important way: they detect overloads that threaten to tear muscles and tendons and can cause a reflexive relaxation of the affected muscles, protecting the muscle (and causing you to drop that book). Another familiar example of a stretch reflex is the knee jerk (or patellar) reflex that we discussed in Chapter 3 (see Figure 3.14).

Classic studies in physiology emphasized the importance of information from muscle spindles and Golgi tendon organs for controlling movement. Mott (1895) and Sherrington (1898) showed that severing the sensory fibers from a monkey's arm muscles causes the monkey to stop using the affected limb, even if the connections from motoneurons to the muscles are preserved. The arm dangles, apparently useless, but if the good arm is restrained the animal soon learns to use the affected arm, and indeed it can become quite dexterous (Taub, 1976). Monkeys manage to do this the same way Ian does, by guiding their movements with visual feedback about how the arm is moving. In fact, we all supplement our proprioceptive information with feedback from other sensory channels, like vision.

The spinal cord mediates "automatic" responses and receives inputs from the brain

To really understand the physiology of movement, we need to understand how the "final common pathway" is controlled by CNS systems. The lowest level of this hierarchy is the spinal cord, where relatively simple circuits produce reflexive behavioral responses to sensory stimuli. A straightforward example is the **stretch reflex**, illustrated in **Figure 5.22**, that can be elicited by stretching any muscle. In this case, dropping a

stretch reflex   The contraction of a muscle in response to stretch of that muscle.

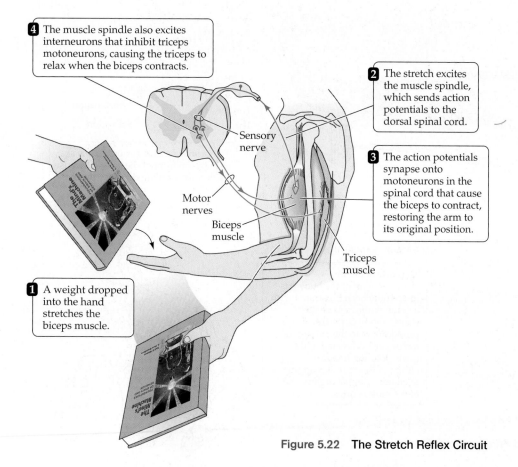

4 The muscle spindle also excites interneurons that inhibit triceps motoneurons, causing the triceps to relax when the biceps contracts.

2 The stretch excites the muscle spindle, which sends action potentials to the dorsal spinal cord.

3 The action potentials synapse onto motoneurons in the spinal cord that cause the biceps to contract, restoring the arm to its original position.

Sensory nerve

Motor nerves

Biceps muscle

Triceps muscle

1 A weight dropped into the hand stretches the biceps muscle.

To see an animation of this figure, go to

mindsmachine.com/5.4
The Stretch Reflex Circuit

Figure 5.22   The Stretch Reflex Circuit

pyramidal system or corticospinal system The motor system that includes neurons within the cerebral cortex and their axons, which form the pyramidal tract.

load into the outstretched hand causes a sudden stretch of the biceps muscle, which is detected by muscle spindles. In the spinal cord, the incoming sensory information from the spindles has two immediate effects: it stimulates motoneurons of the biceps, causing a contraction; and it simultaneously inhibits the antagonistic motoneurons that connect to the triceps muscle on the back of the arm. The reflex thus generates a compensatory movement to bring the hand and arm back to their intended position. Not all spinal circuits are quite this simple; for example, the rhythmic movements of walking are governed by spinal circuits that may involve many neurons across multiple spinal segments.

Although muscles of the head are controlled directly by the brain, via the cranial nerves (see Figure 2.7), the muscles of the rest of the body are ultimately controlled by commands from the brain, via the spinal cord. The brain sends these commands to the spinal cord through two major pathways: the pyramidal system and the extrapyramidal system. The **pyramidal** (or **corticospinal**) **system** consists of neuronal cell bodies within the cerebral cortex and their axons, which pass through the brainstem, forming the pyramidal tract to the spinal cord (**Figure 5.23a**). In a cross section of the medulla, the tract

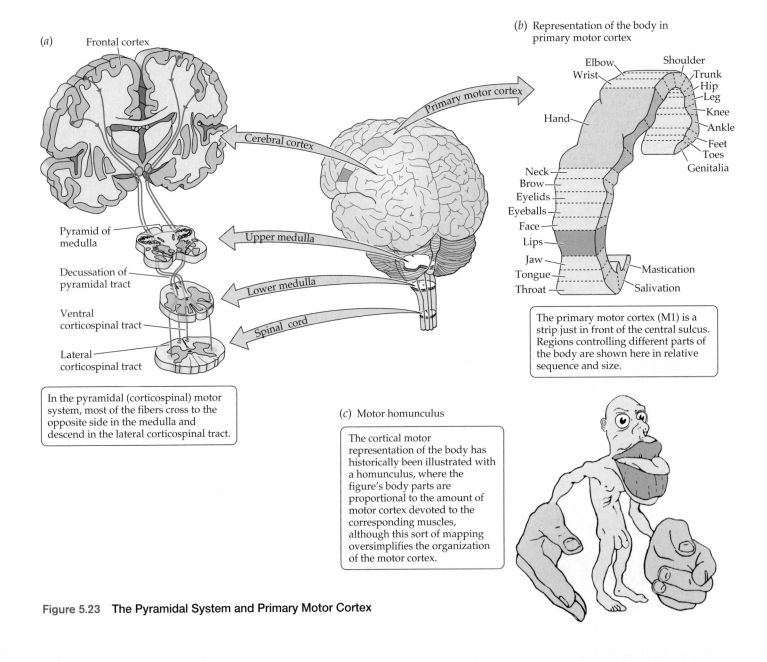

(a) Frontal cortex

Primary motor cortex

Cerebral cortex

Upper medulla

Pyramid of medulla

Decussation of pyramidal tract

Lower medulla

Ventral corticospinal tract

Lateral corticospinal tract

Spinal cord

In the pyramidal (corticospinal) motor system, most of the fibers cross to the opposite side in the medulla and descend in the lateral corticospinal tract.

(b) Representation of the body in primary motor cortex

Elbow, Shoulder, Trunk, Hip, Leg, Knee, Ankle, Feet, Toes, Genitalia

Wrist, Hand

Neck, Brow, Eyelids, Eyeballs, Face, Lips, Jaw, Tongue, Throat

Mastication, Salivation

The primary motor cortex (M1) is a strip just in front of the central sulcus. Regions controlling different parts of the body are shown here in relative sequence and size.

(c) Motor homunculus

The cortical motor representation of the body has historically been illustrated with a homunculus, where the figure's body parts are proportional to the amount of motor cortex devoted to the corresponding muscles, although this sort of mapping oversimplifies the organization of the motor cortex.

Figure 5.23 The Pyramidal System and Primary Motor Cortex

is a wedge-shaped anterior protuberance (pyramid) on each side of the midline. Because the left and right pyramidal tracts each cross over to the other side, the right cortex controls the left side of the body while the left cortex controls the right. Lesions anywhere in the pyramidal tract will cause paralysis in the muscle targets of the damaged axons. Many of the axons of the pyramidal tract originate from neurons in the primary motor cortex (M1), which consists mainly of the precentral gyrus, just anterior to the central sulcus (**Figure 5.23b**). We will return to the topic of motor cortex a little later.

Many other axon pathways run from the forebrain to the brainstem and spinal cord. Because these tracts are outside the pyramids of the medulla, they and their connections are lumped together as the **extrapyramidal system**. In general, lesions of the extrapyramidal system do not prevent the movement of individual joints and limbs, but they do interfere with spinal reflexes, usually exaggerating them, and with systems that regulate and fine-tune motor behavior. Many of these extrapyramidal projections pass to the spinal cord via specialized motor regions (the *reticular formation* and *red nucleus*) of the midbrain and brainstem; as we'll see shortly, the basal ganglia are an important point of origin for extrapyramidal projections.

Reading the Mind   Matt Nagle, who was paralyzed from the neck down, had 96 recording electrodes implanted into his motor cortex. With the aid of a computer, Matt was subsequently able to steer a computer cursor around on a display monitor, simply by imagining the movement (Hochberg et al., 2006). Although these are early days, prosthetic devices may someday become sophisticated enough to help people like Matt effortlessly put thoughts into action. (Photo © Rick Friedman.)

Spinal injuries due to vehicular accidents, violence, falls, and sports injuries are all too common, and they often cause heartbreaking disabilities. Because the spinal cord carries all of the instructions from the brain to the muscles, an injury that completely severs the cord results in immediate and permanent paralysis below the level of injury. Depending on the extent of destruction of the spinal cord below the injury site, spinal reflexes may or may not be lost as well (in fact, reflexes may become *stronger* because of the loss of descending inhibition from the brain). An estimated 250,000–400,000 individuals in the United States have spinal cord injuries, and thousands more occur each year, mostly in young people. Although much remains to be discovered, the hope of reconnecting the injured spinal cord no longer seems far-fetched, as discussed in **A Step Further 5.4**, on the website.

Motor cortex plans and executes movements—and more

The **primary motor cortex** of humans—**M1**—is a major source of axons forming the pyramidal tract. Like S1, the primary somatosensory cortex that we discussed earlier in the chapter, M1 occupies a single large cortical gyrus: the **precentral gyrus**, located immediately in front of the central sulcus (M1 is thus a part of the frontal lobe) (see Figure 5.23b). And like S1, M1 is organized as a map of the contralateral side of the body. So, electrical stimulation of a discrete region of the left M1 will cause movement in the corresponding region of the right side of the body. Once again, the map is distorted, in the sense that the parts of the body that we control most precisely—hands, lips, tongue—are overrepresented in M1. **Figure 5.23c** shows the *motor homunculus*, a figure drawn using the body proportions represented in M1. But although the M1 map helps us understand the basic organization of motor cortex, recent research indicates that the map is really an oversimplification. The mapping of individual body regions in M1 isn't nearly as clear-cut and discrete as traditional M1 maps suggest. In fact, there is a fair bit of intermingling of body regions in the map, because many body parts coordinate with one another across regions of M1 (Rathelot and Strick, 2006; Schieber and Hibbard, 1993).

extrapyramidal system   A motor system that includes the basal ganglia and some closely related brainstem structures. Axons of this system pass into the spinal cord outside the pyramids of the medulla.

primary motor cortex (M1)   The apparent executive region for the initiation of movement; primarily the precentral gyrus.

precentral gyrus   The strip of frontal cortex, just in front of the central sulcus, that is crucial for motor control.

By recording from M1 neurons in monkeys making arm movements (Georgopoulos et al., 1993), we can eavesdrop on the commands originating there (**Figure 5.24a**). Many M1 cells change their firing rates according to the direction of the movement, but for any one cell, discharge rates are highest in one particular direction (**Figure 5.24b**). Only by averaging the activity of hundreds of M1 neurons at once can we predict the direction of arm movements with reasonable accuracy. But of course, *millions*

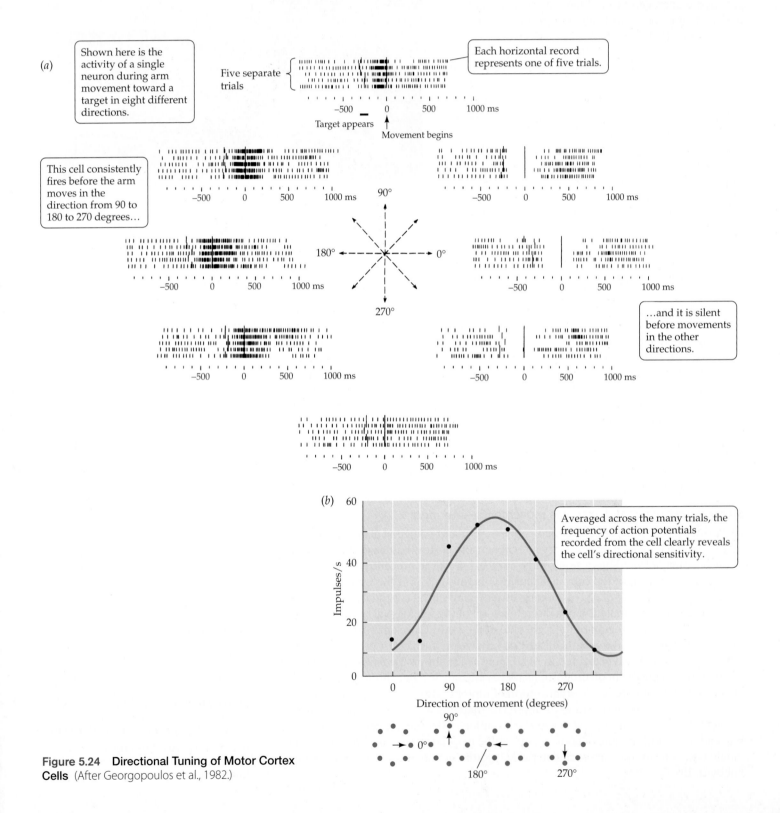

Figure 5.24 Directional Tuning of Motor Cortex Cells (After Georgopoulos et al., 1982.)

(*a*) Before training

This map illustrates forelimb control in a rat's motor cortex, prior to training (green areas: digits and wrist; blue areas: shoulder and elbow).

(*b*) After training

After 10 days of training on a task requiring precise reaching and grasping, the representation of the digits and wrist (green) has expanded into areas previously associated with the shoulder and elbow.

The black line indicates the position of a skull landmark.

Figure 5.25 Motor Learning Causes Remapping of Motor Cortex (Courtesy of J. Kleim.)

of M1 neurons are available, so in principle a larger sampling would provide a more accurate prediction.

One source of controversy is the question of whether it's *muscles* or *movements* that are primarily represented in M1. In other words, when a cortical motor neuron becomes active, is it signaling for contraction of a particular *muscle*, or does it provide a higher-level behavioral command for a particular *movement* in space? Both, it turns out. Direct recordings from cells in monkey M1 indicate that a substantial proportion of the neurons (32%) encode *muscle contractions*, but an even larger proportion (50%) showed activity that corresponded to *particular movements*. Recording enough of the activity of motor cortex to predict what movement a person is calling for might make it possible to guide a robotic arm.

Motor representations in M1 are not static; they change as a result of training. For example, M1 is wider in piano players, especially in the hand area, than in nonmusicians. The younger the musician was at the start of musical training, the larger the gyrus is in adulthood (Amunts et al., 1997), so this expansion of M1 seems to be in response to the experience of musical training. Studies using *transcranial magnetic stimulation* (*TMS*) (see Chapter 2) to noninvasively stimulate cortical neurons have shown that the movements produced by a patch of M1 may change with repeated use (Classen et al., 1998) or as a result of motor learning. In rats, this cortical plasticity associated with motor learning has been directly observed by means of sophisticated mapping of the motor cortex before and after extended training of a new skill (Monfils et al., 2005) (**Figure 5.25**).

Just anterior to M1 are cortical regions, collectively known as **nonprimary motor cortex**, that make additional crucial contributions to motor control. Nonprimary motor systems can contribute to behavior directly, through communication with lower levels of the motor hierarchy in the brainstem and spinal cord systems, as well as indirectly, through M1. The traditional account of nonprimary motor cortex emphasizes two main regions: the **supplementary motor area** (**SMA**), which lies mainly on the medial aspect of the hemisphere; and the **premotor cortex**, which is anterior to the primary motor cortex (**Figure 5.26**).

The SMA seems important for the initiation of movement sequences, especially when they're being executed according to an internal preprogrammed plan (Tanji,

nonprimary motor cortex Frontal lobe regions adjacent to the primary motor cortex that contribute to motor control and modulate the activity of the primary motor cortex.

supplementary motor area (SMA) A region of nonprimary motor cortex that receives input from the basal ganglia and modulates the activity of the primary motor cortex.

premotor cortex A region of nonprimary motor cortex just anterior to the primary motor cortex.

Figure 5.26 Human Motor Cortical Areas

(*a*) Lateral view

(*b*) Medial view

Supplementary motor area

Premotor cortex

Primary motor cortex

The SMA lies mainly on the medial surface of the cerebral hemispheres.

Primary motor cortex (M1) lies just anterior to the central sulcus. Farther forward, the premotor cortex and the supplementary motor area (SMA) together make up the nonprimary motor cortex. Shown here as one area for clarity, the premotor cortex is actually a mosaic of subareas with distinct properties.

How's it going?

1. Describe the arrangement of muscles and joints that allows movement.

2. Briefly describe the main components of a motor unit.

3. Define *proprioception*. Explain how two specialized sensors in muscle provide feedback about the muscle's current state.

4. Provide a summary of the path taken by motor fibers innervating the skeletal musculature—from the level of the brain, through the spinal cord, to the muscle targets.

5. Where is primary motor cortex located, and how is it organized?

6. Distinguish between the pyramidal and extrapyramidal systems.

7. What are some of the contributions of nonprimary motor cortex?

plegia Paralysis, the loss of the ability to move.

paresis Muscular weakness, often the result of damage to motor cortex.

apraxia An impairment in the ability to carry out complex movements, even though there is no muscle paralysis.

mirror neuron A neuron that is active both when an individual makes a particular movement and when that individual sees another individual make the same movement.

2001). In contrast, the premotor cortex seems to be activated when motor sequences are guided by *external* events (Halsband et al., 1994; Larsson et al., 1996). However, evidence is mounting that premotor cortex is not a single system, but really a mosaic of different units, controlling groups of motor behaviors that cluster together into major categories: defensive movements, feeding behavior, and so on (Graziano, 2006; Graziano and Aflalo, 2007). This organization reinforces the idea that motor and premotor areas mostly map *behaviors*, rather than mapping specific *movements*, as in M1.

Strokes or other injuries in motor areas of the cortex tend to result in paralysis (**plegia**) or weakness (**paresis**) of voluntary movements, usually on the contralateral side of the body (*hemiplegia* or *hemiparesis*). Damage to nonmotor zones of the cerebral cortex, such as some regions of parietal or frontal association cortex, produces more-complicated changes in motor control, such as **apraxia** (from the Greek *a*-, "not," and *praxis*, "action"), the inability to carry out complex movements even though paralysis or weakness is not evident and language comprehension and motivation are intact. There are several subtypes of apraxia, but in general it's as though the patient is unable to work out the sequence of movements required to perform a desired behavior—a high-level motor programming problem.

RESEARCHERS AT WORK

Mirror neurons in premotor cortex track movements in others

Recent research has discovered that a subregion of premotor cortex (called *F5*), may contain a population of remarkable neurons that seem to fulfill two functions. These neurons fire shortly before a monkey makes a very particular movement of the hand and arm to reach for an object; different neurons fire during different reaching movements. The data thus suggest that these neurons trigger specific movements. But these neurons also seem to fire whenever the monkey sees *another* monkey (or a human) make that same movement (**Figure 5.27**). These cells are called **mirror neurons**

Figure 5.27 Mirror Neurons

Question

The researchers hypothesized that neurons of the premotor cortex, in a ventral subregion called *F5*, encode specific and detailed movements rather than muscle contractions.

(a) Ventral premotor cortex

F5

Experiment

The activity of single F5 neurons was recorded while the monkey made reaching movements.

Result

The neurons fired shortly before the monkey made a specific movement, in accordance with the initial hypothesis. But to the experimenters' surprise, the neurons also became active when the monkey simply watched an experimenter perform the same movement, as if the monkey was *imagining* making the movement.

(b) Monkey picks up raisin.

Monkey watches human pick up raisin.

Neuronal activity

Monkey mirror neuron responses

Time

(c) Monkey watches human's hand movements.

The neuron is less responsive if there is no object to be picked up.

Conclusion

These "mirror neurons" may be part of a system for analyzing the behavior of others (Umilta et al., 2001).

because they fire as though the monkey were imagining doing the same thing as the other individual. Mirror neurons are also found in adult humans (Buccino et al., 2004) and children (Lepage and Theoret, 2006), both in premotor and in other cortical locations.

Because the activity of these neurons suggests that they are important in the understanding of other individuals' actions (Rizzolatti and Craighero, 2004), an intriguing notion is that mirror neurons could be part of a neural system for empathy. Thus, there has been a great deal of speculation about the function of mirror neurons in the imitating behavior of human infants, the evolution of language, and other behavior. Some have speculated that people with autism, which is characterized by a failure to anticipate other people's thinking and actions, may have a deficit in mirror neuron activity (J. H. Williams et al., 2006). Note, however, that the specific functions ascribed to mirror neurons (and indeed whether they really exist as described) remain somewhat controversial.

Extrapyramidal systems regulate and fine-tune motor commands

Earlier we noted that extrapyramidal projections—the motor fibers outside the pyramidal tracts—are especially important in modulation and ongoing control of movement. Two of the most important sources of extrapyramidal fibers are the basal ganglia and the cerebellum.

As we saw in Chapter 2, the **basal ganglia** are a group of interconnected forebrain nuclei (especially the caudate nucleus, putamen, and globus pallidus, among others), with strong inputs from the substantia nigra and the subthalamic nucleus (**Figure 5.28**). The basal ganglia receive inputs from wide expanses of the cortex via the thalamus, forming a loop from the cortex through the basal ganglia and thalamus and back to the cortex. The basal ganglia help control the amplitude and direction of movement, and changes in activity in regions of the basal ganglia appear to be important for the initiation of movement. Much of the motor function of the basal ganglia appears to be the modulation of activity started by other brain circuits, such as the motor pathways of the cortex (see Figure 5.23). The basal ganglia are especially

basal ganglia   A group of forebrain nuclei, including caudate nucleus, globus pallidus, and putamen, found deep within the cerebral hemispheres.

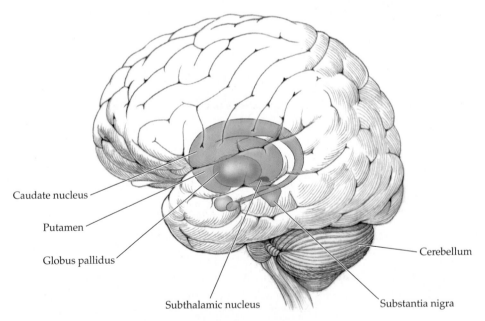

Caudate nucleus

Putamen

Globus pallidus

Subthalamic nucleus

Cerebellum

Substantia nigra

Figure 5.28   Subcortical Systems Involved in Movement

Research Champions Parkinson's disease usually afflicts people aged 65 and older, and it affects almost 1% of the U.S. population in that age category. Sometimes, however, it unaccountably occurs in younger people, such as actor Michael J. Fox, who was just 30 years old when he was diagnosed with Parkinson's, in 1991. Shown here testifying before a U.S. Senate health committee with fellow Parkinson's sufferer Muhammad Ali, Fox heads a research foundation (http://www.michaeljfox.org) that provides funding and advocacy for Parkinson's disease research.

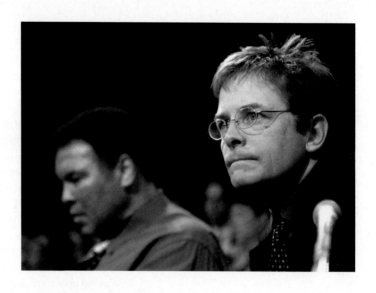

important for movements performed by memory, in contrast to those guided by sensory control (Graybiel et al., 1994).

Inputs to the **cerebellum** come both from sensory sources and from other brain motor systems. Sensory inputs include the muscle and joint receptors, and the vestibular, somatosensory, visual, and auditory systems. Both pyramidal and nonpyramidal pathways contribute inputs to the cerebellum and in turn receive outputs—all of which are inhibitory—from the deep nuclei of the cerebellum. The cerebellum appears to help establish and fine-tune neural programs for *skilled* movements, especially the kinds of rapid, repeated movements that become automatic. In fact, we now know that the cerebellum is crucial for a wide variety of motor and nonmotor learning (Katz and Steinmetz, 2002), as discussed in more detail in Chapter 13.

The basal ganglia and cerebellar systems thus make distinct but complementary contributions to regulating motor behavior. Studying people who were given two similar objects to hold and manipulate, and who were then asked to judge whether the objects were identical, researchers found that different aspects of this motor behavior differentially activated the basal ganglia and cerebellum in fMRI scans. Evidence showed that cerebellar activity correlated with activity of the SMA but not M1, whereas basal ganglia activity during the task correlated more strongly with activity of M1 than of the SMA. So, although the task required activity in all these brain regions, the contributions from the cerebellum and the basal ganglia differ both temporally and anatomically (Y. Liu et al., 1999).

Damage to extrapyramidal systems impairs movement

Different constellations of symptoms are associated with damage to the various extrapyramidal motor structures. The exact consequences of cerebellar damage depend on the part of the cerebellum that has been damaged, but common motor symptoms include characteristic abnormalities of gait and posture, especially **ataxia** (loss of coordination) of the legs. Other cerebellar lesions may cause **decomposition of movement** (in which gestures are broken up into individual segments instead of being executed smoothly) or difficulties with gaze and visual tracking of objects. The anatomy of the cerebellum and the symptomatology of cerebellar disease are discussed in more detail in **A Step Further 5.5**, on the website.

Two diseases that target the basal ganglia reveal important aspects of extrapyramidal contributions to motor control. Patients with **Parkinson's disease** show progressive degeneration of dopamine-containing cells in the **substantia nigra**. Loss of these neurons, which particularly project to the caudate nucleus and putamen, is associated with a cluster of symptoms that are all too familiar: slow movement, tremors of the hands and face while at rest, a rigid bearing, and diminished facial expressions. Patients who suffer from Parkinson's show few spontaneous actions and have great difficulty in all motor efforts, no matter how routine.

Whereas damage to the basal ganglia in Parkinson's disease *slows* movement, other kinds of basal ganglia disorders cause *excessive* movement. The first symptoms of **Huntington's disease** are subtle behavioral changes: clumsiness, and twitches in the fingers and face. Subtlety is rapidly lost as the illness progresses; a continuing stream of involuntary

cerebellum A structure located at the back of the brain, dorsal to the pons, that is involved in the central regulation of movement.

ataxia A loss of movement coordination, often caused by disease of the cerebellum.

decomposition of movement Difficulty of movement in which gestures are broken up into individual segments instead of being executed smoothly; it is a symptom of cerebellar lesions.

Parkinson's disease A degenerative neurological disorder, characterized by tremors at rest, muscular rigidity, and reduction in voluntary movement, caused by loss of the dopaminergic neurons of the substantia nigra.

substantia nigra A brainstem structure in humans that innervates the basal ganglia and is named for its dark pigmentation.

Huntington's disease A genetic disorder, with onset in middle age, in which the destruction of basal ganglia results in a syndrome of abrupt, involuntary writhing movements and changes in mental functioning.

How's it going?

1. What are mirror neurons, and what is their significance?

2. Compare and contrast the motor programming functions of the basal ganglia and the cerebellum.

3. What symptoms arise from damage to the basal ganglia and cerebellum? How do these symptoms compare to the consequences of lesions in M1?

4. How does learning influence the efficient production of movements?

jerks engulfs the entire body. Aimless movements of the eyes, jerky leg movements, and writhing of the body make even routine activity a major challenge, much exacerbated in later stages of the disease by intellectual deterioration. The neuroanatomical basis of this disorder is the progressive destruction of the basal ganglia, especially the caudate nucleus and the putamen, as well as impairment of the cerebral cortex. Several types of cells are particularly vulnerable, including neurons that contain the transmitter GABA.

The sensorimotor system is a very large and complex network that is vulnerable to a wide variety of injuries and diseases. Disease processes that target various parts of the network—ranging from viral infections of motoneurons, to autoimmune, genetic, and other pathological processes that attack the brain and spinal cord motor system—are covered in detail in **A Step Further 5.6**, on the website.

Although much remains to be discovered, there is more reason than ever to look forward to the introduction of effective treatments for motor disorders. Scientists are learning more and more about what goes wrong in Parkinson's and Huntington's diseases, and their continuing research efforts may pave the way to new therapies. Furthermore, it now seems likely that people with paralyzing spinal cord injuries will one day be able to manipulate robotic arms and legs with their minds.

Recommended Reading

Ballantyne, J. C., and Fishman, S. M. (Eds.). (2010). *Bonica's Management of Pain* (4th ed.). Philadelphia, PA: Lippincott.

Basbaum, A. I., and Bushnell, M. C. (2008). *Science of Pain.* New York, NY: Academic Press.

Cytowic, R. E., and Eagleman, D. M. (2009). *Wednesday Is Indigo Blue.* Cambridge, MA: MIT Press.

Graziano, M. (2006). "The Organization of Behavioral Repertoire in Motor Cortex." *Annual Review of Neuroscience, 29,* 105–134.

Lumpkin, E. A., and Caterina, M. J. (2007). "Mechanisms of Sensory Transduction in the Skin." *Nature, 445,* 858–865.

Melzack, R., and Wall, P. D. (2002). *The Challenge of Pain* (2nd ed.). London, England: Penguin Global.

Merchant, H., and Georgopoulos, A. P. (2006). "Neurophysiology of Perceptual and Motor Aspects of Interception." *Journal of Neurophysiology, 95,* 1–13.

Purves, D., Augustine, G. J., Fitzpatrick, D., Hall, W., et al. (Eds.). (2012). *Neuroscience* (5th ed.). Sunderland, MA: Sinauer. (See Unit III: "Movement and Its Central Control," Chapters 16–21.)

Wolfe, J. M., Kluender, J. R., Levi, D. M., Bartoshuk, L. M., et al. (2012). *Sensation & Perception* (3rd ed.). Sunderland, MA: Sinauer.

mindsmachine.com/vs5

CHAPTER 5 VISUAL SUMMARY

You should be able to relate each summary to the adjacent illustration, including structures and processes. If you need to review, go to the figures indicated and read the accompanying text.

1 **Receptor cells** in sensory organs furnish only selected information to the brain. For example, our skin contains four kinds of touch receptors, each specialized for detecting a specific **stimulus**. Species tend to sense only those environmental stimuli that are biologically important to them. Review **Figures 5.2 and 5.4, Animation 5.2, Activity 5.1**

2 **Sensory transduction** is the conversion of an environmental stimulus into a **generator potential** in sensory receptors, leading to the activation of sensory neurons. The **receptive field** of a neuron is the region in space where a stimulus will change the firing of that cell. The receptive fields of neurons may be very different at successive levels of the sensory pathway. Review **Figures 5.5** and **5.6, Animation 5.3**

3 The succession of levels in a sensory pathway allows for increasingly elaborate kinds of processing. Touch information from the skin courses through a distinct spinal pathway, the **dorsal column system**. Review **Figure 5.8**

4 At the level of the cerebral cortex are multiple maps of the body surface. **Primary somatosensory cortex**, or **S1**, located in the postcentral gyrus, contains a map of the contralateral body, which overrepresents highly sensitive body regions. Review **Figures 5.9** and **5.10**

5 **Free nerve endings** detect mechanical damage or temperature changes because they have specialized receptor proteins (**nociceptors**) that detect these conditions. **Pain**, temperature, and itch information enters the spinal cord, crosses the midline, and ascends through the **anterolateral (spinothalamic) system** to the brain. Review **Figures 5.12** and **5.13**, **Activity 5.2**

6 Pain sensation, detected by nociceptors, is subject to many modulating influences, including regions of the brain and spinal cord that employ opioids. Opioid systems are also active in the **placebo effect**, and in other techniques, like **acupuncture**. Review **Figure 5.15**

7 There are two broad categories of motor activity: **movements** and **acts**. In **closed-loop motor control**, movements may be corrected while being produced, on the basis of feedback from sensory systems. Some behaviors are so rapid, however, that they are governed by **open-loop motor control**; that is, the pattern is preset and not modified by feedback once it has started. Review **Figure 5.17**

8 Motor control systems are organized into a hierarchy that consists of the skeletal system and associated muscles, the spinal cord, the brainstem, and various parts of the brain, including the **primary (M1)** and **nonprimary motor cortices**, the **cerebellum**, and the **basal ganglia**. Review **Figure 5.18**

9 Muscles around a joint work in pairs. **Antagonists** work in opposition; **synergists** work together. Action potentials travel over motor nerve fibers (axons from **motoneurons**) and reach muscle fibers at the **neuromuscular junction**, releasing **acetylcholine (Ach)** to trigger muscle contraction. Review **Figures 5.19** and **5.20**

10 **Muscle spindles** and **Golgi tendon organs**—sensory receptors in the muscles and tendons, respectively-transmit crucial information about muscle activities to the central nervous system. The sensitivity of the muscle spindle can be adjusted by efferent impulses that control the length of the spindle. Review **Figures 5.21** and **5.22**, **Animation 5.4**

11 The fibers of the **pyramidal (corticospinal) system** originate mainly in the primary motor cortex (M1) and adjacent regions, and run directly to spinal motoneurons or to interneurons in the spinal cord. Disproportionate amounts of M1, in the **precentral gyrus**, are devoted to finely controlled muscles. Review **Figures 5.23** and **5.26**

12 The **extrapyramidal system**, consisting of brain regions that modulate movement, includes the basal ganglia (caudate nucleus, putamen, and globus pallidus), some major brainstem nuclei (**substantia nigra**, thalamic nuclei, reticular formation, and red nucleus), and the cerebellum. Review **Figure 5.28**, **Activity 5.3**

6

Hearing, Balance, Taste, and Smell

Hold the Phone

I t's a classic horror movie scene: a scientist using amazing technology in an attempt to reanimate parts of dead bodies, seeking out nature's secrets. But when the young Hungarian engineer Georg von Békésy embarked on his experiments on cadavers in 1928, he was not trying to create life. He was seeking an answer to a practical question: How can the human ear pick up sounds so much better than most microphones? Békésy thought that learning how the human ear detects sounds might allow him to make a better microphone for his employer, the Hungarian phone company. He gathered cadavers from local hospitals and came up with a clever dissection that would reveal the inner ear without destroying it. (His work was not always appreciated by his fellow engineers; they didn't like finding their drill press full of human bone dust in the morning.)

Bringing his background in physics to bear on the question, Békésy devised exquisitely precise physical models and biophysical experiments that let him measure extremely brief, minuscule movements in the inner ear. His subsequent discoveries provided us with the key to understanding how we translate a stream of auditory data—sounds—into meaningful neural activity that the brain can understand.

In the end, Békésy did not come up with a better microphone, but his discoveries have helped restore hearing to thousands of people who once were deaf, as we'll see in this chapter.

To see a video, go to

mindsmachine.com/6.1
Inside the Ear

Your existence is directly attributable to the keen senses possessed by your distant ancestors—senses that enabled them to find food and mates, and to avoid predators and other dangers. In this chapter we consider some of the incredible sensors that let us monitor important signals from distant sources, especially sounds (audition) and smells (olfaction). We also discuss related systems for detecting position and movement of the body (the vestibular system, related to the auditory system) and tastes of foods (the gustatory or taste sense, which, like olfaction, is a chemical sense). We begin with hearing because audition evolved from special mechanical receptors related to the touch system that we discussed in Chapter 5.

To see the brain in 3D, go to

mindsmachine.com/6.2
Brain Explorer

decibel (dB)   A measure of sound intensity, perceived as loudness.

hertz (Hz)   Cycles per second, as of an auditory stimulus. Hertz is a measure of frequency.

PART I Hearing and Balance

Hearing is vital for the survival of many animals. Humans can produce an impressive variety of vocalizations—from barely audible murmurs to soaring flights of song—but we especially rely on speech sounds to provide a basis for our social relations and for the transmission of knowledge between individuals. The sounds produced and perceived by other animals—from insects to whales—also have a wide range of complexity, in keeping with their adaptive significance for each species. Birds sing and crickets chirp in order to attract mates; monkeys grunt and screech and burble to signal comfort, danger, and pleasure; owls and bats exploit the directional property of sound to locate prey and avoid obstacles in the dark; and whales produce sounds that can travel hundreds of miles in the ocean. In every case, we find that species have unique auditory capabilities that helped their ancestors solve important problems of survival.

Your auditory system detects changes in the vibration of air molecules that are caused by sound sources, detecting both the *intensity* of sounds (measured in **decibels** [**dB**] and perceived as loudness) and their *frequency* (measured in cycles per second, or **hertz** [**Hz**], and perceived as pitch). Your ear is so good at detecting sounds in the range of normal speech that, if it were any more sensitive, you would be distracted by the noise of air molecules bouncing against each other in your ear canal! **Box 6.1** describes some basic properties of sound.

BOX 6.1 The Basics of Sound

We perceive a repetitive pattern of local increases and decreases in air pressure as sound. Usually this oscillation is caused by a vibrating object, such as a loudspeaker or a person's larynx during speaking. A single alternation of compression and expansion of air is called one *cycle*.

The figure illustrates the changes in pressure produced by a vibrating loudspeaker. Because the sound produced by a loudspeaker has only one frequency of vibration, it is called a **pure tone** and can be represented by a sine wave. A pure tone is described physically in terms of two measures:

1. **Amplitude**, or intensity—usually measured as sound pressure, or force per unit area, in dynes per square centimeter (dyn/cm²). Our perception of amplitude is termed *loudness*, expressed as decibels (dB). The decibel scale is logarithmic: one dB is the threshold for human hearing; a whisper is about 20 dB, and a departing jetliner a couple of hundred feet overhead—a sound that is almost a million times more intense—is about 120 dB.

2. **Frequency**, or the number of cycles per second, measured in hertz (Hz). For example, middle A on a piano has a frequency of 440 Hz. Our perception of frequency is termed *pitch*.

Most sounds are more complicated than a pure tone. For example, a sound made by a musical instrument contains a fundamental frequency and harmonics. The **fundamental** is the basic frequency, and the **harmonics** are multiples of the fundamental. For example, if the fundamental is 440 Hz, the harmonics are 880, 1,320, 1,760, and so on. When different instruments play the same note, the notes differ in the relative intensities of the various harmonics; this difference is what gives each instrument its characteristic sound quality, or **timbre**.

Amplitude and frequency of sound waves

Vibrating body (loudspeaker)

Compression and expansion of air molecules produced by the loudspeaker's vibration

Amplitude: Sine wave representation of the pressure waves above

Wavelength, one cycle

Greater amplitude of movement

Amplitude doubled; frequency same as above

Greater frequency of movement

Amplitude same as original; frequency doubled

Wavelength, one cycle

Each Part of the Ear Performs a Specific Function in Hearing

How do small vibrations in air become the speech, music, and other sounds we hear? The outer ears have been shaped through evolution to capture biologically important sound vibrations and direct them into the inner parts of the ear, where the mechanical force of sound is **transduced** into neural activity.

The external ear captures, focuses, and filters sound

The oddly shaped fleshy objects that most people call "ears" are properly known as **pinnae** (singular *pinna*). Aside from their occasional utility as handles and jewelry hangers, the pinnae funnel sound waves into the second part of the external ear: the **ear canal** (or *auditory canal*). The pinna is a distinctly mammalian characteristic, and mammals show a wide array of ear shapes and sizes. Furthermore, although some humans can move their ears only enough to entertain children, many other mammals deftly shape and swivel their pinnae to help determine the source of a sound. Animals with exceptional auditory localization abilities, such as bats, may have especially mobile ears.

The "hills and valleys" of the pinna modify the character of sound that reaches the middle ear. Some frequencies of sound are enhanced; others are suppressed. For example, the shape of the human ear especially increases the reception of sounds between 2,000 and 5,000 Hz—a frequency range that is important for speech perception. The shape of the external ear is also important in identifying

A Touching Friendship   Helen Keller, who was both blind and deaf, said, "Blindness deprives you of contact with things; deafness deprives you of contact with people"—a poignant reminder of the importance of speech for our social lives. Here, Keller communicates with her young friend by feeling the boy's face as he speaks and makes facial expressions. Rather than living in sensory and social isolation, Keller honed her intact senses to such a degree that she was able to become a noted teacher and writer.

transduction   The conversion of one form of energy to another.

pinna   The external part of the ear.

ear canal   Also called *auditory canal*. The tube leading from the pinna to the tympanic membrane.

The Ears Have It   The external ears, or pinnae, of mammals come in a variety of shapes, each adapted to a particular niche. Many mammals can move their ears to direct them toward a particular sound. In such cases, the brain must account for the position of the ear to judge where a particular sound came from.

inner ear The cochlea and vestibular apparatus.

middle ear The cavity between the tympanic membrane and the cochlea.

tympanic membrane Also called *eardrum*. The partition between the external ear and the middle ear.

ossicles Three small bones (incus, malleus, and stapes) that transmit vibration across the middle ear, from the tympanic membrane to the oval window.

the direction and distance of the source of a sound, as we will discuss later in this chapter.

The middle ear concentrates sound energies

A collection of tiny structures made of membrane, muscle, and bone—essentially a tiny biological microphone—links the ear canal to the neural receptor cells of the **inner ear** (**Figure 6.1a**). This **middle ear** (**Figure 6.1b**) consists of the taut **tympanic membrane** (*eardrum*) sealing the end of the ear canal, and a chain of tiny bones, called **ossicles**, that mechanically couple the tympanic membrane to the inner ear at a specialized patch of membrane called

Figure 6.1 External and Internal Structures of the Human Ear

To see an animation of this figure, go to

mindsmachine.com/6.3
Sound Transduction

(*a*) Orientation

External ear (pinna)

Inner ear

Middle ear

Tympanic membrane (eardrum)

Vestibulocochlear nerve (VIII)

Ear canal

Ossicles

Cochlea

Round window

Eustachian tube

Oval window

(*c*) Cochlea

Scala media (middle canal)

Scala vestibuli (vestibular canal)

Scala tympani (tympanic canal)

Vestibulo-cochlear nerve (VIII)

(*b*) The middle ear

Tensor tympani muscle

Nerve to tensor tympani

Ossicles:
Malleus
Incus
Stapes

Tympanic membrane (eardrum)

Oval window

Branch to stapedius muscle

Stapedius muscle

Round window

(*d*) Organ of Corti

Scala media

Tectorial membrane

Basilar membrane

Outer hair cells

Nerve fibers

Inner hair cell

Scala vestibuli

Scala tympani

(*e*) Inner hair cell

Hairs (stereocilia)

Inner hair cell

Afferent nerve ending

Efferent nerve ending

the **oval window**. These ossicles, the smallest bones in the body, are called the **malleus** (Latin for "hammer"), the **incus** (Latin for "anvil"), and the **stapes** (Latin for "stirrup").

Sound waves in the air strike the tympanic membrane and cause it to vibrate with the same frequency as the sound; as a result, the ossicles start moving too. Because of how they are attached to the eardrum, the ossicles concentrate and amplify the vibrations, focusing the pressures collected from the relatively large tympanic membrane onto the small oval window. This amplification is crucial for converting vibrations in air into movements of fluid in the inner ear, as we'll see shortly.

To help protect against the damaging forces of extremely loud noises, the middle ear is equipped with the equivalent of a built-in volume control. Two tiny muscles—one called the *tensor tympani* and the other the *stapedius*, because of their proximity to the tympanic membrane and the stapes, respectively (see Figure 6.1b)—attach to each end of the chain of ossicles. Within 200 milliseconds of the arrival of a loud sound, the brain signals the muscles to contract, which stiffens the chain of ossicles and reduces the effectiveness of the sounds. Interestingly, the middle-ear muscles activate just *before* we produce self-made sounds like speech or coughing, which is why we don't perceive our own sounds as distractingly loud.

RESEARCHERS AT WORK

The cochlea converts vibrational energy into neural activity

The part of the inner ear that ultimately converts vibrations from sound into neural activity—the coiled, fluid-filled **cochlea** (from the Greek *kochlos*, "snail")—is a marvel of miniaturization (**Figures 6.1c, d**). In an adult, the cochlea measures only about 4 millimeters in diameter—about the size of a pea. Fully unrolled, the cochlea would be about 35–40 millimeters long.

The cochlea is a coil of three parallel canals: (1) the **vestibular canal** (also called the *scala vestibuli*), (2) the **middle canal** (*scala media*), and (3) the **tympanic canal** (*scala tympani*). The oval window is adjacent to the *base* of the spiral; the distant end, like the tip of a snail's shell, is referred to as the *apex*. Because the canals are filled with noncompressible fluid, movement inside the cochlea in response to a push from the stapes onto the oval window requires a second membrane-covered window that can bulge outward a bit. That second membrane is the **round window**, which separates the tympanic canal from the middle ear (see Figure 6.1b).

The portion of the cochlea that converts sounds into neural activity is known as the **organ of Corti** (see Figure 6.1d). It consists of three main structures: (1) the sensory cells (**hair cells**) (**Figure 6.1e**), (2) an elaborate framework of supporting cells, and (3) the terminations of the auditory nerve fibers. The base of the organ of Corti is the **basilar membrane**. When the stapes moves in and out as a result of sound waves hitting the eardrum, it sets in motion waves or ripples in the fluid of the vestibular canal, which in turn cause the basilar membrane to ripple, like shaking out a rug. The basilar membrane is tapered—it's about 5 times wider at the apex of the cochlea than at the base. (It may seem counterintuitive for the basilar membrane to be narrowest at the *base* of the cochlea, where the canals are *widest*, but that's how it is; see Figure 6.1d). The different parts of the basilar membrane, as it grows from narrow at the base of the cochlea to wide at the apex, show their strongest responses to different frequencies of sound (**Figure 6.2**). High frequencies have their greatest effect near the base, where the membrane is narrow; low-frequency sounds produce a larger response near the apex, where the membrane is wider (Ashmore, 1994). The discovery of the mechanics of the basilar membrane garnered a Nobel Prize for Georg von Békésy.

oval window The opening from the middle ear to the inner ear.

malleus Latin for "hammer." A middle-ear bone that is connected to the tympanic membrane.

incus Latin for "anvil." A middle-ear bone situated between the malleus and the stapes.

stapes Latin for "stirrup." A middle-ear bone that is connected to the oval window.

cochlea A snail-shaped structure in the inner ear that contains the primary receptor cells for hearing.

vestibular canal Also called *scala vestibuli*. One of three principal canals running along the length of the cochlea.

middle canal Also called *scala media*. The central of the three spiraling canals inside the cochlea, situated between the vestibular canal and the tympanic canal.

tympanic canal Also called *scala tympani*. One of three principal canals running along the length of the cochlea.

round window A membrane separating the tympanic canal from the middle ear.

organ of Corti A structure in the inner ear that lies on the basilar membrane of the cochlea and contains the hair cells and terminations of the auditory nerve.

hair cell One of the receptor cells for hearing in the cochlea.

basilar membrane A membrane in the cochlea that contains the principal structures involved in auditory transduction.

Figure 6.2   Georg von Békésy and the Cochlear Wave

Question

How does the cochlea determine the frequency of sounds?

Hypothesis

Sound waves cause the basilar membrane to ripple.

Experimental Setup

(1) Partially dissect a human cochlea, replacing cochlear fluid with a gel containing particles of coal and aluminum.

(2) Bounce intense flash of light off the basilar membrane during vibration at the oval window. Record the displacement of aluminum particles to measure how much the basilar membrane has deformed.

"Unrolling" of cochlea

High frequencies displace basilar membrane in base of cochlea.

Low frequencies displace basilar membrane in apex of cochlea.

A flash of intense light is bounced off the basilar membrane…

Cochlear base

Cochlear apex

100 Hz

…and recorded by a camera to measure membrane displacement at different frequencies.

Direction of sound movement

"Unrolled" cochlea

Basilar membrane

Relative amplitude of movement (μm)

3

0

1600 Hz

3

0

100 Hz

3

0

50 Hz

0   10   20   30

Distance from stapes (mm)

Results

"Standing waves" are observed on the basilar membrane, their position corresponding to frequency of the vibration.

Conclusion

The frequency of a sound is encoded by the specific location on the basilar membrane that shows the largest vibration in response to the sound. High frequencies displace the basilar membrane at the base of the cochlea; low frequencies cause displacement at the apex. This differential response depending on location along the membrane has become known as *place coding*.

The hair cells transduce movements of the basilar membrane into electrical signals

It is the rippling of the basilar membrane that is converted into neural activity, through the actions of hair cells. Each hair cell features a sloping brush of minuscule hairs (hence the name) called **stereocilia** (singular *stereocilium*) on its upper surface. In Figure 6.1d you'll notice that, although the bases of hair cells are implanted in the basilar membrane, their stereocilia penetrate the tectorial membrane that lies above. The hair cells—and especially the hairs themselves—thus form a mechanical bridge between the two membranes.

How do hair cells turn movement into neural activity? When sounds induce the basilar membrane to ripple, the movement of the hair cell bases relative to the tectorial

stereocilium   A relatively stiff hair that protrudes from a hair cell in the auditory or vestibular system.

Figure 6.3 **How Auditory Stimulation Affects the Stereocilia on Cochlear Hair Cells**
(After Beurg et al., 2009; micrograph courtesy of A. J. Hudspeth.)

Tip links connect to large, nonselective ion channels on adjacent stereocilia.

Bending of the stereocilia tightens tip links and opens the channels, allowing K$^+$ and Ca^{2+} to enter the stereocilia. The resulting depolarization opens Ca^{2+} channels in the cell's base, causing the release of neurotransmitter that excites nearby nerves, resulting in the transmission of action potentials to the brain.

This micrograph of stereocilia shows the threadlike tip links.

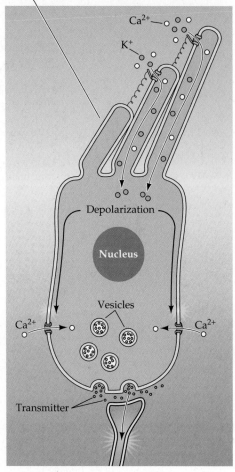

membrane causes the stereocilia to bend. Even a tiny deflection of stereocilia is enough to produce a large depolarization of hair cells, because of a remarkable structural feature of stereocilia. Each stereocilium contains one or two large, nonselective ion channels—imagine trap doors in the membrane. Fine, threadlike fibers called *tip links* connect the channels to the tips of neighboring stereocilia (**Figure 6.3**). As the stereocilia bend, even only very slightly, the tension on the tip links physically pops open the ion channels to which they are attached (Hudspeth, 1997; Hudspeth et al., 2000). The sudden opening of the channels allows potassium (K$^+$) and calcium (Ca^{2+}) ions to rush into the hair cell, causing a rapid depolarization. Just as it works in neurons (see Chapter 3), this depolarization leads to a rapid influx of Ca^{2+} at the base of the hair cell, which in turn causes synaptic vesicles there to fuse with the presynaptic membrane and release neurotransmitter, stimulating adjacent nerve fibers. The stereocilia channels snap shut again in a fraction of a millisecond as the hair cell sways back. This ability to rapidly switch on and off allows hair cells to accurately track the rapid oscillations of the basilar membrane with exquisite sensitivity.

In the human cochlea, the hair cells are organized into a single row of about 3,500 **inner hair cells** (**IHCs**; called *inner* because they are closer to the central axis of the coiled cochlea) and about 12,000 **outer hair cells** (**OHCs**) in three rows (see Figure 6.1d). Fibers of the **vestibulocochlear nerve** (cranial nerve VIII) contact the base of the hair cells (see Figures 6.1e and 6.3). Some of these fibers do indeed convey sound information to the brain, but the neural connections of the cochlea are a little more complicated than just

inner hair cell (IHC) One of the two types of receptor cells for hearing in the cochlea. Compared to outer hair cells, IHCs are positioned closer to the central axis of the coiled cochlea.

outer hair cell (OHC) One of the two types of receptor cells for hearing in the cochlea. Compared to inner hair cells, OHCs are positioned farther from the central axis of the coiled cochlea.

vestibulocochlear nerve Cranial nerve VIII, which runs from the cochlea to the brainstem auditory nuclei.

Figure 6.4 **Auditory Nerve Fibers and Synapses in the Organ of Corti**

(a)

The inner and outer hair cells form synaptic connections to and from the brain.

Inner hair cell

Tectorial membrane

Outer hair cells

1. IHC afferent, to brain

2. IHC efferent, from brain

3. OHC afferent, to brain

4. OHC efferent, from brain

(b)

Inner hair cell

Glutamate

ACh

Outer hair cell

ACh

GABA

Different synaptic transmitters are hypothesized to be active at the synapses of inner and outer hair cells in the organ of Corti.

tuning curve A graph of the responses of a single auditory nerve fiber or neuron to sounds that vary in frequency and intensity.

Figure 6.5 **Tuning Curves of Auditory Nerve Cells** (After Kiang, 1965.)

Responses of six different neurons to sounds of different intensities and frequencies. Because this is a threshold measure, the lowest points—indicated by arrows on the *x*-axis—correspond to the neurons' preferred frequencies.

Sound intensity (threshold in dB)

Frequency of tone stimuli (kHz)

that. In fact, there are four kinds of neural connections with hair cells, each relying on a different neurotransmitter (Eybalin, 1993), as you can see in **Figure 6.4**.

The fibers are distinguished as follows:

1. *IHC afferents* convey to the brain the action potentials that provide the perception of sounds. IHC afferents make up about 95% of the fibers leading to the brain.

2. *IHC efferents* lead from the brain to the IHCs—through which the brain can control the responsiveness of IHCs.

3. *OHC afferents* are thought to convey information to the brain about the mechanical state of the basilar membrane, but *not* the perception of sounds themselves.

4. *OHC efferents* lead from the brain to the OHCs, allowing the brain to activate a remarkable property of OHCs. The OHCs don't detect sound. Instead, OHCs appear to change their length in response to commands from the brain (Zheng et al., 2000). The mechanical responses of the OHCs allow them to control of the stiffness of regions of the basilar membrane to sharpen its tuning (Ashmore, 1994; Hubbard, 1993).

If we record from IHC afferents sending auditory information to the brain, we find that each one has a maximum sensitivity to sound of a particular frequency, but will also respond to neighboring frequencies if the sound is loud enough. For example, the auditory neuron whose responses are shown in red in **Figure 6.5** has its *best frequency* at 1,200 Hz (1.2 kHz)—that is, it is sensitive to even a very weak tone at 1,200 Hz—but for sounds that are 20 dB louder, the cell will respond to frequencies from 500 to 1,800 Hz. We call this the cell's **tuning curve**. If the brain received a signal from only one such fiber, it would not be able to tell whether the stimulus was a weak tone of 1,200 Hz or a stronger tone of 500 or 1,800 Hz, or any frequency in between. Instead, the brain analyzes the activity from thousands of such units simultaneously to calculate the intensity and frequency of each sound.

Auditory System Pathways Run from the Brainstem to the Cortex

Most of the auditory part of the vestibulocochlear nerve is made up of nerve fibers carrying information from the IHCs to the brainstem. Here the auditory fibers terminate in the (sensibly named) **cochlear nuclei**, where some initial processing occurs. Output from the cochlear nuclei projects to the **superior olivary nuclei**, each of which receives inputs from both right and left cochlear nuclei. This bilateral input makes the superior olivary nucleus the first brain site at which *binaural* (two-ear) processing occurs. As you might expect, this mechanism plays a key role in localizing sounds by comparing the two ears, as we'll discuss shortly. The auditory projections within the brain are depicted in **Figure 6.6**.

The superior olivary nuclei pass information derived from both ears to the **inferior colliculi**, which are the primary auditory centers of the midbrain. Outputs of the inferior colliculi go to the **medial geniculate nuclei** of the thalamus. At least two different pathways from the medial geniculate extend to several auditory cortical areas.

At every level of the auditory system, from cochlea to auditory cortex, auditory pathways display **tonotopic organization**; that is, they are spatially arranged like a map from low frequency (sounds that we perceive as *bass*) to high frequency (perceived as *treble*). Furthermore, at the higher levels of the auditory system, auditory neurons are not only excited by certain frequencies, but also *inhibited* by neighboring frequencies, resulting in

cochlear nucleus Either of two brainstem nuclei—left and right—that receive input from auditory hair cells and send output to the superior olivary nuclei.

superior olivary nucleus Either of two brainstem nuclei—left and right—that receive input from both right and left cochlear nuclei, and provide the first binaural analysis of auditory information.

inferior colliculi Paired gray matter structures of the dorsal midbrain that process auditory information.

medial geniculate nucleus Either of two nuclei—left and right—in the thalamus that receive input from the inferior colliculi and send output to the auditory cortex.

tonotopic organization A major organizational feature in auditory systems, in which neurons are arranged as an orderly map of stimulus frequency, with cells responsive to high frequencies located at a distance from those responsive to low frequencies.

To see an animation of this figure, go to

mindsmachine.com/6.4
Mapping Auditory Frequencies

Auditory cortex

Medial geniculate nucleus

Inferior colliculus

Cochlear nucleus Superior olivary nucleus Pons Cochlea

Brainstem

Binaural (two-ear) interactions commence in the brainstem superior olivary nucleus. Most (but not all) of the information from each ear projects to the cortex on the opposite side of the brain.

Figure 6.6 Auditory Pathways of the Human Brain

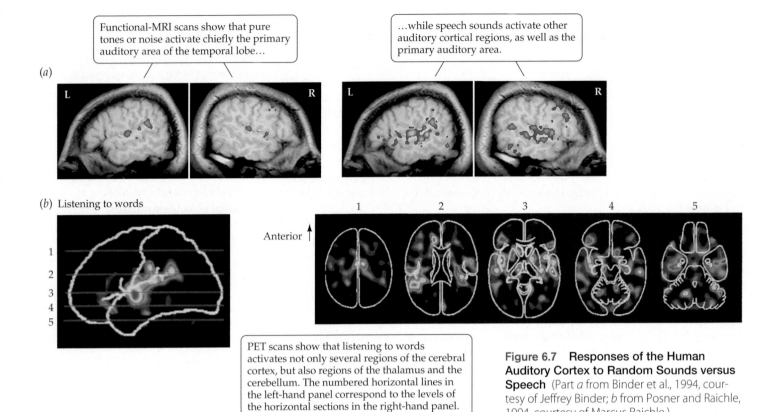

Functional-MRI scans show that pure tones or noise activate chiefly the primary auditory area of the temporal lobe...

...while speech sounds activate other auditory cortical regions, as well as the primary auditory area.

(a)

L   R   L   R

(b) Listening to words

Anterior ↑

PET scans show that listening to words activates not only several regions of the cerebral cortex, but also regions of the thalamus and the cerebellum. The numbered horizontal lines in the left-hand panel correspond to the levels of the horizontal sections in the right-hand panel.

Figure 6.7   Responses of the Human Auditory Cortex to Random Sounds versus Speech (Part *a* from Binder et al., 1994, courtesy of Jeffrey Binder; *b* from Posner and Raichle, 1994, courtesy of Marcus Raichle.)

How's it going?

1. Identify the major components of the external ear. What does the external ear do?

2. Identify the three ossicles, and explain their function. To what structures do the ossicles connect, and how is their action moderated?

3. Provide a brief description of the organ of Corti, naming the components that are most important for the perception of sound.

4. Explain how the movement of hair cells transduces movement into action potentials. Compare and contrast the functions of inner hair cells and outer hair cells.

5. Sketch the major anatomical components of the auditory projections in the brain. Where does binaural processing first occur? What is tonotopic organization? What kind of processing does auditory cortex perform?

much sharper tuning of the frequency responses of these cells. This precision helps us discriminate tiny differences in the frequencies of sounds.

Brain-imaging studies in humans have confirmed that many sounds (tones, noises, and so on) activate the primary auditory cortex, which is located on the upper surface of the temporal lobes (**Figure 6.7a**). Speech sounds produce similar activation, but also activate other, more specialized auditory areas (**Figure 6.7b**). Interestingly, at least some of these regions are activated when normal subjects try to lip-read—that is, to understand someone by watching that person's lips without auditory cues (L. E. Bernstein et al., 2002; Calvert et al., 1997). This result suggests that the auditory cortex integrates other, nonauditory, information with sounds. (The organization of auditory cortical areas in other species is described in **A Step Further 6.1**, on the website.)

Our Sense of Pitch Relies on Two Signals from the Cochlea

At least when we're young, most of us can hear sounds ranging from 20 Hz to about 20,000 Hz, and within this range we can distinguish between sounds that differ by just a few hertz. Differences in frequency are important for our sense of pitch, but *pitch* and *frequency* are not synonymous. *Frequency* describes a *physical* property of sounds (see Box 6.1), but *pitch* relates solely to our subjective *perception* of those sounds. This is an important distinction because frequency is not the sole determinant of perceived pitch; at some frequencies, higher-intensity sounds may seem higher-pitched, and changes in pitch do not precisely parallel changes in frequency.

How do we distinguish pitches? Two signals from the cochlea appear to inform the brain about the pitch of sounds:

1. In **place coding**, the pitch of a sound is determined by the location of activated hair cells along the length of the basilar membrane, as we discussed in this

chapter's "Researchers at Work" feature. So, activation of receptors near the base of the cochlea (which is narrow and responds to high frequencies) signals *treble*, and activation of receptors nearer the apex (which is wide and responds to low frequencies) signals *bass*.

2. A complementary process, known as **temporal coding**, encodes the frequency of auditory stimuli in the rate of firing of auditory neurons. For example, a 500-Hz sound might cause some auditory neurons to fire 500 action potentials per second. *Volleys* of action potentials being produced at this rate, by a number of neurons with similar tunings, provide the auditory cortex with a reliable additional source of pitch information.

Experimental evidence indicates that we rely on both of these processes to discriminate the pitch of sounds. Temporal coding is especially emphasized at the lower end of the hearing range, up to about 4,000 Hz—auditory neurons can fire a maximum of only about 1,000 action potentials per second, but to a limited extent they can encode sound frequencies that are multiples of the action potential frequency. Beyond about 4,000 Hz, however, this encoding becomes impossible, and pitch discrimination relies on place coding of pitch along the basilar membrane.

Some species are sensitive to sounds with very high frequencies (**ultrasound**) or very low frequencies (**infrasound**), and make use of them in special ways. For example, many species of bats produce loud vocalizations in the range of 50,000–100,000 Hz, and they listen to the echoes reflected back from objects in order to navigate and hunt in the dark. At the other end of the spectrum, homing-pigeon races are severely disrupted if the birds encounter the sonic-boom shock wave of a supersonic jet (an infrasound pulse that can travel hundreds of miles), suggesting that the pigeons use infrasound cues to establish where they are relative to home (Hagstrum, 2000).

Listen Up! Because the brain has had no experience with the shapes of the horns and the distances between them, we would expect these contraptions to produce confusion with regard to sound localization—not to mention being pretty darn loud!

Brainstem Systems Compare the Ears to Localize Sounds

Being able to quickly identify where a sound is coming from—whether it is the crack of a twig under a predator's foot, or the sweet tones of a would-be mate—is a matter of great evolutionary significance. So it's no surprise that we are remarkably good at locating a sound source (our accuracy is about ±1 degree horizontally around the head, and many animals are even better). The auditory system accomplishes this feat by analyzing two kinds of binaural cues that signal the location of a sound source.

1. **Intensity differences** are differences in *loudness* at the two ears. Depending on the species—and the placement and characteristics of their pinnae—intensity differences occur because one ear is pointed more directly toward the sound source, or because the head casts a *sound shadow* (**Figure 6.8a**), blocking sounds originating on one side (called *off-axis sounds*) from reaching both ears with equal loudness. The head shadow effect is most pronounced for higher-frequency sounds (**Figure 6.8b**).

2. **Latency differences** are differences between the two ears in the *time of arrival* of sounds. They arise because one ear is always a little closer to an off-axis sound than the other ear is. Two kinds of latency differences are present in a sound: *onset disparity*, which is the difference between the two ears in hearing the beginning of the sound; and *ongoing phase disparity*, which is the continual mismatch between the two ears in the arrival of all the peaks and troughs that make up the sound wave. These cues are illustrated in **Figure 6.8c**.

Both types of cues are employed in sound localization. At low frequencies, no matter where sounds are presented horizontally around the head, there are virtually no intensity differences between the ears. For these frequencies, differences in times of arrival

place coding Frequency discrimination in which the pitch of a sound is determined by the location of activated hair cells along the length of the basilar membrane.

temporal coding Frequency discrimination in which the pitch of a sound is determined by the rate of firing of auditory neurons.

ultrasound High-frequency sound; in general, above the threshold for human hearing, at about 20,000 Hz.

infrasound Very low frequency sound; in general, below the threshold for human hearing, at about 20 Hz.

intensity difference A perceived difference in loudness between the two ears, which the nervous system can use to localize a sound source.

latency difference A difference between the two ears in the time of arrival of a sound, which the nervous system can use to localize a sound source.

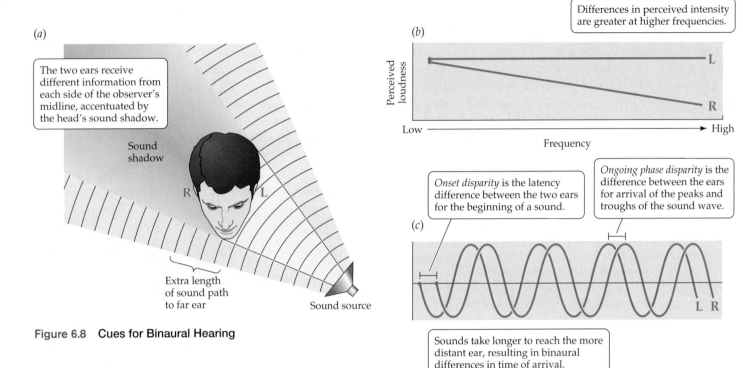

(a)

The two ears receive different information from each side of the observer's midline, accentuated by the head's sound shadow.

Sound shadow

R   L

Extra length of sound path to far ear

Sound source

Figure 6.8   Cues for Binaural Hearing

(b)

Differences in perceived intensity are greater at higher frequencies.

Perceived loudness

Low ———————————————→ High

Frequency

L

R

(c)

Onset disparity is the latency difference between the two ears for the beginning of a sound.

Ongoing phase disparity is the difference between the ears for arrival of the peaks and troughs of the sound wave.

L R

Sounds take longer to reach the more distant ear, resulting in binaural differences in time of arrival.

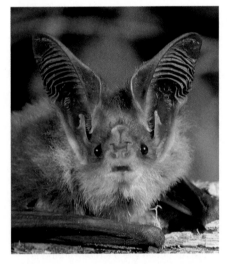

All Ears   Like other mammals, including humans, this bat has ridges and valleys in its outer ear that produce precise changes, through *spectral filtering*, in the sounds being funneled into the ear. This process provides additional cues about the location of a sound source. Some moths produce ultrasonic clicks that interfere with these signals (Corcoran et al., 2009), confusing the bat about where to find that tasty moth.

....

spectral filtering   The process by which the hills and valleys of the external ear alter the amplitude of some, but not all, frequencies in a sound.

are the principal cues for sound position (and at very low frequencies, neither cue is much help; this is why you can place the subwoofer of an audio system anywhere you want). At higher frequencies, however, the sound shadow cast by the head produces significant binaural intensity differences. Of course, we can't perceive which types of processing we're relying on for any given sound; in general, we are aware of the *results* of neural processing but not the processing itself. (You can learn about brain mechanisms of auditory localization in **A Step Further 6.2**, on the website.)

The structure of the external ear provides yet another localization cue. As we mentioned earlier, the hills and valleys of the external ear selectively reinforce some frequencies in a complex sound and diminish others. This process is known as **spectral filtering**, and the frequencies that are affected depend on the angle at which the sound arrives at those peaks and valleys. That angle varies, of course, depending on where the sound came from (Kulkarni and Colburn, 1998); these spectral cues provide critical information about the vertical localization (or *elevation*) of a sound source. Without them, you would have a hard time knowing whether a sound from straight in front of you came from the ground or from the treetops.

The Auditory Cortex Performs Complex Tasks in the Perception of Sound

In some sensory areas of the brain, lesions cause the loss of basic perceptions. For example, lesions of visual cortex result in blind spots, as we discuss in Chapter 7. But the auditory cortex is different: early research revealed that simple pure tones can be detected and discriminated even after the auditory cortex has been surgically removed (Neff and Casseday, 1977; Rosenzweig, 1946). So if the auditory cortex is not involved in these basic kinds of auditory perception, then what does it do? The auditory cortex seems to be specialized for the detection of more complex "biologically relevant" sounds, of the sort we mentioned earlier—vocalizations of animals, footsteps, snaps, crackles, and pops—containing many frequencies and complex patterns (Masterton, 1997; Neff and Casseday, 1977). In other words, the auditory cortex evolved to process the sounds of everyday life.

The unique capabilities of the auditory cortex result from a sensitivity that is fine-tuned by experience as we grow (Kandler et al., 2009). Human infants have diverse hearing capabilities at birth, but their hearing for complex speech sounds in particular becomes more precise and rapid through exposure to the speech of their family and other people. Newborns can distinguish all the different sounds that are made in any human language. But as they develop, they get better and better at distinguishing sounds in the language(s) they hear, and worse at distinguishing sounds that occur in other languages. Similarly, early experience with binaural hearing, compared to equivalent monaural (one-eared) hearing, has a significant effect on the ability of children to localize sound sources later in life (Beggs and Foreman, 1980). Studies with lab animals confirm that experience with sounds of a particular frequency can cause a rapid retuning of auditory neurons (**Figure 6.9**) (N. M. Weinberger, 1998; Fritz et al., 2003). You can learn more about the role of experience in auditory localization in owls in **A Step Further 6.3**, on the website.

Music also shapes the responses of auditory cortex. It might not surprise you to learn that the auditory cortex of trained musicians shows a bigger response to musical sounds than does the same cortex in nonmusicians. After all, when two people differ in any skill, their brains *must* be different in some way, and maybe people born with brains that are more responsive to complex sounds are also more likely to become musicians. The surprising part is that the extent to which a musician's brain is extra sensitive to musical notes is *correlated with the age at which she began her serious training in music*: the earlier the training began, the bigger the difference in auditory cortex in adulthood (Pantev et al., 1998). This finding indicates that intensive musical experience in development alters the functioning of auditory cortex later in life. By adulthood, the portion of primary auditory cortex where music is first processed, called *Heschl's gyrus*, is more than twice as large in professional musicians as in nonmusicians, and more than twice as strongly activated by music (P. Schneider et al., 2002). As we've discussed, at least part of this difference is attributable to early experience with music, but how much is innate?

Some people show a lifelong inability to discern tunes or sing (called **amusia**). Amusia is associated with subtly abnormal function in the right frontal lobe (K. L. Hyde et al., 2006) and relatively few connections between frontal and temporal cortex

amusia A disorder characterized by the inability to discern tunes accurately or to sing.

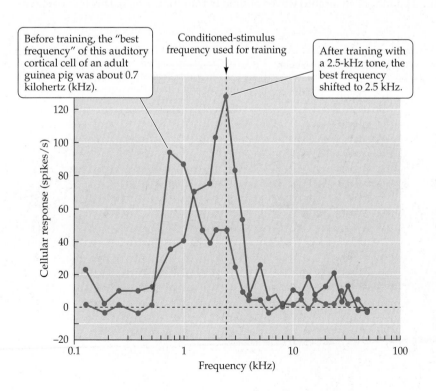

Before training, the "best frequency" of this auditory cortical cell of an adult guinea pig was about 0.7 kilohertz (kHz).

Conditioned-stimulus frequency used for training

After training with a 2.5-kHz tone, the best frequency shifted to 2.5 kHz.

Figure 6.9 Long-Term Retention of a Trained Shift in the Tuning of an Auditory Receptive Field (From N. M. Weinberger, 1998.)

Diffusion tensor imaging (DTI) of axon projections reveals the arcuate fasciculus (yellow), a pathway connecting the frontal cortex, which is active during pitch discrimination, to the temporal lobe, where auditory processing begins (arrows).

The arcuate fasciculus is much more prominent in these four control subjects…

…than in these four people who are tone-deaf.

Figure 6.10 Brain Connections in Tone-Deaf Subjects (Courtesy of Psyche Loui; from Loui et al., 2009.)

(**Figure 6.10**) (Loui et al., 2009), indicating that at least the rudiments of a musical sense are innate (Münte, 2002). Interestingly, studies of people with amusia suggest that, when listening to music, we process pitch and rhythm quite separately (K. L. Hyde and Peretz, 2004).

Deafness Is a Widespread Problem

Whether it's a bit of trouble following quiet conversations, or the profound silence of total hearing loss, some degree of deafness afflicts more than 3% of the population—some 11 million people in the United States alone (Mitchell, 2006). By now, you may have recognized that there are three main ways that sound waves in the air may fail to be transformed into conscious perceptions in the cortex (**Figure 6.11**):

1. Before anything even happens in the nervous system, the ear may fail to convert the sound vibrations in air into waves of fluid within the cochlea. This form of hear-

Figure 6.11 Types of Hearing Loss

Conduction deafness usually involves a middle ear problem that blocks sound vibrations from reaching the inner ear.

In *sensorineural deafness*, there is a problem with the structures— especially the cochlea—that convert sound vibrations into neural activity and project to the brain.

In *central deafness*, damage to auditory brain structures can affect hearing in various ways.

(a)

(b)

(c)

The Destructive Effects of Loud Noise (*a*) In a normal cochlea, hair cells line the organ of Corti throughout its length (*top*). Scanning electron microscopy reveals the stereocilia as very orderly rows of bristles protruding into the tectorial membrane (*bottom*). (*b*) Exposure to excessively loud sounds can have rapid destructive effects in the cochlea. Here, the hair cells are completely missing from a wide extent of the cochlea (*top*) corresponding to the frequencies of the intense sounds that the person was exposed to. The stereocilia (*bottom*) have been crushed and flattened by the noise exposure, like trees blown down in a windstorm. (Micrographs by H. Engstrom and B. Engstrom, courtesy of Widex.)

(*a*) Normal cochlea

(*b*) Severe noise damage

ing loss, called **conduction deafness** (**Figure 6.11a**), often comes about when the ossicles of the middle ear become fused together, so that the vibrations of the eardrum can no longer be conveyed to the oval window of the cochlea.

2. Even if the vibration is successfully conducted to the cochlea, the sensory apparatus of the cochlea—the hair cells—may fail to respond to the ripples created in the basilar membrane, and thus fail to create the action potentials to inform the brain about sounds. This form of hearing loss, termed **sensorineural deafness** (**Figure 6.11b**), is most often due to the permanent damage or destruction of hair cells by any of variety of causes. Some people are born with genetic abnormalities that interfere with the function of hair cells (Cryns and Van Camp, 2004; Petit and Richardson, 2009). Many more people acquire sensorineural deafness during their lives as a result of being exposed to extremely loud sounds—overamplified music, nearby gunshots, and industrial noise are important examples—or because of medical problems such as infections and adverse drug effects (certain antibiotics, such as streptomycin, are particularly *ototoxic*). If you don't think it can happen to you, think again. Anyone listening to something for more than 5 hours per week at 89 dB or louder is already exceeding workplace limits for hearing safety (SCENIHR, 2008). Yet many personal music players can produce sound levels well in excess of 100 dB via headphones. Long-term exposure to loud sounds can cause hearing problems such as **tinnitus**—persistent ringing in the ears—and/or a profound loss of hearing for the frequencies being listened to at such high volumes.

3. For the action potentials sent from the cochlea to be of any use, the auditory areas of the brain must process and interpret them in meaningful ways. **Central deafness** (**Figure 6.11c**) occurs when auditory brain areas are damaged, such as by strokes, tumors, or traumatic injuries. As you might expect from our earlier discussion of auditory processing in the brain, this type of deafness almost never involves a simple loss of auditory sensitivity. Afflicted individuals can often hear a normal range of pure tones but are impaired in the perception of complex, behaviorally relevant sounds. An example in humans is **word deafness**: selective trouble with speech sounds despite normal speech and normal hearing for nonverbal sounds. In **cortical deafness**—a rare syndrome involving bilateral lesions of auditory cortex—patients have more-complete impairment, struggling to recognize all complex sounds, whether verbal or nonverbal.

Although treatments for deafness have been greatly refined in the last few decades, they generally offer only partial restoration of the lost hearing. In cases of conduction deafness, it is sometimes possible to surgically free up the fused ossicles and restore the transmission of sound vibrations to the cochlea. But sensorineural deafness presents a much thornier problem, because neural elements have been destroyed (or were absent from birth). Can new hair cells be grown? Fishes and amphibians produce new hair

conduction deafness A hearing impairment in which the sound vibrations in air fail to be converted into waves of fluid in the cochlea. It is associated with defects of the external ear or middle ear.

sensorineural deafness A hearing impairment most often caused by the permanent damage or destruction of hair cells, or by interruption of the vestibulocochlear nerve that carries auditory information to the brain.

tinnitus A sensation of noises or ringing in the ears not caused by external sound.

central deafness A hearing impairment in which the auditory areas of the brain fail to process and interpret action potentials from sound stimuli in meaningful ways. It is related to damage in auditory brain areas, such as by strokes, tumors, or traumatic injuries.

word deafness A form of central deafness that is characterized by the specific inability to hear words, although other sounds can be detected.

cortical deafness A form of central deafness, caused by damage to both sides of the auditory cortex, that is characterized by difficulty in recognizing all complex sounds, whether verbal or nonverbal.

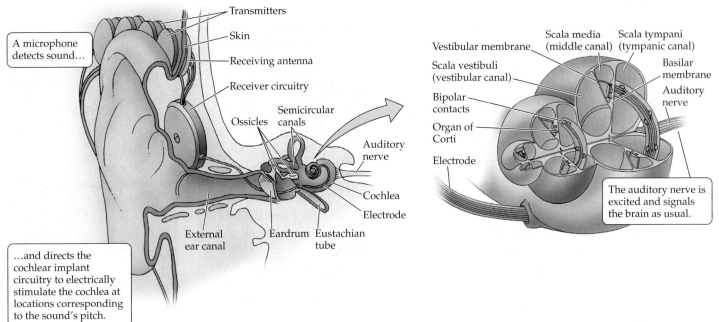

A microphone detects sound…

…and directs the cochlear implant circuitry to electrically stimulate the cochlea at locations corresponding to the sound's pitch.

The auditory nerve is excited and signals the brain as usual.

Figure 6.12 Cochlear Implants Provide Hearing in Some Deaf People

How's it going?

1. Compare and contrast the two important signals about pitch that the brain receives from the cochlea: place coding and temporal coding. How do they work together to give us our sense of pitch?

2. Discuss the sensory capabilities of different species as examples of adaptation through natural selection.

3. Provide an account of sound localization, identifying the several sources of information that we use to determine the source of a sound.

4. Discuss the types of processing that are performed by primary auditory cortex. Is experience with sound an important part of the development of cortical auditory systems?

5. Name and describe the three major forms of deafness, and discuss some possible approaches to restoring hearing in each case.

cochlear implant An electromechanical device that detects sounds and selectively stimulates nerves in different regions of the cochlea via surgically implanted electrodes.

cells throughout life, but mammals historically have been viewed as incapable of regenerating hair cells. This conclusion may have been too hasty, however (Brigande and Heller, 2009). Using several different genetic manipulations, researchers have succeeded in inducing the cochlea of normal and deafened lab animals to produce new hair cells (Izumikawa et al., 2005; Zheng and Gao, 2000). There is thus good reason to hope that a combination of these approaches may provide an effective gene therapy for deaf people someday.

For now, treatments for deafness focus on the use of prostheses. Traditional hearing aids detect and amplify sounds to provide extra stimulation to an impaired—but still functional—auditory system. In recent years, implantable devices called **cochlear implants** have been used to directly stimulate the auditory nerve fibers of the cochlea, bypassing the ossicles and hair cells altogether, and offering partial restoration of hearing even in cases of complete deafness (**Figure 6.12**) (Loeb, 1990; J. M. Miller and Spelman, 1990). You may have had doubts about the value of Békésy's work with cadavers that we described at the start of this chapter. If so, consider this: the cochlear implants that have brought hearing to thousands of deaf people work by reproducing the phenomena Békésy discovered. In other words, the device sends information about low frequencies to electrodes stimulating nerves at the apex of the cochlea, and information about high frequencies to electrodes stimulating nerves at the base.

As you might predict from our discussion of the importance of experience in shaping auditory responsiveness, the earlier these devices are implanted, the better the person will be able to understand complex sounds (Grieco-Calub et al., 2009). So in a sense, the success of these implants is due in part to the cleverness of the brain.

The Inner Ear Provides Our Sense of Balance

When you use an elevator, you feel yourself being lifted up. When you turn your head, take a tight curve in your car, or bounce through the seas in a boat, your continual awareness of motion allows you to plan further movements and anticipate changes in perception due to movement of your head. And of course, too much of this sort of stimulation can make you feel distinctly queasy.

Like hearing, our sense of balance is the product of the inner ear, relying on several small structures that adjoin the cochlea and are known collectively as the **vestibular system** (from the Latin *vestibulum*, "entrance hall," reflecting the fact that the system lies in hollow spaces in the temporal bone). In fact, it is generally accepted that the auditory organ evolved from the vestibular system, although the ossicles probably evolved from parts of the jaw. The most obvious component of the vestibular system is the trio of fluid-filled **semicircular canals**, connected at their ends to two bulbs, called the *saccule* and the *utricle* (**Figure 6.13a**). Notice that the three canals are oriented in the three different planes in which the head can rotate (**Figure 6.13b**)—nodding up and down (technically known as *pitch*, around the y-axis), shaking side-to-side (*yaw*, around the z-axis), and tilting left or right (*roll*, around the x-axis).

The receptors of the vestibular system are hair cells—just like the ones in the cochlea—whose bending ultimately produces action potentials. The cilia of these hair cells are embedded in a gelatinous mass, inside an enlarged region called the **ampulla** (plural *ampullae*) that lies at the base of the semicircular canals (see Figure 6.13b). Movement of the head in one axis sets up a flow of the fluid in the semicircular canal that lies in the same plane, deflecting the stereocilia in the ampulla and signaling the brain that the head has moved. Working together, the three semicircular canals accurately track the rotation of the head. Specialized receptors in the utricle and saccule provide the remaining signals—straight-line acceleration and deceleration—that the brain needs in order to track the precise position and movement of the body in three-dimensional space.

vestibular system   The sensory system that detects balance. It consists of several small inner-ear structures that adjoin the cochlea.

semicircular canal   Any one of the three fluid-filled tubes in the inner ear that are part of the vestibular system. Each of the tubes, which are at right angles to each other, detects angular acceleration in a particular direction.

ampulla   An enlarged region of each semicircular canal that contains the receptor cells (hair cells) of the vestibular system.

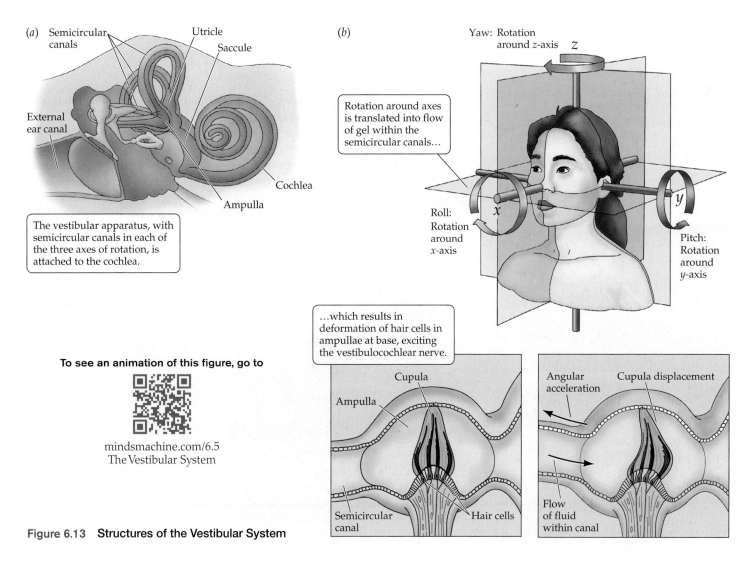

(a) Semicircular canals   Utricle   Saccule

External ear canal

Cochlea

Ampulla

The vestibular apparatus, with semicircular canals in each of the three axes of rotation, is attached to the cochlea.

To see an animation of this figure, go to

mindsmachine.com/6.5
The Vestibular System

(b) Yaw: Rotation around z-axis z

Rotation around axes is translated into flow of gel within the semicircular canals…

Roll: Rotation around x-axis

x y

Pitch: Rotation around y-axis

…which results in deformation of hair cells in ampullae at base, exciting the vestibulocochlear nerve.

Cupula

Ampulla

Semicircular canal

Hair cells

Angular acceleration   Cupula displacement

Flow of fluid within canal

Figure 6.13   Structures of the Vestibular System

vestibular nucleus A brainstem nucleus that receives information from the vestibular organs through cranial nerve VIII (the vestibulocochlear nerve).

The Vestibulo-Ocular Reflex One of the many important functions of the vestibular system is the precise control of eye movements. Try moving your head around while staring at a particular spot on the wall. It seems almost effortless to maintain your gaze on the fixation point, as the model in the photos illustrates. But in reality, it is a very complex processing problem: the six muscles that control the movement of each eye must rapidly and precisely counter the movements of the head as they occur. This function is called the vestibulo-ocular reflex (VOR), involving a high-speed network within the brainstem that uses vestibular information about head rotations to move the eyes in compensation. The VOR functions accurately even when the eyes are closed, showing that vestibular inputs—rather than visual ones—control the accuracy of gaze as we move through the world.

How's it going?

1. Use a diagram to explain how the general layout of the vestibular system allows it to track movement in three axes. Where are the receptors for head movement located? Do they resemble other types of sensory receptors?

2. Where are the vestibular nuclei located? What nerve provides inputs to these nuclei?

3. How is vestibular information used in ongoing behavior?

4. Discuss the role of the vestibular system in motion sickness.

Because vestibular information is crucial for programming movements of the body, maintaining balance against gravity, and smoothly directing sensory organs like the eyes and ears toward specific locations, the nerve pathways from the vestibular system preferentially connect to motor control systems of the brain. On entering the brainstem, many of the vestibular fibers of the vestibulocochlear nerve terminate in the **vestibular nuclei**, while some project directly to the cerebellum to aid in motor programming there. Outputs from the vestibular nuclei project in a complex manner to motor areas throughout the brain, including motor nuclei of the eye muscles, the thalamus, and the cerebral cortex, among others.

The Vomit Comet By following a parabolic flight trajectory, this NASA aircraft is able to simulate the weightless conditions of outer space (zero gravity, or zero-g) for about 30 seconds at a time. These zero-g segments alternate with two-g segments (in which apparent weight is doubled), with up to 30 such cycles occurring during a single training flight. The response of the vestibular system to this unusual stimulation is responsible for the plane's nickname: The Vomit Comet. (Judging from their happy expressions, these trainees must be in the early part of their mission.)

Some Forms of Vestibular Excitation Produce Motion Sickness

There is one aspect of vestibular activation that many of us would gladly do without. Too much strong vestibular stimulation—think of boats and roller coasters—can produce the misery of **motion sickness**. Motion sickness is caused by movements of the body that we cannot control. For example, passengers in a car are more likely to suffer from motion sickness than is the driver.

Why do we experience motion sickness? The **sensory conflict theory** argues that we feel bad when we receive contradictory sensory messages, especially a discrepancy between vestibular and visual information. When an airplane bounces around in turbulence, for instance, the vestibular system signals that various changes in direction and accelerations are occurring, but as far as the visual system is concerned, nothing is happening; the plane's interior is a constant. One hypothesis is that the stimulation is activating a system that originally evolved to rid the body of swallowed poison (M. Treisman, 1977). According to this hypothesis, discrepancies in sensory information might normally signal a dangerous neurological problem, triggering dizziness and vomiting to get rid of potentially toxic food. While this action has obvious protective benefits in an ancestral environment, it sure can interfere with our enjoyment of more contemporary activities!

motion sickness   The experience of nausea brought on by unnatural passive movement, as in a car or boat.

sensory conflict theory   A theory of motion sickness suggesting that discrepancies between vestibular information and visual information simulate food poisoning and therefore trigger nausea.

taste   Any of the five basic sensations detected by the tongue: sweet, salty, sour, bitter, and umami.

flavor   The sense of taste combined with the sense of smell.

papilla   A small bump that projects from the surface of the tongue. Papillae contain most of the taste receptor cells.

taste bud   A cluster of 50–150 cells that detects tastes. Taste buds are found in papillae.

PART II The Chemical Senses: Taste and Smell

Delicious foods, poisons, dangerous adversaries, and fertile mates—these are just a few of the sources of chemical signals in the environment. Being able to detect these signals is vital for survival and reproduction in organisms throughout the animal kingdom. The sense of taste provides an immediate assessment of foods (Lindemann, 1995). But it is the sense of smell that is critical for distinguishing individual foods, as well as discriminating the scent of friend versus foe. In this section we will look at how the sense of taste and smell work together to analyze the chemical signals all around us.

The Human Tongue Detects Five Basic Chemical Tastes

Most people derive great pleasure from eating delicious food, and because we recognize many substances by their distinct flavor, we tend to think that we can discriminate many tastes. In reality, though, humans detect only five basic **tastes**: salty, sour, sweet, bitter, and umami. (*Umami*, Japanese for "delicious taste," is the savory, meaty taste that is characteristic of gravy or soy sauce.) The sensations uniquely aroused by an apple, a steak, or an olive are **flavors** rather than simple tastes; they involve smell as well as taste. To understand the importance of smell to a flavor, block your nose while eating first some raw potato and then some apple, and you'll see that, without olfactory input, you can't tell the difference between them.

Tastes excite specialized receptor cells on the tongue

Many people think that the myriad little bumps on their tongues are taste buds, but they aren't. They are actually **papillae** (singular *papilla*) (**Figure 6.14**), tiny lumps of tissue that increase the surface area of the tongue. There are three kinds of taste papillae—*circumvallate, foliate,* and *fungiform* papillae—occurring in different locations on the tongue (**Figure 6.15c**).

Taste buds, each consisting of a cluster of 50–150 taste receptor cells (**Figure 6.15a**), are found buried within the walls

Figure 6.14   **A Cross Section of the Tongue**

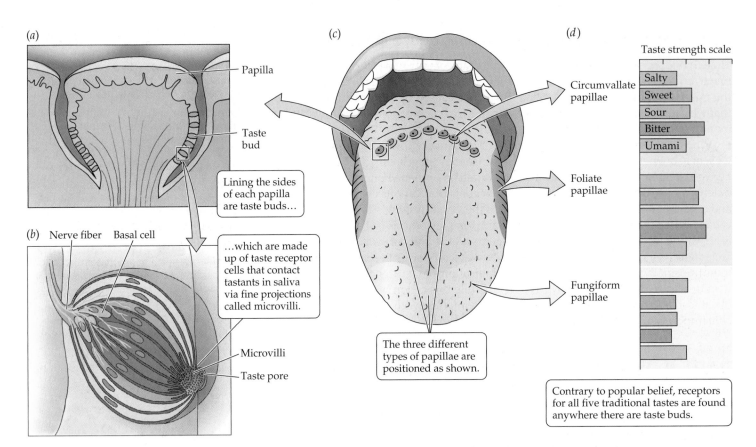

Figure 6.15 A Taste Bud and Taste Receptor Cells (Part *a* after McLaughlin et al., 1994; *c* after Bartoshuk, 1993, and Chandrashekar et al., 2006.)

of the papillae (a single papilla may house several such taste buds; see Figure 6.14). Fine fibers, called *microvilli*, extend from the taste receptor cells into a tiny pore, where they can come into contact with *tastants* (substances that can be tasted) (**Figure 6.15b**). Each taste cell is sensitive to just one of the five basic tastes, and with a life span of only 10–14 days, taste cells are constantly being replaced. But as our varied experience with hot drinks, frozen flag poles, or spicy foods informs us, taste is not the only sensory capability of the tongue. It also possesses sensory cells for pain and touch.

Many books show a map of the tongue indicating that each taste is perceived mainly in one region (sweet at the tip of the tongue, bitter at the back, and so on), but this map is a myth propagated by sloppy textbook writers (which we are not!). All five basic tastes can be perceived *anywhere* on the tongue where there are taste receptors (Chandrashekar, 2006). Those areas do not differ greatly in the strength of taste sensations that they mediate (**Figure 6.15d**).

Different cellular processes transduce the basic tastes

The tastes salty and sour are evoked when taste cells are stimulated by simple ions acting on ion channels in the membranes of the taste cells. Sweet and bitter tastes are perceived by specialized receptor molecules and communicated by second messengers. And at least two types of receptors may be involved in the perception of umami.

SALTY The transduction of the taste of salt (NaCl) is perhaps the easiest to understand, because it relies mostly on ion channels of the sort we have seen in previous chapters. Sodium ions (Na^+) from salty food enter taste cells via sodium channels in the cell membrane, causing a depolarization of the cell and release of neurotransmitter. We know that this is a crucial mechanism for perceiving saltiness, because blocking the sodium channels with a drug greatly reduces—but does not eliminate—our ability to taste salt (Schiffman et al., 1986). The rest of our ability to taste salt comes from a second salt sensor, a variant of a receptor called *TRPV1* (*transient receptor potential vanilloid type 1*), that not only gives us a bit of extra sensitivity to Na⁺, but also detects the positively charged ions (cations) of other salts in food, such as potassium (K⁺) (Treesukosol et al., 2007). Depolarization of the salt-sensitive taste cells causes them to release neurotransmitters that stimulate afferent neurons that relay the information to the brain.

SOUR   Acids in food taste sour—the more acidic the food, the sourer it tastes—but no one knows exactly how sour tastants are detected. Researchers think that the hydrogen ions (H⁺) that all acids release may interact with special acid-sensing ion channels (like the ionotropic receptors in Chapters 3 and 4) to change the polarity of taste cells and alter transmitter release. It seems that all sour-sensitive taste cells contain a particular type of ion channel (Huang et al., 2006) that also detects the sensation and taste of carbonation in drinks (Chandrashekar et al., 2009).

SWEET   The receptors for sweet, bitter, and umami tastes are more like metabotropic receptors than ionotropic receptors (see Figure 4.2), because the binding of tastant molecules to a complex receptor protein on the taste cell's surface activates a second messenger within the cell. These receptors are made up of simpler proteins belonging to two families—designated **T1R** and **T2R**—that are combined in various ways.

When two members of the T1R family—T1R2 and T1R3—combine (heterodimerize), they make a receptor that selectively detects sweet tastants (Nelson et al., 2001). Mice engineered to lack either T1R2 or T1R3 are insensitive to sweet tastes (Zhao et al., 2003). And if you've spent any time around cats, you may be aware that they couldn't care less about sweets. It turns out that all cats, from house cats to leopards, share a mutation in the gene that encodes T1R2; their sweet receptors don't work (X. Li et al., 2009).

BITTER   In nature, bitter tastes often signal the presence of toxins, so it's not surprising that a high sensitivity to different kinds of bitter tastes has evolved (Lush, 1989; McBurney et al., 1972), although individuals vary significantly in their taste sensitivity (**Figure 6.16**). Members of the T2R family of receptor proteins appear to function as bitter receptors (Adler et al., 2000; Chandrashekar et al., 2000). The T2R family has about 30 members, and this large number may reflect the wide variety of bitter substances encountered in the environment, as well as the adaptive importance of being able to detect and avoid them. Interestingly, each bitter-sensing taste cell produces most or all of the different types of T2R bitter receptors (Adler et al., 2000). So bitter-sensing taste cells exhibit broadly tuned sensitivity to *any* bitter-tasting substances (Brasser et al., 2005)—just what you'd expect in a sensory system that has evolved to act as a poison detector.

UMAMI   The fifth basic taste, **umami**—the meaty, savory flavor—is detected by at least two kinds of receptors. One of these is a variant of the metabotropic glutamate receptor

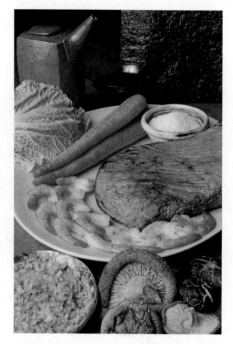

Umami   Meaning "delicious taste" in Japanese, the savory, meaty taste of umami is exemplified by some of the foods (and additives) pictured here.

T1R   A family of taste receptor proteins that, when particular members bind together, form taste receptors for sweet flavors and umami flavors.

T2R   A family of bitter taste receptors.

umami   One of the five basic tastes—the meaty, savory flavor. (The other four tastes are salty, sour, sweet, and bitter.)

Certain substances that taste unpleasantly bitter to most people can't be tasted at all by some people.

(a)

Nontasters have far fewer papillae...

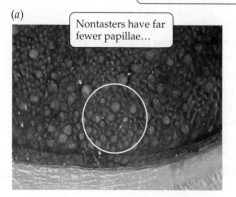

(b)

...than supertasters, who are extra sensitive to bitter and sweet tastants.

Figure 6.16   It's All a Matter of Taste Buds (From Bartoshuk and Beauchamp, 1994; courtesy of Linda Bartoshuk and the Bartoshuk Lab.)

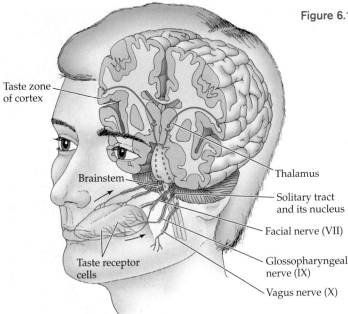

Taste zone of cortex

Brainstem

Taste receptor cells

Thalamus

Solitary tract and its nucleus

Facial nerve (VII)

Glossopharyngeal nerve (IX)

Vagus nerve (X)

Figure 6.17 Anatomy and Main Pathways of the Human Gustatory System

(Chaudhari et al., 2000; Maruyama et al., 2006) and most likely responds to the amino acid *glutamate*, which is found in high concentrations in meats, cheeses, kombu, and other savory foodstuffs (that's why MSG—monosodium glutamate—is used as a "flavor enhancer"). The second probable umami receptor, a combination of T1R1 and T1R3 proteins, responds to most of the dietary amino acids (Nelson et al., 2002). Considering this receptor's similarity to the T1R2+T1R3 sweet receptor, there is reason to suppose that receptors for things that taste good may have shared evolutionary origins. The hunt for other types of taste receptors continues.

Taste information is transmitted to several parts of the brain

Taste projections of the **gustatory system** (from the Latin *gustare*, "to taste") extend from the tongue to several brainstem nuclei, then to the thalamus, and ultimately to gustatory regions of the somatosensory cortex (**Figure 6.17**). Because there are only five basic tastes, and because each taste cell detects just one of the five, the encoding of taste perception is quite simple: the brain monitors which specific axons are active in order to determine which tastes are present (Chandrashekar et al., 2006). In such a simple arrangement—sometimes called a *labeled-line system*—there is no need to analyze complex patterns of activity across multiple kinds of taste receptors. Experimental evidence supports this conclusion: selectively inactivating taste cells that express receptors for just one of the five tastes tends to completely eradicate sensitivity to that one taste while leaving the other four tastes unaffected (Huang et al., 2006).

Chemicals in the Air Elicit Odor Sensations

Our ability to respond to many **odors**—it is estimated that humans can detect more than 10,000 different odors and can discriminate as many as 5,000 (Ressler et al., 1994)—is what produces the complex array of flavors that we normally think of as tastes. While that number may sound impressive, human **olfaction** (sense of smell) is far inferior to that of many other mammals, such as dogs and rabbits; in fact, partial **anosmia** (odor blindness) is quite prevalent among humans, with men exhibiting slightly worse olfaction than women (Gilbert and Wysocki, 1987). Most birds have only basic olfactory abilities, and dolphins don't have olfactory receptors at all (Freitag et al., 1998). These differences evolved because of differences between species in the importance of smell for survival and reproduction.

The sense of smell starts with receptor neurons in the nose

In humans, a sheet of cells called the **olfactory epithelium** (**Figure 6.18**) lines part of the nasal cavities. Within the 5–10 square centimeters of olfactory epithelium that we possess, three types of cells are found: supporting cells, basal cells, and about 10 million olfactory receptor cells. Each olfactory receptor cell is a complete neuron, with a long, slender apical dendrite that divides into branches (cilia) that extend into the moist mucosal surface. *Odorants* (substances that we can smell) from the air that we inhale or sniff, when trapped and dissolved in the mucosal layer, are thus able to interact with receptors studding the dendritic cilia of the olfactory neurons (Farbman, 1994). These olfactory receptor proteins are G protein–coupled receptors (GPCRs), much like the

---

How's it going?

1. What are the five basic tastes?
2. Generate a map of the human tongue, showing how sensitive each region is to the five basic tastes.
3. Compare and contrast taste buds and papillae.
4. Identify the cellular mechanisms underlying each of the five tastes. Discuss the evolution of taste sensitivity: Why do we have these five tastes?

---

gustatory system   The sensory system that detects taste.

odor   The sensation of smell.

olfaction   The sensory system that detects smell; the act of smelling.

anosmia   The inability to detect odors.

olfactory epithelium   A sheet of cells, including olfactory receptors, that lines the dorsal portion of the nasal cavities and adjacent regions, including the septum that separates the left and right nasal cavities.

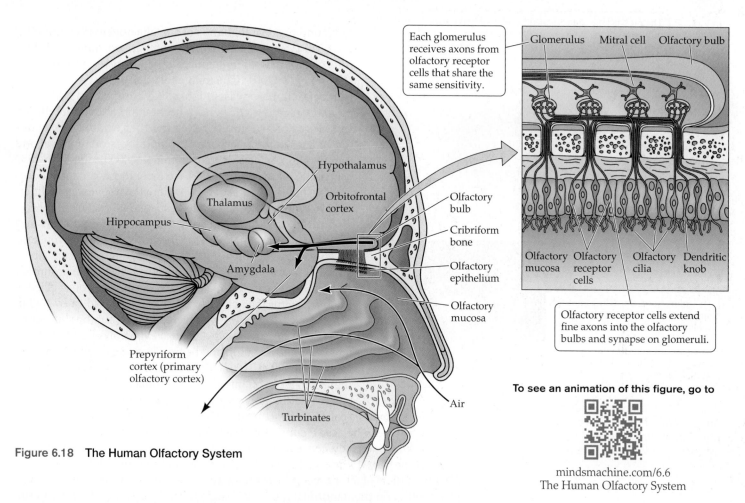

Each glomerulus receives axons from olfactory receptor cells that share the same sensitivity.

Glomerulus   Mitral cell   Olfactory bulb

Olfactory bulb

Cribriform bone

Olfactory epithelium

Olfactory mucosa

Air

Olfactory mucosa   Olfactory receptor cells   Olfactory cilia   Dendritic knob

Olfactory receptor cells extend fine axons into the olfactory bulbs and synapse on glomeruli.

Hypothalamus

Orbitofrontal cortex

Thalamus

Hippocampus

Amygdala

Prepyriform cortex (primary olfactory cortex)

Turbinates

Figure 6.18   The Human Olfactory System

To see an animation of this figure, go to

mindsmachine.com/6.6
The Human Olfactory System

metabotropic neurotransmitter receptors found on neurons of the brain (see Figure 4.2), employing a second-messenger system to respond to the presence of odorants. However, despite these similarities, olfactory neurons also differ from the neurons of the brain in several ways.

One way in which olfactory neurons are distinct from their cousins in the brain relates to the production of receptors: there is an incredible diversity of olfactory receptor protein subtypes. So, while there may be up to a dozen or so subtypes of receptors for a given neurotransmitter in the brain, there are hundreds or even thousands of subtypes within the family of odorant receptors, depending on the species under study. The Nobel Prize–winning discovery of the genes encoding this odorant receptor superfamily (Buck and Axel, 1991) provided one of the most important advances in the history of olfaction research.

Mice have about 2 million olfactory receptor cells, each of which expresses only one of about 1,000 different receptor proteins. These receptor proteins can be divided into four different subfamilies of about 250 receptors each (Mori et al., 1999). Within each subfamily, members have similar structure and presumably recognize chemically similar odorants. Olfactory neurons expressing members of each of the subfamilies of receptors

Moses's Nose Knows   Meet Moses the bloodhound. With some 200 million olfactory receptor neurons, compared to the paltry few million that humans possess, a bloodhound's sense of smell is many times more sensitive than ours. This is why Moses and his cousins are so effective as trackers and as search and rescue dogs. People can be trained to follow a scent trail too (Porter et al., 2007), but they won't work as hard for a biscuit as Moses does.

(a)

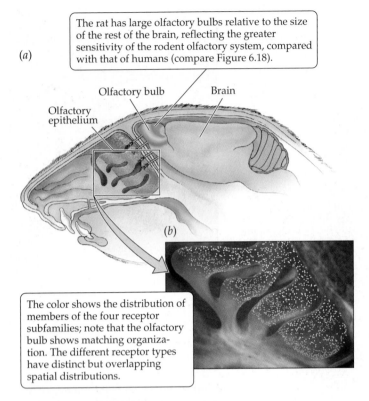

The rat has large olfactory bulbs relative to the size of the rest of the brain, reflecting the greater sensitivity of the rodent olfactory system, compared with that of humans (compare Figure 6.18).

Olfactory epithelium

Olfactory bulb

Brain

(b)

The color shows the distribution of members of the four receptor subfamilies; note that the olfactory bulb shows matching organization. The different receptor types have distinct but overlapping spatial distributions.

Figure 6.19 Different Kinds of Olfactory Receptor Molecules on the Olfactory Epithelium (After Vassar et al., 1993; photo courtesy of Robert Vassar.)

olfactory bulb An anterior projection of the brain that terminates in the upper nasal passages and, through small openings in the skull, provides receptors for smell.

glomerulus A complex arbor of dendrites from a group of olfactory cells.

are found in separate bands of the olfactory epithelium (**Figure 6.19**) (Vassar et al., 1993). By comparison, humans make a total of about 350 different kinds of olfactory receptor proteins (Crasto et al., 2001; Glusman et al., 2001). That's still a large number, but in our case it looks like hundreds of additional olfactory receptor genes have become nonfunctional during the course of evolution, indicating that whatever they detected ceased to be important to our ancestors' survival and reproduction. To be able to discriminate 5,000 odors using 350 functional olfactory receptors, we must recognize most odorants by their activation of a characteristic *combination* of different kinds of receptor molecules (Duchamp-Viret et al., 1999).

Another big difference between olfactory neurons and central neurons is that olfactory neurons die and are replaced in adulthood (Costanzo, 1991). This regenerative capacity is almost certainly an adaptation to the hazardous environment that olfactory neurons inhabit. If an olfactory neuron is killed—say, by the virus that gave you that darn head cold, or by a whiff of something toxic while you were cleaning out the shed, or by some other misadventure—an adjacent basal cell will soon differentiate into a neuron and begin extending a dendrite and an axon (Leung et al., 2007). Each olfactory neuron extends a fine, unmyelinated axon into the nearby **olfactory bulb** of the brain, where it terminates on a specific **glomerulus** (plural *glomeruli*) (from the Latin *glomus*, "ball")—a structure that receives information from one specific class of odorant receptors (see Figure 6.18; we'll return to glomeruli shortly).

No one knows exactly *how* the extending axon knows where to go to find its glomerulus, or how it knows where to form synapses within the glomerulus. One possibility is that olfactory receptor proteins that are found on the *axons* of these cells (as well as on the dendrites) guide the axons to their corresponding glomeruli (Barnea et al., 2004; Imai et al., 2009). But whatever may be the exact mechanisms of neuroplasticity in these cells, better understanding of the process of olfactory neuroregeneration may someday help us develop methods for restoring damaged regions of the brain and spinal cord.

Olfactory information projects from the olfactory bulbs to several brain regions

Each glomerulus within the olfactory bulb is a tight little sphere of neural circuitry that receives inputs exclusively from olfactory neurons that are expressing the same type of olfactory receptor. The glomerulus then actively tunes and sharpens the neural activity associated with the corresponding odorants (Aungst et al., 2003). The glomeruli are organized within the olfactory bulb according to an orderly, topographic map of smells, with neighboring glomeruli receiving inputs from receptors that are closely related. And, as Figure 6.19 shows, the spatial organization of glomeruli within the olfactory bulbs reflects the segregation of the four receptor protein subfamilies in the olfactory epithelium (Mori et al., 1999). In fact, this *olfactotopic* organization is maintained within the olfactory projections throughout the brain.

Olfactory information is conveyed to the brain via the axons of *mitral cells* (see Figure 6.18), which extend from the glomeruli in the olfactory bulbs to various regions of the forebrain (smell is the only sensory modality that synapses directly in the cortex rather than having to pass through the thalamus). Important targets for olfactory inputs include the hypothalamus, the amygdala, and the prepyriform cortex (**Figure 6.20**). The olfactory projections form highly complex maps in the cortex, with structurally related receptors represented in neighboring regions (Zou et al., 2005). Interestingly, the olfactory cortex also contains neurons that respond selectively to *mixtures* of receptor-specific odorants, but not to the odorants individually (Zou and Buck, 2006). This sensitivity

Figure 6.20 **Components of the Brain's Olfactory System**

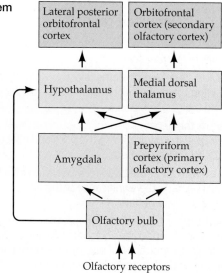

to mixtures may explain why blends of substances, as in perfume, can create unique olfactory experiences.

Many vertebrates possess a vomeronasal system

Though many have tried, no human perfume inventor has concocted a fragrance with even a fraction of the attractive power that the natural scents governing mating and other behaviors in so many species have. The majority of terrestrial vertebrates—mammals, amphibians, and reptiles—possess a secondary chemical detection system that is specialized for detecting these **pheromones**. The system is called the **vomeronasal system** (**Figure 6.21**), and its receptors are found in a **vomeronasal organ** (**VNO**) of epithelial cells near the olfactory epithelium.

In rodents, the sensory neurons of the VNO make hundreds of different vomeronasal receptor proteins, belonging to two large families called V1R and V2R (Dulac and Torello, 2003). These receptors are extremely sensitive, able to detect very low levels of the pheromone signals—such as sex hormone metabolites and signals of genetic relatedness—that are released by other individuals (Leinders-Zufall et al., 2000; Loconto et al., 2003). From the VNO, information extends to the accessory olfactory bulb (adjacent to the main olfactory bulb), which projects to the medial amygdala and hypothalamus, structures that play crucial roles in governing emotional and sexual behaviors, and in regulating hormone secretion. Hamsters and mice can distinguish relatives from nonrelatives just by smell, even if they were raised by foster parents (Isles et al., 2001; Mateo and Johnston, 2000), allowing these animals to select genetically compatible mates and avoid inbreeding.

Do humans have a functional VNO, and do we sense pheromones? On molecular and anatomical bases, the answer to this question would seem to be no: although we possess a vestigial VNO, the genes that encode the V1R and V2R vomeronasal receptor proteins have become nonfunctional "pseudogenes" in humans over evolutionary time. But despite our apparent lack of a functional VNO, some behavioral evidence indicates that humans are sensitive to certain pheromones. For example, applying an extract of sweat to a woman's upper lip causes her menstrual cycle to shift toward synchronization with the menstrual phase of the sweat *donor*, even though the recipient and donor have never met (Stern and McClintock, 1998). This change could be the result of an ancient adaptation that would synchronize the cycles of females living together, resulting in synchronized births of offspring (an antipredator strategy employed by various other species).

The recent discovery of a new class of olfactory receptors within the main olfactory epithelium of mice (Liberles and Buck, 2006) may finally resolve the question of human pheromone sensitivity. Called **TAARs** (for **trace amine–associated receptors**), these receptors are expressed in specific olfactory neurons within the main olfactory epithelium, just like the regular olfactory receptors, but they seem to respond to sex-specific pheromones instead of odorants. Thus it seems the old notion that the olfactory epithelium detects odors while the VNO detects pheromones is an oversimplification, even in rodents, and the apparent ability of humans to respond to pheromones no longer presents a paradox. If rodents can detect pheromones through the olfactory epithelium, perhaps we can too.

pheromone A chemical signal that is released outside the body of an animal and affects other members of the same species.

vomeronasal system A specialized sensory system that detects pheromones and transmits information to the brain.

vomeronasal organ (VNO) A collection of specialized receptor cells, near to but separate from the olfactory epithelium, that detect pheromones and send electrical signals to the accessory olfactory bulb in the brain.

trace amine–associated receptor (TAAR) Any one of a family of probable pheromone receptors produced by neurons in the main olfactory epithelium.

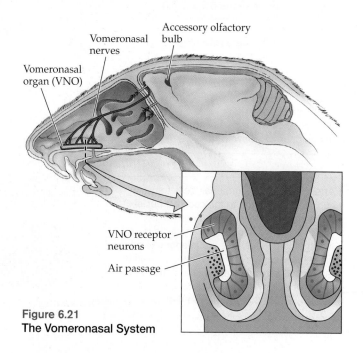

Figure 6.21
The Vomeronasal System

How's it going?

1. Discuss odor sensitivity in humans. How do we compare to other species?

2. Provide a brief sketch of the olfactory epithelium, showing the major cell types and their relationship to the brain.

3. Discuss the genetics of odor receptors, as well as their spatial organization in the nose and olfactory bulbs. What is a glomerulus?

4. Which regions of the brain receive strong olfactory inputs? What is the significance of this arrangement for the animal's behavior?

5. Discuss the structures and receptors associated with pheromone sensitivity, and speculate about the ecological importance of pheromone sensitivity in humans and other animals. Are humans even sensitive to pheromones?

Recommended Reading

Bartoshuk, L. M., and Beauchamp, G. K. (2005). *Tasting and Smelling* (2nd ed.). New York, NY: Academic Press.

Doty, R. L. (2003). *Handbook of Gustation and Olfaction* (2nd ed.). New York, NY: Dekker.

Menini, A. (2009). *The Neurobiology of Olfaction.* Boca Raton, FL: CRC Press.

Musiek, F. E., and Baran, J. A. (2007). *The Auditory System: Anatomy, Physiology, and Clinical Correlates.* Boston, MA: Pearson.

Palmer, A., and Rees, A. (2010). *Oxford Handbook of Auditory Science.* Oxford, England: Oxford University Press.

Wilson, D. A., and Stevenson, R. J. (2006). *Learning to Smell: Olfactory Perception from Neurobiology to Behavior.* Baltimore, MD: Johns Hopkins University Press.

Wolfe, J. M., Kluender, K. R., and Levi, D. M. (2012). *Sensation & Perception* (3rd ed.). Sunderland, MA: Sinauer.

Yost, W. A. (2006). *Fundamentals of Hearing* (5th ed.). San Diego, CA: Academic Press.

CHAPTER **6** VISUAL SUMMARY

mindsmachine.com/vs6

You should be able to relate each summary to the adjacent illustration, including structures and processes. If you need to review, go to the figures indicated and read the accompanying text.

1 The **pinna** (external ear) captures, focuses, and filters sound. The sound arriving at the **tympanic membrane** (eardrum) is focused by the three **ossicles** of the **middle ear** onto the **oval window** to stimulate the fluid-filled **inner ear** (specifically, the **cochlea**). Review **Figure 6.1**, **Animations 6.2** and **6.3**

2 Sound arriving at the oval window causes traveling waves to sweep along the **basilar membrane** of the cochlea. For sounds of high **frequency**, the largest displacement of the basilar membrane is at the base of the cochlea, near the oval window; for low-frequency sounds, the largest **amplitude** is near the apex of the cochlea. Review **Figure 6.2**, **Box 6.1**

3 Movement of the **stereocilia** of the **hair cells** causes the opening and closing of ion channels, thereby **transducing** mechanical movement into changes in electrical potential. These changes in potential stimulate the nerve cell endings that contact the hair cells. Review **Figure 6.3**

4 The **organ of Corti** has both **inner hair cells** (IHCs, about 3,500 in humans) and **outer hair cells** (OHCs, about 12,000 in humans). The inner hair cells convey most of the information about sounds. The outer hair cells change their length under the control of the brain, amplifying the movements of the basilar membrane in response to sound and sharpening the frequency tuning of the cochlea. Review **Figure 6.4**, **Activity 6.1**

5 Afferents from the inner hair cells transmit auditory information to the **cochlear nuclei** of the brainstem. Cochlear neurons project bilaterally to the **superior olivary nucleus**, which in turn innervates the **inferior colliculus**. From there auditory information is relayed to the **medial geniculate nucleus** and then the primary auditory cortex in the temporal lobe. Review **Figure 6.6**, **Animation 6.4**

6 Auditory localization depends on differences in the sounds arriving at the two ears. For low-frequency sounds, differences in time of arrival at the two ears (**latency differences**) are especially important. For high-frequency sounds, **intensity differences** are especially important, and **spectral filtering** provides cues about elevation. Review **Figure 6.8**

7 Primary auditory cortex is specialized for processing complex, biologically important sounds, rather than **pure tones**. Experiences with sound early in life can influence later auditory localization and the responses of neurons in auditory pathways. Experiences later in life can also lead to changes in the responses of auditory neurons. Review **Figures 6.7** and **6.9**

8 Deafness can be caused by changes at any level of the auditory system. **Conduction deafness** consists of impairments in the transmission of sound through the external or middle ear to the cochlea. **Sensorineural deafness** arises in the cochlea, often because of the destruction of hair cells, or in the auditory nerve. **Central deafness** stems from brain damage. Review **Figure 6.11**

9 Some forms of deafness may be alleviated by direct electrical stimulation of the auditory nerve by a **cochlear implant**. Genetic manipulations can induce new hair cell growth in laboratory animals, raising hope of a gene therapy for sensorineural deafness. Review **Figure 6.12**

10 The receptors of the **vestibular system** that detect movement of the head lie within the inner ear next to the cochlea. In mammals the vestibular system consists of three **semicircular canals**, plus the utricle and the saccule. The semicircular canals use hair cells to detect rotation of the body in three planes, and the utricle and saccule sense static positions and linear accelerations. Review **Figure 6.13, Animation 6.5**

11 Humans detect only five main **tastes**—salty, sour, sweet, bitter, and **umami**—using taste receptor cells located in clusters called **taste buds**. Taste cells extend fine filaments into the taste pore of each bud, where tastants come into contact with them. The taste buds are situated on small projections from the surface of the tongue called **papillae**. The tastes of salty and sour are evoked primarily by the action of simple ions on ion channels in the membranes of taste cells. Sweet, umami, and bitter tastes are perceived by specialized receptor molecules belonging to the **T1R** and **T2R** families, which are coupled to G proteins. Review **Figure 6.15, Activity 6.2**

12 Each taste cell transmits information via cranial nerves to brainstem nuclei. This **gustatory system** extends from the taste receptor cells through brainstem nuclei to the thalamus and then to the cerebral cortex. Each taste axon responds most strongly to one category of tastes, providing a labeled line to the brain. Review **Figure 6.17**

13 In contrast to being able to detect only a few tastes, humans can detect thousands of different **odors**. Olfactory receptor cells are small neurons whose dendrites in the **olfactory epithelium** express olfactory receptor proteins. The fine, unmyelinated axons of olfactory neurons run to the **olfactory bulbs** and synapse within **glomeruli**. If an olfactory receptor cell dies, an adjacent cell will replace it. Review **Figure 6.18, Animation 6.6**

14 There is a large family of odor receptor molecules, each of which utilizes G proteins and second messengers. Large subfamilies of receptors are synthesized in distinct bands of the olfactory epithelium. Review **Figure 6.19**

15 Outputs from the olfactory bulb extend to prepyriform cortex, amygdala, and hypothalamus, among other brain regions. Olfactory projections to the cortex maintain a stereotyped olfactory map of slightly overlapping projections from the glomeruli. Review **Figure 6.20**

16 The **vomeronasal organ (VNO)** contains receptors to detect pheromones released from other individuals of the species. These receptors transmit signals to the accessory olfactory bulb, which in turn communicates with the amygdala. **Pheromones** can also be detected by specialized receptors in the main olfactory epithelium. Review **Figure 6.21**

7

Vision: From Eye to Brain

When Seeing Isn't Seeing

It was cold in the bathroom, so the young woman turned on a small heater before she got in the shower. She didn't know that the heater was malfunctioning, filling the room with deadly, odorless carbon monoxide gas. Her husband found her unconscious on the floor and called for an ambulance to rush her to the emergency room. When she regained consciousness, "D.F." seemed to have gotten off lightly, avoiding what could have been a fatal accident. She could understand the doctors' questions and reply sensibly, move all her limbs, and perceive touch on her skin. But something was wrong with her sight.

D.F. had lost the ability to identify things that she viewed. Even the faces of family members had become unfamiliar. To this day, more than a decade later, D.F. still cannot recognize commonplace objects. Yet she is not entirely blind. Show her a flashlight and she can tell you that it's made of shiny aluminum with some red plastic, but she doesn't recognize it ("Is it a kitchen utensil?"). Without telling her what it is, if you ask her to pick it up, her hand goes directly to the flashlight and holds it exactly as one normally holds a flashlight. Show D.F. a slot in a piece of plastic and she cannot tell you whether the slot is oriented vertically, horizontally, or diagonally; but if you hand her a disk and ask her to put it through the hole, D.F. invariably turns the disk so that it goes smoothly through the slot (Goodale et al., 1991).

Can D.F. see or not?

To see a video, go to

mindsmachine.com/7.1
Object Recognition

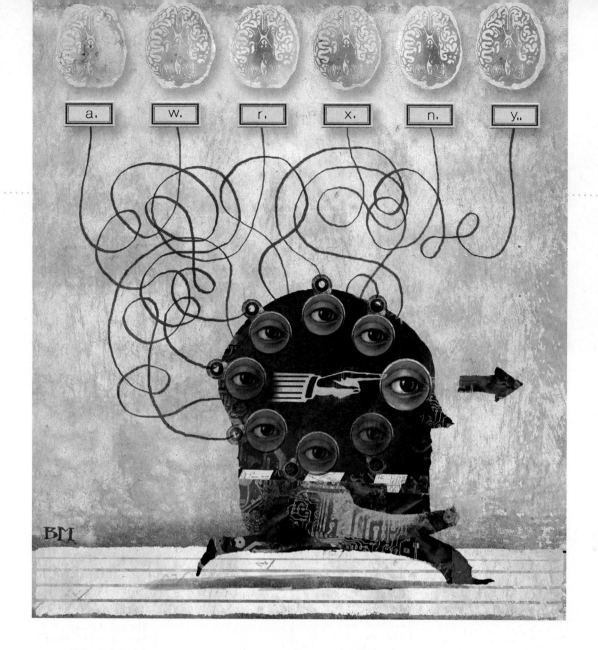

M any species rely on vision for finding food, avoiding predators, finding mates, and locating shelter. And we humans are especially visual, using our sense of sight to enjoy nature and art, to read and write, to watch films and TV. So it's no surprise that we put a lot of effort into improving vision, preventing its deterioration, or even restoring sight to the blind.

However, the sheer volume of visual information poses a serious problem. Viewing the surrounding world has been compared to drinking from a waterfall. How does the visual system avoid being overwhelmed by the flood of information entering the eyes? One answer is that visual systems are especially sensitive to detecting movement, because moving objects are the most likely to represent the danger of predators or the good fortune of prey or mates. So the visual system often ignores information about stationary objects, which is why we have a harder time seeing them.

Another way to deal with information overload is for each species to evolve visual capabilities that are tailored to that species' particular lifestyle. No species can see everything. Most nocturnal species have better night vision than do animals that are active during the day, like us. Most rodent species, such as rats and mice, which live in tunnels and close quarters, have poor vision for distant objects, while daytime hunters like hawks have incredibly keen distance vision. Our vision for distant objects falls somewhere in between. Birds and bees can detect ultraviolet light, allowing them to see patterns in flowers that most mammals, including humans, cannot see. But even within our limits of sight, we humans process a remarkable amount of visual information, which keeps about one-third of our cerebral cortex busy analyzing it.

This chapter is organized according to the stages of visual processing that pull out information from the light around us. We'll begin by tracing the path of visual information in the brain, and then we'll move on to consider how we develop perceptions of form, color, and motion of objects. Later we'll turn to some of the enduring mysteries of visual perception, including how D.F. can see *where* an object is placed in front of her and describe in fine detail what it looks like, yet be unable to say *what* that object is.

The Visual System Extends from the Eye to the Brain

To understand how the visual system constructs our vision, let's follow the path of information triggered by light entering the visual system, starting with the optical properties of the eye and the neural processes in the back of the eye (a region called the *retina*). We'll find that there are two types of light-detecting cells, and they can work in an astonishingly wide range of light intensities, from the dim interior of a movie theater to the beach on a sunny day. Then we'll examine different parts of the retina to understand why our vision is so much better for some parts of the visual scene than for others.

The vertebrate eye acts in some ways like a camera

The eye is an elaborate structure with optical functions, capturing light and projecting detailed images of the external world onto the back of the eye. There a layer of neurons,

Image Enhancement Beyond making a fashion statement, the primary purpose of eyeglasses (and contact lenses) is to "prebend" light rays so that images focus precisely on the retina, restoring sharpness to our vision.

To see the brain in 3D, go to

mindsmachine.com/7.2
Brain Explorer

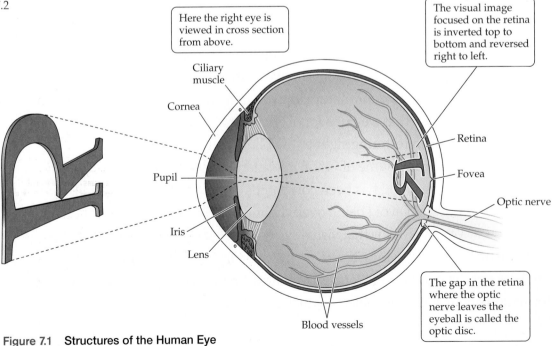

Figure 7.1 **Structures of the Human Eye**

called the **retina**, turns the light into neural signals, in a process called **transduction**. So, good vision requires an accurate optical image focused on the retina. In other words, light from a point on a target object must end up as a point—rather than a blur—in the retinal image.

To produce this sharply focused optical image, the eye has many of the features of a camera, starting with the transparent outer layer of the eye, called the **cornea** (**Figure 7.1**). Light travels in a straight line until it encounters a change in the density of the medium, which causes light rays to bend. This bending of light rays, called **refraction**, is the basis of such instruments as eyeglasses, telescopes, and microscopes. The curvature of the cornea, which does not change shape, refracts light rays and is primarily responsible for focusing on the retina. Light passing through the cornea is further refracted by the **lens**, which changes its shape to fine-tune that image on the retina.

The change in the shape of the lens is controlled by the **ciliary muscles** inside the eye. Changes in contraction of the ciliary muscles alter the focal distance of the eye, causing nearer or farther images to come into focus on the retina; this process is called **accommodation**. As mammals age, their lenses become less elastic and therefore less able to bring nearby objects into focus. Aging humans correct this problem either by holding books and menus farther away from their eyes, or by wearing reading glasses. In young people, the most common vision problem is **myopia** (nearsightedness), which is difficulty seeing distant objects. Myopia develops if the eyeball is too long, causing the cornea and lens to focus images in front of the retina rather than on it (**Figure 7.2**). Distance vision can be restored in such cases by glasses that correct refraction of the visual image onto the retina.

If you've ever played around with a magnifying glass, you've probably noticed that if you hold the lens at arm's length, you can see a clearly focused image of a distant scene through the glass but that scene is upside down and reversed. The lens of the eye has the same shape as a magnifying glass (it bulges out a bit on both sides), so the visual scene that is focused on the retina is also upside down and reversed compared to the real world (see Figure 7.1).

When we look at a complex organ like the eye of a mammal, it is hard at first to understand how it could have evolved something so fully formed as a lens to focus

Come into Focus The lens in our eye is shaped like a magnifying glass, so it reverses and inverts images the way a magnifying glass does when held out about an arm's length.

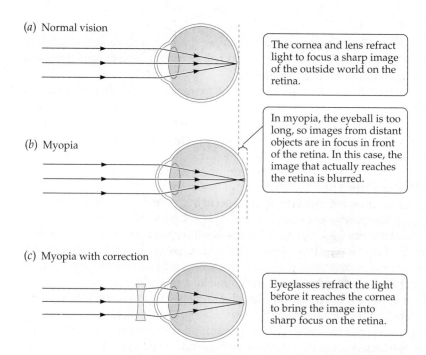

(*a*) Normal vision

> The cornea and lens refract light to focus a sharp image of the outside world on the retina.

(*b*) Myopia

> In myopia, the eyeball is too long, so images from distant objects are in focus in front of the retina. In this case, the image that actually reaches the retina is blurred.

(*c*) Myopia with correction

> Eyeglasses refract the light before it reaches the cornea to bring the image into sharp focus on the retina.

Figure 7.2 Focusing Images on the Retina

retina The receptive surface inside the eye that contains photoreceptors and other neurons.

transduction The conversion of one form of energy to another, as converting light into neuronal activity.

cornea The transparent outer layer of the eye, whose curvature is fixed. The cornea bends light rays and is primarily responsible for forming the image on the retina.

refraction The bending of light rays by a change in the density of a medium, such as the cornea and the lens of the eyes.

lens A structure in the eye that helps focus an image on the retina.

ciliary muscle One of the muscles that control the shape of the lens inside the eye, focusing an image on the retina.

accommodation The process by which the ciliary muscles adjust the lens to focus a sharp image on the retina.

myopia Nearsightedness; the inability to focus the retinal image of objects that are far away.

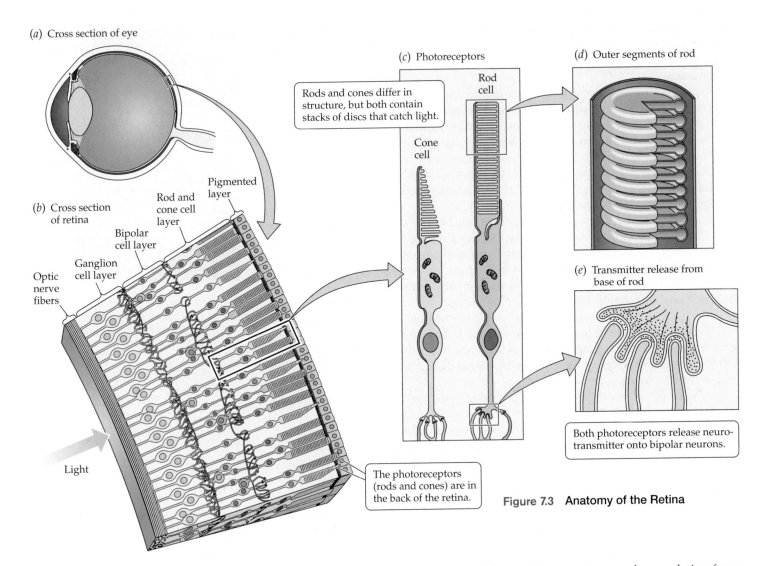

(a) Cross section of eye

(b) Cross section of retina

Optic nerve fibers

Ganglion cell layer

Bipolar cell layer

Rod and cone cell layer

Pigmented layer

Light

(c) Photoreceptors

Rod cell

Cone cell

Rods and cones differ in structure, but both contain stacks of discs that catch light.

(d) Outer segments of rod

(e) Transmitter release from base of rod

Both photoreceptors release neurotransmitter onto bipolar neurons.

The photoreceptors (rods and cones) are in the back of the retina.

Figure 7.3 Anatomy of the Retina

extraocular muscle One of the muscles attached to the eyeball that control its position and movements.

photoreceptor A neural cell in the retina that responds to light.

rod A photoreceptor cell in the retina that is most active at low levels of light.

cone Any of several classes of photoreceptor cells in the retina that are responsible for color vision.

bipolar cell An interneuron in the retina that receives information from rods and cones and passes the information to retinal ganglion cells.

ganglion cell Any of a class of cells in the retina whose axons form the optic nerve.

images on the retina. But comparing different living species reveals a gradation from very simple light-sensitive cells to increasingly complex organs with focusing devices, as discussed in **A Step Further 7.1**, on the website.

The movement of the eyes is controlled by the **extraocular muscles**, three pairs of muscles that extend from the outside of the eyeball to the bony socket of the eye. Fixating still or moving targets requires delicate control of these muscles to anchor the visual image on the retina. Let's talk about how that sharply focused visual image is processed in the retina.

Visual processing begins in the retina

The first stages of visual-information processing occur in the retina, the receptive surface inside the back of the eye (**Figure 7.3a**). The retina is only 200–300 micrometers thick—not much thicker than the edge of a razor blade—but it contains several types of cells in distinct layers (**Figure 7.3b**). Sensory neurons that detect light are called **photoreceptors**. There are two types of photoreceptors in the retina, called **rods** and **cones** in recognition of their respective shapes (**Figure 7.3c**). Cones come in several different varieties, which respond differently to light of varying wavelengths, providing us with color vision (as described later in the chapter). Rods respond to any visible light, regardless of wavelength.

Both rod and cone photoreceptors release neurotransmitter molecules that control the activity of the **bipolar cells** that synapse with them (see Figure 7.12). The bipolar cells, in turn, connect with **ganglion cells**. The axons of the ganglion cells form the **optic**

TABLE 7.1 Properties of the Human Photopic and Scotopic Visual Systems

Property	Photopic system	Scotopic system
Receptors[a]	Cones	Rods
Approximate number of receptors per eye	4 million	100 million
Photopigments[b]	Three classes of cone opsins; the basis of color vision	Rhodopsin
Sensitivity	Low; needs relatively strong stimulation; used for day vision	High; can be stimulated by weak light intensity; used for night vision
Location in retina[c]	Concentrated in and near fovea; present less densely throughout the retina	Outside fovea
Receptive-field size and visual acuity	Small in fovea, so acuity is high; larger outside fovea	Larger, so acuity is lower
Response time	Relatively rapid	Slow

[a]Cones and rods are illustrated in Figure 7.3c.
[b]Figure 7.25 shows the spectral sensitivities of the photopigments.
[c]See Figure 7.7.

nerve, which carries information to the brain. Two additional types of cells—**horizontal cells** and **amacrine cells**—are especially significant in interactions within the retina, as we'll see shortly. The horizontal cells make contacts among the receptor cells and bipolar cells; the amacrine cells contact both the bipolar cells and the ganglion cells.

Interestingly, the rods, cones, bipolar cells, and horizontal cells generate only graded, local potentials; they do not produce action potentials. Unlike most neurons, these cells affect each other through the *graded* release of neurotransmitters in response to *graded* changes in electrical potentials. The ganglion cells, on the other hand, conduct action potentials in the same way that most other neurons do. From the receptor cells to the ganglion cells, enormous amounts of data converge and are compressed; the human eye contains about 100 million rods and 4 million cones, but there are only 1 million ganglion cells to transmit that information to the brain. Thus, a great deal of information processing is done inside the eye, as information from over 100 million photoreceptors is compressed into the action potentials of 1 million ganglion cells.

The two different populations of photoreceptors (rods and cones) provide input to two different functional systems in the retina. A rod-based system, called the **scotopic system** (from the Greek *skotos*, "darkness," and *ops*, "eye"), is very sensitive and thus works especially well in low light—we use rod vision to detect objects in dim light—but it is insensitive to color. That's why in the darkness of night, when only our rods can detect light, we can't tell colors apart. This is the basis for the saying "At night, all cats are gray." There is a lot of **convergence** in the scotopic system, because the information from many rods *converges* onto each ganglion cell.

The other system uses cones, which are less sensitive than rods (that is, they have a higher threshold to respond), and therefore requires more light to function. This **photopic system** (which, like the term *photon*, gets its name from the Greek *phos*, "light") shows differential sensitivity to wavelengths, enabling our color vision. Compared to the scotopic system, the photopic system has less convergence, with some ganglion cells reporting information from only a single cone. At moderate levels of illumination, both the rods and the cones function, and some ganglion cells receive input from both types of receptors. **Table 7.1** summarizes the characteristics of the photopic and scotopic systems.

Photoreceptors respond to light by releasing less neurotransmitter

Rods and cones owe their extraordinary sensitivity to their unusual structure and biochemistry. A portion of their structure, when magnified, looks like a large stack of pancakes or discs (**Figure 7.3d**). The stacking of discs increases the probability that they will capture light particles. This is especially important because light is reflected in many

optic nerve Cranial nerve II; the collection of ganglion cell axons that extend from the retina to the brain.

horizontal cell A specialized retinal cell that contacts both receptor cells and bipolar cells.

amacrine cell A specialized retinal cell that contacts both bipolar cells and ganglion cells, and is especially significant in inhibitory interactions within the retina.

scotopic system A system in the retina that operates at low levels of light and involves the rods.

convergence The phenomenon of neural connections in which many cells send signals to a single cell.

photopic system A system in the retina that operates at high levels of light, shows sensitivity to color, and involves the cones.

(a) Rod photoreceptor

Rod cell outer segment

Rod photoreceptors are hyperpolarized when stimulated by light.

Amplifier

Microelectrode

Rod cell inner segment

Light

(b) Stimulation hyperpolarizes receptor

Light flash

Dim light

Medium light

Bright light

Electrical potential (mV)

−35

−45

−55

Time (ms)

0   100   200

Figure 7.4 Hyperpolarization of Photoreceptors

directions by the surface of the eyeball, the lens, and the fluid inside the eye, so only a fraction of the light that strikes the cornea actually reaches the retina.

The light particles, called *quanta* or *photons*, that strike the discs are captured by special photopigment receptor molecules. In the rods this photopigment is **rhodopsin** (from the Greek *rhodon*, "rose," and *opsis*, "vision"). Cones use similar photopigments, as we'll see later. Curiously enough, photoreceptors in the dark continually release neurotransmitter onto bipolar cells. When light hits photopigment in the photoreceptor, it triggers a cascade of chemical reactions that *hyperpolarize* the cell, causing the cell to release *less* neurotransmitter onto bipolar cells (**Figure 7.4**). You can learn the details of this process in **A Step Further 7.2**, on the website. It may seem puzzling that light causes photoreceptors to release less neurotransmitter, but remember that the visual system responds to *changes* in light. Either an increase or a decrease in the intensity of light can stimulate the visual system, and hyperpolarization is just as much a neural signal as depolarization is.

This change of potential in photoreceptors is the initial electrical signal in the visual pathway. Stimulation of rhodopsin by light hyperpolarizes the rods, just as stimulation of the cone pigments by light hyperpolarizes the cones. For both rods and cones, the size of the hyperpolarizing photoreceptor potential determines how much less transmitter will be released (**Figure 7.3e**). Another important feature of photoreceptors is that their sensitivity to light is constantly changing, depending on how much light is available. This feature, called *adaptation*, allows us to see over wide ranges of light, as discussed next.

Different mechanisms enable the eyes to work over a wide range of light intensities

Our visual system must be able to respond to stimuli of vastly different intensities: a very bright light is about 10 billion times as intense as the weakest lights we can see. At any given time, however, we discriminate over only a small fraction of this range of light intensity (**Figure 7.5**).

One way the visual system deals with a large range of intensities is by adjusting the size of the **pupil**, which is an opening in the colorful disc called the **iris** (see Figure 7.1). In Chapter 2 we mentioned that dilation of the pupils is controlled by the sympathetic division of the autonomic system, and constriction by the parasympathetic division. Because usually both divisions are active, pupil size reflects a balance of influences. During an eye exam, the doctor may use a drug to block acetylcholine transmission in the parasympathetic synapses of your iris; this drug relaxes the muscle fibers and opens the pupil widely. One drug that has this effect—*belladonna*—got its name (Italian for "beautiful lady") because it was thought to make a woman more beautiful by giving her the wide-open pupils of an attentive person. Other drugs, such as morphine, constrict the pupils.

rhodopsin The photopigment in rods that responds to light.

pupil The opening, formed by the iris, that allows light to enter the eye.

iris The circular structure of the eye that provides an opening to form the pupil.

Figure 7.5 **The Wide Range of Sensitivity to Light Intensity**

Our visual system works over a remarkably broad range of light intensities. Even within the photopic range, where cones are active, we can see over a million-fold range of brightness.

In low light, we rely on the scotopic system activated by rods, so color discrimination is weak or absent.

In bright light the pupil contracts quickly to admit only about one-sixteenth as much light as when illumination is dim (**Figure 7.6**). Although rapid, the 16-fold difference in light controlled by the pupil doesn't come close to accounting for the *billion*fold range of visual sensitivity. Another mechanism for handling different light intensities is **range fractionation**, the handling of different intensities by different receptors—some with low thresholds (rods) and others with high thresholds (cones) (see Figure 7.5). But the main reason we can see over such a vast range of light is **photoreceptor adaptation**: each photoreceptor adjusts its sensitivity to match the average level of ambient illumination, over a tremendous range. Thus, the visual system is concerned with *differences*, or changes, in brightness—not with the absolute level of illumination.

At any given time, a photoreceptor operates over a range of intensities of about a hundredfold; that is, it is completely depolarized by a stimulus about one-tenth the ambient level of illumination, and a light ten times more intense than the ambient level will completely hyperpolarize it. The receptors constantly shift their whole range of response to work around the prevailing level of illumination. Further adaptation, controlled by neural circuits, occurs in the brain.

Acuity is best in foveal vision

Visual acuity, commonly known as the sharpness of vision, is a measure of how much detail we can see. Our visual acuity is especially fine in the center of the visual field and falls off rapidly toward the periphery. That's why when we want to look at something closely, we center our visual field on the object of interest.

(*a*) Bright illumination

(*b*) Dark

While the size of the pupil can change rapidly, it affects light entry by only about 16-fold. So it cannot possibly account for our ability to see over a billionfold range of illumination.

Figure 7.6 **The Iris Controls the Size of the Pupil Opening**

range fractionation The means by which sensory systems cover a wide range of intensity values, as each sensory receptor cell specializes in just one part of the overall range of intensities.

photoreceptor adaptation The tendency of rods and cones to adjust their light sensitivity to match ambient levels of illumination.

visual acuity Sharpness of vision.

(a) Distributions of rods and cones across the retina

(b) Variation of visual acuity across the retina

The variation of visual acuity across the retina reflects the distribution of cones.

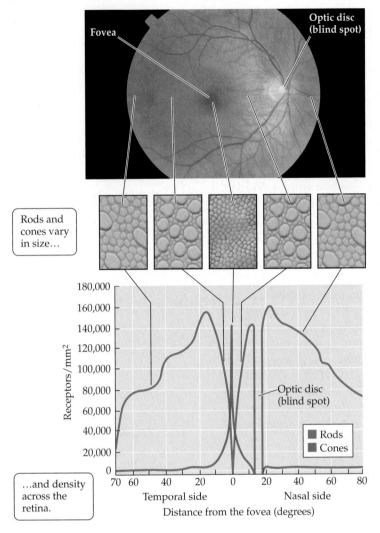

Rods and cones vary in size…

…and density across the retina.

Figure 7.7   Densities of Retinal Receptors and Visual Acuity

The fine structure of the retina explains why our acuity is best in the center of the visual field. **Figure 7.7a** shows a photograph of the back of the eye, taken through the pupil. The central region of the retina, called the **fovea**, has a dense concentration of cones, absorbing so much light that the region looks dark in the photo. Also notice how much smaller cones are in the fovea than in other parts of the retina. That smaller size allows cones to be packed closer together in the fovea and is one reason visual acuity is so high in this region (**Figure 7.7b**). People differ in their concentrations of cones (Curcio et al., 1987), and this variation may be related to individual differences in visual acuity. Species differences in visual acuity also reflect the density of cones in the fovea. For example, hawks, whose acuity is much greater than that of humans, have much narrower and more densely packed cones in the fovea than we do. In the human retina, both cones and rods are larger toward the periphery. Therefore, our acuity falls off about as rapidly in the horizontal direction as in the vertical direction. But species that live in open, flat environments (such as the cheetah and the rabbit) have fields of acute vision that extend farther horizontally than vertically.

The rods show a different distribution from the cones: they are absent in the fovea but more numerous than cones in the periphery of the retina (see Figure 7.7a). This is why, if you want to see a dim star, you do best to search for it a little off to the side of your center of gaze. Not only are rods more sensitive than cones to dim light but, as we mentioned earlier, input from many rods converges on each ganglion cell in the scotopic system, further increasing the system's sensitivity to weak stimuli. But that greater convergence of rods comes at the cost of diminished acuity compared to the fovea. Rods provide high sensitivity with limited acuity; cones provide high acuity with limited sensitivity. Thus, really fine vision requires good lighting.

We noted earlier that rods cannot contribute to color vision. Yet the few cones scattered in the periphery of our gaze enable us to detect color there. That's why peripheral cones are large: so that they're likely to get some color information. We are not aware that most of our peripheral vision lacks color information, because the brain "fills in," assuming that the light striking a rod is of the same wavelength as light hitting a neighboring cone.

Another reason why acuity is greater in the fovea than elsewhere on the retina is that in this region light reaches the cones directly, without having to pass through other

fovea   The central portion of the retina, which is packed with the highest density of photoreceptors and is the center of our gaze.

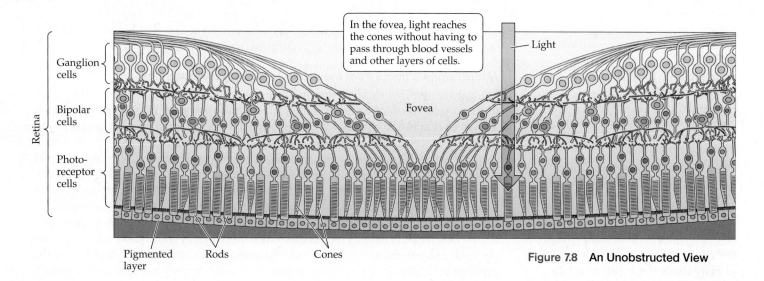

In the fovea, light reaches the cones without having to pass through blood vessels and other layers of cells.

Light

Fovea

Ganglion cells

Retina

Bipolar cells

Photo-receptor cells

Pigmented layer   Rods   Cones

Figure 7.8   An Unobstructed View

layers of cells and blood vessels (**Figure 7.8**). In the rest of the retina, many light particles hit those upper layers without reaching the photoreceptors. This is why the surface of the retina is depressed at the fovea (see Figure 7.1a), giving the structure its name (*fovea* means "pit" in Latin).

The **optic disc**, to the nasal side of the fovea, is where blood vessels and ganglion cell axons leave the eye (see Figure 7.7a). There are no photoreceptors at the optic disc, so there is a **blind spot** here that we normally do not notice. You can locate your blind spot, and experience firsthand some of its interesting features, in **Figure 7.9**. The blind spot is much bigger than we usually appreciate; it is about ten times larger than the image of a full moon, yet we typically don't even notice it! Again, brain systems "fill in" the missing information so that we perceive an uninterrupted visual scene.

How's it going?

1. Describe how structures of the eye refract light to focus an image on the retina.
2. How do the photopic and scotopic visual systems vary?
3. How are we able to discriminate differences in light over such a wide range of illumination?
4. Why is our vision so much more acute at the fovea than it is elsewhere?

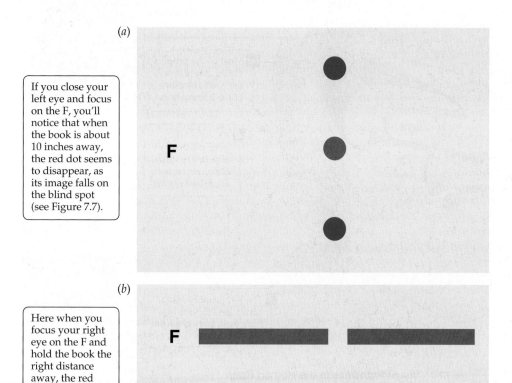

(a)

If you close your left eye and focus on the F, you'll notice that when the book is about 10 inches away, the red dot seems to disappear, as its image falls on the blind spot (see Figure 7.7).

F

(b)

Here when you focus your right eye on the F and hold the book the right distance away, the red line appears unbroken.

F

Figure 7.9   Experiencing the Blind Spot

optic disc   The region of the retina that is devoid of receptor cells because ganglion cell axons and blood vessels exit the eyeball there.

blind spot   The portion of the visual field from which light falls on the optic disc. Because there are no receptors in this region, light striking the blind spot cannot be seen.

occipital cortex   Also called *visual cortex*. The cortex of the occipital lobe of the brain.

optic chiasm   The point at which the two optic nerves meet.

optic tract   The axons of retinal ganglion cells after they have passed the optic chiasm; most of these axons terminate in the lateral geniculate nucleus.

lateral geniculate nucleus (LGN)   The part of the thalamus that receives information from the optic tract and sends it to visual areas in the occipital cortex.

optic radiation   Axons from the lateral geniculate nucleus that terminate in the primary visual areas of the occipital cortex.

primary visual cortex (V1) or striate cortex   Also called *area 17*. The region of the occipital cortex where most visual information first arrives.

....

To see an animation of this figure, go to

mindsmachine.com/7.3
Visual Pathways in the Human Brain

Before we consider how information is processed at different levels of the visual system, we need to describe the pathway from the eye to the cortex.

Neural signals travel from the retina to several brain regions

The ganglion cells in each eye produce action potentials that are conducted along their axons to send visual information to the brain. These axons make up the optic nerve (also known as cranial nerve II), which brings visual information into the brain on each side, eventually reaching the **occipital cortex** at the back of the brain.

In all vertebrates, some or all of the axons of each optic nerve cross to the opposite cerebral hemisphere (**Figure 7.10**). The optic nerves cross the midline at the **optic chiasm** (named for the Greek letter **X** [chi] because of its crossover shape). In humans, axons from the half of the retina toward your nose (the *nasal retina*) cross over to the opposite side of the brain (step 3 in Figure 7.10). The half of the retina toward your temple (the *temporal retina*) projects its axons to its own side of the brain. After they pass the optic chiasm, the axons of the retinal ganglion cells are known collectively as the **optic tract**. Proportionally more axons cross the midline in prey animals, such as rabbits, that have laterally placed eyes with little overlap in their fields of vision.

Most axons of the optic tract terminate on cells in the **lateral geniculate nucleus** (**LGN**) (step 4a in Figure 7.10), which is the visual part of the thalamus. Axons of the LGN neurons form the **optic radiations** (step 5), which terminate in the **primary visual cortex** (**V1**) of the occipital cortex at the back of the brain (step 6). The primary visual cortex is sometimes called **striate cortex** because cross sections of brain tissue from this

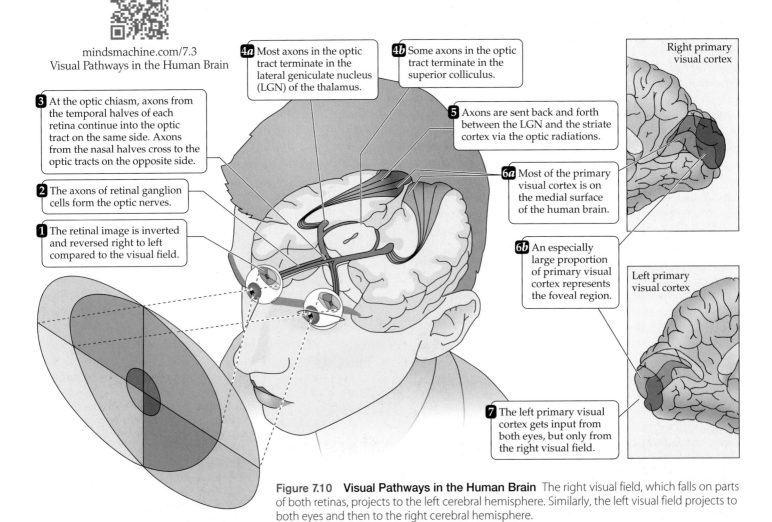

3 At the optic chiasm, axons from the temporal halves of each retina continue into the optic tract on the same side. Axons from the nasal halves cross to the optic tracts on the opposite side.

2 The axons of retinal ganglion cells form the optic nerves.

1 The retinal image is inverted and reversed right to left compared to the visual field.

4a Most axons in the optic tract terminate in the lateral geniculate nucleus (LGN) of the thalamus.

4b Some axons in the optic tract terminate in the superior colliculus.

5 Axons are sent back and forth between the LGN and the striate cortex via the optic radiations.

6a Most of the primary visual cortex is on the medial surface of the human brain.

6b An especially large proportion of primary visual cortex represents the foveal region.

7 The left primary visual cortex gets input from both eyes, but only from the right visual field.

Right primary visual cortex

Left primary visual cortex

Figure 7.10 Visual Pathways in the Human Brain The right visual field, which falls on parts of both retinas, projects to the left cerebral hemisphere. Similarly, the left visual field projects to both eyes and then to the right cerebral hemisphere.

region feature a prominent stripe, or *striation*, corresponding to convergent **binocular** ("two-eyed") inputs. The binocular input to layer IV of the primary visual cortex is important for depth perception. You can learn details about the organization of inputs to primary visual cortex in **A Step Further 7.3**, on the website.

As Figure 7.10 shows, the visual cortex in the right cerebral hemisphere receives its input from the left half of the visual field, and the visual cortex in the left hemisphere receives its input from the right half of the visual field. The figure shows that some retinal ganglion cells send their optic-tract axons to the superior colliculus in the midbrain (step 4b). The superior colliculus helps coordinate rapid movements of the eyes toward a target, and it controls the pupil's response to light levels.

In addition to the primary visual cortex (V1) shown in Figure 7.10, numerous surrounding regions of the cortex are largely visual in function. These visual cortical areas outside the striate cortex are sometimes called **extrastriate cortex**. Working in parallel, these cortical regions process different aspects of visual perception, such as form, color, location, and movement, as we'll discuss later in this chapter. The striate cortex, as well as most extrastriate regions, contains a topographic projection of the retina, which means there's a topographic projection of the visual field, discussed next.

The retina projects to the brain in a topographic fashion

The whole area that you can see without moving your head or eyes is called your **visual field**. The retina represents a two-dimensional map of the visual field. As this information courses through the brain, the point-to-point correspondence between neighboring parts of visual space is maintained, forming a maplike projection (see Figure 7.10). Much of this **topographic projection** of visual space is devoted to the foveal region (**Figure 7.11a**) (Tootell et al., 1982). Although monkey V1 is located on the lateral surface

binocular Two-eyed.

extrastriate cortex Visual cortex outside of the primary visual (striate) cortex.

visual field The whole area that you can see without moving your head or eyes.

topographic projection A mapping that preserves the point-to-point correspondence between neighboring parts space. For example, the retina extends a topographic projection onto the cortex.

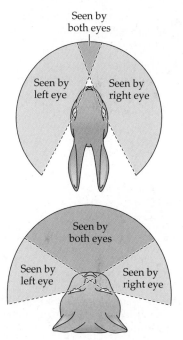

Visual Fields In general, prey species such as rabbits (*top*) have wider fields of vision and a greater proportion of retinal fibers crossing the midline than do predatory species such as cats (*bottom*). In any case, information from the left visual field reaches the right brain, and vice versa.

(a) Monkey

> A pattern of flickering lights was shown in a monkey's visual field…

> …and a map of the visual field was revealed by autoradiography in a flattened portion of the primary visual cortex.

1 cm

> The small central region of the visual field projects to a large part of primary visual cortex.

(b) Human

> Maps of human visual cortex from fMRI show primary visual cortex as the innermost yellow region in each of these medial views.

Figure 7.11 Location of the Primary Visual Cortex (Part *a* from Tootell et al., 1988; *b* from Tootell et al., 1998; both courtesy of Roger Tootell.)

of the occipital area, human V1 is located mainly on the medial surface of the cortex (**Figure 7.11b**; see also Figure 7.10). The fact that about half of the human V1 is devoted to the fovea and the retinal region just around the fovea does not mean that our spatial perception is distorted. Rather, this representation makes possible the great acuity of spatial discrimination in the central part of the visual field. In other words, another reason why our vision is so much more acute in the foveal region is that we devote proportionally more brain regions to analyzing information from that region.

Because of the orderly mapping of the visual field (known as *retinotopic mapping*) at the various levels of the visual system, damage to parts of the visual system can be diagnosed from defects in perception of the visual field. If we know the site of injury in the visual pathway, we can predict the location of such a perceptual gap, or **scotoma**, in the visual field. Although the word *scotoma* comes from the Greek *skotos*, meaning "darkness," a scotoma is not perceived as a dark patch in the visual field; rather, it is a spot where nothing can be perceived, and usually rigorous testing is required to demonstrate its existence. Like the blind spots we all have, people may not be aware of scotomas that arise.

Within a scotoma, a person cannot *consciously* perceive visual cues, but some visual discrimination in this region may still be possible; this paradoxical phenomenon has been called **blindsight**. People with blindsight say they cannot see, but when asked to *guess* whether a stimulus is present, they're correct more often than could be expected by chance alone, or they may walk down a corridor strewn with objects without running into them (de Gelder et al., 2008).

Neurons at Different Levels of the Visual System Have Very Different Receptive Fields

As we noted in Chapter 5, the **receptive field** of a sensory cell consists of the stimulus region and the features that excite or inhibit the cell. The nature of the receptive field of a cell gives us good clues about the cell's function(s) in perception. Cells in the retina or LGN can be activated by simple spots of light, but many cells in the visual cortex are more demanding and respond only to more-complicated stimuli. In this section we will see that neurons at lower levels in the visual system seem to account for some perceptual phenomena while neurons at higher levels account for others.

Photoreceptors excite some retinal neurons and inhibit others

At rest, both rod and cone photoreceptors steadily release the synaptic neurotransmitter glutamate. Light always hyperpolarizes the photoreceptors, causing them to release less glutamate. But the *response* of the bipolar cells that receive this glutamate differs, depending on the type of glutamate receptor they possess. Glutamate depolarizes one group of bipolar cells but hyperpolarizes another group. These groups differ in their receptive fields.

One group of bipolar cells consists of **on-center bipolar cells**; turning on a light in the center of an on-center bipolar cell's receptive field *excites* the cell because it receives less glutamate, which *inhibits* this type of bipolar cell (**Figure 7.12**, left). The second group consists of **off-center bipolar cells**; light hitting the center of an off-center bipolar cell's field *inhibits* it because glutamate *excites* this type of cell (**Figure 7.12**, right). It's called an off-center bipolar cell because turning *off* a light in the center of its receptive field excites it.

Bipolar cells also *release* glutamate, which always depolarizes ganglion cells. Therefore, when light is turned on, on-center bipolar cells depolarize (excite) **on-center ganglion cells**; and when light is turned off, off-center bipolar cells depolarize (excite) **off-center ganglion cells** (see Figure 7.12). The stimulated on-center and off-center ganglion cells then fire nerve impulses and report "light" or "dark" to higher visual centers.

scotoma   A region of blindness within the visual fields, caused by injury to the visual pathway or brain.

blindsight   The paradoxical phenomenon whereby, within a scotoma, a person cannot *consciously* perceive visual cues but may still be able to make some visual discrimination.

receptive field   The stimulus region and features that affect the activity of a cell in a sensory system.

on-center bipolar cell   A retinal bipolar cell that is excited by light in the center of its receptive field.

off-center bipolar cell   A retinal bipolar cell that is inhibited by light in the center of its receptive field.

on-center ganglion cell   A retinal ganglion cell that is activated when light is presented to the center, rather than the periphery, of the cell's receptive field.

off-center ganglion cell   A retinal ganglion cell that is activated when light is presented to the periphery, rather than the center, of the cell's receptive field.

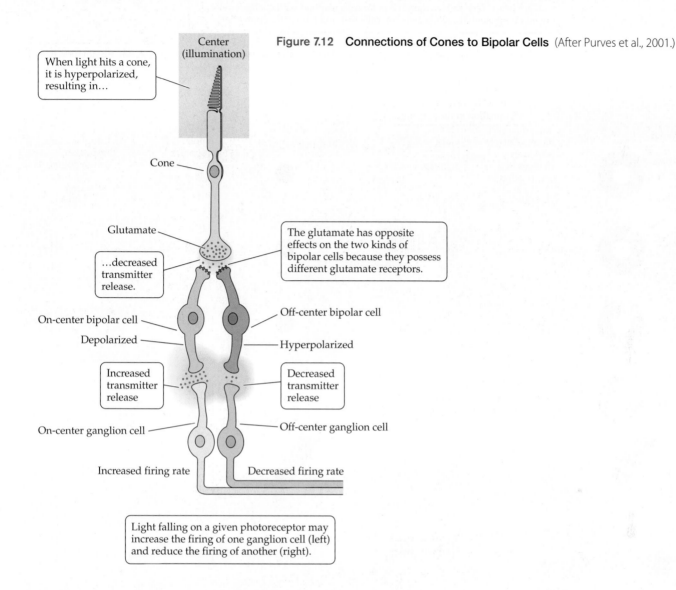

Figure 7.12   Connections of Cones to Bipolar Cells (After Purves et al., 2001.)

Center
(illumination)

When light hits a cone, it is hyperpolarized, resulting in…

Cone

Glutamate

…decreased transmitter release.

The glutamate has opposite effects on the two kinds of bipolar cells because they possess different glutamate receptors.

On-center bipolar cell

Off-center bipolar cell

Depolarized

Hyperpolarized

Increased transmitter release

Decreased transmitter release

On-center ganglion cell

Off-center ganglion cell

Increased firing rate

Decreased firing rate

Light falling on a given photoreceptor may increase the firing of one ganglion cell (left) and reduce the firing of another (right).

Neurons in the retina and the LGN have concentric receptive fields

The pattern of connections between photoreceptors and bipolar cells shapes the receptive fields of the ganglion cell. Scientists can record from single ganglion cells while moving a small spot of light across the visual field, keeping the animal's eye still. These studies show that the receptive fields of retinal ganglion cells are *concentric*, consisting of a roughly circular central area and a ring around it, which is usually called a *surround* because it surrounds the central patch. Through various retinal connections, the photoreceptors in the central area and those in the ring surrounding it tend to have opposite effects on the next cells in the circuit. Thus, both bipolar cells and ganglion cells have two basic types of retinal receptive fields: **on-center/off-surround** (**Figure 7.13a**) and **off-center/on-surround** (**Figure 7.13b**). These antagonistic effects of the center and its surround explain why uniform illumination of the visual field has little effect on ganglion cell activity, compared to a well-placed small spot of light on the cell's receptive field. Neurons in the LGN, which are stimulated by retinal ganglion cells, also have these concentric on-center/off-surround or off-center/on-surround receptive fields. In other words, on-center/off-surround LGN neurons respond best to a small spot of light on the retina, and expanding the spot to the surrounding retina reduces that response.

To understand why the effect of light falling on the surround of a firing ganglion cell is opposite to the effect of light falling in the center, we need to discuss the concept of

on-center/off-surround   Referring to a concentric receptive field in which stimulation of the center excites the cell of interest while stimulation of the surround inhibits it.

off-center/on-surround   Referring to a concentric receptive field in which stimulation of the center inhibits the cell of interest while stimulation of the surround excites it.

Each retinal bipolar cell and ganglion cell has a concentric receptive field, with antagonistic center and surround. Bipolar cells respond with changes in local membrane potentials, while ganglion cells respond with action potentials.

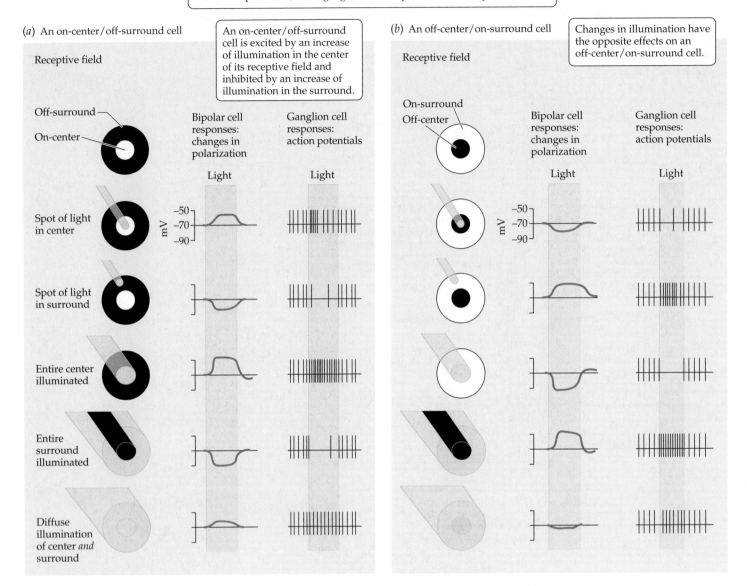

(a) An on-center/off-surround cell

An on-center/off-surround cell is excited by an increase of illumination in the center of its receptive field and inhibited by an increase of illumination in the surround.

Receptive field

Off-surround
On-center

Bipolar cell responses: changes in polarization

Ganglion cell responses: action potentials

Spot of light in center

Spot of light in surround

Entire center illuminated

Entire surround illuminated

Diffuse illumination of center *and* surround

(b) An off-center/on-surround cell

Changes in illumination have the opposite effects on an off-center/on-surround cell.

Receptive field

On-surround
Off-center

Bipolar cell responses: changes in polarization

Ganglion cell responses: action potentials

Figure 7.13   Receptive Fields of Retinal Cells

To see an animation of this figure, go to

mindsmachine.com/7.4
Receptive Fields in the Retina

. . . .

lateral inhibition   The phenomenon by which interconnected neurons inhibit their neighbors, producing contrast at the edges of regions.

lateral inhibition, in which sensory receptor cells inhibit the reporting of information from neighboring receptor cells. As illustrated in **Figure 7.14**, the bipolar cells that relay information from photoreceptors to ganglion cells also inhibit one another. Generally these connections are inhibitory synapses, so when one bipolar cell is active, it inhibits its neighbors.

Because of this lateral inhibition, the ganglion cells stimulated by the right-hand edge of each dark band in **Figure 7.15a** are inhibited by the neighboring photoreceptors stimulated by the lighter band next door. Thus, ganglion cells stimulated by the right edge of each bar report receiving less light than they actually do (that is, that edge looks darker to us). Conversely, the left edge of each bar looks lighter than the rest of the bar.

Again in **Figure 7.15b**, two indicated patches, which clearly differ in the brightness we perceive, *reflect the same amount of light*. If you use your finger to cover the edge where the two squares meet, you'll see that the two patches are the same shade of gray. How are such puzzling effects produced? Although the contrast effect in Figure 7.15a is determined, at least in part, by lateral inhibition among adjacent retinal cells, the entire areas indicated in Figure 7.15b, not just the edges, appear different, so the effect must be produced higher in the visual system. One explanation is that we are accustomed to

Figure 7.14 Lateral Inhibition in the Retina

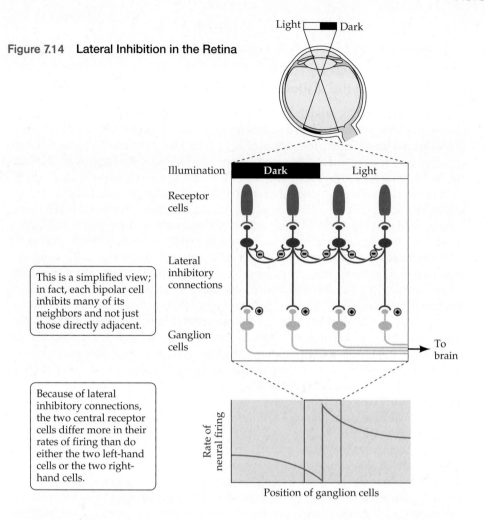

This is a simplified view; in fact, each bipolar cell inhibits many of its neighbors and not just those directly adjacent.

Because of lateral inhibitory connections, the two central receptor cells differ more in their rates of firing than do either the two left-hand cells or the two right-hand cells.

How's it going?

1. Given that *all* photoreceptors are hyperpolarized by light, how can the same photoreceptor excite some bipolar cells while inhibiting others?

2. What is a receptive field, and what two kinds of receptive fields are displayed by retinal ganglion cells?

3. Describe lateral inhibition in the retina and how it can sharpen our vision yet make us susceptible to optical illusions like that in Figure 7.15a.

light sources coming from overhead (such as the sun, or a room light), so our brain assumes that the upper patch must actually be darker than the lower patch, because the upper one should be receiving more light than the lower one.

Whether or not that particular explanation is correct, the important point is that our *visual experience is not a simple reporting of the physical properties of light.* Rather, our perception of light versus dark is created by the brain in response to many factors, including surrounding stimuli. For example, if you read this book in bright sunlight, the black ink reflects far more light to your eyes than the blank parts of the page do indoors. Yet, whether you're in sunlight or indoors, you perceive the ink as black and the blank parts as white. Later in the chapter we'll find that our experience of color is also created by the visual system, and is not a simple reporting of the wavelengths of light.

(a)

(b)

Figure 7.15 The Effect of Context on the Perception of Brightness (Part *b* from Purves and Lotto, 2011.)

Each strip is uniform, yet they all look lighter on the left edge and darker on the right edge.

Of the two indicated patches, the upper one looks darker, even though they are in fact the same shade of gray. If you don't believe this, use your finger to cover up the line where they meet. See?

RESEARCHERS AT WORK

Neurons in the visual cortex have varied receptive fields

Neurons from the LGN send their axons to cells in the primary visual cortex (V1), but the *spots* of light that are effective stimuli for LGN cells (**Figure 7.16a**; see also Figure 7.13a) are not very effective for cortical cells. In 1959, David Hubel and Torsten Wiesel reported that visual cortical cells require more-specific, elongated stimuli than those that activate LGN cells and ganglion cells. Most cells in area V1 respond best to *lines* or bars in a particular position and at a particular orientation in the visual field (**Figure 7.16b**). Some cortical cells also require *movement* of the stimulus to make them respond actively. For some of these cells, any movement in their field is sufficient; others are more demanding, requiring motion in a specific direction (**Figure 7.16c**).

Hubel and Wiesel categorized cortical cells according to the types of stimuli required to produce maximum responses. So-called **simple cortical cells** responded best to an edge or a bar that had a particular width and a particular orientation and location in the visual field. These cells were therefore sometimes called *bar detectors* or *edge detectors*. Like the simple cells, **complex cortical cells** had elongated receptive fields, but they also showed some latitude for location; that is, they responded to a bar of a particular size and orientation anywhere within a larger area of the visual field. Hubel and Wiesel's theoretical model can be described as hierarchical; that is, more-complex receptive fields are built up from inputs of simpler ones. For example, a simple cortical cell can be thought of as receiving input from a row of LGN cells (**Figure 7.17**), and a complex cortical cell can be thought of as receiving input from a row of simple cortical cells.

Other theorists extrapolated from this hierarchical model, suggesting that higher-order circuits of cells could detect any possible form. Thus it was suggested that, by integration of enough successive levels of analysis, a neuron could respond only to a person's grandmother, and such hypothetical "grandmother cells" were frequently mentioned in the literature. According to this view, whenever such a cell was excited, up would pop a mental picture of one's grandmother. This hypothesis was given as a possible explanation for facial recognition.

Critics soon pointed out both theoretical and empirical problems with the hierarchical model. For one thing, a hierarchical system like this would require a *vast* number of cells—perhaps more neurons than the cortex possesses—in order to account for all the visual objects we might encounter. Although some neurons are indeed activated by the sight of very specific faces (e.g., "Halle Berry neurons" were found, which are activated by photos of that actress) in both humans (Pedreira et al., 2010) and monkeys (Freiwald et al., 2009), these neurons do not respond to specific features of the face, as we would expect if they were built up from feature detectors. Rather, they respond only when the *whole face* or most of the face is presented (Freiwald et al., 2009).

To get around the problems of the hierarchical model, there arose an alternative model of vision, known as the **spatial-frequency model** (F. W. Campbell and Robson, 1968; R. L. DeValois and DeValois, 1988), that is not at all intuitive. This model proposes that the visual system analyzes the number of cycles of light-dark (or color) patches in any stimulus. Some cycles are narrow, others broad. Some cycles of light-dark are oriented vertically, others horizontally, and others somewhere in between. If cortical neurons are indeed optimized to detect light-dark cycles, then they should respond to repeating bars of light, as in the examples shown in **Figure 7.18**, even better than to a single bar of light. And that's precisely what researchers found.

The suggestion of multiple spatial-frequency channels had a revolutionary impact because it led to entirely different conceptions of how the visual system might work. The idea suggests that, rather than specifically detecting such seminaturalistic

simple cortical cell   Also called *bar detector* or *edge detector*. A cell in the visual cortex that responds best to an edge or a bar that has a particular width, as well as a particular orientation and location in the visual field.

complex cortical cell   A cell in the visual cortex that responds best to a bar of a particular size and orientation anywhere within a particular area of the visual field.

spatial-frequency model   A model of vision that emphasizes the analysis of different spatial frequencies, of various orientations and in various parts of the visual field, as the basis of visual perception of form.

Figure 7.16 Receptive Fields of Cells at Various Levels in the Cat Visual System

Hypothesis
Cells at higher levels of the visual system respond to progressively more complex stimuli.

Test
Compare receptive fields of neurons at each level, and see how they relate to one another.

Examples of receptive fields of brain cells:

(*a*) Lateral geniculate cell with concentric field; on-center/off-surround.

    1. Response to light in center of cell's field

    2. Response to light in periphery of cell's field

(*b*) A simple cortical cell is sensitive to orientation. This particular cell responds strongly only when the stimulus is a vertical stripe.

(*c*) A complex cortical cell is also sensitive to motion. This particular cell responds strongly only when the stimulus moves down. It responds weakly to upward motion and does not respond at all to sideways motion.

Results
(*a*) Visual cells in the LGN have concentric receptive fields.
(*b*) Visual cells in the cerebral cortex may show orientation specificity or respond only to motion, or…
(*c*) …they may respond only to motion in a particular direction.

Conclusion
Neurons at each level of the visual system combine input from neurons at lower levels to make progressively more complex receptive fields. Thus, retinal and LGN neurons respond best to spots of light on the retina, while cortical cells respond best to lines of particular orientation, or lines that move in a particular direction.

(a)

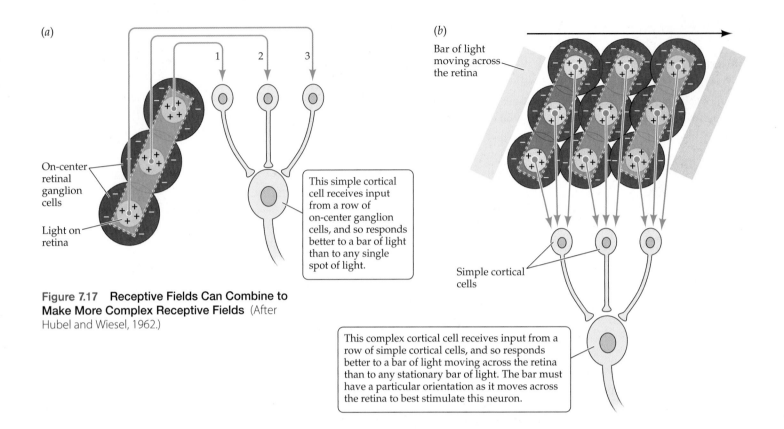

On-center retinal ganglion cells

Light on retina

This simple cortical cell receives input from a row of on-center ganglion cells, and so responds better to a bar of light than to any single spot of light.

Figure 7.17 Receptive Fields Can Combine to Make More Complex Receptive Fields (After Hubel and Wiesel, 1962.)

(b)

Bar of light moving across the retina

Simple cortical cells

This complex cortical cell receives input from a row of simple cortical cells, and so responds better to a bar of light moving across the retina than to any stationary bar of light. The bar must have a particular orientation as it moves across the retina to best stimulate this neuron.

features as bars and edges, the system is breaking down complex stimuli into their individual spatial-frequency components (R. L. DeValois and DeValois, 1988, p. 320). In such a system, we might require a view of the whole face, which includes the low-frequency components, for recognition. This could explain why "Halle Berry neurons" do not respond to small portions of a face, because such snippets contain only high-frequency components. The spatial-frequency approach has proven useful in the analysis of many aspects of human pattern vision (K. K. DeValois et al., 1979), and it provides the basis of high-definition television (HDTV). If you would like to know more about how the spatial-frequency model works, see **A Step Further 7.4**, on the website.

To see an animation, go to

mindsmachine.com/7.5
Spatial Frequencies

Cortical cells respond even better to these repeating patterns of light than to single bars of light.

Figure 7.18 Examples of Spatial Frequencies in Vision The brain combines information about all these spatial frequencies to give us our perception of the scene.

Each cortical cell fires best to such patterns in a particular orientation—vertical…

…horizontal…

…or somewhere in between— with a particular frequency (narrow or wide bars), and in a particular part of the visual field.

(a) Macaque brain, lateral view

Macaque visual areas in occipital and temporal cortex are shown in pink.

(b) Macaque brain, medial view

(c) Visual areas

All the known visual areas in the macaque are indicated in color here on a flattened cortex.

Dorsal prefrontal — Cingulate

Frontal eye fields

Motor

V2

V1

Lateral prefrontal

Somatosensory

Orbito-frontal

Olfactory

Auditory

V3

Medial temporal (V5)

V4

V1

Inferior temporal

V2

V1

Lateral geniculate

Pulvinar

Eyeball

Superior colliculus

Optic nerve

Retina

(d)

The occipital regions of human brain shown in Figure 7.11b were "flattened" virtually, to reveal that V1 is larger than secondary visual cortex regions (V2, V3, etc.).

V3A

V3

V2

Representation of the center of the fovea

V1 ✱

V2

VP

V4V

Figure 7.19   Main Visual Areas in Monkey and Human Brains (Parts *a–c* after Van Essen and Drury, 1997; *d* from Tootell et al., 1998, courtesy of Roger Tootell.)

Neurons in the visual cortex beyond area V1 have complex receptive fields and help identify forms

Area V1 represents only a small fraction of the total amount of cortex that is devoted to vision. From area V1, axons extend to cortical areas involved in the perception of form: V2, V4, and the inferior temporal area (**Figure 7.19a–c**). The receptive fields of the cells in many of these extrastriate visual areas are even more complex than those of area V1.

The visual areas of the human brain (**Figure 7.19d**) have been less thoroughly mapped than those of the monkey brain, and mainly by neuroimaging (the spatial resolution of which is not as fine as that of the electrophysiological recording used in the monkey brain), but the general layout appears similar in the two species, especially for V1 (Tootell et al., 2003).

An astonishing proportion of primate cortex analyzes visual information. The areas that are largely or entirely visual in function occupy about 55% of the surface of the macaque cortex (Van Essen and Drury, 1997), and about 30% of human cortex (Tootell et al., 2003). We will discuss only a few of the main visual cortical areas and their functions.

Area V2 is adjacent to V1, and many of its cells have receptive fields similar to those of V1 cells. Many V2 cells can respond to illusory contours, such as the boundaries of the upright triangle in **Figure 7.20** (Peterhans and von der Heydt, 1989). Clearly, such cells respond to complex relations among the parts of their receptive fields.

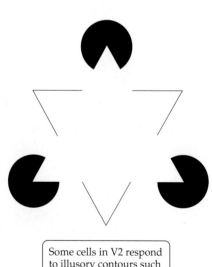

Some cells in V2 respond to illusory contours such as those of the upright triangle shown here.

Figure 7.20   A Geometric Figure with "Illusory" or "Subjective" Contours

(a)

(b)

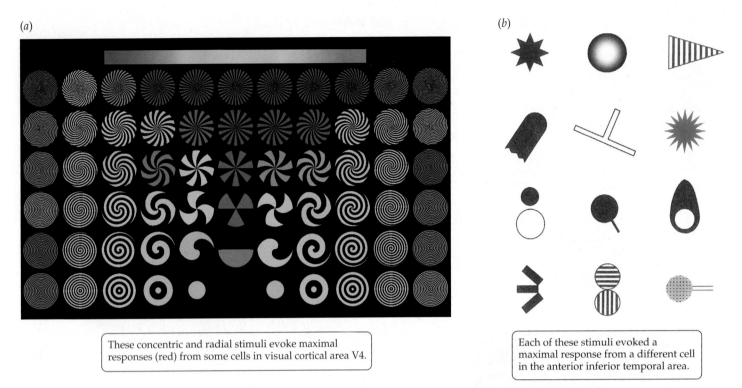

These concentric and radial stimuli evoke maximal responses (red) from some cells in visual cortical area V4.

Each of these stimuli evoked a maximal response from a different cell in the anterior inferior temporal area.

Figure 7.21 Complex Stimuli Evoke Strong Responses in Visual Cortex
(Part *a* from Gallant et al., 1993, courtesy of Jack Gallant; *b* from Tanaka, 1993, courtesy of Keiji Tanaka.)

Area V4 cells give their strongest responses to the frequency gratings that we discussed earlier (see Figure 7.18). However, many V4 cells give even stronger responses to concentric and radial stimuli, such as those in **Figure 7.21a** (Gallant et al., 1993). Area V4 also has many cells that respond most strongly to color differences, as we will see later, when we discuss color vision.

The inferior temporal (IT) visual cortex has many cells that respond best to particular complex forms, sometimes combined with color or texture, such as those in **Figure 7.21b**. The complex receptive fields in IT cortex probably develop through experience and learning (Desimone et al., 1984). After a monkey was trained for a year to discriminate a set of 28 moderately complex shapes, 39% of the cells in its anterior IT cortex responded significantly to some of these shapes. In control monkeys, on the other hand, only 9% of the cells responded strongly to these forms (Kobatake and Tanaka, 1994).

The prefrontal cortex also contains a restricted region of neurons that are activated by faces but not by other visual stimuli (Scalaidhe et al., 1997; Ungerleider et al., 1998). These findings indicate that a pathway mediating visual recognition extends from V1 through temporal cortex to the prefrontal cortex. Later we'll see that this pathway was damaged in D.F., the woman described at the start of the chapter.

Perception of visual motion is analyzed by a special system that includes cortical area V5

In area V5 (also called the *medial temporal area* or *MT*; see Figure 7.19c) of monkeys, all neurons respond to moving visual stimuli, indicating that they are specialized for the perception of motion and its direction. Imaging studies show that moving stimuli also evoke responses in human area V5.

Experimental lesions of area V5 in monkeys trained to report the direction of perceived motion impaired their performance, at least temporarily (Newsome et al., 1985). Conversely, electrically *stimulating* an area of V5 that normally responds to stimuli moving up in other monkeys caused them to report that dots on the screen were moving up even when they were actually moving to the right. In other words, the electrical stimulation appeared to alter the monkey's *experience* of the motion.

One striking report described a woman who had lost the ability to perceive motion after a stroke damaged her area V5 (Zihl et al., 1983). The woman was unable to perceive continuous motion and saw only separate, successive static images. This impairment led to many problems in her daily life. She had difficulty crossing streets because she could not follow the positions of automobiles in motion: "When I'm looking at the car at first, it seems far away. But then when I want to cross the road, suddenly the car is very near." She also complained of difficulties in following conversations because she could not see the movements of speakers' lips. Except for her inability to perceive motion, this woman's visual perception appeared normal.

Color Vision Depends on Special Channels from the Retinal Cones through Cortical Area V4

For most people, color is a striking aspect of vision. We will discuss four stages of color perception. In the first stage the cones—the retinal receptor cells that are specialized to respond to certain wavelengths of light—receive visual information. In the second stage this information is processed by neurons in the local circuits of the retina, leading to retinal ganglion cells that are excited by light of some wavelengths and inhibited by light of other wavelengths. The ganglion cells send the wavelength information via their axons to the LGN. From there this information goes to area V1, which relays it to other visual cortical areas, where the third and fourth stages of color perception take place.

Color is created by the visual system

For most of us, the visible world has several distinguishable hues: blue, green, yellow, red, and their intermediates. These hues appear different because every light particle, or photon, vibrates as it travels across space, behaving like a sinusoidal wave. Photons vary in the frequency of vibration and therefore the **wavelength** (the distance between two adjacent peaks of the wave) of the light, and we can detect some of these differences, perceiving faster-vibrating (thus shorter-wavelength) photons as blue and green, and slower-vibrating (longer-wavelength) photons as more orange and red. The human visual system responds only to particles whose wavelengths lie within a very narrow section of the total electromagnetic range, from about 400 to 700 nanometers, as **Figure 7.22** shows. If particles have shorter or longer wavelengths than this narrow range, we no longer call them photons, but give them names like X-rays or radio waves. The color of an object depends on which wavelengths of light are absorbed

How's it going?

1. How could information from LGN neurons with simple concentric receptive fields be combined in a cortical cell such that it now responds best to a line of light?
2. How could information from simple cortical cells be combined in another cortical cell so that it now responds best to a moving line of light?
3. Describe the spatial-frequency hypothesis of vision.
4. What are some examples of visual receptive fields outside of V1 that respond to very complex stimuli?
5. What kind of stimuli affect the firing of neurons in V5 (also known as area MT)?

wavelength The length between two peaks in a repeated stimulus such as a wave, light, or sound.

Only a narrow range of the entire electromagnetic spectrum is visible, and we refer to particles in that range as photons or light particles.

Figure 7.22 **The Wavelengths of Light**

Sunlight consists of photons of all wavelengths.

S M L

This patch looks "blue" because it absorbs/subtracts most of the long wavelengths and some of the medium wavelengths. The short- and medium-wavelength light that is reflected to the eye appears blue.

Figure 7.23   Colored Objects Reflect Different Wavelengths of Light

S M L

This patch looks "yellow" because it reflects best in the middle range of wavelengths and absorbs the other wavelengths.

S M L

Mix the two pigments together, and what you have left when each has absorbed its wavelengths are some remaining medium wavelengths that look "green."

versus which wavelengths are reflected. Our eyes detect these reflected wavelengths to distinguish different colors (**Figure 7.23**).

The color solid shown in **Figure 7.24** illustrates the basic dimensions of our perception of light; the figure is deliberately asymmetrical, for reasons we will explain. The three dimensions of color perception are

1. **Brightness**, which varies from dark to light. It is represented by the vertical dimension in Figure 7.24a, and planes are shown intersecting the figure at different levels of brightness. The planes are tipped up for yellow and down for blue because yellow is perceived as lighter and blue as darker than the other hues.

2. **Hue**, which varies continuously around the color circle through blue, green, yellow, orange, and red. (Hue is what most people mean when they use the term *color*.)

3. **Saturation**, which varies from rich, full colors at the periphery of the color solid to gray at the center. For example, starting with red at the periphery, the colors become paler toward the center, going through pink to gray. Yellow is shown closer to the central axis than the other saturated hues because yellow is perceived as less saturated than the other hues.

It is important to understand that the perception of a particular hue is *not* a simple function of the wavelength of light. For example, a patch reflecting light of a particular wavelength is perceived as various different hues, depending on several factors, including the intensity of illumination, prior exposure to a different stimulus, or the surrounding field.

As illumination fades, the blues in a painting or a rug appear more prominent and the reds appear duller, even though the wavelength distribution in the light reflecting off those objects has not changed. In addition, the hue perceived at a particular point is strongly affected by the pattern of wavelengths and intensities in other parts of the visual field, as **Figure 7.24b** illustrates. To understand how the visual system creates our experience of color, we must understand how cone photoreceptors work.

Color perception requires receptor cells that differ in their sensitivities to different wavelengths

Artists have long known that all the hues can be obtained from a small number of primary colors. On the basis of observations of mixing pigments and lights, scientists at the start of the nineteenth century hypothesized that three separate kinds of receptors in the retina provide the basis for color vision. Endorsed in 1852 by the great physiologist-physicist-psychologist Hermann von Helmholtz, this **trichromatic hypothesis** (from the Greek *tri-*, "three," and *chroma*, "color") became the dominant position.

Helmholtz predicted that blue-sensitive, green-sensitive, and red-sensitive receptors would be found, that each would be sharply tuned to its part of the spectrum, and

brightness   One of three basic dimensions of light perception, varying from dark to light.

hue   One of three basic dimensions of light perception, varying around the color circle through blue, green, yellow, orange, and red.

saturation   One of three basic dimensions of light perception, varying from rich to pale.

trichromatic hypothesis   A hypothesis of color perception stating that there are three different types of cones, each excited by a different region of the spectrum and each having a separate pathway to the brain.

(a)

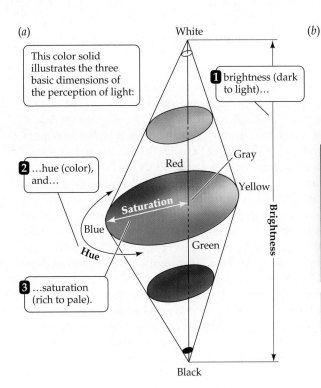

White

This color solid illustrates the three basic dimensions of the perception of light:

1 brightness (dark to light)…

2 …hue (color), and…

3 …saturation (rich to pale).

Red

Gray

Saturation

Yellow

Blue

Green

Hue

Brightness

Black

(b)

Color perception is *not* a simple function of the wavelength of light reaching the eye. The dotted squares in the center of each grid reflect the *same wavelength of light*, yet most of us perceive one as green and the other as yellow.

Color perception is affected by inferences about the color of light shining on an object. As the object on the right seems to be bathed in blue light, our visual system infers that the dotted square must actually be yellow, and so we perceive it as yellow.

Figure 7.24 Color Perception (Part *b* from Purves and Lotto, 2011.)

that each type would have a separate path to the brain. The color of an object would be recognized, then, on the basis of which color receptor(s) were activated. This system would be like the mechanisms for discriminating touch and temperature on the basis of which skin receptors and labeled neural lines are activated (see Chapter 5).

Later in the nineteenth century, physiologist Ewald Hering proposed a different explanation. He argued, on the basis of visual experience, that there are four unique hues (blue, green, yellow, red) and three *opposed pairs of colors*—blue versus yellow, green versus red, and black versus white—and that three physiological processes with opposed positive and negative values must therefore be the basis of color vision. As we will see, both this **opponent-process hypothesis** and the trichromatic hypothesis are encompassed in current color vision theory, but neither of the old hypotheses is sufficient by itself.

Measurements of photopigments in cones have borne out the trichromatic hypothesis in part. Each cone of the human retina has one of three classes of pigments (each pigment has a name, but we'll just refer to them as *opsins*). The response of the cone depends on which wavelength of light its pigment absorbs to start the process depicted in Figure 7.4. These pigments do not, however, have the narrow spectral distributions that Helmholtz predicted.

Despite what you may have heard in other classes (or even read in other textbooks!), the human visual system does *not* have receptors that are sensitive to only a narrow part of the visible spectrum, such as "red" cones and "green" cones; instead, the receptor pigments exhibit broad sensitivity that substantially overlaps between the different receptor types. In fact, two of the three retinal cone pigments show some response to light of almost *any* wavelength. The pigments have different *peaks* of sensitivity, but even the peaks are not as far apart as Helmholtz predicted, and those peaks don't always correspond to a particular color. As **Figure 7.25** shows, the cone pigment peaks occur at about 420 nanometers, abbreviated nm (in the part of the spectrum where we usually see violet under daylight conditions), about 530 nm (where most of us see green), and about 560 nm (where most of us see yellow-green). Despite Helmholtz's prediction, *none* of the curves peak in the long-wavelength part of the spectrum, where most of us see red (about 630 nm).

Color Varies with Light If you really want to know what color that paint will look like in your room, take the sample home and view it there.

opponent-process hypothesis A hypothesis of color perception stating that different systems produce opposite responses to light of different wavelengths.

Each pigment has a peak sensitivity but responds to a wide range of wavelengths.

S, short-wavelength
M, medium-wavelength
L, Long-wavelength

Knowing only that an M cone is active, you cannot tell whether it was stimulated by weak light at 530 nm ("green"), or by strong light anywhere from 450 nm ("blue") to 620 nm ("red"). Only by *comparing* responses of *different* cones can the brain extract color information.

Figure 7.25 Spectral Sensitivities of Human Photopigments

Under ordinary conditions, almost any object, no matter what color it is, stimulates at least two kinds of cones, thus ensuring high visual acuity and good perception of form. It is the subsequent processing performed by the nervous system, comparing the *degree* of activation across receptors that differ in peak wavelength sensitivity, that extracts color information about the light falling on the retina. Thus, certain ganglion cells and certain neurons at higher stations in the visual system are color-specific, even though the receptor cells are not. In a similar manner, photoreceptors are not form-specific (they respond to single points of light), but form is detected later in the system, by comparison of the outputs of different receptors.

Because the cones are not color detectors, the most appropriate brief names for them can be taken from their peak areas of wavelength sensitivity: *short* (S) for the receptor with peak sensitivity at about 420 nm, *medium* (M) for 530 nm, and *long* (L) for 560 nm (see Figure 7.25). There are typically twice as many L as M receptors, but far fewer S receptors (Brainard et al., 2000; Carroll et al., 2000; Hagstrom et al., 1998); this difference explains why acuity is much lower with short-wavelength illumination (blue light) than in the other parts of the visible spectrum. In some insects, including bees, the short-wavelength receptors respond to ultraviolet wavelengths that we humans cannot see. This ability permits bees to see color patterns in flowers that are invisible to us (**Figure 7.26**). Most birds have not three but four different types of cones, and they can also detect ultraviolet light (Osorio and Vorobyev, 2008). Likewise, even those mammalian species with weak color vision can discriminate some colors, as we discuss in **Box 7.1**.

The genes for wavelength-sensitive pigments in the retina have been analyzed, and the similarities in structure of the three genes suggest that they are all derived from a common ancestral gene (Nathans, 1987). In addition, the genes for the medium- and long-wavelength pigments occupy adjacent positions on the X chromosome and are much more similar to each other than either is to the gene for the short-wavelength pigment on chromosome 7. Probably our primate ancestors had only one photopigment gene on the X chromosome, which became duplicated. Then mutations caused the two genes to become more and more different, until their responses to various wavelengths of light were no longer the same. Thus, our ancestors went from having only two cone pigments (one on the X chromosome and the S pigment on chromosome 7) to three, with an associated improvement in color vision.

Certain evidence suggests that this evolution of a third photopigment may have happened recently (in evolutionary terms); for example, most South American monkeys have only a single longer-wavelength pigment. The fact that the genes for the M

Figure 7.26 How Flowers Look to the Birds and the Bees

When we humans look at flowers, we cannot see the reflected ultraviolet light…

…which may reveal patterns visible only to animals, like birds and bees, that detect light in that range.

and L pigments are on the X chromosome also explains why defects of red-green color vision are much more frequent in human males (about 8%) than in human females (about 0.5%). Because males have only one X chromosome, a mutation in the genes for the M or L pigments can impair color vision. But if a female has a defective phot-opigment gene in one of her two X chromosomes, a normal copy of the gene on the

BOX 7.1 Most Mammalian Species Have Some Color Vision

Animals exhibit different degrees of color vision. Many species of birds, fishes, and insects have excellent color vision. Humans and Old World monkeys also have an excellent ability to discriminate wavelengths, but many other mammals (e.g., cats) cannot discriminate wavelengths very well. Still, most mammals have at least some degree of color vision (G. H. Jacobs, 1993). Although only certain primates have good *tri*chromatic color vision (vision based on *three* classes of cone photopigments), most mammalian species have at least *di*chromatic color vision (based on *two* classes of cone pigments). Most so-called color-blind humans (actually color-*deficient* humans) have dichromatic vision and can distinguish short-wavelength

stimuli (blue) from long-wavelength stim-uli (not blue). When a gene carrying a third photopigment was introduced into photore-ceptors of adult male squirrel monkeys with such dichromatic vision, they soon displayed excellent trichromatic vision (Mancuso et al., 2009). Likewise, introducing photopigment genes in mice enabled them to discriminate colors they normally cannot see (G. H. Jacobs et al., 2007), so it may be possible to correct dichromatic vision in humans.

There is a continuum of color vision capabilities, including at least four categories among mammalian species:

1. Excellent trichromatic color vision is found in diurnal primates such as humans and the rhesus monkey.

2. Robust dichromatic color vision is found in species that have two kinds of cone photopigments and a reasonably large population of cones. Examples of such species include the dog, the pig, and many male South American monkeys, such as the squirrel monkey and the mar-moset monkey.

3. Feeble dichromatic color vision occurs in species that have two kinds of cone pigments but very few cones. Examples include the domestic cat and the coati.

4. Minimal color vision is possessed by species that have only a single kind of cone pigment and that must rely on interactions between rods and cones to discriminate wavelength.

(Continued on next page)

(A)

(B)

Simulating Color Blindness (A) The photograph on the right has been adjusted to simulate the experience of the most common form of color blindness in humans, which is the absence of cones sensitive to medium-wavelength light (M cones). For such individuals, the world's colors consist of blue (detected by short-wavelength photopigment encoded on the seventh chromosome) and not blue (detected by the long-wavelength photopigment encoded on the X chromosome). (B) In a typical test for color vision, dichromats may have a difficult time detecting the numerals displayed in figures like this. (A [right] was produced by software available from Vischeck [www.vischeck.com]).

BOX 7.1   *(continued)*

Examples include the owl monkey and the raccoon. When you compare diurnal and nocturnal species of a given taxonomic family (e.g., the coati and the raccoon), the diurnal species (in this case the coati) usually has the better color vision.

Among those species of South American monkeys that are generally dichromats, some females are actually trichromatic. Why? Because the gene encoding one photopigment is on the X chromosome. Since females have two X chromosomes, if the two chromosomes carry *different* genes for the photopigment, the female will possess a total of three different kinds of cones, and will therefore have trichromatic vision.

Unlike South American monkeys that carry a single gene on the X for photopigment, many other primates, like humans, have two photopigment genes on the X chromosome: one for medium- and one for long-wavelength cones. The short-wavelength photopigment gene is on an autosome rather than on the X. Women are less likely than men to have color deficiency because if one of their X chromosomes has a defective gene for a photopigment, the copy on the other X is likely to be fine. Because men have only one X, if they have a defective copy of the gene for the medium- or long-wavelength pigment, there's no backup copy to compensate. They will see blue (light

stimulating the short-wavelength cones) and not blue (light stimulating the other functioning cones), as the figure illustrates.

Interestingly, a woman may carry slightly different genes for the long-wavelength photopigment on her two X chromosomes (Neitz et al., 1998), and therefore have *four* different kinds of cones. Such so-called *tetrachromats* tend to be very good at discriminating colors and very sensitive to clashing colors. It's interesting to speculate whether such women have a different experience of, for example, green, than those of us who are trichromats and dichromats. We will take up the question of our subjective experience of color again in Chapter 14.

other X chromosome can compensate. Even though the term *color blindness* is commonly used, most people with impaired color vision are able to distinguish some hues. Complete color blindness can be caused by brain lesions or by the congenital absence of *any* cones, but in humans it is extremely rare.

Some retinal ganglion cells and LGN cells show spectral opponency

Recordings made from retinal ganglion cells in monkeys that can discriminate colors as humans do reveal the second stage in the processing of color vision. Most ganglion cells and LGN cells are excited and fire in response to some wavelengths and are inhibited by other wavelengths.

Figure 7.27a shows the response of an LGN cell as a large spot of light centered on its receptive field changes from one wavelength to another. Firing is stimulated by wavelengths above 600 nm, where the L cones are most sensitive; and then inhibited at shorter wavelengths, where the L cones are less sensitive than the M cones. A cell exhibiting this response pattern is therefore called a *plus L/minus M cell* (+L/–M). This is an example of a **spectrally opponent cell** (or *color-opponent cell*) because two regions of the spectrum have opposite effects on the cell's rate of firing. Figure 7.27 shows the responses of the four main kinds of spectrally opponent cells.

Each spectrally opponent ganglion cell receives input from two or three different kinds of cones through bipolar cells. The connections from at least one type of cone are excitatory, and those from at least one other type are inhibitory. The spectrally opponent ganglion cells thus record the *difference* in stimulation of different types of cones. For example, a +M/–L cell responds to the difference in the excitation of M and L cones.

The peaks of the sensitivity curves of the M and L cones are not very different (see Figure 7.25). However, whereas the M-minus-L *difference* curve (**Figure 7.27b**) shows a clear peak at about 500 nm (in the green part of the spectrum), the L-minus-M difference function (see Figure 7.27a) shows a peak at about 650 nm (in the red part of the spectrum). Thus, +M/–L and +L/–M cells yield distinctly different neural response curves. LGN cells that are excited by the L and M cells, but inhibited by S cells—that is, +(L+M)/–S cells—peak in the red range (**Figure 7.27c**); while cells excited by S but inhibited by L and M—that is, +S/–(L+M) cells—peak in the blue-violet range (**Figure 7.27d**).

Spectrally opponent neurons are the second stage in the system for color perception, but they still cannot be called *color cells*, because (1) they send their outputs into

spectrally opponent cell   A visual receptor cell that has opposite firing responses to different regions of the spectrum.

Spectral Opponency If you stare at the central dot in this image for 30 seconds or so and then look at a blank page, you'll see a colorful picture. In that afterimage, the colors you perceive are the opposite of those in the figure. The colors are reversed because staring at the image fatigues some cones, causing the brain, comparing input from different cones, to perceive the opponent color in that part of the visual field.

many higher circuits—for detection of form, depth, and movement, as well as hue; and (2) their peak wavelength sensitivities do not correspond precisely to the wavelengths that we see as the principal hues. **Figure 7.28** diagrams the presumed inputs to not only the four kinds of spectrally opponent ganglion cells, but also the ganglion cells that detect brightness and darkness. The brightness detectors receive stimulation from both M and L cones (+M/+L); the darkness detectors are inhibited by those same cones (–M/–L).

In the monkey LGN, 70–80% of the cells are spectrally opponent; in the cat, very few spectrally opponent cells are found—only about 1%. This difference explains why monkeys so easily distinguish between colors and it's so difficult to train cats to discriminate even large differences in color.

Some visual cortical cells and regions appear to be specialized for color perception

In the cortex, spectral information appears to be used for various kinds of information processing. Forms are segregated from their background by differences in color or intensity (or both). The most important role that color plays in our perception is to denote which parts of a complex image belong to one object and

Figure 7.27 Responses by the Four Main Types of Spectrally Opponent Cells in Monkey LGN

The four main types of spectrally opponent cells are:

(*a*) +L/–M

1 +L/–M peaks in the red range…

(*b*) +M/–L

2 +M/–L peaks in the green range…

(*c*) +(L+M)/–S

3 +(L+M)/–S peaks in the red range…

(*d*) +S/–(L+M)

4 …and +S/–(L+M) peaks in the blue-violet range.

Wavelength (nm)

Each type is excited by one band of wavelengths and inhibited by another.

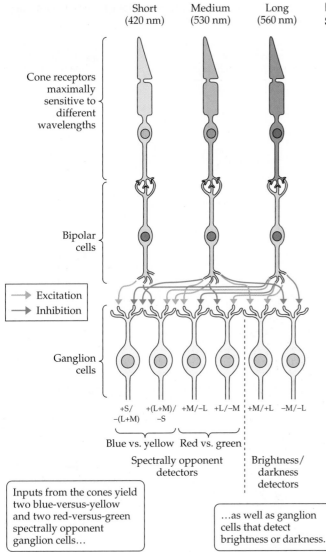

Short (420 nm)   Medium (530 nm)   Long (560 nm)

Cone receptors maximally sensitive to different wavelengths

Bipolar cells

→ Excitation
→ Inhibition

Ganglion cells

+S/ –(L+M)   +(L+M)/ –S   +M/–L   +L/–M   +M/+L   –M/–L

Blue vs. yellow   Red vs. green

Spectrally opponent detectors

Brightness/ darkness detectors

Inputs from the cones yield two blue-versus-yellow and two red-versus-green spectrally opponent ganglion cells…

…as well as ganglion cells that detect brightness or darkness.

Figure 7.28   A Model of the Connections of Wavelength Discrimination Systems in the Primate Retina (After R. L. De Valois and De Valois, 1980.)

which belong to another. Some animals use displays of brightly colored body parts to call attention to themselves, but color can also be used as camouflage.

Some spectrally opponent cortical cells contribute to the perception of color, providing the third stage of the color vision system. These cells are not just responding to the differences between two types of cones, as retinal ganglion cells and LGN cells do. Rather, they are responding to differences in colors that we *perceive*; in other words, they are perceptually opponent: red versus green, blue versus yellow, and black versus white (R. L. De Valois and De Valois, 1993). The spectral responses of these cells correspond to the wavelengths of the principal hues specified by human observers, and their characteristics also help explain other color phenomena.

Visual cortical region V4 is particularly rich in color-sensitive cells; each of these cells truly responds best to a particular hue, including the four that Hering postulated (blue, green, yellow, red). V4 cells respond best if the color outside the receptive field is different from the color preferred inside the receptive field (Schein and Desimone, 1990). These cells provide a fourth stage of color perception that may be important for color constancy and for discrimination between a figure and background (Zeki et al., 1991). It would probably be wrong, however, to think of area V4 as devoted *exclusively* to color perception, because cells there are also tuned for orientation of the stimuli (Desimone and Schein, 1987).

The Many Cortical Visual Areas Are Organized into Two Major Streams

Many investigators have wondered why primate visual systems contain so many distinct regions. Certain regions specialize in processing different attributes of visual experience (such as shape, location, color, motion, and orientation). But there are more than 30 cortical areas analyzing vision, which is larger than the number of basic attributes we can identify. Perhaps the reason so many separate visual regions have been found is simply that investigators, being visually oriented primates themselves, have lavished special attention on the visual system.

Mortimer Mishkin and Leslie Ungerleider (1982) proposed that primates have two main cortical processing streams, both originating in primary visual cortex: a ventral processing stream responsible for visually *identifying* objects, and a dorsal stream responsible for appreciating the spatial *location* of objects and for visually guiding our movement toward them (**Figure 7.29**). They called these processing streams, respectively, the *what* and *where* streams.

PET studies, as well as brain lesions in patients, indicate that the human brain possesses *what* and *where* visual

How's it going?

1. What two main hypotheses were developed to explain our ability to discriminate colors? Which aspects of the visual system appear to match each hypothesis?

2. Describe some examples in which our perception of color is not simply the detection of particular wavelengths of light.

3. Why do we label cones as S cones, M cones, and L cones rather than blue, green, and red cones?

4. Why are men more likely than women to have difficulty distinguishing some colors?

Dorsal stream: vision for movement, location

Right

The ventral (*what*) pathway, shown in yellow and red, and the dorsal (*where*) pathway, shown in green and blue, serve different functions.

Occipital lobe

Ventral stream: vision for recognition (objects, faces)

Frontal lobe

Figure 7.29 Parallel Processing Pathways in the Visual System (Courtesy of Leslie Ungerleider.)

processing streams similar to those that have been found in monkeys (Ungerleider et al., 1998). The two streams are not completely separate, because there are normally many cross-connections between them. In the ventral stream, including regions of the occipitotemporal, inferior temporal, and inferior frontal areas, information about faces becomes more specific as one proceeds farther forward. PET studies show that, whereas general information about facial features and gender is extracted more posteriorly, the more anterior parts of the stream provide representations of individual faces (Courtney et al., 1996).

Discovery of these separate visual cortical streams helps us understand the case of patient D.F., described at the start of this chapter. Recall that, after carbon monoxide poisoning, D.F. lost the ability to perceive faces and objects while retaining the ability to reach and grasp those same objects under visual control. The investigators who studied her (A. D. Milner et al., 1991) hypothesized that D.F.'s visual ventral (*what*) stream had been devastated but that her dorsal (*where*) stream was unimpaired. An opposite kind of dissociation had already been reported: damage to the dorsal parietal cortex often results in **optic ataxia**, in which patients have difficulty using vision to reach for and grasp objects, yet some of these patients can still identify objects correctly (Perenin and Vighetto, 1988).

Studies of D.F. support the idea that her ventral stream is impaired but her dorsal stream remains relatively normal (T. W. James et al., 2003). High-resolution MRI of her brain (**Figure 7.30a**) reveals diffuse damage concentrated in the ventrolateral occipital cortex. Throughout the brain there is evidence of atrophy, indicated by shrunken gyri and enlarged sulci. **Figure 7.30b** shows the area activated in fMRI recordings when normal subjects viewed pictures of objects; it corresponds to D.F.'s lateral occipital lesion. When D.F. reached for and grasped objects, her fMRI activation in the parietal lobe was similar to that of normal subjects, indicating that her dorsal stream is largely intact. D.F.'s intact dorsal pathway not only tells her where objects are but also guides her movements to use these objects properly.

It is still puzzling that one part of D.F. knows exactly how to grasp a pencil held in front of her, yet another part of her—the part that talks to you—has no idea whether the object she's holding is a pencil, a ruler, or a bouquet of flowers. This condition is reminiscent of the cortical damage that causes *blindsight*, mentioned earlier: people with such damage report being unable to see, but they show evidence that they can. In later chapters we'll learn about other people who can see only one thing at a time, or who can see faces but cannot recognize anyone. Imagining what such disjointed visual experience must be like helps us appreciate how effortlessly our brains usually bind together information with our marvelous sense of sight.

optic ataxia Spatial disorientation in which the patient is unable to accurately reach for objects using visual guidance.

(a) Lesions in subject D.F.

The brain region that was damaged in patient D.F. is seen from lateral views…

…and from below (outlined in orange).

(b) Areas activated in control subjects while visually identifying objects

This same brain region is activated (yellow) when control subjects look at intact pictures of various objects rather than at scrambled pictures.

D.F.'s inability to recognize the objects she sees appears to be due to damage in this region on the border of the occipital and temporal cortex.

Figure 7.30   Object Recognition Centers in the Brain (From T. W. James et al., 2003; courtesy Thomas James.)

Visual Neuroscience Can Be Applied to Alleviate Some Visual Deficiencies

Vision is so important that many investigators have sought ways to prevent its impairment, to improve inadequate vision, and to restore sight to the blind. In the United States, half a million people are blind. Recent medical advances have reduced some causes of blindness but have increased blindness from other causes. For example, medical advances permit people with diabetes to live longer, but because we don't know how to prevent blindness associated with diabetes, there are more people alive today with diabetes-induced blindness. In the discussion that follows, we will first consider ways of avoiding the impairment of vision. Then we will take up ways of improving an impaired visual system.

Impairment of vision often can be prevented or reduced

Studies of the development of vision show that the incidence of myopia (nearsightedness) can be reduced. Myopia develops if the eyeball is too long, causing the eye to focus images in front of the retina rather than on the retina (see Figure 7.2). As a result, distant objects appear blurred. Considerable evidence suggests that the reason some children develop myopia is that certain environmental factors cause the eyeball to grow excessively. Previously it was thought that the modern habit of looking closely at nearby objects (books, computer screens, and so on) might be responsible for myopia (Marzani and Wallman, 1997), but mounting evidence suggests that indoor lighting may be to blame.

Before civilization, most people spent the bulk of their time outdoors, looking at objects illuminated by sunlight. But with the advent of indoor lighting, we've come to spend a lot of time looking at things with light that, while containing many wavelengths, does not exactly match the composition of sunlight. Several studies have found that children with myopia spend less time outdoors than do other children, but that correlation could be caused by genes that favor both myopia and indoor activities, like reading. Indeed, the advent of public schools in various nations is accompanied by increased rates of myopia. However, one of these studies focused on people of Chinese origin who lived in either Singapore, where crowded conditions mean that people spend little time outdoors, or Sydney, Australia. Even though these populations should be genetically very similar, 30% of the Chinese children living in Singapore, who average only 30 minutes a day outdoors, were myopic, versus only 3% of those living in Sydney, who average 2 hours a day outdoors (Rose et al., 2008). What's more, in these populations myopia correlates much more strongly with time spent indoors than with time spent reading.

Of course, too much sunlight can be a bad thing, especially for our skin. But the researchers note that almost all children in Australia wear hats to shield their faces when outdoors, yet they still benefit from being outdoors in terms of avoiding myopia. Likewise, there's no evidence that wearing glasses blocks the benefit of light from the sun. The next challenge will be determining what it is about indoor lighting, as opposed to sunlight, that encourages the eyeball in children to grow excessively, leading to myopia.

Increased exercise can restore function to a previously deprived or neglected eye

The misalignment of the two eyes (*lazy eye*), can lead to a condition called **amblyopia**, in which acuity is poor in one eye, even though the eye and retina are normal. If the two eyes are not aligned properly during the first few years of life, the primary visual cortex of the child tends to suppress the information traveling to the cortex from one eye, and that eye becomes functionally blind. Studies of the development of vision in children and other animals show that most cases of amblyopia are avoidable.

The balance of the eye muscles can be surgically adjusted to bring the two eyes into better alignment. Alternatively, if the weak eye is given regular practice, with the good eye covered (**Figure 7.31**), vision can be preserved in both eyes. Attempts to alleviate amblyopia by training alone, however, have produced mixed results. The optimal treatment appears to be a combination of both surgical correction *and* eye patches and visual exercises (Pediatric Eye Disease Investigator Group, 2005).

Some studies have reported considerable improvement, even with adults, if the eye is exercised sufficiently and if the amblyopia is not too severe. Michael May, who was blind from the age of 3 to 43, regained some aspects of vision quickly after he underwent surgery to let light back into one of his eyes. Other aspects, such as his perception of faces and objects, remain severely impaired—but nevertheless show improvement with practice.

Frequent causes of visual impairment, especially with age, include *cataracts*, cloudy portions of the lens. Surgically removing the entire lens and replacing it with a prosthetic lens can restore sight in these cases. Diseases such as *macular degeneration* damage the rods and cones. These diseases leave the ganglion cells and the higher neural pathways largely intact. Scientists are working on arrays of electrodes to be placed within the eye in contact with the ganglion cells. These electrodes would be stimulated by a small camera and radio frequency transmitter lodged in the patient's eyeglasses. "The aim is to bring a blind person to the point where he or she can read, move around objects in the house, and do basic household chores," says project leader Kurt Wessendork. "They won't be able to drive cars, at least in the near future … But people who are blind will see" (N. Singer, 2002, p. 1).

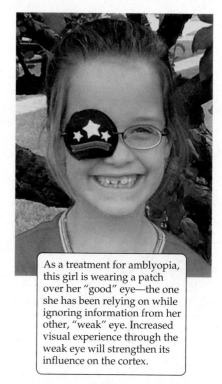

As a treatment for amblyopia, this girl is wearing a patch over her "good" eye—the one she has been relying on while ignoring information from her other, "weak" eye. Increased visual experience through the weak eye will strengthen its influence on the cortex.

Figure 7.31   Hey There, You with the Stars over Your Eye

How's it going?

1. What are the two main streams of visual processing in the cortex, and what aspects of vision does each stream support?

2. Describe D.F.'s symptoms, and relate them to the brain damage revealed by MRIs.

3. What is the evidence that indoor lighting may cause myopia in children?

amblyopia Reduced visual acuity that is not caused by optical or retinal impairments.

Recommended Reading

De Valois, R. L., and De Valois, K. K. (1988). *Spatial Vision.* New York, NY: Oxford University Press.

Ings, S. (2008). *A Natural History of Seeing: The Art and Science of Vision.* New York, NY: Norton.

Purves, D., and Lotto, R. B. (2011). *Why We See What We Do Redux: A Wholly Empirical Theory of Vision.* Sunderland, MA: Sinauer.

Rodieck, R. W. (1998). *The First Steps in Seeing.* Sunderland, MA: Sinauer.

Wandell, B. A. (1995). *Foundations of Vision.* Sunderland, MA: Sinauer.

Wolfe, J. M., Kluender, K. R., Levi, D. M., Bartoshuk, L. M., et al. (2012). *Sensation & Perception* (3rd ed.). Sunderland, MA: Sinauer.

mindsmachine.com/vs7

CHAPTER **7** VISUAL SUMMARY

You should be able to relate each summary to the adjacent illustration, including structures and processes. If you need to review, go to the figures indicated and read the accompanying text.

1 Light is bent, or **refracted**, by the transparent outer layer of the eye, the **cornea**, focusing an image on the **retina** in the back of the eye. We vary the thickness of the **lens** to fine-tune that refraction, sharpening the focus of the image. The refracted light forms an image on the retina that is upside down and reversed. Review **Figures 7.1** and **7.2**, **Animation 7.2, Activity 7.1**

2 The retina contains two different types of **photoreceptors** to detect light forming the focused image. **Rods** are very sensitive, working even in very low light, and they respond to light of any **wavelength**. Rods drive the **scotopic** system, which can work in dim light. Each of the three different types of **cones** responds better to some wavelengths of light than others, allowing us to detect colors. The cones provide information for the **photopic** system, which needs more light to function. Photoreceptors **adapt** to function across a wide range of light intensities. Review **Figures 7.3–7.6, Table 7.1**

3 The retina consists of layers of neurons, with the photoreceptors in the very back stimulating **bipolar cells**, which stimulate **ganglion cells**. The ganglion cells of the retina project their axons to the brain via the **optic nerve**. **Amacrine cells** and **horizontal cells** communicate across the retina, using processes such as **lateral inhibition** to analyze **brightness**. Review **Figures 7.3, 7.14,** and **7.15**

4 The center of our **visual field** lands on the **fovea**, the portion of the retina with the greatest density of photoreceptors, an absence of overlying cell layers, and more direct synaptic connections to ganglion cells, providing us with our greatest **visual acuity** (sharpness of vision). Cones are concentrated in the fovea, and rods are concentrated in the peripheral retina, so our peripheral vision is best for seeing dim objects, but it provides no color information. Review **Figures 7.7–7.9**

5 The left visual field falls on the nasal retina of the left eye and the temporal retina of the right eye. Only nasal retinal ganglion cells of each eye send their axons across the midline, forming the **optic chiasm**, so the left visual field projects to the right hemisphere and the right visual field projects to the left hemisphere. Review **Figures 7.10** and **7.11**, **Animation 7.3**

6 Ganglion cells of the retina synapse on neurons in the **lateral geniculate nucleus (LGN)** of the thalamus. The LGN neurons send axons to synapse on neurons in layer IV of the **primary visual cortex** (also called **striate cortex** or **V1**) in the **occipital cortex**. V1 sends information to many different cortical areas, called **extrastriate cortex** (nearly one-third of the human cortex), to further analyze visual information. Review **Figures 7.10** and **7.19**

7 The **receptive fields** of bipolar cells and ganglion cells consist of a circular center and a surround that have opposing effects: either **on-center/off-surround** or **off-center/on-surround**. Review **Figures 7.12** and **7.13**, **Animation 7.4**

8 Receptive fields of cells at successively higher levels in the visual cortex change in two main ways: (1) they become larger (occupy larger parts of the visual field), and (2) they require increasingly specific stimuli to evoke responses. For example, they respond best to a bar of light at a particular angle, or to bars that move in a particular direction. Review **Figures 7.16–7.21**, **Animation 7.5**

9 Rods detect light using a pigment called **rhodopsin**. Our detection of **hue** (color) depends on the three different cone photopigments (opsins). Each cone responds to wide range of wavelengths, not just a single color. Our perception of hue results from the *relative activity* of each type of cone. One way of assessing this relative activity is by retinal connections that yield **spectrally opponent** neurons. Review **Figures 7.22–7.28**

10 Visual cortical areas are organized into two main streams: a ventral *what* stream that serves in the recognition of faces and objects, and a dorsal *where* stream that serves in location and visuomotor skills. Review **Figures 7.29** and **7.30**

Go to **mindsmachine.com** for study questions, quizzes, flashcards, and other resources.

8 Hormones and Sex

Genitals and Gender: What Makes Us Male and Female?

Few aspects of human biology are as impressive and humbling as the making of a baby; it is a developmental ballet of staggering complexity and critical timing. Given the countless processes that must unfold perfectly and in precisely the right order, it is a marvel that, in the great majority of cases, development proceeds without a hitch. Inevitably, though, there are times when a crucial part of the program is derailed along the way and a baby is born with a heartbreaking deformity.

Such is the case with **cloacal exstrophy**, a developmental defect that affects about one in 400,000 babies. As a consequence of abnormal development of the pelvic region, a genetic male with this condition is typically born with normal testes but a very short, split penis or no penis at all. It isn't really possible to surgically fashion a normal penis in these cases, so the parents are faced with a terrible dilemma. Is it better to raise the child as a boy without a penis, despite the emotional costs of the deformity? Or would the outcome be better if the child were assigned to the female gender, underwent early surgery to remove the testes and fashion female-looking genitals, and then was raised as a girl? Which would you choose?

Arguments for each course of action boil down to different opinions about the extent to which our gender identity is shaped through nurturing and socialization, rather than biological factors. In other words, we need to consider the larger question of why men and women behave differently. Is it because as boys and girls they were treated differently and trained to grow into their gender roles, or do the forces that provide a fetus with testes or ovaries also induce the developing brain to take on a masculine or feminine form?

To see a video, go to

mindsmachine.com/8.1
Gender

In this chapter we'll discuss research that informs us about this long-standing question: How do biological and social forces combine to direct development in male-typical and female-typical ways? In Part I we'll learn how hormones can affect the brain to influence behavior. Part II will explain how hormones act on different parts of the brain to influence sexual behavior and parental behavior in particular. Part III will take up the question of how the fetus normally develops into either a male or a female form, not just in terms of the body, but also in terms of the brain and behavior. In animals, prenatal hormones have a tremendous influence on the brain and sexual behaviors. We'll close by reviewing growing evidence that those same prenatal hormones also affect our development into boys or girls, men or women, as well as our sexual orientation.

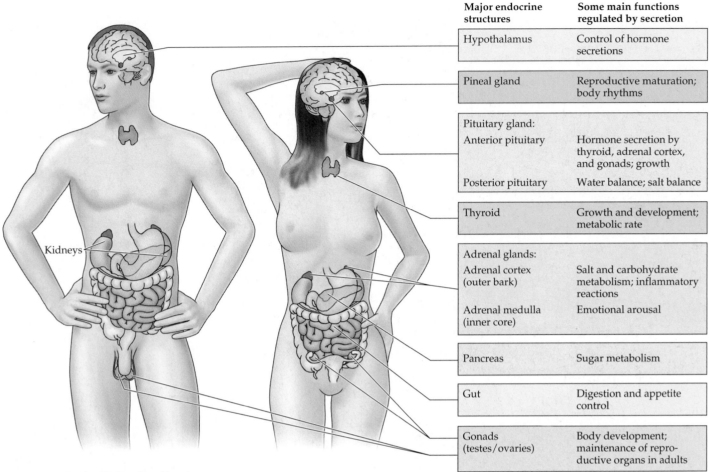

Major endocrine structures	Some main functions regulated by secretion
Hypothalamus	Control of hormone secretions
Pineal gland	Reproductive maturation; body rhythms
Pituitary gland: Anterior pituitary	Hormone secretion by thyroid, adrenal cortex, and gonads; growth
Posterior pituitary	Water balance; salt balance
Thyroid	Growth and development; metabolic rate
Adrenal glands: Adrenal cortex (outer bark)	Salt and carbohydrate metabolism; inflammatory reactions
Adrenal medulla (inner core)	Emotional arousal
Pancreas	Sugar metabolism
Gut	Digestion and appetite control
Gonads (testes / ovaries)	Body development; maintenance of reproductive organs in adults

Figure 8.1 Major Endocrine Glands and Their Functions

To see the brain in 3D, go to

mindsmachine.com/8.2
Brain Explorer

cloacal exstrophy A rare medical condition in which XY individuals are born completely lacking a penis.

hormone A chemical secreted by an endocrine gland that is conveyed by the bloodstream and regulates target organs or tissues.

endocrine gland A gland that secretes products into the bloodstream to act on distant targets.

castration Removal of the gonads, usually the testes.

PART I The Endocrine System

The body's cells use chemicals to communicate, including an extensive array of **hormones**, chemicals secreted by one group of cells and carried through the bloodstream to other parts of the body, where they act on specific target tissues to produce physiological effects. Changes in hormone levels can produce striking changes in brain function. Cognitive abilities, emotions, our appetite for food or drink or sex, our aggressiveness or submissiveness, our care for children—the scope of hormonal influences on behavior is vast.

Hormones Act in a Great Variety of Ways throughout the Body

Most hormones are produced by **endocrine glands** (from the Greek *endon*, "within," and *krinein*, "to secrete"), so called because they release their hormones *within* the body (**Figure 8.1**). Endocrine glands are sometimes contrasted with *exocrine glands* (tear glands, salivary glands, sweat glands), which use ducts to secrete fluid *outside* the body.

RESEARCHERS AT WORK

Our current understanding of hormones developed in stages

Ancient civilizations understood the importance of hormones. In the fourth century BCE, Aristotle accurately described the effects of **castration** (removal of the testes) in chickens, and he compared the behavioral and bodily effects with those seen in *eunuchs* (castrated men). The ancient Greeks emphasized four body *humors*, or fluids, as an explanation of temperament and emotions. Today we know there are a lot more than four hormones.

The first major endocrine experiment was carried out in 1849 by German physician Arnold Berthold (1803–1861). Aristotle noted that when roosters are castrated as juveniles, they fail to develop normal reproductive behavior and secondary sexual characteristics, such as the rooster's comb, in adulthood. Berthold observed, however, that *returning one testis back into the body cavity* of these young castrates allowed them to develop normal male anatomy and behavior. In adulthood, these animals showed the usual male sexual behaviors of mounting hens, fighting, and crowing (**Figure 8.2**). Because no nerves had reestablished contact with the transplanted testis, the organ could not be communicating to the brain through nerves. Berthold (1849) concluded that the testes release a chemical into the blood that affects both male

Figure 8.2 **Berthold's (1849) experiment demonstrated the importance of hormones for behavior.**

Question

Male chicks that are castrated grow up to have small wattles and combs, and they show little interest in mounting hens, fighting, or crowing. What causes these changes—the loss of a nerve connection between the testes and the body, or the loss of a chemical signal released from the testes?

Experiment

Berthold removed the testes from their normal position but then reimplanted them elsewhere in the abdomen, disconnected from normal innervation.

Group 1	Group 2	Group 3
Left undisturbed, young roosters grow up to have large red wattles and combs, to mount and mate with hens readily, and to fight one another and crow loudly.	Animals whose testes were removed during development displayed neither the appearance nor the behavior of normal roosters as adults.	However, if one of the testes was reimplanted into the abdominal cavity immediately after its removal, the rooster developed normal wattles and normal behavior.

	Group 1	Group 2	Group 3
Comb and wattles:	Large	Small	Large
Mount hens?	Yes	No	Yes
Aggressive?	Yes	No	Yes
Crowing?	Normal	Weak	Normal

Outcome

The animals with the reimplanted testes grew up to look and act like normal males. Berthold reasoned that the testes must have secreted a signal, which today we would call a hormone, that has widespread effects on the body and brain. Today we know that the hormone is testosterone.

behavior and male body structures. Today we know that the testes make and release the hormone *testosterone*, which exerts these effects.

Although Berthold didn't know it, experiments like this also illustrate another principle of hormone action. If he had waited until the castrated chicks were adults before transplanting the testes, Berthold would have seen little effect. The testosterone must be present *early* in life to have such dramatic effects on the body and behavior. We'll return to this point in the final section of this chapter. For now, let's see how hormones fit into the grand scheme of chemical signaling in the body.

Hormones are one of several types of chemical communication

People had long suspected that special substances circulate to carry messages through the body, but as we discussed above, it wasn't until nineteenth-century scientists started experimenting with hormone-secreting glands that details of chemical communication began to emerge. Reviewing several categories of chemical signals used by the body, we can look at how hormonal communication compares to other methods of communication:

- *Endocrine communication.* In **endocrine** communication, our topic for this chapter, the chemical signal is a hormone released into the bloodstream to selectively affect distant target organs (**Figure 8.3a**).

- *Synaptic communication.* Communication via **synapses** was described in Chapters 3 and 4. In typical synaptic transmission, the released chemical signal diffuses a tiny distance across the synaptic cleft and causes a change in the postsynaptic membrane (**Figure 8.3b**).

- *Pheromone communication.* Chemicals can be used for communication not only within an individual, but also *between* individuals. **Pheromones** are chemicals that are released outside the body to affect other individuals of the same species (**Figure 8.3c**). For example, ants produce pheromones that identify the route to a rich food source (to the annoyance of picnickers). Dogs and wolves urinate on landmarks to designate their territory, and other members of the species smell the pheromones in the urine and either respect or challenge the territory. In Chapter 6 we discuss pheromones in more detail.

endocrine   Referring to glands that release chemicals to the interior of the body. These glands secrete the principal hormones used by the body.

synapse   The cellular location at which information is transmitted from a neuron to another cell.

pheromone   A chemical signal that is released outside the body of an animal and affects other members of the same species.

(*a*) Endocrine function

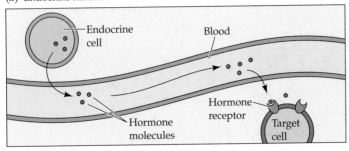

(*b*) Neural function (synaptic transmission)

Figure 8.3   Chemical Communication Systems

(*c*) Pheromone function

(*d*) Allomone function

To see an animation of this figure, go to

mindsmachine.com/8.3
Chemical Communication Systems

- *Allomone communication.* Some chemical signals are released by members of one species to affect the behavior of individuals of *another* species. These substances are called **allomones** (**Figure 8.3d**). Flowers exude scented allomones to attract insects and birds in order to distribute pollen. And the bolas spider—nature's femme fatale—releases a moth sex pheromone to lure male moths to their doom (Haynes et al., 2002).

Let's review the basic types of hormones and how they influence cells.

Hormones can be classified by chemical structure

Most hormones fall into one of three categories: protein hormones, amine hormones, or steroid hormones. Like any other protein, a **protein hormone** (or **peptide hormone**) is composed of a string of amino acids (**Figure 8.4a**). (Recall that a peptide is simply a small protein—that is, a shorter string of amino acids.) Different protein hormones consist of different combinations of amino acids. **Amine hormones** are smaller and simpler, consisting of a modified version of a single amino acid (hence their alias, *monoamine hormones*) (**Figure 8.4b**). The amine hormone melatonin is discussed in **A Step Further 8.1**, on the website.

Scents and Sensibility   Skunks produce a very effective allomone.

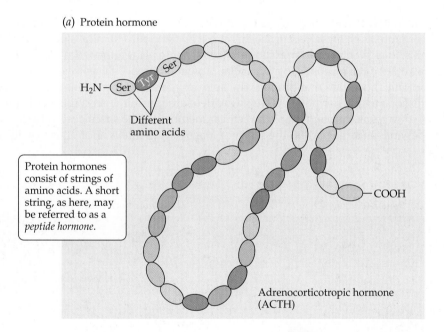

(*a*) Protein hormone

H_2N — Ser — Tyr — Ser

Different amino acids

Protein hormones consist of strings of amino acids. A short string, as here, may be referred to as a *peptide hormone.*

— COOH

Adrenocorticotropic hormone (ACTH)

(*b*)

Amine hormones such as thyroxine are modified single amino acids.

HO — ⬡ — O — ⬡ — $CH_2CHCOOH$
                               |
                               NH_2

(I atoms shown on rings)

Thyroxine (tetraiodothyronine)

(*c*)

Steroid hormones are derived from cholesterol and consist of four interconnected rings of carbon atoms, with various chemical attachments.

OH
CH_3

HO

Estradiol

Figure 8.4   Chemical Structures of the Three Main Hormone Types

allomone   A chemical signal that is released outside the body by one species and affects the behavior of other species.

protein hormone or peptide hormone   A hormone that consists of a string of amino acids.

amine hormone   Also called *monoamine hormone.* A hormone composed of a single amino acid that has been modified into a related molecule, such as melatonin or epinephrine.

steroid hormone   Any of a class of hormones, each of which is composed of four interconnected rings of carbon atoms.

second messenger   A slow-acting substance in a target cell that amplifies the effects of synaptic or hormonal activity and regulates activity within the target cell.

Steroid hormones are derivatives of cholesterol and thus share its structure of four rings of carbon atoms (**Figure 8.4c**). Different steroid hormones vary in the number and kinds of atoms attached to the rings. Because steroids dissolve readily in lipids, they can pass through membranes easily (recall from Chapter 2 that cell membranes consist of a lipid bilayer). **Table 8.1** gives examples of each class of hormones.

The distinction between protein or amine hormones and steroid hormones is important because the different types of hormones interact with different types of receptors, as we discuss next.

Hormones Act on a Wide Variety of Cellular Mechanisms

To prepare for later discussions of specific hormonal effects on behavior, let's look briefly at two aspects of hormone activity: first the mechanisms of hormone action, then the types of changes that hormones cause in target cells, including neurons.

Hormones initiate actions by binding to receptor molecules

The three classes of hormones exert their influences on target organs in two different ways. As we'll see next, protein and amine hormones use one mode of action, while steroid hormones use another.

PROTEIN AND AMINE HORMONES   Protein and amine hormones bind to specific receptor proteins *on the surface* of the target cell and activate chemical signals inside the cell that are called **second messengers** (see Chapter 4) (**Figure 8.5a**). What determines whether a cell responds to a particular protein hormone? Receptors are highly specific, so only those cells that produce the appropriate receptor proteins for a hormone can respond to that hormone. As we saw with neurotransmitter receptors in Chapters 3 and 4, the receptor protein spans the cellular membrane. The specific effect of the hormone depends in large part on the receptor it activates. Protein hormones usually act rela-

To see an animation of this figure, go to

mindsmachine.com/8.4
Mechanisms of Hormone Action

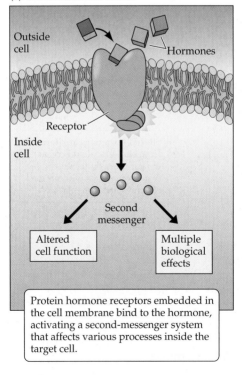

(a) Protein hormone action

Protein hormone receptors embedded in the cell membrane bind to the hormone, activating a second-messenger system that affects various processes inside the target cell.

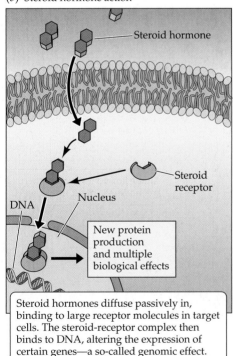

(b) Steroid hormone action

Steroid hormones diffuse passively in, binding to large receptor molecules in target cells. The steroid-receptor complex then binds to DNA, altering the expression of certain genes—a so-called genomic effect.

Figure 8.5   Two Main Mechanisms of Hormone Action

TABLE 8.1 Examples of Major Classes of Hormones

Class	Hormone
Protein hormones	Adrenocorticotropic hormone (ACTH)
	Follicle-stimulating hormone (FSH)
	Luteinizing hormone (LH)
	Thyroid-stimulating hormone (TSH)
	Growth hormone (GH)
	Prolactin
	Insulin
	Glucagon
	Oxytocin
	Vasopressin (arginine vasopressin, AVP; antidiuretic hormone, ADH)
	Releasing hormones, such as:
	Corticotropin-releasing hormone (CRH)
	Gonadotropin-releasing hormone (GnRH)
Amine hormones	Epinephrine (adrenaline)
	Norepinephrine (NE)
	Thyroid hormones
	Melatonin
Steroid hormones	Estrogens (e.g., estradiol)
	Progestins (e.g., progesterone)
	Androgens (e.g., testosterone, dihydrotestosterone)
	Glucocorticoids (e.g., cortisol)
	Mineralocorticoids (e.g., aldosterone)

tively rapidly, within seconds to minutes. (Although rapid for a hormone, this action is much slower than neural activity.)

STEROID HORMONES   We mentioned earlier that steroid hormones easily pass through cell membranes, so their receptors are generally located *inside* the target cell. Different classes of steroids have their own specific receptors; for example, estrogens selectively interact with estrogen receptors, and androgens like testosterone bind to androgen receptors. When a steroid molecule and a receptor molecule combine, the steroid-receptor complex enters the nucleus of the cell to bind specific regions of the DNA, controlling the expression of specific genes (**Figure 8.5b**), increasing or decreasing the rate of protein production (see the Appendix). Because they involve multiple steps and the synthesis of large new molecules, steroid hormone actions are typically slower-acting than those of protein or amine hormones. Steroid effects may take hours, days, or even years to fully unfold.

We can study where a steroid hormone is active by injecting radioactively tagged molecules of the steroid and observing where they accumulate. For example, tagged estrogens accumulate not only in the uterus (as you might expect), but also in the nuclei of some neurons throughout the hypothalamus. Because neurons that produce hormone receptors are found in only a limited number of brain regions, we can begin to learn how hormones affect behavior by finding those brain sites and asking what happens when the hormone arrives there. This strategy for learning about hormones and behavior is discussed in **Box 8.1**.

By altering protein production, steroids have slow but long-lasting effects on the development or adult function of cells. We will discuss such effects of steroids further in the next two sections of this chapter.

BOX 8.1 Techniques of Modern Behavioral Endocrinology

To establish that a particular hormone affects behavior, investigators usually begin with the type of experiment that Arnold Berthold performed in the nineteenth century: observing the behavior of the intact animal, and then removing the endocrine gland and looking for a change in behavior (see Figure 8.2). Berthold was limited to this type of experiment, but modern scientists have many additional options available. Let's imagine that we're investigating a particular effect of hormones on behavior to see how we might proceed.

Which Hormones Affect Which Behaviors?

First we must carefully observe the behavior of several individuals, seeking ways to classify and quantify the different types of behavior and to place them in the context of the behavior of other individuals. For example, most adult male rats will try to mount and copulate with a receptive female placed in their cage. If the testes are removed from the male rat, he will eventually stop copulating with females. We know that one of the hormones produced by the testes is testosterone. Is it the loss of testosterone that causes the loss of male copulatory behavior?

To explore this question, we inject some testosterone into castrated males and observe whether the copulatory behavior returns. (It does.) Another way to ask whether a steroid hormone is affecting a particular behavior is to examine the behavior of animals that lack the receptors for that steroid. We can delete the gene for a given hormone receptor, making a **knockout organism** (so called because the gene for the receptor has been "knocked out"), and ask which behaviors are different in the knockouts versus normal animals.

1 A rat is injected with molecules of testosterone (an androgen) that have been radioactively labeled.

2 The testosterone molecules enter the bloodstream and accumulate in those cells that have androgen receptors.

3 The brain is removed and frozen to keep the testosterone molecules inside the target cells.

Film

4 The brain is thinly sliced and film is placed on top in the dark. The radioactive molecules release particles that "expose" the film just as light would.

Exposure

5 When the film is developed, small black dots form on the film where the testosterone has accumulated in target cells.

(A) Steps in steroid autoradiography.

Next we might examine individual male rats and ask whether the ones that copulate a lot have more testosterone circulating in their blood than those that copulate only a little. To investigate this question, we measure individual differences in the amount of copulatory behavior, take a sample of blood from each individual, and measure levels of testosterone. It turns out that individual differences in the sexual behavior of normal male

rats (and normal male humans) do *not* correlate with differences in testosterone levels in the blood. In both rats and humans, a drastic loss of testosterone, as after castration, results in a gradual decline in sexual behavior. All normal males, however, appear to make more than enough testosterone to maintain sexual behavior, so something else must modulate this behavior. In other words, the hormone acts in a *permissive* manner: it permits the display of the behavior, but something else determines how much of the behavior each individual exhibits.

Where Are the Target Cells?

What does testosterone do to permit sexual behavior? One step toward answering this question is to ask another question: Which parts of the brain are normally affected by this hormone? We have several methods at our disposal for investigating this question.

First we might inject a castrated animal with radioactively labeled testosterone and wait for the hormone to accumulate in the brain regions that have receptors for the hormone. Then we could sacrifice the animal, remove the brain, freeze it, cut thin sections from it, and place the thin sections on photographic film. Radioactive emissions from the tissue expose the film, revealing which brain regions accumulated the most labeled testosterone. This method is known as **autoradiography** because the tissue "takes its own picture" with radioactivity (Figure A).

When the labeled hormone is a steroid like testosterone, the radioactivity accumulates in the nuclei of neurons and leaves small black specks on the film (Figure B). When the radiolabeled hormone is a protein hormone such as oxytocin, the radioactivity accumulates in the membranes of cells and appears in particular layers of the brain. Computers can generate

(Continued on next page)

BOX 8.1 *(continued)*

(B) An autoradiogram showing that spinal motoneurons (purple cell profiles) accumulate radioactive testosterone (small dots).

(C) An autoradiogram showing the concentration of oxytocin receptors in the ventromedial hypothalamus (oval outlines).

(D) Immunocytochemistry revealing cells with nuclei that contain androgen receptors (dark circles), to which testosterone can bind. The cell bodies of these neurons have been labeled with two different tracers, one white and the other red.

color maps that highlight regions with high densities of receptors (Figure C).

Another method for detecting hormone receptors is **immunocytochemistry**, or **ICC** (described in more detail in Box 2.1). ICC enables us to map the distribution of hormone receptors in the brain. We allow specific antibodies to seek out and bind to receptors on slices of brain tissue, and then we use chemical methods to make the antibodies visible, leaving a dark color in the nuclei of target brain cells (Figure D). We can also use *in situ* hybridization (see Box 2.1) to look for the neurons that make the mRNA for the steroid receptor. Because these cells make the transcript for the receptor, they are likely to possess the receptor protein itself.

What Happens at the Target Cells?

Once we've used autoradiography, immunocytochemistry, or *in situ* hybridization (or, better yet, all three) to identify brain regions that have receptors for the hormone, those regions become candidates for the places at which the hormone works to change behavior. Now we can take castrated males, implant tiny pellets of testosterone into one of those brain regions, and see whether the behavior is restored. If not, then in other animals we can implant pellets in a different region or try placing implants in a combination of brain sites.

It turns out that such implants can restore male sexual behavior in rats only if they are placed in the medial preoptic area (mPOA)

of the hypothalamus. So far, we've found that testosterone does something to the mPOA to permit individual males to display sexual behavior. Now we can examine the mPOA in detail to learn what changes in the anatomy, physiology, or protein production of this region are caused by testosterone. And with that, we have more or less caught up to modern-day scientists who work on this very question, as described in this chapter. (Figure C courtesy of Bruce McEwen; D courtesy of Cynthia Jordan.)

Hormones can have different effects on different target organs

Virtually all hormones, whether protein or steroid, act on more than one target organ. What's more, a given hormone may have one type of effect on one organ, and a quite different effect on another organ. This means hormones often act to *coordinate different parts of the body*, causing diverse changes to several different parts of the body, all of which prepare the animal for a particular activity (**Figure 8.6**). For example, the testes secrete testosterone, which acts in the testes themselves to drive sperm production but also acts to masculinize the body in diverse ways, favoring muscle development and, in humans, beard growth. In this and numerous other cases we'll discuss, the same hormone also acts on the brain—in the case of testosterone, to promote sexual behavior and aggression in many animal species.

How is the same hormone able to cause many different responses in different organs? First, often more than one receptor responds to a given hormone. For example, there are at least two different receptors for estrogens, and for other hormones there may be four or more. In addition, sometimes the same receptor, in response to the same hormone, will have a different effect because the target cell responds differently.

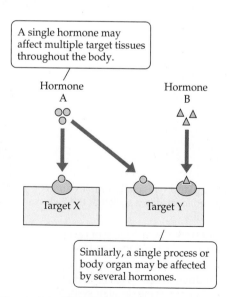

A single hormone may affect multiple target tissues throughout the body.

Similarly, a single process or body organ may be affected by several hormones.

Figure 8.6 The Multiplicity of Hormone Action

How's it going?

1. What are hormones, and how do they act?
2. Describe Berthold's experiment with young roosters, and explain how it indicated hormonal effects.
3. Compare and contrast the mechanisms by which protein/amine hormones versus steroid hormones act on cells.
4. Why are hormones effective for coordinating different changes in different parts of the body?

Another principle of hormone action is that it is rare for a hormone to act alone. Rather, a target organ that is responding to one hormone is likely responding to other hormones too (see Figure 8.6). Nowhere is the principle of several different hormones acting in a coordinated fashion on an organ more common than in the brain. As we'll see later, the brain maintains strict control over all hormone secretion, which means, among other things, that the brain has receptors to detect almost all hormones, in order to monitor their release.

Each Endocrine Gland Secretes Specific Hormones

Now we'll discuss the specific hormones that endocrine glands secrete. To cover all the hormones would require an entire book (e.g., Hadley and Levine, 2006), so we will restrict our discussion to only some of the main endocrine glands. **A Step Further 8.2**, on the website, gives a fuller (though far from complete) listing of hormones and their functions. Hormones involved in thirst and hunger are discussed in Chapter 9.

We must begin with the pituitary because it regulates so many other endocrine glands. Resting in a socket in the base of the skull, the **pituitary gland** is about the size of a garden pea, weighing about 1 gram (see Figure 8.1). The hypothalamus sits just above the pituitary and is connected to the gland by a slender thread called the **pituitary stalk**. The term *pituitary* comes from the Latin *pituita*, "mucus," reflecting the outmoded belief that waste products dripped down from the brain into the pituitary, which then secreted them out through the nose. (The ancients may have thought you could literally sneeze your brains out!) Because the pituitary regulates most other endocrine glands, it is sometimes referred to as the *master gland*. But the pituitary is itself enslaved by the hypothalamus above it, as we'll see.

To understand how the pituitary works, we need to consider a special category of cells that are something of a blend of neuronal cells and endocrine cells, called **neuroendocrine cells**. On the one hand, neuroendocrine cells receive synaptic input from other neurons and, if they are excited past threshold, produce action potentials. But unlike regular neurons, which release a neurotransmitter into a synapse when they fire, neuroendocrine cells release a hormone into the bloodstream (**Figure 8.7**).

To understand the pivotal role of such neuroendocrine cells in hormone release from the pituitary, we need to consider separately the two parts of the pituitary: the *anterior pituitary* and the *posterior pituitary*. These two halves of the pituitary develop from different embryonic tissues and are completely separate in function. The mechanism of hormone release is simpler in the posterior pituitary, so let's discuss that first.

pituitary gland A small, complex endocrine gland located in a socket at the base of the skull.

pituitary stalk A thin piece of tissue that connects the pituitary gland to the hypothalamus.

neuroendocrine cell A neuron that releases hormones into local or systemic circulation.

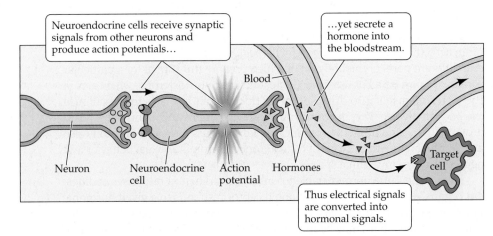

Neuroendocrine cells receive synaptic signals from other neurons and produce action potentials…

…yet secrete a hormone into the bloodstream.

Blood

Thus electrical signals are converted into hormonal signals.

Neuron   Neuroendocrine cell   Action potential   Hormones   Target cell

Figure 8.7 Neuroendocrine Cells Are the Interface between Neurons and Endocrine Glands

The posterior pituitary releases two hormones directly into the bloodstream

Although it is called a gland, the **posterior pituitary** does not itself produce hormones. Rather, the hormones are produced by neuroendocrine cells in two hypothalamic regions: the *supraoptic* and *paraventricular nuclei*. These neuroendocrine cells transport hormones down their axons, which extend along the pituitary stalk to terminate in the posterior pituitary. When the hypothalamic neuroendocrine cells are excited by synaptic input, they produce action potentials that travel down the axons and release hormone directly onto *capillaries* (small blood vessels) in the posterior pituitary, allowing the hormone to enter circulation immediately (**Figure 8.8**).

In this fashion, the neuroendocrine cells in the hypothalamus produce and release two peptide hormones from the posterior pituitary: **oxytocin** and **arginine vasopressin** (**AVP**), often called just **vasopressin**. Some of the signals that activate the nerve cells

posterior pituitary   The rear division of the pituitary gland.

oxytocin   A hormone, released from the posterior pituitary, that triggers milk letdown in the nursing female.

arginine vasopressin (AVP) or vasopressin   Also called *antidiuretic hormone*. A peptide hormone from the posterior pituitary that promotes water conservation and increases blood pressure.

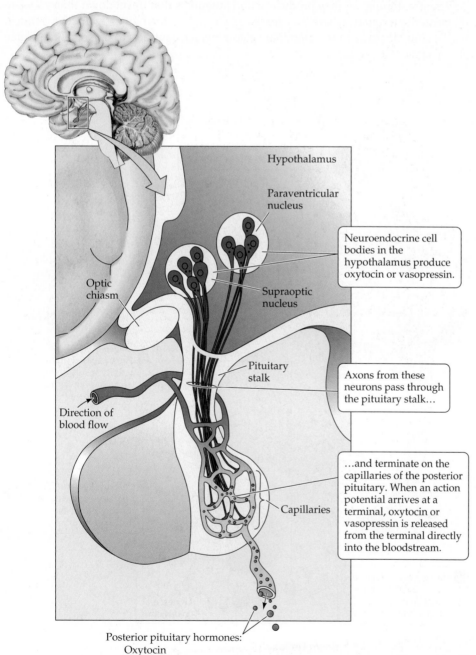

Hypothalamus

Paraventricular nucleus

Neuroendocrine cell bodies in the hypothalamus produce oxytocin or vasopressin.

Supraoptic nucleus

Optic chiasm

Pituitary stalk

Axons from these neurons pass through the pituitary stalk...

Direction of blood flow

...and terminate on the capillaries of the posterior pituitary. When an action potential arrives at a terminal, oxytocin or vasopressin is released from the terminal directly into the bloodstream.

Capillaries

Posterior pituitary hormones:
Oxytocin
Vasopressin

Figure 8.8   **Hormone Production by the Posterior Pituitary**

of the supraoptic and paraventricular nuclei are related to thirst and water regulation; vasopressin is involved in these interactions, which will be discussed in Chapter 9. Oxytocin is involved in many aspects of reproductive and parental behavior. One of its functions is to stimulate contractions of the uterus in childbirth. Injections of oxytocin (or a synthetic version) are frequently used in hospitals to induce or accelerate labor and delivery.

Oxytocin also triggers the **milk letdown reflex**, the contraction of mammary gland cells that ejects milk into the breast ducts. This reflex exemplifies the reciprocal relationship between behavior and hormone release. When an infant first begins to suckle, the arrival of milk at the nipple is delayed by 30–60 seconds. This delay is caused by the sequence of steps that precedes letdown. Stimulation of the nipple activates receptors in the skin, which transmit this information through a chain of neurons and synapses to hypothalamic cells that contain oxytocin. Once these neuroendocrine cells have been sufficiently stimulated, they produce action potentials that travel down their axons to the posterior pituitary, where they release oxytocin into the bloodstream. The oxytocin reaches muscle tissue in the mammary glands, which contracts to make milk available at the nipple (**Figure 8.9**).

Peptide Hormones in the Hypothalamus
This section of the paraventricular nucleus reveals cells that make oxytocin (red) or vasopressin (green), hormones that are released from the posterior pituitary. (Courtesy of V. Tobin and M. Ludwig.)

milk letdown reflex   The reflexive release of milk by the mammary glands of a nursing female in response to suckling, or to stimuli associated with suckling.

1 Stimulation of the mother's nipple by the infant's suckling response produces brain activity in the mother.

Nerve impulses to hypothalamus

5 The baby, rewarded with milk, continues suckling until sated.

2 The increased brain activity results in inputs to the hypothalamus.

Hypothalamus

3 Cells in the hypothalamus produce oxytocin and release it from the posterior pituitary.

Posterior pituitary

4 The oxytocin causes the cells of the mammary glands to contract, thereby releasing milk.

Release of oxytocin

Figure 8.9   The Milk Letdown Reflex

(a)

Prairie voles form long-lasting pair-bonds.

(b)

Monogamy in male prairie voles seems to be due to the dense concentration of vasopressin receptors in the ventral pallidum (VP).

(c)

Males of the closely related meadow vole species have fewer vasopressin receptors in the VP, which may explain why they are not monogamous.

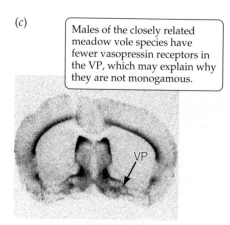

Figure 8.10 Vasopressin and the Monogamous Brain (Photographs courtesy of Miranda Lim and Larry Young.)

For mothers, this reflex response to suckling frequently becomes conditioned to baby cries, so that milk appears promptly at the start of nursing. Because the mother learns to release oxytocin *before* the suckling begins, sometimes the cries of *someone else's baby* in public trigger an inconvenient release of milk.

Posterior pituitary hormones can affect social behavior

We've already seen the role of oxytocin in the interaction of nursing babies and their mothers (see Figure 8.9). It turns out that this hormone is involved in several other social behaviors too. For one thing, a pulse of oxytocin is released during orgasm in both men and women (Carmichael et al., 1994), adding to the pleasurable feelings accompanying sexual encounters.

In nonhuman animals, oxytocin and vasopressin facilitate many social processes (Lim and Young, 2006). Rodents given supplementary doses of oxytocin spend more time in physical contact with one another (Carter, 1992). Male mice that have the oxytocin gene knocked out and are therefore unable to produce the hormone display social amnesia: they seem unable to recognize the scent of female mice that they have met before (Ferguson et al., 2000). These oxytocin knockout males can be cured of their social amnesia with brain infusions of oxytocin (Winslow and Insel, 2002).

In prairie voles (*Microtus ochrogaster*), couples form stable **pair-bonds**, and oxytocin infusions in the brains of females help them bond to their mates. In *male* prairie voles, it is vasopressin rather than oxytocin that facilitates the formation of a preference for female partners. In fact, the distribution of vasopressin receptors in the brains of male prairie voles may be what makes them monogamous. Supporting this idea is the finding that the closely related meadow voles (*Microtus pennsylvanicus*), which do not form pair-bonds and instead have multiple mating partners, have far fewer vasopressin receptors in certain brain regions than prairie voles have (**Figure 8.10**) (Lim et al., 2004). Thus, oxytocin and vasopressin regulate a range of social behaviors, and natural selection appears to alter the social behaviors of a species by changing the brain distribution of receptors for these peptides (Donaldson and Young, 2008).

Feedback control mechanisms regulate the secretion of hormones

All hormone release is carefully controlled by the brain, which monitors internal and external cues to decide whether and how much hormone should be released. Brain regulation of posterior pituitary hormone release is readily understood, because the neuroendocrine cells secrete hormone only when they are excited synaptically. For example, sensory information from a child's suckling at the breast reaches the brain and excites hypothalamic neuroendocrine cells, which fire action potentials and release oxytocin. Once the baby is satisfied, the suckling stops, so the brain stops exciting the neuroendocrine cells and oxytocin release ceases.

pair-bond A durable and exclusive relationship between a male and a female.

This is an example of the basic mechanism that regulates all hormone secretion, called **negative feedback**: output of the hormone *feeds back* to inhibit the drive for more of that same hormone (**Figure 8.11a**). This negative feedback action of a hormonal system is like that of a thermostat, and just as the thermostat can be set to different temperatures at different times, the set points of a person's endocrine feedback systems can change to meet varying circumstances. We'll discuss negative feedback regulation of other processes in Chapter 9 (see Figure 9.1).

Hormone secretion from the *anterior* pituitary is also regulated by negative feedback, but the mechanism is a bit more complicated, as we'll see next.

Hypothalamic releasing hormones govern the anterior pituitary

The **anterior pituitary** consists of many different endocrine cells, each secreting a different protein/peptide hormone. So, unlike the posterior half of the pituitary, the anterior pituitary actually synthesizes the hormones it releases. The anterior pituitary hormones are called **tropic hormones**. (*Tropic* is pronounced with a long *o* as in *toe*; there is nothing "tropical" about these hormones.) The term *tropic* means "directed toward," because each tropic hormone acts on a different endocrine gland, such as the thyroid or ovaries, as if the tropic hormone were directed at that gland. Actually the tropic hormone travels throughout the bloodstream, reaching *all* glands, but only the *target glands* have the appropriate receptors to respond to it. Once the tropic hormone reaches a target gland, it drives the gland to produce its own hormone. For example, one anterior pituitary tropic hormone acts on the thyroid gland to make it secrete thyroid hormones.

To regulate secretions of tropic hormones from the anterior pituitary, the hypothalamus uses another whole set of hormones, called **releasing hormones**. The cells that synthesize the different releasing hormones are neuroendocrine cells residing in various regions of the hypothalamus. The axons of these neuroendocrine cells converge on the **median eminence**, just above the pituitary stalk. This region contains an elaborate

To see an animation, go to

mindsmachine.com/8.5
The Hypothalamus and
Endocrine Function

negative feedback The property by which some of the output of a system feeds back to reduce the effect of input signals.

anterior pituitary The front division of the pituitary gland; it secretes tropic hormones.

tropic hormone Any of a class of anterior pituitary hormones that affect the secretion of hormones by other endocrine glands.

releasing hormone Any of a class of hormones, produced in the hypothalamus, that traverse the hypothalamic-pituitary portal system to control the pituitary's release of tropic hormones.

median eminence A midline feature on the base of the brain that marks the point at which the pituitary stalk exits the hypothalamus to connect to the pituitary. The median eminence contains elements of the hypothalamic-pituitary portal system.

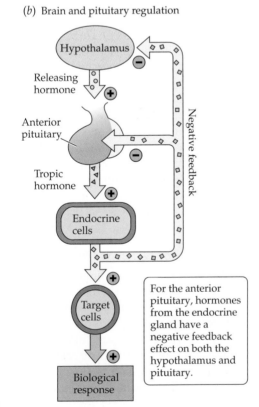

Figure 8.11 Endocrine Feedback Loops

profusion of blood vessels that form the **hypothalamic-pituitary portal system**. Here, in response to inputs from the rest of the brain, the axon terminals of the hypothalamic neuroendocrine cells secrete their releasing hormones into the *local* bloodstream (**Figure 8.12**). Blood carries the various releasing hormones only a very short distance, into the anterior pituitary. The rate at which releasing hormones arrive at the anterior pituitary controls the rate at which the anterior pituitary cells, in turn, release their tropic hormones into the *general* circulation. These tropic hormones then regulate the activity of major endocrine organs throughout the body. Thus, the brain's releasing hormones affect the anterior pituitary's tropic hormones, which affect the release of hormones from endocrine glands. Failure to properly regulate these hormone levels can lead to psychiatric symptoms, as detailed in **A Step Further 8.3**, on the website.

The hypothalamic neuroendocrine cells that synthesize the releasing hormones are themselves subject to two kinds of influences. First, they are directly affected by *circulating messages*, such as other hormones, especially hormones that were secreted in response to tropic hormones (**Figure 8.11b**). This hormone sensitivity of the hypothalamic neurons is an important part of the negative feedback we mentioned earlier, because typically the hormones secreted from an endocrine gland feed back to inhibit

hypothalamic-pituitary portal system
An elaborate bed of blood vessels leading from the hypothalamus to the anterior pituitary.

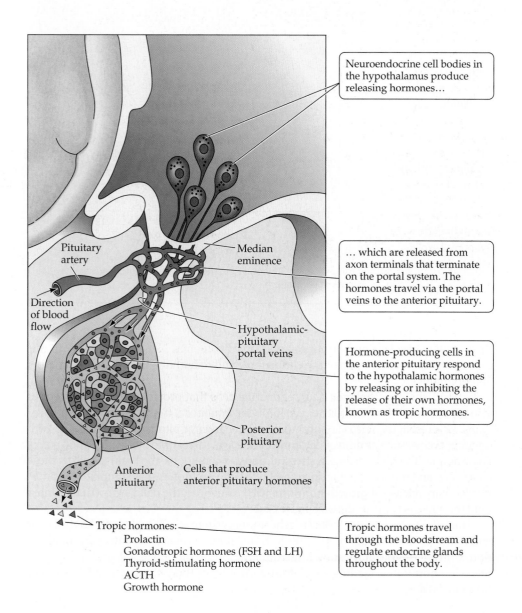

Neuroendocrine cell bodies in the hypothalamus produce releasing hormones…

Pituitary artery

Median eminence

… which are released from axon terminals that terminate on the portal system. The hormones travel via the portal veins to the anterior pituitary.

Direction of blood flow

Hypothalamic-pituitary portal veins

Hormone-producing cells in the anterior pituitary respond to the hypothalamic hormones by releasing or inhibiting the release of their own hormones, known as tropic hormones.

Posterior pituitary

Anterior pituitary

Cells that produce anterior pituitary hormones

Tropic hormones:
Prolactin
Gonadotropic hormones (FSH and LH)
Thyroid-stimulating hormone
ACTH
Growth hormone

Tropic hormones travel through the bloodstream and regulate endocrine glands throughout the body.

Figure 8.12 Hormone Release by the Anterior Pituitary

BOX 8.2 Stress and Growth: Psychosocial Dwarfism

Genie had a horrifically deprived childhood. For over 10 years, starting from the age of 20 months, she was isolated in a small, closed room, and much of the time she was tied to a potty chair. Her disturbed parents provided food, but nobody held Genie or spoke to her. When she was released from her confinement and observed by researchers at the age of 13, her size made her appear only 6 or 7 years old (Rymer, 1993).

Other, less horrendous forms of family deprivation also result in failure of growth. This syndrome is referred to as **psychosocial dwarfism** to emphasize that the growth failure arises from psychological and social factors mediated through the central nervous system and its control over endocrine functions (W. H. Green et al., 1984). Often when children suffering from psychosocial dwarfism are removed from stressful circumstances, they begin to grow rapidly. The growth rates of five such children, before and after periods of emotional deprivation, are shown in the figure. Following their removal from the abusive situation, these children seem to have compensated for much of the growth deficit that occurred during prolonged stress periods (Sirotnak et al., 2004).

How do stress and emotional deprivation impair growth? Growth impairments appear to be mediated by changed outputs of several hormones, including growth hormone (GH), cortisol, and other hormones,

known as *somatomedins* (which are ordinarily released by the liver in response to GH). GH and the somatomedins normally stimulate cell growth.

Some children with psychosocial dwarfism show almost a complete lack of GH release (Albanese et al., 1994). Disturbed sleep has also been suggested as a cause of this failure, because GH is typically released during certain stages of sleep, and children under stress show disturbed sleep patterns (L. I. Gardner, 1972). Other children who exhibit psychosocial dwarfism show normal levels of GH but low levels of somatomedins, and these hormones, along with GH, appear to be necessary for normal growth. Still other children with this condition show elevated levels of cortisol, probably as a result of stress, that inhibit growth. Finally, some affected children show none of these hormonal disturbances, so there must also be other routes through which emotional experiences affect growth.

Growth is an example of a process that involves many factors—hormonal, metabolic, and dietary—and can therefore malfunction in a variety of ways. Cases of psychosocial dwarfism are more common than once was thought, and investigators who study this syndrome are calling for heightened awareness of and attention to it (W. H. Green et al., 1984). For Genie, relief came in time to restore much of her *body* growth, but her mental development remains severely limited; she has never learned to say more than a few words and, now in her fifties, she lives in an institution.

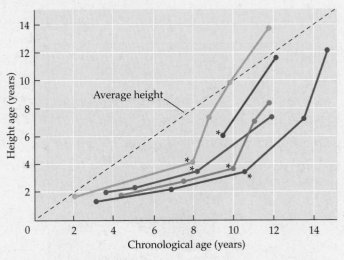

Growth rates of abused children before and after removal from the abusive situation. Removal from the abusive situation is indicated by the asterisk in each case.

How's it going?

1. How do hormones and behaviors interact in the course of the milk letdown reflex?
2. Describe the system regulating hormone release from the anterior pituitary, and explain how that system controls other endocrine glands.

growth hormone (GH)   Also called *somatotropin* or *somatotropic hormone*. A tropic hormone, secreted by the anterior pituitary, that influences the growth of cells and tissues.

the secretion of releasing hormones and tropic hormones. Negative feedback in this case goes from the hormone of the endocrine gland to both the hypothalamus and the anterior pituitary.

Second, the hypothalamic neuroendocrine cells that provide releasing hormones also receive *synaptic inputs* (either excitatory or inhibitory) from many other brain regions. As a result, the release of hormones by the anterior pituitary is coordinated with ongoing events, such as time of day, time of the year, safety of the individual, and so on. For example, if a child is living in stressful, abusive conditions, the brain monitors these conditions and reduces the production of releasing hormones that stimulate the anterior pituitary release of **growth hormone** (GH). Therefore, the child's growth is stunted until the stress is lifted, as detailed in **Box 8.2**.

Thus, the hypothalamic-releasing-hormone system exerts high-level control over endocrine organs throughout the body, translating brain activity into hormonal action. Cutting the pituitary stalk interrupts the portal blood vessels and the flow of releasing hormones, leading to profound atrophy of the pituitary, as well as major hormonal disruptions.

Two anterior pituitary tropic hormones act on the gonads

Driven by various releasing hormones from the hypothalamus, the anterior pituitary gland secretes at least six different tropic hormones. We don't really need to go into all these hormones and the glands they control right now, but you can learn more about them in **A Step Further 8.4**, on the website. Here we will concentrate on the tropic hormones that affect male and female **gonads** (the *testes* and *ovaries*, respectively), because the hormones produced by gonads play a role in the rest of this chapter.

In the hypothalamus, neuroendocrine cells produce **gonadotropin-releasing hormone (GnRH)**, which is secreted into the capillaries of the median eminence, traveling via the hypothalamic-pituitary portal system to arrive at the anterior pituitary. In response to this GnRH, anterior pituitary cells release one or both of the tropic hormones that act on the gonads, which are thus collectively known as **gonadotropins**:

1. **Follicle-stimulating hormone (FSH)** gets its name from its actions in the ovary, where it stimulates the growth and maturation of egg-containing **follicles** and the secretion of estrogens from the follicles. In males, FSH governs sperm production.

2. **Luteinizing hormone (LH)** stimulates the follicles of the ovary to rupture, release their eggs, and form into structures called **corpora lutea** (singular *corpus luteum*) that secrete the sex steroid hormone progesterone. In males, LH stimulates the testes to produce testosterone.

Since both of the gonadotropins drive the release of gonadal steroids, we'll turn our attention to those hormones next.

The gonads produce steroid hormones, regulating reproduction

Almost all aspects of reproductive behavior, including mating and parental behaviors, depend on hormones, as we'll see later in this chapter. Each ovary or testis consists of two different subcompartments—one to produce hormones (the sex steroids we mentioned earlier) and another to produce *gametes* (eggs or sperm). The gonadal hormones are critical for triggering both reproductive behavior controlled by the brain and gamete production.

THE TESTES Within the **testes** (singular *testis*) are Sertoli cells, which produce sperm, and Leydig cells, which produce and secrete the steroid **testosterone**. Testosterone and other male hormones are called **androgens** (from the Greek *andro-*, "man," and *gennan*, "to produce").

Testosterone controls a wide range of bodily changes that become visible at puberty, including changes in voice, hair growth, and genital size. In species that breed only in certain seasons of the year, testosterone has especially marked effects on appearance

gonad Any of the sexual organs (ovaries in females, testes in males), which produce gametes for reproduction.

gonadotropin-releasing hormone (GnRH) A hypothalamic hormone that controls the release of luteinizing hormone and follicle-stimulating hormone from the pituitary.

gonadotropin An anterior pituitary hormone that selectively stimulates the cells of the gonads to produce sex steroids and gametes.

follicle-stimulating hormone (FSH) A gonadotropin, named for its actions on ovarian follicles.

follicle The structure of the ovary that contains immature ova.

luteinizing hormone (LH) A gonadotropin, named for its stimulatory effects on the ovarian corpora lutea.

corpus luteum The structure that forms from the collapsed ovarian follicle after ovulation. The corpora lutea are a major source of progesterone.

testes The male gonads, which produce sperm and androgenic steroid hormones.

testosterone A hormone, produced by male gonads, that controls a variety of bodily changes that become visible at puberty. One of a class of hormones called androgens.

androgen Any of a class of hormones that includes testosterone and other male hormones.

The Influence of a Hormone The antlers and combative behavior of the North American elk are both seasonally affected by testosterone.

and behavior—for example, the antlers and fighting between males that are displayed by many species of deer. **Figure 8.13a** summarizes the regulation of testosterone secretion. As men age, testosterone levels tend to decline. Although elderly men who happen to maintain high levels of circulating testosterone perform better on tests of memory and attention than do those with low levels (Yaffe et al., 2002), there have been too few studies to tell whether taking supplemental testosterone actually helps aging men (Harder, 2003; Nair et al., 2006). Furthermore, taking supplemental testosterone can sometimes increase aggressive or manic behaviors (Pope et al., 2000), as well as possibly increasing prostate cancer risk.

(a) Male

(b) Female

Figure 8.13   Regulation of the Gonadal Steroid Hormones

THE OVARIES The paired female gonads, the **ovaries**, also produce both the mature female gametes—called *ova* (singular *ovum*) or eggs—and sex steroid hormones. However, hormone secretion is more complicated in ovaries than in testes. Ovarian hormones are produced in cycles, the duration of which varies with the species. Human ovarian cycles last about 4 weeks; rat cycles last only 4 days.

Normally the ovary produces two major classes of steroid hormones: **progestins** (from the Latin *pro*, "favoring," and *gestare*, "to bear," because these hormones help to maintain pregnancy) and **estrogens** (from the Latin *oestrus*, "gadfly" or "frenzy"—*estrus* is the scientific term for the periodic sexual receptivity of females in many species). The most important naturally occurring estrogen is **estradiol** (specifically, 17-beta-estradiol). The primary progestin is **progesterone**.

The **ovulatory cycle** begins when FSH stimulates ovarian follicles to grow and secrete estrogens (**Figure 8.13b**). The estrogens induce the hypothalamus and pituitary to release LH, which triggers ovulation (the release of an egg) and causes the follicles to develop as corpora lutea. The corpora lutea then secrete progesterone to maintain the uterus for pregnancy. If the female does not become pregnant, the cycle starts over again.

Oral contraceptives contain small doses of synthetic estrogens and/or progestins, which exert a negative feedback effect on the hypothalamus, inhibiting the release of GnRH. The lack of GnRH prevents the release of FSH and LH from the pituitary, and therefore the ovary fails to release an egg for fertilization.

Estrogens may improve aspects of cognitive functioning (Maki and Resnick, 2000), although this topic is still debated (Dohanich, 2003). Estrogens may also protect the brain from some of the effects of stress and stroke (S. Suzuki et al., 2009). For these reasons and others, estrogen replacement therapy has been a popular postmenopausal treatment, but the possibility that these treatments increase the risk of serious diseases like cancer and heart disease (Christensen, 1999; Turgeon et al., 2004) makes the decision of whether to take the hormones difficult for postmenopausal women.

RELATIONS AMONG GONADAL HORMONES All steroid hormones—including androgens, estrogens, and progestins—are based on the chemical structure of cholesterol (see Figure 8.4c). Glands manufacture steroid hormones by using enzymes to modify cholesterol, step by step, into different steroids. For example, ovaries first convert cholesterol into progestins, and then they convert those progestins into androgens, which are then converted into estrogens.

Different organs—and the two sexes—differ in the *relative* amounts of gonadal steroids that they produce. For example, whereas the testes convert only a relatively small proportion of testosterone into estradiol, the ovaries convert most of the testosterone they make into estradiol. What's important to understand is that *no steroid is found exclusively in either males or females*.

Hormonal and neural systems interact to produce integrated responses

In many ways, the endocrine system and the nervous system can be viewed simply as divisions of a single master control mechanism. The two divisions work together, each affecting the other, seamlessly integrating various body systems to produce adaptive responses to the environment. So, for example, if our sensory system tells us that a stimulus calls for action—perhaps that faint buzzing sound you're hearing turns out to be coming from a nest of angry wasps—hormones can be released to provide energy to fuel appropriate behaviors (sprinting away, yelling, cursing maybe).

Four kinds of signals are possible between neurons and endocrine cells: neural-to-neural, neural-to-endocrine, endocrine-to-endocrine, and endocrine-to-neural. All four types are illustrated in the courtship behavior of the ringdove. The visual processing that occurs when a male dove sees an attractive female involves neural-to-neural

ovaries The female gonads, which produce eggs (ova) for reproduction.

progestin Any of a major class of steroid hormones that are produced by the ovary, including progesterone.

estrogen Any of a class of steroid hormones produced by female gonads.

estradiol The primary type of estrogen that is secreted by the ovary. Its formal name is *17-beta-estradiol*.

progesterone The primary type of progestin that is secreted by the ovary.

ovulatory cycle The periodic occurrence of ovulation in females.

oral contraceptive A birth control pill, typically consisting of steroid hormones to prevent ovulation.

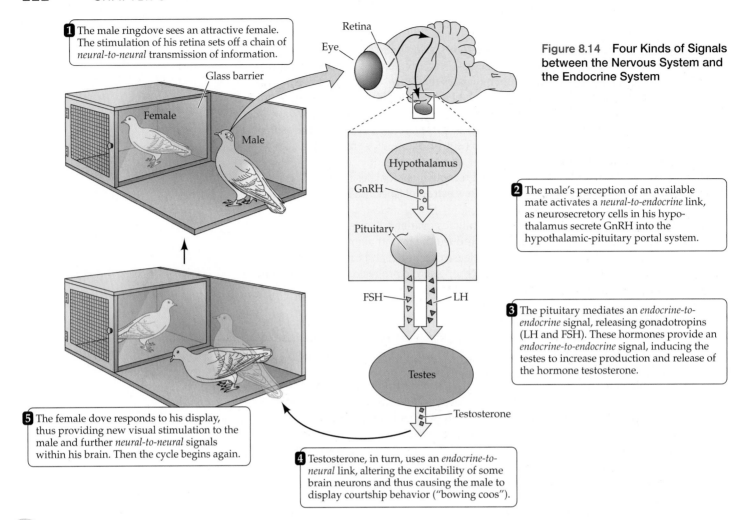

1 The male ringdove sees an attractive female. The stimulation of his retina sets off a chain of *neural-to-neural* transmission of information.

Retina
Eye

Glass barrier

Female

Male

Figure 8.14   Four Kinds of Signals between the Nervous System and the Endocrine System

Hypothalamus

GnRH

Pituitary

FSH   LH

Testes

Testosterone

2 The male's perception of an available mate activates a *neural-to-endocrine* link, as neurosecretory cells in his hypothalamus secrete GnRH into the hypothalamic-pituitary portal system.

3 The pituitary mediates an *endocrine-to-endocrine* signal, releasing gonadotropins (LH and FSH). These hormones provide an *endocrine-to-endocrine* signal, inducing the testes to increase production and release of the hormone testosterone.

5 The female dove responds to his display, thus providing new visual stimulation to the male and further *neural-to-neural* signals within his brain. Then the cycle begins again.

4 Testosterone, in turn, uses an *endocrine-to-neural* link, altering the excitability of some brain neurons and thus causing the male to display courtship behavior ("bowing coos").

How's it going?

1. Describe the role of the hypothalamus and the anterior pituitary in regulating gonadal hormones.
2. What hormones are found in birth control pills, and how do they prevent pregnancy?
3. Describe the interplay of neural and hormonal signaling in the human milk letdown reflex and the male ringdove's courtship behavior.

transmission (step 1 in **Figure 8.14**). The details of the particular visual stimulus—namely, an opportunity to mate—activate a neural-to-endocrine link (step 2), which causes neuroendocrine cells in the male's hypothalamus to secrete GnRH. The GnRH provides an endocrine-to-endocrine signal (step 3), stimulating the pituitary to release gonadotropins, which induce the testes to release more testosterone. Testosterone in turn alters the excitability of neurons in the male's brain through an endocrine-to-neural link (step 4), causing the male to display courtship behavior. The female dove responds to this display (step 5), thus providing new visual stimulation to the male, which triggers another cycle of signaling in him.

The interactions between endocrine activity and behavior are cyclical, as depicted by the circle schema in **Figure 8.15**. The levels of circulating hormones can also be altered by experience, which in turn can affect future behavior and future experience. For example, men rooting for a sports team will produce more testosterone if their team wins (Bernhardt et al., 1998). Physical stresses, pain, and unpleasant emotional situations trigger the release of steroids from the adrenal gland (see Chapter 11).

Conversely, each of these hormonal events will affect the brain, shaping behavior, which will once more affect the person's future hormone production, and so on. It will be important to keep in mind these interactions between hormones and behavior as we consider reproductive behavior in the next section.

Change in hormone release

Change in experience

Change in behavior

Figure 8.15   The Reciprocal Relations between Hormones and Behavior

PART II Reproductive Behavior

Sexual behaviors are almost as diverse as the species that employ them. But in every case, males and females must produce a specific set of behaviors, in a precise and intricately coordinated sequence, to reproduce successfully. In this section we review sexual behaviors, which include the sex act itself (copulation), as well as the parental behaviors that the newborns of many species require to survive. The final section of the chapter will cover sexual differentiation, the process by which an individual's body and brain develop in a male or female fashion.

We wish we could explain exactly why and how humans and other animals engage in the three *C*s—courting, copulating, and cohabiting—but relatively little practical knowledge of such matters exists. Two barriers have blocked our understanding of sexual behavior: (1) cultural barriers to disseminating information about sexual behavior and (2) the remarkable variety of sexual behaviors.

Reproductive Behavior Can Be Divided into Four Stages

Taking a broad view of reproductive behavior, we recognize four distinct stages: (1) sexual attraction, (2) appetitive behavior, (3) copulation, and (4) postcopulatory behavior (**Figure 8.16**).

Sexual attraction is the first stage in bringing males and females together. In many species, sexual attraction is closely synchronized with physiological readiness to reproduce. In experiments, we gauge an individual's attractiveness by observing the responses of potential mates: how rapidly they approach, how hard they work to gain access, and so on. By manipulating the appearance of individuals, we can deduce which special features are most attractive. For example, males of many primate species are strongly attracted to the "sex skin," which swells on a female's rump when her ovaries are secreting estrogenic hormones. Most male mammals are attracted by particular female odors, which also tend to reflect estrogen levels.

Because estrogen secretion is associated with the release of eggs, these mechanisms tend to synchronize female sexual attractiveness with

sexual attraction The first step in the mating behavior of many animals, in which animals emit stimuli that attract members of the opposite sex.

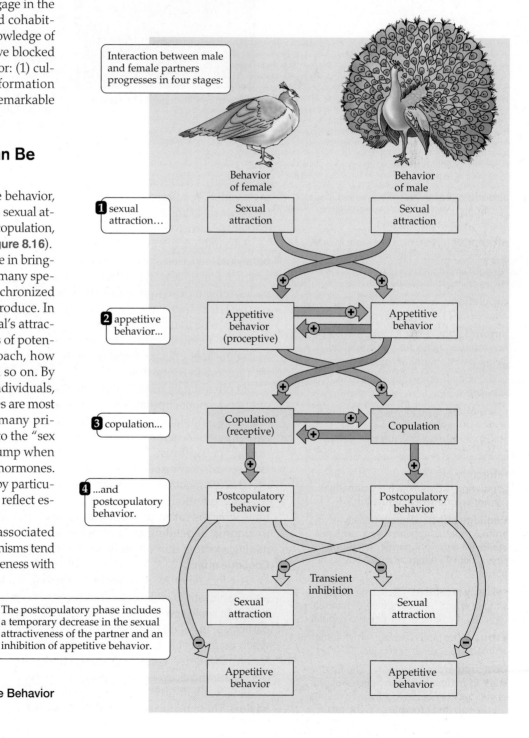

Interaction between male and female partners progresses in four stages:

1 sexual attraction…

2 appetitive behavior…

3 copulation…

4 …and postcopulatory behavior.

The postcopulatory phase includes a temporary decrease in the sexual attractiveness of the partner and an inhibition of appetitive behavior.

Figure 8.16 Stages of Reproductive Behavior (After Beach, 1977.)

The Coolidge Effect   By reducing the refractory phase, when a sexually exhausted male encounters an unfamiliar female the Coolidge effect permits him to take advantage of a new reproductive opportunity and sire more offspring. (Of course, encountering 24 lovelorn females at once is a situation few males—guinea pig or otherwise—could even dream of.)

Sooty enjoyed two nights of passion among 24 females.

Guinea pig Don Juan sires 43 offspring in 2 nights

PONTYPRIDD, WALES, 1 DECEMBER 2000

HAVING ESCAPED from captivity at Little Friend's Farm earlier this year, a male guinea pig named Sooty chose to re-enter captivity immediately—in the nearby cage housing 24 females. Two months later he is now the father of 43 offspring.

According to his owner, Carol Feehan, Sooty was missing for two whole days before the staff checked the females' pen. "We did a head count and found 25 guinea pigs," she told the press. "Sooty was fast asleep in the corner.

"He was absolutely shattered. We put him back in his cage and he slept for two days."

---

appetitive behavior   The second stage of mating behavior; it helps establish or maintain sexual interaction.

proceptive   Referring to a state in which an animal advertises its readiness to mate through species-typical behaviors, such as ear wiggling in the female rat.

copulation   Also called *coitus*. The sexual act.

intromission   Insertion of the erect penis into the vagina during copulation.

vagina   The opening from the outside of the body to the cervix and uterus in females.

ejaculation   The forceful expulsion of semen from the penis.

semen   A mixture of fluid, including sperm, that is released during ejaculation.

refractory phase   A period following copulation during which an individual cannot recommence copulation.

Coolidge effect   The propensity of an animal that has appeared sexually satiated with a present partner to resume sexual activity when provided with a new partner.

sexually receptive   Referring to the state in which an individual (in mammals, typically the female) is willing to copulate.

estrus   The period during which female animals are sexually receptive.

postcopulatory behavior   The final stage in mating behavior. Species-specific postcopulatory behaviors include rolling (in the cat) and grooming (in the rat).

peak fertility. Of course, the female may find a particular male unattractive and refuse to mate with him. Although apparent rape has been described in some nonhuman species (Maggioncalda and Sapolsky, 2002), for most species copulation is not possible without the female's active cooperation.

If the animals are mutually attracted, they may progress to the next stage: **appetitive behaviors**—species-specific behaviors that establish, maintain, or promote sexual interaction. A female displaying these behaviors is said to be **proceptive**: she may approach males, remain close to them, or show alternating approach and retreat behaviors. Proceptive female rats typically exhibit "ear wiggling" and a hopping and darting gait to induce a male to mount. Male appetitive behaviors usually consist of staying near the female. In many mammals the male may sniff around the female's face and vagina. Male birds may engage in elaborate songs or nest-building behaviors, as illustrated for the ringdove in Figure 8.14.

If both animals display appetitive behaviors, they may progress to the third stage of reproduction: **copulation**, also known as *coitus*. In many vertebrates, including all mammals, copulation involves one or more **intromissions**, in which the male inserts his penis into the female's **vagina**, followed by a variable amount of stimulation, usually through pelvic thrusting. When stimulation reaches a threshold level, the male **ejaculates** sperm-bearing **semen** into the female; the length of time and quantity of stimulation that are required vary greatly between species and between individuals.

After one bout of copulation, the animals will not mate again for a period of time, which is called the **refractory phase**. The refractory phase varies from minutes to months, depending on the species and circumstances. Many animals will resume mating sooner if they are provided with a new partner—a phenomenon known as the **Coolidge effect**.

The female often appears to be the one to choose whether copulation will take place; when she is willing to copulate, she is said to be **sexually receptive**, in heat, or in **estrus**. In some species the female may show proceptive behaviors days before she will participate in copulation itself. In most (but not all) species, females are receptive only when mating is likely to produce offspring. Most species are seasonal breeders, with females that are receptive only during the breeding season; and some—such as salmon, octopuses, and cicadas—reproduce only once, at the end of life.

Finally, the fourth stage of reproductive behavior consists of **postcopulatory behaviors**. These behaviors are especially varied, having been strongly shaped by diverse evolutionary pressures related to the different species' mating systems. For example, in some mammals, like dogs and southern grasshopper mice, the male's penis swells so much after ejaculation that he can't remove it from the female for a while. In species like these, where multiple males may copulate with an ovulating female in quick succession, this **copulatory lock** prevents other males from mating, at least for a while (Dewsbury, 1972). Despite wild stories you may have heard or read, humans *never* experience copulatory lock; that urban myth started in 1884 when a physician submitted a fake report as a practical joke (Nation, 1973). For mammals and birds, postcopulatory behavior includes extensive *parental behaviors* to nurture the offspring, as we describe later in this chapter.

Copulation brings gametes together

All mammals, birds, and reptiles employ internal fertilization: the fusion of their **gametes**—**sperm** and **ovum**—within the female's body to form a **zygote**. Most of what we know about the copulatory behavior of mammals comes from studies of lab animals, especially rats. Like most other rodents, rats do not engage in lengthy courtship, nor do the partners tend to remain together after copulation. Rats are attracted to each other largely through odors. Female rats, like humans, are spontaneous ovulators; that is, even when left alone they **ovulate** (release eggs from the ovary). Rats ovulate every 4 days, and for a few hours around the time of ovulation the female seeks out a male and displays proceptive behaviors, including vocalizations at frequencies too high for humans to detect but audible to other rats.

These behaviors prompt the male to mount the female from the rear, grasp her flanks with his forelegs, and rhythmically thrust his hips against her rump. If she is receptive, the female adopts a stereotyped posture called **lordosis** (**Figure 8.17**), elevating her rump and moving her tail to one side to allow intromission. Once intromission has been achieved, the male rat makes a single deep thrust and then springs back off the female. During the next 6–7 minutes the male and female orchestrate seven to nine such intromissions; then, instead of springing away, the male raises the front half of his body up for a second or two while he ejaculates. Finally, he falls backward off the female.

After copulation, the male and female separately engage in grooming their own genitalia, and the male pays little attention to the female for the next 5 minutes or so, until, often in response to the female's proceptive behaviors, the two engage in another bout of intromissions and ejaculation. The cycle may repeat five or six times in one mating session.

There is plenty of variation in the details of rodent sexual behavior. The northern pygmy mouse, for example, has only a single ejaculation during a mating session (talk about pressure!). In some rodent species, such as the prairie voles we discussed earlier, a male and a female live together before and long after copulation, forming a pair-bond.

RESEARCHERS AT WORK

Gonadal steroids activate sexual behavior

Hormones play an important role in rat mating behaviors. Testosterone drives the male's interest in copulation: if he is castrated (his testes removed), he will stop ejaculating within a few weeks and will eventually stop mounting receptive females. Although testosterone disappears from the bloodstream within a few hours after castration, the hormone's effects on the nervous system take days or weeks to dissipate. Treating a castrated male with testosterone eventually restores mating behavior; if testosterone treatment is stopped, the mating behavior fades again. This is an example of a hormone exerting an **activational effect**: the hormone transiently promotes certain behaviors. In normal development, the rise of androgen secretion at puberty activates masculine behavior in males.

Although individual male rats and guinea pigs differ considerably in how eagerly they will mate, blood levels of testosterone clearly are *not* responsible for these

The raised rump and deflected tail of the female (the lordosis posture) make intromission possible in rats.

Figure 8.17   Copulation in Rats

copulatory lock   Reproductive behavior in which the male's penis swells after ejaculation so that the male and female are forced to remain joined for 5–10 minutes; it occurs in dogs and some rodents, but not in humans.

gamete   A sex cell (sperm or ovum) that contains only unpaired chromosomes and therefore has only half of the usual number of chromosomes.

sperm   The gamete produced by males for the fertilization of eggs (ova).

ovum   An egg, the female gamete.

zygote   The fertilized egg.

ovulation   The production and release of an egg (ovum).

lordosis   A female receptive posture in four-legged animals in which the hindquarter is raised and the tail is turned to one side, facilitating intromission by the male.

activational effect   A temporary change in behavior resulting from the administration of a hormone to an adult animal.

differences. For one thing, animals displaying different levels of sexual vigor do not show reliable differences in blood levels of testosterone. Furthermore, when these males are castrated and subsequently all treated with exactly the same doses of testosterone, their precastration differences in sexual activity persist (**Figure 8.18**).

Figure 8.18   Androgens Permit Male Copulatory Behavior (After Grunt and Young, 1953.)

Hypothesis

Individual differences in the vigor with which male guinea pigs mate are caused by differences in testosterone secretion.

Test

Classify individual males by mating vigor, then castrate and provide them all with the same dose of testosterone.

Result

A few weeks after castration, all males stopped mating. But when provided the same dose of testosterone, males returned to their previous levels of mating vigor. Giving a higher dose of testosterone did not eliminate these differences.

Conclusion

Although androgens—especially testosterone—are important for normal male sexual function, individual differences in sexual activity are not determined by differences in androgen levels.

Furthermore, it turns out that a very small amount of testosterone—one-tenth the amount normally produced by the animals—is enough to fully maintain the mating behavior of male rats. Thus, since all male rats make more testosterone than is required to maintain their copulatory behavior, some other factor, which we can call "drive," must differ across individual males.

Estrogens secreted at the beginning of the 4- to 5-day ovulatory cycle facilitate proceptive behavior in female rats, and the subsequent production of progesterone increases proceptive behavior and activates receptivity (**Figure 8.19**). An adult female whose ovaries have been removed will show neither proceptive nor receptive behaviors. However, 2 days of estrogen treatment followed by a single injection of progesterone will, about 6 hours later, make the female rat proceptive and receptive for a few hours. Only the correct combination of estrogens and progesterone will fully activate copulatory behaviors in female rats—another example illustrating the activational effects of gonadal steroids.

Next we'll discuss how steroid hormones affect the brain to activate mating behavior.

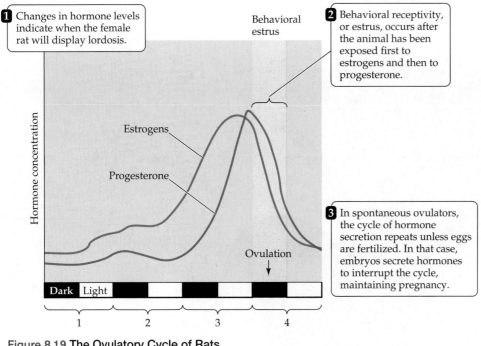

1 Changes in hormone levels indicate when the female rat will display lordosis.

2 Behavioral receptivity, or estrus, occurs after the animal has been exposed first to estrogens and then to progesterone.

Behavioral estrus

Estrogens

Progesterone

3 In spontaneous ovulators, the cycle of hormone secretion repeats unless eggs are fertilized. In that case, embryos secrete hormones to interrupt the cycle, maintaining pregnancy.

Ovulation

Hormone concentration

Dark Light

1   2   3   4

Figure 8.19 The Ovulatory Cycle of Rats

How's it going?

1. What are the four stages of reproductive behavior?
2. Describe a typical mating session in laboratory rats.
3. Describe the activational effects of gonadal steroids on mating behaviors in rodents.
4. Are differences in testosterone secretion responsible for individual differences in male reproductive behavior?

The Neural Circuitry of the Brain Regulates Reproductive Behavior

Although most of what we know about the neural circuitry of sexual behavior comes from studies of rats, steroid receptors are found in the same specific brain regions across a wide variety of vertebrate species. Steroid-sensitive regions include the cortex, brainstem nuclei, medial amygdala, hippocampus, and many others. And, as we'll see, the hypothalamus plays a particularly important role in regulating copulatory behavior.

Ovarian steroids act on a lordosis circuit that spans from brain to muscle

Scientists have exploited the steroid sensitivity of the rat lordosis response to develop a map of the neural circuitry that controls this behavior. Using steroid autoradiography (see Box 8.1), investigators identified hypothalamic nuclei containing many estrogen- and progesterone-sensitive neurons. In particular, the **ventromedial hypothalamus** (**VMH**) is crucial for lordosis because lesions there abolish the response. Furthermore, tiny quantities of estradiol implanted directly into the brain can induce receptivity in females, but only when the hormone is placed in the VMH (Lisk, 1962).

One action of estrogen treatment is to cause dendrites of VMH neurons to grow and become more complex (Meisel and Luttrell, 1990). Another important action of estrogens is to stimulate the production of progesterone receptors so that the animal will become more responsive to that hormone. Activated progesterone receptors in turn help mediate the lordosis reflex (Mani et al., 2000).

The VMH sends axons to the **periaqueductal gray** region of the midbrain, where again, lesions greatly diminish lordosis. The periaqueductal gray neurons project to other brain regions and the spinal cord. In the spinal cord the sensory information provided by the mounting male will now evoke the motor response of lordosis. Thus, the role of the VMH is to monitor steroid hormone concentrations and, at the right time in the ovulatory cycle, activate a neural circuit that allows a lordosis response to occur in response to a mounting male (Pfaff, 1997). **Figure 8.20b** schematically represents this neural pathway and its steroid-responsive components.

ventromedial hypothalamus (VMH) A hypothalamic region involved in eating and sexual behaviors.

periaqueductal gray The region of the midbrain surrounding the cerebral aqueduct that connects the third and fourth ventricles; rich in neuronal cell bodies, it is involved in pain perception and reproductive behaviors.

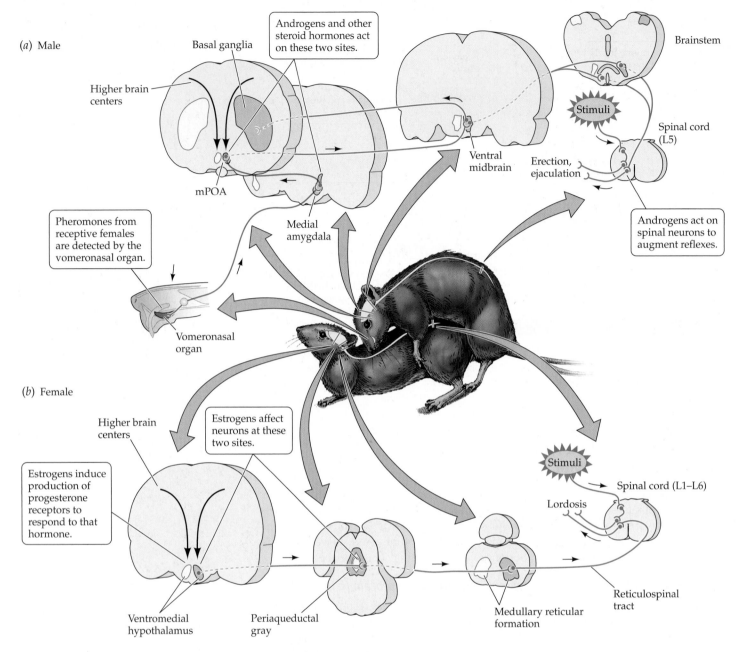

(a) Male

Basal ganglia

Androgens and other steroid hormones act on these two sites.

Brainstem

Higher brain centers

mPOA

Ventral midbrain

Stimuli

Spinal cord (L5)

Erection, ejaculation

Androgens act on spinal neurons to augment reflexes.

Medial amygdala

Pheromones from receptive females are detected by the vomeronasal organ.

Vomeronasal organ

(b) Female

Higher brain centers

Estrogens affect neurons at these two sites.

Stimuli

Estrogens induce production of progesterone receptors to respond to that hormone.

Spinal cord (L1–L6)

Lordosis

Reticulospinal tract

Ventromedial hypothalamus

Periaqueductal gray

Medullary reticular formation

Figure 8.20 Neural Circuits for Reproduction in Rodents (After Pfaff, 1980.)

medial preoptic area (mPOA) A region of the anterior hypothalamus implicated in the control of many behaviors, including thermoregulation, sexual behavior, and gonadotropin secretion.

Androgens activate a neural system for male reproductive behavior

Steroid hormones also activate male copulatory behavior in rodents (**Figure 8.20a**), and other animals, and again the sites of steroid action provide important clues about the neural circuitry involved. The hypothalamic **medial preoptic area** (**mPOA**) is chock-full of steroid-sensitive neurons, and lesions of the mPOA abolish male copulatory behavior in a wide variety of vertebrate species (Meisel and Sachs, 1994). Note that lesions of the mPOA do not interfere with males' *motivation* for females; males will still press a bar to gain access to a receptive female (Everitt and Stacey, 1987), but they seem unable to commence mounting. Furthermore, mating can be reinstated in castrated males by small implants of testosterone in the mPOA, but not in other brain regions. Thus, the mPOA seems to provide "higher-order" control of male copulatory behaviors.

The mPOA coordinates copulatory behavior by sending axons to the ventral midbrain (which innervates several brain regions to coordinate mounting behaviors) and, via a multisynaptic pathway, to the spinal cord (Hamson and Watson, 2004), which mediates various genital reflexes, such as ejaculation. Brainstem projections of serotonergic fibers to the spinal cord normally hold the penile erection reflex in check (McKenna, 1999). Antidepressant drugs that boost serotonergic activity in the brain—for example, selective serotonin reuptake inhibitors like Prozac (see Chapter 12)—can produce side effects that include difficulty achieving erection, ejaculation, and/or orgasm, probably by enhancing serotonergic inhibition of the spinal cord.

Because the reflex circuits and ejaculation generator are in the lumbar spinal cord, men with damage at higher levels of the spinal cord often remain capable of copulation and ejaculation. (If you're wondering, the drug sildenafil, better known as Viagra, acts directly on tissue in the penis, not in the spinal cord or brain, to promote erection [Boolell et al., 1996].)

We can also learn about male copulatory mechanisms by tracing a sensory system that activates male arousal in rodents: the vomeronasal system. The **vomeronasal organ**, or **VNO** (see Chapter 9) consists of specialized receptor cells near to, but separate from, the olfactory epithelium. These sensory cells detect chemicals, called pheromones (see Figure 8.3c and Chapter 6) that are released by other individuals. Vomeronasal receptor neurons send their axons to the accessory olfactory bulb in the brain, which then projects elsewhere in the brain to govern sexual behavior. For example, receptive female rats release pheromones that male rats find arousing, as evidenced by penile erections. (You can learn more about the role of pheromones in reproductive behavior **A Step Further 8.5**, on the website.) Humans also respond to pheromones, but we detect them with our olfactory system, since the vomeronasal organ is absent in our species.

In rats, an important target for vomeronasal information is the **medial amygdala**, which depends on adult circulating levels of sex steroids to maintain a masculine form and function (Cooke et al., 2003). Lesions here will abolish the penile erections that normally occur around receptive females (Kondo et al., 1997). The medial amygdala, in turn, sends axons to the mPOA. So the mPOA appears to integrate hormonal and sensory information such as pheromones, and to coordinate the motor patterns of copulation. Figure 8.20a summarizes the neural circuitry for male rat copulatory behavior.

We will see later that testosterone activates sexual arousal in humans too.

Parental behaviors are governed by several sex-related hormones

In many vertebrate species, copulation is not enough to ensure reproduction. Many young vertebrates, and all newborn mammals, need parental attention to survive. Earlier we discussed the milk letdown reflex, when the infant's suckling on the nipple triggers the secretion of oxytocin to promote the release of milk (see Figure 8.9). In rats, the pregnant female prepares for her pups by licking all of her nipples. Doing so probably helps clean the nipples before the pups arrive, but it also makes them more sensitive to touch. This self-grooming actually expands the amount of sensory cortex that responds to skin surrounding the nipples (Xerri et al., 1994), setting the stage for the letdown reflex. This is a wonderful example of an animal's behavior altering its own brain and therefore changing its future behavior.

Rat mothers (called *dams*) show four easily measured **parental behaviors**: nest building, crouching over pups, retrieving pups, and nursing (**Figure 8.21**). Neither virgin female rats nor male rats normally show these behaviors toward rat pups. In fact, a virgin female finds the smell of newborn pups aversive. Information about the odor from pups projects via the olfactory bulb to the medial amygdala and on to the VMH. Lesions anywhere along that path will cause a virgin rat to show maternal behavior right away (Numan and Numan, 1991), because she no longer detects the smell.

However, if a virgin female is exposed to newborn pups a few hours a day for several days in a row, she (or almost any adult rat—male or female) will start building a nest, crouching over pups, and retrieving them. As the rat gradually habituates to the smell of the pups, it starts taking care of them. But the rat dam that gives birth to her first litter will *instantly* show these behaviors. It turns out that the rather complicated pattern of hormones during pregnancy shapes her brain to display maternal behaviors *before* she is exposed to the pups.

vomeronasal organ (VNO) A collection of specialized receptor cells, near to but separate from the olfactory epithelium, that detect pheromones and send electrical signals to the accessory olfactory bulb in the brain.

medial amygdala A portion of the amygdala that receives olfactory and pheromonal information.

parental behavior Behavior of adult animals that has the goal of enhancing the well-being of their own offspring, often at some cost to the parents.

Rat dams clean their pups…

…crouch over them to allow them to nurse…

…and will retrieve them if they stray from the nest.

Figure 8.21 **Parental Behavior in Rats**

A pregnant rat dam will instantly show maternal behavior when her pups arrive.

These animals are connected parabiotically, sharing all hormones in circulation.

A virgin female, which would normally avoid pups, will show maternal behavior if she has been exposed to the hormones circulating in a pregnant female.

Figure 8.22 Parabiotic Exchange Facilitates Maternal Behavior (After Terkel and Rosenblatt, 1972.)

The effect of pregnancy hormones on a rat's maternal behaviors is demonstrated by a **parabiotic** preparation in which two female rats are surgically joined, sharing a single blood supply, such that each is exposed to any hormones secreted by the other (**Figure 8.22**). If one of those females is pregnant, then at the end of her pregnancy the other female, who was never pregnant but was exposed to the pregnant rat's hormones, will also immediately show maternal behavior (Terkel and Rosenblatt, 1972). Which hormone is responsible for promoting maternal behavior? No single hormone alone can do it; the combination of several hormones, including estrogens, progesterone, oxytocin, and prolactin, is required. There is ample evidence that the hormones of pregnancy also prepare human mothers to nurture their newborns (Fleming et al., 2002). Compared to other women, mothers who have recently given birth are better at distinguishing odors from different newborns, and they can even recognize odors from their own newborn. This increased ability to discriminate odors correlates with hormone levels after delivery (Fleming et al., 1997).

The Hallmark of Human Sexual Behavior Is Diversity

How much of what we've described so far about sexual behavior in animals is relevant to human sexuality? Until the 1940s, when biology professor Alfred Kinsey began to ask friends and colleagues about their sexual histories, there was virtually no scientific study of human sexual behavior. Kinsey constructed a standardized set of questions and procedures to get information. Eventually, he and his collaborators published extensive surveys (based on tens of thousands of respondents) on the sexual behavior of American males (Kinsey et al., 1948) and females (Kinsey et al., 1953).

Controversial in their time, these surveys indicated that nearly all men masturbated, that college-educated people were more likely to engage in oral sex than were non-college-educated people, that many people had at one time or another engaged in homosexual behaviors, and that as much as 10% of the population preferred homosexual sex. Although it has since been shown that the last figure is an overestimate, these surveys opened our eyes about human sexual behavior.

Another way to investigate human sexual behavior is to make behavioral and physiological observations of people engaged in sexual intercourse or masturbation, but the squeamishness of the general public impeded such research for many years. Finally, after Kinsey's surveys were published, physician William Masters and psychologist Virginia Johnson began a large, famous project of this kind (Masters and Johnson, 1970; Masters et al., 1994), documenting the impressively diverse sexuality of humans.

Among most mammalian species, including most nonhuman primates, the male mounts the female from the rear; but among humans, face-to-face postures are most common. A great variety of coital positions have been described, and many couples vary their positions from session to session or even within a session. It is this variety in reproductive behaviors, rather than differences in reproductive anatomy, that distinguishes human sexuality from that of most other species.

Another difference between species is that, unlike other animals, humans can report their subjective reactions to sexual behavior—specifically **orgasm**, the brief, extremely pleasurable sensations experienced by most men during ejaculation and by most women during copulation. In the original conceptual model of human sexuality, Masters and Johnson (1966) summarized the typical response patterns of both men and

parabiotic Referring to a surgical preparation that joins two animals to share a single blood supply.

orgasm The climax of sexual behavior, marked by extremely pleasurable sensations.

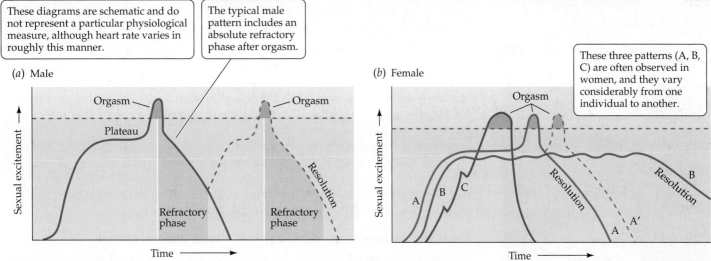

These diagrams are schematic and do not represent a particular physiological measure, although heart rate varies in roughly this manner.

The typical male pattern includes an absolute refractory phase after orgasm.

These three patterns (A, B, C) are often observed in women, and they vary considerably from one individual to another.

(a) Male

Sexual excitement →

Orgasm

Plateau

Refractory phase

Refractory phase

Resolution

Time →

(b) Female

Sexual excitement →

Orgasm

A   B   C

Resolution

Resolution

A

A′

B

Time →

Figure 8.23   Human Sexual Response Cycles (After Masters and Johnson, 1966.)

women as consisting of four phases: increasing excitement, plateau, orgasm, and resolution (**Figure 8.23**).

During the excitement phase, the **phallus** (the **penis** in men, the **clitoris** in women) becomes engorged with blood, making it erect. In women, parasympathetic activity during the excitement phase causes changes in vaginal blood vessels, producing lubricating fluids that facilitate intromission. Stimulation of the penis, clitoris, and vagina during rhythmic thrusting accompanying intromission may lead to orgasm. In both men and women, orgasm is accompanied by waves of contractions of genital muscles (mediating ejaculation in men and contractions of the uterus and vagina in women).

In spite of some basic similarities, the sexual responses of men and women differ in important ways. For one thing, women show a much greater variety of commonly observed copulatory sequences. Whereas men have only one basic pattern, captured by the linear model of Masters and Johnson (see Figure 8.23a), women have at least three typical patterns (see Figure 8.23b). Another important aspect of human sexuality is that most men, but not most women, have an absolute refractory phase following orgasm (also illustrated in Figure 8.23a). That is, most men cannot achieve full erection and another orgasm until some time has elapsed—the length of time varying from minutes to hours, depending on individual differences and other factors. Many women, on the other hand, can have multiple orgasms in rapid succession. Functional imaging of the brains of men and women during sexual activity suggests that, although the brain circuitry associated with orgasm itself is quite similar between the sexes, substantially different networks are active in men's and women's brains during sexual activity *prior* to orgasm (Georgiadis et al., 2009).

Taking a broader perspective on sexuality reveals additional distinctions between men and women (Peplau, 2003). Basic sex drive seems to be greater in men, reflected in more frequent masturbation, sexual fantasies, and pursuit of sexual contacts. There are closer links between sexuality and aggression in men than in women, ranging from differences in sexual assertiveness to the most extreme manifestation: rape.

In women's sex lives, emotional components and cognitive factors play a stronger role than in men. In addition to having a somewhat flexible sexuality that adapts to new experiences and situations over time, women place more emphasis on sexual intimacy within the context of committed relationships. These observations and others have led sex researchers to adopt a more nuanced view of female sexuality. While Masters and Johnson simply adapted the linear model of male sexuality to women, the more modern perspective views women's sexuality as a cycle, governed in large measure by emotional factors (Basson, 2001, 2008). According to this model, emotional intimacy and desire (more than physiological arousal) are crucial in the initiation of sexual responses, and following a sexual encounter, a combination of both emotional and physical satisfaction affects the likelihood of subsequent sexual activity.

phallus   The clitoris or penis.
penis   The male phallus.
clitoris   The female phallus.

Testosterone Patches These patches can revive libido in men who have lost their testes through accident or disease.

How's it going?

1. What brain regions appear to be involved in male and female sexual behaviors?

2. Compare and contrast the maternal behavior of a female rat that has just undergone pregnancy with that of a naive female. What factor is responsible for the differences?

3. Compare and contrast the patterns of sexual arousal in men and women.

4. What are the effects of gonadal steroids on human sexual behavior?

double-blind test   A test of a drug or treatment in which neither the subjects nor the attending researchers know which subjects are receiving the drug (treatment) and which are receiving the placebo (control).

sexual differentiation   The process by which individuals develop either malelike or femalelike bodies and behavior.

Although male and female sexuality may bear the imprint of our evolutionary history, on an individual basis it is also shaped by sociocultural pressures and experience. Sexual therapy, for example, usually consists of helping the person to relax, to recognize the sensations associated with coitus, and to learn the behaviors that produce the desired effects in both partners. Masturbation during adolescence, rather than being harmful as suggested in previous times, may help avoid sexual problems in adulthood. As with other behaviors, practice, practice, practice helps.

Sexual behavior may also aid overall health; epidemiological studies indicate that men who have frequent sex tend to live longer than men who do not (Davey-Smith et al., 1997). Of course, it is also important to one's health to take precautions (such as using condoms) to avoid contracting sexually transmitted infections.

Hormones play only a permissive role in human sexual behavior

We have already seen that a little bit of testosterone must be in circulation to activate male-typical mating behavior in rodents. The same relation seems to hold for human males. For example, boys who fail to produce testosterone at puberty show little interest in dating unless they receive androgen treatments. These males, as well as men who have lost their testes as a result of cancer or accident, made it possible to conduct double-blind tests demonstrating that testosterone indeed stimulates sexual interest and activity in men. (In **double-blind tests**, neither the subjects nor the investigators know which subjects are receiving the drug and which are receiving a placebo, until after the treatment is over.) Despite the double-blind design of the experiment, men sometimes know when they're getting the testosterone treatment, because they feel more energetic (Davidson et al., 1979).

Recall that, in rats, *additional* testosterone has no effect on the vigor of mating. Consequently, there is no correlation between the amount of androgens produced by an individual male rat and his tendency to copulate. In humans, too, just a little testosterone is sufficient to restore behavior fully, and there is no correlation between systemic androgen levels and sexual activity among men who have at least *some* androgen.

Some women experience sexual dysfunction after menopause, reporting decreased sexual desire and difficulty achieving comfortable coitus. There are many possible reasons for such a change, including several hormonal changes. Evidence is accumulating that providing postmenopausal women with low doses of both estrogens and androgens can have beneficial effects on the genital experience of sex and also on women's sexual interest (Basson, 2008; Sherwin, 1998, 2002).

There have been several attempts to determine whether women's interest or participation in sexual behavior varies with the menstrual cycle. Some researchers have found a slight increase in sexual behavior around the time of ovulation, but the effect is small, and several studies have failed to see any significant change in interest in sex across the menstrual cycle.

Now that we've discussed some of the unique aspects of male and female sexuality, let's look at some of the developmental processes that cause the growing individual to take on male-typical or female-typical forms and functions in the first place.

PART III Sexual Differentiation and Orientation

For species such as our own, in which the only kind of reproduction is sexual reproduction (so far), each individual must become either a male or a female to reproduce. **Sexual differentiation** is the process by which individuals develop either male or female bodies and behaviors. In mammals this process begins before birth and continues into adulthood. As we'll see, some people may be very malelike (masculine) in some parts of the body and very femalelike (feminine) in others, so that a person can't be said to be either male or female, but may be a blend of the two sexes.

Genetic and Hormonal Mechanisms Guide the Development of Masculine and Feminine Structures

In mammals, every egg carries an X chromosome from the mother; the penetration of the egg by a sperm carrying either a second X or a Y chromosome is the key event in **sex determination**, the developmentally early event that decides whether the new individual will develop as a male or a female. Mammals that receive an X chromosome from the father will become females with an XX sex chromosome complement; those that receive the father's Y chromosome will become XY males. From that point on, the path of sexual differentiation is set, with only occasional exceptions.

In vertebrates, the first major consequence of sexual determination is in the gonads. Very early in development, each individual has a pair of **indifferent gonads**, glands that vaguely resemble both testes and ovaries. During the first month of gestation in humans, the indifferent gonads begin changing into either ovaries or testes.

Sex chromosomes direct sexual differentiation of the gonads

In mammals, the Y chromosome contains the **SRY gene** (for *s*ex-determining *r*egion on the *Y* chromosome), which is responsible for the development of testes. If an individual has a Y chromosome, the cells of the indifferent gonad begin making the Sry protein, which induces the indifferent gonad to develop into a testis.

If the individual has no Y chromosome (or if it has a Y chromosome but the *SRY* gene is defective), no Sry protein is produced, and the indifferent gonad becomes an ovary. This early event of forming either testes or ovaries has a domino effect, setting off a chain of actions that usually results in either a male or a female.

Gonadal hormones direct sexual differentiation of the body

For all mammals, including humans, the gonads secrete hormones to direct sexual differentiation of the body. Fetal ovaries produce very little hormone, but fetal testes produce several hormones. If other embryonic cells are exposed to the testicular hormones, they begin developing masculine characters; if the cells are not exposed to testicular hormones, they develop feminine characters.

We can chart masculine or feminine development by examining the structures that connect the gonads to the outside of the body: these are quite different in adult males and females, but at the embryonic stage all individuals have the precursor tissues of both systems. The early fetus has a **genital tubercle** (a "bump" between the legs) that can form either a clitoris or a penis, as well as two sets of ducts that connect the indifferent gonads to the outer body wall: the **wolffian ducts** and the **müllerian ducts** (**Figure 8.24a**). In females, the müllerian ducts develop into the oviducts (or fallopian tubes), uterus, and inner vagina (**Figures 8.24b, c**, right), and only a remnant of the wolffian ducts remains. In males, hormones secreted by the testes orchestrate the converse outcome: the wolffian ducts develop into epididymis, vas deferens, and seminal vesicles (**Figures 8.24b, c**, left), while the müllerian ducts shrink to mere remnants.

The system is masculinized by two testicular secretions: testosterone, which promotes development of the wolffian system; and **anti-müllerian hormone** (**AMH**), which causes regression of the müllerian system. In the absence of testosterone and AMH, the genital tract develops in a feminine pattern, in which the wolffian ducts regress and the müllerian ducts develop into components of the female internal reproductive tract.

Testosterone also masculinizes other structures, acting on the fetal genitalia to form a scrotum and penis. These effects are aided by the local conversion of testosterone into a more potent androgen, **dihydrotestosterone** (**DHT**), promoted by an enzyme that is found in the genital skin, **5-alpha-reductase**. We'll see later that without the local production of DHT, testosterone alone is able to masculinize the genitalia only partially. If androgens are absent altogether, the genital tissues grow into the female labia and clitoris.

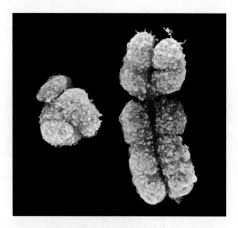

Mammalian Sex Chromosomes The Y chromosome (left) is much shorter than the X (right) because it carries far fewer genes. But one of those genes, *SRY*, is critical for masculine development.

sex determination   The process by which it is established that a fetus will develop as a male or a female.

indifferent gonads   The undifferentiated gonads of the early mammalian fetus, which will eventually develop into either testes or ovaries.

SRY gene   A gene on the Y chromosome that directs the developing gonads to become testes. The name *SRY* stands for *s*ex-determining *r*egion on the *Y* chromosome.

genital tubercle   In the early fetus, a "bump" between the legs that can develop into either a clitoris or a penis.

wolffian duct   A duct system in the embryo that will develop into male reproductive structures (epididymis, vas deferens, and seminal vesicles) if testes are present in the embryo.

müllerian duct   A duct system in the embryo that will develop into female reproductive structures (oviduct, uterus, and upper vagina) if testes are not present in the embryo.

anti-müllerian hormone (AMH)   Also called *müllerian regression hormone*. A protein hormone secreted by the fetal testes that inhibits müllerian duct development.

dihydrotestosterone (DHT)   The 5-alpha-reduced metabolite of testosterone; DHT is a potent androgen that is principally responsible for the masculinization of the external genitalia in mammalian sexual differentiation.

5-alpha-reductase   An enzyme that converts testosterone into dihydrotestosterone.

(*a*) 6 weeks of gestation (undifferentiated fetus)

Gonad
Wolffian duct
Müllerian duct
Kidney
Urogenital sinus
Genital tubercle
Genital fold

Figure 8.24 Sexual Differentiation in Humans

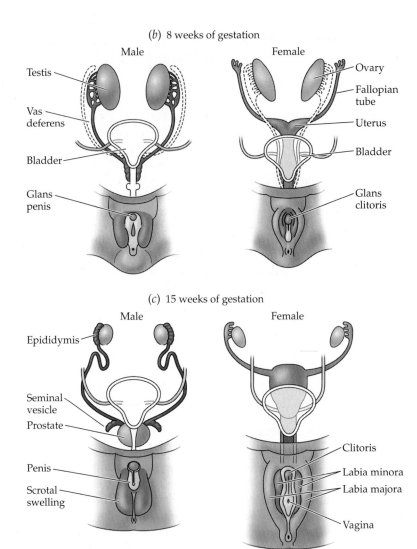

(*b*) 8 weeks of gestation

Male

Testis
Vas deferens
Bladder
Glans penis

Female

Ovary
Fallopian tube
Uterus
Bladder
Glans clitoris

(*c*) 15 weeks of gestation

Male

Epididymis
Seminal vesicle
Prostate
Penis
Scrotal swelling

Female

Clitoris
Labia minora
Labia majora
Vagina

Turner's syndrome A condition, seen in individuals carrying a single X chromosome but no other sex chromosome, in which an apparent female has underdeveloped but recognizable ovaries.

congenital adrenal hyperplasia (CAH) Any of several genetic mutations that can cause a female fetus to be exposed to adrenal androgens, resulting in partial masculinization at birth.

intersex Referring to an individual with atypical genital development and sexual differentiation that generally resembles a form intermediate between typical male and typical female genitals.

Changes in the sequence of sexual differentiation result in predictable changes in development

Some people have only one sex chromosome: a single X (embryos containing only single Y chromosomes do not survive). This genetic makeup results in **Turner's syndrome**, in which an apparent female has underdeveloped but recognizable ovaries, as you might expect because no *SRY* gene is available. In general, unless the indifferent gonad becomes a testis and begins secreting hormones, immature mammals develop as females in most respects, including women with Turner's syndrome. So the sex chromosomes determine the sex of the gonad, and gonadal hormones then drive sexual differentiation of the rest of the body (**Figure 8.25**).

Sometimes XX individuals with well-formed ovaries are exposed to androgens *in utero*, and depending on the degree of exposure, they may be masculinized. In humans, **congenital adrenal hyperplasia** (**CAH**) causes developing females to be exposed to excess androgens before birth. In CAH, the adrenal glands produce considerable amounts of androgens, somewhere between those of normal females and males, so the newborn often has an **intersex** appearance: a phallus that is intermediate in size between a normal clitoris and a normal penis, and skin folds that resemble both labia and scrotum (**Figure 8.26**). Such individuals are usually recognizable at birth because, even in severe cases in which penis and scrotum appear well formed, no testes are present inside the "scrotum"; instead, these individuals have normal abdominal ovaries, as you would

Figure 8.25   The Sequence of Sexual Differentiation

1 The presence of a Y chromosome will direct indifferent gonads to develop as testes.

2 Without a Y chromosome, the indifferent gonads develop as ovaries.

3 Hormones from the fetal testes masculinize the body…

4 …and the brain (at least in nonhuman animals).

5 The fetal ovaries do not secrete androgens, so the body develops in a feminine fashion…

6 …as does the brain.

expect. Once born, CAH children are given medicine to prevent further androgen production. There is controversy, however, over whether the best course of action for the parents of CAH girls is to opt for immediate surgical modification of the genitalia, or to wait until adulthood, when the CAH-affected individuals can decide for themselves whether to have surgery that is purely cosmetic.

In spotted hyenas, females are always exposed to prenatal androgens, resulting in highly masculinized genitalia. You can read about these fascinating animals in **A Step Further 8.6**, on the website.

Dysfunctional androgen receptors can block the masculinization of males

An interesting demonstration of the influence of androgens on sexual differentiation is provided by the condition known as **androgen insensitivity syndrome** (**AIS**). AIS is caused when an XY zygote inherits a dysfunctional gene for the androgen receptor, so the embryo's tissues cannot respond to androgenic hormones like testosterone. The gonads of such people develop as normal testes (as directed by Sry), and the testes produce AMH (which inhibits müllerian duct structures) and plenty of testosterone.

In the absence of working androgen receptors, however, the wolffian ducts fail to develop and the external tissue forms labia and a clitoris. Such individuals look like other females at birth, and at puberty they develop breasts, but they fail to start

androgen insensitivity syndrome (AIS) A syndrome caused by a mutation of the androgen receptor gene that renders tissues insensitive to androgenic hormones like testosterone. Affected XY individuals are phenotypic females, but they have internal testes and regressed internal genital structures.

Enlarged clitoris

Fused labia

The partially masculinized genitalia of this girl with CAH are the result of excessive androgen production by the adrenals.

Figure 8.26   An Intersex Phenotype

Figure 8.27   Androgen-Insensitive Women (Photos courtesy of Jane Goto and Cindy Stone.)

Although these women have Y chromosomes and were born with testes, because they are insensitive to androgen their bodies developed in a feminine fashion. Their behavior is feminine too.

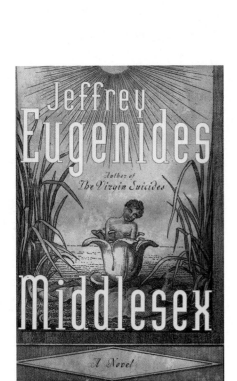

A Confusing Adolescence   In his novel *Middlesex*, Jeffrey Eugenides portrays the life of a person with 5-alpha-reductase deficiency who is raised as a girl in Detroit and grows a penis at puberty.

guevedoces   Literally, "eggs at 12" (in Spanish). A nickname for individuals who are raised as girls but at puberty change appearance and begin behaving as boys.

menstruating because neither ovaries nor uterus are present. Women with AIS are infertile, but otherwise they look like other women (**Figure 8.27**) and, as we'll detail later, behave like other women.

Some people seem to change sex at puberty

Babies are occasionally born with a rare genetic mutation that disables the enzyme (5-alpha-reductase) that converts testosterone to dihydrotestosterone (DHT). An XY individual with this condition will develop testes and normal male internal reproductive structures (because testosterone and AMH function normally), but the external genitalia will fail to masculinize fully (**Figure 8.28**). The reason for this failure is that the genital epithelium, which normally possesses 5-alpha-reductase, is unable to amplify the androgenic signal by converting testosterone to the more active DHT. Consequently, the phallus is only slightly masculinized and resembles a large clitoris, and the genital folds resemble labia, although they contain the testes. Usually there is no vaginal opening.

A particular village in the Dominican Republic is home to several families that carry the mutation causing 5-alpha-reductase deficiency. Children born with this appearance seem to be regarded as girls in the way they are dressed and raised (Imperato-McGinley et al., 1974). At puberty, however, the testes increase androgen production, and the external genitalia become more fully masculinized. The phallus grows into a small but recognizable penis; the body develops narrow hips and a muscular build, without breasts; and the individuals begin acting like young men. The villagers have nicknamed such individuals *guevedoces*, meaning "eggs (testes) at 12 (years)." These men never develop beards, but they usually have girlfriends, indicating that they are sexually interested in women. We will discuss the sexual behavior of *guevedoces*, as well as women with CAH or AIS, later.

How should we define gender—by genes, gonads, genitals?

Most humans are either male or female, and whether we examine their chromosomes, gonads, external genitalia, or internal structures, we see a consistent pattern: each one is either feminine or masculine in character. But as the various syndromes we've been discussing demonstrate, different physical features in a single person can be either masculine or feminine, so from a scientific perspective, legal efforts to categorize all people as either male or female are doomed to failure. Androgen-insensitive women have male

(a) Newborn

In the Dominican Republic, some individuals, called *guevedoces*, are born with ambiguous genitalia and are raised as girls.

(b) Adolescent

At puberty, however, the phallus grows into a recognizable penis, and the individuals begin acting like young men.

Figure 8.28 *Guevedoces* (Courtesy of Julianne Imperato-McGinley.)

XY sex chromosomes and internal testes, and like most males they do not have fallopian tubes or a uterus. But they do have a vagina and breasts, and in most respects their behavior is typical of females: they dress like females, they are attracted to and marry males, and perhaps most important, even after they learn the details of their condition they strongly identify themselves as women (Money and Ehrhardt, 1972). They are males in some respects, but females in others. If laws define marriage as only between a man and a woman, whom should these individuals, carrying a Y chromosome and born with testes, be allowed to marry? How about XY individuals with 5-alpha-reductase deficiency, born and raised as girls—with a birth certificate to prove it? Should they be restricted to marrying men, even if, at 12 years of age, they sprout a penis?

This recognition that a single individual may be masculine in some regards and feminine in others is especially important as we consider hormonal effects on the brain in the next section.

How's it going?

1. Describe the process of fetal sexual differentiation in males and females, especially the role of hormones.

2. Does it make sense to you that a single signal, such as androgens, would masculinize the entire body?

3. What are some of the syndromes that can affect sexual differentiation, and what do they tell us about the problems of defining a person's gender?

RESEARCHERS AT WORK

Gonadal hormones direct sexual differentiation of behavior and the brain

As scientists began discovering that testicular hormones direct masculine development of the fetal body, behavioral researchers found evidence for a similar influence on the fetal brain. A female guinea pig, like most other rodents, normally displays the lordosis posture in response to male mounting (see Figure 8.17) for only a short period around the time of ovulation, when her fertility is highest. If a male mounts her at other times, she does not show lordosis. Experimenters can induce female rodents to display lordosis by injecting ovarian steroids in the sequence they normally follow during ovulation—giving the animals estrogens for a few days and then progesterone (see Figure 8.19). A few hours after the progesterone injection, the female will display lordosis in response to male mounting.

Phoenix et al. (1959) exposed female guinea pigs to testosterone *in utero*. As adults, these females did *not* show lordosis. Even if their ovaries were removed and

To see an animation, go to

mindsmachine.com/8.6
Organizational Effects of Testosterone

Figure 8.29 **Organizational Effects of Testosterone on Rodent Behavior** (After Phoenix et al., 1959.)

Hypothesis
Androgens early in life organize the brain, and therefore adult behavior, in a masculine fashion.

Test
Manipulate androgen exposure in genetic male and female rodents early in life, then ask whether hormones in adulthood can elicit male and/or female behaviors.

	Tested with male	Tested with receptive female
(a) Untreated male	No lordosis	Mounts

Conception — Birth — Adult
Sensitive period

Results
- Normally male rodents eagerly mount receptive females but do not show lordosis behavior in response to another male, even when given ovarian steroids.

(b) Untreated female	Lordosis	Does not mount

- Conversely, female rodents show little masculine sexual behavior, but they display lordosis when treated with an estrogen and progesterone.

(c) Treated female

Treated with testosterone during the sensitive period…

…and treated with steroids again in adulthood.

Testosterone

No lordosis	Mounts

- However, female rodents exposed to testosterone early in life show little or no lordosis, even when given steroids that activate that behavior in normal females. When given testosterone, these androgenized females eagerly mount other females.

(d) Castrated male

Castrated (i.e., deprived of testosterone) at birth.

Estradiol

Lordosis	Does not mount

Conception — Birth — Adult
Sensitive period

- Conversely, males deprived of androgens early in life are demasculinized as adults, showing little copulatory behavior, and are also feminized, displaying lordosis when given the proper steroids to activate that behavior.

Conclusion
When the developing brain is exposed to androgens, the animal's brain is organized in a masculine fashion, so that, as an adult, it is more likely to show malelike behaviors, and less likely to show femalelike behaviors.

organizational effect A permanent alteration of the nervous system, and thus permanent change in behavior, resulting from the action of a steroid hormone on an animal early in its development.

sensitive period The period during development in which an organism can be permanently altered by a particular experience or treatment.

neonatal Referring to newborns.

they were given the steroid regimen that reliably activated lordosis in normal females, these fetally androgenized females did not show lordosis. From these data the researchers inferred that the same testicular steroids that masculinize the genitalia during early development also masculinize the developing brain. In other words, they proposed that the brain was just one more target tissue that is masculinized by androgens acting early in life (see Figure 8.25). This type of lasting change due to steroid exposure is known as an **organizational effect**.

A steroid has an organizational effect only when present during a specific **sensitive period**, generally in early development. Unlike the transient nature that characterizes the activational effects of hormones, which we discussed earlier, the organizational effects of hormones tend to be permanent (**Figure 8.29a–c**). The exact boundaries of the sensitive period of development depend on which behavior and which species are being studied. For rats, androgens given just after birth (the **neonatal** period) can affect later behavior. Guinea pigs, however, must be exposed to androgens *before* birth for adult lordosis behavior to be affected. In mammals, puberty can be viewed as a second sensitive period; for example, steroid exposure during puberty causes the addition of new cells (an organizational effect) to sex-related brain regions of rats (Ahmed et al., 2008).

Early testicular secretions result in masculine behavior in adulthood

The organizational hypothesis provides a unitary explanation for sexual differentiation: a single steroid signal (androgen) masculinizes the body, the brain, and behavior (see Figure 8.25). From this point of view the nervous system is just another type of tissue listening for the androgenic signal that will instruct it to organize itself in a masculine fashion. If the nervous system does not detect androgens, it will organize itself in a mostly feminine fashion. With their capacity to infiltrate the entire body, steroids have a unique ability to communicate a single message to disparate parts of the body to coordinate an integrated response.

What was demonstrated originally for the lordosis behavior of guinea pigs has been observed in a variety of vertebrate species and for many behaviors. Exposing female rat pups to testosterone either just before birth or during the first 10 days after birth greatly reduces their lordosis responsiveness as adults. This explains the observation that adult male rats show very little lordosis, even when given estrogens and progesterone. However, male rats that are castrated during the first week of life display excellent lordosis responses in adulthood if injected with estrogens and progesterone (**Figure 8.29d**). In rats, many behaviors conform to the organizational hypothesis: animals exposed to either endogenous or exogenous androgens early in life behave like males, whereas animals not exposed to androgens early in life behave like females.

In most cases, full masculine behavior requires androgens both during development (to organize the nervous system to enable the later behavior) and in adulthood (to activate that behavior). For example, the copulatory behavior of male rats can be quantified in terms of how often they mount a receptive female and how often such mounting results in intromission. Androgens must be present in adulthood to activate this behavior: adult males that have been castrated stop mounting in a few weeks; injecting them with testosterone eventually restores masculine copulatory behavior (see Figure 8.18). Such androgen treatment has some effect on adult female rats as well, causing them to mount other females more often, but they rarely manage intromission of their phallus (the clitoris) into the stimulus female's vagina. Only animals exposed to androgen both in development and in adulthood show fully masculine behavior.

Several regions of the nervous system display prominent sexual dimorphism

The fact that male and female rats behave differently means that their brains must be different in some way, and according to the organizational hypothesis this difference results primarily from androgenic masculinization of the developing brain. The exact form of these neural sex differences can be very subtle; the same basic circuit of neurons will produce very different behavior if the pattern of synapses varies. Sex differences in the number of synapses were identified in the preoptic area (POA) of the hypothalamus (Raisman and Field, 1971). But scientists soon found that, in a wide variety of species, including humans, there are much more obvious sex differences in the brain. Darwin coined a term, **sexual dimorphism**, to describe the condition in which males and females show pronounced sex differences in structure. Many examples of sexual dimorphism in the nervous system were found, including differences in the number, size, and shape of neurons. In all animal models studied so far, androgens masculinize the brain region, and the absence of androgen leads to a female-typical brain anatomy. We'll discuss two well-studied models.

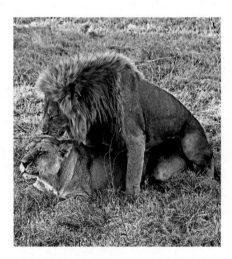

Sexual dimorphism Adult male and female lions differ in both anatomy and behavior.

sexual dimorphism The condition in which males and females of the same species show pronounced sex differences in appearance.

Figure 8.30 The Sexually Dimorphic Nucleus of the Preoptic Area (Courtesy of Roger Gorski.)

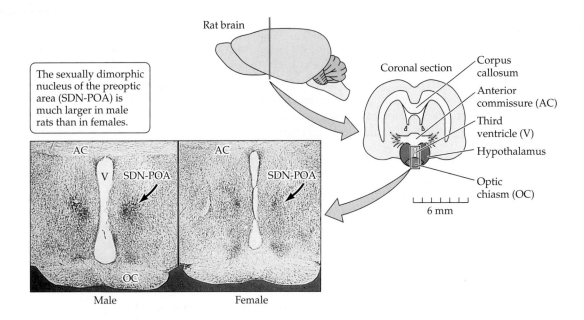

The sexually dimorphic nucleus of the preoptic area (SDN-POA) is much larger in male rats than in females.

Male   Female

THE PREOPTIC AREA OF RATS Roger Gorski et al. (1978) examined the preoptic area (POA) of the hypothalamus in rats because of the earlier reports that the number of synapses in this region was different in males and females, and because lesions of the POA disrupt ovulatory cycles in female rats and reduce copulatory behavior in males, as we mentioned earlier. Sure enough, the investigators found a nucleus within the POA that has a much larger volume in males than in females.

This nucleus, dubbed the **sexually dimorphic nucleus of the POA** (**SDN-POA**), is much more evident in male rats than in females (**Figure 8.30**). The SDN-POA conformed beautifully to the organizational hypothesis: males castrated at birth had much smaller SDN-POAs in adulthood, while females androgenized at birth had large, malelike SDN-POAs as adults. Castrating male rats in adulthood, however, did not alter the size of the SDN-POA. Thus, testicular androgens somehow alter the development of the SDN-POA, resulting in a nucleus permanently larger in males than in females (**Figure 8.31**).

One quirk of sexual dimorphism in the brains of some lab species, including rodents, is that testosterone reaching the brain is converted into estrogens that act on estrogen receptors, not androgen receptors, to masculinize the SDN-POA and some other brain regions. For example, XY rats that are androgen-insensitive (like the people with AIS discussed earlier) have testes but a feminine exterior. These rats have a masculine SDN-POA because their estrogen receptors are normal. Androgen-insensitive rats also do not display lordosis in response to estrogens and progesterone, because the testosterone that they secreted early in life was converted to an *estrogen* in the brain and masculinized their behavior (Olsen, 1979). Instead, the androgen-insensitive rats show normal male attraction to receptive females, with whom they may attempt to mate, despite the lack of a penis (Hamson et al., 2009). Estrogenic metabolites of testosterone do not seem to play a role in masculinizing the primate brain (Grumbach and Auchus, 1999), so we won't deal with that mechanism any further, but you can learn more about it in **A Step Further 8.7**, on the website.

THE SPINAL CORD IN MAMMALS In rats, the bulbocavernosus (BC) muscles that surround the base of the penis are innervated by motoneurons in the **spinal nucleus of the bulbocavernosus** (**SNB**). Male rats have about 200 SNB cells, but females have far fewer motoneurons in this region of the spinal cord.

On the day before birth, female rats have BC muscles attached to the base of the clitoris that are nearly as large as those of males and that are innervated by motoneurons in the SNB region (Rand and Breedlove, 1987). In the days just before and after birth, however, many SNB cells die, especially in females (Nordeen et al., 1985), and the BC muscles of females die (**Figure 8.32**).

sexually dimorphic nucleus of the preoptic area (SDN-POA) A region of the preoptic area that is five to six times larger in volume in male rats than in females.

spinal nucleus of the bulbocavernosus (SNB) A group of motoneurons in the spinal cord of rats that innervate striated muscles controlling the penis.

Rat brain

Coronal section

Corpus callosum
Anterior commissure (AC)
Third ventricle (V)
Hypothalamus
Optic chiasm (OC)

6 mm

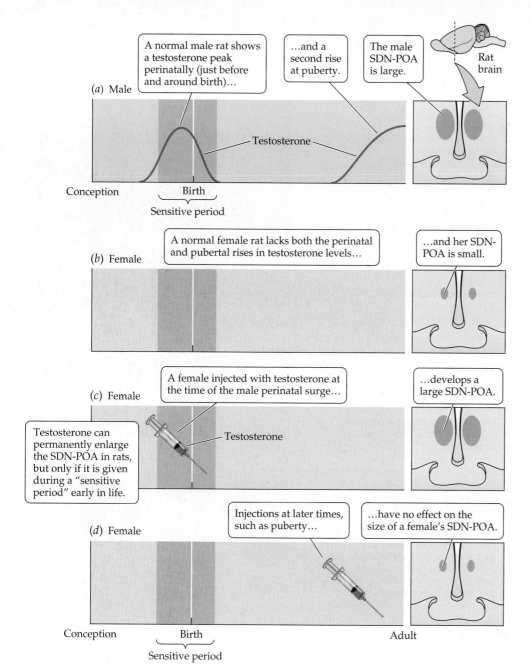

A normal male rat shows a testosterone peak perinatally (just before and around birth)…

…and a second rise at puberty.

The male SDN-POA is large.

Rat brain

(a) Male

Testosterone

Conception

Birth

Sensitive period

A normal female rat lacks both the perinatal and pubertal rises in testosterone levels…

…and her SDN-POA is small.

(b) Female

A female injected with testosterone at the time of the male perinatal surge…

…develops a large SDN-POA.

(c) Female

Testosterone can permanently enlarge the SDN-POA in rats, but only if it is given during a "sensitive period" early in life.

Testosterone

Injections at later times, such as puberty…

…have no effect on the size of a female's SDN-POA.

(d) Female

Conception

Birth

Sensitive period

Adult

Figure 8.31 Organization of the SDN-POA

A single injection of androgens delivered to a newborn female rat permanently spares some SNB motoneurons and their muscles. Castration of newborn males, accompanied by prenatal blockade of androgen receptors, causes the BC muscles and SNB motoneurons to die as in females. The system also dies in newborn androgen-insensitive rats, so estrogens seem to be unimportant for masculine development of the SNB.

Androgens act on the BC muscles to prevent their demise, and this sparing of the muscles causes the innervating SNB motoneurons to survive (Fishman et al., 1990; C. L. Jordan et al., 1991). Thus the developmental rescue of SNB motoneurons is accomplished indirectly as a consequence of actions on muscle, but androgens can also directly affect the neurons themselves. SNB neurons contain androgen receptors and retain androgen sensitivity throughout life. In adulthood, androgen acts directly on the neurons to cause them to grow (Watson et al., 2001) and to start expressing genes that help new connections to form (Monks and Watson, 2001).

In nonrodents, the BC motoneurons are found in a slightly different spinal location and are known as **Onuf's nucleus**. Surprisingly, most female mammals retain a BC muscle into adulthood; in women, for example, the bulbocavernosus (or *constrictor*

Onuf's nucleus The human homolog of the spinal nucleus of the bulbocavernosus (SNB) in rats.

Figure 8.32 Sexual Differentiation of the SNB

Spinal cord

Motoneuron

1 In both sexes, spinal motoneurons make connections with the bulbocavernosus muscle early in development.

Neuromuscular junction

Bulbocavernosus muscle

Androgen receptor

2 In both sexes, the muscle expresses androgen receptors.

Male   Female

Testosterone

3 In males, circulating testosterone binds to the androgen receptors. In females, the receptors remain unoccupied.

Factors

4 In males, the activated receptors promote the survival of the muscle and cause it to secrete unknown factors, which are picked up by the motoneurons. In females, the lack of receptor activation causes the muscle to die, and no factors are produced.

5 In males, the factors picked up by the motoneurons promote their survival. In females, the lack of these factors causes the motoneurons to die.

Male rat

SNB

Female rat

vestibule) helps constrict the vaginal opening. But, as in rodents, the system is profoundly sexually dimorphic. Men have larger BC muscles and more Onuf's motoneurons than do women, probably because of androgen exposure during fetal development (Forger and Breedlove, 1986, 1987).

These systems and several others all demonstrate the power of androgens to affect the gender of the brain. By controlling the amount and timing of testosterone exposure, researchers can make the various brain structures as masculine or feminine as they like. However, despite the crucial role of androgens in masculinizing sexually dimorphic nuclei in the nervous system, there's evidence that experience affects them too.

Social influences also affect sexual differentiation of the nervous system

Environmental factors of many sorts, including social experience, can modulate the masculinization produced by steroids. The development of the SNB offers a clear example. Celia Moore et al. (1992) noticed that rat dams spend more time licking the anogenital regions of male pups than of females. If the dam is anosmic (unable to smell), she licks all the pups less and does not distinguish between males and females. Males raised by anosmic mothers thus receive less anogenital licking, and remarkably, fewer of their SNB cells survive the period around birth. The dam's stimulation of a male's anogenital region helps to masculinize his spinal cord.

On the one hand, this masculinization is still an effect of androgens, because the dam identifies male pups by detecting androgen metabolites in their urine. On the other hand, this effect is clearly the result of a social influence: the dam treats a pup differently because he's a male, and this differential treatment masculinizes his developing nervous system. Perhaps this example illustrates the futility of trying to distinguish "biological" from "social" influences.

Attention from the dam has a different organizing effect on female rat pups. In adulthood, females that were licked frequently as pups show enhanced estrogen and oxytocin sensitivity in brain regions associated with maternal behavior, and they tend to be attentive mothers themselves. Females that were licked less as pups are less attentive mothers later (Champagne et al., 2001).

What about humans? (No, no, not the licking part—the social influence part.) Humans are at least as sensitive to social influences as rats are. In every culture, most people treat boys and girls differently, even when they are infants. Such differential treatment undoubtedly has some effect on the developing human brain and contributes to later sex differences in behavior. Of course, this is a social influence, but testosterone instigated the influence when it induced the formation of a penis.

If prenatal androgens have even a very subtle effect on the fetal brain, then adults interacting with a baby might detect such differences and treat the baby differently. Thus, originally subtle sex differences might be magnified by social experience, especially early in life. Such interactions of steroidal and social influences are probably the norm in the sexual differentiation of human behavior. So does fetal testosterone play a role in masculinizing human behavior? Let's examine that question by zeroing in on human sexual orientation, the final topic of this chapter.

How's it going?

1. How does exposure to androgens early in life masculinize the brain and spinal cord in rats?

2. Why is it difficult to distinguish between social and biological influences on sexual differentiation?

Do Fetal Hormones Masculinize Human Behaviors in Adulthood?

As with rats and other animals, the fact that men and women behave differently implies that something about them, probably something about their brains, must also be different. Indeed, many parts of the brain are different between men and women (**Figure 8.33**). But are these sexual dimorphisms in the human brain caused by prenatal exposure to hormones, as in other animals, or by social influences? In other words, does prenatal exposure to steroids affect the adult behavior of humans? This is a tricky problem because, although prenatal androgens may act on the human brain, they certainly act on the rest of the body too.

For example, recall that females with androgen insensitivity syndrome (AIS) are usually raised as girls, because their XY genotype is not discovered until puberty. We said earlier that androgen-insensitive women tend to be very feminine, including being sexually attracted to men and often seeking a family through adoption. Are they feminine because they received the social tutoring to be females, or because their brains, without

This composite image is based on data obtained from MRI scans of numerous male and female volunteers. Overall, sex differences tend to be evident in regions that are known to possess receptors for sex steroids.

☐ Structures that are larger in the healthy female brain, relative to cerebrum size

☐ Structures that are larger in the healthy male brain, relative to cerebrum size

Figure 8.33 Sexual Dimorphism in the Human Brain (Courtesy of Jill Goldstein, based on data from Goldstein et al., 2001.)

Training Girls to Be Verbal   Adults tend to spend more time talking to a baby if they believe the baby is a girl (whether it actually is a girl or not) (Seavey et al., 1975).

androgen receptors, could not respond to testosterone? Their behavior is consistent with either hypothesis.

What about females with CAH, who are exposed to androgens before birth? In fact, girls with CAH are much more likely to be described by their parents (and themselves) as tomboys than are other girls, and they exhibit enhanced spatial abilities on cognitive tests that usually favor males (Berenbaum, 2001). In adulthood, most CAH females describe themselves as heterosexual, but they are more likely to report a homosexual orientation than are other women. Interestingly, as females with CAH grow older, the proportion who report homosexual attractions increases to as much as 40% (Dittmann et al., 1992), suggesting that they start off trying to follow the socially approved role of heterosexual female but then become more comfortable with a homosexual orientation later in life. Do women with CAH exhibit those behaviors because early androgens partially masculinized their brains? Or did their ambiguous genitalia cause parents and others to treat them differently from infancy?

The *guevedoces* of the Dominican Republic, who are raised as girls but grow a penis at puberty, behave like males as adults, dressing like men and seeking girlfriends. There are two competing explanations for why these people raised as girls later behave as men. First, prenatal testosterone may masculinize their brains; thus, despite being raised as girls, when they reach puberty their brains lead them to seek out females for mates. This explanation suggests that the social influences of growing up—assigning oneself to a gender and mimicking role models of that gender, as well as gender-specific playing and dressing—are unimportant for later behavior and sexual orientation.

An alternative explanation is that early hormones have no effect—that the local culture simply recognizes and teaches children that some people can start out as girls and change to boys later. If so, then the social influences on gender role development might be completely different in this society from those in ours. Of course, a third option is that both mechanisms contribute to the final outcome; for example, early androgens may affect the brain to masculinize the child's behavior and predispose later sexual orientation toward females, and these masculine qualities of the child could alter the behavior of parents and others in ways that promote the emergence of male gender identity as the child develops.

At the opening of the chapter we discussed the dilemma of cloacal exstrophy, in which genetic boys are born with functional testes but without penises. Historically in these cases, neonatal sex reassignment has been recommended on the assumption that unambiguously raising these children as girls, and surgically providing them with the appropriate external genitalia, could produce a more satisfactory outcome. In a long-term follow-up of 14 such cases, however, Reiner and Gearhart (2004) found that 8 of these "girls" eventually declared themselves to be boys, even though several were unaware that they had ever been operated on. Although this finding indicates that prenatal exposure to androgens strongly predisposes subsequent male gender identity, 5 of the remaining 6 cases were apparently content with their female identities, suggesting that socialization can also play a strong role. In most people, gender identity is presumably established by nature and nurture working in conjunction.

Although far from conclusive, the studies of people with these various conditions are part of a growing body of evidence suggesting that prenatal testosterone does in fact influence sexual orientation in humans, as we'll see next.

What determines a person's sexual orientation?

There are two kinds of developmental influences that could shape human sexual orientation. Sociocultural influences may instruct developing children about how they should behave when they grow up (think of all those charming princes wooing princesses in Disney movies). But, as we discussed in the previous section, differences in fetal exposure to testosterone could also organize developing brains to be attracted to females or males in adulthood. For that great majority of people who are heterosexual, there's no way to distinguish between these two influences, because they both favor the same outcome. However, people who are homosexual provide a test. Is there evidence that early hormones are responsible for causing some people to ignore society's prescription and become gay? If so, then maybe hormones play a role in heterosexual development too.

Homosexual behavior is certainly seen in other species—mountain sheep, swans, gulls, and dolphins, to name a few (Bagemihl, 1999). Interestingly, homosexual behavior is more common among apes and monkeys than in prosimian primates like lemurs and lorises (Vasey, 1995), so perhaps greater complexity of the brain makes homosexual behavior more likely. In the most studied animal model—sheep—some rams consistently refuse to mount females but prefer to mount other rams. There is growing evidence of differences in the POA (preoptic area) of "gay" versus "straight" rams (Roselli et al., 2004), apparently organized by testosterone acting on the brain during fetal development (Roselli and Stormshak, 2009).

Simon LeVay (1991) performed postmortem examinations of the POA in humans and found a nucleus (the third interstitial nucleus of the anterior hypothalamus, or INAH-3) (**Figure 8.34a**) that is larger in men than in women, and larger in heterosexual men than in homosexual men (**Figure 8.34b**). All but one of the gay men in the study had died of AIDS, but the brain differences could not be due to AIDS pathology, because straight men with AIDS still had a significantly larger INAH-3 than did the gay men. To the press and the public, this finding sounded like strong evidence that sexual orientation is "built in." It's still possible, however, that early social experience affects the development of INAH-3 to determine later sexual orientation. Furthermore, sexual experiences as an adult could affect INAH-3 structure, so the smaller nucleus in some homosexual men may be the *result* of their homosexuality, rather than the *cause*, as LeVay himself was careful to point out.

In women, purported markers of exposure to androgen as a fetus—sounds emitted from the ears (McFadden and Pasanen, 1998), finger length patterns (T. J. Williams et al., 2000), patterns of eye blinks (Rahman, 2005), and skeletal features (J. T. Martin and Nguyen, 2004)—all indicate that lesbians, on average, were exposed to slightly more fetal androgen than were heterosexual women. These findings suggest that fetal exposure to androgen increases the likelihood that a girl will grow up to be gay. There is always considerable overlap between the two groups, so you cannot use these features to predict whether a particular woman is gay, and clearly fetal androgens cannot account for all lesbians. Likewise, the finding that homosexual people are more likely to be left-handed than are individuals of the general population (Lalumiere et al., 2000) suggests that androgens cannot be the whole story, because there is no known effect of early androgens on handedness. However, handedness does seem to be established early in life, so this correlation, too, indicates that early events influence adult sexual orientation.

Those same markers of fetal androgen do not provide for a consensus about gay versus straight men; some markers suggest that gay men were exposed to less prenatal testosterone, and others suggest that they were exposed to *more* prenatal testosterone than were straight men. However, another

Figure 8.34 Interstitial Nuclei of the Anterior Hypothalamus

(a)

1 These nuclei in humans are seen in the same part of the hypothalamus where the SDN-POA is found in rats.

Third ventricle
INAH-4
INAH-3
INAH-2
INAH-1
Supraoptic nucleus
Paraventricular nucleus
Optic chiasm

3 Although most of the gay men in this study had died of AIDS, note that heterosexual men who died of AIDS still had a larger INAH-3, indicating that the differences between straight and gay men are not due to AIDS.

(b)

2 INAH-3 is larger in men than in women, and larger in straight men than in gay men.

= AIDS victims

Size of INAH-3 (mm³)

Females   Males   Homosexual males

fraternal birth order effect   A phenomenon in human populations, such that the more older biological brothers a boy has, the more likely he is to develop a homosexual orientation.

nonsocial factor influences the probability of homosexuality in men: the more older brothers a boy has, the more likely he is to grow up to be gay (Blanchard et al., 2006). Your first guess might be that this is a social influence of older brothers, but it turns out that older stepbrothers that are raised with the boy have no effect, while biological brothers (sharing the same mother) increase the probability of the boy's being gay *even if they are raised apart* (Bogaert, 2006). Furthermore, this **fraternal birth order effect** is seen in boys who are right-handed, but not in left-handed boys (Blanchard et al., 2006; Bogaert, 2007), providing another indication of differences in early development between the two sexual-orientation groups. Statistically, the birth order effect is strong enough that about one in every seven homosexual men in North America—about a million people—is gay because his mother had sons before him (Cantor et al., 2002).

There is good evidence that human sexual orientation is at least partly heritable, reinforcing the notion that both biological and social factors have a say. About 50% of variability in human sexual orientation is accounted for by genetic factors, leaving ample room for early social influences. Monozygotic twins, who have exactly the same genes, do not always have the same sexual orientation (J. M. Bailey et al., 1993). In the unusual case of two nontwin brothers who are both homosexual, genetic evidence suggests that they are much more likely than chance would dictate to have both inherited the same X chromosome region (called Xq28) from their mother (Hamer et al., 1993); but again the genetic explanation accounts for only some, not all, of the cases. It seems clear that there are several different pathways to homosexuality.

From a political viewpoint, the controversy—whether sexual orientation is determined before birth or determined by early social influences—is irrelevant. Laws and prejudices against homosexuality are based primarily on religious views that homosexuality is a sin that some people "choose." But almost all homosexual and heterosexual men report that, from the beginning, their interests and romantic attachments matched their adult orientation. So any social influence would have to be acting very early in life and without any conscious awareness (do you remember "choosing" whom to find attractive?). Furthermore, despite extensive efforts, no one has come up with a reliable way to change sexual orientation (LeVay, 1996). These findings, added to evidence that older brothers and prenatal androgens affect the probability of being gay, have convinced most scientists that we do not choose our sexual orientation.

How's it going?

1. What does the sexual orientation of people with various syndromes of sexual differentiation suggest about hormonal influences on human sexual orientation?

2. If human sexual orientation were shown definitively to be influenced by prenatal factors such as hormones and the fraternal birth order effect, would you be more or less inclined to accept homosexuality?

Recommended Reading

Becker, J. B., Breedlove, S. M., Crews, D., and McCarthy, M. M. (Eds.). (2002). *Behavioral Endocrinology* (2nd ed.). Cambridge, MA: MIT Press.

Colapinto, J. (2000). *As Nature Made Him.* New York, NY: HarperCollins.

Eugenides, J. (2002). *Middlesex: A Novel.* New York, NY: Farrar, Straus, Giroux.

Hadley, M. E., and Levine, J. (2006). *Endocrinology* (6th ed.). Englewood Cliffs, NJ: Prentice Hall.

LeVay, S., and Baldwin, J. (2012). *Human Sexuality* (4th ed.). Sunderland, MA: Sinauer.

Nelson, R. J. (2011). *An Introduction to Behavioral Endocrinology* (4th ed.). Sunderland, MA: Sinauer.

CHAPTER 8 VISUAL SUMMARY

You should be able to relate each summary to the adjacent illustration, including structures and processes. If you need to review, go to the figures indicated and read the accompanying text.

mindsmachine.com/vs8

1 **Hormones** are chemicals that are secreted by **endocrine glands** into the bloodstream and are taken up by receptor molecules in target cells. Unlike neuronal signaling, hormones spread more slowly and act throughout the body. Review **Figures 8.1–8.3**, **Table 8.1**, **Activity 8.1**, **Animations 8.2 and 8.3**

2 Most hormones act on receptors in a wide variety of cells, coordinating influences throughout the body. **Protein hormones** and **amine hormones** bind to receptor molecules at the surface of the target cell membrane and activate **second-messenger** molecules inside the cell. **Steroid hormones** pass through the membrane and bind to receptor molecules inside the cell, ultimately regulating gene expression. Review **Figures 8.4–8.7**, **Animation 8.4**

3 **Negative feedback** systems control hormone secretion. **Neuroendocrine cells** in the hypothalamus send axons down the **pituitary stalk** to the **posterior pituitary**, releasing two hormones—**oxytocin** and **vasopressin**—into the bloodstream. Release of the hormones is regulated by **synaptic** influences on those neuroendocrine cells. Review **Figures 8.8–8.10**

4 Other hormones are controlled by a **releasing hormone** from the hypothalamus that stimulates the **anterior pituitary** to release **tropic hormones**, which in turn control the secretion of hormones by endocrine glands. The endocrine gland hormone then provides negative feedback to the hypothalamus and pituitary. Review **Figures 8.11–8.13**, **Animation 8.5**

5 Many behaviors require the coordination of neural and hormonal components. Messages may be transmitted in the body via neural-to-neural, neural-to-endocrine, endocrine-to-endocrine, or endocrine-to-neural links. *There are continual, reciprocal influences between the endocrine system and the nervous system*: experience affects hormone secretion, and hormones affect behavior and therefore future experiences. Review **Figures 8.14–8.16**

6 In animals, reproductive behaviors are regulated by hormones. In female rats, a steroid-sensitive **lordosis** circuit extends from the **ventromedial hypothalamus (VMH)** to the spinal cord. In male rats, **medial preoptic area (mPOA)** neurons integrate inputs from the **medial amygdala** and **vomeronasal organ (VNO)**, and they project axons widely to regulate copulatory behavior. Review **Figures 8.17–8.20**

7 In humans, very low levels of **testosterone** are required for either men or women to display a full interest in sex, but additional testosterone has no additional effect. In animals, hormones significantly influence **parental behavior** by acting on the same brain regions that are important for sexual behavior (mPOA, VMH). Review **Figures 8.18** and **8.21–8.23**

8 Genes (XX or XY chromosomes) **determine sex** by controlling whether the **indifferent gonads** of an individual develop as **testes** or **ovaries**. Then, hormonal secretions from the testes masculinize the rest of the body in males. This means that some people may be masculine in some parts of the body but feminine in others, as, for example, women who carry a Y chromosome but have **androgen insensitivity syndrome (AIS)**. Review **Figure 8.24–8.28**

9 In animals, **androgens** also organize the developing brain, masculinizing regions such as the **sexually dimorphic nucleus of the preoptic area (SDN-POA)** and the **spinal nucleus of the bulbocavernosus (SNB)**. There is evidence that prenatal androgens also masculinize the human brain. Review **Figures 8.29–8.33**, **Animation 8.6**

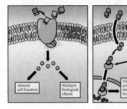

10 Several regions of the human brain are **sexually dimorphic**, but we do not know whether these dimorphisms are organized by fetal steroids or by sex differences in the social environment. No perfect animal model of sexual orientation has been developed, but research indicates that human sexual orientation is determined early in life and is not simply a matter of individual choice. Review **Figures 8.33** and **8.34**

Go to **mindsmachine.com** for study questions, quizzes, flashcards, and other resources.

chapter 9

Homeostasis:
Active Regulation of the Internal Environment

A Love–Hate Relationship with Food

Six-hundred ninety calories—that's what this milkshake represented to me.

But to Kitty it was the object of her deepest fear and loathing. "You're trying to make me fat," she said in a high-pitched, distorted voice that made the hairs on the back of my neck stand up. She rocked, clutching her stomach, chanting over and over: "I'm a fat pig. I'm so fat."

> — Harriet Brown, "One Spoonful at a Time,"
> New York Times Magazine, November 6, 2006

How does food become an object of "fear and loathing" for some people? Harriet Brown paints a harrowing portrait of the "demon" of anorexia nervosa that seemed to possess her daughter, Kitty. This disorder completely deranges the sufferer's relationship with food. Obsession with food, lost appetite, starvation, fear, and distorted self-perception are hallmarks of anorexia nervosa. In Kitty's case, these symptoms developed like a gathering storm, from the first hints of unusual fascination with food, poring over *Gourmet* magazine, to the loss of appetite and relentless exercising, until the day when 14-year-old Kitty lay in bed a mere 71 pounds, every bone sharply evident beneath her skin, her hair falling out in clumps, her breath laden with the pearlike scent of ketones as her body metabolized itself for fuel. Still, Kitty considered herself "a fat pig," sobbing and terrified at the prospect of drinking a milkshake or eating a piece of birthday cake. Kitty's parents faced uncertainty and difficult decisions. What was the best way to strike back at the demon?

To see a video, go to

mindsmachine.com/9.1
Anorexia

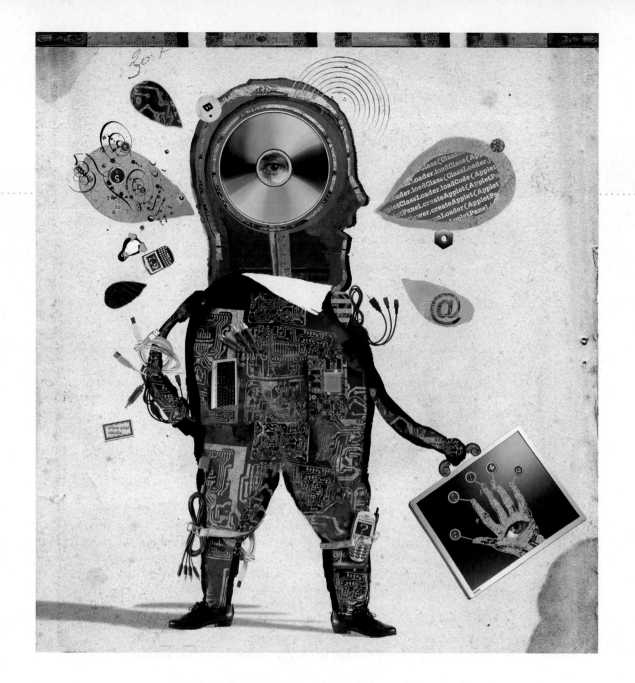

Millions of years of evolution have endowed our bodies with complex physiological mechanisms, and multiple backup systems, devoted to producing a stable internal environment. Food energy, body temperature, fluid balance, fat storage, nutrients—all of the conditions required for optimal cellular functioning—are carefully regulated by the brain at every stage. But in the context of modern society, some of these ancient systems are making trouble for us; obesity, for example, is reaching epidemic proportions and placing a severe burden on health care resources. The physiological and behavioral processes governing the internal environment, and their role when things go wrong, are our topic in this chapter.

To see the brain in 3D, go to

mindsmachine.com/9.2
Brain Explorer

PART I Principles of Homeostasis

Scientists in the nineteenth century realized that the body is a self-contained environment, providing optimal conditions for cells to live and grow. This perspective made it easier to understand many physiological and behavioral systems, whose job it is to prevent internal conditions from varying to any great extent. Variables such as acidity, saltiness, water level, oxygen supply, temperature, and energy availability, among others, are carefully monitored and maintained by elaborate physiological systems. Collectively, these systems are responsible for **homeostasis**, the maintenance of a relatively stable, balanced internal environment.

Alterations in the internal environment can have an effect on **motivation**, the psychological process that induces or sustains a particular behavior. According to this view, the mismatch between the actual internal state (e.g., being dehydrated) and the regulated, intended state produces a *drive* to restore balance (in this case by having a drink of water). And as we all know, drive can rapidly escalate as the mismatch worsens, from a minor distraction (like the desire for a couple of sips if a glass of water happens to be present) to an overwhelming, all-consuming desire (like the raging thirst of someone lost in the desert).

Because homeostasis is a relatively simple system, we'll start by using thermoregulation (the regulation of body temperature) to look at some important general concepts of homeostasis: negative feedback, redundancy, and behavioral homeostasis. These concepts will arise again when we talk about the regulation of body fluids and body weight in the second and third parts of the chapter.

Homeostatic Systems Share Several Key Features

We mammals are **endotherms**, species that make our own heat from *inside* our body, using metabolism and muscular activity (and if our muscles aren't making enough heat, we can shiver them to make more). Endothermy gives us a couple of advantages over **ectotherms** (animals that get their heat mostly from *outside* their body—the environment), by allowing us to roam more widely. Ectotherms, such as lizards and snakes, need to stay nearer sources of warmth. Endothermy allows our muscles to work hard for longer periods of time. So it's no surprise that our body temperature is carefully regulated. The systems that govern body temperature operate according to several general principles common to almost all homeostatic systems. (For more on the pros and cons of endothermy and ectothermy, see **A Step Further 9.1**, on the website).

Internal states are governed through negative feedback

The homeostatic mechanisms that regulate temperature, body fluids, and metabolism are primarily **negative feedback** systems, in which deviation from a desired value, called the **set point**, triggers a compensatory action of the system. Restoring the desired value turns *off* the response (this is why it is called "negative" feedback). A simple analogy is a household thermostat (**Figure 9.1**): a temperature drop below the set point activates the thermostat, which turns on the heating system. The heat that is produced has a negative feedback effect on the thermostat, so it stops calling for heat. Most heating systems have at least a little bit of tolerance built in—otherwise the system would be going on and off too frequently—so there is generally a **set zone** rather than a rigid set *point*.

The set zone for body temperature operates in a manner similar to a thermostat. For example, your body temperature drops at night for much the same reason that people turn down their home thermostats at night: to conserve energy. Or your set zone may be temporarily elevated, producing a fever to help your body fight off an infection. But in either case there are narrow limits. Too cool, and chemical reactions of the body occur too slowly; too hot, and proteins begin to lose their correct shape, link together, and malfunction (this modification of proteins is called denaturing or, if it is really hot, *cooking*).

homeostasis   The active process of maintaining a particular physiological parameter relatively constant.

motivation   The psychological process that induces or sustains a particular behavior.

endotherm   An animal whose body temperature is regulated chiefly by internal metabolic processes. Examples include mammals and birds.

ectotherm   An animal whose body temperature is regulated by, and whose heat comes mainly from, the environment. Examples include snakes and bees.

negative feedback   The property by which some of the output of a system feeds back to reduce the effect of input signals.

set point   The point of reference in a feedback system. An example is the temperature at which a thermostat is set.

set zone   The range of a variable that a feedback system tries to maintain.

Figure 9.1 Negative Feedback

To see an animation of this figure, go to

mindsmachine.com/9.3
Negative Feedback

The thermostat controlling a household heating system employs negative feedback. All such systems have a sensor (in this example a thermometer) to monitor the variable (temperature), and a device (the heating system) to change the variable (e.g., by heating the room).

Heat from the heating system provides negative feedback, inhibiting the thermostat from calling for more heat.

Redundancy is a feature of many homeostatic systems

Just as human engineers equip critical equipment with several backup systems, our bodies tend to have multiple mechanisms for monitoring our stores, conserving remaining supplies, obtaining new resources, and shedding excesses. Loss of function in one part of the system usually can be compensated for by the remaining parts. This redundancy attests to the importance of maintaining our inner environment, but it also complicates the lives of scientists who are trying to figure out exactly how the body normally regulates temperature, water balance, and food intake.

It has long been known that the hypothalamus senses and controls body temperature, but lesion experiments eventually showed that different hypothalamic sites control two separate thermoregulatory systems. In these studies, lesions in the preoptic area (POA) of rats impaired the physiological responses to cold, such as shivering and constriction of the blood vessels, but did not interfere with such behaviors as pressing levers to control heating lamps or cooling fans (Satinoff and Rutstein, 1970; Van Zoeren and Stricker, 1977). Lesions in the lateral hypothalamus of rats abolished behavioral regulation of temperature but did not affect the physiological responses (Satinoff and Shan, 1971; Van Zoeren and Stricker, 1977). This is a clear example of homeostatic redundancy: two different systems for regulating the same variable. Furthermore, there

Redundancy Highly critical systems—like the flight control system for the International Space Station, pictured here—are generally engineered with multiple "fail-safe" redundancies. That way, if one system fails, other independent mechanisms monitoring and adjusting the same parameter can easily compensate for the failure. Multiple redundancy is a feature of many of the body's homeostatic systems, because maintaining a constant internal environment is a basic requirement for survival.

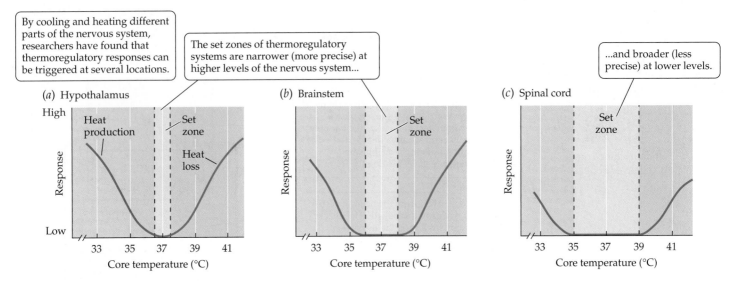

Figure 9.2 Multiple Thermostats in the Nervous System (After Satinoff, 1978.)

seems to be a hierarchy of thermoregulatory circuits—some located at the spinal level, some centered in the brainstem, and others situated in the hypothalamus (**Figure 9.2**).

Behavioral mechanisms are crucial for homeostasis

Organisms use behavior to help them regulate and acquire more heat, water, or food. In general, ectotherms and endotherms behaviorally regulate their temperature in one or more of three ways: (1) by changing *exposure* of the body surface—for example, by huddling or extending limbs; (2) by changing external *insulation*, such as by using clothing or nests; or (3) by changing *surroundings*, moving into the sun, into the shade, or into a burrow.

Because ectotherms generate little heat through metabolism, behavioral methods of thermoregulation are especially important to them. In the laboratory, iguanas carefully regulate their temperature by moving toward or away from a heat lamp, and when infected by bacteria they even produce a fever through such behavioral means (**Figure 9.3**). We endotherms use internal processes to generate a fever when fighting infections, which boosts our immune system response. Unfortunately, sometimes the body goes too far, as a fever

(a) Heat source

The lizard controls its body temperature by moving around the cage.

Temperature gradient (°C)

Injection of bacteria

Day 1 shows the normal daily cycle of body temperature.

On day 2, the iguanas were injected with bacteria, and they reacted by moving closer to the heat source to create a "behavioral fever" like the fever that endotherms use to help fight off infection.

Figure 9.3 Behavioral Thermoregulation in Bacteria-Challenged Lizards (After Kluger, 1978.)

(a) *(b)*

Behavioral Control of Body Temperature (*a*) A Galápagos marine iguana, upon emerging from the cold sea, raises its body temperature by hugging a warm rock and lying broadside to the sun. (*b*) Once its temperature is sufficiently high, the iguana reduces its surface contact with the rock and faces the sun to minimize its exposure. These behaviors control body temperature. (Photographs by Mark R. Rosenzweig.)

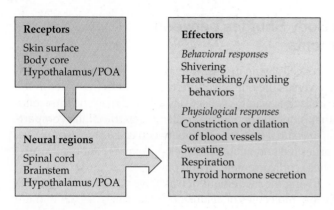

Receptors	Effectors
Skin surface	*Behavioral responses*
Body core	Shivering
Hypothalamus/POA	Heat-seeking/avoiding behaviors
	Physiological responses
Neural regions	Constriction or dilation of blood vessels
Spinal cord	Sweating
Brainstem	Respiration
Hypothalamus/POA	Thyroid hormone secretion

Figure 9.4 Basic Elements of Mammalian Thermoregulatory Systems

To see an animation, go to

mindsmachine.com/9.4
Thermoregulation in Humans

How's it going?

1. Define homeostasis, and discuss its relation to the psychological concept of motivation.

2. Distinguish between endotherms and ectotherms, and give a few examples of each.

3. Briefly describe each of the three key features of homeostatic systems that we have discussed, illustrated by examples. What is the significance of each?

4. Why do homeostatic systems tend to have a set *zone* instead of a set *point*?

above 40°C (104°F), especially in younger animals does more harm than good (see **A Step Further 9.2**, on the website).

Figure 9.4 summarizes the basic mammalian thermoregulatory system: receptors in the skin, body core, and hypothalamus detect temperature and transmit that information to three neural regions (spinal cord, brainstem, and hypothalamus). If the body temperature moves outside the set zone, each of these neural regions can initiate physiological and behavioral responses to return it to the set zone. As we will see next, other sensors and responses regulate our internal fluid and energy balance. The regulation of these internal resources is complicated by the fact that staying alive requires us to use up some of those resources. Our homeostatic mechanisms are continually challenged by these unavoidable losses (sometimes called *obligatory losses*), which require us to regain the lost resources from the external environment. Restoring expended water and food takes up much of an animal's waking life, so we turn to those activities next.

PART II Fluid Regulation

The water you drink on a hot day is carefully measured and partitioned by the brain. A precise balance of fluids and dissolved salts bathes the cells of the body and enables them to function. The composition of this fluid provides an echo of our evolutionary past: for most organisms, the fluid of the body is strikingly similar to dilute seawater (**Figure 9.5**). Because the basic physiology of cells was established in ancient single-celled ocean-dwelling organisms, later species evolved methods for providing body cells with the proper marine environment in which to operate (Bourque, 2008). Such methods became even more crucial for land animals, which face the constant threat of dehydration. Even relatively minor deviation from optimal water and salt balance can be lethal. It is for this reason that we each carry a tiny ocean within us.

Because we cannot seal our bodies from the outside world, we experience constant obligatory losses of water and salts. Many body functions require us to use up some water (and some salt molecules), as, for example, when we produce urine to get rid of waste molecules. In this section we discuss how the brain monitors and controls the precise composition of body fluids that cells require in order to function.

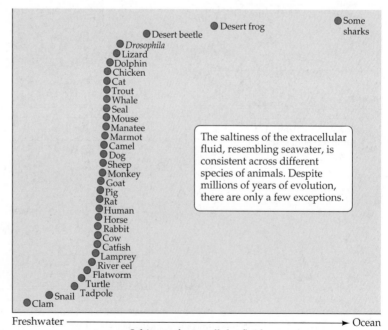

The saltiness of the extracellular fluid, resembling seawater, is consistent across different species of animals. Despite millions of years of evolution, there are only a few exceptions.

Figure 9.5 Each Animal Contains a Tiny Sea (After Bourque, 2008.)

Water in the Human Body Shuttles between Two Major Compartments

intracellular compartment The fluid space of the body that is contained within cells.

extracellular compartment The fluid space of the body that exists outside the cells.

diffusion The spontaneous spread of solute molecules through a solvent until a uniform solute concentration is achieved.

osmosis The passive movement of a solvent, usually water, through a semipermeable membrane until a uniform concentration of solute (often salt) is achieved on both sides of the membrane.

Because we consist of trillions of cells living in a seawater bath, we describe water balance by contrasting the inside versus the outside of our cells. Most of the water in the body is contained within our cells; this water is collectively referred to as the **intracellular compartment**. The fluid that is outside of our cells, called the **extracellular compartment**, is divided between the *interstitial fluid* (the fluid between cells) and *blood plasma* (the protein-rich fluid that carries red and white blood cells). Water is continually moving back and forth between these compartments, in and out of cells.

To understand the forces driving the movement of water, we must understand diffusion and osmosis. In **diffusion**, molecules of a substance like salt (a *solute*) that are dissolved in a quantity of another substance, such as a glass of water (a *solvent*), will passively spread through the water because of the random jiggling and movement of the molecules, until they are more or less uniformly distributed throughout the glass. If we divide a container of water with a membrane that is impermeable to water and salt, and we put the salt in the water on one side, the molecules diffuse only within that half. If instead the membrane impedes salt molecules only a little, then the salt will distribute itself evenly within the initial half but will also—more slowly—invade and distribute itself across the other half. A membrane that is permeable to some molecules but not others is referred to as *selectively permeable* or *semipermeable*. As we saw in Chapter 3, selective permeability of cell membranes is what lets neurons create and transmit electrical potentials.

Osmosis, illustrated in **Figure 9.6**, is the movement of water molecules that occurs when a semipermeable membrane separates solutions containing different concentrations of solute and the solute cannot cross the membrane to spread itself evenly across both sides. This is the case we examine in **Figure 9.6b**, in which the semipermeable membrane blocks the passage of salt molecules. Here the water molecules are moving

Figure 9.6 Osmosis

into the compartment where they are less concentrated (because the salt molecules are there), eventually resulting in equal concentrations of solution on both sides of the membrane. The physical force that pushes or pulls water across the membrane is called **osmotic pressure**.

Normally the concentration of salt (NaCl) in the extracellular fluid of mammals is about 0.9% (which means there's about 0.9 gram of NaCl for every 100 milliliters of water). A solution with this concentration of salt is called *physiological saline* or described as *isotonic*. Because water moves so as to produce uniform saltiness (see Figure 9.6b), cells will lose water if placed in a saltier solution and will gain water in a less salty solution. If excessive, this movement of water will damage or kill the cell. To prevent such damage, the extracellular fluid serves as a *buffer*, a reservoir of isotonic fluid that provides and accepts water molecules so that cells can maintain proper internal conditions. The nervous system uses two cues to ensure that the extracellular compartment has about the right amount of water and solute to allow cells to absorb or shed water molecules readily, as we'll see next.

Two Internal Cues Trigger Thirst

In addition to acting as a buffer, the extracellular fluid is an indicator of conditions in the intracellular compartment. In fact, the nervous system carefully monitors the extracellular compartment to determine whether we should seek water. Two different states can signal that more water is needed: (1) low extracellular volume (**hypovolemic thirst**), resulting from the loss of a quantity of body fluids; or (2) high extracellular solute concentration (**osmotic thirst**) (**Figure 9.7**)—a consequence of our body fluids becoming too salty. We'll consider each in turn.

Hypovolemic thirst is triggered by a loss of water volume

The example of hypovolemic thirst that is most easily understood is one we hope you never experience: serious blood loss (*hemorrhage*). Any animal that loses a lot of blood has a lowered total blood volume (*hypovolemic* means literally "low volume"). In this condition, blood vessels that would normally be full and slightly stretched no longer contain their full capacity. Blood pressure drops, and the individual becomes thirsty; in fact, powerful thirst is one of the most noticeable symptoms of serious blood loss.

Note that losing fluids from blood loss (or from diarrhea or vomiting) does not change the *concentration* of the extracellular fluid, because salts and other ions are lost along with the water (**Figure 9.7a**). The initial drop in extracellular volume is detected by pressure receptors, called **baroreceptors**, which are located in major blood vessels and in the heart. Reacting to the signal from the baroreceptors, the brain activates a variety of responses, such as thirst (to replace the lost water) and salt hunger (to replace the solutes that have been lost along with the water). Replacing the water without also replacing the salts would result in *hypotonic* extracellular fluid. The sympathetic nervous system also stimulates muscles in the artery walls to constrict, reducing the size of the vessels and partly compensating for the reduced volume. Finally, several hormonal systems are activated.

osmotic pressure The tendency of a solvent to move across a membrane in order to equalize the concentration of solute on both sides of the membrane.

hypovolemic thirst A desire to ingest fluids that is stimulated by a reduction in volume of the extracellular fluid.

osmotic thirst A desire to ingest fluids that is stimulated by loss of water from the extracellular compartment.

baroreceptor A pressure receptor in the heart or a major artery that detects a change in blood pressure.

Figure 9.7 Two Kinds of Thirst

(*a*) Hypovolemic thirst

Extracellular compartment

Intracellular compartment

Hypovolemic thirst results from loss of fluids containing both water and solutes, such as through hemorrhage, intense sweating, or diarrhea. Baroreceptors in major blood vessels detect the resultant drop in blood pressure.

(*b*) Osmotic thirst

In *osmotic thirst*, a change in the balance of water to salt in the extracellular fluid (from gaining salt or losing water) pulls water out of the intracellular compartment. Osmosensory neurons in the brain detect the increased saltiness of the extracellular fluid.

atrial natriuretic peptide (ANP) A hormone, secreted by the heart, that normally reduces blood pressure, inhibits drinking, and promotes the excretion of water and salt at the kidneys.

vasopressin or arginine vasopressin Also called *antidiuretic hormone* (*ADH*). A peptide hormone from the posterior pituitary that promotes water conservation and increases blood pressure.

angiotensin II A hormone that is produced in the blood by the action of renin and that may play a role in the control of thirst.

circumventricular organ Any of multiple distinct sites that lie in the wall of a cerebral ventricle and monitor the composition of the cerebrospinal fluid.

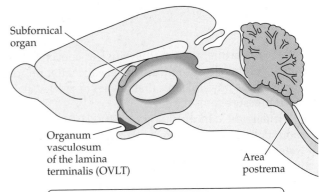

Figure 9.8
Circumventricular Organs

True to their name, the circumventricular organs lie in the walls of the ventricular system (blue). Thanks to a diminished blood-brain barrier, neurons of the circumventricular organs can monitor salt and other components of blood.

Physiological responses to a drop in blood volume are coordinated by a set of peptide hormones originating in several different organs. Immediately after the baroreceptors detect a drop in blood pressure, the heart decreases its secretion of **atrial natriuretic peptide** (**ANP**), which normally reduces blood pressure, inhibits drinking, and promotes the excretion of water and salt at the kidneys. At the same time, the brain's posterior pituitary gland steps up its release of the hormone **vasopressin** (more formally known as **arginine vasopressin**). Vasopressin acts on the kidneys to slow the production of urine (which is why this hormone is also known as *antidiuretic hormone; diuresis* is the production of urine). A third hormonal response is governed by the kidneys, which respond to lowered blood volume by triggering the production of **angiotensin II** (from the Greek *angeion*, "blood vessel," and the Latin *tensio*, "tension" or "pressure") from a precursor circulating in the bloodstream.

Angiotensin II (AII) has several water-conserving actions. By directly constricting blood vessels, AII increases blood pressure, ensuring that the brain and vital organs continue to receive essential materials for as long as possible. AII stimulates the release of vasopressin and aldosterone (to be discussed shortly). And AII acts directly on the brain, at the preoptic area (POA) and at distinct sites called **circumventricular organs** (**Figure 9.8**), to stimulate drinking behavior (Epstein et al., 1970; Fitzsimmons, 1998). Evidence suggests that the AII mechanism is just one of several redundant systems for provoking thirst, and is not active under all conditions (Fitzsimmons, 1998; McKinley and Johnson, 2004).

Osmotic thirst occurs when the extracellular fluid becomes too salty

For most of us, severe hypovolemic thirst is a relatively uncommon event. Thirst is more commonly triggered by obligatory water losses—respiration, urination, and so on—in which more water is lost than salt. In this case, not only is the *volume* of the extracellular fluid decreased, triggering the responses described in the previous section, but also the solute *concentration* of the extracellular fluid increases (that is, the fluid becomes hypertonic). As a result of this increased extracellular saltiness, water is pulled out of cells through osmosis.

Another thing that can make the extracellular fluid more concentrated is eating a lot of salty food. Once again, water will be drawn out of cells through osmosis. This loss of intracellular water triggers osmotic thirst (**Figure 9.7b**): we want to drink water in order to return the extracellular fluid to a comfortable isotonic state.

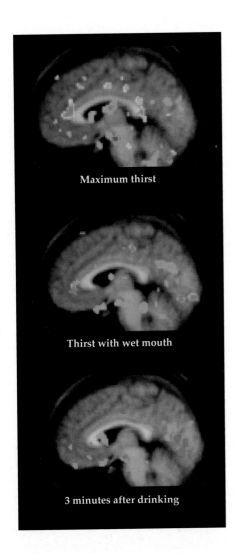

Maximum thirst

Thirst with wet mouth

3 minutes after drinking

Ahhhhhhh! The experience of strong thirst, induced by the injection of hypertonic saline, is associated with activity in several brain regions, especially the cingulate cortex and cerebellum (*top*). Wetting the mouth reduces this activation only slightly (*middle*), but drinking a glass of water (*bottom*) reduces activation in these brain regions dramatically. (From Denton et al., 1999.)

Figure 9.9   An Overview of Fluid Regulation

Electrical recordings from single neurons have revealed that there are specialized **osmosensory neurons**—neurons that specifically monitor the concentration of the extracellular fluid—in numerous regions of the hypothalamus, including the preoptic area, the anterior hypothalamus, and the supraoptic nucleus. Osmosensory neurons are also found in the *organum vasculosum of the lamina terminalis (OVLT)*, a circumventricular organ (see Figure 9.8).

Thirst is a homeostatic signal that intrudes forcefully into consciousness, with associated strong activation of certain brain regions, particularly in the limbic system (Denton et al., 1999). The two types of thirst (hypovolemic and osmotic), the two fluid compartments (extracellular and intracellular), and the multiple redundant methods to conserve water make for a fairly complicated system that is not yet fully understood. The current conceptualization of this system is depicted in **Figure 9.9.**

We don't stop drinking just because the throat and mouth are wet

Although plausible, the most obvious explanation of why we stop drinking—that we have dampened our previously dry throat and mouth—is all wet (sorry). In a classic test of this idea, thirsty animals were allowed to drink water, but the water they consumed was diverted out of the esophagus through a small tube. They remained thirsty and continued drinking.

Furthermore, we stop drinking before water has left the gastrointestinal tract and entered the extracellular compartment. Somehow we monitor how much water we have ingested and stop in *anticipation* of correcting the extracellular volume and/or the concentration of solutes. Experience may teach us and other animals how to gauge accurately whether we've ingested enough to counteract our thirst (hypovolemic or osmotic). Normally, all the signals—blood volume, solute concentration, moisture in the mouth, estimates of the amount of water we've ingested that's "on the way"—agree, but the cessation of one signal alone will not stop thirst; in this way, animals ensure against dehydration.

osmosensory neuron   A specialized neuron that monitors the concentration of the extracellular fluid by measuring the movement of water into and out of the intracellular compartment.

Water Balance Depends on the Regulation of Salt in the Body

Animals may travel great distances to eat salt (NaCl), and the sodium ion (Na⁺) is particularly important to fluid balance. We cannot maintain water in the extracellular compartment without solutes; if the extracellular compartment contained pure water, osmotic pressure would drive it into the cells until they ruptured and died. The amount of water that we can retain is determined primarily by the number of Na⁺ ions we possess. That's why thirst is quenched more effectively by very slightly salty drinks (like sports drinks) than by pure water. But saltier water, like seawater, has the reverse effect. Seawater is hypertonic, so just like eating salty food, drinking seawater causes ever-worsening osmotic thirst. We simply can't get rid of the excess salt fast enough.

Excretion of Excess Salt
Marine birds, such as this giant petrel, have only seawater to drink for long periods of time. To compensate, they have salt glands that pull excess salt out of plasma and release it out the nostrils (Schmidt-Nielsen, 1960).

aldosterone A mineralocorticoid hormone, secreted by the adrenal cortex, that promotes the conservation of sodium by the kidneys.

nutrient A chemical that is needed for growth, maintenance, and repair of the body but is not used as a source of energy.

glucose An important sugar molecule used by the body and brain for energy.

glycogen A complex carbohydrate made by the combining of glucose molecules for a short-term store of energy.

insulin A pancreatic hormone that lowers blood glucose, promotes energy storage, and facilitates glucose utilization by cells.

glucagon A pancreatic hormone that converts glycogen to glucose, and thus increases blood glucose.

lipid A large molecule (commonly called a *fat*) that consists of fatty acids and glycerol that are insoluble in water.

adipose tissue Commonly called *fat tissue*. Tissue made up of fat cells.

ketone A compound, liberated by the breakdown of body fats and proteins, that is a metabolic fuel source.

basal metabolism The consumption of energy to fuel processes such as heat production, maintenance of membrane potentials, and all the other basic life-sustaining functions of the body.

Some Na⁺ loss is inevitable, as during urination or sweating. But when water is at a premium, the body tries to conserve Na⁺ in order to retain water. In addition to its effects on thirst and vasopressin secretion, angiotensin II stimulates the release of the steroid hormone **aldosterone** from the adrenal glands. Aldosterone directly stimulates the kidneys to conserve Na⁺. Nonetheless, animals must find additional salt in their environments in order to retain sufficient water to survive.

Our need to compensate for obligatory losses is also crucial to understanding energy regulation, as we'll see in the next section.

PART III Food and Energy Regulation

Feast or famine—these are poles of human experience. Hunger for the food that we need to build, maintain, and fuel our bodies is a compelling drive; and flavors are powerful reinforcements. The behaviors involved in obtaining and consuming food shape our daily schedules, and mass media feed us a steady diet of information about food: crop reports, stories about famines and droughts, cooking shows, and restaurant ads.

Our reliance on food for energy and nutrition is shared with all other animals. In the remainder of this chapter we look at the regulation of feeding and energy expenditure, as well as some aspects of food-related behavior.

Nutrient Regulation Helps Prepare for Future Needs

The regulation of eating and of body energy, compared to that of drinking, involves numerous redundant mechanisms and a more complex set of homeostatic mechanisms. The added complexity is due to the fact that the brain must monitor and regulate a wide range of **nutrients** (chemicals required for the effective functioning, growth, and maintenance of the body): 20 amino acids (of which 9 *essential amino acids* cannot be synthesized by the body), several fatty acids, about 15 vitamins, and a variety of minerals, carbohydrates for energy, and so on. No animal can afford to run out of energy or nutrients, so we need systems to anticipate future needs and keep a reserve on hand (but not *too* much!). (For more information about the complexity and variation in the nutrient needs of different species, see **A Step Further 9.3**, on the website).

The principal fuel for the cells of the body is **glucose**, a simple sugar that is obtained through the breakdown of more complex molecules. Because we need a steady supply of glucose between meals and may also experience elevated demand for fuel at other times—for example, during intense physical activity—several mechanisms have evolved for short- and long-term storage of excess fuel. For shorter-term storage, glucose can be converted into a more complicated molecule called **glycogen** and stored as reserve fuel in several locations, most notably the liver and skeletal muscles. This process is promoted by the hormone **insulin**, which is synthesized and released by the pancreas. When blood glucose levels drop too low, a second pancreatic hormone, **glucagon**, converts glycogen back into glucose (**Figure 9.10**). For longer-term storage, molecules of **lipid** (fat) from dietary sources or created from surplus sugars and other nutrients are stored in **adipose tissue** (commonly called *fat tissue*). Under conditions of prolonged food deprivation, fat can be converted into glucose and a secondary form of fuel, called **ketones**, which can similarly be utilized by the body and brain.

Only about 10–20% of the energy in food is used for active behavioral processes. The majority of food energy is spent on **basal metabolism**: the basic physiological processes of life, like heat production (the price we pay for endothermy), cellular activity, maintenance of membrane potentials, and so on. Metabolism is under homeostatic control and can be adjusted to a surprising extent. An all-too-familiar consequence of this metabolic flexibility is that people and animals tend to resist either losing or gaining weight following dietary changes (**Figure 9.11**). To the frustration of dieters everywhere, many studies show that a calorie-reduced diet prompts a reduction in basal metabolic

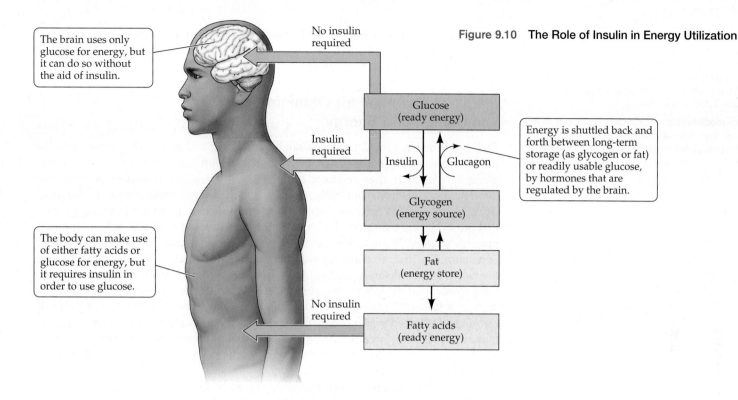

Figure 9.10 **The Role of Insulin in Energy Utilization**

The brain uses only glucose for energy, but it can do so without the aid of insulin.

No insulin required

Insulin required

The body can make use of either fatty acids or glucose for energy, but it requires insulin in order to use glucose.

No insulin required

Glucose (ready energy)

Insulin   Glucagon

Glycogen (energy source)

Fat (energy store)

Fatty acids (ready energy)

Energy is shuttled back and forth between long-term storage (as glycogen or fat) or readily usable glucose, by hormones that are regulated by the brain.

rate in order to prevent the loss of weight, regardless of whether the dieter is initially of normal weight or obese (Bray, 1969; C. K. Martin et al., 2007). Mice whose basal metabolic rate has been increased (by an induced increase in the energy used by mitochondria) eat more yet weigh less than normal mice, without increased locomotor activity (Clapham et al., 2000). Perhaps someday a drug will be developed to exert this effect on human mitochondria and produce such wonderful results in humans as well.

In the meantime, the debate about the most effective ways to decrease fat deposition through dieting continues to be immensely popular in the mass media. Although it is counterintuitive, some evidence suggests that diets low in carbohydrates, and correspondingly high in proteins and fats, can help people lose weight and also may increase serum levels of "good" cholesterol while decreasing fats (G. D. Foster et al., 2003; Samaha et al., 2003). However, long-term studies will be required to establish the overall safety of low-carbohydrate diets; after all, plenty of evidence already indicates that people with diets high in fat have more heart disease. For now, the only certain way

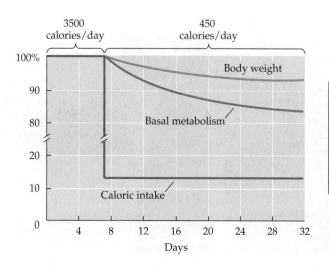

After 7 days on a rich 3,500-calorie diet, six obese subjects reduced their daily calories by 87%, to 450 calories per day. However, basal metabolism also declined by 15%; so after 3 weeks on the new diet, body weight had declined by only 6%.

Figure 9.11 **Why Losing Weight Is So Difficult** (After Bray, 1969.)

diabetes mellitus A condition, characterized by excessive glucose in the blood and urine and by reduced glucose utilization by body cells, that is caused by the failure of insulin to induce glucose absorption.

glucodetector A specialized type of liver cell that detects and informs the nervous system about levels of circulating glucose.

to lose weight is to decrease the number of calories eaten and/or increase the number of calories spent in physical activity. For the weight loss to be permanent, these changes in diet and activity must be permanent too.

Insulin Is Essential for Obtaining, Storing, and Using Food Energy

Each time you eat a meal, the foods are broken down and glucose is released into the bloodstream. We have already mentioned that insulin converts surplus glucose into glycogen, which can then be stored for later use. But insulin has another, more immediately critical function: your body needs insulin in order to make any use of the circulating glucose. That's because *glucose transporters*—the membrane-spanning proteins that most cells use to import glucose from the blood—need insulin in order to function properly (brain cells are an important exception; they can use glucose without the aid of insulin). The disease **diabetes mellitus** results from a lack of insulin production (in the *type 1*, or *juvenile-onset*, variety of the disease) or from greatly reduced tissue sensitivity to insulin (*type 2*, or *adult-onset*, diabetes, which is often associated with obesity). Although the brain can still make use of glucose from the diet, the rest of the body cannot and is forced to use energy from fatty acids. An untreated person with diabetes may eat a great deal because the body cannot make efficient use of the ingested food, and the long-term reliance on fatty acids for energy can result in severe damage of various tissues.

Insulin release around mealtimes is so important that it is triggered by several different mechanisms at different points in time. First, simply seeing, smelling, or tasting stimuli associated with food evokes a conditioned release of insulin in anticipation of glucose arrival in the blood. This release, because it is mediated by the brain, is called the *cephalic phase* of insulin release (recall that *cephalic* means "of the head"). Then, during the *digestive phase* (if you were lucky enough to get something to eat), food entering the digestive tract prompts an additional release of insulin. Finally, during the *absorptive phase*, as digested food is absorbed into the bloodstream, specialized liver cells called **glucodetectors** detect the increase in circulating glucose and signal the pancreas to release still more insulin. Information from the liver's glucodetectors is also conveyed directly to the hypothalamus via the vagus nerve (Powley, 2000), and the brain uses this information about circulating glucose to help control the pancreas and to stimulate feelings of hunger.

Given the crucial role of insulin in mobilizing and distributing food energy, you might think that the primary way the brain decides when it's time to eat (and when to stop) is by monitoring circulating insulin levels; high levels of insulin, signaling the presence of food in the gut, could provoke satiety (feeling "full") and low levels

(*a*) (*b*)

Not Too Sweet People with type 1 diabetes mellitus must receive insulin in order to utilize glucose. Taking insulin requires careful monitoring of blood glucose and, as shown here, self-administration via (*a*) daily injections or (*b*) drug pumps to infuse insulin throughout the day. Until the 1920s, when insulin was discovered as a result of experiments on dogs, this form of diabetes was a dreaded killer of children. In an especially dramatic moment in science, three of the discoverers of insulin—Frederick Banting, James Collip, and Charles Best—went through a hospital ward full of dying diabetic children, injecting them with the newly purified hormone. By the time the last child had been injected, the first was already waking up from diabetic coma. The discovery saved millions of lives and garnered Banting and another colleague a Nobel Prize in 1923.

of insulin between meals could make us feel hunger. Indeed, lowering an animal's blood insulin level causes it to become hungry and eat a large meal, and injecting some insulin causes the animal to eat much less. But injecting a larger dose of insulin doesn't produce fully satiated animals; instead, they become hungry again and eat a large meal! The reason for this surprising result is that the high insulin levels direct much of the blood glucose into storage, which means that there is *less* glucose in circulation. The brain learns of this glucose deficit directly via glucodetectors, leading to a hunger response.

Do these observations mean that the hunger signal might be circulating glucose rather than insulin? While it is certainly important, glucose can't be the sole appetite signal either, because people with untreated diabetes have very high levels of circulating glucose yet are constantly hungry. Somehow the brain integrates insulin and glucose levels with other sources of information to decide whether to initiate eating. As we'll see next, this has become a central theme in research on appetite control—that the brain integrates many different signals rather than relying exclusively on any single signal to trigger hunger.

The Hypothalamus Coordinates Multiple Systems That Control Hunger

Although no single brain region has exclusive control of appetite, many findings have confirmed that the hypothalamus is critically important for regulating metabolic rate, food intake, and body weight. In classic research, scientists found that lesions in the hypothalamus could induce either chronic hunger and massive weight gain, or chronic satiety and severe weight loss, depending on the location of the lesion. Next we'll review the experiments that led to these conclusions.

RESEARCHERS AT WORK

Lesion studies showed that the hypothalamus is crucial for appetite

Early researchers made discrete bilateral lesions in the hypothalamus—in either the **ventromedial hypothalamus** (**VMH**) or the **lateral hypothalamus** (**LH**) (**Figure 9.12a**). After recovery, VMH-lesioned rats ate to excess and became obese (Hetherington and Ranson, 1940), leading researchers to suggest that the VMH is the *satiety center* of the brain (because the rats ceased to experience satiety once the VMH was gone). Rats with LH lesions, conversely, ceased eating and rapidly lost weight, suggesting that the LH acts as a *hunger center* (Anand and Brobeck, 1951). A simple *dual-center hypothesis* derived from these results proposed that the VMH and LH act in opposition, integrating signals from the gut and elsewhere, to provide minute-to-minute appetite control.

Subsequent research provided a more refined view. For one thing, although the VMH was identified as a satiety center, its destruction did not create out-of-control feeding machines. Instead, VMH-lesioned animals exhibited a period of rapid weight gain but then stabilized at a new, higher body weight. When obese VMH-lesioned animals are forced to either gain or lose weight through dietary manipulation, they return to their new "normal" weight as soon as they are allowed to eat freely again (**Figure 9.12b**). So, because VMH-lesioned rats experience satiety, the VMH cannot be the sole satiety controller.

Similarly, the LH can't be the sole hunger center. Although they initially stopped eating, LH-lesioned rats that were kept alive with a feeding tube soon resumed eating and drinking, and eventually stabilized their body weight at a new, lower level. As with the VMH-lesioned animals, LH-lesioned animals can be forced to lose or

How's it going?

1. Provide a review of how glucose is used, stored, and retrieved from storage. Be sure to identify the roles of pancreatic hormones in each step.

2. What is basal metabolism? How is it affected by homeostatic processes, and how does the homeostatic regulation of metabolism frustrate efforts to lose weight?

3. Define and discuss the types and causes of diabetes mellitus. What are some of the ways that insulin release is normally controlled?

4. Discuss the evidence that insulin directly controls hunger.

ventromedial hypothalamus (VMH) A hypothalamic region involved in eating and sexual behaviors.

lateral hypothalamus (LH) A hypothalamic region involved in the control of appetite and other functions.

Figure 9.12   Lesion Studies Revealed That the Hypothalamus Is Involved in Appetite

Hypothesis

The hypothalamus contains discrete systems for controlling hunger and satiety.

Test

Place small lesions in target areas within the hypothalamus.

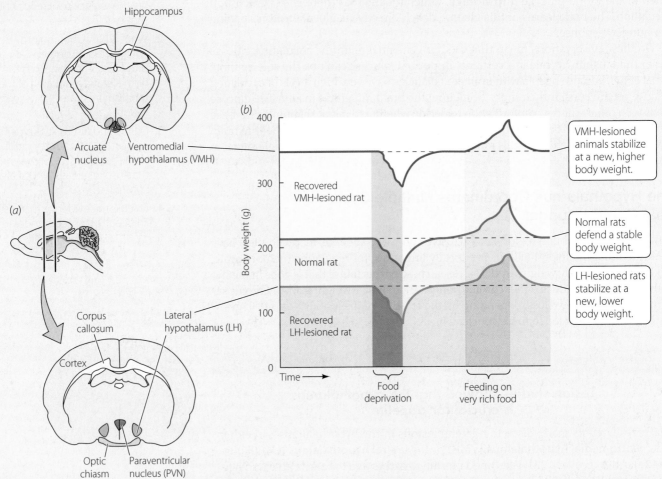

VMH-lesioned animals stabilize at a new, higher body weight.

Normal rats defend a stable body weight.

LH-lesioned rats stabilize at a new, lower body weight.

Result

Animals with lesions of the lateral hypothalamus (LH) decrease their food intake and rapidly lose weight, but they eventually stabilize at a new, lower weight. Following recovery, LH-lesioned animals forced to gain or lose weight return to the new lower weight when allowed to feed freely. Animals with lesions of the ventromedial hypothalamus (VMH) increase their food intake and rapidly gain weight, but they eventually stabilize at a new, higher weight. Following recovery, VMH-lesioned animals forced to gain or lose weight return to their new higher weight when allowed to feed freely.

Conclusion

The LH and VMH appear to play a role in appetite and body weight control, but because LH- and VMH-lesioned animals eventually show hunger and satiety, these two hypothalamic centers alone cannot constitute the entire appetite control system.

gain weight, but when returned to their standard diet they will precisely regulate their body weight at the new, lower set point (see Figure 9.12b) (Keesey, 1980).

The research program thus demonstrated that the hypothalamus contains distinct components of an appetite control network. This perspective provided a framework for subsequent findings. For example, fMRI studies show that elevations in circulating glucose after a period of fasting produce large changes in the activity of the human hypothalamus (**Figure 9.13**) (Y. Liu et al., 2000), probably acting via hypothalamic glucodetector neurons that directly monitor blood levels of glucose (Parton et al., 2007).

Today it is clear that hypothalamic control of feeding is quite complicated and, like other homeostatic systems, exhibits redundancy as a safety measure. However, researchers have uncovered many of the details of the hypothalamic appetite control network, and its integration of multiple signals, as we'll see next.

Hormones from the body drive a hypothalamic appetite controller

A spate of discoveries has sharpened our understanding of the hypothalamic control of appetite. This evidence indicates that a circuit within the **arcuate nucleus** of the hypothalamus is the key element in a highly specialized appetite network integrating peptide hormone signals from several sites in the body. One important source of information about energy stores is the pancreas; we have already discussed how the pancreatic hormone insulin signals the state of glucose circulating in the blood. Other information about energy balance—especially short-term and long-term reserves—comes in the form of hormonal secretions from elsewhere in the body, particularly the digestive organs and fat tissue.

You may be surprised to learn that the fat cells that make up adipose tissue are endocrine; in fact, they release a hormone called **leptin** (from the Greek *leptos*, "thin") into the bloodstream (Y. Zhang et al., 1994). Genetically modified mice carrying two copies of the aptly named *obese* gene fail to produce leptin—and they do indeed become obese (**Figure 9.14**). The fat mice will stay that way even if they are given only unpalatable food, or if they are required to work hard to obtain food (Cruce et al., 1974). And mice that make normal amounts of leptin but have nonfunctional leptin receptors likewise become obese (al-Barazanji et al., 1997; L. M. Zucker and Zucker, 1961). It appears that the brain senses circulating leptin levels to monitor the body's longer-term energy reserves in the form of fat. Defective leptin production or impaired leptin sensitivity causes a false underreporting of body fat, leading the animals to overeat, especially high-fat or sugary foods.

Shorter-term energy balance—the presence or absence of food in the gut—is reported by hormones from the digestive organs. Two such hormones that seem to be especially important for appetite control are **ghrelin**, synthesized and released into the bloodstream by endocrine cells of the stomach, and the awkwardly named **PYY$_{3-36}$**, a small peptide released by intestinal cells. Ghrelin reaches high concentrations during fasting and powerfully stimulates appetite (Wren et al., 2000, 2001), dropping sharply after a meal is eaten (Nakazato et al., 2001). PYY$_{3-36}$ shows the converse pattern, spiking to higher levels on ingestion of a meal and providing a potent appetite-*suppressing* satiety signal (see Karra et al., 2009, for a review). Injections of ghrelin cause increased appetite and feeding in rats or humans, and injections of PYY$_{3-36}$ into the bloodstream or directly into the arcuate nucleus curb appetite (Batterham and Bloom, 2003; Baynes et al., 2006; Chelikani et al., 2005). Furthermore, ghrelin is chronically slightly elevated in obese people, and PYY$_{3-36}$ is chronically lowered—possibly causing continual hunger (English et al., 2002). All of these hormone signals appear

> Following glucose ingestion, changes in activity in the hypothalamus are evident in this midsagittal fMRI image.

Figure 9.13   Sweet Spot (From Y. Liu et al., 2000.)

arcuate nucleus   An arc-shaped hypothalamic nucleus implicated in appetite control.

leptin   A peptide hormone released by fat cells.

ghrelin   A peptide hormone produced and released by the gut.

PYY$_{3-36}$ A peptide hormone, secreted by the intestines, that probably acts on hypothalamic appetite control mechanisms to suppress appetite.

> This mouse has two copies of the *obese* gene, impairing the production of leptin by fat cells, and it weighs 67 grams.

> This mouse has the same two copies of the *obese* gene, but following treatment with leptin its weight is much closer to normal. Few cases of human obesity are due to leptin deficiency, so such treatment is not generally effective in people.

Figure 9.14   Inherited Obesity Can Be Overcome

NPY neuron A neuron, involved in the hypothalamic appetite control system, that produces both neuropeptide Y and agouti-related peptide.

POMC neuron A neuron, involved in the hypothalamic appetite control system, that produces both pro-opiomelanocortin and cocaine- and amphetamine-related transcript.

to converge on an appetite controller in the arcuate nucleus, so next we'll have a look at how that system seems to work.

The current model of the organization of appetite control neurons in the arcuate nucleus is illustrated in **Figure 9.15**. The system relies on two types of neurons with opposite effects, named after the types of signaling substances they produce. Neurons that produce the peptides neuropeptide Y and agouti-related peptide—**NPY neurons**—act as hunger neurons, stimulating appetite and reducing metabolism when activated. Neurons that produce the peptides pro-opiomelanocortin (POMC) and cocaine- and amphetamine-regulated transcript—**POMC neurons**—act as satiety neurons when activated, inhibiting appetite and increasing metabolism. The two types of neurons interact and influence each other, and their projections to regions outside the arcuate nucleus ultimately control food intake (see Figure 9.15b), as we'll see shortly. But first, let's consider what is known about how the peripheral hormones interact with this appetite controller.

As we've discussed, leptin (and to a lesser extent, insulin) conveys information about the body's longer-term energy reserves, stored away within fat cells. Leptin affects both types of arcuate appetite neurons, but in opposite ways. High circulating levels of leptin activate the POMC satiety neurons but simultaneously inhibit the NPY

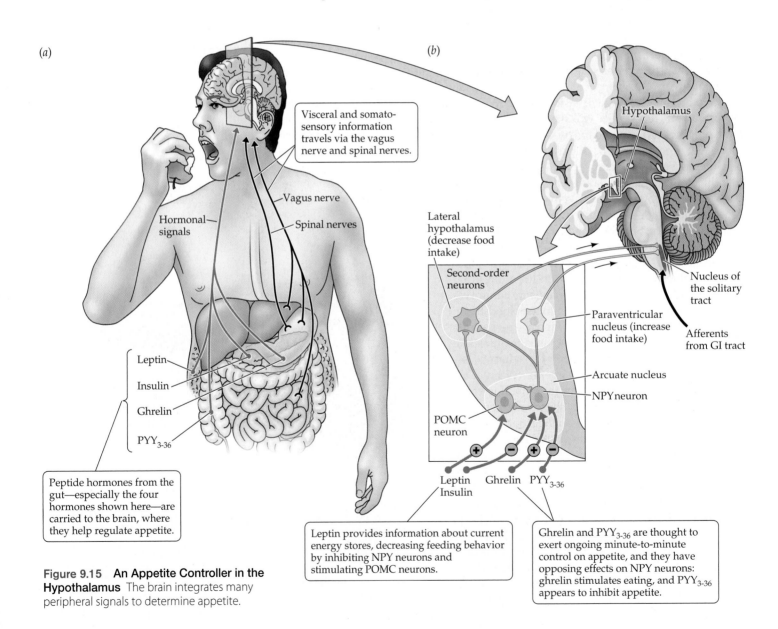

Figure 9.15 An Appetite Controller in the Hypothalamus The brain integrates many peripheral signals to determine appetite.

(a)

Visceral and somato-sensory information travels via the vagus nerve and spinal nerves.

Vagus nerve

Hormonal signals

Spinal nerves

Leptin

Insulin

Ghrelin

PYY$_{3-36}$

Peptide hormones from the gut—especially the four hormones shown here—are carried to the brain, where they help regulate appetite.

(b)

Hypothalamus

Lateral hypothalamus (decrease food intake)

Second-order neurons

Nucleus of the solitary tract

Paraventricular nucleus (increase food intake)

Afferents from GI tract

Arcuate nucleus

NPY neuron

POMC neuron

(+) (−) (+) (−)

Leptin Ghrelin PYY$_{3-36}$
Insulin

Leptin provides information about current energy stores, decreasing feeding behavior by inhibiting NPY neurons and stimulating POMC neurons.

Ghrelin and PYY$_{3-36}$ are thought to exert ongoing minute-to-minute control on appetite, and they have opposing effects on NPY neurons: ghrelin stimulates eating, and PYY$_{3-36}$ appears to inhibit appetite.

hunger neurons—so in both systems leptin is working to suppress hunger. In contrast to leptin, ghrelin and PYY$_{3-36}$ provide shorter-term hour-to-hour hunger signals from the gut. Both of these peptides act primarily on the appetite-stimulating NPY neurons of the arcuate. Ghrelin stimulates these cells, leading to a corresponding increase in appetite. PYY$_{3-36}$ works in opposition, inhibiting the same cells to *reduce* appetite. Thus, short-term control of appetite seems to reflect a balance between ghrelin and PYY$_{3-36}$ concentrations in circulation.

The net result of all this is a constant balancing act between the appetite-stimulating effects of the NPY system and the appetite-suppressing effects of the POMC system, spread across the hypothalamus. The peptide **orexin**, produced by neurons in the lateral hypothalamus, appears to participate in the subsequent control of feeding behavior (**Figure 9.16**) (Sakurai et al., 1998).

Other systems also play a role in hunger and satiety

Appetite signals from the hypothalamus converge on the **nucleus of the solitary tract (NST)** in the brainstem (see Figure 9.15b). The NST can be viewed as part of a common pathway for feeding behavior, receiving appetite signals from a variety of sources in addition to the hypothalamus. For example, the sensation of hunger is affected by a wide variety of peripheral sensory inputs, such as oral stimulation and the feeling of stomach distension, transmitted via spinal and cranial nerves. Information about nutrient levels is conveyed directly from the body to the NST via the vagus nerve (Tordoff et al., 1991). For example, the gut peptide **cholecystokinin (CCK)**, released by the gut after feeding, acts directly on receptors of the vagus nerve to inhibit appetite (H. Fink et al., 1998).

A variety of other brain locations also participate in feeding behavior, either directly or through indirect effects on other processes. For example, as you might expect, the brain's reward system appears to be intimately involved with feeding. Activity of a circuit including the amygdala and the dopamine-mediated reward system in the nucleus accumbens (see Chapter 4) is hypothesized to mediate pleasurable aspects of feeding (Ahn and Phillips, 2002; Volkow and Wise, 2005).

The **endocannabinoid** system is also emerging as a major regulator of appetite and feeding. Endocannabinoids, such as *anandamide*, are endogenous substances that act much like the active ingredient in marijuana (*Cannabis sativa*) and, like marijuana, can potently stimulate hunger. Acting both in the brain and in the periphery, endocannabinoids are thought to stimulate feeding by affecting the mesolimbic dopamine reward system, as well as hypothalamic appetite mechanisms, while also inhibiting satiety signals from the gut (Di Marzo and Matias, 2005).

orexin Also called *hypocretin*. A neuropeptide produced in the hypothalamus that is involved in switching between sleep states, in narcolepsy, and in the control of appetite.

nucleus of the solitary tract (NST) A complicated brainstem nucleus that receives visceral and taste information via several cranial nerves.

cholecystokinin (CCK) A peptide hormone that is released by the gut after ingestion of food that is high in protein and/or fat.

endocannabinoid An endogenous ligand of cannabinoid receptors; thus, a marijuana analog that is produced by the brain.

Orexin mRNA (white spots) is present only in the lateral hypothalamus. Infusion of orexin into this region causes rats to eat more food.

Figure 9.16 Neuropeptides That Induce Hunger? (Courtesy of Masashi Yanagisawa.)

How's it going?

1. Review the early work implicating the LH and VMH in appetite control. Why did researchers abandon the view that the LH and VMH were the sole controllers of appetite and satiety?

2. Sketch or briefly describe the major components of the hypothalamic appetite controller, as currently understood.

3. Describe how the hypothalamic appetite controller functions during hunger, in contrast to just after a meal.

4. What is leptin? Discuss its origins in the body and its effects on feeding behavior.

5. What are some of the gut hormones that may be involved in appetite control, and what are they thought to do?

6. Briefly describe some of the additional (redundant) mechanisms of appetite control that supplement the hypothalamic appetite system. What is the basis of the increased appetite frequently experienced after use of marijuana?

TABLE 9.1 Body Mass Index (BMI)

Value	Body weight category
<15	Starvation
15–18.5	Underweight
18.5–25	Ideal weight
25–30	Overweight
30–40	Obese
>40	Morbidly obese

Note:

$$BMI = \frac{weight\ (kg)}{height \times height\ (m \times m)}\ or$$

$$BMI = 703\frac{weight\ (lb)}{height \times height\ (in. \times in.)}$$

Hypothalamic feeding control must be strongly influenced by inputs from higher brain centers, but little is known about these mechanisms. During development, for example, our feeding patterns are increasingly influenced by social factors such as parental and peer group pressures (Birch et al., 2003). Understanding the nature of cortical influences on feeding mechanisms is a major challenge for the future. The list of participants in appetite regulation is long and growing longer each day, revealing overlapping and complex controls with a high degree of redundancy, as befits a behavioral function of such critical importance to the health and survival of the individual. With each new discovery, we draw nearer to finally developing safe and effective treatments for eating disorders, as we discuss next.

Obesity Is Difficult to Treat

Unfortunately, effective treatments to aid weight loss have been elusive. Our multiple redundant systems for energy management work all too well in fighting against weight loss: like it or not, evolution has optimized our bodies for obtaining and storing energy, and accumulating *too much* energy was not much of a concern for our ancestors. The tendency to accumulate excess energy is exacerbated by our increasingly sedentary lifestyles. Obesity has certainly reached epidemic proportions: a majority of the adults in the United States are overweight—about 61%—and about one in three qualify as obese (Flegal et al., 2002), as defined by body mass index (BMI; **Table 9.1**). The higher incidence of cardiovascular disease, diabetes, and other disorders that accompany obesity will be an increasingly heavy burden on health care services in the future.

In Lewis Carroll's *Alice's Adventures in Wonderland*, Alice quaffs the contents of a small bottle in order to shrink. The quest for a real-life shrinking potion—but one that makes you thin rather than short—is the subject of intense scientific activity, and several major strategies or targets are emerging.

1. *Appetite control.* Hopes are high that drugs designed to dampen the hypothalamic appetite controller will be safe and potent obesity treatments. Alteration of leptin levels has not proven to be very effective (Montague et al., 1997). But drugs that directly interfere with endocannabinoid activity, which is normally regulated by leptin in the hypothalamus, effectively produce "anti-munchies"—the reverse of the hunger experienced by marijuana users (Thornton-Jones et al., 2006; Van Gaal et al., 2005). Significant mood problems (an "anti-high"?) also occur, however, so the search continues for drugs that can selectively modify the signaling systems in the arcuate appetite controller. Many experimental treatments are being studied, such as a PYY_{3-36}-based nasal spray—recall that PYY_{3-36} from the gut normally triggers satiety neurons of the arcuate (Batterham et al., 2003; Chelikani et al., 2005)—as well as drugs that mimic other signaling peptides (Neary and Batterham, 2009).

2. *Increased metabolism.* An alternative approach to treating obesity involves treatments that cause the body's metabolic rate to increase and thus expend extra calories in the form of heat. For example, metabolic rate is controlled by the thyroid hormones, so scientists are trying to design drugs that will increase the rate at which energy is used by cells without producing harmful side effects (Grover et al., 2003).

3. *Inhibition of fat tissue.* A third approach to treating obesity involves interference with the formation of new fat tissue. For example, in order for fat tissue to grow, it must be able to recruit and develop new blood vessels. Drugs that block this process inhibit weight gain in mice and may have similar anti-obesity benefits in humans (Rupnick et al., 2002; Tam et al., 2009).

4. *Reduced absorption.* One of the few currently approved obesity medications—orlistat (Xenical)—works by interfering with the digestion of fat. However, this approach has generally produced only modest weight loss, and it often causes intestinal discomfort.

5. *Reduced reward.* A different perspective on treating obesity focuses on the rewarding properties of food. Not only is food delicious, but "comfort foods" also directly reduce

circulating stress hormones, thereby providing another reward. Drugs that affect the brain's reward circuitry (see Chapter 4), reducing the rewarding properties of food, may promote weight loss (Volkow and Wise, 2005).

6. *Anti-obesity surgery.* The surgical removal of fat tissue, particularly through **liposuction**, is a popular approach to controlling weight, but it is generally only moderately successful, and it is temporary. Because of the propensity of fat tissue to regrow after excision, some people are turning to more invasive **bariatric** procedures that bypass part of the intestinal tract or stomach in order to reduce the absorptive capacity of the digestive system (**Figure 9.17**). As the only current intervention that produces significant and lasting weight loss, bariatric surgery can offer hope of substantial weight loss and reversal of co-morbid conditions like type 2 diabetes and hypertension, but it is accompanied by significant risk of complications, even death (Flum et al., 2005).

Eating Disorders Can Be Life-Threatening

Sometimes people shun food, despite having no apparent aversion to it. Like Kitty, whom we met at the opening of the chapter, these people are usually young, become obsessed with their body weight, and become extremely thin—generally by eating very little and sometimes also by regurgitating food, taking laxatives, overexercising, or drinking large amounts of water to suppress appetite. This condition, which is more common in adolescent and adult women than in men, is called **anorexia nervosa**. The name of the disorder indicates (1) that the patients have no appetite (*anorexia*) and (2) that the disorder originates in the nervous system (*nervosa*).

The liner is inserted through the mouth via an endoscope and is guided into position by use of a ball and catheter.

The sleeve lines the small intestine and is held in place with a spiked attachment. It serves as a barrier to prevent food from being absorbed along much of the small intestine, so fewer calories are absorbed from the diet.

Figure 9.17 A Fat-Busting Liner for the Intestine

People who suffer from anorexia nervosa tend to think about food a good deal, and physiological evidence suggests that they respond even *more* than normal subjects to the presentation of food (Broberg and Bernstein, 1989); for example, food stimuli provoke a large release of insulin, despite cognitive denial of any feelings of hunger. So, in a physiological sense their hunger may be normal or even exaggerated, but this hunger is somehow absent from their conscious perceptions and they refuse to eat. The idea that anorexia nervosa is primarily a nervous system disorder stems from this mismatch between physiology and cognition, and from the distorted body image of the patients (they may consider themselves fat when others see them as emaciated). There may also be abnormalities in the functioning of the dopamine-based reward system that signals pleasurable aspects of eating, persisting even after recovery (Kaye et al., 2009).

Anorexia nervosa is notoriously difficult to treat because it appears to involve an unfortunate combination of genetic, endocrine, personality, cognitive, and environmental variables. One approach that is successful in some cases is *family-based treatment (FBT)*, a therapy that deemphasizes the identification of causal factors and instead focuses on intensive, parent-led "refeeding" of the anorexic person (Le Grange, 2005). This approach (sometimes also called *Maudsley therapy* after the hospital where it was introduced) was effective in returning Kitty to her normal weight (H. Brown, 2006).

Bulimia (or *bulimia nervosa*, from the Greek *boulimia*, "great hunger") is a related disorder. Like those who suffer from anorexia nervosa, people with bulimia may believe themselves fatter than they are, but they periodically gorge themselves, usually

liposuction The surgical removal of fat tissue.

bariatric Having to do with obesity.

anorexia nervosa A syndrome in which individuals severely deprive themselves of food.

bulimia Also called *bulimia nervosa*. A syndrome in which individuals periodically gorge themselves, usually with "junk food," and then either vomit or take laxatives to avoid weight gain.

Changing Ideals of Female Beauty   Actress Keira Knightley (left) provides an extreme example of modern society's emphasis on thinness as an aspect of beauty. In contrast, Flemish painter Peter Paul Rubens' wife (right), pictured here in *Helena Fourment as Aphrodite* (circa 1630), exemplifies the very different ideal for the feminine form during her era. Are our modern weight-conscious notions of female beauty responsible for some cases of anorexia nervosa and bulimia?

with "junk food," and then either vomit the food or take laxatives to avoid weight gain. Also like sufferers of anorexia nervosa, people with bulimia may be obsessed with food and body weight, but not all of them become emaciated. Both anorexia nervosa and bulimia can be fatal because the patient's lack of nutrient reserves damages various organ systems and/or leaves the body unable to battle otherwise mild diseases.

In **binge eating**, people spontaneously gorge themselves with far more food than is required to satisfy hunger, often to the point of illness. Such people are often obese, and the causes of the bingeing are not fully understood. In susceptible people, the strong pleasure associated with food activates opiate and dopaminergic reward mechanisms to such an extent that bingeing resembles drug addiction.

Despite the epidemic of obesity in our society, or perhaps because of it, our present culture emphasizes that women, especially young women, must be thin to be attractive. This cultural pressure is widely perceived as one of the causes of eating disorders. In earlier times, however, when plump women were considered the most beautiful, some women still fasted severely and may have suffered from anorexia nervosa. The origins of these disorders remain elusive, and to date, the available therapies help only a minority of patients like Kitty.

How's it going?

1. What proportion of adults in the United States are overweight or obese? How might homeostasis be part of the problem?

2. If you were designing drugs to combat obesity, what specific parts of the hypothalamic appetite controller might you target? Why?

3. Discuss nonpharmacological methods of weight reduction. Is surgery a good option?

4. Compare and contrast anorexia nervosa and bulimia. Are people with anorexia interested in food at all? Briefly discuss possible methods of treating anorexia.

5. Discuss the likely contributions of cultural versus biological factors in various eating disorders.

binge eating   The rapid intake of large quantities of food, often poor in nutritional value and high in calories.

Recommended Reading

Agras, W. S. (Ed.). (2010). *Oxford Handbook of Eating Disorders.* New York, NY: Oxford University Press.

Blumberg, M. S. (2009). *Body Heat.* Cambridge, MA: Harvard University Press.

Brown, H. N. (2010) *Brave Girl Eating.* New York, NY: Morrow.

Kirkham, T., and Cooper, S. J. (Eds.). (2006). *Appetite and Body Weight: Integrative Systems and the Development of Anti-obesity Drugs.* Burlington, MA: Academic Press.

Power, M. L., and Schulkin, J. (2009). *The Evolution of Obesity.* Baltimore, MD: Johns Hopkins University Press.

CHAPTER 9 VISUAL SUMMARY

mindsmachine.com/vs9

You should be able to relate each summary to the adjacent illustration, including structures and processes. If you need to review, go to the figures indicated and read the accompanying text.

1 **Homeostatic systems**, such as the processes regulating body temperature (thermoregulation), work to maintain a constant internal environment. Like other homeostatic system, thermoregulation employs **negative feedback** control: the resulting heat inhibits the system from calling for more. Review **Figure 9.1, Animations 9.2** and **9.3**

2 Critical homeostatic mechanisms tend to exhibit multiple redundancy. For example, redundant thermoregulatory controls with slightly different features can be found in the spinal cord, the brainstem, and the hypothalamus. Review **Figure 9.2, Animation 9.4**

3 Homeostatic systems rely on specialized behaviors to help regulate physiological parameters. For example, most species have specialized behaviors to help warm or cool the body. Review **Figure 9.3**

4 Our cells function properly only when the concentration of salts and other ions of the **intracellular compartment** of the body is within a critical range. The **extracellular compartment** is a source of replacement water and a buffer between the intracellular compartment and the outside world. Review **Figure 9.6**

5 Thirst is a powerful motivator, triggered either by decreased volume of the extracellular fluid (**hypovolemic thirst**) or by increased extracellular saltiness (**osmotic thirst**). Because of the importance of solute concentration, we must regulate salt intake in order to regulate water balance effectively. Review **Figure 9.7**

6 Specialized **osmosensory neurons** detect the concentration of extracellular fluid. **Baroreceptors** in the major blood vessels monitor blood pressure and volume. Review **Figure 9.8**

7 Hypovolemic and osmotic thirsts are triggered by different mechanisms, and differ in their immediate effects, but both forms of thirst ultimately trigger a complex shared thirst network. Review **Figure 9.9**

8 Our digestive system breaks down food and uses most of it for energy. **Insulin** helps most body cells to use **glucose** for fuel (the brain can use glucose directly), and promotes the storage of excess food energy. Another pancreatic hormone, **glucagon**, helps liberate glucose from storage. Review **Figure 9.10**

9 To the dismay of dieters, the body responds to caloric restriction by reducing metabolism, thus limiting weight loss. Review **Figure 9.11**

10 In **endotherms**, most food energy is used for **basal metabolism**. Metabolism readily shifts to compensate for changes in the availability of food. Review **Figure 9.12**

11 An appetite controller located in the **arcuate nucleus** of the hypothalamus responds to levels of several peptide gut hormones. When activated, arcuate **POMC neurons** act to decrease appetite, and arcuate **NPY neurons** act to stimulate appetite. **Leptin** and **insulin** provide important hormonal signals about longer-term energy storage. **Ghrelin** and **PYY$_{3-36}$** provide more-acute signals from the gut. Ghrelin stimulates and PYY$_{3-36}$ inhibits the arcuate appetite control system. Review **Figure 9.15, Activity 9.1**

12 Obesity is a pervasive problem that is difficult to treat through diet, drugs, or surgery. The only long-lasting medical intervention for obesity is **bariatric** surgery, but several drug strategies based on a new understanding of appetite control offer promise. Review **Figure 9.17**

chapter 10

Biological Rhythms and Sleep

When Sleep Gets Out of Control

Starting college always brings its share of new experiences and adjustments, but "Barry" knew something was wrong freshman year when he seemed to be sleepy all the time (S. Smith, 1997). Barry napped so often that his friends called him the hibernating bear. Of course, college can be exhausting, and many students seek refuge in long snooze sessions. But one day while Barry was camping with his pals, an even odder thing happened: "I laughed really hard, and I kind of fell on my knees ... After that, about every week I'd have two or three episodes where if I'd laugh ... my arm would fall down or my muscles in my face would get weak. Or if I was running around playing catch and someone said something, I would get weak in the knees. And there was a time there that my friends kinda used it as a joke. If they're going to throw me the ball and they didn't want me to catch it, they'd tell me a joke and I'd fall down and miss it."

It was as if any big surge in emotion in Barry might trigger a sudden paralysis lasting anywhere from a few seconds to a few minutes, affecting either a body part or his whole body. Sex became something of a challenge because sometimes during foreplay, Barry's body would just collapse. "Luckily, you're probably laying down, so it's not that big a deal. But it just puts a damper on the whole thing."

What was happening to Barry? By the end of this chapter, we'll know a lot more about sleep and what went wrong in Barry's brain to cause these problems.

To see a video, go to

mindsmachine.com/10.1
Narcolepsy

All living systems show repeating, predictable changes over time. Some rhythms, like brain potentials, are rapid; other rhythms, like annual hibernations, are slow. Daily rhythms, the first topic of this chapter, have an intriguing clocklike regularity and are seen in virtually every physiological measure, including body temperature and hormone secretion. The second topic of the chapter is that familiar daily rhythm known as the sleep-waking cycle. By age 60, most humans have spent 20 years asleep (some, alas, on one side or the other of the classroom podium). We'll find that sleep is not a passive state of "nonwaking," but rather the interlocking of several different states controlled by distinct brain regions.

To see the brain in 3D, go to

mindsmachine.com/10.2
Brain Explorer

PART I Biological Rhythms

Biological rhythms are regular fluctuations in any living process. Almost all physiological processes—hormone levels, body temperature, drug sensitivity—change over the course of the day. Because such rhythms last about a day, they are called **circadian rhythms** (from the Latin *circa*, "about," and *dies*, "day"). Circadian rhythms are by far the most studied of the biological rhythms, and they will be our major concern in this chapter.

While circadian rhythms are the most familiar, you should know that some biological rhythms are shorter than a day. Such rhythms are referred to as **ultradian** (because they repeat more than once per day; the Latin *ultra* means "beyond"), and they vary from several minutes to hours long. Ultradian rhythms are seen in such behaviors as bouts of activity, feeding, and hormone release. For example, humans show a 90-minute cycle of daydreaming (P. Lavie and Kripke, 1981).

Biological rhythms that take *more* than a day are called **infradian** rhythms because they repeat less than once per day (the Latin *infra* means "below"). A familiar infradian rhythm is the 28-day human menstrual cycle. Many animal behaviors vary across the year; for example, most animals breed only during a particular season. There's also growing evidence of annual rhythms in the onset of human behavioral disorders, such as depression (see Chapter 12). (By the way, despite the urban myth that cases of depression peak around the holiday season, in fact they peak in the spring.) You might think that breeding seasons in animals would be triggered by changes in temperatures or food availability, but experiments suggest that the duration of light each day might be the real trigger because in the laboratory, animals exposed to short days and long nights (mimicking wintertime conditions) will often change to the nonbreeding condition (**Figure 10.1**).

Next we'll concentrate on the best-studied biological rhythms—circadian rhythms—in which light also plays a crucial role.

Many Animals Show Daily Rhythms in Activity

Humans and many other primates are **diurnal**—active during the day. But most other mammals, including most rodents, are **nocturnal**—active during dark periods. These circadian activities are extraordinarily precise: the beginning of activity may vary only a

biological rhythm   A regular fluctuation in any living process.

circadian rhythm   A pattern of behavioral, biochemical, or physiological fluctuation that has a 24-hour period.

ultradian   Referring to a rhythmic biological event whose period is shorter than that of a circadian rhythm, usually from several minutes to several hours long.

infradian   Referring to a rhythmic biological event whose period is longer than that of a circadian rhythm—that is, longer than a day.

diurnal   Active during the light periods of the daily cycle.

nocturnal   Active during the dark periods of the daily cycle.

Siberian hamsters in the wild suppress their reproductive systems and develop a silvery fur coat for camouflage in the snow each fall.

In the laboratory, they undergo identical changes, despite warm temperatures and abundant food, if the lights are on only 10 hours per day. Their brains seem to interpret these short days as an indication that winter is coming.

Figure 10.1   A Hamster for All Seasons
(Photo by Carol D. Hegstrom.)

1 A running wheel in a hamster's cage is monitored by a computer-linked device. Each revolution of the wheel is displayed as a dark mark that can be printed out on paper. The paper strips are cut apart, and each subsequent day's activity is aligned underneath. Nowadays, computers record the activity and print out plots.

2 This hamster's activity record shows that it becomes active shortly before the start of the dark phase of the daily cycle and remains active during the dark period.

Continuous activity record

Paper

Day 1 Day 2   Day 3   Day 4

24:00   24:00   24:00

Time of day

24:00   24:00

Day 1
     2
     3
     4

3 When the timing of the light was shifted, so that the lights came on later and went off later each day, the hamster also showed a phase shift of activity.

Phase shift

Light   Dark

Light-dark cycle

Constant dim light

4 In constant dim light, the hamster became active a few minutes later each day. This free-running activity rhythm indicates that the hamster has an endogenous clock that has a period slightly greater than 24 hours.

Figure 10.2 How Activity Rhythms Are Measured (After I. Zucker, 1976; based on Rusak and Zucker, 1979.)

few minutes from one day to another. For humans equipped with watches and clocks, this regularity may seem uninteresting, but other animals achieve such remarkable regularity using only a built-in *biological clock*.

Circadian rhythms are generated by an endogenous clock

A favorite way to study circadian rhythms exploits rodents' love of running wheels. A switch attached to the wheel connects to a computer that registers each turn, revealing an activity rhythm as in **Figure 10.2a**. A hamster placed in a dimly lit room continues to show a daily rhythm in wheel running despite the absence of day versus night, suggesting that the animal has an internal clock. But even when the light is constantly dim, it is always possible that the animal detects other external cues (e.g., outside noises, temperature, barometric pressure—who knows?) signaling the time of day. Arguing for a biological clock, however, is the fact that in constant light or dark the circadian cycle is not *exactly* 24 hours: activity starts a few minutes later each day, so eventually the normally nocturnal hamster is active while it is daytime outside (**Figure 10.2b**, bottom). The animal is said to be **free-running**, maintaining its own personal cycle, which, in the absence of external cues, is a bit more than 24 hours long.

The free-running **period**, the time between two similar points of successive cycles (such as sunset to sunset), differs from one hamster to another. If two hamsters are placed in constant dim light next door to each other, eventually one may be active when

To see an animation of this figure, go to

mindsmachine.com/10.3
Biological Rhythms

free-running   Referring to a rhythm of behavior shown by an animal deprived of external cues about time of day.

period   The interval of time between two similar points of successive cycles, such as sunset to sunset.

phase shift   A shift in the activity of a biological rhythm, typically provided by a synchronizing environmental stimulus.

entrainment   The process of synchronizing a biological rhythm to an environmental stimulus.

zeitgeber   Literally, "time-giver" (in German). The stimulus (usually the light-dark cycle) that entrains circadian rhythms.

suprachiasmatic nucleus (SCN)   A small region of the hypothalamus above the optic chiasm that is the location of a circadian clock.

the other is asleep—further evidence that they are not detecting some mysterious external cue. Rather, every animal has its own endogenous clock, with periods that vary from one animal to another.

Normally this internal clock is reset by light. If we expose a free-running nocturnal animal to periods of light and dark, the animal soon synchronizes its wheel running to the beginning of the dark period. The shift of activity produced by a synchronizing stimulus is referred to as a **phase shift** (see Figure 10.2b, middle), and the process of shifting the rhythm is called **entrainment**. Any cue that an animal uses to synchronize its activity with the environment is called a **zeitgeber** (German for "time giver"). Light acts as a powerful zeitgeber, and we can easily manipulate it in the lab. Because light stimuli can entrain circadian rhythms, the endogenous clock must receive input from the visual system, as we'll confirm shortly. We humans experience a phase shift (we call it "jet lag") when we fly from one time zone to another. Flying three time zones east (say, from California to New York) means that sunlight arrives 3 hours sooner than our brain expects. The next morning we'll probably have a hard time waking up at 7:00 AM New York time, because it's 4:00 AM California time.

In the absence of jet travel, the major value of circadian rhythms is obvious: they enable us to *anticipate* an event, such as sunrise or sunset, and to begin physiological and behavioral preparations *before* that event. Let's talk about how this circadian clock works.

The Hypothalamus Houses a Circadian Clock

Where is the biological clock that drives circadian rhythms, and how does it work? Early research showed that while removing various endocrine glands has little effect on the free-running rhythm of rats, large lesions of the hypothalamus interfere with circadian rhythms (Richter, 1967). It was subsequently discovered that a tiny subregion of the hypothalamus—the **suprachiasmatic nucleus** (**SCN**), named for its location above the optic chiasm— serves as a biological clock. Lesions confined to the SCN portion of the hypothalamus interfere with circadian rhythms of drinking and locomotor behavior (**Figure 10.3**) (Stephan and Zucker, 1972), and of hormone secretion (R. Y. Moore and Eichler, 1972).

The clocklike nature of the SCN is also evident in its metabolic activity (**Figure 10.4**). If we take SCN cells out of the brain and put them in a dish (Earnest et al., 1999; Yamazaki et al., 2000), their electrical activity remains synchronized to the light-dark cycle that the animal had previously experienced. This striking evidence supports the idea that the SCN contains an endogenous clock. But even stronger proof that the SCN generates a circadian rhythm comes from transplanting the SCN from one animal to another, as we'll see next.

Circadian rhythms in the hamster whose activity is plotted here were normal and synchronized to the light-dark period before an SCN lesion was made (asterisk).

After the lesion, the animal continued being more active when the lights were out...

...but when placed in continuous (dim) light, the animal's activity became completely random, indicating that the lesion had eliminated the endogenous rhythm.

Figure 10.3   **The Effects of Lesions in the SCN** (From I. Zucker, 1976; based on Rusak and Zucker, 1979.)

Figure 10.4   The Circadian Rhythm of the SCN's Metabolic Activity (From Schwartz et al., 1979.)

Eye

SCN

(*a*) Light phase

In a section taken from an animal during a light phase, greater metabolic activity in the SCN is represented by the dark circles at the base of the brain.

(*b*) Dark phase

The SCN shows a lower metabolic rate in a section taken from an animal during a dark phase.

RESEARCHERS AT WORK

Transplants prove that the SCN produces a circadian rhythm

Ralph and Menaker (1988) found a male hamster that exhibited an unusually short free-running activity rhythm in constant conditions. Normally, hamsters free-run at a period slightly longer than 24 hours, but this male showed a free-running period of 22 hours. Half of his offspring also had a shorter circadian rhythm, indicating that he had a genetic mutation affecting the endogenous clock. Grandchildren inheriting two copies of this mutation had an even shorter period: 20 hours. The mutation was named *tau*, after the Greek symbol used by scientists to represent time. These hamsters entrained to a normal 24-hour light-dark cycle just fine; their abnormal endogenous circadian rhythm was revealed only in constant conditions.

Dramatic evidence that the SCN is a master clock was provided by transplant experiments. When nonmutant hamsters with lesions of the SCN were placed in constant conditions, their circadian activity rhythms were abolished, as expected **(Figure 10.5)**. The hamsters then received a transplant into the hypothalamus of an SCN taken from a fetal hamster with two copies of the mutant *tau* gene. About a week later the hamsters that had received the transplants began showing a free-running activity rhythm again, but the new rhythm matched that of the *donor* SCN: it was about 20 hours rather than the original 24.05 (Ralph et al., 1990).

Reciprocal transplants gave comparable results: the endogenous rhythm following the transplant was always that of the *donor* SCN, not the recipient, so the SCN must be driving the circadian rhythms. This remains the only known case of transplanting brain tissue from one individual to another in which the recipient subsequently displayed the donor's behavior!

Figure 10.5 Brain Transplants Prove That the SCN Contains a Clock
(From Ralph et al., 1990.)

Hypothesis

The endogenous clock determining an individual hamster's circadian rhythm is in the suprachiasmatic nucleus (SCN).

Test

The SCN is lesioned in several normal hamsters, rendering them arrhythmic.

These hamsters receive SCN transplants from newborn hamsters. Some receive SCN from mutant hamsters that have a period of about 20 hours. Others receive SCN from normal hamsters, which have a period of just over 24 hours.

Alternative Outcomes

- If the endogenous circadian rhythm is generated outside the SCN, then when the hamster recovers, it should return to its original period of just over 24 hours.
- If the endogenous circadian rhythm is controlled by the SCN, then when the adult hamster recovers, its period should match that of the donor—about 20 hours.

Result

When the adult hamster recovered, it did not show its original circadian rhythm of about 24 hours, but displayed a rhythm that matched that of its donor, about 20 hours.

Conclusion

Within the SCN itself there must be a mechanism that can drive a circadian rhythm in activity, and this biological clock is affected by mutation of the gene *tau*.

In mammals, light information from the eyes reaches the SCN directly

Most vertebrates have photoreceptors *outside the eye* that are part of the mechanism of light entrainment (Rusak and Zucker, 1979). For example, the pineal gland of some birds and amphibians is itself sensitive to light (Jamieson and Roberts, 2000) and helps entrain circadian rhythms to light. Because the skull over the pineal is especially thin in some species, we can think of those species as having a primitive "third eye" in the back of the head (some elementary school teachers also seem to have an eye in the back of the head, but this has not been proven to be the pineal gland). At night, the pineal gland secretes a hormone, **melatonin**, that informs the brain about daylight. For more on the nocturnal secretion of melatonin, see Chapter 8, Part I.

In mammals, however, cells in the eye tell the SCN when it is light out. Certain retinal ganglion cells send their axons along the **retinohypothalamic pathway**, veering out of the optic chiasm to synapse directly within the SCN. This short pathway carries information about light to the hypothalamus (R.Y. Moore, 1983) to entrain rhythms (**Figure 10.6**). Most of the retinal ganglion cells that extend their axons to the SCN do not rely on the traditional photoreceptors—rods and cones—to learn about light. Rather, these retinal ganglion cells themselves contain a special photopigment, called **melanopsin**, that makes them sensitive to light (Do et al., 2009). Transgenic mice that lack retinal photoreceptors, and so are blind in every other respect, will still entrain their behavior to light (Freedman et al., 1999), if the specialized melanopsin-containing ganglion cells are present.

Unfortunately, those melanopsin-containing retinal ganglion cells appear to be absent or dysfunctional in most totally blind humans, because people who are blind often show a free-running circadian rhythm, with difficulties getting to sleep at night and staying awake during the day (Sack, Lewy, et al., 1992). Taking melatonin at bedtime, thus mimicking the normal nightly release of the hormone from the pineal gland, helps blind people to entrain to daylight (Sack et al., 2000). This result suggests that while humans rely primarily on light stimulation of the retinohypothalamic tract to the SCN in order to entrain to light, our brains have retained enough sensitivity to melatonin that we can use that cue in the absence of information about light.

Circadian rhythms have been genetically dissected in flies and mice

Like humans, the fruit fly *Drosophila melanogaster* displays a diurnal circadian rhythm in activity. Flies with a mutation that disabled the gene called *period* (*per*) were arrhythmic when transferred to constant dim light, indicating that their internal clock wasn't running (Konopka and Benzer, 1971). Eventually, more genes were discovered that affect the circadian cycle in *Drosophila*, and mammals were found to have their own versions of each of those genes, paving the way for understanding the molecular basis of the circadian clock.

Cells in the mammalian SCN make two proteins, named Clock and Cycle, that bind together to form a dimer (a pair of proteins attached to each other). The Clock/

melatonin   An amine hormone that is secreted by the pineal gland at night, thereby signaling day length to the brain.

retinohypothalamic pathway   The route by which retinal ganglion cells send their axons to the suprachiasmatic nuclei.

melanopsin   A photopigment found within particular retinal ganglion cells that projects to the suprachiasmatic nucleus.

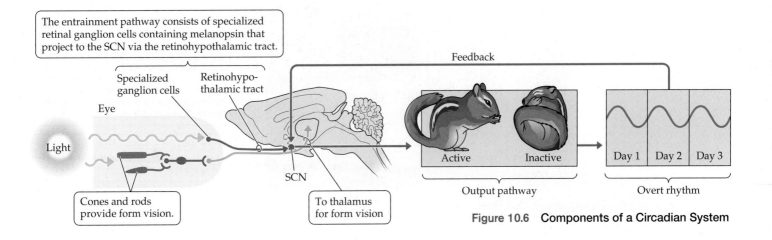

Figure 10.6 **Components of a Circadian System**

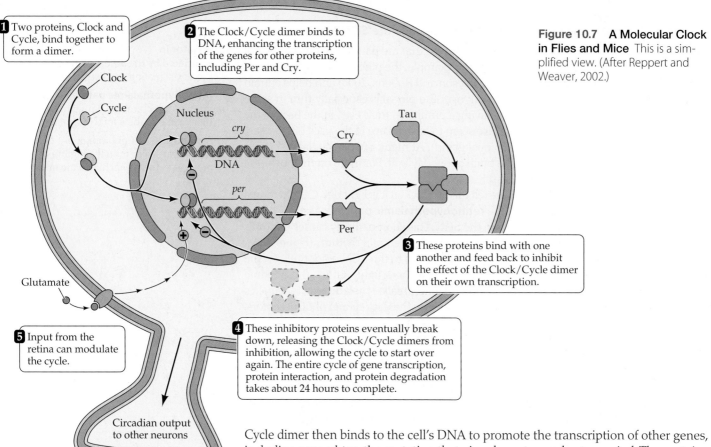

1 Two proteins, Clock and Cycle, bind together to form a dimer.

2 The Clock/Cycle dimer binds to DNA, enhancing the transcription of the genes for other proteins, including Per and Cry.

Figure 10.7 A Molecular Clock in Flies and Mice This is a simplified view. (After Reppert and Weaver, 2002.)

Clock

Cycle

Nucleus

cry

DNA

per

Cry

Per

Tau

3 These proteins bind with one another and feed back to inhibit the effect of the Clock/Cycle dimer on their own transcription.

Glutamate

5 Input from the retina can modulate the cycle.

4 These inhibitory proteins eventually break down, releasing the Clock/Cycle dimers from inhibition, allowing the cycle to start over again. The entire cycle of gene transcription, protein interaction, and protein degradation takes about 24 hours to complete.

Circadian output to other neurons

To see an animation of this figure, go to

mindsmachine.com/10.4
A Molecular Clock

Cycle dimer then binds to the cell's DNA to promote the transcription of other genes, including *per* and *tau*, the mutation that gives hamsters a shorter period. The proteins made from these other genes go back to inhibit the action of Clock and Cycle, which started the whole process. Because those inhibitory proteins degrade with time, eventually the inhibition is lifted, starting the whole cycle over again (**Figure 10.7**). The entire cycle takes about 24 hours to complete, and it is this 24-hour molecular cycle that drives the 24-hour activity cycle of SCN cells. You can learn more about the molecular basis of the circadian clock in **A Step Further 10.1**, on the website.

One indication of the importance of the molecular clock in controlling circadian behavior is the effect of mutations in the genes involved in the clock. We've already seen that hamsters with a mutation in *tau* have a free-running rhythm that is shorter than normal. Mice in which both copies of the *Clock* gene are disrupted show severe arrhythmicity under constant conditions (**Figure 10.8**). People who feel energetic in the morning ("larks") are likely to carry a different version of the *Clock* gene than "night

Dark   Light

Days

Time (h)

This homozygous *Clock/Clock* mouse showed a normal circadian rhythm when given light cues.

In constant dim light, it maintained an activity period of 27 hours for a few days but then lost circadian rhythmicity.

Note, however, that an ultradian rhythm (that is, a rhythm that has a frequency of more than once a day) remains.

Figure 10.8 When the Endogenous Clock Goes Kaput (From J. S. Takahashi, 1995.)

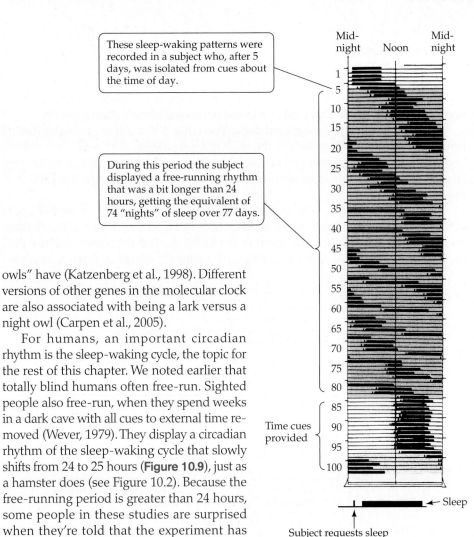

These sleep-waking patterns were recorded in a subject who, after 5 days, was isolated from cues about the time of day.

During this period the subject displayed a free-running rhythm that was a bit longer than 24 hours, getting the equivalent of 74 "nights" of sleep over 77 days.

Time cues provided

Sleep

Subject requests sleep

Figure 10.9 Humans Free-Run Too
(From Weitzman et al., 1981.)

owls" have (Katzenberg et al., 1998). Different versions of other genes in the molecular clock are also associated with being a lark versus a night owl (Carpen et al., 2005).

For humans, an important circadian rhythm is the sleep-waking cycle, the topic for the rest of this chapter. We noted earlier that totally blind humans often free-run. Sighted people also free-run, when they spend weeks in a dark cave with all cues to external time removed (Wever, 1979). They display a circadian rhythm of the sleep-waking cycle that slowly shifts from 24 to 25 hours (**Figure 10.9**), just as a hamster does (see Figure 10.2). Because the free-running period is greater than 24 hours, some people in these studies are surprised when they're told that the experiment has ended. The person may have experienced only 74 sleep-waking cycles during a 77-day study.

Now that you understand some of the mechanisms that enforce our daily rhythm of sleep and waking, we'll spend the rest of the chapter exploring that mysterious state of consciousness called sleep.

How's it going?

1. What are circadian rhythms, and how can they be studied and manipulated in lab animals?

2. Describe experiments that established which parts of the brain control circadian rhythms.

3. How does information about day and night reach the mammalian brain?

4. Give some examples of ultradian and infradian rhythms.

PART II Sleeping and Waking

Perhaps the simplest explanation for why we sleep is that the brain gets tired from all that activity and just stops working for a while. But in fact our brains are quite active and go through many remarkable changes in the course of a night's sleep. We'll begin by describing the study of brain activity during sleep that revealed the different types of sleep. Then we'll talk about how sleep changes as we grow up (and grow old), before considering the effects of sleep deprivation and the perplexing question of why we sleep at all. That will lead to a discussion of the brain mechanisms underlying sleep, and we'll conclude by reviewing sleep disorders, including the one afflicting Barry, the sleepy college student we met at the start of the chapter.

Human Sleep Exhibits Different Stages

In the 1930s, experimenters found that brain potentials recorded from electrodes on the scalp (by **electroencephalography**, or **EEG**; see Figure 3.15a) provide a way to define, describe, and classify levels of arousal and states of sleep. In sleep studies, eye

electroencephalography (EEG) The recording and study of gross electrical activity of the brain via large electrodes placed on the scalp.

slow-wave sleep (SWS) Also called *non-REM sleep*. Sleep, divided into stages 1–3, that is defined by the presence of slow-wave EEG activity.

rapid-eye-movement (REM) sleep Also called *paradoxical sleep*. A stage of sleep characterized by small-amplitude, fast-EEG waves, no postural tension, and rapid eye movements. REM rhymes with "gem."

desynchronized EEG Also called *beta activity*. A pattern of EEG activity comprising a mix of many different high frequencies with low amplitude.

alpha rhythm A brain potential of 8–12 hertz that occurs during relaxed wakefulness.

movements and muscle tension are monitored in addition to the EEG. Together, these measures led to the groundbreaking discovery that there are two distinct classes of sleep: **slow-wave sleep** (**SWS**) and **rapid-eye-movement sleep**, or **REM sleep** (Aserinsky and Kleitman, 1953). **Table 10.1** compares the properties of SWS and REM sleep. In humans, SWS can be divided further into distinct stages, as we'll discuss shortly.

What are the electrophysiological distinctions that define different sleep states? To begin, the pattern of EEG activity in the brain of a fully awake, alert person is a mixture of many relatively fast frequencies (greater than 15–20 cycles per second, or hertz [Hz]) and low amplitude, sometimes referred to as *beta activity* or a **desynchronized EEG** (**Figure 10.10a**).

When you relax and close your eyes, a distinctive rhythm appears in the EEG, consisting of a regular oscillation at a frequency of 8–12 Hz, known as the **alpha rhythm**. As drowsiness sets in, the time spent in the alpha rhythm decreases, and the EEG shows waves of smaller amplitude and irregular frequency, as well as sharp waves called

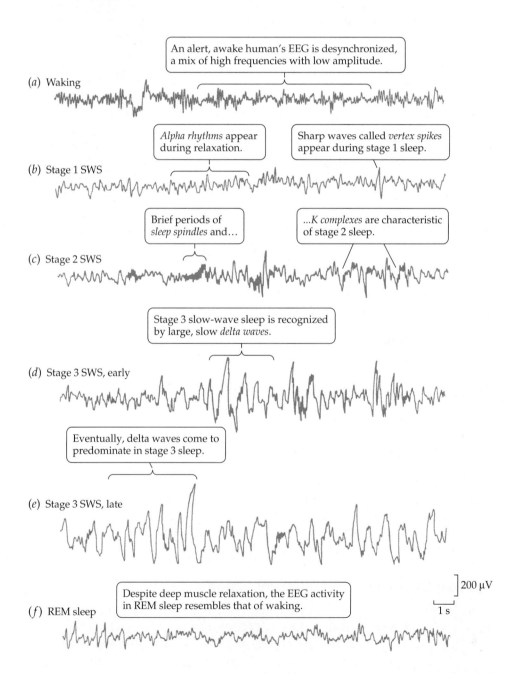

(*a*) Waking

> An alert, awake human's EEG is desynchronized, a mix of high frequencies with low amplitude.

(*b*) Stage 1 SWS

> *Alpha rhythms* appear during relaxation.

> Sharp waves called *vertex spikes* appear during stage 1 sleep.

(*c*) Stage 2 SWS

> Brief periods of *sleep spindles* and...

> ...*K complexes* are characteristic of stage 2 sleep.

(*d*) Stage 3 SWS, early

> Stage 3 slow-wave sleep is recognized by large, slow *delta waves*.

(*e*) Stage 3 SWS, late

> Eventually, delta waves come to predominate in stage 3 sleep.

(*f*) REM sleep

> Despite deep muscle relaxation, the EEG activity in REM sleep resembles that of waking.

200 μV
1 s

Figure 10.10 Electrophysiological Correlates of Sleep and Waking (After Rechtschaffen and Kales, 1968.)

vertex spikes. This is the beginning of SWS, called **stage 1 sleep** (**Figure 10.10b**), which is accompanied by slowing of the heart rate and relaxation of the muscles; in addition, under the closed eyelids the eyes may roll about slowly. Stage 1 sleep usually lasts several minutes and gives way to **stage 2 sleep** (**Figure 10.10c**), which is defined by waves of 12–14 Hz called **sleep spindles** that occur in periodic bursts, and by **K complexes**. If awakened during these first two stages of sleep, many subjects deny that they have been asleep, even though they failed to respond to signals while in those stages.

Stage 2 sleep leads to (can you guess?) **stage 3 sleep** (**Figure 10.10d**), which is defined by the appearance of large-amplitude, *very* slow waves (so-called **delta waves**, about one per second). As the night progresses, the delta waves become even more prominent (**Figure 10.10e**). (Previously, SWS with delta waves at least half the time was called stage 4 sleep, but that distinction is no longer followed. Now all SWS with delta waves is called stage 3.) The slow waves of electrical potential that give SWS its name represent a widespread synchronization of cortical activity that has been likened to a room of people who are all chanting the same phrase over and over. From a distance you would be able to hear the rise and fall of the cadence of speech in a slow rhythm. But if each person were saying something *different*, you would hear only a buzz—the rapid frequencies of many desynchronized speakers, which is like the desynchronized EEG of wakefulness, when many parts of the cortex are saying different things. In contrast, during SWS neighboring cortical neurons have synchronized activity (Poulet and Petersen, 2008), as if they were all "chanting" together, rather than fulfilling different functions as they do in waking.

After about an hour—the typical time to progress through these SWS stages, with a brief return to stage 2—something totally different occurs: REM sleep. Quite abruptly, the EEG displays a pattern of small-amplitude, high-frequency activity similar in many ways to the pattern of an awake individual (**Figure 10.10f**), except the eyes are darting rapidly about under their lids (the *r*apid *e*ye *m*ovements that give REM sleep its name). Aside from those muscles moving the eyes, all other skeletal muscles are not just relaxed, but completely limp. The active-looking EEG coupled with deeply relaxed muscles is typical of REM sleep. If you see a cat sleeping in the sitting, sphinx position, it cannot be in REM sleep; in REM, it will be sprawled limply on the floor. For the same reason, a student sleeping while sitting upright in class cannot be in REM sleep.

Wired for Sleep   Machines measure electrical activity across the various electrodes to monitor EEG, eye movements, and muscle tension across sleep stages.

TABLE 10.1 Properties of Slow-Wave versus REM Sleep

Property	Slow-wave sleep	REM sleep
AUTONOMIC ACTIVITIES		
Heart rate	Slow decline	Variable, with high bursts
Respiration	Slow decline	Variable, with high bursts
Brain temperature	Decreased	Increased
Cerebral blood flow	Reduced	High
SKELETAL MUSCULAR SYSTEM		
Postural tension	Progressively reduced	Eliminated
Knee jerk reflex	Normal	Suppressed
Twitches	Reduced	Increased
Eye movements	Infrequent, slow, uncoordinated	Rapid, coordinated
COGNITIVE STATE	Vague thoughts	Vivid dreams, well organized
HORMONE SECRETION		
Growth hormone secretion	High	Low
NEURAL FIRING RATES		
Cerebral cortex activity	Many cells reduced	Increased firing rates

vertex spike   A sharp-wave EEG pattern that is seen during stage 1 sleep.

stage 1 sleep   The initial stage of slow-wave sleep, which is characterized by small-amplitude EEG waves of irregular frequency, slow heart rate, and reduced muscle tension.

stage 2 sleep   A stage of slow-wave sleep that is defined by bursts of regular 14- to 18-hertz EEG waves called sleep spindles.

sleep spindle   A characteristic 14- to 18-hertz wave in the EEG of a person said to be in stage 2 sleep.

K complex   A sharp, negative EEG potential that is seen in stage 2 sleep.

stage 3 sleep   A stage of slow-wave sleep that is defined by the presence of large amplitude, slow delta waves.

delta wave   The slowest type of EEG wave, characteristic of stage 3 sleep.

(a)

(b)

Postural Cues to Sleep States The kitten in (*a*) must be in SWS, because its body is not limp, as it would be if it was in REM sleep, like the kitten in (*b*).

This flaccid muscle state appears despite intense brain activity because during this stage of sleep, brainstem regions are profoundly inhibiting motoneurons. This seeming contradiction—the brain waves look awake, but the muscles are flaccid and unresponsive—is what gives REM sleep its other name: *paradoxical sleep*. Unlike SWS, REM sleep is accompanied by irregular breathing and pulse rate, as in wakefulness. It is also during REM sleep that we experience vivid dreams, as we'll discuss shortly.

The EEG portrait in Figure 10.10 shows that sleep consists of a complex series of brain states, not just an "inactive" period. The total sleep time of young adults usually ranges from 7 to 8 hours, about half of it in stage 2 sleep. REM sleep accounts for about 20% of total sleep. A typical night of adult human sleep shows repeating cycles approximately 90–110 minutes long, recurring four or five times in a night. These cycles change in a subtle but regular manner through the night. Stage 3 SWS is more prominent early in the night (**Figure 10.11**), and then it tapers off as the night progresses. In contrast, REM sleep is more prominent in the later cycles of sleep. The first REM period is the shortest, while the last REM period, just before waking, may last up to 40 minutes.

Brief arousals (yellow bars in Figure 10.11) occasionally occur immediately after a REM period, and the sleeper may shift posture at this time (Aaronson et al., 1982). The sleep cycle of 90–110 minutes suggests that there is a basic ultradian rest-activity cycle (Kleitman, 1969), reflected in the 90-minute cycles of daydreaming mentioned earlier.

At puberty, most people shift their circadian rhythm of sleep so that they get up later in the day (**Figure 10.12**), but many school systems require students to come to school *earlier* in the day when they hit adolescence. One group of high schools shifted their morning start from 7:15 to 8:40 and noted improved student attendance and enrollment, with (big surprise!) less sleeping in class and, more important, a reduced incidence of depression (Wahlstrom, 2002). You can see that sleep is a remarkably complex, multifaceted set of behaviors. Now let's consider an even more fascinating aspect of sleep: dreaming.

We do our most vivid dreaming during REM sleep

We can record the EEGs of subjects, awaken them at a particular stage—1, 2, 3, or REM—and question them about thoughts or perceptions they were having. Early studies of this sort suggested that dreams happen only during REM sleep, but we now know that dreams also occur in other sleep stages. What is distinctive about dreams during REM sleep is that they are characterized by visual imagery, whereas dreams during non-REM sleep are of a more "thinking" type. REM dreams are apt to include a story that involves odd perceptions and the sense that the dreamer "is there" experiencing sights, sounds, smells, and emotions. Subjects awakened from non-REM sleep report thinking about problems rather than seeing themselves in a stage presentation. The dreams of these two states are so different that people can be trained to predict accurately whether

Figure 10.11   A Typical Night of Sleep in a Young Adult (After Kales and Kales, 1970.)

a described dream occurred during REM sleep or SWS (Cartwright, 1979).

Almost everyone has terrifying dreams on occasion (Hartmann, 1984). **Nightmares** are defined as long, frightening dreams that awaken the sleeper from REM sleep. They are occasionally confused with **night terror**, which is a sudden arousal from stage 3 SWS marked by intense fear and autonomic activation. In night terror the sleeper does not recall a vivid dream but may remember a sense of a crushing feeling on the chest, as though being suffocated (**Figure 10.13**). Night terrors are common in children during the early part of an evening's sleep.

Many medications, including antidepressants and drugs that control blood pressure, make nightmares more frequent (Pagel and Helfter, 2003), but nightmares are quite prevalent even without such influences. At least 25% of college students report having one or more nightmares per month. Have you had the common one, which Sigmund Freud had, of suddenly remembering that you're supposed to be taking a final exam that is already in progress?

As fascinating as they are, we still do not know what function, if any, is fulfilled by dreams. Later we'll discuss evidence that at least some other animals experience dreaming, which suggests that dreaming either fulfills an important function or is an unavoidable consequence of some other function of REM sleep.

Different species provide clues about the evolution of sleep

With the aid of behavioral and EEG techniques, sleep has been studied in a wide assortment of mammals and, to a lesser extent, in reptiles, birds, and amphibians (S. S. Campbell and Tobler, 1984). Nearly all mammalian species that have been investigated thus far, including our most distant relatives, such as the platypus (Siegel, Manger, et al., 1999), display both REM sleep and SWS. Among the other vertebrates, only birds display clear signs of both SWS and REM sleep. These comparisons suggest that either REM sleep was present in an ancestor common to birds and mammals, or that REM sleep evolved independently in mammals and birds.

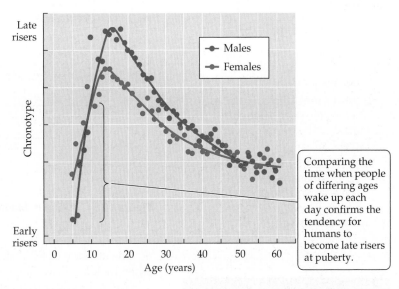

Comparing the time when people of differing ages wake up each day confirms the tendency for humans to become late risers at puberty.

Figure 10.12 How I Hate to Get Out of Bed in the Morning! (After Roenneberg et al., 2004.)

nightmare A long, frightening dream that awakens the sleeper from REM sleep.

night terror A sudden arousal from stage 3 sleep that is marked by intense fear and autonomic activation.

Figure 10.13 Night Terror This 1781 painting by Henry Fuseli is called *The Nightmare*. It also aptly illustrates night terror, or even sleep paralysis, discussed later in the chapter, as the demon crushes the breath from his victim.

How's it going?

1. What are the different stages of sleep, and what measures define them?

2. What happens to our muscles during the sleep stage characterized by the most vivid dreams?

3. Describe one way that certain species manage to remain active around the clock and still sleep.

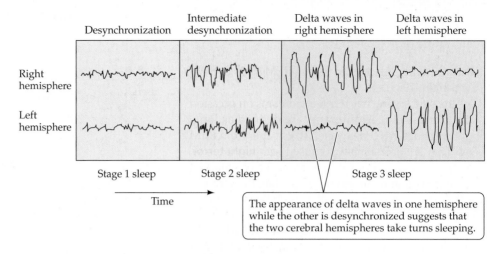

Figure 10.14 **Sleep in Marine Mammals** (From Mukhametov, 1984.)

Sleeping on the Go A female bar-tailed godwit flew over 10,000 miles, nonstop, from Alaska to Australia in a week. Were both sides of its brain awake the entire time?

The absence of REM sleep in dolphins is probably a late adaptation that evolved when their land-dwelling ancestors took to the water, because they must come to the surface of the water to breathe. That requirement may be incompatible with the deep relaxation of muscles during REM sleep. Another dolphin adaptation to living in water is that only one side of the dolphin brain engages in SWS at a time (Mukhametov, 1984). It's as if one whole hemisphere is asleep while the other is awake (**Figure 10.14**). During these periods of "unilateral sleep," the animals continue to come up to the surface occasionally to breathe. Birds can also display unilateral sleep—one hemisphere sleeping while the other hemisphere watches for predators (Rattenborg, 2006). Unilateral sleep while gliding may also enable birds to fly long distances without stopping; for example, a bar-tailed godwit flew nonstop more than 10,000 miles, from Alaska to Australia, in a week (Gill et al., 2009). You can learn more about comparing patterns of sleep in different species in **A Step Further 10.2**, on the website.

Our Sleep Patterns Change across the Life Span

How much sleep and what kind of sleep we get changes across our lifetime. As infants, we sleep a lot; but as we grow we sleep less and less until we hit adolescence, when once again sleep seems precious. After that, we sleep less and less as we age, sometimes to our disappointment. These changes as we grow up and grow old suggest that the function(s) of sleep are more important during some stages of life than others.

Mammals sleep more during infancy than in adulthood

A clear cycle of sleeping and waking takes several weeks to become established in human infants (**Figure 10.15**). A 24-hour rhythm is generally evident by 16 weeks of age. Infant sleep is characterized by shorter sleep cycles than those of adults, probably reflecting the relative immaturity of the brain, since sleep cycles in prematurely born infants are even shorter than in full-term newborns.

Infant mammals also show a large percentage of REM sleep. In humans, for example, half of sleep in the first 2 weeks of life is REM sleep. The prominence of REM sleep is even greater in premature infants, accounting for up to 80% of total sleep. Unlike normal adults, human infants can move directly from an awake state to REM sleep. The REM sleep of infants is quite active, accompanied by muscle twitching, smiles, grimaces, and vocalizations. The preponderance of REM sleep early in life (**Figure 10.16**) suggests that this state provides stimulation that is essential to maturation of the nervous system. By contrast, killer whales and bottlenose dolphins appear to spend little or no time sleeping for the first month of life (Lyamin et al., 2005), presumably because they have to surface often to breathe. So, either REM sleep does not fill a crucial need in all mammalian infants, or dolphin and whale infants have evolved a different way to fill that need.

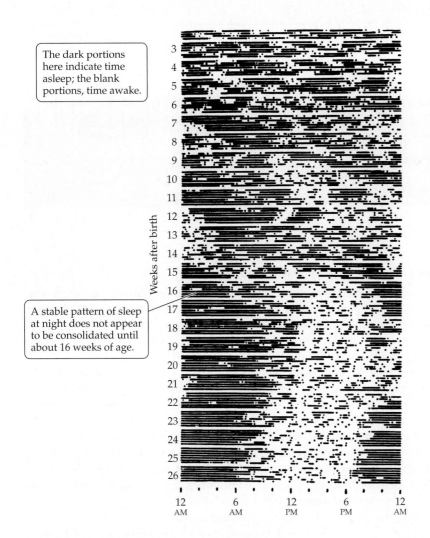

The dark portions here indicate time asleep; the blank portions, time awake.

A stable pattern of sleep at night does not appear to be consolidated until about 16 weeks of age.

Figure 10.15   The Trouble with Babies (From Kleitman and Engelmann, 1953.)

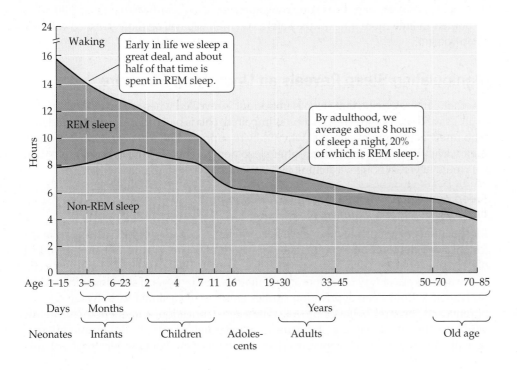

Early in life we sleep a great deal, and about half of that time is spent in REM sleep.

By adulthood, we average about 8 hours of sleep a night, 20% of which is REM sleep.

Figure 10.16   Human Sleep Patterns Change with Age (After Roffwarg et al., 1966.)

Figure 10.17 The Typical Pattern of Sleep in an Elderly Person Compare this recording with the young-adult sleep pattern shown in Figure 10.11. (After Kales and Kales, 1974.)

Most people sleep appreciably less as they age

The character of sleep changes more slowly in old age than in early development. **Figure 10.17** shows the sleep pattern typical of an elderly person. The total amount of sleep declines, while the number of awakenings increases (compare with Figure 10.11). Lack of sleep, or *insomnia* (which we discuss at the end of this chapter), is a common complaint of the elderly (Miles and Dement, 1980).

In humans and other mammals, the most dramatic decline is in stage 3 sleep; 60-year-old people spend only about half as much time in stage 3 as they did at age 20 (Bliwise, 1989). By 90 years of age, stage 3 sleep has disappeared. This decline in stage 3 sleep with age may be related to diminished cognitive functioning, since an especially marked reduction of stage 3 SWS characterizes the sleep of people who suffer from senile dementia. Growth hormone is secreted primarily during stage 3 SWS (see Table 10.1), so perhaps the loss of growth hormone from disrupted sleep in the elderly leads to the cognitive deficits. Most elderly people fall asleep easily enough, but then they may have a hard time staying asleep, causing sleep "dissatisfaction."

As in so many things, attitude may be important for how you experience sleep loss as you age. Objective measures of sleep suggest that elderly people who complain of poor sleep may actually sleep *more* than those who are satisfied with their sleep (McCrae et al., 2005). Perhaps if, as you grow older, you can regard waking up at 3:00 AM as a "bonus" (a little more time awake before you die), you will be more satisfied with the sleep you get.

sleep deprivation The partial or total prevention of sleep.

Manipulating Sleep Reveals an Underlying Structure

Another persuasive clue that sleep is important is revealed when we go without it. First of all, as we'll see, our mental function is impaired. This is bad news for college students, who rarely get enough sleep, just when they're supposed to be learning how to make their way in the world. In addition, after sleep deprivation we tend to sleep more than we would have, as though "catching up" on something we need, as we'll see.

Sleep deprivation impairs cognitive functioning but does not cause insanity

Most of us at one time or another have been willing or not-so-willing participants in informal **sleep deprivation** experiments. Thus, most of us are aware of the primary effect of partial or total sleep deprivation: it makes us sleepy (**Figure 10.18**). The study of sleep deprivation is also a way to explore the regulatory mechanisms of sleeping and waking. Early reports from sleep deprivation studies emphasized a similarity between schizophrenia and "bizarre" behavior provoked by sleep deprivation. A frequent theme in this work was the functional role of dreams as a "guardian of sanity." But examination of patients suffering from schizophrenia does not fit this view. For example, these patients

Going without sleep has one clear effect: you feel sleepy.

Figure 10.18 I Need Sleep!

can show sleep-waking cycles similar to those of normal adults, and sleep deprivation does not exacerbate their symptoms.

The behavioral effects of prolonged, total sleep deprivation vary appreciably and may depend on some general personality factors and on age. In studies employing prolonged total deprivation—205 hours (8.5 days)—a few subjects showed occasional episodes of hallucinations. But the most common behavior changes noted in these experiments were increases in irritability, difficulty in concentrating, and episodes of disorientation. The subject's ability to perform tasks was summed up like this: "His performance is like a motor that after much use misfires, runs normally for a while, then falters again" (L. C. Johnson, 1969, p. 216).

You don't need to resort to total sleep deprivation to see effects. Moderate *sleep debt* can accumulate with successive nights of little sleep. Voluntary experimental subjects who got 6 or 4 hours sleep per night for 2 weeks showed ever-mounting deficits in attention tasks and in speed of reaction compared to those sleeping 8 hours per night (Van Dongen et al., 2003). Interestingly, the sleep-deprived subjects often reported not feeling sleepy, yet they still exhibited behavioral deficits. By the end of the study, the subjects getting less than 8 hours of sleep per night had cognitive deficits equivalent to subjects who had been totally sleep-deprived for 3 days!

Finally, it is clear that prolonged, total sleep deprivation in mammals compromises the immune system and leads to death (**Box 10.1**). Even fruit flies need sleep, as evidenced by the fact that a particular mutation of the *Cycle* gene (part of the circadian molecular clock; see Figure 10.7) causes flies to die after only 10 hours of sleep deprivation (P. J. Shaw et al., 2002).

Sleep recovery may take time

One of the most famous cases of sleep deprivation began as a high school student's science project. Researchers became involved only after Randy Gardner had started his deprivation schedule, which is why we have no data about his sleep before he decided to stay awake for … 11 days! As in other studies, Randy's performance on some tests was impaired, but he could still hold a conversation and was articulate and clear in a press conference at the end of his experiment. In other words, he showed no signs of insanity—he just acted really, really sleepy.

Randy's **sleep recovery** after 11 days of sleep deprivation, depicted in **Figure 10.19**, shows the same pattern of sleep recovery as in controlled studies with shorter periods of deprivation. In the first night of sleep recovery, stage 3 sleep shows the greatest relative difference from normal. This increase in stage 3 sleep is usually at the expense

sleep recovery The process of sleeping more than normally after a period of sleep deprivation, as though in compensation.

Skipping Sleep for Science As a young man, Randy Gardner decided to see how long he could stay awake as a science fair project. The answer? Just over 11 days. Is that a record for the most demanding science fair project?

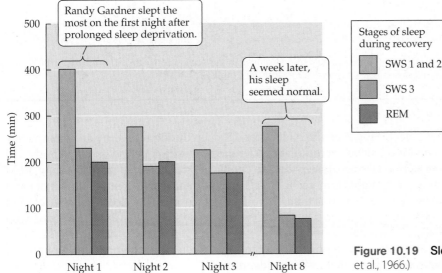

Figure 10.19 **Sleep Recovery after 11 Days Awake** (After Gulevich et al., 1966.)

BOX 10.1 Sleep Deprivation Can Be Fatal

Sleep that knits up the ravell'd sleave of care.

— *William Shakespeare,*
Macbeth, Act II, Scene 2

Although some people seem to need very little sleep, most of us feel the need to sleep 7–8 hours a night. In fact, sustained sleep deprivation in rats causes them to increase their metabolic rate, lose weight, and, within an average of 19 days, die (Everson et al., 1989). Allowing them to sleep prevents their death.

After the fatal effect of sleep deprivation had been shown, researchers undertook studies in which they terminated the sleep deprivation before the fatal end point and looked for pathological changes in different organ systems (Rechtschaffen and Bergmann, 1995). No single organ system seems affected in chronically sleep-deprived animals, but early in the deprivation they develop sores on their bodies. These sores mark the beginning of the end; shortly thereafter, blood tests reveal infections from a host of bacteria, which probably enter through the sores (Everson, 1993).

These bacteria are not normally fatal, because the rat's immune system and body defenses keep the bacteria in check; but severely sleep-deprived rats fail to develop a fever in response to these infections. (Fever helps the body fight infection.) In fact, the sleep-deprived animals show a *drop* in body temperature, which probably speeds bacterial infections that in turn cause diffuse organ damage. The decline of these severely sleep-deprived rats is complicated, but it seems clear that getting sleep improves immune system function (Bryant et al., 2004). So perhaps Shakespeare's folk theory of the function of sleep, quoted above, isn't so far from the truth.

What about the rare humans who sleep only 1 or 2 hours a night? Why aren't their immune systems and inflammatory responses compromised? We don't know, but since the distinguishing trait of these people is that they don't need much sleep, perhaps their immune systems and inflammatory responses don't need much sleep either. Or perhaps the small amount of sleep they have almost every night is more efficient at doing whatever sleep does.

Some unfortunate humans inherit a defect in the gene for the prion protein (which can transmit mad cow disease, discussed in Chapter 12), and although they sleep normally at the beginning of life, in midlife they simply stop sleeping—with fatal effect. People with this disease, called **fatal familial insomnia**, die 7–24 months after the insomnia begins (Mastrianni et al., 1999; Medori et al., 1992). Autopsy reveals degeneration in the cerebral cortex (shown in the figure) and thalamus, which may cause the insomnia (Almer et al., 1999). (Electrical stimulation of the thalamus can induce sleep in animals.) Like sleep-deprived rats, sleep-deprived humans with this disorder don't have obvious damage to any single organ system, but they suffer from diffuse bacterial infections. Apparently these patients die because they are chronically sleep-deprived, and these results, combined with research on rats, certainly support the idea that prolonged insomnia is fatal.

Note the large holes (arrows) that have developed in this section of frontal cortex from a victim of fatal familial insomnia. (Micrograph courtesy of H. Budka.)

How's it going?

1. Describe how sleep changes as we grow up and grow old.
2. What happens when we are deprived of sleep?
3. Describe the outcome of Randy Gardner's famous self-study.

of stage 2 sleep. However, the added stage 3 sleep during recovery never completely makes up for the deficit accumulated over the deprivation period. In fact, Randy had no more additional stage 3 sleep than do people deprived of sleep for half as long. REM sleep in recovery nights is more "intense" than normal, with a greater number of rapid eye movements per period of time. So you never recover all the sleep time you lost, but you may make up for the loss by having more intense sleep for a while. The sooner you get to sleep, the sooner you recover.

The effects of sleep deprivation suggest that sleep plays an important function, or even several functions, that we'll consider next.

What Are the Biological Functions of Sleep?

Doesn't it seem like a big waste of time to spend one-third of our lifetime asleep? Most of us have fantasized about how great it would be if we could stay awake and chipper all the time, but we've seen that it's just not possible. What is so important about sleep that we can't seem to live without it? Let's consider the four functions that are most often ascribed to sleep:

1. Energy conservation
2. Niche adaptation
3. Body restoration
4. Memory consolidation

Sleep conserves energy

We use up less energy when we sleep than when we're awake. For example, slow-wave sleep (SWS) is marked by reduced muscular tension, lowered heart rate, reduced blood pressure, reduced body temperature, and slower respiration. This diminished metabolic activity during sleep suggests that one role of sleep is to conserve energy. We can see the importance of this function by considering small animals. Small mammals and birds have very high metabolic rates (see Chapter 9), so activity for them is metabolically expensive. In general, the smaller the mammal, the higher the metabolic rate and the more time it spends asleep. That correlation supports the idea that sleep helps conserve energy.

Sleep enforces niche adaptation

Almost all animals are either nocturnal or diurnal. This specialization for either nighttime or daytime activity is part of each species' **ecological niche**, that unique assortment of environmental opportunities and challenges to which each organism is adapted (**Figure 10.20**). Thanks to these adaptations, each species is better at gathering food either at night or in the daytime, and it is also better at avoiding predators either during the day or at night. If you're a nocturnal mammal, like a mouse, you are adept at sneaking around in the dark, using your acute senses of hearing and smell to navigate and find food. The rest of the time, during daylight, you should spend holed up somewhere safe to stay away from keen-eyed predators. So, one important function of sleep is to force the individual to conform to a particular ecological niche for which it is well adapted (Meddis, 1975). From this perspective, sleep debt and the unpleasant feelings of sleepiness are simply tools that natural selection has evolved to enforce a circadian rhythm in activity. Ensuring that activity fits a particular ecological niche certainly is a function of sleep, and it must have played an important role in the evolution of sleep, but is it the *only* function?

Sleep restores the body

If someone asked you why you wanted to go to sleep, you might answer that you "feel worn out." Indeed, one of the proposed functions of sleep is simply the rebuilding or restoration of materials used during waking, such as proteins (Moruzzi, 1972). Maybe this is why most growth hormone release happens during slow-wave sleep.

If simple wear and tear from activity triggered the need for sleep, we would expect exercise to result in more sleep. But while exercise often causes people to fall asleep more quickly, it generally does *not* help them sleep longer. We've seen that prolonged and total sleep deprivation—either forced on rats or, in humans, a result of inherited pathology—interferes with the immune system and leads to death (see Box 10.1). Even relatively mild deprivation, having sleep shortened or disrupted (e.g., by a nurse taking vital signs every hour), makes people more sensitive to pain the following day (Edwards et al., 2009). A study of over a million Americans found that those sleeping less than 6 hours per night were more likely to die over the next 6 years, although interestingly, people who slept *more than 8* hours per night were also at greater risk

Figure 10.20 Sleep Helps Animals to Adapt an Ecological Niche These Honduran white bats (*Ectophylla alba*) sleep together in a large leaf each day, waiting until dusk, when they can use their many nocturnal adaptations, to feed. They chew a line along the leaf to create a flap to cover them while they sleep.

ecological niche The unique assortment of environmental opportunities and challenges to which each organism is adapted.

(Kripke et al., 2002). People who sleep less than 5 hours per night are more likely to develop diabetes (Gangwisch et al., 2007). Perhaps the most alarming link between sleep and health are findings that people who work at night and sleep in the daytime are more likely to develop cancer (Erren et al., 2009). So the widespread belief that sleep helps the body ward off illness is well supported by research (S. Cohen et al., 2009; Imeri and Opp, 2009).

Sleep may aid memory consolidation

A peculiar property of dreams is that, unless we describe them to someone or write them down soon after waking, we tend to forget them (Dement, 1974), as though the brain refuses to store anything that we experience during REM sleep. This seems like a good idea—why waste memory storage space on something that never happened? Similarly, and despite ads you might read in the backs of magazines, you cannot learn new material while you're sleeping (Druckman and Bjork, 1994). Putting a speaker under your pillow to recite material for a final exam will not help you ... unless you stay awake to listen (J. M. Wood et al., 1992).

Sleep seems important for learning in another way, however. In 1924 an experiment suggested that sleep helps you learn or remember material or events experienced *before* you go to bed (Jenkins and Dallenbach, 1924). Some subjects were trained in a verbal learning task at bedtime and tested 8 hours later on rising from sleep; other subjects were trained early in the day and tested 8 hours later (with no intervening sleep). The results showed better retention when a period of sleep intervened between a learning period and tests of recall. A recent surge of supporting evidence has shown that sleep helps with memory formation in many domains, not just verbal memory (Ellenbogen et al., 2007; Korman et al., 2007; U. Wagner et al., 2004).

When researchers deliberately deprive subjects of either REM sleep or SWS, results suggest that REM sleep improves performance on tests that involve learning perceptual skills. For example, humans learning to make difficult visual discriminations show little improvement in a single training session, but they show considerable improvement 8–10 hours after the session. If deprived of REM sleep after a training session, however, people fail to show the later improvement (Karni et al., 1994; C. Smith, 1995). In contrast, consolidation of "declarative" memory tasks (the kind of memories that you can declare to others; see Chapter 13), such as in the original 1924 study, and of complicated motor skills, seems to benefit from SWS (Nishida and Walker, 2007). In fact, consolidation of a declarative memory task was even better if the subject's cortical slow-wave oscillations during SWS were boosted by electrically stimulating electrodes over the skull (Marshall et al., 2006). (Don't try this at home.)

Jerome Siegel (2001) remains skeptical, however, that sleep is essential for learning. He points out that any sleep deprivation is necessarily stressful, which might be the real cause of memory disruption. He also notes that there is no correlation across species between time spent in REM sleep and obvious learning capacity. In humans, there is no correlation between the amount of REM sleep and either IQ or academic achievement (Borrow et al., 1980). Finally, one man who had brainstem injuries that seemed to eliminate REM sleep could still learn, and he earned a law school degree (P. Lavie, 1996). So even if REM sleep *aids* learning, clearly it is not absolutely *necessary* for learning.

Some humans sleep remarkably little, yet function normally

One challenge to all the theories about the function of sleep is the existence of a few people who seem perfectly normal and healthy, yet sleep hardly at all. These cases are more than just folktales. A Stanford University professor slept only 3–4 hours a night for more than 50 years and lived to be 80 (Dement, 1974). Sleep researcher Ray Meddis (1977) found a cheerful 70-year-old retired nurse who said she had slept little since childhood. She was a busy person who easily filled up her 23 hours of daily wakefulness. During the night she sat in bed reading or writing, and at about 2:00 AM she fell asleep for an hour or so, after which she readily awakened.

Figure 10.21 A Nonsleeper When Ray Meddis brought this 70-year-old nurse into the lab for sleep recording, he confirmed that she slept only about an hour per night. Yet she was a healthy and energetic person. Here she's touring a garden with Meddis's son. (Photo courtesy of Ray Meddis.)

For her first two nights in Meddis's laboratory, she did not sleep at all, because it was all so interesting to her. On the third night she slept a total of 99 minutes, and her sleep contained both SWS and REM sleep periods. Later her sleep was recorded for 5 days. She never slept the first night, but on subsequent nights she slept an average of 67 minutes. She never complained about not sleeping more, and she did not feel drowsy during either the day or the night (**Figure 10.21**). Meddis described several other people who slept only an hour or two per night. Some of these people reported having parents who slept little, so there may be a genetic tendency for little sleep. Whatever the function of sleep is, such people have some way of fulfilling it with a brief nap. They show less stages 1 and 2 sleep, so perhaps they are more efficient sleepers. Importantly, though, no healthy person has ever been found who does not sleep at all.

At Least Four Interacting Neural Systems Underlie Sleep

At one time sleep was regarded as a passive state, as though most of the brain simply stopped working while we slept, leaving us unaware of events around us. We now know that sleep is an active state mediated by at least four interacting neural systems:

1. A *forebrain* system that generates SWS
2. A *brainstem* system that activates the sleeping forebrain into wakefulness
3. A *pontine* system that triggers REM sleep
4. A *hypothalamic* system that coordinates the other three brain regions to determine which state we're in

Let's examine each of these systems in some detail.

RESEARCHERS AT WORK

The forebrain generates slow-wave sleep

Some of the earliest studies of sleep indicated that a system in the forebrain promotes SWS. These are experiments in which the brain is transected—literally cut into two parts: an upper part and a lower part. The entire brain can be isolated from the body by an incision between the medulla and the spinal cord. This preparation was first studied by the Belgian physiologist Frédéric Bremer (1892–1982), who called it the **isolated brain** (Bremer, 1938).

The EEGs of such animals showed signs of waking alternating with sleep (**Figure 10.22a**). During EEG-defined wakeful periods, the pupils were dilated and the eyes followed moving objects. During EEG-defined sleep, the pupils were small, as in normal sleep. REM sleep can also be detected in the isolated brain. These results demonstrated that wakefulness, SWS, and REM sleep are all mediated by *networks within the brain*.

When Bremer made the transection higher along the brainstem—in the midbrain—a very different result was seen. Bremer referred to such a preparation as an **isolated forebrain**, and he found that the EEG from the brain in front of the cut displayed constant SWS (**Figure 10.22b**), with no indications of wakefulness or REM sleep. This result demonstrates that the forebrain alone can generate SWS, without contributions from the lower brain regions.

The constant SWS seen in the cortex of the isolated forebrain appears to be generated by the **basal forebrain** in the ventral frontal lobe and anterior hypothalamus (**Figure 10.23a**). Electrical stimulation of the basal forebrain can induce SWS activity (Clemente and Sterman, 1967), while lesions there suppress sleep (McGinty and Sterman, 1968). Neurons in this region become active at sleep onset and release gamma-aminobutyric acid (GABA) (Gallopin et al., 2000) to stimulate GABA$_A$

How's it going?

1. Describe the four most prominent theories about the function of sleep and the evidence to support them.

2. What can we conclude about the function of sleep when we consider people who sleep very little?

3. What happens when we stop sleeping altogether?

isolated brain An experimental preparation in which an animal's brainstem has been separated from the spinal cord by a cut below the medulla.

isolated forebrain An experimental preparation in which an animal's nervous system has been cut in the upper midbrain, dividing the forebrain from the brainstem.

basal forebrain A ventral region in the forebrain that has been implicated in sleep.

Figure 10.22 Transecting the Brain at Different Levels

Hypothesis

The forebrain contains a neural system promoting SWS.

Test

Bremer transected the brain at one of two levels: between the spinal cord and medulla, or between the midbrain and the forebrain. If neural systems in the forebrain generate SWS, then the isolated forebrain should show SWS.

Result

Waking

SWS

REM

Transection of the lower brainstem produces an isolated brain, which exhibits signs of alternating between wakefulness, SWS, and REM sleep, showing that systems controlling sleep are found in the brain.

Transection of the brainstem at the midbrain produces an isolated forebrain, which exhibits signs of constant SWS, showing that a forebrain system promotes SWS and that brainstem systems promote wakefulness and REM sleep.

SWS

(a) Isolated brain

Cerebral cortex

Midbrain

Cerebellum

Basal forebrain

Optic chiasm

Pons

Medulla

(b) Isolated forebrain

Cerebral cortex

Midbrain

Cerebellum

Basal forebrain

Optic chiasm

Pons

Medulla

Forebrain

Conclusion

The mechanism mediating SWS is in the forebrain and needs input from the brainstem to be roused from sleep.

---

receptors in the nearby **tuberomammillary nucleus** in the posterior hypothalamus. These same GABA$_A$ receptors are stimulated by **general anesthetics**—drugs such as barbiturates and anesthetic gases that render people unconscious during surgery. Thus, general anesthetics produce slow waves in the EEG that resemble those seen in SWS (Franks, 2008). So the basal forebrain promotes SWS by releasing GABA into the nearby tuberomammillary nucleus, and if left alone, this system would keep the cortex asleep forever. But as we'll see next, the brainstem contains a system that arouses the forebrain from slumber.

tuberomammillary nucleus   A region of the basal hypothalamus, near the pituitary stalk, that plays a role in generating slow-wave sleep.

general anesthetic   A drug that renders an individual unconscious.

reticular formation   Also called *reticular activating system*. An extensive region of the brainstem (extending from the medulla through the thalamus) that is involved in arousal (waking).

The reticular formation wakes up the forebrain

In the late 1940s, scientists found that they could wake sleeping animals by electrically stimulating an extensive region of the brainstem known as the **reticular formation (Figure 10.23b)** (Moruzzi and Magoun, 1949). The reticular formation is a diffuse group of cells whose axons and dendrites course in many directions, extending from the medulla through the thalamus. Because electrical stimulation anywhere along this region activates the forebrain, the reticular formation is sometimes called the *reticular activating system* of the brainstem. Conversely, lesions of these regions produced persistent sleep in the animals. So the basal forebrain region actively imposes SWS on the brain, and the brainstem reticular formation seems to push the brain from SWS to wakefulness. What system imposes REM sleep?

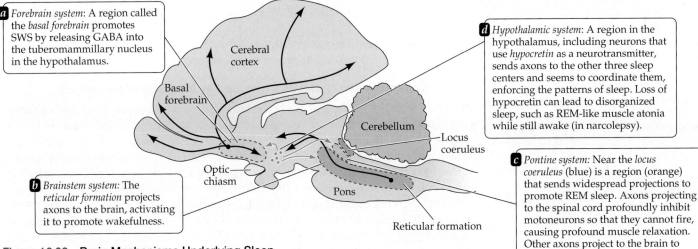

a *Forebrain system:* A region called the *basal forebrain* promotes SWS by releasing GABA into the tuberomammillary nucleus in the hypothalamus.

d *Hypothalamic system:* A region in the hypothalamus, including neurons that use *hypocretin* as a neurotransmitter, sends axons to the other three sleep centers and seems to coordinate them, enforcing the patterns of sleep. Loss of hypocretin can lead to disorganized sleep, such as REM-like muscle atonia while still awake (in narcolepsy).

b *Brainstem system:* The *reticular formation* projects axons to the brain, activating it to promote wakefulness.

c *Pontine system:* Near the *locus coeruleus* (blue) is a region (orange) that sends widespread projections to promote REM sleep. Axons projecting to the spinal cord profoundly inhibit motoneurons so that they cannot fire, causing profound muscle relaxation. Other axons project to the brain to activate other regions.

Cerebral cortex

Basal forebrain

Cerebellum

Optic chiasm

Locus coeruleus

Pons

Reticular formation

Figure 10.23 **Brain Mechanisms Underlying Sleep**

The pons triggers REM sleep

Several experiments indicated that a region of the pons is important for REM sleep. Lesions of the region just ventral to the **locus coeruleus** abolish REM sleep (**Figure 10.23c**) (Friedman and Jones, 1984). Electrical stimulation of the same region, or pharmacological stimulation of this region with cholinergic agonists, can induce or prolong REM sleep. Finally, some neurons in this region seem to be active only during REM sleep (Siegel, 1994). So the pons has a REM sleep center near the locus coeruleus.

One important job of the pontine REM sleep center is to prevent motoneurons from firing. During REM sleep, the inhibitory transmitters GABA and glycine produce powerful inhibitory postsynaptic potentials (discussed in Chapter 3) in spinal motoneurons, preventing them from reaching threshold and producing an action potential (Kodama et al., 2003). Thus, the dreamer's muscles are not just relaxed, but flaccid. This loss of muscle tone during REM sleep can be abolished by small lesions that damage only a part of the REM center, suggesting that this subregion is what normally disables the motor system during REM.

Cats with such lesions seem to act out their dreams. They enter SWS as they normally would, but when they begin to display the EEG signs of REM sleep, instead of becoming completely limp as normal cats do, these cats stagger to their feet (A. R. Morrison, 1983; A. R. Morrison et al., 1995). Are they awake or in REM sleep? They move their heads as though visually tracking moving objects (that aren't there), bat with their forepaws at nothing, and ignore objects that are present (**Figure 10.24**). In addition, the cats' *inner eyelids*, the translucent nictitating membranes, partially cover the eyes. Thus, the cats appear to be in REM sleep, but motor activity is not being inhibited by the brain. These results

locus coeruleus A small nucleus in the brainstem whose neurons produce norepinephrine and modulate large areas of the forebrain.

(a) This cat received a small lesion near the locus coeruleus that blocked the completely limp muscles (atonia) that normally accompanies REM sleep.

(b) The cat stands up wobbly, "looking" at something we cannot see. These behaviors indicate the cat is dreaming—seeing and interacting with objects that aren't really there.

Following a bout of SWS, the cat in REM rises up as though about to pounce, but its eyes are nearly closed and nothing is there.

To see a video of this figure, go to

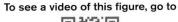

mindsmachine.com/10.5
Animal Sleep Activity

Figure 10.24 **Acting Out a Dream** (From A. R. Morrison et al., 1995.)

narcolepsy   A disorder that involves frequent, intense episodes of sleep, which last from 5 to 30 minutes and can occur anytime during the usual waking hours.

cataplexy   Sudden loss of muscle tone, leading to collapse of the body without loss of consciousness. Cataplexy is sometimes a common component of narcoleptic attacks.

strongly suggest that animals dream too. What do cats dream of? If their actions while sleeping are any indication, they dream of stalking prey, perhaps a mouse or a ball of yarn.

A hypothalamic sleep center was revealed by the study of narcolepsy

So far we've described three interacting brain systems controlling sleep: an SWS-promoting region in the forebrain, an arousing reticular formation in the brainstem, and a system in the pons that triggers REM sleep, including paralysis of the body during that state. There is a fourth important system, which seems to act as a "coordinating center" among these three centers, in the hypothalamus (**Figure 10.23d**). To understand how we learned about this fourth system, we need to consider a rare but fascinating condition.

You might not consider getting lots of sleep an affliction, but some people are either drowsy all the time or suffer sudden attacks of sleep. At the extreme of such tendencies is **narcolepsy**, an unusual disorder in which the person is afflicted by frequent, intense attacks of sleep that last 5–30 minutes and can occur at any time during usual waking hours. These sleep attacks occur several times a day—usually about every 90 minutes (Dantz et al., 1994).

Most people display SWS for an hour or more before entering REM; individuals who suffer from narcolepsy, however, tend to enter REM in the first few minutes of sleep. People with this disorder exhibit an otherwise normal sleep pattern at night, but they suffer abrupt, overwhelming sleepiness during the day. Many people with narcolepsy also show **cataplexy**, a sudden loss of muscle tone, leading to collapse of the body *without loss of consciousness*. Cataplexy can be triggered by sudden, intense emotional stimuli, including both laughter and anger. Narcolepsy usually manifests itself between the ages of 15 and 25 years and continues throughout life. Remember Barry from the start of this chapter? His narcolepsy symptoms began in his freshman year of college, when he started showing the classic signs of excessive daytime sleepiness and cataplexy.

Several strains of dogs exhibit narcolepsy (Aldrich, 1993), complete with sudden collapse and very rapid sleep onset (**Figure 10.25**). Just like humans who suffer from

To see a video, go to

mindsmachine.com/10.6
Narcoleptic Dachshund

Figure 10.25   Canine Narcolepsy
(Courtesy of Seiji Nishino.)

(a) Normal   (b) Narcoleptic

Immunocytochemistry reveals hypocretin-containing neurons in the lateral hypothalamus of a person who did not have narcolepsy.

This same region of the brain from someone who suffered from narcolepsy has far fewer hypocretin neurons.

Figure 10.26   Neural Degeneration in Humans with Narcolepsy (Courtesy of Jerome Siegel.)

narcolepsy, these dogs often show REM signs immediately upon falling asleep. Abrupt collapse in these dogs is suppressed by the same drugs (discussed shortly) that are used to treat human cataplexy.

The mutant gene responsible for one of these narcoleptic strains of dogs was found to be the gene for receptors for the neuropeptide **hypocretin** (also known as orexin) (L. Lin et al., 1999). Mice with the *hypocretin* gene knocked out also display narcolepsy (Chemelli et al., 1999). Genetically normal rats can be made narcoleptic if injected with a toxin that destroys neurons possessing hypocretin receptors (Gerashchenko et al., 2001). The narcoleptic dogs show signs of neural degeneration in forebrain structures at about the age when symptoms of narcolepsy appear (Siegel, Nienhuis, et al., 1999).

Similarly, humans with narcolepsy have lost about 90% of their hypocretin neurons (**Figure 10.26**) (Thannickal et al., 2000). This degeneration of hypocretin neurons seems to cause inappropriate activation of the cataplexy pathway that normally happens only during REM sleep. So, hypocretin normally keeps sleep at bay and prevents the transition from wakefulness directly into REM sleep.

The neurons that produce hypocretin are found almost exclusively in the hypothalamus. Where do these neurons send their axons to release the hypocretin? Not so coincidentally, the axons go to each of the three brain centers that we mentioned before: basal forebrain, reticular formation, and locus coeruleus (Sutcliffe and de Lecea, 2002). The hypocretin neurons also project axons to the hypothalamic tuberomammillary nucleus—the same structure that is inhibited by the basal forebrain to induce SWS. So, it looks as if the hypothalamus contains a hypocretin-based sleep center that controls whether we are awake, in SWS sleep, or in REM sleep (see Figure 10.23).

The traditional treatment for narcolepsy was the use of amphetamines in the daytime. The drug GHB (gamma-hydroxybutyrate, trade name Xyrem), helps some narcoleptics (although there are concerns about potential abuse of this drug [Tuller, 2002]). A newer drug, modafinil (Provigil), is sometimes effective for preventing narcoleptic attacks and has been proposed as an "alertness drug" for people with attention deficit disorder. There is also debate about whether modafinil should be available to anyone who feels sleepy or needs to stay awake (Pack, 2003), but at least one study found the drug no more effective than caffeine in this regard (Wesensten et al., 2002). Our friend Barry, from the chapter opener, eventually found a combination of mild stimulants that worked for him, and he ultimately earned an MD degree. Now that narcolepsy is known to be caused by a loss of hypocretin signaling, there is hope of developing synthetic drugs to stimulate hypocretin receptors, both for the relief of symptoms in narcolepsy and to combat sleepiness in people without narcolepsy.

Many people who do not suffer from narcolepsy nevertheless occasionally experience the cataplexy that accompanies narcolepsy (Fukuda et al., 1998). **Sleep paralysis** is the temporary inability to move or talk either just before dropping off to sleep, or, more often, just after waking. In this state people may experience sudden sensory hallucinations (Cheyne, 2002), including the belief that something is crushing their chest (see Figure 10.13). Sleep

hypocretin   Also called *orexin*. A neuropeptide produced in the hypothalamus that is involved in switching between sleep states, in narcolepsy, and in the control of appetite.

sleep paralysis   A state, during the transition to or from sleep, in which the ability to move or talk is temporarily lost.

How's it going?

1. Describe the four brain systems that control different stages of the sleep-waking cycle, discussing the experiments that revealed each.

2. What happens when brainstem systems to inhibit movement during REM sleep are damaged?

3. What is narcolepsy, and what brain systems seem to be responsible for this disorder?

To see a video, go to

mindsmachine.com/10.7
REM Behavior Disorder

sleep enuresis   Bed-wetting.

somnambulism   Sleepwalking.

REM behavior disorder (RBD)   A sleep disorder in which a person physically acts out a dream.

sleep-onset insomnia   Difficulty in falling asleep.

sleep-maintenance insomnia   Difficulty in staying asleep.

paralysis never lasts more than a few minutes, so it's best to relax and avoid panic. One hypothesis is that sleep paralysis results when the pontine center (see Figure 10.23c) continues to impose paralysis for a short while after a person awakes from a REM episode.

Sleep Disorders Can Be Serious, Even Life-Threatening

Narcolepsy is just one of several sleep disorders (**Table 10.2**) that have made sleep disorder clinics common in major medical centers. For some people, the peace and comfort of regular, uninterrupted sleep is routinely disturbed by the inability to fall asleep, by prolonged sleep, or by unusual awakenings.

Some minor dysfunctions are associated with sleep

Some dysfunctions associated with sleep are much more common in children than in adults. Two sleep disorders in children—night terrors (described earlier) and **sleep enuresis** (bed-wetting)—are associated with SWS. Most people grow out of these conditions without intervention, but pharmacological approaches can be used to reduce the amount of stage 3 sleep (as well as REM time) while increasing stage 2 sleep. For sleep enuresis, some doctors prescribe a nasal spray of the hormone vasopressin (see Chapter 9) before bedtime, which decreases urine production.

Somnambulism (sleepwalking) consists of getting out of bed, walking around the room, and appearing awake. Although more common in childhood, it sometimes persists into adulthood. These episodes last a few seconds to minutes, and the person usually does not remember the experience. Because such episodes occur during stage 3 SWS, they are more common in the first half of the night (when that stage predominates).

Most sleepwalkers are not acting out a dream (Parkes, 1985). The main problem is the inability of sleepwalkers to wake into full contact with their surroundings. At least one person was acquitted of murder after suggesting that he had suffered from "homicidal somnambulism," but such claims are difficult to evaluate (Broughton et al., 1994). Some people, however, do seem to be acting out their dreams in bed. **REM behavior disorder (RBD)** is characterized by organized behavior—such as fighting an imaginary foe, eating a meal, or acting like a wild animal—from a person who appears to be asleep (Schenck and Mahowald, 2002). Sometimes the person remembers a dream that fits well with his behavior (C. Brown, 2003). This disorder usually begins after the age of 50 and is more common in men than in women. Individuals with RBD are reminiscent of the cats with a lesion near the locus coeruleus, mentioned earlier, that were no longer paralyzed during REM and so acted out their dreams. Unfortunately, the onset of RBD is often followed by the early symptoms of Parkinson's disease and dementia (Postuma et al., 2009), suggesting that the disorder marks the beginning of widespread neurodegeneration. RBD may be controlled by antianxiety drugs (benzodiazepines like Valium) taken at bedtime.

Insomniacs have trouble falling asleep or staying asleep

Almost all of us have trouble falling asleep on occasion, but many people persistently find it difficult to get as much sleep as they would like. Estimates of the prevalence of insomnia range from 15% to 30% of the adult population (Parkes, 1985). Insomnia is commonly reported by people who are older, female, and/or users of drugs like tobacco, caffeine, and alcohol. It is not a trivial disorder; recall that adults who regularly sleep for short periods show a higher mortality rate than those who regularly sleep 7–8 hours each night (Kripke et al., 2002).

Insomnia seems to be the final common outcome for various conditions. Situational factors such as shift work, time zone changes, and changes in the daily routine (that hard motel bed) can lead to insomnia. Usually these conditions produce transient **sleep-onset insomnia**, a difficulty in falling asleep. Drugs, as well as neurological and psychiatric factors, seem to cause **sleep-maintenance insomnia**, a difficulty in remaining asleep. In this type of insomnia, sleep is punctuated by frequent nighttime arousals. This form of insomnia is especially evident in disorders of the respiratory system.

TABLE 10.2 Classification of Sleep Disorders

Disorders of initiating and maintaining sleep (insomnia)

Ordinary, uncomplicated insomnia

Drug-related insomnia caused by:

Use of stimulants

Withdrawal of depressants

Chronic alcoholism

Insomnia associated with psychiatric disorders

Insomnia associated with sleep-induced respiratory impairment (sleep apnea)

Disorders of excessive drowsiness

Narcolepsy

Drowsiness associated with psychiatric problems

Drug-related drowsiness

Drowsiness associated with sleep-induced respiratory impairment (sleep apnea)

Disorders of sleep-waking schedule

Temporary disruption caused by:

Time zone change by airplane flight (jet lag)

Shift work, especially night work

Persistent disruption (irregular rhythm)

Dysfunctions associated with sleep, sleep stages, or partial arousals

Sleepwalking (somnambulism)

Sleep enuresis (bed-wetting)

Night terror

Nightmares

Sleep-related seizures

Teeth grinding

REM behavior disorder (RBD)

Source: After Weitzman, 1981.

Back to Sleep Placing infants on their backs for sleep reduces the risk of sudden infant death syndrome (SIDS) by half.

In some people, respiration becomes unreliable during sleep. Breathing may cease for a minute or so, or it may slow alarmingly; blood levels of oxygen drop markedly. This syndrome, called **sleep apnea**, arises either from the progressive relaxation of muscles of the chest, diaphragm, and throat cavity or from changes in the pacemaker respiratory neurons of the brainstem. In the former instance, relaxation of the throat obstructs the airway—a kind of self-choking. This mode of sleep apnea is common in very obese people, but it also occurs, often undiagnosed, in non-obese people. Sleep apnea is frequently accompanied by loud, interrupted snoring, so loud snorers should consult a physician about the possibility that they suffer from sleep apnea.

Investigators have speculated that **sudden infant death syndrome** (**SIDS**, or *crib death*) arises from sleep apnea as a result of immature systems that normally control respiration. Autopsies of SIDS victims reveal abnormalities in brainstem serotonin systems (Kinney, 2009); interfering with this system in mice renders them unable to regulate respiration effectively. What's more, some of these young mice spontaneously stop breathing and die (Audero et al., 2008). The incidence of SIDS has been cut almost in half by the "Back to Sleep" campaign, which urges parents to place infants on their backs to sleep rather than on their stomachs. Placing the baby face down may lead to suffocation if the baby cannot regulate breathing or arouse properly. Exposure to cigarette smoke also increases the risk of crib death.

People with **sleep state misperception** (McCall and Edinger, 1992) *report* that they didn't sleep even when the EEG showed signs of sleep and they failed to respond to stimuli. They are sleeping without knowing it. Sometimes these people, upon learning that they really are sleeping, are more satisfied with the sleep they get.

sleep apnea A sleep disorder in which respiration slows or stops periodically, waking the patient. Excessive daytime sleepiness results from the frequent nocturnal awakening.

sudden infant death syndrome (SIDS) Also called *crib death*. The sudden, unexpected death of an apparently healthy human infant who simply stops breathing, usually during sleep.

sleep state misperception Commonly, a person's perception that he has not been asleep when in fact he has. It typically occurs at the start of a sleep episode.

Sleepy College Students   Many students have difficulty staying awake in class (and the professor isn't always to blame). Uneven sleep schedules—waking up early on some days of the week while sleeping late on others—can make it hard to get enough sleep before class.

How's it going?

1. Sleepwalking tends to happen during what stage of sleep? During what time of night?

2. Describe REM behavior disorder.

3. What are the different types of insomnia, and why are sleeping pills an imperfect long-term solution?

Although many drugs affect sleep, there is no perfect sleeping pill

Throughout recorded history, humans have reached for substances to enhance sleep. Ancient Greeks used the juice of the poppy to obtain opium and used products of the mandrake plant to aid sleep (Hartmann, 1978). The preparation of barbituric acid in the mid–nineteenth century started the development of many drugs—*barbiturates*—that were widely used to combat insomnia.

Most modern sleeping pills—including benzodiazepines (see Chapter 4) like triazolam (Halcion), and nonbenzodiazepine sedatives like zolpidem (Ambien) and eszopiclone (Lunesta)—bind to GABA receptors, inhibiting broad regions of the brain. But reliance on sleeping pills poses many problems (Rothschild, 1992). Viewed solely as a way to deal with sleep problems, current drugs fall far short of being a suitable remedy, for several reasons. First, none of them provide a completely normal night of sleep in terms of time spent in various sleep states, such as REM sleep. Second, continued use of sleeping pills causes them to lose effectiveness, and this declining ability to induce sleep often leads to increased self-prescribed dosages that can be dangerous. Another major drawback is that sleeping pills produce marked changes in the pattern of sleep, both while the drug is being used and for days afterward.

Use of sleeping pills may lead to a persistent "sleep drunkenness," coupled with drowsiness, that impairs waking activity; or to memory gaps about daily activity. Police report cases of "the Ambien driver," a person who took a sleeping pill and then got up a few hours later to go for a spin, with sometimes disastrous results, while apparently asleep (Saul, 2006). In other cases, people taking such medicines eat snacks, shop over the Internet, or even have sex, with no memory of these events the next day (Dolder and Nelson, 2008).

Certainly, the treatment for insomnia that has the fewest side effects, and that is very effective for most people, is not to use any drug, but to develop a regular routine to exploit the body's circadian clock. The best advice for insomniacs is to use an alarm clock to wake up faithfully at the same time each day (weekends included) and then simply go to bed *once they feel sleepy* (Webb, 1992). They should also avoid daytime naps and having caffeine at night. Going through a bedtime routine in a quiet, dark environment can also help to condition sleep onset. These steps will let you get the sleep you need, and sleeping pills will not (no matter what the $600 million in annual pharmaceutical advertising might say).

Unfortunately, many college students adopt schedules that virtually guarantee they won't get enough sleep. Waking up early on Monday and Wednesday to attend one class, sleeping a bit later on Tuesday and Thursday, and then sleeping a *lot* later on weekends disrupts your circadian sleep cycle. That makes it hard to fall asleep when you should on the nights before an early class. It's unpopular advice, but if you want enough sleep, get up at the same time *every* day, not just the day you have that early class, and go to bed about the same time each night. True, you'll miss out on some late-night activities with your friends, but you'll get to feel so self-righteous being awake and working while they are sleeping in. Plus you'll stay awake in lectures (we hope).

Recommended Reading

Aserinsky, E., and Kleitman, N. (1955). "Regularly Occurring Periods of Eye Motility, and Concomitant Phenomena, during Sleep." *Science, 118*, pp. 273–274.

Dunlap, J. C., Loros, J. J., and DeCoursey, P. J. (2004). *Chronobiology: Biological Timekeeping.* Sunderland, MA: Sinauer.

Kryger, M. K., Roth, T., and Dement, W. C. (Eds.). (2011). *Principles and Practice of Sleep Medicine* (5th ed.). Philadelphia, PA: Saunders/Elsevier.

Lavie, P. (2003). *Restless Nights: Understanding Snoring and Sleep Apnea.* New Haven, CT: Yale University Press.

Max, D. T. (2007). *The Family That Couldn't Sleep: A Medical Mystery.* New York, NY: Random House.

Schenk, C. H. (2008). *Sleep: A Groundbreaking Guide to the Mysteries, the Problems, and the Solutions.* New York, NY: Avery.

CHAPTER **10** VISUAL SUMMARY

You should be able to relate each summary to the adjacent illustration, including structures and processes.
If you need to review, go to the figures indicated and read the accompanying text.

mindsmachine.com/vs10

1 Animals show **circadian rhythms** of activity that can be **entrained** by light. These rhythms synchronize behavior to changes in the environment. In constant dim light, animals **free-run**, displaying a period of just over 24 hours. Review **Figures 10.2** and **10.9**, **Animations 10.2** and **10.3**

2 Lesions of the **suprachiasmatic nucleus (SCN)** abolish activity rhythms in constant conditions. Transplanting the SCN from one animal into another results in a free-running rhythm of the donor, demonstrating that the SCN contains a clock that can drive circadian activity. Several proteins (including Clock and Cycle) interact, increasing and decreasing in a cyclic fashion that takes about 24 hours. This molecular clock, pooled from many SCN neurons, drives circadian rhythms. Review **Figures 10.3–10.8, Animation 10.4**

3 Almost all mammals show two sleep states: **slow-wave sleep (SWS)** and **rapid-eye-movement (REM) sleep**. Human SWS has three distinct stages (**stages 1, 2, 3**) defined by **electroencephalography (EEG)** criteria, including **sleep spindles** and large, slow **delta waves**. During SWS, the body shows decreases in muscle tension, heart rate, respiratory rate, and temperature. Review **Figure 10.10, Table 10.1, Activity 10.1**

4 REM sleep is characterized by rapid, low-amplitude EEG (almost like an EEG while awake), but also by profound muscle relaxation because motoneurons are inhibited. People awakened from REM frequently report vivid dreams, while people awakened from SWS report ideas or thinking. Review **Table 10.1**

5 Sleep stages cycle through the night, with stage 3 SWS prominent early, while REM predominates later. Infants sleep a lot, with lots of REM, but as we grow up we sleep less, with less REM. Elderly people sleep even less, and stage 3 sleep eventually disappears. Review **Figures 10.11, 10.12,** and **10.15–10.17**

6 Four proposed functions of sleep are *energy conservation*, **ecological niche** *adaptation*, *body restoration*, and *memory consolidation*. A few people sleep only an hour per night, suggesting that they accomplish the function(s) of sleep very efficiently, but all healthy people sleep. Review **Figures 10.19–10.21**

7 **Sleep deprivation** leads to impairments in vigilance and reaction times. It also incurs sleep debt, although the lost SWS and REM may be partially restored in subsequent nights. Prolonged sleep deprivation compromises the immune system and leads to death. Review **Box 10.1**

8 Four brain systems control sleep and waking. The **basal forebrain** promotes SWS, the brainstem **reticular formation** promotes arousal, a pontine system triggers REM sleep, and hypothalamic neurons releasing **hypocretin** regulate these three centers. Review **Figures 10.22–10.24, Activity 10.2, Video 10.5**

9 **Narcolepsy** is characterized by sudden, uncontrollable periods of sleep, which may be accompanied by **cataplexy**, paralysis while remaining conscious. Disruption of hypocretin signaling causes narcolepsy. Review **Figure 10.26, Video 10.6**

10 Sleep disorders fall into four categories: trouble falling or staying asleep (insomnia); excessive drowsiness (e.g., narcolepsy); disruption of the sleep-waking schedule; and dysfunctions associated with sleep, sleep stages, or partial arousals (e.g., **somnambulism**). No pill guarantees a normal night's sleep. Review **Figure 10.25, Table 10.2, Video 10.7**

Go to **mindsmachine.com** for study questions, quizzes, flashcards, and other resources.

chapter 11 Emotions, Aggression, and Stress

Trouble in Paradise

You might think the life of a baboon on the Serengeti Plain of Africa is sheer bliss. After all, these highly social animals have so many vigilant eyes that predators almost never manage to sneak up close, and if one does, it may regret it when a whole troop of adults fights back. Food is relatively plentiful, so the baboons need to work only about 3 hours a day to get all the calories they need. Yet these baboons lead highly stressful lives. Why? Because, as Robert Sapolsky (2008) puts it, if you spend only three hours per day working, then "you've got nine hours of free time every day to devote to making somebody else just *miserable*." Like modern humans, these individuals experience stress that comes almost exclusively from their own species.

When Sapolsky began studying a group of baboons he named the Forest Troop, the animals' life was dominated by the hyperaggressive interactions of the oldest, strongest, meanest males. These males were constantly picking fights with each other, resulting occasionally in injuries, even for the "winner." But it wasn't just the rowdy males who were affected. When one of those males was in a bad mood—after losing a fight with another male, for example—he might attack females or even young baboons. These attacks, too, could be quite serious, taking off a strip of skin or part of an ear. The behavior of these snarly, aggressive males required everyone in the troop to be constantly vigilant, not for lions or food, but for other baboons.

Physiological examination of the baboons confirmed what behavioral observations had suggested: the whole troop was *stressed out*. Their blood had high levels of hormones that are released from the adrenal glands during times of stress. The blood samples also revealed that these baboons had fewer immune system cells to ward off illness (Sapolsky, 2001). That lowered immunity may have played a role in the disaster that befell the troop when it came across some tainted meat, which brought an agonizing death to some of the baboons (Angier, 2004). As the survivors deal with the new social landscape, what will become of the Forest Troop?

To see a video, go to

mindsmachine.com/11.1
Stress

The sound of unexpected footsteps in the eerie quiet of the night brings fear to many of us. But a particular piece of music or a loved one's voice summons feelings of comfort or happiness. For some of us, feelings and emotions can become vastly exaggerated; fears may become paralyzing attacks of anxiety and panic. No story about human behavior is complete without considering these powerful feelings.

Baboons Experience Stress Too The baboons of the Forest Troop in Kenya went through a drastic social reorganization.

Our chapter begins with emotions, the bodily responses and brain mechanisms underlying happiness and joy, fear and loathing. We'll discuss both the development of emotions in individuals and the evolution of emotions. The first section's examination of brain mechanisms related to emotional states emphasizes fear and aggression because both are important for survival and they are readily studied in animals. That discussion will lead us to the second section, where we'll see that fear and aggression are often associated with stress. Stress, in turn, is associated with a variety of health problems, because it involves not only the nervous and endocrine systems but also the immune system. We'll find that the nervous, endocrine, and immune systems interact extensively.

PART I Emotional Processing

The topic of emotions is complicated by the fact that we apply the word *emotion* to several different things. Emotion is a private, subjective *feeling* that we may have without anyone else being aware of it. But the word *emotional* is also used to describe many *behaviors* that people show, such as fearful facial expressions, frantic arm movements, or angry shouting. Furthermore, during strong emotion we often experience *physiological* changes, such as a rapidly beating heart, shortness of breath, or excessive sweating. To encompass all three of these aspects, we will define **emotion** as a *subjective mental state* that is usually accompanied by *distinctive behaviors* as well as *involuntary physiological changes*. Typically we experience an emotion for only a brief time, but we'll see in the second part of the chapter that prolonged experience of negative emotions, which is the hallmark of stress, can be very bad for our health.

We begin this chapter by discussing the major theories of how we experience emotions, including efforts to figure out whether emotional experience causes the physiological arousal or vice versa. Then we'll discuss the different types of emotions and how they relate to one another. Normally we display very distinctive facial expressions that differ for each of the emotions, and we'll see that people from very different cultures recognize these expressions. This near-universal recognition of emotional faces suggests that emotions evolved and that the facial displays of emotional experience may help us get along with others. We'll conclude this section by considering brain circuits for emotion, including a rather specialized brain circuit for fear. That topic will serve as a transition to the next part of the chapter, where we consider two consequences of fear: aggression and stress.

Broad Theories of Emotion Emphasize Bodily Responses

In many emotional states the heart races, the hands and face become warm, the palms sweat, and the stomach feels queasy. Common expressions capture this association: "my hair stood on end," "a sinking feeling in my stomach." These sensations are the result of activation of the autonomic nervous system—either the **sympathetic nervous system** (the "fight or flight" system that generally activates the body for action) or the **parasympathetic nervous system** (which generally prepares the body to relax and recuperate) (see Figure 2.9).

Several theories have tried to explain the close ties between the subjective feelings of emotions and the activity of the autonomic nervous system. Folk wisdom suggests

To see the brain in 3D, go to

mindsmachine.com/11.2
Brain Explorer

emotion A subjective mental state that is usually accompanied by distinctive behaviors as well as involuntary physiological changes.

sympathetic nervous system The part of the autonomic nervous system that acts as the "fight or flight" system, generally activating the body for action.

parasympathetic nervous system The part of the autonomic nervous system that generally prepares the body to relax and recuperate.

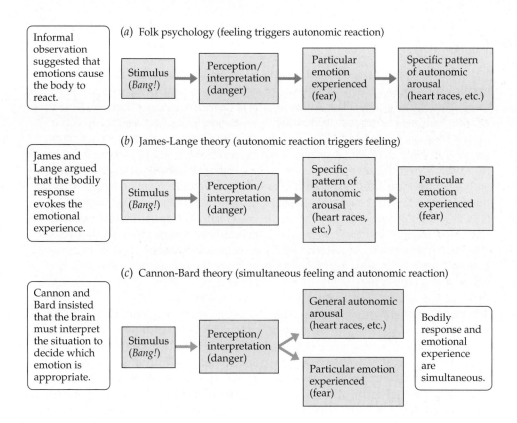

that the autonomic reactions are *caused* by the emotion—"I was so angry my stomach was churning"—as though the anger produces the churning sensation (**Figure 11.1a**). Yet research indicates that the relationship between emotion and physiological arousal is more subtle.

Do emotions cause bodily changes, or vice versa?

William James (1842–1910) and Carl Lange (1834–1900) turned the folk notion on its head, suggesting that the emotions we experience are caused by the bodily changes. From this perspective, we experience fear because we perceive the activity that dangerous conditions trigger in our body (**Figure 11.1b**). Different emotions thus feel different because they are generated by a different constellation of physiological responses.

The James-Lange theory inspired many attempts to link specific emotions to specific bodily responses. These attempts mostly failed, because it turns out that there is no distinctive autonomic pattern for each emotion. Fear, surprise, and anger, for example, tend to be accompanied by sympathetic activation, while parasympathetic activation tends to accompany both joy and sadness.

In addition, the physiological reactions are rather slow, as physiologists Walter Cannon (1871–1945) and Philip Bard (1898–1977) pointed out (Cannon, 1929). In Cannon and Bard's view, it is the brain's job to decide which particular emotion is an appropriate response to the stimuli. According to this model, the cerebral cortex *simultaneously* decides on the appropriate emotional experience (fear, surprise, joy) and activates the autonomic nervous system to appropriately prepare the body, using either the parasympathetic system to help the body rest, or the sympathetic system to ready the body for action (**Figure 11.1c**). It is because the sympathetic system is activated by any threatening situation that so-called lie detectors are very poor at distinguishing liars from truthful people who are anxious (**Box 11.1**).

BOX 11.1 Lie Detector?

One of the most controversial attempts to apply biomedical science is the so-called lie detector test. In this procedure, properly known as a **polygraph** test (from the Greek *polys*, "many," and *graphein*, "to write"), multiple physiological measures are recorded in an attempt to detect lying during a carefully structured interview. The test is based on the assumption that people have emotional responses when lying because they fear detection and/or feel guilty about lying. Emotions are usually accompanied by bodily responses that are difficult to control, such as changes in respiratory rate, heart rate, blood pressure, skin conductance (a measure of sweating), and so on. In polygraph recordings like the one in Figure A, each wiggly line, or *trace*, provides a measurement of one of these physiological variables, and taken together, the measures are assumed to track the subject's physiological arousal over time. When subjects lie in response to a direct question (arrows), momentary changes in several of the measured variables may occur.

People who administer polygraph examinations for a living claim that polygraphs are accurate in 95% of tests, but the estimate from impartial research is an overall accuracy of about 65% (Nietzel, 2000; Eriksson and Lacerda, 2007). Even if the higher figure were correct, the fact that these tests are widely used means that thousands of truthful people could be branded as liars and fired, disciplined, or not hired. On the other hand, many criminals and spies have been able to pass the tests without detection. For example, longtime CIA agent Aldrich Ames, who was sentenced in 1995 to life in prison for espionage, successfully passed polygraph tests after becoming a spy. In the wake of the terrorist attacks of 2001, a federally appointed panel of scientists noted that even if polygraphs were correct 80% of the time (which is much higher than impartial research suggests), then giving the test to 10,000 people that included 10 spies would condemn 1,600 innocent people, and let 2 spies go free (National Academy of Sciences, 2003)!

Some scientists believe that modern neuroscience may provide new methods of lie detection someday. Conscious lying may trigger unusual activation of executive control mechanisms of the prefrontal cortex (Figure B) (Abe et al., 2007). Fear results in activation of the amygdala (as we'll discuss later in this chapter) that, in the case of deception, also might be visible with fMRI (see Chapter 2). Functional MRI shows that the anterior cingulate cortex (another region associated with executive control) becomes more active when subjects are lying (Langleben et al., 2002). Although such initial results from brain-imaging studies of deception are intriguing, much more work will be required to establish that brain imaging can detect lies with enough reliability to be useful in making important decisions about individual people. And of course, even if they are validated, such lie detectors will be more costly and less widely available than polygraphs. (Figure B from Abe et al., 2007.)

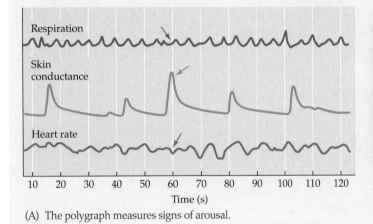

(A) The polygraph measures signs of arousal.

(B) Your cheatin' brain. PET images reveal selective activation of prefrontal cortex in a subject engaged in lying (relative to a control scan). (Courtesy of Nobuhito Abe.)

RESEARCHERS AT WORK

Stanley Schachter proposed a cognitive interpretation of stimuli and visceral states

Like Cannon and Bard, Stanley Schachter (1975) emphasized cognitive mechanisms in emotion. Under Schachter's model, however, emotional labels (e.g., *anger, fear, joy*) are attributed to relatively nonspecific feelings of physiological arousal. Which emotion we experience depends on cognitive systems that assess the *context*—our current social, physical, and psychological situation.

In a famous test of this idea, people were injected with epinephrine (adrenaline) and told either that there would be no effect or that their heart would race (Schachter and Singer, 1962) (**Figure 11.2**).

Figure 11.2   The Classic Schacter and Singer Experiment

Hypothesis

We experience a particular emotion as a result of the activity of the autonomic nervous system (the James-Lange theory).

Test

Activate the sympathetic nervous system with an injection of epinephrine to see whether the subjects experience one particular emotion as they fill out some forms. To test the alternative hypothesis—that our emotional experience is determined by cognitive processes—expose the subjects to a confederate who acts either angry or happy while filling out the forms.

(a)

Happy confederate

Some subjects are exposed to a happy confederate while filling out the form

Angry confederate

Other subjects are exposed to an angry confederate while filling out the form

These subjects were more likely to report feeling elated.

These subjects were more likely to report feeling angry and frustrated.

Outcome

Subjects who were warned that the injection might affect heart rate reported no emotional reaction. Subjects who were not warned about the sympathetic arousal reported more intense emotional reactions than subjects given a control injection. However, among the subjects who were not warned about the effects of the injection, *which* emotion they experienced (angry or happy) tended to match that of the confederate.

Conclusion

While autonomic responses can *intensify* our emotional experience, they cannot explain why we have different emotional experiences in different situations. Rather, our cognitive analysis of the environment affects which emotion we experience.

(b) Schachter's cognitive theory

General autonomic arousal (heart races, etc.)

Stimulus (forms)

Stimulus (forms to fill)

Perception/ interpretation

Context (angry peer)

Autonomic responses contribute to the intensity of emotional experience.

Emotion experienced will affect future interpretations of stimuli and continuing autonomic arousal.

Particular emotion experienced (anger)

Feedback

Participants who were warned of the reaction reported no emotional experience, but some participants who were not forewarned experienced emotions when their bodies responded to the drug.

However, *which* emotion was experienced could be affected by whether a confederate in the room acted angry or happy. The unsuspecting subjects injected with epinephrine were much more likely to report feeling angry when in the presence of an "angry" confederate, and more likely to report feeling elated when with a "happy" confederate (**Figure 11.2a**). These findings contradict the James-Lange prediction that feelings of anger or elation should each be associated with a unique profile of autonomic reactions. Schachter and Singer concluded that the misinformed subjects experienced their physiological arousal as whichever emotion seemed appropriate. "My heart's really pounding—I'm so angry!" or, "My heart's really pounding—I'm so elated!" depending on the environment. Thus, our emotional state is the result of an interaction between physiological arousal and cognitive interpretation of that arousal. This cognitive theory of emotions emphasizes that our interpretation of the context, including social factors such as other people's emotions, determines which emotion we'll experience. The cognitive theory also suggests that our emotional experience at one time may affect how we interpret later events (**Figure 11.2b**).

Another interesting outcome of the experiment is that the subjects receiving epinephrine reported experiencing *more intense* emotions than those given saline, as would be predicted by the James-Lange theory that bodily reactions are experienced as emotion. The autonomic responses did not specify *which* emotion was being experienced, but our awareness of the body's autonomic responses intensifies our experience of emotion (G. W. Hohmann, 1966).

How's it going?

1. Compare and contrast the folk psychology view of bodily responses to emotions with the James-Lange theory.

2. What two findings cast doubt on the James-Lange theory of emotions?

3. Describe the results of Schachter and Singer's experiment. What do these findings suggest about how autonomic reactions, emotional experience, and cognitive processing are related?

Facial Expressions Suggest a Core Set of Emotions

Just as the colors of the spectrum combine into subtle hues, researchers think there may be a basic core set of emotions underlying the more varied and delicate nuances of our world of feelings. One theory (Plutchik, 1994) proposes there are eight basic emotions, grouped in four pairs of opposites—joy/sadness, affection/disgust, anger/fear, and expectation/surprise—with all other emotions arising from combinations of this basic array (**Figure 11.3**). But investigators do not yet agree about the number of basic emotions (six, seven, eight?). While there is no way to determine once and for all the number of basic emotions, one clue comes from examining the number of different kinds of facial expressions that we produce and can recognize in others.

Facial expressions have complex functions in communication

How many different emotions can be detected in facial expressions? According to Paul Ekman and collaborators, there are distinctive expressions for anger, sadness, happiness, fear, disgust, surprise, contempt, and embarrassment (**Figure 11.4**) (Keltner and Ekman, 2000). Facial expressions of these emotions are interpreted similarly across many cultures without explicit training. (In case you're keeping track, whereas Plutchik included affection and expectation in his eight basic emotions, Keltner and Ekman include, instead, facial expressions of contempt and embarrassment. The other six emotions—anger, sadness, happiness, fear, disgust, and surprise—are the same in both schemes.)

Cross-cultural similarity is also noted in the *production* of expressions specific to particular emotions. For example, people in a preliterate New Guinea society show emotional facial expressions like those of people in industrialized societies. However, facial expressions are not unfailingly universal. For example, although Russell (1994) found significant agreement across cultures in the recognition of most emotional states from facial expressions, isolated nonliterate groups did not agree with Westerners about

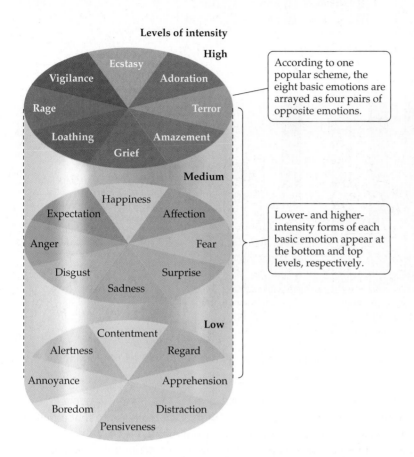

Levels of intensity

According to one popular scheme, the eight basic emotions are arrayed as four pairs of opposite emotions.

Lower- and higher-intensity forms of each basic emotion appear at the bottom and top levels, respectively.

Figure 11.3   One Classification of Basic Emotions
(Modified from Plutchik, 1994.)

Figure 11.4   The Eight Universal Facial Expressions of Emotion

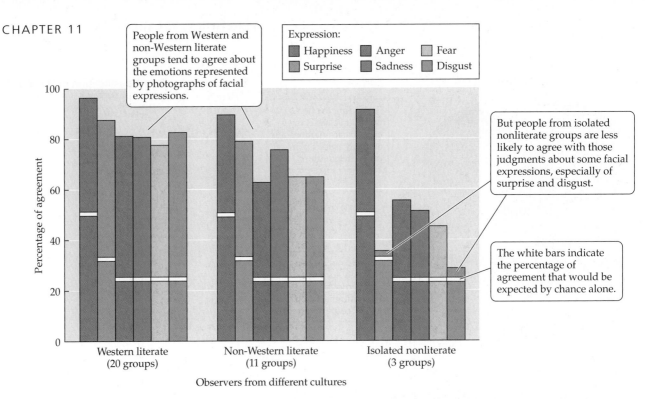

Figure 11.5   Cultural Differences in Recognizing Facial Expressions of Emotion (After Russell, 1994.)

recognizing expressions of surprise and disgust (**Figure 11.5**), suggesting that different cultures have adopted different ways to express those emotions.

These subtle cultural differences suggest that cultures prescribe rules for facial expression, and that they control and enforce those rules by cultural conditioning. Everyone agrees that cultures affect the facial display of emotion; the remaining controversy is over the extent of that cultural influence (**Figure 11.6**).

Facial expressions are mediated by muscles, cranial nerves, and CNS pathways

The human face is a complicated object, a network of small muscles that are carefully controlled by the nervous system. We use subsets of those muscles to produce nuanced facial expressions, from grimace to grin, alongside less subtle facial behaviors, like eating and speaking. Facial muscles can be divided into two categories:

1. *Superficial facial muscles*, most of which attach only between different points of facial skin (**Figure 11.7**); so when they contract, they change the shape of the mouth, eyes, or nose, or maybe create a dimple.

2. *Deep facial muscles* that attach to bone and produce larger-scale movements, like chewing.

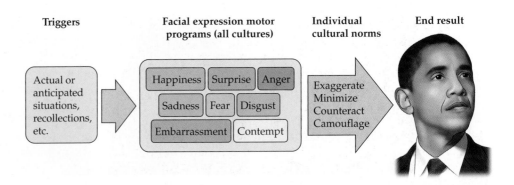

Figure 11.6   A Model for Emotional Facial Expressions across Cultures

Branches of the facial nerve

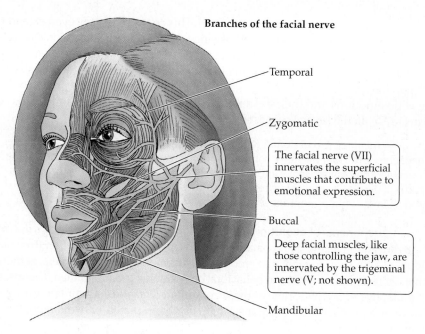

Temporal

Zygomatic

The facial nerve (VII) innervates the superficial muscles that contribute to emotional expression.

Buccal

Deep facial muscles, like those controlling the jaw, are innervated by the trigeminal nerve (V; not shown).

Mandibular

Figure 11.7 Superficial Facial Muscles and Their Neural Control

These facial muscles are innervated by two cranial nerves: (1) the facial nerve (VII), which innervates the superficial muscles of facial expression; and (2) the motor branch of the trigeminal nerve (V), which innervates muscles that move the jaw (see Figure 2.7). The activity of the cranial nerves is governed by the face area of motor cortex: this is a disproportionately large brain region in humans (see Figure 5.10), probably reflecting the importance of emotional expression in our species.

Lending support to the James-Lange notion that sensations from our body inform us about our emotions, the **facial feedback hypothesis** suggests that sensory feedback from our facial expressions can affect our mood. In the best tests of this idea, people are given a task, such as holding a pencil either under their nose or between their teeth (**Figure 11.8**), that effectively has them take on a sad or happy face, respectively. The subjects are then probed to see how happy or sad they feel, or how funny they find a cartoon. Typically, people who have been simulating a smile report more positive feelings than the folks who have been simulating a frown (Davis et al., 2009). So it is possible that forcing yourself to take on a cheerful expression may actually help you feel happier, and the old song that advises "just put on a happy face" may have its basis in fact. Conversely, people who receive Botox injections, paralyzing facial muscles to relieve wrinkles and look younger, experience emotions less intensely after the treatment than before (Davis et al., 2010).

How did emotion and emotional displays evolve?

In his book *The Expression of the Emotions in Man and Animals* (1872), Charles Darwin presented evidence that certain expressions of emotions are universal among people of all regions of the world, anticipating by more than a century the studies of facial expressions that we reviewed earlier (see Figure 11.5). Furthermore, Darwin asserted that some nonhuman animals show comparable expressions of some emotions, suggesting that aspects of emotional expression may have originated in a common ancestor.

Disputing earlier scholars, Darwin emphasized that nonhuman primates have the same facial muscles that humans have. A century later, Redican (1982) noted distinct facial expressions in nonhuman primates, including a *play face*,

facial feedback hypothesis The idea that sensory feedback from our facial expressions can affect our mood.

(a)

Several studies indicate that, when subjects are manipulated into mimicking facial expressions of sadness...

...or happiness, their emotional mood is actually affected.

(b)

So putting on a happy, cheerful expression may actually help you to feel better.

Figure 11.8 Facial Feedback Hypothesis

evolutionary psychology   A field of study devoted to asking how natural selection has shaped behavior in humans and other animals.

homologous to the human laugh (**Figure 11.9**). This connection may even extend beyond primates: for example, tickling and playing with rats can elicit ultrasonic vocalizations that may be analogous to laughter. Expression of positive emotions of this sort may facilitate social contact and learning in a variety of species (Burgdorf et al., 2008; Panksepp, 2007).

How do emotions and their expression help individuals survive and reproduce? Darwin (1872) offered several suggestions:

> The movements of expression in the face and body [are important] for our welfare. They serve as the first means of communication between the mother and her infant; she smiles approval, and thus encourages her child on the right path, or frowns disapproval. We readily perceive sympathy in others by their expression … and mutual good feeling is thus strengthened. (p. 365)

Current proponents of **evolutionary psychology** point to additional ways in which emotions are adaptive and could have developed through natural selection (Cosmides and Tooby, 2000). They suggest that emotions act as motivational programs, gathering together distinct physiological and behavioral components to form unified responses to specific adaptive problems. Some of these coordinated responses maintain good relations with other people; other responses help us obtain mates, or avoid predators, or find food, and so forth.

Most of us have experienced the frightening nighttime perception of being stalked by a predator—real or imagined, human or nonhuman. The intensity of the experience may be a legacy of the ancestral environment in which our behavioral systems evolved, where the presence of an unseen predator would be a situation of utmost urgency. Back then, as with most kinds of behavior, individuals differed in their responses to this life-threatening situation. Some individuals made poor choices resulting in reduced reproductive success. Others made more-effective choices, and to the extent that this behavior was heritable, their descendants were also more likely to survive in similar situations.

Thus, through natural selection, a program for dealing with this situation evolved: we call that program *fear*. The emotion of fear shifts our perception, attention, cognition, and action to focus on avoiding danger and seeking safety, while preparing us physiologically for fighting or for flight. Other activities, such as seeking food, sleep, or mates, are suppressed. In the face of an imminent threat to life it is better to be afraid, calling on this recipe for action, developed and tested over the ages, than to ad-lib something.

Viewed in this way, emotions can be seen as evolved preprogramming that helps us deal quickly and effectively with a wide variety of situations. As another example,

How's it going?

1. List some examples of particular facial expressions that are associated with particular emotions.

2. What evidence suggests that facial expressions of emotional state are inherited rather than taught by culture?

3. Describe the facial feedback hypothesis of emotion, and give an example of an experiment supporting this hypothesis.

4. What is the evidence that emotions, and the facial expressions that accompany them, evolved by natural selection?

(a)

An adult female chimpanzee screams at another female, who is pulling at her food. Screaming is used in submission and protest.

(b)

A juvenile chimpanzee shows a play face while being tickled. He also makes a guttural laughing sound.

(c)

A Tibetan macaque bares his teeth, grinning to signal submission to a dominant animal. In humans, teeth baring has gained a different, friendlier meaning.

Figure 11.9   Facial Expression of Emotions in Nonhuman Primates (Photographs by Frans de Waal, from de Waal, 2003.)

feelings of disgust for body fluids may help us avoid exposure to germs (Curtis et al., 2004), so it may be wise to recognize disgust in others. Our unfortunate tendency to make snap judgments about other people, based on their appearance and facial expressions, may be an overgeneralization of mechanisms that evolved to help us recognize signs of threat or danger in others (Todorov et al., 2008).

Do Distinct Brain Circuits Mediate Emotions?

The question of whether specific brain circuits have control over emotions has been explored in studies using either brain lesions or electrical stimulation. The evidence confirms not only that some brain regions do specialize in emotions, but also that the same regions may be involved in multiple emotions.

Electrical stimulation of the brain can produce emotional effects

One way to study the neuroanatomy of emotion is to electrically stimulate brain sites in conscious animals and then observe the effects on behavior. Classic work in the 1950s produced an intriguing finding: rats will enthusiastically press a lever in order to give themselves brief electrical stimulation in a brain region called the *septum* (**Figure 11.10**) (Olds and Milner, 1954). This phenomenon, called **brain self-stimulation**, can also happen in humans. Patients receiving electrical stimulation in the septum feel a sense of pleasure or warmth, or sometimes sexual excitement (Heath, 1972).

A rush of experimentation soon mapped brain sites that yield self-stimulation responses. Almost all of these sites are subcortical, especially in the hypothalamus and extending into the brainstem. We now know that a bundle of axons that ascends from the midbrain through the hypothalamus—the **medial forebrain bundle**—may be affected at many of the self-stimulation sites. One important target for the axons of the median forebrain bundle is the **nucleus accumbens**, a major component of the brain's reward circuitry (see Chapter 4). The release of dopamine into the nucleus accumbens appears to produce very pleasurable feelings.

One theory is that electrical stimulation taps into dopaminergic circuits that are normally activated by behaviors that produce pleasurable feelings, such as feeding or sexual activity (White and Milner, 1992). As we discussed in Chapter 4, researchers have proposed that drugs of abuse are addictive because they activate these same neural circuits with an artificial intensity (R. C. Pierce and Kumaresan, 2006).

Brain lesions also affect emotions

Early in the twentieth century, dogs in which the cortex had been removed were found to respond to routine handling with sudden intense **decorticate rage**—snarling, biting, and so on—sometimes referred to as *sham rage* because it lacks well-directed attack. Clearly, then, emotional behaviors of this type must be organized at a subcortical level, with the cerebral cortex normally *inhibiting* rage responses. On the basis of studies such as these, combined with observations from brain autopsies of

Wow, That Feels Great! As Larry Niven's novel *Ringworld* opens, the hero Louis Wu is addicted to electrical stimulation of his brain.

brain self-stimulation The process in which animals will work to provide electrical stimulation to particular brain sites, presumably because the experience is very rewarding.

medial forebrain bundle A collection of axons traveling in the midline region of the forebrain.

nucleus accumbens A region of the forebrain that receives dopaminergic innervation from the ventral tegmental area.

decorticate rage Also called *sham rage*. Sudden intense rage characterized by actions (such as snarling and biting in dogs) that lack clear direction.

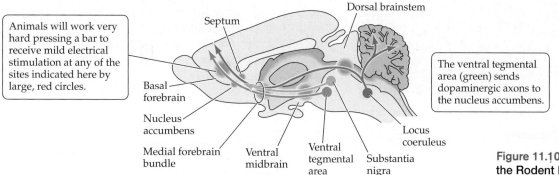

Animals will work very hard pressing a bar to receive mild electrical stimulation at any of the sites indicated here by large, red circles.

Dorsal brainstem

Septum

Basal forebrain

Nucleus accumbens

Medial forebrain bundle

Ventral midbrain

Ventral tegmental area

Substantia nigra

Locus coeruleus

The ventral tegmental area (green) sends dopaminergic axons to the nucleus accumbens.

Figure 11.10 Self-Stimulation Sites in the Rodent Brain

limbic system   A loosely defined, widespread group of brain nuclei that innervate each other to form a network. These nuclei are implicated in emotions.

Klüver-Bucy syndrome   A condition, brought about by bilateral amygdala damage, that is characterized by dramatic emotional changes including reduction in fear and anxiety.

fear conditioning   A form of classical conditioning in which a previously neutral stimulus is repeatedly paired with an unpleasant stimulus, like foot shock, until the previously neutral stimulus alone elicits the responses seen in fear.

amygdala   A group of nuclei in the medial anterior part of the temporal lobe.

people with emotional disorders, James Papez (1937) proposed a subcortical circuit of emotion. Noting associations between emotional changes and specific sites of brain damage, Papez (which rhymes with "capes") concluded that destruction of a set of interconnected pathways in the brain would impair emotional processes. These interconnected regions, known as the **limbic system** (MacLean, 1949), include the mammillary bodies of the hypothalamus, the anterior thalamus, the cingulate cortex, the hippocampus, the amygdala, and the fornix. The arrows in **Figure 11.11** schematically depict the interconnections of this circuit.

Early support for the limbic model of emotion came from studies of monkeys following removal of their temporal lobes (Klüver and Bucy, 1938). The animals' behavior changed dramatically after surgery; the highlight of this behavioral change was an extraordinary taming effect known as the **Klüver-Bucy syndrome**. Animals that had been wild and fearful of humans before surgery became tame and showed neither fear nor aggression afterward. In addition, they showed strong oral tendencies, eating a variety of objects, including rocks. Frequent and often inappropriate sexual behavior was also observed. Because this type of behavior is also seen in monkeys in which only the left and right amygdalas have been destroyed—without damaging any adjacent tissue (Emery et al., 2001)—it appears that the amygdala is a key structure in the behavioral changes in Klüver-Bucy syndrome, specifically the loss of fear. Let's take a closer look at the role of the amygdala in fear.

The amygdala governs a fear circuit

There is nothing subtle about fear. Conditions that provoke fear elicit similar behaviors from individuals of many different species. This lack of subtlety and the similarity of fear-related behavior across species may explain why we know much more about the neural circuitry of fear than of any other emotion (LeDoux, 1995). For example, it is very easy to reliably elicit fear by using classical conditioning, in which the person or animal is presented with a stimulus such as light or sound that is paired with a brief aversive stimulus such as mild electric shock (**Figure 11.12a**). After several such pairings, the response to the sound or light itself is the typical fear portrait, including freezing in position and autonomic signs such as more rapid heart rate and breathing.

Studies of such **fear conditioning** have provided a map of the neural circuitry, with the **amygdala** as a key structure in the mediation of fear (**Figure 11.12b**). Located at the anterior medial portion of each temporal lobe, the amygdala is composed of about a dozen different nuclei, each with a distinctive set of connections. Lesioning just the central nucleus of the amygdala in rats prevents blood pressure increases and freezing behavior in response to a conditioned fear stimulus.

On its way to the amygdala, via various sensory channels, information about fear-provoking stimuli reaches a fork in the road at the level of the thalamus (recall from Chapter 2 that the thalamus acts like a switchboard, directing sensory information to specific brain regions). A direct projection from the thalamus to the amygdala, nicknamed the "low road" for fear responses, bypasses conscious processing and allows for immediate reactions to fearful stimuli (LeDoux, 1996). An alternate "high road" pathway routes the incoming information through sensory cortex, allowing for processing that, while slower, is conscious, fine-grained,

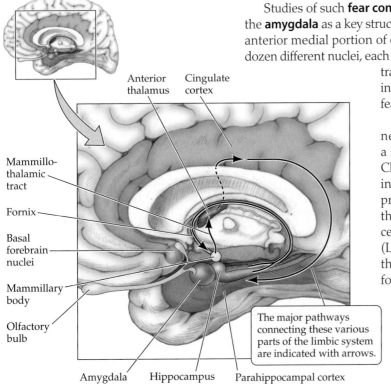

Anterior thalamus

Cingulate cortex

Mammillo-thalamic tract

Fornix

Basal forebrain nuclei

Mammillary body

Olfactory bulb

Amygdala   Hippocampus   Parahippocampal cortex

The major pathways connecting these various parts of the limbic system are indicated with arrows.

Figure 11.11   The Limbic System: Medial Brain Regions Involved in Emotions

(a) In one classical-conditioning procedure, called fear conditioning, a tone is associated with a mild electrical shock, which causes increased blood pressure and "freezing."

Eventually the tone alone elicits these responses.

Grid electrified

(b) A fear-inducing stimulus reaches the thalamus and is relayed either directly to the amygdala (the "low road" for unconscious reactions to threat) or via the cortex and hippocampus (the "high road," involving more detailed and conscious processing of stimuli).

(c) The information ultimately reaches the amygdala's central nucleus, which projects to different brain nuclei to produce different components of the fear response.

Figure 11.12 The Circuitry of Fear (After LeDoux, 1994, 1996.)

and integrated with higher-level cognitive processes, such as memory (**Figure 11.12c**). You can learn more details about the amygdala circuitry for fear and other emotions in **A Step Further 11.1**, on the website.

The data from rats and mice implicating the amygdala fit well with observations in humans. For example, when people are shown visual stimuli associated with pain or fear, blood flow to the amygdala increases (LaBar et al., 1998), even if the person is not consciously aware of the stimuli (Pegna et al., 2005). People who suffer from temporal lobe seizures that include the amygdala commonly report that intense fear precedes the start of a seizure (Engel, 1992). Likewise, stimulation of temporal lobe sites may elicit feelings of fear in patients (Bancaud et al., 1994).

The case of a woman, referred to as S.M., who suffered a rare genetic disease that damaged both amygdalas, shows the value of being afraid (Feinstein et al., 2011). Not only is S.M. unafraid of snakes or spiders, but she once walked right up to a knife-wielding drug addict who was trying to rob her. He was so disquieted by her strange response that *he* was the one who ran away. Once she was nearly killed in an act of domestic violence. While her behavioral responses and self-report appear typical for other emotions, S.M. shows very little sympathetic response to fearful stimuli, and produces almost no startle response to a sudden, loud noise. Shown movie clips that other people find frightening, S.M. reports being unmoved (**Figure 11.13**). S.M. is also very poor at recognizing the facial expressions of fear in other people, but she recognizes other emotional expressions—a pattern seen in other people with damaged amygdalas (Adolphs et al., 2005).

In short, both experimental and clinical observations, in both animals and people, confirm that the amygdala is crucial not only for generating fear in ourselves but also for recognizing fear in others.

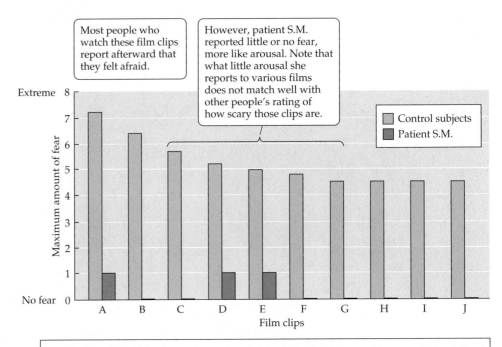

A – *The Ring* (2002) The ghost of a murdered child infiltrates the lives of her soon-to-be victims.
B – *Blair Witch Project* (1999) Campers are attacked by an unknown apparition during the middle of the night.
C – *CSI* (2009) A man struggles to survive after being buried alive.
D – *The English Patient* (1996) A man is tortured by the Germans during World War II.
E – *Seven* (1995) A mutilated man awakes from the dead.
F – *Cry Freedom* (1987) Armed trespassers attack a woman who is home alone during the night.
G – *Arachnophobia* (1990) A large poisonous spider attacks a girl in the shower.
H – *Halloween* (1978) A woman is being chased by a murderer.
I – *The Shining* (1980) A young boy hears voices in the hallway of a haunted hotel.
J – *The Silence of the Lambs* (1991) A female FBI agent tries to capture a twisted serial killer who is hiding in a dark basement.

Figure 11.13 The Woman Who Was Never Afraid (After Feinstein et al., 2011.)

The two cerebral hemispheres process emotion differently

Experimental and clinical observations indicate that the two cerebral hemispheres play different roles in cognitive processes in humans (see Chapter 15). There appear to be similar hemispheric differences in emotion processing. Patients suffering strokes in the left cerebral hemisphere are more likely to have depressive symptoms, independent of any trouble they may be having with speech (Starkstein and Robinson, 1994). In contrast, patients with lesions of the right parietal or temporal cortex are described as unduly cheerful and indifferent to their loss. **A Step Further 11.2**, on the website, details some of the emotional changes resulting from brain damage. Injection of the anesthetic sodium amytal into just one side—either the left or the right carotid artery (the Wada test, described in Box 15.1)—causes one entire cerebral hemisphere to go to sleep for a short time. As with the people who have left-hemisphere damage, injection of anesthetic into the left hemisphere causes depressed mood, whereas right-sided injections elicit smiling and a feeling of euphoria (Terzian, 1964).

Differences in the contributions of the two hemispheres to emotion are also evident in the asymmetry of facial expressions. By cutting a photograph of the face of a person who is displaying an emotion down the exact middle of the face, we can create two new composite photos: one that combines two left sides of the face (one of which is printed in mirror image), and another that combines two right sides. The results reveal that facial expressions are not symmetrical (**Figure 11.14**). Most observers judge the left-sides photos as more emotional than the right-sides photos. Because the left side of the face is controlled by the right hemisphere (and vice versa), this observation again suggests that the right hemisphere is especially important for emotional processing (Borod et al., 1997).

Different emotions activate different regions of the human brain

Several forebrain areas have been consistently implicated in various emotions. Bartels and Zeki (2000) recruited volunteers who professed to be "truly, deeply, and madly in love." Each participant furnished four color photographs: one photo of his or her boy- or girlfriend, and three photos of friends who were the same sex as the loved partner and were similar in age and length of friendship. Functional-MRI brain scans were made while each participant was shown counterbalanced sequences of the four photographs. Brain activity elicited by viewing the loved person was compared with that elicited by viewing friends. Love, compared with friendship, involved *increased* activity

Composite faces reveal differences between left and right in the level of intensity of emotional expression.

Photographs constructed from only the left side of the face are judged to be more emotional than either the original face or a composite based on just the right side of the face.

(*a*) Left sides   (*b*) Original   (*c*) Right sides

Figure 11.14 Emotions and Facial Asymmetry

(a) Brain regions implicated in emotions are depicted here in midsagittal...

Orbitofrontal region of prefrontal cortex   Anterior cingulate cortex   Posterior cingulate cortex

(b) ...anterior coronal...

Orbitofrontal region of prefrontal cortex

(c) ...and posterior coronal sections.

Anterior cingulate cortex   Amygdala

Insula

Figure 11.15 The Emotional Brain (From Dolan, 2002.)

How's it going?

1. Describe brain self-stimulation and what this phenomenon suggests about emotional experience.

2. What is the limbic system, and what happens when portions of this system are damaged, such as in Klüver-Bucy syndrome?

3. Describe fear conditioning and the evidence that the amygdala plays a role in this process.

4. What evidence suggests that the amygdala mediates fear in humans?

5. Describe the evidence that one hemisphere of the brain is more involved than the other in the display of emotions.

in the insula and anterior cingulate cortex, and *reduced* activity in the posterior cingulate and prefrontal cortex (**Figure 11.15**). Given its role in fear, you won't be surprised to learn that the amygdala also showed *reduced* activity when people were contemplating their romantic partner.

Another study compared brain activation during four different kinds of emotion, and again the insula, cingulate cortex, and prefrontal cortex were among the regions implicated. These studies indicate that *there is no simple, one-to-one relation between a specific emotion and changed activity of a brain region.* There is no "happy center" or "sad center." Instead, each emotion involves differential patterns of activation across a network of brain regions associated with emotion, as you can see in **A Step Further 11.3**, on the website. For example, activity of the cingulate cortex is altered in sadness, happiness, and anger; and the left somatosensory cortex is deactivated in both anger and fear. Although different emotions are associated with different patterns of activation, there is a good deal of overlap among patterns for different emotions (A. R. Damasio et al., 2000).

In the next section of this chapter we'll focus on the darker side of human emotional experience: aggression, stress, and the toll these negative experiences take on our health.

PART II Aggression and Stress

Violence, assaults, and homicide exact a high price in modern society, and physical assault is not the only form of aggression. Verbal and symbolic aggression—name calling, horn honking, angry glares—also take their toll. We begin this section by examining the biological factors that influence aggression in animals and humans. Then we'll conclude the chapter by discussing a consequence of being the target of aggression: stress. As we noted at the start of the chapter, most of our stress today is caused by the behavior of other people. We'll learn that the body's hormonal responses to stress, an adaptation to the brief crises of our ancestral environment, can be disastrous in the face of the long-lasting stresses of modern-day life. In learning how chronic stress compromises the immune system, we'll learn that the nervous system, the endocrine system, and the immune system are constantly regulating each other to preserve our health.

Neural Circuitry, Hormones, and Synaptic Transmitters Mediate Violence and Aggression

We can define **aggression** as behavior that is intended to cause pain or harm to others. In the discussion that follows, we focus primarily on physical aggression between individuals, excluding the aggression of predators toward their prey, which is perhaps better viewed as feeding behavior (Glickman, 1977). **Intermale aggression** (aggression between males of the same species) is observed in most vertebrates. The relevance to humans is reflected in the fact that males are 5 times as likely as females to be arrested on charges of murder in the United States. Further, aggressive behavior between boys, in contrast to that between girls, is evident early, in the form of vigorous and destructive play behavior (J. Archer, 2006). Whatever we may think about aggression, it seems clear that in many species aggressive behavior in males is adaptive for gaining access to food and mates. We'll find that the hormone that prepares males for reproduction—testosterone—also makes them more aggressive. We'll also discuss certain neurotransmitters that play a role in aggression, as well as the controversial idea of using surgery to control violence.

aggression Behavior that is intended to cause pain or harm to others.

intermale aggression Aggression between males of the same species.

testosterone A hormone, produced by male gonads, that controls a variety of bodily changes that become visible at puberty. One of a class of hormones called androgens.

Androgens seem to increase aggression

At sexual maturity, as the testes begin secreting the steroid hormone **testosterone**, intermale aggression markedly increases in many species (McKinney and Desjardins, 1973). In seasonally breeding species as diverse as birds and primates, intermale aggression waxes and wanes in concert with seasonal changes in levels of testosterone (Wingfield et al., 1987). Conversely, castrating males to remove the source of testosterone usually reduces aggressive behavior profoundly. Treating castrated males with testosterone restores fighting behavior (**Figure 11.16**).

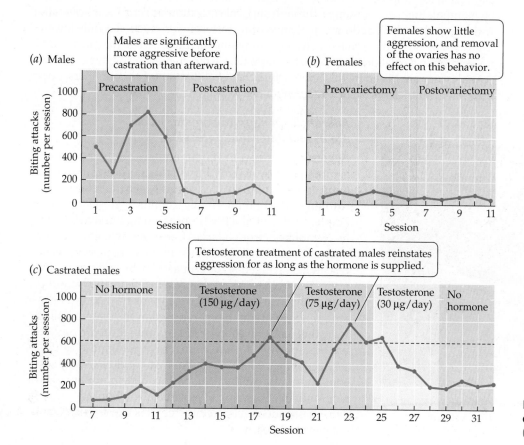

Figure 11.16 **The Effects of Androgens on the Aggressive Behavior of Mice** (After G. C. Wagner et al., 1980.)

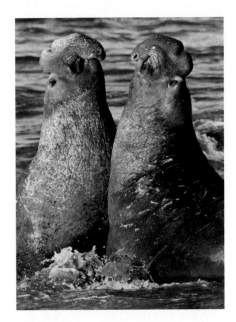

Nature Red in Tooth and Flipper Fighting male elephant seals draw blood. In most mammalian species, males must compete with one another, often in the form of physical aggression, for the chance to mate with females.

serotonin A synaptic transmitter that is produced in the raphe nuclei and is active in structures throughout the central nervous system.

The relationship between testosterone and aggression in humans is less clear-cut. Treating adult volunteers with extra testosterone does not increase their aggression (O'Connor et al., 2004). Similarly, young men going through puberty experience a sudden large increase in circulating testosterone, yet they do not show a correlated increase in aggressive behavior (J. Archer, 2006). Nevertheless, some human studies report a positive correlation between testosterone levels and the magnitude of hostility, as measured by behavior rating scales (Dabbs and Morris, 1990). Nonaggressive tendencies in males are associated with satisfaction in family functioning and with lower levels of serum testosterone (Julian and McKenry, 1979). Among female convicts, testosterone concentrations are highest in women convicted of unprovoked violence and lowest among women convicted of defensive violent crimes (Dabbs and Hargrove, 1997; Dabbs et al., 1988).

At least two variables confound the correlations between testosterone and aggression. First is the observation that experience can affect testosterone levels. In mice and monkeys, the loser in aggressive encounters shows reduced androgen levels (I. S. Bernstein and Gordon, 1974; Lloyd, 1971), so measured levels of testosterone sometimes may be a *result*, rather than a cause, of behavior. In men, testosterone levels rise in the winners and fall in the losers after competitions ranging from wrestling to chess (van Anders and Watson, 2006). Male sports fans even show a vicarious competition effect in response to simply watching "their" team win or lose a sporting event (Bernhardt, 1997), and during the 2008 U.S. presidential election, men who voted for McCain experienced a sharp drop in circulating testosterone, compared to Obama backers (Stanton et al., 2009).

These observations suggest that a second confounding variable between testosterone and aggression is dominance (Mazur and Booth, 1998), since most chess players could hardly be said to be aggressive, at least not physically. According to this model, testosterone levels should be associated with behaviors that confer or protect the individual's social status (and thus reproductive fitness). These behaviors may *sometimes*, but not always, involve overt aggression. Despite the lack of a close relationship between aggression and androgens, people have tried to modify the behavior of male criminals by manipulating sex hormones, through surgical castration or "chemical" castration with drugs that block androgen receptors or testosterone production. While lowered testosterone may reduce violence in some sex offenders (Brain, 1994), the main effect is a reduction in sexual drive and interest more than a direct effect on aggression. Many ethical issues are raised by this approach to the rehabilitation of sex offenders, not to mention the intricacies of such intervention, have yet to be worked out.

Alterations in neurotransmitter levels are associated with aggression

Aggressive behavior in various animals, including humans, is modulated by activity in several neurotransmitter systems. In particular, studies suggest that the release of **serotonin** in the brain normally inhibits aggression. For example, Higley et al. (1992) observed aggressive behavior in 28 monkeys from a large, free-ranging colony, and he ranked the animals from least to most aggressive. When researchers gauged serotonin activity by measuring serotonin metabolites in the cerebrospinal fluid, they found evidence that the most aggressive monkeys had the lowest amount of serotonin being released in the brain. Similarly, mice that lack one subtype of serotonin receptor, and thus are less sensitive to serotonin, are hyperaggressive (Bouwknecht et al., 2001)—just what we would expect if serotonin normally inhibits aggression. This inhibitory role of serotonin in aggression is probably evolutionarily ancient, since it is evident even in invertebrates like crayfish (Panksepp et al., 2003).

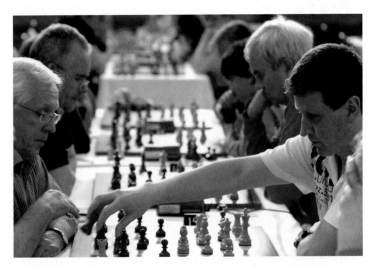

Chess Tournaments and Testosterone Because no physical violence is involved, the rise in testosterone seen in men who win chess games seems more related to dominance than aggression.

Indicators of diminished serotonin activity are seen in humans who become violent with alcohol use (Virkkunen and Linnoila, 1993), in U.S. marines expelled for excessive violence (G. L. Brown et al., 1979), in children who torture animals (Kruesi, 1979), and in children whose poor impulse control produces disruptive behavior. Taken together, the evidence suggests that serotonin is a key participant in networks that are responsible for high-level control of aggressive behavior (Siever, 2008).

Other neurotransmitters have also been implicated in aggression, including gamma-aminobutyric acid (GABA) (Lieving et al., 2008) and a variety of peptide hormones, including vasopressin, oxytocin, and the endogenous opioids (Siever, 2008). The development of antiaggression treatments based on these mechanisms is an active area of research.

The biopsychology of human violence is a topic of controversy

Some forms of human violence are characterized by sudden, intense physical assaults. A long-standing controversy surrounds the idea that some forms of intense human violence are caused by temporal lobe disorders (Mark and Ervin, 1970). Aggression is sometimes a prominent symptom in patients with temporal lobe seizures, and a significant percentage of people arrested for violent crimes have abnormal EEGs or other indicators of temporal lobe dysfunction (D. O. Lewis, 1990; D. O. Lewis et al., 1979; D. Williams, 1969).

Psychopaths are often intelligent individuals with superficial charm who have poor self-control, a grandiose sense of self-worth, and little or no feelings of remorse (Hare et al., 1990), and who sometimes commit very violent acts. Compared to controls, psychopaths do not react as negatively to words about violence (Gray et al., 2003). PET studies suggest that psychopaths have reduced activity in the prefrontal cortex (Raine et al., 1998), and it is hypothesized that this lower activity may impair their ability to control impulsive behavior. An MRI follow-up indicated that the prefrontal cortex of psychopaths is smaller than in controls (Raine et al., 2000)—another finding that is consistent with this hypothesis.

Undoubtedly, human violence and aggression stem from many sources. Biological studies of aggression have been vigorously criticized by some politicians and social scientists. These critics argue that, as a result of emphasizing biological factors such as genetics or brain mechanisms, the *preventable* origins of human violence and aggression, such as poverty and child neglect, might be overlooked. But as we have seen throughout the book, the brain is a malleable organ that is shaped by experience—and violent behavior *must* have its origins in the brain—so in principle it could be possible to reshape or at least moderate brain mechanisms of violence. The quality of life of some violent persons might be significantly improved if biological problems could be identified and addressed. For example, treatments that enhance serotonin activity in the brain might be a useful adjunct to psychotherapeutic intervention (Hollander, 1999).

Next we'll consider one consequence of suffering from aggression: stress.

Psychopathic Impulsivity   Serial killer Theodore Bundy displayed many characteristics of a psychopath. He was superficially charming and, as shown here acting out in the courtroom when the judge was away, impulsive in nature. This scene also hints that, like other psychopaths, Bundy felt little or no remorse for his actions.

How's it going?

1. Why is intermale aggression common in so many species?
2. What is the relationship between androgens and aggression?
3. Which neurotransmitter has been most consistently implicated in aggression?

Stress Activates Many Bodily Responses

We all experience stress, but what is it? Attempts to define this term have a certain vagueness. Hans Selye (1907–1982), whose work launched the modern field of stress research, broadly defined *stress* as "the rate of all the wear and tear caused by life" (Selye, 1956). Nowadays, researchers try to sharpen their focus by treating **stress** as a multidimensional concept that encompasses stressful stimuli, the stress-processing system (including cognitive assessment of the stimuli), and responses to stress.

The stages of the stress response

Selye emphasized a close connection between stress and disease that he termed "general adaptation syndrome." He called the initial response to stress the **alarm reaction**. As one part of the alarm reaction, the hypothalamus activates the sympathetic nervous system to ready the body for action; this is the "fight or flight" system we mentioned

psychopath   An individual incapable of experiencing remorse.

stress   Any circumstance that upsets homeostatic balance.

alarm reaction   The initial response to stress.

Figure 11.17 The Alarm Reaction to Stress

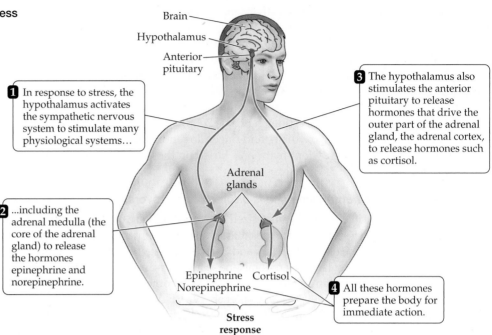

1 In response to stress, the hypothalamus activates the sympathetic nervous system to stimulate many physiological systems…

2 …including the adrenal medulla (the core of the adrenal gland) to release the hormones epinephrine and norepinephrine.

3 The hypothalamus also stimulates the anterior pituitary to release hormones that drive the outer part of the adrenal gland, the adrenal cortex, to release hormones such as cortisol.

4 All these hormones prepare the body for immediate action.

Brain

Hypothalamus

Anterior pituitary

Adrenal glands

Epinephrine   Cortisol
Norepinephrine

Stress response

adrenal medulla The inner core of the adrenal gland.

epinephrine Also called *adrenaline*. A compound that acts both as a hormone (secreted by the adrenal medulla under the control of the sympathetic nervous system) and as a synaptic transmitter.

norepinephrine Also called *noradrenaline*. A neurotransmitter produced and released by sympathetic postganglionic neurons to accelerate organ activity.

adrenal cortex The outer rind of the adrenal gland.

adrenal steroid hormone A steroid hormone that is secreted by the adrenal cortex.

cortisol A glucocorticoid stress hormone of the adrenal cortex.

adaptation stage The second stage in the stress response, including successful activation of the appropriate response systems and the reestablishment of homeostatic balance.

exhaustion stage A stage in the response to stress that is caused by prolonged or frequently repeated stress and is characterized by increased susceptibility to disease.

at the start of the chapter. The "fight or flight" response includes sympathetic stimulation of the core of the adrenal gland, which is called the **adrenal medulla**, to release the hormones **epinephrine** (also known as *adrenaline*) and **norepinephrine** (*noradrenaline*). These hormones act on many parts of the body to boost heart rate, breathing, and other physiological processes that prepare the body for action. As another part of the alarm reaction, the hypothalamus stimulates the anterior pituitary to release a hormone that drives the outer layer of the adrenal gland, the **adrenal cortex**, to release **adrenal steroid hormones** such as **cortisol** (**Figure 11.17**). These hormones act more slowly than epinephrine, but they also ready the body for action, including releasing body stores of energy.

In Selye's scheme, the alarm reaction is followed by the **adaptation stage**, which brings the body back to normal, reestablishing physiological balance. Thus a single, short-lived stressor can be successfully handled. But prolonged or frequently repeated stress leads to the **exhaustion stage**, which is characterized by increased susceptibility to disease. Uncertainty or unpredictability about how to gain positive outcomes when confronted with stressful situations—that is, poor coping strategies—may exacerbate the health consequences of stress (S. Levine and Ursin, 1980).

These stages of hormonal response to stress were studied in a group of young recruits in the Norwegian military both before and during scary parachute training (Ursin et al., 1978). On each jump day, the anterior pituitary released enhanced levels of hormones, and both the sympathetic and parasympathetic systems were activated (**Figure 11.18a**). Initially, cortisol levels were elevated in the blood before each jump, but with more and more successful jumps over successive days, the pituitary-adrenal response soon declined. Epinephrine and norepinephrine were also elevated before the first jumps, but eventually they returned to normal before jumps. Testosterone showed the reverse pattern, falling far below control levels on the first day of training, but returning to normal with subsequent jumps (**Figure 11.18b**). Once the soldiers mastered the jumps, they no longer showing increased hormonal responses, having reached the adaptation stage, so they avoided the exhaustion phase that Selye had described.

Less-dramatic real-life situations also evoke clear endocrine responses (Frankenhaeuser, 1978). For example, riding in a commuter train provokes the release of epinephrine; the longer the ride and the more crowded the train, the greater the hormonal

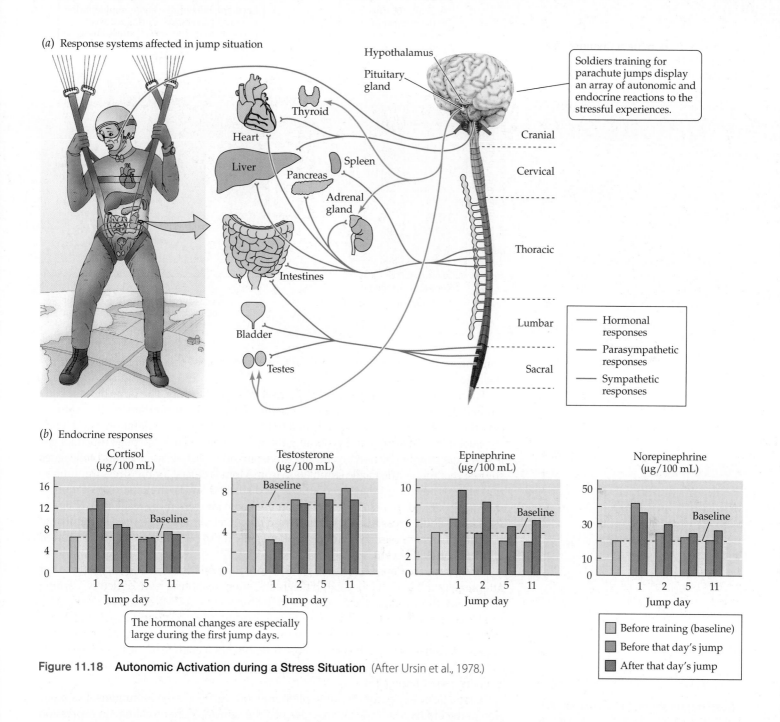

(*a*) Response systems affected in jump situation

Soldiers training for parachute jumps display an array of autonomic and endocrine reactions to the stressful experiences.

Hypothalamus
Pituitary gland
Thyroid
Heart
Liver
Spleen
Pancreas
Adrenal gland
Intestines
Bladder
Testes

Cranial
Cervical
Thoracic
Lumbar
Sacral

— Hormonal responses
— Parasympathetic responses
— Sympathetic responses

(*b*) Endocrine responses

Cortisol (µg/100 mL)
Baseline
Jump day

Testosterone (µg/100 mL)
Baseline
Jump day

Epinephrine (µg/100 mL)
Baseline
Jump day

Norepinephrine (µg/100 mL)
Baseline
Jump day

The hormonal changes are especially large during the first jump days.

☐ Before training (baseline)
☐ Before that day's jump
☐ After that day's jump

Figure 11.18 **Autonomic Activation during a Stress Situation** (After Ursin et al., 1978.)

response (**Figure 11.19a**). Factory work likewise leads to the release of epinephrine; the shorter the work cycle—that is, the more frequently the person has to repeat the same operations—the higher the levels of epinephrine. The stress of a PhD oral exam leads to a dramatic increase in both epinephrine and norepinephrine (**Figure 11.19b**).

Individual differences in the stress response

Why do individuals differ in their responses to stress? One hypothesis focuses on early experience. Rat pups clearly find it stressful to have a human pick them up and handle them. Yet Seymour Levine et al. (1967) found that rats that had been briefly handled as pups were less susceptible to adult stress than were rats that had been left alone as pups. For example, the previously handled rats secreted lower adrenal steroid amounts in response to a wide variety of adult stressors. This effect was termed **stress**

Figure 11.19 Hormonal Changes in Humans in Response to Social Stresses (After Frankenhaeuser, 1978.)

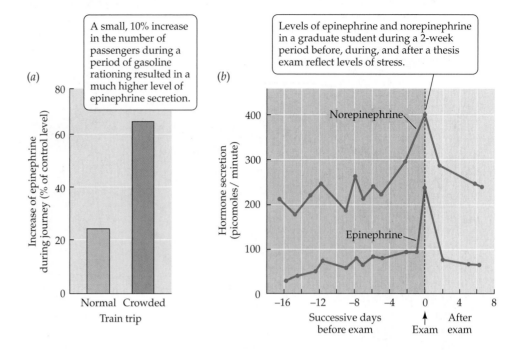

(a) A small, 10% increase in the number of passengers during a period of gasoline rationing resulted in a much higher level of epinephrine secretion.

(b) Levels of epinephrine and norepinephrine in a graduate student during a 2-week period before, during, and after a thesis exam reflect levels of stress.

immunization because a little stress early in life seemed to make the animals more resilient to later stress.

Follow-up research suggests that there is more to the story. The pups did not benefit because they were stressed; they benefited because their mothers *comforted* them *after* the stress. When pups are returned to their mother after a separation, she spends considerable time licking and grooming them. And she will lick the pups much longer if they were handled by humans during the separation. Michael Meaney and colleagues suggest that this gentle tactile stimulation from Mom is crucial for the stress immunization effect. They found that, even among undisturbed litters, the offspring of mother rats that exhibited more licking and grooming behavior were more resilient in their responses to adult stress than other rats were (D. Liu et al., 1997). So the "immunizing" benefit of early stressful experience happens only if the pups are promptly comforted after each stressful event.

If the pups are deprived of their mother for long periods, receiving very little of her attention, then as adults they exhibit a greater stress response, have difficulty learning mazes, and show reduced neurogenesis in the hippocampus (Mirescu et al., 2004). Maternal deprivation exerts this negative effect on adult stress responses by causing long-lasting changes in the expression of adrenal steroid receptors in the brain. This change is termed **epigenetic regulation** because it represents a change in the *expression* of the gene, rather than a change in the encoding region of the gene (*epigenetic* means "above genetics"; see Chapter 13).

Dramatic evidence for the same phenomenon has been seen in humans. Examination of the brains of suicide victims revealed the same epigenetic change in expression of the adrenal steroid receptor, but only in those victims who had a history of being abused or neglected as children (McGowan et al., 2009). The implication is that the early abuse epigenetically modified expression of the gene, making the person less able to handle stress, and thus more likely to become depressed and commit suicide. Suicide victims who had no history of early neglect did not show the epigenetic change, so their depression may have been a response to other influences.

Stress and emotions influence the immune system

The field of **psychosomatic medicine** emphasizes that distinctive behaviors, psychological characteristics, and personality factors may affect either susceptibility or resistance to diverse illnesses. The related field called **health psychology** (or *behavioral medicine*) has developed to focus on identifying ways in which specific emotions and social

stress immunization The concept that mild stress early in life makes an individual better able to handle stress later in life.

epigenetic regulation Changes in gene expression that are due to environmental effects rather than to changes in the nucleotide sequence of the gene.

psychosomatic medicine A field of study that emphasizes the role of psychological factors in disease.

health psychology Also called *behavioral medicine*. A field of study that focuses on psychological influences on health-related processes, such as why people become ill or how they remain healthy.

Figure 11.20   Factors That Interact during the Development and Progression of Disease

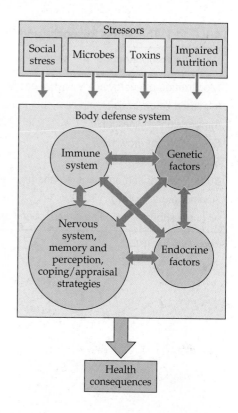

contexts affect health outcomes and disease processes (Baum and Posluszny, 1999; Schwartzer and Gutiérrez-Doña, 2000).

The field of **psychoneuroimmunology** studies how the immune system—with its collection of cells that recognize and attack intruders—interacts with other organs, especially hormonal systems and the nervous system (Ader, 2001). Studies of both human and nonhuman subjects clearly show psychological and neurological influences on the immune system. For example, people with happy social lives are less likely to develop a cold when exposed to the virus (S. Cohen et al., 2006). Likewise, people who tend to feel positive emotions will also produce more antibodies in response to a flu vaccination (Rosenkranz et al., 2003), which should help them fight off sickness. These interactions go both ways: the brain influences responses of the immune system, and immune cells and their products affect brain activities, as **Figure 11.20** shows. You can learn details of how the immune system, endocrine system, and nervous system communicate with one another in **A Step Further 11.4**, on the website.

As an example, stressful exam periods usually suppress the immune system (Glaser et al., 1986). Importantly, the student's *perception* of the stress of the academic program is a predictor of immune system suppression: those who perceive a program as stressful show the most suppression. One experiment considered the effects of university examinations on wound healing in dental students (Marucha et al., 1998). Two small wounds were placed on the roof of the mouth of 11 dental students (sounds like revenge, doesn't it?). The first wound was timed during summer vacation; the second was inflicted 3 days before the first major examination of the term. Two independent daily measures showed that no student healed as rapidly during the exam period, when healing took 40% longer. One measure of immunological response declined 68% during the exam period. The experimenters concluded that even something as transient, predictable, and relatively benign (do students agree with this description?) as final exams can have significant consequences for wound healing.

Why does stress suppress the immune system?

Under stressful conditions, as noted earlier, the brain causes adrenal steroid hormones such as cortisol to be released from the adrenal cortex. These adrenal steroids directly suppress the immune system. But doesn't it seem like a bad idea to suppress immunity just when you are more likely to sustain an injury, and maybe an infection? Modern evolutionary theory offers some possible explanations for this seemingly maladaptive situation (for a very readable account, see Sapolsky, 2004).

To the extent that stress might be a sudden emergency, the *temporary* suppression of immune responses makes some sense because the stress response demands a rapid mobilization of energy. Slow and long-lasting immune responses consume energy that otherwise could be used for dealing with the emergency at hand. A zebra wounded by a lion must first escape and hide, and only then does infection of the wound pose a threat. So the stress of the encounter first suppresses the immune system, conserving resources until a safe haven is found. Later the animal can afford to mobilize the immune system to heal the wound. The adrenal steroids also suppress the swelling (inflammation) of injuries, especially of joints, to help the animal remain mobile long enough to find refuge. It is precisely this action that makes adrenal steroids like prednisone such useful medicines.

In the wild, animals are under stress for only a short while; any animal stressed for a *prolonged* period dies. So natural selection favored stress reactions as a drastic effort to deal with a short-term problem. What makes humans and baboons "special" is that, with our highly social lives and keen analytical minds, we are capable of experiencing stress for prolonged periods—months or even years. The bodily reactions to stress, which evolved to deal with short-term problems, become a handicap when extended

How's it going?

1. What are the stages of stress response as described by Selye?

2. What are the hormonal responses to stressful events, and how do those change as individuals adapt to those events?

3. What is stress immunization, and how is it mediated by epigenetic events?

4. Why do we suppress the immune system in times of stress, and how does that suppression impair health in brainy, social animals like us?

psychoneuroimmunology   The study of the immune system and its interaction with the nervous system and behavior.

TABLE 11.1 The Stress Response and Consequences of Prolonged Stress

Principal components of the stress response	Common pathological consequences of prolonged stress
Mobilization of energy at the cost of energy storage	Fatigue, muscle wasting, diabetes
Increased cardiovascular and cardiopulmonary tone	Hypertension (high blood pressure)
Suppression of digestion	Ulcers
Suppression of growth	Psychogenic dwarfism, bone decalcification
Suppression of reproduction	Suppression of ovulation, impotency, loss of libido
Suppression of immunity and of inflammatory response	Impaired disease resistance
Analgesia (pain-killing)	Apathy
Neural responses, including altered cognition and sensory thresholds	Accelerated neural degeneration during aging

Source: Sapolsky, 1992.

Baboons Can Peacefully Coexist

too long (Sapolsky, 2004). **Table 11.1** lists a variety of stress responses that are beneficial in the short term but detrimental in the long term.

What we have described so far is a really depressing picture. If you are stressed for long periods of time, your health suffers, which brings another source of stress to your life. But don't give up hope. Remember the Forest Troop of baboons we met at the start of the chapter? Perhaps it was fortunate that only the meanest, most aggressive males of the troop got access to the tainted meat. It was mostly those males who died horrible, agonizing deaths, while about half the males and most of the females and youngsters survived. This loss of the most aggressive males had a remarkable effect on the social life of Forest Troop. The surviving males, which had always been a little easier to get along with than most males, never ramped up their aggression to the levels that had been seen before. They might occasionally tussle with one another, but hostilities usually ended before anyone got hurt, and the baboons rarely took out their aggression on the innocent bystanders—the females and the young. Now, everyone spent much more time grooming each other, and otherwise spending "quality baboon time" in peaceful pursuits. Twenty years later, members of the troop still show fewer physiological signs of stress than before.

Perhaps the most important lesson these animals have for us is that most of the stress we experience is avoidable. If we all treat each other better, everyone can benefit. These animals also make it clear that aggression, fighting, and stress are not inevitable consequences of biology. If baboons can, in a short time, convert from a fractious, stressed-out society to a more peaceful, nurturing society, and can maintain that new social order for generations, shouldn't an even more intelligent species like humans be able to follow suit?

Recommended Reading

Ekman, P. (2007). *Emotions Revealed: Recognizing Faces and Feelings to Improve Communication and Emotional Life* (2nd ed.) New York, NY: Owl Books.

Hodgins, S., Viding, E., and Plodowski, A. (2009). *The Neurobiological Basis of Violence: Science and Rehabilitation.* New York, NY: Oxford University Press.

Nelson, R. J. (2006). *The Biology of Aggression.* New York, NY: Oxford University Press.

Nettle, D. (2006). *Happiness: The Science behind Your Smile.* New York, NY: Oxford University Press.

Oatley, K., Keltner, D., and Jenkins, J. M. (2006). *Understanding Emotions* (2nd ed.). Oxford, England: Blackwell.

Panksepp, J. (2004). *Affective Neuroscience: The Foundations of Human and Animal Emotions.* New York, NY: Oxford University Press.

Sapolsky, R. (2004). *Why Zebras Don't Get Ulcers* (3rd ed.). New York, NY: Holt.

CHAPTER **11** VISUAL SUMMARY

You should be able to relate each summary to the adjacent illustration, including structures and processes. If you need to review, go to the figures indicated and read the accompanying text.

mindsmachine.com/vs11

1 **Emotions** are feelings, actions, physiological arousal, and motivational programs. The James-Lange theory considered emotions to be the perceptions of stimulus-induced bodily changes. The Cannon-Bard theory emphasized simultaneous emotional experience and bodily response. In Schachter's cognitive theory, we attribute visceral arousal to specific emotions by analyzing the physical and social context. Review **Figures 11.1** and **11.2**, **Animation 11.2**

2 Distinct facial expressions represent anger, sadness, happiness, fear, disgust, surprise, contempt, and embarrassment, which are interpreted similarly across many cultures. **Polygraphs** actually measure activation of the **sympathetic nervous system**, and therefore reflect stress, not lying. Review **Figures 11.3–11.6, Box 11.1**

3 Facial expressions are controlled by distinct sets of facial muscles controlled by the facial and trigeminal nerves. Emotions evolved as adaptations, and our expression of emotions helps in social relations. The left side of the face, controlled by the right hemisphere of the brain, is more emotionally expressive than the right side of the face Review **Figures 11.7–11.9**

4 Lesions revealed an interconnected brain circuit, the **limbic system** (which includes the amygdala) that mediates and controls emotions. Electrical **self-stimulation** of some brain regions is rewarding. The right cerebral hemisphere is better than the left at interpreting emotional expressions and stimuli. Review **Figures 11.10–11.11**

5 Fear is mediated by circuitry involving the **amygdala**, which receives information both through a rapid direct route and via cortical sensory regions, allowing for both immediate responses and cognitive processing. Review **Figures 11.12** and **11.13, Activity 11.1**

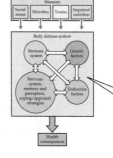

6 **Aggression** is increased by androgens such as **testosterone**. Stimulation of some limbic system regions elicits a species-typical pattern of aggression. **Serotonin** levels are negatively correlated with aggression. Review **Figure 11.16**

7 **Stress** elevates levels of hormones from the **adrenal cortex** (**cortisol**) and the **adrenal medulla** (**epinephrine** and **norepinephrine**), while suppressing other hormones (testosterone). While these responses to stress are adaptive in the short run, in socially complex species that can experience stress for long periods, these hormonal responses decrease immune system competence, damaging our health. Review **Figures 11.17–11.19, Table 11.1, Activity 11.2**

8 The nervous, endocrine, and immune systems interact reciprocally to monitor and maintain health. Emotional traits such as aggressive and depressive characteristics can damage our health by, for example, increasing the risk of heart attack. Review **Figure 11.20**

Go to **mindsmachine.com** for study questions, quizzes, flashcards, and other resources.

chapter 12

Psychopathology:
The Biology of Behavioral Disorders

"My Lobotomy"

Howard Dully's biological mother died unexpectedly when he was 4, and 3 years later his father married a woman named Lucille. For whatever reasons, Howard and Lucille did not get along. Howard was rebellious in the way that virtually all kids are—sassing back, breaking curfew, skipping out on church. But Howard was never violent with his stepmother (or anyone else). He sometimes got in trouble at school, for not paying attention in class or smoking in the bathroom, but not for fighting or damaging school property. Howard's grades were erratic—an A on a test one day, an F on a test the next—but he was not flunking out.

Still, Lucille, frustrated with a headstrong boy in her house, took Howard to six different psychiatrists to find out "what was wrong with him." All concluded that his behavior was normal. But doctor number seven, the famous Walter Freeman diagnosed the boy as *schizophrenic*. In 1960, Freeman gave 12-year-old Howard a *lobotomy*. First Freeman sedated the boy by giving him electroshocks—jolts of electricity across the skull that induce a seizure and render the patient unconscious. Then he lifted the boy's upper eyelids and used a hammer on an ice pick–like device to punch holes in the skull above each eye. He then inserted a device to cut off some of Howard's prefrontal cortex from the rest of his brain. Freeman was an old hand at the procedure, having lobotomized thousands of people, so the procedure itself took only 10 minutes. The total hospital charge was $200.

Family members report that Howard acted like a zombie for several days, and then he was so lethargic and disinterested in the events around him that, according to Freeman's notes, they called Howard "lazy, stupid, dummy, and so on." One aunt said he acted like he was permanently tranquilized. And yet Lucille *still* wanted Howard out of her house. Soon Howard was institutionalized, and he would spend decades in various mental wards. Not until he was 50 was Howard able to find out what had happened to him as a child, a journey he recounts movingly in his memoir, *My Lobotomy*.

To see a video, go to

mindsmachine.com/12.1
Lobotomy

Debilitating mental afflictions have plagued humankind throughout history, plunging their victims into disordered thought and emotional chaos. Despite rapid advances in our understanding of the causes and treatment of schizophrenia, depression, and anxiety disorders, the emotional and economic costs of these illnesses remain great.

delusion A false belief that is strongly held in spite of contrary evidence.

To see the brain in 3D, go to

mindsmachine.com/12.2
Brain Explorer

Changed for Life Twelve-year-old Howard Dully before, during, and after his transorbital lobotomy. The swelling around his eyes eventually went away, but Howard would spend the next four decades in various mental institutions.

In this chapter we survey the major categories of psychiatric disorders and explore their biological underpinnings. Although no single remedy has been found that cures all who suffer from any of these disorders, modern discoveries have restored millions of people to normal life.

The Toll of Psychiatric Disorders Is Huge

The classification of psychiatric disorders is an evolving science and subject to periodic revision, but we know that psychiatric disorders are startlingly prevalent in modern society. About one-third of the U.S. population reports symptoms of a major psychiatric disorder at some point in life (Robins and Regier, 1991). As much as 19% of the adult population experiences psychiatric symptoms in the course of a year (Narrow et al., 2002), and it's estimated that at any given moment nearly 5% of Americans are suffering from a serious mental illness. As shown in **Figure 12.1**, these rates are higher for females than for males, primarily because females are more likely to be depressed. (On the other hand, drug dependency and alcoholism, which are not reflected in Figure 12.1, are much more frequent in males.) Note also that the peak is in 18- to 25-year-olds, because certain psychiatric disorders—for example, schizophrenia—tend to appear in adolescence and young adulthood. Clearly, mental disorders exact an enormous toll on our lives.

The seeds for a biological perspective in psychiatry were sown at the start of the twentieth century. At that time, almost a quarter of the patients in mental hospitals suffered from so-called *paralytic dementia*, featuring sudden onset of **delusions** (false beliefs strongly held in spite of contrary evidence), grandiosity (boastful self-importance), euphoria, poor judgment, impulsive behavior, disordered thought, and physiological signs like abnormal pupillary constriction (Argyll-Robertson, 1869). This disorder, which had been noted in all societies of the world for centuries, was believed to be caused by "weak character."

But in 1911, Hideyo Noguchi (1876–1928) discovered that the brains of people suffering from this disorder had been extensively damaged by syphilis, a sexually

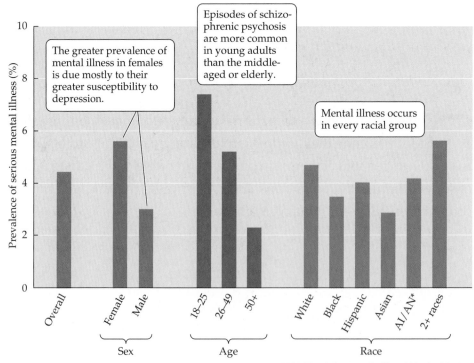

Prevalence is the percentage of people suffering from a disorder at any one point in time.

The greater prevalence of mental illness in females is due mostly to their greater susceptibility to depression.

Episodes of schizophrenic psychosis are more common in young adults than the middle-aged or elderly.

Mental illness occurs in every racial group

Figure 12.1 Prevalence of Serious Mental Illness among U.S. Adults (From the National Institute of Mental Health: http://www.nimh.nih.gov/statistics/SMI_AASR.shtml.)

*AI/AN = American Indian/Alaska Native

transmitted disease. The disease got a new name, *syphilitic psychosis*. Upon the discovery of antibiotics to combat the bacteria that cause the disease, syphilitic psychosis became a rarity. This success encouraged researchers to study other forms of psychopathology in hopes of finding similarly effective treatments.

Schizophrenia is a major neurobiological challenge in psychiatry

Throughout the world and across the centuries, some people have been recognized as unusual because they hear voices that others don't, feel intensely frightened, sense persecution from unseen enemies, and generally act strangely (Bark, 2002; Heinrichs, 2003). For many, this disordered state—now known as **schizophrenia**—lasts a lifetime. For others, it appears and disappears unpredictably. Schizophrenia is also a public health problem, because all too many of the people who suffer from it become homeless on our streets.

Schizophrenia is characterized by an unusual array of symptoms

The term *schizophrenia* (from the Greek *schizein*, "to split," and *phren*, "mind") was introduced early in the twentieth century to convey the idea that various functions of the mind—like memory, perception, and thinking—were split from each other (Bleuler, 1950, originally published in 1911). This poetic but vague description of schizophrenia has been replaced in modern times with more-objective and reliable definitions of the symptoms (K. Schneider, 1959), focusing on "first-rank symptoms," which include (1) auditory hallucinations, (2) highly personalized delusions, and (3) changes in affect (emotion).

Some investigators have proposed a major division of schizophrenic symptoms into two separate groups: positive and negative (**Table 12.1**) (Andreasen, 1991). **Positive symptoms** are abnormal behavioral states that have been *gained*; examples include hallucinations, delusions, and excited motor behavior. **Negative symptoms** are abnormalities resulting from normal functions that have been *lost*—for example, slow and impoverished thought and speech, emotional and social withdrawal, or blunted affect. The fact that positive and negative symptoms respond differently to drug treatments suggests that they arise from different neural abnormalities. Likewise, there are probably several different kinds of schizophrenia, varying in the relative degree of delusions, blunted affect, or cognitive impairment.

Schizophrenia has a heritable component

For many years, genetic studies of schizophrenia were controversial because some early researchers failed to understand that genes need not act in an all-or-none fashion. For any genotype there is often a large range of alternative outcomes determined by both developmental and environmental factors, as we'll see.

FAMILY STUDIES   If schizophrenia is inherited, relatives of people with schizophrenia should show a higher incidence of the disorder than is found in the general population. In addition, the risk of schizophrenia among relatives should increase with the closeness

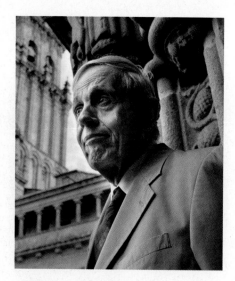

Not So Beautiful Voices   Mathematician John Nash's struggle with schizophrenia is depicted in the Academy Award–winning movie *A Beautiful Mind*. The movie portrays him having elaborate visual hallucinations, but in fact his hallucinations were exclusively auditory, consisting of taunting voices that fueled his paranoid thinking. Auditory hallucinations are common in schizophrenia; visual hallucinations are quite rare.

schizophrenia   A severe psychopathological disorder characterized by negative symptoms such as emotional withdrawal and impoverished thought, and by positive symptoms such as hallucinations and delusions.

positive symptom   In psychiatry, an abnormal behavioral state. Examples include hallucinations, delusions, and excited motor behavior.

negative symptom   In psychiatry, an abnormality that reflects insufficient functioning. Examples include emotional and social withdrawal, blunted affect, and slow and impoverished thought and speech.

TABLE 12.1 Symptoms of Schizophrenia

Positive symptoms	Negative symptoms
Hallucinations, most often auditory	Social withdrawal
Delusions of grandeur, persecution, etc.	Flat affect (blunted emotional responses)
Disordered thought processes	Anhedonia (loss of pleasurable feelings)
Bizarre behaviors	Reduced motivation; poor focus on tasks
	Alogia (reduced speech output)
	Catatonia (reduced movement)

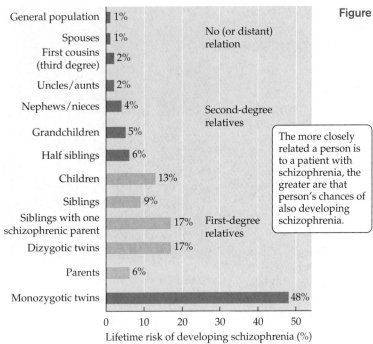

General population 1%
Spouses 1%
First cousins (third degree) 2%
Uncles/aunts 2%
Nephews/nieces 4%
Grandchildren 5%
Half siblings 6%
Children 13%
Siblings 9%
Siblings with one schizophrenic parent 17%
Dizygotic twins 17%
Parents 6%
Monozygotic twins 48%

No (or distant) relation

Second-degree relatives

First-degree relatives

The more closely related a person is to a patient with schizophrenia, the greater are that person's chances of also developing schizophrenia.

Lifetime risk of developing schizophrenia (%)

Figure 12.2   The Heritability of Schizophrenia (After Gottesman, 1991.)

of the relationship because closer relatives share a greater number of genes. Indeed, parents and siblings of people with schizophrenia have a higher risk of becoming schizophrenic than do individuals in the general population (**Figure 12.2**) (Gottesman, 1991). However, the mode of inheritance of schizophrenia is not simple; that is, it does not involve a single recessive or dominant gene (Tamminga and Schulz, 1991). Rather, multiple genes play a role in the emergence of schizophrenia.

ADOPTION STUDIES   It is easy to find fault with family studies. They confuse hereditary and environmental factors because members of a family share both. But what about children who are not raised with their biological parents? In fact, studies of adopted persons confirm a strong genetic factor in schizophrenia. The biological parents of adoptees who suffer from schizophrenia are far more likely to have suffered from this disorder than are the adopting parents (Kety et al., 1975, 1994).

TWIN STUDIES   In twins, nature provides researchers with an excellent opportunity for a genetic experiment. Human twins from the same fertilized egg—called **monozygotic** (*identical*) twins—share an identical set of genes. Twins from two different eggs—**dizygotic** (*fraternal*) twins—have only half of their genes in common, like any pair of siblings. In monozygotic twins, if one of the twins develops schizophrenia, the other twin has a roughly 50-50 chance of also developing the disorder. But in dizygotic twin pairs, this **concordance** (shared characteristic) drops to just 17% or so (see Figure 12.2) (Cardno and Gottesman, 2000). The much higher concordance in the genetically identical, monozygotic twins is strong evidence of a genetic factor. After all, environmental variables like family structure and socioeconomic stress would presumably be comparable for the two kinds of twins. Even with identical twins, however, the concordance rate for schizophrenia is only about 50% (see Figure 12.2), so *genes alone cannot fully explain whether a person will develop schizophrenia*.

What accounts for the 50% of monozygotic twins who are unafflicted? The answer to this question could provide crucial clues about the environmental factors that lead to schizophrenia, and it might suggest ways to protect susceptible people. In these discordant cases, the twin who goes on to develop schizophrenia tends to have an abnormal developmental history in general: lower birth weight; more physiological distress in early life (Torrey et al., 1994; Wahl, 1976); and behavior that seems more submissive, tearful, and sensitive than that of the unaffected twin. The affected twin also may show subtle neurological signs, such as impaired motor coordination (Torrey et al., 1994). Trained observers watching old films of the twins as children can pick out, with uncanny accuracy, which twin went on to suffer from schizophrenia in adulthood (Walker, 1991). People with schizophrenia find it difficult to use normal smooth movements of the eyes to follow a moving target (Avila et al., 2006), and instead show rapid, jerky eye movements (**Figure 12.3**), confirming that motor abnormalities are associated with schizophrenia.

While studies of twins indicate that genes alone cannot account for the development of schizophrenia, they make it clear that genetics contributes to schizophrenia. But which genes are related to this disorder, and what processes do they control?

INDIVIDUAL GENES   It has been difficult to identify any single gene that causes schizophrenia to develop or increases susceptibility (Mowry et al., 2004). In fact, genetic

monozygotic   Referring to twins derived from a single fertilized egg (*identical* twins). Such individuals share an identical set of genes.

dizygotic   Referring to twins derived from separate eggs (*fraternal* twins). Such twins are no more closely related genetically than are other full siblings.

concordance   A characteristic that is seen in both individuals of a pair of twins.

Eye movement recording

Smooth-pursuit response of eyes to moving target in a control subject

Patients with schizophrenia have difficulty making smooth-pursuit movements with their eyes.

Tracking of a patient with schizophrenia

Figure 12.3   Eye Tracking in Patients with Schizophrenia versus Control Subjects

analyses suggest that genes influencing the development of schizophrenia are scattered across many different human chromosomes (Stefansson et al., 2009). Nonetheless, a few genes have been identified that appear to be abnormal in a small proportion of schizophrenia cases, including genes that are known to participate in synaptic plasticity (Kennedy et al., 2003; Mei and Xiong, 2008). In one large Scottish family, the several members who had schizophrenia also carried a mutant, disabled version of a gene, which was therefore named *disrupted in schizophrenia 1* (*DISC1*). We'll discuss *DISC1* further a little later in the chapter.

An interesting *epigenetic factor* (see Chapter 13) in schizophrenia is paternal age: older men are more likely than younger men to have children with schizophrenia (Rosenfield et al., 2010). It is thought that, because the sperm of older men are the product of more cell divisions than the sperm of younger men, they have thus had more opportunity to accumulate mutations caused by errors in copying the chromosomes; these mutations may contribute to the development of schizophrenia in some cases.

Taken together, the studies make it clear that certain genes can indeed increase the risk of developing schizophrenia, but that the environment also matters. As we'll see next, a big factor in whether a person will develop schizophrenia is stress.

RESEARCHERS AT WORK

An integrative model of schizophrenia emphasizes the interaction of multiple factors

We've established that there is genetic influence on schizophrenia, but also that genes alone cannot account for the disorder. What environmental factors contribute to the probability of developing schizophrenia? Research suggests that a variety of stressful events significantly increase the risk. For example, schizophrenia usually appears during a time in life that many people find stressful—the transition from childhood to adulthood, when people deal with physical, emotional, and lifestyle changes (e.g., going away to college). Note that the peak in prevalence of mental illness in Figure 12.1 is seen in the 18- to 25-year-old group.

Prenatal stress—for example, if the mother has an infection while carrying the child—is also a risk factor. The baby of a pregnant woman who contracts influenza in the first trimester of pregnancy is 7 times more likely to develop schizophrenia (P. H. Patterson, 2007). Several other maternal infections also increase chances that the fetus will develop schizophrenia one day (A. S. Brown, 2011). This correlation may be why people born in late winter and early spring are more likely to develop schizophrenia (Messias et al., 2004): their mothers may be more likely to have gotten sick during the winter before, when the fetus was vulnerable. Likewise, if the mother and baby have incompatible blood types, the baby is more likely to develop schizophrenia. Birth complications that deprive the baby of oxygen also increase the probability of schizophrenia (Clarke et al., 2011).

Another risk factor seen in multiple studies is the stress of city living. As **Figure 12.4** shows, people living in a medium-sized city are about one and a half times more likely to develop schizophrenia than are people living in the country. What's more, the earlier in life a person begins living in the city, the greater the risk. People living in a *big* city are even more likely to develop the disorder (Pedersen and Mortensen, 2001). We don't know what it is about living in a city that makes schizophrenia more likely. Pollutants, greater exposure to minor diseases, crowded conditions, tense social interactions—all of these could be considered stressful.

Because we know that some people are genetically more susceptible to schizophrenia than others, these findings suggest that relatively minor stress during development can make the difference in whether schizophrenia develops. It is fascinating, and frightening, to think that events in the womb or early childhood can affect the outcome 16 or 20 years later, when the schizophrenia appears.

Figure 12.4   City Living Increases the Risk of Schizophrenia

Hypothesis
Stress increases the risk of schizophrenia.

Test
Find a data set that lets you compare people from a relatively homogeneous culture and genetic background, such as Denmark. Assuming that city living is more stressful than living in the country, determine whether populations living in a big city, in other (smaller) cities, or in the country differ in the proportion of people diagnosed with schizophrenia.

Result

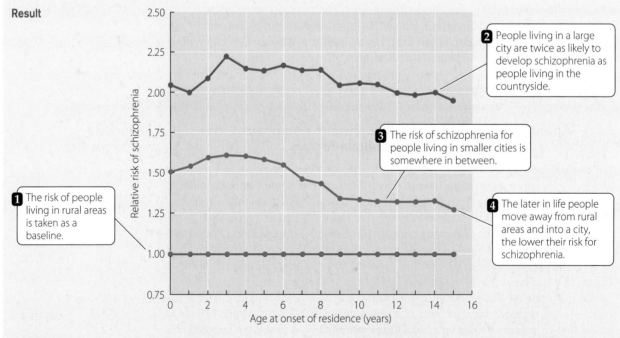

Conclusion
Some aspect of city living, perhaps generalized stress, increases the probability that a person will develop schizophrenia.

Thus the modern view is that schizophrenia is caused by the *interaction of genetic factors and stress*. Each life stage has its own specific features that increase vulnerability to schizophrenia: infections before birth, complications at delivery, urban living in childhood and adulthood (Powell, 2010). From this perspective, the emergence of schizophrenia and related disorders depends on whether a person who is genetically susceptible to schizophrenia is subjected to environmental stressors (**Figure 12.5**). The models of genes interacting with environmental stressors also suggest that we may someday be able to reduce the likelihood that a child at risk will develop schizophrenia. New biological aids, such as functional brain imaging and genetic tools, might help us identify and understand the at-risk child early in life, when interventions to reduce stress might prevent schizophrenia later in life.

Once the interaction of genetic susceptibility and stress results in schizophrenia, the condition affects not only the person's behavior but also the physical state of the brain, as we'll see next.

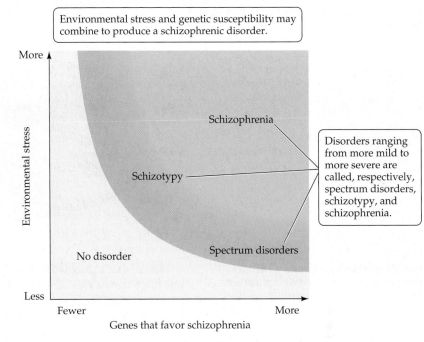

Figure 12.5   **A Model of the Interaction between Stress and Genetic Influences in Schizophrenia** (After Mirsky and Duncan, 1986.)

The brains of some patients with schizophrenia show structural changes

Because the symptoms of schizophrenia can be so marked and persistent, investigators hypothesized early on that the brains of people with this illness would show distinctive and measurable structural abnormalities. Later, CT and MRI scans confirmed this idea, revealing significant, consistent anatomical differences in the brains of many patients with schizophrenia (Trimble, 1991). Interestingly, these scans also confirm the idea that genes alone cannot account for whether a person will develop schizophrenia.

VENTRICULAR ABNORMALITIES   Most patients with schizophrenia have enlarged cerebral ventricles, especially the lateral ventricles (T. M. Hyde and Weinberger, 1990; Vita et al., 2000). An important distinction is that twins with schizophrenia have decidedly enlarged lateral ventricles compared to their well counterparts, whose ventricles are of normal size (**Figure 12.6**) (Torrey et al., 1994). Among people with schizophrenia, those with larger ventricles benefit less from antipsychotic drugs (Garver et al., 2000).

Figure 12.6   **Identical Genes, Different Fates** (After Torrey et al., 1994; MRIs courtesy of E. Fuller Torrey.)

Figure 12.7   Enlarged Ventricles in a Mouse Model (From Pletnikov et al., 2008.)

Transgenic mice expressing the *DISC1* mutation associated with schizophrenia in humans develop enlarged lateral ventricles (green) reminiscent of those in people with schizophrenia.

Control

Mutant

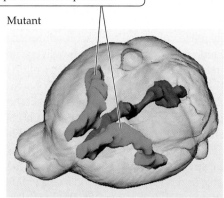

hypofrontality hypothesis   The idea that schizophrenia may reflect underactivation of the frontal lobes.

Recall that a disabled version of the gene *DISC1* is associated with schizophrenia in one large family. The DISC1 protein normally interacts with a bewildering array of neuronal proteins, but one function seems to relate to glutamatergic synapses (Hayashi-Takagi et al., 2010). Creating mice that express the mutant version of *DISC1* that is associated with schizophrenia in humans has a dramatic effect: the mice develop enlarged lateral ventricles (**Figure 12.7**) (Pletnikov et al., 2008) that are very reminiscent of the enlarged ventricles in people with schizophrenia.

What is the significance of enlarged ventricles? Because overall brain size does not seem to be affected in people with schizophrenia or in mice expressing mutant *DISC1*, the enlarged ventricles must come at the expense of brain tissue. Therefore, interest has centered on brain structures that run alongside the lateral ventricles, as discussed in **A Step Further 12.1**, on the website.

CORTICAL ABNORMALITIES   Chronic sufferers of schizophrenia whose disorder started early in life have a thicker corpus callosum, both in anatomical preparations and in CT scans (Bigelow et al., 1983). One postmortem study of frontal cortex from people who had schizophrenia found evidence that neuronal migration had been abnormal during fetal development (Akbarian et al., 1996). Several studies reported a loss of gray matter in schizophrenia patients (M. Suzuki et al., 2002; P. M. Thompson et al., 2001), with a wave of cortical gray matter loss occurring during adolescence in the case of early-onset schizophrenia (**Figure 12.8**).

Although some researchers report that the frontal lobes are especially different in people with schizophrenia, other studies fail to find abnormalities there (Highley et al., 2001; Wible et al., 1995). So if the frontal lobes of people suffering from schizophrenia are not very different in their *structure*, what about the *activity* of the frontal cortex?

Functional maps reveal differences in schizophrenic brains

People with schizophrenia tend to be impaired on neuropsychological tests that are sensitive to frontal cortical lesions. These findings raised the possibility of frontal cortical abnormality as an important component of schizophrenia. Early observations using PET indicated that patients with schizophrenia show relatively less metabolic activity in the frontal lobes (compared with their posterior lobes), while control subjects have more-equal activation of frontal and posterior cortex (M. S. Buchsbaum et al., 1984). This observation led to the **hypofrontality hypothesis** that the frontal lobes are underactive in people with schizophrenia. A review of many studies over the past 25 years seems to support this idea (Minzenberg et al., 2009).

Blood flow levels in the frontal cortex are lower in monozygotic twins who suffer from schizophrenia than in their unaffected twin (Andreasen et al., 1986; Morihisa and McAnulty, 1985). Some experiments show the hypofrontality effect only during difficult

How's it going?

1. What are the first-order symptoms of schizophrenia, and at what stage of life does schizophrenia usually appear?

2. What are the positive and negative symptoms of schizophrenia?

3. Review the evidence that heredity plays a role in schizophrenia.

4. What is the evidence that stress can affect whether a person will develop schizophrenia?

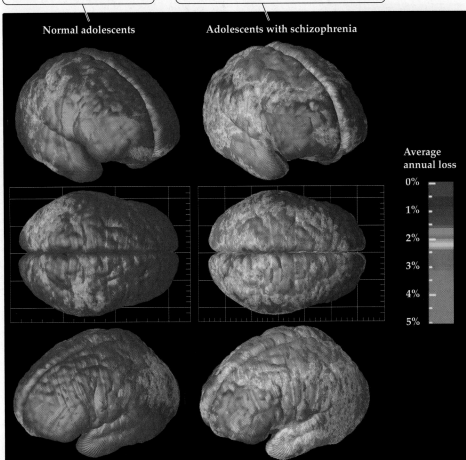

Although neuron loss is a normal part of development…

…adolescents with schizophrenia lose gray matter over wide regions at a faster rate.

Normal adolescents   Adolescents with schizophrenia

Average annual loss

0%

1%

2%

3%

4%

5%

Figure 12.8   Accelerated Loss of Gray Matter in Adolescents with Schizophrenia (From P. M. Thompson et al., 2001; courtesy of Paul Thompson.)

cognitive tasks that particularly depend on the frontal lobes for accurate performance, such as the Wisconsin Card Sorting Task (**Figure 12.9**). Unlike control subjects, subjects with schizophrenia show little increase in their prefrontal activation during the task (D. R. Weinberger et al., 1994). Treatment with drugs that alleviate symptoms of schizophrenia, discussed next, also increase the activation of frontal cortex (Honey et al., 1999).

Figure 12.9   Hypofrontality in Schizophrenia (Courtesy of Karen Berman.)

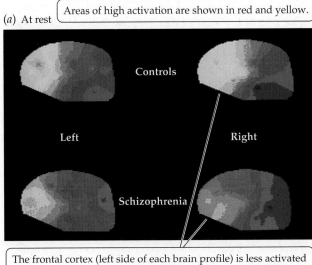

(a) At rest

Areas of high activation are shown in red and yellow.

Controls

Left   Right

Schizophrenia

The frontal cortex (left side of each brain profile) is less activated in patients with schizophrenia compared to their twins who don't have schizophrenia ("controls") both at rest…

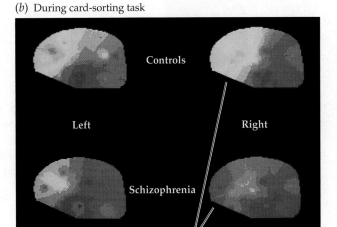

(b) During card-sorting task

Controls

Left   Right

Schizophrenia

…and during the Wisconsin Card Sorting Task, which is very difficult for people with damage to the frontal lobes.

Bedlam   The word *bedlam*, meaning "confusion and uproar," is derived from the name "Bethlem," a hospital for the mentally ill in eighteenth-century London where visitors could, for a penny, peer into rooms to laugh at the suffering of the mentally ill. ("The Interior of Bedlam," from A *Rake's Progress* by William Hogarth, 1763. McCormick Library, Northwestern University.)

Antipsychotic medications revolutionized the treatment of schizophrenia

In the 1930s, there were no effective treatments for schizophrenia. Because patients were often unable to take care of themselves, they were placed in caregiving institutions. In many cases, the health and welfare of patients in these (poorly funded) institutions were badly neglected, leading to recurrent scandals. So perhaps it was in desperation that psychiatrists turned to **lobotomy**, the surgical separation of a portion of the frontal lobes from the rest of the brain, as a treatment for schizophrenia. Certainly there was little scientific evidence to think the surgery would be effective. But early practitioners reported nearly miraculous recoveries that, in retrospect, must be regarded as wishful thinking on the part of the physicians. The surgery may well have made the patients easier to handle, but they were rarely able to leave the mental institution. Used for almost any mental disorder, not just schizophrenia, lobotomies were performed on some 40,000 people in the United States alone (Kopell et al., 2005).

By the 1950s, more and more physicians were skeptical that lobotomy was effective for any disorder, and in 1954 a drug—**chlorpromazine** (trade name Thorazine)—was discovered that quickly replaced lobotomy as a treatment for schizophrenia. Although chlorpromazine was originally developed as an anesthetic, a lucky observation revealed that it could powerfully reduce the "positive" symptoms of schizophrenia, including auditory hallucinations, delusions, and disordered thinking. Ironically, the drug was first promoted as "a lobotomy in a bottle" because at the time, that was viewed as a good thing! But chlorpromazine was much better than a lobotomy, not only because drug treatment is reversible while lobotomy is not, but because the drug actually worked. In fact, the symptoms of schizophrenia that responded to chlorpromazine were exactly those that kept people in mental institutions. The introduction of chlorpromazine truly revolutionized psychiatry, relieving symptoms for millions of sufferers and freeing them from long-term beds in psychiatric hospitals. Unfortunately, sometimes people taking antipsychotics develop undesireable side effects in movement (**Box 12.1**).

Poor Howard Dully, whom we met at the start of the chapter, was very unlucky to run into a physician still performing lobotomies as late as the 1960s. Why didn't Dr. Freeman try giving Howard chlorpromazine? For one thing, the drug helps only positive symptoms, and Howard didn't have any of those—he wasn't hearing voices, experiencing delusions, or suffering disordered thinking at school. For that matter, there's little reason to think the boy had *any* symptoms of schizophrenia (six psychiatrists had declared him "normal"). Unfortunately for Howard, his stepmother just happened upon the wrong physician at the wrong time.

THE DOPAMINE HYPOTHESIS   Chlorpromazine and other **antipsychotic** drugs (also known as **neuroleptics**) that came along a little later were eventually found to share

lobotomy   The surgical separation of a portion of the frontal lobes from the rest of the brain, once used as a treatment for schizophrenia and many other ailments.

chlorpromazine   An antipsychotic drug that replaced lobotomy as a treatment for schizophrenia.

antipsychotic or neuroleptic   Any of a class of drugs that alleviate symptoms of schizophrenia, typically by blocking dopamine receptors.

Another Victim of Lobotomy   Rosemary Kennedy, the younger sister of President John F. Kennedy, shown here with her father, Joseph P. Kennedy, in 1938, when she was 20. Although it is unclear what psychological problems she had, if any, at age 23 she was given a lobotomy and permanently incapacitated. She then lived in private institutions until her death at age 86.

a specific action: they block postsynaptic dopamine receptors, particularly *dopamine D₂ receptors*. Because *all* of the earliest antipsychotic drugs blocked dopamine D_2 receptors, researchers proposed the **dopamine hypothesis**: that people with schizophrenia suffer from an excess of either dopamine release or dopamine receptors.

At about the same time, support for the dopamine hypothesis came from another source: people who were abusing drugs. As a consequence of drug tolerance (see Chapter 4), some daily users of amphetamine reach the point of taking astonishingly high doses—as much as 3,000 milligrams per day—in order to experience the drug's "high." (Compare this with the normal 5-milligram dose used to combat sleepiness.) Many individuals taking these large doses of amphetamine develop symptoms of paranoia, often involving delusions of persecution with auditory hallucinations, and they exhibit suspiciousness and bizarre motor behavior. These symptoms strikingly resemble those of schizophrenia and are referred to as **amphetamine psychosis**. What's more, amphetamine exacerbates the symptoms of schizophrenia. It turns out that amphetamine promotes the release of dopamine and prolongs the action of the released transmitter by blocking reuptake (see Chapter 4). And finally, chlorpromazine treatment rapidly reverses amphetamine psychosis.

In contrast, while drugs such as LSD and mescaline produce some perceptual, cognitive, and emotional changes that resemble psychosis in some ways, the resemblance is superficial at best. For instance, the hallucinations produced by these drugs

dopamine hypothesis   The idea that schizophrenia results from either excessive levels of synaptic dopamine or excessive postsynaptic sensitivity to dopamine.

amphetamine psychosis   A delusional and psychotic state, closely resembling acute schizophrenia, that is brought on by repeated use of high doses of amphetamine.

To see a video, go to

mindsmachine.com/12.3
Tardive Dyskinesia

BOX 12.1 Long-Term Effects of Antipsychotic Drugs

Few people would deny that neuroleptic drugs have revolutionized the treatment of schizophrenia. With such treatment, many people who might otherwise have been in mental hospitals their whole lives can take care of themselves in nonhospital settings. Drugs of this class can justly be regarded as "miracle drugs."

Unfortunately, traditional antipsychotic drugs can have other, undesirable effects as well. Soon after beginning to take these drugs, some people develop maladaptive motor symptoms (**dyskinesia**, from the Greek *dys*, "bad," and *kinesis*, "motion"). Although many of these symptoms are transient and disappear when the dosage of drug is reduced, some drug-induced motor changes emerge only after prolonged drug treatment—after months, sometimes years—and are effectively permanent. The condition, called **tardive dyskinesia** (the Latin *tardus* means "slow"), is characterized by repetitive, involuntary movements, especially involving the face, mouth, lips, and tongue (see the figure). Elaborate, uncontrollable movements of the tongue are particularly prominent, including incessant rolling movements and sucking or smacking of the lips. Some patients show twisting and sudden jerking movements of the arms or legs (Casey, 1989). The atypical

Tardive dyskinesia is a late onset of involuntary movements, often of the lower face. This woman with tardive dyskinesia suffers from involuntary facial movements such as her tongue popping out (*left*) and intense grimacing (*right*).

neuroleptics discussed in the text have fewer dyskinesia side effects than traditional neuroleptics have, but unfortunately they are more likely to lead to weight gain.

The underlying mechanism for tardive dyskinesia continues to be a puzzle. It may arise from the chronic blocking of dopamine receptors, which results in *receptor supersensitivity*. However, tardive dyskinesia frequently takes a long time to develop and tends to be irreversible—a time course that is different from dopamine receptor supersensitivity.

The dopamine receptor supersensitivity resulting from long-term treatment with traditional antipsychotic drugs can have another unusual effect. In some patients, *discontinuation* of the drugs or a lowering of the dosage results in a sudden, marked increase in positive symptoms of schizophrenia, such as delusions or hallucinations. This **supersensitivity psychosis** can often be reversed by the administration of increased dosages of dopamine receptor–blocking agents.

typical neuroleptic An antischizophrenic drug that shows antagonist activity at dopamine D_2 receptors.

atypical neuroleptic An antipsychotic drug that has actions other than or in addition to the dopamine D_2 receptor antagonism that characterizes the typical neuroleptics.

clozapine An atypical neuroleptic.

are usually visual, in contrast to the predominantly auditory hallucinations of schizophrenia. Patients with schizophrenia who are given LSD report that the experience produced by the drug is very different from the experiences of their disorder.

All of the various antipsychotic drugs that are now classified as **typical neuroleptics** are D_2 receptor antagonists (**Figure 12.10a**). In fact, the clinically effective dose of a typical neuroleptic can be predicted from its affinity for D_2 receptors, as the dopamine hypothesis would predict (**Figure 12.10b**). For example, *haloperidol*, discovered a few years after chlorpromazine, has a greater affinity for D_2 receptors and quickly became the more widely used drug. Over the years, other clinical and experimental findings have bolstered the dopamine hypothesis; for example, treating patients who suffer from Parkinson's disease with L-dopa (the metabolic precursor of dopamine) may induce schizophrenia-like symptoms, presumably by boosting the synaptic availability of dopamine.

Although some evidence supports the dopamine hypothesis of schizophrenia, there are also several problems with the hypothesis. For example, there is no correspondence between the speed with which drugs block dopamine receptors (quite rapidly—within hours) and how long it takes for the symptoms to diminish (usually on the order of weeks). Thus, the relation of dopamine to schizophrenia is more complex than just hyperactive dopamine synapses.

Another weakness of the dopamine model of schizophrenia is that some patients don't respond to dopamine antagonists (Alpert and Friedhoff, 1980). Additional problems for the dopamine hypothesis were raised by the search for new neuroleptics to avoid motor side effects (see Box 12.1). Called **atypical neuroleptics**, these drugs generally don't have the selective high affinity for dopamine receptors that is the hallmark of the typical neuroleptics. Atypical neuroleptic drugs such as **clozapine** selectively block

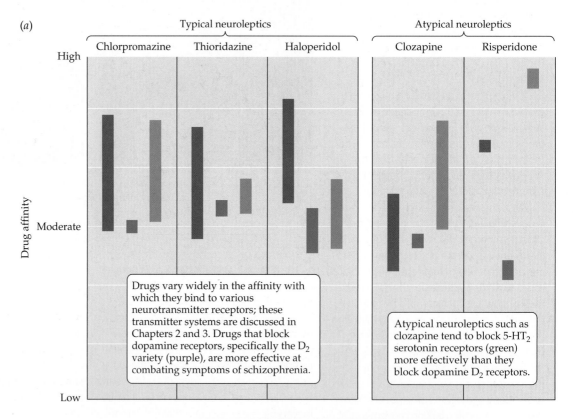

Figure 12.10 Typical Antipsychotic Drugs Affect Dopamine Receptors (Part *a* After Seeman, 1990; *b* after Seeman and Tallerico, 1998.)

serotonin receptors (especially 5-HT$_{2A}$ receptors), as well as other receptor types (see Figure 12.10).

Atypical neuroleptics are just as effective as the older generation of drugs for relieving the symptoms of schizophrenia. So, if the problem is as simple as an overstimulation of dopamine receptors, why are the atypical neuroleptics effective? For example, clozapine can *increase* dopamine release in frontal cortex (Hertel et al., 1999)—hardly what we would expect if excess dopaminergic activity lies at the root of schizophrenia. In fact, it seems that supplementing neuroleptic treatments with L-dopa (thereby increasing dopaminergic activity) actually helps reduce symptoms of schizophrenia (Jaskiw and Popli, 2004).

Until recently, almost all clinicians believed that atypical antipsychotics were more effective than typical antipsychotics for treating schizophrenia, especially for relieving negative symptoms. But a large British study comparing the outcome for patients who had been given the two types of drugs found no difference (Jones et al., 2006). Although the atypical neuroleptics are less likely than typical neuroleptics to cause side effects in motor function (see Box 12.1), they are more likely to cause weight gain (Sikich et al., 2008). So the overall outcome for quality of life appears equivalent for the two types of drugs (Heres et al., 2006).

THE GLUTAMATE HYPOTHESIS   Another drug that, like chlorpromazine, was initially developed as an anesthetic has a much different relationship to schizophrenia. **Phencyclidine (PCP)** was soon found to be a potent **psychotomimetic**; that is, PCP produces phenomena strongly resembling both the positive and negative symptoms of schizophrenia. Users of PCP often experience auditory hallucinations, strange depersonalization, and disorientation; and they may become violent as a consequence of their drug-induced delusions. Prolonged psychotic states can develop with chronic use of PCP.

phencyclidine (PCP)   Also called *angel dust*. An anesthetic agent that is also a psychedelic drug. PCP makes many people feel dissociated from themselves and their environment.

psychotomimetic   A drug that induces a state resembling schizophrenia.

(b)

The effective dose of neuroleptics correlates with their affinity for dopamine D$_2$ receptors.

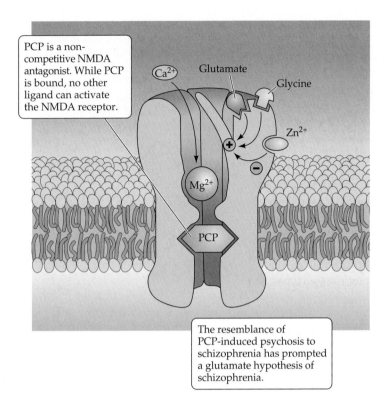

PCP is a non-competitive NMDA antagonist. While PCP is bound, no other ligand can activate the NMDA receptor.

The resemblance of PCP-induced psychosis to schizophrenia has prompted a glutamate hypothesis of schizophrenia.

Figure 12.11 The Effects of PCP on the NMDA Receptor

As illustrated in **Figure 12.11**, PCP acts as an NMDA receptor antagonist. PCP blocks the NMDA receptor's central calcium channel, thereby preventing the endogenous ligand—glutamate—from having its usual effects. Treating monkeys with PCP for 2 weeks produces a schizophrenia-like syndrome, including poor performance on a test that is sensitive to prefrontal damage (Jentsch et al., 1997). Other antagonists of NMDA receptors, such as **ketamine**, have similar effects. These and other observations prompted researchers to propose a **glutamate hypothesis** of schizophrenia (Moghaddam and Adams, 1998), which suggests that schizophrenia results from an *under*activation of glutamate receptors (Coyle et al., 2003). If this hypothesis is true, you might ask whether compounds that increase glutamatergic activity would be effective antischizophrenic drugs. Unfortunately, selective NMDA receptor agonists tend to produce seizures, so glutamatergic-boosting compounds are not an option.

The glutamate hypothesis has been expanded to suggest that underactivation of *all glutamate receptors*, not just the NMDA subtype, contributes to schizophrenia. This possibility might help explain the effectiveness of the atypical neuroleptics, which act on 5-HT_{2A} serotonin receptors, because some metabotropic glutamate receptors (mGluR's) (see Chapter 4) form complexes with 5-HT_{2A} receptors. Atypical neuroleptics, which block 5-HT_{2A} receptors, seem to make nearby mGluR's more effective (González-Maeso et al., 2008), so perhaps they reduce schizophrenia symptoms indirectly, by boosting mGluR responsiveness. If so, then direct stimulation of the proper class of mGluR's (there are at least eight different subtypes; Mueller et al., 2004) might someday provide a third generation of antipsychotics.

Mood Disorders Are a Major Psychiatric Category

Disturbances of mood are a fact of life for humans; most of us experience periods of unhappiness that we commonly describe as depression. But for some people, an unhappy mood state is more than a passing phase. This condition is more common in women than in men. A higher level of education makes depression less likely, but depression can and does afflict people of every race and ethnicity (CDC, 2010).

Depression is the most prevalent mood disorder

Clinically, **depression** is characterized not just by sadness, but by a combination of unhappy mood, loss of interests, reduced energy, changes in appetite and sleep patterns, and a loss of pleasure in most things. Difficulty in concentration and restless agitation or torpor are common; the person may dwell on thoughts of death or even contemplate suicide. Pessimism seems to seep into every act (Solomon, 2001). Periods of such **unipolar depression** (depression that alternates with normal emotional states) can occur with no readily apparent stress. Without treatment, the depression often lasts several months (Cassens et al., 1990). A second major type of mood disorder is *bipolar disorder* (formerly known as *manic-depressive illness*), which is characterized by repeated fluctuation between depressive periods and episodes of euphoric, sometimes grandiose, positive mood (or *mania*). We'll discuss bipolar disorder a little later.

Depression can be lethal, as it may lead to suicide. Most estimates indicate that about 80% of all suicide victims are profoundly depressed. Whether or not the person

How's it going?

1. Compare the evidence supporting the dopamine hypothesis of schizophrenia, and the evidence casting doubt on this hypothesis.

2. What distinguishes typical neuroleptics from atypical neuroleptics?

3. Which drugs can induce a psychosis resembling schizophrenia? What receptor(s) do these drugs act on?

ketamine A dissociative anesthetic drug, similar to PCP, that acts as an NMDA receptor antagonist.

glutamate hypothesis The idea that schizophrenia may be caused, in part, by understimulation of glutamate receptors.

depression A psychiatric condition characterized by such symptoms as an unhappy mood; loss of interests, energy, and appetite; and difficulty concentrating.

unipolar depression Depression that alternates with normal emotional states.

is depressed, many suicides appear to be impulsive acts. For example, one classic study found that of over 500 people who were prevented from jumping off the Golden Gate Bridge in San Francisco, only 6% later went on to commit suicide (Seiden, 1978). Similarly, suicide rates went down by a third in Britain when that country switched from using coal gas, which contains lots of deadly carbon monoxide, to natural gas for heating. The suicide rate has remained at that reduced level in the 40+ years since. Apparently those thousands of Britons who would have found it easy to follow a suicidal impulse by turning on the kitchen oven, did not kill themselves when more planning was required. Thus, it is important for society to erect barriers, either literally (e.g., on bridges) or metaphorically, to make it difficult for people suffering from depression to kill themselves. If suicide is averted the first time it is seriously attempted, the person is very unlikely to ever try it again.

Inheritance is an important determinant of depression

Genetic studies of depressive disorders reveal strong hereditary contributions. The concordance rate for monozygotic twins (about 60%) is substantially higher than for dizygotic twins (about 20%) (Kendler et al., 1999). The concordance rates for monozygotic twins are similar whether the twins are reared apart or together. Although several early studies implicated specific chromosomes, subsequent research has failed to identify any particular gene (Risch et al., 2009). So, as is the case for schizophrenia, there probably is no single gene for depression. Rather, *many* genes contribute to making a person more or less susceptible, and environmental factors determine whether depression results.

The brain changes with depression

Most reports of differences in the brains of depressed people focus on functional changes. PET scans of depressed patients show increases in blood flow, suggesting greater activity, in the prefrontal cortex and the amygdala compared to control subjects (**Figure 12.12**) (Drevets, 1998). In addition to increasing in the prefrontal cortex, blood flow decreases in the parietal and posterior temporal cortex and in the anterior cingulate—systems that have been implicated in attention (see Chapter 14). The increase in blood flow in the amygdala—a structure involved in mediating fear (see Chapter 11)—persists even after the depression has lifted.

People at risk for depression (because they are descendants of someone with severe depression) also have a thinner cortex across large swaths of the right hemisphere than do control subjects (B. S. Peterson et al., 2009), which might make them vulnerable to depression. There is also evidence that people who are depressed have difficulties regulating stress hormone release, as discussed in **A Step Further 12.2**. However, whether the change in stress hormone response is a *cause* or a *result* of depression is unknown.

Despite the many unknowns about the cause of depression, several treatments are effective for some people, as we discuss next.

A wide variety of treatments are available for depression

Electroconvulsive shock therapy (**ECT**)—the intentional induction of a large-scale seizure (Weiner, 1994)—was originally deployed during the 1930s in a desperate and unsuccessful attempt to relieve the symptoms of schizophrenia. (Recall that Howard Dully was given several ECT treatments by Dr. Freeman simply to anesthetize him long enough to receive a lobotomy.) Despite its failure at helping sufferers of schizophrenia, clinical observations soon revealed that ECT *could* rapidly reverse severe depression. The advent of antidepressant drugs has made ECT less common, but ECT remains an important tool for treating severe, drug-resistant depression (M. Fink and Taylor, 2007). A more modern technique for altering cortical electrical activity, called *transcranial magnetic stimulation* (*TMS*; see Chapter 2), is also being explored as a treatment for depression (D. R. Kim et al., 2009).

Today, the most common treatment for depression is the use of drugs that affect the monoamine transmitters: norepinephrine, dopamine, and serotonin. The first

PET scans reveal increased activity in the prefrontal cortex and the amygdala of depressed patients.

Figure 12.12 Brain Activity Patterns in Depression (Courtesy of Wayne C. Drevets.)

electroconvulsive shock therapy (ECT) A last-resort treatment for unmanageable depression in which a strong electrical current is passed through the brain, causing a seizure.

TABLE 12.2 Drugs Used to Treat Depression

Drug class	Mechanism of action	Examples[a]
Monoamine oxidase (MAO) inhibitors	Inhibit the enzyme monoamine oxidase, which breaks down serotonin, norepinephrine, and dopamine	Marplan, Nardil, Parnate
Tricyclics and heterocyclics	Inhibit the reuptake of norepinephrine, serotonin, and/or dopamine	Elavil, Wellbutrin, Aventyl, Ludiomil, Norpramin
Selective serotonin reuptake inhibitors (SSRIs)	Block the reuptake of serotonin, having little effect on norepinephrine or dopamine synapses	Prozac, Paxil, Zoloft

[a]We give here the more commonly used trade names rather than chemical names.

antidepressants were inhibitors of **monoamine oxidase** (**MAO**), the enzyme that normally inactivates monoamines (Schildkraut and Kety, 1967). The fact that MAO inhibitors raise the level of monoamines present in synapses suggests that depressed people do not get enough stimulation at monoamine synapses (the so-called *monoamine hypothesis of depression*). A second generation of antidepressants, called *tricyclics*, inhibits the reuptake of monoamines, which similarly boosts their synaptic activity. ECT may help depression by inducing the release of monoamines.

Among the monoamines, serotonin seems to play an especially important role in depression (Asberg et al., 1986; L. Du et al., 2000; Svenningsson et al., 2006). The most recently developed class of antidepressants—**selective serotonin reuptake inhibitors** (**SSRIs**), such as Prozac (**Table 12.2**) (see Chapter 4), are more effective than MAO inhibitors and tricyclics, and they have fewer side effects. In rats, SSRIs increase the birth of new neurons in the hippocampus (Sahay and Hen, 2007), which may mediate some of the mood effects of the drugs.

However, there is a problem with the idea that reduced serotonin stimulation causes depression. We know that SSRI drugs increase synaptic serotonin within hours of administration. Yet it typically takes *several weeks* of SSRI treatment before people feel better. This paradox suggests that it is the brain's *response* to increased synaptic serotonin that relieves the symptoms, and that this response takes time. So even though boosting serotonin helps some people, their depression may originally have been caused by other factors in the brain.

While SSRIs help many people who are depressed, they do not help everyone. In placebo-controlled trials, although a slightly higher proportion of people report relief among those taking the drug (Turner et al., 2008), about a third of the people taking the *placebo* also feel better. This result suggests that some people helped by SSRI treatment are actually benefiting from a placebo effect (Berton and Nestler, 2006). One review concluded that only a minority of depressed patients, the 13% constituting the most severe cases, responded significantly better to SSRIs than to placebos (Fournier et al., 2010). Furthermore, only about half of the people getting the drug are completely "cured," and about 20% show no improvement at all.

Finally, there is no evidence that SSRIs or any other antidepressant drugs do better than placebos when given to children or teenagers (Bower, 2006), yet millions of American children have been given prescriptions for SSRIs. This is unfortunate, because evidence suggests that SSRIs actually increase the risk of suicide in children and adolescents (Olfson et al., 2006), and that drug companies have concealed these troubling data (Ramchandani, 2004). Other drugs being studied as potential antidepressants are the glutamate receptor antagonist ketamine (see Chapter 4), which relieves depression almost instantly (Machado-Viera et al., 2009); and leptin (Lu, 2007), the hormone normally secreted by fat cells (see Chapter 9).

An unusual treatment for depression involves stimulation of the vagus nerve (cranial nerve X; see Chapter 2). In this treatment, a pacemaker periodically applies mild stimulation to the nerve via implanted electrodes. The treatment is offered for people who have

monoamine oxidase (MAO)   An enzyme that breaks down and thereby inactivates monoamine transmitters.

selective serotonin reuptake inhibitor (SSRI)   A drug that blocks the reuptake of transmitter at serotonergic synapses. SSRIs are commonly used to treat depression.

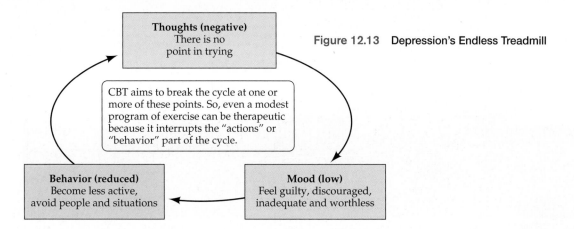

Figure 12.13   Depression's Endless Treadmill

Thoughts (negative)
There is no
point in trying

CBT aims to break the cycle at one or
more of these points. So, even a modest
program of exercise can be therapeutic
because it interrupts the "actions" or
"behavior" part of the cycle.

Behavior (reduced)
Become less active,
avoid people and situations

Mood (low)
Feel guilty, discouraged,
inadequate and worthless

not gotten relief through drugs or ECT, but it is an expensive procedure and there is little evidence that it actually works (Boodman, 2006; Grimm and Bajbouj, 2010). Because the electrodes, once implanted, cannot be safely removed, it is also an irreversible step. Likewise, **deep brain stimulation** (**DBS**), mild electrical stimulation of brain sites through a surgically implanted electrode, is being directed at the cingulate cortex to treat depression that resists other treatments (Kringelbach et al., 2007). The effectiveness of DBS or vagal nerve stimulation for depression is difficult to evaluate because trials have few subjects and most studies have no placebo control (R. Robinson, 2009). The lack of such controls is unfortunate because we know depression is very susceptible to placebo effects. Patients may be reluctant to have a wire permanently implanted in their neck or head if there's a chance that they will be receiving only sham stimulation.

Despite the overwhelming popularity of SSRIs for treating depression, 20 or so sessions of **cognitive behavioral therapy** (**CBT**), psychotherapy aimed at correcting negative thinking (**Figure 12.13**) and improving interpersonal relationships, is about as effective as SSRI treatment (Butler et al., 2006). Furthermore, the rate of relapse is lower for CBT than for SSRI treatment (DeRubeis et al., 2008). Interestingly, CBT and SSRI treatment *together* are more effective in combating depression than either one is alone (March et al., 2004).

Why do more females than males suffer from depression?

Studies all over the world show that more women than men suffer from major depression. In the United States, women are twice as likely as men to suffer major depression (Robins and Regier, 1991). Some researchers suggest that the apparent sex difference reflects patterns of help-seeking by males and females—that women are willing to use health facilities, while men see that as a sign of weakness. But sex differences in the incidence of depression also are evident in door-to-door surveys (Robins and Regier, 1991), which would appear to rule out the simple explanation that women seek treatment more often than men do.

Some researchers have emphasized gender differences in endocrine physiology. The appearance of clinical depression often is related to events in the female reproductive cycle—for example, before menstruation, during use of contraceptive pills, following childbirth, and during menopause. Although there is little relation between circulating levels of individual hormones and measures of depression, the phenomenon of **postpartum depression**, a bout of depression immediately preceding and/or following childbirth, suggests that some combination of hormones can precipitate depression. About one out of every seven pregnant women will show symptoms of depression (Dietz et al., 2007). Because postpartum depression may affect the mother's relationship with her child and may have long-lasting deleterious effects on the child's behavior (Tronick and Reck, 2009), there is growing alarm about this problem. No one knows how SSRIs and other antidepressants taken by the mother would affect breast-fed infants, so CBT is the preferred treatment for postpartum depression.

Depression   For reasons that are not understood, women are more likely than men to suffer from depression.

deep brain stimulation (DBS)   Mild electrical stimulation through an electrode that is surgically implanted deep in the brain.

cognitive behavioral therapy (CBT)   Psychotherapy aimed at correcting negative thinking and consciously changing behaviors as a way of changing feelings.

postpartum depression   A bout of depression that afflicts a woman either immediately before or after giving birth.

(*a*) Sleep pattern of a patient with depression

(*b*)

Figure 12.14 **Sleep and Depression** (Part *b* after Gillin et al., 1981 and Kupfer et al., 1982.)

Sleep characteristics change in affective disorders

Difficulty falling asleep and inability to maintain sleep are common in depression. In addition, EEG sleep studies of depressed patients show certain abnormalities that go beyond difficulty falling asleep. The sleep of patients with major depressive disorders is marked by a striking reduction in stage 3 of slow-wave sleep (see Chapter 10) and a corresponding increase in stages 1 and 2 (**Figure 12.14a**). In addition, depressed patients enter rapid-eye-movement sleep (REM sleep) much sooner after sleep onset (**Figure 12.14b**); the length of time before REM sleep begins correlates with the severity of depression. Furthermore, the distribution of REM sleep across the night is altered, with an increased amount of REM sleep occurring during the first half of sleep, as though REM sleep were displaced toward an earlier period in the night (Wehr et al., 1985).

In addition to these links between the daily rhythm of sleep and depression, seasonal rhythms have been implicated in a particular depressive condition known as *seasonal affective disorder* (*SAD*), which is described in **A Step Further 12.3**.

Scientists are still searching for animal models of depression

Everyone agrees that an animal model of depression could be invaluable, as it might reveal underlying mechanisms, or offer a convenient way to screen potential treatments (Lachman et al., 1993). But it's not clear that any animal model has lived up to this promise so far (O'Neil and Moore, 2003). If depression were caused by the mutation of a particular gene, it might be possible to create a model by introducing that mutated gene in mice. But in fact, it appears that human depression is influenced by many genes, each having a modest effect alone. Plus, some of the most powerful effects of depression are internal—apathy and a feeling of hopelessness—and thus are difficult to assess in species we can't talk to.

Still, many of the signs of depression—such as decreased social contact, problems with eating, and changes in activity—are observable behaviors. So researchers have used these behaviors to evaluate animal models of depression. In one stress model—**learned helplessness**—an animal is exposed to a repetitive stressful stimulus, such as an electrical shock, that it cannot escape. Like depression, learned helplessness has been linked to a decrease in serotonin function (Petty et al., 1994). Removing the olfactory bulb from rodents also creates a model of depression: the animals display irritability, preferences for alcohol, and elevated levels of corticosteroids—all of which are reversed by many antidepressants. A strain of rats created through selective breeding—the Flinders-sensitive line—has been proposed as a model of depression because these animals show reduced overall activity, reduced body weight, increased REM sleep, learning difficulties, and exaggerated response to chronic stress (Overstreet, 1993).

learned helplessness A learning paradigm in which individuals are subjected to inescapable, unpleasant conditions.

(*a*) Manic phase

(*b*) Depressive phase

Figure 12.15   Functional Images of Bipolar Disorder (Courtesy of Dr. Robert G. Kohn, Brain-Spect.com.)

There are dramatic differences in brain activity between the manic (*a*) and depressive (*b*) phases of this person's bipolar disorder. White indicates the greatest brain activity, while blue indicates the lowest.

These varied animal models may be useful in finding the essential mechanisms that cause and maintain depression in humans.

People with bipolar disorder show repeating mood cycles

Bipolar disorder is characterized by periods of depression alternating with periods of excessively expansive mood (or *mania*) that includes sustained overactivity, talkativeness, strange grandiosity, and increased energy (**Figure 12.15**). The rate at which the alternation occurs varies between individuals: some patients exhibit *rapid-cycling* bipolar disorder, defined as consisting of four or more distinct cycles in one year (and some individuals have many more cycles than that; some may even show several cycles per *day*).

Men and women are equally affected by bipolar disorder, and the age of onset is usually much earlier than that of unipolar depression. Bipolar disorder is clearly heritable, with several different genes affecting the probability of the disorder (Faraone et al., 2004; Smoller and Finn, 2003).

The neural basis of bipolar disorder is not fully understood, but since the 1980s it has been known that patients with bipolar disorder exhibit enlarged ventricles on brain scans. As in schizophrenia (see Figure 12.6), this enlargement probably indicates reduced gray matter, although the specific regions affected may differ (Arnone et al., 2009). The more manic episodes the person has experienced, the greater the reduction in gray matter, suggesting an accumulation of brain loss over time (Moorhead et al., 2007).

These changes in the brain are similar to those seen in people with schizophrenia, and some researchers believe that bipolar disorder has more in common with schizophrenia than with unipolar depression. (This is one reason why old terms for bipolar disorder—*bipolar depression* and *manic depression*—are falling out of favor.) For example, the self-aggrandizing delusions and extreme talkativeness of people in the manic phase of bipolar disorder may have frank delusions (e.g., "The president called me this morning to thank me for my efforts") that resemble those in schizophrenia. In addition, families in which some individuals have been diagnosed with bipolar disorder are more likely than other families to have individuals with a diagnosis of schizophrenia (Lichtenstein et al., 2009; van Os and Kapur, 2009). And although typical antipsychotics do not seem to help people with bipolar disorder, the newer, atypical antipsychotics seem to help dampen the manic phase in people with bipolar disorder.

However, most people suffering from bipolar disorder benefit from treatment with the element **lithium** (Kingsbury and Garver, 1998). The effect of lithium on bipolar disorder was discovered by accident when it was intended as an inert "control" for another drug, so the mechanism of action is not understood. Lithium has wide-ranging effects

A Disturbance in the Force Actress Carrie Fisher, who played Princess Leia in the original *Star Wars* series, has written about her struggles with bipolar disorder.

bipolar disorder Also called *manic-depressive illness*. A psychiatric disorder characterized by periods of depression that alternate with excessive, expansive moods.

lithium An element that, administered to patients, often relieves the symptoms of bipolar disorder.

How's it going?

1. What are the symptoms of depression, and how does depression differ from simple sadness?

2. What treatments for depression arose in the twentieth century, and which treatment is used most often today?

3. What is bipolar disorder, and how does it compare to unipolar depression and to schizophrenia. How is it treated?

on the brain, including interacting with a protein that is part of the circadian molecular clock (see Chapter 10) (L. Yin et al., 2006). Because lithium has a narrow range of safe doses (see Chapter 4), care must be taken to avoid toxic side effects of an overdose. Nevertheless, well-managed lithium treatment produces marked relief for many patients and even has been reported to increase the volume of gray matter in the human brain (G. J. Moore et al., 2000).

The fact that the manic phases blocked by lithium are so exhilarating may be the reason that some bipolar clients stop taking the medication. Unfortunately, doing so means that the depressive episodes return as well. As in unipolar depression, transcranial magnetic stimulation may provide a nonpharmacological treatment alternative in difficult cases of bipolar disorder (Michael and Erfurth, 2004). Furthermore, mounting evidence suggests that some forms of CBT for mild cases of bipolar disorder can be as effective as drug treatments (Hollon et al., 2002), and perhaps can be beneficially combined with other forms of treatment.

There Are Several Types of Anxiety Disorders

All of us have at times felt apprehensive and fearful. But some people experience this state with an intensity that is overwhelming and includes irrational fears, a sense of terror, body sensations such as dizziness, difficulty breathing, trembling, shaking, and a feeling of loss of control. Anxiety can be lethal: men with panic disorder are more likely than controls to die from cardiovascular disease or suicide (Coryell et al., 1986).

The American Psychiatric Association distinguishes several major types of **anxiety disorders**. *Phobic disorders* are intense, irrational fears that become centered on a specific object, activity, or situation that the person feels compelled to avoid. Anxiety disorders also include *panic disorder*, characterized by recurrent transient attacks of intense fearfulness, as well as *generalized anxiety disorder*, in which persistent, excessive anxiety and worry are experienced for months. Other anxiety disorders that we'll consider are posttraumatic stress disorder and obsessive-compulsive disorder. There is a strong genetic contribution to each of these disorders (Shih et al., 2004).

Some patients who suffer from recurrent panic attacks have temporal lobe abnormalities (Ontiveros et al., 1989). Overall volume of the temporal lobes tends to be lower in patients with panic disorder (Vythilingam et al., 2000). Given the special role of the amygdala in mediating fear (see Chapter 11), changes may be particularly evident in the amygdala and associated circuitry (Rauch et al., 2003).

Drug treatment of anxiety provides clues to the mechanisms of this disorder

Throughout history, people have consumed all sorts of substances in the hopes of controlling anxiety. The list includes alcohol, bromides, scopolamine, opiates, and barbiturates. In the 1950s the drug meprobamate (Miltown) was introduced as a tranquilizer, and it became an instant best seller, ushering in the modern age of anxiety pharmacotherapy. Soon researchers discovered a new class of drugs called **benzodiazepines**, which quickly replaced Miltown as the favored drugs for treating anxiety. One type of benzodiazepine—diazepam (trade name Valium)—is one of the most prescribed drugs in history. Other commonly prescribed benzodiazepines include Xanax, Halcion, and Ativan. Such drugs that combat anxiety are commonly described as **anxiolytic** ("anxiety-dissolving"), although at high doses they also have anticonvulsant and sleep-inducing properties. The anxiolytic drugs are also discussed in Chapter 4.

Anxiolytic benzodiazepines bind to GABA receptors, where they act as noncompetitive agonists. Recall from Chapter 4 that GABA is the most common inhibitory transmitter in the brain. When GABA is released from a presynaptic terminal and activates postsynaptic receptors, it hyperpolarizes the target neuron and therefore inhibits it from firing. Benzodiazepines alone have little effect on the GABA receptor, but in the presence of GABA they markedly enhance the GABA-provoked hyperpolarization. In other words, benzodiazepines boost GABA-mediated postsynaptic inhibition.

anxiety disorder   Any of a class of psychological disorders that include recurrent panic states, generalized persistent anxiety disorders, and posttraumatic stress disorder.

benzodiazepine   Any of a class of antianxiety drugs are agonists of GABA receptors in the central nervous system. One example is diazepam (Valium).

anxiolytic   A substance that is used to combat anxiety. Examples include alcohol, opiates, barbiturates, and the benzodiazepines.

Figure 12.16   The Distribution of Benzodiazepine Receptors in the Human Brain (Courtesy of Goran Sedvall.)

This PET scan of benzodiazepine receptors shows their wide distribution in the brain, especially the cortex. Highest concentrations are in red; lowest concentrations are in blue.

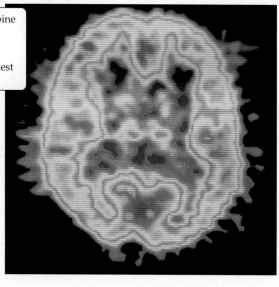

Interestingly, the brain probably makes its own anxiety-relieving substances that interact with the benzodiazepine-binding site on the GABA receptor; the neurosteroid allopregnanolone is a prime candidate for this function. Drugs developed to act at this site are effective anxiolytics in both rats and humans (Rupprecht et al., 2009). These GABA receptors are widely distributed throughout the brain, especially in the cerebral cortex (**Figure 12.16**) and some subcortical areas, such as the hippocampus and the amygdala.

Although the benzodiazepines remain an important category of anxiolytics, especially for acute attacks, other anxiety-relieving drugs have been developed. A notable example is the drug buspirone (Buspar), an agonist at serotonin 5-HT$_{1A}$ receptors that can provide relief from anxiety. This effect is consistent with functional-imaging research that reveals an abnormal density of 5-HT$_{1A}$ receptors in the brains of people with anxiety disorders (Neumeister et al., 2004). SSRI antidepressants, such as paroxetine (Paxil) and fluoxetine (Prozac), which increase the stimulation of serotonin receptors, are also sometimes effective treatments for anxiety disorders.

In posttraumatic stress disorder, horrible memories won't go away

Some people experience especially awful moments in life that seem indelible, resulting in vivid impressions that persist the rest of their lives. The kind of event that seems particularly likely to produce subsequent stress disorders is intense and usually associated with witnessing abusive violence and/or death. Examples include the sudden loss of a close friend, rape, torture, kidnapping, or profound social dislocation, such as in forced migration. In these cases, memories of horrible events intrude into consciousness and produce the same intense visceral arousal—the fear and trembling and general autonomic activation—that the original event caused. These traumatic memories are easily reawakened by stressful circumstances and even by harmless stimuli that somehow prompt recollection of the original event. An ever-watchful and fearful stance becomes the portrait of individuals afflicted with what is called **posttraumatic stress disorder (PTSD)**, formerly called *combat fatigue*, *war neurosis*, or *shell shock*.

Analysis of a random sample of Vietnam War veterans indicates that 19% had PTSD at some point after service. This was the rate for *all* Vietnam veterans; of those exposed to intense war zone stressors, more than 35% developed PTSD at some point, and most of them were still suffering from the disorder *decades* later (Dohrenwend et al., 2006). Gulf War veterans may be even more likely to suffer from PTSD (Institute of Medicine, 2010).

Genetic factors affect vulnerability to PTSD, as indicated in twin studies of Vietnam War veterans who had seen combat, which showed that monozygotic twins were more similar than dizygotic twins. People who display combat-related PTSD show (1) memory changes such as amnesia for some war experiences, (2) flashbacks, and (3) deficits in short-term memory (Bremner et al., 1993). These memory disturbances suggest involvement of the hippocampus (see Chapter 13), and indeed the volume of the right hippocampus is smaller in combat veterans with PTSD than in controls, with no differences in other brain regions (Bremner et al., 1995). It was once widely assumed that the stressful episode caused the hippocampus to shrink, but some veterans suffering PTSD left a monozygotic twin at home, and it turns out that the nonstressed twins without PTSD also tend to have a smaller hippocampus (Gilbertson et al., 2002). So some inherited characteristic that's associated with having a small hippocampus may also be associated with susceptibility to developing PTSD if exposed to stress.

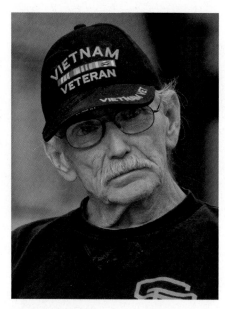

Delayed Reaction   Many combat veterans suffer from PTSD for years afterward.

posttraumatic stress disorder (PTSD)
Formerly called *combat fatigue*, *war neurosis*, or *shell shock*. A disorder in which memories of an unpleasant episode repeatedly plague the victim.

Figure 12.17 A Neural Model of Post-traumatic Stress Disorder

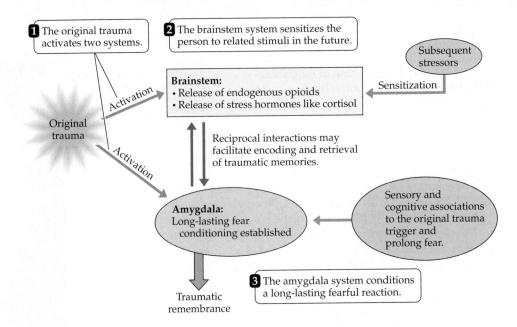

A comprehensive psychobiological model of the development of PTSD draws connections among the symptoms and the neural mechanisms of fear conditioning, behavioral sensitization, and extinction (Charney et al., 1993). Work in animals revealed that this type of memory—**fear conditioning**—is very persistent and involves the amygdala and brainstem pathways that are part of a circuit of startle response behavior (see Chapter 11). The persistence of memory and fear in PTSD may depend on the failure of mechanisms to *forget*. There is also a hormonal link, because PTSD sufferers exhibit a paradoxical long-term *reduction* in stress hormone (cortisol) levels (Yehuda, 2002), perhaps due to persistent increases in *sensitivity* to cortisol. If, as a result, they feel the effect of stress hormones more strongly than other people do, that greater effect might repeatedly retrigger the fear response, making it harder for them to forget stressful events (**Figure 12.17**). In Chapter 13 we will discuss research-based methods that have been proposed to help people forget traumatic life events by recalling the event while under the influence of a drug that dampens the stress response.

In obsessive-compulsive disorder, thoughts and acts keep repeating

Most of us aspire to be neat and clean, especially when we discover a thick layer of dust under the furniture, or perhaps realize we've created yet another tottering pile of papers and bills. And of course, having certain small rituals in our lives—making coffee a certain way in the morning, wishing everyone good night before going to bed—can be a comfort amid the chaos of daily life. But when does orderliness and routine cross the line into pathology? People with **obsessive-compulsive disorder** (**OCD**) lead lives riddled with repetitive rituals and persistent thoughts that they feel powerless to control or stop, despite recognizing that the behaviors are abnormal. In OCD patients, routine acts that we all engage in, such as checking whether the door is locked when we leave our home, become *compulsions* that are repeated over and over. Recurrent thoughts, or *obsessions*, such as fears of germs or other potential harms in the world, invade the consciousness. These symptoms progressively isolate a person from ordinary social engagement with the world. For many patients, hours each day are consumed by compulsive acts such as repetitive hand washing. **Table 12.3** summarizes some of the symptoms of OCD.

Determining the number of people afflicted with OCD is difficult, especially because people with this disorder tend to hide their symptoms (Rapoport, 1989). In many cases, the initial symptoms of this disorder appear in childhood; the peak age group for onset of OCD, however, is 25–44 years. PET scan studies of patients with OCD consistently report increased metabolic rates in the orbitofrontal cortex, cingulate cortex, and caudate nuclei (Chamberlain et al., 2008; Rauch et al., 1994; Saxena and Rauch, 2000).

Happily, OCD responds to drug treatment in most cases. What do effective OCD drugs—like fluoxetine (Prozac), fluvoxamine (Luvox), and clomipramine

fear conditioning A form of learning in which fear comes to be associated with a previously neutral stimulus.

obsessive-compulsive disorder (OCD) An anxiety disorder in which the affected individual experiences recurrent unwanted thoughts and engages in repetitive behaviors without reason or the ability to stop.

TABLE 12.3 Symptoms of Obsessive-Compulsive Disorder

Symptoms	Percentage of patients exhibiting symptom
OBSESSIONS (thoughts)	
Dirt, germs, or environmental toxins	40
Something terrible happening (e.g., fire, death or illness of self or loved one)	24
Symmetry, order, or exactness	17
Religious obsessions	13
Body wastes or secretions (urine, stool, saliva, etc.)	8
Lucky or unlucky numbers	8
Forbidden, aggressive, or perverse sexual thoughts, images, or impulses	4
Fear of harming self or others	4
Household items	3
Intrusive nonsense sounds, words, or music	1
COMPULSIONS (acts)	
Performing excessive or ritualized hand washing, showering, bathing, tooth brushing, or grooming	85
Repeating rituals (e.g., going in or out of a door, getting up from or sitting down on a chair)	51
Checking (doors, locks, stove, appliances, emergency brake on car, paper route, homework, etc.)	46
Engaging in miscellaneous rituals (such as writing, moving, speaking)	26
Decontaminating	23
Touching	20
Counting	18
Ordering or arranging	17
Preventing harm to self or others	16
Hoarding or collecting	11
Cleaning household or inanimate objects	6

(Anafranil)—tend to have in common? They share the ability to inhibit the reuptake of serotonin at serotonergic synapses, thereby increasing the synaptic availability of serotonin. This observation suggests that the dysfunction of serotonergic neurotransmission plays a central role in OCD. Recall that we already discussed SSRIs like Prozac that inhibit the reuptake of serotonin when we discussed treatments for depression. How can the same drug help two disorders that seem so different? For one thing, depression often accompanies OCD, so the two disorders may be related. Furthermore, functional brain imaging suggests that the same SSRI drugs alter the activity of the orbitofrontal prefrontal cortex in people with OCD (Saxena et al., 2001), while affecting primarily ventrolateral prefrontal cortex in people with depression (see Figure 12.12).

Many researchers also believe that OCD and another disease involving repetitive behaviors, *Tourette's syndrome*, are part of a spectrum of related disorders (Olson, 2004). OCD and Tourette's are often **co-morbid** (occurring together), and both disorders involve abnormalities of the basal ganglia. However, drug therapy in Tourette's syndrome has typically focused on modifying the actions of dopamine rather than of serotonin (**Box 12.2**).

There is a heritable genetic component to OCD; as with schizophrenia and depression, several genes may contribute to susceptibility to this disorder (Grados et al., 2003; Hall et al., 2003), including the gene encoding the serotonin 5-HT$_{2A}$ receptor (Enoch et al., 1998). There is evidence that OCD can be triggered by infections. Upon observing that numerous children exhibiting OCD symptoms had recently been treated for strep throat,

co-morbid Referring to the tendency of certain diseases or disorders to occur together in individuals.

BOX 12.2 Tics, Twitches, and Snorts: The Unusual Character of Tourette's Syndrome

Their faces twitch in an insistent way, and every now and then, out of nowhere, they blurt out an odd sound. At times they fling their arms, kick their legs, or make violent shoulder movements. Sufferers of **Tourette's syndrome** also exhibit heightened sensitivity to tactile, auditory, and visual stimuli (A. J. Cohen and Leckman, 1992). Many patients report that an urge to emit verbal or phonic tics builds up and that giving in to the urge brings relief. Although popular media often portray people with Tourette's shouting out insults and curse words (a symptom called *coprolalia*), verbal tics of that sort are rare.

Tourette's syndrome begins early in life; the mean age of diagnosis is 6–7 years (de Groot et al., 1995), and the syndrome is 3–4 times more common in males than in females. Figure A draws a portrait of the chronology of symptoms. Often people with Tourette's also exhibit attention deficit hyperactivity disorder (ADHD) or obsessive-compulsive disorder (OCD) (Park et al., 1993).

Children with Tourette's display a thinning of primary somatosensory and motor cortex representing facial, oral, and laryngeal structures (Sowell et al., 2008), suggesting that the tics mediated by these regions may be underinhibited by cortex.

Family studies indicate that genetics plays an important role in this disorder. Twin studies of the disorder reveal a concordance rate among monozygotic twins of 53–77%, contrasted with a concordance rate among dizygotic twins of 8–23% (T. M. Hyde et al., 1992). Among discordant monozygotic twin pairs, the twin with Tourette's has a greater density of dopamine D_2 receptors in the caudate nucleus of the basal ganglia than the unaffected twin has (Wolf et al., 1996). This observation suggests that differences in the dopaminergic system, especially in the basal ganglia, may be important (D_2 receptor binding in an affected twin is illustrated in Figure B). The contemporary view is that Tourette's syndrome is mediated in a complex manner by more than one gene, but the precise

genes that are involved remain unidentified (Abelson et al., 2005).

Administration of haloperidol, a dopamine D_2 receptor antagonist that is better known as an effective antischizophrenic drug, significantly reduces tic frequency and is a primary treatment for Tourette's syndrome. Unfortunately, this treatment has some unpleasant side effects (as noted in Box 12.1) but, as with people who suffer from schizophrenia, some people with Tourette's respond well to the atypical antipsychotics, which bring fewer side effects. Behavior modification techniques aimed at reducing the frequency of some symptoms, especially tics, help some patients learn to substitute more-subtle or more socially acceptable behaviors in place of the more obvious tics (Himle et al., 2006).

Deep brain stimulation (DBS), which we mentioned in the text as a treatment for depression, may also benefit people with Tourette's. Neurosurgeons implant bilateral stimulating electrodes within the thalamus, in regions associated with the control of movement. The stimulators are controlled by pacemakers and batteries implanted near the collarbone. One person with Tourette's, Jeff Matovic, reported that within hours after the stimulators were activated, his symptoms completely abated. For the first time in 25 years he was free of the motor and vocal tics that had threatened to ruin his life. A group of 15 people with Tourette's who, like Jeff, did not respond to medication, received thalamic implants and reported reduced symptoms 24 months later (Porta et al., 2009). (Figure B courtesy of Steven Wolf.)

(A) The chronology of Tourette's symptoms

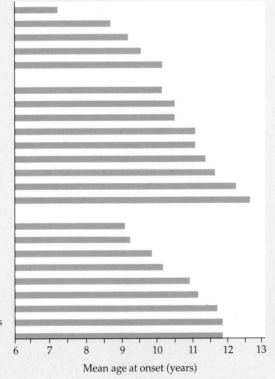

Motor tics
- Eyes, face, head
- Shoulder, neck
- Arms, hands
- Trunk
- Legs

Vocal tics
- Low noises
- Loud noises
- Stuttering
- Repetition
- Obscenities
- Syllables
- Blocking
- Words out of context
- Repeating others

Compulsive actions
- Head banging
- Kissing
- Touching objects
- Kicking
- Tapping
- Touching self or others
- Biting self
- Touching sexual organs
- Mimicking others

Mean age at onset (years)

(B) D_2 receptor binding in Tourette's syndrome

These MRIs show the brain of a patient who underwent a cingulotomy—the disruption of cingulate cortex connections—in an attempt to treat OCD.

Figure 12.18   Neurosurgery to Treat Obsessive-Compulsive Disorder (From Martuza et al., 1990; courtesy of Robert L. Martuza.)

(*a*) Horizontal view

(*b*) Sagittal view

Dale et al. (2005) found that many children with OCD are producing antibodies to brain proteins. Dale's team theorizes that, in mounting an immune response to the streptococcal bacteria, these children also make antibodies that attack their own brains. The genetic link may be that some people are more likely than others to produce antibodies to the brain proteins. This theory suggests that measures designed to block antibody production or antibody access to the brain might relieve OCD symptoms someday.

In the meantime, people with OCD that does not respond to other treatments sometimes resort to psychosurgery. Unlike lobotomies, these surgeries target much smaller regions. For example, about one-third of severely disabled OCD patients who underwent *cingulotomy* (lesions that interrupt pathways in the cingulate cortex) (**Figure 12.18**) benefited substantially (S. Rasmussen et al., 2000; Shah et al., 2008). A different type of surgery, in which small, discrete lesions are placed in the anterior part of the internal capsule (the white matter projections underlying the cortex), reportedly benefits some cases of severe anxiety disorders (Ruck et al., 2003). Note that these psychosurgeries involve relatively small areas of the brain. Frontal lobotomy, which causes much more extensive damage to the brain, is virtually never performed today. So we can hope that no one else will suffer the fate of Howard Dully, lobotomized for being a teenager.

How's it going?

1. What is the main division of anxiety disorders?
2. What class of drugs is the most common anxiolytic, and what effect do these drugs have on transmitter systems?
3. Describe PTSD and the hypothesis that the disorder is a special case of fear conditioning.
4. What is OCD, and what treatments are available to combat it?

Recommended Reading

Charney, D., and Nestler E. J. (Eds.). (2011). *Neurobiology of Mental Illness* (3rd ed.). New York, NY: Oxford University Press.

Cichetti, D., and Walker, E. F. (Eds.). (2003). *Neurodevelopmental Mechanisms in Psychopathology.* Cambridge, England: Cambridge University Press.

Hersen, M., Turner, S. M., and Beidel, D. C. (2007). *Adult Psychopathology and Diagnosis* (2nd ed.). New York, NY: Wiley.

Huettel, S. A., Song, A. W., and McCarthy, G. (2009). *Functional Magnetic Resonance Imaging* (2nd ed.). Sunderland, MA: Sinauer.

Meyer, J. S., and Quenzer, L. F. (2005). *Psychopharmacology: Drugs, the Brain, and Behavior.* Sunderland, MA: Sinauer.

Solomon, A. (2001). *The Noonday Demon: An Atlas of Depression.* New York, NY: Scribner.

Steketee, G. (Ed.) (2011). *The Oxford Handbook of Obsessive Compulsive and Spectrum Disorders.* New York, NY: Oxford University Press.

Walkup, J. T., Mink, J. W., and Hollenbeck, P. J. (2006). *Advances in Neurology: Vol. 99. Tourette Syndrome.* New York, NY: Lippincott Williams & Wilkins.

CHAPTER **12** VISUAL SUMMARY

You should be able to relate each summary to the adjacent illustration, including structures and processes. If you need to review, go to the figures indicated and read the accompanying text.

1 Population studies find that psychiatric disorders are prevalent in modern society. Studies of families, twins, and adoptees demonstrate a strong role of genetic factors in schizophrenia. Rather than a single gene determining whether a person will develop **schizophrenia**, several genes contribute to the risk. Review **Figures 12.1** and **12.2**, **Table 12.1**, **Animation 12.2**

2 Structural changes in the brains of patients with schizophrenia—including enlarged ventricles—may arise from early developmental problems. The emergence of schizophrenia depends on the interaction of genes that make a person vulnerable to environmental stressors. Review **Figures 12.3–12.8**

3 The frontal lobes are less active in people with schizophrenia than in control subjects. Biochemical theories of schizophrenia emphasize the importance of the dopamine, glutamate, and serotonin receptors. **Typical neuroleptics** block *dopamine D_2 receptors*, while **atypical neuroleptics** block 5-HT_{2A} receptors. Review **Figures 12.9–12.11**, **Box 12.1**, **Video 12.3**

4 **Depression** also has a strong genetic factor. Serotonin has been implicated in this disorder. In general, females are more likely than males to suffer from depression. People suffering from depression show increased activity in the frontal cortex and the amygdala, as well as disrupted sleep patterns. Review **Figures 12.12** and **12.14**

5 The most effective treatment for most cases of depression is a combination of **cognitive behavioral therapy (CBT)** and a **selective serotonin reuptake inhibitor (SSRI)**. Review **Table 12.2**

6 **Bipolar disorder** is characterized by extreme mood swings and subtle changes in the brain, and it has a complex genetic component. The disorder is commonly treated with **lithium**. Review **Figure 12.15**

7 Anxiety states are characterized by functional changes in the temporal lobes, particularly the amygdala. **Benzodiazepine** antianxiety drugs **(anxiolytics)** enhance the inhibitory effects of receptors for the transmitter GABA. Drugs affecting serotonergic synapses may also reduce anxiety. Review **Figure 12.16**

8 **Posttraumatic stress disorder (PTSD)** is characterized by an inability to forget horrible experiences. Temporal lobe atrophy in this disorder may be caused by exposure to stress hormones such as cortisol, and prolonged sensitivity to those hormones. Review **Figure 12.17**

9 **Obsessive-compulsive disorder (OCD)** is characterized by changes in basal ganglia and frontal cortex and linked to serotonin. A restricted type of neurosurgery is sometimes used to treat the most severe cases of anxiety disorders. In **Tourette's syndrome**, overstimulation of dopamine receptors induces motor and verbal tics and compulsions. Review **Figure 12.18**, **Table 12.3**, **Box 12.2**, **Activity 12.1**

Go to **mindsmachine.com** for study questions, quizzes, flashcards, and other resources.

chapter 13
Memory, Learning, and Development

Trapped in the Eternal Now

Henry Molaison, known as "patient H.M." in a classic series of research articles, was probably the most famous research subject in the history of brain science. Henry started to suffer seizures during adolescence, and by his late twenties, in 1953, his epilepsy was out of control. Because tests showed that Henry's seizures began in both temporal lobes, a neurosurgeon removed most of the anterior temporal lobe on both sides.

After the operation, Henry's seizures were milder, and could be controlled by medication. But this relief came at a terrible, unforeseen price: He couldn't seem to form new memories (Scoville and Milner, 1957). For more than 50 years after the surgery, until his death in 2008, Henry could retain any new fact only briefly; as soon as he was distracted, the newly acquired information vanished. He didn't know his age or the current date, or that his parents (with whom he lived well into adulthood) had died years previously. Henry knew that something was wrong with him, because he had no memories from the years since his surgery, or even memories from earlier the same day.

Every day is alone in itself, whatever enjoyment I've had, and whatever sorrow I've had. ... Right now, I'm wondering, have I done or said anything amiss? You see, at this moment everything looks clear to me, but what happened just before? That's what worries me. It's like waking from a dream. I just don't remember. (B. Milner, 1970, p. 37)

Henry's inability to form new memories meant that he couldn't have a lasting relationship with anybody new. No matter what experiences he might share with someone he met, Henry would have to start the acquaintance anew the following day, because he would have no recollection of ever meeting the person before. In some ways, this dreadful loss of memory ended Henry's journey as a human being—he could no longer grow in his experience of historical events, friendships, or even a sense of his own life story.

What happened to Henry, and what does his experience teach us about learning and memory?

To see a video, go to

mindsmachine.com/13.1
Memory

All the distinctively human aspects of our behavior are learned: the languages we speak, how we dress, the foods we eat and how we eat them, our skills and the ways we reach our goals. So much of our own individuality depends on **learning**, the process of acquiring new information; and **memory**, the ability to store and retrieve that information. We begin this chapter with a discussion of memory because research in the twentieth century revealed that there are fundamentally different types of memory. Then we delve into what we know about how learning alters the structure of the brain, which differs for different types of memory. The final section of the chapter takes up the fascinating story of brain development, as our brains grow at a stupendous rate so we can learn and remember the masses of information that make us into unique human beings.

PART I Types of Learning and Memory

We can discover a great deal about learning and memory by examining how they fail. Clinical case studies teach us that memory can fail in very different ways, revealing different forms of learning and memory. The clinical research also guides studies with animal models and brain-imaging technology; together, these diverse approaches are providing a comprehensive picture of the brain's mechanisms of learning and memory.

There Are Several Kinds of Memory and Learning

The terms *learning* and *memory* are so often paired that it sometimes seems as if one necessarily implies the other. We cannot be sure that learning has occurred unless a memory can be elicited later. Many kinds of brain damage, caused by disease or accident, impair learning and memory. We'll start by looking at some brain damage cases that revealed different classes of learning and memory.

For patient H.M., the present vanished into oblivion

Amnesia (Greek for "forgetfulness"), is a severe impairment of memory, usually as a result of accident or disease. Loss of memories that formed prior to an event (such as surgery or trauma)—called **retrograde amnesia** (from the Latin *retro-*, "backward," and *gradi*, "to go")—is not uncommon. After an accident that damages the brain, people often have retrograde amnesia with regard to events that happened a few hours or days before the accident, or even a year, but despite dramatic depictions you may see on TV, it is unlikely that longer-term (or "complete") retrograde memory loss has ever occurred.

Patient H.M.—Henry Molaison, whom we met at the start of the chapter—suffered from a far more unusual symptom. In Henry's case, most old memories remained intact, but he had difficulty recollecting any events that took place *after* his surgery. What's more, he was unable to retain any new material for more than a brief period. The inability

To see the brain in 3D, go to

mindsmachine.com/13.2
Brain Explorer

(a)

Hippocampus is Latin for "sea horse," and you can see how the brain structure resembles that animal.

Hippocampus

Temporal lobe

Mammillary body

Cerebellum

(b) Ventral view

Normal   H.M.

1 cm

Coronal view

As a young man, Henry Molaison (patient H.M.) had the hippocampus (H) from both hemispheres surgically removed, with disastrous results. The surgeons did not remove the cerebellum (Cer), but the loss of hippocampal inputs caused it to shrink as he aged.

Figure 13.1 Brain Regions Crucial for Forming New Memories (From Corkin et al., 1997; photos courtesy of Suzanne Corkin.)

to form new memories after an event is called **anterograde amnesia** (the Latin *antero-* means "forward").

Over the very short term, Henry's memory was normal. If given a series of six or seven digits, he could immediately repeat the list without error. But if he was given a list of words to study and then tested on them after being distracted by another task, he could not repeat the list or even recall that there *was* a list. So Henry's case provided clear neuroanatomical evidence that *short-term memory* differs from *long-term memory*—a distinction, long recognized by psychologists on behavioral grounds (W. James, 1890), that we will discuss in more depth later in this chapter.

Henry's surgery removed the amygdala, most of the hippocampus, and some surrounding cortex from both temporal lobes (**Figure 13.1**). The memory deficit seemed to be caused by loss of the **hippocampus**, because surgical patients who had other nearby structures removed had no memory impairment. But to the puzzlement of researchers, experimental bilateral hippocampal lesions in laboratory animals seemed not to produce widespread memory deficits (Isaacson, 1972). What might account for this discrepancy?

Early in their work, Henry's research team found that he showed noticeable improvement over days of practice on a mirror-tracing task (**Figure 13.2a**) (B. Milner, 1965). Each day, when asked if he remembered the test, Henry said no, yet his performance was better than at the start of the first day (**Figure 13.2b**). So, was Henry's memory loss limited to tasks that relied on verbal processing? Not quite. For example, patients with amnesia like Henry's can learn the skill of *reading* mirror-reversed text (**Figure 13.3**), which is a verbal task.

(a)

Henry was given this mirror-tracing task to test motor skill.

(b)

Although Henry never recognized the task, his performance progressively improved over successive days, demonstrating a type of long-term memory.

Trial number

learning The process of acquiring new and relatively enduring information, behavior patterns, or abilities, characterized by modifications of behavior as a result of practice, study, or experience.

memory 1. The ability to retain information, based on the mental process of learning or encoding, retention across some interval of time (consolidation), and retrieval or reactivation of the memory. 2. The specific information that is stored in the brain.

amnesia Severe impairment of memory.

retrograde amnesia Difficulty in retrieving memories formed before the onset of amnesia.

patient H.M. A patient who, because of damage to medial temporal lobe structures, was unable to encode new declarative memories. Upon his death we learned his name was Henry Molaison.

anterograde amnesia Difficulty in forming new memories beginning with the onset of a disorder.

hippocampus A medial temporal lobe structure that is important for learning and memory.

Henry Molaison Henry was a young man when he had the surgery that disrupted his memory, as described in the famous studies of patient "H. M." (Photo courtesy of Dr. Suzanne Corkin, MIT.)

Figure 13.2 Henry's Performance on a Mirror-Tracing Task (After B. Milner, 1965.)

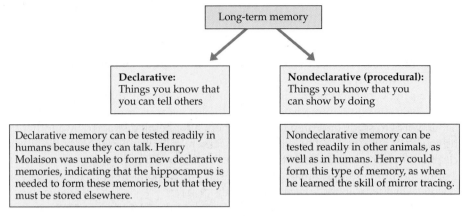

If you practice reading text that is mirror-reversed, you will become better and better at deciphering the text quickly. This is an example of learning a perceptual skill, and does not require an intact hippocampus.

Patients like Henry can learn to read mirror-reversed text quite well, even though they don't remember practicing it. This ability shows that their problem is not in learning verbal material, but in forming new declarative memories.

Figure 13.3 Reading Mirror-Reversed Text

declarative memory A memory that can be stated or described.

nondeclarative memory or procedural memory A memory that is shown by performance rather than by conscious recollection.

delayed non-matching-to-sample task A test in which the subject must respond to the unfamiliar stimulus of a pair.

Long-term memory

Declarative: Things you know that you can tell others

Nondeclarative (procedural): Things you know that you can show by doing

Declarative memory can be tested readily in humans because they can talk. Henry Molaison was unable to form new declarative memories, indicating that the hippocampus is needed to form these memories, but that they must be stored elsewhere.

Nondeclarative memory can be tested readily in other animals, as well as in humans. Henry could form this type of memory, as when he learned the skill of mirror tracing.

Figure 13.4 Two Main Kinds of Memory: Declarative and Nondeclarative

Subsequent research showed that the important distinction is not between motor and verbal performances, but rather between two general categories of memory:

1. **Declarative memory** is what we usually think of as memory: facts and information acquired through learning. It is memory we are aware of accessing, which we can *declare* to others. This is the type of memory that was so profoundly impaired by Henry's surgery. Tests of declarative memory take the form of requests for specific information that was learned previously, such as a story or word list. It is the type of memory we use to answer "what" questions—and thus is difficult to test in animals.

2. **Nondeclarative memory**, or **procedural memory**—that is, memory about perceptual or motor procedures—is shown by *performance* rather than by conscious recollection. Examples of procedural memory include learning the mirror-tracing task at which Henry excelled, and the skill of mirror reading. It is the type of memory we use to answer "how" questions. **Figure 13.4** illustrates this basic division in memory type.

Once researchers caught on to this distinction, they came up with a clever way to measure declarative memory in monkeys. The **delayed non-matching-to-sample task** (**Figure 13.5**) is a test of *object recognition* memory that requires monkeys to declare what they remember. In this task the monkeys must identify which of two objects was *not* seen previously, with delays ranging from 8 seconds to 2 minutes (Spiegler and Mishkin, 1981). Monkeys that have extensive damage to the medial temporal lobe, and thus are similar to Henry, are severely impaired on this task, especially with the longer delays. But which specific temporal lobe structures are most important?

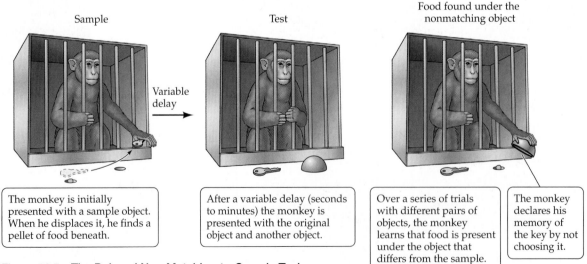

Sample — Test — Food found under the nonmatching object

Variable delay

The monkey is initially presented with a sample object. When he displaces it, he finds a pellet of food beneath.

After a variable delay (seconds to minutes) the monkey is presented with the original object and another object.

Over a series of trials with different pairs of objects, the monkey learns that food is present under the object that differs from the sample.

The monkey declares his memory of the key by not choosing it.

Figure 13.5 The Delayed Non-Matching-to-Sample Task

RESEARCHERS AT WORK

Which brain structures are important for declarative memory?

To determine which parts of the temporal lobe are crucial for declarative memory, researchers selectively removed specific parts of the medial temporal lobes of monkeys to confirm that the amygdala—one of the structures removed in Henry's surgery—is not crucial for performance on tests of declarative memory. However, removal of the adjacent hippocampus significantly impaired performance on these tests and, as shown in **Figure 13.6**, the deficit was even more pronounced when the hippocampal damage was paired with lesions of nearby cortical regions that communicate with the hippocampus: entorhinal and parahippocampal cortex, and perirhinal cortex (Zola-Morgan et al., 1994). Human patients similarly show larger impairments when both the hippocampus and medial temporal cortex are damaged (Rempel-Clower et al., 1996; Zola-Morgan and Squire, 1986). So Henry's symptoms were probably caused by loss of the hippocampus and nearby cortex on both sides of the brain.

The experiments with monkeys, together with Henry's case, indicate that we need at least one intact hippocampus in order to make new declarative memories. But the hippocampus isn't the only brain structure needed for new declarative memories, as we'll see next.

Figure 13.6   Memory Performance after Medial Temporal Lobe Lesions

Hypothesis

Particular portions of the temporal lobe are required for the formation of new declarative memories.

Test

Selectively remove different portions of the temporal lobe from both sides of the brain, and test for declarative memories using the delayed non-matching-to-sample task (see Figure 13.5).

Result

(a) Ventral view of monkey brain showing areas of different medial temporal lesions

- Entorhinal cortex
- Hippocampus
- Perirhinal cortex
- Parahippocampal cortex

(b) Scores of groups with different lesions

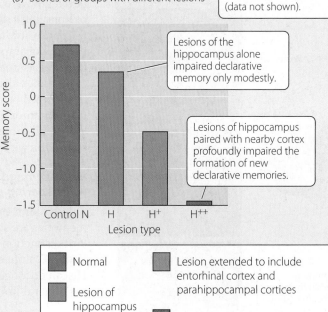

Lesions of the amygdala had no effect on declarative memories (data not shown).

Lesions of the hippocampus alone impaired declarative memory only modestly.

Lesions of hippocampus paired with nearby cortex profoundly impaired the formation of new declarative memories.

Legend:
- Normal
- Lesion of hippocampus
- Lesion extended to include entorhinal cortex and parahippocampal cortices
- Lesion extended forward to include the anterior entorhinal and perirhinal cortices

Conclusion

The severe disruption of new declarative memories in Henry Molaison and patients like him is due to damage to both the hippocampus itself and to nearby cortex.

patient N.A.   A patient who is unable to encode new declarative memories, because of damage to the dorsomedial thalamus and the mammillary bodies.

dorsomedial thalamus   A limbic system structure that is connected to the hippocampus.

mammillary body   One of a pair of limbic system structures that are connected to the hippocampus.

Korsakoff's syndrome   A memory disorder, related to a thiamine deficiency, that is generally associated with chronic alcoholism. It is commonly accompanied by confabulation.

confabulate   To fill in a gap in memory with a falsification. Confabulation is often seen in Korsakoff's syndrome.

patient K.C.   A patient who sustained damage to the cortex that renders him unable to form and retrieve new episodic memories.

Damage to the mammillary bodies can also cause amnesia

In 1960, a young man now known to brain researchers as **patient N.A.** had a bizarre accident in which a miniature sword entered his nostril and injured his brain. Like Henry, N.A. has shown profound anterograde amnesia ever since his accident, primarily for verbal material (Squire and Moore, 1979), and he can give little information about events since his accident, although his memory for earlier events is near normal (Kaushall et al., 1981). MRI study of N.A. (**Figure 13.7**) shows damage to several limbic system structures that have connections to the hippocampus: the **dorsomedial thalamus** and the **mammillary bodies** (so called because they are shaped like a pair of breasts—see Figure 13.1a). Like Henry Molaison, N.A. shows normal short-term memory and can gain new nondeclarative/procedural memories, but he is impaired in forming declarative long-term memories. The similarity in symptoms suggests that the medial temporal lobe damaged in Henry's brain and these midline regions damaged in N.A. are parts of a larger memory system.

That idea is reinforced by studies of people with **Korsakoff's syndrome**, a degenerative disease in which damage is found in some parts of the limbic system, especially the mammillary bodies and dorsomedial thalamus (Mair et al., 1979), but not in temporal lobe structures like the hippocampus. The mammillary bodies may serve as a processing system connecting the hippocampus and nearby cortex (which were removed from Henry Molaison) to the thalamus and, from there, to other cortical sites (Vann and Aggleton, 2004). People with Korsakoff's syndrome often fail to recognize or sense any familiarity with some items, even when presented repeatedly, yet frequently they deny that anything is wrong with them. They often **confabulate**—that is, fill a gap in memory with a falsification that they seem to accept as true. Damage to the frontal cortex, also found in patients suffering from Korsakoff's syndrome, probably causes the denial and confabulation that differentiates them from other patients who have amnesia, such as Henry.

The main cause of Korsakoff's syndrome is lack of the vitamin thiamine. Alcoholics who obtain most of their calories from alcohol and neglect their diet often suffer this deficiency. Treating them with thiamine can prevent further deterioration of memory functions but will not reverse the damage already done. If alcoholic beverages were supplemented with thiamine, then many new cases of Korsakoff's syndrome might be prevented.

These studies make it clear that a brain circuit that includes the hippocampus, the mammillary bodies, and the dorsomedial thalamus is needed to *form* new declarative memories. But these case studies also clearly show that established declarative memories, formed before brain damage, are not *stored* in these structures. If the memories had been stored there, they would have been lost when the structures were damaged. So where are memories stored? As we'll see next, a leading candidate is the cerebral cortex.

Brain damage can destroy autobiographical memories while sparing general memories

One striking case study suggests that at least some declarative memories are stored in the cortex, and it also illustrates an important distinction between two *subtypes* of declarative memory. **Patient K.C.** suffered brain damage in a motorcycle accident at age 30. He can no longer retrieve any *personal memory* of his past, although his general knowledge remains good. He converses easily and

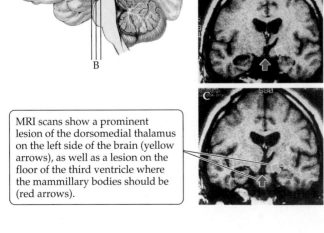

MRI scans show a prominent lesion of the dorsomedial thalamus on the left side of the brain (yellow arrows), as well as a lesion on the floor of the third ventricle where the mammillary bodies should be (red arrows).

Figure 13.7   The Brain Damage in Patient N.A. (From Squire et al., 1989; MRI scans courtesy of Larry Squire.)

plays a good game of chess, but he cannot remember where he learned to play chess or who taught him the game. Detailed autobiographical declarative memory of this sort is known as **episodic memory**; you show episodic memory when you recall a specific *episode* in your life or relate an event to a particular time and place. In contrast, **semantic memory** is generalized declarative memory, such as knowing the meaning of a word without knowing where or when you learned that word (Tulving, 1972). If care is taken to space out the trials, K.C. can acquire new semantic knowledge (Tulving et al., 1991). But even with this method, K.C. cannot acquire new *episodic* knowledge—he won't remember where he learned that new material.

Brain scans of K.C. reveal extensive damage to the left frontoparietal and the right parieto-occipital cerebral cortex, as well as severe shrinkage of the hippocampus and nearby cortex (Rosenbaum et al., 2005). As with Henry, the bilateral hippocampal damage probably accounts for K.C.'s anterograde declarative amnesia. But hippocampal damage cannot account for K.C.'s selective loss of nearly all his autobiographical memory, because other patients with damage restricted to the hippocampus and nearby cortex lack this symptom. K.C.'s inability to recall any autobiographical details of his life from many years before his accident may instead be a consequence of injuries to frontal and parietal cortex (Tulving, 1989). (Unlike dramatic portrayals of retrograde amnesia in fiction, K.C. knows his name and recognizes his family, although he can't remember any particular events with those people).

Brain-imaging studies in normal subjects confirm the distinction between *semantic* (general) and *episodic* (autobiographical) declarative memories, exemplified by patient K.C. Subjects listening to passages about themselves show greater activation of right frontal and temporal lobe regions (G. R. Fink et al., 1996) than when listening to other people's stories (**Figure 13.8**). Thus, autobiographical memories and semantic memories appear to be processed in different locations and are probably stored in different parts of the cortex.

episodic memory Also called *autobiographical memory*. Memory of a particular incident or a particular time and place.

semantic memory Generalized declarative memory, such as knowing the meaning of a word without knowing where or when you learned that word.

How's it going?

1. What are the two main types of amnesia, and which type did Henry Molaison exhibit?
2. What are the two main types of memory, and which type was affected in Henry?
3. How did research with animals help pin down the brain regions required for forming new memories that we can declare to others?
4. What are the two main types of declarative memory?

(*a*) Your story

Right hemisphere · Posterior · Frontal cortex

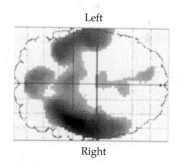

Left · Right · Anterior

Different parts of the brain are activated if the story you are listening to is about yourself (as opposed to someone else's story), suggesting that autobiographical memories are processed in different parts of the brain from other memories.

(*b*) Their story

Sagittal section

Frontal cortex · Coronal section

Horizontal section

Figure 13.8 Your Story versus Their Story

skill learning The process of learning to perform a challenging task simply by repeating it over and over.

basal ganglia A group of forebrain nuclei, including the caudate nucleus, globus pallidus, and putamen, found deep within the cerebral hemispheres. They are crucial for skill learning.

priming Also called *repetition priming*. The phenomenon by which exposure to a stimulus facilitates subsequent responses to the same or a similar stimulus.

associative learning A type of learning in which an association is formed between two stimuli or between a stimulus and a response. It includes both classical and instrumental conditioning.

classical conditioning Also called *Pavlovian conditioning*. A type of associative learning in which an originally neutral stimulus (the conditioned stimulus, or CS)—through pairing with another stimulus (the unconditioned stimulus, or US) that elicits a particular response—acquires the power to elicit that response when presented alone. A response elicited by the US is called an unconditioned response (UR); a response elicited by the CS alone is called a conditioned response (CR).

cerebellum A structure located at the back of the brain, dorsal to the pons, that is involved in the central regulation of movement and in classical conditioning.

off the mark by Mark Parisi

Biological Psychologists at Work We don't all like weird hairdos. Or mazes.

Different Forms of Nondeclarative Memory Involve Different Brain Regions

So far, we've seen that there are two different kinds of declarative memory: semantic and episodic. There are also different types of nondeclarative (procedural) memory, and we'll see that different brain regions are involved in these different forms.

Different types of nondeclarative memory serve varying functions

Skill learning is the process of learning how to perform a challenging task simply by repeating it over and over. Experimental tests like the mirror-tracing task performed by Henry Molaison (see Figure 13.2) or learning to read mirror-reversed text (see Figure 13.3) are examples of skill learning. So, too, is the acquisition of everyday skills like learning to ride a bike or to juggle (well, okay, maybe juggling isn't an "everyday" skill, but you get the idea).

Imaging studies have investigated learning and memory for different kinds of skills, including *sensorimotor skills* (e.g., mirror tracing), *perceptual skills* (e.g., learning to read mirror-reversed text), and *cognitive skills* (tasks involving planning and problem solving, common in puzzles like the Tower of Hanoi problem, which you can play on the website). All three kinds of skill learning are impaired in people with damage to the **basal ganglia** (see Figure 2.14a). Damage to other brain regions, especially the motor cortex and cerebellum, also affects aspects of some skills. Neuroimaging studies confirm that the basal ganglia, cerebellum, and motor cortex are important for sensorimotor skill learning in normal people (Grafton et al., 1992; Hazeltine et al., 1997).

Priming (or *repetition priming*) is a change in the way you process a stimulus, usually a word or a picture, because you've seen it, or something similar, previously. For example, if a person is shown the word *stamp* in a list and later is asked to complete the word stem *STA-*, she becomes more likely to reply "stamp," rather than, say, "start." Priming does not require declarative memory of the stimulus—Henry Molaison and other patients with amnesia show priming for words they don't remember having seen. In contrast with skill learning, tests of priming are not impaired by damage to the basal ganglia. In functional-imaging studies, perceptual priming (priming based on the visual *form* of words) is related to *reduced* activity in bilateral occipitotemporal cortex (Schacter et al., 1996), while conceptual priming (priming based on word *meaning*) is associated with reduced activation of the left frontal cortex (A. D. Wagner et al., 1997). So priming appears to be at least partly a function of the cortex.

Learning that involves relations between events—for example, between two or more stimuli, between a stimulus and a response, or between a response and its consequence—is called **associative learning**. In the best-studied form (**classical conditioning**), an initially neutral stimulus comes to predict an event. In famous experiments, Ivan Pavlov (1849–1936) found that a dog would learn to salivate when presented with an auditory or visual stimulus, if the stimulus came to predict the presentation of food. So, repeatedly ringing a bell before putting meat powder in a dog's mouth will eventually cause the dog to start salivating when it hears the bell alone. In this case the meat powder in the mouth is the *unconditioned stimulus* (US), which already evokes an *unconditioned response* (UR; salivation in the example). The sound of the bell is the *conditioned stimulus* (CS), and the learned response to the CS alone (salivation in response to the bell) is called the *conditioned response* (CR) (**Figure 13.9**).

Experimental evidence in lab animals, which we will discuss later in the chapter, shows that circuits in the **cerebellum** are crucial for simple eye-blink conditioning, in which a tone or other stimulus is associated with eye blinking in response to a puff of air. A PET study in humans confirmed this idea by showing a progressive increase in activity in the cerebellum during eye-blink conditioning (Logan and Grafton, 1995). Patients with hippocampal lesions can acquire the conditioned eye-blink response, but patients with damage to the cerebellum on one side can acquire a conditioned eye-blink response *only on the side where the cerebellum is intact* (Papka et al., 1994).

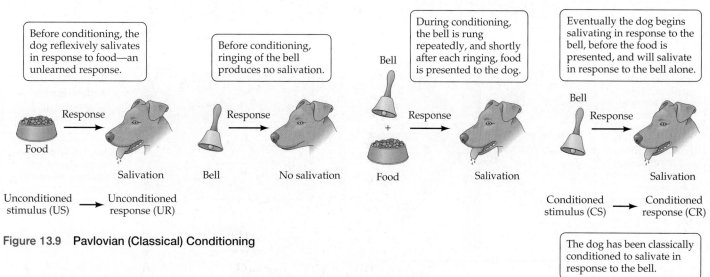

Figure 13.9   Pavlovian (Classical) Conditioning

In **instrumental conditioning** (also called **operant conditioning**), an association is formed between the animal's behavior and the consequence(s) of that behavior. An example of an apparatus designed to study instrumental conditioning is the *Skinner box*, named for its originator, B. F. Skinner (**Figure 13.10**). In a common setup, the animal learns that performing a certain action (e.g., pressing a bar) is followed by a reward (such as a food pellet). Research in animals has not pinpointed the brain regions that are crucial for instrumental conditioning, perhaps because this behavior taps so many different aspects of behavior.

Animal research confirms the various brain regions involved in different attributes of memory

The caricature of the white-coated biopsychologist watching rats run in mazes, a staple of cartoonists to this day, has its origins in the intensive memory research of the early twentieth century. The early work indicated that rats and other animals don't just learn a series of turns but instead form a **cognitive map** (an understanding of the relative spatial organization of objects and information) in order to solve a maze (Tolman, 1949). Animals apparently learn at least some of these details of their spatial environment simply by moving through it (Tolman and Honzik, 1930).

We now know that, in parallel with its role in other types of declarative memory, the hippocampus is crucial for spatial learning. The rat hippocampus contains many neurons that selectively encode spatial location (Leutgeb et al., 2005; O'Keefe and Dostrovsky, 1971). These **place cells** become active when the animal is in—or moving toward—a particular location. If the animal is moved to a new environment, place cell activity indicates that the hippocampus remaps to the new locations (Moita et al., 2004). Bird species that hide food in many locations have a larger hippocampus than other birds have (Krebs et al., 1989), indicating that natural selection favors enlargement of the hippocampus to enhance spatial learning, as we discuss in **A Step Further 13.1**, on the website.

Researchers devised tasks that selectively tap different attributes of memory, in order to assess the relative contributions of different regions of the brain (Kesner, 1998; Kesner et al., 1993). An eight-arm radial maze was used to test memory of *spatial* location. To solve this task correctly and receive a food reward, rats must recognize and enter an arm of the maze that they followed shortly beforehand. Rats were tested following surgical lesions of the hippocampus, the basal ganglia (specifically the caudate nucleus), or the extrastriate cortex (visual cortex outside the primary visual area). Only the animals with

instrumental conditioning or operant conditioning   A form of associative learning in which the likelihood that an act (instrumental response) will be performed depends on the consequences (reinforcing stimuli) that follow it.

cognitive map   A mental representation of the relative spatial organization of objects and information.

place cell   A neuron in the hippocampus that selectively fires when the animal is in a particular location.

Figure 13.10   A Skinner Box

(*a*) Spatial-location recognition memory

In the study phase of each trial, the rat can choose any of the eight arms. In the test phase, doors block all but two arms: the arm entered in the study phase and one other. The rat obtains food only if it chooses the arm it entered in the study phase.

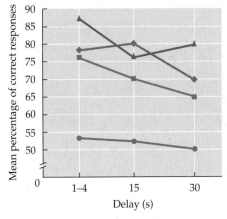

Brain region lesioned
● Hippocampus
■ Control
▲ Basal ganglia
◆ Extrastriate visual cortex

Only rats with hippo-campal lesions are impaired, relative to controls.

(*b*) Response recognition memory

In the first part of each trial, the rat is placed in the middle compartment on one side (2), and it finds food if it enters the compartment to either its right (1) or its left (3). In the second part of the trial, it is placed in the middle compartment on the other side (5), and it finds food only if it turns to the same side of its body as in the first part.

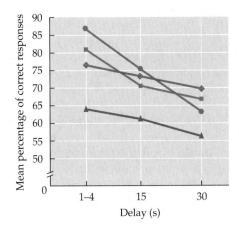

Brain region lesioned
● Hippocampus
■ Control
▲ Basal ganglia
◆ Extrastriate visual cortex

Only rats with basal ganglia lesions are impaired, relative to controls.

(*c*) Object recognition memory (non-matching-to-sample)

In the study phase of each trial, the rat obtains food by displacing a sample object over a small food well (top). In the test phase (bottom), the rat chooses between two objects and obtains food only if it chooses the object that does *not* match the sample.

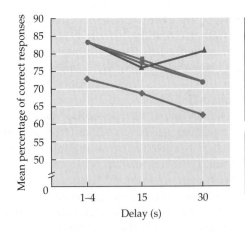

Brain region lesioned
● Hippocampus
■ Control
▲ Basal ganglia
◆ Extrastriate visual cortex

Only rats with lesions of the extrastriate visual cortex are impaired, relative to controls.

Figure 13.11 Testing Specific Attributes of Memory (After Kesner et al., 1993.)

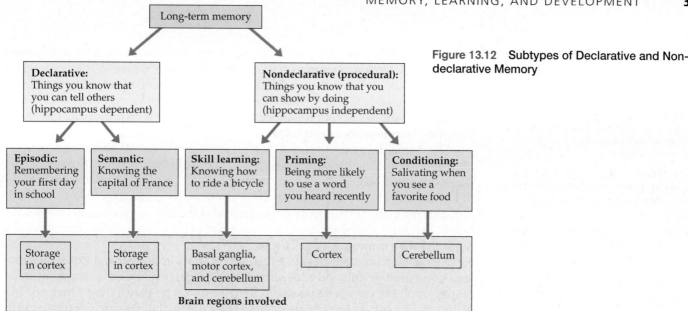

Figure 13.12 Subtypes of Declarative and Non-declarative Memory

hippocampal lesions were impaired on this predominantly spatial task—a result that is consistent with the role of the hippocampus in spatial cognition (**Figure 13.11a**).

The test shown in **Figure 13.11b** was used to assess the memory of the same rats for their own *motor* behavior. In this task the animal must remember whether it made a left or right turn a few moments earlier, and it receives a food reward only if it makes a turn in the same direction on a follow-up trial. Only the animals with lesions of the basal ganglia were significantly impaired on this task.

Finally, in the test depicted in **Figure 13.11c**, rats were required to hold in memory the *sensory* attributes of presented stimuli, identifying the novel stimulus in each pair of stimuli presented. Here, only the rats with cortical lesions were significantly impaired. This impressive lack of overlap in the symptoms of the different lesions nicely illustrates how memories involving different attributes are parceled out to diverse brain regions for storage.

Brain regions involved in learning and memory: A summary

Figure 13.12 updates and summarizes the classification of long-term memory that we've been discussing. Several major conclusions should be apparent by now, especially (1) that many regions of the brain are involved in learning and memory; (2) that different forms of memory rely on at least partly different brain mechanisms, which may include several different regions of the brain; and (3) that the same brain structure can be a part of the circuitry for several different forms of learning. Next we'll discuss the stages by which memories, of any sort, can be preserved for a lifetime.

Successive Processes Capture, Store, and Retrieve Information in the Brain

The span of time over which a piece of information is retained in the brain varies. There are at least three different stages of memory. The briefest memories are called **iconic memories** (from the Greek *eikon*, "image"); an example is the fleeting impression of a glimpsed scene that vanishes from memory seconds later. These brief memories are thought to be residual activity in sensory neurons—the so-called sensory buffers.

Somewhat longer than iconic memories are **short-term memories** (STMs). If you look up a phone number and keep it in mind (perhaps through rehearsal) just until you make the phone call, you are using STM. In the absence of rehearsal, STMs last only about 30 seconds (J. Brown, 1958; L. R. Peterson and Peterson, 1959). With rehearsal, you may be able to retain an STM until you turn to a new task a few minutes later; but

How's it going?

1. Name three different types of nondeclarative memories, and give an example of each.

2. What are hippocampal place cells, and why do they suggest a role for the hippocampus in spatial learning?

3. What different parts of the brain have been implicated in the nondeclarative tasks of skill learning, priming, and classical conditioning?

4. Describe how animal research implicated different brain regions in learning different attributes of a task.

iconic memory   A very brief type of memory that stores the sensory impression of a scene.

short-term memory (STM) or working memory   A form of memory that usually lasts only seconds, or as long as rehearsal continues.

long-term memory (LTM) An enduring form of memory that lasts days, weeks, months, or years and has a very large capacity.

encoding The first process in the memory system, in which the information entering sensory channels is passed into short-term memory.

consolidation The second process in the memory system, in which information in short-term memory is transferred to long-term memory.

retrieval The third process of the memory system, in which a stored memory is used by an organism.

when the STM is gone, it's gone for good. Many researchers now refer to this form of memory as **working memory**, in recognition of the way we use it. This is where we hold information while we're working with it to solve a problem or are otherwise actively manipulating the information. Eventually, some memories become really long-lasting—the address of your childhood home, how to ride a bike, your first love—and are called **long-term memories (LTMs)**.

The memory system consists of at least three processes: (1) **encoding** of raw information from sensory channels into STM, (2) **consolidation** of the volatile STM into more durable LTM, and (3) eventual **retrieval** of the stored information from LTM for use (**Figure 13.13**). A problem at any stage can cause us to lose information. Although not depicted in the figure, this model suggests that the flow of information into and out of working memory is supervised by another part of the brain, a *central executive*, which we will discuss in more detail in Chapter 14.

Not all memories are created equal. We all know from firsthand experience that emotion can powerfully enhance our memory for past events. For example, an emotionally arousing story is remembered significantly better than a closely matched but emotionally neutral story (Reisberg and Heuer, 1995). But if people are treated with propranolol (a beta-adrenergic antagonist, or "beta-blocker," that blocks the effects of epinephrine), this emotional enhancement of memory vanishes. It's not that treated subjects perceive the story as being any less emotional; in fact, treated subjects rate the emotional content of the stories just the same as untreated subjects do. Instead, the drug seems to directly interfere with the ability of adrenal stress hormones to act on the brain to enhance memory (Cahill et al., 1994). **Box 13.1** delves further into this topic.

STM and LTM appear to be different processes

Henry Molaison's case and the research it inspired have already told us several ways in which STM and LTM differ from one another. While the hippocampus is not needed to encode sensory information into STM, or to retrieve that information from STM

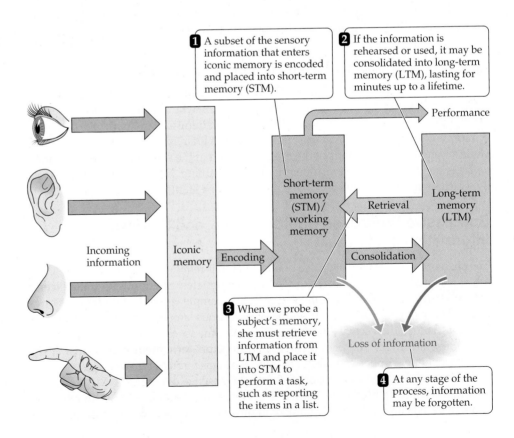

1 A subset of the sensory information that enters iconic memory is encoded and placed into short-term memory (STM).

2 If the information is rehearsed or used, it may be consolidated into long-term memory (LTM), lasting for minutes up to a lifetime.

3 When we probe a subject's memory, she must retrieve information from LTM and place it into STM to perform a task, such as reporting the items in a list.

4 At any stage of the process, information may be forgotten.

Performance

Incoming information · Iconic memory · Encoding · Short-term memory (STM)/ working memory · Retrieval · Consolidation · Long-term memory (LTM) · Loss of information

Figure 13.13 The Stages of Memory

BOX 13.1 Emotions and Memory

Almost everyone knows from personal experience that strong emotions can affect memory formation and retrieval. Examples of memories enhanced in this way might include a strong association between special music and a first kiss, or uncomfortably vivid recollection of the morning of September 11, 2001. A large-scale research effort in many labs has identified a suite of biochemical agents that participate in the emotional enhancement of memory.

Epinephrine (adrenaline), released from the adrenal glands in large quantities during times of stress and strong emotion, appears to affect memory formation by influencing the amygdala, a brain region that is critical for fear conditioning (see Chapter 11). Electrical stimulation or lesions of the amygdala potently alter the memory-enhancing effects of epinephrine injections (Cahill and McGaugh, 1991), and tiny doses of epinephrine injected directly into the amygdala enhance memory formation in the same way that systemic injections do. This treatment appears to cause the release of norepinephrine within the amygdala, as do emotional experiences. Injecting propranolol, a blocker of beta-adrenergic receptors, into the amygdala blocks the memory-enhancing effects. In humans, the same drug can ease fears that have been conditioned in the lab (Kindt et al., 2009).

Can we develop pharmacological treatments to weaken or erase unwanted memories outside the lab? Some disorders would benefit greatly from such treatments. For example, people who have had life-threatening or other catastrophic experiences often develop **posttraumatic stress disorder** (**PTSD**) (see Chapter 12), characterized as "reliving experiences such as intrusive thoughts, nightmares, dissociative flashbacks to elements of the original traumatic event, and … preoccupation with that event" (Keane, 1998, p. 398). In PTSD, each recurrence of the strong emotions and memories of the traumatic event may reactivate memories that, when reconsolidated in the presence of stress signals like epinephrine, become even stronger. Therefore, one strategy to prevent PTSD formation could be to block the effects of epinephrine in the amygdala by treating victims with antiadrenergic drugs either shortly before a traumatic experience (e.g., in rescue workers) or as quickly as possible after it (in the case of victims of violence, for example) (Cahill, 1997). This treatment would not delete memories of the event but might diminish the traumatic aspects, and it might also be useful for weakening existing traumatic memories.

Perhaps one day it will be possible to selectively interfere with other neurotransmitters at work in the amygdala to provide more-specific and more-complete relief from traumatic memories. Whatever that treatment might be, it will probably have to be administered soon after the accident to effectively dull the painful memories.

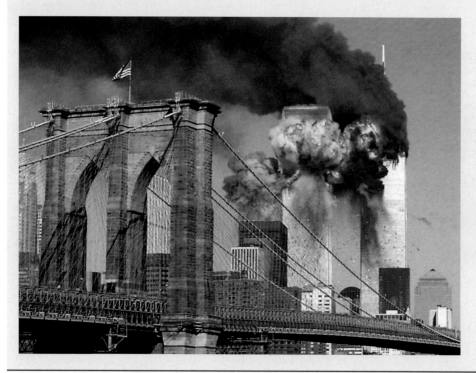

Flashbulb Memories Many people have vivid, detailed memories of where they were when they learned of the September 11, 2001, terrorist attack on the World Trade Center towers in New York City.

(Henry could repeat back to you a list of words or numbers), the hippocampus is crucial for moving information from STM into LTM. In terms of the model, an intact hippocampus is required to *consolidate* declarative STMs into LTMs, indicating that the information is somehow transformed into a different format, one that may make it available for a lifetime.

Likewise, the fact that brain trauma often causes retrograde amnesia (the inability to retrieve memories of events just before the accident) without affecting older memories suggests that STMs are more vulnerable to trauma—more likely to be lost—than are LTMs. When the retrograde amnesia stretches to several days before the accident, some recently acquired LTMs have been lost too. These cases suggest that, even after

primacy effect The superior performance seen in a memory task for items at the start of a list; it is usually attributed to long-term memory.

recency effect The superior performance seen in a memory task for items at the end of a list; it is usually attributed to short-term memory.

information has been consolidated into LTM, older memories are more "secure"—less likely to be lost—than freshly consolidated LTMs.

Another indication that STM and LTM rely on different processes to store information comes from a classic demonstration of learning lists of words or numbers. If you hear a list of ten words and then try to repeat them back after a 30-second delay, you will probably do especially well with the earliest few words (this effect is termed a **primacy effect** because these words came first) and with the last few words (this effect is termed a **recency effect** because you heard these words most recently), compared to words in the middle of the list. The blue curve in **Figure 13.14a** shows typical results from such an experiment: a U-shaped *serial position curve*. If the delay prior to recall is extended from a few seconds to a few minutes, the recency effect goes away, while the primacy effect is still seen (**Figure 13.14b**). Because the recency effect is short-lived, lost in just a few minutes, it is attributed to STM. Conversely, the primacy effect is seen only if there is a delay in responding (see Figure 13.14b), suggesting that time is needed to get the early items into LTM. Similarly, patients with amnesia caused by impairment of the hippocampus show a reduced primacy effect, despite retaining the recency effect (the red curve in Figure 13.14a). Other animals also show primacy and recency effects too, but only if shorter delays are used, as if STM lasts longer in humans than in other species.

Figure 13.14 Serial Position Curves (Part *a* after Baddeley and Warrington, 1970; *b* after A. A. Wright et al., 1985.)

(a)

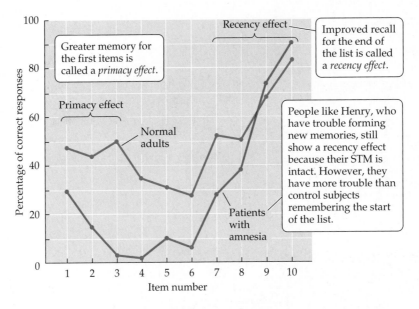

When people listen to a list of items and then, after a short delay, are asked to repeat those items, they tend to remember those at the start and end of the series better than those in the middle.

Greater memory for the first items is called a *primacy effect*.

Improved recall for the end of the list is called a *recency effect*.

People like Henry, who have trouble forming new memories, still show a recency effect because their STM is intact. However, they have more trouble than control subjects remembering the start of the list.

(b)

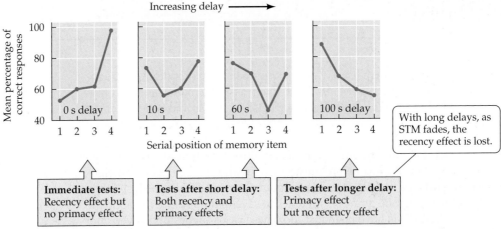

When we vary how long we wait between providing a series of items, we can eliminate primacy and recency effects. The primacy effect is lost if we have no delay between presentation of the list and testing, perhaps because there wasn't enough time for the items at the start of the list to enter LTM.

Increasing delay ⟶

With long delays, as STM fades, the recency effect is lost.

Immediate tests: Recency effect but no primacy effect

Tests after short delay: Both recency and primacy effects

Tests after longer delay: Primacy effect but no recency effect

A Prodigious Memory   The model for the fictional film *Rain Man*, the late Kim Peek, was a *savant* (from the French for "knowing"), a person with an unusually well developed ability or skill. Born with several brain deformities, including an absence of the corpus callosum (Treffert and Christensen, 2005), Kim eventually memorized about 9,000 books, each taking about an hour. For example, he read the novel *The Hunt for Red October* in 75 minutes, and when asked, 4 months later, to name a minor character, not only did he know the name, but he cited the page number where the character appeared and he quoted several passages on the page verbatim!

Long-term memory has vast capacity but is subject to distortion

How much information can be stored in LTM? There must be a limit, but no one has been able to come up with a way to measure it. In one classic experiment, people viewed long sequences of color photos of various scenes; several days later, they were shown pairs of images—in each case a new image plus one from the previous session—and asked to identify the images seen previously. Astonishingly, subjects performed with a high degree of accuracy for series of up to 10,000 different stimuli! The researcher concluded that, for all practical purposes, "there is no upper bound to memory capacity" (Standing, 1973).

We take this capacity for granted and barely notice, for example, that knowledge of a language involves remembering at least 100,000 pieces of information. Most of us also store a huge assortment of information about faces, tunes, odors, skills, stories, and so on. Pigeons have a similarly impressive visual memory (Vaughan and Greene, 1984). Case studies of individuals with exceptional memory indicate that without the usual process of pruning out unimportant memories, continual perfect recall can become uncontrollable, distracting, and exhausting (Luria, 1987; Parker et al., 2006).

Despite the vast capacity of LTM, forgetting is a normal aspect of memory, helping to filter out unimportant information and freeing up needed cognitive resources (Kuhl et al., 2007). Interestingly, research indicates that the **memory trace** (the record laid down in memory by a learning experience) doesn't simply deteriorate from disuse and the passage of time; instead, memories tend to suffer interference from events before or after their formation.

For example, several studies have found that the process of retrieving information from LTM causes the memories to become temporarily unstable, and susceptible to disruption or alteration before undergoing **reconsolidation** and returning to stable status (Nader and Hardt, 2009). Thus we can create *false memories* by asking people to retrieve a memory with a leading question—"Did you see the broken headlight?" rather than "Was the headlight broken?" (Loftus, 2003)—incorporating the false detail as the memory is reconsolidated. This possibility of planting false memories clouds the issue of "recovered memories" of childhood sexual or physical abuse, because controversial therapeutic methods such as hypnosis or guided imagery (in which the patient is encouraged to imagine hypothetical abuse scenarios) can inadvertently plant false memories.

On the other hand, you can use the power of reconsolidation when studying—as long as you're careful to check your facts. One of the best ways to improve learning is simply repeated retrieval (and thus, repeated reconsolidation) of the stored information with feedback to let you know what you got right or wrong (Karpicke and Roediger, 2008). In other words, test yourself repeatedly, as with the "How's it going?" questions in this book. For your next exam, try making up some additional practice tests for yourself, or have a friend quiz you, instead of simply "cramming."

We still haven't talked about the nitty-gritty of memory in the brain—what exactly changes in the brain when we learn? That's what we'll take up in Part II.

Kim Peek memorized an estimated 9,000 books, revealing the vast capacity of his long-term memory.

9,000 books

1,250 feet

Empire State Building

memory trace   A persistent change in the brain that reflects the storage of memory.

reconsolidation   The return of a memory trace to stable long-term storage after it has been temporarily made changeable during the process of recall.

How's it going?

1. What are the stages of memory, and what do we call the processes by which information moves from one stage to the next?

2. What are the serial position effects of memory?

3. Explain how reconsolidation makes us vulnerable to distorted memories.

neuroplasticity or neural plasticity
The ability of the nervous system to change in response to experience or the environment.

. . . .

PART II Neural Mechanisms of Memory

What are the basic cellular, synaptic, and molecular events that store information in the nervous system? In this next part of the chapter we will look at some of the ways in which new learning involves changes in the strength of existing synapses, and the biochemical signals that may produce those changes. We'll consider how the formation of memories may require the formation of new synapses, or even the birth of new neurons. This **neuroplasticity** (or **neural plasticity**) is found in virtually all animals, indicating that it is an ancient and vital product of evolution.

Memory Storage Requires Neuronal Remodeling

In introducing the term *synapse*, Charles Sherrington (1897) speculated that synaptic alterations might be the basis of learning. Sherrington's speculation anticipated an area of research that remains one of the most intensive efforts in all of neuroscience, since most theories of learning focus on plasticity of the structure and function of synapses.

Figure 13.15 Synaptic Changes That May Store Memories

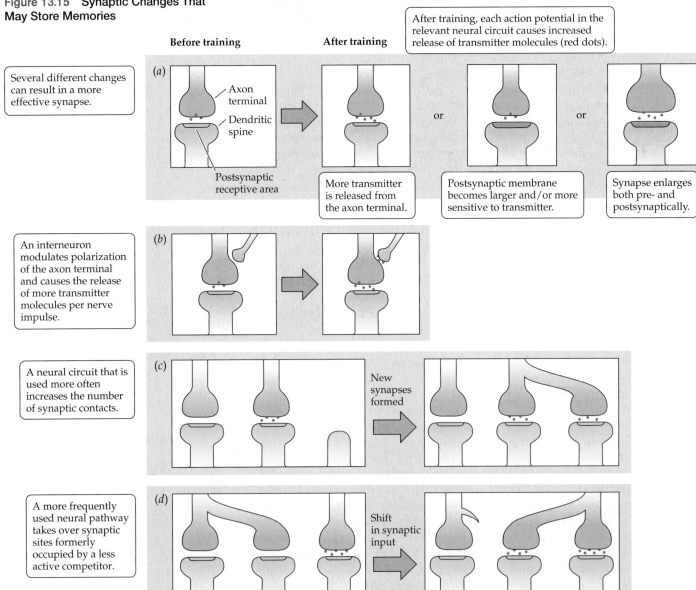

After training, each action potential in the relevant neural circuit causes increased release of transmitter molecules (red dots).

Before training   After training

(a) Several different changes can result in a more effective synapse.

Axon terminal
Dendritic spine
Postsynaptic receptive area

More transmitter is released from the axon terminal.

or

Postsynaptic membrane becomes larger and/or more sensitive to transmitter.

or

Synapse enlarges both pre- and postsynaptically.

(b) An interneuron modulates polarization of the axon terminal and causes the release of more transmitter molecules per nerve impulse.

(c) A neural circuit that is used more often increases the number of synaptic contacts.

New synapses formed

(d) A more frequently used neural pathway takes over synaptic sites formerly occupied by a less active competitor.

Shift in synaptic input

Plastic changes at synapses can be physiological or structural

Synaptic changes that may store information can be measured physiologically. The changes could be presynaptic, postsynaptic, or both (**Figure 13.15a**). They might include changes in the amount of neurotransmitter released and/or changes in the number or sensitivity of the postsynaptic receptors, resulting in larger (or smaller) postsynaptic potentials. Inhibiting inactivation of the transmitter (by altering reuptake or enzymatic degradation) could produce a similar effect. Synaptic activity could also be influenced by inputs from other neurons, causing extra depolarization or hyperpolarization of the axon terminals and therefore changes in the amount of neurotransmitter released (**Figure 13.15b**).

Long-term memories may require changes in the nervous system so substantial that they can be directly observed (with the aid of a microscope, of course). After all, structural changes resulting from use are apparent in other parts of the body, as when exercise tones and shapes muscle. In a similar way, new synapses can form (or old synapses may die back) as a result of use (**Figure 13.15c**).

Training could also lead to the reorganization of synaptic connections. For example, it could cause a more active pathway to take over sites formerly occupied by a less active competitor (**Figure 13.15d**).

Varied experiences and learning cause the brain to change and grow

The remarkable plasticity of the brain is not all that difficult to demonstrate. Simply living in a complex environment, with its many opportunities for new learning, produces pronounced biochemical and anatomical changes in the brains of rats (Renner and Rosenzweig, 1987).

In standard studies of environmental enrichment, rats are randomly assigned to one of three housing conditions:

1. **Standard condition (SC)**. Animals are housed in small groups in standard lab cages (**Figure 13.16a**). This is the typical environment for laboratory animals.

2. **Impoverished condition (IC)**. Animals are housed individually in standard lab cages (**Figure 13.16b**).

3. **Enriched condition (EC)**. Animals are housed in large social groups in special cages containing various toys and other interesting features (**Figure 13.16c**). This condi-

standard condition (SC) The usual environment for laboratory rodents, with a few animals in a cage and adequate food and water, but no complex stimulation.

impoverished condition (IC) Also called *isolated condition*. An environment for laboratory rodents in which animals are housed singly in a small cage without complex stimuli.

enriched condition (EC) Also called *complex environment*. An environment for laboratory rodents in which animals are group-housed with a wide variety of stimulus objects.

(*a*) Standard condition

(*b*) Impoverished condition

Figure 13.16 Experimental Environments to Test the Effects of Enrichment on Learning and Brain Measures

(*c*) Enriched condition

Interaction with an enriched environment has measurable effects on the brain, on stress reactions, and on learning.

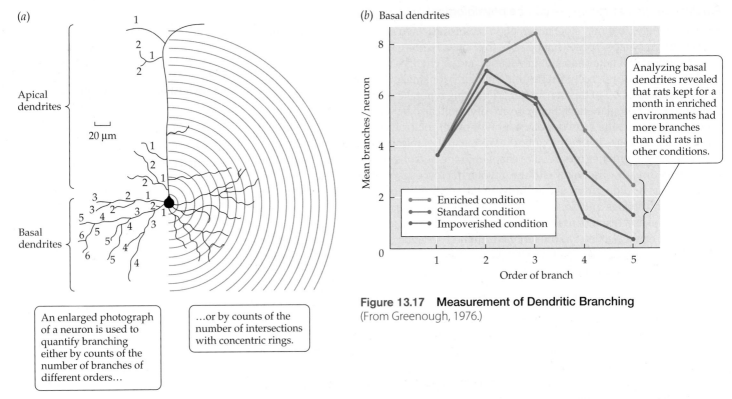

(a)

Apical dendrites

20 μm

Basal dendrites

An enlarged photograph of a neuron is used to quantify branching either by counts of the number of branches of different orders...

...or by counts of the number of intersections with concentric rings.

(b) Basal dendrites

Mean branches/neuron

Order of branch

- Enriched condition
- Standard condition
- Impoverished condition

Analyzing basal dendrites revealed that rats kept for a month in enriched environments had more branches than did rats in other conditions.

Figure 13.17 **Measurement of Dendritic Branching** (From Greenough, 1976.)

tion provides enhanced opportunities for learning perceptual and motor skills, social learning, and so on.

In dozens of studies over several decades, a variety of changes in the brain were linked to environmental enrichment. For example, compared to IC animals:

- EC animals have a heavier, thicker cortex, especially in somatosensory and visual cortical areas (M. C. Diamond, 1967).
- EC animals show enhanced cholinergic activity throughout the cortex (Rosenzweig et al., 1961).
- EC animals have more dendritic branches on cortical neurons, and many more dendritic spines on those branches (**Figure 13.17**) (Greenough, 1976).
- EC animals have *larger* cortical synapses (M. C. Diamond et al., 1975), consistent with the storage of long-term memory in cortical areas through changes in synapses and circuits.
- EC animals have more neurons in the hippocampus because newly generated neurons (a topic of the next section of this chapter) live longer (Kempermann et al., 1997).
- EC animals show enhanced recovery from brain damage (Will et al., 2004).

These cerebral effects of experience, which were surprising when first reported for rats in the early 1960s, are now seen to occur widely in the animal kingdom—from flies to philosophers (Mohammed, 2001). But how can we study the physiology of learning when the mammalian cortex has many billions of neurons, organized in vast networks, and upwards of a billion synapses per cubic centimeter (Merchán-Pérez et al., 2009)? Researchers made progress by studying simple learning circuits, in various species including mammals, uncovering basic cellular principles of memory formation that may generalize to neurons throughout the brain.

Invertebrate nervous systems show synaptic plasticity

As we've discussed, neuroplasticity and the ability to learn are ancient adaptations found throughout the animal kingdom. At the neuronal level, even species that are only remotely related likely share the same basic cellular processes for information storage.

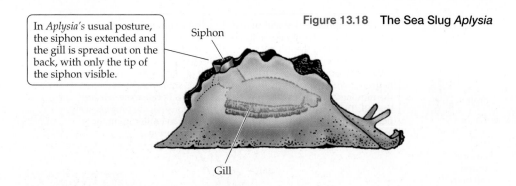

In *Aplysia*'s usual posture, the siphon is extended and the gill is spread out on the back, with only the tip of the siphon visible.

Siphon

Gill

Figure 13.18 The Sea Slug *Aplysia*

Indeed, one fruitful research strategy has been to focus on memory mechanisms in the very simple nervous systems of certain invertebrates. Invertebrate nervous systems have relatively few neurons (on the order of hundreds to tens of thousands). Because these neurons are arranged identically in different individuals, it is possible to construct detailed neural circuit diagrams for particular behaviors and study the same few neurons in multiple individuals.

Even in these "simple" organisms, the search for memory mechanisms began with the simplest types of learning. Earlier we discussed one of the most basic forms of learning—associative learning about two stimuli, such as the case of a dog learning to associate the sound of a bell with food. Even simpler than associative learning are the types of learning that involve only *one* stimulus, called **nonassociative learning**. Perhaps the simplest form of nonassociative learning is **habituation**—a decrease in response to a stimulus as it is repeated. To be true habituation, the decreased response cannot be due to failure of the sensory system to detect the stimulus, or an inability of the motor system to respond. Sitting in a café, you may stop noticing the door chime when someone enters. Your ears still detect the chime, and your body is perfectly capable of looking up to see what happened, but you've habituated to the sound.

Scientists uncovered how the sea slug *Aplysia* learns to habituate to a stimulus (Kandel, 2009). If you squirt water at the slug's *siphon*—a tube through which it draws water—the animal protectively retracts its delicate gill (**Figure 13.18**). But with repeated stimulation the animal retracts the gill less and less, as it learns that the stimulation represents no danger to the gill. Eric Kandel and associates demonstrated that this *short-term habituation* is caused by changes in the synapse between the sensory cell that detects the squirt of water and the motoneuron that retracts the gill. As less and less transmitter is released at this synapse, the gill withdrawal in response to the stimulation slowly fades (**Figure 13.19a**) (M. Klein et al., 1980).

The number and size of synapses can also vary with training in *Aplysia*. For example, if an *Aplysia* is tested in the habituation paradigm over a series of days, each successive day the animal habituates faster than it did the day before. This phenomenon represents *long-term habituation* (as opposed to the short-term habituation that we just described), and in this case there is a reduction in the *number of synapses* between the sensory cell and the motoneuron (**Figure 13.19b**) (C. H. Bailey and Chen, 1983).

A similar research program aimed at understanding simple learning in much more complicated species—mammals—found that learning also alters the strength of synaptic connections, as we'll see next.

Classical conditioning relies on circuits in the mammalian cerebellum

Success at studying the more complicated mammalian brain came when researchers probed simple associative learning: classical conditioning of the eye-blink reflex (Lavond et al., 1993; R. F. Thompson, 1990; R. F. Thompson and Steinmetz, 2009).

When a puff of air is aimed at the cornea of a rabbit, the animal reflexively blinks. The eye-blink reflex can be classically conditioned: over several trials, if the air puff (US) immediately follows an acoustic tone (CS), a simple conditioned response (CR)

nonassociative learning A type of learning in which presentation of a particular stimulus alters the strength or probability of a response according to the strength and temporal spacing of that stimulus. It includes habituation and sensitization.

habituation A form of nonassociative learning in which an organism becomes less responsive following repeated presentations of a stimulus.

Figure 13.19 **Synaptic Plasticity Underlying Habituation in *Aplysia***

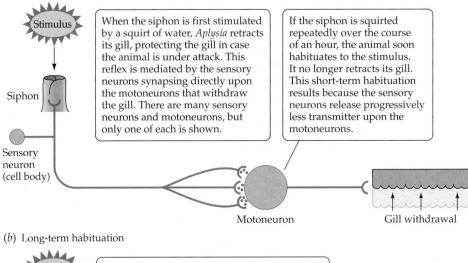

(a) Short-term habituation

Stimulus

Siphon

Sensory neuron (cell body)

When the siphon is first stimulated by a squirt of water, *Aplysia* retracts its gill, protecting the gill in case the animal is under attack. This reflex is mediated by the sensory neurons synapsing directly upon the motoneurons that withdraw the gill. There are many sensory neurons and motoneurons, but only one of each is shown.

If the siphon is squirted repeatedly over the course of an hour, the animal soon habituates to the stimulus. It no longer retracts its gill. This short-term habituation results because the sensory neurons release progressively less transmitter upon the motoneurons.

Motoneuron

Gill withdrawal

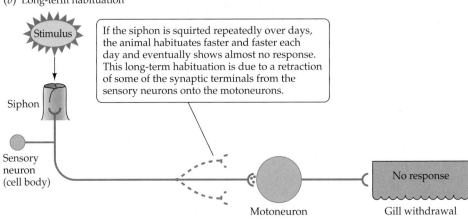

(b) Long-term habituation

Stimulus

Siphon

Sensory neuron (cell body)

If the siphon is squirted repeatedly over days, the animal habituates faster and faster each day and eventually shows almost no response. This long-term habituation is due to a retraction of some of the synaptic terminals from the sensory neurons onto the motoneurons.

Motoneuron

No response

Gill withdrawal

How's it going?

1. What are some of the ways that learning could alter synaptic structure or function?

2. Describe the effects of different environments on the brains of rats.

3. How does the circuitry in *Aplysia* change in the course of short-term and long-term habituation?

4. Which brain region is crucial for classical conditioning, and how does it play its role?

develops rapidly: the rabbit comes to blink when the tone is sounded (to review these terms and the basics of conditioning, see Figure 13.9). The neural circuit of the eye-blink reflex is also simple, involving cranial nerves and some interneurons that connect their nuclei (**Figure 13.20a**). Sensory fibers from the cornea run along cranial nerve V (the trigeminal nerve) to its nucleus in the brainstem. From there, some interneurons send axons to synapse on other cranial nerve motor nuclei (VI and VII), which in turn activate the muscles of the eyelids, causing the blink.

Early studies showed that destruction of the hippocampus has little effect on the conditioned eye-blink response in rabbits (Lockhart and Moore, 1975). Therefore, the hippocampus is *not* required for this conditioning. Instead, as we mentioned earlier, researchers found that a *cerebellar* circuit is both necessary and sufficient for eye-blink conditioning.

The trigeminal (V) pathway that carries information about the corneal stimulation (the US) to the cranial motor nuclei also sends axons to the brainstem. These brainstem neurons, in turn, send axons called *climbing fibers* to synapse on cerebellar neurons. The same cerebellar cells also receive information about the auditory CS by a pathway through the auditory nuclei (**Figure 13.20b**). So information about the US and CS converges in the cerebellum. After conditioning, the occurrence of the CS—the tone—has an enhanced effect on the cerebellar neurons, so they now trigger eye blink even in the absence of an air puff (**Figure 13.20c**). Imaging studies confirm that the cerebellum is important for conditioning of the eye-blink reflex and other simple conditioning in humans (Timmann et al., 2010). How does the training change the strength of those synapses, so that now the tone triggers a blink? At least some of these plastic changes in the cerebellar neurons rely on a special synaptic mechanism that has been best studied in the hippocampus (Mao and Evinger, 2001), and that's where we turn our attention next.

(a) Before

1 Before training, a puff of air on the surface of the eye triggers a reflexive eye blink.

2 Information about the puff of air is also sent to the cerebellum. Although the cerebellum can send information to the cranial motor nuclei that trigger the eye blink, at this stage those synapses are inactive.

Cerebellum

Reflex pathway

Corneal air puff (US) → Trigeminal nucleus → Cranial motor nuclei → Eye blink

(b) Training

3 During conditioning, information about the sound of the bell also reaches the cerebellum. There, impulses from this auditory signal and the air puff converge on particular neurons. Repeated pairings of bell (CS) and air puff (US) strengthen particular synapses within the cerebellum.

Bell (CS) → → Cerebellum

Reflex pathway

Corneal air puff (US) → Trigeminal nucleus → Cranial motor nuclei → Eye blink

(c) After

4 After training is complete, the sound of the bell now triggers activity in the cerebellum that drives the cranial motor nuclei to trigger an eye blink even if the air puff never happens. This is a conditioned response. The animal has learned that the ringing of the bell predicts that an air puff will soon hit the eye.

Bell (CS) → → Cerebellum

5 Repeated presentation of the bell without the air puff begins to weaken the cerebellar connections so that eventually the bell stops eliciting an eye blink. The animal has now learned that the bell no longer predicts an air puff.

Reflex pathway

No corneal air puff (US) → Trigeminal nucleus → Cranial motor nuclei → Eye blink

Figure 13.20   The Neural Circuit for Conditioning the Eye-Blink Reflex (After R. F. Thompson and Krupa, 1994.)

Synaptic Plasticity Can Be Measured in Simple Hippocampal Circuits

Modern ideas about synaptic plasticity have their origins in the theories of Donald Hebb, who proposed that when a presynaptic and a postsynaptic neuron are repeatedly activated together, the synaptic connection between them will become stronger and more stable (the phrase "cells that fire together wire together" captures the basic idea). These **Hebbian synapses** could then act together to store memory traces (Hebb, 1949).

This idea was eventually confirmed in various brain tissues. Most prominently, researchers in the 1970s discovered an impressive form of neuroplasticity in the hippocampus that appeared to confirm Hebb's theories about synaptic changes (Bliss and Lømo, 1973; Schwartzkroin and Wester, 1975). In such experiments, electrodes are placed within the rat hippocampus, positioned so that the researchers can stimulate a group of *presynaptic* axons and immediately record the electrical response of a group of *postsynaptic* neurons. Normal, low-level activation of the presynaptic cells produces stable and predictable excitatory postsynaptic potentials (EPSPs) (see Chapter 3), as expected. But when a brief high-frequency burst of electrical stimuli (called a **tetanus**) is applied to the presynaptic neurons, causing them to produce a high rate of action potentials, the response of the postsynaptic neurons changes. Now the postsynaptic

Donald O. Hebb (1904–1985)   "When an axon of cell A is near enough to excite cell B and repeatedly or persistently takes part in firing it, some growth process or metabolic change takes place in one or both cells such that A's efficiency, as one of the cells firing B, is increased" (Hebb, 1949). (Photo courtesy of Ms. Mary Ellen Hebb and Dr. Richard Brown.)

Hebbian synapse   A synapse that is strengthened when it successfully drives the postsynaptic cell.

tetanus   An intense volley of action potentials.

Figure 13.21 Long-Term Potentiation Occurs in the Hippocampus

If axons in the circuit are stimulated only once every second, the size of the response in the postsynaptic neurons is quite stable.

After a brief tetanus, however, the excitatory post-synaptic potential (EPSP) response increases markedly and remains high. This greater responsiveness is called *long-term potentiation (LTP).*

Tetanus

Potentiation

long-term potentiation (LTP) A stable and enduring increase in the effectiveness of synapses following repeated strong stimulation.

cells respond to normal levels of presynaptic activity by producing much larger EPSPs; in other words, the synapses appear to have become stronger, more effective. This stable and long-lasting enhancement of synaptic transmission, termed **long-term potentiation** (**LTP**; *potentiation* means a "strengthening"), is illustrated in **Figure 13.21**.

We now know that LTP can be generated in conscious and freely behaving animals, in anesthetized animals, and in tissue slices, and that LTP is evident in a variety of invertebrate and vertebrate species. LTP can also last for weeks or more (Bliss and Gardner-Medwin, 1973). So, at least superficially, LTP appears to have the hallmarks of a cellular mechanism of memory. This hint at a cellular origin prompted research into the molecular and physiological mechanisms underlying LTP.

(a) Normal synaptic transmission

Axon terminal

1 Normally, the NMDA channel is blocked by a Mg^{2+} molecule and only the AMPA channel functions in exciting the neuron.

Glu
Mg^{2+} Glu Na^+

NMDA receptor, inactive because of block by Mg^{2+} ion

AMPA receptor, when activated, depolarizes cell

Latent AMPA receptor

CaMKII

PKC TK

Dendritic spine

CREB

3 The rapid entry of Ca^{2+} ions triggers second messenger systems that lead to LTP, increasing the conductance of existing AMPA receptors and moving more into the membrane.

(b) Induction of LTP

2 With repeated activation of AMPA receptors, depolarization of the neuron drives Mg^{2+} out of the NMDA channel, allowing Ca^{2+} ions in.

Enhances subsequent transmitter release

Ca^{2+} Glu Na^+
Mg^{2+}

Increased Ca^{2+} concentration leads to activation of second messengers

CaMKII

Second-messenger systems

PKC TK

CREB

Retrograde signal generator

4 Retrograde transmitters, perhaps nitric oxide, reach the presynaptic terminal to enhance neurotransmitter release.

NMDA receptors and AMPA receptors collaborate in LTP

The *hippocampal formation* consists of two interlocking C-shaped structures: the hippocampus itself and the **dentate gyrus**. At least three different pathways in the hippocampal formation display LTP, and it is seen in other brain regions too (Malenka and Bear, 2004). The most studied form of hippocampal LTP occurs at synapses that use the excitatory neurotransmitter **glutamate**, and it is critically dependent on a glutamate receptor subtype called the **NMDA receptor** (after its selective ligand, *N-m*ethyl-*D-a*spartate). Treatment with drugs that selectively block NMDA receptors completely prevents new LTP in this region, but it does not affect synaptic changes that have already been established. As you might expect, these postsynaptic NMDA receptors—working in conjunction with other glutamate receptors called **AMPA receptors**—have some unique characteristics, which are responsible for LTP.

During normal, low-level activity, the release of glutamate at a CA1 synapse activates only the AMPA receptors. The NMDA receptors cannot respond to the glutamate, because magnesium ions (Mg^{2+}) block the NMDA receptor's calcium ion (Ca^{2+}) channel (**Figure 13.22a**); thus, few Ca^{2+} ions can enter the neuron. The situation changes, however, if larger quantities of glutamate are released—say, in response to a barrage of action potentials caused by a tetanus. That stronger stimulation of the AMPA receptors depolarizes the postsynaptic membrane so much that the Mg^{2+} plug is driven from the central channels of the NMDA receptors (**Figure 13.22b**). Now the NMDA receptors are also able to respond to glutamate, admitting large amounts of Ca^{2+} into the postsynaptic neuron. Thus, NMDA receptors are fully active only when "gated" by a combination of strong depolarization (via AMPA receptors) and the ligand (glutamate).

dentate gyrus   A strip of gray matter in the hippocampal formation.

glutamate   An amino acid transmitter; the most common excitatory transmitter.

NMDA receptor   A glutamate receptor that also binds the glutamate agonist NMDA (*N*-methyl-D-aspartate), and that is both ligand-gated and voltage-sensitive.

AMPA receptor   A glutamate receptor that also binds the glutamate agonist AMPA.

(*c*) Enhanced synapse, after induction of LTP

To see an animation of this figure, go to

mindsmachine.com/13.3
AMPA and NMDA Receptors

5 These changes make the synapse more responsive.

6 The postsynaptic cell now has a stronger response, as more transmitter is released and more AMPA receptors are present.

Glu

Mg^{2+} Glu   Na+   Na+

NMDA receptor

AMPA receptors

Figure 13.22   Roles of the NMDA and AMPA Receptors in the Induction of LTP in the CA1 Region   CaMKII, calcium/calmodulin-dependent protein kinase II; CREB, cAMP responsive element–binding protein; Glu, glutamate; PKC, protein kinase C; TK, tyrosine kinase.

retrograde transmitter A neurotransmitter that is released by the postsynaptic region, diffuses back across the synapse, and alters the functioning of the presynaptic neuron.

The large influx of Ca²⁺ at NMDA receptors activates a variety of intracellular enzymes that affect AMPA receptors in several important ways (**Figure 13.22c**) (Kessels and Malinow, 2009; Lisman et al., 2002). First, the enzymes cause existing nearby AMPA receptors to move to the active synapse (T. Takahashi et al., 2003), and modify the AMPA receptors to increase their conductance of Na⁺ and K⁺ ions (Sanderson et al., 2008). In addition, more AMPA receptors are produced and inserted into the postsynaptic membrane. Thus, after the tetanus there are more AMPA receptors, and those receptors are more effective, so the synaptic response to glutamate is strengthened (see Figure 13.22b).

There are *presynaptic* changes in LTP too. When the postsynaptic cell is strongly stimulated and its NMDA receptors become active and admit Ca²⁺, an intracellular process causes the postsynaptic cell to release a **retrograde transmitter**—often a diffusible gas—that travels back across the synapse and alters the functioning of the presynaptic neuron (see Figure 13.22b). By affecting the presynaptic cell, the retrograde transmitter ensures that more glutamate will be released into the synapse than previously, thereby strengthening the synapse some more. So, LTP involves active changes on both sides of the synapse.

So far, we've talked about how activity can make existing Hebbian synapses stronger. However, evidence suggests that the same mechanisms can affect whether new synapses are formed and old synapses retracted. As depicted in **Figure 13.23**, in these systems it appears that when a group of presynaptic neurons fire at the same time, they "gang up" on the postsynaptic cell, depolarizing it enough that the NMDA receptors are activated to strengthen the connections. Conversely, any presynaptic neurons that tend to fire out of synchrony with the other inputs are not likely to depolarize the postsynaptic neurons enough to activate NMDA receptors. Eventually, the strengthened inputs seem to sprout new, additional connections, while the weakened synapses fade away.

Many scientists are excited about LTP because this momentary burst of neural activity, the tetanus, can change synaptic strength for a long time. It's easy to imagine how another momentary burst of neural activity, in this case triggered by a learning experience, could change synaptic strength, and that change in synaptic strength might be memory trace. But is this just a case of an overactive imagination, or is LTP truly involved in learning?

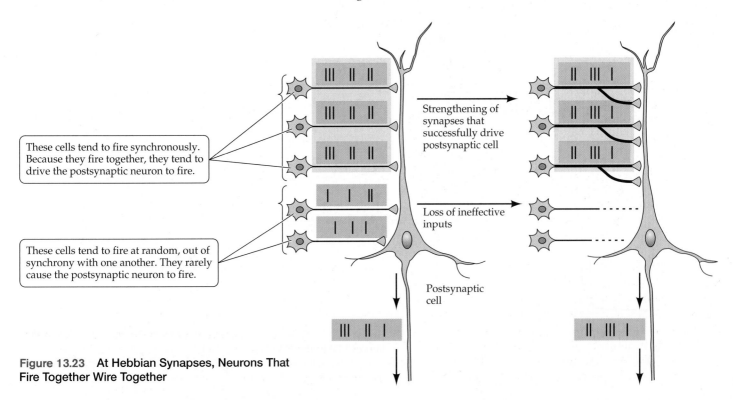

These cells tend to fire synchronously. Because they fire together, they tend to drive the postsynaptic neuron to fire.

These cells tend to fire at random, out of synchrony with one another. They rarely cause the postsynaptic neuron to fire.

Strengthening of synapses that successfully drive postsynaptic cell

Loss of ineffective inputs

Postsynaptic cell

Figure 13.23 At Hebbian Synapses, Neurons That Fire Together Wire Together

Is LTP a mechanism of memory formation?

Even the simplest learning involves circuits of multiple neurons and many synapses, and more-complex declarative and procedural memory traces must involve vast networks of neurons, so we are unlikely to conclude that LTP is the *only* mechanism of learning. However, evidence from several research perspectives implicates LTP in memory:

1. *Correlational observations.* The time course of LTP bears strong similarity to the time course of memory formation (Lynch et al., 1991; Staubli, 1995). Covarying with memory, LTP can be induced within seconds, may last for days or weeks, and shows a vulnerable period that lasts for several minutes after induction. In that way, LTP resembles the vulnerability of STM to loss from accident or disease.

2. *Somatic intervention experiments.* In general, pharmacological treatments that interfere with LTP also tend to impair learning. So, for example, NMDA receptor blockade interferes with performance in the Morris water maze (a test of spatial memory) and other types of memory tests (R. G. Morris et al., 1989). Drugs that inhibit the enzymes activated by NMDA receptors also generally interfere with aspects of memory formation (Frankland et al., 2001). And knockout mice that lack functional NMDA receptors only in CA1 appear normal in many respects, but their hippocampi are incapable of LTP and their declarative memory is impaired (Rampon et al., 2000). In a clever reversal, researchers have also shown that mice engineered to *overexpress* NMDA receptors in the hippocampus have enhanced LTP and better-than-normal long-term memory (Y. P. Tang et al., 2001). (For the full story of these mice, see **A Step Further 13.2**, on the website.)

3. *Behavioral intervention experiments.* In principle, the most convincing evidence for a link between LTP and learning would be "behavioral LTP": a demonstration that training an animal in a memory task induces LTP somewhere in the brain. Such research is difficult because of uncertainty about exactly where to put the recording electrodes in order to detect any induced LTP. Nevertheless, several examples of successful behavioral LTP have been reported. Fear conditioning—for example, the repeated pairing of an aversive stimulus and a tone, eventually resulting in fearful responses to the tone alone—produces clear LTP specifically in fear circuits in the amygdala and not elsewhere (McKernan and Shinnick-Gallagher, 1997; Rogan et al., 1997). And in one region of the hippocampus, a different form of aversive learning in rats produces exactly the same changes in electrophysiology and changes in AMPA receptors that are seen with LTP induced by electrodes (Whitlock et al., 2006).

Taken together, these findings support the idea that LTP is a kind of synaptic plasticity that underlies (or is very similar to) certain forms of learning and memory.

Thus it seems that Henry's tragic amnesia may have been the loss of hippocampal mechanisms like LTP to consolidate short-term memories into long-term memories. It's strange to think that such microscopic changes in synapses in a particular brain region could be so crucial for living a full human life. Eventually Henry seemed to stop being shocked when he saw his reflection, and he learned he was no longer in his mid-twenties. But it's not clear whether he understood, for long, that his parents had passed away. As a final act of generosity to a field of science that he helped launch, Henry arranged to donate his brain for further study after he died. Through webcasting technology, the dissection of Henry's brain was viewed live by thousands of people (see http://thebrainobservatory.ucsd.edu), and a series of more than 2,000 brain sections will eventually be made available.

To the end, although Henry could remember so little of his entire adult life, he was courteous and concerned about other people. Henry remembered the surgeon he had met several times before his operation: "He did medical research on people … What he learned about me helped others too, and I'm glad about that" (Corkin, 2002, p. 158). Henry never knew how famous he was, or how much his dreadful condition taught us about learning and memory; yet despite being deprived of one of the most important characteristics of a human being, he held fast to his humanity.

To see a video, go to

mindsmachine.com/13.4
Morris Water Maze

How's it going?

1. Describe how LTP is measured in the hippocampus.

2. What happens to AMPA receptors and NMDA receptors during LTP?

3. What evidence suggests that LTP may underlie some forms of learning and memory?

PART III Development of the Brain

Age puts its stamp on us all. Although the rate, progression, and orderliness of changes in the brain are especially prominent early in life, change is a feature of the entire life span. In this final part of the chapter we describe brains in terms of their progress through life from the womb to the tomb. The fertilization of an egg leads to a body with a brain that contains billions of neurons with an incredible number of connections. The pace of this process is extraordinary: during the height of prenatal growth of the human brain, more than 250,000 neurons are added per minute! We will describe the emergence of nerve cells, the formation of their connections, and the role of genes in shaping the nervous system. But we'll see that experience, gained through behavioral interactions with the environment, also sculpts the developing brain.

Growth and Development of the Brain Are Orderly Processes

Picture, if you can, the number of neurons in the mature human brain—about 100 billion. There are many types of neurons, each forming a vast array of hundreds or thousands of connections. Overall, the brain contains more than 100 trillion connections. If each synapse were represented by a grain of sand, the collected grains would form a cube longer than a football field on each edge! Yet each of us began as a single microscopic cell, the fertilized egg. How can one cell divide and grow to form the most complicated machines on Earth, perhaps in the universe?

Within 12 hours after a human egg is fertilized, the single cell begins dividing, forming a small mass of homogeneous cells, like a cluster of grapes, that is a mere 200 micrometers in diameter. Within a week the emerging human embryo shows three distinct cell layers (**Figure 13.24a**)—the beginnings of all the tissues of the body. The nervous system develops from the outer layer, called the **ectoderm** (from the Greek *ektos*, "out," and *derma*, "skin"). As the cell layers thicken, they grow to form a groove that will become the midline. At the head end of this neural groove, a thickened collection of cells forms (**Figure 13.24b**).

The tops of the neural ridges come together to form the **neural tube** (**Figure 13.24c**). At the anterior part of the neural tube, three subdivisions become apparent. These subdivisions correspond to the future **forebrain** (cortical regions, thalamus, and hypothalamus), **midbrain**, and **hindbrain** (cerebellum, pons, and medulla) (**Figure 13.24d**), which were discussed in Chapter 2. The interior of the neural tube becomes the fluid-filled cerebral ventricles of the brain, the central canal of the spinal cord, and the passages that connect them.

By the end of the eighth week, the human embryo shows the rudimentary beginnings of most body organs. The rapid development of the brain is reflected in the fact that by this time the head is half the total size of the embryo! (Note that the developing human is called an **embryo** during the first 10 weeks after fertilization; thereafter it is called a **fetus**.) **Figure 13.24e** shows the prenatal development of the human brain from weeks 10–41. Even after birth, there are dramatic local changes as some brain regions grow more than others, as we'll see later.

Development of the Nervous System Can Be Divided into Six Distinct Stages

From a cellular viewpoint it is useful to consider brain development as a sequence of six distinct stages, most of which occur during prenatal life:

1. *Neurogenesis*, the mitotic division of nonneuronal cells to produce neurons
2. *Cell migration*, the massive movements of nerve cells or their precursors to establish distinct nerve cell populations (nuclei in the CNS, layers of the cerebral cortex, and so on)
3. *Cell differentiation*, the refining of cells into distinctive types of neurons or glial cells

ectoderm The outer cellular layer of the developing fetus, giving rise to the skin and the nervous system.

neural tube An embryonic structure with subdivisions that correspond to the future forebrain, midbrain, and hindbrain.

forebrain The front division of the brain, which, in the mature vertebrate, contains the cerebral hemispheres, the thalamus, and the hypothalamus.

midbrain The middle division of the brain.

hindbrain The rear division of the brain, which, in the mature vertebrate, contains the cerebellum, pons, and medulla.

embryo The earliest stage in a developing animal.

fetus A developing individual after the embryo stage.

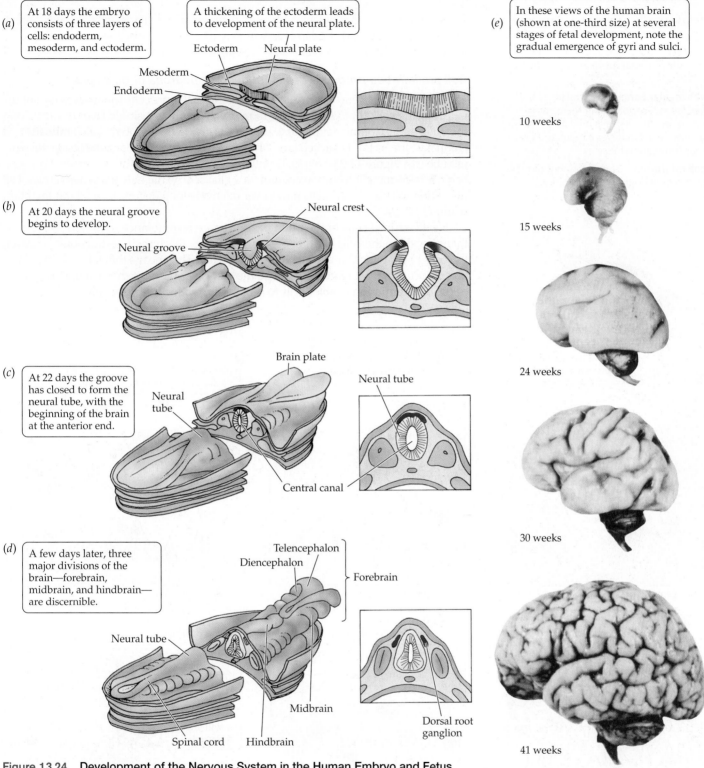

(a) At 18 days the embryo consists of three layers of cells: endoderm, mesoderm, and ectoderm.

A thickening of the ectoderm leads to development of the neural plate.

Ectoderm   Neural plate

Mesoderm

Endoderm

(e) In these views of the human brain (shown at one-third size) at several stages of fetal development, note the gradual emergence of gyri and sulci.

10 weeks

(b) At 20 days the neural groove begins to develop.

Neural crest

Neural groove

15 weeks

(c) At 22 days the groove has closed to form the neural tube, with the beginning of the brain at the anterior end.

Brain plate

Neural tube

Neural tube

Central canal

24 weeks

(d) A few days later, three major divisions of the brain—forebrain, midbrain, and hindbrain—are discernible.

Telencephalon

Diencephalon

Forebrain

30 weeks

Neural tube

Midbrain

Dorsal root ganglion

Spinal cord   Hindbrain

41 weeks

Figure 13.24   Development of the Nervous System in the Human Embryo and Fetus
(Part *e* from Larroche, 1977.)

To see an animation, go to

mindsmachine.com/13.5
Stages of Neuronal Development

4. *Synaptogenesis*, the establishment of synaptic connections as axons and dendrites grow

5. *Neuronal cell death*, the selective death of many nerve cells

6. *Synapse rearrangement*, the loss of some synapses and the development of others, to refine synaptic connections

neurogenesis The mitotic division of nonneuronal cells to produce neurons.

mitosis The process of division of somatic cells that involves duplication of DNA.

ventricular zone Also called *ependymal layer*. A region lining the cerebral ventricles that displays mitosis, providing neurons early in development and glial cells throughout life.

cell migration The movement of cells from site of origin to final location.

The six stages proceed at different rates and times in different parts of the nervous system. Some of the stages may overlap even within a region. In the discussion that follows, we will take up each stage in succession. This sequence is portrayed in **Figure 13.25**.

Cell proliferation produces cells that become neurons or glial cells

The production of neurons is called **neurogenesis**. Nerve cells themselves do not divide, but the cells that will give rise to neurons begin as a single layer of cells along the inner surface of the neural tube. These cells divide (in a process called **mitosis**) and gradually form a closely packed layer of cells called the **ventricular zone** inside the neural tube (see Figure 13.25, step 1). Eventually, some cells leave the ventricular zone and begin transforming into either a neuron or a glial cell. As the nervous system grows, **cell migration** follows, as the cells move over relatively long distances to fill out the brain (Figure 13.25, step 2).

Newly arrived cells in the brain bear no more resemblance to mature nerve cells than they do to the cells of other organs. Once they reach their destinations, however, the cells begin to use, or **express**, particular genes. This means that the cells make use of a particular subset of genes to make the particular proteins they need. This process of **cell differentiation** enables cells to acquire the distinctive appearance and functions

1 Cells of the neural tube divide to provide progeny cells.

Neural tube

Central canal

Neurogenesis

2 The cells produced migrate to their appropriate regions.

Ventricular zone

Cell migration

3 Each cell *differentiates*, expressing a particular subset of genes, to become a particular type of neuron or glial cell.

Cell differentiation

4 Neurons extend their axons and dendrites and form many synapses with one another.

Synaptogenesis

5 Many neurons normally die early in development.

Cell death

6 Many of the synapses initially formed…

…will later be retracted,…

…while other, later-appearing synapses form (shown in blue).

Synapse rearrangement

Figure 13.25 The Six Stages of Neural Development

of neurons characteristic of that particular region (Figure 13.25, step 3). Once they take on the characteristics of neurons, they begin making synaptic connections with one another, in the process of **synaptogenesis** (Figure 13.25, step 4).

The particular fate of a differentiating cell depends on where in the brain the cell happens to be and what the cell's neighbors are doing. Cells in the developing brain are constantly sending chemical signals to one another, each shaping the development of the other. This is the hallmark of vertebrate development: cells sort themselves out via **cell-cell interactions**, taking on fates that are appropriate in the context of what neighboring cells are doing. When the negotiations are all over, if things go properly, a new person is formed with all the types of cells in the brain that she or he needs to live.

This system of cell-cell interactions determining how brain cells develop has an important consequence: If cells that have not yet differentiated extensively can be obtained and placed in a particular brain region, they will differentiate in an appropriate way and become properly integrated. Such undifferentiated cells, called **stem cells**, are present throughout embryonic tissues, so they can be gathered from umbilical-cord blood, miscarried embryos, or unused embryos produced during *in vitro* fertilization. It may even be possible someday to take cells from adult tissue and, by treating them with various factors in a dish, transform them into stem cells (Palmer et al., 2001). It is hoped that placing stem cells in areas of brain degeneration, such as loss of myelin in multiple sclerosis, or loss of dopaminergic neurons in Parkinson's disease (see Chapter 5), might reverse such degeneration as the implanted cells differentiate to fill in for the missing components (S. Liu et al., 2000).

In the adult brain, newly born neurons aid learning

At birth, mammals have already produced most of the neurons they will ever have. The postnatal increase of human brain weight is due primarily to growth in the size of neurons, branching of dendrites, elaboration of synapses, increase in myelin, and addition of glial cells. But research in the last decade or so has shown that we are also capable of **adult neurogenesis**, the generation of new neurons in adulthood, primarily in the dentate gyrus of the hippocampal formation (**Figure 13.26**) (Gould, Reeves, et al., 1999; Magavi et al., 2000). Anatomically, the new neurons appear to integrate into the functional circuitry of the hippocampus and adjacent cortex (Bruel-Jungerman et al., 2007), which we've seen to play a role in forming new memories.

Indeed, although the new neurons acquired in adulthood represent just a tiny minority of the total, there's reason to think they are important. In experimental animals, the birth and/or survival of new neurons is enhanced by factors like exercise,

gene expression The process by which a cell makes an mRNA transcript of a particular gene.

cell differentiation The developmental stage in which cells acquire distinctive characteristics, such as those of neurons, as a result of expressing particular genes.

synaptogenesis The establishment of synaptic connections as axons and dendrites grow.

cell-cell interaction The general process during development in which one cell affects the differentiation of other, usually neighboring, cells.

stem cell A cell that is undifferentiated and therefore can take on the fate of any cell that a donor organism can produce.

adult neurogenesis The creation of new neurons in the brain of an adult.

To see a video, go to

mindsmachine.com/13.6
Migration of a Neuron along a
Radial Glial Cell

(a) BrdU *(b)* NeuN *(c)* Merged

20 µm

BrdU (bromodeoxyuridine) is a label that is selectively incorporated into the DNA of cells that are about to divide.

NeuN selectively labels neurons (green cells), in order to distinguish them from other nearby cells, such as glial cells.

Merging the two images makes it clear that some of the newly born cells are, in fact, neurons.

Figure 13.26 Neurogenesis in the Dentate Gyrus (Courtesy of Elodie Bruel-Jungerman and Serge Laroche, from Bruel-Jungerman et al., 2007.)

cell death or apoptosis The developmental process during which "surplus" cells die.

death gene A gene that is expressed only when a cell becomes committed to natural cell death (apoptosis).

neurotrophic factor Also called *trophic factor*. A target-derived chemical that acts as if it "feeds" certain neurons to help them survive.

environmental enrichment, and training (Gould, Beylin, et al., 1999; Waddell and Shors, 2008). Neurogenesis appears to enhance various forms of hippocampus-dependent learning, such as spatial memory and fear conditioning in some (but not all) studies (Kee et al., 2007; Saxe et al., 2006; Winocur et al., 2006). Mice with a genetic manipulation that turns off neurogenesis in the brains of adults showed a marked impairment in spatial learning with little effect on other behaviors (C. L. Zhang et al., 2008).

So by studying this chapter, you may be giving your brain a few more neurons to use on exam day! Physical exercise also boosts neurogenesis in rats—an effect that can be blocked by stressors such as social isolation (Stranahan et al., 2006)—so invest in exercise and a network of friends too.

The death of many neurons is a normal part of development

As strange as it may seem, cell death is a crucial phase of brain development, especially during embryonic stages (see Figure 13.25, step 5). This developmental stage is not unique to the nervous system. Naturally occurring **cell death**, also called **apoptosis** (from the Greek *apo*, "away from," and *ptosis*, "act of falling"), is evident as a kind of sculpting process in the emergence of other tissues in both animals and plants.

The number of neurons that die during early development is quite large. In some regions of the brain and spinal cord, *most* of the young nerve cells die during prenatal development. In 1958, Viktor Hamburger (1900–2001) first described naturally occurring neuronal cell death in chicks, in which nearly half the originally produced spinal motoneurons die before the chick hatches. A similar loss of spinal motoneurons was later reported in developing humans (**Figure 13.27**) (Forger and Breedlove, 1987).

These cells are not dying because of a defect. Rather, it appears that these cells have "decided" to die, as a consequence of complex interactions with surrounding cells, and are actively "committing suicide." Your chromosomes carry **death genes**—genes that are expressed only when a cell undergoes apoptosis (Peter et al., 1997). Genetically interfering with death genes in fetal mice causes them to grow brains that are too large to fit in the skull (Depaepe et al., 2005), so we can see how vital it is that some cells die.

Neurons compete for connections to target structures (other nerve cells or end organs, such as muscle). Cells that make adequate synapses remain; those without a place to form synaptic connections die. Apparently the cells compete not just for synaptic sites, but for a chemical that the target structure makes and releases (**Figure 13.28**). Neurons that receive enough of the chemical survive; those that do not, die. Such target-derived chemicals are called **neurotrophic factors** (or simply *trophic factors*) because they act as if they "feed" the neurons to help them survive (in Greek, *trophe* means "nourishment").

Figure 13.27 Many Neurons Die during Normal Early Development (Part *a* from Hamburger, 1975; *b* from Forger and Breedlove, 1987.)

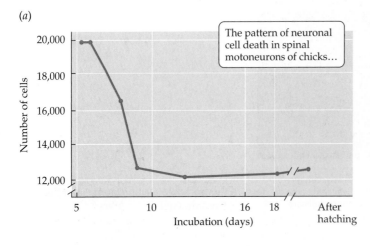

(a)

The pattern of neuronal cell death in spinal motoneurons of chicks…

(b)

…resembles that of humans. Many other neuronal populations show a similar pattern of apoptosis.

Figure 13.28 A Model for the Action of Neurotrophic Factors

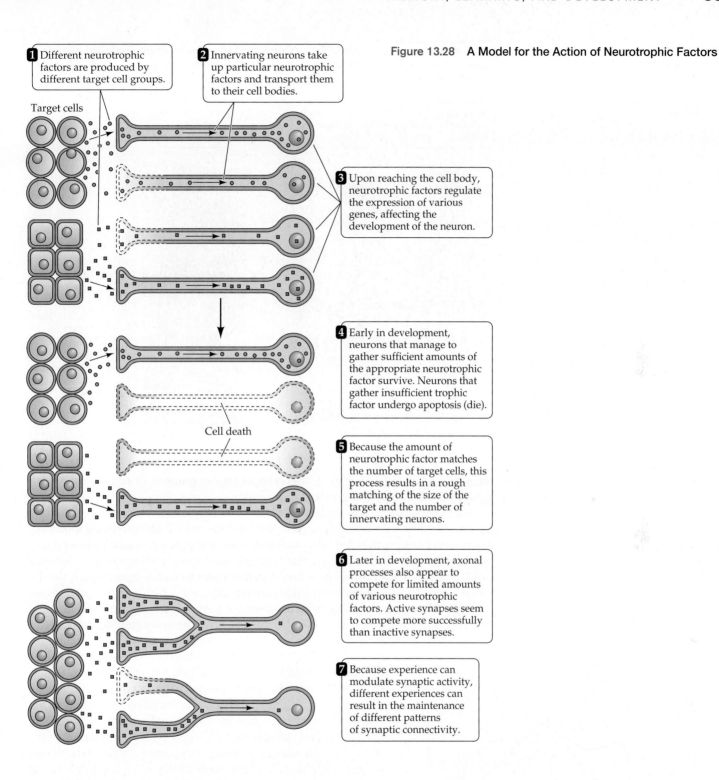

1 Different neurotrophic factors are produced by different target cell groups.

2 Innervating neurons take up particular neurotrophic factors and transport them to their cell bodies.

Target cells

3 Upon reaching the cell body, neurotrophic factors regulate the expression of various genes, affecting the development of the neuron.

4 Early in development, neurons that manage to gather sufficient amounts of the appropriate neurotrophic factor survive. Neurons that gather insufficient trophic factor undergo apoptosis (die).

Cell death

5 Because the amount of neurotrophic factor matches the number of target cells, this process results in a rough matching of the size of the target and the number of innervating neurons.

6 Later in development, axonal processes also appear to compete for limited amounts of various neurotrophic factors. Active synapses seem to compete more successfully than inactive synapses.

7 Because experience can modulate synaptic activity, different experiences can result in the maintenance of different patterns of synaptic connectivity.

An explosion of synapse formation is followed by synapse rearrangement

Before birth and after, neurons in the human cortex grow ever longer and more elaborate dendrites, as shown in **Figure 13.29**, each jammed with synapses. As we noted earlier, this massive increase in dendrites and synapses is responsible for most of the increase in brain size after birth. But just as not all the neurons produced by a developing individual are kept into adulthood, some of the synapses formed early in development are later retracted. Some original synapses are lost, and many, many new synapses are

synapse rearrangement   Also called *synaptic remodeling*. The loss of some synapses and the development of others; a refinement of synaptic connections that is often seen in development.

These representations of cerebral cortex show the extent of neural connections and neuronal differentiation at birth…

…at 3 months of age…

…and at 2 years of age.

The mature cerebral cortex contains six layers.

Figure 13.29   Cerebral Cortex Tissue in the Early Development of Humans (From Conel, 1939, 1947, 1959.)

formed (see Figure 13.25, step 6). This **synapse rearrangement**, or *synaptic remodeling*, typically takes place after the period of cell death.

For example, as we learned already, about half of the spinal motoneurons that form die later (see Figure 13.27). By the end of the cell death period, each surviving motoneuron innervates many muscle fibers, and every muscle fiber is innervated by several motoneurons. But later the surviving motoneurons retract many of their axon collaterals, until each muscle fiber comes to be innervated by only one motoneuron. Again, the decision about which synaptic connections are retained, and which new connections are formed, is thought to result from competition for trophic factors during development (see Figure 13.28) and/or competition between Hebbian synapses (see Figure 13.23).

Similar events have been documented in several neural regions, including the cerebellum (Mariani and Changeaux, 1981), the brainstem (Jackson and Parks, 1982), the visual cortex (Hubel et al., 1977), and the autonomic nervous system (Lichtman and Purves, 1980). In human cerebral cortex there seems to be a net loss of synapses from late childhood until midadolescence (**Figure 13.30**). This synaptic remodeling is evident in thinning of the cortical gray matter as pruning of dendrites and axon terminals progresses. The thinning process continues in a caudal–rostral (posterior–anterior) direction during maturation (**Figure 13.31**), so prefrontal cortex is affected last (Gogtay et al., 2004). Since prefrontal cortex is important for inhibiting behavior (see Chapter 14), this delayed brain maturation may contribute to teenagers' impulsivity and lack of control (Paus et al., 2008).

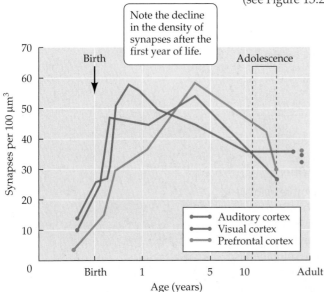

Note the decline in the density of synapses after the first year of life.

Figure 13.30   The Postnatal Development of Synapses In Human Cortex (From Huttenlocher et al., 1982.)

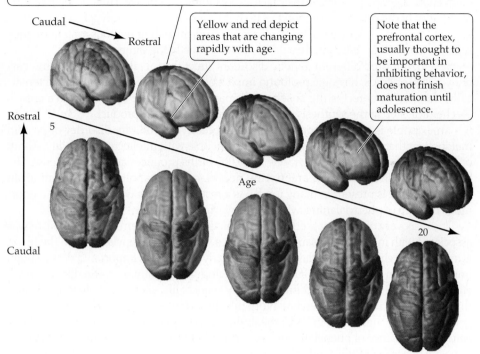

Repeated measures from many subjects reveal that the layer of gray matter on the surface of the cortex gets thinner throughout development, as synapses are retracted. Purple and blue depict regions with little change in cortical thickness.

Yellow and red depict areas that are changing rapidly with age.

Note that the prefrontal cortex, usually thought to be important in inhibiting behavior, does not finish maturation until adolescence.

Figure 13.31 Synapse Rearrangement in the Developing Human Brain (From Gogtay et al., 2004, courtesy of Nitin Gogtay.)

What determines which synapses are kept and which are lost? Although we don't know all the factors, one important influence is neural activity. One theory is that active synapses take up some neurotrophic factor that maintains the synapse, while inactive synapses get too little trophic factor to remain stable (see Figure 13.28). Intellectual stimulation probably contributes, as suggested by the fact that teenagers with the highest IQ show an especially prolonged period of cortical thinning (P. Shaw et al., 2006). Another stage of brain development, the formation of myelin sheaths for axons, is discussed in **A Step Further 13.3**, on the website.

This influence of experience on the developing brain brings us to the question of how both genes and the environment affect human intelligence.

Genes Interact with Experience to Guide Brain Development

Many factors influence the emergence of the form, arrangements, and connections of the developing brain. One influence is genes, which direct the production of every protein the cell can make. An individual who has inherited an altered gene will make an altered protein, which will affect any cell structure that includes that protein. Thus, every neuronal structure, and therefore every behavior, can be altered by changes in the appropriate gene(s). It is useful to think of genes as *intrinsic* factors—that is, factors that originate within the developing cell itself. All other influences we can consider *extrinsic*—originating outside of the developing cell.

Genotype is fixed at birth, but phenotype changes throughout life

Two terms help illustrate how these intrinsic and extrinsic factors interact. The sum of all the intrinsic, genetic information that an individual has is its **genotype**. The sum of all the physical characteristics that make up an individual is its **phenotype**. Your genotype

How's it going?

1. What six stages of cellular processes take place in the developing brain?

2. What is cell differentiation, and what guides this process in each cell in the developing brain?

3. Brain development is not always an increase in cell numbers or connections, as some cells and synapses are lost. Speculate about why these "regressive" events might be important.

genotype All the genetic information that one specific individual has inherited.

phenotype The sum of an individual's physical characteristics at one particular time.

Be Careful What You Eat Millie Lonergan, who has phenylketonuria, eats fruit and protein-free rice and pasta (without cheese) for a diet low in phenylalanine.

was determined at the moment of fertilization and remains the same throughout your life. But your phenotype changes constantly, as you grow up and grow old and even, in a tiny way, as you take each breath. In other words, phenotype is determined by the interaction of genotype and extrinsic factors, including experience. Thus, as we'll see, individuals who have identical genotypes do not have identical phenotypes, because they have not received identical extrinsic influences. And since their nervous system phenotypes are somewhat different, they do not behave exactly the same.

Several hundred different genetic disorders affect the metabolism of proteins, carbohydrates, or lipids, having a profound impact on the developing brain. Characteristically, the genetic defect is the absence of a particular enzyme that controls a critical biochemical step in the synthesis or breakdown of a vital body product.

An example is **phenylketonuria** (**PKU**), a recessive hereditary disorder of protein metabolism that at one time resulted in many people with intellectual disability. About one out of 100 persons is a carrier; one in 10,000 births produces an affected victim. The basic defect is the absence of an enzyme necessary to metabolize phenylalanine, an amino acid that is present in many foods. As a result, the brain is damaged by an enormous buildup of phenylalanine, which becomes toxic.

The discovery of PKU marked the first time that an inborn error of metabolism was associated with intellectual disability. These days, the level of phenylalanine in the blood is measured in children a few days after birth. Early detection is important because brain impairment can be prevented simply by reducing phenylalanine in the diet. Such dietary control of PKU is critical during the early years of life, especially before age 2; after that, diet can be relaxed somewhat. Note this important example of the interaction of genes and the environment in PKU: the dysfunctional gene causes intellectual disability *only* in the presence of phenylalanine. Reducing phenylalanine consumption reduces or prevents this effect of the gene.

PKU illustrates one reason why, despite the importance of genes for nervous system development, understanding the genotype alone could never enable an understanding of the developing brain. Knowing that a baby is born with PKU doesn't tell you anything about how that child's brain will develop *unless* you also know something about the child's diet. Another reason why genes alone cannot tell the whole story is that experience can affect the activity of genes, as we discuss next.

Experience regulates gene expression in the developing and mature brain

Genetically identical animals, called **clones**, used to be known mainly in science fiction and horror films. But life imitates art. In grasshopper clones, the basic shape of larger cells is similar in all clones, but many neurons show differences in neural connections despite the identical genotypes (Goodman, 1979). Likewise, genetically identical cloned pigs show as much variation in behavior and temperament as do normal siblings (G. S. Archer et al., 2003), and genetically identical mice raised in different laboratories behave very differently on a variety of tests (Finch and Kirkwood, 2000). If genes are so important to the developing nervous system, how can genetically identical individuals differ in their behavior?

EPIGENETICS Recall that although nearly all of the cells in your body have a complete copy of your genotype, each cell uses only a small subset of those genes at any one time. We mentioned earlier that when a cell transcribes a particular gene and makes the encoded protein, we say the cell has *expressed* that gene. **Epigenetics** is the study of factors that affect gene expression without making any changes in the nucleotide sequence of the genes themselves. We've already seen one example of epigenetic effects in PKU, where the consequences of a missing gene—effects on mental capacity—depend on the child's diet.

Another important epigenetic factor affecting the developing brain in mice is the mothering they receive. If genetically identical embryos of one mouse strain are implanted into the womb of a foster mother of either their own strain or another strain, their behavior is affected (Francis et al., 2003). Strain B6 males carried and raised by mothers from the

phenylketonuria (PKU) An inherited disorder of protein metabolism in which the absence of an enzyme leads to a toxic buildup of certain compounds, causing intellectual disability.

clones Asexually produced organisms that are genetically identical.

epigenetics The study of factors that affect gene expression without making any changes in the nucleotide sequence of the genes themselves.

other strain (Balb) show significant differences in several behaviors, including maze running and measures of anxiety (**Figure 13.32**). Since the various males are *genetically identical* to one another, their different behaviors must be due to the effect of different prenatal environments and postnatal experiences on how those genes are expressed.

One particular influence of mothering on gene expression has been well documented. **Methylation** is a chemical modification of DNA that does not affect the nucleotide sequence of a gene but makes that gene less likely to be expressed. Michael Meaney and colleagues demonstrated that rodent pups provided with inattentive

methylation A chemical modification of DNA that does not affect the nucleotide sequence of a gene but makes that gene less likely to be expressed.

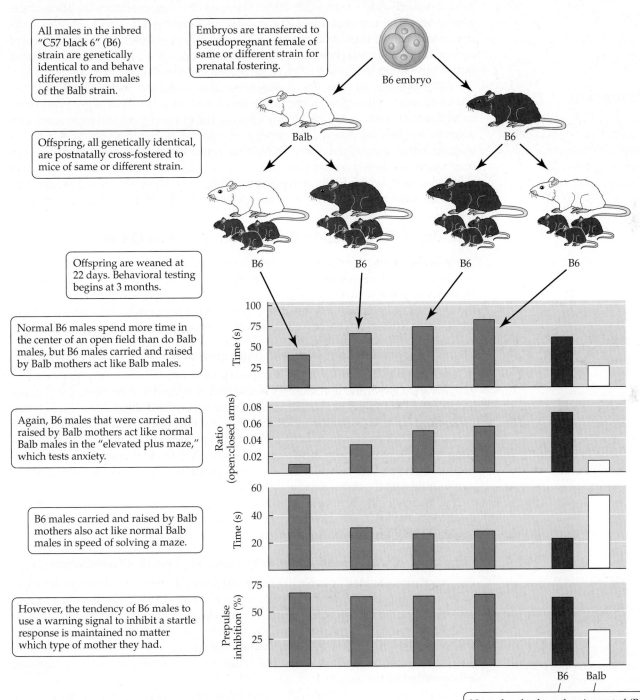

All males in the inbred "C57 black 6" (B6) strain are genetically identical to and behave differently from males of the Balb strain.

Embryos are transferred to pseudopregnant female of same or different strain for prenatal fostering.

Offspring, all genetically identical, are postnatally cross-fostered to mice of same or different strain.

Offspring are weaned at 22 days. Behavioral testing begins at 3 months.

Normal B6 males spend more time in the center of an open field than do Balb males, but B6 males carried and raised by Balb mothers act like Balb males.

Again, B6 males that were carried and raised by Balb mothers act like normal Balb males in the "elevated plus maze," which tests anxiety.

B6 males carried and raised by Balb mothers also act like normal Balb males in speed of solving a maze.

However, the tendency of B6 males to use a warning signal to inhibit a startle response is maintained no matter which type of mother they had.

Normal males from the pigmented (B6) and albino (Balb) strains differ in these different behaviors.

Figure 13.32 Epigenetic Effects on Mouse Behavior
(From Francis et al., 2003.)

mothers, or subjected to interruptions in maternal care, secrete more glucocorticoids in response to stress as adults (T. Y. Zhang and Meaney, 2010). Poor maternal care programs this heightened stress hormone response by inducing methylation of the glucocorticoid receptor gene in the brain, making the pups hyperresponsive to stress for the rest of their lives.

A similar mechanism may apply to humans, because this same gene is also more likely to be methylated in the postmortem brains of suicide victims than of controls, *but only in those victims who were subjected to childhood abuse.* Suicide victims that did not suffer childhood abuse were no more likely to have the gene methylated than were control subjects (McGowan et al., 2009). These results suggest that methylation of the gene in abused children may make them hyperresponsive to stress as adults—a condition that may lead them to take their own lives. This is a powerful demonstration of epigenetic influences on behavior. Other developmental disorders are also influenced by both genes and the environment, as we discuss in **A Step Further 13.4**, on the website.

Taken together, all these bits of evidence lead us to the conclusion that the incredible intelligence of the adult human is due not only to the inheritance of genes provided us by natural selection, but also to the effect of the environment and experience that determines where and when those genes are expressed in the brain, especially in development, but also throughout life. We wish we could tell you that, once your brain has been sharpened by experience (including what you gain by reading this book), you will remain brilliant forever. Sadly, development continues relentlessly toward old age. Just as our faces and bodies weaken and fade, the brain also declines, as we discuss next.

The Brain Continues to Change as We Grow Older

The passage of time brings us an accumulation of joys and sorrows—perhaps riches and fame—and a progressive decline in many of our abilities. Although slower responses seem inevitable with aging, many of our cognitive abilities show little change during the adult years, until we reach an advanced age. What happens to brain structure from adolescence to the day when we all become a little forgetful and walk more hesitantly?

Memory impairment correlates with hippocampal shrinkage during aging

In a study of healthy and cognitively normal people aged 55–87, investigators asked whether mild impairment in memory is specifically related to reduction in size of the hippocampal formation or is better explained by generalized shrinkage of brain tissue (Golomb et al., 1994). Volunteers took a series of memory tests and were scored for both immediate recall and delayed recall, and their brains were measured from MRI images (**Figure 13.33**). When effects of sex, age, IQ, and overall brain atrophy were eliminated statistically, hippocampal formation volume was the only brain measure that correlated significantly with the delayed memory score.

PET scans of elderly people reveal that cerebral metabolism normally remains almost constant as we age. This stability is in marked contrast to the dramatic decline of cerebral metabolism in Alzheimer's disease, which we will consider next.

Alzheimer's disease is associated with a decline in cerebral metabolism

The population of elderly people in the United States is increasing dramatically. Most people reaching an advanced age lead happy, productive lives, although at a slower pace than they did in their earlier years. In a growing number of elderly people, however, age has brought a particular agony: the disorder called **Alzheimer's disease**, named after Alois Alzheimer (1864–1915), the neurologist who first described a type of **dementia** (drastic failure of cognitive ability, including memory failure and loss of orientation) appearing before the age of 65.

Over 4 million Americans suffer from Alzheimer's disease, and the progressive aging of our population means that these ranks will continue to swell. This disorder is found worldwide with almost no geographic differences. The frequency of Alzheimer's

How's it going?

1. Compare changes in genotype and phenotype in an individual during development and aging.
2. Describe two examples of epigenetic effects on development.

Alzheimer's disease   A form of dementia that may appear in middle age but is more frequent among the aged.

dementia   Drastic failure of cognitive ability, including memory failure and loss of orientation.

Figure 13.33   Hippocampal Shrinkage Correlates with Memory Decline in Aging (From Golomb et al., 1994; MRI courtesy of James Golomb.)

MRI images illustrate the hippocampal formation (red), the supratemporal gyrus (orange), and the space between brain and skull (yellow-green). Only shrinkage of the hippocampal formation correlated with memory decline.

increases with aging up to age 85–90 (Rocca et al., 1991), but people who reach that age *without* symptoms become increasingly *less* likely ever to develop them (Breitner et al., 1999). This last finding indicates that Alzheimer's is in fact a disease, and not simply the result of wear and tear in the brain. The fact that remaining physically and mentally active reduces the risk of developing Alzheimer's disease (Smyth et al., 2004) also refutes the notion that brains simply "wear out" with age. Extensive use of the brain makes Alzheimer's *less* likely.

Alzheimer's disease begins as a loss of memory of recent events. Eventually this memory impairment becomes all-encompassing, so extensive that Alzheimer's patients cannot maintain any form of conversation, because both context and prior information are rapidly lost. They cannot answer simple questions such as, What year is it? Who is the president of the United States? or Where are you now? Cognitive decline is progressive and relentless. In time, patients become disoriented and easily lose themselves even in familiar surroundings.

Observations of the brains of patients with Alzheimer's reveal striking cortical atrophy, especially in the frontal, temporal, and parietal areas. PET scans show marked reduction of metabolism in posterior parietal cortex and some portions of the temporal lobe (N. L. Foster et al., 1984). The brains of individuals suffering from Alzheimer's also reveal progressive changes at the cellular level (**Figure 13.34**):

- Strange patches termed **amyloid plaques** appear in frontal and temporoparietal cortex, the hippocampus, and associated limbic system sites. The plaques are formed by the buildup of a substance called **beta-amyloid** (Selkoe, 1991), which is how amyloid plaques get their name.

- Some cells show abnormalities called **neurofibrillary tangles**, which are abnormal whorls of neurofilaments, including a protein called **tau**, that form a tangled array inside the cell. The number of neurofibrillary tangles is directly related to the magnitude of cognitive impairment, and they are probably a secondary response to amyloid plaques.

- Patients with Alzheimer's gradually lose many of the neurons, located in the basal forebrain, that make the transmitter acetylcholine. Drugs that slow this loss may reduce some of the symptoms of Alzheimer's for a time.

One hypothesis about how these processes are related to each other is offered in **A Step Further 13.5**, on the website.

amyloid plaque   Also called *senile plaque*. A small area of the brain that has abnormal cellular and chemical patterns. Amyloid plaques correlate with dementia.

beta-amyloid   A protein that accumulates in amyloid plaques in Alzheimer's disease.

neurofibrillary tangle   An abnormal whorl of neurofilaments within nerve cells that is seen in Alzheimer's disease.

tau   A protein associated with neurofibrillary tangles in Alzheimer's disease.

(a)

Cerebral cortex

Basal forebrain nuclei

Hippocampus

(b)

Neurofibrillary tangles…

…and amyloid plaques are visible in this section of cerebral cortex from a patient with Alzheimer's.

The basal forebrain nuclei project their axons, which use acetylcholine as a neurotransmitter, widely across the brain. These cells seem to disappear in Alzheimer's patients.

Figure 13.34   Patients with Alzheimer's Show Structural Changes in the Brain (After Roses, 1995; micrograph courtesy of Gary W. Van Hoesen.)

Figure 13.35 Imaging Amyloid Plaques in the Brain (Courtesy of the University of Pittsburgh Amyloid Imaging Group; from Wolk et al., 2009.)

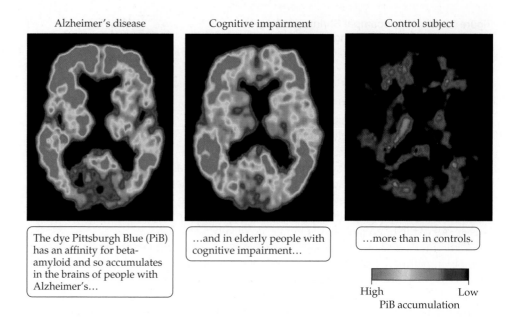

Alzheimer's disease   Cognitive impairment   Control subject

The dye Pittsburgh Blue (PiB) has an affinity for beta-amyloid and so accumulates in the brains of people with Alzheimer's...

...and in elderly people with cognitive impairment...

...more than in controls.

High   Low
PiB accumulation

At present, the only surefire diagnosis for Alzheimer's is postmortem examination of the brain revealing amyloid plaques and neurofibrillary tangles. But one innovative approach is to inject a dye, called Pittsburgh Blue (PiB) that has an affinity for beta-amyloid. Then a PET scan determines whether the dye accumulates in the brain (Wolk et al., 2009). The brain of virtually every patient diagnosed with Alzheimer's accumulates the dye, as do the brains of many elderly people showing mild cognitive impairment (**Figure 13.35**).

Our current understanding of Alzheimer's disease suggests several treatment strategies, such as injection of antibodies that will bind beta-amyloid and slow the formation of plaques, but that does not seem to be effective (Holmes et al., 2008). Another strategy is to develop drugs that interfere with enzymes that favor beta-amyloid production (O. Singer et al., 2005). In the meantime, and in keeping with the repeated theme of this chapter—that genes and experience interact—there is good evidence that physical activity (LaFerla et al., 2007), mental activity (Willis et al., 2006), and adequate sleep (J.-E. Kang et al., 2009) can postpone the appearance of Alzheimer's disease. So unless you want to pin your hopes on medical miracles in the future, the best way to avoid suffering from Alzheimer's is to remain physically and mentally active. Perhaps you should consider a career in neuroscience research...

How's it going?

1. What is Alzheimer's disease, and how is it diagnosed?

2. Although genes clearly influence the risk of Alzheimer's, what epigenetic factors can postpone its onset?

Recommended Reading

Baddeley, A. D., Eysenck, M., and Anderson, M. C. (2009). *Memory.* London, England: Psychology Press.

Gilbert, S. F. (2010). *Developmental Biology* (9th ed.). Sunderland, MA: Sinauer.

Kesner, R. P., and Martinez, J. L. (Eds.). (2007). *The Neurobiology of Learning and Memory* (2nd ed.). San Diego, CA: Elsevier.

Marcus, G. (2004). *The Birth of the Mind: How a Tiny Number of Genes Creates the Complexities of Human Thought.* New York, NY: Basic Books.

Rudy, J. W. (2008). *The Neurobiology of Learning and Memory.* Sunderland, MA: Sinauer.

Sanes, D. H., Reh, T. A., and Harris, W. A. (2012). *Development of the Nervous System* (3rd ed.). San Diego, CA: Academic Press.

Squire, L. R., and Kandel, E. R. (2008). *Memory: From Mind to Molecules.* Greenwood Village, CO: Roberts.

Thompson, R. F., and Madigan, S. A. (2005). *Memory: The Key to Consciousness.* Washington, DC: Joseph Henry Press.

CHAPTER 13 VISUAL SUMMARY

You should be able to relate each summary to the adjacent illustration, including structures and processes. If you need to review, go to the figures indicated and read the accompanying text.

mindsmachine.com/vs13

1 The **hippocampus**, **mammillary bodies**, and **dorsomedial thalamus** are part of a network that must be intact to form new **declarative memories**—memories that we can declare to others. Damage to these regions can cause **amnesia**, the impairment of memory. Review **Figure 13.1, Animation 13.2**

2 Removal of the hippocampus and nearby cortex left **patient H.M.** unable to form declarative memories that lasted more than a few minutes. He could, however, learn new skills, such as mirror tracing, showing that his **nondeclarative** (or **procedural**) **memory** for perceptual and motor behaviors, was intact. Review **Figures 13.2–13.4**

3 Declarative memory consists of **semantic memory** of facts, and **episodic memory** of particular incidents in the past. Brain damage can remove one type of declarative memory without affecting the other, indicating that the two kinds of memories are stored separately. Review **Figures 13.4 and 13.12, Activity 13.1**

4 Nondeclarative memory, which includes **skill learning**, **priming**, and conditioning, is demonstrated through performance. In nonhuman animals, most tests of memory measure nondeclarative memory, an exception being the **delayed non-matching-to-sample task** in monkeys. Review **Figures 13.3–13.6, Activity 13.2**

5 **Nonassociative learning** includes **habituation**, while **associative learning** includes **classical conditioning** (*Pavlovian conditioning*) and **instrumental conditioning** (**operant conditioning**). In the slug *Aplysia*, habituation is due to a weakening of the synapse between the sensory neuron and the motoneuron. In mammals, classical conditioning happens through changes in synaptic strength in the **cerebellum**. Review **Figure 13.9, 13.18–13.20**

6 Different kinds of learning depend on different brain regions. Spatial learning requires an intact hippocampus, while skill learning relies on the **basal ganglia**, and recognition relies on the cortex. Review **Figures 13.11** and **13.12**

7 Memories are classified by how long they last. **Iconic memory** is a very brief recollection of sensations. **Short-term memory** (**STM**; sometimes called **working memory**) lasts only a few minutes. Then the memory is either lost or transferred to **long-term memory** (**LTM**), which may last a lifetime. The successive processes transferring information from one store to the other are **encoding**, **consolidation**, and **retrieval**. Memories are subject to distortion during recall and reconsolidation. Strong emotion can affect the strength of memories, as in **posttraumatic stress disorder** (**PTSD**). Review **Figures 13.12–13.14, Box 13.1**

8 **Long-term potentiation** (**LTP**) is a lasting increase in amplitude of the response of neurons caused by brief high-frequency stimulation of their afferents (tetanus). In the hippocampus, LTP depends on the activation of **NMDA receptors**, which induces an increase in the number of postsynaptic **AMPA receptors** and greater neurotransmitter release. These are examples of **Hebbian synapses**, which become stronger if they successfully drive the postsynaptic cell, and weaker if they are unsuccessful. Review **Figures 13.21–13.23, Animation 13.3, Video 13.4**

9 The brain develops in six stages: (1) **neurogenesis**, (2) **cell migration**, (3) **cell differentiation**, (4) **synaptogenesis**, (5) **cell death** (**apoptosis**), and (6) **synapse rearrangement**. In adulthood, synapse rearrangement continues throughout the brain, and experience guides this process. Some neurogenesis also occurs in adults. Review **Figures 13.24–13.31, Animation 13.5, Video 13.6, Activity 13.3**

10 While genes play an important role in brain development, the environment and experience, such as mothering, can affect **gene expression**. Thus, development is an **epigenetic** process, so genetically identical individuals may behave very differently from one another. For example, the severe mental impairment that may accompany **phenylketonuria** (**PKU**) is avoided by controlling diet. While genes affect the buildup of **beta-amyloid** in **amyloid plaques** and therefore increase the risk of **Alzheimer's disease**, mental and physical activity postpone the onset of the disease. Review **Figures 13.32–13.35**

Go to **mindsmachine.com** for study questions, quizzes, flashcards, and other resources.

14 Attention and Consciousness

Lost in Space

To see a video, go to

mindsmachine.com/14.1
Attention and Perception

Betty's family had an unhappy medical history; several close relatives had suffered multiple strokes as they grew older, and at age 67 Betty shared that fate. In the span of just 6 months, blood clots from Betty's heart had caused strokes in each hemisphere. And in a million-to-one coincidence, the two strokes resulted in damage to identical regions of the left and right parietal lobes.

Betty's unlikely lesions produced equally unlikely symptoms. A few weeks after her second stroke, Betty had regained many of her intellectual powers—she could converse normally and remember things. Her visual fields were apparently normal too, but her visual *perception* was anything but normal. Betty had lost the ability to perceive more than one thing at a time. For example, she could see her husband's face just fine, but she couldn't judge whether he had glasses on or not. It turned out that she could see the glasses *or* she could see the face, but couldn't perceive them *both* at the same time. When shown a drawing of several overlapping items, she could perceive and name only one at a time. Furthermore, she couldn't understand where the objects she saw were located. It was as if Betty was lost in space, able to focus on only one object at a time, apparently alone in a world of its own. What could explain Betty's symptoms?

Although she may delight in pretending otherwise, the average 5-year-old knows exactly what it means when her exasperated parents shout, "Pay attention!" We all share an intuitive understanding of the term *attention*, but it is tricky to formally define. A definition provided in the nineteenth century by the great American psychologist William James is a good place to start:

> *Everyone knows what attention is. It is the taking possession by the mind, in clear and vivid form, of one out of what seem several simultaneously possible objects or trains of thought. Focalization, concentration, of consciousness are of its essence. It implies withdrawal from some things in order to deal effectively with others, and is a condition which has a real opposite in the confused, dazed, scatterbrained state. (W. James, 1890, pp. 403–404)*

Clearly, James understood that attention can be effortful, improves perception, and acts as a filter. This continual shifting of our focus from one interesting stimulus to the next lies at the heart of our experience of consciousness. So we open this chapter by considering modern approaches to understanding attention, which will lead us to the fascinating topic of consciousness. We'll find discomforting evidence that consciousness, the part of our mind that seems so central to who we are, may not always decide how we behave.

Attention Focuses Cognitive Processing on Specific Objects

In general, **attention** (or *selective attention*) is the process by which we select or focus on one or more specific stimuli—either external phenomena or internal processes—for enhanced study and analysis. Most of the time we use **overt attention**, focusing our attention along with our sensory orientation. For example, as you read this sentence, it is both the center of your visual gaze and (we hope) the main item that your brain has selected for attention. But if we choose to, we can also shift the focus of our visual attention without changing the direction of visual gaze, keeping our eyes fixed on one location while "secretly" scrutinizing a different location in peripheral vision (Helmholtz, 1962; original work published in 1894). Remember that teacher who, even when looking out the window, somehow knew instantly when someone passed a note? That's an example of what is known as **covert attention** (**Figure 14.1**).

Selective attention isn't restricted to visual stimuli. Imagine you're at a noisy party, chatting with an old friend. Despite the background noise, you would probably find it relatively easy to focus on what your friend was saying, even if she was speaking quietly, because attention aids your sensory perception—paying close attention to your friend enhances your processing of her speech and helps filter out distracters. This phenomenon, known as the **cocktail party effect**, illustrates how attention *focuses cognitive processing resources on a particular target*—in this case a single speech source. If your attention shifts to a different stimulus—for example, if you start eavesdropping on a more interesting conversation nearby—it becomes almost impossible to simultaneously follow what your friend is saying.

To see the brain in 3D, go to

mindsmachine.com/14.2
Brain Explorer

attention Also called *selective attention*. A state or condition of selective awareness or perceptual receptivity, by which specific stimuli are selected for enhanced processing.

overt attention Attention in which the focus coincides with sensory orientation (e.g., you're attending to the same thing you're looking at).

covert attention Attention in which the focus can be directed independently of sensory orientation (e.g., you're attending to one sensory stimulus while looking at another).

cocktail party effect The selective enhancement of attention in order to filter out distracters, such as while listening to one person talking in the midst of a noisy party.

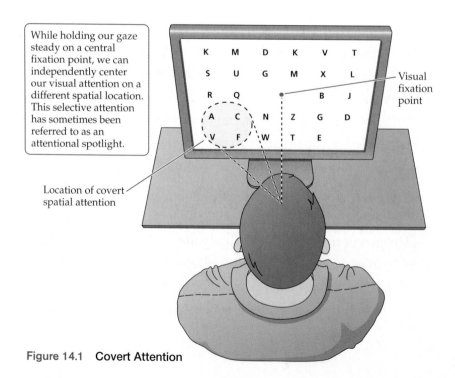

While holding our gaze steady on a central fixation point, we can independently center our visual attention on a different spatial location. This selective attention has sometimes been referred to as an attentional spotlight.

Visual fixation point

Location of covert spatial attention

Figure 14.1 Covert Attention

There are limits on attention

The powers of attention that help you to focus on a conversation with a friend in a noisy room normally use several types of sensory cues, such as where her speech sounds are coming from, how her face moves as she speaks, what unique sounds her voice makes, and so on. But what if we restrict our attention to just one type of stimulus?

In **shadowing** experiments, subjects must focus their attention on just one out of two or more simultaneous streams of stimuli. In a classic example of this technique, Cherry (1953) presented different streams of speech simultaneously to people's left and right ears via headphones—the technique is called *dichotic presentation*—and asked them to focus their attention on one ear or the other and report what they heard. Subjects were able to accurately report what they heard in the attended ear, but they reported very little about what was said in the *nonattended* ear, aside from simple characteristics, such as the sex of the speaker. In fact, if a shadowing task is difficult enough, people may fail to detect even their own names in the unattended ear about two-thirds of the time (N. Wood and Cowan, 1995)!

Similar restrictions of attention can be seen in other sensory modalities, such as musical notes (Zendel and Alain, 2009) and visual stimuli. Subjects closely attending to one complex visual event against a background of other moving stimuli—dancers weaving through a basketball game, for example—may show **inattentional blindness**: a surprising failure to perceive nonattended stimuli. And the unperceived stimuli can be things that you might think impossible to miss, like a gorilla strolling across a movie screen out of the blue (Simons and Chabris, 1999; Simons and Jensen, 2009). You can try out some examples on the website.

In general, **divided-attention tasks**—in which the subject is asked to process two or more simultaneous stimuli—confirm that *attention is a limited resource* and that it's very difficult to attend to more than one thing at a time, particularly if the stimuli are spatially separated (Bonnel and Prinzmetal, 1998). So, our limited selective attention generally acts like an **attentional spotlight**, shifting around the environment, highlighting stimuli for enhanced processing. It's an adaptation that we share with many other species because, like us, they are confronted with the problem of extracting important signals from a noisy background (Bee and Micheyl, 2008). Birds, for example, have to be able to isolate the vocalizations of specific individuals from a cacophony of calls and other noises in the environment—an avian version of the cocktail party problem (Benney and Braaten, 2000). Having a single attentional spotlight helps us focus cognitive resources and behavioral responses toward the most important things in the environment at any given moment (the smell of smoke, the voice of a potential mate, a glimpse of a big spotted cat), while filtering out extraneous information.

Attention filters information early or late in sensory processing

In a sense, attention protects the brain from being overwhelmed by the world. Attentional processes provide a strict filter, sifting through the torrent of information coming in through our senses and selecting only the most important events for special processing. But the details of this **attentional bottleneck** have been elusive. Some researchers have argued that the filtering occurs at the level of the sensory inputs, and that unattended information simply never reaches higher cognitive levels (Broadbent, 1958). The basic shadowing experiment that we described earlier is consistent with this **early-selection model of attention**, because the subjects didn't appear to process much about the dialog in the unattended ear. But this can't be a complete account of the attentional control of information flow, because, as we noted earlier, some important but unattended stimuli (such as your name) are sometimes processed right up to the level of semantic meaning and awareness, at which point they can suddenly capture attention (N. Wood and Cowan, 1995). Observations of this sort gave rise to **late-selection models of attention**, which suggest that the processing bottleneck imposed by the nervous system occurs later in the processing pathway, filtering out stimuli only after substantial analysis has occurred.

To see a video, go to

mindsmachine.com/14.3
Inattentional Blindness

shadowing   A task in which the subject is asked to focus attention on one ear or the other while stimuli are being presented separately to both ears, and to repeat aloud the material presented to the attended ear.

inattentional blindness   The failure to perceive nonattended stimuli that seem so obvious as to be impossible to miss.

divided-attention task   A task in which the subject is asked to focus attention on two or more stimuli simultaneously.

attentional spotlight   The shifting of our limited selective attention around the environment to highlight stimuli for enhanced processing.

attentional bottleneck   A filter that results from the limits intrinsic to our attentional processes, with the result that only the most important stimuli are selected for special processing.

early-selection model of attention
A theory postulating that the attentional bottleneck imposed by the nervous system can exert control early in the processing pathway, filtering out stimuli before even preliminary perceptual analysis has occurred.

late-selection model of attention   A theory postulating that the attentional bottleneck imposed by the nervous system exerts control late in the processing pathway, filtering out stimuli only after substantial analysis has occurred.

Many models of attention contain both early- and late-selection mechanisms (e.g., Wolfe, 1994), and vigorous debate continues over their relative importance (for a classic demonstration, see **A Step Further 14.1**, on the website). A possible resolution to this debate involves **perceptual load**—the immediate processing demands presented by a stimulus. According to this view, when we focus on a very complex stimulus, the load on our perceptual processing resources is so great that there is nothing left over. We are thus unable to process competing unattended items, so those extra stimuli are excluded from the outset (N. Lavie, 1995; N. Lavie et al., 2004). But when we focus on stimuli that are easier to process, we may have enough perceptual resources left over that we can simultaneously process additional stimuli, right up to the level of semantic meaning and awareness. In this case the result is a late selection of stimuli to attend to (N. Lavie et al., 2009). According to this model, attention involves a continual balancing act, varying between early and late selection, depending on the difficulty and specific features of the task at hand.

Attention May Be Endogenous or Exogenous

We've now seen that through an act of willpower we can direct our attention to specific stimuli without moving our eyes or otherwise reorienting. Early experiments on this phenomenon employed **sustained-attention tasks**, like the one depicted in Figure 14.1, where a single stimulus location must be held in the attentional spotlight for an extended period. Although these tasks are useful for studying basic phenomena, several key questions about attention require another approach. For example, how do we *shift* our attention around? *How* does attention enhance the processing of stimuli, and *which brain regions* are involved? To answer these questions, researchers devised clever tasks that employ stimulus cuing to control attention, which revealed two general categories of attention: endogenous and exogenous. Let's consider these different forms of attention.

RESEARCHERS AT WORK

We can choose which stimuli we will attend to

So far, our discussion of attention has focused mostly on what researchers call **endogenous** (or *voluntary*) **attention**. As its name (from the Greek *endon*, "within," and *genes*, "born") implies, endogenous attention comes from within; it is the voluntary, or *top-down*, direction of attention toward specific aspects of the environment, according to our interests and goals. **Figure 14.2** features the *symbolic cuing task*, developed by Michael Posner and used extensively to study endogenous attention. Studies using cuing tasks have confirmed that consciously directing your attention to the correct location or stimulus substantially improves processing speed and accuracy. Conversely, directing your attention to an *incorrect* location or stimulus impairs processing efficiency.

How much does it help to shift your attention to a location before a stimulus occurs there? Posner's (1980) **symbolic cuing** task allows us to quantify how endogenous attention benefits processing. In a symbolic cuing task, the subject is instructed to keep his eyes fixed on a point in the center of a computer screen, and to press a key as quickly as possible when a *specific* target appears on the screen (this technique measures *reaction time*, as described in **Box 14.1**). The stimulus is preceded by a cue that briefly flashes on the screen, telling the subject where the stimulus will appear. In most trials, like the one shown in **Figure 14.2a**, the cue gives a valid hint; for example a rightward arrow flashes on the screen, and a few moments later the stimulus appears on the right side of the screen. In a few trials, like the one in **Figure 14.2b**, the cue points the *wrong* way and thus is *invalid*. And in "neutral" control

---

perceptual load   The immediate processing demands presented by a stimulus.

sustained-attention task   A task in which a single stimulus source or location must be held in the attentional spotlight for a protracted period.

endogenous attention   Also called *voluntary attention*. The voluntary direction of attention toward specific aspects of the environment, in accordance with our interests and goals.

symbolic cuing   A technique for testing endogenous attention in which a visual stimulus is presented and subjects are asked to respond as soon as the stimulus appears on a screen. Each trial is preceded by a meaningful symbol used as a cue to hint at where the stimulus will appear.

trials (**Figure 14.2c**), the cue doesn't provide any hint at all. Both the cue and the stimulus are on the screen so briefly that the subject doesn't have time to shift his gaze to them (and in any case, he has been told to stare at the fixation point).

When Posner averaged the effects of valid and invalid cues on reaction time over many trials, he found that cued shifts in endogenous attention had powerful effects on stimulus processing. As you can see in **Figure 14.2d**, subjects swiftly learn to use cues to predict stimulus location, shifting their attention in the cued direction—*without shifting their gaze*—anticipating the appearance of the target stimulus. Reaction time is thus significantly faster for validly cued trials, compared to the uncued neutral condition. And subjects clearly pay a price for misdirecting their attention on those few trials in which the cue is invalid, pointing to the wrong side of the display. Many variants of the symbolic cuing paradigm—changing the timing of the stimuli, altering their complexity, choosing between different responses (as in Box 14.1), and so on—have been used to study the neurophysiological mechanisms of attention (R. D. Wright and Ward, 2008), as we'll discuss a little later in the chapter.

Figure 14.2   Measuring the Effects of Endogenous Shifts of Attention

Question

Does shifting your attention to a location improve your processing of stimuli that appear there?

Hypothesis

Cued attention will improve subsequent processing—as measured by reaction time—if the stimulus appears at the cued location, but not if the stimulus appears elsewhere.

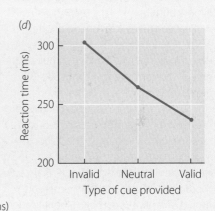

Results

Processing is improved for stimuli appearing at the cued location, and impaired for stimuli appearing at an uncued location.

Conclusion

Endogenous attention enhances processing independent of gaze.

exogenous attention   Also called *reflexive attention*. The involuntary reorienting of attention toward a specific stimulus source, cued by an unexpected object or event.

Some stimuli are hard to ignore

There is a second way in which we pay attention to the world, involving more than just consciously steering our attentional spotlight around. Flashes, bangs, sudden movements—important changes generally—can instantly snatch our attention away from whatever we're doing, unless we are very focused. Drop a glass in a restaurant sometime to hear the silence as every conversation stops, and watch every head in the place swivel toward the source of the sound (you, embarrassingly). This sort of involuntary reorientation toward a sudden or important event is an example of **exogenous** (or *reflexive*) **attention**. It is considered to be a *bottom-up* process, because attention is being

---

BOX 14.1 Reaction-Time Responses, from Input to Output

Reaction-time measures are a mainstay of cognitive neuroscience research. In tests of *simple reaction time*, subjects make a single response—for example, pressing a button—in response to experimental stimuli (the appearance of a target, the solution to a problem, a tone, or whatever the experiment is testing). In tests of *choice reaction time*, the situation is slightly more complicated: a person is presented with alternatives and has to choose among them (e.g., right versus wrong, same versus different) by pressing one of two or more buttons.

Reaction times in an uncomplicated choice-reaction-time test, in which the subject indicates whether two stimuli are the same or different, average about 300–350 milliseconds (ms). The delay between stimulus and response varies depending on the amount of neural processing required between input and output. The stations involved in our sample task, and the timing of events, are illustrated in the figure. Brain activity proceeds from the primary visual cortex through a ventral visual object identification pathway (see Chapter 7) to prefrontal cortex, and then through premotor and primary motor cortex, down to the spinal motoneurons and out to the finger muscles. In the sequence shown in the figure—proceeding from the presentation of visual stimuli to a discrimination response—notice that it takes about 110 ms for the sensory system to recognize the stimulus (somewhere in

the inferior temporal lobe), and about 35 ms more for that information to reach the prefrontal cortex, which then takes about 30 ms to determine which button to push. After that, it takes another 75 ms or so for the movement to be executed (that is, 75 ms of time elapses between the moment the signal from the prefrontal cortex arrives in premotor cortex and the moment the finger pushes the button). It is fascinating to think that something like this sequence of neural events

happens over and over in more-complicated behaviors, such as recognizing a long lost friend or composing an opera.

To see an animation of this figure, go to

mindsmachine.com/14.4
From Input to Output

A Reaction-Time Circuit in the Brain   The sequence and timing of brain events that determine reaction time. LGN, lateral geniculate nucleus; V1, primary visual cortex; V2 and V4, extrastriate visual areas. (Timings based on Thorpe and Fabre-Thorpe, 2001.)

(a) Exogenous attention

In valid trials, a momentary flash appears in the location where a stimulus will appear moments later.

Fixation | Unexpected stimulus | Delay | Target

Valid trial

Fixation point

Invalid trial

In invalid trials, the stimulus appears somewhere else.

(b) Inhibition of return

At short delays, a valid unexpected stimulus enhances the detection of targets…

Reaction time (ms)

- Valid
- Invalid

Cue-to-target interval (ms)

…but with greater delays, the subject takes *longer* to detect a target in the cued region, because of *inhibition of return*. Reaction times show that attention is focused on the cued location for less than about 200 ms.

Figure 14.3 Exogenous Attention and Inhibition of Return (After R. M. Klein, 2000.)

controlled by sensory inputs from lower levels of the nervous system, rather than by voluntary, conscious cognitive control by the forebrain.

Researchers study exogenous attention using a different kind of cuing task, called **peripheral spatial cuing** (**Figure 14.3a**). In this task, instead of a meaningful symbol like an arrow, the cue that is presented is a simple sensory stimulus, such as a flash of light, occurring *in the location to which attention is to be drawn*. As you can see in **Figure 14.3b**, a valid exogenous cue enhances the processing of subsequent stimuli at the same location, provided that the target stimulus closely follows the cue. At longer cue-to-target intervals, from about 200 milliseconds onward, a curious phenomenon is observed: detection of stimuli at the location where the cue occurred is increasingly *impaired* (R. M. Klein, 2000; Posner and Cohen, 1984). It's as though attention has moved on from the flash and is reluctant to return to that location. This **inhibition of return** probably evolved to prevent exogenously controlled attention from settling on unimportant stimuli for more than an instant.

Normally, exogenous and endogenous attention work together to control cognitive activities (**Figure 14.4**), probably relying on somewhat overlapping neural mechanisms.

peripheral spatial cuing A technique for testing exogenous attention in which a visual stimulus is preceded by a simple task-irrelevant sensory stimulus either in the location where the stimulus will appear or in an incorrect location.

inhibition of return The phenomenon, observed in peripheral spatial cuing tasks and occurring when the interval between cue and target stimulus is 200 milliseconds or more, in which the detection of stimuli at the former location of the cue is increasingly impaired.

Endogenous attention is consciously controlled, so it is slower, but it can be maintained longer and coordinated with exogenous attention to analyze our surroundings.

Exogenous attention rapidly orients to interesting stimuli, but it fades quickly unless the stimulus is important (dashed line).

Target-processing efficiency

Time (ms)

Figure 14.4 Exogenous and Endogenous Attention Are Complementary

feature search   A search for an item in which the target pops out right away, because it possesses a unique attribute, no matter how many distracters are present.

conjunction search   A search for an item that is based on two or more features (e.g., size and color) that together distinguish the target from distracters that may share some of the same attributes.

binding problem   The question of how the brain understands which individual attributes blend together into a single object, when these different features are processed by different regions in the brain.

Where's Waldo?   Puzzles like the "Where's Waldo?" series are classic examples of conjunction searches: You can find Waldo only if you search for the right combination of striped sweater, hat, glasses, and slightly goofy expression. Imagine how much easier it would be to find Waldo if everyone else in the store was wearing green! In that case, finding Waldo would be a feature search (the only person *not* dressed in green) and he would "pop out" in the picture … but what fun would that be?

Anyone who has watched a squirrel at work has seen that twitchy interplay. When it comes to single-mindedly searching for tasty tidbits, a squirrel has few rivals, yet even slight noises and movements will cause the squirrel to stop and scan its surroundings—a sensible precaution if, like a squirrel, you are yourself a tasty tidbit.

We use visual search to make sense of a cluttered world

Another familiar way in which we use attention in our daily lives is to try to find specific objects that are surrounded by similar others—your car in a parking lot, for example, or your friend's face in a crowd. If the sought-after item varies in just one key attribute, the task can be pretty easy—searching for your red car among a bunch of silver and black ones, for example. In a simple **feature search** like this (**Figure 14.5a**), the sought-after item "pops out" immediately, no matter how many distracters are present (Joseph et al., 1997); effortful voluntary attention isn't needed. But that's something of a luxury.

More commonly we must use a **conjunction search**—searching for an item on the basis of a *combination* of two or more features, such as size and color (**Figure 14.5b**). This can become very difficult when, for example, you must simultaneously consider the hair, nose, eyes, and smile of your friend's face in a crowd—and the bigger the crowd grows, the harder the task becomes (unless your friend waves, in which case you can fall back on using a feature search—phew!).

Experimental results (**Figure 14.5c**) confirm what you probably already intuitively know: conjunction searches can be relatively slow and laborious. That's because your brain has to deal with what is known as the **binding problem** (A. M. Treisman, 1996), which is this: How do we know which different features, processed by different regions of the brain, are bound together in a single object? And if those objects appear only infrequently—say, weapons in luggage or tumors in X-rays—they may go undetected with alarmingly high frequency, even by highly trained screeners (Wolfe et al., 2005). Sustained vigilance and attention of this sort always requires a large cognitive effort—our innate tendency is to let our covert attention wander between the various sources of stimuli in our environment. Suppressing that tendency in fast-changing, high-stakes situations, such as air traffic control, can be exhausting.

(*a*) Feature search

Find a green object

Find a square

> In these two feature search arrays, targets "pop out" because they differ from all other stimuli on one key feature, such as color or shape.

(*b*) Conjunction search

Find a red circle

Find a green square

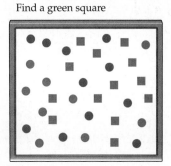

> Conjunction searches are harder because several target features must be considered simultaneously. Here, only one array actually contains the target.

Figure 14.5 Visual Search (After A. M. Treisman and Gelade, 1980.)

(*c*) Data for three types of visual search

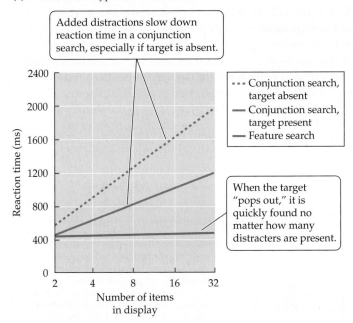

> Added distractions slow down reaction time in a conjunction search, especially if target is absent.

- - - Conjunction search, target absent
— Conjunction search, target present
— Feature search

> When the target "pops out," it is quickly found no matter how many distracters are present.

To uncover finer details of attentional mechanisms, neuroscientists use two general experimental strategies. First, we can look at *consequences of attention* in the brain, asking how selective attention to stimuli modifies brain activity and thus enhances stimulus processing. To do this, we need techniques with excellent **temporal resolution**—the ability to track changes in the brain that occur very quickly, in fractions of a second. Electrophysiological measures are commonly used for this purpose, because they can track rapid oscillations in brain areas involved in stimulus processing. A second class of questions is concerned with the *mechanisms of attention*, the brain regions that produce and control attention, shifting it between different stimuli in different sensory modalities. For this approach we need the excellent **spatial resolution** of anatomical and brain-imaging studies in order to observe the detailed structure of the brain. We discuss the two types of questions individually in the following sections.

The Electrical Activity of the Brain Provides Clues about Mechanisms of Attention

When many cortical neurons work together on a specific task, their activity becomes synchronized to some degree. You might think this would be easy to see in a standard

How's it going?

1. Summarize Posner's symbolic cuing task. What did this task reveal?

2. Compare and contrast endogenous attention and exogenous attention. What are three important ways in which they differ? What is inhibition of return, and does it relate to endogenous attention or to exogenous attention?

3. While conducting a visual search for something, we sometimes experience "pop-out." What is it? Is pop-out more closely associated with feature search or with conjunction search, and how do those differ?

4. Distinguish between temporal resolution and spatial resolution as they apply to brain-imaging techniques. How are they related?

temporal resolution The ability to track changes in the brain that occur very quickly.

spatial resolution The ability to observe the detailed structure of the brain.

EEG recording (that is, an *electroencephalogram*, the recording of the brain's electrical activity that we described in Chapter 3), but it isn't. Because of variation in the firing of the neurons, not to mention regional differences in the timing of brain activity, a "real-time" EEG recorded during an attention task looks surprisingly random. So instead, researchers have subjects do the same task over and over again, and they *average* all the EEGs recorded during the repeated trials (**Figure 14.6**). Over enough trials, the random variation averages out, and what's left is the overall electrical activity specifically associated with task performance (**Figure 14.6c**). This averaged activity, called the **event-related potential** (**ERP**) (Luck, 2005), tracks regional changes in brain activity much faster than brain-imaging techniques like fMRI do. For this reason, ERP has become the favorite tool of neuroscientists studying moment-to-moment consequences of attention in the brain, as we'll see.

Distinctive patterns of brain electrical activity mark voluntary shifts of attention

Consciously directing your attention to a particular auditory stimulus—for example, shadowing one ear, as we described earlier—has a predictable effect on the ERP. Between about 100 and 150 milliseconds after the onset of a sound stimulus, two large waves are seen in the ERP from the auditory cortex: an initial positive-going wave called *P1*, immediately followed by a larger negative-going wave called *N1* (see Figure 14.6c). The N1 wave reflects an important aspect of auditory attention: it is much larger following a stimulus that is being attended to than it is for the very same stimulus presented at the same ear but *not* attended to (**Figure 14.7**) (Hillyard et al., 1973). Because the only thing that changes between conditions is the subjects' attention to the stimuli, this **auditory N1 effect** must be a result of selective attention somehow acting on neural mechanisms to enhance processing of the sound.

event-related potential (ERP)   Also called *evoked potential*. Averaged EEG recordings measuring brain responses to repeated presentations of a stimulus. Components of the ERP tend to be reliable because the background noise of the cortex has been averaged out.

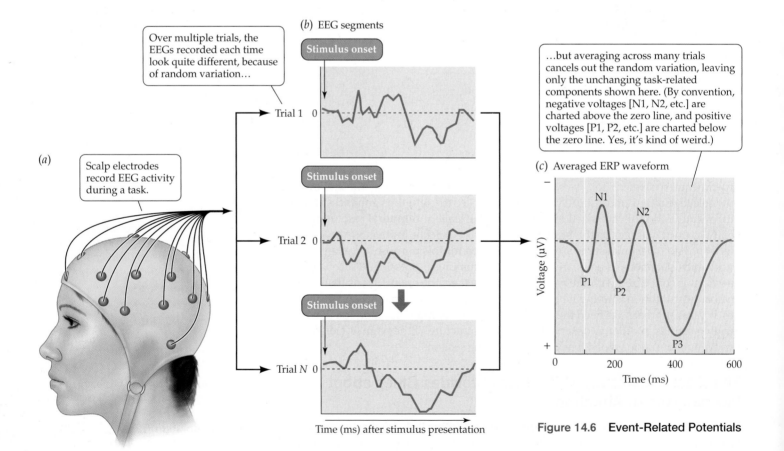

(a) Scalp electrodes record EEG activity during a task.

Over multiple trials, the EEGs recorded each time look quite different, because of random variation…

(b) EEG segments

Stimulus onset

Trial 1   0

Stimulus onset

Trial 2   0

Stimulus onset

Trial N   0

Time (ms) after stimulus presentation

…but averaging across many trials cancels out the random variation, leaving only the unchanging task-related components shown here. (By convention, negative voltages [N1, N2, etc.] are charted above the zero line, and positive voltages [P1, P2, etc.] are charted below the zero line. Yes, it's kind of weird.)

(c) Averaged ERP waveform

Voltage (μV)

N1   N2

P1   P2

P3

0   200   400   600
Time (ms)

Figure 14.6   Event-Related Potentials

(a)

ERP signal averager

The subject attends to stimuli in one ear, while ignoring the other ear.

(b)

A larger N1 component is observed in the ERP for the attended ear, showing that attention can have a direct effect on neural processing.

— Attended ear
— Unattended ear

−2 μV

N1 effect

0

+2 μV

0   100   200

Time (ms)

Figure 14.7   Enhancement of N1 in Auditory Attention (After Hillyard et al., 1973.)

The N1 wave isn't the only ERP feature that is affected by endogenous auditory attention. Just 20–50 milliseconds after an attended stimulus occurs, an enhanced positive-going wave is seen (Woldorff and Hillyard, 1991). Called the **P20–50 effect**, this component occurs so soon after onset that researchers think it must represent a subconscious, early-selection aspect of attention. There simply hasn't been enough time for the auditory stimuli to have been processed to the level of speech cues or meaning. Conversely, auditory attention also enhances much later ERP components, especially a wave called P3 (or *auditory P300*) (see Figure 14.6). P3 is believed to reflect higher-order cognitive processing of the stimulus (Herrmann and Knight, 2001), so the **P3 effect** is an example of a late-selection effect of attention. Abnormal P3 responses are a reliable finding in people with schizophrenia, consistent with their difficulty in filtering out distracting information (Ford, 1999).

What about effects of attention on ERPs from *visual* stimuli? Because the neural systems involved in visual perception are different from those involved in audition, endogenous visual attention causes its own distinctive changes in the ERP. We can study these visual effects by collecting ERP data over occipital cortex—the primary visual area of the brain—while a subject performs a symbolic cuing task. **Figure 14.8** depicts this sort of experiment. On valid trials (remember, this is when the target appears as expected, in the location indicated by the cue, as in **Figure 14.8a**), electrodes over occipital cortex show a substantial enhancement of the ERP component called P1, the positive wave that occurs over auditory cortex about 70–100 milliseconds after stimulus onset, often carrying over into an enhancement of the N1 component immediately afterward (**Figure 14.8c**). Notice that the enhancement occurs over the *contralateral* occipital cortex; this is because information from the left visual fields is processed in right occipital cortex, and vice versa, as we discussed in Chapter 7.

For invalid trials (**Figure 14.8b**), where attention is being directed elsewhere, the **visual P1 effect** isn't evident, even though the visual stimulus is identical and in the same location as in the valid trials. Interestingly, the P1 effect is evident only in visual tasks involving manipulations of *spatial* attention (*where* is the target?)—not other features, like color, orientation, or more complex properties that would be characteristic of late-selection tasks. These later-occurring aspects of endogenous visual attention may be evident in other types of tasks, affecting the later-occurring ERP component P3, as we discussed earlier (see Figure 14.6). Some of the neural mechanisms of visual attention are plastic to a degree; for example, experience with fast-paced "first-person shooter"

auditory N1 effect   A negative deflection of the event-related potential, occurring about 100 milliseconds after stimulus presentation, that is enhanced for selectively attended auditory input compared to ignored input.

P20–50 effect   A positive deflection of the event-related potential, occurring about 20–50 milliseconds after stimulus presentation, that is enhanced for selectively attended auditory input compared to ignored input.

P3 effect   A positive deflection of the event-related potential, occurring about 300 milliseconds after stimulus presentation, that is associated with higher-order auditory stimulus processing and late attentional selection.

visual P1 effect   A positive deflection of the event-related potential, occurring 70–100 milliseconds after stimulus presentation, that is enhanced for selectively attended visual input compared to ignored input.

The subject fixates on the red point and covertly orients attention (dashed circle) in the direction indicated by a prior symbolic cue (such as an arrow), pressing a key as soon as a stimulus appears.

(*a*) Valid cue: attend left

In most trials the cue is valid...

(*b*) Invalid cue: attend right

...but sometimes it misdirects attention to another location.

Attention enhances contralateral occipital activity.

Correct direction of attention enhances neural processing, resulting in larger P1 and N1 components in the corresponding ERP. Note that neither the stimulus nor the subject's gaze differs between conditions; the change in *attention* is solely responsible for the ERP effect.

(*c*) Right occipital ERP

N1 component

P1 component

Voltage (μV)

Time (ms)

Valid cue
Invalid cue

Figure 14.8 ERP Changes in Endogenous Visual Attention

video games can cause some of the longer-latency ERP components to change (C. S. Green and Bavelier, 2003).

Reflexive visual attention has its own electrophysiological signature

When an external event captures our attention—that is, when we experience an exogenous shift of attention—what brain regions are involved, and how do they differ from those involved in voluntary shifts of attention? Determining whether exogenous attention involves the same brain mechanisms as endogenous attention is an interesting topic (to cognitive neuroscientists, anyway) that can be addressed using ERP.

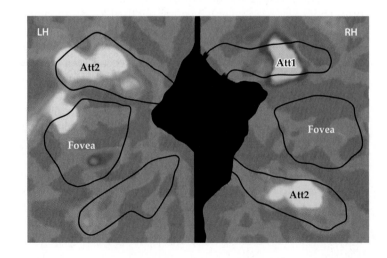

Event-Related fMRI Lets Us See Attention at Work in the Visual Cortex This map of a subject's visual cortex is arranged according to visual space. With gaze fixated on one spot, a cue directed covert attention to a location away from central vision. As a result, activation was enhanced in the cortical region corresponding to that location (Att1; activity in blue), well away from central vision (the fovea). When the subject's attention was split between two visual locations (Att2), enhancement was seen over both corresponding locations in visual cortex (activity in yellow-orange). (Image courtesy of David Somers.)

Figure 14.9 ERP Maps in Exogenous Visual Attention
(Courtesy of Joe Hopfinger.)

The same right-sided stimulus was presented in each case, but in some trials the stimulus was preceded by an unexpected flash in the location where the stimulus then appeared (valid trials). In other trials the flash drew attention to a different location (invalid trials).

(*a*) Short delay

For short delays between cue and stimulus, an enhancement in P1 is evident (yellow) over left occipital cortex.

(*b*) Long delay

At longer delays, the P1 response in the cued location is blunted because of inhibition of return, and it may even be larger for *invalid* cues!

In exogenous spatial cuing tasks, where a simple flash (or similar cue) draws attention to the location to be attended to (as in Figure 14.3), a visual P1 effect is seen in the contralateral ERP (Hopfinger and Mangun, 1998, 2001). This augmented P1 is just the same as what we saw for endogenous visual attention in the previous section, and it is associated with enhanced processing by the visual cortex. At least, that's what happens when the target stimulus follows closely after the sensory cue. But as the delay between the sensory cue and the target lengthens, the P1 enhancement is reduced and even becomes inverted, as **Figure 14.9** shows; this is the electrophysiological manifestation of inhibition of return, which we discussed earlier. In contrast, the experience of "pop-out" in visual search tasks is associated with a unique ERP component called the N2pc wave, an enhancement of N2 (Luck and Hillyard, 1994).

Attention affects the activity of individual neurons

PET and fMRI operate too slowly to track the rapid changes in brain activity that occur in reaction-time tests. Instead, researchers have used "sustained-attention tasks" to confirm that attention enhances neural activity in specific anatomical regions that process particular stimulus features. So, for example, when subjects are presented with stimuli made up of faces overlaid on pictures of houses, and asked to focus and sustain their attention only on the faces, fMRI reveals enhanced activation of a part of the brain (called the *fusiform face area*) that is specialized for face processing (O'Craven et al., 1999). A different brain area (the *parahippocampal place area*) is activated if attention is instead focused on the houses, within the same stimuli. Results like these suggest that attention somehow acts directly on neurons, boosting the activity of those brain regions that process whichever stimulus characteristic has been targeted.

In Chapter 7 we discussed the distinctive receptive fields of visual neurons, and how stimuli falling within these fields can excite or inhibit the neurons, causing them to produce more or fewer action potentials. In an important early study (**Figure 14.10**), Moran and Desimone (1985) recorded the activity of neurons in visual cortex while attention was shifted *within the cell's receptive field*. Using a system of rewards, the researchers trained monkeys to covertly attend to one spatial location or another while recordings were made from single neurons in visual cortex. A display was presented that included the cell's most preferred stimulus, as well as a nonpreferred stimulus a short distance away but still within the cell's receptive field. As long as attention was covertly directed at the preferred stimulus, the cell responded by producing a high volume of action potentials. But when the monkey's attention was shifted elsewhere within the cell's receptive field, even though the animal's gaze had not shifted, that same stimulus provoked far fewer action potentials from the neuron. Only the shift in attention could account for this sort of modulation of the cell's excitability. Subsequent work has confirmed that attention can remold the receptive fields of neurons in a variety of ways (Mounts, 2000; Womelsdorf et al., 2008).

How's it going?

1. Define *EEG* and *ERP*, and explain how ERPs are measured. Why is the ERP a favored technique in cognitive neuroscience?

2. Match each of the following ERP phenomena—N1, P20–50, P1, P3, N2pc—with one of these terms: *pop-out*, *early selection*, *auditory attention*, *late selection*, *visual attention*.

3. Describe an experimental procedure that can demonstrate the effects of selective attention on the activity of an individual neuron.

Figure 14.10 Effect of Selective Attention on the Activity of Single Visual Neurons (After Moran and Desimone, 1985.)

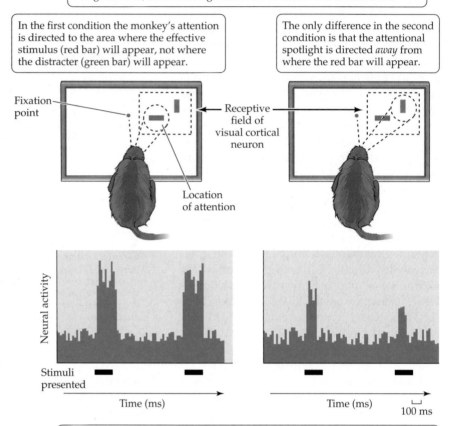

Here, a monkey has been trained to maintain central fixation while moving covert attention. Within the receptive field for the particular cortical neuron being recorded, the area being attended to is shown as a dashed circle.

In the first condition the monkey's attention is directed to the area where the effective stimulus (red bar) will appear, not where the distracter (green bar) will appear.

The only difference in the second condition is that the attentional spotlight is directed *away* from where the red bar will appear.

Fixation point

Receptive field of visual cortical neuron

Location of attention

Neural activity

Stimuli presented

Time (ms)

Time (ms)

100 ms

The red bar is less effective at firing the cell in the second condition. Because (1) the stimuli are identical in both conditions, (2) the fixation point hasn't changed, and (3) the same cell is being recorded in both conditions, attentional mechanisms must have directly altered the individual neuron's responsiveness.

Many Brain Regions Are Involved in Processes of Attention

The research that we've discussed so far confirms that attention alters neural processing, and it also indicates that endogenous and exogenous attention may share much the same kinds of effects on sensory analysis mechanisms. That doesn't mean that the *sources* of the different forms of attention are identical, however, or even that they are similar—just that their *consequences* are somewhat comparable. So let's turn to some of the details of the brain mechanisms that are the *source* of attention. Our moment-to-moment engagement with the world may seem effortless, but it requires a complex network of specialized subcortical and cortical systems, working together to extract a few important stimuli from a chaotic background.

Two subcortical systems guide shifts of attention

Subcortical structures can be difficult to study with minimally invasive techniques because, deep in the center of the brain and skull, they are difficult to probe using EEG or neuroimaging techniques. Our knowledge of their role in attention thus comes mostly from work with animals.

Single-cell recordings have implicated the **superior colliculus**, a midbrain structure (**Figure 14.11**), in the movement of the eyes toward objects of attention. Neurons of the superior colliculus are selectively activated during eye movements toward objects that are

superior colliculus A gray matter structure of the dorsal midbrain that processes visual information and is involved in direction of visual gaze and visual attention to intended stimuli.

Figure 14.11 Subcortical Sites Implicated in Visual Attention

- Pulvinar
- Superior colliculus
- Thalamus

also the focus of attention, especially overt attention (Wurtz et al., 1982). When the same eye movements are made but attention is directed elsewhere, a lower rate of firing by the collicular neurons is recorded. And in patients with lesions in one superior colliculus, inhibition of return was reduced for visual stimuli on the affected side (Sapir et al., 1999). So it seems that the superior colliculus helps direct our gaze to attended objects, and it ensures that we don't return to them too soon after our gaze has moved on.

Making up about the posterior quarter of the thalamus in humans (see Figure 14.11), the **pulvinar** is heavily involved in visual processing, with widespread interconnections between lower visual pathways, the superior colliculus, and many cortical areas. The pulvinar is important for the orienting and shifting of attention, and it is particularly crucial for the filtering of stimuli. In monkeys, treatment with a drug that inhibits the pulvinar causes them to have great difficulty orienting *covert* attention toward visual targets (D. L. Robinson and Petersen, 1992); the pulvinar is also needed to filter out and ignore distracting stimuli while we're engaged in covert attention tasks. In humans, attention tasks with larger numbers of distracters induce greater activation of the pulvinar as seen by fMRI (M. S. Buchsbaum et al., 2006), indicating that this nucleus is also important for human attention.

Several cortical areas are crucial for generating and directing attention

The extensive connections between subcortical mechanisms of attention and the parietal lobes, along with observations from clinical cases that we will discuss shortly, point to a special role of the parietal lobes for attentional control. Evidence is mounting that two integrated networks—dorsal frontoparietal and right temporoparietal—work together to give us our seamless experience of the world, continually selecting and shifting between objects of interest, in coordination with subcortical mechanisms of attention.

A DORSAL FRONTOPARIETAL SYSTEM FOR CONSCIOUS CONTROL OF ATTENTION In monkeys, recordings from single cells show that a region called the **lateral intraparietal area**, or just **LIP**, is crucial for endogenous attention. LIP neurons increase their firing rate when attention—not gaze—is directed to particular locations, and it doesn't matter whether the endogenous attention is being directed toward visual or auditory targets (Bisley and Goldberg, 2003; Gottlieb, 2007). So it's the "top-down" steering of the attentional spotlight that is important to LIP neurons, not the sensory characteristics of the stimuli.

pulvinar In humans, the posterior portion of the thalamus. It is heavily involved in visual processing and direction of attention.

lateral intraparietal area (LIP) A region in the monkey parietal lobe, homologous to the human intraparietal sulcus, that is especially involved in voluntary, top-down control of attention.

Figure 14.12   Cortical Regions Implicated in the Top-Level Control of Attention

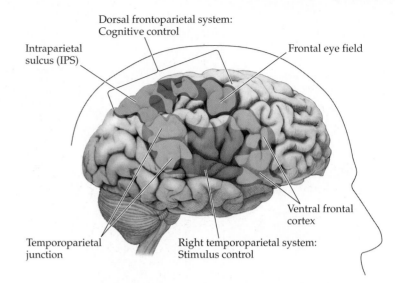

intraparietal sulcus (IPS)   A region in the human parietal lobe, homologous to the monkey lateral intraparietal area, that is especially involved in voluntary, top-down control of attention.

frontal eye field (FEF)   An area in the frontal lobe of the brain that contains neurons important for establishing gaze in accordance with cognitive goals (top-down processes) rather than with any characteristics of stimuli (bottom-up processes).

temporoparietal junction (TPJ)   The point in the brain where the temporal and parietal lobes meet. It plays a role in shifting attention to a new location after target onset.

The human equivalent of this system is a region around the **intraparietal sulcus (IPS)** (**Figure 14.12**) that behaves much like the monkey LIP. For example, on tasks designed so that covert attention can be sustained long enough to make fMRI images, enhanced activity in the IPS is associated with the control of attention (Corbetta and Shulman, 1998). And when researchers used transcranial magnetic stimulation (see Chapter 2) to interfere with the IPS in normal humans, the subjects found it difficult to voluntarily shift attention (Koch et al., 2005).

People with damage to a frontal lobe region called the **frontal eye field** (**FEF**) (see Figure 14.12) struggle to prevent their gaze from being drawn away toward peripheral distracters while they're performing an endogenous attention task (Paus et al., 1991). Neurons of the FEF appear to be crucial for ensuring that our gaze is directed among stimuli according to cognitive goals rather than being guided by any characteristics of stimuli. In effect, the FEF ensures that cognitively controlled top-down attention gets priority. It's no surprise, then, that the FEF is closely connected to the superior colliculus, which, as we discussed earlier, is important for planned eye movements.

A modified form of fMRI that allows partial tracking of activity during rapid events (called, unsurprisingly, *event-related fMRI*, or *ER-fMRI*) enables us to visualize network activities during top-down attentional processing (Corbetta et al., 2000; Hopfinger et al., 2000). **Figure 14.13** shows patterns of activation uniquely evident while endogenous attention is shifting in response to a symbolic cue. Enhanced activity is evident in the vicinity of the frontal eye fields (dorsolateral frontal cortex) and, simultaneously, in the IPS.

A RIGHT TEMPOROPARIETAL SYSTEM FOR REFLEXIVE SHIFTS OF ATTENTION   A second attention system, located at the border of the temporal and parietal lobes of the right hemisphere—and named, a little unimaginatively, the **temporoparietal junction** (**TPJ**) (see Figure 14.12)—is crucial for shifting attention in response to the intrinsic properties of stimuli (flashes, color, and so on). Brain images created with ER-fMRI (**Figure 14.14**) confirm that subjects show a spike in right-hemisphere TPJ activity if a relevant stimulus suddenly appears in an unexpected location (Corbetta and Shulman, 2002; Corbetta et al., 2000). Neurological patients with TPJ damage may fail to react

During conscious shifts of covert attention, ER-fMRI shows activation of the frontal eye field and the intraparietal sulcus (along with some activation of the temporal lobe).

Figure 14.13   The Frontoparietal Attention Network (Image courtesy of Joe Hopfinger and George Mangun.)

Intraparietal sulcus (IPS)

Temporoparietal junction (TPJ)

When attention is captured by the sudden appearance of stimuli (exogenous attention), activity is evident in this right-hemisphere system.

Figure 14.14   The Right Temporoparietal System and Endogenous Attention (Image courtesy of Maurizio Corbetta.)

Diagnostic Test for Hemispatial Neglect
When asked to duplicate drawings of common symmetrical objects, patients suffering from hemispatial neglect ignore the left side of the model that they're copying.

to unanticipated targets (Friedrich et al., 1998). Interestingly, the TPJ system receives direct input from the visual cortex, presumably providing direct access for information about visual stimuli. The TPJ also has strong connections with the ventral frontal cortex (VFC), a region that is involved in working memory (see Chapter 13). Because working memory tracks sensory inputs over short time frames, the VFC's contribution may be to analyze *novelty*, by comparing present stimuli with those of the recent past. Overall, the ventral TPJ system seems to act as an alerting signal, or "circuit breaker," overriding our current attentional priority if something new and unexpected happens.

Ultimately, the dorsal and ventral attentional control networks have to function as a single interactive system. According to one influential model (Corbetta and Shulman, 2002), the more dorsal stream of processing is responsible for *endogenous attention*, enhancing neural processing of stimuli and interacting with the pulvinar and superior colliculus to steer the attentional spotlight around. At the same time, the right-sided ventral system scans for novel salient stimuli (drawing *exogenous attention*), rapidly reassigning attention as interesting stimuli pop up. This basic model seems to apply across sensory modalities (Kanwisher and Wojciulik, 2000), including visual and auditory stimuli (Brunetti et al., 2008; Walther et al., 2010).

Brain disorders can cause specific impairments of attention

One way to learn about attention systems in the brain is to note the behavioral consequences of damage to discrete neuroanatomical regions. Research with neurological patients shows that damage of cortical or subcortical attention mechanisms can dramatically alter the ability to understand and interact with the environment.

RIGHT-HEMISPHERE LESIONS   We've discussed evidence that the right hemisphere normally plays a special role in attention (see Figure 14.14). Unfortunately, it is not uncommon for people to suffer strokes or other types of brain damage that particularly affect this part of the brain. The result—**hemispatial neglect**—is an extraordinary attention syndrome in which the patient tends to completely disregard the left side of the world. People and objects to the left of the person's midline may be completely ignored, as if unseen, despite the absence of any visual-field defects (Rafal, 1994). The patient may fail to dress the left side of her body, will not notice visitors if they approach from the left, and may fail to eat the food on the left side of her dinner plate. If touched lightly on both hands at the same moment, the patient may notice only the right-hand touch—a symptom called *simultaneous extinction*. She may even deny ownership of her left arm or leg—"My sister must've left that arm in my bed; wasn't that an awful thing to do?!"—despite normal sensory function and otherwise intact intellectual capabilities.

It is as if the normally balanced competition for attention between the two sides has become skewed, so that the input from the right side now overrules or extinguishes

How's it going?

1. Identify two subcortical structures that are implicated in the control of attention. What functions do they perform? Which one is damaged in PSP, and what are the symptoms of that disorder?

2. What is the general name for the cortical system responsible for conscious shifts of attention? What are its components, and what happens when those components are damaged in neurological patients?

3. Name the cortical system implicated in exogenous shifts of attention. Which specific regions are part of this system, and what happens if they are damaged?

hemispatial neglect   Failure to pay any attention to objects presented to one side of the body. Patients exhibiting this symptom may even deny connection with that side.

(a) Critical areas damaged in hemispatial neglect

This brain map is an average of the lesions of several people with hemispatial neglect.

(b) Model of cortical attention control network

Intraparietal   Frontal eye field   Ventral frontal
sulcus (IPS)   cortex

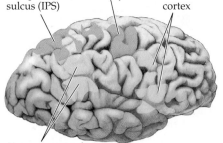

Temporoparietal
junction

Note how the hemispatial-neglect lesions overlap with the proposed attentional networks discussed in the text and shown here.

Figure 14.15   Brain Damage in Hemispatial Neglect

Balint's syndrome   A disorder, caused by damage to both parietal lobes, that is characterized by difficulty in steering visual gaze (oculomotor apraxia), in accurately reaching for objects using visual guidance (optic ataxia), and in directing attention to more than one object or feature at a time (simultagnosia).

simultagnosia   A profound restriction of attention, often limited to a single item or feature.

progressive supranuclear palsy (PSP) A rare, degenerative disease of the brain that begins with marked, persistent visual symptoms and leads to more widespread intellectual deterioration.

attention deficit hyperactivity disorder (ADHD) A syndrome characterized by distractibility, impulsiveness, and hyperactivity that, in children, interferes with school performance.

the input from the left. Lesions in hemispatial neglect patients (**Figure 14.15a**) neatly overlap the frontoparietal attention network that we discussed earlier (shown again in **Figure 14.15b**). This overlap suggests that hemispatial neglect is a disorder of attention itself, and not a problem with processing spatial relationships, as was once thought (Bartolomeo, 2007; Mesulam, 1985).

BILATERAL LESIONS   Betty, the stroke victim we met at the beginning of the chapter, had bilateral lesions of the parietal lobe regions that are implicated in the attention network. While rare, this sort of biparietal damage can result in a dramatic disorder made up of three principal symptoms. People with this disorder, called **Balint's syndrome**, have great difficulty steering their visual gaze appropriately (a symptom called *oculomotor apraxia*), and they are unable to accurately reach for objects using visual guidance (*optic ataxia*). But the most striking symptom is a profound restriction of attention, to the point that only one object or feature can be consciously observed at any moment. This problem, called **simultagnosia**, can be likened to an extreme narrowing of the attentional spotlight, to the point that it can't encompass more than one object at a time. Hold up a comb or a pencil, and Betty has no trouble identifying the object. But hold up both the comb *and* the pencil, and she can identify only one or the other. It's as though she is simply unable to see more than one thing at a time, despite having little or no loss of vision. Balint's syndrome thus illustrates the coordination of attention and awareness with mechanisms that orient us within our environment.

SUBCORTICAL DAMAGE   A rare, degenerative disease of the brain called **progressive supranuclear palsy (PSP)** begins with marked impairment of gaze control; specifically, the superior colliculi are damaged. In the early phases of the disease, before more-widespread mental deterioration becomes evident, PSP patients have trouble with visual tasks such as moving the eyes voluntarily, and with converging the two eyes to view close-up objects. But patients with PSP also experience problems with covert attention; they find it increasingly difficult to switch attention between different *attentional* targets, even without eye movements. So, damage to the human superior colliculus appears to impair a mechanism for shifting the attentional spotlight (Rafal et al., 1988; R. D. Wright and Ward, 2008), which echoes work in monkeys indicating that the superior colliculus plays a role in shifting visual attention.

Difficulty with sustained attention can sometimes be relieved with stimulants

About 5% of all children are diagnosed with **attention deficit hyperactivity disorder (ADHD)**, and three-fourths of these are male. Children with ADHD have trouble paying attention, and they are more impulsive than other children of the same age. Although diagnosis of ADHD is complicated and controversial, evidence has accumulated suggesting that there are some neurological changes in the disorder. Affected children tend to have slightly reduced overall brain volumes (about 3–4% smaller than in unaffected children), with reductions most evident in the cerebellum and the frontal lobes (Castellanos et al., 2002; Arnsten, 2006). As we discuss later in the chapter, frontal lobe function is important for myriad complex cognitive processes, including the inhibition of impulsive behavior.

In addition to structural changes, children with ADHD may have abnormal activity levels in some brain locations, such as the system that signals the rewarding aspects of activities (Volkow et al., 2009). For this reason, some researchers advocate treating ADHD children with stimulant drugs like methylphenidate (Ritalin). Stimulant treatment often improves the focus and performance of ADHD children in traditional school settings, but this treatment remains controversial because of the significant risk of side effects, and because some researchers view ADHD as being simply one extreme on a continuum of normal behavior. You can read more about ADHD and another developmental disorder—autism—in **A Step Further 13.4**, on the website.

Consciousness and Attention Are Closely Linked

So far, this chapter has been about attention, but when you think about it (no joke intended), consciousness is completely dependent on attention. Whenever we are conscious, we're attending to *something*, be it internal or external. William James (1890) tried to capture the relationship between attention and consciousness when he wrote, "My experience is what I agree to attend to. Only those items which I notice shape my mind—without selective interest, experience is an utter chaos." We all experience consciousness, so we know what it is, but that experience is so personal, so subjective, that it's difficult to come up with an objective definition. Perhaps a reasonable attempt is to say that **consciousness** is the state of being *aware* that we are conscious, coupled with our perception of what is going on in our minds. However, a lot of different activities are embedded in the phrase "perception of what is going on in our minds." It includes our perception of what's going on around us, our sense of time passing, our sense of being aware, our recollection of events that happened in the past, and our imaginings about what might happen in the future. Add to that our belief that we are free to direct our attention and make decisions, and we have a concept of immense scope.

Despite the definitional complexities, consciousness is an active area of research. So far, there are numerous competing theoretical models—neuroscientists like to spin a yarn as much as anyone!—but there isn't much in the way of hard physiological data. One practical approach has been to study consciousness by focusing on people who lack it—people in comas or other states of reduced consciousness. Maps of brain activity in such people—or more precisely, maps of *deactivated* areas (Tsuchiya and Adolphs, 2007)—suggest that consciousness depends on a specific frontoparietal network (**Figure 14.16**) that includes much of the cortical attention network we've been discussing, along with regions of medial frontal cortex and the cingulate.

consciousness The state of awareness of one's own existence, thoughts, emotions, and experiences.

These fMRI studies range from the temporary unconsciousness we all experience (sleep) to the profound and long-lasting unconsciousness of a persistent vegetative state. They share reduced activity of a frontoparietal network that includes dorsolateral prefrontal cortex (F), medial frontal cortex (MF), posterior parietal cortex (P), and posterior cingulate (Pr).

Sleep

General anesthesia

Coma

Persistent vegetative state

Deeper degrees of unconsciousness

Figure 14.16   The Unconscious Brain (Courtesy of Ralph Adolphs.)

Figure 14.17   Communication in "Unconscious" Patients (Image courtesy of Adrian Owen.)

Functional MRI shows the brain activity of a normal control subject asked to use two different mental images (playing tennis versus navigating) to signal "yes" or "no" answers to questions.

"YES"   "NO"

Control

Patient

The strikingly similar brain activity of a patient in a persistent vegetative state raises questions about the definition of unconsciousness. The patient was able to correctly answer a variety of questions using this technique, despite being in a state of apparently deep unconsciousness due to profound brain damage (black regions on MRI scan) and lacking behavioral responses.

But perhaps it's not that simple. For one thing, some patients in apparently deep and unresponsive coma can be instructed to use two different forms of mental imagery to create distinct "yes" and "no" patterns of activity on fMRI, and then to use this mental activity to answer questions (**Figure 14.17**) (Monti et al., 2010). Although this ability is observed in only a small number of coma patients—most people in a coma give no evidence of responding to their environments—studies like this suggest that it isn't accurate to view a coma as an exact inverse of what we experience as consciousness. In any case, there seems to be more to consciousness than just being awake, aware, and attending. How can we identify and study the additional dimensions of consciousness?

Some aspects of consciousness are easier to study than others

Most of the activity of the central nervous system is unconscious. Scientists say that these brain functions are **cognitively impenetrable**: they involve basic neural processing operations that cannot be experienced through introspection. For example, we see whole objects and can't even imagine what the primitive visual precursors of those perceptions could look like. Sweet food tastes sweet, and we can't mentally break it down any further. But those simpler mechanisms, operating below the surface of awareness, are the foundation that conscious experiences are built on.

In principle, then, we might someday develop technology that would let us directly reconstruct people's conscious experience—read their minds—by decoding the primitive neural activity and assembling identifiable patterns from it. This is sometimes called the **easy problem of consciousness**: understanding how particular patterns of neural activity create *specific* conscious experiences. Of course, it's almost a joke to call this problem "easy," but at least we can fairly say that, someday, the necessary technology and knowledge may be available to accomplish the task of eavesdropping on large networks of neurons, in real time.

cognitively impenetrable   Involving basic neural processing operations that cannot be experienced through introspection—that is, that are unconscious.

easy problem of consciousness   Understanding how particular patterns of neural activity create specific conscious experiences by reading brain activity directly from people's brains as they're having particular experiences.

Present-day technology offers a glimpse of that possible future. For example, if subjects are repeatedly scanned while viewing several distinctive scenes, a computer can eventually learn to identify which of the scenes the subject is viewing on each trial, solely on the basis of the pattern of brain activation (**Figure 14.18a**) (Kay et al., 2008). Of course, this outcome relies on having the subjects repeatedly view the same static images—hardly a normal state of consciousness. A much more difficult problem is to reconstruct conscious experience from neural activity during a person's initial exposure to a stimulus; so far, this has been accomplished for only very simple visual stimuli (**Figure 14.18b**) (Miyawaki et al., 2008). But at least it's a start.

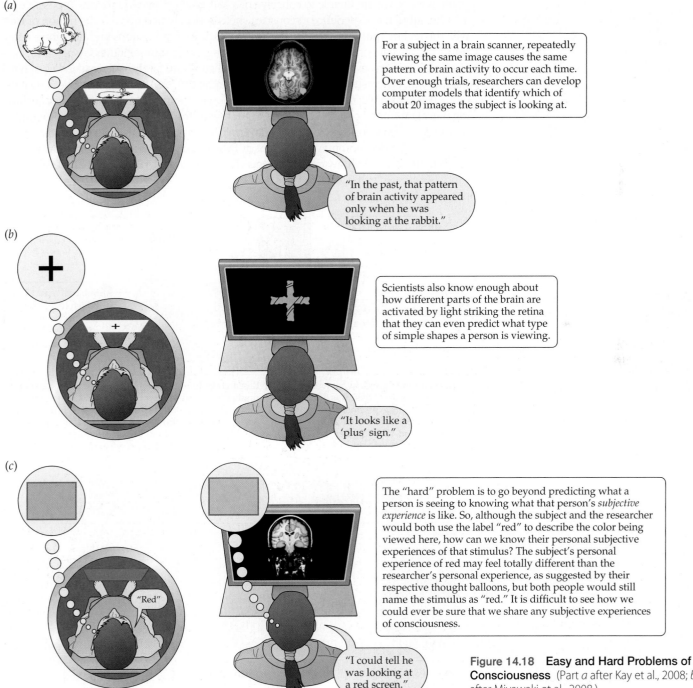

Figure 14.18 Easy and Hard Problems of Consciousness (Part *a* after Kay et al., 2008; *b* after Miyawaki et al., 2008.)

hard problem of consciousness Understanding the brain processes that produce people's subjective experiences of their conscious perceptions—that is, their qualia.

quale A purely subjective experience of perception.

free will The feeling that our conscious self is the author of our actions and decisions.

Alas, there is also the **hard problem of consciousness**, and it may prove impossible to crack. How can we understand the brain processes that produce people's *subjective experiences* of their conscious perceptions? To use a simple example, everyone with normal vision will agree that a ripe tomato is "red"; that's the label that, as children, we all learned to apply to the particular pattern of information, entering our consciousness from the color-processing areas of visual cortex, that is provoked by looking at something like a tomato. But that doesn't mean that your friend's internal *personal* experience of "red" is the same as yours. These purely subjective experiences of perceptions are referred to as **qualia** (singular *quale*). Because they are subjective and impossible to communicate to others—how can your friend know if "redness" feels the same in your mind as it does in hers?—qualia may prove impossible to study (**Figure 14.18c**). At this point anyway, we are unable to conceive of a technology that would make it possible.

Our subjective experience of consciousness is closely tied up with the notion of **free will**: the feeling that our conscious self is the author of our actions and decisions. After hundreds of years of argument, there's still no agreement on whether we actually have free will, but in any event there must be a neural substrate for the universal *feeling* of having free will. When subjects *intend* to act (push a button, say), there is selective activation of the IPS (which we implicated earlier in top-down attention) and frontal regions including dorsal prefrontal cortex (Lau et al., 2004), suggesting that these regions are important for our feelings of control over our behavior. But consider this: brain activity associated with making a decision may be evident in fMRI scans as much as 5–10 seconds *before* subjects are consciously aware of making a choice (**Figure 14.19**) (Soon et al., 2008)!

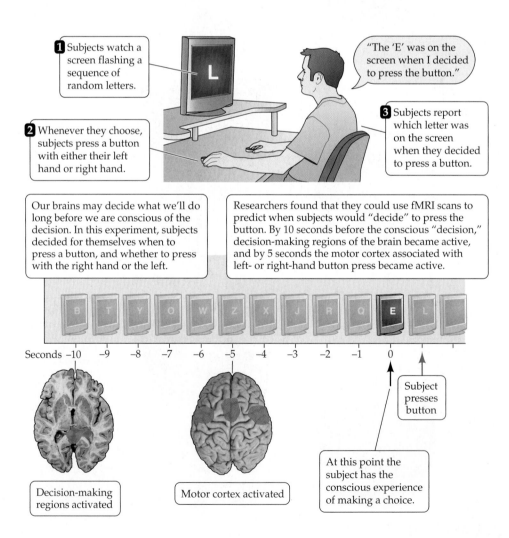

Figure 14.19 **Reading the Future** (After Soon et al., 2008.)

BOX 14.2 Neuroeconomics Identifies Brain Regions Active during Decision Making

The waiter has brought over the dessert trolley, and it's decision time: do you go with the certain delight of the chocolate cake, or do you succumb to the glistening allure of the sticky toffee pudding? Or, do you allow yourself only a cup of black coffee, for the sake of

Amygdala   Orbitofrontal cortex

A Poor Choice   A costly decision is associated with activation of the amygdala and orbitofrontal cortex, signaling diminished reward and aversion to loss. (From Coricelli et al., 2005; courtesy of Angela Sirigu.)

your waistline? What happens in your brain when you finally make your difficult choice?

In the lab, researchers usually evaluate decision making by using monetary rewards (instead of desserts, darn it) because money is convenient: you can vary how much money is at stake, how great a reward is offered, and so on, to accurately gauge how we really make economic decisions. These studies show that most of us are very averse to loss and risk: we are more sensitive to losing a certain amount of money than we are to gaining that amount. In other words, losing $20 makes us feel a lot worse than gaining $20 makes us feel good. From a strictly logical point of view, the value of money, whether lost or gained, should be exactly the same. Our tendency to overemphasize loss is just one of several ways in which people fail to act rationally in the marketplace.

Neuroeconomics is the study of brain mechanisms at work during economic decision making, and our attention to environmental factors and evaluation of rewards has a tremendous impact on these decisions. In general, findings from human and animal research suggest that two main

systems underlie decision processes (Kable and Glimcher, 2009). The first, consisting of the ventromedial prefrontal cortex (including the anterior cingulate) plus the dopamine-based reward system of the brain (see Chapter 4), is a *valuation system*, a network that ranks choices on the basis of their perceived worth and potential reward. The second system, involving mostly dorsolateral prefrontal cortex and parietal regions (like the LIP or IPS discussed in the text), is thought to be a *choice system*, sifting through the valuated alternatives and producing the conscious decision.

Neuroeconomics research is also confirming that the prefrontal cortex inhibits impulsive decision making as a way to avoid loss (Tom et al., 2007). As people are faced with more and more uncertainty, the prefrontal cortex becomes more and more active (Hsu et al., 2005; Huettel et al., 2006). Likewise, when people have made wrong, costly decisions that they regret, activity increases in the amygdala and in the orbitofrontal aspect of the prefrontal cortex as shown in the figure (Coricelli et al., 2005), probably reflecting the subject's perception of diminished reward and increasing aversion to loss.

In any event, the earliest indications of the decision-making process are found in frontal cortex (**Box 14.2**). Such involvement of prefrontal systems in most aspects of attention and consciousness, regardless of sensory modality or emotional tone, suggests that the frontal cortex is the main source of goal-driven behaviors (E. K. Miller and Cohen, 2001), as we discuss next.

The Frontal Lobes Govern Our Most Complex Behaviors

How do we decide what to do, and when to do it? Humans are distinctive among mammals for the comparatively large size of our prefrontal cortex—about a third of the entire cortex (**Figure 14.20a**) (Semendeferi et al., 2002). Perhaps it reflects a bit of vanity about our species, but size is one reason why researchers have long viewed the frontal cortex as the source of intelligence, abstract thinking, and self-awareness. Adding to the mystery of frontal lobe function is the unusual assortment of behavioral changes that accompany damage to the frontal lobe.

The posterior portion of the frontal cortex includes motor and premotor regions (see Chapter 5). The anterior portion, usually referred to as **prefrontal cortex**, is immensely interconnected with the rest of the brain (Fuster, 1990; Mega and Cummings, 1994), and it is usually subdivided into *dorsolateral* and *orbitofrontal* regions (**Figure 14.20b**). The study of prefrontal cortical function began with Carlyle Jacobsen's work in the 1930s on delayed-response learning in chimpanzees. The animals were shown where food was

prefrontal cortex   The anteriormost region of the frontal lobe.

(a)

The relative percentage of prefrontal cortex is greatest in humans and the great apes, such as the chimpanzees, but it decreases successively in monkeys, carnivores (such as cats), and rodents (not shown). The brains here are drawn to different scales.

Squirrel monkey   Cat   Rhesus monkey

Chimpanzee   Human

Figure 14.20   The Prefrontal Cortex

(b)

The human prefrontal cortex can be subdivided into a dorsolateral region (blue) and an orbitofrontal region (green). Lesions in these different areas of prefrontal cortex have different effects on behavior.

hidden, but they had to wait before being allowed to reach for it. Chimps with prefrontal lesions were strikingly impaired on this simple task, compared to animals that sustained lesions in other brain regions. Jacobsen believed the impairment was caused by memory problems. But subsequent observations, which we'll discuss next, suggest that the chimps' problems were with directing attention and formulating a plan of action.

Frontal lobe injury in humans leads to emotional, motor, and cognitive changes

Because they are large, the frontal lobes are vulnerable to injury; frontal lobe damage is a common consequence of strokes, tumors, and trauma. The exact symptoms induced by frontal lobe damage depend to some extent on the lesion location, but they include an unusual collection of emotional, motor, and cognitive changes. A common symptom in patients with frontal lobe damage is a persistent strange apathy, broken by bouts of

Phineas Gage Phineas P. Gage was a sober, polite, and capable member of a rail-laying crew, responsible for placing the charges used to blast rock from new rail beds. That's Gage on the left, in a newly discovered daguerreotype, holding a meter-long steel tamping rod. Perhaps the image on the right can help you guess why there appears to be something wrong with the left side of his face. In a horrific accident in 1848, a premature detonation blew that rod right through Gage's skull, on the trajectory shown in red, severely damaging both frontal lobes, especially in the orbitofrontal regions. Amazingly, Gage could speak shortly after the accident, and he walked to the doctor's office, although no one expected him to live (Macmillan, 2000). In fact, Gage survived another 12 years, but he was definitely a changed man, so rude and aimless, and his powers of attention so badly impaired, "that his friends and acquaintances said that he was 'no longer Gage.'" The historical account of Gage's case, now a neuroscience classic, was eventually found to closely agree with the symptoms of modern patients with frontal damage (Damasio et al., 1994; Wallis, 2007).

euphoria (an exalted sense of well-being). Ordinary social conventions are readily cast aside by impulsive behavior. Concern for the past or the future is absent (Duffy and Campbell, 1994; Petrides and Milner, 1982). Frontal lobe patients often show shallow emotions, even including reduced responsiveness to pain. Forgetfulness is shown in many tasks requiring sustained attention. And yet, standard IQ test performance shows only slight changes after injury or stroke.

Clinical examination of patients with frontal lesions also reveals an array of strange impairments in their behavior, especially in the realm of **executive function**, the high-level control of other cognitive functions in order to attend to important stimuli and make suitable "plans" for action. For example, a frontal lobe patient given a simple set of errands may be unable to complete them without numerous false starts, back-tracking, and confusion (Shallice and Burgess, 1991). Regions of dorsolateral prefrontal cortex, along with anterior portions of the cingulate, are closely associated with executive control. Dorsolateral prefrontal cortex is also crucial for working memory, the ability to hold information in mind while processing it or using the information to solve problems.

Frontal lobe patients often struggle with *task shifting* and tend to **perseverate** (continue beyond a reasonable degree) in any activity (Alvarez and Emory, 2006; B. Milner, 1963). Similarly, frontal lobe patients may show motor perseveration, repeating a simple movement over and over. However, the overall level of ordinary spontaneous motor activity is often quite diminished in these patients. Along with movement of the head and eyes, facial expression of emotions may be greatly reduced. Frontal lobe lesions also produce systematic problems with memory.

One explanation for these disparate effects of prefrontal lesions is that this region of cortex may be important for organizing different aspects of goal-directed behavior; crucial components include the capacity for prolonged attention and sensitivity to potential rewards and punishments. Patients with prefrontal lesions, like the famous Phineas Gage, often have an inability to plan acts and use foresight. Their social skills may decline, especially the ability to inhibit inappropriate behaviors, and they may be unable to stay focused on any but short-term projects. They may agonize over even

executive function A neural and cognitive system that helps develop plans of action and organizes the activities of other high-level processing systems.

perseverate To continue to show a behavior repeatedly.

Man of Mystery Our inability to perceive the conscious experiences of our fellow humans—and the fact that we will never make perfect predictions about their behavior—is one of the things that make humans so much more interesting than even the most complex robots.

How's it going?

1. Define *consciousness* (or at least try!).

2. Discuss unconsciousness in states like deep coma. Is this unconsciousness the inverse of consciousness?

3. Contrast the easy and hard problems of consciousness, giving examples of each. What are "qualia"?

4. Name the two main parts of the prefrontal cortex. How do they differ in function?

5. What are some of the main symptoms of frontal lobe lesions?

6. What are the two main neural systems that are thought to operate in the process of decision making, as identified in neuro-economics research?

simple decisions. (**A Step Further 14.2** summarizes the results of damage to different parts of prefrontal cortex).

In normal subjects, it seems that prefrontal cortex—especially the orbitofrontal region—controls goal-directed behaviors. For example, monkeys that must make decisions that could lead to rewards show increased orbitofrontal activation (Matsumoto et al., 2003); in general, orbitofrontal cortex seems to link pleasant experiences (e.g., eating a delicious meal) with reward signals (dopamine release in the reward pathway) generated elsewhere in the brain (Kringelbach, 2005). In humans performing tasks in which some stimuli have more reward value than others, the level of activation in prefrontal cortex correlates with how rewarding the stimulus is (Gottfried et al., 2003). This relationship seems to be a significant factor in gambling behavior and, more generally, is important for our decision-making processes. In fact, progress in understanding the decision-making process has spawned a new field, *neuroeconomics*, discussed in Box 14.2.

We may never have a full understanding of the deepest secrets of consciousness, or an answer to the question of whether we possess free will. But that doesn't prevent us from marveling that our consciousness has become so self-aware that it can study itself to a high degree. Perhaps it's best to allow ourselves at least one or two mysteries, if only for the sake of art. Would life seem as rich if we could predict other people's behavior, or even our own, with perfect accuracy?

Recommended Reading

Bernat, J. L. (2009). "Chronic Consciousness Disorders." *Annual Review of Medicine, 60*, pp. 381–392.

Chun, M. M., Golomb, J. D., and Turk-Browne, N. B. (2011). "A Taxonomy of External and Internal Attention." *Annual Review of Psychology, 62*, 73–101.

Glimcher, P. W., Camerer, C., Poldrack, R. A., and Fehr, E. (2008). *Neuroeconomics: Decision Making and the Brain.* San Diego, CA: Academic Press.

Goldberg, E. (2009). *The New Executive Brain: Frontal Lobes in a Complex World.* Oxford, England: Oxford University Press.

Itti, L., Rees, G., and Tsotsos, J. K. (2005). *Neurobiology of Attention.* Amsterdam, Netherlands: Elsevier.

Koch, C. (2004). *The Quest for Consciousness: A Neurobiological Approach.* Englewood, CO: Roberts.

Posner, M. I. (Ed.). (2012). *Cognitive Neuroscience of Attention* (2nd ed.). New York, NY: Guilford Press.

Stuss, D. T., and Knight, R. T. (2002). *Principles of Frontal Lobe Function.* Oxford, England: Oxford University Press.

Wright, R. D., and Ward, L. M. (2008). *Orienting of Attention.* Oxford, England: Oxford University Press.

CHAPTER **14** VISUAL SUMMARY

You should be able to relate each summary to the adjacent illustration, including structures and processes. If you need to review, go to the figures indicated and read the accompanying text.

mindsmachine.com/vs14

1 Although we pay mostly **overt attention** to stimuli, we can also pay **covert attention** to stimuli or locations of our choosing. **Attention** has been likened to a spotlight, helping us to distinguish stimuli from distracters. Review **Figure 14.1, Animations 14.2** and **14.3**

2 In **endogenous attention** we voluntarily select objects to attend to; it is studied using **symbolic cuing** tasks. **Exogenous attention** is the involuntary capture of attention by stimuli studied using **peripheral spatial cuing** tasks. Review **Figures 14.2–14.4, Animation 14.4**

3 In visual search, targets may pop out if they are distinctive for a particular feature (**feature search**). More often, though, we use **conjunction searches**, identifying target stimuli on the basis of two or more features. Review **Figure 14.5**

4 **Event-related potentials (ERPs)** are created by the averaging of many EEG recordings from repeated experimental trials. ERPs can track neural operations with excellent **temporal resolution**. Review **Figure 14.6**

5 Endogenous and exogenous attention enhance various ERP components. The specific ERP components that are affected depends on the sensory modality (for example, audition versus vision) and the task employed. Review **Figures 14.6–14.9**

6 Single-cell recordings in lab animals confirm that attention affects the responses of individual neurons. Review **Figure 14.10**

7 Subcortical mechanisms involving the **superior colliculi** and the **pulvinar** are crucial for shifting visual attention and gaze between important objects of attention. Review **Figure 14.11, Activity 14.1**

8 A dorsal frontoparietal system directs voluntary, endogenous attention. A right-sided temporoparietal attention system is responsible for detecting and shifting attention to novel stimuli. The two networks interact extensively. Review **Figures 14.12–14.15, Activity 14.2**

9 People in various unconscious states show reduced activity of frontoparietal regions. Review **Figures 14.16** and **14.17**

10 The **easy problem of consciousness** is how to read specific current conscious experiences directly from people's brains as they're happening. The **hard problem of consciousness** is how to read people's subjective experience of consciousness and determine the **qualia** that accompany perception. Review **Figure 14.18**

11 Feelings of **free will** may rely on the activity of specific frontal lobe mechanisms. But even if that's true, it's possible that unconscious mechanisms make many of our decisions well before we are consciously aware of them. Review **Figure 14.19**

12 Prefrontal cortex consists of dorsolateral and orbitofrontal divisions. Damage in these regions produces a distinctive set of symptoms. Medial aspects of the frontal lobes, including anterior cingulate regions, are associated with **executive function**. Review **Figure 14.20**

Go to **mindsmachine.com** for study questions, quizzes, flashcards, and other resources.

15

Language and Our Divided Brain

Putting a Name to a Face

Humpty Dumpty, the famously grouchy egg in Lewis Carroll's *Through the Looking-Glass, and What Alice Found There*, was grumbling to Alice about his problem distinguishing between people:

"The face is what one goes by, generally," Alice remarked in a thoughtful tone.

"That's just what I complain of," said Humpty Dumpty. "Your face is the same as everybody has—the two eyes, so—" (marking their places in the air with his thumb) "nose in the middle, mouth under. It's always the same. Now, if you had the two eyes on the same side of the nose, for instance—or the mouth at the top—that would be of some help."

Brian can relate. Throughout his 54 years of life, Brian has had great difficulty distinguishing between people. He regularly fails to recognize his seven children, his wife, or even himself reflected in a mirror. He relies on name badges to identify colleagues he has worked with for years. Yet Brian can make out other people's features perfectly well, because he can describe the color of the eyes, the shape of the nose and mouth, and so on, and is otherwise just like anyone else.

Intriguingly, sometimes people who suffer a stroke, especially in the right hemisphere, have difficulty recognizing faces, but there's no evidence that Brian ever had a stroke. What might account for Brian's—and Humpty's—difficulty with putting a name to a face?

To see a video, go to

mindsmachine.com/15.1
Face Blindness

Some of the most fascinating findings of twentieth-century neuroscience were built on the observation that brain damage can have very different effects on behavior, depending on whether it happens in the left or right hemisphere. For example, the left hemisphere of the brain is specialized for verbal processing, that quintessentially human capability, while the right hemisphere is specialized for **spatial cognition**, our ability to navigate and to understand the spatial relationships between objects. These discoveries propelled research on the many ways in which the left and right sides of the human brain perform different but complementary functions. In this chapter we survey the neuroscience of asymmetry in cerebral function. Because much of what we know about human brain organization comes from studies of people who have suffered strokes and other forms of brain injury, we also consider evidence that some recovery of function is possible even after severe brain damage.

To see the brain in 3D, go to

mindsmachine.com/15.2
Brain Explorer

PART I Speech and Language

Some Aspects of Language Are Innate, but Others Must Be Learned

A few years ago, researchers discovered a most unusual family in England. Across at least three generations, about half of the members of the KE family suffered from a severe language disorder. Affected family members take a long time to learn to speak and have difficulty with particular language tasks, such as learning verb tenses (Lai et al., 2001). Brain activation during language tasks is altered too (Liégeois et al., 2003).

By studying the KE family's pedigree, researchers soon identified a gene, called *FOXP2*, that must be important for the normal acquisition of human language, because affected members of the KE family all share a mutation in this gene (**Figure 15.1**). Similarly, **stuttering**—the tendency of otherwise normal people to produce speech sounds only haltingly, tripping over certain syllables or unable to start vocalizing certain words—is at least partly heritable (C. Kang et al., 2010).

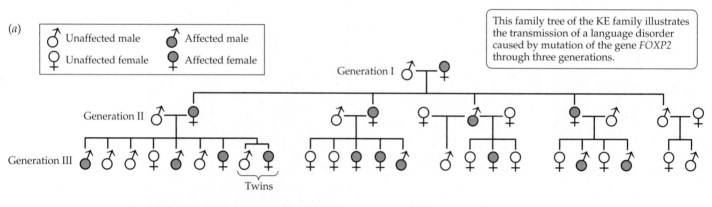

(a)

This family tree of the KE family illustrates the transmission of a language disorder caused by mutation of the gene *FOXP2* through three generations.

(b)   Caudate nucleus   Inferior cerebellum

Regions of reduced gray matter are evident in these MRI scans of the brains of affected members of the KE family. (Crossed reference lines indicate the affected regions.)

Inferior frontal gyrus from two perspectives

Figure 15.1   A Heritable Language Disorder (Part *b* images courtesy of Dr. Faraneh Vargha-Khadem.)

The King's Speech England's King George VI—shown here during a wartime radio broadcast—suffered from severe stuttering. His struggle and eventual success in coping with speech difficulties, as portrayed in the film *The King's Speech*, shows that despite the possible genetic bases of the condition, effective therapy is possible.

On the flip side of the coin, children born with **Williams syndrome**—caused by the deletion of 28 genes from chromosome 7—have various intellectual deficits but excellent verbal skills. No one knows exactly what developmental mechanism results in this hyperverbal behavior (Paterson et al., 1999), but possession of *extra* copies of the identified genes on chromosome 7—rather than deletions of these genes—produces a syndrome of very poor expressive language that is, in many ways, the converse of Williams syndrome (Somerville et al., 2005).

These findings confirm that basic mechanisms of language are heritable components of the human brain, and the product of a long evolutionary history. Indeed, the use of language is one of the key adaptations of our species, with basic capabilities probably arising in an ancient ancestor of our species. For example, the Neandertals shared our version of *FOXP2* (Krause et al., 2007), so perhaps major differences in just a few genes like *FOXP2* and the stuttering genes are enough to explain why we write books and give speeches and chimps do not, despite our otherwise great genetic similarity.

The basic mechanisms of language may be universal, but the particular *forms* of language we use must be learned in childhood, and they are incredibly diverse: about 7,000 different languages, most of which have never been formally studied (Wuethrich, 2000). Nevertheless, all languages share certain basic features. Each language has basic speech sounds, or **phonemes**, that are assembled into simple units of meaning called **morphemes**. Morphemes are assembled into words (the word *unfathomable*, for example, consists of the morphemes *un*, *fathom*, and *able*), which have meaning (termed *semantics*). In turn, the words are assembled into meaningful strings (which may be complete sentences or just phrases) according to the language's *syntax* (rules for constructing phrases—an element of grammar). So anyone who knows the sounds, symbols, and rules of a particular language can generate sentences that convey information to others who have similar knowledge of the language.

spatial cognition The ability to navigate and to understand the spatial relationship between objects.

stuttering The tendency of otherwise normal people to produce speech sounds only haltingly, tripping over certain syllables or unable to start vocalizing certain words.

Williams syndrome A disorder characterized by impairments of spatial cognition and IQ, but superior linguistic abilities.

phoneme A sound that is produced for language.

morpheme The smallest grammatical unit of a language; a word or meaningful part of a word.

The Appearance of Williams Syndrome Children with Williams syndrome often have a characteristic facial shape, caused by the loss of a copy of the *elastin* gene. The loss of copies of other nearby genes is thought to cause mild mental disability paired with verbal fluency. (Photo courtesy of the Williams Syndrome Association.)

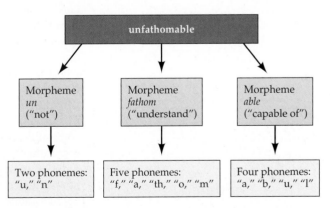

It's All in a Word A morpheme is not the same as a syllable; "fathom" has two syllables but only one meaning (here, "understand"). In English, some phonemes are depicted as a combination of letters, as "th." Words are strung together according to the rules of a language, the syntax, to communicate meaning to others. (Note: Linguists use a very specific notation to identify phonemes that we are not using here.)

Hand and Mouth   Hand gestures and speaking go together so naturally that it seems difficult not to gesture while speaking, even (as here) when the person you're talking to can't see you. This relationship has led theorists to surmise that as speech evolved, it built upon more-ancient systems specialized for gestural communication; perhaps millions of years ago our distant evolutionary ancestors used a sort of prehistoric sign language to communicate important information.

sensitive period or critical period   The period during development in which an organism can be permanently altered by a particular experience or treatment.

A child's brain is an incredible linguistic machine, rapidly acquiring the phonemes, vocabulary, and grammar of the local language without need of formal instruction. A human baby starts out babbling nearly all the phonemes known in all human languages, but she soon comes to use only the subset of phonemes that she hears in use around her. And the baby's developing language abilities are especially shaped by "parentese," the singsong speech of parents that helps babies to attach emotion and meaning to speech sounds (Falk, 2004). By 7 months of age, infants already have a sense of the grammar of the language used in their homes, and they react to exceptions (Marcus et al., 1999).

The human brain contains specialized mechanisms for language acquisition that show a clear-cut **sensitive period** (or **critical period**): a limited span of time during which exposure and practice with language must occur in order for language skills to develop normally. This sensitive period tapers down from the maximal sensitivity of early childhood to an eventual end of special sensitivity around puberty. Individuals that are exposed to language only late in the sensitive period or after it has ended show much-reduced language development (Curtiss, 1989). And as many of us know from first-hand experience, learning a second language is much more difficult in adulthood, after the sensitive period has closed. In fact, people learning a second language later than age 11 apparently use different brain regions for each language (K. H. Kim et al., 1997), unlike those who learn multiple languages early in life.

Speech mechanisms may have evolved from more-ancient systems controlling gestures of the face and hands (Corballis, 2002; Hewes, 1973). Even today there is a close relationship between speaking and gesturing with the hands (Krauss, 1998); in fact, most people find it difficult *not* to gesture when speaking. An evolutionary origin of brain mechanisms of gesturing and speaking suggests that the rudiments of language—or at least some capacity to learn language-like behavior—may be shared with our closest primate relatives. If so, perhaps modern-day nonhuman primates could learn enough grammar to engage in linguistic behavior—an idea we take up next.

Can nonhuman primates acquire language with training?

Nonhuman primates make a variety of vocalizations—shrieks, purring, peeping, growling and so on (Ploog, 1992)—that appear to be mostly preprogrammed and emotional, but that sometimes also communicate semantic information about the environment to others (Seyfarth and Cheney, 2003). Electrical stimulation of the brain indicates that vocal behavior in monkeys and apes relies primarily on subcortical systems, especially sites in the limbic system, rather than on cortex. The vocalizations elicited by subcortical stimulation are associated with strongly emotional behaviors such as defense, attack, feeding, sex, and so on (**Figure 15.2**). Vocalizations are more common if subcortical stimulation is provided to the left hemisphere, indicating a special role of the left hemisphere in the communicative behavior of monkeys and apes (Meguerditchian and Vauclair, 2006; Taglialatela et al., 2006)—an idea that has been amply confirmed in humans, where the cortex is also important for speech.

Because both the vocal tracts and the vocal repertoires of nonhuman primates are very different from those of humans, scientists long ago gave up trying to train animals to produce human speech. But can nonhuman primates be taught other forms of communication, with features similar to those of human language? Can they learn to represent objects with symbols and to manipulate those symbols according to rules of order? Can animals other than humans generate a novel string of symbols, such as a new sentence, in a grammatical form?

In evolutionary terms, our nearest primate relatives are the great apes: chimpanzees and gorillas. Apes are capable of learning many of the hand gestures of American Sign Language (ASL) (see Figure 15.8), the standardized sign language used by deaf people in most of North America (R. A. Gardner and Gardner, 1969, 1984; F. Patterson and Linden, 1981). Through extensive practice, apes can also be trained to communicate by assembling abstract symbols, such as colored plastic chips or computerized symbols, into new sentences (Premack, 1971; Rumbaugh, 1977).

Figure 15.2 **Electrical Stimulation of the Monkey Brain Elicits Vocalizations** (After Ploog, 1992; spectrograms courtesy of Uwe Jürgens.)

Some researchers conclude that apes are able to acquire words (or equivalent symbols; **Figure 15.3**) and then string them together into novel, meaningful chains; that is, they seem to employ a grammar to communicate ideas. Other researchers argue that these sequences may simply be subtle forms of imitation (Terrace, 1979), perhaps unconsciously cued by the experimenter who is providing the training. Native ASL users dispute the linguistic validity of the signs generated by apes; and Pinker (1994) concludes that "even putting aside vocabulary, phonology, morphology, and syntax, what impresses one the most about chimpanzee signing is that fundamentally, deep down, chimps just don't get it" (p. 349).

Nevertheless, considering that apes can comprehend spoken words, produce novel combinations of words, and respond appropriately to sentences arranged according to a syntactic rule, it seems likely that the capabilities of apes have been underestimated (Savage-Rumbaugh, 1993). For example, a bonobo (or pygmy chimpanzee) named Kanzi, the focus of a long-term research program (Savage-Rumbaugh and Lewin, 1994), reportedly learned numerous symbols and ways to assemble them in novel combinations, entirely through observational learning rather than the usual intensive training. And in natural settings, monkeys combine certain vocalizations into higher-order, more complex calls, suggesting the presence of both syntax and semantic meaning, at least on a rudimentary level (K. Arnold and Zuberbühler, 2006; Ouattara, et al., 2009).

Vocal behavior is a feature of many different species

In addition to primates, many other species of animals use vocalizations—chirps, barks, meows, songs, and more—to communicate important information to members of their own or other species. Although these communication sounds do not constitute language, in that they lack the features of language that we've discussed earlier, such sounds nevertheless broadcast crucial signals about

These spectrograms show a variety of typical monkey vocalizations.

● Purring

● Trilling

● Shrieking

● Alarm peeping

● Cackling

Each type of vocalization can be elicited through electrical stimulation of the specific brain sites illustrated in these coronal sections of the monkey brain.

Anterior coronal section

Posterior section

Chimpanzees can learn to use arbitrary signs and/or symbols to communicate, but it is questionable whether this usage is equivalent to human language.

Figure 15.3 **Chimpanzee Using Symbols** (Photo courtesy of Sue Savage-Rumbaugh.)

Talk to the Animals   People and animals can clearly communicate: anyone who has watched a sheepdog at work has to acknowledge that the dog's human handler is transmitting lots of information to his highly intelligent companion. Instilling *language* in a nonhuman is a different matter, however. Every day, you utter sentences that you've never said before, yet the meaning is clear to both you and your listener because you both understand the rules. Animals generally are incapable of similar feats, instead requiring extensive training with each specific utterance (e.g., each voice command to the sheepdog) in order for communication to occur at all. In other words, most animals appear to lack grammar.

readiness to mate, danger, territorial defense, emotional state, and so on. Whales sing and may imitate songs that they hear from distant oceans (Noad et al., 2000), and some seal mothers recognize their pups' vocalizations even after 4 years of separation (Insley, 2000). In fact, many species—from elephants to bats to birds to dolphins—are capable of vocal learning and use their vocalizations to help form social bonds and identify individuals (Poole et al., 2005; Tyack, 2003).

In the lab, measurement with special instruments reveals that rats and mice produce complex ultrasonic vocalizations that they use to communicate emotional information (Panksepp, 2005). These ultrasonic vocalizations are impaired in mice with mutations in the *FOXP2* gene (Shu et al., 2005), providing an intriguing parallel to the situation in humans that we discussed at the beginning of the chapter.

Birds are particularly vocal animals. Many bird species produce only simple vocalizations, but songbirds like canaries and zebra finches produce rich and melodious vocalizations that are critical components for reproductive behavior. Although birdsong has evolved quite independently of human speech, there are some interesting parallels between the two (Marler, 1970). For example, the songbird brain contains a specialized neural system for the control of vocal behavior (**Figure 15.4**) and, as in humans, damage to the left hemisphere has a greater effect on vocal behavior. What's more, the juvenile bird must be exposed to the songs of adults during a distinct critical period in order for its own singing behavior to develop normally (DeVoogd, 1994)—a requirement that also parallels human language. And yes, once again, the *FOXP2* gene has been implicated: when *FOXP2* expression is blocked in parts of the song control system, young males fail to properly learn and recite their tutor's song, producing errors that in some ways resemble those in the humans with abnormal *FOXP2* that we described earlier (Haesler et al., 2007).

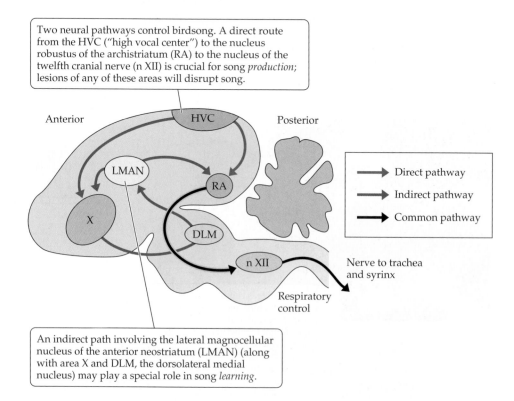

Two neural pathways control birdsong. A direct route from the HVC ("high vocal center") to the nucleus robustus of the archistriatum (RA) to the nucleus of the twelfth cranial nerve (n XII) is crucial for song *production*; lesions of any of these areas will disrupt song.

Anterior   Posterior

HVC

LMAN

RA

X

DLM

n XII

Nerve to trachea and syrinx

Respiratory control

→ Direct pathway
→ Indirect pathway
→ Common pathway

An indirect path involving the lateral magnocellular nucleus of the anterior neostriatum (LMAN) (along with area X and DLM, the dorsolateral medial nucleus) may play a special role in song *learning*.

Figure 15.4   Song Control Nuclei of the Songbird Brain (After A. P. Arnold, 1980.)

In many important ways, the birdsong system is also dramatically different from the human speech system. For one thing, because it is a sexually selected trait, most birdsong is produced by males. In humans, of course, both sexes use language (in fact, women outperform men on some verbal tasks; see Chapter 8). Also in stark contrast to the human system, the birdsong system "crystallizes" after the sensitive period ends; from then on, the bird's singing becomes highly stereotyped, and he fixedly produces the same unchanging song for the rest of his life (not something that humans do, although sometimes it can seem that way!). (For more on birdsong and its social roles, see **A Step Further 15.1**, on the website.)

Language Disorders Result from Region-Specific Brain Injuries

For thousands of years, dating back to the earliest medical records and beyond, people have known that a selective impairment of language abilities, known as **aphasia**, could result from injury to specific regions of the brain, especially the left hemisphere (Finger, 1994). Left-hemisphere damage can impair language to varying degrees, depending on the location and extent of the injury. In cases of severe damage, people may lose the ability to produce any speech whatsoever. In less severe cases, patients may exhibit speech with **paraphasia**—insertion of incorrect sounds or words—along with labored, effortful speech production.

Most patients with aphasia also show some impairment in writing (**agraphia**) and disturbances in reading (**alexia**). Brain damage that produces aphasia also produces a distinctive motor impairment called **apraxia** (see Chapter 5), characterized by great difficulty in making a sequence of movements, despite the absence of weakness or paralysis. In fact, as we discuss later, some theorists view aphasia as primarily a disorder of motor control. Research has distinguished several major categories of aphasia, differing from one another in the pattern of symptoms that occur.

Linking these distinctive language disorders to specific regions of brain damage has uncovered details of a left-hemisphere language network (**Figure 15.5**). The specific language deficit experienced depends on which particular components are compromised, as we discuss in the following sections.

How's it going?

1. Why do researchers think that a capacity for language is innate in the human brain? Briefly describe some pertinent research findings that support this position, including genetic evidence.

2. What are the basic linguistic components of verbal language?

3. Discuss the process of language acquisition in infants. What is the significance of the term *critical period* in this regard?

4. Survey some of the ways in which studies of nonhuman animals help us understand the neural mechanisms of language.

Figure 15.5   Left-Hemisphere Speech and Language Areas in Humans

*Labels in figure:*
Primary motor cortex
Supramarginal gyrus
Broca's area
Damage to the supramarginal gyrus interferes with repetition of heard speech.
Angular gyrus
Lesions in the left anterior frontal *Broca's area* interfere with speech production.
Damage to the temporoparietal *Wernicke's area* interferes with language comprehension.
Primary auditory area
Wernicke's area

aphasia   An impairment in language understanding and/or production that is caused by brain injury.

paraphasia   A symptom of aphasia that is distinguished by the substitution of a word by a sound, an incorrect word, an unintended word, or a neologism (a meaningless word).

agraphia   The inability to write.

alexia   The inability to read.

apraxia   An impairment in the ability to carry out complex sequential movements, even though there is no muscle paralysis.

Damage to a left anterior speech zone causes nonfluent (or Broca's) aphasia

A modern era of understanding the brain mechanisms of language dawned in 1861, when French neurologist Paul Broca (1824–1880) reported that damage to the left inferior frontal region that now bears his name—**Broca's area** (see Figure 15.5)—tended to result in a severe speech impairment. Anterior lesions that include Broca's area often produce a type of aphasia known as **nonfluent**, or **Broca's**, **aphasia**. Patients with nonfluent aphasia have a lot of difficulty producing speech, talking only in a labored and hesitant manner. Reading and writing are also impaired. The ability to utter automatic speech, however, is often preserved. Such speech includes greetings ("Hello"); short, common expressions ("Oh, my God!"); and swear words.

Compared to the difficulty that these patients have expressing themselves, their *comprehension* of language remains relatively good. Because primary and supplementary motor cortex are located in anterior portions of the hemisphere (see Chapter 5), many people who suffer from nonfluent aphasia also have **hemiplegia**—paralysis of one side of the body (usually the right side, which is controlled by the left hemisphere). Sometimes there is unilateral weakness, termed **hemiparesis**, rather than full paralysis.

The CT scans in **Figures 15.6a, b** reveal lesion sites in patients with nonfluent aphasia. Seven years after a stroke, one such patient still spoke slowly, used mainly nouns and very few verbs or function words (a selective loss of action words, called *averbia*, sometimes occurs in nonfluent aphasia), and spoke only with great effort. When asked to repeat the phrase "Go ahead and do it if possible," she could say only, "Go to do it," with pauses between each word. People who suffer brain lesions as extensive as hers show little recovery of speech with the passing of time, but people with milder cases can show some recovery.

Damage to a left posterior speech zone causes fluent (or Wernicke's) aphasia

German neurologist Carl Wernicke (pronounced "VER-nih-keh") (1848–1905), described a different form of aphasia, resulting from damage to a region of the left posterior temporal cortex, now known as **Wernicke's area** (see Figure 15.5). Unlike nonfluent aphasics, people with this **fluent**, or **Wernicke's**, **aphasia** produce plenty of verbal output, but their utterances, although speechlike, tend to contain many paraphasias, such as sound substitutions (e.g., "girl" becomes "curl") and/or word substitutions (e.g., *bread* becomes *cake*). Some fluent aphasias are marked by difficulty in naming persons or objects—an impairment referred to as **anomia**. The ability to repeat words and sentences is impaired. For this reason, people with fluent aphasia are believed to have difficulty *understanding* what they read or hear.

Lesions that produce fluent aphasia usually include the posterior parts of the superior left temporal lobe, extending into adjacent regions of parietal cortex (Damasio, 1995). Examples of lesions causing fluent aphasia are shown in **Figure 15.6c**. Sometimes stroke victims experience *word deafness* (the inability to understand spoken words), which usually means that auditory regions of the temporal lobe are particularly affected. Other patients may instead experience *word blindness* (the inability to understand written words), usually indicating damage that includes connections to visual regions (via the angular gyrus; see Figure 15.5). And because the typical lesion is posterior, postcentral somatosensory cortex is more likely to be damaged than precentral motor cortex, so patients are more likely to have a right-sided numbness than a right-sided weakness.

Widespread left-hemisphere damage can obliterate language capabilities

In some patients, brain injury or disease results in total loss of the ability to understand or produce language, called **global aphasia**. Patients suffering from global aphasia may retain some ability for automatic speech, especially emotional exclamations. But they can utter very few words, and no semblance of syntax is evident in their vocalizations. Global aphasia generally results from very large left-hemisphere lesions that encompass both anterior and posterior language zones. Frontal, temporal, and parietal cortex—including Broca's area, Wernicke's area, and the supramarginal gyrus (see Figure 15.5)—are usually affected (**Figure 15.6d**). The prognosis for language recovery in these

---

Broca's area   A region of the frontal lobe of the brain that is involved in the production of speech.

nonfluent aphasia or Broca's aphasia   A language impairment characterized by difficulty with speech production but not with language comprehension. It is related to damage in Broca's area.

hemiplegia   Partial paralysis involving one side of the body.

hemiparesis   Weakness of one side of the body.

Wernicke's area   A region of temporo-parietal cortex in the brain that is involved in the perception and production of speech.

fluent aphasia or Wernicke's aphasia   A language impairment characterized by fluent, meaningless speech and little language comprehension. It is related to damage in Wernicke's area.

anomia   The inability to name persons or objects readily.

global aphasia   The total loss of ability to understand language, or to speak, read, or write.

Primary motor cortex
Somatosensory cortex

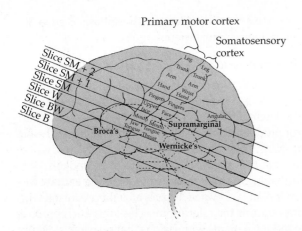

Figure 15.6 Brain Lesions That Produce Aphasia (After Naeser and Hayward, 1978; CT scans courtesy of Margaret Naeser.)

To make the maps shown below, brain CT scan "slices" were labeled according to the brain language regions shown in each slice: B, Broca's area; SM, supramarginal gyrus; W, Wernicke's area.

(a) This 51-year-old patient had nonfluent (Broca's) aphasia as a result of a stroke that included Broca's area.

(b) Here the lesions (in blue) of four patients with nonfluent (Broca's) aphasia are drawn as overlapping maps.

(c) Lesion sites for four cases of fluent (Wernicke's) aphasia are mapped on these drawings.

(d) These drawings show lesion sites for five cases of global aphasia. Large lesions are present in every language area.

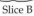

| Slice B | Slice BW | Slice W | Slice SM | Slice SM + 1 | Slice SM + 2 |

connectionist model of aphasia   Also called *Wernicke-Geschwind model*. A theory proposing that left-hemisphere language deficits result from disconnection between the brain regions in a language network, each of which serves a particular linguistic function.

arcuate fasciculus   A fiber tract classically viewed as a connection between Wernicke's speech area and Broca's speech area.

conduction aphasia   An impairment in the ability to repeat words and sentences.

patients is quite poor, and because of the extent of their lesions, the aphasia is generally accompanied by other debilitating neurological impairments.

Disconnection of language regions may result in specific verbal problems

The traditional **connectionist model of aphasia**—also known as the *Wernicke-Geschwind model*—views language deficits as resulting from *disconnection* between the brain regions in a language network. Each of these regions is proposed to serve a particular feature of language analysis or production. So, when a word or sentence is heard, the auditory cortex transmits information about the sounds to Wernicke's area, where the sounds are analyzed to decode what they mean. For the word to be spoken, Wernicke's area must transmit this information, via a fiber pathway called the **arcuate fasciculus**, to Broca's area, where a speech plan is activated. Broca's area then transmits this plan to adjacent motor cortex, which controls the relevant muscles for speech production (**Figure 15.7**). According to the model, patients with lesions that selectively disrupt the connection between the posterior speech reception zone (Wernicke's area) and the anterior speech production zone (Broca's area) will especially struggle with repetition of words and phrases that they hear, despite good speech comprehension and production—a condition termed **conduction aphasia**. **Table 15.1** summarizes the main features of the aphasias that we've discussed.

Figure 15.7   The Connectionist Model of Aphasia (After Geschwind, 1976.)

(a) Speaking a *heard* word

1 Information about the sound is analyzed by primary auditory cortex and transmitted to Wernicke's area.

2 Wernicke's area analyzes the sound information to determine the word that was said.

3 Under the connectionist model this information is transmitted via the arcuate fasciculus. (Note, however, that anatomical research casts doubt on this projection.)

4 Broca's area forms a motor plan to repeat the word and sends that information to motor cortex.

5 Motor cortex implements the plan, manipulating the larynx and related structures to say the word.

Lesions of the arcuate fasciculus disrupt the transfer from Wernicke's area to Broca's area, so the patient has difficulty repeating spoken words (so-called conduction aphasia), but may retain comprehension of spoken language (because of intact Wernicke's area) and may still be able to speak spontaneously (because of intact Broca's area).

(b) Speaking a *written* word

1 Visual cortex analyzes the image and transmits the information about the image to the angular gyrus.

2 The angular gyrus decodes the image information to recognize the word and associate this visual form with the spoken form in Wernicke's area.

3 Information about the word is transmitted via the arcuate fasciculus to Broca's area.

4 Broca's area formulates a motor plan to say the appropriate word and transmits that plan to motor cortex for implementation.

5 Motor cortex implements the plan, manipulating the larynx and related structures to say the word.

A lesion of the angular gyrus disrupts the flow of information from visual cortex, so the person has difficulty saying words he has seen but not words he has heard.

In ASL, letters, words, and concepts are communicated via different configurations (*signs*) of the hands and arms, as these three examples illustrate.

Feeling

Be quiet

Secret

Figure 15.8 American Sign Language

Critics of the connectionist model argue that it oversimplifies the neural mechanisms of language and prematurely attaches functional labels to anatomical structures. And brain-imaging studies indicate that the left hemisphere contains several speech areas well outside of the classical Broca's and Wernicke's areas (Bates et al., 2003; Dronkers et al., 2004), implying greater complexity than was previously supposed. For example, detailed brain-imaging research suggests that so-called conduction aphasia results from a specific type of lesion of superior temporal cortex, rather than the disruption of white matter pathways as proposed under the connectionist model (B. R. Buchsbaum et al., 2011). So it remains to be seen exactly how the various mechanisms of the left hemisphere collaborate to give us the vocal abilities that seem so effortless.

An alternative model of speech mechanisms—the **motor theory of language** (Kimura, 1993; Lieberman, 1985)—suggests that the anterior and posterior left-hemisphere language zones are both specialized for motor control. According to the motor theory, when we listen to speech we simply process the speech sounds using the same neural systems that we would use to *make* the same sounds: an anterior system for programming simple phonemic units, and a posterior system stringing speech sounds together into long sequences of movements (Kimura and Watson, 1989). Interestingly, people who use sign language (**Figure 15.8**)—a language based entirely on movements—employ the same language-related regions of the left hemisphere as people who use spoken lan-

motor theory of language The theory of speech mechanisms proposing that the left-hemisphere language zones are motor control systems that are concerned with both the precise production and the perception of the extremely complex movements that go into speech.

TABLE 15.1 Language Symptomatology in Aphasia

Type of aphasia	Brain area affected	Spontaneous speech	Comprehension	Paraphasia	Repetition	Naming
Nonfluent (Broca's) aphasia		Nonfluent	Good	Uncommon	Poor	Poor
Fluent (Wernicke's) aphasia		Fluent	Poor	Common	Poor	Poor
Global aphasia		Nonfluent	Poor	Variable	Poor	Poor
Conduction aphasia		Fluent	Good	Common	Poor	Poor

How's it going?

1. Distinguish among aphasia, agraphia, and alexia.

2. Identify the main types of aphasia, and summarize the distinctive symptoms of each. Which type of aphasia is most often associated with paralysis?

3. Provide a brief outline of the traditional "connectionist" model of aphasia. How does it get its name, and what shortcomings of the model have been identified by critics?

4. Briefly describe the motor theory of language. Can you think of ways that this theory may relate to the evolutionary origins of language?

Overcoming Dyslexia   Many highly intelligent, highly successful people—like self-made billionaire Richard Branson, pictured here—have coped with dyslexia on their way to fame and fortune.

dyslexia   Also called *alexia*. A reading disorder attributed to brain impairment.

deep dyslexia   Acquired dyslexia in which the patient reads a word as another word that is semantically related.

surface dyslexia   Acquired dyslexia in which the patient seems to attend only to the fine details of reading.

guage (Neville et al., 1998; Petitto et al., 2000), and they show comparable aphasia-like symptoms after focal left-hemisphere damage (Bellugi et al., 1983; Kimura, 1981).

Reading Skills Are Difficult to Acquire and Frequently Impaired

Why is it so much harder to learn to read and write than to speak? Compared to speech, the written word is a relatively new development, so we haven't had enough time to evolve brain mechanisms for reading and writing of the sort we have for speech. Therefore, learning the written form of a language is a slow and laborious chore of childhood, and vulnerable to developmental disruptions that result in **dyslexia** (from the Greek *dys*, "bad," and *lexis*, "word"), a mild to severe difficulty with reading.

Brain damage may cause specific impairments in reading

Sometimes people who learned to read just fine as children suddenly become dyslexic in adulthood as a result of disease or injury, usually to the left hemisphere. This *acquired dyslexia* (sometimes called *alexia*) offers hints about how the brain processes written language. One type of acquired dyslexia, known as **deep dyslexia**, is characterized by semantic errors (that is, errors related to the *meaning* of words); for example, the printed word *cow* is read as *horse*. These patients are also unable to read aloud words that are abstract as opposed to concrete, and they make frequent errors in which they seem to fail to see small differences in words. It's as though they grasp words whole, without noting the details of the letters, so they have a hard time reading nonsense words.

In another form of acquired dyslexia, **surface dyslexia**, the patient makes different types of errors when reading. These patients can read nonsense words without problems, indicating that they understand which letters make which sounds. But they find it difficult to recognize words in which the letter-to-sound rules are irregular. *The Tough Coughs as He Ploughs the Dough* by Dr. Seuss (1987), for example, would utterly confound them. In contrast to patients with deep dyslexia, those with surface dyslexia seem restricted to the details and sounds of letters. Interestingly, surface dyslexia doesn't occur in native speakers of languages that are perfectly phonetic (such as Italian, where every letter is pronounced). This finding indicates that what's lost in speakers of non-phonetic languages, like English, is purely a learned aspect of language. In contrast, deep dyslexia probably involves language mechanisms that are more hardwired.

Some people struggle throughout their lives to read

Some children seem to take forever to learn to read, and not even extended practice can make their reading easy and accurate. Affecting about 5% of children—especially boys and left-handers—this *developmental dyslexia* is a problem unique to written language, and not a general cognitive deficit. (Indeed, some children with dyslexia have a high IQ (B. Morris, 2002); several notable examples have grown up to amass billion-dollar fortunes). Instead, the problem seems to lie in connecting written language with the brain mechanisms for speech that have evolved.

Developmental dyslexia has been associated with several types of neurological abnormalities (**Figure 15.9**). Either in postmortem investigations or using MRI, anatomical studies of the brains of dyslexic people have found aberrant layering of the neurons of the cerebral cortex, along with excessive cortical folding and clusters of extra neurons in unexpected locations (Chang et al., 2005; Galaburda, 1994). Cortical abnormalities are especially evident in the frontal and temporal lobes, possibly because of defective migration of newborn neurons during fetal development (Galaburda et al., 2006). Studies using fMRI confirm that people with dyslexia show impaired neural activity in left posterior regions (Pugh et al., 2000; Shaywitz et al., 1998, 2003), while displaying a relative overactivation of anterior regions. Abnormality in the nearby temporoparietal region has been linked to the phonological (phoneme-processing) aspects of dyslexia (Hoeft et al., 2006). And it looks like some of these abnormalities have genetic bases; for example,

In these drawings of the left and right upper temporal lobe from the brain of a dyslexic person, the planum temporale is nearly symmetrical; in most people the left planum temporale is considerably larger. The dots and the shaded area represent regions where cellular disorganization has been found in the brains of individuals with dyslexia.

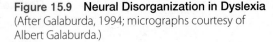

Figure 15.9 **Neural Disorganization in Dyslexia**
(After Galaburda, 1994; micrographs courtesy of Albert Galaburda.)

(a)

View from above

Heschl's gyrus (primary auditory cortex)

Temporal lobes

Planum temporale

L   R

Plane of section

Occipital lobes

Structural abnormalities in patients with dyslexia are much more common in the left hemisphere.

Left   Right

(b) Area of micropolygyria, excessive cortical folding

(c) Ectopias, clusters of neurons in unusual locations

disruption of genes involved in brain development and the migration of neurons into adult positions are associated with developmental dyslexia (Cope et al., 2005; Meng et al., 2005; Harold et al., 2006).

Taken together, imaging and behavioral studies indicate that our brains rely on two different language systems during reading: one focused on the sounds of letters, the other on the meanings of whole words (McCarthy and Warrington, 1990). Presumably, these systems are shaped by training: as with learning any highly skilled behavior, our brains mold themselves to accommodate our acquired expertise with written language. For example, remedial training in people with dyslexia induces changes in the left-hemisphere systems that are used for reading (Temple et al., 2003). Perhaps, then, coupling education interventions with early genetic screening for dyslexia will help affected people overcome their trouble with words completely.

Brain Mapping Helps Us Understand the Organization of Language in the Brain

Researchers have exploited two complementary experimental approaches to explore the neural systems underlying human language. In cortical stimulation studies, discrete cortical regions are directly activated, and the resultant changes in language function are measured. In functional brain-imaging studies the approach is reversed: subjects engage in language behaviors, and associated changes in brain activity are measured. Together, these techniques have extended our understanding of the neural bases of language.

Cortical stimulation mapping shows localized functions within language areas

Early studies of the organization of language areas in the brain used cortical stimulation mapping, in which discrete regions of cortex are electrically stimulated and the effect on behavior is observed. The subjects were neurosurgical patients undergoing surgery to remove a tumor or epileptic tissue. Once the brain was exposed, small stimulating electrodes were touched to the surface, disrupting the normal functioning of neurons in the immediate vicinity. Because patients were given only local anesthesia, they were conscious and able to perform various cognitive tests (the main aim of the procedure was to identify tissue that could be removed without impairing language). The data from numerous patients provided a map of language-related zones of the left hemisphere (**Figure 15.10a**) (Penfield and Roberts, 1959). Stimulation anywhere within a large anterior zone stopped speech, and other forms of language interference, such as misnaming or impaired repetition of words, occurred with stimulation of both this region and more-posterior cortical regions.

Later cortical stimulation studies revealed anatomical compartmentalization of linguistic systems such as naming, reading, speech production, and verbal memory. An interesting example of the effects of cortical stimulation on naming is illustrated in **Figure 15.10b**, which shows the different places where stimulation caused naming errors in English and Spanish in a bilingual subject. Presumably this person learned the two languages sequentially, for if they had been learned simultaneously, a more complete overlap of the English and Spanish language zones would be expected (Perani and Abutalebi, 2005). More recent studies (featured in the next section) employ a noninvasive cortical stimulation technology called transcranial magnetic stimulation (TMS) to further probe the organization of language areas in normal subjects. These studies have confirmed the general organization of the left-hemisphere language network and have revealed new details about the compartmentalization of functions within traditional speech areas.

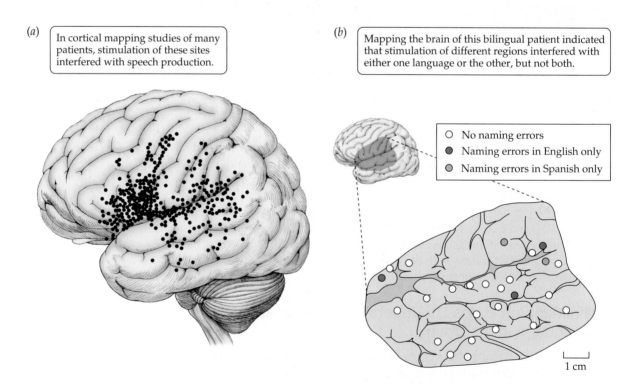

(a) In cortical mapping studies of many patients, stimulation of these sites interfered with speech production.

(b) Mapping the brain of this bilingual patient indicated that stimulation of different regions interfered with either one language or the other, but not both.

○ No naming errors
● Naming errors in English only
● Naming errors in Spanish only

1 cm

Figure 15.10 Electrical Stimulation of Some Brain Sites Can Interfere with Language (Part *a* after Penfield and Roberts, 1959; *b* after Ojemann and Mateer, 1979.)

RESEARCHERS AT WORK

Noninvasive stimulation mapping shows that the language areas of the normal brain may contain a variety of functional zones

Transcranial magnetic stimulation (TMS) is a relatively new technology that allows the researcher to stimulate small clusters of cortical neurons with good precision, from outside the scalp (see Figure 2.20). By using MRI scans to select targets, TMS provides a noninvasive method for inducing a sort of temporary brain lesion, disrupting the activity of the selected brain region for up to an hour. Alternatively, TMS can be used along with PET or fMRI to precisely map regions of increased activity.

Using TMS mapping, researchers have generally replicated and extended the earlier findings regarding the cortical organization of language functions. For example, Ingo Meister and coworkers (2003) found that speech production activates not only face areas in motor cortex but also hand areas, confirming the linkage and possible evolutionary relationship of hand gestures and speech. Sophie Scott and Richard Wise (2004) used TMS to show that speech *perception* apparently activates specific regions that TMS shows to be involved with speech *production*, providing support for the motor theory of speech, which we discussed earlier.

Impressively, the TMS temporary-lesion approach has revealed previously unknown distinct regional differences *within* Broca's area (**Figure 15.11**), in experiments by Patricia Gough and her colleagues (2005). Gough's team found that anterior parts of Broca's area are involved in the semantic *meaning* of words, while a more posterior part of Broca's area is important for the patterning of speech *sounds*. Other research has shown that the posterior speech zone likewise contributes to both semantic and phonological aspects of language (Stoeckel et al., 2009). So the TMS procedure is providing new insights into the fine details of the cortical organization of language, especially in conjunction with traditional neuroimaging techniques (Devlin and Watkins, 2007).

Figure 15.11 **Subregions of Broca's Area Revealed by TMS**

Question

Does Broca's area perform a single language function (as proposed in classical models of language organization), or is Broca's a collection of structures with differing linguistic functions?

Test

Guided by precise structural MRI scans, apply transcranial magnetic stimulation (TMS) to activate discrete regions within Broca's area.

Broca's area

Semantic processing (meanings)

Phonological processing (sounds)

Result

Anterior regions of Broca's area appear to be important for semantic processing (word meanings), while more posterior regions within Broca's area specialize in phonological processing (sounds of words).

Functional neuroimaging technologies identify brain regions that are active during specific language tasks

PET scans of normal subjects (described in Chapter 2) reveal patterns of brain activation during different types of verbal behavior (Posner and Raichle, 1994). These behaviors included (1) passively viewing words, (2) passively listening to words, (3) orally repeating words, and (4) generating semantic associations to words. The experimental conditions, and the patterns of brain activation observed in each condition, are shown in **Figure 15.12**. The researchers found that passive viewing of words activates a posterior area

Figure 15.12 PET Scans of Brain Activation in Progressively More Complex Language Tasks (After Posner and Raichle, 1994; PET scans courtesy of Marcus Raichle.)

(*a*) Passively viewing words

(*b*) Listening to words

(*c*) Speaking words

(*d*) Generating a verb associated with each noun shown

Each series of PET scans shows the pattern of brain activity associated with the verbal task depicted at left.

within the left hemisphere (**Figure 15.12a**). Passive hearing of words shifts the maximum brain activation to the temporal lobes (**Figure 15.12b**). Repeating words orally activates the motor cortex of both sides, along with supplementary motor cortex and some of the cerebellum (**Figure 15.12c**). Thus, during word repetition or reading aloud, little activity was seen in Broca's area. But when subjects were required to provide a verb appropriate for a presented noun, language-related regions in the left hemisphere, including Broca's area, suddenly became markedly activated (**Figure 15.12d**).

Even languages that sound very, very different tend to activate much the same brain regions in native speakers. Silbo Gomero is a very unusual whistled language of the Canary Islands, used by shepherds (known as *silbadores*) to communicate over long distances. In Silbo, whistled notes serve as the phonemes and morphemes of a stripped-down form of Spanish (for an audio sample of Silbo, with translation, see **A Step Further 15.2**, on the website). Functional MRI reveals that silbadores process Silbo using the same left-hemisphere mechanisms that they (and everyone else) use to process spoken language (Carreiras et al., 2005). Nonsilbadore controls, in contrast, process the whistle sounds of Silbo using completely different regions of the brain. So the brain's left-hemisphere language systems appear to be sufficiently plastic to adapt to many types of signals, provided that they're heard early enough. Even 3-month-old infants, when exposed to speech, show more metabolic activity in the left hemisphere than in the right (Dehaene-Lambertz et al., 2002).

Event-related potentials (ERPs; see Chapters 3 and 14) also provide hints about the brain's language network, by revealing the time base for language processing by the brain. Subjects are asked to read a sentence in which they encounter a word that is grammatically correct but, because of its meaning, doesn't fit—for example, "The man started the car engine and stepped on the pancake." About 400 milliseconds after the subject reads the word *pancake*, a negative wave is detected on the scalp (Kutas and Hillyard, 1980). Such "N400" responses (*N* denotes "negative," and the number represents the response time in milliseconds) to word meanings seem to be centered over the temporal lobe (Neville et al., 1992) and therefore may originate from temporoparietal cortex (including Wernicke's area). But *grammatically* inappropriate words elicit a positive potential about 600 milliseconds after they are encountered (a "P600" response), indicating that detection of this level of error requires an extra 200 milliseconds of brain processing by other components of the language network (Osterhout, 1997).

How's it going?

1. Why do researchers believe that it is so much harder to learn to read than to learn to speak?

2. What are the two principal types of acquired dyslexia? Summarize their respective features.

3. What is developmental dyslexia, and what are some of the neurological findings associated with this form of reading disorder?

4. Summarize and discuss the organization of language systems in the human brain, as revealed by stimulation mapping. Include TMS mapping in this discussion.

5. Discuss the patterns of brain activity that are observed in various verbal tasks, using functional-imaging technologies and ERPs. How well do these results align with traditional models of the organization of language areas in the brain?

PART II Cerebral Asymmetry

One of the major advances of twentieth-century biological psychology was the realization that in controlling ongoing behavior, the two cerebral hemispheres are not necessarily doing the same things. Instead, prompted by the discovery that most language functions are contained within the left hemisphere, researchers started to think in terms of hemispheric specialization, or lateralization (Finger, 1994). While we'll see plenty of evidence that the two sides of the brain differ in how readily they handle various tasks, keep in mind that normally the two halves work together. Claims that some people are especially "right-brained" (supposedly more random, intuitive, and creative), while others are more "left-brained" (supposedly logical, sequential, and analytical), have little scientific basis.

The Left and Right Brains Are Different

Lateralization of function is not really such a surprising idea; other body organs also show considerable asymmetry between the right and left sides. But when we study the *behavior* of normal people, cerebral lateralization of function is masked by the rich neural connections between the hemispheres: the hemispheres communicate with each other so quickly and so thoroughly that they seem to act as one. So researchers had to develop clever techniques to study the functioning of each hemisphere in isolation from the other.

Disconnection of the cerebral hemispheres reveals their individual processing specializations

Some rare and unfortunate people develop epilepsy that becomes very difficult to control with medication. They experience frequent seizures that start in one hemisphere and then spread through the corpus callosum—the huge axon pathway connecting the two hemispheres—to involve the whole brain. One last-ditch approach to controlling unmanageable epilepsy was to cut the corpus callosum, preventing the spread of the seizure discharges from one hemisphere to the other. When it was first developed, this operation greatly reduced the severity of seizures in patients, but it also created a research opportunity. Because the hemispheres were now isolated from one another, detailed behavioral testing of these **split-brain individuals** could allow researchers to document cerebral hemispheric specialization in cognitive, perceptual, emotional, and motor activities.

In Nobel Prize–winning research starting in the 1960s, Roger Sperry and his collaborators began using behavioral techniques that he had perfected in split-brain cats to study split-brain humans. Sperry realized that by exploiting the organization of the sensory systems, stimuli could be directed exclusively to one hemisphere or the other. For example, objects felt with the left hand, or seen only in the left visual fields, are first processed in the sensory cortex of the **contralateral** (opposite side) hemisphere (in this case, the right hemisphere). Normally, information about the object would be passed to the other hemisphere immediately, via the corpus callosum. But in split-brain individuals, the sensory information remains trapped within the receiving hemisphere, so the patient's response to the stimuli reflects the processing specializations of that hemisphere in isolation.

In some of Sperry's studies, words were projected visually to either the left or the right hemisphere. The results were dramatic. Split-brain subjects could easily read and verbally report words projected to the left hemisphere, but not words directed to the right hemisphere (**Figure 15.13**). In subsequent work, Zaidel (1976) showed that the right hemisphere does have a limited amount of linguistic ability; for example, it can recognize simple words and the emotional content of verbal material. But in most people, vocabulary and grammar are the exclusive domain of the left hemisphere (left-handers occasionally show a reversed asymmetry).

The specializations of the "mute" right hemisphere had to be tested by nonverbal means. For example, a picture of a key might be projected to the left visual field and so reach only the right visual cortex. The subject would then be asked to touch several different objects that she could not see and hold up the correct one. Such a task could be performed correctly by the left hand (controlled by the right hemisphere) but not by the right hand (controlled by the left hemisphere). So in this case, the left hemisphere literally does not know what the left hand is doing! In general, these and other studies with split-brain individuals provided evidence that, in most people, the right hemisphere is specialized for processing spatial information. Right-hemisphere mechanisms are also crucial for face perception, for processing emotional aspects of language, and for controlling attention (as we discuss in Chapter 14).

The dramatic findings of split-brain research prompted a lot of commentary and theory. One common view of lateralization is that the left hemisphere provides analytical and sequential processing, while the right hemisphere offers a more holistic, general analysis of information (**Table 15.2**). But many untested or inconsistent ideas about laterality are also in circulation, in various formats like self-help books and instructional materials. For example, the notion that the two hemispheres are so different that they need separate instruction lacks any scientific basis, as does the idea that people can have "left-brain" or "right-brain" personalities. Almost all behavior, from manual skills

To see a video, go to

mindsmachine.com/15.3
Split-Brain Research

split-brain individual   An individual whose corpus callosum has been severed, halting communication between the right and left hemispheres.

contralateral   In anatomy, pertaining to a location on the opposite side of the body.

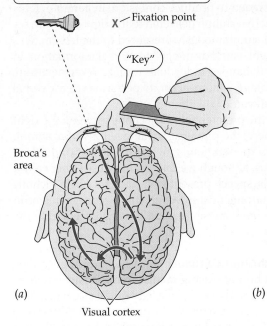

Words or pictures projected to the left visual field activate the right visual cortex. In normal individuals, activation of the right visual cortex excites corpus callosum fibers, which transmit the visual information to the left hemisphere, where its verbal content is analyzed and language is produced.

(a)

In split-brain patients, stimuli from the left visual field reach the right-hemisphere visual cortex (visual inputs are independent of the corpus callosum), but the split corpus callosum prevents the visual information from getting from the right hemisphere to the language areas of the left hemisphere, making verbal responses to the stimuli impossible.

(b)

Split-brain individuals can respond verbally to stimuli appearing in the *right* visual field because interhemispheric transfer is not required in this case.

(c)

Figure 15.13 Testing a Split-Brain Individual

to intellectual activity, is performed better by the two hemispheres working together than by either hemisphere working alone. For this reason, and because better medical options have also been developed, the split-brain surgery has remained a very rare procedure, and the modern form of the operation generally transects only about a third of the corpus callosum.

The two hemispheres process information differently in normal humans

Almost all the research on hemispheric differences in information processing has concentrated on two sensory modalities: hearing and vision. In each modality, researchers can detect differences in behavioral responses to confirm that, in most people, the left cerebral hemisphere is specialized to process language.

TABLE 15.2 Proposed Cognitive Modes of the Two Cerebral Hemispheres in Humans

Left hemisphere	Right hemisphere
Phonetic	Nonlinguistic
Sequential	Holistic
Analytical	Synthetic
Propositional	Gestalt
Discrete temporal analysis	Form perception
Linguistic	Spatial

(a)

Wernicke's area

Auditory cortex

"ma"

ma

ma

ma

Brainstem auditory regions

Left   Right

Information to the left ear goes to right auditory cortex and then to Wernicke's area in the left hemisphere. Subject repeats word.

Figure 15.14 **The Right-Ear Advantage in Dichotic Presentation** (After Kimura, 1973.)

(b)

"pa"

pa

pa

Information to the right ear goes to left auditory cortex and then to Wernicke's area. Subject repeats word.

(c)

"pa"

ma

pa ma   ma

pa

When conflicting information goes to both ears, the information to the right ear reaches Wernicke's area first. Subject repeats only the right-ear information.

THE RIGHT-EAR ADVANTAGE   Through earphones, we can present different sounds to each ear at the same time; this technique is called **dichotic presentation**. The subject hears a particular speech sound in one ear and, at the same time, a different vowel, consonant, or word in the other ear. The subject is asked to identify or recall both sounds. Although this technique may seem designed to produce confusion, in general, right-handed people identify verbal stimuli delivered to the right ear more accurately than the stimuli simultaneously presented to the left ear. This result is described as a right-ear "advantage" for verbal information. In contrast, about 50% of left-handed individuals reveal a reverse pattern, showing a left-ear advantage—more-accurate performance for verbal stimuli delivered to the left ear.

As a consequence of the preferential connections between the right ear and the left hemisphere, the right-ear advantage for verbal stimuli is probably a reflection of the left hemisphere's specialization for language (**Figure 15.14**). Thus, although we can normally use either ear for processing speech sounds, speech presented to the right ear in dichotic presentation tests exerts stronger control over language mechanisms in the left hemisphere than does speech simultaneously presented to the left ear (Kimura, 1973).

VISUAL PERCEPTION OF LINGUISTIC STIMULI   We can study hemispheric specialization in normal humans using **tachistoscope tests**, in which stimuli are very briefly presented to either the left or right visual half field (see Figures 7.10 and 15.13). If the stimulus exposure lasts less than 150 milliseconds or so, input is restricted to one hemisphere because there is not enough time for the eyes to shift their direction. In intact humans, of course, further processing may involve the transmission of information through the corpus callosum to the other hemisphere.

Most studies show that verbal stimuli (words and letters) presented to the right visual field (going to the left hemisphere) are better recognized than the same input presented to the left visual field (going to the right hemisphere). On the other hand, nonverbal visual stimuli (such as faces or geometric forms) presented to the left visual field are better recognized than the same stimuli presented to the right visual field. Simpler visual processing, such as the detection of light, hue, or simple patterns, is equivalent in the two hemispheres.

Does the left hemisphere hear words and the right hemisphere hear music?

The left and right auditory cortical areas appear to play somewhat different roles in the human perception of speech and music. An early clue to this difference came from a postmortem study of adult temporal lobe anatomy (Geschwind and Levitsky, 1968): In 65% of the brains examined, the upper surface of the lobe—a region known as the **planum temporale**—was larger in the left hemisphere than in the right (**Figure 15.15a**). In only 11% of adults was the right side larger. And in the remaining subjects, the left and right sides were equivalent. Because the planum temporale includes part of Wernicke's area, some researchers argued that the larger left planum temporale is related to the known left-hemisphere specialization for language. However, no direct link between language function and the leftward asymmetry of the planum

Figure 15.15 **Structural Asymmetry of the Human Planum Temporale** (After Schlaug et al., 1995; *b* courtesy of Gottfried Schlaug.)

temporale has been shown. For example, structural MRI measurements failed to find a relationship between asymmetry of the planum temporale and the lateralization of language functions in the brain (Dorsaint-Pierre et al., 2006).

Asymmetry of the planum temporale is also evident in infant brains (Wada et al., 1975). In fact, by just 12–14 weeks of gestation, a variety of genes show asymmetrical expression in the fetal human brain (Sun et al., 2005). The planum temporale tends to be larger on the left than on the right in chimpanzees (Gannon et al., 1998), and Broca's area is larger on the left than on the right in chimps, bonobos, and gorillas, as well as in humans (Cantalupo and Hopkins, 2001). Furthermore, just as our left hemisphere is more activated than the right when we hear speech rather than other sounds, the left hemisphere of monkeys is more activated than the right when they hear monkey vocalizations rather than human speech (Poremba et al., 2004). These results suggest that other primates also possess a left-hemisphere specialization for communication.

In contrast, the auditory areas of the *right* hemisphere play a major role in the perception of music. Musical perception is especially impaired after damage to the right hemisphere (Samson and Zatorre, 1994), and many aspects of music activate the right hemisphere more than the left (Zatorre et al., 1994). In musicians, however, perfect pitch (the ability to accurately name a musical note just by listening to it) appears to strongly rely on left-hemisphere mechanisms (**Figure 15.15b**) (Schlaug et al., 1995), perhaps owing to its verbal aspects.

Despite these data, we cannot assign the perception of speech and pitch entirely to the left hemisphere and the perception of music entirely to the right hemisphere. We have seen that the right hemisphere can play a role in speech perception even in people in whom the left hemisphere is speech-dominant. In addition, the perception of emotional tone-of-voice aspects of language, termed **prosody**, is a *right*-hemisphere specialization. Furthermore, although damage to the right hemisphere can impair the perception of music, it does not abolish it. Damage to *both* sides of the brain can completely wipe out musical perception (Samson and Zatorre, 1991). Thus, even though each hemisphere plays a greater role than the other in different kinds of auditory perception, the two hemispheres appear to collaborate in these functions, as well as in many others.

Do left-handed people have unusual brain organization?

About 10% of the population is left-handed, although the estimated prevalence seems to vary somewhat through history and across geographic regions (Leask and Beaton, 2007). Surveys of left-handed writing in American college populations indicate an incidence of 13.8% in that group (Spiegler and Yeni-Komshian, 1983). This is nothing new. Artifacts from prehistoric human societies suggest that a predominance of

dichotic presentation The simultaneous delivery of different stimuli to both the right and the left ears at the same time.

tachistoscope test A test in which stimuli are very briefly presented to either the left or right visual half field.

planum temporale An auditory region of superior temporal cortex.

prosody The perception of emotional tone-of-voice aspects of language.

Whorls Apart Because of the relationship between handedness and features such as the whorl of hair at the crown of the scalp—the whorl is clockwise in 93% of right-handers but randomly clockwise or counterclockwise in non-right-handers—it has been suggested that a single gene has a major (but not absolute) influence on asymmetries throughout the body (Klar, 2003). Other aspects of development presumably account for the remaining variability in hand preference.

right-handedness is probably an ancient human characteristic, possibly in concert with hemispheric specializations for throwing and speech (Watson, 2001). Some researchers even argue that hemispheric asymmetry and limb preferences reflect a left-right division of labor that, as a matter of processing efficiency, arose in the first vertebrates, hundreds of millions of years ago (MacNeilage et al., 2009). (For other examples of the evolution of asymmetry, see **A Step Further 15.3**, on the website.)

Geneticists have established that handedness is indeed influenced by heredity, but it is not a simple effect. Genes that play a role in asymmetry throughout the body, ranging from the shape of internal organs to the pattern of hair whorls on the scalp, may be involved. But in any case, just as in right-handers, language is vested in the *left* hemisphere in the great majority of left-handers. Only in those very rare cases where the right hemisphere is dominant for language is the person more likely to be left-handed than right-handed.

In a tiny minority of cases, early brain injuries may be responsible for a shift to left-handedness (Silva and Satz, 1979). Simply because most people are right-handed, early one-sided brain injury is more likely to cause a change from right-handedness to left-handedness than the reverse. Other, rare circumstances can also cause a change in handedness in adults. Two right-handed people who received double hand transplants after losing their own hands in accidents reportedly both became left-handers after the surgery (Vargas et al., 2009). One speculation is that the right hemisphere required less reorganization in order to take control of its contralateral hand, whereas reconnection of the left hemisphere to the new right hand was initially hampered by the strong cortical representation of the former right hand. After getting an early start, perhaps the right hemisphere–left hand combo simply outcompeted the left hemisphere–right hand combo. Of course, no one yet knows whether this process bears any relationship whatsoever to the normal establishment of hand preference, but it does suggest a surprising degree of flexibility.

Deficits in Spatial Perception Follow Right-Hemisphere Damage

Normal people studied with procedures such as tachistoscope tests reliably demonstrate a right-hemisphere advantage for processing spatial stimuli. Some examples include processing of geometric shapes and relations, direction sense and navigation, face processing, and the mental rotation of objects held in the mind's eye. Unsurprisingly, then, right-hemisphere lesions—especially more-posterior lesions that involve the temporal and parietal lobes—tend to produce a variety of striking visuospatial impairments, such as inability to recognize faces, spatial disorientation, inability to recognize objects placed in the hand, or complete neglect of one side of the body, as we discussed in Chapter 14.

The diversity of behavioral changes following injury to the parietal lobe is related partly to the large expanse of this lobe and its critical position, abutting all three of the other major lobes of the brain. The anterior end of the parietal region includes the postcentral gyrus, which is the primary cortical receiving area for somatic sensation. Brain injury in these areas can produce impairments beyond simple numbness, instead causing changes in complex sensory processing. In one example, objects placed in the hand opposite the injured somatosensory area can be *felt* but cannot be identified by touch and active manipulation. This deficit is called **astereognosis** (from the Greek *a-*, "not"; *stereos*, "solid"; and *gnosis*, "knowledge").

How's it going?

1. Summarize the cardinal differences between the left and right hemispheres of the human brain. How were these functional differences first identified?

2. Describe the dichotic listening task and tachistoscope testing. How do these tasks reveal lateralization of function in normal people?

3. Discuss the representation of music in the human brain. What is the planum temporale, and how does its structure relate to musical experience?

4. Provide a survey of the neural underpinnings of left-handedness. Do left-handers generally show reversed asymmetry, with language vested in the *right* hemisphere?

astereognosis The inability to recognize objects by touching and feeling them.

More-extensive injuries in the parietal cortex, beyond the somatosensory cortex, affect interactions between or among sensory modalities, such as visual or tactile matching tasks, which require the subject to visually identify an object that is touched or to reach for an object that is identified visually.

prosopagnosia or face blindness A condition characterized by the inability to recognize faces.

In prosopagnosia, faces are unrecognizable

Suppose that one day when you looked in the mirror, the person looking back at you wasn't familiar. As incredible as this scenario might seem, it's a fate that some individuals suffer following very specific brain damage. In this rare syndrome, called **prosopagnosia** (from the Greek *prosop-*, "face"; *a-*, "not"; and *gnosis*, "knowledge") or **face blindness**, afflicted individuals fail to recognize not only their own faces but also the faces of relatives and friends. No amount of remedial training restores their ability to recognize anyone's face. In contrast, the ability to visually recognize *objects* may be retained, and the patient may be able to easily identify familiar voices.

To people with prosopagnosia, faces simply lack meaning. No disorientation or confusion accompanies this condition, nor is there evidence of diminished intellectual abilities, or significant visual impairment. Most research indicates that the right hemisphere is especially important for recognizing faces. For example, using the Wada test (see **Box 15.1**) to anesthetize the right hemisphere causes patients to have difficulty recognizing

BOX 15.1 The Wada Test

Given the incidence of aphasia after unilateral brain damage, scientists estimate that 90–95% humans have a left-hemisphere specialization for language. But how can we be certain which hemisphere is dominant for language (or other functions, such as spatial memory or music perception) in people who haven't had a stroke? For example, it can be crucial to understand an individual's specific lateralization prior to brain surgery.

By injecting a short-acting anesthetic (sodium amytal) into the carotid artery—first on one side (as shown in the figure) and then, several minutes later, on the other—it is possible to simulate a massive stroke, shutting down the entire hemisphere for a few minutes (Wada and Rasmussen, 1960). This is just long enough to use behavioral measures to document the specializations of each hemisphere.

This **Wada Test** confirms that most people have left-hemisphere specialization for language, regardless of handedness. The reverse pattern (right-hemisphere dominance for language) is very rare, but when it occurs it is more common in left-handed people. Similar results can be obtained in healthy people using transcranial magnetic stimulation (TMS) (Knecht et al., 2002) or fMRI.

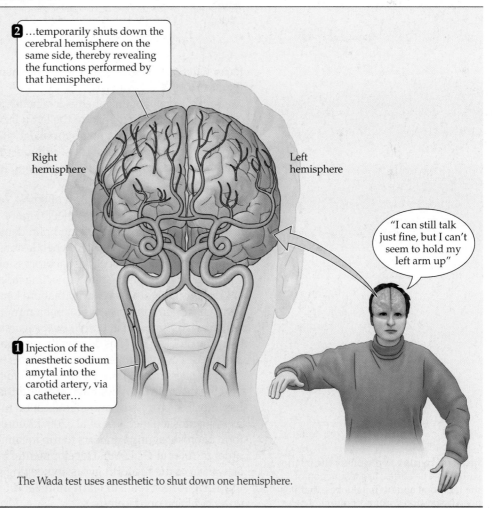

2 …temporarily shuts down the cerebral hemisphere on the same side, thereby revealing the functions performed by that hemisphere.

Right hemisphere

Left hemisphere

"I can still talk just fine, but I can't seem to hold my left arm up"

1 Injection of the anesthetic sodium amytal into the carotid artery, via a catheter…

The Wada test uses anesthetic to shut down one hemisphere.

Self   Celebrity

Figure 15.16   Use of the Right Hemisphere for Facial Recognition (From Keenan et al., 2001; courtesy of Julian Keenan.)

Anesthetizing the left hemisphere in a Wada test (see Box 15.1) does not interfere with a subject's ability to recognize her own face in a picture that is a composite of her face and the face of a celebrity…

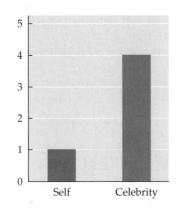

…but when the right hemisphere is anesthetized, the subject interprets the composite face as that of the celebrity.

Left hemisphere anesthetized   Composite face presented to subject   Right hemisphere anesthetized

faces, whereas anesthetizing the left hemisphere has less effect on facial recognition (**Figure 15.16**).

Similarly, split-brain patients do a better job of recognizing faces that are presented to the right hemisphere than to the left (Gazzaniga and Smylie, 1983). Still, split-brain patients and functional imaging make it clear that both hemispheres have *some* capacity for recognizing faces. Thus, although damage restricted to the right hemisphere can impair face processing, the most complete cases of prosopagnosia are caused by *bilateral* damage.

The **fusiform gyrus**, a region of cortex on the inferior surface of the brain where occipital and temporal cortices meet (**Figure 15.17**), is crucial for face recognition, and cases of prosopagnosia following brain damage almost always involve damage here. Symptoms may be exacerbated when lesions also include a nearby occipital area that performs initial face-specific visual processing, as well as the superior temporal sulcus, which has been implicated in connecting faces with speech and facial expressions.

Until recently, it was believed that prosopagnosia occurred solely as a result of brain damage (*acquired prosopagnosia*), but a number of cases of *developmental* (or *congenital*, which means "present at birth") *prosopagnosia* have now been identified. This is apparently the problem that has dogged Brian, whom we met at the beginning of the chapter; and the discovery that he's not alone in this problem has been a huge relief to him (we can only guess how Humpty Dumpty would feel about it).

Unexpectedly, surveys have revealed that about 2.5% of the general population has impaired processing and identification of faces that meet the criteria for congenital prosopagnosia (Duchaine et al., 2007; Kennerknecht et al., 2006). The developmental form of prosopagnosia appears to run in families, indicating a genetic aspect to the disorder (Grüter et al., 2008). Developmental prosopagnosia is associated with reduced activation of the fusiform gyrus, in keeping with the anatomical findings in acquired prosopagnosia. (You can learn more, and test yourself for prosopagnosia, online at www.faceblind.org/facetests.)

fusiform gyrus   A region on the inferior surface of the cortex, at the junction of the temporal and occipital lobes, that has been associated with recognition of faces.

In this view from below the brain, the cerebellum has been removed to reveal the region of cortex that normally lies opposite to it.

Frontal lobe

Temporal lobe

Brainstem

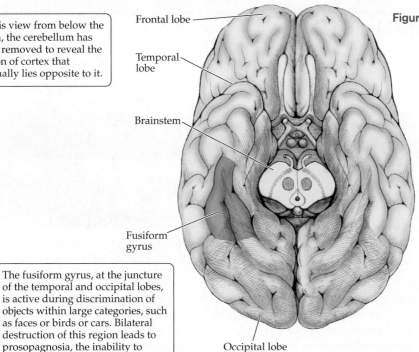

Figure 15.17   The Fusiform Gyrus

Fusiform gyrus

The fusiform gyrus, at the juncture of the temporal and occipital lobes, is active during discrimination of objects within large categories, such as faces or birds or cars. Bilateral destruction of this region leads to prosopagnosia, the inability to recognize individual faces.

Occipital lobe

How's it going?

1. In general, what are the behavioral consequences of right-hemisphere damage in humans?

2. Define, compare, and contrast two of the most striking symptoms of right-hemisphere damage: astereognosis and prosopagnosia. Which areas of the brain appear to be involved in each?

3. Is prosopagnosia always associated with brain damage? What other behavioral abnormalities may co-occur with prosopagnosia?

Prosopagnosia of both types may be accompanied by additional forms of **agnosia**, an inability to identify individual items—makes of cars, tools, bird species, sounds, and so on—in the absence of any specific sensory deficits or memory problems (Gauthier et al., 1999). Functional-MRI studies of healthy subjects show that, as with face recognition, the fusiform gyrus is important for identifying individual members of large categories (e.g., faces or birds or cars) in which all members have many things in common (Gauthier et al., 2000).

PART III Recovery of Function

Because of the brain's extreme complexity, high metabolic demands, delicate structure, and vulnerable location, disabling brain injuries are all too common. In the United States alone, according to the 2009 National Health Interview Survey (*Summary Health Statistics*, 2010), about 6 million people are survivors of stroke, and many more are living with the consequences of other disease processes, such as tumors and brain trauma. In addition to diseases, motor vehicle accidents, horseback riding, diving, and contact sports such as boxing are major causes of injuries to the brain and spinal cord (**Box 15.2**). So it's no surprise that discovering the mechanisms mediating **recovery of function** after brain damage, and developing new treatments to exploit those mechanisms, are topics of intense research activity. But in spite of encouraging recent developments, prevention is clearly better than treatment.

Stabilization and Reorganization Are Crucial for Recovery of Function

In the months following a brain injury, patients may improve considerably, probably because of physiological stabilization of the injury site. We now know that the nervous system has much more potential for plasticity and recovery than was previously believed. For example, damaged neurons can regrow their connections under some

agnosia   The inability to recognize objects, despite being able to describe them in terms of form and color. Agnosia may occur after localized brain damage.

recovery of function   The recovery of behavioral capacity following brain damage from stroke or injury.

BOX 15.2 Contact Sports Can Be Costly

Jarring blows to the body are common in a number of sports—football, hockey, and wrestling, for example—and when the part of the body receiving the impact is the head, a minor brain injury called a **concussion** may result. Even one concussion, and certainly repeated concussion, places the athlete at risk of permanent brain injury. Although uncomplicated concussions generally clear up with time, up to 25% of concussion cases may experience persistent cognitive symptoms (Ponsford, 2005), some of which may not become evident until later in an athlete's life (Thornton et al., 2008).

Nowhere is the risk of brain injury more evident than in boxing, where the whole goal of the contest is to rain blows upon the head of the opponent. For too many boxers, the result of so many blows to the head is a debilitated state that was historically called *dementia pugilistica* (the Latin *pugil* means "boxer") or *punch-drunk* (Erlanger et al., 1999), but nowadays is known as **chronic traumatic encephalopathy (CTE)**. Punch-drunk boxers have markedly impaired cognitive abilities, and it is all too common for serious boxers to show marked abnormalities in the brain.

Casson et al. (1982) studied ten active professional boxers who had been knocked out, including some of championship caliber, as well as mediocre and poor boxers. At least

Tau Protein in the Brain of a Boxer Suffering from CTE (*Left*) Unmagnified section of cortex. (*Right*) Cortical gray matter magnified 350×. (Courtesy of Ann McKee.)

five of the group had definitely abnormal CT scans, such as generalized cortical atrophy, which in some cases included ventricular dilation. Only one boxer had a clearly normal brain picture. Sadly, the most successful boxers may have the most profound cortical atrophy: successful boxers have had the greatest number of high-caliber fights, and thus may have sustained the most punishment (A. H. Roberts, 1969) because they participate in more matches. A large-scale CT study of 338 active boxers showed that scans were abnormal in 7% (showing brain atrophy) and borderline in 12% (B. D. Jordan et al., 1992).

Neuropathological evidence indicates that, like Alzheimer's disease, CTE in athletes

is a type of *tauopathy*, in which excess Tau protein within neurons interferes with their functioning (McKee et al., 2009). The photos in the figure show the brain of a former boxer who, by his mid-thirties, was experiencing punch-drunk symptoms including memory loss, confusion, and a tendency to fall. As in other cases of CTE, an excessive amount of Tau (brown in the photos) is evident in the brain, and it is found forming tangles within many neurons. While CTE may occur in other sports, only in boxing is significant head trauma an explicit goal—no small reason why many believe that boxing is a sport whose time has passed.

---

circumstances, through a process called collateral sprouting. (For more information on collateral sprouting, see **A Step Further 15.4**, on the website.) And, as we've discussed in several places in this book, it has become evident that the adult brain is capable of producing new neurons; although this neurogenesis normally plays a minimal role in recovery from brain damage, perhaps we will learn how to bend these new neurons to our will and use them to replace missing cells.

Possibly the most exciting prospect for brain repair following stroke, injury, or many other neurological conditions is the use of **embryonic stem cells** (Lindvall and Kokaia, 2006). Derived from embryos, these cells have not yet differentiated into specific roles and therefore seem to be able to develop, under local chemical cues, into the type of neuron needed. At present, the use of human embryos as cell donors is controversial, so researchers hope to find ways of creating stem cells from other sources, such as skin, that can then be induced to form into new neurons.

Several factors determine how thoroughly a person will recover from a brain injury. One of these is simply the passage of time. Immediate medical treatment at the onset of a stroke can greatly limit the extent of damage, reducing cell death and inflammation. (Mechanisms of brain damage, and the mitigation of brain injuries, are discussed in **A Step Further 15.5**, on the website.) However, it takes months for the extent of recovery to become evident. For stroke patients with aphasia, most recovery occurs during the

embryonic stem cell   A cell, derived from an embryo, that has the capacity to form any type of tissue.

Figure 15.18 Courses of Recovery for Patients with Aphasia (Parts *a* and *b* after Kertesz et al., 1979; *c* after Naeser et al., 1990.)

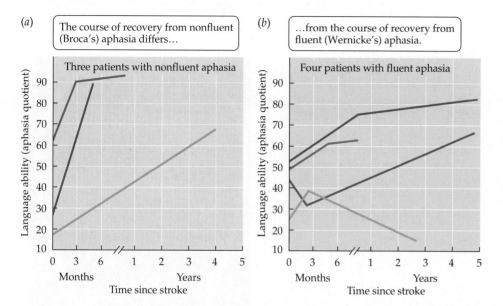

(a)

The course of recovery from nonfluent (Broca's) aphasia differs…

(b)

…from the course of recovery from fluent (Wernicke's) aphasia.

(c)

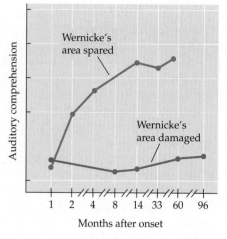

The recovery of auditory speech comprehension after a stroke in which Wernicke's area was damaged is compared here with the course of recovery after a stroke in which Wernicke's area was spared.

first 3 months following brain damage, but recovery continues for 1–1.5 years (**Figure 15.18**) (Kertesz et al., 1979).

Most studies find little improvement after 18 months, but this may have more to do with the need for better therapeutic tools than any absolute limit on the capacity for recovery. New rehabilitation therapies may extend the recovery period; for example, using alternate communication channels, such as singing, can help in some cases (Racette et al., 2006). Age is also a factor. As in adults, left-hemisphere damage can cause aphasia in children, but they often show rapid and full recovery. In fact, children can recover their language function even if they lose the *entire* left hemisphere (**Box 15.3**), powerfully demonstrating that the right hemisphere *can* take over the language function if the left-hemisphere damage occurs early in life. Unfortunately, as we age, our capacity for this sort of plastic reorganization of the brain diminishes.

Statistically, several additional factors help determine the degree of impairment and extent of recovery that a brain injury patient can expect. In neurological disorders such as stroke and tumors, **lesion momentum** is important: patients experience less impairment when the lesion develops more gradually than when it occurs suddenly. So, for example, two or three sequential strokes may have less impact than a single stroke even if they damage as much or more cortex, probably because there is enough time for compensatory reorganization to occur in between the strokes.

In general, recovery is also better in survivors of brain damage due to trauma, such as a blow to the head, than in those whose brain damage is caused by stroke; this difference may be due to the generation of cell-damaging signaling chemicals in cells that have been starved of oxygen during a stroke. Patients with more-severe initial language loss recover less completely. And left-handed people show better recovery than those who are right-handed, perhaps because of reduced lateralization of function in left-handers.

Rehabilitation and Retraining Can Help Recovery from Brain and Spinal Cord Injury

Cognitive and/or perceptual handicaps that develop from brain impairments can be modified by training; similarly, intensive training may restore some measure of walking ability after certain spinal cord injuries (Barbeau et al., 1998). But it is important to

lesion momentum The phenomenon in which the brain is impaired more by a lesion that develops quickly than by a lesion that develops slowly.

BOX 15.3 The Amazing Resilience of a Child's Brain

Complications in pregnancy and fetal development occasionally result in children that are born with a terrible kind of epilepsy that can't be controlled by medication. These children may suffer paralysis on one side of the body, along with almost continual seizures. Sometimes, in these extreme cases, the only way to save the life of the child is to remove an entire brain hemisphere, as shown in this scan of a girl whose left hemisphere was completely removed when she was 7 years old.

Hemispherectomy surgery removes the malfunctioning brain tissue and saves the life of the child, but it also produces severe symptoms of its own, such as complete paralysis of one side, speech loss, or visual impairments. However, provided the surgery occurs early enough, the child may show almost complete recovery of function over a long period of time. The girl whose brain scan is

shown in the figure experienced paralysis and complete speech loss after her surgery, but at follow-up a few years later she had recovered normal language function, and her paralysis had resolved almost completely.

Other childhood hemispherectomy patients have gone on to develop above-average IQs in adulthood, along with superior language and cognitive abilities (A. Smith and Sugar, 1975). So, although extensive hemispheric damage in an adult usually results in drastic and largely permanent functional and intellectual impairments, cases of childhood hemispherectomy vividly illustrate the amazing plasticity of the young brain.

The brain can compensate even for the loss of a whole hemisphere, provided that this radical surgery is performed early enough in the patient's development. (From Borgstein and Grootendorst, 2002.)

---

constraint-induced movement therapy A therapy for recovery of movement after stroke or injury in which the person's unaffected limb is constrained while he is required to perform tasks with the affected limb.

distinguish restoration of function from compensation. Practice can significantly reduce the impact of brain injury by fostering compensatory behavior. For example, vigorous eye movements can make up for large blind spots that result from injury to the visual pathways. Behavior strategies can be changed after a brain injury to enable successful performance on a variety of tests.

Previous generations may have been too pessimistic about recovery from stroke. A growing body of evidence indicates that people can substantially regain the use of limbs affected by stroke, if they are forced to use the limb repeatedly. **Constraint-induced movement therapy** persuades stroke patients to use the affected arm by simply tying the "good" arm to a splint for up to 90% of waking hours (Taub et al., 2002). But immobilizing the good arm isn't enough; such patients are subjected to rehabilitation therapy 6 hours a day to practice moving the affected limb repeatedly (**Figure 15.19**). In a study conducted by Liepert et al. (2000), most patients who received this treatment had regained 75% of normal use of the paralyzed arm after only 2 weeks of therapy, and there was evidence of a remapping of the motor cortex.

Another surprising use of experience for rehabilitation involves a simple mirror. Altschuler et al. (1999) treated stroke patients who had reduced

> In this therapy, an unaffected limb is gently restrained (in this case in a white mitten) so that the patient must use the limb that was affected by the stroke in a series of repetitive tasks.

Figure 15.19 Constraint-Induced Movement Therapy (Photo courtesy of Edward Taub.)

Perseverance and Plasticity   Despite suffering a severe gunshot wound to the left cerebral hemisphere during an assassination attempt, former U.S. Representative Gabrielle Giffords has made striking progress in regaining her language and cognitive functions, thanks to intensive rehabilitation therapy and strategies for compensating for the damage.

use of one arm by placing them before a mirror with only their "good" arm visible. To the patients, it looked as though they were seeing the entire body, but now both arms were the good arm. The patient was told to make symmetrical fluid motions with both arms. In the mirror, the motions looked perfectly symmetrical (of course), but surprisingly, most of the patients soon learned to use the "weak" arm more extensively. It was as though the visible feedback, indicating that the weak arm was moving perfectly, overcame the brain's reluctance to use that arm. It is likely that the mirror neurons of the brain, discussed in Chapter 5, mediate some of the beneficial effects of this sort of rehearsal (Buccino et al., 2006).

Brain damage will remain a serious problem for the foreseeable future—one that will affect most of us in some way as our friends and relatives go through their lives. Perhaps the most important message to convey to victims of stroke and other nervous system damage is the encouragement that, with effort and perseverance, they can help their remarkably plastic brains to regain a significant amount of the lost behavioral capacity.

Recommended Reading

Bradbury, J. W., and Vehrencamp, S. L. (2011). *Principles of Animal Communication* (2nd ed.). Sunderland, MA: Sinauer.

Deutscher, G. (2005). *The Unfolding of Language: An Evolutionary Tour of Mankind's Greatest Invention.* New York, NY: Metropolitan Books.

Ellard, C. (2009). *You Are Here: Why We Can Find Our Way to the Moon, but Get Lost in the Mall.* New York, NY: Doubleday.

Gazzaniga, M. S. (2008). *Human: The Science behind What Makes Us Unique.* New York, NY: HarperCollins.

Kolb, B., and Whishaw, I. Q. (2008). *Fundamentals of Human Neuropsychology* (6th ed.). New York, NY: Worth.

McManus, I. C. (2003). *Right Hand, Left Hand: The Origins of Asymmetry in Brains, Bodies, Atoms, and Cultures.* Cambridge, MA: Harvard University Press.

Patel, A. (2007). *Music, Language, and the Brain.* Oxford, England: Oxford University Press.

Purves, D., Brannon, E. M., Cabeza, R., Huettel, S. A., et al. (2008). *Principles of Cognitive Neuroscience.* Sunderland, MA: Sinauer.

Tomasello, M. (2010). *Origins of Human Communication.* Cambridge, MA: Bradford Books/MIT Press.

Zeigler, H. P., and Marler, P. (2008). *Neuroscience of Birdsong.* Cambridge, England: Cambridge University Press.

How's it going?

1. Just how prevalent is brain damage due to stroke, and to other diseases? Once the brain is damaged, is recovery more or less complete in a matter of hours, days, or months?

2. Discuss some of the factors that determine how thoroughly a person will recover from brain injury.

3. Explain the concept of lesion momentum.

4. Is recovery better when brain damage is caused by trauma, or when the damage is caused by stroke? What is believed to be responsible for the difference?

5. Discuss some of the types of therapy that appear to help maximize recovery following brain damage.

CHAPTER 15 VISUAL SUMMARY

mindsmachine.com/vs15

You should be able to relate each summary to the adjacent illustration, including structures and processes. If you need to review, go to the figures indicated and read the accompanying text.

1 Languages are made up of speech sounds, called **phonemes** and **morphemes**, that are assembled into words and sentences according to *syntax*. Humans acquire language during an early **sensitive period**, involving genes like *FOXP2*, suggesting that mechanisms of language acquisition are innate. Review **Figure 15.1, Animation 15.2**

2 Monkeys produce emotional vocalizations but cannot produce speech. Certain species of apes can learn American Sign Language, but it is not clear that this use constitutes language. Review **Figures 15.2** and **15.3**

3 Many species use vocalizations for communication (but not *language*); for example, birdsong is controlled by a lateralized system in the brains of some species of songbirds, and early experience is essential for proper song development. Review **Figure 15.4, Activity 15.1**

4 The left hemisphere of the human brain contains a network of structures specialized for processing speech and language. Damage in this network can cause the language impairment **aphasia**. Review **Figure 15.5, Activity 15.2**

5 Left inferior frontal lesions produce an impairment in speech production called **nonfluent (or Broca's) aphasia**. More-posterior lesions, involving the temporo-parietal cortex, cause **fluent (or Wernicke's) aphasia**. Extensive destruction of the left hemisphere causes a more complete loss of language called **global aphasia**. Review **Figure 15.6**

6 The **connectionist model of aphasia** involves a loop from a posterior speech reception zone to an anterior expressive zone that, when severed, may produce a **conduction aphasia**. However, the **motor theory of language** suggests that the entire circuit serves motor control and is used for both production and perception. Review **Figure 15.7, Activity 15.3**

7 Left-hemisphere lesions in users of sign language produce impairments in the use of sign language that are similar to impairments in spoken language shown by nondeaf individuals suffering from aphasia. Review **Figure 15.8**

8 *Acquired dyslexia* is a difficulty with reading due to brain damage; in **deep dyslexia** there is a disturbance in reading whole words; **surface dyslexia** involves a difficulty with the sounds of words. *Developmental dyslexia* is a congenital difficulty with reading that is associated with brain abnormalities. Review **Figure 15.9**

9 Noninvasive stimulation has confirmed the left-hemisphere organization for language functions. Stimulation of anterior regions causes speech arrest, while stimulation in other locations causes misnaming and other speech errors. Transcranial magnetic stimulation indicates that the anterior speech zone contains further subdivisions. Review **Figures 15.10** and **15.11**

10 Studies using PET and fMRI reveal that distinct regions of the left hemisphere are active during viewing, hearing, repeating, or assembling of verbal material. ERP studies have documented differential left-hemisphere processing of speech sounds versus speech meanings Review **Figure 15.12**

11 **Split-brain individuals** show striking examples of hemispheric specialization (lateralization). Most words projected only to the right hemisphere, for example, cannot be read, but the same stimuli directed to the left hemisphere can be read. Spatial tasks, however, are performed better by the right hemisphere than by the left. Review **Figure 15.13, Video 15.3**

12 Normal humans show many forms of cognitive specialization of the cerebral hemispheres. For example, most normal humans show an advantage for verbal stimuli presented to the right ear or right visual field. Review **Figure 15.14**

13 Anatomical asymmetry of the hemispheres is seen in some brain regions, such as the **planum temporale** (larger in the left hemisphere than in the right hemisphere of most right-handed individuals). Perfect pitch in musicians is also associated with a larger left planum temporale, but the right hemisphere is dominant for many other aspects of music processing. Review **Figure 15.15**

14 In most patients, parietal cortical injuries produce perceptual changes, including alterations in sensory and spatial processing. Damage including the **fusiform gyrus** can produce acquired **prosopagnosia**, a dramatic inability to recognize the faces of familiar people. A developmental form of prosopagnosia affects about 2.5% of the population. Review **Figures 15.16** and **15.17**

15 Much of the damage following brain injury can show at least partial **recovery of function**, especially during the first year or so, as the damaged brain stabilizes and reorganizes. Retraining is a significant part of functional recovery and may involve both compensation, by establishing new solutions to adaptive demands, and reorganization of surviving networks. Review **Figure 15.18**

Go to **mindsmachine.com** for study questions, quizzes, flashcards, and other resources.

Molecular Biology:
Basic Concepts and Important Techniques

Appendix

Genes Carry Information That Encodes the Synthesis of Proteins

The most important thing about **genes** is that they are pieces of information, inherited from parents, that affect the development and function of our cells. Information carried by the genes is a very specific sort: each gene codes for the construction of a specific string of amino acids to form a **protein** molecule. This is *all* that genes do; they do not *directly* encode intelligence, or memories, or any other sort of complex behavior. The various proteins, each encoded by its own gene, make up the physical structure and most of the constituents of cells, such as enzymes. These proteins make complex behavior possible, and in that context they are also the targets upon which the forces of evolution act.

Enzymes are proteins that enable particular chemical reactions in our cells. For example, only cells that have liver-typical proteins will look like liver cells and be able to perform liver functions. Neurons are cells that make neuron-typical proteins so that they can look and act like neurons. The genetic information for making these various proteins is crucial for an animal to live and for a nervous system to work properly.

One thing we hope this book will help you understand is that everyday experience can affect whether and when particular genetic recipes for making various proteins are used. To aid those discussions, let's review how genetic information is stored and how proteins are made. Our discussion will be brief, but many online tutorials can provide you with more detailed information (see **A Step Further A.1**, on the website).

Genetic information is stored in molecules of DNA

The information for making all of our proteins could, in theory, be stored in any sort of format—on sheets of paper, magnetic tape, a DVD, an iPod—but creatures on this planet store their genetic information in a chemical called **deoxyribonucleic acid**, or **DNA**. Each molecule of DNA consists of a long strand of chemicals called **nucleotides** strung one after the other. DNA has only four nucleotides: guanine, cytosine, thymine, and adenine (abbreviated G, C, T, and A). The particular sequence of nucleotides (e.g., GCTTACC or TGGTCC or TGA) holds the information that will eventually make a protein. Because many millions of these nucleotides can be joined one after the other, a tremendous amount of information can be stored in very little space—on a single molecule of DNA.

A set of nucleotides that has been strung together can snuggle tightly against another string of nucleotides if it has the proper sequence: T nucleotides preferentially link with A nucleotides, and G nucleotides link with C nucleotides. Thus, T nucleotides are said to be complementary to A nucleotides, and C nucleotides are complementary to G nucleotides. In fact, most of the time our DNA consists not of a single strand of nucleotides, but of two complementary strands of nucleotides wrapped around one another.

gene   A length of DNA that encodes the information for constructing a particular protein.

protein   A long string of amino acids. Proteins are the basic building material of organisms.

enzyme   A complicated protein whose action increases the probability of a specific chemical reaction.

deoxyribonucleic acid (DNA)   A nucleic acid that is present in the chromosomes of cells and codes hereditary information.

nucleotide   A portion of a DNA or RNA molecule that is composed of a single base and the adjoining sugar-phosphate unit of the strand.

Figure A.1   Duplication of DNA Before cell division, all of the chromosomes in the cell must be duplicated as illustrated here so that each daughter cell has the full complement of genetic information.

hybridization   The process by which one string of nucleotides becomes linked to a complementary series of nucleotides.

chromosome   A complex of condensed strands of DNA and associated protein molecules. Chromosomes are found in the nucleus of cells.

eukaryote   Any organism whose cells have the genetic material contained within a nuclear envelope.

cell nucleus   The spherical central structure of a cell that contains the chromosomes.

ribonucleic acid (RNA)   A nucleic acid that implements information found in DNA.

transcription   The process during which mRNA forms bases complementary to a strand of DNA. The resulting message (called a *transcript*) is then used to translate the DNA code into protein molecules.

messenger RNA (mRNA) or transcript   Also sometimes called *message*. A strand of RNA that carries the code of a section of a DNA strand to the cytoplasm.

ribosome   An organelle in the cell body where genetic information is translated to produce proteins.

translation   The process by which amino acids are linked together (directed by an mRNA molecule) to form protein molecules.

codon   A set of three nucleotides that uniquely encodes one particular amino acid.

peptide   A short string of amino acids. Longer strings of amino acids are called *proteins*.

The two strands of nucleotides are said to **hybridize** with one another, coiling slightly to form the famous double helix. The double-stranded DNA twists and coils further, becoming visible in microscopes as **chromosomes**, which resemble twisted lengths of yarn. Humans and many other organisms are known as **eukaryotes** because we store our chromosomes in a membranous sphere called a **nucleus** (plural *nuclei*) inside each cell. The ability of DNA to exist as two complementary strands of nucleotides is crucial for the duplication of the chromosomes (**Figure A.1**), but the details of that story will not concern us. Just remember that, with very few exceptions, every cell in your body has a faithful copy of all the DNA you received from your parents.

DNA is transcribed to produce messenger RNA

The information from DNA is used to assemble another molecule—**ribonucleic acid**, or **RNA**—that serves as a template for later steps in protein synthesis. Like DNA, RNA is made up of a long string of four different nucleotides. For RNA, those nucleotides are G and C (which, recall, are complementary to each other), and A and U (uracil), which are also complementary to each other. Note that the T nucleotide is found only in DNA, and the U nucleotide is found only in RNA.

When a particular gene becomes active, the double strand of DNA unwinds enough so that one strand becomes free of the other and becomes available to special cellular machinery (including an enzyme called *transcriptase*) that begins **transcription**—the construction of a specific string of RNA nucleotides that are complementary to the exposed strand of DNA (**Figure A.2**). This length of RNA goes by several names: **messenger RNA (mRNA)**, **transcript**, or sometimes *message*. Each DNA nucleotide encodes a specific RNA nucleotide (an RNA G for every DNA C, an RNA C for every DNA G, an RNA U for every DNA A, and an RNA A for every DNA T). This transcript is made in the nucleus where the DNA resides; then the mRNA molecule moves to the cytoplasm, where protein molecules are assembled.

RNA molecules direct the formation of protein molecules

In the cytoplasm are special organelles, called **ribosomes**, that attach themselves to a molecule of RNA, "read" the sequence of RNA nucleotides, and, using that information, begin linking together amino acids to form a protein molecule. The structure and function of a protein molecule depend on which particular amino acids are put together and in what order. The decoding of an RNA transcript to manufacture a particular protein is called **translation** (see Figure A.2), as distinct from *transcription*, the construction of the mRNA molecule.

Each trio of RNA nucleotides, or **codon**, encodes one of 20 or so different amino acids. Special molecules associated with the ribosome recognize the codon and bring a molecule of the appropriate amino acid so that the ribosome can fuse that amino acid to the previous one. If the resulting string of amino acids is short (say, 50 amino acids or less), it is called a **peptide**; if it is long, it is called a *protein*. Thus the ribosome assembles a very particular sequence of amino acids at the behest of a very particular sequence of RNA nucleotides, which were themselves encoded in the DNA inherited from our parents. In short, the secret of life is that DNA makes RNA, and RNA makes protein.

There are fascinating additions to this short story. Often the information from separate stretches of DNA is spliced together to make a single transcript; so-called alternative splicing can create different transcripts from the same gene. Sometimes a protein is modified extensively after translation ends; special chemical processes can cleave long proteins to create one or several active peptides.

Keep in mind that each cell has the complete library of genetic information (collectively known as the **genome**) but makes only a fraction of all the proteins encoded in that DNA. In modern biology we say that each cell **expresses** only some genes; that is, the cell transcribes certain genes and makes the corresponding gene products (protein molecules). Thus, each cell must come to express all the genes needed to perform its function. Modern biologists refer to the expression of a particular subset of the genome as **cell differentiation**: the process by which different types of cells acquire their unique appearance and function. During development, individual cells appear to become more and more specialized, expressing progressively fewer genes. Many molecular biologists are striving to understand which cellular and molecular mechanisms "turn on" or "turn off" gene expression, in order to understand development and pathologies such as cancer, or to provide crucial proteins to afflicted organs in a variety of diseases.

Molecular Biologists Have Craftily Enslaved Microorganisms and Enzymes

Many basic methods of molecular biology are not explicitly discussed in the text, so we will not describe them in detail here. However, you should understand what some of the terms *mean*, even if you don't know exactly how the methods are performed.

Molecular biologists have found ways to incorporate DNA from other species into the DNA of microorganisms such as bacteria and viruses. After the foreign DNA is incorporated, the microorganisms are allowed to reproduce rapidly, producing more and more copies of the (foreign) gene of interest. At this point the gene is said to be **cloned** because researchers can make as many copies as they want. To ensure that the right gene is being cloned, the researcher generally clones many, many different genes—each into different bacteria—and then "screens" the bacteria rapidly to find the rare one that has incorporated the gene of interest.

When enough copies of the DNA have been made, the microorganisms are ground up and the DNA extracted. If sufficient DNA has been generated, chemical steps can then determine the exact sequence of nucleotides found in that stretch of DNA—a process known as **DNA sequencing**. Once the sequence of nucleotides has been determined, the sequence of complementary nucleotides in the messenger RNA for that gene can be inferred. The sequence of mRNA nucleotides tells the investigator the sequence of amino acids that will be made from that transcript because biologists know which amino acid is encoded by each trio of DNA nucleotides. For

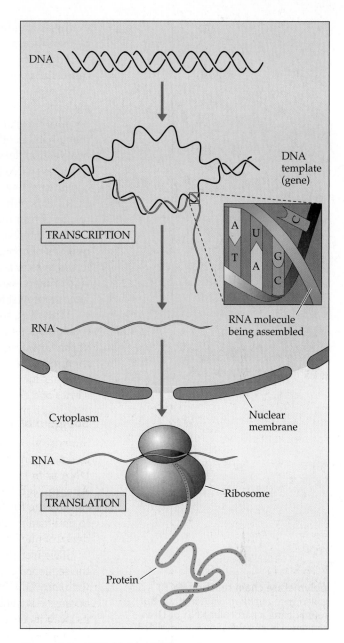

Figure A.2   DNA Makes RNA, and RNA Makes Protein

genome   Also called *genotype*. All the genetic information that one specific individual has inherited.

gene expression   The process by which a cell makes an mRNA transcript of a particular gene.

cell differentiation   The developmental stage in which cells acquire distinctive characteristics, such as those of neurons, as the result of expressing particular genes.

clones   Asexually produced organisms that are genetically identical.

DNA sequencing   The process by which the order of nucleotides in a gene is identified.

example, scientists discovered the amino acid sequence of neurotransmitter receptors by this process.

The business of obtaining many copies of DNA has been boosted by a technique called the **polymerase chain reaction**, or **PCR**. This technique exploits a special type of polymerase enzyme that, like other such enzymes, induces the formation of a DNA molecule that is complementary to an existing single strand of DNA (see Figure A.1). Because this particular polymerase enzyme (called *Taq polymerase*) evolved in bacteria that inhabit geothermal hot springs, it can function in a broad range of temperatures. By heating double-stranded DNA, we can cause the two strands to separate, making each strand available to polymerase enzymes that, when the temperature is cooled enough, construct a new "mate" for each strand so that they are double-stranded again. The first PCR yields only double the original number of DNA molecules; repeating the process results in four times as many molecules as at first. Repeatedly heating and cooling the DNA of interest in the presence of this heat-resistant polymerase enzyme soon yields millions of copies of the original DNA molecule, which is why this process is also referred to as *gene amplification*. In practice, PCR usually requires the investigator to provide primers—short nucleotide sequences synthesized to hybridize on either side of the gene of interest to amplify that particular gene more than others.

With PCR, sufficient quantities of DNA are produced for chemical analysis or other manipulations, such as introducing DNA into cells. For example, we might inject some of the DNA encoding a protein of interest into a fertilized mouse egg (a zygote) and then return the zygote to a pregnant mouse to grow. Occasionally the injected DNA becomes incorporated into the zygote's genome, resulting in a **transgenic** mouse that carries and expresses the foreign gene.

Southern blots identify particular genes

Suppose we want to know whether a particular individual or a particular species carries a certain gene. Because all cells contain a complete copy of the genome, we can gather DNA from just about any kind of cell population: blood, skin, or muscle, for example. After the cells are ground up, a chemical extraction procedure isolates the DNA (discarding the RNA and protein). Finding a particular gene in that DNA boils down just to finding a particular sequence of DNA nucleotides. To do that, we can exploit the tendency of nucleic acids to hybridize with one another.

If we were looking for the DNA sequence GCT, for example, we could manufacture the sequence CGA (there are machines to do that), which would then stick to (hybridize with) any DNA sequence of GCT. The manufactured sequence CGA is called a **probe** because it is made to include a label (a colorful or radioactive molecule) that lets us track its location. Of course, such a short length of nucleotides will be found in many genes. In order for a probe to recognize one particular gene, it has to be about 15 nucleotides long.

When we extract DNA from an individual, it's convenient to let enzymes cut up the very long stretches of DNA into more manageable pieces of 1,000–20,000 nucleotides each. A process called **gel electrophoresis** uses electrical current to separate these millions of pieces more or less by size (**Figure A.3**). Large pieces move slowly through a tube of gelatin-like material, and small pieces move rapidly. The tube of gel is then sliced and placed on top of a sheet of paperlike material called *nitrocellulose*. When fluid is allowed to flow through the gel and nitrocellulose, DNA molecules are pulled out of the gel and deposited on the waiting nitrocellulose. This process of making a "sandwich" of gel and nitrocellulose and using fluid to move molecules from the former to the latter is called **blotting** (see Figure A.3).

If the gene we're looking for is among those millions of DNA fragments sitting on the nitrocellulose, our labeled probe should recognize and hybridize to the sequence. The nitrocellulose sheet is soaked in a solution containing our labeled probe; we wait for the probe to find and hybridize with the gene of interest (if it is present), and we rinse the sheet to remove probe molecules that did not find the gene. Then we *visualize*

polymerase chain reaction (PCR) Also called *gene amplification*. A method for reproducing a particular RNA or DNA sequence manyfold, allowing amplification for sequencing or manipulating the sequence.

transgenic Referring to an animal in which a new or altered gene has been deliberately introduced into the genome.

probe In molecular biology, a manufactured sequence of DNA that is made to include a label (a colorful or radioactive molecule) that lets us track its location.

gel electrophoresis A method of separating molecules of differing size or electrical charge by forcing them to flow through a gel.

blotting Transferring DNA, RNA, or protein fragments to nitrocellulose following separation via gel electrophoresis. The blotted substance can then be labeled.

Gel electrophoresis

Wells are filled with DNA solutions.

Gel support

Gel

Buffer solution

Electrical current is applied to the gel.

DNA samples

Later

Still later

Bands of DNA fragments, bearing a negative charge, move toward the positive electrode.

Smaller fragments move more rapidly than larger ones.

Movement continues as long as the electrical current is maintained.

Southern blotting

Weight

Absorbent paper

Wick

Nitrocellulose sheet

Buffer solution (to transfer DNA)

Support

Gel (with DNA fragments)

To see an animation, go to

mindsmachine.com/A.1
Gel Electrophoresis

Hybridization

Add labeled probe.

Rinse off unattached probe and make chemical label visible.

Chemical labels

Nitrocellulose sheet

Figure A.3   Gel Electrophoresis and Southern Blotting

the probe, either by causing the label to show its color or, if radioactive, by letting the probe expose photographic film to identify the locations where the probe has accumulated. In either case, if the probe found the gene, a labeled band will be evident, corresponding to the size of DNA fragment that contained the gene (see Figure A.3).

Southern blot A method of detecting a particular DNA sequence in the genome of an organism, by separating DNA with gel electrophoresis, blotting the separated DNA molecules onto nitrocellulose, and then using a nucleotide probe to hybridize with, and highlight, the gene of interest.

Northern blot A method of detecting a particular RNA transcript in a tissue or organ, by separating RNA from that source with gel electrophoresis, blotting the separated RNA molecules onto nitrocellulose, and then using a nucleotide probe to hybridize with, and highlight, the transcript of interest.

***in situ* hybridization** A method for detecting particular RNA transcripts in tissue sections by providing a nucleotide probe that is complementary to, and will therefore hybridize with, the transcript of interest.

This process of looking for a particular sequence of DNA is called a **Southern blot**, named after the man who developed the technique, Edward Southern. Southern blots are useful for determining whether related individuals share a particular gene or for assessing the evolutionary relatedness of different species. The developed blots, with their lanes of labeled bands (see Figure A.3), are often seen in popular-media accounts of "DNA fingerprinting" of individuals.

Northern blots identify particular mRNA transcripts

A method more relevant for our discussions is the **Northern blot** (whimsically named as the opposite of the Southern blot). A Northern blot can identify which tissues are making a particular RNA transcript. If liver cells are making a particular protein, for example, then some transcripts for the gene that encodes that protein should be present. So we can take the liver, grind it up, and use chemical processes to isolate most of the RNA (discarding the DNA and protein). The resulting mixture consists of RNA molecules of many different sizes: long, medium, and short transcripts. Gel electrophoresis will separate the transcripts by size, and we can blot the size-sorted mRNA molecules onto nitrocellulose sheets; the process is very similar to the Southern blot procedure.

To see whether the particular transcript we're looking for is among the mRNAs, we construct a labeled probe (of either DNA nucleotides or RNA nucleotides) that is complementary to the mRNA transcript of interest and long enough that it will hybridize only to that particular transcript. We incubate the nitrocellulose in the probe, allow time for the probe to hybridize with the targeted transcript (if present), rinse off any unused probe molecules, and then visualize the probe as before. If the transcript of interest is present, we should see a band on the film (see Figure A.3). The presence of several bands indicates that the probe has hybridized to more than one transcript and we may need to make a more specific probe or alter chemical conditions to make the probe less likely to bind similar transcripts.

Because different gene transcripts have different lengths, the transcript of interest should have reached a particular point in the electrophoresis gel: small transcripts should have moved far; large transcripts should have moved only a little. If our probe has found the right transcript, the single band of labeling should be at the point that is appropriate for a transcript of that length.

In situ *hybridization localizes mRNA transcripts within specific cells*

Northern blots can tell us whether a particular *organ* has transcripts for a particular gene product. For example, Northern blot analyses have indicated that thousands of genes are transcribed only in the brain. Presumably the proteins encoded by these genes are used exclusively in the brain. But such results alone are not very informative, because the brain consists of so many different kinds of glial and neuronal cells. We can refine Northern blot analyses somewhat, by dissecting out a particular part of the brain—say, the hippocampus—to isolate mRNAs. Sometimes, though, it is important to know *exactly which cells* are making the transcript. In that case we use ***in situ* hybridization**.

With *in situ* hybridization we use the same sort of labeled probe, constructed of nucleotides that are complementary to (and will therefore hybridize with) the targeted transcript, as in Northern blots. Instead of using the probe to find and hybridize with the transcript on a sheet of nitrocellulose, however, we use the probe to find the transcripts "in place" (*in situ* in Latin)—that is, on a section of tissue. After rinsing off the probe molecules that didn't find a match, we visualize the probe right in the tissue section. Any cells in the section that were transcribing the gene of interest will have transcripts in the cytoplasm that should have hybridized with our labeled probe. *In situ* hybridization therefore can tell us exactly which cells are expressing a particular gene (**Figure A.4**; see also Box 2.1).

Western blots identify particular proteins

Sometimes we wish to study a particular protein rather than its transcript. In such cases we can use antibodies. **Antibodies** are large, complicated molecules (proteins, in fact) that our immune system adds to the bloodstream to identify and fight invading microbes, thereby arresting and preventing disease. But if we inject a rabbit or mouse with a sample of a protein of interest, we can induce the animal to create antibodies that recognize and attach to that particular protein, just as if it were an invader.

Once these antibodies have been purified and chemically labeled, we can use them to search for the target protein. We grind up an organ, isolate the proteins (discarding the DNA and RNA), and separate them by means of gel electrophoresis. Then we blot these proteins out of the gel and onto nitrocellulose. Next we use the antibodies to tell us whether the targeted protein is among those made by that organ. If the antibodies identify only the protein we care about, there should be a single band of labeling (if there are two or more, then the antibodies recognize more than one protein). Because proteins come in different sizes, the single band of label should be at the position corresponding to the size of the protein that we're studying. Such blots are called **Western blots**.

To review, Southern blots identify particular DNA pieces (genes), Northern blots identify particular RNA pieces (transcripts), and Western blots identify particular proteins (sometimes called *products*).

Antibodies can also tell us which cells possess a particular protein

If we need to know which particular cells within an organ such as the brain are making a particular protein, we can use the same sorts of antibodies that we use in Western blots, but in this case directed at that protein in tissue sections. We slice up the brain, expose the sections to the antibodies, allow time for them to find and attach to the protein, rinse off unattached antibodies, and use chemical treatments to visualize the antibodies. Cells that were making the protein will be labeled from the chemical treatments (see Box 2.1).

Because antibodies from the *immune* system are used to identify *cells* with the aid of *chemical* treatment, this method is called **immunocytochemistry**, or **ICC**. This technique can even tell us where, within the cell, the protein is found. Such information can provide important clues about the function of the protein. For example, if the protein is found in axon terminals, it may be a neurotransmitter.

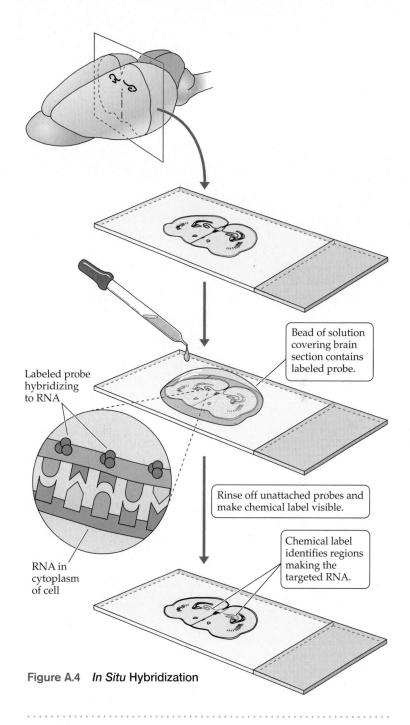

Figure A.4 *In Situ* Hybridization

Bead of solution covering brain section contains labeled probe.

Labeled probe hybridizing to RNA

RNA in cytoplasm of cell

Rinse off unattached probes and make chemical label visible.

Chemical label identifies regions making the targeted RNA.

antibody Also called *immunoglobulin*. A large protein that recognizes and permanently binds to particular shapes, normally as part of the immune system attack on foreign particles.

Western blot A method of detecting a particular protein molecule in a tissue or organ, by separating proteins from that source with gel electrophoresis, blotting the separated proteins onto nitrocellulose, and then using an antibody that binds, and highlights, the protein of interest.

immunocytochemistry (ICC) A method for detecting a particular protein in tissues in which an antibody recognizes and binds to the protein and then chemical methods are used to leave a visible reaction product around each antibody.

Glossary

Numbers in brackets refer to the chapter(s), Appendix (App), or A Step Further (ASF) where the term is introduced.

5-alpha-reductase An enzyme that converts testosterone into dihydrotestosterone. [8]

5-HT See *serotonin*. [4]

17-beta-estradiol See *estradiol*. [8]

A

A delta (Aδ) fiber A moderately large, myelinated, and therefore fast-conducting, axon, usually transmitting pain information. Compare *C fiber*. [5]

absence attack See *petit mal seizure*. [3]

absolute refractory phase A brief period of complete insensitivity to stimuli. Compare *relative refractory phase*. [3]

accommodation The process by which the ciliary muscles adjust the lens to focus a sharp image on the retina. [7]

acetylcholine (ACh) A neurotransmitter that is produced and released by parasympathetic postganglionic neurons, by motoneurons, and by neurons throughout the brain. See Figure 4.3; Table 4.1. [3–5]

acetylcholinesterase (AChE) An enzyme that inactivates the transmitter acetylcholine. [3, ASF 4.1]

ACh See *acetylcholine*. [3–5]

AChE See *acetylcholinesterase*. [3, ASF 4.1]

acid See *LSD*. [4]

act Complex behavior, as distinct from a simple *movement*. [5]

ACTH See *adrenocorticotropic hormone*. [8]

action potential Also called *spike*. A rapid reversal of the membrane potential that momentarily makes the inside of the membrane positive with respect to the outside. See Figures 3.6, 3.7. [3]

activational effect A temporary change in behavior resulting from the administration of a hormone to an adult animal. Compare *organizational effect*. [8]

acupuncture The insertion of needles at designated points on the skin to alleviate pain or neurological malfunction. [5]

adaptation 1. In the context of sensory processing, the progressive loss of receptor sensitivity as stimulation is maintained. See Figure 5.7. [5] 2. In the context of evolution, a trait that increases the probability that an individual will leave offspring in subsequent generations.

adaptation stage The second stage in the stress response, including successful activation of the appropriate response systems and the reestablishment of homeostatic balance. [11]

addiction See *dependence*. [4]

ADH See *antidiuretic hormone*. [8, 9]

ADHD See *attention deficit hyperactivity disorder*. [14, ASF 13.4]

adipose tissue Commonly called *fat tissue*. Tissue made up of fat cells. [9]

adrenal cortex The outer rind of the adrenal gland. Each of the cellular layers of the adrenal cortex produces different hormones. See Figure 8.1. Compare *adrenal medulla*. [11]

adrenal gland An endocrine gland atop the kidney. See Figure 8.1.

adrenal medulla The inner core of the adrenal gland. The adrenal medulla secretes epinephrine and norepinephrine. See Figure 8.1. Compare *adrenal cortex*. [11]

adrenal steroid hormone Also called *adrenocorticoid*. A steroid hormone that is secreted by the adrenal cortex. [11]

adrenaline See *epinephrine*. [11]

adrenocorticoid See *adrenal steroid hormone*. [11]

adrenocorticotropic hormone (ACTH) A tropic hormone, secreted by the anterior pituitary gland, that controls the production and release of hormones of the adrenal cortex. [ASF 8.4]

adult neurogenesis The creation of new neurons in the brain of an adult. [1, 13]

afferent In reference to an axon, carrying nerve impulses from a sensory organ to the central nervous system, or from one region to another region of interest. See Box 2.2. Compare *efferent*. [2]

affinity See *binding affinity*. [4]

afterpotential The positive or negative change in membrane potential that may follow an action potential. [3]

aggression Behavior that is intended to cause pain or harm to others. [11]

agnosia The inability to recognize objects, despite being able to describe them in terms of form and color. Agnosia may occur after localized brain damage. [15]

agonist A molecule, usually a drug, that binds a receptor molecule and initiates a response like that of another molecule, usually a neurotransmitter. Compare *antagonist* (definition 1). [3, 4]

agraphia The inability to write. Compare *alexia*. [15]

AIS See *androgen insensitivity syndrome*. [8]

alarm reaction The initial response to stress. [11]

alcohol A neuroactive compound (primarily the ethyl alcohol found in various beverages) that first stimulates and then depresses neural activity, with varied behavioral consequences. [4]

aldosterone A mineralocorticoid hormone, secreted by the adrenal cortex, that promotes the conservation of sodium by the kidneys. [9]

alexia The inability to read. See also *dyslexia*. Compare *agraphia*. [15]

all-or-none property The fact that the size (amplitude) of the action potential is independent of the size of the stimulus. See Table 3.2. Compare *postsynaptic potential*. [3]

allele Any particular version of a gene.

allomone A chemical signal that is released outside the body by one species and affects the behavior of other species. See Figure 8.3. Compare *pheromone*. [8]

alpha-fetoprotein A protein found in the plasma of fetuses. In rodents, alpha-fetoprotein binds estrogens and prevents them from entering the brain. [ASF 8.7]

alpha rhythm A brain potential of 8–12 hertz that occurs during relaxed wakefulness. See Figure 10.10. Compare *desynchronized EEG*. [10]

alpha-synuclein A protein that has been implicated in Parkinson's disease. [ASF 5.6]

ALS See *amyotrophic lateral sclerosis*. [ASF 5.6]

Alzheimer's disease A form of dementia that may appear in middle age but is more frequent among the aged. [13]

amacrine cell A specialized retinal cell that contacts both *bipolar cells* and *ganglion cells*, and is especially significant in inhibitory interactions within the retina. Compare *horizontal cell*. [7]

amblyopia Reduced visual acuity that is not caused by optical or retinal impairments. [7, ASF 13.4]

AMH See *anti-müllerian hormone*. [8]

amine hormone Also called *monoamine hormone*. A hormone composed of a single amino acid that has been modified into a related molecule, such as melatonin or epinephrine. Compare *protein hormone* and *steroid hormone*. [8]

amine neurotransmitter A neurotransmitter based on modifications of a single amino acid nucleus. Examples include acetylcholine, serotonin, and dopamine. See Table 4.1. Compare *amino acid neurotransmitter*, *gas neurotransmitter*, and *peptide neurotransmitter*. [4]

amino acid neurotransmitter A neurotransmitter that is itself an amino acid. Examples include GABA, glycine, and glutamate. See Table 4.1. Compare *amine neurotransmitter*, *gas neurotransmitter*, and *peptide neurotransmitter*. [4]

amnesia Severe impairment of memory. [13]

AMPA receptor A glutamate receptor that also binds the glutamate agonist AMPA. The AMPA receptor is responsible for most of the activity at glutamatergic synapses. Compare *NMDA receptor*. [4, 13]

amphetamine A molecule that resembles the structure of the catecholamine transmitters and enhances their activity. [4]

amphetamine psychosis A delusional and psychotic state, closely resembling acute schizophrenia, that is brought on by repeated use of high doses of amphetamine. [12]

amplitude Also called *intensity*. The force that sound exerts per unit area, usually measured as dynes per square centimeter. In practical terms, amplitude corresponds to the volume of a sound. See Box 6.1. [6]

ampulla (pl. ampullae) An enlarged region of each semicircular canal that contains the receptor cells (hair cells) of the vestibular system. See Figure 6.13. [6]

amusia A disorder characterized by the inability to discern tunes accurately or to sing. [6]

amygdala A group of nuclei in the medial anterior part of the temporal lobe. See Figure 2.14. [2, 11]

amyloid plaque Also called *senile plaque*. A small area of the brain that has abnormal cellular and chemical patterns. Amyloid plaques correlate with dementia. See Figure 13.34. [13]

amyloid precursor protein (APP) A protein that, when cleaved by several enzymes, produces beta-amyloid, which can lead to Alzheimer's disease. [ASF 13.4]

amyotrophic lateral sclerosis (ALS) Also called *Lou Gehrig's disease*. A disease in which motoneurons and their target muscles waste away. [ASF 5.6]

analgesia Absence of or reduction in pain. [5]

analgesic Having painkilling properties. [4]

anandamide An endogenous substance that binds the cannabinoid receptor molecule. [4]

androgen Any of a class of hormones that includes testosterone and other male hormones. See Figure 8.13. [8]

androgen insensitivity syndrome (AIS) A syndrome caused by a mutation of the androgen receptor gene that renders tissues insensitive to androgenic hormones like testosterone. Affected XY individuals are phenotypic females, but they have internal testes and regressed internal genital structures. See Figure 8.27. [8]

angel dust See *phencyclidine*. [12]

angiotensin II A hormone that is produced in the blood by the action of renin and that may play a role in the control of thirst. [9]

angular gyrus A brain region in which strokes can lead to word blindness.

anion A negatively charged ion, such as a protein or a chloride ion. Compare *cation*. [3]

anomia The inability to name persons or objects readily. [15]

anorexia nervosa A syndrome in which individuals severely deprive themselves of food. [9]

anosmia The inability to detect odors. [6]

ANP See *atrial natriuretic peptide*. [9]

antagonist 1. A molecule, usually a drug, that interferes with or prevents the action of a neurotransmitter. Compare *agonist*. [3, 4] 2. A muscle that counteracts the effect of another muscle. Compare *synergist*. [5]

anterior Also called *rostral*. In anatomy, toward the head end of an organism. See Box 2.2. Compare *posterior*. [2]

anterior cerebral artery Either of two large arteries, arising from the carotid arteries, that provide blood to the anterior poles and medial surfaces of the cerebral hemispheres. Compare *middle cerebral artery* and *posterior cerebral artery*. [ASF 2.1]

anterior pituitary Also called *adenohypophysis*. The front division of the pituitary gland; it secretes tropic hormones. See Figures 8.1, 8.12. Compare *posterior pituitary*. [8]

anterograde amnesia Difficulty in forming new memories beginning with the onset of a disorder. Compare *retrograde amnesia*. [13]

anterolateral system Also called *spinothalamic system*. A somatosensory system that carries most of the pain information from the body to the brain. See Figure 5.13. Compare *dorsal column system*. [5]

antibody Also called *immunoglobulin*. A large protein that recognizes and permanently binds to particular shapes, normally as part of the immune system attack on foreign particles. [11, App]

antidepressant A drug that relieves the symptoms of depression. Major categories include monoamine oxidase inhibitors, tricyclics, and selective serotonin reuptake inhibitors. [4]

antidiuretic hormone (ADH) See *arginine vasopressin*. [8, 9]

anti-müllerian hormone (AMH) Also called *müllerian regression hormone*. A protein hormone secreted by the fetal testes that inhibits müllerian duct development. [8]

antipsychotic See *neuroleptic*. [4, 12]

anxiety disorder Any of a class of psychological disorders that include recurrent panic states, generalized persistent anxiety disorders, and posttraumatic stress disorder. [12]

anxiolytic A substance that is used to combat anxiety. Examples include alcohol, opiates, barbiturates, and the benzodiazepines. [4, 12]

aphasia An impairment in language understanding and/or production that is caused by brain injury. [15]

ApoE See *apolipoprotein E*. [ASF 13.1]

apolipoprotein E (ApoE) A protein that may help break down beta-amyloid. Individuals carrying the *ApoE4* allele are more likely to develop Alzheimer's disease. [ASF 13.1]

apoptosis See *cell death*. [13]

APP See *amyloid precursor protein*. [13]

appetitive behavior The second stage of mating behavior; it helps establish or maintain sexual interaction. See Figure 8.16. [8]

apraxia An impairment in the ability to carry out complex sequential movements, even though there is no muscle paralysis. [5, 15]

arachnoid The thin covering (one of the three meninges) of the brain that lies between the *dura mater* and the *pia mater*. See Figure 2.8. [2]

arcuate fasciculus A fiber tract classically viewed as a connection between Wernicke's speech area and Broca's speech area. See Figure 15.7. [15]

arcuate nucleus An arc-shaped hypothalamic nucleus implicated in appetite control. See Figure 9.12.

area 17 See *primary visual cortex*. [7]

arginine vasopressin (AVP) Also called *antidiuretic hormone* or simply *vasopressin*. A peptide hormone from the posterior pituitary that promotes water conservation and increases blood pressure. [8, 9]

aromatase An enzyme that converts many androgens into estrogens. [ASF 8.7]

aromatization The chemical reaction that converts testosterone to estradiol, and other androgens to other estrogens. [ASF 8.7]

aromatization hypothesis The hypothesis that testicular androgens enter the brain and are converted there into estrogens to masculinize the developing nervous system of some rodents. [ASF 8.7]

arousal The global, nonselective level of alertness of an individual.

Asperger's syndrome Also called *high-functioning autism*. A syndrome characterized by difficulties in social cognitive processing; it is usually accompanied by strong language skills. Compare *autism*. [ASF 13.4]

associative learning A type of learning in which an association is formed between two stimuli or between a stimulus and a response. It includes both classical and instrumental conditioning. Compare *non-associative learning*. [13]

astereognosis The inability to recognize objects by touching and feeling them. [15]

astrocyte A star-shaped glial cell with numerous processes (extensions) that run in all directions. Astrocyte extensions provide structural support for the brain and may isolate receptive surfaces. See Figure 2.5. [2]

ataxia A loss of movement coordination, often caused by disease of the cerebellum. [5]

atrial natriuretic peptide (ANP) A hormone, secreted by the heart, that normally reduces blood pressure, inhibits drinking, and promotes the excretion of water and salt at the kidneys. [9]

attention Also called *selective attention*. A state or condition of selective awareness or perceptual receptivity, by which specific stimuli are selected for enhanced processing. [14]

attention deficit hyperactivity disorder (ADHD) A syndrome characterized by distractibility, impulsiveness, and hyperactivity that, in children, interferes with school performance. [14, ASF 13.4]

attentional blink The reduced ability of subjects to detect a target stimulus if it follows another target stimulus by about 200–450 milliseconds.

attentional bottleneck A filter that results from the limits intrinsic to our attentional processes, with the result that only the most important stimuli are selected for special processing. [14]

attentional spotlight The shifting of our limited selective attention around the environment to highlight stimuli for enhanced processing. [14]

atypical neuroleptic An antipsychotic drug that has actions other than or in addition to the dopamine D_2 receptor antagonism that characterizes the *typical neuroleptics*. Atypical neuroleptics often feature selective antagonism of serotonin receptors. [4, 12]

auditory canal See *ear canal*. [6]

auditory N1 effect A negative deflection of the event-related potential, occurring about 100 milliseconds after stimulus presentation, that is enhanced for selectively attended auditory input compared to ignored input. Compare *visual P1 effect*. [14]

auditory P300 See *P3 effect*. [14]

aura In epilepsy, the unusual sensations or premonition that may precede the beginning of a seizure. [3]

autism A disorder, arising during childhood, that is characterized by social withdrawal and perseverative behavior. Compare *Asperger's syndrome*. [ASF 13.4]

autobiographical memory See *episodic memory*. [13]

autocrine Referring to a signal that is secreted by a cell into its environment and that feeds back to the same cell.

autoimmune disorder A disorder caused when the immune system mistakenly attacks a person's own body, thereby interfering with normal functioning. [ASF 5.6]

autonomic ganglion A collection of nerve cell bodies, belonging to the autonomic division of the peripheral nervous system, that is found in any of various locations and contributes to the innervation of major organs.

autonomic nervous system The part of the peripheral nervous system that supplies neural connections to glands and

to smooth muscles of internal organs. Its two divisions (sympathetic and parasympathetic) act in opposite fashion. See Figure 2.9. [2]

autoradiography A staining technique that shows the distribution of radioactive chemicals in tissues. See Boxes 2.1, 8.1. [2, 8]

autoreceptor A receptor for a synaptic transmitter that is located in the presynaptic membrane and tells the axon terminal how much transmitter has been released. [4]

AVP See *arginine vasopressin*. [8, 9]

axo-axonic synapse A synapse at which a presynaptic axon terminal synapses onto the axon terminal of another neuron. Compare *axo-dendritic synapse*, *axo-somatic synapse*, and *dendro-dendritic synapse*. [3]

axo-dendritic synapse A synapse at which a presynaptic axon terminal synapses onto a dendrite of the postsynaptic neuron, either via a dendritic spine or directly onto the dendrite itself. Compare *axo-axonic synapse*, *axo-somatic synapse*, and *dendro-dendritic synapse*. [3]

axo-somatic synapse A synapse at which a presynaptic axon terminal synapses onto the cell body (soma) of the postsynaptic neuron. Compare *axo-axonic synapse*, *axo-dendritic synapse*, and *dendro-dendritic synapse*. [3]

axon Also called *nerve fiber*. A single extension from the nerve cell that carries action potentials from the cell body toward the axon terminals. Functionally, the axon is the *conduction zone* of the neuron. See Figures 2.1, 2.3. [2]

axon collateral A branch of an axon. [2]

axon hillock The cone-shaped area on the cell body from which the axon originates. See Figure 2.4. [2, 3]

axon terminal Also called *synaptic bouton*. The end of an axon or axon collateral, which forms a synapse on a neuron or other target cell. Functionally, the axon terminals are the *output zone* of the neuron. See Figures 2.1, 2.3 [2]

axonal transport The transportation of materials from the neuronal cell body to distant regions in the dendrites and axons, and from the axon terminals back to the cell body. [2]

B

B cell See *B lymphocyte*. [11]

B lymphocyte Also called *B cell*. An immune system cell, formed in the bone marrow (hence the *B*), that mediates humoral immunity. Compare *T lymphocyte*. [11]

Balint's syndrome A disorder, caused by damage to both parietal lobes, that is characterized by difficulty in steering visual gaze (oculomotor ataxia), in accurately reaching for objects using visual guidance (optic ataxia), and in directing attention to more than one object or feature at a time (simultagnosia). [14]

ballistic Referring to a rapid muscular movement that is generally fully preprogrammed and thus not susceptible to error correction during execution. [5]

bar detector See *simple cortical cell*. [7]

barbiturate An early anxiolytic drug and sleep aid that has depressant activity in the nervous system. [4]

bariatric Having to do with obesity. [9]

baroreceptor A pressure receptor in the heart or a major artery that detects a change in blood pressure. [9]

basal forebrain A region, ventral to the basal ganglia, that is the major source of acetylcholine in the brain and has been implicated in sleep. [4, 10]

basal ganglia A group of forebrain nuclei, including the caudate nucleus, globus pallidus, and putamen, found deep within the cerebral hemispheres. See Figures 2.14, 2.15, 5.28. [2, 5, 13]

basal metabolism The consumption of energy to fuel processes such as heat production, maintenance of membrane potentials, and all the other basic life-sustaining functions of the body. [9]

basilar artery An artery, formed by the fusion of the vertebral arteries, that supplies blood to the brainstem and to the posterior cerebral arteries. [ASF 2.1]

basilar membrane A membrane in the cochlea that contains the principal structures involved in auditory transduction. See Figures 6.1, 6.2. [6]

behavioral intervention An approach to finding relations between body variables and behavioral variables that involves intervening in the behavior of an organism and looking for resultant changes in body structure or function. See Figure 1.8. Compare *somatic intervention*. [1]

behavioral medicine See *health psychology*. [11]

behavioral neuroscience See *biological psychology*. [1]

benzodiazepine Any of a class of antianxiety drugs that are agonists of $GABA_A$ receptors in the central nervous system. One example is diazepam (Valium). [4, 12]

beta activity See *desynchronized EEG*. [10]

beta-amyloid A protein that accumulates in amyloid plaques in Alzheimer's disease. [13]

beta-secretase An enzyme that cleaves amyloid precursor protein, forming beta-amyloid, which can lead to Alzheimer's disease. See also *presenilin*. [ASF 13.4]

between-subjects experiment An experiment in which a group of experimental subjects is compared with a control group of individuals who have been treated identically in every way except that they haven't received the experimental manipulation. Compare *within-subjects experiment*. [1]

binaural Pertaining to two ears. Compare *monaural*.

binding affinity Also called simply *affinity*. The propensity of molecules of a drug (or other ligand) to bind to receptors. Drugs with high affinity for their receptors are effective even at low doses. [4]

binding problem The question of how the brain understands which individual attributes blend together into a single object, when these different features are processed by different regions in the brain. [14]

binge eating The rapid intake of large quantities of food, often poor in nutritional value and high in calories. [9]

binocular Two-eyed. [7]

binocular deprivation Depriving both eyes of form vision, as by sealing the eyelids. Compare *monocular deprivation*. [ASF 13.4]

bioavailable Referring to a substance, usually a drug, that is present in the body in a form that is able to interact with physiological mechanisms. [4]

biological psychology Also called *behavioral neuroscience, brain and behavior*, and *physiological psychology*. The study of the biological bases of psychological processes and behavior. [1]

biological rhythm A regular fluctuation in any living process. [10]

biotransformation The process in which enzymes convert a drug into a metabolite that is itself active, possibly in ways that are substantially different from the actions of the original substance. [4]

bipolar cell An interneuron in the retina that receives information from rods and cones and passes the information to retinal *ganglion cells*. See Figure 7.3. Compare *amacrine cell* and *horizontal cell*. [7]

bipolar disorder Also called *manic-depressive illness*. A psychiatric disorder characterized by periods of depression that alternate with excessive, expansive moods. Compare *unipolar depression*. [12]

bipolar neuron A nerve cell that has a single dendrite at one end and a single axon at the other end. See Figure 2.3. Compare *unipolar neuron* and *multipolar neuron*. [2]

blind spot The portion of the visual field from which light falls on the optic disc. Because there are no receptors in this region, light striking the blind spot cannot be seen. [7]

blindsight The paradoxical phenomenon whereby, within a scotoma, a person cannot *consciously* perceive visual cues but may still be able to make some visual discrimination. [7]

blood-brain barrier The mechanisms that make the movement of substances from blood vessels into brain cells more difficult than exchanges in other body organs, thus affording the brain greater protection from exposure to some substances found in the blood. [2, 4]

blotting Transferring DNA, RNA, or protein fragments to nitrocellulose following separation via gel electrophoresis. The blotted substance can then be labeled. See Appendix Figure A.3. [App]

brain and behavior See *biological psychology*. [1]

brain self-stimulation The process in which animals will work to provide electrical stimulation to particular brain sites, presumably because the experience is very rewarding. [11]

brainstem The region of the brain that consists of the midbrain, the pons, and the medulla. [2]

brightness One of three basic dimensions of light perception, varying from dark to light. See Figure 7.24. Compare *hue* and *saturation*. [7]

Broca's aphasia See *nonfluent aphasia*. [15]

Broca's area A region of the frontal lobe of the brain that is involved in the production of speech. See Figures 15.5, 15.6, 15.7. Compare *Wernicke's area*. [15]

brown fat Also called *brown adipose tissue*. A specialized type of fat tissue that generates heat through intense metabolism. [9]

bulimia Also called *bulimia nervosa*. A syndrome in which individuals periodically gorge themselves, usually with "junk food," and then either vomit or take laxatives to avoid weight gain.

bungarotoxin A neurotoxin, isolated from the venom of the banded krait, that selectively blocks acetylcholine receptors. [3]

C

C fiber A small, unmyelinated axon that conducts pain information slowly and adapts slowly. Compare *A delta fiber*. [5]

c-fos An immediate early gene commonly used to identify activated neurons. See Box 2.1.

caffeine A stimulant compound found in coffee, cacao, and other plants. [4]

CAH See *congenital adrenal hyperplasia*. [8]

calcium ion (Ca²⁺) A calcium atom that carries a double positive charge because it has lost two electrons. [3]

capsaicin A compound synthesized by various plants to deter predators by mimicking the experience of burning. Capsaicin is responsible for the burning sensation in chili peppers.

carotid artery Either of the two major arteries that ascend the left and right sides of the neck to the brain, supplying blood to the anterior and middle cerebral arteries. The branch that enters the brain is called the internal carotid artery. [ASF 2.1]

CART See *cocaine- and amphetamine-regulated transcript*.

castration Removal of the gonads, usually the testes. [8]

CAT See *computerized axial tomography*. [2]

cataplexy Sudden loss of muscle tone, leading to collapse of the body without loss of consciousness. Cataplexy is sometimes a component of narcoleptic attacks. [10]

cation A positively charged ion, such as a potassium or sodium ion. Compare *anion*. [3]

cauda equina Literally, "horse's tail" (in Latin). The caudalmost spinal nerves, which extend beyond the spinal cord proper to exit the spinal column.

caudal See *posterior*. [2]

caudate nucleus One of the basal ganglia; it has a long extension or tail. See Figure 2.14. [2]

causality The relation of cause and effect, such that we can conclude that an experimental manipulation has specifically caused an observed result. [1]

CBT See *cognitive behavioral therapy*. [12]

CCK See *cholecystokinin*. [9]

cell body Also called *soma*. The region of a neuron that is defined by the presence of the cell nucleus. Functionally, the cell body is the *integration zone* of the neuron. See Figures 2.1, 2.3. [2]

cell-cell interaction The general process during development in which one cell affects the differentiation of other, usually neighboring, cells. [13]

cell death Also called *apoptosis*. The developmental process during which "surplus" cells die. See Figure 13.25. [13]

cell differentiation The developmental stage in which cells acquire distinctive characteristics, such as those of neurons, as a result of expressing particular genes. See Figure 13.25. [13, App]

cell membrane The lipid bilayer that ensheathes a cell. [3]

cell migration The movement of cells from site of origin to final location. See Figure 13.25. [13]

cell nucleus The spherical central structure of a cell that contains the chromosomes. [App]

central deafness A hearing impairment in which the auditory areas of the brain fail to process and interpret action potentials from sound stimuli in meaningful ways. It is related to damage in auditory brain areas, such as by strokes, tumors, or traumatic injuries. Cortical deafness and word deafness are two examples of central deafness. See Figure 6.11. Compare *conduction deafness* and *sensorineural deafness*. [6]

central modulation of sensory information The process in which higher brain centers, such as the cortex and thalamus, suppress some sources of sensory information and amplify others. [5]

central nervous system (CNS) The portion of the nervous system that includes the brain and the spinal cord. See Figures 2.6, 2.12. Compare *peripheral nervous system*. [2]

central sulcus A fissure that divides the frontal lobe from the parietal lobe. See Figure 2.10. [2]

cerebellum A structure located at the back of the brain, dorsal to the pons, that is involved in the central regulation of movement. See Figures 2.10, 2.12, 2.16, 5.28. [2, 5, 13]

cerebral cortex Sometimes called simply *cortex*. The outer covering of the cerebral hemispheres, which consists largely of nerve cell bodies and their branches. In mammals, the cerebral cortex has six distinct layers. See Figure 2.13. [2]

cerebral hemisphere One of the two halves—right or left—of the forebrain. See Figure 2.12. [2]

cerebrocerebellum The lowermost part of the cerebellum, consisting especially of the lateral parts of each cerebellar hemisphere. It is implicated in planning complex movements. Compare *spinocerebellum* and *vestibulocerebellum*. [ASF 5.5]

cerebrospinal fluid (CSF) The fluid that fills the cerebral ventricles. See Figure 2.17. [2]

cerveau isolé See *isolated forebrain*. [10]

cervical Referring to the topmost 8 segments of the spinal cord, in the neck region. See Figures 2.8, 2.9. Compare *thoracic*, *lumbar*, *sacral*, and *coccygeal*. [2]

change blindness A failure to notice changes in comparisons of two alternating static visual scenes.

ChAT See *choline acetyltransferase*. [ASF 4.1]

chemical transmitter See *neurotransmitter*. [2, 3]

chloride ion (Cl⁻) A chlorine atom that carries a negative charge because it has gained one electron. [3]

chlorpromazine An antipsychotic drug that replaced lobotomy as a treatment for schizophrenia. [12]

cholecystokinin (CCK) A peptide hormone that is released by the gut after ingestion of food that is high in protein and/or fat. [9]

choline acetyltransferase (ChAT) An important enzyme involved in the synthesis of the neurotransmitter acetylcholine. [ASF 4.1]

cholinergic Referring to cells that use acetylcholine as their synaptic transmitter. [3, 4]

choroid plexus A specialized membrane lining the ventricles that produces cerebrospinal fluid by filtering blood. [2]

chromosome A complex of condensed strands of DNA and associated protein molecules. Chromosomes are found in the nucleus of cells. [App]

chronic traumatic encephalopathy (CTE) Also called *dementia pugilistica* or *punch-drunk*. The dementia that develops in boxers and other athletes engaged in contact sports. CTE is especially prominent in successful boxers, because they participate in more bouts. [15]

ciliary muscle One of the muscles that control the shape of the lens inside the eye, focusing an image on the retina. See Figure 7.1. [7]

cingulate cortex See *cingulate gyrus*. [5]

cingulate gyrus Also called *cingulate cortex* or *cingulum*. A strip of cortex, found in the frontal and parietal midline, that is part of the limbic system and is implicated in many cognitive functions. See Figures 2.14, 2.16. [2, 5]

cingulum (pl. cingula) See *cingulate gyrus*. [5]

circadian rhythm A pattern of behavioral, biochemical, or physiological fluctuation that has a 24-hour period. [10]

circle of Willis A structure at the base of the brain that is formed by the joining of the carotid and basilar arteries. [ASF 2.1]

circumventricular organ Any of multiple distinct sites that lie in the wall of a cerebral ventricle and monitor the composition of the cerebrospinal fluid. See Figure 9.8. [9]

classical conditioning Also called *Pavlovian conditioning*. A type of associative learning in which an originally neutral stimulus (the conditioned stimulus, or CS)—through pairing with another stimulus (the unconditioned stimulus, or US) that elicits a particular response—acquires the power to elicit that response when presented alone. A response elicited by the US is called an unconditioned response (UR); a response elicited by the CS alone is called a conditioned response (CR). See Figure 13.9. Compare *instrumental conditioning*. [13]

clitoris The female phallus. Compare *penis*. [8]

cloacal exstrophy A rare medical condition in which XY individuals are born completely lacking a penis. [8]

clones Asexually produced organisms that are genetically identical. [13, App]

closed-loop motor control A control mechanism that provides a flow of information from whatever is being controlled to the device that controls it. See Figure 5.17. Compare *open-loop motor control*. [5]

clozapine An atypical neuroleptic. [12]

CNS See *central nervous system*. [2]

cocaine A drug of abuse, derived from the coca plant, that acts by enhancing catecholamine neurotransmission. [4]

cocaine- and amphetamine-regulated transcript (CART) A peptide produced in the brain when an animal is injected with either cocaine or amphetamine. It is also associated with the appetite control circuitry of the hypothalamus.

coccygeal Referring to the lowest spinal vertebra (the *coccyx*, also known as the *tailbone*). See Figure 2.9. Compare *cervical*, *thoracic*, *lumbar*, and *sacral*. [2]

cochlea A snail-shaped structure in the inner ear that contains the primary receptor cells for hearing. See Figure 6.1. [6]

cochlear implant An electromechanical device that detects sounds and selectively stimulates nerves in different regions of the cochlea via surgically implanted electrodes. [6]

cochlear nucleus Either of two brainstem nuclei—left and right—that receive input from auditory hair cells and send output to the superior olivary nuclei. See Figure 6.6. [6]

cocktail party effect The selective enhancement of attention in order to filter out distracters, such as while listening to one person talking in the midst of a noisy party. [14]

coding The rules by which action potentials in a sensory system reflect a physical stimulus.

codon A set of three nucleotides that uniquely encodes one particular amino acid. A series of codons determines the structure of a peptide or protein. [App]

cognitive behavioral therapy (CBT) Psychotherapy aimed at correcting negative thinking and consciously changing behaviors as a way of changing feelings. [12]

cognitive map A mental representation of the relative spatial organization of objects and information. [13]

cognitively impenetrable Involving basic neural processing operations that cannot be experienced through introspection—that is, that are unconscious. [14]

coitus See *copulation*. [8]

collateral sprouting The formation of a new branch on an axon, usually in response to the uncovering of unoccupied postsynaptic sites. [ASF 15.4]

combat fatigue See *posttraumatic stress disorder*. [12, 13]

co-morbid Referring to the tendency of certain diseases or disorders to occur together in individuals. [12]

complex cortical cell A cell in the visual cortex that responds best to a bar of a particular size and orientation anywhere within a particular area of the visual field. Compare *simple cortical cell*. [7]

complex environment See *enriched condition*. [13]

complex partial seizure In epilepsy, a type of seizure that doesn't involve the entire brain, and therefore can cause a wide variety of symptoms. [3]

computerized axial tomography (CAT or CT) A noninvasive technique for examining brain structure through computer analysis of X-ray absorption at several positions around the head. CT affords a virtual direct view of the brain. The resulting images are referred to as *CAT scans* or *CT scans*. See Figure 2.18. Compare *magnetic resonance imaging*. [2]

concordance A characteristic that is seen in both individuals of a pair of twins. [12]

concussion A form of closed head injury caused by a jarring blow to the head, resulting in damage to the tissue of the brain with short- or long-term consequences for cognitive function. [15]

conduction aphasia An impairment in the ability to repeat words and sentences. [15]

conduction deafness A hearing impairment in which the sound vibrations in air fail to be converted into waves of fluid in the cochlea. It is associated with defects of the external ear or middle ear. See Figure 6.11. Compare *central deafness* and *sensorineural deafness*. [6]

conduction velocity The speed at which an action potential is propagated along the length of an axon (or section of peripheral nerve). [3]

conduction zone The part of a neuron over which the nerve's electrical signal may be actively propagated. This zone usually corresponds to the cell's *axon*. See Figures 2.1, 2.3. Compare *input zone*, *integration zone*, and *output zone*. [2]

cone Any of several classes of photoreceptor cells in the retina that are responsible for color vision. See Figure 7.3. Compare *rod*. [7]

confabulate To fill in a gap in memory with a falsification. Confabulation is often seen in Korsakoff's syndrome. [13]

congenital adrenal hyperplasia (CAH) Any of several genetic mutations that can cause a female fetus to be exposed to adrenal androgens, resulting in partial masculinization at birth. [8]

conjunction search A search for an item that is based on two or more features (e.g., size and color) that together distinguish the target from distracters that may share some of the same attributes. Compare *feature search*. [14]

connectionist model of aphasia Also called *Wernicke-Geschwind model*. A theory proposing that left-hemisphere language deficits result from disconnection between the brain regions in a language network, each of which serves a particular linguistic function. Compare *motor theory of language*. [15]

consciousness The state of awareness of one's own existence, thoughts, emotions, and experiences. [1, 14]

conserved In the context of evolution, referring to a trait that is passed on from a common ancestor to two or more descendant species. [1]

consolidation The second process in the memory system, in which information in short-term memory is transferred to long-term memory. See Figure 13.13. Compare *encoding* and *retrieval*. [13]

constraint-induced movement therapy A therapy for recovery of movement after stroke or injury in which the person's unaffected limb is constrained while he is required to perform tasks with the affected limb. [15]

contralateral In anatomy, pertaining to a location on the opposite side of the body. See Box 2.2. Compare *ipsilateral*. [2, 15]

control group A group of research subjects that are identical to an experimental (or test) group in every way except that they do not receive the experimental treatment or manipulation. The experimental group is then compared to the control group to assess the effect of the treatment. [1]

convergence The phenomenon of neural connections in which many cells send signals to a single cell. Compare *divergence*. [3, 7]

Coolidge effect The propensity of an animal that has appeared sexually satiated with a present partner to resume sexual activity when provided with a new partner. [8]

copulation Also called *coitus*. The sexual act. [8]

copulatory lock Reproductive behavior in which the male's penis swells after ejaculation so that the male and female are forced to remain joined for 5–10 minutes; it occurs in dogs and some rodents, but not in humans. [8]

cornea The transparent outer layer of the eye, whose curvature is fixed. The cornea bends light rays and is primarily responsible for forming the image on the retina. See Figure 7.1. [7]

coronal plane Also called *frontal plane* or *transverse plane*. The plane that divides the body or brain into front and back parts. See Box 2.2. Compare *horizontal plane* and *sagittal plane*. [2]

corpus callosum The main band of axons that connects the two cerebral hemispheres. See Figures 2.11, 2.16. [2]

corpus luteum (pl. corpora lutea) The structure that forms from the collapsed ovarian follicle after ovulation. The corpora lutea are a major source of progesterone. [8, ASF 8.4]

correlation The covariation of two measures. [1]

cortex (pl. cortices) The outer layer of a structure. See also *cerebral cortex* and *neocortex*.

cortical column One of the vertical columns that constitute the basic organization of the cerebral cortex. [2]

cortical deafness A form of central deafness, caused by damage to both sides of the auditory cortex, that is characterized by difficulty in recognizing all complex sounds, whether verbal or nonverbal. [6]

corticospinal system See *pyramidal system*. [5]

cortisol A glucocorticoid stress hormone of the adrenal cortex. [11]

covert attention Attention in which the focus can be directed independently of sensory orientation (e.g., you're attending to one sensory stimulus while looking at another). Compare *overt attention*. [14]

cranial nerve A nerve that is connected directly to the brain. Composed of a set of pathways concerned mainly with sensory and motor systems associated with the head, the cranial nerves together constitute one of the three main subdivisions of the peripheral nervous system. There are 12 cranial nerves, typically designated by Roman numerals I–XII. See Figure 2.7. Compare *spinal nerve*. [2]

crib death See *sudden infant death syndrome*. [10]

critical period See *sensitive period*. [15]

cross-tolerance A condition in which the development of tolerance for one drug causes an individual to develop tolerance for another drug. [4]

crystallization The final stage of birdsong formation, in which fully formed adult song is achieved. [ASF 15.1]

CSF See *cerebrospinal fluid*. [2]

CT See *computerized axial tomography*. [2]

CTE See *chronic traumatic encephalopathy*. [15]

curare A neurotoxin that causes paralysis by blocking acetylcholine receptors in muscle. [3]

Cushing's syndrome A condition in which levels of adrenal glucocorticoids are abnormally high. [12, ASF 8.3]

cytokine A protein that induces the proliferation of other cells, as in the immune system. Examples include interleukins and interferons. [11]

cytoplasm See *intracellular fluid*. [3]

D

DA See *dopamine*. [4]

dB See *decibel*. [6]

DBS See *deep brain stimulation*. [12]

death gene A gene that is expressed only when a cell becomes committed to natural cell death (apoptosis). [13]

decibel (dB) A measure of sound intensity, perceived as loudness. See Box 6.1. [6]

declarative memory A memory that can be stated or described. See Figures 13.4, 13.12. Compare *nondeclarative memory*. [13]

decomposition of movement Difficulty of movement in which gestures are broken up into individual segments instead of being executed smoothly; it is a symptom of cerebellar lesions. [5]

decorticate rage Also called *sham rage*. Sudden intense rage characterized by actions (such as snarling and biting in dogs) that lack clear direction. [11]

deep brain stimulation (DBS) Mild electrical stimulation through an electrode that is surgically implanted deep in the brain. [12]

deep dyslexia Acquired dyslexia in which the patient reads a word as another word that is semantically related. Compare *surface dyslexia*. [15]

degradation The chemical breakdown of a neurotransmitter into inactive metabolites. [3]

dehydration Excessive loss of water.

delayed non-matching-to-sample task A test in which the subject must respond to the unfamiliar stimulus of a pair. See Figure 13.5. [13]

delta-9-tetrahydrocannabinol (THC) The major active ingredient in marijuana. [4]

delta wave The slowest type of EEG wave, characteristic of stage 3 sleep. See Figure 10.10. [10]

delusion A false belief strongly held in spite of contrary evidence. [12]

dementia Drastic failure of cognitive ability, including memory failure and loss of orientation. [13]

dementia pugilistica See *chronic traumatic encephalopathy*. [15]

dendrite An extension of the cell body that receives information from other neurons. Functionally, the dendrites are the *input zone* of the neuron. See Figures 2.1, 2.3. [2]

dendritic spine An outgrowth along the dendrite of a neuron. See Figure 2.4.

dendro-dendritic synapse A synapse at which a synaptic connection forms between the dendrites of two neurons. Compare *axo-axonic synapse*, *axo-dendritic synapse*, and *axo-somatic synapse*. [3]

dentate gyrus A strip of gray matter in the hippocampal formation. [13]

deoxyribonucleic acid (DNA) A nucleic acid that is present in the chromosomes of cells and codes hereditary information. Compare *ribonucleic acid*. [App]

dependence Also called *addiction*. In the context of substance-related disorders, the strong desire to self-administer a drug of abuse. To be diagnosed as dependent, a person must meet at least three of seven criteria relating to patterns of consumption, craving, expenditure of time and energy in serving the addiction, and impact on other aspects of the person's life. See Box 4.1. Compare *substance abuse*. [4]

dependent variable The factor that an experimenter measures to monitor a change in response to changes in an *independent variable*. [1]

depolarization A decrease in membrane potential (the interior of the neuron becomes less negative). See Figure 3.5. Compare *hyperpolarization*. [3]

depressant A drug that reduces the excitability of neurons. Compare *stimulant*. [4]

depression A psychiatric condition characterized by such symptoms as an unhappy mood; loss of interests, energy, and appetite; and difficulty concentrating. See also *bipolar disorder* and *unipolar depression*. [12]

dermatome A strip of skin innervated by a particular spinal nerve. [5]

desynchronized EEG Also called *beta activity*. A pattern of EEG activity comprising a mix of many different high frequencies with low amplitude. Compare *alpha rhythm*. [10]

dexamethasone suppression test A test of pituitary-adrenal function in which the subject is given dexamethasone, a synthetic glucocorticoid hormone, which should cause a decline in the production of adrenal corticosteroids. [12]

DHT See *dihydrotestosterone*. [8]

diabetes mellitus A condition, characterized by excessive glucose in the blood and urine and by reduced glucose utilization by body cells, that is caused by the failure of insulin to induce glucose absorption. [9]

dichotic presentation The simultaneous delivery of different stimuli to both the right and the left ears at the same time. See Figure 15.14. [15]

diencephalon The posterior part of the fetal forebrain, which will become the thalamus and hypothalamus in the adult brain. See Figures 2.12, 13.24. Compare *telencephalon*. [2]

differentiation See *cell differentiation*. [13, App]

diffusion The spontaneous spread of molecules until a uniform concentration is achieved. See Figure 3.3. Compare *osmosis*. [3, 9]

digestion The process by which food is broken down to provide energy and nutrients. [9]

dihydrotestosterone (DHT) The 5-alpha-reduced metabolite of testosterone; DHT is a potent androgen that is principally responsible for the masculinization of the external genitalia in mammalian sexual differentiation. [8]

dissociative A type of drug that produces a dreamlike state in which consciousness is partly separated from sensory inputs. In contrast to *hallucinogens*, dissociatives produce feelings of depersonalization and detachment from reality, rather than primary sensory alterations. [4]

distal In anatomy, toward the periphery of an organism or toward the end of a limb. See Box 2.2. Compare *proximal*. [2]

diurnal Active during the light periods of the daily cycle. Compare *nocturnal*. [10]

divergence The phenomenon of neural connections in which one cell sends signals to many other cells. Compare *convergence*. [3]

divided-attention task A task in which the subject is asked to focus attention on two or more stimuli simultaneously. Compare *sustained-attention task*. [14]

dizygotic Referring to twins derived from separate eggs (*fraternal* twins). Such twins are no more closely related genetically than are other full siblings. Compare *monozygotic*. [12]

DNA See *deoxyribonucleic acid*. [App]

DNA sequencing The process by which the order of nucleotides in a gene is identified. [App]

dopamine (DA) A monoamine transmitter found in the midbrain—especially the substantia nigra—and in the basal forebrain. See Figure 4.4; Table 4.1. [4]

dopamine hypothesis The idea that schizophrenia results from either excessive levels of synaptic dopamine or excessive postsynaptic sensitivity to dopamine. [12]

dopaminergic Referring to cells that use dopamine as their synaptic transmitter. [4]

dorsal In anatomy, toward the back of the body or the top of the brain. See Box 2.2. Compare *ventral*. [2]

dorsal column system A somatosensory system that delivers most touch stimuli via the dorsal columns of spinal white matter to the brain. See Figure 5.8. Compare *anterolateral system*. [5]

dorsomedial thalamus A limbic system structure that is connected to the hippocampus. [13]

dose-response curve (DRC) A formal graph of a drug's effects (on the y-axis) versus the dose given (on the x-axis). Analysis of dose-response curves can provide a range of information about the drug, such as its efficacy, potency, and safety. See Figure 4.6. [4]

double-blind test A test of a drug or treatment in which neither the subjects nor the attending researchers know which subjects are receiving the drug (treatment) and which are receiving the placebo (control). [8]

down-regulation A compensatory decrease in receptor availability at the synapses of a neuron. Compare *up-regulation*. [4]

DRC See *dose-response curve*. [4]

drug tolerance Also called simply *tolerance*. A condition in which, with repeated exposure to a drug, an individual becomes less responsive to a constant dose. [4]

dualism The notion, promoted by René Descartes, that the mind has an immaterial aspect that is distinct from the material body and brain. [1]

duplex theory A theory that we localize sound by combining information about intensity differences and latency differences between the two ears. [6]

dura mater The outermost of the three meninges that surround the brain and spinal cord. See also *pia mater* and *arachnoid*. See Figure 2.8. [2]

dynorphin One of the three kinds of endogenous opioids. Compare *endorphin* and *enkephalin*. See Table 4.1. [4]

dyskinesia Difficulty or distortion in voluntary movement. [12]

dyslexia Also called *alexia*. A reading disorder attributed to brain impairment. [15]

dysphoria Unpleasant feelings; the opposite of euphoria. [4]

dystrophin A protein that is needed for normal muscle function. Dystrophin is defective in some forms of muscular dystrophy. [ASF 5.6]

E

ear canal Also called *auditory canal*. The tube leading from the pinna to the tympanic membrane. [6]

eardrum See *tympanic membrane*. [6]

early-selection model of attention A theory postulating that the attentional bottleneck imposed by the nervous system can exert control early in the processing pathway, filtering out stimuli before even preliminary perceptual analysis has occurred. Compare *late-selection model of attention*. [14]

easy problem of consciousness Understanding how particular patterns of neural activity create specific conscious experiences by reading brain activity directly from people's brains as they're having particular experiences. Compare *hard problem of consciousness*. [14]

EC See *enriched condition*. [13]

ecological niche The unique assortment of environmental opportunities and challenges to which each organism is adapted. [10]

Ecstasy See *MDMA*. [4]

ECT See *electroconvulsive shock therapy*. [12]

ectoderm The outer cellular layer of the developing fetus, giving rise to the skin and the nervous system. [13]

ectotherm An animal whose body temperature is regulated by, and whose heat comes mainly from, the environment. Examples include snakes and bees. Compare *endotherm*. [9]

ED$_{50}$ Effective dose 50%; the dose of a drug that is required to produce half of its maximal effect. See Figure 4.6. Compare *LD$_{50}$*.

edema The swelling of tissue, especially in the brain, in response to injury. [2]

edge detector See *simple cortical cell*. [7]

EEG See *electroencephalography*. [3, 10]

efferent In reference to an axon, carrying information from the nervous system to the periphery, or from a region of interest to another region. See Box 2.2. Compare *afferent*. [2]

efficacy Also called *intrinsic activity*. The extent to which a drug activates a response when it binds to a receptor. Receptor antagonist drugs have low efficacy; receptor agonists have high efficacy. See Figure 4.6. [4]

egg See *ovum*. [8]

ejaculation The forceful expulsion of semen from the penis. [8]

electrical synapse Also called *gap junction*. The region between neurons where the presynaptic and postsynaptic membranes are so close that the action potential can jump to the postsynaptic membrane without first being translated into a chemical message. [ASF 3.1]

electroconvulsive shock therapy (ECT) A last-resort treatment for unmanageable depression in which a strong electrical current is passed through the brain, causing a seizure. Rapid relief from depressive symptoms often results, associated with improved accumulation of monoamine neurotransmitters in the brain. [12]

electroencephalography (EEG) The recording and study of gross electrical activity of the brain via large electrodes placed on the scalp. The abbreviation EEG may refer either to the process of encephalography or to its product, the encephalogram. See Figures 3.15, 10.10. [3, 10]

electromyography (EMG) The electrical recording of muscle activity. See Figure 5.16. [5]

electrostatic pressure The propensity of charged molecules or ions to move, via diffusion, toward areas with the opposite charge. [3]

embryo The earliest stage in a developing animal. Humans are considered to be embryos until 8–10 weeks after conception. Compare *fetus*. [13]

embryonic stem cell A cell, derived from an embryo, that has the capacity to form any type of tissue. [15]

EMG See *electromyography*. [5]

emotion A subjective mental state that is usually accompanied by distinctive behaviors as well as involuntary physiological changes. [11]

encéphale isolé See *isolated brain*. [10]

encoding The first process in the memory system, in which the information entering sensory channels is passed into short-term memory. See Figure 13.13. Compare *consolidation* and *retrieval*. [13]

endocannabinoid An endogenous ligand of cannabinoid receptors; thus, a marijuana analog that is produced by the brain. [4, 9]

endocrine Referring to glands that release chemicals to the interior of the body. These glands secrete the principal hormones used by the body. See Figure 8.3. [8]

endocrine gland A gland that secretes products into the bloodstream to act on distant targets. See Figure 8.1. [8]

endogenous Produced inside the body. Compare *exogenous*. [4]

endogenous attention Also called *voluntary attention*. The voluntary direction of attention toward specific aspects of the environment, in accordance with our interests and goals. Compare *exogenous attention*. [14]

endogenous ligand Any substance, produced within the body, that selectively binds to the type of receptor that is under study. Compare *exogenous ligand*.

endogenous opioid Any of a class of opium-like peptide transmitters that have been called the body's own narcotics. The three kinds are enkephalins, endorphins, and dynorphins. See Table 4.1. [4]

endorphin One of the three kinds of endogenous opioids. Compare *dynorphin* and *enkephalin*. See Table 4.1. [4, 5]

endotherm An animal whose body temperature is regulated chiefly by internal metabolic processes. Examples include mammals and birds. Compare *ectotherm*. [9]

enkephalin One of the three kinds of endogenous opioids. Compare *dynorphin* and *endorphin*. See Table 4.1. [4]

enriched condition (EC) Also called *complex environment*. An environment for laboratory rodents in which animals are group-housed with a wide variety of stimulus objects. See Figure 13.16. Compare *impoverished condition* and *standard condition*. [13]

entrainment The process of synchronizing a biological rhythm to an environmental stimulus. See Figure 10.2. [10]

enzyme A complicated protein whose action increases the probability of a specific chemical reaction. [App]

ependymal layer See *ventricular zone*. [13]

epigenetic regulation Changes in gene expression that are due to environmental effects rather than to changes in the nucleotide sequence of the gene. [11]

epigenetics The study of factors that affect gene expression without making any changes in the nucleotide sequence of the genes themselves. [1, 13]

epilepsy A brain disorder marked by major, sudden changes in the electrophysiological state of the brain that are referred to as seizures. See Figure 3.16. [3]

epinephrine Also called *adrenaline*. A compound that acts both as a hormone (secreted by the adrenal medulla under the control of the sympathetic nervous system) and as a synaptic transmitter. See Tables 4.1, 8.1. [11]

episodic memory Also called *autobiographical memory*. Memory of a particular incident or a particular time and place. Compare *semantic memory*. [13]

EPSP See *excitatory postsynaptic potential*. [3]

equilibrium potential The point at which the movement of ions across the cell membrane is balanced, as the electrostatic pressure pulling ions in one direction is offset by the diffusion force pushing them in the opposite direction. [3]

ERP See *event-related potential*. [3, 14]

estradiol The primary type of estrogen that is secreted by the ovary. Its formal name is *17-beta-estradiol*. [8]

estrogen Any of a class of steroid hormones produced by female gonads. See Figure 8.13. [8]

estrus The period during which female animals are sexually receptive. [8]

eukaryote Any organism whose cells have the genetic material contained within a nuclear envelope. [App]

event-related potential (ERP) Also called *evoked potential*. Averaged EEG recordings measuring brain responses to repeated presentations of a stimulus. Components of the ERP tend to be reliable because the background noise of the cortex has been averaged out. See Figures 3.15, 14.6. [3, 14]

evoked potential See *event-related potential*. [3, 14]

evolution by natural selection The Darwinian theory that evolution proceeds by differential success in reproduction.

evolutionary psychology A field of study devoted to asking how natural selection has shaped behavior in humans and other animals. [1, 11]

excitatory postsynaptic potential (EPSP) A depolarizing potential in the postsynaptic neuron that is caused by excitatory presynaptic potentials. EPSPs increase the probability that the postsynaptic neuron will fire an action potential. See Figure 3.9. Compare *inhibitory postsynaptic potential*. [3]

excitotoxicity The property by which neurons die when overstimulated, as with large amounts of glutamate. [ASF 15.5]

executive function A neural and cognitive system that helps develop plans of action and organizes the activities of other high-level processing systems. [14]

exhaustion stage A stage in the response to stress that is caused by prolonged or frequently repeated stress and is characterized by increased susceptibility to disease. [11]

exocytosis A cellular process that results in the release of a substance into the extracellular space. [4]

exogenous Arising from outside the body. Compare *endogenous*. [4]

exogenous attention Also called *reflexive attention*. The involuntary reorienting of attention toward a specific stimulus source, cued by an unexpected object or event. Compare *endogenous attention*. [14]

exogenous ligand Any substance, originating from outside the body, that selectively binds to the type of receptor that is under study. Compare *endogenous ligand*.

expression See *gene expression*. [1, 13, App]

external ear The part of the ear that we readily see (the pinna) and the canal that leads to the eardrum. See Figure 6.1.

extracellular compartment The fluid space of the body that exists outside the cells. See Figure 9.7. Compare *intracellular compartment*. [9]

extracellular fluid The fluid in the spaces between cells (interstitial fluid) and in the vascular system. Compare *intracellular fluid*. [3]

extraocular muscle One of the muscles attached to the eyeball that control its position and movements. [7]

extrapyramidal system A motor system that includes the basal ganglia and some closely related brainstem structures. Axons of this system pass into the spinal cord outside the pyramids of the medulla. Compare *pyramidal system*. [5]

extrastriate cortex Visual cortex outside of the primary visual (striate) cortex. [7]

F

face blindness See *prosopagnosia*. [15]

facial feedback hypothesis The idea that sensory feedback from our facial expressions can affect our mood. [11]

fat See *lipid*. [9]

fat tissue See *adipose tissue*. [9]

fatal familial insomnia An inherited disorder in which humans sleep normally at the beginning of their life but in midlife stop sleeping and, 7–24 months later, die. See Box 10.1. [10]

fear conditioning A form of classical conditioning in which a previously neutral stimulus is repeatedly paired with an unpleasant stimulus, like foot shock, until the previously neutral stimulus alone elicits the responses seen in fear. [11, 12]

feature search A search for an item in which the target pops out right away, because it possesses a unique attribute, no matter how many distracters are present. Compare *conjunction search*. [14]

FEF See *frontal eye field*. [14]

fetal alcohol syndrome A disorder, including intellectual disability and characteristic facial abnormalities, that affects children exposed to too much alcohol (through maternal ingestion) during fetal development. [4]

fetus A developing individual after the embryo stage. Humans are considered to be fetuses from 10 weeks after fertilization until birth. Compare *embryo*. [13]

final common pathway The motoneurons of the spinal cord, so called because they receive and integrate all motor signals from the brain and then direct movement accordingly. [5]

flavor The sense of taste combined with the sense of smell. Compare *taste*. [6]

fluent aphasia Also called *Wernicke's aphasia*. A language impairment characterized by fluent, meaningless speech and little language comprehension. It is related to damage in Wernicke's area. See Figure 15.6. Compare *nonfluent aphasia*. [15]

fMRI See *functional MRI*. [2]

follicle The structure of the ovary that contains immature ova. [8, ASF 8.4]

follicle-stimulating hormone (FSH) A gonadotropin, named for its actions on ovarian follicles. See Figure 8.13. [8, ASF 8.4]

forebrain The front division of the brain, which, in the mature vertebrate, contains the cerebral hemispheres, the thalamus, and the hypothalamus. See Figures 2.12, 13.24. Compare *hindbrain* and *midbrain*. [2, 13]

fornix A fiber tract that extends from the hippocampus to the mammillary body. See Figures 2.14, 2.16. [2]

Fourier analysis The analysis of a complex pattern into the sum of sine waves. [6, ASF 7.4]

fourth ventricle The passageway within the pons that receives cerebrospinal fluid from the third ventricle and releases it to surround the brain and spinal cord. See Figure 2.17. Compare *lateral ventricle* and *third ventricle*. [2]

fovea The central portion of the retina, which is packed with the highest density of photoreceptors and is the center of our gaze. See Figure 7.1. [7]

fragile X syndrome A condition that is a frequent cause of inherited intellectual disability; produced by a fragile site on the X chromosome that seems prone to breaking because the DNA there is unstable.

fraternal birth order effect A phenomenon in human populations, such that the more older biological brothers a boy has, the more likely he is to develop a homosexual orientation. [8]

free nerve ending An axon that terminates in the skin and has no specialized cell associated with it. Free nerve endings detect pain and/or changes in temperature. See Figure 5.4. [5]

free-running Referring to a rhythm of behavior shown by an animal deprived of external cues about time of day. See Figure 10.2. [10]

free will The feeling that our conscious self is the author of our actions and decisions. [14]

frequency The number of cycles per second in a sound wave, measured in hertz. See Box 6.1. [6]

frontal eye field (FEF) An area in the frontal lobe of the brain that contains neurons important for establishing gaze in accordance with cognitive goals (top-down processes) rather than with any characteristics of stimuli (bottom-up processes). [14]

frontal lobe The most anterior portion of the cerebral cortex. See Figure 2.10. Compare *occipital lobe*, *parietal lobe*, and *temporal lobe*. [2]

frontal plane See *coronal plane*. [2]

FSH See *follicle-stimulating hormone*. [8]

functional MRI (fMRI) Magnetic resonance imaging that detects changes in blood flow and therefore identifies regions of the brain that are particularly active during a given task. See Figure 2.18. Compare *positron emission tomography*. [2]

functional tolerance The form of drug tolerance that arises when repeated exposure to the drug causes receptors to be up-regulated or down-regulated. Compare *metabolic tolerance*. [4]

fundamental The predominant frequency of an auditory tone or a visual scene. Compare *harmonic*. See Box 6.1. [6]

fusiform gyrus A region on the inferior surface of the cortex, at the junction of the temporal and occipital lobes, that has been associated with recognition of faces. See Figure 15.17. [15]

G

GABA See *gamma-aminobutyric acid*. [4]

gamete A sex cell (sperm or ovum) that contains only unpaired chromosomes and therefore has only half of the usual number of chromosomes. [8]

gamma-aminobutyric acid (GABA) A widely distributed amino acid transmitter, and the main inhibitory transmitter in the mammalian nervous system. See Table 4.1. [4]

ganglion (pl. ganglia) A collection of nerve cell bodies outside the central nervous system. Compare *nucleus* (definition 1).

ganglion cell Any of a class of cells in the retina whose axons form the optic nerve. See Figure 7.14. Compare *amacrine cell*, *bipolar cell*, and *horizontal cell*. [7]

gap junction See *electrical synapse*. [3]

gas neurotransmitter A neurotransmitter that is a soluble gas. Examples include nitric oxide and carbon monoxide. Usually gas neurotransmitters act, in a retrograde fashion, on presynaptic neurons. See Table 4.1. Compare *amine neurotransmitter*, *amino acid neurotransmitter*, and *peptide neurotransmitter*. [4]

gel electrophoresis A method of separating molecules of differing size or electrical charge by forcing them to flow through a gel. See Appendix Figure A.3. [App]

gene A length of DNA that encodes the information for constructing a particular protein. [App]

gene amplification See *polymerase chain reaction*. [App]

gene expression The turning on or off of specific genes. The process by which a cell makes an mRNA transcript of a particular gene. [1, 13, App]

general anesthetic A drug that renders an individual unconscious. [10]

generator potential A local change in the resting potential of a receptor cell that mediates between the impact of stimuli and the initiation of action potentials. [5]

genital tubercle In the early fetus, a "bump" between the legs that can develop into either a clitoris or a penis. [8]

genome See *genotype*. [App]

genotype Also called *genome*. All the genetic information that one specific individual has inherited. Compare *phenotype*. [13, App]

GH See *growth hormone*. [8]

ghrelin A peptide hormone produced and released by the gut. See Figure 9.15. Compare PYY_{3-36}. [9]

glial cells Also called *glia*. Nonneuronal brain cells that provide structural, nutritional, and other types of support to the brain. See Figure 2.5. [2]

global aphasia The total loss of ability to understand language, or to speak, read, or write. See Figure 15.6. [15]

globus pallidus One of the basal ganglia. See Figure 2.14. [2]

glomerulus (pl. glomeruli) A complex arbor of dendrites from a group of olfactory cells. [6]

glucagon A pancreatic hormone that converts glycogen to glucose, and thus increases blood glucose. Compare *insulin*. [9]

glucocorticoid Any of a class of steroid hormones, released by the adrenal cortex, that affect carbohydrate metabolism and inflammation.

glucodetector A specialized type of liver cell that detects and informs the nervous system about levels of circulating glucose. [9]

glucose An important sugar molecule used by the body and brain for energy. [9]

glutamate An amino acid transmitter, the most common excitatory transmitter. See Table 4.1. [4, 13]

glutamate hypothesis The idea that schizophrenia may be caused, in part, by understimulation of glutamate receptors. [12]

glutamatergic Referring to cells that use glutamate as their synaptic transmitter.

glycine An amino acid transmitter, often inhibitory. See Table 4.1.

glycogen A complex carbohydrate made by the combining of glucose molecules for a short-term store of energy. [9]

GnRH See *gonadotropin-releasing hormone*. [8]

Golgi stain A tissue stain that fills a small proportion of neurons with a dark, silver-based precipitate. See Box 2.1. [2]

Golgi tendon organ Any of the receptors within tendons that send impulses to the

central nervous system when a muscle contracts. See Figure 5.21. Compare *muscle spindle*. [5]

gonad Any of the sexual organs (ovaries in females, testes in males), which produce gametes for reproduction. See Figure 8.1. [8]

gonadotropin An anterior pituitary hormone that selectively stimulates the cells of the gonads to produce sex steroids and gametes. See *luteinizing hormone* and *follicle-stimulating hormone*. [8, ASF 8.4]

gonadotropin-releasing hormone (GnRH) A hypothalamic hormone that controls the release of luteinizing hormone and follicle-stimulating hormone from the pituitary. See Figure 8.13. [8]

grammar All of the rules for usage of a particular language.

grand mal seizure A type of generalized epileptic seizure in which nerve cells fire in high-frequency bursts, usually accompanied by involuntary rhythmic contractions of the body. See Figure 3.16. Compare *petit mal seizure*. [3]

gray matter Areas of the brain that are dominated by cell bodies and are devoid of myelin. Gray matter mostly receives and processes information. See Figure 2.11. Compare *white matter*. [2]

gross neuroanatomy Anatomical features of the nervous system that are apparent to the naked eye. [2]

growth hormone (GH) Also called *somatotropin* or *somatotropic hormone*. A tropic hormone, secreted by the anterior pituitary, that influences the growth of cells and tissues. [8, ASF 8.4]

guevedoces Literally, "eggs at 12" (in Spanish). A nickname for individuals who are raised as girls but at puberty change appearance and begin behaving as boys. [8]

gustatory system The sensory system that detects taste. See Figure 6.17. [6]

gyrus (pl. gyri) A ridged or raised portion of a convoluted brain surface. Compare *sulcus*. [2]

H

habituation A form of nonassociative learning in which an organism becomes less responsive following repeated presentations of a stimulus. See Figure 13.19. [13]

hair cell One of the receptor cells for hearing in the cochlea. Displacement of hair cells by sound waves generates nerve impulses that travel to the brain. See Figures 6.1, 6.3. [6]

hallucinogen A drug that alters sensory perception and produces peculiar experiences. Compare *dissociative*. [4]

hard problem of consciousness Understanding the brain processes that produce people's subjective experiences of their conscious perceptions—that is, their qualia. Compare *easy problem of consciousness*. [14]

harmonic A multiple of a particular frequency called the *fundamental*. See Box 6.1. [6]

health psychology Also called *behavioral medicine*. A field of study that focuses on psychological influences on health-related processes, such as why people become ill or how they remain healthy. [11]

Hebbian synapse A synapse that is strengthened when it successfully drives the postsynaptic cell. [13, ASF 13.4]

hemiparesis Weakness of one side of the body. Compare *hemiplegia*. [15]

hemiplegia Partial paralysis involving one side of the body. Compare *hemiparesis*. [15]

hemispatial neglect Failure to pay any attention to objects presented to one side of the body. Patients exhibiting this symptom may even deny connection with that side. [14]

hermaphrodite An individual possessing the reproductive organs of both sexes, either simultaneously or at different points in time. [ASF 8.6]

heroin Diacetylmorphine; an artificially modified, very potent form of morphine. [4]

hertz (Hz) Cycles per second, as of an auditory stimulus. Hertz is a measure of frequency. See Box 6.1. [6]

high-functioning autism See *Asperger's syndrome*. [ASF 13.4]

hindbrain The rear division of the brain, which, in the mature vertebrate, contains the cerebellum, pons, and medulla. See Figures 2.12, 13.24. Compare *forebrain* and *midbrain*. [2, 13]

hippocampus (pl. hippocampi) A medial temporal lobe structure that is important for learning and memory. See Figures 2.14, 13.1, 13.21. [2, 13]

histology The study of tissue structure.

homeostasis The active process of maintaining a particular physiological parameter relatively constant. [9]

horizontal cell A specialized retinal cell that contacts both receptor cells and *bipolar cells*. Compare *amacrine cell* and *ganglion cell*. [7]

horizontal plane The plane that divides the body or brain into upper and lower parts. See Box 2.2. Compare *coronal plane* and *sagittal plane*. [2]

hormone A chemical secreted by an endocrine gland that is conveyed by the bloodstream and regulates target organs or tissues. See Table 8.1.

horseradish peroxidase (HRP) An enzyme found in horseradish and other plants that is used to determine the cells of origin of a particular set of axons. See Box 2.1. [2]

HRP See *horseradish peroxidase*. [2]

hue One of three basic dimensions of light perception, varying around the color circle through blue, green, yellow, orange, and red. See Figure 7.24. Compare *brightness* and *saturation*. [7]

hunger The internal state of an animal seeking food. Compare *satiety*.

huntingtin A protein produced by a gene (called *HTT*) that, when containing too many trinucleotide repeats, results in Huntington's disease in a carrier. [ASF 5.6]

Huntington's disease A genetic disorder, with onset in middle age, in which the destruction of basal ganglia results in a syndrome of abrupt, involuntary writhing movements and changes in mental functioning. Compare *Parkinson's disease*. [5]

hybridization The process by which one string of nucleotides becomes linked to a complementary series of nucleotides. [App]

hyperpolarization An increase in membrane potential (the interior of the neuron becomes even more negative). See Figure 3.5. Compare *depolarization*. [3]

hypertonic Referring to a solution with a higher concentration of salt than that found in interstitial fluid and blood plasma (more than about 0.9% salt). Compare *hypotonic* and *isotonic*.

hypocretin Also called *orexin*. A neuropeptide produced in the hypothalamus that is involved in switching between sleep states, in narcolepsy, and in the control of appetite. [9, 10]

hypofrontality hypothesis The idea that schizophrenia may reflect underactivation of the frontal lobes. [12]

hypothalamic-pituitary portal system An elaborate bed of blood vessels leading from the hypothalamus to the anterior pituitary. [8]

hypothalamus Part of the diencephalon, lying ventral to the thalamus. See Figures 2.12, 2.14, 2.16. [2]

hypotonic Referring to a solution with a lower concentration of salt than that found in interstitial fluid and blood plasma (less than about 0.9% salt). Compare *hypertonic* and *isotonic*.

hypovolemic thirst A desire to ingest fluids that is stimulated by a reduction in volume of the extracellular fluid. Compare *osmotic thirst*. [9]

Hz See *hertz*. [6]

I

IC See *impoverished condition*. [13]

ICC See *immunocytochemistry*. [2, 8, App]

iconic memory A very brief type of memory that stores the sensory impression of a scene. Compare *long-term memory* and *short-term memory*. See Figure 13.13. [13]

IEG See *immediate early gene*. [2]

IHC See *inner hair cell*. [6]

immediate early gene (IEG) A gene that shows rapid but temporary increases in expression in cells that have become activated. See Box 2.1. [2]

immunocytochemistry (ICC) A method for detecting a particular protein in tissues in which an antibody recognizes and binds to the protein and then chemical methods are used to leave a visible reaction product around each antibody. See Boxes 2.1, 8.1. [2, 8, App]

immunoglobulin See *antibody*. [11, App]

impoverished condition (IC) Also called *isolated condition*. An environment for laboratory rodents in which animals are housed singly in a small cage without complex stimuli. See Figure 13.16. Compare *enriched condition* and *standard condition*. [13]

***in situ* hybridization** A method for detecting particular RNA transcripts in tissue sections by providing a nucleotide probe that is complementary to, and will therefore hybridize with, the transcript of interest. See Box 2.1; Appendix Figure A.4. [2, 8, App]

in vitro Literally, "in glass" (in Latin). Usually, in a laboratory dish; outside the body.

inattentional blindness The failure to perceive nonattended stimuli that seem so obvious as to be impossible to miss. [14]

incus Latin for "anvil." A middle-ear bone situated between the *malleus* (attached to the tympanic membrane) and the *stapes* (attached to the cochlea). It is one of the three ossicles that conduct sound across the middle ear. See Figure 6.1. [6]

independent variable The factor that is manipulated by an experimenter. Compare *dependent variable*. [1]

indifferent gonads The undifferentiated gonads of the early mammalian fetus, which will eventually develop into either testes or ovaries. See Figure 8.24. See also *gonads*.

indoleamines A class of monoamines that serve as neurotransmitters, including serotonin and melatonin. See Table 4.1.

inferior In anatomy, below. See Box 2.2. Compare *superior*. [2]

inferior colliculi (sing. colliculus) Paired gray matter structures of the dorsal midbrain that process auditory information. See Figure 2.16. Compare *superior colliculi*. [2, 6]

infradian Referring to a rhythmic biological event whose period is longer than that of a circadian rhythm—that is, longer than a day. Compare *ultradian*. [10]

infrasound Very low frequency sound; in general, below the threshold for human hearing, at about 20 Hz. Compare *ultrasound*. [6]

infundibulum See *pituitary stalk*. [8]

inhibition of return The phenomenon, observed in peripheral spatial cuing tasks and occurring when the interval between cue and target stimulus is 200 milliseconds or more, in which the detection of stimuli at the former location of the cue is increasingly impaired. [14]

inhibitory postsynaptic potential (IPSP) A hyperpolarizing potential in the postsynaptic neuron that is caused by inhibitory connections. IPSPs decrease the probability that the postsynaptic neuron will fire an action potential. See Figure 3.9. Compare *excitatory postsynaptic potential*. [3]

inner ear The cochlea and vestibular apparatus. See Figure 6.1. [6]

inner hair cell (IHC) One of the two types of receptor cells for hearing in the cochlea. Compared to *outer hair cells*, IHCs are positioned closer to the central axis of the coiled cochlea. See Figure 6.1. [6]

innervate To provide neural input to. [2]

input zone The part of a neuron that receives information, from other neurons or from specialized sensory structures. This zone usually corresponds to the cell's *dendrites*. See Figures 2.1, 2.3. Compare *conduction zone*, *integration zone*, and *output zone*. [2]

instrumental conditioning Also called *operant conditioning*. A form of associative learning in which the likelihood that an act (instrumental response) will be performed depends on the consequences (reinforcing stimuli) that follow it. Compare *classical conditioning*. [13]

insula A region of cortex lying below the surface, within the lateral sulcus, of the frontal, temporal, and parietal lobes. [4]

insulin A pancreatic hormone that lowers blood glucose, promotes energy storage, and facilitates glucose utilization by cells. Compare *glucagon*. [9]

integration zone The part of a neuron that initiates nerve electrical activity. This zone usually corresponds to the neuron's *cell body*. See Figures 2.1, 2.3. Compare *conduction zone*, *input zone*, and *output zone*. [2]

intensity See *amplitude*. [6]

intensity difference A perceived difference in loudness between the two ears, which the nervous system can use to localize a sound source. Compare *latency difference*. [6]

intermale aggression Aggression between males of the same species. [11]

interneuron A nerve cell that is neither a sensory neuron nor a motoneuron; interneurons receive input from and send output to other neurons. Compare *motoneuron* and *sensory neuron*. [2]

intersex Referring to an individual with atypical genital development and sexual differentiation that generally resembles a form intermediate between typical male and typical female genitals. [8]

intracellular compartment The fluid space of the body that is contained within cells. See Figure 9.7. Compare *extracellular compartment*. [9]

intracellular fluid Also called *cytoplasm*. The watery solution found within cells. Compare *extracellullar fluid*. [3]

intrafusal fiber Any of the small muscle fibers that lie within each muscle spindle. See Figure 5.21. [5]

intraparietal sulcus (IPS) A region in the human parietal lobe, homologous to the monkey *lateral intraparietal area*, that is especially involved in voluntary, top-down control of attention. [14]

intrinsic activity See *efficacy*. [4]

intromission Insertion of the erect penis into the vagina during copulation. [8]

inverse agonist A substance that binds to a receptor and causes it to do the opposite of what the naturally occurring transmitter does.

ion An atom or molecule that has acquired an electrical charge by gaining or losing one or more electrons. [3]

ion channel A pore in the cell membrane that permits the passage of certain ions through the membrane when the channels are open. See Figure 3.2. [3]

ionotropic receptor Also called *ligand-gated ion channel*. A receptor protein containing an ion channel that opens when the receptor is bound by an agonist. See Figure 4.2. Compare *metabotropic receptor*. [4]

IPS See *intraparietal sulcus*. [14]

ipsilateral In anatomy, pertaining to a location on the same side of the body. See Box 2.2. Compare *contralateral*. [2]

IPSP See *inhibitory postsynaptic potential*. [3]

iris (pl. irides) The circular structure of the eye that provides an opening to form the pupil. See Figure 7.1. [7]

isocortex See *neocortex*.

isolated brain An experimental preparation in which an animal's brainstem has been separated from the spinal cord by a cut below the medulla. Sometimes referred to by the French term, *encéphale isolé*. See Figure 10.22. Compare *isolated forebrain*. [10]

isolated condition See *impoverished condition*. [13]

isolated forebrain An experimental preparation in which an animal's nervous system has been cut in the upper midbrain, dividing the forebrain from the brainstem. Sometimes referred to by the French term, *cerveau isolé*. See Figure 10.22. Compare *isolated brain*. [10]

isotonic Referring to a solution with a concentration of salt that is the same as that found in interstitial fluid and blood plasma (about 0.9% salt). Compare *hypertonic* and *hypotonic*.

K

K complex A sharp, negative EEG potential that is seen in stage 2 sleep. [10]

kcal See *kilocalorie*. [9]

ketamine A dissociative anesthetic drug, similar to PCP, that acts as an NMDA receptor antagonist. [12]

ketone A compound, liberated by the breakdown of body fats and proteins, that is a metabolic fuel source. [9]

kilocalorie (kcal) A measure of energy commonly applied to food; formally defined as the quantity of heat required to raise the temperature of 1 kilogram of water by 1°C. [9]

Klüver-Bucy syndrome A condition, brought about by bilateral amygdala damage, that is characterized by dramatic emotional changes including reduction in fear and anxiety. [11]

knee jerk reflex A variant of the stretch reflex in which stretching of the tendon beneath the knee leads to an upward kick of the leg. See Figure 3.14. [3]

knockout organism An individual in which a particular gene has been disabled by an experimenter. See Box 8.1. [8]

Korsakoff's syndrome A memory disorder, related to a thiamine deficiency, that is generally associated with chronic alcoholism. It is commonly accompanied by confabulation. [13]

L

L-dopa The immediate precursor of the transmitter dopamine. It is known to markedly reduce symptoms in patients with Parkinson's, decreasing tremors and increasing the speed of movements. [ASF 5.6]

labeled lines The concept that each nerve input to the brain reports only a particular type of information. [5]

lamellated corpuscle See *Pacinian corpuscle*. [5]

late-selection model of attention A theory postulating that the attentional bottleneck imposed by the nervous system exerts control late in the processing pathway,

filtering out stimuli only after substantial analysis has occurred. Compare *early-selection model of attention*. [14]

latency difference A difference between the two ears in the time of arrival of a sound, which the nervous system can use to localize a sound source. Compare *intensity difference*. [6]

lateral In anatomy, toward the side of the body. See Box 2.2. Compare *medial*. [2]

lateral geniculate nucleus (LGN) The part of the thalamus that receives information from the optic tract and sends it to visual areas in the occipital cortex. [7]

lateral hypothalamus (LH) A hypothalamic region involved in the control of appetite and other functions. See Figure 9.12. [9]

lateral inhibition The phenomenon by which interconnected neurons inhibit their neighbors, producing contrast at the edges of regions. See Figure 7.14. [7]

lateral intraparietal area (LIP) A region in the monkey parietal lobe, homologous to the human *intraparietal sulcus*, that is especially involved in voluntary, top-down control of attention. [14]

lateral sulcus See *Sylvian fissure*. [2]

lateral tegmental area A brainstem region that provides some of the norepinephrine-containing projections of the brain. [4]

lateral ventricle A complexly shaped lateral portion of the ventricular system within each hemisphere of the brain. See Figures 2.15, 2.17. Compare *fourth ventricle* and *third ventricle*. [2]

lateralization The tendency for the right and left halves of a system to differ from one another.

LD$_{50}$ Lethal dose 50%; the dose of a drug at which half the treated animals will die. See Figure 4.6. Compare *ED$_{50}$*.

learned helplessness A learning paradigm in which individuals are subjected to inescapable, unpleasant conditions. [12]

learning The process of acquiring new and relatively enduring information, behavior patterns, or abilities, characterized by modifications of behavior as a result of practice, study, or experience. [13]

lens A structure in the eye that helps focus an image on the retina. See Figure 7.1. [7]

leptin A peptide hormone released by fat cells. [9]

lesion momentum The phenomenon in which the brain is impaired more by a lesion that develops quickly than by a lesion that develops slowly. [15]

levels of analysis The scope of experimental approaches. A scientist may try to understand behavior by monitoring molecules, nerve cells, brain regions, or social environments, or using some combination of these levels of analysis. [1]

LGN See *lateral geniculate nucleus.* [7]

LH 1. See *lateral hypothalamus.* [9] 2. See *luteinizing hormone.* [8, ASF 8.4]

lie detector See *polygraph.* [11]

ligand A substance that binds to receptor molecules, such as a neurotransmitter or drug that binds postsynaptic receptors. [3, 4]

ligand-gated ion channel See *ionotropic receptor.* [4]

limbic system A loosely defined, widespread group of brain nuclei that innervate each other to form a network. These nuclei are implicated in emotions. See Figure 2.14. [2, 11]

LIP See *lateral intraparietal area.* [14]

lipid A large molecule (commonly called a *fat*) that consists of fatty acids and glycerol that are insoluble in water. [9]

liposuction The surgical removal of fat tissue. [9]

lithium An element that, administered to patients, often relieves the symptoms of bipolar disorder. [12]

lobotomy The surgical separation of a portion of the frontal lobes from the rest of the brain, once used as a treatment for schizophrenia and many other ailments. [12]

local anesthetic A drug, such as procaine or lidocaine, that blocks sodium channels to stop neural transmission in pain fibers.

local potential An electrical potential that is initiated by stimulation at a specific site, which is a graded response that spreads passively across the cell membrane, decreasing in strength with time and distance. Postsynaptic potentials are a type of local potential. [3]

localization of function The concept that different brain regions specialize in specific behaviors. [1]

locus coeruleus A small nucleus in the brainstem whose neurons produce norepinephrine and modulate large areas of the forebrain. Compare *substantia nigra.* [4, 10]

long-term memory (LTM) An enduring form of memory that lasts days, weeks, months, or years and has a very large capacity. Compare *iconic memory* and *short-term memory.* See Figure 13.13. [13]

long-term potentiation (LTP) A stable and enduring increase in the effectiveness of synapses following repeated strong stimulation. See Figures 13.21, 13.22. [13]

lordosis A female receptive posture in four-legged animals in which the hindquarter is raised and the tail is turned to one side, facilitating intromission by the male. See Figures 8.17, 8.20. [8]

Lou Gehrig's disease See *amyotrophic lateral sclerosis.* [ASF 5.6]

LSD Also called *acid.* Lysergic acid diethylamide, a hallucinogenic drug. [4]

LTM See *long-term memory.* [13]

LTP See *long-term potentiation.* [13]

lumbar Referring to the 5 spinal segments that make up the upper part of the lower back. See Figures 2.8, 2.9. Compare *cervical,* *thoracic,* *sacral,* and *coccygeal.* [2]

luteinizing hormone (LH) A gonadotropin, named for its stimulatory effects on the ovarian corpora lutea. See Figure 8.13. [8, ASF 8.4]

lysergic acid diethylamide See *LSD.* [4]

M

M1 See *primary motor cortex.* [5]

magnetic resonance imaging (MRI) A noninvasive technique for examining brain structure that uses magnetic energy to generate images that reveal some structural details in the living brain. See Figures 1.5, 2.18. Compare *computerized axial tomography.* [2]

magnetoencephalography (MEG) A passive and noninvasive technique for examining brain function that measures the tiny magnetic fields produced by active neurons, in order to identify regions of the brain that are particularly active during a given task. Compare *transcranial magnetic stimulation.* [2]

malleus Latin for "hammer." A middle-ear bone that is connected to the tympanic membrane. It is one of the three ossicles that conduct sound across the middle ear. See Figure 6.1. Compare *incus* and *stapes.* [6]

mammillary body One of a pair of limbic system structures that are connected to the hippocampus. See Figure 2.14. [13]

manic-depressive illness See *bipolar disorder.* [12]

MAO See *monoamine oxidase.* [4, ASF 4.1, 12]

marijuana A dried preparation of the *Cannabis sativa* plant, usually smoked to obtain THC. [4]

MD See *muscular dystrophy.* [ASF 5.6]

MDMA Also called *Ecstasy.* 3,4-Methylenedioxymethamphetamine, a drug of abuse. [4]

medial In anatomy, toward the middle of an organ or organism. See Box 2.2. Compare *lateral.* [2]

medial amygdala A portion of the amygdala that receives olfactory and pheromonal information. [8]

medial forebrain bundle A collection of axons traveling in the midline region of the forebrain. See Figure 4.17. [11]

medial geniculate nucleus Either of two nuclei—left and right—in the thalamus

that receive input from the inferior colliculi and send output to the auditory cortex. See Figure 6.6. [6]

medial preoptic area (mPOA) A region of the anterior hypothalamus implicated in the control of many behaviors, including thermoregulation, sexual behavior, and gonadotropin secretion. [8]

median eminence A midline feature on the base of the brain that marks the point at which the pituitary stalk exits the hypothalamus to connect to the pituitary. The median eminence contains elements of the hypothalamic-pituitary portal system. See Figure 8.12. [8]

medulla The posterior part of the hindbrain, continuous with the spinal cord. See Figures 2.12, 2.16. [2]

MEG See *magnetoencephalography.* [2]

Meissner's corpuscle Also called *tactile corpuscle.* A skin receptor cell type that detects light touch, responding especially to changes in stimuli. See Figures 5.4, 5.5. Compare *Merkel's disc,* *Pacinian corpuscle,* and *Ruffini corpuscle.* [5]

melanopsin A photopigment found within particular retinal ganglion cells that project to the suprachiasmatic nucleus. See Figure 10.6. [10]

melatonin An amine hormone that is secreted by the pineal gland at night. See Table 4.1. [10, ASF 8.1]

memory 1. The ability to retain information, based on the mental process of learning or encoding, retention across some interval of time (consolidation), and retrieval or reactivation of the memory. 2. The specific information that is stored in the brain. [13]

memory trace A persistent change in the brain that reflects the storage of memory. [13]

meninges The three protective membranes—dura mater, pia mater, and arachnoid—that surround the brain and spinal cord. See Figure 2.8. [2]

meningioma A noninvasive tumor of the meninges. [2]

meningitis An acute inflammation of the meninges, usually caused by a viral or bacterial infection. [2]

Merkel's disc A skin receptor cell type that detects light touch, responding especially to edges and isolated points on a surface. See Figures 5.4, 5.5. Compare *Meissner's corpuscle,* *Pacinian corpuscle,* and *Ruffini corpuscle.* [5]

message See *messenger RNA.* [App]

messenger RNA (mRNA) Also called *transcript* or *message.* A strand of RNA that carries the code of a section of a DNA strand to the cytoplasm. See the Appendix. [App]

metabolic tolerance The form of drug tolerance that arises when repeated exposure to the drug causes the metabolic machinery of the body to become more efficient at clearing the drug. Compare *functional tolerance*. [4]

metabolism The breakdown of complex molecules into smaller molecules. [ASF 9.1]

metabotropic receptor A receptor protein that does not contain ion channels but may, when activated, use a G protein system to open nearby ion channels or to produce other cellular effects. See Figure 4.2. Compare *ionotropic receptor*. [4]

methylation A chemical modification of DNA that does not affect the nucleotide sequence of a gene but makes that gene less likely to be expressed. [13]

microelectrode An especially small electrode used to record electrical potentials in living cells. [3]

microglial cells Also called *microglia*. Extremely small glial cells that remove cellular debris from injured or dead cells. [2]

midbrain The middle division of the brain. See Figures 2.12, 13.24. Compare *forebrain* and *hindbrain*. [2, 13]

middle canal Also called *scala media*. The central of the three spiraling canals inside the cochlea, situated between the *vestibular canal* and the *tympanic canal*. See Figure 6.1.

middle cerebral artery Either of two large arteries, arising from the carotid arteries, that provide blood to most of the lateral surfaces of the cerebral hemispheres. Compare *anterior cerebral artery* and *posterior cerebral artery*. [ASF 2.1]

middle ear The cavity between the tympanic membrane and the cochlea. See Figure 6.1. [6]

milk letdown reflex The reflexive release of milk by the mammary glands of a nursing female in response to suckling, or to stimuli associated with suckling. The mechanism involves release of the hormone oxytocin. See Figure 8.9. [8]

millivolt (mV) A thousandth of a volt. [3]

mirror neuron A neuron that is active both when an individual makes a particular movement and when that individual sees another individual make the same movement. [5]

mitochondrion (pl. mitochondria) A cellular organelle that provides metabolic energy for the cell's processes. See Figure 2.4. [2]

mitosis The process of division of somatic cells that involves duplication of DNA. [13]

monaural Pertaining to one ear. Compare *binaural*.

monoamine hormone See *amine hormone*. [8]

monoamine oxidase (MAO) An enzyme that breaks down and thereby inactivates monoamine transmitters. [4, 12, ASF 4.1]

monocular deprivation Depriving one eye of form vision. Compare *binocular deprivation*. [ASF 13.4]

monopolar neuron See *unipolar neuron*. [2]

monozygotic Referring to twins derived from a single fertilized egg (*identical* twins). Such individuals share an identical set of genes. Compare *dizygotic*. [12]

morpheme The smallest grammatical unit of a language; a word or meaningful part of a word. [15]

morphine An opiate compound derived from the poppy flower. [4]

motion sickness The experience of nausea brought on by unnatural passive movement, as in a car or boat. [6]

motivation The psychological process that induces or sustains a particular behavior. [9]

motoneuron Also called *motor neuron*. A neuron that transmits neural messages to muscles (or glands). See Figure 5.20. Compare *interneuron* and *sensory neuron*. [2, 5]

motor nerve A nerve that transmits information from the central nervous system to the muscles and glands. Compare *sensory nerve*. [2]

motor neuron See *motoneuron*. [2]

motor plan Also called *motor program*. A plan for a series of muscular contractions, established in the nervous system prior to its execution. [5]

motor theory of language The theory of speech mechanisms proposing that the left-hemisphere language zones are motor control systems that are concerned with both the precise production and the perception of the extremely complex movements that go into speech. Compare *connectionist model of aphasia*. [15]

motor unit A single motor axon and all the muscle fibers that it innervates. [5]

movement A single relocation of a body part, usually resulting from a brief muscle contraction; less complex than an *act*. [5]

mPOA See *medial preoptic area*. [8]

MRI See *magnetic resonance imaging*. [2]

mRNA See *messenger RNA*. [App]

müllerian duct A duct system in the embryo that will develop into female reproductive structures (oviduct, uterus, and upper vagina) if testes are not present in the embryo. See Figure 8.24. Compare *wolffian duct*. [8]

müllerian regression hormone See *antimüllerian hormone*. [8]

multiple sclerosis Literally, "many scars"; a disorder characterized by the widespread degeneration of myelin. [2, 3, ASF 13.3]

multipolar neuron A nerve cell that has many dendrites and a single axon. See Figure 2.3. Compare *bipolar neuron* and *unipolar neuron*. [2]

multisensory See *polymodal*. [ASF 6.3]

muscarinic Referring to cholinergic receptors that respond to the chemical muscarine as well as to acetylcholine. Muscarinic receptors mediate chiefly the inhibitory activities of acetylcholine. Compare *nicotinic*.

muscle fiber Large, cylindrical cells, making up most of a muscle, that can contract in response to neurotransmitter released from a motoneuron. See Figures 5.20, 5.21. See also *intrafusal fiber*.

muscle spindle A muscle receptor that lies parallel to a muscle and sends impulses to the central nervous system when the muscle is stretched. See Figure 5.24. Compare *Golgi tendon organ*. [5]

muscular dystrophy (MD) A disease that leads to degeneration of and functional changes in muscles. [ASF 5.6]

musth An annual period of heightened aggressiveness and sexual activity in male elephants. [ASF 8.7]

mV See *millivolt*. [3]

myasthenia gravis A disorder characterized by a profound weakness of skeletal muscles; it is caused by a loss of acetylcholine receptors. [ASF 5.6]

myelin The fatty insulation around an axon, formed by glial cells. This sheath boosts the speed at which nerve impulses are conducted. See Figures 2.5, 3.8. [2, 3]

myelination The process by which myelin sheaths develop around axons. See Figure 2.5. [ASF 13.3]

myopia Nearsightedness; the inability to focus the retinal image of objects that are far away. [7]

N

N1 effect See *auditory N1 effect*. [14]

naloxone A potent antagonist of opiates that is often administered to people who have taken drug overdoses. It binds to receptors for endogenous opioids. [5]

narcolepsy A disorder that involves frequent, intense episodes of sleep, which last from 5 to 30 minutes and can occur anytime during the usual waking hours. [10]

NE See *norepinephrine*. [11]

negative correlation A covariation of two measures in which one of the two usually goes up when the other goes down (and vice versa). Compare *positive correlation*. [1]

negative feedback The property by which some of the output of a system feeds back to reduce the effect of input signals. Compare *positive feedback*. [8, 9]

negative symptom In psychiatry, an abnormality that reflects insufficient functioning. Examples include emotional and social withdrawal, blunted affect, and slow and impoverished thought and speech. Compare *positive symptom*. [12]

neocortex Also called *isocortex* or simply *cortex*. Cerebral cortex that is made up of six distinct layers.

neonatal Referring to newborns. [8]

nerve A collection of axons bundled together outside of the central nervous system. See Figures 2.6, 2.7. Compare *tract*. [2]

nerve cell See *neuron*. [1, 2]

nerve fiber See *axon*. [2]

neural chain A simple kind of neural circuit in which neurons are attached linearly, end-to-end. [ASF 3.2]

neural groove In the developing embryo, the groove between the neural folds. See Figure 13.24.

neural plasticity Also called *neuroplasticity*. The ability of the nervous system to change in response to experience or the environment. [1, 2, 13]

neural tube An embryonic structure with subdivisions that correspond to the future forebrain, midbrain, and hindbrain. The cavity of this tube will include the cerebral ventricles and the passages that connect them. See Figure 13.24. [2, 13]

neuroeconomics The study of brain mechanisms at work during economic decision making. [1, 14]

neuroendocrine cell Also called *neurosecretory cell*. A neuron that releases hormones into local or systemic circulation. [8]

neurofibrillary tangle An abnormal whorl of neurofilaments within nerve cells that is seen in Alzheimer's disease. See Figure 13.34. [13]

neurogenesis The mitotic division of nonneuronal cells to produce neurons. See Figure 13.25. [13]

neuroleptic Also called *antipsychotic*. Any of a class of drugs that alleviate symptoms of schizophrenia, typically by blocking dopamine receptors. [4, 12]

neuromuscular junction The region where the motoneuron terminal and the adjoining muscle fiber meet; the point where the nerve transmits its message to the muscle fiber. [5]

neuron Also called *nerve cell*. The basic unit of the nervous system, each composed of receptive extensions called dendrites, an integrating cell body, a conducting axon, and a transmitting axon terminal. See Figures 2.2, 2.3. [1, 2]

neuron doctrine The hypothesis that the brain is composed of separate cells that are distinct structurally, metabolically, and functionally.

neuropathic pain Pain that persists long after the injury that started it has healed. It is caused by damage to peripheral nerves and is often difficult to treat. [5]

neuropeptide See *peptide transmitter*. [4]

neurophysiology The study of the life processes of neurons. [3]

neuroplasticity See *neural plasticity*. [1, 2, 13]

neuroscience The scientific study of the nervous system. [1]

neurosecretory cell See *neuroendocrine cell*. [8]

neurotransmitter Also called simply *transmitter*. A signaling chemical, released by a presynaptic neuron, that diffuses across the synaptic cleft to alter the functioning of the postsynaptic neuron. See Figure 3.11; Table 4.1. [2, 3, 4]

neurotransmitter receptor Also called simply *receptor*. A protein that captures and reacts to molecules of a neurotransmitter or hormone. [2, 3, 4]

neurotrophic factor Also called *trophic factor*. A target-derived chemical that acts as if it "feeds" certain neurons to help them survive. See Figure 13.28. [13]

nicotine A compound found in plants, including tobacco, that acts as an agonist on a large class of cholinergic receptors. [4]

nicotinic Referring to cholinergic receptors that respond to nicotine as well as to acetylcholine. Nicotinic receptors mediate chiefly the excitatory activities of acetylcholine, including at the neuromuscular junction. Compare *muscarinic*.

night terror A sudden arousal from stage 3 sleep that is marked by intense fear and autonomic activation. Compare *nightmare*. [10]

nightmare A long, frightening dream that awakens the sleeper from REM sleep. Compare *night terror*. [10]

Nissl stain A tissue stain that outlines all cell bodies because the dyes are attracted to RNA, which encircles the nucleus. See Box 2.1. [2]

NMDA receptor A glutamate receptor that also binds the glutamate agonist NMDA (*N*-methyl-D-aspartate), and that is both ligand-gated and voltage-sensitive, so it can participate in a wide variety of information processing. Compare *AMPA receptor*. [13, ASF 4.2]

nociceptor A receptor that responds to stimuli (e.g., pain or changes in temperature) that produce tissue damage or pose the threat of damage. [5]

nocturnal Active during the dark periods of the daily cycle. Compare *diurnal*. [10]

node of Ranvier A gap between successive segments of the myelin sheath where the axon membrane is exposed. See Figures 2.5, 3.8. [2, 3]

nonassociative learning A type of learning in which presentation of a particular stimulus alters the strength or probability of a response according to the strength and temporal spacing of that stimulus. It includes habituation and sensitization. See Figure 13.19. Compare *associative learning*. [13]

noncompetitive ligand A drug that affects a transmitter receptor while binding at a site other than that bound by the endogenous ligand.

nondeclarative memory Also called *procedural memory*. A memory that is shown by performance rather than by conscious recollection. See Figures 13.4, 13.12. Compare *declarative memory*. [13]

nonfluent aphasia Also called *Broca's aphasia*. A language impairment characterized by difficulty with speech production but not with language comprehension. It is related to damage in Broca's area. See Figure 15.6. Compare *fluent aphasia*. [15]

nonprimary motor cortex Frontal lobe regions adjacent to the primary motor cortex that contribute to motor control and modulate the activity of the *primary motor cortex*. See Figure 5.26. [5]

nonprimary sensory cortex Also called *secondary sensory cortex*. For a given sensory modality, the cortical regions receiving direct projections from primary sensory cortex for that modality. Compare *primary sensory cortex*. [5]

non-REM sleep See *slow-wave sleep*. [10]

noradrenaline See *norepinephrine*. [4, 11]

noradrenergic Referring to cells using norepinephrine (noradrenaline) as a transmitter. [4]

norepinephrine (NE) Also called *noradrenaline*. A neurotransmitter that is produced and released by sympathetic postganglionic neurons to accelerate organ activity. It is also produced in the brainstem and found in projections throughout the brain. See Figure 4.4; Table 4.1. [4, 11]

Northern blot A method of detecting a particular RNA transcript in a tissue or organ, by separating RNA from that source with gel electrophoresis, blotting the separated RNA molecules onto nitrocellulose, and then using a nucleotide probe to hybridize with, and highlight, the transcript of interest. Compare *Southern blot* and *Western blot*. [App]

notochord A midline structure arising early in the embryonic development of vertebrates. See Figure 13.24.

NPY neuron A neuron, involved in the hypothalamic appetite control system, that produces both neuropeptide Y and agouti-related peptide. Compare *POMC neuron*. [9]

NST See *nucleus of the solitary tract*. [9]

nucleotide A portion of a DNA or RNA molecule that is composed of a single base and the adjoining sugar-phosphate unit of the strand. [App]

nucleus (pl. nuclei) 1. A collection of neuronal cell bodies within the central nervous system (e.g., the caudate nucleus). Compare *ganglion*. [2] 2. See *cell nucleus*. [App]

nucleus accumbens A region of the forebrain that receives dopaminergic innervation from the ventral tegmental area. Dopamine release in this region may mediate the reinforcing qualities of many activities, including drug abuse. [4, 11]

nucleus of the solitary tract (NST) A complicated brainstem nucleus that receives visceral and taste information via several cranial nerves. See Figure 9.15. [9]

nutrient A chemical that is needed for growth, maintenance, and repair of the body but is not used as a source of energy. [9]

O

obsessive-compulsive disorder (OCD) An anxiety disorder in which the affected individual experiences recurrent unwanted thoughts and engages in repetitive behaviors without reason or the ability to stop. [12]

occipital cortex Also called *visual cortex*. The cortex of the occipital lobe of the brain. See Figure 7.10. [7]

occipital lobe A large region of cortex that covers much of the posterior part of each cerebral hemisphere. It is specialized for visual processing. See Figure 2.10. Compare *frontal lobe, parietal lobe,* and *temporal lobe*. [2]

OCD See *obsessive-compulsive disorder*. [12]

ocular dominance column A region of cortex in which one eye or the other provides a greater degree of synaptic input. [ASF 7.3]

ocular dominance histogram A graph that plots how strongly a brain neuron responds to stimuli presented to either the left eye or the right eye. Ocular dominance histograms are used to determine the effects of manipulating visual experience. [ASF 13.4]

ocular dominance slab A slab of visual cortex, about 0.5 millimeters wide, in which the neurons of all layers respond preferentially to stimulation of one eye. [ASF 7.3]

odor The sensation of smell. [6]

off-center bipolar cell A retinal bipolar cell that is inhibited by light in the center of its receptive field. See Figures 7.12, 7.13. Compare *on-center bipolar cell*. [7]

off-center ganglion cell A retinal ganglion cell that is activated when light is presented to the periphery, rather than the center, of the cell's receptive field. See Figures 7.12, 7.13. Compare *on-center ganglion cell*. [7]

off-center/on-surround Referring to a concentric receptive field in which stimulation of the center inhibits the cell of interest while stimulation of the surround excites it. See Figure 7.13. Compare *on-center/off-surround*. [7]

OHC See *outer hair cell*. [6]

olfaction The sensory system that detects smell; the act of smelling. [6]

olfactory bulb An anterior projection of the brain that terminates in the upper nasal passages and, through small openings in the skull, provides receptors for smell. See Figures 2.10, 2.16, 6.19. [2, 6]

olfactory epithelium (pl. epithelia) A sheet of cells, including olfactory receptors, that lines the dorsal portion of the nasal cavities and adjacent regions, including the septum that separates the left and right nasal cavities. See Figures 6.18, 6.19. [6]

oligodendrocyte A type of glial cell that forms myelin in the central nervous system. See Figure 2.5. Compare *Schwann cell*. [2]

on-center bipolar cell A retinal bipolar cell that is excited by light in the center of its receptive field. See Figures 7.12, 7.13. Compare *off-center bipolar cell*. [7]

on-center ganglion cell A retinal ganglion cell that is activated when light is presented to the center, rather than the periphery, of the cell's receptive field. See Figures 7.12, 7.13. Compare *off-center ganglion cell*. [7]

on-center/off-surround Referring to a concentric receptive field in which stimulation of the center excites the cell of interest while stimulation of the surround inhibits it. See Figure 7.13. Compare *off-center/on-surround*. [7]

ontogeny The process by which an individual changes in the course of its lifetime—that is, grows up and grows old. [1]

Onuf's nucleus The human homolog of the *spinal nucleus of the bulbocavernosus* in rats. [8]

open-loop motor control A control mechanism in which feedback from the output of the system is not provided to the input control. Compare *closed-loop motor control*. [5]

operant conditioning See *instrumental conditioning*. [13]

opiate Any of a class of compounds that exert an effect like that of opium, including reduced pain sensitivity. Compare *opioids*.

opioid Any of a class of peptides produced in various regions of the brain that bind to opioid receptors and act like *opiates*.

opioid peptide A type of endogenous peptide that mimics the effects of morphine in binding to opioid receptors and producing marked analgesia and reward. See Table 4.1. [4]

opioid receptor A receptor that responds to endogenous opioids and/or exogenous opiates. [4]

opium An extract of the seedpod juice of the opium poppy, *Papaver somniferum*. Drugs based on opium are potent painkillers. [4]

opponent-process hypothesis A hypothesis of color perception stating that different systems produce opposite responses to light of different wavelengths. See Figures 7.23, 7.25. [7]

opsin One of the two components of photopigments in the retina. The other is RETINAL. [ASF 7.2]

optic ataxia Spatial disorientation in which the patient is unable to accurately reach for objects using visual guidance. [7]

optic chiasm The point at which the two optic nerves meet. See Figure 7.10. [7]

optic disc The region of the retina that is devoid of receptor cells because ganglion cell axons and blood vessels exit the eyeball there. See Figure 7.7. [7]

optic nerve Cranial nerve II; the collection of ganglion cell axons that extend from the retina to the brain. See Figures 2.7, 7.10. [7]

optic radiation Axons from the lateral geniculate nucleus that terminate in the primary visual areas of the occipital cortex. See Figure 7.10. [7]

optic tract The axons of retinal ganglion cells after they have passed the optic chiasm; most of these axons terminate in the lateral geniculate nucleus. See Figure 7.10. [7]

oral contraceptive A birth control pill, typically consisting of steroid hormones to prevent ovulation. [8]

orexin See *hypocretin*. [10]

organ of Corti A structure in the inner ear that lies on the basilar membrane of the cochlea and contains the hair cells and terminations of the auditory nerve. See Figure 6.1. [6]

organizational effect A permanent alteration of the nervous system, and thus permanent change in behavior, resulting from the action of a steroid hormone on an animal early in its development. Compare *activational effect*. [8]

orgasm The climax of sexual behavior, marked by extremely pleasurable sensations. [8]

orientation column A column of visual cortex that responds to rod-shaped stimuli of a particular orientation. [ASF 7.3]

osmosensory neuron A specialized neuron that monitors the concentration of the extracellular fluid by measuring the movement of water into and out of the intracellular compartment. See Figures 9.7, 9.9. [9]

osmosis The passive movement of a solvent, usually water, through a semipermeable membrane until a uniform concentration of solute (often salt) is achieved on both sides of the membrane. See Figure 9.6. Compare *diffusion*. [9]

osmotic pressure The tendency of a solvent to move across a membrane in order to equalize the concentration of solute on both sides of the membrane. [9]

osmotic thirst A desire to ingest fluids that is stimulated by loss of water from the extracellular compartment. Compare *hypovolemic thirst*. [9]

ossicles Three small bones (incus, malleus, and stapes) that transmit vibrations across the middle ear, from the tympanic membrane to the oval window. See Figure 6.1. [6]

otolith A small crystal on the gelatinous membrane in the vestibular system.

outer hair cell (OHC) One of the two types of receptor cells for hearing in the cochlea. Compared to *inner hair cells*, OHCs are positioned farther from the central axis of the coiled cochlea. See Figure 6.1. [6]

output zone The part of a neuron at which the cell sends information to another cell. This zone usually corresponds to the *axon terminals*. See Figures 2.1, 2.3. Compare *conduction zone*, *input zone*, and *integration zone*. [2]

oval window The opening from the middle ear to the inner ear. See Figure 6.1. [6]

ovaries The female gonads, which produce eggs (ova) for reproduction. See Figure 8.1. Compare *testes*. [8]

overt attention Attention in which the focus coincides with sensory orientation (e.g., you're attending to the same thing you're looking at). Compare *covert attention*. [14]

ovulation The production and release of an egg (ovum). [8]

ovulatory cycle The periodic occurrence of ovulation in females. See Figure 8.19. [8]

ovum (pl. ova) An egg, the female gamete. Compare *sperm*. [8]

oxytocin A hormone, released from the posterior pituitary, that triggers milk letdown in the nursing female. See Figures 8.8, 8.9. [8]

P

P1 effect See *visual P1 effect*. [14]

P3 effect A positive deflection of the event-related potential, occurring about 300 milliseconds after stimulus presentation, that is associated with higher-order auditory stimulus processing and late attentional selection. P3 is also called *auditory P300*. [14]

P20–50 effect A positive deflection of the event-related potential, occurring about 20–50 milliseconds after stimulus presentation, that is enhanced for selectively attended auditory input compared to ignored input. [14]

Pacinian corpuscle Also called *lamellated corpuscle*. A skin receptor cell type that detects vibration and pressure. See Figures 5.4, 5.5. Compare *Meissner's corpuscle*, *Merkel's disc*, and *Ruffini corpuscle*. [5]

pain The discomfort normally associated with tissue damage. [5]

pair-bond A durable and exclusive relationship between a male and a female. [8]

Papez circuit A group of brain regions within the limbic system. [8]

papilla (pl. papillae) A small bump that projects from the surface of the tongue. Papillae contain most of the taste receptor cells. See Figure 6.14. [6]

parabiotic Referring to a surgical preparation that joins two animals to share a single blood supply. [8]

paradoxical sleep See *rapid-eye-movement sleep*. [10]

paraphasia A symptom of aphasia that is distinguished by the substitution of a word by a sound, an incorrect word, an unintended word, or a neologism (a meaningless word). [15]

parasympathetic nervous system The division of the autonomic nervous system that arises from both the cranial nerves and the sacral spinal cord. This division helps the body to relax, recuperate, and prepare for future action. See Figure 2.9. Compare *sympathetic nervous system*. [2, 11]

parental behavior Behavior of adult animals that has the goal of enhancing the well-being of their own offspring, often at some cost to the parents. [8]

paresis Muscular weakness, often the result of damage to motor cortex. Compare *plegia*. [5]

parietal lobe The large region of cortex lying between the *frontal* and *occipital lobes* in each cerebral hemisphere. See Figure 2.10. Compare also *temporal lobe*. [2]

parkin A protein that has been implicated in Parkinson's disease. [ASF 5.6]

Parkinson's disease A degenerative neurological disorder, characterized by tremors at rest, muscular rigidity, and reduction in voluntary movement, caused by loss of the dopaminergic neurons of the substantia nigra. Compare *Huntington's disease*. [5]

partial agonist A drug that, when bound to a receptor, has less effect than the endogenous ligand would. The term *partial antagonist* is equivalent.

patient H.M. A patient who, because of damage to medial temporal lobe structures, was unable to encode new declarative memories. Upon his death we learned his name was Henry Molaison. See Figure 13.1. [13]

patient K.C. A patient who sustained damage to the cortex that renders him unable to form and retrieve new episodic memories. [13]

patient N.A. A patient who is unable to encode new declarative memories, because of damage to the dorsomedial thalamus and the mammillary bodies. [13]

Pavlovian conditioning See *classical conditioning*. [13]

PCP See *phencyclidine*. [12]

PCR See *polymerase chain reaction*. [App]

penis The male phallus. Compare *clitoris*. [8]

peptide A short string of amino acids. Longer strings of amino acids are called *proteins*. [App]

peptide hormone See *protein hormone*. [8]

peptide neurotransmitter Also called *neuropeptide*. A neurotransmitter consisting of a short chain of amino acids. See Table 4.1. Compare *amine neurotransmitter*, *amino acid neurotransmitter*, and *gas neurotransmitter*. [4]

perceptual load The immediate processing demands presented by a stimulus. [14]

periaqueductal gray The neuronal body–rich region of the midbrain surrounding the cerebral aqueduct that connects the third and fourth ventricles; it is involved in pain perception. [4, 8]

period The interval of time between two similar points of successive cycles, such as sunset to sunset. [10]

peripheral nervous system The portion of the nervous system that includes all the nerves and neurons outside the brain and spinal cord. See Figures 2.6, 2.12. Compare *central nervous system*. [2]

peripheral spatial cuing A technique for testing exogenous attention in which a visual stimulus is preceded by a simple task-irrelevant sensory stimulus either in the location where the stimulus will appear or in an incorrect location. Compare *symbolic cuing*. [14]

perseverate To continue to show a behavior repeatedly. Perseveration is commonly seen in autism and in frontal lobe damage. [14, ASF 13.4]

PET See *positron emission tomography*. [2]

petit mal seizure Also called *absence attack*. A seizure that is characterized by a spike-and-wave EEG and often involves a loss of awareness and inability to recall events surrounding the seizure. See Figure 3.16. Compare *grand mal seizure*. [3]

phagocyte An immune system cell that engulfs invading molecules or microbes. [11]

phallus The clitoris or penis. [8]

phase shift A shift in the activity of a biological rhythm, typically provided by a synchronizing environmental stimulus. [10]

phasic receptor A receptor in which the frequency of action potentials drops rapidly as stimulation is maintained. Compare *tonic receptor*. [5]

phencyclidine (PCP) Also called *angel dust*. An anesthetic agent that is also a psychedelic drug. PCP makes many people feel dissociated from themselves and their environment. [12]

phenotype The sum of an individual's physical characteristics at one particular time. Compare *genotype*. [13]

phenylketonuria (PKU) An inherited disorder of protein metabolism in which the absence of an enzyme leads to a toxic buildup of certain compounds, causing intellectual disability. [13]

pheromone A chemical signal that is released outside the body of an animal and affects other members of the same species. See Figure 8.3. Compare *allomone*. [6, 8]

phoneme A sound that is produced for language. [15]

photopic system A system in the retina that operates at high levels of light, shows sensitivity to color, and involves the cones. See Table 7.1. Compare *scotopic system*. [7]

photoreceptor A neural cell in the retina that responds to light. [7]

photoreceptor adaptation The tendency of rods and cones to adjust their light sensitivity to match ambient levels of illumination. [7]

phrenology The belief that bumps on the skull reflect enlargements of brain regions responsible for certain behavioral faculties. See Figure 1.4. [1]

physiological psychology See *biological psychology*. [1]

pia mater The innermost of the three meninges that surround the brain and spinal cord. See also *dura mater* and *arachnoid*. See Figure 2.8. [2]

pineal gland A secretory gland in the brain midline that is the source of melatonin release. See Figure 8.1. [8, ASF 8.1]

pinna (pl. pinnae) The external part of the ear. [6]

pitch A dimension of auditory experience in which sounds vary from low to high.

pituitary gland Also called *hypophysis*. A small, complex endocrine gland located in a socket at the base of the skull. The *anterior pituitary* and *posterior pituitary* are separate in function. See Figures 2.16, 8.8, 8.12. [8]

pituitary stalk Also called *infundibulum*. A thin piece of tissue that connects the pituitary gland to the hypothalamus. [8]

PKU See *phenylketonuria*. [13]

place cell A neuron in the hippocampus that selectively fires when the animal is in a particular location. [13]

place coding Frequency discrimination in which the pitch of a sound is determined by the location of activated hair cells along the length of the basilar membrane. Compare *temporal coding*. [6]

place theory A theory of frequency discrimination stating that pitch perception depends on the place of maximal displacement of the basilar membrane produced by a sound. Compare *volley theory*.

placebo effect Relief of a symptom, such as pain, that results following a treatment that is known to be ineffective or inert. [5]

planum temporale An auditory region of superior temporal cortex. See Figure 15.15. [15]

plegia Paralysis, the loss of the ability to move. Compare *paresis*. [5]

polarized Exhibiting a difference in electrical charge between the inside and outside of the cell. [3]

poliovirus A virus that destroys motoneurons of the spinal cord and brainstem, causing permanent paralysis. [ASF 5.6]

polygraph Popularly known as a *lie detector*. A device that measures several bodily responses, such as heart rate and blood pressure. [11]

polymerase chain reaction (PCR) Also called *gene amplification*. A method for reproducing a particular RNA or DNA sequence manyfold, allowing amplification for sequencing or manipulating the sequence. [App]

polymodal Also called *multisensory*. Involving several sensory modalities. [ASf 6.3]

polymodal neuron A neuron upon which information from different sensory systems converges. [5]

POMC neuron A neuron, involved in the hypothalamic appetite control system, that produces both pro-opiomelanocortin and cocaine- and amphetamine-related transcript. Compare *NPY neuron*. [9]

pons The portion of the brainstem that connects the midbrain to the medulla. See Figures 2.12, 2.16. [2]

positive correlation A covariation of two measures in which they both usually increase together, or decrease together. Compare *negative correlation*. [1]

positive feedback The property by which some of the output of a system feeds back to increase the effect of input signals. Positive feedback is rare in biological systems. Compare *negative feedback*.

positive symptom In psychiatry, an abnormal behavioral state. Examples include hallucinations, delusions, and excited motor behavior. Compare *negative symptom*. [12]

positron emission tomography (PET) A technique for examining brain function that combines tomography with injections of radioactive substances used by the brain. Analysis of the metabolism of these substances reflects regional differences in brain activity. See Figure 2.18. Compare *functional MRI*. [2]

postcentral gyrus The strip of parietal cortex, just behind the central sulcus, that receives somatosensory information from the entire body. See Figure 2.10. Compare *precentral gyrus*. [2]

postcopulatory behavior The final stage in mating behavior. Species-specific postcopulatory behaviors include rolling (in the cat) and grooming (in the rat). See Figure 8.16. [8]

posterior Also called *caudal*. In anatomy, toward the tail end of an organism. See Box 2.2. Compare *anterior*. [2]

posterior cerebral artery Either of two large arteries, arising from the basilar artery, that provide blood to posterior aspects of the cerebral hemispheres, cerebellum, and brainstem. Compare *anterior cerebral artery* and *middle cerebral artery*. [ASF 2.1]

posterior pituitary Also called *neurohypophysis*. The rear division of the pituitary gland. See Figures 8.1, 8.8. Compare *anterior pituitary*. [8]

postganglionic Literally, "after the ganglion." Referring to neurons in the autonomic nervous system that run from the autonomic ganglia to various targets in the body. See Figure 2.9. Compare *preganglionic*.

postpartum depression A bout of depression that afflicts a woman either immediately before or after giving birth. [12]

postsynaptic Referring to the region of a synapse that receives and responds to neurotransmitter. See Figure 2.4. Compare *presynaptic*. [2, 3, 4]

postsynaptic membrane The specialized membrane on the surface of a nerve cell that receives information by responding to neurotransmitter from a presynaptic neuron. This membrane contains specialized receptor proteins that allow it to respond to neurotransmitter molecules. See Figure 2.4. Compare *presynaptic membrane*. [2]

postsynaptic potential A local potential that is initiated by stimulation at a synapse, can vary in amplitude, and spreads passively across the cell membrane, decreasing in strength with time and distance. Compare *all-or-none property*. [3]

posttraumatic stress disorder (PTSD) Formerly called *combat fatigue, war neurosis*, or *shell shock*. A disorder in which memories of an unpleasant episode repeatedly plague the victim. See Box 13.1. [12, 13]

potassium ion (K⁺) A potassium atom that carries a positive charge because it has lost one electron. [3]

precentral gyrus The strip of frontal cortex, just in front of the central sulcus, that is crucial for motor control. See Figure 2.10. Compare *postcentral gyrus*. [2, 5]

prefrontal cortex The anteriormost region of the frontal lobe. [14]

preganglionic Literally, "before the ganglion." Referring to neurons in the autonomic nervous system that run from the central nervous system to the autonomic ganglia. See Figure 2.9. Compare *postganglionic*. [2]

premotor cortex A region of nonprimary motor cortex just anterior to the primary motor cortex. See Figure 5.26. [5]

presenilin An enzyme that cleaves amyloid precursor protein, forming beta-amyloid, which can lead to Alzheimer's disease. See also *beta-secretase*. [ASF 13.5]

presynaptic Referring to the region of a synapse that releases neurotransmitter. See Figure 2.4. Compare *postsynaptic*. [2, 3, 4]

presynaptic membrane The specialized membrane on the axon terminal of a nerve cell that transmits information by releasing neurotransmitter. Vesicles bearing neurotransmitter can bind to this membrane and release their contents, thus affecting the *postsynaptic membrane*. See Figure 2.4. [2]

primacy effect The superior performance seen in a memory task for items at the start of a list; it is usually attributed to long-term memory. See Figure 13.14. Compare *recency effect*. [13]

primary motor cortex (M1) The apparent executive region for the initiation of movement; primarily the precentral gyrus. Compare *nonprimary motor cortex*. [5]

primary sensory cortex For a given sensory modality, the region of cortex that receives most of the information about that modality from the thalamus or, in the case of olfaction, directly from the secondary sensory neurons. Compare *nonprimary sensory cortex*. [5]

primary somatosensory cortex Also called *somatosensory 1*. The gyrus just posterior to the central sulcus where sensory receptors on the body surface are mapped. Primary cortex for receiving touch and pain information, in the parietal lobe. See Figures 5.8, 5.10. [5]

primary visual cortex (V1) Also called *striate cortex* or *area 17*. The region of the occipital cortex where most visual information first arrives. See Figures 7.10, 7.11, 7.19. [7]

priming Also called *repetition priming*. In memory, the phenomenon by which exposure to a stimulus facilitates subsequent responses to the same or a similar stimulus. [13]

probe In molecular biology, a manufactured sequence of DNA that is made to include a label (a colorful or radioactive molecule) that lets us track its location. [App]

procedural memory See *nondeclarative memory*. [13]

proceptive Referring to a state in which an animal advertises its readiness to mate through species-typical behaviors, such as ear wiggling in the female rat. [8]

progesterone The primary type of progestin that is secreted by the ovary. See Figure 8.13. [8]

progestin Any of a major class of steroid hormones that are produced by the ovary, including progesterone. See Figure 8.13. [8]

progressive supranuclear palsy (PSP) A rare, degenerative disease of the brain that begins with marked, persistent visual symptoms and leads to more widespread intellectual deterioration. [14]

prolactin A protein hormone, produced by the anterior pituitary, that promotes mammary development for lactation in female mammals. [ASF 8.4]

proprioception Body sense; information about the position and movement of the body that is sent to the brain. [5]

prosody The perception of emotional tone-of-voice aspects of language. [15]

prosopagnosia Also called *face blindness*. A condition characterized by the inability to recognize faces. [15]

protein A long string of amino acids. Proteins are the basic building material of organisms. Compare *peptide*. [App]

protein hormone Also called *peptide hormone*. A hormone that consists of a string of amino acids. Compare *amine hormone* and *steroid hormone*. [8]

proximal In anatomy, near the trunk or center of an organism. See Box 2.2. Compare *distal*. [2]

PSP See *progressive supranuclear palsy*. [14]

psychoneuroimmunology The study of the immune system and its interaction with the nervous system and behavior. [11]

psychopath An individual incapable of experiencing remorse. [11]

psychosocial dwarfism Reduced stature caused by stress early in life. See Box 8.2. [8]

psychosomatic medicine A field of study that emphasizes the role of psychological factors in disease. [11]

psychosurgery Surgery in which brain lesions are produced to modify severe psychiatric disorders.

psychotomimetic A drug that induces a state resembling schizophrenia. [12]

PTSD See *posttraumatic stress disorder*. [12, 13]

pulvinar In humans, the posterior portion of the thalamus. It is heavily involved in visual processing and direction of attention. [14]

punch-drunk See *chronic traumatic encephalopathy*. [15]

pupil The opening, formed by the iris, that allows light to enter the eye. See Figures 7.1, 7.6. [7]

pure tone A tone with a single frequency of vibration. See Box 6.1. [6]

Purkinje cell A type of large nerve cell in the cerebellar cortex.

putamen One of the basal ganglia. See Figure 2.14. [2]

pyramidal cell A type of large nerve cell that has a roughly pyramid-shaped cell body and is found in the cerebral cortex. See Figure 2.13. [2]

pyramidal system Also called *corticospinal system*. The motor system that includes neurons within the cerebral cortex and their axons, which form the pyramidal tract. See Figure 5.23. Compare *extrapyramidal system*. [5]

PYY₃₋₃₆ A peptide hormone, secreted by the intestines, that probably acts on hypothalamic appetite control mechanisms to suppress appetite. Compare *ghrelin*. [9]

Q

quale (pl. qualia) A purely subjective experience of perception. [14]

R

range fractionation The means by which sensory systems cover a wide range of intensity values, as each sensory receptor cell specializes in just one part of the overall range of intensities. [5, 7]

raphe nuclei A string of nuclei in the midline of the midbrain and brainstem that contain most of the serotonergic neurons of the brain. [4]

rapid-eye-movement (REM) sleep Also called *paradoxical sleep*. A stage of sleep characterized by small-amplitude, fast-EEG waves, no postural tension, and rapid eye movements. REM rhymes with "gem." See Figure 10.10. Compare *slow-wave sleep*. [10]

RBD See *REM behavior disorder*. [10]

recency effect The superior performance seen in a memory task for items at the end of a list; it is usually attributed to short-term memory. See Figure 13.14. Compare *primacy effect*. [13]

receptive field The stimulus region and features that affect the activity of a cell in a sensory system. See Figures 5.6, 7.13, 7.16. [5, 7]

receptor See *neurotransmitter receptor*. [2, 3, 4]

receptor cell A specialized cell that responds to a particular energy or substance in the internal or external environment, and converts this energy into a change in the electrical potential across its membrane. [5]

receptor subtype Any type of receptor having functional characteristics that distinguish it from other types of receptors for the same neurotransmitter. For example, at least 15 different subtypes of receptor molecules respond to serotonin.

reconsolidation The return of a memory trace to stable long-term storage after it has been temporarily made changeable during the process of recall. [13]

recovery of function The recovery of behavioral capacity following brain damage from stroke or injury. [15]

red nucleus A brainstem structure related to motor control.

reductionism The scientific strategy of breaking a system down into increasingly smaller parts in order to understand it. [1]

reflex A simple, highly stereotyped, and unlearned response to a particular stimulus (e.g., an eye blink in response to a puff of air). See Figures 3.14, 5.22. [5]

reflexive attention See *exogenous attention*. [14]

refraction The bending of light rays by a change in the density of a medium, such as the cornea and the lens of the eyes. [7]

refractory Temporarily unresponsive or inactivated. [3]

refractory phase 1. A period during and after a nerve impulse in which the responsiveness of the axonal membrane is reduced. A brief period of complete insensitivity to stimuli (*absolute refractory phase*) is followed by a longer period of reduced sensitivity (*relative refractory phase*) during which only strong stimulation produces an action potential. [3] 2. A period following copulation during which an individual cannot recommence copulation. See Figure 8.23. [8]

relative refractory phase A period of reduced sensitivity during which only strong stimulation produces an action potential. Compare *absolute refractory phase*. [3]

releasing hormone Any of a class of hormones, produced in the hypothalamus, that traverse the hypothalamic–pituitary portal system to control the pituitary's release of tropic hormones. See Figure 8.12. [8]

REM behavior disorder (RBD) A sleep disorder in which a person physically acts out a dream. [10]

REM sleep See *rapid-eye-movement sleep*. [10]

repetition priming See *priming*. [13]

resting potential A difference in electrical potential across the membrane of a nerve cell during an inactive period. See Figures 3.1, 3.5. [3]

reticular formation Also called *reticular activating system*. An extensive region of the brainstem (extending from the medulla through the thalamus) that is involved in sleep and arousal. See Figure 10.23. [2, 10]

retina The receptive surface inside the eye that contains photoreceptors and other neurons. See Figures 7.1, 7.3. [7]

RETINAL One of the two components of photopigments in the retina. The other is *opsin*. (The term is printed in small capital letters in this text to distinguish it from the adjective retinal, meaning "pertaining to the retina.") [ASF 7.2]

retinohypothalamic pathway The route by which retinal ganglion cells send their axons to the suprachiasmatic nuclei. [10]

retrieval The third process of the memory system, in which a stored memory is used by an organism. See Figure 13.13. Compare *encoding* and *consolidation*. [13]

retrograde amnesia Difficulty in retrieving memories formed before the onset of amnesia. Compare *anterograde amnesia*. [13]

retrograde transmitter A neurotransmitter that is released by the postsynaptic region, diffuses back across the synapse, and alters the functioning of the presynaptic neuron. [4, 13]

reuptake The process by which released synaptic transmitter molecules are taken up and reused by the presynaptic neuron, thus stopping synaptic activity. [3, 4]

rhodopsin The photopigment in rods that responds to light. [7]

ribonucleic acid (RNA) A nucleic acid that implements information found in DNA. Compare *deoxyribonucleic acid*. [App]

ribosome An organelle in the cell body where genetic information is translated to produce proteins. See Appendix Figure A.2. [App]

RNA See *ribonucleic acid*. [App]

rod A photoreceptor cell in the retina that is most active at low levels of light. See Figure 7.3. Compare *cone*. [7]

root Either of two distinct branches of a spinal nerve, each of which serves a separate function. The dorsal root enters the dorsal horn of the spinal cord and carries sensory information from the peripheral nervous system to the spinal cord. The ventral root arises from the ventral horn of the spinal cord and carries motor messages from the spinal cord to the peripheral nervous system. See Figure 2.8. [2]

rostral See *anterior*. [2]

round window A membrane separating the tympanic canal from the middle ear. See Figure 6.1. [6]

Ruffini corpuscle A skin receptor cell type that detects stretching of the skin. See Figure 5.4. Compare *Meissner's corpuscle*, *Merkel's disc*, and *Pacinian corpuscle*. [5]

S

S1 See *somatosensory 1*. [5]

sacral Referring to the 5 spinal segments that make up the lower part of the lower back. See Figures 2.8, 2.9. Compare *cervical*, *thoracic*, *lumbar*, and *coccygeal*. [2]

SAD See *seasonal affective disorder*. [ASF 12.3]

sagittal plane The plane that divides the body or brain into right and left portions. See Box 2.2. Compare *coronal plane* and *horizontal plane*. [2]

saltatory conduction The form of conduction that is characteristic of myelinated axons, in which the action potential jumps from one node of Ranvier to the next. [3]

satiety A feeling of fulfillment or satisfaction. Compare *hunger*.

saturation One of three basic dimensions of light perception, varying from rich to pale. See Figure 7.24. Compare *brightness* and *hue*. [7]

SC See *standard condition*. [13]

scala media See *middle canal*. [6]

scala tympani See *tympanic canal*. [6]

scala vestibuli See *vestibular canal*. [6]

schizophrenia A severe psychopathological disorder characterized by negative symptoms such as emotional withdrawal and impoverished thought, and by positive symptoms such as hallucinations and delusions. [12]

Schwann cell A type of glial cell that forms myelin in the peripheral nervous system. Compare *oligodendrocyte*. [2]

SCN See *suprachiasmatic nucleus*. [10]

scotoma A region of blindness within the visual fields, caused by injury to the visual pathway or brain. [7]

scotopic system A system in the retina that operates at low levels of light and involves the rods. See Table 7.1. Compare *photopic system*. [7]

SDN-POA See *sexually dimorphic nucleus of the preoptic area*. [8]

seasonal affective disorder (SAD) A depression putatively brought about by the short days of winter. [ASF 12.3]

second messenger A slow-acting substance in a target cell that amplifies the effects of synaptic or hormonal activity and regulates activity within the target cell. [8]

secondary sensory cortex See *nonprimary sensory cortex*. [5]

seizure An epileptic episode. See Figure 3.16. [3]

selective attention See *attention*. [14]

selective permeability The property of a membrane that allows some substances to pass through, but not others. [3]

selective serotonin reuptake inhibitor (SSRI) A drug that blocks the reuptake of transmitter at serotonergic synapses, commonly used to treat depression. [4, 12]

semantic memory Generalized declarative memory, such as knowing the meaning of a word without knowing where or when you learned that word. Compare *episodic memory*. [13]

semantics The meanings or interpretation of words and sentences in a language.

semen A mixture of fluid, including sperm, that is released during ejaculation. [8]

semicircular canal Any one of the three fluid-filled tubes in the inner ear that are part of the vestibular system. Each of the tubes, which are at right angles to each other, detects angular acceleration in a particular direction. See Figure 6.13. [6]

senile dementia A neurological disorder of the aged that is characterized by progressive behavioral deterioration, including personality change and profound intellectual decline. It includes, but is not limited to, Alzheimer's disease.

senile plaque See *amyloid plaque*. [13]

sensitive period Also called *critical period*. The period during development in which an organism can be permanently altered by a particular experience or treatment. [8, 15, ASF 13.4]

sensorineural deafness A hearing impairment most often caused by the permanent damage or destruction of hair cells, or by interruption of the vestibulocochlear nerve that carries auditory information to the brain. See Figure 6.11. Compare *central deafness* and *conduction deafness*. [6]

sensory conflict theory A theory of motion sickness suggesting that discrepancies between vestibular information and visual information simulate food poisoning and therefore trigger nausea. [6]

sensory nerve A nerve that conveys information from the body to the central nervous system. Compare *motor nerve*. [2]

sensory neuron A nerve cell that is directly affected by changes in the environment, such as light, odor, or touch. Compare *interneuron* and *motoneuron*. [2]

sensory transduction The process in which a receptor cell converts the energy in a stimulus into a change in the electrical potential across its membrane. [5]

serotonergic Referring to cells that use serotonin as their synaptic transmitter. [4]

serotonin (5-HT) A synaptic transmitter that is produced in the raphe nuclei and is active in structures throughout the central nervous system. See Figure 4.4; Table 4.1. [4, 11]

set point The point of reference in a feedback system. An example is the temperature at which a thermostat is set. Compare *set zone*. [9]

set zone The range of a variable that a feedback system tries to maintain. Compare *set point*. [9]

sex determination The process by which it is established that a fetus will develop as a male or a female. In mammals, sex determination is under genetic control; but in some groups of animals, environmental variables like incubation temperature determine the sex of the offspring. [8]

sexual attraction The first step in the mating behavior of many animals, in which animals emit stimuli that attract members of the opposite sex. See Figure 8.16. [8]

sexual differentiation The process by which individuals develop either malelike or femalelike bodies and behavior. See Figure 8.24. [8]

sexual dimorphism The condition in which males and females of the same species show pronounced sex differences in appearance. [8]

sexually dimorphic nucleus of the preoptic area (SDN-POA) A region of the preoptic area that is five to six times larger in volume in male rats than in females. See Figure 8.30. [8]

sexually receptive Referring to the state in which an individual (in mammals, typically the female) is willing to copulate. In many species, no sexual activity is possible other than during the period of sexual receptivity in the female, which generally corresponds to ovulation. [8]

shadowing A task in which the subject is asked to focus attention on one ear or the other while stimuli are being presented separately to both ears, and to repeat aloud the material presented to the attended ear. [14]

sham rage See *decorticate rage*. [11]

shell shock See *posttraumatic stress disorder*. [12, 13]

shivering Rapid involuntary muscle contractions that generate heat in hypothermic animals. [9]

short-term memory (STM) Also called *working memory*. A form of memory that usually lasts only seconds, or as long as rehearsal continues. See Figure 13.13. Compare *iconic memory* and *long-term memory*. [13]

SIDS See *sudden infant death syndrome*. [10]

simple cortical cell Also called *bar detector* or *edge detector*. A cell in the visual cortex that responds best to an edge or a bar that has a particular width, as well as a particular orientation and location in the visual field. Compare *complex cortical cell*. [7]

simultagnosia A profound restriction of attention, often limited to a single item or feature. Simultagnosia is one of the three primary symptoms of Balint's syndrome. [14]

skeletal muscle A muscle that is used for movement of the skeleton, typically under our conscious control. [5]

skill learning The process of learning to perform a challenging task simply by repeating it over and over. [13]

sleep apnea A sleep disorder in which respiration slows or stops periodically, waking the patient. [10]

sleep cycle A period of slow-wave sleep followed by a period of REM sleep. In humans, a sleep cycle lasts 90–110 minutes.

sleep deprivation The partial or total prevention of sleep. [10]

sleep enuresis Bed-wetting. [10]

sleep-maintenance insomnia Difficulty in staying asleep. Compare *sleep-onset insomnia*. [10]

sleep-onset insomnia Difficulty in falling sleep. Compare *sleep-maintenance insomnia*. [10]

sleep paralysis A state, during the transition to or from sleep, in which the ability to move or talk is temporarily lost. [10]

sleep recovery The process of sleeping more than normally after a period of sleep deprivation, as though in compensation. [10]

sleep spindle A characteristic 14- to 18-hertz wave in the EEG of a person said to be in stage 2 sleep. See Figure 10.10. [10]

sleep state misperception Commonly, a person's perception that he has not been asleep when in fact he has. It typically occurs at the start of a sleep episode. [10]

slow-wave sleep (SWS) Also called *non-REM sleep*. Sleep, divided into stages 1–3, that is defined by the presence of slow-wave EEG activity. See Figure 10.10. Compare *rapid-eye-movement sleep*. [10]

SMA See *supplementary motor area*. [5]

SNB See *spinal nucleus of the bulbocavernosus*. [8]

social neuroscience A field of study that uses the tools of neuroscience to discover the biological bases of social behavior, and the effects of social circumstances on brain activity. [1]

sodium ion (Na⁺) A sodium atom that carries a positive charge because it has lost one electron. [3]

sodium-potassium pump The energetically expensive mechanism that pushes sodium ions out of a cell, and potassium ions in. [3]

solute A solid compound that is dissolved in a liquid. Compare *solvent*.

solvent The liquid (often water) in which a compound is dissolved. Compare *solute*.

soma (pl. somata) See *cell body*. [2]

somatic intervention An approach to finding relations between body variables and behavioral variables that involves manipulating body structure or function and looking for resultant changes in behavior. See Figure 1.8. Compare *behavioral intervention*. [1]

somatic nerve See *spinal nerve*. [2]

somatosensory 1 (S1) See *primary somatosensory cortex*. [5]

somatosensory system A set of specialized receptors and neural mechanisms responsible for body sensations such as touch and pain. [5]

somatotropic hormone or somatotropin See *growth hormone*. [8]

somnambulism Sleepwalking. [10]

Southern blot A method of detecting a particular DNA sequence in the genome of an organism, by separating DNA with gel electrophoresis, blotting the separated DNA molecules onto nitrocellulose, and then using a nucleotide probe to hybridize with, and highlight, the gene of interest. See Appendix Figure A.3. Compare *Northern blot* and *Western blot*. [App]

spasticity Markedly increased rigidity in response to forced movement of the limbs.

spatial cognition The ability to navigate and to understand the spatial relationship between objects. [15]

spatial-frequency model A model of vision that emphasizes the analysis of different spatial frequencies, of various orientations and in various parts of the visual field, as the basis of visual perception of form. [7, ASF 7.4]

spatial resolution The ability to observe the detailed structure of the brain. Compare *temporal resolution*. [14]

spatial summation The summation of postsynaptic potentials that reach the axon hillock from different locations across the cell body. If this summation reaches threshold, an action potential is triggered. See Figure 3.10. Compare *temporal summation*. [3]

spectral filtering The process by which the hills and valleys of the external ear

alter the amplitude of some, but not all, frequencies in a sound. When performed by the irregular shapes of the external ear, this process is a source of information that assists in the localization of sound sources. [6]

spectrally opponent cell A visual receptor cell that has opposite firing responses to different regions of the spectrum. See Figures 7.25, 7.26. [7]

sperm The gamete produced by males for the fertilization of eggs (*ova*). [8]

spike See *action potential*. [3]

spinal nerve Also called *somatic nerve*. A nerve that emerges from the spinal cord. There are 31 pairs of spinal nerves. Compare *cranial nerve*. See Figure 2.8. [2]

spinal nucleus of the bulbocavernosus (SNB) A group of motoneurons in the spinal cord of rats that innervate striated muscles controlling the penis. See Figure 8.32. See also *Onuf's nucleus*. [8]

spinocerebellum The uppermost part of the cerebellum, consisting mostly of the vermis and the anterior lobe. It receives sensory information about the current spatial location of the parts of the body and anticipates subsequent movement. Compare *cerebrocerebellum* and *vestibulocerebellum*. [ASF 5.5]

spinothalamic system See *anterolateral system*. [5]

split-brain individual An individual whose corpus callosum has been severed, halting communication between the right and left hemispheres. [15]

***SRY* gene** A gene on the Y chromosome that directs the developing gonads to become testes. The name *SRY* stands for *s*ex-determining *r*egion on the *Y* chromosome. [8]

SSRI See *selective serotonin reuptake inhibitor*. [4, 12]

stage 1 sleep The initial stage of slow-wave sleep, which is characterized by small-amplitude EEG waves of irregular frequency, slow heart rate, and reduced muscle tension. See Figure 10.10. [10]

stage 2 sleep A stage of slow-wave sleep that is defined by bursts of regular 14- to 18-hertz EEG waves called sleep spindles. See Figure 10.10. [10]

stage 3 sleep A stage of slow-wave sleep that is defined by the presence of large-amplitude, slow delta waves. See Figure 10.10. [10]

standard condition (SC) The usual environment for laboratory rodents, with a few animals in a cage and adequate food and water, but no complex stimulation. See Figure 13.16. Compare *enriched condition* and *impoverished condition*. [13]

stapedius A middle-ear muscle that is attached to the stapes. See Figure 6.1.

stapes Latin for "stirrup." A middle-ear bone that is connected to the oval window. It is one of the three ossicles that conduct sounds across the middle ear. See Figure 6.1. [6]

stem cell A cell that is undifferentiated and therefore can take on the fate of any cell that a donor organism can produce. [13]

stereocilium (pl. stereocilia) A relatively stiff hair that protrudes from a hair cell in the auditory or vestibular system. See Figure 6.1. [6]

steroid hormone Any of a class of hormones, each of which is composed of four interconnected rings of carbon atoms. Compare *amine hormone* and *protein hormone*. [8]

stimulant A drug that enhances the excitability of neurons. Compare *depressant*. [4]

stimulus (pl. stimuli) A physical event that triggers a sensory response. [5]

stimulus cuing A technique for testing reaction time to sensory stimuli in which a cue to the location in which the stimulus will be presented is provided before the stimulus itself.

STM See *short-term memory*. [13]

stress Any circumstance that upsets homeostatic balance. Examples include exposure to extreme cold or heat or an array of threatening psychological states. [11]

stress immunization The concept that mild stress early in life makes an individual better able to handle stress later in life. [11]

stretch reflex The contraction of a muscle in response to stretch of that muscle. See Figure 5.22. [5]

striate cortex See *primary visual cortex*. [7]

striate muscle A type of muscle that has a striped appearance; it is generally under voluntary control. Skeletal muscle is one type of striate muscle. [5]

striatum The caudate nucleus and putamen together.

stroke Damage to a region of brain tissue that results from the blockage or rupture of vessels that supply blood to that region. [2]

stuttering The tendency of otherwise normal people to produce speech sounds only haltingly, tripping over certain syllables or unable to start vocalizing certain words. [15]

substance abuse A maladaptive pattern of substance use that has lasted more than a month but does not fully meet the criteria for *dependence*. See Box 4.1. [4]

substance P A peptide transmitter that is involved in pain transmission. [5]

substantia nigra A brainstem structure that innervates the basal ganglia and is the source of all dopaminergic projections. Compare *locus coeruleus*. [2, 4, 5]

sudden infant death syndrome (SIDS) Also called *crib death*. The sudden, unexpected death of an apparently healthy human infant who simply stops breathing, usually during sleep. [10]

sulcus (pl. sulci) A crevice or valley of a convoluted brain surface. Compare *gyrus*. [2]

superior In anatomy, above. See Box 2.2. Compare *inferior*. [2]

superior colliculi (sing. colliculus) Paired gray matter structures of the dorsal midbrain that process visual information. See Figures 2.16, 7.10. Compare *inferior colliculi*. [2, 7]

superior olivary nucleus Either of two brainstem nuclei—left and right—that receive input from both right and left cochlear nuclei, and provide the first binaural analysis of auditory information. See Figure 6.6. [6]

supersensitivity psychosis An exaggerated psychosis that may emerge when doses of antipsychotic medication are reduced, probably as a consequence of the up-regulation of receptors that occurred during drug treatment. [12]

supplementary motor area (SMA) A region of nonprimary motor cortex that receives input from the basal ganglia and modulates the activity of the primary motor cortex. See Figure 5.26. [5]

suprachiasmatic nucleus (SCN) A small region of the hypothalamus above the optic chiasm that is the location of a circadian clock. [10]

surface dyslexia Acquired dyslexia in which the patient seems to attend only to the fine details of reading. Compare *deep dyslexia*. [15]

sustained-attention task A task in which a single stimulus source or location must be held in the attentional spotlight for a protracted period. Compare *divided-attention task*. [14]

SWS See *slow-wave sleep*. [10]

Sylvian fissure Also called *lateral sulcus*. A deep fissure that demarcates the temporal lobe. See Figure 2.10. [2]

symbolic cuing A technique for testing endogenous attention in which a visual stimulus is presented and subjects are asked to respond as soon as the stimulus appears on a screen. Each trial is preceded by a meaningful symbol used as a cue to hint at where the stimulus will appear. Compare *peripheral spatial cuing*. [14]

sympathetic nervous system The division of the autonomic nervous system that arises from the thoracic and lumbar spinal cord. This division prepares the body for immediate action. See Figure 2.9. Compare *parasympathetic nervous system*. [2, 11]

synapse The location at which information flows between a presynaptic neuron and a postsynaptic neuron, often through the conversion of electrical activity in the presynaptic neuron into a secretion of chemical neurotransmitter that alters the functioning of the postsynaptic neuron. See Figure 2.4. [2, 4, 8]

synapse rearrangement Also called *synaptic remodeling*. The loss of some synapses and the development of others; a refinement of synaptic connections that is often seen in development. See Figure 13.25. [13]

synaptic bouton See *axon terminal*. [2]

synaptic cleft The space between the presynaptic and postsynaptic neurons at a synapse. This gap measures about 20–40 nm. See Figures 2.2, 2.4, 3.11. [2, 3]

synaptic delay The brief delay between the arrival of an action potential at the axon terminal and the creation of a postsynaptic potential. The delay is caused by the translation of an electrical event into a secretory event, and back to an electrical event on the postsynaptic side. [3]

synaptic remodeling See *synapse rearrangement*. [13]

synaptic transmitter See *neurotransmitter*. [2, 3]

synaptic vesicle A small, spherical structure that contains molecules of neurotransmitter. See Figure 2.4. [3]

synaptogenesis The establishment of synaptic connections as axons and dendrites grow. See Figure 13.25. [13]

synergist A muscle that acts together with another muscle. Compare *antagonist* (definition 2). [5]

synesthesia A condition in which stimuli in one modality evoke the involuntary experience of an additional sensation in another modality. [5]

syrinx The vocal organ in birds. [ASF 15.1]

T

T cell See *T lymphocyte*. [11]

T lymphocyte Also called *T cell*. An immune system cell, formed in the thymus (hence the *T*), that attacks foreign microbes or tissue; "killer cell." Compare *B lymphocyte*. [11]

T1R A family of taste receptor proteins that, when particular members bind together, form taste receptors for sweet flavors and umami flavors. Compare *T2R*. [6]

T2R A family of bitter taste receptors. Compare *T1R*. [6]

TAAR See *trace amine–associated receptor*. [6]

tachistoscope test A test in which stimuli are very briefly presented to either the left or right visual half field. [15]

tactile Referring to touch.

tactile corpuscle See *Meissner's corpuscle*. [5]

tailbone See *coccygeal*. [2]

tardive dyskinesia A disorder characterized by involuntary movements, especially involving the face, mouth, lips, and tongue; related to prolonged use of antipsychotic drugs, such as chlorpromazine. See Box 12.1. [12]

taste Any of the five basic sensations detected by the tongue: sweet, salty, sour, bitter, and umami. Compare *flavor*. [6]

taste bud A cluster of 50–150 cells that detects tastes. Taste buds are found in papillae. See Figure 6.15. [6]

tau A protein associated with neurofibrillary tangles in Alzheimer's disease. [13]

tectorial membrane A membrane that sits atop the organ of Corti in the cochlear duct. See Figure 6.1. [6]

tectum The dorsal portion of the midbrain consisting of the inferior and superior colliculi. [2]

telencephalon The anterior part of the fetal forebrain, which will become the cerebral hemispheres in the adult brain. See Figure 2.12, 13.24. Compare *diencephalon*. [2, 13]

temporal coding Frequency discrimination in which the pitch of a sound is determined by the rate of firing of auditory neurons. Compare *place coding*. [6]

temporal lobe The large lateral region of cortex in each cerebral hemisphere. It is continuous with the *parietal lobe* posteriorly and separated from the *frontal lobe* by the Sylvian fissure. The temporal lobes contain the hippocampus and amygdala, and are involved in a variety of functions, including memory, emotional processing, and the olfactory and auditory senses. See Figure 2.10. Compare also *occipital lobe*. [2]

temporal resolution The ability to track changes in the brain that occur very quickly. Compare *spatial resolution*. [14]

temporal summation The summation of postsynaptic potentials that reach the axon hillock at different times. The closer in time the potentials occur, the more complete the summation is. Compare *spatial summation*. [3]

temporoparietal junction (TPJ) The point in the brain where the temporal and parietal lobes meet. It plays a role in shifting attention to a new location after target onset. [14]

TENS See *transcutaneous electrical nerve stimulation*. [5]

testes (sing. testis) The male gonads, which produce sperm and androgenic steroid hormones. See Figure 8.1. Compare *ovaries*. [8]

testosterone A hormone, produced by male gonads, that controls a variety of bodily changes that become visible at puberty. One of a class of hormones called androgens. See Figure 8.13. [8, 11]

tetanus An intense volley of action potentials. [13]

tetrahydrocannabinol (THC) See *delta-9-tetrahydrocannabinol*. [4]

thalamus (pl. thalami) The brain regions at the top of the brainstem that trade information with the cortex. See Figures 2.14, 2.15, 2.16. [2, 5]

THC See *delta-9-tetrahydrocannabinol*. [4]

therapeutic index The margin of safety for a given drug, expressed as the distance between effective doses and toxic doses. See Figure 4.6. [4]

third ventricle The midline ventricle that conducts cerebrospinal fluid from the lateral ventricles to the fourth ventricle. See Figure 2.17. Compare *fourth ventricle* and *lateral ventricle*. [2]

thoracic Referring to the 12 spinal segments below the cervical (neck) portion of the spinal cord, corresponding to the chest. See Figures 2.8, 2.9. Compare *cervical, lumbar, sacral,* and *coccygeal*. [2]

threshold The stimulus intensity that is just adequate to trigger an action potential at the axon hillock. [3, 5]

thrombolytic A substance that is used to unblock blood vessels and restore circulation. [ASF 15.5]

thyroid-stimulating hormone (TSH) A tropic hormone, released by the anterior pituitary gland, that signals the thyroid gland to secrete its hormones. [8]

timbre The characteristic sound quality of a musical instrument, as determined by the relative intensities of its various harmonics. See Box 6.1. [6]

tinnitus A sensation of noises or ringing in the ears not caused by external sound. [6]

tip link A fine, threadlike fiber that runs along and connects the tips of stereocilia. See Figure 6.3. [6]

TMS See *transcranial magnetic stimulation*. [2]

tobacco A highly addictive North American plant whose leaves (usually dried and smoked) are a major source of nicotine. [4]

tolerance See *drug tolerance*. [4]

tonic receptor A receptor in which the frequency of action potentials declines slowly or not at all as stimulation is maintained. Compare *phasic receptor*. [5]

tonotopic organization A major organizational feature in auditory systems, in which neurons are arranged as an orderly map of stimulus frequency, with cells responsive to high frequencies located at a distance from those responsive to low frequencies. [6]

topographic projection A mapping that preserves the point-to-point correspondence between neighboring parts space. For example, the retina extends a topographic projection onto the cortex. [7]

Tourette's syndrome A disorder that is characterized by heightened sensitivity to tactile, auditory, and visual stimuli that may be accompanied by the buildup of an urge to emit verbal or phonic tics. See Box 12.2. [12]

TPJ See *temporoparietal junction*. [14]

trace amine–associated receptor (TAAR) Any one of a family of probable pheromone receptors produced by neurons in the main olfactory epithelium. TAARs are candidate pheromone receptors, despite being situated outside the vomeronasal organ. [6]

tract A bundle of axons found within the central nervous system. Compare *nerve*. [2]

transcranial magnetic stimulation (TMS) A noninvasive technique for examining brain function that applies strong magnetic fields to stimulate cortical neurons, in order to identify discrete areas of the brain that are particularly active during specific behaviors. Compare *magnetoencephalography*. [2]

transcript See *messenger RNA*. [App]

transcription The process during which mRNA forms bases complementary to a strand of DNA. The resulting message (called a *transcript*) is then used to translate the DNA code into protein molecules. See Appendix Figure A.2. Compare *translation*. [App]

transcutaneous electrical nerve stimulation (TENS) The delivery of electrical pulses through electrodes attached to the skin, which excite nerves that supply the region to which pain is referred. TENS can relieve the pain in some instances. [5]

transduction The conversion of one form of energy to another, as converting light into neuronal activity. [6, 7]

transgenic Referring to an animal in which a new or altered gene has been deliberately introduced into the genome. See the Appendix. [App]

transient receptor potential 2 (TRP2) A receptor, found in some free nerve endings, that opens its channel in response to rising temperatures. [5]

translation The process by which amino acids are linked together (directed by an mRNA molecule) to form protein molecules. See Appendix Figure A.2. Compare *transcription*. [App]

transmitter See *neurotransmitter*. [2, 3, 4]

transporter A specialized receptor in the presynaptic membrane that recognizes transmitter molecules and returns them to the presynaptic neuron for reuse. [3, 4]

transverse plane See *coronal plane*. [2]

trichromatic hypothesis A hypothesis of color perception stating that there are three different types of cones, each excited by a different region of the spectrum and each having a separate pathway to the brain. [7]

tricyclic antidepressant An antidepressant that acts by increasing the synaptic accumulation of serotonin and norepinephrine. [4]

trinucleotide repeat Repetition of the same three nucleotides within a gene, which can lead to dysfunction, as in Huntington's disease. [5]

trophic factor See *neurotrophic factor*. [13]

tropic hormone Any of a class of anterior pituitary hormones that affect the secretion of hormones by other endocrine glands. See Figure 8.12. [8]

TRP2 See *transient receptor potential 2*. [5]

TSH See *thyroid-stimulating hormone*. [8]

tuberomammillary nucleus A region of the basal hypothalamus, near the pituitary stalk, that plays a role in generating slow-wave sleep. [10]

tuning curve A graph of the responses of a single auditory nerve fiber or neuron to sounds that vary in frequency and intensity. See Figure 6.5. [6]

Turner's syndrome A condition, seen in individuals carrying a single X chromosome but no other sex chromosome, in which an apparent female has underdeveloped but recognizable ovaries. [8]

tympanic canal Also called *scala tympani*. One of three principal canals running along the length of the cochlea. Compare *middle canal* and *vestibular canal*. See Figure 6.1. [6]

tympanic membrane Also called *eardrum*. The partition between the external ear and the middle ear. See Figure 6.1. [6]

typical neuroleptic An antischizophrenic drug that shows antagonist activity at dopamine D_2 receptors. Compare *atypical neuroleptic*. [12]

U

ultradian Referring to a rhythmic biological event whose period is shorter than that of a circadian rhythm, usually from several minutes to several hours long. Compare *infradian*. [10]

ultrasound High-frequency sound; in general, above the threshold for human hearing, at about 20,000 Hz. Compare *infrasound*. [6]

umami One of the five basic tastes—the meaty, savory flavor. (The other four tastes are salty, sour, sweet, and bitter.) [6]

unipolar depression Depression that alternates with normal emotional states. Compare *bipolar disorder*. [12]

unipolar neuron Also called *monopolar neuron*. A nerve cell with a single branch that leaves the cell body and then extends in two directions; one end is the input zone, and the other end is the output zone. See Figure 2.3. Compare *bipolar neuron* and *multipolar neuron*. [2]

up-regulation A compensatory increase in receptor availability at the synapses of a neuron. Compare *down-regulation*. [4]

V

V1 See *primary visual cortex*. [7]

vagina The opening from the outside of the body to the cervix and uterus in females. [8]

vagus nerve Cranial nerve X, which provides extensive innervation of the viscera (organs). The vagus both regulates visceral activity and transmits signals from the viscera to the brain. See Figures 2.7, 9.15. [2, 9]

vasopressin See *arginine vasopressin*. [8, 9]

ventral In anatomy, toward the belly or front of the body, or the bottom of the brain. See Box 2.2. Compare *dorsal*. [2]

ventral tegmental area (VTA) A portion of the midbrain that projects dopaminergic fibers to the nucleus accumbens. [4]

ventricular system A system of fluid-filled cavities inside the brain. See Figure 2.17. [2]

ventricular zone Also called *ependymal layer*. A region lining the cerebral ventricles that displays mitosis, providing neurons early in development and glial cells throughout life. See Figure 13.25. [13]

ventromedial hypothalamus (VMH) A hypothalamic region involved in eating and sexual behaviors. See Figures 8.20, 9.12. [8, 9]

vertex spike A sharp-wave EEG pattern that is seen during stage 1 sleep. See Figure 10.10. [10]

vestibular canal Also called *scala vestibuli*. One of three principal canals running along the length of the cochlea. See Figure 6.1. Compare *middle canal* and *tympanic canal*. [6]

vestibular nucleus A brainstem nucleus that receives information from the vestibular organs through cranial nerve VIII (the vestibulocochlear nerve). [6]

vestibular system The sensory system that detects balance. It consists of several small inner-ear structures that adjoin the cochlea. [6]

vestibulocerebellum The middle portion of the cerebellum, sandwiched between the *spinocerebellum* and the *cerebrocerebellum* and consisting of the nodule and the flocculus. It helps the motor systems to maintain posture and appropriate orientation toward the external world. [ASF 5.5]

vestibulocochlear nerve Cranial nerve VIII, which runs from the cochlea to the brainstem auditory nuclei. See Figures 2.7, 6.1. [6]

visual acuity Sharpness of vision. [7]

visual cortex See *occipital cortex*. [7]

visual field The whole area that you can see without moving your head or eyes. [7]

visual P1 effect A positive deflection of the event-related potential, occurring 70–100 milliseconds after stimulus presentation, that is enhanced for selectively attended visual input compared to ignored input. Compare *auditory N1 effect*. [14]

VMH See *ventromedial hypothalamus*. [8, 9]

VNO See *vomeronasal organ*. [6, 8]

volley theory A theory of frequency discrimination that emphasizes the relation between sound frequency and the firing pattern of nerve cells. For example, a 500-hertz tone would produce 500 neural discharges per second by a nerve cell or group of nerve cells. Compare *place theory*.

voltage-gated Na+ channel A Na+-selective channel that opens or closes in response to changes in the voltage of the local membrane potential; it mediates the action potential. Compare *ligand-gated ion channel*. [3]

voluntary attention See *endogenous attention*. [14]

vomeronasal organ (VNO) A collection of specialized receptor cells, near to but separate from the olfactory epithelium, that detect pheromones and send electrical signals to the accessory olfactory bulb in the brain. [6, 8]

vomeronasal system A specialized sensory system that detects pheromones and transmits information to the brain. [6]

VTA See *ventral tegmental area*. [4]

W

Wada test A test in which a short-lasting anesthetic is delivered into one carotid artery to determine which cerebral hemisphere principally mediates language. See Box 15.1. [15]

war neurosis See *posttraumatic stress disorder*. [12, 13]

wavelength The length between two peaks in a repeated stimulus such as a wave, light, or sound. See Figure 7.21. [7]

Wernicke-Geschwind model See *connectionist model of aphasia*. [15]

Wernicke's aphasia See *fluent aphasia*. [15]

Wernicke's area A region of temporoparietal cortex in the brain that is involved in the perception and production of speech. See Figures 15.5, 15.6, 15.7. Compare *Broca's area*. [15]

Western blot A method of detecting a particular protein molecule in a tissue or organ, by separating proteins from that source with gel electrophoresis, blotting the separated proteins onto nitrocellulose, and then using an antibody that binds, and highlights, the protein of interest. Compare *Northern blot* and *Southern blot*. [App]

white matter A lighter-colored layer of tissue, consisting mostly of myelin-sheathed axons, that lies underneath the gray matter of the cortex. White matter mostly transmits information. See Figures 2.8, 2.11. Compare *gray matter*. [2]

Williams syndrome A disorder characterized by impairments of spatial cognition and IQ, but superior linguistic abilities. [15]

withdrawal symptom An uncomfortable symptom that arises when a person stops taking a drug that he or she has used frequently, especially at high doses. [4]

within-subjects experiment An experiment in which the same set of subjects is compared before and after an experimental manipulation. The subjects thus serve as their own controls. Compare *between-subjects experiment*. [1]

wolffian duct A duct system in the embryo that will develop into male reproductive structures (epididymis, vas deferens, and seminal vesicles) if testes are present in the embryo. See Figure 8.24. Compare *müllerian duct*. [8]

word deafness A form of central deafness that is characterized by the specific inability to hear words, although other sounds can be detected. [6]

working memory See *short-term memory*. [13]

Z

zeitgeber Literally, "time-giver" (in German). The stimulus (usually the light-dark cycle) that entrains circadian rhythms. [10]

zygote The fertilized egg. [8]

Illustration Credits

Chapter 1

1.2: Reproduced with gracious permission of Her Majesty Queen Elizabeth II, copyright reserved. 1.3: Bettmann/Corbis. 1.4a: © The Print Collector/Alamy. p. 6 top: © Scala/Art Resource, NY. p. 13: © Roman Sigaev/istockphoto.com. p. 18: © Caters News/Zuma Press.

Chapter 2

2.4c: © Dennis Kunkel Microscopy, Inc. 2.6a: From *Gray's Anatomy*, 35th ed., Figure 2.9, page 807. Reprinted with permission of the publisher, Churchill Livingstone. (Dissection by M. C. E. Hutchinson, photograph by Kevin Fitzpatrick, Guy's Hospital Medical School, London.) 2.18a: © Living Art Enterprises, LLC/Photo Researchers, Inc. 2.18b: © Guy Croft SciTech/Alamy. 2.18d: Courtesy of Jamie Eberling. 2.18e: © Shutterstock. 2.21b: Courtesy of Dr. Mario Liotti and Anthony Herdman, Simon Fraser University, and Down Syndrome Research Foundation. p. 27: Reproduced with permission from www.brains.rad.msu.edu, and brainmuseum.org, supported by the US National Science Foundation.

Chapter 3

3.15a: Courtesy of Neuroscan Labs, a division of Neurosoft, Inc. 3.16c: Courtesy of Hal Blumenfeld, Rik Stokking, Susan Spencer, and George Zubal, Yale School of Medicine. p. 52: Photographs of events and activities documenting Yale University, Manuscripts and Archives, Yale University Library. p. 73: © Globe Photos/Zuma Press.

Chapter 4

4.10: Courtesy of E. Riley. p. 93: © Featureflash/Shutterstock. p. 94: © Alfred Eisenstaedt/Time & Life Pictures/Getty Images. p. 95: © South West Images Scotland/Alamy. p. 96 bottom: Courtesy of the U.S. Food and Drug Administration. p. 98: © Jason Bye/Alamy. p. 100 bottom: Art by Wes Black, courtesy of www.blotterart.com. p. 102: © ejwhite/Shutterstock.

Chapter 5

5.1a: © The Natural History Museum/Alamy. 5.1b: Courtesy of Matthew Haskins and Brianna Matthews. 5.1c: © Vitaly Titov/istockphoto. 5.1d: © Stockbyte/PictureQuest. 5.15: © al wekelo/istockphoto. p. 137: © Danita Delimont/Alamy.

Chapter 6

6.14: © Astrid & Hanns-Frieder Michler/Photo Researchers, Inc. p. 143 top: © Bradley Smith/Corbis. p. 143 opossums: © Stuart Elflett/ShutterStock. p. 143 rabbit: © Heather Craig/istockphoto.com. p. 143 elephant: © Gerry Ellis/DigitalVision. p. 143 chimp: © Holger Ehlers/ShutterStock. p. 152: © Dave Watts/Naturepl.com. p. 158 top: David McIntyre. p. 158 bottom: Courtesy of NASA. p. 161: David McIntyre.

Chapter 7

7.7: © Paul Parker/SPL/Photo Researchers, Inc. 7.26: Courtesy of Thomas Eisner. 7.31: Courtesy of Patch Pals, www.PatchPals.com. Box 7.1A: Photo by David McIntyre; simulation created using software from Vischeck (www.vischeck.com). Box 7.1B: © Brand X Pictures/Alamy. p. 170: © Ahowden–Japan Stock Photography/Alamy. p. 171: David McIntyre. p. 191: © Victoria Short/Shutterstock. p. 195: © Dynamic Graphics Group/Creatas/Alamy. p. 199: Courtesy of Patch Pals, www.PatchPals.com.

Chapter 8

8.26: © The Wellcome Photo Library. p. 207: © Tom Vezo/Nature Picture Library. p. 214: Image by Vicky Tobin and Mike Ludwig, Centre for Integrative Physiology, University of Edinburgh. p. 219: © nouseforname/Shutterstock. p. 224: © Jane Burton/Naturepl.com. p. 232: David McIntyre. p. 233: © Biophoto Associates/Photo Researchers, Inc. p. 239: Courtesy of Andrew D. Sinauer. p. 244: © Murat Sarica/istock.

Chapter 9

9.14: © John Sholtis/Rockefeller University. p. 251: Courtesy of NASA. p. 257: © Don Paulson/Alamy. p. 260a: © Dmitry Lobanov/Shutterstock. p. 260b: © Ace Stock Limited/Alamy. p. 268 left: © Ash Knotek/Zuma Press. p. 268 right: Kunsthistorisches Museum, Vienna.

Chapter 10

10.18: © petech/istockphoto. 10.20: © Jouan & Rius/Naturepl.com. p. 297: Courtesy of Joanne Delphia. p. 281: © Hank Morgan/Photo Researchers, Inc. p. 282a: © Tomo Jesenicnik/istockphoto. p. 282b: © Ira Bachinskaya/istockphoto. p. 284: © Robin Chittenden/Alamy. p. 287: © San Diego History Center. p. 298: © Wavebreakmedia Ltd./Shutterstock.

Chapter 11

11.4: © Sinauer Associates. 11.8a: © Richard Green/Commercial/Alamy. 11.8b: Courtesy of Jennifer Basil-Whitaker. 11.14: © Sinauer Associates. p. 302: © blickwinkel/Alamy. p. 311: © Zephyr/Photo Researchers, Inc. p. 318 top: © David Osborn/Alamy. p. 318 bottom: © Neil Lloyd/Alamy. p. 319: © Bill Frakes/Time & Life Pictures/Getty Images. p. 324: © Richard Garvey-Williams/Alamy.

Chapter 12

Box 12.1: Courtesy of Steven J Frucht. p. 328: Courtesy of Howard Dully. p. 329: © EFE/Zuma Press. p. 336 bottom: © Bettmann/Corbis. p. 343: © MBI/Alamy. p. 345: © AF archive/Alamy. p. 347: © Jimmy Urquhart/Zuma Press.

References

A

Aaronson, S. T., Rashed, S., Biber, M. P., and Hobson, J. A. (1982). Brain state and body position. A time-lapse video study of sleep. *Archives of General Psychiatry, 39*, 330–335.

Abe, N., Suzuki, M., Mori, E., Itoh, M., et al. (2007). Deceiving others: Distinct neural responses of the prefrontal cortex and amygdala in simple fabrication and deception with social interactions. *Journal of Cognitive Neuroscience, 19*, 287–295.

Abelson, J. F., Kwan, K.Y., O'Roak, B. J., Baek, D.Y., et al. (2005). Sequence variants in *SLITRK1* are associated with Tourette's syndrome. *Science, 310*, 317–320.

Absil, P., Pinxten, R., Balthazart, J., and Eens, M. (2003). Effect of age and testosterone on autumnal neurogenesis in male European starlings (*Sturnus vulgaris*). *Behavioural Brain Research, 143*, 15–30.

Ader, R. (2001). Psychoneuroimmunology. *Current Directions in Psychological Science, 10*, 94–98.

Adler, E., Hoon, M. A., Mueller, K. L., Chandrashekar, J., et al. (2000). A novel family of mammalian taste receptors. *Cell, 100*, 693–702.

Adolphs, R., Gosselin, F., Buchanan, T. W., Tranel, D., et al. (2005). A mechanism for impaired fear recognition after amygdala damage. *Nature, 433*, 68–72.

Agarwal, N., Pacher, P., Tegeder, I., Amay, F., et al. (2007). Cannabinoids mediate analgesia largely via peripheral type cannabinoid receptors in nociceptors. *Nature Neuroscience, 10*, 870–878.

Agmon-Snir, H., Carr, C. E., and Rinzel, J. (1998). The role of dendrites in auditory coincidence detection. *Nature, 393*, 268–272.

Ahmed, E. I., Zehr, J. L., Schulz, K. M., Lorenz, B. H., et al. (2008). Pubertal hormones modulate the addition of new cells to sexually dimorphic brain regions. *Nature Neuroscience, 11*, 995–997.

Ahn, S., and Phillips, A. G. (2002). Modulation by central and basolateral amygdalar nuclei of dopaminergic correlates of feeding to satiety in the rat nucleus accumbens and medial prefrontal cortex. *Journal of Neuroscience, 22*, 10958–10965.

Akbarian, S., Kim, J. J., Potkin, S. G., Hetrick, W. P., et al. (1996). Maldistribution of interstitial neurons in prefrontal white matter of the brains of schizophrenic patients. *Archives of General Psychiatry, 53*, 425–436.

Albanese, A., Hamill, G., Jones, J., Skuse, D., et al. (1994). Reversibility of physiological growth hormone secretion in children with psychosocial dwarfism. *Clinical Endocrinology (Oxford), 40*, 687–692.

al-Barazanji, K. A., Buckingham, R. E., Arch, J. R., Haynes, A., et al. (1997). Effects of intracerebroventricular infusion of leptin in obese Zucker rats. *Obesity Research, 5*, 387–394.

Alberts, J. R. (1978). Huddling by rat pups: Multisensory control of contact behavior. *Journal of Comparative and Physiological Psychology, 92*, 220–230.

Aldrich, M. A. (1993). The neurobiology of narcolepsy-cataplexy. *Progress in Neurobiology, 41*, 533–541.

Almer, G., Hainfellner, J. A., Brücke, T., Jellinger, K., et al. (1999). Fatal familial insomnia: A new Austrian family. *Brain, 122*, 5–16.

Alpert, M., and Friedhoff, A. J. (1980). An un-dopamine hypothesis of schizophrenia. *Schizophrenia Bulletin, 6*, 387–390.

Altschuler, E. L., Wisdom, S. B., Stone, L., Foster, C., et al. (1999). Rehabilitation of hemiparesis after stroke with a mirror. *Lancet, 353*, 2035–2036.

Alvarez, J. A., and Emory, E. (2006). Executive function and the frontal lobes: A meta-analytic review. *Neuropsychology Review, 16*, 17–42.

American Psychiatric Association. (2000). *Diagnostic and statistical manual of mental disorders: DSM IV-TR* (4th ed., text revision). Washington, DC: American Psychiatric Association.

Amunts, K., Schlaug, G., Jaencke, L., Steinmetz, H., et al. (1997). Motor cortex and hand motor skills: Structural compliance in the human brain. *Human Brain Mapping, 5*, 206–215.

Anand, B. K., and Brobeck, J. R. (1951). Localization of a "feeding center" in the hypothalamus of the rat. *Proceedings of the Society for Experimental Biology and Medicine, 77*, 323–324.

Andersen, B. B., Korbo, L., and Pakkenberg, B. (1992). A quantitative study of the human cerebellum with unbiased stereological techniques. *Journal of Comparative Neurology, 326*, 549–560.

Andersen, P. M., Nilsson, P., Ala-Hurula, V., Keranen, M. L., et al. (1995). Amyotrophic lateral sclerosis associated with homozygosity for an Asp90Ala mutation in CuZn-superoxide dismutase. *Nature Genetics, 10*, 61–66.

Andreasen, N. C. (1991). Assessment issues and the cost of schizophrenia. *Schizophrenia Bulletin, 17*, 475–481.

Andreasen, N. C., Flaum, M., Swayze, V. O. D. S., Alliger, R., et al. (1993). Intelligence and brain structure in normal individuals. *American Journal of Psychiatry, 150*, 130–134.

Andreasen, N., Nassrallah, H. A., Dunn, V., Olson, S. C., et al. (1986). Structural abnormalities in the frontal system in schizophrenia. *Archives of General Psychiatry, 43*, 136–144.

Angier, N. (2004, April 13). No time for bullies: Baboons retool their culture. *The New York Times*.

Apkarian, A. V., Sosa, Y., Sonty, S., Levy, R. M., et al. (2004). Chronic back pain is associated with decreased prefrontal and thalamic gray matter density. *Journal of Neuroscience, 24,* 10410–10415.

Archer, G. S., Friend, T. H., Piedrahita, J., Nevill, C. H., et al. (2003). Behavioral variation among cloned pigs. *Applied Animal Behaviour Science, 82,* 151–161.

Archer, J. (2006). Testosterone and human aggression: An evaluation of the challenge hypothesis. *Neuroscience and Biobehavioral Reviews, 30,* 319–345.

Argyll-Robertson, D. M. C. L. (1869). On an interesting series of eye symptoms in a case of spinal disease, with remarks on the action of belladonna on the iris. *Edinburgh Medical Journal, 14,* 696–708.

Arnold, A. P. (1980). Sexual differences in the brain. *American Scientist, 68,* 165–173.

Arnold, A. P., and Schlinger, B. A. (1993). Sexual differentiation of brain and behavior: The zebra finch is not just a flying rat. *Brain, Behavior and Evolution, 42,* 231–241.

Arnold, K., and Zuberbühler, K. (2006). Language evolution: Semantic combinations in primate calls. *Nature, 441,* 303.

Arnone, D., Cavanagh, J., Gerber, D., Lawrie, S. M., et al. (2009). Magnetic resonance imaging studies in bipolar disorder and schizophrenia: Meta-analysis. *British Journal of Psychiatry, 195,* 194–201.

Arnsten, A. F. (2006). Fundamentals of attention-deficit/hyperactivity disorder: Circuits and pathways. *Journal of Clinical Psychiatry, 67,* 7–12.

Asberg, M., Nordstrom, P., and Traskman-Bendz, L. (1986). Cerebrospinal fluid studies in suicide. An overview. *Annals of the New York Academy of Sciences, 487,* 243–255.

Aschner, M., and Ceccatelli, S. (2010). Are neuropathological conditions relevant to ethylmercury exposure? *Neurotoxicity Research, 18,* 59–68.

Aserinsky, E., and Kleitman, N. (1953). Regularly occurring periods of eye motility, and concomitant phenomena, during sleep. *Science, 118,* 273–274.

Ashmore, J. F. (1994). The cellular machinery of the cochlea. *Experimental Physiology, 79,* 113–134.

Ashtari, M., Kumra, S., Bhaskar, S. L., Clarke, T., et al. (2005). Attention-deficit/hyperactivity disorder: A preliminary diffusion tensor imaging study. *Biological Psychiatry, 57,* 448–455.

Audero, E., Coppi, E., Mlinar, B., Rossetti, T., et al. (2008). Sporadic autonomic dysregulation and death associated with excessive serotonin autoinhibition. *Science, 321,* 130–133.

Aungst, J. L., Heyward, P. M., Puche, A. C., Karnup, S.V., et al. (2003). Centre-surround inhibition among olfactory bulb glomeruli. *Nature, 426,* 623–629.

Avila, M. T., Hong, L. E., Moates, A., Turano, K. A., et al. (2006). Role of anticipation in schizophrenia-related pursuit initiation deficits. *Journal of Neurophysiology, 95,* 593–601.

B

Baddeley, A. D., and Warrington, E. K. (1970). Amnesia and the distinction between long- and short-term memory. *Journal of Verbal Learning and Verbal Behavior, 9,* 176–189.

Bagemihl, B. (1999). *Biological exuberance: Animal homosexuality and natural diversity.* New York, NY: St. Martin's Press.

Bailey, C. H., and Chen, M. (1983). Morphological basis of long-term habituation and sensitization in *Aplysia. Science, 220,* 91–93.

Bailey, J. M., Pillard, R. C., Neale, M. C., and Agyei,Y. (1993). Heritable factors influence sexual orientation in women. *Archives of General Psychiatry, 50,* 217–223.

Bakker, J., De Mees, C., Douhard, Q., Balthazart, J., et al. (2006). Alpha-fetoprotein protects the developing female mouse brain from masculinization and defeminization by estrogens. *Nature Neuroscience, 9,* 220–226.

Ball, G. F., and Hulse, S. H. (1998). Birdsong. *American Psychologist, 53,* 37–58.

Bancaud, J., Brunet-Bourgin, F., Chauvel, P., and Halgren, E. (1994). Anatomical origin of deja vu and vivid "memories" in human temporal lobe. *Brain, 117,* 71–90.

Bao, S., Chan, V.T., and Merzenich, M. M. (2001). Cortical remodelling induced by activity of ventral tegmental dopamine neurons. *Nature, 412,* 79–83.

Baptista, L. F. (1996). Nature and its nurturing in avian vocal development. In D. E. Kroodsma and E. H. Miller (Eds.), *Ecology and evolution of acoustic communication in birds* (pp. 39–60). Ithaca, NY: Cornell University Press.

Baptista, L., and Petrinovich, L. (1986). Song development in the white-crowned sparrow: Social factors and sex differences. *Animal Behaviour, 34,* 1359–1371.

Barbeau, H., Norman, K., Fung, J., Visintin, M., et al. (1998). Does neurorehabilitation play a role in the recovery of walking in neurological populations? *Annals of the New York Academy of Sciences, 860,* 377–392.

Bark, N. (2002). Did schizophrenia change the course of English history? The mental illness of Henry VI. *Medical Hypotheses, 59,* 416–421.

Barkow, J. H., Cosmides, L., and Tooby, J. (1992). *The adapted mind: Evolutionary psychology and the generation of culture.* New York, NY: Oxford University Press.

Barnea, G., O'Donnell, S., Mancia, F., Sun, X., et al. (2004). Odorant receptors on axon termini in the brain. *Science, 304,* 1468.

Baron-Cohen, S. (2003). *The essential difference: Men, women and the extreme male brain.* London, England: Allen Lane.

Bartels, A., and Zeki, S. (2000). The neural basis of romantic love. *Neuroreport, 11,* 3829–3834.

Bartfai, T. (2001). Telling the brain about pain. *Nature, 410,* 425–426.

Bartolomeo, P. (2007). Visual neglect. *Current Opinion in Neurology, 20,* 381–386.

Bartoshuk, L. M. (1993). Genetic and pathological taste variation: What can we learn from animal models and human disease? In D. Chadwick, J. Marsh, and J. Goode (Eds.), *The molecular basis of smell and taste transduction* (pp. 251–267). New York, NY: Wiley.

Bartoshuk, L. M., and Beauchamp, G. K. (1994). Chemical senses. *Annual Review of Psychology, 45,* 419–449.

Basson, R. (2001). Human sex-response cycles. *Journal of Sex & Marital Therapy, 27,* 33–43.

Basson, R. (2008). Women's sexual function and dysfunction: Current uncertainties, future directions. *International Journal of Impotence Research, 20,* 466–478.

Bates, E., Wilson, S. M., Saygin, A. P., Dick, F., et al. (2003). Voxel-based lesion-symptom mapping. *Nature Neuroscience, 6,* 448–450.

Batterham, R. L., and Bloom, S. R. (2003). The gut hormone peptide YY regulates appetite. *Annals of the New York Academy of Sciences, 994,* 162–168.

Batterham, R. L., Cohen, M. A., Ellis, S. M., Le Roux, C. W., et al. (2003). Inhibition of food intake in obese subjects by peptide YY_{3-36}. *New England Journal of Medicine, 349,* 941–948.

Baum, A., and Posluszny, D. M. (1999). Health psychology: Mapping biobehavioral contributions to health and illness. *Annual Review of Psychology, 50,* 137–163.

Bautista, D. M., Siemens, J., Glazer, J. M., Tsuruda, P. R., et al. (2007). The menthol receptor TRPM8 is the principal detector of environmental cold. *Nature, 448,* 204–208.

Baynes, K. C., Dhillo, W. S., and Bloom, S. R. (2006). Regulation of food intake by gastrointestinal hormones. *Current Opinion in Gastroenterology, 22,* 626–631.

Beach, F. A. (1977). *Human sexuality in four perspectives.* Baltimore, MD: Johns Hopkins University Press.

Bee, M. A., and Micheyl, C. (2008). The cocktail party problem: What is it? How can it be solved? And why should animal behaviorists study it? *Journal of Comparative Psychology, 122,* 235–251.

Beeli, G., Esslen, M., and Jäncke, L. (2005). When coloured sounds taste sweet. *Nature, 434,* 38.

Beggs, W. D., and Foreman, D. L. (1980). Sound localization and early binaural experience in the deaf. *British Journal of Audiology, 14,* 41–48.

Bellinger, D. L., Ackerman, K. D., Felten, S. Y., and Felten, D. L. (1992). A longitudinal study of age-related loss of noradrenergic nerves and lymphoid cells in the rat spleen. *Experimental Neurology, 116,* 295–311.

Bellugi, U., Poizner, H., and Klima, E. S. (1983). Brain organization for language: Clues from sign aphasia. *Human Neurobiology, 2,* 155–171.

Bennett, A. F., and Ruben, J. A. (1979). Endothermy and activity in vertebrates. *Science, 206,* 649–654.

Bennett, M. V. (2000). Electrical synapses, a personal perspective (or history). *Brain Research Reviews, 32,* 16–28.

Bennett, W. (1983). The nicotine fix. *Rhode Island Medical Journal, 66,* 455–458.

Benney, K. S., and Braaten, R. F. (2000). Auditory scene analysis in estrildid finches (*Taeniopygia guttata* and *Lonchura striata domestica*): A species advantage for detection of conspecific song. *Journal of Comparative Psychology, 114,* 174–182.

Berenbaum, S. A. (2001). Cognitive function in congenital adrenal hyperplasia. *Endocrinology and Metabolism Clinics of North America, 30,* 173–192.

Bernhardt, P. C. (1997). Influences of serotonin and testosterone in aggression and dominance: Convergence with social psychology. *Current Directions in Psychological Science, 2*(6), 44–48.

Bernhardt, P. C., Dabbs, J. M., Jr., Fielden, J. A., and Lutter, C. D. (1998). Testosterone changes during vicarious experiences of winning and losing among fans at sporting events. *Physiology & Behavior, 65,* 59–62.

Bernstein, I. S., and Gordon, T. P. (1974). The function of aggression in primate societies. *American Scientist, 62,* 304–311.

Bernstein, L. E., Auer, E. T., Jr., Moore, J. K., Ponton, C. W., et al. (2002). Visual speech perception without primary auditory cortex activation. *Neuroreport, 13,* 311–315.

Bernstein-Goral, H., and Bregman, B. S. (1993). Spinal cord transplants support the regeneration of axotomized neurons after spinal cord lesions at birth: A quantitative double-labeling study. *Experimental Neurology, 123,* 118–132.

Berthold, A. (1849). Transplantation der Hoden. *Archiv für Anatomie, Physiologie und Wissenschaftliche Medicin, 16,* 42–46.

Berton, O., and Nestler, E. J. (2006). New approaches to antidepressant drug discovery: Beyond monoamines. *Neuroscience, 7,* 137–151.

Bertram, L., and Tanzi, R. E. (2008). Thirty years of Alzheimer's disease genetics: The implications of systematic meta-analyses. *Nature Reviews. Neuroscience, 9,* 768–778.

Besedovsky, H. O., and del Rey, A. (1992). Immune-neuroendocrine circuits: Integrative role of cytokines. *Frontiers of Neuroendocrinology, 13,* 61–94.

Beurg, M., Fettiplace, R., Nam, J.-H., and Ricci, A. J. (2009). Localization of inner hair cell mechanotransducer channels using high-speed calcium imaging. *Nature Neuroscience, 12,* 553–558.

Bigelow, L., Nasrallah, H. A., and Rauscher, F. P. (1983). Corpus callosum thickness in chronic schizophrenia. *British Journal of Psychiatry, 142,* 284–287.

Binder, J. R., Rao, S. M., Hammeke, T. A., Yetkin, F. Z., et al. (1994). Functional magnetic resonance imaging of human auditory cortex. *Annals of Neurology, 35,* 662–672.

Birch, L. L., Fisher, J. O., and Davison, K. K. (2003). Learning to overeat: Maternal use of restrictive feeding practices promotes girls' eating in the absence of hunger. *American Journal of Clinical Nutrition, 78,* 215–220.

Bisley, J. W., and Goldberg, M. E. (2003). Neuronal activity in the lateral intraparietal area and spatial attention. *Science, 299,* 81–86.

Blake, D. J., Weir, A., Newey, S. E., and Davies, K. E. (2002). Function and genetics of dystrophin and dystrophin-related proteins in muscle. *Physiology Review, 82,* 291–329.

Blake, D. T., Heiser, M. A., Caywood, M., and Merzenich, M. M. (2006). Experience-dependent adult cortical plasticity requires cognitive association between sensation and reward. *Neuron, 52,* 371–381.

Blakemore, C., and Campbell, F. W. (1969). On the existence of neurones in the human visual system selectively sensitive to the orientation and size of retinal images. *Journal of Physiology (London), 203,* 237–260.

Blanchard, R., Cantor, J. M., Bogaert, A. F., Breedlove, S. M., et al. (2006). Interaction of fraternal birth order and handedness in the development of male homosexuality. *Hormones and Behavior, 49,* 405–414.

Blehar, M. C., and Rosenthal, N. E. (1989). Seasonal affective disorders and phototherapy. Report of a National Institute of Mental Health-sponsored workshop. *Archives of General Psychiatry, 46,* 469–474.

Bleuler, E. (1950). *Dementia praecox; or, The group of schizophrenias* (J. Zinkin, Trans.). New York, NY: International Universities Press.

Bliss, T. V. P., and Gardner-Medwin, A. R. (1973). Long-lasting potentiation of synaptic transmission in the dentate area of the unanaesthetized rabbit following stimulation of the perforant path. *Journal of Physiology (London), 232,* 357–374.

Bliss, T. V. P., and Lømo, T. (1973). Long-lasting potentiation of synaptic transmission in the dentate area of the anaesthetized rabbit following stimulation of the perforant path. *Journal of Physiology (London), 232,* 331–356.

Bliwise, D. L. (1989). Neuropsychological function and sleep. *Clinics in Geriatric Medicine, 5,* 381–394.

Blumberg, M. S., Sokoloff, G., and Kirby, R. F. (1997). Brown fat thermogenesis and cardiac rate regulation during cold challenge in infant rats. *American Journal of Physiology, 272,* R1308–R1313.

Bogaert, A. F. (2006). Biological versus nonbiological older brothers and men's sexual orientation. *Proceedings of the National Academy of Sciences, USA, 103,* 10771–10774.

Bogaert, A. F. (2007). Extreme right-handedness, older brothers, and sexual orientation in men. *Neuropsychology, 21,* 141–148.

Bolhuis, J. J., and Gahr, M. (2006). Neural mechanisms of birdsong memory. *Nature Reviews. Neuroscience, 7,* 347–357.

Bonhoeffer, T., and Grinvald, A. (1991). Iso-orientation domains in cat visual cortex are arranged in pinwheel-like patterns. *Nature, 353,* 429–431.

Bonnel, A. M., and Prinzmetal, W. (1998). Dividing attention between the color and the shape of objects. *Perception & Psychophysics, 60,* 113–124.

Boodman, S. G. (2006, March 21). Mood machine: Now there's a device to treat depression. If only there were solid evidence that it works. *Washington Post,* p. HE01.

Boolell, M., Gepi-Attee, S., Gingell, J. C., and Allen, M. J. (1996). Sildenafil, a novel effective oral therapy for male erectile dysfunction. *British Journal of Urology, 78,* 257–261.

Borgstein, J., and Grootendorst, C. (2002). Clinical picture: Half a brain. *Lancet, 359,* 473.

Borod, J. C., Haywood, C. S., and Koff, E. (1997). Neuropsychological aspects of facial asymmetry during emotional expression: A review of the normal adult literature. *Neuropsychology Review, 7,* 41–60.

Borrow, S. J., Adam, K., Chapman, K., Oswald, I., et al. (1980). REM sleep and normal intelligence. *Biological Psychiatry, 15,* 165–169.

Bottjer, S. W., Miesner, E. A., and Arnold, A. P. (1984). Forebrain lesions disrupt development but not maintenance of song in passerine birds. *Science, 224,* 901–903.

Bourque, C. W. (2008). Central mechanisms of osmosensation and systemic osmoregulation. *Nature Reviews. Neuroscience, 9,* 519–531.

Bouwknecht, J. A., Hijzen, T. H., van der Gugten, J., Maes, R. A., et al. (2001). Absence of 5-HT(1B) receptors is associated with impaired impulse control in male 5-HT(1B) knockout mice. *Biological Psychiatry, 49,* 557–568.

Bower, B. (2006). Prescription for controversy: Medications for depressed kids spark scientific dispute. *Science News, 169,* 168–172.

Brain, P. F. (1994). Neurotransmission, the individual and the alcohol/aggression link. Commentary on Miczek et al. "Neuropharmacological characteristics of individual differences in alcohol effects on aggression in rodents and primates." *Behavioural Pharmacology, 5,* 422–424.

Brainard, D. H., Roorda, A., Yamauchi, Y., Calderone, J. B., et al. (2000). Functional consequences of the relative numbers of L and M cones. *Journal of the Optical Society of America. Part A, Optics, Image Science and Vision, 17,* 607–614.

Brasser, S. M., Mozhui, K., and Smith, D. V. (2005). Differential covariation in taste responsiveness to bitter stimuli in rats. *Chemical Senses, 30,* 793–799.

Bray, G. A. (1969). Effect of caloric restriction on energy expenditure in obese patients. *Lancet, 2,* 397–398.

Breitner, J. C., Wyse, B. W., Anthony, J. C., Welsh-Bohmer, K. A., et al. (1999). APOE-epsilon4 count predicts age when prevalence of AD increases, then declines: The Cache County Study. *Neurology, 53,* 321–331.

Bremer, F. (1938). L'activité électrique de l'écorce cérébrale. *Actualités Scientifiques et Industrielles, 658,* 3–46.

Bremner, J. D., Randall, P., Scott, T. M., Bronen, R. A., et al. (1995). MRI-based measurement of hippocampal volume in patients with combat-related posttraumatic stress disorder. *American Journal of Psychiatry, 152,* 973–981.

Bremner, J. D., Scott, T. M., Delaney, R. C., Southwick, S. M., et al. (1993). Deficits in short-term memory in posttraumatic stress disorder. *American Journal of Psychiatry, 150,* 1015–1019.

Brennan, P., Kaba, H., and Keverne, E. B. (1990). Olfactory recognition: A simple memory system. *Science, 250,* 1223–1226.

Brigande, J. V., and Heller, S. (2009). *Quo vadis,* hair cell regeneration? *Nature Neuroscience, 12,* 679–685.

Broadbent, D. A. (1958). *Perception and communication.* New York, NY: Pergamon Press.

Broberg, D. J., and Bernstein, I. L. (1989). Cephalic insulin release in anorexic women. *Physiology and Behavior, 45,* 871–874.

Broughton, R., Billings, R., Cartwright, R., Doucette, D., et al. (1994). Homicidal somnambulism: A case report. *Sleep, 17,* 253–264.

Brown, A. S. (2011). The environment and susceptibility to schizophrenia. *Progress in Neurobiology, 93,* 23–58.

Brown, C. (2003, February 2). The man who mistook his wife for a deer. *The New York Times,* Section 6, p. 32.

Brown, G. L., Goodwin, F. K., Ballenger, J. C., Goyer, P. F., et al. (1979). Aggression in humans correlates with cerebrospinal fluid amine metabolites. *Psychiatry Research, 1,* 131–139.

Brown, H. (2006, November 26). One spoonful at a time. *New York Times Magazine.*

Brown, J. (1958). Some tests of the decay theory of immediate memory. *Quarterly Journal of Experimental Psychology, 10,* 12–21.

Brownlee, S., and Schrof, J. M. (1997). The quality of mercy. Effective pain treatments already exist. Why aren't doctors using them? *U.S. News & World Report, 122,* 54–67.

Bruel-Jungerman, E., Rampon, C., and Laroche S. (2007). Adult hippocampal neurogenesis, synaptic plasticity and memory: Facts and hypotheses. *Review in the Neurosciences, 18,* 93–114.

Brunetti, M., Della Penna, S., Ferretti, A., Del Gratta, C., et al. (2008). A fronto-parietal network for spatial attention reorienting in the auditory domain: A human fMRI/MEG study of functional and temporal dynamics. *Cerebral Cortex, 18,* 1139–1147.

Bryant, P., Trinder, J., and Curtis, N. (2004). Sick and tired: Does sleep have a vital role in the immune system? *Nature Reviews. Immunology, 4,* 457–467.

Bu, G. (2009). Apolipoprotein E and its receptors in Alzheimer's disease: Pathways, pathogenesis and therapy. *Nature Reviews. Neuroscience, 10,* 333–344.

Buccino, G., Lui, F., Canessa, N., Patteri, I., et al. (2004). Neural circuits involved in the recognition of actions performed by nonconspecifics: An fMRI study. *Journal of Cognitive Neuroscience, 16,* 114–126.

Buccino, G., Solodkin, A., and Small, S. L. (2006). Functions of the mirror neuron system: Implications for neurorehabilitation. *Cognitive and Behavioral Neurology, 19,* 55–63.

Buchsbaum, B. R., Baldo, J., Okada, K., Berman, K. F., et al. (2011). Conduction aphasia, sensory-motor integration, and phonological short-term memory—An aggregate analysis of lesion and fMRI data. *Brain and Language, 119,* 119–128.

Buchsbaum, M. S., Buchsbaum, B. R., Chokron, S., Tang, C., et al. (2006). Thalamocortical circuits: fMRI assessment of the pulvinar and medial dorsal nucleus in normal volunteers. *Neuroscience Letters, 404,* 282–287.

Buchsbaum, M. S., Mirsky, A. F., DeLisi, L. E., Morihisa, J., et al. (1984). The Genain quadruplets: Electrophysiological, positron emission and X-ray tomographic studies. *Psychiatry Research, 13,* 95–108.

Buck, L., and Axel, R. (1991). A novel multigene family may encode odorant receptors: A molecular basis for odor recognition. *Cell, 65,* 175–187.

Burgdorf, J., Kroes, R. A., Moskal, J. R., Pfaus, J. G., et al. (2008). Ultrasonic vocalizations of rats (*Rattus norvegicus*) during mating, play, and aggression: Behavioral concomitants, relationship to reward, and self-administration of playback. *Journal of Comparative Psychology, 122,* 357–367.

Buss, D. M. (2000). *The dangerous passion: Why jealousy is as necessary as love and sex.* New York, NY: Free Press.

Butler, A. C., Chapman, J. E., Forman, E. M., and Beck, A. T. (2006). The empirical status of cognitive-behavioral therapy: A review of meta-analyses. *Clinical Psychology Review, 26,* 17–31.

C

Cahill, L. (1997). The neurobiology of emotionally influenced memory: Implications for understanding traumatic memory. In R. Yehuda and A. C. McFarlane (Eds.), *Annals of the New York Academy of Sciences: Vol. 41. Psychobiology of traumatic stress disorder* (pp. 238–246). New York, NY: New York Academy of Sciences.

Cahill, L., and McGaugh, J. L. (1991). NMDA-induced lesions of the amygdaloid complex block the retention-enhancing effect of posttraining epinephrine. *Psychobiology, 19,* 206–210.

Cahill, L., Prins, B., Weber, M., and McGaugh, J. L. (1994). Beta-adrenergic activation and memory for emotional events. *Nature, 371,* 702–704.

Calder, A. J., Keane, J., Manes, F., Antoun, N., et al. (2000). Impaired recognition and experience of disgust following brain injury. *Nature Neuroscience, 3,* 1077.

Calvert, G. A., Bullmore, E. T., Brammer, M. J., Campbell, R., et al. (1997). Activation of auditory cortex during silent lipreading. *Science, 276,* 593–596.

Campbell, F. W., and Robson, J. G. (1968). Application of Fourier analysis to the visibility of gratings. *Journal of Physiology (London), 197,* 551–566.

Campbell, S. S., and Tobler, I. (1984). Animal sleep: A review of sleep duration across phylogeny. *Neuroscience and Biobehavioral Reviews, 8,* 269–301.

Cannon, W. B. (1929). *Bodily changes in pain, hunger, fear and rage.* New York, NY: Appleton.

Cantalupo, C., and Hopkins, W. D. (2001). Asymmetric Broca's area in great apes. *Nature, 414,* 505.

Cantor, J. M., Blanchard, R., Paterson, A. D., and Bogaert, A. F. (2002). How many gay men owe their sexual orientation to fraternal birth order? *Archives of Sexual Behavior, 31,* 63–71.

Cao, Y. Q., Mantyh, P. W., Carlson, E. J., Gillespie, A. M., et al. (1998). Primary afferent tachykinins are required to experience moderate to intense pain. *Nature, 392,* 390–394.

Cardno, A. G., and Gottesman, I. I. (2000). Twin studies of schizophrenia: From bow-and-arrow concordances to star wars Mx and functional genomics. *American Journal of Medical Genetics, 97,* 12–17.

Carmichael, M. S., Warburton, V. L., Dixen, J., and Davidson, J. M. (1994). Relationships among cardiovascular, muscular, and oxytocin responses during human sexual activity. *Archives of Sexual Behavior, 23,* 59–79.

Carpen, J. D., Archer, S. N., Skene, D. J., Smits, M., et al. (2005). A single-nucleotide polymorphism in the 5'-untranslated region of the *hPER2* gene is associated with diurnal preference. *Journal of Sleep Research, 14,* 293–297.

Carreiras, M., Lopez, J., Rivero, F., and Corina, D. (2005). Linguistic perception: Neural processing of a whistled language. *Nature, 433,* 31–32.

Carroll, J., McMahon, C., Neitz, M., and Neitz, J. (2000). Flicker-photometric electroretinogram estimates of L:M cone photoreceptor ratio in men with photopigment spectra derived from genetics. *Journal of the Optical Society of America. Part A, Optics, Image Science, and Vision, 17,* 499–509.

Carter, C. S. (1992). Oxytocin and sexual behavior. *Neuroscience and Biobehavioral Reviews, 16,* 131–144.

Cartwright, R. D. (1979). The nature and function of repetitive dreams: A survey and speculation. *Psychiatry, 42,* 131–137.

Casey, D. E. (1989). Clozapine: Neuroleptic-induced EPS and tardive dyskinesia. *Psychopharmacology (Berlin), 99,* S47–S53.

Cassens, G., Wolfe, L., and Zola, M. (1990). The neuropsychology of depressions. *Journal of Neuropsychiatry and Clinical Neurosciences, 2,* 202–213.

Casson, I. R., Sham, R., Campbell, E. A., Tarlau, M., et al. (1982). Neurological and CT evaluation of knocked-out boxers. *Journal of Neurology, Neurosurgery and Psychiatry, 45,* 170–174.

Castellanos, F. X., Lee, P. P., Sharp, W., Jeffries, N. O., et al. (2002). Developmental trajectories of brain volume abnormalities in children and adolescents with attention-deficit/hyperactivity disorder. *Journal of the American Medical Association, 288,* 1740–1748.

Caterina, M. J., Leffler, A., Malmberg, A. B., Martin, W. J., et al. (2000). Impaired nociception and pain sensation in mice lacking the capsaicin receptor. *Science, 288,* 306–313.

Caterina, M. J., Schumacher, M. A., Tominaga, M., Rosen, T. A., et al. (1997). The capsaicin receptor: A heat-activated ion channel in the pain pathway. *Nature, 389,* 816–824.

CDC (Centers for Disease Control and Prevention). (2010). Current depression among adults—United States, 2006 and 2008. *Morbidity and Mortality Weekly Report, 59,* 1229–1235 (http://www.cdc.gov/mmwr/preview/mmwrhtml/mm5938a2.htm).

Chamberlain, S. R., Menzies, L., Hampshire, A., Suckling, J., et al. (2008). Orbitofrontal dysfunction in patients with obsessive-compulsive disorder and their unaffected relatives. *Science, 321,* 421–422.

Champagne, F., Diorio, J., Sharma, S., and Meaney, M. J. (2001). Naturally occurring variations in maternal behavior in the rat are associated with differences in estrogen-inducible central oxytocin receptors. *Proceedings of the National Academy of Sciences, USA, 98,* 12736–12741.

Chandrashekar, J., Hoon, M. A., Ryba, N. J., and Zuker, C. S. (2006). The receptors and cells for mammalian taste. *Nature, 444,* 288–294.

Chandrashekar, J., Mueller, K. L., Hoon, M. A., Adler, E., et al. (2000). T2Rs function as bitter taste receptors. *Cell, 100,* 703–711.

Chandrashekar, J., Yarmolinsky, D., von Buchholtz, L., Oka, Y., et al. (2009). The taste of carbonation. *Science, 326,* 443–445.

Chang, B. S., Ly, J., Appignani, B., Bodell, A., et al. (2005). Reading impairment in the neuronal migration disorder of periventricular nodular heterotopia. *Neurology, 64,* 799–803.

Charney, D. S., Deutch, A. Y., Krystal, J. H., Southwick, S. M., et al. (1993). Psychobiologic mechanisms of posttraumatic stress disorder. *Archives of General Psychiatry, 50,* 295–305.

Chaudhari, N., Landin, A. M., and Roper, S. D. (2000). A metabotropic glutamate receptor variant functions as a taste receptor. *Nature Neuroscience, 3,* 113–119.

Chelikani, P. K., Haver, A. C., and Reidelberger, R. D. (2005). Intravenous infusion of peptide YY(3-36) potently inhibits food intake in rats. *Endocrinology, 146,* 879–888.

Chemelli, R. M., Willie, J. T., Sinton, C. M., Elmquist, J. K., et al. (1999). Narcolepsy in orexin knockout mice: Molecular genetics of sleep regulation. *Cell, 98,* 437–451.

Chen, L., and Feany, M. B. (2005). α-Synuclein phosphorylation controls neurotoxicity and inclusion formation in a *Drosophila* model of Parkinson disease. *Nature Neuroscience, 8,* 657–663.

Cherry, E. C. (1953). Some experiments on the recognition of speech, with one and with two ears. *Journal of the Acoustical Society of America, 25,* 975–979.

Cheyne, J. A. (2002). Situational factors affecting sleep paralysis and associated hallucinations: Position and timing effects. *Journal of Sleep Research, 11,* 169–177.

Christensen, D. (1999). Designer estrogens: Getting all the benefits, few of the risks. *Science News, 156,* 252–254.

Ciccocioppo, R., Martin-Fardon, R., and Weiss, F. (2004). Stimuli associated with a single cocaine experience elicit long-lasting cocaine-seeking. *Nature Neuroscience, 7,* 495–496.

Clapham, J. C., Arch, J. R. S., Chapman, H., Haynes, A., et al. (2000). Mice overexpressing human uncoupling protein-3 in skeletal muscle are hyperphagic and lean. *Nature, 406,* 415–418.

Clarke, M. C., Tanskanen, A., Huttunen, M., Leon, D. A., et al. (2011). Increased risk of schizophrenia from additive interaction between infant motor developmental delay and obstetric complications: Evidence from a population-based longitudinal study. *American Journal of Psychiatry, 168,* 1295–1302.

Classen, J., Liepert, J., Wise, S. P., Hallett, M., et al. (1998). Rapid plasticity of human cortical movement representation induced by practice. *Journal of Neurophysiology, 79,* 1117–1123.

Clemente, C. D., and Sterman, M. B. (1967). Limbic and other forebrain mechanisms in sleep induction and behavioral inhibition. *Progress in Brain Research, 27,* 34–37.

Coghill, R. C., McHaffie, J. G., and Yen, Y.-F. (2003). Neural correlates of interindividual differences in the subjective experience of pain. *Proceedings of the National Academy of Sciences, USA, 100,* 8538–8542.

Cohen, A. H., Baker, M. T., and Dobrov, T. A. (1989). Evidence for functional regeneration in the adult lamprey spinal cord following transection. *Brain Research, 496,* 368–372.

Cohen, A. J., and Leckman, J. F. (1992). Sensory phenomena associated with Gilles de la Tourette's syndrome. *Journal of Clinical Psychiatry, 53,* 319–323.

Cohen, S., Alper, C. M., Doyle, W. H., Treanor, J. J., et al. (2006). Positive emotional style predicts resistance to illness after experimental exposure to Rhinovirus or Influenza A virus. *Psychosomatic Medicine, 68,* 809–815.

Cohen, S., Doyle, W. J., Alper, C. M., Janicki-Deverts, D., et al. (2009). Sleep habits and susceptibility to the common cold. *Archive of Internal Medicine, 169,* 62–67.

Cohen, S., Lichtenstein, E., Prochaska, J. O., Rossi, J. S., et al. (1989). Debunking myths about quitting: Evidence from 10 perspective studies of persons who attempt to quit smoking by themselves. *American Psychologist, 44,* 1355–1365.

Cole, J. (1995). *Pride and a daily marathon.* Cambridge, MA: MIT Press.

Colom, R., Haier, R. J., Head, K., Álvarez-Linera, J., et al. (2009). Gray matter correlates of fluid, crystallized, and spatial intelligence: Testing the P-FIT model. *Intelligence, 37,* 124–135.

Conel, J. L. (1939). *The postnatal development of the human cerebral cortex: Vol. 1. The cortex of the newborn.* Cambridge, MA: Harvard University Press.

Conel, J. L. (1947). *The postnatal development of the human cerebral cortex: Vol. 3. The cortex of the three-month infant.* Cambridge, MA: Harvard University Press.

Conel, J. L. (1959). *The postnatal development of the human cerebral cortex: Vol. 6. The cortex of the twenty-four-month infant.* Cambridge, MA: Harvard University Press.

Conrad, A. J., Abebe, T., Austin, R., Forsythe, S., et al. (1991). Hippocampal pyramidal cell disarray in schizophrenia as a bilateral phenomenon. *Archives of General Psychiatry, 48,* 413–417.

Cooke, B. M., Breedlove, S. M., and Jordan, C. L. (2003). Both estrogen receptors and androgen receptors contribute to testosterone-induced changes in the morphology of the medial amygdala and sexual arousal in male rats. *Hormones and Behavior, 43,* 336–346.

Cooke, B. M., Chowanadisai, W., and Breedlove, S. M. (2000). Post-weaning social isolation of male rats reduces the volume of the medial amygdala and leads to deficits in adult sexual behavior. *Behavioural Brain Research, 117,* 107–113.

Cope, N., Harold, D., Hill, G., Moskvina, V., et al. (2005). Strong evidence that KIAA0319 on chromosome 6p is a susceptibility gene for developmental dyslexia. *American Journal of Human Genetics, 76,* 581–591.

Corballis, M. C. (2002). *From hand to mouth: The origins of language.* Princeton, NJ: Princeton University Press.

Corbetta, M., Kincade, J. M., Ollinger, J. M., McAvoy, M. P., et al. (2000). Voluntary orienting is dissociated from target detection in human posterior parietal cortex. *Nature Neuroscience, 3,* 292–297.

Corbetta, M., and Shulman, G. L. (1998). Human cortical mechanisms of visual attention during orienting and search. *Philosophical Transactions of the Royal Society of London. Series B: Biological Sciences, 353,* 1353–1362.

Corbetta, M., and Shulman, G. L. (2002). Control of goal-directed and stimulus-driven attention in the brain. *Nature Reviews. Neuroscience, 3,* 201–215.

Corcoran, A. J., Barber, J. R., and Conner, W. E. (2009). Tiger moth jams bat sonar. *Science, 325,* 325–327.

Coricelli, G., Critchley, H. D., Joffily, M., O'Doherty, J. P., et al. (2005). Regret and its avoidance: A neuroimaging study of choice behavior. *Nature Neuroscience, 8,* 1255–1262.

Corkin, S. (2002). What's new with the amnesic patient H.M.? *Neuroscience, 3,* 153–159.

Corkin, S., Amaral., D. G., Gonzalez, R. G., Johnson, K. A., et al. (1997). H.M.'s medial temporal lobe lesion: Findings from Magnetic resonance imaging. *Journal of Neuroscience, 17,* 3964–3979.

Coryell, W., Noyes, R., Jr., and House, J. D. (1986). Mortality among outpatients with anxiety disorders. *American Journal of Psychiatry, 143,* 508–510.

Cosmides, L., and Tooby, J. (2000). Evolutionary psychology and the emotions. In M. Lewis and J. M. Haviland-Jones (Eds.), *Handbook of emotions* (2nd ed., pp. 91–115). New York, NY: Guilford Press.

Costanzo, R. M. (1991). Regeneration of olfactory receptor cells. *CIBA Foundation Symposium, 160,* 233–242.

Courtney, S., Ungerleider, L., Keil, K., and Haxby, J. (1996). Object and spatial visual working memory activate separate neural systems in human cortex. *Cerebral Cortex, 6,* 39–49.

Cox, J. J., Reimann, F., Nicholas, A. K., Thornton, G., et al. (2006). An SCN9A channelopathy causes congenital inability to experience pain. *Nature, 444,* 894–898.

Coyle, J. T., Tsai, G., and Goff, D. (2003). Converging evidence of NMDA receptor hypofunction in the pathophysiology of schizophrenia. *Annals of the New York Academy of Sciences, 1003,* 318–327.

Cragg, B. G. (1975). The development of synapses in the visual system of the cat. *Journal of Comparative Neurology, 160,* 147–166.

Crasto, C., Singer, M. S., and Shepherd, G. M. (2001). The olfactory receptor family album. *Genome Biology, 2,* reviews1027.1–reviews1027.4.

Cruce, J. A. F., Greenwood, M. R. C., Johnson, P. R., and Quartermain, D. (1974). Genetic versus hypothalamic obesity: Studies of intake and dietary manipulation in rats. *Journal of Comparative and Physiological Psychology, 87,* 295–301.

Cryns, K., and Van Camp, G. (2004). Deafness genes and their diagnostic applications. *Audiology & Neurootology, 9,* 2–22.

Cummings, J. L. (1995). Dementia: The failing brain. *Lancet, 345,* 1481–1484.

Curcio, C. A., Sloan, K. R., Packer, O., Hendrickson, A. E., et al. (1987). Distribution of cones in human and monkey retina: Individual variability and radial asymmetry. *Science, 236,* 579–582.

Curtis, V., Aunger, R., and Rabie, T. (2004). Evidence that disgust evolved to protect from risk of disease. *Proceedings. Biological Sciences, 271*(Suppl. 4), S131–S133.

Curtiss, S. (1989). The independence and task-specificity of language. In M. H. Bornstein and J. S. Bruner (Eds.),

Interaction in human development (pp. 105–137). Hillsdale, NJ: Erlbaum.

Cytowic, R. E., and Eagleman, D. M. (2009). *Wednesday is indigo blue: Discovering the brain of synaesthesia.* Cambridge, MA: MIT Press.

D

Dabbs, J. M., Jr., and Hargrove, M. F. (1997). Age, testosterone, and behavior among female prison inmates. *Psychosomatic Medicine, 59,* 477–480.

Dabbs, J. M., and Morris, R. (1990). Testosterone, social class, and antisocial behavior in a sample of 4,462 men. *Psychological Science, 1,* 209–211.

Dabbs, J. M., Ruback, R. B., Frady, R. L., Hopper, C. H., et al. (1988). Saliva testosterone and criminal violence among women. *Personality and Individual Differences, 9,* 269–275.

Dale, R. C., Heyman, I., Giovannoni, G., and Church, A. W. (2005). Incidence of anti-brain antibodies in children with obsessive-compulsive disorder. *British Journal of Psychiatry, 187,* 314–319.

Dalton, K. M., Nacewicz, B. M., Johnstone, T., Schaefer, H. S., et al. (2005). Gaze fixation and the neural circuitry of face processing in autism. *Nature Neuroscience, 8,* 519–526.

Damasio, H. (1995). *Human brain anatomy in computerized images.* New York, NY: Oxford University Press.

Damasio, H., Grabowski, T., Frank, R., Galaburda, A. M., et al. (1994). The return of Phineas Gage: Clues about the brain from the skull of a famous patient. *Science, 264,* 1102–1105.

Daniele, C. A., and MacDermott, A. B. (2009). Low-threshold primary afferent drive onto GABAergic interneurons in the superficial dorsal horn of the mouse. *Journal of Neuroscience, 29,* 686–695.

Dantz, B., Edgar, D. M., and Dement, W. C. (1994). Circadian rhythms in narcolepsy: Studies on a 90 minute day. *Electroencephalography and Clinical Neurophysiology, 90,* 24–35.

Dantzer, R., O'Connor, J. C., Freund, G. G., Johnson, R. W., et al. (2008). From inflammation to sickness and depression: When the immune system subjugates the brain. *Nature Reviews. Neuroscience, 9,* 46–56.

Dapretto, M., Davies, M. S., Pfeifer, J. H., Scott, A. A., et al. (2006). Understanding emotions in others: Mirror neuron dysfunction in children with autism spectrum disorders. *Nature Neuroscience, 9,* 28–30.

D'Ardenne, K., McClure, S. M., Nystrom, L. E., and Cohen, J. D. (2008). BOLD responses reflecting dopaminergic signals in the human ventral tegmental area. *Science, 319,* 1264–1267.

Darian-Smith, I., Davidson, I., and Johnson, K. O. (1980). Peripheral neural representations of the two spatial dimensions of a textured surface moving over the monkey's finger pad. *Journal of Physiology (London), 309,* 135–146.

Dark, J., Forger, N. G., and Zucker, I. (1984). Rapid recovery of body mass after surgical removal of adipose tissue in ground squirrels. *Proceedings of the National Academy of Sciences, USA, 81,* 2270–2272.

Darwin, C. (1872). *The expression of the emotions in man and animals.* London, England: J. Murray.

Davalos, D., Grutzendler, J., Yang, G., Kim, J. V., et al. (2005). ATP mediates rapid microglial response to local brain injury in vivo. *Nature Neuroscience, 8,* 752–758.

Davey-Smith, G., Frankel, S., and Yarnell, J. (1997). Sex and death: Are they related? Findings from the Caerphilly Cohort Study. *British Medical Journal (Clinical Research Edition), 315,* 1641–1644.

Davidson, J. M., Camargo, C. A., and Smith, E. R. (1979). Effects of androgen on sexual behavior in hypogonadal men. *Journal of Clinical Endocrinology and Metabolism, 48,* 955–958.

Davis, J. I., Senghas, A., Brandt, F., and Ochsner, K. N. (2010). The effects of BOTOX injections on emotional experience. *Emotion, 10,* 433–440.

Davis, J. I., Senghas, A., and Ochsner, K. N. (2009). How does facial feedback modulate emotional experience? *Journal of Research in Personality, 43,* 822–829.

Dawson, T. M., and Dawson, V. L. (2003). Molecular pathways of neurodegeneration in Parkinson's disease. *Science, 302,* 819–822.

Dearborn, G. V. N. (1932). A case of congenital general pure analgesia. *Journal of Nervous and Mental Disease, 75,* 612–615.

De Felipe, C., Herrero, J. F., O'Brien, J. A., Palmer, J. A., et al. (1998). Altered nociception, analgesia and aggression in mice lacking the receptor for substance P. *Nature, 392,* 394–397.

de Gelder, B., Tamietto, M., van Boxtel, G., Goebel, R., et al. (2008). Intact navigation skills after bilateral loss of striate cortex. *Current Biology, 18,* R1128–R1129.

de Groot, C. M., Janus, M. D., and Bornstein, R. A. (1995). Clinical predictors of psychopathology in children and adolescents with Tourette syndrome. *Journal of Psychiatric Research, 29,* 59–70.

Dehaene-Lambertz, G., Dehaene, S., and Hertz-Pannier, L. (2002). Functional neuroimaging of speech perception in infants. *Science, 298,* 2013–2015.

Delgado, J. M. R. (1969). *Physical Control of the Mind: Toward a Psychocivilized Society.* New York, NY: Harper and Row.

Dement, W. C. (1974). *Some must watch while some must sleep.* San Francisco, CA: Freeman.

Dennis, S. G., and Melzack, R. (1983). Perspectives on phylogenetic evolution of pain expression. In R. L. Kitchell, H. H. Erickson, E. Carstens, and L. E. Davis (Eds.), *Animal pain* (pp. 151–161). Bethesda, MD: American Physiological Society.

Denton, D., Shade, R., Zamarippa, F., Egan, G., et al. (1999). Neuroimaging of genesis and satiation of thirst and an interoceptor-driven theory of origins of primary consciousness. *Proceedings of the National Academy of Sciences, USA, 96,* 5304–5309.

Depaepe, V., Suarez-Gonzalez, N., Dufour, A., Passante, L., et al. (2005). Ephrin signalling controls brain size by regulating apoptosis of neural progenitors. *Nature, 435,* 1244–1250.

DeRubeis, R. J., Siegle, G. J., and Hollon, S. D. (2008). Cognitive therapy versus medication for depression: Treatment outcomes and neural mechanisms. *Nature, 9,* 788–796.

Desimone, R., Albright, T. D., Gross, C. G., and Bruce, C. (1984). Stimulus-selective properties of inferior temporal neurons in the macaque. *Journal of Neuroscience, 4,* 2051–2062.

Desimone, R., and Schein, S. J. (1987). Visual properties of neurons in area V4 of the macaque: Sensitivity to stimulus form. *Journal of Neurophysiology, 57,* 835–868.

De Valois, K. K., De Valois, R. L., and Yund, E. W. (1979). Responses of striate cortex cells to grating and checkerboard patterns. *Journal of Physiology (London), 291,* 483–505.

De Valois, R. L., and De Valois, K. K. (1980). Spatial vision. *Annual Review of Psychology, 31,* 309–341.

De Valois, R. L., and De Valois, K. K. (1988). *Spatial vision.* New York, NY: Oxford University Press.

De Valois, R. L., and De Valois, K. K. (1993). A multi-stage color model. *Vision Research, 33,* 1053–1065.

Devane, W. A., Dysarz, F. A., Johnson, M. R., Melvin, L. S., et al. (1988). Determination and characterization of a cannabinoid receptor in rat brain. *Molecular Pharmacology, 34,* 605–613.

Devane, W. A., Hanus, L., Breuer, A., Pertwee, R. G., et al. (1992). Isolation and structure of a brain constituent that binds the cannabinoid receptor. *Science, 258,* 1946–1949.

Devlin, J. T., and Watkins, K. E. (2007). Stimulating language: Insights from TMS. *Brain, 130*(Pt. 3), 610–622.

DeVoogd, T. J. (1994). Interactions between endocrinology and learning in the avian song system. *Annals of the New York Academy of Sciences, 743,* 19–41.

de Waal, F. B. M. (2003). Darwin's legacy and the study of primate visual communication. *Annals of the New York Academy of Sciences, 1000,* 7–31.

de Win, M. M., Jager, G., Booij, J., Reneman, L., et al. (2008). Sustained effects of ecstasy on the human brain: A prospective neuroimaging study in novel users. *Brain, 131*(Pt. 11), 2936–2945.

Dewsbury, D. A. (1972). Patterns of copulatory behavior in male mammals. *Quarterly Review of Biology, 47,* 1–33.

Diamond, J., Cooper, E., Turner, C., and Macintyre, L. (1976). Trophic regulation of nerve sprouting. *Science, 193,* 371–377.

Diamond, M. C. (1967). Extensive cortical depth measurements and neuron size increases in the cortex of environmentally enriched rats. *Journal of Comparative Neurology, 131,* 357–364.

Diamond, M. C., Lindner, B., Johnson, R., Bennett, E. L., et al. (1975). Differences in occipital cortical synapses from environmentally enriched, impoverished, and standard colony rats. *Journal of Neuroscience Research, 1,* 109–119.

Dichgans, J. (1984). Clinical symptoms of cerebellar dysfunction and their topodiagnostical significance. *Human Neurobiology, 2,* 269–279.

Di Chiara, G., Tanda, G., Bassareo, V., Pontieri, F., et al. (1999). Drug addiction as a disorder of associative learning. Role of nucleus accumbens shell/extended amygdala dopamine. *Annals of the New York Academy of Sciences, 877,* 461–485.

Dietz, P. M., Williams, S. B., Callaghan, W. M., Bachman, D. J., et al. (2007). Clinically identified maternal depression before, during, and after pregnancies ending in live births. *American Journal of Psychiatry, 164,* 1457–1459.

Di Marzo, V., and Matias, I. (2005). Endocannabinoid control of food intake and energy balance. *Nature Neuroscience, 8,* 585–589.

Dittmann, R. W., Kappes, M. E., and Kappes, M. H. (1992). Sexual behavior in adolescent and adult females with congenital adrenal hyperplasia. *Psychoneuroendocrinology, 17,* 153–170.

Do, M. T. H., Kang, S. H., Zue, T., Zhong, H., et al. (2009). Photon capture and signalling by melanopsin retinal ganglion cells. *Nature, 457,* 281–287.

Dohanich, G. (2003). Ovarian steroids and cognitive function. *Current Directions in Psychological Science, 12,* 57–61.

Dohrenwend, B. P., Turner, J. B., Turse, N. A., Adams, B. G., et al. (2006). The psychological risks of Vietnam for U.S. veterans: A revisit with new data and methods. *Science, 313,* 979–982.

Dolan, R. J. (2002). Emotion, cognition, and behavior. *Science, 298,* 1191–1194.

Dolder, C. R., and Nelson, M. H. (2008). Hypnosedative-induced complex behaviours: Incidence, mechanisms and management. *CNS Drugs, 22,* 1021–1036.

Domjan, M., and Purdy, J. E. (1995). Animal research in psychology: More than meets the eye of the general psychology student. *American Psychologist, 50,* 496–503.

Donaldson, Z. R., and Young, L. J. (2008). Oxytocin, vasopressin, and the neurogenetics of sociality. *Science, 322,* 900–903.

Dorsaint-Pierre, R., Penhune, V. B., Watkins, K. E., Neelin, P., et al. (2006). Asymmetries of the planum temporale and Heschl's gyrus: Relationship to language lateralization. *Brain, 129,* 1164–1176.

Drea, C. M., Weldele, M. L., Forger, N. G., Coscia, E. M., et al. (1998). Androgens and masculinization of genitalia in the spotted hyaena (*Crocuta crocuta*). 2. Effects of prenatal anti-androgens. *Journal of Reproduction and Fertility, 113,* 117–127.

Drevets, W. C. (1998). Functional neuroimaging studies of depression: The anatomy of melancholia. *Annual Review of Medicine, 49,* 341–361.

Drickamer, L. C. (1992). Behavioral selection of odor cues by young female mice affects age of puberty. *Developmental Psychobiology, 25,* 461–470.

Dronkers, N. F., Wilkins, D. P., Van Valin, R. D., Jr., Redfern, B. B., et al. (2004). Lesion analysis of the brain areas involved in language comprehension. *Cognition, 92,* 145–177.

Druckman, D., and Bjork, R. A. (1994). *Learning, remembering, believing: Enhancing human performance.* Washington, DC: National Academy Press.

Du, J. L., and Poo, M. M. (2004). Rapid BDNF-induced retrograde synaptic modification in a developing retinotectal system. *Nature, 429,* 878–882.

Du, L., Bakish, D., Lapierre, Y. D., Ravindran, A. V., et al. (2000). Association of polymorphism of serotonin 2A receptor gene with suicidal ideation in major depressive disorder. *American Journal of Medical Genetics, 96,* 56–60.

Duchaine, B., Germine, L., and Nakayama, K. (2007). Family resemblance: Ten family members with prosopagnosia and within-class object agnosia. *Cognitive Neuropsychology, 24,* 419–430.

Duchamp-Viret, P., Chaput, M. A., and Duchamp, A. (1999). Odor response properties of rat olfactory receptor neurons. *Science, 284,* 2171–2174.

Duffy, J. D., and Campbell, J. J. (1994). The regional prefrontal syndromes: A theoretical and clinical overview. *Journal of Neuropsychiatry and Clinical Neurosciences, 6,* 379–387.

Dulac, C., and Torello, A. T. (2003). Molecular detection of pheromone signals in mammals, from genes to behaviour. *Nature Reviews. Neuroscience, 4,* 551–562.

Dunah, A. W., Hyunkyung, J., Griffin, A., Kim, Y.-M., et al. (2002). Sp1 and TAFII130 transcriptional activity disrupted in early Huntington's disease. *Science, 296,* 2238–2242.

E

Earnest, D. J., Liang, F. Q., Ratcliff, M., and Cassone, V. M. (1999). Immortal time: Circadian clock properties of rat suprachiasmatic cell lines. *Science, 283,* 693–695.

Ebbinghaus, H. (1908). *Psychology: An elementary textbook.* Boston: Heath.

Edelsohn, G. A. (2006). Hallucinations in children and adolescents: Considerations in the emergency setting. *American Journal of Psychiatry, 163,* 781–785.

Edwards, R. R., Grace, E., Peterson, S., Klick, B., et al. (2009). Sleep continuity and architecture: Associations with pain-inhibitory processes in patients with temporomandibular joint disorder. *European Journal of Pain, 13,* 1043–1047.

Egaas, B., Courchesne, E., and Saitoh, O. (1995). Reduced size of corpus callosum in autism. *Archives of Neurology, 52,* 794–801.

Elbert, T., Pantev, C., Wienbruch, C., Rockstroh, B., et al. (1995). Increased cortical representation of the fingers of the left hand in string players. *Science, 270,* 305–307.

Ellenbogen, J. M., Hu, P. T., Payne, J. D., Titone, D., et al. (2007). Human relational memory requires time and sleep. *Proceedings of the National Academy of Sciences, USA, 104,* 7317–7318.

Elster, A. D., and Burdette, J. H. (2001). *Magnetic resonance imaging.* Philadelphia, PA: Mosby.

Emery, N. J., Capitanio, J. P., Mason, W. A., Machado, C. J., et al. (2001). The effects of bilateral lesions of the amygdala on dyadic social interactions in rhesus monkeys (*Macaca mulatta*). *Behavioral Neuroscience, 115,* 515–544.

Engel, J., Jr. (1992). Recent advances in surgical treatment of temporal lobe epilepsy. *Acta Neurologica Scandinavica. Supplementum, 140,* 71–80.

English, P. J., Ghatei, M. A., Malik, I. A., Bloom, S. R., et al. (2002). Food fails to suppress ghrelin levels in obese humans. *Journal of Clinical Endocrinology and Metabolism, 87,* 2984–2987.

Enoch, M. A., Kaye, W. H., Rotondo, A., Greenberg, B. D., et al. (1998). 5-HT2A promoter polymorphism -1438G/A, anorexia nervosa, and obsessive-compulsive disorder. *Lancet, 351,* 1785–1786.

Epstein, A. N., Fitzsimons, J. T., and Rolls, B. J. (1970). Drinking induced by injection of angiotensin into the brain of the rat. *Journal of Physiology (London), 210,* 457–474.

Erhardt, V. R., and Goldman, M. B. (1992). Adverse endocrine effects. In M. S. Keshavan and J. S. Kennedy (Eds.), *Drug-induced dysfunction in psychiatry* (pp. 293–310). New York, NY: Hemisphere.

Eriksson, A., and Lacerda, F. (2007). Charlantry in forensic speech science: A problem to be taken seriously. *International Journal of Speech Language and the Law, 14,* 169–193.

Erlanger, D. M., Kutner, K. C., Barth, J. T., and Barnes, R. (1999). Neuropsychology of sports-related head injury: Dementia pugilistica to post concussion syndrome. *Clinical Neuropsychologist, 13,* 193–209.

Ernst, T., Chang, L., Leonido-Yee, M., and Speck, O. (2000). Evidence for long-term neurotoxicity associated with methamphetamine abuse: A 1H MRS study. *Neurology, 54,* 1344–1349.

Erren, T. C., Morfeld, P., Stork, J., Knauth, P., et al. (2009). Shift work, chronodisruption and cancer?—The IARC 2007 challenge for research and prevention and 10 theses from the Cologne Colloquium 2008. *Scandinavian Journal of Work, Environment & Health, 35,* 74–79.

Everitt, B. J., and Stacey, P. (1987). Studies of instrumental behavior with sexual reinforcement in male rats (*Rattus norvegicus*): II. Effects of preoptic area lesions, castration, and testosterone. *Journal of Comparative Psychology, 101,* 407–419.

Everson, C. A. (1993). Sustained sleep deprivation impairs host defense. *American Journal of Physiology, 265,* R1148–R1154.

Everson, C. A., Bergmann, B. M., and Rechtschaffen A. (1989). Sleep deprivation in the rat: III. Total sleep deprivation. *Sleep, 12,* 13–21.

Eybalin, M. (1993). Neurotransmitters and neuromodulators of the mammalian cochlea. *Physiological Reviews, 73,* 309–373.

F

Falk, D. (2004). Prelinguistic evolution in early hominins: Whence motherese? *Behavioral and Brain Sciences, 27,* 491–503.

Faraone, S.V., Glatt, S. J., Su, J., and Tsuang, M. T. (2004). Three potential susceptibility loci shown by a genome-wide scan for regions influencing the age at onset of mania. *American Journal of Psychiatry, 161,* 625–630.

Farbman, A. I. (1994). The cellular basis of olfaction. *Endeavour, 18,* 2–8.

Feder, H. H., and Whalen, R. E. (1965). Feminine behavior in neonatally castrated and estrogen-treated male rats. *Science, 147,* 306–307.

Feinstein, J. S., Adolphs, R., Damasio, A., and Tranel, D. (2011). The human amygdala and the induction and experience of fear. *Current Biology, 21,* 34–38.

Fenstemaker, S. B., Zup, S. L., Frank, L. G., Glickman, S. E., et al. (1999). A sex difference in the hypothalamus of the spotted hyena. *Nature Neuroscience, 2,* 943–945.

Ferguson, J. N., Young, L. J., Hearn, E. F., Matzuk, M. M., et al. (2000). Social amnesia in mice lacking the oxytocin gene. *Nature Genetics, 25,* 284–288.

Fernald, R. D. (2000). Evolution of eyes. *Current Opinion in Neurobiology, 10,* 444–450.

Fields, R. D., and Stevens-Graham, B. (2002). New insights into neuron-glia communication. *Science, 298,* 556–562.

Fields, S. (1990). Pheromone response in yeast. *Trends in Biochemical Sciences, 15,* 270–273.

Finch, C. E., and Kirkwood, T. B. L. (2000). *Chance, development, and aging.* New York, NY: Oxford University Press.

Finger, S. (1994). *Origins of neuroscience: A history of explorations into brain function.* New York, NY: Oxford University Press.

Fink, G. R., Markowitsch, H. J., Reinkemeier, M., Bruckbauer, T., et al. (1996). Cerebral representation of one's own past: Neural networks involved in autobiographical memory. *Journal of Neuroscience, 16,* 4275–4282.

Fink, H., Rex, A., Voits, M., and Voigt, J. P. (1998). Major biological actions of CCK—A critical evaluation of research findings. *Experimental Brain Research, 123,* 77–83.

Fink, M., and Taylor, M. A. (2007). Electroconvulsive therapy: Evidence and challenges. *JAMA, 298,* 330–332.

Fischer, C., Hatzidimitriou, G., Wlos, J., Katz, J., et al. (1995). Reorganization of ascending 5-HT axon projections in animals previously exposed to the recreational drug (+/–)3,4-methylenedioxymethamphetamine (MDMA, "ecstasy"). *Journal of Neuroscience, 15,* 5476–5485.

Fishman, R. B., Chism, L., Firestone, G. L., and Breedlove, S. M. (1990). Evidence for androgen receptors in sexually dimorphic perineal muscles of neonatal male rats. Absence of androgen accumulation by the perineal motoneurons. *Journal of Neurobiology, 21,* 694–704.

Fitzsimmons, J. T. (1998). Angiotensin, thirst, and sodium appetite. *Physiological Reviews, 78,* 583–686.

Flegal, K. M., Carroll, M. D., Ogden, C. L., and Johnson, C. L. (2002). Prevalence and trends in obesity among US adults, 1999–2000. *Journal of the American Medical Association, 288,* 1723–1727.

Fleming, A. S., Kraemer, G. W., Gonzalez, A., Lovic, V., et al. (2002). Mothering begets mothering: The transmission of behavior and its neurobiology across generations. *Pharmacology, Biochemistry, and Behavior, 73,* 61–75.

Fleming, A. S., Ruble, D., Krieger, H., and Wong, P.Y. (1997). Hormonal and experiential correlates of maternal responsiveness during pregnancy and the puerperium in human mothers. *Hormones and Behavior, 31,* 145–158.

Florence, S. L., Taub, H. B., and Kaas, J. H. (1998). Large-scale sprouting of cortical connections after peripheral injury in adult macaque monkeys. *Science, 282,* 1117–1121.

Flum, D. R., Salem, L., Elrod, J. A., Dellinger, E. P., et al. (2005). Early mortality among Medicare beneficiaries undergoing bariatric surgical procedures. *JAMA, 294,* 1903–1908.

Foerster, O., and Penfield, W. (1930). The structural basis of traumatic epilepsy and results of radical operation. *Brain, 53,* 8–119.

Ford, J. M. (1999). Schizophrenia: The broken P300 and beyond. *Psychophysiology, 36,* 667–682.

Forger, N. G., and Breedlove, S. M. (1986). Sexual dimorphism in human and canine spinal cord: Role of early androgen. *Proceedings of the National Academy of Sciences, USA, 83,* 7527–7531.

Forger, N. G., and Breedlove, S. M. (1987). Seasonal variation in mammalian striated muscle mass and motoneuron morphology. *Journal of Neurobiology, 18,* 155–165.

Forger, N. G., Frank, L. G., Breedlove, S. M., and Glickman, S. E. (1996). Sexual dimorphism of perineal muscles and motoneurons in spotted hyenas. *Journal of Comparative Neurology, 375,* 333–343.

Foster, G. D., Wyatt, H. R., Hill, J. O., Mc-Guckin, B. G., et al. (2003). A randomized trial of a low-carbohydrate diet for obesity. *New England Journal of Medicine, 348,* 2082–2090.

Foster, N. L., Cahse, T. N., Mansi, L., Brooks, R., et al. (1984). Cortical abnormalities in Alzheimer's disease. *Annals of Neurology, 16,* 649–654.

Foster, R. G., and Soni, B. G. (1998). Extra-retinal photoreceptors and their regulation of temporal physiology. *Reproduction, 3,* 145–150.

Fournier, J. C., DeRubeis, R. J., Hollon, S. D., Dimidjian, S., et al. (2010). Antidepressant drug effects and depression severity: A patient-level meta-analysis. *JAMA, 303,* 47–53.

Francis, D. D., Szegda, K., Campbell, G., Martin, W. D., et al. (2003). Epigenetic sources of behavioral differences in mice. *Nature Neuroscience, 6,* 445–446.

Frank, L. G., Glickman, S. E., and Licht, P. (1991). Fatal sibling aggression, precocial development, and androgens in neonatal spotted hyenas. *Science, 252,* 702–704.

Frank, M. J., Samanta, J., Moustafa, A. A., and Sherman, S. J. (2007). Hold your horses: Impulsivity, deep brain stimulation, and medication in parkinsonism. *Science, 318,* 1309–1312.

Frankenhaeuser, M. (1978). Psychoneuroendocrine approaches to the study of emotion as related to stress and coping. *Nebraska Symposium on Motivation, 26,* 123–162.

Frankland, P. W., O'Brien, C., Masuo, O., Kirkwood, A., et al. (2001). α-CaMKII-dependent plasticity in the cortex is required for permanent memory. *Nature, 411,* 309–312.

Franklin, T. R., Acton, P. D., Maldjian, J. A., Gray, J. D., et al. (2002). Decreased gray matter concentration in the insular, orbitofrontal, cingulate, and temporal cortices of cocaine patients. *Biological Psychiatry, 51,* 134–142.

Franks, N. P. (2008). General anaesthesia: From molecular targets to neuronal pathways of sleep and arousal. *Nature, 9,* 370–386.

Freed, C. R., Greene, P. E., Breeze, R. E., Tsai, W.-Y., et al. (2001). Transplantation of embryonic dopamine neurons for severe Parkinson's disease. *New England Journal of Medicine, 344,* 710–719.

Freedman, M. S., Lucas, R. J., Soni, B., von Schantz, M., et al. (1999). Regulation of mammalian circadian behavior by non-rod, non-cone, ocular photoreceptors. *Science, 284,* 502–504.

Freitag, J., Ludwig, G., Andreini, P., Roessler, P., et al. (1998). Olfactory receptors in aquatic and terrestrial vertebrates. *Journal of Comparative Physiology, 183,* 635–650.

Freiwald, W. A., Tsao, D.Y., and Livingstone, M. S. (2009). A face feature space in the macaque temporal lobe. *Nature Neuroscience, 12,* 1187–1196.

Frey, S. H., Bogdanov, S., Smith, J. C., Watrous, S., et al. (2008). Chronically deafferented sensory cortex recovers a grossly typical organization after allogenic hand transplantation. *Current Biology, 18,* 1530–1534.

Fried, I., Wilson, C. L., MacDonald, K. A., and Behnke, E. J. (1998). Electric current stimulates laughter. *Nature, 391,* 650.

Friedman, L., and Jones, B. E. (1984). Study of sleep-wakefulness states by computer graphics and cluster analysis before and after lesions of the pontine tegmentum in the cat. *Electroencephalography and Clinical Neurophysiology, 57,* 43–56.

Friedrich, F. J., Egly, R., Rafal, R. D., and Beck, D. (1998). Spatial attention deficits in humans: A comparison of superior parietal and temporal-parietal junction lesions. *Neuropsychology, 12,* 193–207.

Fritz, J., Shamma, S., Elhilali, M., and Klein, D. (2003). Rapid task-related plasticity of spectrotemporal receptive fields in primary auditory cortex. *Nature Neuroscience, 6,* 1216–1223.

Frost, B., Jacks, R. L., and Diamond, M. I. (2009). Propagation of Tau misfolding from the outside to the inside of a cell. *Journal of Biological Chemistry, 284,* 12845–12852.

Fukuda, K., Ogilvie, R. D., Chilcott, L., Vendittelli, A.-M., et al. (1998). The prevalence of sleep paralysis among Canadian and Japanese college students. *Dreaming: Journal of the Association for the Study of Dreams, 8*(2), 59–66.

Fuster, J. M. (1990). Prefrontal cortex and the bridging of temporal gaps in the perception-action cycle. *Annals of the New York Academy of Sciences, 608,* 318–336.

G

Galaburda, A. M. (1994). Developmental dyslexia and animal studies: At the interface between cognition and neurology. *Cognition, 56,* 833–839.

Galaburda, A. M., LoTurco, J., Ramus, F., Fitch, R. H., et al. (2006). From genes to behavior in developmental dyslexia. *Nature Neuroscience, 9,* 1213–1217.

Gallant, J. L., Braun, J., and Van Essen, D. C. (1993). Selectivity for polar, hyperbolic, and Cartesian gratings in macaque visual cortex. *Science, 259,* 100–103.

Gallopin, T., Fort, P., Eggermann, E., Cauli, B., et al. (2000). Identification of sleep-promoting neurons *in vitro. Nature, 404,* 992–995.

Gangwisch, J. E., Heymsfield, S. B., Boden-Albala, B., Buijs, R. M., et al. (2007). Sleep duration as a risk factor for diabetes incidence in a large U.S. sample. *Sleep, 30,* 1667–1673.

Gannon, P. J., Holloway, R. L., Broadfield, D. C., and Braun, A. R. (1998). Asymmetry of chimpanzee planum temporale: Humanlike pattern of brain language area homolog. *Science, 279,* 220–222.

Gaoni, Y., and Mechoulam, R. (1964). Isolation, structure, and partial synthesis of an active constituent of hashish. *Journal of the American Chemical Society, 86,* 1646–1647.

Gardner, L. I. (1972). Deprivation dwarfism. *Scientific American, 227*(1), 76–82.

Gardner, R. A., and Gardner, B. T. (1969). Teaching sign language to a chimpanzee. *Science, 165,* 664–672.

Gardner, R. A., and Gardner, B. T. (1984). A vocabulary test for chimpanzees (*Pan troglodytes*). *Journal of Comparative Psychology, 98,* 381–404.

Gardner, T. J., Naef, F., and Nottebohm, F. (2005). Freedom and rules: The acquisition and reprogramming of a bird's learned song. *Science, 308,* 1046–1049.

Garver, D. L., Holcomb, J. A., and Christensen, J. D. (2000). Heterogeneity of response to antipsychotics from multiple disorders in the schizophrenia spectrum. *Journal of Clinical Psychiatry, 61,* 964–972.

Gaulin, S. J. C, and Fitzgerald, R. W. (1989). Sexual selection for spatial-learning ability. *Animal Behaviour, 37,* 322–331.

Gauthier, I., Behrmann, M., and Tarr, M. J. (1999). Can face recognition really be dissociated from object recognition? *Journal of Cognitive Neuroscience, 11,* 349–370.

Gauthier, I., Skudlarski, P., Gore, J. C., and Anderson, A. W. (2000). Expertise for cars and birds recruits brain areas involved in face recognition. *Nature Neuroscience, 3,* 191–197.

Gazzaniga, M. S., and Smylie, C. S. (1983). Facial recognition and brain asymmetries: Clues to underlying mechanisms. *Annals of Neurology, 13,* 536–540.

Georgiadis, J. R., Reinders, A. A., Paans, A. M., Renken, R., et al. (2009). Men versus women on sexual brain function: Prominent differences during tactile genital stimulation, but not during orgasm. *Human Brain Mapping, 10,* 3089–3101.

Georgopoulos, A. P., Kalaska, J. F., Caminiti, R., and Massey, J. T. (1982). On the relations between the direction of two-dimensional arm movements and cell discharge in primate motor cortex. *Journal of Neuroscience, 2,* 1527–1537.

Georgopoulos, A. P., Taira, M., and Lukashin, A. (1993). Cognitive neurophysiology of the motor cortex. *Science, 260,* 47–52.

Gerashchenko, D., Kohls, M. D., Greco, M. A., Waleh, N. S., et al. (2001). Hypocretin-2-saporin lesions of the lateral hypothalamus produce narcoleptic-like sleep behavior in the rat. *Neuroscience, 21,* 7273–7283.

Geschwind, N. (1976). Language and cerebral dominance. In T. N. Chase (Ed.), *Nervous system: Vol. 2. The clinical neurosciences* (pp. 433–439). New York, NY: Raven Press.

Geschwind, N., and Levitsky, W. (1968). Human brain: Left-right asymmetries in temporal speech region. *Science, 161,* 186–187.

Gilbert, A. N., and Wysocki, C. J. (1987). The smell survey results. *National Geographic, 172,* 514–525.

Gilbertson, M. W., Shenton, M. E., Ciszewski, A., Kasai, K., et al. (2002). Smaller hippocampal volume predicts pathologic vulnerability to psychological trauma. *Nature Neuroscience, 5,* 1242–1247.

Gill, R. E., Tibbitts, T. L., Douglas, D. C., Hanel, C. M., et al. (2009). Extreme endurance flights by landbirds crossing the Pacific Ocean: Ecological corridor rather than barrier? *Proceedings. Biological Sciences, 276,* 447–457.

Gillin, J. C., Duncan, W. C., Murphy, D. L., Post, R. M., et al. (1981). Age-related changes in sleep in depressed and normal subjects. *Psychiatry Research, 4,* 73–78.

Glantz, M., and Pickens, R. (1992). *Vulnerability to drug abuse.* Washington, DC: American Psychological Association.

Glaser, R., Rice, J., Speicher, C. E., Stout, J. C., et al. (1986). Stress depresses interferon production by leukocytes concomitant with a decrease in natural killer cell activity. *Behavioral Neuroscience, 100,* 675–678.

Glickman, S. E. (1977). Comparative psychology. In P. Mussen and M. R. Rosenzweig (Eds.), *Psychology: An introduction* (2nd ed., pp. 625–703). Lexington, MA: Heath.

Glickman, S. E., Frank, L. G., Davidson, J. M., Smith, E. R., et al. (1987). Androstenedione may organize or activate sex-reversed traits in female spotted hyenas. *Proceedings of the National Academy of Sciences, USA, 84,* 344–347.

Glusman, G., Yanai, I., Rubin, I., and Lancet D. (2001). The complete human olfactory subgenome. *Genome Research, 11,* 685–702.

Goel, V., and Dolan, R. J. (2001). The functional anatomy of humor: Segregating cognitive and affective components. *Nature Neuroscience, 4,* 237–238.

Gogtay, N., Giedd, J. N., Lusk, L., Hayashi, K. M., et al. (2004). Dynamic mapping of human cortical development during childhood through early adulthood. *Proceedings of the National Academy of Sciences, USA, 101,* 8174–8179.

Golden, R. N., Gaynes, B. N., Ekstrom, R. D., Hamer, R. M., et al. (2005). The efficacy of light therapy in the treatment of mood disorders: A review and meta-analysis of the evidence. *American Journal of Psychiatry, 162,* 656–662.

Goldstein, J. M., Seidman, L. J., Horton, N. J., Makris, N., et al. (2001). Normal sexual dimorphism of the adult human brain assessed by in vivo magnetic resonance imaging. *Cerebral Cortex, 11,* 490–497.

Golomb, J., de Leon, M. J., George, A. E., Kluger, A., et al. (1994). Hippocampal atrophy correlates with severe cognitive impairment in elderly patients with suspected normal pressure hydrocephalus. *Journal of Neurology, Neurosurgery and Psychiatry, 57,* 590–593.

Gonzáles-Maeso, J., Ang, R. L., Yuen, T., Chan, P., et al. (2008). Identification of a serotonin/glutamate receptor complex implicated in psychosis. *Nature, 452,* 93–97.

Goodale, M. A., Milner, A. D., Jakobson, L. S., and Carey, D. P. (1991). A neurological dissociation between perceiving objects and grasping them. *Nature, 349,* 154–156.

Goodman, C. (1979). Isogenic grasshoppers: Genetic variability and development of identified neurons. In X. O. Breakefeld (Ed.), *Neurogenetics* (pp. 101–151). New York, NY: Elsevier.

Gordon, N. S., Burke, S., Akil, H., Watson, S. J., et al. (2003). Socially-induced brain "fertilization": Play promotes brain derived neurotrophic factor transcription in the amygdala and dorsolateral frontal cortex in juvenile rats. *Neuroscience Letters, 341,* 17–20.

Gorski, R. A., Gordon, J. H., Shryne, J. E., and Southam, A. M. (1978). Evidence for a morphological sex difference within the medial preoptic area of the rat brain. *Brain Research, 148,* 333–346.

Gorzalka, B. B., Mendelson, S. D., and Watson, N. V. (1990). Serotonin receptor subtypes and sexual behavior. *Annals of the New York Academy of Sciences, 600,* 435–444.

Gottesman, I. I. (1991). *Schizophrenia genesis: The origins of madness.* New York, NY: Freeman.

Gottfried, J. A., O'Doherty, J., and Dolan, R. J. (2003). Encoding predictive reward value in human amygdala and orbito-frontal cortex. *Science, 301,* 1104–1107.

Gottlieb, J. (2007). From thought to action: The parietal cortex as a bridge between perception, action, and cognition. *Neuron, 53,* 9–16.

Gough, P. M., Nobre, A. C., and Devlin, J. T. (2005). Dissociating linguistic processes in the left inferior frontal cortex with transcranial magnetic stimulation. *Journal of Neuroscience, 25,* 8010–8016.

Gould, E., Beylin, A., Tanapat, P., Reeves, A., et al. (1999). Learning enhances adult neurogenesis in the hippocampal formation. *Nature Neuroscience, 2,* 260–265.

Gould, E., Reeves, A. J., Graziano, M. S., and Gross, C. G. (1999). Neurogenesis in the neocortex of adult primates. *Science, 286,* 548–552.

Grados, M. A., Walkup, J., and Walford, S. (2003). Genetics of obsessive-compulsive disorders: New findings and challenges. *Brain & Development, 25*(Suppl. 1), S55–S61.

Grafton, S. T., Mazziotta, J. C., Presty, S., Friston, K. J., et al. (1992). Functional anatomy of human procedural learning determined with regional cerebral blood flow and PET. *Journal of Neuroscience, 12,* 2542–2548.

Graham, R. K., Deng, Y., Slow, E. J., Haigh, B., et al. (2006). Cleavage at the caspase-6 site is required for neuronal dysfunction and degeneration due to mutant huntingtin. *Cell, 125,* 1179–1191.

Gray, N. S., MacCulloch, M. J., Smith, J., Morris, M., et al. (2003). Violence viewed by psychopathic murderers. *Nature, 423,* 497.

Graybiel, A. M., Aosaki, T., Flaherty, A. W., and Kimura, M. (1994). The basal ganglia and adaptive motor control. *Science, 265,* 1826–1831.

Graziano, M. (2006). The organization of behavioral repertoire in motor cortex. *Annual Review of Neuroscience, 29,* 105–134.

Graziano, M. S., and Aflalo, T. N. (2007). Mapping behavioral repertoire onto the cortex. *Neuron, 56,* 239–251.

Green, C. S., and Bavelier, D. (2003). Action video game modifies visual selective attention. *Nature, 423,* 534–537.

Green, W. H., Campbell, M., and David, R. (1984). Psychosocial dwarfism: A critical review of the evidence. *Journal of the American Academy of Child Psychiatry, 23,* 39–48.

Greenewalt, C. H. (1968). *Bird song: Acoustics and physiology.* Washington, DC: Smithsonian Institution Press.

Greenough, W. T. (1976). Enduring brain effects of differential experience and training. In M. R. Rosenzweig and E. L. Bennett (Eds.), *Neural mechanisms of learning and memory* (pp. 255–278). Cambridge, MA: MIT Press.

Grieco-Calub, T. M., Saffran, J. R., and Litovsky, R. Y. (2009). Spoken word recognition in toddlers who use cochlear implants. *Journal of Speech, Language, and Hearing Research, 52,* 1390–1400.

Grimm, S., and Bajbouj, M. (2010). Efficacy of vagus nerve stimulation in the treatment of depression. *Expert Review of Neurotherapeutics, 19,* 87–92.

Grothe, B. (2003). New roles for synaptic inhibition in sound localization. *Nature Reviews. Neuroscience, 4,* 540–550.

Grover, G. J., Mellstrom, K., Ye, L., Malm, J., et al. (2003). Selective thyroid hormone receptor-β activation: A strategy for reduction of weight, cholesterol, and lipoprotein (a) with reduced cardiovascular liability. *Proceedings of the National Academy of Sciences, USA, 100,* 10067–10072.

Grumbach, M. M., and Auchus, R. J. (1999). Estrogen: Consequences and implications of human mutations in synthesis and action. *Journal of Clinical Endocrinology and Metabolism, 84,* 4677–4694.

Grunt, J. A., and Young, W. C. (1953). Consistency of sexual behavior patterns in individual male guinea pigs following castration and androgen therapy. *Journal of Comparative and Physiological Psychology, 46,* 138–144.

Grüter, T., Grüter, M., and Carbon, C. C. (2008). Neural and genetic foundations of face recognition and prosopagnosia. *Journal of Neuropsychology, 2,* 79–97.

Gulevich, G., Dement, W., and Johnson, L. (1966). Psychiatric and EEG observations on a case of prolonged (264 hours) wakefulness. *Archives of General Psychiatry, 15,* 29–35.

Gurney, M. E., Pu, H., Chiu, A. Y., Dal Canto, M. C., et al. (1994). Motor neuron degeneration in mice that express a human Cu,Zn superoxide dismutase mutation. *Science, 264,* 1772–1775.

Gusella, J. F., and MacDonald, M. E. (1993). Hunting for Huntington's disease. *Molecular Genetic Medicine, 3,* 139–158.

H

Hadley, M. E., and Levine, J. E. (2006). *Endocrinology* (6th ed.). Upper Saddle River, NJ: Prentice Hall.

Haesler, S., Rochefort, C., Georgi, B., Licznerski, P., et al. (2007). Incomplete and inaccurate vocal imitation after knockdown of FoxP2 in songbird basal ganglia nucleus Area X. *PLoS Biology, 5,* e321.

Haesler, S., Wada, K., Nshdejan, A., Morrisey, E. E., et al. (2004). FoxP2 expression in avian vocal learners and non-learners. *Journal of Neuroscience, 24,* 3164–3175.

Hagstrom, S. A., Neitz, J., and Neitz, M. (1998). Variations in cone populations for red-green color vision examined by analysis of mRNA. *Neuroreport, 9,* 1963–1967.

Hagstrum, J. T. (2000). Infrasound and the avian navigational map. *Journal of Experimental Biology, 203,* 1103–1111.

Hall, D., Dhilla, A., Charalambous, A., Gogos, J. A., et al. (2003). Sequence variants of the brain-derived neurotrophic factor (BDNF) gene are strongly associated with obsessive-compulsive disorder. *American Journal of Human Genetics, 73,* 370–376.

Halsband, U., Matsuzaka, Y., and Tanji, J. (1994). Neuronal activity in the primate supplementary, pre-supplementary and premotor cortex during externally and internally instructed sequential movements. *Neuroscience Research, 20,* 149–155.

Hamburger, V. (1958). Regression versus peripheral control of differentiation in motor hypoplasia. *American Journal of Anatomy, 102,* 365–410.

Hamburger, V. (1975). Cell death in the development of the lateral motor column of the chick embryo. *Journal of Comparative Neurology, 160,* 535–546.

Hamer, D. H., Hu, S., Magnuson, V. L., Hu, N., et al. (1993). A linkage between DNA markers on the X chromosome and male sexual orientation. *Science, 261,* 321–327.

Hamson, D. K., Csupity, A. S., Ali, F. M., and Watson, N. V. (2009). Partner preference and mount latency are masculinized in androgen insensitive rats. *Physiology & Behavior, 98,* 25–30.

Hamson, D. K., and Watson, N. V. (2004). Regional brainstem expression of Fos associated with sexual behavior in male rats. *Brain Research, 1006,* 233–240.

Hanaway, J., Woolsey, T. A., Gado, M. H., and Roberts, M. P. (1998). *The brain atlas.* Bethesda, MD: Fitzgerald Science.

Harder, B. (2003). Unproven elixir: Hormone therapy tempts aging men, but its risks haven't yet been reckoned. *Science News, 163,* 296–301.

Hare, R. D., Harpur, T. J., Hakstian, A. R., Forth, A. E., et al. (1990). The revised psychopathy checklist: Descriptive statistics, reliability, and factor structure. *Psychological Assessment, 2,* 338–341.

Harel, N. Y., and Strittmatter, S. M. (2006). Can generating axons recapitulate developmental guidance during recovery from spinal cord injury? *Nature Reviews. Neuroscience, 7,* 603–616.

Harold, D., Paracchini, S., Scerri, T., Dennis, M., et al. (2006). Further evidence that the KIAA0319 gene confers susceptibility to developmental dyslexia. *Molecular Psychiatry, 11,* 1085–1091, 1061.

Hart, B. L. (1988). Biological basis of the behavior of sick animals. *Neuroscience and Biobehavioral Reviews, 12,* 123–137.

Hartmann, E. (1978). *The sleeping pill.* New Haven, CT: Yale University Press.

Hartmann, E. (1984). *The nightmare: The psychology and biology of terrifying dreams.* New York, NY: Basic Books.

Hauser, P., Zametkin, A. J., Martinez, P., Vitiello, B., et al. (1993). Attention deficit-hyperactivity disorder in people with generalized resistance to thyroid hormone. *New England Journal of Medicine, 328,* 997–1001.

Hayashi-Takagi, A., Takaki, M., Graziane, N., Seshadri, S., et al. (2010). Disrupted-in-Schizophrenia 1 (DISC1) regulates spines of the glutamate synapse via Rac1. *Nature Neuroscience, 13,* 327–332.

Haynes, K. F., Gemeno, C., Yeargan, K. V., Millar, J. G., et al. (2002). Aggressive chemical mimicry of moth pheromones by a bolas spider: How does this specialist predator attract more than one species of prey? *Chemoecology, 12,* 99–105.

Hazeltine, E., Grafton, S. T., and Ivry, R. (1997). Attention and stimulus characteristics determine the locus of motor-sequence encoding. A PET study. *Brain, 120,* 123–140.

Heath, R. G. (1972). Pleasure and brain activity in man. *Journal of Nervous and Mental Diseases, 154,* 3–18.

Hebb, D. O. (1949). *The organization of behavior.* New York, NY: Wiley.

Heinrichs, R. W. (2003). Historical origins of schizophrenia: Two early madmen and their illness. *Journal for the History of Behavioral Sciences, 39,* 349–363.

Heit, S., Owens, M. J., Plotsky, P., and Nemeroff, C. B. (1997). Corticotropin-releasing factor, stress, and depression. *Neuroscientist, 3,* 186–194.

Held, R. (1993). Binocular vision—Behavioral and neuronal development. In M. H. Johnson (Ed.), *Brain development and cognition: A reader* (pp. 152–166). Oxford, England: Blackwell.

Helmholtz, H. von. (1962). *Treatise on physiological optics* (J. P. C. Southall, Trans.). New York, NY: Dover. (Original work published 1894)

Hemmingsen, A. M. (1960). Energy metabolism as related to body size and respiratory surfaces, and its evolution. *Reports of Steno Memorial Hospital, Copenhagen, 9,* 1–110.

Hendriks, W. T., Ruitenberg, M. J., Blits, B., Boer, G. J., et al. (2004). Viral vector-mediated gene transfer of neurotrophins to promote regeneration of the injured spinal cord. *Progress in Brain Research, 146,* 451–476.

Heres, S., Davis, J., Maino, K., Jetzinger, E., et al. (2006). Why olanzapine beats risperidone, risperidone beats quetiapine, and quetiapine beats olanzapine: An exploratory analysis of head-to-head comparison studies of second-generation antipsychotics. *American Journal of Psychiatry, 163,* 185–194.

Hernandez, T. L., Kittelson, J. M., Law, C. K., Ketch, L. L., et al. (2011). Fat redistribution following suction lipectomy: Defense of body fat and patterns of restoration. *Obesity (Silver Spring), 19,* 1388–1395.

Herrmann, C., and Knight, R. (2001). Mechanisms of human attention: Event-related potentials and oscillations. *Neuroscience and Biobehavioral Reviews, 25,* 465–476.

Hertel, P., Fagerquist, M. V., and Svensson, T. H. (1999). Enhanced cortical dopamine output and antipsychotic-like effects of raclopride by alpha-2 adrenoceptor blockade. *Science, 286,* 105–107.

Hetherington, A. W., and Ranson, S. W. (1940). Hypothalamic lesions and adiposity in the rat. *Anatomical Record, 78,* 149–172.

Hewes, G. (1973). Primate communication and the gestural origin of language. *Current Anthropology, 14,* 5–24.

Hickmott, P. W., and Steen, P. A. (2005). Large-scale changes in dendritic structure during reorganization of adult somatosensory cortex. *Nature Neuroscience, 8,* 140–142.

Highley, J. R., Walker, M. A., Esiri, M. M., McDonald, B., et al. (2001). Schizophrenia and the frontal lobes: Post-mortem stereological study of tissue volume. *British Journal of Psychiatry, 178,* 337–343.

Higley, J. D., Mehlman, P. T., Taub, D. M., Higley, S. B., et al. (1992). Cerebrospinal fluid monoamine and adrenal correlates of aggression in free-ranging rhesus monkeys. *Archives of General Psychiatry, 49,* 436–441.

Hillyard, S. A., Hink, R. F., Schwent, V. L., and Picton, T. W. (1973). Electrical signs of selective attention in the human brain. *Science, 182,* 177–180.

Himle, M. B., Woods, D. W., Piacentini, J. C., and Walkup, J. T. (2006). Brief review of habit reversal training for Tourette syndrome. *Journal of Child Neurology, 21,* 719–725.

Hirsch, E., Moye, D., and Dimon, J. H. (1995). Congenital indifference to pain: Long-term follow-up of two cases. *Southern Medical Journal, 88,* 851–857.

Hirtz, D., Thurman, D. J., Gwinn-Hardy, K., Mohamed, M., et al. (2007). How common are the "common" neurologic disorders? *Neurology, 68,* 326–337.

Hitt, E. (2007). Careers in neuroscience: From protons to poetry. *Science, 318,* 661–665.

Hochberg, L. R., Serruya, M. D., Friehs, G. M., Mukand, J. A., et al. (2006). Neuronal ensemble control of prosthetic devices by a human with tetraplegia. *Nature, 442,* 164–171.

Hodgkin, A. L., and Katz, B. (1949). The effect of sodium ions on the electrical activity of the giant axon of the squid. *Journal of Physiology (London), 108,* 37–77.

Hoeft, F., Hernandez, A., McMillon, G., Taylor-Hill, H., et al. (2006). Neural basis of dyslexia: A comparison between dyslexic and nondyslexic children equated for reading ability. *Journal of Neuroscience, 26,* 10700–10708.

Hohmann, A. G., Suplita, R. L., Bolton, N. M., Neely, M. H., et al. (2005). An endocannabinoid mechanism for stress-induced analgesia. *Nature, 435,* 1108–1112.

Hohmann, G. W. (1966). Some effects of spinal cord lesions on experienced emotional feelings. *Psychophysiology, 3,* 143–156.

Hollander, E. (1999). Managing aggressive behavior in patients with obsessive-compulsive disorder and borderline personality disorder. *Journal of Clinical Psychiatry, 60*(Suppl.), 38–44.

Hollon, S. D., Thase, M. E., and Markowitz, J. C. (2002). Treatment and prevention of depression. *Psychological Science in the Public Interest, 3,* 39–77.

Holman, B. L., Mendelson, J., Garada, B., Teoh, S. K., et al. (1993). Regional cerebral blood flow improves with treatment in chronic cocaine polydrug users. *Journal of Nuclear Medicine, 34,* 723–727.

Holmes, C., Boche, D., Wilkinson, D., Yadegarfar, G., et al. (2008). Long-term effects of Abeta42 immunisation in Alzheimer's disease: Follow-up of a randomized, placebo-controlled phase I trial. *Lancet, 372,* 216–223.

Honey, G. D., Bullmore, E. T., Soni, W., Varatheesan, M., et al. (1999). Differences in frontal cortical activation by a working memory task after substitution of risperidone for typical antipsychotic drugs in patients with schizophrenia. *Proceedings of the National Academy of Sciences, USA, 96,* 13432–13437.

Hopfinger, J. B., Buonocore, M. H., and Mangun, G. R. (2000). The neural mechanisms of top-down attentional control. *Nature Neuroscience, 3,* 284–291.

Hopfinger, J., and Mangun, G. (1998). Reflexive attention modulates processing of visual stimuli in human extrastriate cortex. *Psychological Science, 6,* 441–447.

Hopfinger, J., and Mangun, G. (2001). Tracking the influence of reflexive attention on sensory and cognitive processing. *Cognitive, Affective & Behavioral Neuroscience, 1,* 56–65.

Horton, J. C., and Adams, D. L. (2005). The cortical column: A structure without a function. *Philosophical Transactions of the Royal Society of London. Series B: Biological Sciences, 360,* 837–862.

Hsu, M., Bhatt, M., Adolphs, R., Tranel, D., et al. (2005). Neural systems responding to degrees of uncertainty in human decision-making. *Science, 310,* 1680–1683.

Huang, A. L., Chen, X., Hoon, M. A., Chandrashekar, J., et al. (2006). The cells and logic for mammalian sour taste detection. *Nature, 442,* 934–938.

Hubbard, A. (1993). A traveling-wave amplifier model of the cochlea. *Science, 259,* 68–71.

Hubel, D. H., and Wiesel, T. N. (1959). Receptive fields of single neurones in the cat's striate cortex. *Journal of Physiology (London), 148,* 573–591.

Hubel, D. H., and Wiesel, T. N. (1962). Receptive fields, binocular interaction and functional architecture in the cat's visual cortex. *Journal of Physiology (London), 160,* 106–154.

Hubel, D. H., and Wiesel, T. N. (1965). Binocular interaction in striate cortex kittens reared with artificial squint. *Journal of Neurophysiology, 28,* 1041–1059.

Hubel, D. H., Wiesel, T. N., and LeVay, S. (1977). Plasticity of ocular dominance in monkey striate cortex. *Philosophical Transactions of the Royal Society of London. Series B: Biological Sciences, 278,* 377–409.

Hudspeth, A. J. (1997). How hearing happens. *Neuron, 19,* 947–950.

Hudspeth, A. J., Choe, Y., Mehta, A. D., and Martin, P. (2000). Putting ion channels to work: Mechanoelectrical transduction, adaptation, and amplification by hair cells. *Proceedings of the National Academy of Sciences, USA, 97,* 11765–11772.

Huettel, S. A., Stowe, C. J., Gordon, E. M., Warner, B. T., et al. (2006). Neural signatures of economic preferences for risk and ambiguity. *Neuron, 49,* 765–775.

Hughes, J., Smith, T. W., Kosterlitz, H. W., Fothergill, L. A., et al. (1975).

Identification of two related pentapeptides from the brain with potent opiate agonist activity. *Nature, 258,* 577–580.

Huntington, G. (1872). On chorea. *Medical and Surgical Reporter, 26,* 317–321.

Hyde, K. L., and Peretz I. (2004). Brains that are out of tune but in time. *Psychological Science, 15,* 356–360.

Hyde, K. L., Zatorre, R. J., Griffiths, T. D., Lerch, J. P., et al. (2006). Morphometry of the amusic brain: A two-site study. *Brain, 129,* 2562–2570.

Hyde, T. M., and Weinberger, D. R. (1990). The brain in schizophrenia. *Seminars in Neurology, 10,* 276–286.

Hyde, T. M., Aaronson, B. A., Randolph, C., Rickler, K. C., et al. (1992). Relationship of birth weight to the phenotypic expression of Gilles de la Tourette's syndrome in monozygotic twins. *Neurology, 42,* 652–658.

I

Imai, T., Yamazaki, T., Kobayakawa, R., Kobayakawa, K., et al. (2009). Pre-target axon sorting establishes the neural map topography. *Science, 325,* 585–590.

Imeri, L., and Opp, M. R. (2009). How (and why) the immune system makes us sleep. *Nature Reviews. Neuroscience, 10,* 199–210.

Imperato-McGinley, J., Guerrero, L., Gautier, T., and Peterson, R. E. (1974). Steroid 5α-reductase deficiency in man: An inherited form of male pseudohermaphroditism. *Science, 86,* 1213–1215.

Insley, S. J. (2000). Long-term vocal recognition in the northern fur seal. *Nature, 406,* 404–405.

Institute of Medicine. (1990). *Broadening the base of treatment for alcohol problems.* Washington, DC: National Academy Press.

Institute of Medicine. (2010). *Gulf War and health: Vol. 8. Update of health effects of serving in the Gulf War.* Washington, DC: National Academy Press.

Isaacson, R. L. (1972). Hippocampal destruction in man and other animals. *Neuropsychologia, 10,* 47–64.

Isacson, O., Bjorklund, L., and Sanchez Pernaute, R. (2001). Parkinson's disease: Interpretations of transplantation study erroneous. *Nature Neuroscience, 4,* 533.

Isles, A. R., Baum, M. J., Ma, D., Keverne, E. B., et al. (2001). Urinary odour preferences in mice. *Nature, 409,* 783–784.

Iwamura, Y., and Tanaka, M. (1978). Postcentral neurons in hand region of area 2: Their possible role in the form discrimination of tactile objects. *Brain Research, 150,* 662–666.

Izumikawa, M., Minoda, R., Kawamoto, K., Abrashkin, K. A., et al. (2005). Auditory hair cell replacement and hearing improvement by *Atoh1* gene therapy in deaf mammals. *Nature Medicine, 11,* 271–276.

J

Jackson, H., and Parks, T. N. (1982). Functional synapse elimination in the developing avian cochlear nucleus with simultaneous reduction in cochlear nerve axon branching. *Journal of Neuroscience, 2,* 1736–1743.

Jacobs, G. H. (1993). The distribution and nature of colour vision among the mammals. *Biological Reviews of the Cambridge Philosophical Society, 68,* 413–471.

Jacobs, G. H., Williams, G. A., Cahill, H., and Nathans, J. (2007). Emergence of novel color vision in mice engineered to express a human cone photopigment. *Science, 315,* 1723–1725.

Jacobs, L. F., Gaulin, S. J., Sherry, D. F., and Hoffman, G. E. (1990). Evolution of spatial cognition: Sex-specific patterns of spatial behavior predict hippocampal size. *Proceedings of the National Academy of Sciences, USA, 87,* 6349–6352.

Jacobs, L. F., and Spencer, W. D. (1994). Natural space-use patterns and hippocampal size in kangaroo rats. *Brain, Behavior and Evolution, 44,* 125–132.

James, T. W., Culham, J., Humphery, G. K., Milner, A. D., et al. (2003). Ventral occipital lesions impair object recognition but not object-directed grasping: An fMRI study. *Brain, 126,* 2464–2475.

James, W. (1890). *Principles of psychology.* New York, NY: Holt.

Jamieson, D., and Roberts, A. (2000). Responses of young *Xenopus laevis* tadpoles to light dimming: Possible roles for the pineal eye. *Journal of Experimental Biology, 203,* 1857–1867.

Jaskiw, G. E., and Popli, A. P. (2004). A meta-analysis of the response to chronic L-dopa in patients with schizophrenia: Therapeutic and heuristic implications. *Psychopharmacology (Berlin), 171,* 365–374.

Jasper, H., and W. Penfield. (1954). *Epilepsy and the functional anatomy of the human brain* (2nd ed.). New York, NY: Little, Brown.

Jeffress, L. A. (1948). A place theory of sound localization. *Journal of Comparative and Physiological Psychology, 41,* 35–39.

Jenkins, J., and Dallenbach, K. (1924). Oblivescence during sleep and waking. *American Journal of Psychology, 35,* 605–612.

Jentsch, J. D., Redmond, D. E., Jr., Elsworth, J. D., Taylor, J. R., et al. (1997). Enduring cognitive deficits and cortical dopamine dysfunction in monkeys after long-term administration of phencyclidine. *Science, 277,* 953–955.

Johansson, R. S., and Flanagan, J. R. (2009). Coding and use of tactile signals from the fingertips in object manipulation tasks. *Nature Reviews. Neuroscience, 10,* 345–358.

Johnson, K. O., and Hsiao, S. S. (1992). Neural mechanisms of tactual form and texture perception. *Annual Review of Neuroscience, 15,* 227–250.

Johnson, L. C. (1969). Psychological and physiological changes following total sleep deprivation. In A. Kales (Ed.), *Sleep: Physiology & pathology; a symposium* (pp. 206–220). Philadelphia, PA: Lippincott.

Jones, P. B., Barnes, T. R. E., Davies, L., Dunn, G., et al. (2006). Randomized controlled trial of the effect on Quality of Life of second- vs first-generation antipsychotic drugs in schizophrenia. *Archives of General Psychiatry, 39,* 1079–1087.

Jordan, B. D., Jahre, C., Hauser, W. A., Zimmerman, R. D., et al. (1992). CT of 338 active professional boxers. *Radiology, 185,* 509–512.

Jordan, C. L., Breedlove, S. M., and Arnold, A. P. (1991). Ontogeny of steroid accumulation in spinal lumbar motoneurons of the rat: Implications for androgen's site of action during synapse elimination. *Journal of Comparative Neurology, 313,* 441–448.

Jordt, S.-E., Bautista, D. M., Chuang, H., McKemy, D. D., et al. (2004). Mustard oils and cannabinoids excite sensory nerve fibres through the TRP channel ANKTM1. *Nature, 427,* 260–265.

Joseph, J. S., Chun, M. M., and Nakayama, K. (1997). Attentional requirements in a "preattentive" feature search task. *Nature, 387,* 805–807.

Julian, T., and McKenry, P. C. (1979). Relationship of testosterone to men's family functioning at mid-life: A research note. *Aggressive Behavior, 15,* 281–289.

K

Kaar, G. F., and Fraher, J. P. (1985). The development of alpha and gamma motoneuron fibres in the rat. I. A comparative ultrastructural study of their central and peripheral axon growth. *Journal of Anatomy, 141,* 77–88.

Kaas, J. H., Nelson, R. J., Sur, M., Lin, C. S., et al. (1979). Multiple representations of the body within the primary somatosensory cortex of primates. *Science, 204,* 521–523.

Kable, J. W., and Glimcher, P. W. (2009). The neurobiology of decision: Consensus and controversy. *Neuron, 63,* 733–745.

Kales, A., and Kales, J. (1970). Evaluation, diagnosis and treatment of clinical conditions related to sleep. *JAMA, 213,* 2229–2235.

Kales, A., and Kales, J. D. (1974). Sleep disorders. Recent findings in the diagnosis and treatment of disturbed sleep. *New England Journal of Medicine, 290,* 487–499.

Kandel, E. R. (2009). The biology of memory: A forty-year perspective. *Journal of Neuroscience, 29,* 12748–12756.

Kandler, K., Clause, A., and Noh, J. (2009). Tonotopic reorganization of developing auditory brainstem circuits. *Nature Neuroscience, 12,* 711–716.

Kang, C., Riazuddin, S., Mundorff, J., Krasnewich, D., et al. (2010). Mutation in the lysosomal enzyme–targeting pathway and persistent stuttering. *New England Journal of Medicine, 362,* 677–685.

Kang, J.-E., Lim, M. M., Bateman, R. J., Lee, J. J., et al. (2009). Amyloid-β dynamics are regulated by orexin and the sleep-wake cycle. *Science, 326,* 1005–1007.

Kanwisher, N., and Wojciulik, E. (2000). Visual attention: Insights from brain imaging. *Nature Reviews. Neuroscience, 1,* 91–100.

Karch, S. B. (2006). *Drug abuse handbook* (2nd ed.). Boca Raton, FL: CRC Press.

Karlin, A. (2002). Emerging structure of the nicotinic acetylcholine receptors. *Nature Reviews. Neuroscience, 3,* 102–114.

Karni, A., Tanne, D., Rubenstein, B. S., Askenasy, J. J., et al. (1994). Dependence on REM sleep of overnight improvement of a perceptual skill. *Science, 265,* 679–682.

Karpicke, J. D., and Roediger, H. L., III. (2008). The critical importance of retrieval for learning. *Science, 319,* 966–968.

Karra, E., Chandarana, K., and Batterham, R. L. (2009). The role of peptide YY in appetite regulation and obesity. *Journal of Physiology, 587,* 19–25.

Katz, D. B., and Steinmetz, J. E. (2002). Psychological functions of the cerebellum. *Behavioral Cognitive Neuroscience Review, 1,* 229–241.

Katzenberg, D., Young, T., Finn, L., Lin, L., et al. (1998). A CLOCK polymorphism associated with human diurnal preference. *Sleep, 21,* 569–576.

Kaushall, P. I., Zetin, M., and Squire, L. R. (1981). A psychosocial study of chronic, circumscribed amnesia. *Journal of Nervous and Mental Disease, 169,* 383–389.

Kay, K. N., Naselaris, T., Prenger, R. J., and Gallant, J. L. (2008). Identifying natural images from human brain activity. *Nature, 452,* 352–355.

Kaye, W. H., Fudge, J. L., and Paulus, M. (2009). New insights into symptoms and neurocircuit function of anorexia nervosa. *Nature Reviews. Neuroscience, 10,* 573–584.

Keane, T. M. (1998). Psychological and behavioral treatments of post-traumatic stress disorder. In P. E. Nathan, and J. M. Gorman (Eds.), *A guide to treatments that work* (pp. 398–407). New York, NY: Oxford University Press.

Kee, N., Teixeira, C. M., Wang, A. H., and Frankland, P. W. (2007). Preferential incorporation of adult-generated granule cells into spatial memory networks in the dentate gyrus. *Nature Neuroscience, 10,* 355–362.

Keenan, J. P., Nelson, A., O'Connor, M., and Pascual-Leone, A. (2001). Self-recognition and the right hemisphere. *Nature, 409,* 305.

Keesey, R. E. (1980). A set-point analysis of the regulation of body weight. In A. J. Stunkard (Ed.), *Obesity* (pp. 144–165). Philadelphia, PA: Saunders.

Keesey, R. E., and Boyle, P. C. (1973). Effects of quinine adulteration upon body weight of LH-lesioned and intact male rats. *Journal of Comparative and Physiological Psychology, 84,* 38–46.

Keesey, R. E., and Corbett, S. W. (1984). Metabolic defense of the body weight set-point. *Research Publications—Association for Research in Nervous and Mental Disease, 62,* 87–96.

Keesey, R. E., and Powley, T. L. (1986). The regulation of body weight. *Annual Review of Psychology, 37,* 109–133.

Keltner, D., and Ekman, P. (2000). Facial expression of emotion. In M. Lewis and J. M. Haviland-Jones (Eds.), *Handbook of emotions* (2nd ed., pp. 236–250). New York, NY: Guilford Press.

Kemp, J. A., and McKernan, R. M. (2002). NMDA receptor pathways as drug targets. *Nature Neuroscience, 5*(Suppl.): 1039–1042.

Kempermann, G., Kuhn, H. G., and Gage, F. H. (1997). More hippocampal neurons in adult mice living in an enriched environment. *Nature, 386,* 493–495.

Kendler, K. S., Gardner, C. O., and Prescott, C. A. (1999). Clinical characteristics of major depression that predict risk of depression in relatives. *Archives of General Psychiatry, 56,* 322–327.

Kenis, G., and Maes, M. (2002). Effects of antidepressants on the production of cytokines. *International Journal of Neuropsychopharmacology, 5,* 401–412.

Kennedy, J. L., Farrer, L. A., Andreasen, N. C., Mayeux, R., et al. (2003). The genetics of adult-onset neuropsychiatric disease: Complexities and conundra? *Science, 302,* 822–826.

Kennerknecht, I., Grueter, T., Welling, B., Wentzek, S., et al. (2006). First report of prevalence of non-syndromic hereditary prosopagnosia (HPA). *American Journal of Medical Genetics. Part A, 140,* 1617–1622.

Kertesz, A., Harlock, W., and Coates, R. (1979). Computer tomographic localization, lesion size, and prognosis in aphasia and nonverbal impairment. *Brain and Language, 8,* 34–50.

Kesner, R. P. (1998). Neurobiological views of memory. In J. L. Martinez, Jr., and R. P. Kesner (Eds.), *Neurobiology of learning and memory* (3rd ed., pp. 361–416). San Diego, CA: Harcourt Brace.

Kesner, R. P., Bolland, B. L., and Dakis, M. (1993). Memory for spatial locations, motor responses, and objects: Triple dissociation among the hippocampus, caudate nucleus, and extrastriate visual cortex. *Experimental Brain Research, 93,* 462–470.

Kessels, H. W., and Malinow, R. (2009). Synaptic AMPA receptor plasticity and behavior. *Neuron, 61,* 340–350.

Kessler, R. C., Berglund, P., Demler, O., Jin, R., et al. (2005). Lifetime prevalence and age-of-onset distributions of DSM-IV disorders in the National Comorbidity Survey Replication. *Archives of General Psychiatry, 62,* 593–602.

Kety, S., Rosenthal, D., Wender, P. H., Schulsinger, F., et al. (1975). Mental illness in the biological and adoptive families of adopted individuals who have become schizophrenic: A preliminary report based on psychiatric interviews. *Proceedings of the Annual Meeting of the American Psychopathological Association, 63,* 147–165.

Kety, S. S., Wender, P. H., Jacobsen, B., Ingraham, L. J., et al. (1994). Mental illness in the biological and adoptive relatives of schizophrenic adoptees. Replication of the Copenhagen Study in the rest of Denmark. *Archives of General Psychiatry, 51,* 442–455.

Kiang, N. Y. S. (1965). *Discharge patterns of single fibers in the cat's auditory nerve.* Cambridge, MA: MIT Press.

Kim, D. R., Pesiridou, A., and O'Reardon, J. P. (2009). Transcranial magnetic stimulation in the treatment of psychiatric disorders. *Current Psychiatry Reports, 11,* 447–452.

Kim, K. H., Relkin, N. R., Lee, K. M., and Hirsch, J. (1997). Distinct cortical areas associated with native and second languages. *Nature, 388,* 171–174.

Kimura, D. (1973). The asymmetry of the human brain. *Scientific American, 228*(3), 70–78.

Kimura, D. (1981). Neural mechanisms in manual signing. *Sign Language Studies, 33,* 291–312.

Kimura, D. (1993). *Neuromotor mechanisms in human communication.* Oxford, England: Oxford University Press.

Kimura, D., and Watson, N. V. (1989). The relation between oral movement control and speech. *Brain and Language, 37,* 565–590.

Kindt, M., Soeter, M., and Vervliet, B. (2009). Beyond extinction: Erasing human fear responses and preventing the return of fear. *Nature Neuroscience, 12,* 256–258.

Kingsbury, S. J., and Garver, D. L. (1998). Lithium and psychosis revisited. *Progress in Neuro-Psychopharmacology & Biological Psychiatry, 22,* 249–263.

Kinney, H. C. (2009). Brainstem mechanisms underlying the sudden infant death syndrome: Evidence from human pathologic studies. *Developmental Psychobiology, 51,* 223–233.

Kinsey, A. C., Pomeroy, W. B., and Martin, C. E. (1948). *Sexual behavior in the human male.* Philadelphia, PA: Saunders.

Kinsey, A. C., Pomeroy, W. B., Martin, C. E., and Gebhard, P. H. (1953). *Sexual behavior in the human female.* Philadelphia, PA: Saunders.

Kirik, D., Georgievska, B., and Björklund, A. (2004). Localized striatal delivery of GDNF as a treatment for Parkinson disease. *Nature Neuroscience, 7,* 105–110.

Klar, A. J. (2003). Human handedness and scalp hair-whorl direction develop from a common genetic mechanism. *Genetics, 165,* 269–276.

Kleiber, M. (1947). Body size and metabolic rate. *Physiological Reviews, 15,* 511–541.

Klein, B. A. (2003). Signatures of sleep in a paper wasp. *Sleep, 26,* A115–A116.

Klein, M., Shapiro, K. M., and Kandel, E. R. (1980). Synaptic plasticity and the modulation of the Ca^{2+} current. *Journal of Experimental Biology, 89,* 117–157.

Klein, R. M. (2000). Inhibition of return. *Trends in Cognitive Science, 4,* 138–147.

Kleitman, N. (1969). Basic rest-activity cycle in relation to sleep and wakefulness. In A. Kales (Ed.), *Sleep: Physiology and pathology* (pp. 33–38). Philadelphia, PA: Lippincott.

Kleitman, N., and Engelmann, T. (1953). Sleep characteristics of infants. *Journal of Applied Physiology, 6,* 269–282.

Kluger, M. J. (1978). The evolution and adaptive value of fever. *American Scientist, 66,* 38–43.

Klüver, H., and Bucy, P. C. (1938). An analysis of certain effects of bilateral temporal lobectomy in the rhesus monkey, with special reference to "psychic blindness." *Journal of Psychology, 5,* 33–54.

Knecht, S., Flöel, A., Dräger, B., Breitenstein, C., et al. (2002). Degree of language lateralization determines susceptibility to unilateral brain lesions. *Nature Neuroscience, 5,* 695–699.

Knibestol, M., and Valbo, A. B. (1970). Single unit analysis of mechanoreceptor activity from the human glabrous skin. *Acta Physiologica Scandinavica, 80,* 178–195.

Knudsen, E. I. (1982). Auditory and visual maps of space in the optic tectum of the owl. *Journal of Neuroscience, 2,* 1177–1194.

Knudsen, E. I. (1984). The role of auditory experience in the development and maintenance of sound localization. *Trends in Neurosciences, 7,* 326–330.

Knudsen, E. I. (1998). Capacity for plasticity in the adult owl auditory system expanded by juvenile experience. *Science, 279,* 1531–1533.

Knudsen, E., and Knudsen, P. (1985). Vision guides adjustment of auditory localization in young barn owls. *Science, 230,* 545–548.

Knudsen, E. I., Knudsen, P. F., and Esterly, S. D. (1984). A critical period for the recovery of sound localization accuracy following monaural occlusion in the barn owl. *Journal of Neuroscience, 4,* 1012–1020.

Knudsen, E. I., and Konishi, M. (1978). A neural map of auditory space in the owl. *Science, 200,* 795–797.

Kobatake, E., and Tanaka, K. (1994). Neuronal selectivities to complex object features in the ventral visual pathway of the macaque cerebral cortex. *Journal of Neurophysiology, 71,* 856–867.

Koch, G., Oliveri, M., Torriero, S., and Caltagirone, C. (2005). Modulation of excitatory and inhibitory circuits for visual awareness in the human right parietal cortex. *Experimental Brain Research, 160,* 510–516.

Kodama, T., Lai, Y. Y., and Siegel, J. M. (2003). Changes in inhibitory amino acid release linked to pontine-induced atonia: An *in vivo* microdialysis study. *Journal of Neuroscience, 23,* 1548–1554.

Koh, K., Joiner, W. J., Wu, M. N., Yue, Z., et al. (2008). Identification of SLEEPLESS, a sleep-promoting factor. *Science, 321,* 372–376.

Kojima, M., Hosoda, H., Date, Y., Nakazato, M., et al. (1999). Ghrelin is a growth-hormone-releasing acylated peptide from stomach. *Nature, 402,* 656–660.

Kolb, B., and Whishaw, I. Q. (1990). *Fundamentals of human neuropsychology.* San Francisco, CA: Freeman.

Kondo, Y., Sachs, B. D., and Sakuma, Y. (1997). Importance of the medial amygdala in rat penile erection evoked by remote stimuli from estrous females. *Behavioural Brain Research, 88,* 153–160.

Konishi, M. (1985). Birdsong: From behavior to neuron. *Annual Review of Neuroscience, 8,* 125–170.

Konopka, R. J., and Benzer, S. (1971). Clock mutants of *Drosophila melanogaster. Proceedings of the National Academy of Sciences, USA, 68,* 2112–2116.

Koob, G. F. (1995). Animal models of drug addiction. In F. E. Bloom and D. J. Kupfer (Eds.), *Psychopharmacology: The fourth generation of progress* (pp. 759–772). New York, NY: Raven Press.

Kopell, B. H., Machado, A. G., and Rezai, A. R. (2005). Not your father's lobotomy: Psychiatric surgery revisited. *Clinical Neurosurgery, 52,* 315–330.

Kordower, J. H., Chu, Y., Hauser, R. A., Freeman, T. B., et al. (2008). Lewy body-like pathology in long-term embryonic nigral transplants in Parkinson's disease. *Nature Medicine, 14,* 504–506.

Korman, M., Doyon, J., Doljansky, J., Carrier, J., et al. (2007). Daytime sleep condenses the time course of motor memory consolidation. *Nature Neuroscience, 10,* 1206–1213.

Kosslyn, S. M., Alpert, N. M., Thompson, W. L., Maljkovic, V., et al. (1993). Visual mental imagery activates topographically organized visual cortex. *Journal of Cognitive Neuroscience, 5,* 263–287.

Kosslyn, S. M., Pascual-Leone, A., Felician, O., Camposano, S., et al. (1999). The role of Area 17 in visual imagery: Convergent evidence from PET and RTMS. *Science, 208,* 167–170.

Kovelman, J. A., and Scheibel, A. B. (1984). A neurohistological correlate of schizophrenia. *Biological Psychiatry, 19,* 1601.

Krause, J., Lalueza-Fox, C., Orlando, L., Enard, W., et al. (2007). The derived FOXP2 variant of modern humans was shared with Neandertals. *Current Biology, 17,* 1908–1912.

Krauss, R. M. (1998). Why do we gesture when we speak? *Current Directions in Psychological Science, 7*(2), 54–60.

Krebs, J. R., Sherry, D. F., Healy, S. D., Perry, V. H., et al. (1989). Hippocampal specialisation of food-storing birds. *Proceedings of the National Academy of Sciences, USA, 86,* 1388–1392.

Kril, J., Halliday, G., Svoboda, M., and Cartwright, H. (1997). The cerebral cortex is damaged in chronic alcoholics. *Neuroscience, 79,* 983–998.

Kringelbach, M. L. (2005). The human orbitofrontal cortex: Linking reward to hedonic experience. *Nature Reviews. Neuroscience, 6,* 691–702.

Kringelbach, M. L., Jenkinson, N., Owen, S. L. F., and Aziz, T. Z. (2007). Translational principles of deep brain stimulation. *Nature Reviews. Neuroscience, 8,* 623–634.

Kripke, D. F., Garfinkel, L., Wingard, D. L., Klauber, M. R., et al. (2002). Mortality associated with sleep duration and insomnia. *Archives of General Psychiatry, 59,* 131–136.

Kruesi, M. J. (1979). Cruelty to animals and CSF 5HIAA. *Psychiatry Research, 28,* 115–116.

Krystal, A., Krishnan, K. R., Raitiere, M., Poland, R., et al. (1990). Differential diagnosis and pathophysiology of Cushing's syndrome and primary affective disorder. *Journal of Neuropsychiatry and Clinical Neurosciences, 2,* 34–43.

Kuhl, B. A., Dudukovic, N. M., Kahn, I., and Wagner, A. D. (2007). Decreased demands on cognitive control reveal the neural processing benefits of forgetting. *Nature Neuroscience, 10,* 908–914.

Kulkarni, A., and Colburn, H. S. (1998). Role of spectral detail in sound-source localization. *Nature, 396,* 747–749.

Kupfer, D. J., Reynolds, C. F., Ulrich, R. F., Shaw, D. H., et al. (1982). EEG sleep, depression, and aging. *Neurobiology of Aging, 3,* 351–360.

Kutas, M., and Hillyard, S. A. (1980). Reading senseless sentences: Brain potentials reflect semantic incongruity. *Science, 207,* 203–205.

L

LaBar, K. S., Gatenby, J. C., Gore, J. C., LeDoux, J. E., et al. (1998). Human amygdala activation during conditioned fear acquisition and extinction: A mixed-trial fMRI study. *Neuron, 20,* 937–945.

Lachman, H. M., Papolos, D. F., Boyle, A., Sheftel, G., et al. (1993). Alterations in glucorticoid inducible RNAs in the limbic system of learned helpless rats. *Brain Research, 609,* 110–116.

LaFerla, F. M., Green, K. N., and Oddo, S. (2007). Intracellular amyloid-β in Alzheimer's disease. (2007). *Nature Reviews. Neuroscience, 8,* 499–508.

Lai, C. S. L., Fisher, S. E., Hurst, J. A., Vargha-Khadem, F., et al. (2001). A forkhead-domain gene is mutated in a severe speech and language disorder. *Nature, 413,* 519–523.

Lalumiere, M. L., Blanchard, R., and Zucker, K. J. (2000). Sexual orientation and handedness in men and women: A meta-analysis. *Psychological Bulletin, 126,* 575–592.

Landau, B., and Levy, R. M. (1993). Neuromodulation techniques for medically refractory chronic pain. *Annual Review of Medicine, 44,* 279–287.

Langleben, D. D., Schroeder, L., Maldjian, J. A., Gur, R. C., et al. (2002). Brain activity during simulated deception: An event-related functional magnetic resonance study. *Neuroimage, 15,* 727–732.

Larroche, J.-C. (1977). *Developmental pathology of the neonate.* Amsterdam, Netherlands: Excerpta Medica.

Larsson, J., Gulyas, B., and Roland, P. E. (1996). Cortical representation of self-paced finger movement. *Neuroreport, 7,* 463–468.

Lau, H. C., Rogers, R. D., Haggard, P., and Passingham, R. E. (2004). Attention to intention. *Science, 303,* 1208–1210.

Laverty, P. H., Leskovar, A., Breur, G. J., Coates, J. R., et al. (2004). A preliminary study of intravenous surfactants in paraplegic dogs: Polymer therapy in canine clinical SCI. *Journal of Neurotrama, 21,* 1767–1777.

Lavie, N. (1995). Perceptual load as a necessary condition for selective attention. *Journal of Experimental Psychology. Human Perception and Performance, 21,* 451–468.

Lavie, N., Hirst, A., de Fockert, J. W., and Viding, E. (2004). Load theory of selective attention and cognitive control. *Journal of Experimental Psychology. General, 133,* 339–354.

Lavie, N., Lin, Z., Zokaei, N., and Thoma, V. (2009). The role of perceptual load in object recognition. *Journal of Experimental Psychology. Human Perception and Performance, 35,* 1346–1358.

Lavie, P. (1996). *The enchanted world of sleep* (A. Berris, Trans.). New Haven, CT: Yale University Press.

Lavie, P., and Kripke, D. F. (1981). Ultradian circa 1 1/2 hour rhythms: A multioscillatory system. *Life Sciences, 29,* 2445–2450.

Lavond, D. G., Kim, J. J., and Thompson, R. F. (1993). Mammalian brain substrates of aversive classical conditioning. *Annual Review of Psychology, 44,* 317–342.

Leask, S. J., and Beaton, A. A. (2007). Handedness in Great Britain. *Laterality, 12,* 559–572.

LeDoux, J. E. (1994). Emotion, memory and the brain. *Scientific American, 270*(6), 50–57.

LeDoux, J. E. (1995). Emotion: Clues from the brain. *Annual Review of Psychology, 46,* 209–235.

LeDoux, J. E. (1996). *The emotional brain: The mysterious underpinnings of emotional life.* London, England: Simon & Schuster.

Le Grange, D. (2005). The Maudsley family-based treatment for adolescent anorexia nervosa. *World Psychiatry, 4,* 142–146.

Leinders-Zufall, T., Lane, A. P., Puche, A. C., Ma, W., et al. (2000). Ultrasensitive pheromone detection by mammalian vomeronasal neurons. *Nature, 405,* 792–796.

Lepage, J. F., and Theoret, H. (2006). EEG evidence for the presence of an action observation-execution matching system in children. *European Journal of Neuroscience, 23,* 2505–2510.

Leroi, I., Sheppard, J. M., and Lyketsos, C. G. (2002). Cognitive function after 11.5 years of alcohol use: Relation to alcohol use. *American Journal of Epidemiology, 156,* 747–752.

Lesné, S., Koh, M. T., Kotilinek, L., Kayed, R., et al. (2006). A specific amyloid-β protein assembly in the brain impairs memory. *Nature, 440,* 352–357.

Leung, C. T., Coulombe, P. A., and Reed, R. R. (2007). Contribution of olfactory neural stem cells to tissue maintenance and regeneration. *Nature Neuroscience, 10,* 720–726.

Leutgeb, S., Leutgeb, J. K., Barnes, C. A., Moser, E. I., et al. (2005). Independent codes for spatial and episodic memory in hippocampal neuronal ensembles. *Science, 309,* 619–623.

LeVay, S. (1991). A difference in hypothalamic structure between heterosexual and homosexual men. *Science, 253,* 1034–1037.

LeVay, S. (1996). *Queer science: The use and abuse of research into homosexuality.* Cambridge, MA: MIT Press.

Levine, J. D., Gordon, N. C., and Fields, H. L. (1978). The mechanism of placebo analgesia. *Lancet, 2,* 654–657.

Levine, S., Haltmeyer, G. C., and Karas, G. G. (1967). Physiological and behavioral effects of infantile stimulation. *Physiology & Behavior, 2,* 55–59.

Levine, S., and Ursin, H. (1980). *Coping and health.* New York, NY: Plenum Press.

Lewis, D. O. (1990). Neuropsychiatric and experiential correlates of violent juvenile delinquency. *Neuropsychology Review, 1,* 125–136.

Lewis, D. O., Shankok, S. S., and Pincus, J. (1979). Juvenile male sexual assaulters. *American Journal of Psychiatry, 136,* 1194–1195.

Lewis, R. (1998). Flies invade human genetics. *Scientist, 12,* 1, 4–5.

Lewy, A. J., Bauer, V. K., Cutler, N. L., Sack, R. L., et al. (1998). Morning vs evening light treatment of patients with winter depression. *Archives of General Psychiatry, 55,* 890–896.

Lewy, A. J., Rough, J. N., Songer, J. B., Mishra, N., et al. (2007). The phase shift hypothesis for the circadian component of winter depression. *Dialogues in Clinical Neuroscience, 9,* 291–300.

Li, J.Y., Englund, E., Holton, J. L., Soulet, D., et al. (2008). Lewy bodies in grafted neurons in subjects with Parkinson's disease suggest host-to-graft disease propagation. *Nature Medicine, 14,* 501–503.

Li, X., Glaser, D., Li, W., Johnson, W. E., et al. (2009). Analyses of sweet receptor gene (Tas1r2) and preference for sweet stimuli in species of Carnivora. *Journal of Heredity, 100*(Suppl. 1), S90–S100.

Liberles, S. D., and Buck, L. B. (2006). A second class of chemosensory receptors in the olfactory epithelium. *Nature, 442,* 645–650.

Licht, P., Frank, L. G., Pavgi, S., Yalcinkaya, T. M., et al. (1992). Hormonal correlates of "masculinization" in female spotted hyenas (*Crocuta crocuta*). 2. Maternal and fetal steroids. *Journal of Reproduction and Fertility, 95,* 463–474.

Lichtenstein, P., Yip, B. H., Björk, C., Pawitan, Y., et al. (2009). Common genetic determinants of schizophrenia and bipolar disorder in Swedish families: A population-based study. *Lancet, 373,* 234–239.

Lichtman, J. W., and Purves, D. (1980). The elimination of redundant preganglionic innervation to hamster sympathetic ganglion cells in early post-natal life. *Journal of Physiology (London), 301,* 213–228.

Lieberman, P. (1985). On the evolution of human syntactic ability: Its pre-adaptive bases—motor control and speech. *Journal of Human Evolution, 14,* 657–668.

Liégeois, F., Baldeweg, T., Connelly, A., Gadian, D. G., et al. (2003). Language fMRI abnormalities associated with FOXP2 gene mutation. *Nature Neuroscience, 6,* 1230–1237.

Liepert, J., Bauder, H., Wolfgang, H. R., Miltner, W. H., et al. (2000). Treatment-induced cortical reorganization after stroke in humans. *Stroke, 31,* 1210–1216.

Lieving, L. M., Cherek, D. R., Lane, S. D., Tcheremissine, O.V., et al. (2008). Effects of acute tiagabine administration on aggressive responses of adult male parolees. *Journal of Psychopharmacology, 22,* 144–152.

Lim, M. M., Wang, Z., Olazabal, D. E., Ren, X., et al. (2004). Enhanced partner preference in a promiscuous species by manipulating the expression of a single gene. *Nature, 429,* 754–757.

Lim, M. M., and Young, L. J. (2006). Neuropeptidergic regulation of affiliative behavior and social bonding in animals. *Hormones and Behavior, 50,* 506–557.

Lin, F. H., Witzel, T., Hamalainen, M. S., Dale, A. M., et al. (2004). Spectral spatiotemporal imaging of cortical oscillations and interactions in the human brain. *Neuroimage, 23,* 582–595.

Lin, L., Faraco, J., Li, R., Kadotani, H., et al. (1999). The sleep disorder canine narcolepsy is caused by a mutation in the hypocretin (orexin) receptor 2 gene. *Cell, 98,* 365–376.

Linde, K., Allais, G., Brinkhaus, B., Manheimer, E., et al. (2009). Acupuncture for tension-type headache. *Cochrane Database of Systematic Reviews, 1,* CD007587.

Lindemann, B. (1995). Sweet and salty: Transduction in taste. *News in Physiological Sciences, 10,* 166–170.

Lindvall, O., and Kokaia, Z. (2006). Stem cells for the treatment of neurological disorders. *Nature, 441,* 1094–1096.

Lindvall, O., Sawle, G., Widner, H., Rothwell, J. C., et al. (1994). Evidence for long-term survival and function of dopaminergic grafts in progressive Parkinson's disease. *Annals of Neurology, 35,* 172–180.

Lisk, R. D. (1962). Diencephalic placement of estradiol and sexual receptivity in the female rat. *American Journal of Physiology, 203,* 493–496.

Lisman, J., Schulman, H., and Cline, H. (2002). The molecular basis of CAMKII function in synaptic and behavioural memory. *Nature Reviews. Neuroscience, 3,* 175–190.

Liu, D., Diorio, J., Tannenbaum, B., Caldji, C., et al. (1997). Maternal care, hippocampal glucocorticoid receptors, and hypothalamic-pituitary-adrenal responses to stress. *Science, 277,* 1659–1662.

Liu, J., Lillo, C., Jonsson, P. A., Vande Velde, C., et al. (2004). Toxicity of familial ALS-linked SOD1 mutants from selective recruitment to spinal mitochondria. *Neuron, 42,* 5–17.

Liu, S., Qu, Y., Stewart, T. J., Howard, M. J., et al. (2000). Embryonic stem cells differentiate into oligodendrocytes and myelinate in culture and after spinal cord transplantation. *Proceedings of the National Academy of Sciences, USA, 97,* 6126–6131.

Liu, Y., Gao, J. H., Liotti, M., Pu, Y., et al. (1999). Temporal dissociation of parallel processing in the human subcortical outputs. *Nature, 400,* 364–367.

Liu, Y., Gao, J.-H., Liu, H.-L., and Fox, P. T. (2000). The temporal response of the brain after eating revealed by functional MRI. *Nature, 405,* 1058–1062.

Livingstone, M. S. (2000). Is it warm? Is it real? Or just low spatial frequency? *Science, 290,* 1299.

Lloyd, J. A. (1971). Weights of testes, thymi, and accessory reproductive glands in relation to rank in paired and grouped house mice (*Mus musculus*). *Proceedings of the Society for Experimental Biology and Medicine, 137,* 19–22.

Lo, E. H., Dalkara, T., and Moskowitz, M. A. (2003). Mechanisms, challenges and opportunities in stroke. *Nature Reviews. Neuroscience, 4,* 399–415.

Lockhart, M., and Moore, J. W. (1975). Classical differential and operant conditioning in rabbits (*Orycytolagus cuniculus*) with septal lesions. *Journal of Comparative and Physiological Psychology, 88,* 147–154.

Loconto, J., Papes, F., Chang, E., Stowers, L., et al. (2003). Functional expression of murine V2R pheromone receptors involves selective association with the M10 and M1 families of MHC class Ib molecules. *Cell, 112,* 607–618.

Loeb, G. E. (1990). Cochlear prosthetics. *Annual Review of Neuroscience, 13,* 357–371.

Loewenstein, W. R. (Ed.) (1971). Mechanoelectric transduction in the Pacinian corpuscle. Initiation of sensory impulses in mechanoreception. In *Handbook of sensory physiology: Vol. 1. Principles of receptor physiology* (pp. 269–290). Berlin, Germany: Springer-Verlag.

Loftus, E. F. (2003). Make-believe memories. *American Psychologist, 58,* 867–873.

Logan, C. G., and Grafton, S. T. (1995). Functional anatomy of human eyeblink conditioning determined with regional cerebral glucose metabolism and positron emission tomography. *Proceedings of the National Academy of Sciences, USA, 92,* 7500–7504.

Long, M. A., Jutras, M. J., Connors, B. W., and Burwell, R. D. (2005). Electrical synapses coordinate activity in the suprachiasmatic nucleus. *Nature Neuroscience, 8,* 61–66.

Loui, P., Alsop, D., and Schlaug, G. (2009). Tone deafness: A new disconnection syndrome? *Journal of Neuroscience, 29,* 10215–10220.

Lu, X.Y. (2007). The leptin hypothesis of depression: A potential link between mood disorders and obesity? *Current Opinion in Pharmacology, 7,* 648–652.

Luck, S. J. (2005). *An introduction to the event-related potential technique.* Cambridge, MA: MIT Press.

Luck, S. J., and Hillyard, S. A. (1994). Electrophysiological correlates of feature analysis during visual search. *Psychophysiology, 31,* 291–308.

Lucking, C. B., Durr, A., Bonifati, V., Vaughan, J., et al. (2000). Association between early-onset Parkinson's disease and mutations in the parkin gene. *New England Journal of Medicine, 342,* 1560–1567.

Luria, A. R. (1987). *The mind of a mnemonist.* Cambridge, MA: Harvard University Press.

Lush, I. E. (1989). The genetics of tasting in mice. VI. Saccharin, acesulfame, dulcin and sucrose. *Genetical Research, 53,* 95–99.

Lyamin, O., Pryaslova, J., Lance, V., and Siegel, J. (2005). Continuous activity in cetaceans after birth: The exceptional wakefulness of newborn whales and dolphins has no ill-effect on their development. *Nature, 435,* 1177.

Lynch, G., Larson, J., Staubli, U., and Granger, R. (1991). Variants of synaptic potentiation and different types of memory operations in hippocampus and related structures. In L. R. Squire, N. M. Weinberger, G. Lynch, and J. L. McGaugh (Eds.), *Memory: Organization and locus of change* (pp. 330–363). New York, NY: Oxford University Press.

M

Mace, G. M., Gittleman, J. L., and Purvis, A. (2003). Preserving the tree of life. *Science, 300,* 1707–1709.

Machado-Vieira, R., Salvador, G., Diazgranados, N., and Zarate, C. A., Jr. (2009). Ketamine and the next generation of antidepressants with a rapid onset of action. *Pharmacology & Therapeutics, 123,* 143–150.

MacLean, P. D. (1949). Psychosomatic disease and the "visceral brain": Recent developments bearing on the Papez theory of emotion. *Psychosomatic Medicine, 11,* 338–353.

MacLeod, C. M. (1991). Half a century of research on the Stroop effect: An integrative review. *Psychological Bulletin, 109,* 163–203.

Macmillan, M. (2000). *An odd kind of fame: Stories of Phineas Gage.* Cambridge, MA: MIT Press.

MacNeilage, P. F., Rogers, L. J., and Vallortigara, G. (2009). Origins of the left & right brain. *Scientific American, 301*(1), 60–67.

Maes, M., Bosmans, E., Suy, E., Vandervorst, C., et al. (1991). Depression-related disturbances in mitogen-induced lymphocyte responses and interleukin-1 beta and soluble interleukin-2 receptor production. *Acta Psychiatrica Scandinavica, 84,* 379–386.

Magavi, S. S., Leavitt, B. R., and Macklis, J. D. (2000). Induction of neurogenesis in the neocortex of adult mice. *Nature, 405,* 951–955.

Maggioncalda, A. N., and Sapolsky, R. M. (2002). Disturbing behaviors of the orangutan. *Scientific American, 286*(6), 60–65.

Magnusson, A., and Stefansson, J. G. (1993). Prevalence of seasonal affective disorder in Iceland. *Archives of General Psychiatry, 50,* 941–946.

Mair, W. G. P., Warrington, E. K., and Wieskrantz, L. (1979). Memory disorder in Korsakoff's psychosis. *Brain, 102,* 749–783.

Mak, G. K., Enwere, E. K., Gregg, C., Pakarainen, T., et al. (2007). Male pheromone-stimulated neurogenesis in the adult female brain: Possible role in mating behavior. *Nature Neuroscience, 10,* 1003–1011.

Maki, P. M., and Resnick, S. M. (2000). Longitudinal effects of estrogen replacement therapy on pet cerebral blood flow and cognition. *Neurobiology of Aging, 21,* 373–383.

Malenka, R. C., and Bear, M. F. (2004). LTP and LTD: An embarrassment of riches. *Neuron, 44,* 5–21.

Mancuso, K., Hauswirth, W. W., Li, Q., Connor, T. B., et al. (2009). Gene therapy for red-green colour blindness in adult primates. *Nature, 461,* 784–788.

Mani, S. K., Fienberg, A. A., O'Callaghan, J. P., Snyder, G. L., et al. (2000). Requirement for DARPP-32 in progesterone-facilitated sexual receptivity in female rats and mice. *Science, 287,* 1053–1056.

Manova, M. G., and Kostadinova, I. I. (2000). Some aspects of the immunotherapy of multiple sclerosis. *Folia Medica, 42*(1), 5–9.

Mantyh, P. W., Rogers, S. D., Honore, P., Allen, B. J., et al. (1997). Inhibition of hyperalgesia by ablation of lamina I spinal neurons expressing the substance P receptor. *Science, 278,* 275–279.

Mao, J. B., and Evinger, C. (2001). Long-term potentiation of the human blink reflex. *Journal of Neuroscience, 21,* RC151.

March, J., Silva, S., Petrychi, S., Curry, J., et al. (2004). Fluoxetine, cognitive-behavioral therapy, and their combination for adolescents with depression: Treatment for adolescents with depression study (TADS) randomized controlled trial. *Journal of the American Medical Association, 292,* 807–820.

Marcus, G. F., Vijayan, S., Bandi Rao, S., and Vishton, P. M. (1999). Rule learning by seven-month-old infants. *Science, 283,* 77–80.

Maren, S., and Quirk, G. J. (2004). Neuronal signalling of fear memory. *Nature, 5,* 844–852.

Mariani, J., and Changeaux, J.-P. (1981). Ontogenesis of olivocerebellar relationships. I. Studies by intracellular recordings of the multiple innervation of Purkinje cells by climbing fibers in the developing rat cerebellum. *Journal of Neuroscience, 1,* 696–702.

Mark, V. H., and Ervin, F. R. (1970). *Violence and the brain.* New York, NY: Harper & Row.

Marler, P. (1970). Birdsong and speech development: Could there be parallels? *American Scientist, 58,* 669–673.

Marler, P. (1991). Song-learning behavior: The interface with neuroethology. *Trends in Neurosciences, 14,* 199–206.

Marler, P., and Peters, S. (1982). Developmental overproduction and selective attrition: New processes in the epigenesis of birdsong. *Developmental Psychobiology, 15,* 369–378.

Marler, P., and Sherman, V. (1983). Song structure without auditory feedback: Emendations of the auditory template hypothesis. *Journal of Neuroscience, 3,* 517–531.

Marler, P., and Sherman, V. (1985). Innate differences in singing behaviour of sparrows reared in isolation from adult conspecific song. *Animal Behavior, 33,* 57–71.

Marshall, L., Helgadóttir, H., Mölle, M., and Born, J. (2006). Boosting slow oscillations during sleep potentiates memory. *Nature, 444,* 610–613.

Marsicano, G., Goodenough, S., Monory, K., Hermann, H., et al. (2003). CB1 cannabinoid receptors and on-demand defense against excitotoxicity. *Science, 302,* 84–88.

Marsicano, G., Wotjak, C. T., Azad, S. C., Bisogno, T., et al. (2002). The endogenous cannabinoid system controls extinction of aversive memories. *Nature, 418,* 530–532.

Martin, C. K., Heilbronn, L., de Jonge, L., Delany, J. P., et al. (2007). Effect of calorie restriction on resting metabolic rate and spontaneous physical activity. *Obesity (Silver Spring), 15,* 2964–2973.

Martin, J. T., and Nguyen, D. H. (2004). Anthropometric analysis of homosexuals and heterosexuals: Implications for early hormone exposure. *Hormones and Behavior, 45,* 31–39.

Martuza, R. L., Chiocca, E. A., Jenike, M. A., Giriunas, I. E., et al. (1990). Stereotactic radiofrequency thermal cingulotomy for obsessive compulsive disorder. *Journal of Neuropsychiatry and Clinical Neurosciences, 2,* 331–336.

Marucha, P.T., Kiecolt-Glaser, J. K., and Favagehi, M. (1998). Mucosal wound healing is impaired by examination stress. *Psychosomatic Medicine, 60,* 362–365.

Maruyama,Y., Pereira, E., Margolskee, R. F., Chaudhari, N., et al. (2006). Umami responses in mouse taste cells indicate more than one receptor. *Journal of Neuroscience, 26,* 2227–2234.

Marzani, D., and Wallman, J. (1997). Growth of the two layers of the chick sclera is modulated reciprocally by visual conditions. *Investigative Ophthalmology & Visual Science, 38,* 1726–1739.

Maskos, U., Molles, B. E., Pons, S., Besson, M., et al. (2005). Nicotine reinforcement and cognition restored by targeted expression of nicotinic receptors. *Nature, 436,* 103–107.

Masters, W. H., and Johnson,V. E. (1966). *Human sexual response.* Boston, MA: Little, Brown.

Masters, W. H., and Johnson,V. E. (1970). *Human sexual inadequacy.* Boston, MA: Little, Brown.

Masters, W. H., Johnson,V. E., and Kolodny, R. C. (1994). *Heterosexuality.* New York, NY: HarperCollins.

Masterton, R. B. (1997). Neurobehavioral studies of the central auditory system. *Annals of Otology Rhinology Laryngology, Supplement, 168,* 31–34.

Mastrianni, J. A., Nixon, R., Layzer, R., Telling, G. C., et al. (1999). Prion protein conformation in a patient with sporadic fatal insomnia. *New England Journal of Medicine, 340,* 1630–1638.

Mateo, J. M., and Johnston, R. E. (2000). Kin recognition and the "armpit effect": Evidence of self-referent phenotype matching. *Proceedings of the Royal Society of London. Series B: Biological Sciences, 267,* 695–700.

Matsumoto, K., Suzuki, W., and Tanaka, K. (2003). Neuronal correlates of goal-based motor selection in the prefrontal cortex. *Science, 301,* 229–232.

Mauch, D. H., Nägler, K., Schumacher, S., Göritz, C., et al. (2001). CNS synaptogenesis promoted by glia-derived cholesterol. *Science, 294,* 1354–1357.

Maurer, P., and Bachmann, M. F. (2007). Vaccination against nicotine: An emerging therapy for tobacco dependence. *Expert Opinion on Investigational Drugs, 16,* 1775–1783.

Mayberg, H. S., Lozano, A. M., Voon,V., McNeely, H. E., et al. (2005). Deep brain stimulation for treatment-resistant depression. *Neuron, 45,* 651–660.

Mazur, A., and Booth, A. (1998). Testosterone and dominance in men. *Behavioral and Brain Sciences, 21,* 353–363.

McAllister, A. K., Katz, L. C., and Lo, D. C. (1997). Opposing roles for endogenous BDNF and NT-3 in regulating cortical dendritic growth. *Neuron, 18,* 767–778.

McAlpine, D., Jiang, D., and Palmer, A. R. (2001). A neural code for low-frequency sound localization in mammals. *Nature Neuroscience, 4,* 396–401.

McBurney, D. H., Smith, D.V., and Shick, T. R. (1972). Gustatory cross adaptation: Sourness and bitterness. *Perception & Psychophysics, 11,* 2228–2232.

McCall, W.V., and Edinger, J. D. (1992). Subjective total insomnia: An example of sleep state misperception. *Sleep, 15,* 71–73.

McCarthy, R. A., and Warrington, E. K. (1990). *Cognitive neuropsychology: A clinical introduction.* San Diego, CA: Academic Press.

McCrae, C. S., Rowe, M. A., Tierney, C. G., Dautovich, N. D., et al. (2005). Sleep complaints, subjective and objective sleep patterns, health, psychological adjustment, and daytime functioning in community-dwelling older adults. *Journals of Gerontology. Series B, Psychological Sciences and Social Sciences, 60*(4), P182–P189.

McDonald, J. J., Teder-Sälejärvi, W. A., and Hillyard, S. A. (2000). Involuntary orienting to sound improves visual perception. *Nature, 407,* 906–908.

McFadden, D., and Pasanen, E. (1998). Comparison of the auditory systems of heterosexuals and homosexuals: Click-evoked otoacoustic emissions. *Proceedings of the National Academy of Sciences, USA, 95,* 2709–2713.

McGinty, D. J., and Sterman, M. B. (1968). Sleep suppression after basal forebrain lesions in the cat. *Science, 160,* 1253–1255.

McGowan, P. O., Sasaki, A., D'Alessio, A. C., Dymov, S., et al. (2009). Epigenetic regulation of the glucocorticoid receptor in human brain associates with childhood abuse. *Nature Neuroscience, 12,* 342–348.

McKee, A. C., Cantu, R. C., Nowinski, C. J., Hedley-Whyte, E.T., et al. (2009). Chronic traumatic encephalopathy in athletes: Progressive tauopathy after repetitive head injury. *Journal of Neuropathology and Experimental Neurology, 68,* 709–735.

McKenna, K. (1999). The brain is the master organ in sexual function: Central nervous system control of male and female sexual function. *International Journal of Impotence Research, 11*(Suppl. 1), S48–S55.

McKernan, M. G., and Shinnick-Gallagher, P. (1997). Fear conditioning induces a lasting potentiation of synaptic currents in vitro. *Nature, 390,* 607–611.

McKim, W. A. (1991). *Drugs and behavior: An introduction to behavioral pharmacology* (2nd ed.). Englewood Cliffs, NJ: Prentice Hall.

McKinley, M. J., and Johnson, A. K. (2004). The physiological regulation of thirst and fluid intake. *News in Physiological Sciences, 19,* 1–6.

McKinney, T. D., and Desjardins, C. (1973). Postnatal development of the testis, fighting behavior, and fertility in house mice. *Biology of Reproduction, 9,* 279–294.

McLaughlin, S. K., McKinnon, P. J., Spickofsky, N., Danho, W., et al. (1994). Molecular cloning of G proteins and phosphodiesterases from rat taste cells. *Physiology & Behavior, 56,* 1157–1164.

Meddis, R. (1975). On the function of sleep. *Animal Behavior, 23,* 676–691.

Meddis, R. (1977). *The sleep instinct.* London, England: Routledge & Kegan Paul.

Mednick, S. A., Huttunen, M. O., and Machon, R. A. (1994). Prenatal influenza infections and adult schizophrenia. *Schizophrenia Bulletin, 20,* 263–267.

Medori, R., Montagna, P., Tritschler, H. J., LeBlanc, A., et al. (1992). Fatal familial insomnia: A second kindred with mutation of prion protein gene at codon 178. *Neurology, 42,* 669–670.

Mega, M. S., and Cummings, J. L. (1994). Frontal-subcortical circuits and neuropsychiatric disorders. *Journal of Neuropsychiatry and Clinical Neurosciences, 6,* 358–370.

Meguerditchian, A., and Vauclair, J. (2006). Baboons communicate with their right hand. *Behavioural Brain Research, 171,* 170–174.

Mei, L., and Xiong, W.-C. (2008). Neuregulin 1 in neural development, synaptic plasticity and schizophrenia. *Nature Reviews. Neuroscience, 9,* 437–452.

Meisel, R. L., and Luttrell,V. R. (1990). Estradiol increases the dendritic length of ventromedial hypothalamic neurons in female Syrian hamsters. *Brain Research Bulletin, 25,* 165–168.

Meisel, R. L., and Sachs, B. D. (1994). The physiology of male sexual behavior. In E. Knobil and J. D. Neill (Eds.), *The physiology of reproduction* (2nd ed.,Vol. 1, pp. 3–105). New York, NY: Raven Press.

Meister, I. G., Boroojerdi, B., Foltys, H., Sparing, R., et al. (2003). Motor cortex hand area and speech: Implications for the development of language. *Neuropsychologia, 41*, 401–406.

Mello, C. V., Vicario, D. S., and Clayton, D. F. (1992). Song presentation induces gene expression in the songbird forebrain. *Proceedings of the National Academy of Sciences, USA, 89*, 6818–6822.

Melzack, R. (1984). Neuropsychological basis of pain measurement. *Advances in Pain Research, 6*, 323–341.

Melzack, R. (1990). The tragedy of needless pain. *Scientific American, 262*(2), 27–33.

Melzack, R., and Wall, P. D. (1965). Pain mechanisms: A new history. *Science, 150*, 971–979.

Meng, H., Smith, S. D., Hager, K., Held, M., et al. (2005). DCDC2 is associated with reading disability and modulates neuronal development in the brain. *Proceedings of the National Academy of Sciences, USA, 102*, 17053–17058.

Menninger, W. C. (1948). Facts and statistics of significance for psychiatry. *Bulletin of the Menninger Clinic, 12*, 1–25.

Merchán-Pérez, A., Rodriguez, J. R., Alonso-Nanclares, L., Schertel, A., et al. (2009). Counting synapses using FIB/SEM microscopy: A true revolution for ultrastructural volume reconstruction. *Frontiers in Neuroanatomy, 3*, 18.

Mersch, P. P., Middendorp, H. M., Bouhuys, A. L., Beersma, D. G., et al. (1999). Seasonal affective disorder and latitude: A review of the literature. *Journal of Affective Disorders, 53*, 35–48.

Merzenich, M. M., Schreiner, C., Jenkins, W., and Wang, X. (1993). Neural mechanisms underlying temporal integration, segmentation, and input sequence representation: Some implications for the origin of learning disabilities. *Annals of the New York Academy of Sciences, 682*, 1–22.

Meshberger, F. L. (1990). An interpretation of Michelangelo's *Creation of Adam* based on neuroanatomy. *Journal of the American Medical Association, 264*, 1837–1841.

Messias, E., Kirkpatrick, B., Bromet, E., Ross, D., et al. (2004). Summer birth and deficit schizophrenia: A pooled analysis from 6 countries. *Archives of General Psychiatry, 61*, 985–989.

Mesulam, M.-M. (1985). Attention, confusional states and neglect. In M.-M. Mesulam (Ed.), *Principles of behavioral neurology*. Philadelphia, PA: Davis.

Michael, N., and Erfurth, A. (2004). Treatment of bipolar mania with right prefrontal rapid transcranial magnetic stimulation. *Journal of Affective Disorders, 78*, 253–257.

Miczek, K. A., Fish, E. W., De Bold, J. F., and De Almeida, R. M. (2002). Social and neural determinants of aggressive behavior: Pharmacotherapeutic targets at serotonin, dopamine and gamma-aminobutyric acid systems. *Psychopharmacology (Berlin), 163*, 434–458.

Miles, L. E., and Dement, W. C. (1980). Sleep and aging. *Sleep, 3*, 1220.

Miller, E. K., and Cohen, J. D. (2001). An integrative theory of prefrontal cortex function. *Annual Review of Neuroscience, 24*, 167–202.

Miller, G. F. (2000). *The mating mind: How sexual choice shaped the evolution of human nature*. New York, NY: Doubleday.

Miller, J. M., and Spelman, F. A. (1990). *Cochlear implants: Models of the electrically stimulated ear*. New York, NY: Springer-Verlag.

Milner, A. D., Perrett, D. I., Johnston, R. S., Benson, P. J., et al. (1991). Perception and action in "visual form agnosia." *Brain, 114*, 405–428.

Milner, B. (1963). Effect of different brain lesions on card sorting. *Archives of Neurology, 9*, 90–100.

Milner, B. (1965). Memory disturbance after bilateral hippocampal lesions. In P. M. Milner and S. E. Glickman (Eds.), *Cognitive processes and the brain; an enduring problem in psychology* (pp. 97–111). Princeton, NJ: Van Nostrand.

Milner, B. (1970). Memory and the medial temporal regions of the brain. In D. H. Pribram and D. E. Broadbent (Eds.), *Biology of memory* (pp. 29–50). New York, NY: Academic Press.

Minzenberg, M. J., Laird, A. R., Thelen, S., Carter, C. S., et al. (2009). Meta-analysis of 41 functional neuroimaging studies of executive function in schizophrenia. *Archives of General Psychiatry, 66*, 811–822.

Mirescu, C., Peters, J. D., and Gould, E. (2004). Early life experience alters response of adult neurogenesis to stress. *Nature Neuroscience, 7*, 841–846.

Mirsky, A. F., and Duncan, C. C. (1986). Etiology and expression of schizophrenia: Neurobiological and psychosocial factors. *Annual Review of Psychology, 37*, 291–321.

Mishkin, M., and Ungerleider, L. (1982). Contribution of striate inputs to the visuospatial functions of parieto-preoccipital cortex in monkeys. *Behavioural Brain Research, 6*, 57–77.

Mitchell, R. E. (2006). How many deaf people are there in the United States? Estimates from the Survey of Income and Program Participation. *Journal of Deaf Studies and Deaf Education, 11*, 112–119.

Miyawaki, Y., Uchida, H., Yamashita, O., Sato, M. A., et al. (2008). Visual image reconstruction from human brain activity using a combination of multiscale local image decoders. *Neuron, 60*, 915–929.

Moghaddam, B., and Adams, B. W. (1998). Reversal of phencyclidine effects by a group II metabotropic glutamate receptor agonist in rats. *Science, 281*, 1349–1352.

Mohammed, A. (2001). *Enrichment and the brain. Plasticity in the adult brain: From genes to neurotherapy.* 22nd International Summer School of Brain Research, Amsterdam, Netherlands.

Moita, M. A., Rosis, S., Zhou, Y., LeDoux, J. E., et al. (2004). Putting fear in its place: Remapping of hippocampal place cells during fear conditioning. *Journal of Neuroscience, 24*, 7015–7023.

Money, J., and Ehrhardt, A. A. (1972). *Man and woman, boy and girl.* Baltimore, MD: Johns Hopkins University Press.

Monfils, M. H., Plautz, E. J., and Kleim, J. A. (2005). In search of the motor engram: Motor map plasticity as a mechanism for encoding motor experience. *Neuroscientist, 11*, 471–483.

Monks, D. A., and Watson N. V. (2001). N-cadherin expression in motoneurons is directly regulated by androgens: A genetic mosaic analysis in rats. *Brain Research, 895*, 73–79.

Montague, C. T., Farooqi, I. S., Whitehead, J. P., Soos, M. A., et al. (1997). Congenital leptin deficiency is associated with severe early-onset obesity in humans. *Nature, 387*, 903–908.

Monti, M. M., Vanhaudenhuyse, A., Coleman, M. R., Boly, M., et al. (2010). Willful modulation of brain activity in disorders of consciousness. *New England Journal of Medicine, 362*, 579–589.

Moore, C. L., Dou, H., and Juraska, J. M. (1992). Maternal stimulation affects the number of motor neurons in a sexually dimorphic nucleus of the lumbar spinal cord. *Brain Research, 572*, 52–56.

Moore, G. J., Bebchuk, J. M., Wilds, I. B., Chen, G., et al. (2000). Lithium-induced increase in human brain grey matter. *Lancet, 356*, 241–242.

Moore, R. Y. (1983). Organization and function of a central nervous system circadian oscillator: The suprachiasmatic nucleus. *Federation Proceedings, 42*, 2783–2789.

Moore, R. Y., and Eichler, V. B. (1972). Loss of circadian adrenal corticosterone rhythm following suprachiasmatic lesions in the rat. *Brain Research, 42,* 201–206.

Moorhead, T. W., McKirdy, J., Sussmann, J. E., Hall, J., et al. (2007). Progressive gray matter loss in patients with bipolar disorder. *Biological Psychiatry, 62,* 894–900.

Moran, J., and Desimone, R. (1985). Selective attention gates visual processing in the extrastriate cortex. *Science, 229,* 782–784.

Mori, K., Nagao, H., and Yoshihara, Y. (1999). The olfactory bulb: Coding and processing of odor molecule information. *Science, 286,* 711–715.

Morihisa, J., and McAnulty, G. B. (1985). Structure and function: Brain electrical activity mapping and computed tomography in schizophrenia. *Biological Psychiatry, 20,* 3–19.

Morris, B. (2002). Overcoming dyslexia. *Fortune, 145*(10), 1–7.

Morris, R. G., Halliwell, R. F., and Bowery, N. (1989). Synaptic plasticity and learning. II: Do different kinds of plasticity underlie different kinds of learning? *Neuropsychologia, 27,* 41–59.

Morrison, A. R. (1983). A window on the sleeping brain. *Scientific American, 248*(4), 94–102.

Morrison, A. R., Sanford, L. D., Ball, W. A., Mann, G. L., et al. (1995). Stimulus-elicited behavior in rapid eye movement sleep without atonia. *Behavioral Neuroscience, 109,* 972–979.

Morrison, R. G., and Nottebohm, F. (1993). Role of a telencephalic nucleus in the delayed song learning of socially isolated zebra finches. *Journal of Neurobiology, 24,* 1045–1064.

Mortensen, P. B., Pedersen, C. B., Westergaard, T., Wohlfahrt, J., et al. (1999). Effects of family history and place and season of birth on the risk of schizophrenia. *New England Journal of Medicine, 340,* 603–608.

Moruzzi, G. (1972). The sleep-waking cycle. *Ergebnisse der Physiologie, biologischen Chemie und experimentellen Pharmakologie, 64,* 1–165.

Moruzzi, G., and Magoun, H. W. (1949). Brain stem reticular formation and activation of the EEG. *Clinical Neurophysiology, 1,* 455–473.

Moscovitch, A., Blashko, C. A., Eagles, J. M., Darcourt, G., et al. (2004). A placebo-controlled study of sertraline in the treatment of outpatients with seasonal affective disorder. *Psychopharmacology (Berlin), 171,* 390–397.

Mott, F. W. (1895). Experimental inquiry upon the afferent tracts of the central nervous system of the monkey. *Brain, 18,* 1–20.

Mountcastle, V. B. (1979). An organizing principle for cerebral function: The unit module and the distributed system. In F. O. Schmitt and F. G. Worden (Eds.), *The neurosciences: Fourth study program* (pp. 21–24). Cambridge, MA: MIT Press.

Mountcastle, V. B. (1984). Central nervous mechanisms in mechanoreceptive sensibility. In I. Darian-Smith (Ed.), *Handbook of physiology, Section 1: Vol. 3. Sensory processes* (pp. 789–878). Bethesda, MD: American Physiological Society.

Mounts, J. R. (2000). Attentional capture by abrupt onsets and feature singletons produces inhibitory surrounds. *Perception & Psychophysics, 62,* 1485–1493.

Mowry, B. J., Holmans, P. A., Pulver, A. E., Gejman, P. V., et al. (2004). Multicenter linkage study of schizophrenia loci on chromosome 22q. *Molecular Psychiatry, 9,* 784–795.

Mueller, H. T., Haroutunian, V., Davis, K. L., and Meador-Woodruff, J. H. (2004). Expression of the ionotropic glutamate receptor subunits and NMDA receptor-associated intracellular proteins in the substantia nigra in schizophrenia. *Brain Research. Molecular Brain Research, 121,* 60–69.

Mukamal, K. J., Conigrave, K. M., Mittleman, M. A., Camargo, C. A., Jr., et al. (2003). Roles of drinking pattern and type of alcohol consumed in coronary heart disease in men. *New England Journal of Medicine, 348,* 109–118.

Mukhametov, L. M. (1984). Sleep in marine mammals. In A. Borbély and J. L. Valatx (Eds.), *Experimental Brain Research: Suppl. 8. Sleep mechanisms* (pp. 227–238). Berlin, Germany: Springer-Verlag.

Münte, T. F. (2002). Brains out of tune. *Nature, 415,* 589–590.

Münte, T. F., Altenmüller, E., and Jäncke, L. (2002). The musician's brain as a model of neuroplasticity. *Nature Reviews. Neuroscience, 3,* 473–478.

Murray, R. M., Morrison, P. D., Henquet, C., and Di Forti, M. (2007). Cannabis, the mind and society: The hash realities. *Nature Reviews. Neuroscience, 8,* 885–895.

N

Nader, K., and Hardt, O. (2009). A single standard for memory: The case for reconsolidation. *Nature Reviews. Neuroscience, 10,* 224–234.

Naeser, M., Gaddie, A., Palumbo, C., and Stiassny-Eder, D. (1990). Late recovery of auditory comprehension in global aphasia. Improved recovery observed with subcortical temporal isthmus lesion vs. Wernicke's cortical area lesion. *Archives of Neurology, 47,* 425–432.

Naeser, M., and Hayward, R. (1978). Lesion localization in aphasia with cranial computed tomography and the Boston Diagnostic Aphasia Exam. *Neurology, 28,* 545–551.

Nair, K. S., Rizza, R. A., O'Brien, P., Dhatariya, K., et al. (2006). DHEA in elderly women and DHEA or testosterone in elderly men. *New England Journal of Medicine, 355,* 1647–1659.

Nakazato, M., Murakami, N., Date, Y., Kojima, M., et al. (2001). A role for ghrelin in the central regulation of feeding. *Nature, 409,* 194–198.

Naqvi, N. H., Rudrauf, D., Damasio, H., and Bechara, A. (2007). Damage to the insula disrupts addiction to cigarette smoking. *Science, 315,* 531–534.

Narrow, W. E., Rae, D. S., Robins, L. N., and Regier, D. A. (2002). Revised prevalence estimates of mental disorders in the United States: Using a clinical significance criterion to reconcile 2 surveys' estimates. *Archives of General Psychiatry, 59,* 115–123.

Nathans, J. (1987). Molecular biology of visual pigments. *Annual Review of Neuroscience, 10,* 163–194.

Nation, E. F. (1973). William Osler on penis captivus and other urologic topics. *Urology, 2,* 468–470.

National Academy of Sciences. (2003). *The polygraph and lie detection.* Washington, DC: National Academies Press (www.nap.edu/openbook.php?isbn=0309084369).

Neary, M. T., and Batterham, R. L. (2009). Gut hormones: Implications for the treatment of obesity. *Pharmacology & Therapeutics, 124,* 44–56.

Neff, W. D., and Casseday, J. H. (1977). Effects of unilateral ablation of auditory cortex on monaural cat's ability to localize sound. *Journal of Neurophysiology, 40,* 44–52.

Neitz, M., Kraft, T. W., and Neitz, J. (1998). Expression of L cone pigment gene subtypes in females. *Vision Research, 38,* 3221–3225.

Nelson, G., Chandrashekar, J., Hoon, M. A., Feng, L., et al. (2002). An amino-acid taste receptor. *Nature, 416,* 199–202.

Nelson, G., Hoon, M. A., Chandrashekar, J., Zhang, Y., et al. (2001). Mammalian sweet taste receptors. *Cell, 106,* 381–390.

Neumeister, A., Bain, E., Nugent, A. C., Carson, R. E., et al. (2004). Reduced serotonin type 1A receptor binding in panic disorder. *Journal of Neuroscience, 24,* 589–591.

Neville, H. J., Bavelier, D., Corina, D., Rauschecker, J., et al. (1998). Cerebral organization for language in deaf and hearing subjects: Biological constraints and effects of experience. *Proceedings of the National Academy of Sciences, USA, 95,* 922–929.

Neville, H. J., Mills, D. L., and Lawson, D. S. (1992). Fractionating language: Different neural subsystems with different sensitive periods. *Cerebral Cortex, 2,* 244–258.

Newsome, W. T., Wurtz, R. H., Dursteler, M. R., and Mikami, A. (1985). Deficits in visual motion processing following ibotenic acid lesions of the middle temporal visual area of the macaque monkey. *Journal of Neuroscience, 5,* 825–840.

Nichols, M. J., and Newsome, W. T. (1999). The neurobiology of cognition. *Nature, 402,* C35–C38.

Nieto-Sampedro, M., and Cotman, C. W. (1985). Growth factor induction and temporal order in central nervous system repair. In C. W. Cotman (Ed.), *Synaptic plasticity* (pp. 407–457). New York, NY: Guilford Press.

Nietzel, M. T. (2000). Police psychology. In A. E. Kazdin (Ed.), *Encyclopedia of psychology* (Vol. 6, pp. 224–226). Washington, DC: American Psychological Association.

Nishida, M., and Walker, M. P. (2007). Daytime naps, motor memory consolidation and regionally specific sleep spindles. *PLoS ONE, 2,* e341.

Nixon, K., and Crews, F. T. (2002). Binge ethanol exposure decreases neurogenesis in adult rat hippocampus. *Journal of Neurochemistry, 83,* 1087–1093.

Noad, M. J., Cato, D. H., Bryden, M. M., Jenner, M.-N., et al. (2000). Cultural revolution in whale songs. *Nature, 408,* 537–538.

Nobelstiftelsen. (1964). *Physiology or medicine: Vol. 3. 1942–1962.* (Nobel Lectures, Including Presentation Speeches and Laureates' Biographies.) Amsterdam, Netherlands: Elsevier.

Noguchi, H. (1911). *Serum diagnosis of syphilis and the butyric acid test for syphilis.* Philadelphia, PA: Lippincott.

Noguchi, Y., Watanabe, E., and Sakai, K. L. (2003). An event-related optical topography study of cortical activation induced by single-pulse transcranial magnetic stimulation. *Neuroimage, 19,* 156–162.

Nordeen, E. J., Nordeen, K. W., Sengelaub, D. R., and Arnold, A. P. (1985). Androgens prevent normally occurring cell death in a sexually dimorphic spinal nucleus. *Science, 229,* 671–673.

Norsell, U. (1980). Behavioral studies of the somatosensory system. *Physiological Reviews, 60,* 327–354.

Nottebohm, F. (1980). Brain pathways for vocal learning in birds: A review of the first 10 years. *Progress in Psychobiology and Physiological Psychology, 9,* 85–124.

Nottebohm, F. (1981). A brain for all seasons: Cyclical anatomical changes in song control nuclei of the canary brain. *Science, 214,* 1368–1370.

Numan, M., and Numan. M. J. (1991). Preoptic-brainstem connections and maternal behavior in rats. *Behavioral Neuroscience, 105,* 1010–1029.

Nutt, J. G., Rufener, S. L., Carter, J. H., Anderson, V. C., et al. (2001). Interactions between deep brain stimulation and levodopa in Parkinson's disease. *Neurology, 57,* 1835–1842.

O

Oades, R. D., and Halliday, G. M. (1987). Ventral tegmental (A10) system: Neurobiology. 1. Anatomy and connectivity. *Brain Research Reviews, 12,* 117–165.

O'Connor, D. B., Archer, J., and Wu, F. C. (2004). Effects of testosterone on mood, aggression, and sexual behavior in young men: A double-blind, placebo-controlled, cross-over study. *Journal of Clinical Endocrinology & Metabolism, 89,* 2837–2845.

O'Craven, K. M., Downing, P. E., and Kanwisher, N. (1999). fMRI evidence for objects as the units of attentional selection. *Nature, 401,* 584–587.

Ojemann, G., and Mateer, C. (1979). Human language cortex: Localization of memory, syntax, and sequential motor-phoneme identification systems. *Science, 205,* 1401–1403.

Okano, H., Ogawa, Y., Nakamura, M., Kaneko, S., et al. (2003). Transplantation of neural stem cells into the spinal cord after injury. *Seminars in Cell and Developmental Biology, 14,* 191–198.

O'Keefe, J., and Dostrovsky, J. (1971). The hippocampus as a spatial map. Preliminary evidence from unit activity in the freely-moving rat. *Brain Research, 34,* 171–175.

Olanow, C. W., Goetz, C. G., Kordower, J. H., Stoessl, A. J., et al. (2003). A double-blind controlled trial of bilateral fetal nigral transplantation in Parkinson's disease. *Annals of Neurology, 54,* 403–414.

Olds, J., and Milner, P. (1954). Positive reinforcement produced by electrical stimulation of septal area and other regions of the rat brain. *Journal of Comparative and Physiological Psychology, 47,* 419–427.

Olfson, M., Marcus, S. C., and Shaffer, D. (2006). Antidepressant drug therapy and suicide in severely depressed children and adults: A case-control study. *Archives of General Psychiatry, 63,* 865–872.

Olsen, K. L. (1979). Androgen-insensitive rats are defeminised by their testes. *Nature, 279,* 238–239.

Olson, S. (2004). Making sense of Tourette's. *Science, 305,* 1390–1392.

Olsson, A., and Phelps, E. A. (2007). Social learning of fear. *Nature Neuroscience, 10,* 1095–1102.

O'Neil, M. F., and Moore, N. A. (2003). Animal models of depression: Are there any? *Human Psychopharmacology, 18,* 239–254.

Ontiveros, A., Fontaine, R., Breton, G., Elie, R., et al. (1989). Correlation of severity of panic disorder and neuroanatomical changes on magnetic resonance imaging. *Journal of Neuropsychiatry and Clinical Neurosciences, 1,* 404–408.

Oppenheim, R. W. (1991). Cell death during development of the nervous system. *Annual Review of Neuroscience, 14,* 453–501.

Osorio, D., and Vorobyev, M. (2008). A review of the evolution of animal colour vision and visual communication signals. *Vision Research, 48,* 2042–2051.

Osterhout, L. (1997). On the brain response to syntactic anomalies: Manipulations of word position and word class reveal individual differences. *Brain and Language, 59,* 494–522.

Ouattara, K., Lemasson, A., and Zuberbühler, K. (2009). Campbell's monkeys concatenate vocalizations into context-specific call sequences. *Proceedings of the National Academy of Sciences, USA, 22,* 22026–22031.

Overstreet, D. H. (1993). The Flinders sensitive line rats: A genetic animal model of depression. *Neuroscience and Biobehavioral Reviews, 17,* 51–68.

Ozelius, L. J., Senthil, G., Saunders-Pullman, R., Ohmann, E., et al. (2006). *LRRK2* G2019S as a cause of Parkinson's disease in Ashkenazi Jews. *New England Journal of Medicine, 354,* 424–425.

P

Pack, A. I. (2003). Should a pharmaceutical be approved for the broad indication of excessive sleepiness? *American Journal of Respiratory and Critical Care Medicine, 167,* 109–111.

Pagel, J. F., and Helfter, P. (2003). Drug induced nightmares—An etiology based review. *Human Psychopharmacology, 18,* 59–67.

Palmer, T. D., Schwartz, P. H., Taupin, P., Kaspar, B., et al. (2001). Progenitor cells from human brain after death. *Nature, 411,* 42–43.

Palmiter, R. D. (2008). Dopamine signaling in the dorsal striatum is essential for motivated behaviors: Lessons from dopamine-deficient mice. *Annals of the New York Academy of Sciences, 1129*, 35–46.

Panksepp, J. (1998). *Affective neuroscience.* New York, NY: Oxford University Press.

Panksepp, J. (2000). Emotions as natural kinds within the mammalian brain. In M. Lewis and J. M. Haviland-Jones (Eds.), *Handbook of emotions* (2nd ed., pp. 137–156). New York, NY: Guilford Press.

Panksepp, J. (2005). Beyond a joke: From animal laughter to human joy? *Science, 308*, 62–63.

Panksepp, J. (2007). Neuroevolutionary sources of laughter and social joy: Modeling primal human laughter in laboratory rats. *Behavioural Brain Research, 182*, 231–244.

Panksepp, J. B., Yue, Z., Drerup, C., and Huber, R. (2003). Amine neurochemistry and aggression in crayfish. *Microscopy Research and Technique, 60*, 360–368.

Panov, A. V., Gutekunst, C.-A., Leavitt, B. R., Hayden, M. R., et al. (2002). Early mitochondrial calcium defects in Huntington's disease are a direct effect of polyglutamines. *Nature Neuroscience, 5*, 731–736.

Pantev, C., Oostenveld, R., Engelien, A., Ross, B., et al. (1998). Increased auditory cortical representation in musicians. *Nature, 392*, 811–814.

Pantle, A., and Sekuler, R. (1968). Size-detecting mechanisms in human vision. *Science, 162*, 1146–1148.

Papez, J. W. (1937). A proposed mechanism of emotion. *Archives of Neurology and Psychiatry, 38*, 725–745.

Papka, M., Ivry, R., and Woodruff-Pak, D. S. (1994). Eyeblink classical conditioning and time production in patients with cerebellar damage. *Society of Neuroscience Abstracts, 20*, 360.

Pare, M., Behets, C., and Cornu, O. (2003). Paucity of presumptive ruffini corpuscles in the index finger pad of humans. *Journal of Comparative Neurology, 456*, 260–266.

Park, S., Como, P. G., Cui, L., and Kurlan, R. (1993). The early course of the Tourette's syndrome clinical spectrum. *Neurology, 43*, 1712–1715.

Parker, G., Cahill, L., and McGaugh, J. L. (2006). A case of unusual autobiographical remembering. *Neurocase, 12*, 35–49.

Parkes, J. D. (1985). *Sleep and its disorders.* Philadelphia, PA: Saunders.

Parton, L. E., Ye, C. P., Coppari, R., Enriori, P. J., et al. (2007). Glucose sensing by POMC neurons regulates glucose homeostasis and is impaired in obesity. *Nature, 449*, 228–232.

Paterson, S. J., Brown, J. H., Gsödl, M. K., Johnson, M. H., et al. (1999). Cognitive modularity and genetic disorders. *Science, 286*, 2355–2358.

Patterson, F., and Linden, E. (1981). *The education of Koko.* New York, NY: Holt, Rinehart, and Winston.

Patterson, P. H. (2007). Maternal effects on schizophrenia risk. *Science, 318*, 576–578.

Paus, T., Kalina, M., Patocková, L., Angerová, Y., et al. (1991). Medial vs lateral frontal lobe lesions and differential impairment of central-gaze fixation maintenance in man. *Brain, 114*, 2051–2067.

Paus, T., Keshavan, M., and Giedd, J. N. (2008). Why do many psychiatric disorders emerge during adolescence? *Nature Reviews. Neuroscience, 9*, 947–956.

Pedersen, C. B., and Mortensen, P. B. (2001). Evidence of a dose-response relationship between urbanicity during upbringing and schizophrenia risk. *Archives of General Psychiatry, 58*, 1039–1046.

Pediatric Eye Disease Investigator Group. (2005). Randomized trial of treatment of amblyopia in children aged 7 to 17 years. *Archives of Ophthalmology, 13*, 437–447.

Pedreira, C., Mormann, F., Kraskov, A., Cerf, M., et al. (2010). Responses of human medial temporal lobe neurons are modulated by stimulus repetition. *Journal of Neurophysiology, 103*, 97–107.

Pegna, A. J., Khateb, A., Lazeyras, F., and Seghier, M. L. (2005). Discriminating emotional faces without primary visual cortices involves the right amygdala. *Nature Neuroscience, 8*, 24–25.

Peña, J. L., and Konishi, M. (2000). Cellular mechanisms for resolving phase ambiguity in the owl's inferior colliculus. *Proceedings of the National Academy of Sciences, USA, 97*, 11787–11792.

Penfield, W., and Rasmussen, T. (1950). *The cerebral cortex in man.* New York, NY: Macmillan.

Penfield, W., and Roberts, L. (1959). *Speech and brain-mechanisms.* Princeton, NJ: Princeton University Press.

Peplau, L. A. (2003). Human sexuality: How do men and women differ? *Current Directions in Psychological Science, 12*, 37–40.

Perani, D., and Abutalebi, J. (2005). The neural basis of first and second language processing. *Current Opinion in Neurobiology, 15*, 202–206.

Perenin, M. T., and Vighetto, A. (1988). Optic ataxia: A specific disruption in visuomotor mechanisms. I. Different aspects of the deficit in reaching for objects. *Brain, 111*, 643–674.

Pernía-Andrade, A. J., Kato, A., Witschi, R., Nyilas, R., et al. (2009). Spinal endocannabinoids and CB$_1$ receptors mediate C-fiber–induced heterosynaptic pain sensitization. *Science, 325*, 760–764.

Peschanski, M., Defer, G., N'Guyen, J. P., Ricolfi, F., et al. (1994). Bilateral motor improvement and alteration of L-dopa effect in two patients with Parkinson's disease following intrastriatal transplantation of foetal ventral mesencephalon. *Brain, 117*, 487–499.

Peter, M. E., Medema, J. P., and Krammer, P. H. (1997). Does the *Caenorhabditis elegans* protein CED-4 contain a region of homology to the mammalian death effector domain? *Cell Death and Differentiation, 4*, 51–134.

Peterhans, E., and von der Heydt, R. (1989). Mechanisms of contour perception in monkey visual cortex. II. Contours bridging gaps. *Journal of Neuroscience, 9*, 1749–1763.

Peters, A., Palay, S. L., and Webster, H. deF. (1991). *The fine structure of the nervous system: Neurons and their supporting cells* (3rd ed.). New York, NY: Oxford University Press.

Peterson, B. S., Warner, V., Bansal, R., Zhu, H., et al. (2009). Cortical thinning in persons at increased familial risk for major depression. *Proceedings of the National Academy of Sciences, USA, 106*, 6273–6278.

Peterson, L. R., and Peterson, M. J. (1959). Short-term retention of individual verbal items. *Journal of Experimental Psychology, 58*, 193–198.

Petit, C., and Richardson, G. P. (2009). Linking genes underlying deafness to hair-bundle development and function. *Nature Neuroscience, 12*, 703–710.

Petitto, L. A., Zatorre, R. J., Gauna, K., Nikelski, E. J., et al. (2000). Speech-like cerebral activity in profoundly deaf people processing signed languages: Implications for the neural basis of human language. *Proceedings of the National Academy of Sciences, USA, 97*, 13961–13966.

Petrides, M., and Milner, B. (1982). Deficits on subject-ordered tasks after frontal- and temporal-lobe lesions in man. *Neuropsychologia, 20*, 249–262.

Petrovic, P., Kalso, E., Petersson, K. M., and Ingvar, M. (2002). Placebo and opioid analgesia imaging—A shared neuronal network. *Science, 295*, 1737–1740.

Pettit, H. O., and Justice, J. B., Jr. (1991). Effect of dose on cocaine self-administration behavior and dopamine levels in the nucleus accumbens. *Brain Research, 539*, 94–102.

Petty, F., Kramer, G., Wilson, L., and Jordan, S. (1994). In vivo serotonin release and learned helplessness. *Psychiatry Research, 52,* 285–293.

Pfaff, D. W. (1980). *Estrogens and brain function: Neural analysis of a hormone-controlled mammalian reproductive behavior.* New York, NY: Springer-Verlag.

Pfaff, D. W. (1997). Hormones, genes, and behavior. *Proceedings of the National Academy of Sciences, USA, 94,* 14213–14216.

Pfefferbaum, A., Sullivan, E.V., Mathalon, D. H., Shear, P. K., et al. (1995). Longitudinal changes in magnetic resonance imaging brain volumes in abstinent and relapsed alcoholics. *Alcoholism: Clinical and Experimental Research, 19,* 1177–1191.

Phillips, M. L., Young, A. W., Scott, S. K., Calder, A. J., et al. (1998). Neural responses to facial and vocal expressions of fear and disgust. *Proceedings of the Royal Society of London. Series B: Biological Sciences, 265,* 1809–1817.

Phoenix, C. H., Goy, R. W., Gerall, A. A., and Young, W. C. (1959). Organizing action of prenatally administered testosterone propionate on the tissues mediating mating behavior in the female guinea pig. *Endocrinology, 65,* 369–382.

Pickens, R., and Thompson, T. (1968). Drug use by U.S. Army enlisted men in Vietnam: A followup on their return home. *Journal of Pharmacology and Experimental Therapeutics, 161,* 122–129.

Pierce, K., Müller, R.-A., Ambrose, J., Allen, G., et al. (2001). Face processing occurs outside the fusiform "face area": Evidence from functional MRI. *Brain, 124,* 2059–2073.

Pierce, R. C., and Kumaresan, V. (2006). The mesolimbic dopamine system: The final common pathway for the reinforcing effect of drugs of abuse? *Neuroscience and Biobehavioral Reviews, 30,* 215–238.

Pinker, S. (1994). *The language instinct.* New York, NY: Morrow.

Pletnikov, M.V., Ayhan,Y., Nikolskaia, O., Xu,Y., et al. (2008). Inducible expression of mutant human DISC1 in mice is associated with brain and behavioral abnormalities reminiscent of schizophrenia. *Molecular Psychiatry, 13,* 13–186.

Ploog, D. W. (1992). Neuroethological perspectives on the human brain: From the expression of emotions to intentional signing and speech. In A. Harrington (Ed.), *So human a brain: Knowledge and values in the neurosciences* (pp. 3–13). Boston, MA: Birkhauser.

Plutchik, R. (1994). *The psychology and biology of emotion.* New York, NY: HarperCollins.

Polymeropoulos, M. H., Lavedan, C., Leroy, E., Ide, S. E., et al. (1997). Mutation in the alpha-synuclein gene identified in families with Parkinson's disease. *Science, 276,* 2045–2047.

Ponsford, J. (2005). Rehabilitation interventions after mild head injury. *Current Opinion in Neurology, 18,* 692–697.

Poole, J. H., Tyack, P. L., Stoeger-Horwath, A. S., and Watwood, S. (2005). Animal behaviour: Elephants are capable of vocal learning. *Nature, 434,* 455–456.

Pope, H. G., Jr., Kouri, E. M., and Hudson, J. I. (2000). Effects of supraphysiologic doses of testosterone on mood and aggression in normal men: A randomized controlled trial. *Archives of General Psychiatry, 57,* 133–140.

Poremba, A., Malloy, M., Saunders, R. C., Carson, R. E., et al. (2004). Species-specific calls evoke asymmetric activity in the monkey's temporal poles. *Nature, 427,* 448–451.

Porta, M., Brambilla, A., Cavanna, A. E., Servello, D., et al. (2009). Thalamic deep brain stimulation for treatment-refractory Tourette syndrome: Two-year outcome. *Neurology, 73,* 1375–1380.

Porter, J., Craven, B., Khan, R. H., Chang, S.-J., et al. (2007). Mechanisms of scent-tracking in humans. *Nature Neuroscience, 10,* 27–29.

Posner, M. I. (1980). Orienting of attention. *Quarterly Journal of Experimental Psychology, 32,* 3–25.

Posner, M. I., and Cohen, Y. (1984). Components of visual orienting. In H. Bouma and D. Bowhuis (Eds.), *Attention and performance: Vol 10. Control of language processes* (pp. 531–556). Hillsdale, NJ: Erlbaum.

Posner, M. I., and Raichle, M. E. (1994). *Images of mind.* New York, NY: Scientific American Library.

Postuma, R. B., Gagnon, J. F., Vendette, M., Fantini, M. L., et al. (2009). Quantifying the risk of neurodegenerative disease in idiopathic REM sleep behavior disorder. *Neurology, 72,* 1296–1300.

Poulet, J. F. A., and Petersen, C. C. H. (2008). Internal brain state regulates membrane potential synchrony in barrel cortex of behaving mice. *Nature, 454,* 881–885.

Powell, S. B. (2010). Models of neurodevelopmental abnormalities in schizophrenia. *Current Topics in Behavioral Neurosciences, 4,* 435–481.

Powley, T. L. (2000). Vagal circuitry mediating cephalic-phase responses to food. *Appetite, 34,* 184–188.

Premack, D. (1971). Language in a chimpanzee? *Science, 172,* 808–822.

Price, M. A., and Vandenbergh, J. G. (1992). Analysis of puberty-accelerating pheromones. *Journal of Experimental Zoology, 264,* 42–45.

Pugh, K. R., Mencl, W. E., Shaywitz, B. A., Shaywitz, S. E., et al. (2000). The angular gyrus in developmental dyslexia: Task-specific differences in functional connectivity within posterior cortex. *Psychological Science, 11,* 51–56.

Purves, D., Augustine, G. J., Fitzpatrick, D., Katz, L., et al. (Eds.). (2001). *Neuroscience* (2nd ed.). Sunderland, MA: Sinauer.

Purves, D., and Lotto, B., 2011. *Why We See What We Do, Redux, A Wholly Empirical Theory of Vision.* Sunderland, MA: Sinauer.

R

Racette, A., Bard, C., and Peretz, I. (2006). Making non-fluent aphasics speak: Sing along! *Brain, 129,* 2571–2584.

Racine, E., Bar-Ilan, O., and Illes, J. (2005). fMRI in the public eye. *Nature Reviews. Neuroscience, 6,* 159–164.

Rafal, R. D. (1994). Neglect. *Current Opinion in Neurobiology, 4,* 231–236.

Rafal, R. D., Posner, M. I., Friedman, J. H., Inhoff, A. W., et al. (1988). Orienting of visual attention in progressive supranuclear palsy. *Brain, 111,* 267–280.

Rahman, Q. (2005). The neurodevelopment of human sexual orientation. *Neuroscience and Biobehavioral Reviews, 29,* 1057–1066.

Raine, A., Lencz, T., Bihrle, S., LaCasse, L., et al. (2000). Reduced prefrontal gray matter volume and reduced autonomic activity in antisocial personality disorder. *Archives of General Psychiatry, 57,* 119–127.

Raine, A., Meloy, J. R., Bihrle, S., Stoddard, J., et al. (1998). Reduced prefrontal and increased subcortical brain functioning assessed using positron emission tomography in predatory and affective murderers. *Behavioral Sciences & the Law, 16,* 319–332.

Rainville, P., Duncan, G. H., Price, D. D., Carrier, B., et al. (1997). Pain affect encoded in human anterior cingulate but not somatosensory cortex. *Science, 277,* 968–971.

Raisman, G. (1978). What hope for repair of the brain? *Annals of Neurology, 3,* 101–106.

Raisman, G., and Field, P. M. (1971). Sexual dimorphism in the preoptic area of the rat. *Science, 173,* 731–733.

Raisman, G., and Li,Y. (2007). Repair of neural pathways by olfactory ensheathing cells. *Nature Reviews. Neuroscience, 8,* 312–319.

Ralph, M. R., Foster, R. G., Davis, F. C., and Menaker, M. (1990). Transplanted suprachiasmatic nucleus determines circadian period. *Science, 247*, 975–978.

Ralph, M. R., and Menaker, M. (1988). A mutation of the circadian system in golden hamsters. *Science, 241*, 1225–1227.

Ramachandran, V. S., and Hubbard, E. M. (2001). Psychophysical investigations into the neural basis of synthaesthesia. *Proceedings of the Royal Society of London. Series B: Biological Sciences, 268*, 979–983.

Ramachandran, V. S., and Rogers-Ramachandran, D. (2000). Phantom limbs and neural plasticity. *Archives of Neurology, 57*, 317–320.

Ramchandani, P. (2004). A question of balance: How safe are the medicines that are prescribed to children? *Nature, 430*, 401–402.

Rampon, C., Tang, Y. P., Goodhouse, J., Shimizu, E., et al. (2000). Enrichment induces structural changes and recovery from nonspatial memory deficits in CA1 NMDAR1-knockout mice. *Nature Neuroscience, 3*, 238–244.

Rand, M. N., and Breedlove, S. M. (1987). Ontogeny of functional innervation of bulbocavernosus muscles in male and female rats. *Brain Research, 430*, 150–152.

Randolph, M., and Semmes, J. (1974). Behavioral consequences of selective subtotal ablations in the postcentral gyrus of *Macaca mulatta*. *Brain Research, 70*, 55–70.

Rao, P. D. P., and Finger, T. E. (1984). Asymmetry of the olfactory system in the brain of the winter flounder *Pseudopleuronectes americanus*. *Journal of Comparative Neurology, 225*, 492–510.

Rapoport, J. L. (1989). The biology of obsessions and compulsions. *Scientific American, 260*(6), 82–89.

Rasmussen, L. E., and Greenwood, D. R. (2003). Frontalin: A chemical message of musth in Asian elephants (*Elephas maximus*). *Chemical Senses, 28*, 433–446.

Rasmussen, L. E., Riddle, H. S., and Krishnamurthy, V. (2002). Chemical communication: Mellifluous matures to malodorous in musth. *Nature, 415*, 975–976.

Rasmussen, S., Greenberg, B., Mindus, P., Friehs, G., et al. (2000). Neurosurgical approaches to intractable obsessive-compulsive disorder. *CNS Spectrums, 5*(11), 23–34.

Rathelot, J. A., and Strick, P. L. (2006). Muscle representation in the macaque motor cortex: An anatomical perspective. *Proceedings of the National Academy of Sciences, USA, 103*, 8257–8262.

Rattenborg, N. C. (2006). Do birds sleep in flight? *Naturwissenschaften, 93*, 413–425.

Rauch, S. L., Jenike, M. A., Alpert, N. M., Baer, L., et al. (1994). Regional cerebral blood flow measured during symptom provocation in obsessive-compulsive disorder using oxygen 15-labeled carbon dioxide and positron emission tomography. *Archives of General Psychiatry, 51*, 62–70.

Rauch, S. L., Shin, L. M., and Wright, C. I. (2003). Neuroimaging studies of amygdala function in anxiety disorders. *Annals of the New York Academy of Sciences, 985*, 389–410.

Recanzone, G. H., Schreiner, D. E., and Merzenich, M. M. (1993). Plasticity in the frequency representation of primary auditory cortex following discrimination training in adult owl monkeys. *Journal of Neuroscience, 13*, 87–103.

Rechtschaffen, A., and Bergmann, B. M. (1995). Sleep deprivation in the rat by the disk-over-water method. *Behavioural Brain Research, 69*, 55–63.

Rechtschaffen, A., and Kales, A. (1968). *A manual of standardized terminology, techniques and scoring system for sleep stages of human subjects.* Bethesda, MD: U.S. National Institute of Neurological Diseases and Blindness, Neurological Information Network.

Redican, W. K. (1982). An evolutionary perspective on human facial displays. In P. Ekman (Ed.), *Emotion in the human face* (2nd ed., pp. 212–280). Cambridge, England: Cambridge University Press.

Rehkamper, G., Haase, E., and Frahm, H. D. (1988). Allometric comparison of brain weight and brain structure volumes in different breeds of the domestic pigeon, *Columba livia* f. d. (fantails, homing pigeons, strassers). *Brain, Behavior and Evolution, 31*, 141–149.

Reiner, W. G., and Gearhart, J. P. (2004). Discordant sexual identity in some genetic males with cloacal exstrophy assigned to female sex at birth. *New England Journal of Medicine, 350*, 333–341.

Reisberg, D., and Heuer, F. (1995). Emotion's multiple effects on memory. In J. L. McGaugh, N. M. Weinberger, and G. Lynch (Eds.), *Brain and memory: Modulation and mediation of neuroplasticity* (pp. 84–92). New York, NY: Oxford University Press.

Rempel-Clower, N. L., Zola, S. M., Squire, L. R., and Amaral, D. G. (1996). Three cases of enduring memory impairment after bilateral damage limited to the hippocampal formation. *Journal of Neuroscience, 16*, 5233–5255.

Renner, M. J., and Rosenzweig, M. R. (1987). *Enriched and impoverished environments: Effects on brain and behavior.* New York, NY: Springer-Verlag.

Reppert, S. M., and Weaver, D. R. (2002). Coordination of circadian timing in mammals. *Nature, 418*, 935–941.

Ressler, K. J., Sullivan, S. L., and Buck, L. B. (1994). A molecular dissection of spatial patterning in the olfactory system. *Current Opinion in Neurobiology, 4*, 588–596.

Reuter, J., Raedler, T., Rose, M., Hand, I., et al. (2005). Pathological gambling is linked to reduced activation of the mesolimbic reward system. *Nature Neuroscience, 8*, 147–148.

Revel, F. G., Masson-Pévet, M., Pévet, P., Mikkelsen, J. D., et al. (2009). Melatonin controls seasonal breeding by a network of hypothalamic targets. *Neuroendocrinology, 90*, 1–14.

Richman, D. P., and Agius, M. A. (2003). Treatment of autoimmune myasthenia gravis. *Neurology, 61*, 1652–1661.

Richter, C. (1967). Sleep and activity: Their relation to the 24-hour clock. *Proceedings of the Association for Research in Nervous and Mental Diseases, 45*, 8–27.

Risch, N., Herrell, R., Lehner, T., Liang, K. Y., et al. (2009). Interaction between the serotonin transporter gene (5-HT-TLPR), stressful life events, and risk of depression: A meta-analysis. *JAMA, 301*, 2462–2471.

Rizzolatti, G., and Craighero, L. (2004). The mirror-neuron system. *Annual Review of Neuroscience, 27*, 169–192.

Rizzolatti, G., Fogassi, L., and Gallese, V. (2006). Mirrors of the mind. *Scientific American, 295*(5), 54–61.

Roberts, A. H. (1969). *Brain damage in boxers.* London, England: Pitman.

Robins, L. N., and Regier, D. A. (1991). *Psychiatric disorders in America: The epidemiologic catchment area study.* New York, NY: Free Press.

Robinson, D. L., and Petersen, S. E. (1992). The pulvinar and visual salience. *Trends in Neuroscience, 15*, 127–132.

Robinson, R. (2009). Intractable depression responds to deep brain stimulation. *Neurology Today, 9*, 7–10.

Rocca, W. A., Hofman, A., Brayne, C., Breteler, M. M., et al. (1991). The prevalence of vascular dementia in Europe: Facts and fragments from 1980–1990 studies. *Annals of Neurology, 30*, 817–824.

Roenneberg, T., Kuehnle, T., Pramstaller, P. P., Ricken, J., et al. (2004). A marker for the end of adolescence. *Current Biology, 14*, R1038–R1039.

Roffwarg, H. P., Muzio, J. N., and Dement, W. C. (1966). Ontogenetic development of the human sleep-dream cycle. *Science, 152*, 604–619.

Rogan, M. T., Staubli, U. V., and LeDoux, J. E. (1997). Fear conditioning induces associative long-term potentiation in the amygdala. *Nature, 390,* 604–607.

Rogawski, M. A., and Löscher, W. (2004). The neurobiology of antiepileptic drugs. *Nature Reviews. Neuroscience, 5,* 553–564.

Roland, E., and Larson, B. (1976). Focal increase of cerebral blood flow during stereognostic testing in man. *Archives of Neurology, 33,* 551–558.

Roland, P. E. (1993). *Brain activation.* New York, NY: Wiley-Liss.

Rose, K. A., Morgan, I. G., Smith, W., Burlutsky, G., et al. (2008). Myopia, lifestyle, and schooling in students of Chinese ethnicity in Singapore and Sydney. *Archives of Ophthalmology, 126,* 527–530.

Roselli, C. E., Larkin, K., Resko, J. A., Stellflug, J. N., et al. (2004). The volume of a sexually dimorphic nucleus in the ovine medial preoptic area/anterior hypothalamus varies with sexual partner preference. *Endocrinology, 145,* 475–477.

Roselli, C. E., and Stormshak, F. (2009). The neurobiology of sexual partner preferences in rams. *Hormones and Behavior, 55,* 611–620.

Rosenbaum, R. S., Köhler, S., Schacter, D. L., Moscovitch, M., et al. (2005). The case of K.C.: Contributions of a memory-impaired person to memory theory. *Neuropsychologia, 43,* 989–1021.

Rosenfield, P. J., Kleinhaus, K., Opler, M., Perrin, M., et al. (2010). Later paternal age and sex differences in schizophrenia symptoms. *Schizophrenia Research, 116,* 191–195.

Rosenkranz, M. A., Jackson, D. C., Dalton, K. M., Dolski, I., et al. (2003). Affective style and in vivo immune response: Neurobehavioral mechanisms. *Proceedings of the National Academy of Sciences, USA, 100,* 11148–11152.

Rosenzweig, M. R. (1946). Discrimination of auditory intensities in the cat. *American Journal of Psychology, 59,* 127–136.

Rosenzweig, M. R., Krech, D., and Bennett, E. L. (1961). Heredity, environment, brain biochemistry, and learning. In *Current trends in psychological theory* (pp. 87–110). Pittsburgh, PA: University of Pittsburgh Press.

Roses, A. D. (1995). On the metabolism of apolipoprotein E and the Alzheimer diseases. *Experimental Neurology, 132,* 149–156.

Rossi, D. J., Oshima, T., and Attwell, D. (2000). Glutamate release in severe brain ischaemia is mainly by reversed uptake. *Nature, 403,* 316–321.

Rothschild, A. J. (1992). Disinhibition, amnestic reactions, and other adverse reactions secondary to triazolam: A review of the literature. *Journal of Clinical Psychiatry, 53,* 69–79.

Rouw, R., and Scholter, H. S. (2007). Increased structural connectivity in grapheme-color synesthesia. *Nature Neuroscience, 10,* 792–797.

Roy, A. (1992). Hypothalamic-pituitary-adrenal axis function and suicidal behavior in depression. *Biological Psychiatry, 32,* 812–816.

Ruck, C., Andreewitch, S., Flyckt, K., Edman, G., et al. (2003). Capsulotomy for refractory anxiety disorders: Long-term follow-up of 26 patients. *American Journal of Psychiatry, 160,* 513–521.

Rumbaugh, D. M. (1977). *Language learning by a chimpanzee: The LANA project.* New York, NY: Academic Press.

Rupnick, M. A., Panigrahy, D., Zhang, C.Y., Dallabrida, S. M., et al. (2002). Adipose tissue mass can be regulated through the vasculature. *Proceedings of the National Academy of Sciences, USA, 99,* 10730–10735.

Rupprecht, R., Rammes, G., Eser, D., Baghai, T. C., et al. (2009). Translocator protein (18 kD) as target for anxiolytics without benzodiazepine-like side effects. *Science, 325,* 490–493.

Rusak, B., and Zucker, I. (1979). Neural regulation of circadian rhythms. *Physiological Reviews, 59,* 449–526.

Russell, J. A. (1994). Is there universal recognition of emotion from facial expressions? A review of the cross-cultural studies. *Psychological Bulletin, 115,* 102–141.

Rymer, R. (1993). *Genie: An abused child's flight from silence.* New York, NY: HarperCollins.

S

Sack, R. L., Blood, M. L., and Lewy, A. J. (1992). Melatonin rhythms in night shift workers. *Sleep, 15,* 434–441.

Sack, R. L., Brandes, R. W., Kendall, A. R., and Lewy, A. J. (2000). Entrainment of free-running circadian rhythms by melatonin in blind people. *New England Journal of Medicine, 343,* 1070–1077.

Sack, R. L., Lewy, A. J., Blood, M. L., Keith, L. D., et al. (1992). Circadian rhythm abnormalities in totally blind people: Incidence and clinical significance. *Journal of Clinical Endocrinology and Metabolism, 75,* 127–134.

Sahay, A., and Hen, R. (2007). Adult hippocampal neurogenesis in depression. *Nature Neuroscience, 10,* 1110–1114.

Sakurai, T., Amemiya, A., Ishii, M., Matsuzaki, I., et al. (1998). Orexins and orexin receptors: A family of hypothalamic neuropeptides and G protein-coupled receptors that regulate feeding behavior. *Cell, 92,* 573–585.

Salazar, H., Llorente, I., Jara-Oseguera, A., García-Villegas, R., et al. (2008). A single N-terminal cysteine in TRPV1 determines activation by pungent compounds from onion and garlic. *Nature Neuroscience, 11,* 255–260.

Salvini-Plawen, L.V., and Mayr, E. (1977). On the evolution of photoreceptors and eyes. *Evolutionary Biology, 10,* 207–263.

Samad, T. A., Moore, K. A., Sapirstein, A., Billet, S., et al. (2001). Interleukin-1β-mediated induction of Cox-2 in the CNS contributes to inflammatory pain hypersensitivity. *Nature, 410,* 471–475.

Samaha, F. F., Iqbal, N., Seshadri, P., Chicano, K. L., et al. (2003). A low-carbohydrate as compared with a low-fat diet in severe obesity. *New England Journal of Medicine, 348,* 2074–2081.

Samson, S., and Zatorre, R. J. (1991). Recognition memory for text and melody of songs after unilateral temporal lobe lesion: Evidence for dual encoding. *Journal of Experimental Psychology. Learning, Memory, and Cognition, 17,* 793–804.

Samson, S., and Zatorre, R. J. (1994). Contribution of the right temporal lobe to musical timbre discrimination. *Neuropsychologia, 32,* 231–240.

Sanderson, D. J., Good, M. A., Seeburg, P. H., Sprengel, R., et al. (2008). The role of the GluR-A (GluR1) AMPA receptor subunit in learning and memory. *Progress in Brain Research, 169,* 159–178.

Sapir, A., Soroker, N., Berger, A., and Henik, A. (1999). Inhibition of return in spatial attention: Direct evidence for collicular generation. *Nature Neuroscience, 2,* 1053–1054.

Sapolsky, R. M. (1992). Neuroendocrinology of the stress-response. In J. B. Becker, S. M. Breedlove, and D. Crews (Eds.), *Behavioral endocrinology* (pp. 287–324). Cambridge, MA: MIT Press.

Sapolsky, R. M. (2001). *A primate's memoir.* New York, NY: Scribner.

Sapolsky, R. M. (2004). *Why zebras don't get ulcers* (3rd ed.). New York, NY: Holt.

Sapolsky, R. (2008, September 23). Stress: Portrait of a killer [National Geographic Special]. [Washington, DC]: National Geographic Television.

Satinoff, E. (1978). Neural organization and evolution of thermal regulation in mammals. *Science, 201,* 16–22.

Satinoff, E., and Rutstein, J. (1970). Behavioral thermoregulation in rats with anterior hypothalamic lesions. *Journal of Comparative and Physiological Psychology, 71,* 77–82.

Satinoff, E., and Shan, S.Y. (1971). Loss of behavioral thermoregulation after lateral hypothalamic lesions in rats. *Journal of Comparative and Physiological Psychology, 77,* 302–312.

Saul, S. (2006, March 8). Some sleeping pill users range far beyond bed. *The New York Times.*

Savage-Rumbaugh, E. S. (1993). *Language comprehension in ape and child.* Chicago: University of Chicago Press.

Savage-Rumbaugh, [E.] S., and Lewin, R. (1994). *Kanzi: The ape at the brink of the human mind.* New York, NY: Wiley.

Saxe, M. D., Battaglia, F., Wang, J. W., Malleret, G., et al. (2006). Ablation of hippocampal neurogenesis impairs contextual fear conditioning and synaptic plasticity in the dentate gyrus. *Proceedings of the National Academy of Sciences, USA, 103,* 17501–17506.

Saxena, S., Brody, A. L., Ho, M. L., Alborzian, S., et al. (2001). Cerebral metabolism in major depression and obsessive-compulsive disorder occurring separately and concurrently. *Biological Psychiatry, 50,* 159–170.

Saxena, S., and Rauch, S. L. (2000). Functional neuroimaging and the neuroanatomy of obsessive-compulsive disorder. *Psychiatric Clinics of North America, 23,* 563–586.

Scalaidhe, S. P. O., Wilson, F. A. W., and Goldman-Rakic, P. S. (1997). Areal segregation of face-processing neurons in prefrontal cortex. *Science, 278,* 1135–1138.

SCENIHR (Scientific Committee on Emerging and Newly Identified Health Risks). (2008, September 23). Scientific opinion on the potential health risks of exposure to noise from personal music players and mobile phones including a music playing function.

Schachter, S. (1975). Cognition and peripheralist-centralist controversies in motivation and emotion. In M. S. Gazzaniga and C. Blakemore (Eds.), *Handbook of psychobiology* (pp. 529–564). New York, NY: Academic Press.

Schachter, S., and Singer, J. (1962). Cognitive, social, and physiological determinants of emotional state. *Psychological Review, 69,* 379–399.

Schacter, D. L., Alpert, N. M., Savage, C. R., Rauch, S. L., et al. (1996). Conscious recollection and the human hippocampal formation: Evidence from positron emission tomography. *Proceedings of the National Academy of Sciences, USA, 93,* 321–325.

Scharff, C., Kirn, J. R., Grossman, M., Macklis, J. D., et al. (2000). Targeted neuronal death affects neuronal replacement and vocal behavior in adult songbirds. *Neuron, 25,* 481–492.

Scheibel, A. B., and Conrad, A. S. (1993). Hippocampal dysgenesis in mutant mouse and schizophrenic man: Is there a relationship? *Schizophrenia Bulletin, 19,* 21–33.

Schein, S. J., and Desimone, R. (1990). Spectral properties of V4 neurons in the macaque. *Journal of Neuroscience, 10,* 3369–3389.

Schenck, C. H., and Mahowald, M. W. (2002). REM sleep behavior disorder: Clinical, developmental, and neuroscience perspectives 16 years after its formal identification in *Sleep. Sleep, 25,* 120–138.

Schieber, M. H, and Hibbard, L. S. (1993). How somatotopic is the motor cortex hand area? *Science, 261,* 489–492.

Schiffman, S. S., Simon, S. A., Gill, J. M., and Beeker, T. G. (1986). Bretylium tosylate enhances salt taste. *Physiology & Behavior, 36,* 1129–1137.

Schildkraut, J. J., and Kety, S. S. (1967). Biogenic amines and emotion. *Science, 156,* 21–30.

Schlaug, G., Jancke, L., Huang, Y., and Steinmetz, H. (1995). In vivo evidence of structural brain asymmetry in musicians. *Science, 267,* 699–701.

Schmidt-Nielsen, K. (1960). *Animal physiology.* Englewood Cliffs, NJ: Prentice-Hall.

Schnapf, J. L., and Baylor, D. A. (1987). How photoreceptor cells respond to light. *Scientific American, 256*(4), 40–47.

Schneider, K. (1959). *Clinical psychopathology.* New York, NY: Grune & Stratton.

Schneider, P., Scherg, M., Dosch, H. G., Specht, H. J., et al. (2002). Morphology of Heschl's gyrus reflects enhanced activation in the auditory cortex of musicians. *Nature Neuroscience, 5,* 688–694.

Schumann, C. M., and Amaral, D. G. (2006). Stereological analysis of amygdala neuron number in autism. *Journal of Neuroscience, 26,* 7674–7679.

Schummers, J., Yu, H., and Sur, M. (2008). Tuned responses of astrocytes and their influence on hemodynamic signals in the visual cortex. *Science, 320,* 1638–1643.

Schuster, C. R. (1970). Psychological approaches to opiate dependence and self-administration by laboratory animals. *Federation Proceedings, 29,* 1–5.

Schwartz, W. J., Smith, C. B., Davidsen, L., Savaki, H., et al. (1979). Metabolic mapping of functional activity in the hypothalamo-neurohypophysial system of the rat. *Science, 205,* 723–725.

Schwartzer, R., and Gutiérrez-Doña, B. (2000). Health psychology. In K. Pawlik and M. R. Rosenzweig (Eds.), *International handbook of psychology* (pp. 452–465). London, England: Sage.

Schwartzkroin, P. A., and Wester, K. (1975). Long-lasting facilitation of a synaptic potential following tetanization in the in vitro hippocampal slice. *Brain Research, 89,* 107–119.

Sclafani, A., Springer, D., and Kluge, L. (1976). Effects of quinine adulteration on the food intake and body weight of obese and nonobese hypothalamic hyperphagic rats. *Physiology & Behavior, 16,* 631–640.

Scott, D. J., Stohler, C. S., Egnatuk, C. M., Wang, H., et al. (2008). Placebo and nocebo effects are defined by opposite opioid and dopaminergic responses. *Archives of General Psychiatry, 65,* 220–231.

Scott, S. K., and Wise, R. J. (2004). The functional neuroanatomy of prelexical processing in speech perception. *Cognition, 92,* 13–45.

Scoville, W. B., and Milner, B. (1957). Loss of recent memory after bilateral hippocampal lesions. *Journal of Neurology, Neurosurgery and Psychiatry, 20,* 11–21.

Seavey, C., Katz, P., and Zalk, S. R. (1975). Baby X: The effects of gender labels on adult responses to infants. *Sex Roles, 2,* 103–109.

Seeman, P. (1990). Atypical neuroleptics: Role of multiple receptors, endogenous dopamine, and receptor linkage. *Acta Psychiatrica Scandinavica. Supplementum, 358,* 14–20.

Seeman, P., and Tallerico, T. (1998). Antipsychotic drugs which elicit little or no parkinsonism bind more loosely than dopamine to brain D2 receptors, yet occupy high levels of these receptors. *Molecular Psychiatry, 3,* 123–134.

Seiden, R. H. (1978). Where are they now? A follow-up study of suicide attempters from the Golden Gate Bridge. *Suicide and Life Threatening Behavior, 8,* 203–216.

Selkoe, D. J. (1991). Amyloid protein and Alzheimer's disease. *Scientific American, 265*(5), 68–71.

Selye, H. (1956). *The stress of life.* New York, NY: McGraw-Hill.

Semendeferi, K., Lu, A., Schenker, N., and Damasio, H. (2002). Humans and great apes share a large frontal cortex. *Nature Neuroscience, 5,* 272–276.

Senju, A., Southgate, V., White, S., and Frith, W. (2009). Mindblind eyes: An absence of spontaneous theory of mind in Asperger syndrome. *Science, 325,* 883–885.

Serviere, J., Webster, W. R., and Calford, M. B. (1984). Isofrequency labelling revealed by a combined [14C]-2-deoxyglucose, electrophysiological, and horseradish peroxidase study of the inferior colliculus of the cat. *Journal of Comparative Neurology, 228,* 463–477.

Seuss, Dr. (1987). *The tough coughs as he ploughs the dough: Early writings and cartoons by Dr. Seuss.* New York, NY: Morrow.

Seyfarth, R. M., and Cheney, D. L. (2003). Meaning and emotion in animal vocalizations. *Annals of the New York Academy of Sciences, 1000,* 32–55.

Shah, D. B., Pesiridou, A., Baltuch, G. H., Malone, D. A., et al. (2008). Functional neurosurgery in the treatment of severe obsessive compulsive disorder and major depression: Overview of disease circuits and therapeutic targeting for the clinician. *Psychiatry (Edgmont), 5*(9), 24–33.

Shallice, T., and Burgess, P. W. (1991). Deficits in strategy application following frontal lobe damage in man. *Brain, 114,* 727–741.

Shammi, P., and Stuss, D. T. (1999). Humour appreciation: A role of the right frontal lobe. *Brain, 122,* 657–666.

Shapiro, R. M. (1993). Regional neuropathology in schizophrenia: Where are we? Where are we going? *Schizophrenia Research, 10,* 187–239.

Shaw, P., Eckstrand, K., Sharp, W., Blumenthal, J., et al. (2007). Attention-deficit/hyperactivity disorder is characterized by a delay in cortical maturation. *Proceedings of the National Academy of Sciences, USA, 104,* 19649–19654.

Shaw, P., Greenstein, D., Lerch, J., Clasen, L., et al. (2006). Intellectual ability and cortical development in children and adolescents. *Nature, 440,* 676–679.

Shaw, P. J., Tononi, G., Greenspan, R. J., and Robinson, D. F. (2002). Stress response genes protect against lethal effects of sleep deprivation in *Drosophila. Nature, 417,* 287–291.

Shaywitz, S. E., Shaywitz, B. A., Fulbright, R. K., Skudlarski, P., et al. (2003). Neural systems for compensation and persistence: Young adult outcome of childhood reading disability. *Biological Psychiatry, 54,* 25–33.

Shaywitz, S. E., Shaywitz, B. A., Pugh, K. R., Fulbright, R. K., et al. (1998). Functional disruption in the organization of the brain for reading in dyslexia. *Proceedings of the National Academy of Sciences, USA, 95,* 2636–2641.

Sherrington, C. S. (1897). *A textbook of physiology. Part III. The central nervous system* (7th ed.), M. Foster (Ed.). London, England: Macmillan.

Sherrington, C. S. (1898). Experiments in examination of the peripheral distribution of the fibres of the posterior roots of some spinal nerves. *Philosophical Transactions, 190,* 45–186.

Sherry, D. F. (1992). Memory, the hippocampus, and natural selection: Studies of food-storing birds. In L. R. Squire and N. Butters (Eds.), *Neuropsychology of memory* (2nd ed., pp. 521–532). New York, NY: Guilford Press.

Sherry, D. F., and Vaccarino, A. L. (1989). Hippocampus and memory for food caches in black-capped chickadees. *Behavioral Neuroscience, 103,* 308–318.

Sherry, D. F., Vaccarino, A. L., Buckenham, K., and Herz, R. S. (1989). The hippocampal complex of food-storing birds. *Brain Behavior and Evolution, 34,* 308–317.

Sherwin, B. B. (1998). Use of combined estrogen-androgen preparations in the postmenopause: Evidence from clinical studies. *International Journal of Fertility and Women's Medicine, 43*(2), 98–103.

Sherwin, B. B. (2002). Randomized clinical trials of combined estrogen-androgen preparations: Effects on sexual functioning. *Fertility and Sterility, 77*(Suppl. 4), 49–54.

Shih, R. A., Belmonte, P. L., and Zandi, P. P. (2004). A review of the evidence from family, twin and adoption studies for a genetic contribution to adult psychiatric disorders. *International Review of Psychiatry, 16,* 260–283.

Shimura, H., Schlossmacher, M. G., Hattori, N., Frosch, M. P., et al. (2001). Ubiquitination of a new form of α-synuclein by parkin from human brain: Implications for Parkinson's disease. *Science, 293,* 263–269.

Shu, W., Cho, J. Y., Jiang, Y., Zhang, M., et al. (2005). Altered ultrasonic vocalization in mice with a disruption in the Foxp2 gene. *Proceedings of the National Academy of Sciences, USA, 102,* 9643–9648.

Siegel, J. M. (1994). Brainstem mechanisms generating REM sleep. In M. H. Kryger, T. Roth, and W. C. Dement (Eds.), *Principles and practice of sleep medicine* (2nd ed., pp. 125–144). Philadelphia, PA: Saunders.

Siegel, J. M. (2001). The REM sleep–memory consolidation hypothesis. *Science, 294,* 1058–1063.

Siegel, J. M. (2005). Clues to the function of mammalian sleep. *Nature, 437,* 1264–1271.

Siegel, J. M., Manger, P. R., Nienhuis, R., Fahringer, H. M., et al. (1999). Sleep in the platypus. *Neuroscience, 91,* 391–400.

Siegel, J. M., Nienhuis, R., Gulyani, S., Ouyang, S., et al. (1999). Neuronal degeneration in canine narcolepsy. *Journal of Neuroscience, 19,* 248–257.

Siever, L. J. (2008). Neurobiology of aggression and violence. *American Journal of Psychiatry, 165,* 429–442.

Sikich, L, Frazier, J. A., McClellan, J., Findling, R. L., et al. (2008). Double-blind comparison of first- and second-generation antipsychotics in early-onset schizophrenia and schizo-affective disorder: Findings from the treatment of early-onset schizophrenia spectrum disorders (TEOSS) study. *American Journal of Psychiatry, 165,* 1420–1431.

Silva, D. A., and Satz, P. (1979). Pathological left-handedness. Evaluation of a model. *Brain and Language, 7,* 8–16.

Simons, D. J., and Chabris, C. F. (1999). Gorillas in our midst: Sustained inattentional blindness for dynamic events. *Perception, 28,* 1059–1074.

Simons, D. J., and Jensen, M. S. (2009). The effects of individual differences and task difficulty on inattentional blindness. *Psychonomic Bulletin & Review, 16,* 398–403.

Singer, N. (2002). Ambitious plan to give sight to the blind. *Sandia Lab News, 54,* 19, 1.

Singer, O., Marr, R. A., Rockenstein, E., Crews, L., et al. (2005). Targeting BACE1 with siRNAs ameliorates Alzheimer disease neuropathology in a transgenic model. *Nature Neuroscience, 8,* 1343–1349.

Singer, P. (1975). *Animal liberation: A new ethics for our treatment of animals.* New York, NY: New York Review.

Singer, T., Seymour, B., O'Doherty, J., Kaube, H., et al. (2004). Empathy for pain involves the affective but not sensory components of pain. *Science, 303,* 1157–1162.

Sirotnak, A. P., Grigsby, T., and Krugman, R. D. (2004). Physical abuse of children. *Pediatrics in Review, 25,* 264–277.

Smale, L. (1988). Influence of male gonadal hormones and familiarity on pregnancy interruption in prairie voles. *Biology of Reproduction, 39,* 28–31.

Smale, L., Holekamp, K. E., and White, P. A. (1999). Siblicide revisited in the spotted hyaena: Does it conform to obligate or facultative models? *Animal Behaviour, 58,* 545–551.

Smith, A., and Sugar, O. (1975). Development of above normal language and intelligence 21 years after hemispherectomy. *Neurology, 25,* 813–818.

Smith, C. (1995). Sleep states and memory processes. *Behavioural Brain Research, 69,* 137–145.

Smith, M. A., Brandt, J., and Shadmehr, R. (2000). Motor disorder in Huntington's disease begins as a dysfunction in error feedback control. *Nature, 403,* 544–549.

Smith, S. (1997, September 2). Dreaming awake Part 1: Living with narcolepsy. *Minnesota Public Radio News* (http://news.minnesota.publicradio.org/features/199709/02_smiths_narcolepsy/narco_1.shtml).

Smoller, J. W., and Finn, C. T. (2003). Family, twin, and adoption studies of bipolar disorder. *American Journal of Medical Genetics. Part C, Seminars in Medical Genetics, 123,* 48–58.

Smyth, K. A., Pritsch, T., Cook, T. B., McClendon, M. J., et al. (2004). Worker functions and traits associated with occupations and the development of AD. *Neurology, 63,* 498–503.

Solomon, A. (2001). *The noonday demon: An atlas of depression.* New York, NY: Scribner.

Somerville, M. J., Mervis, C. B., Young, E. J., Seo, E. J., et al. (2005). Severe expressive-language delay related to duplication of the Williams-Beuren locus. *New England Journal of Medicine, 353,* 1694–1701.

Soon, C. S., Brass, M., Heinze, H. J., and Haynes, J. D. (2008). Unconscious determinants of free decisions in the human brain. *Nature Neuroscience, 11,* 543–545.

Sorensen, P. W., and Goetz, F. W. (1993). Pheromonal and reproductive function of F prostaglandins and their metabolites in teleost fish. *Journal of Lipid Mediators, 6,* 385–393.

Sowell, E. R., Kan, E., Yoshii, J., Thompson, P. M., et al. (2008). Thinning of sensorimotor cortices in children with Tourette syndrome. *Nature Neuroscience, 11,* 637–639.

Spiegler, B. J., and Mishkin, M. (1981). Evidence for the sequential participation of inferior temporal cortex and amygdala in the acquisition of stimulus-reward associations. *Behavioural Brain Research, 3,* 303–317.

Spiegler, B. J., and Yeni-Komshian, G. H. (1983). Incidence of left-handed writing in a college population with reference to family patterns of hand preference. *Neuropsychologia, 21,* 651–659.

Squire, L. R., Amaral, D. G., Zola-Morgan, S., and Kritchevsky, M. P. G. (1989). Description of brain injury in the amnesic patient N.A. based on magnetic resonance imaging. *Experimental Neurology, 105,* 23–35.

Squire, L. R., and Moore, R.Y. (1979). Dorsal thalamic lesion in a noted case of chronic memory dysfunction. *Annals of Neurology, 6,* 503–506.

Squire, L. R., and Zola-Morgan, S. (1991). The medial temporal lobe memory system. *Science, 253,* 1380–1386.

Standing, L. G. (1973). Learning 10,000 pictures. *Quarterly Journal of Experimental Psychology, 25,* 207–222.

Stanovich, K. E. (2009). *What intelligence tests miss: The psychology of rational thought.* New Haven, CT: Yale University Press.

Stanton, S. J., Beehner, J. C., Saini, E. K., Kuhn, C. M., et al. (2009). Dominance, politics, and physiology: Voters' testosterone changes on the night of the 2008 United States presidential election. *PLoS ONE, 4,* e7543.

Starkstein, S. E., and Robinson, R. G. (1994). Neuropsychiatric aspects of stroke. In C. E. Coffey, J. L. Cummings, M. R. Lovell, and G. D. Pearlson (Eds.), *The American Psychiatric Press textbook of geriatric neuropsychiatry* (pp. 457–477). Washington, DC: American Psychiatric Press.

Staubli, U. V. (1995). Parallel properties of long-term potentiation and memory. In J. L. McGaugh, N. M. Weinberger, and G. Lynch (Eds.), *Brain and memory: Modulation and mediation of neuroplasticity* (pp. 303–318). New York, NY: Oxford University Press.

Stefansson, H., Ophoff, R. A., Steinberg, S. Andreassen, O. A., et al. (2009). Common variants conferring risk of schizophrenia. *Nature, 460,* 744–747.

Stein, B. E., and Stanford, T. R. (2008). Multisensory integration: Current issues from the perspective of the single neuron. *Nature Reviews. Neuroscience, 9,* 255–266.

Stein, M., and Miller, A. H. (1993). Stress, the hypothalamic-pituitary-adrenal axis, and immune function. *Advances in Experimental Medicine and Biology, 335,* 1–5.

Stein, M., Miller, A. H., and Trestman, R. L. (1991). Depression, the immune system, and health and illness. Findings in search of meaning. *Archives of General Psychiatry, 48,* 171–177.

Stephan, F. K., and Zucker, I. (1972). Circadian rhythms in drinking behavior and locomotor activity of rats are eliminated by hypothalamic lesions. *Proceedings of the National Academy of Sciences, USA, 69,* 1583–1586.

Stern, K., and McClintock, M. (1998). Regulation of ovulation by human pheromones. *Nature, 392,* 177–179.

Stoeckel, C., Gough, P. M., Watkins, K. E., and Devlin, J. T. (2009). Supramarginal gyrus involvement in visual word recognition. *Cortex, 45,* 1091–1096.

Stranahan, A. M., Khalil, D., and Gould, E. (2006). Social isolation delays the positive effects of running on adult neurogenesis. *Nature Neuroscience, 9,* 526–533.

Substance Abuse and Mental Health Services Administration. (2011). *Results from the 2010 National Survey on Drug Use and Health: Summary of national findings* (NSDUH Series H-41, HHS Publication No. [SMA] 11-4658). Rockville, MD: Substance Abuse and Mental Health Services Administration.

Summary health statistics for U.S. adults: National Health Interview Survey, 2009. (2010). Vital Health Statistics Series 10, No. 249; DHHS Publication No. (PHS) 2011-1577. Hyattsville, MD: U.S. Department of Health and Human Services.

Sumnall, H. R., and Cole, J. C. (2005). Self-reported depressive symptomatology in community samples of polysubstance misusers who report Ecstasy use: A meta-analysis. *Journal of Psychopharmacology, 19,* 84–92.

Sun, T., Patoine, C., Abu-Khalil, A., Visvader, J., et al. (2005). Early asymmetry of gene transcription in embryonic human left and right cerebral cortex. *Science, 308,* 1794–1798.

Sunn, N., Egli, M., Burazin, T. C. D., Burns, P., et al. (2002). Circulating relaxin acts on subfornical organ neurons to stimulate water drinking in the rat. *Proceedings of the National Academy of Sciences, USA, 99,* 1701–1706.

Sunstein, C. R., and Nussbaum, M. C. (Eds.) (2004). *Animal rights: Current debates and new directions.* Oxford, England: Oxford University Press.

Sutcliffe, J. G., and de Lecea, L. (2002). The hypocretins: Setting the arousal threshold. *Nature Reviews. Neuroscience, 3,* 339–349.

Suzuki, M., Nohara, S., Hagino, H., Kurokawa, K., et al. (2002). Regional changes in brain gray and white matter in patients with schizophrenia demonstrated with voxel-based analysis of MRI. *Schizophrenia Research, 55,* 41–54.

Suzuki, S., Brown, C. M., and Wise, P. M. (2009). Neuroprotective effects of estrogens following ischemic stroke. *Frontiers in Neuroendocrinology, 30,* 201–211.

Svenningsson, P., Chergui, K., Rachleff, I., Flajolet, M., et al. (2006). Alterations in 5-HT$_{1B}$ receptor function by p11 in depression-like states. *Science, 311,* 77–80.

Szarfman, A., Doraiswamy, P. M., Tonning, J. M., and Levine, J. G. (2006). Association between pathologic gambling and parkinsonian therapy as detected in the Food and Drug Administration Adverse Event database. *Archives of Neurology, 62,* 299–300.

Szente, M., Gajda, Z., Said Ali, K., and Hermesz, E. (2002). Involvement of electrical coupling in the in vivo ictal epileptiform activity induced by 4-aminopyridine in the neocortex. *Neuroscience, 115,* 1067–1078.

T

Taglialatela, J. P., Cantalupo, C., and Hopkins, W. D. (2006). Gesture handedness predicts asymmetry in the chimpanzee inferior frontal gyrus. *Neuroreport, 17,* 923–927.

Takahashi, J. S. (1995). Molecular neurobiology and genetics of circadian rhythms in mammals. *Annual Review of Neuroscience, 18,* 531–554.

Takahashi, T., Svoboda, K., and Malinow, R. (2003). Experience strengthening transmission by driving AMPA receptors into synapses. *Science, 299,* 1585–1588.

Tam, J., Duda, D. G., Perentes, J.Y., Quadri, R. S., et al. (2009). Blockade of VEGFR2 and not VEGFR1 can limit diet-induced fat tissue expansion: Role of local versus bone marrow-derived endothelial cells. *PLoS One, 4,* e4974.

Tamgüney, G., Miller, M. W., Wolfe, L. L., Sirochman, T. M., et al. (2009). Asymptomatic deer excrete infectious prions in faeces. *Nature, 461,* 529–532.

Tamminga, C. A., and Schulz, S. C. (1991). *Schizophrenia research.* New York, NY: Raven Press.

Tanaka, K. (1993). Neuronal mechanisms of object recognition. *Science, 262,* 685–688.

Tanda, G., Munzar, P., and Goldberg, S. R. (2000). Self-administration behavior is maintained by the psychoactive ingredient of marijuana in squirrel monkeys. *Nature Neuroscience, 3,* 1073–1074.

Tang, N. M., Dong, H. W., Wang, X. M., Tsui, Z. C., et al. (1997). Cholecystokinin antisense RNA increases the analgesic effect induced by electroacupuncture or low dose morphine: Conversion of low responder rats into high responders. *Pain, 71,* 71–80.

Tang, Y. P., Shimizu, E., Dube, G. R., Rampon, C., et al. (1999). Genetic enhancement of learning and memory in mice. *Nature, 401,* 63–69.

Tang, Y. P., Wang, H., Feng, R., Kyin, M., et al. (2001). Differential effects of enrichment on learning and memory function in NR2B transgenic mice. *Neuropharmacology, 41,* 779–790.

Tanji, J. (2001). Sequential organization of multiple movements: Involvement of cortical motor areas. *Annual Review of Neuroscience, 24,* 631–651.

Taub, E. (1976). Movement in nonhuman primates deprived of somatosensory feedback. *Exercise and Sport Sciences Reviews, 4,* 335–374.

Taub, E., Uswatte, G., and Elbert, T. (2002). New treatments in neurorehabilitation founded on basic research. *Nature Reviews. Neuroscience, 3,* 228–235.

Temple, E., Deutsch, G. K., Poldrack, R. A., Miller, S. L., et al. (2003). Neural deficits in children with dyslexia ameliorated by behavioral remediation: Evidence from functional MRI. *Proceedings of the National Academy of Sciences, USA, 100,* 2860–2865.

Templeton, C. N., Greene, E., and Davis, K. (2005). Allometry of alarm calls: Black-capped chickadees encode information about predator size. *Science, 308,* 1934–1937.

Terkel, J., and Rosenblatt, J. S. (1972). Humoral factors underlying maternal behavior at parturition: Cross transfusion between freely moving rats. *Journal of Comparative and Physiological Psychology, 80,* 365–371.

Terpstra, N. J., Bolhuis, J. J., Riebel, K., van der Burg, J. M., et al. (2006). Localized brain activation specific to auditory memory in a female songbird. *Journal of Comparative Neurology, 494,* 784–791.

Terrace, H. S. (1979). *Nim.* New York, NY: Knopf.

Terzian, H. (1964). Behavioural and EEG effects of intracarotid sodium amytal injection. *Acta Neurochirurgica, 12,* 230–239.

Thannickal, T. C., Moore, R.Y., Nienhuis, R., Ramanathan, L., et al. (2000). Reduced number of hypocretin neurons in human narcolepsy. *Neuron, 27,* 469–474.

Thompson, P. M., Giedd, J. N., Woods, R. P., MacDonald, D., et al. (2000). Growth patterns in the developing brain detected by using continuum mechanical tensor maps. *Nature, 404,* 190–193.

Thompson, P. M., Vidal, C., Giedd, J. N., Gochman, P., et al. (2001). Mapping adolescent brain change reveals dynamic wave of accelerated gray matter loss in very early-onset schizophrenia. *Proceedings of the National Academy of Sciences, USA, 98,* 11650–11655.

Thompson, R. F. (1990). Neural mechanisms of classical conditioning in mammals. *Philosophical Transactions of the Royal Society of London. Series B: Biological Sciences, 329,* 161–170.

Thompson, R. F., and Krupa, D. J. (1994). Organization of memory traces in the mammalian brain. *Annual Review of Neuroscience, 17,* 519–549.

Thompson, R. F., and Steinmetz, J. E. (2009). The role of the cerebellum in classical conditioning of discrete behavioral responses. *Neuroscience, 162,* 732–755.

Thompson, T., and Schuster, C. R. (1964). Morphine self-administration, food reinforced and avoidance behaviour in rhesus monkeys. *Psychopharmacologia, 5,* 87–94.

Thornton, A. E., Cox, D. N., Whitfield, K., and Fouladi, R. T. (2008). Cumulative concussion exposure in rugby players: Neurocognitive and symptomatic outcomes. *Journal of Clinical and Experimental Neuropsychology, 30,* 398–409.

Thornton-Jones, Z. D., Kennett, G. A., Benwell, K. R., Revell, D. F., et al. (2006). The cannabinoid CB1 receptor inverse agonist, rimonabant, modifies body weight and adiponectin function in diet-induced obese rats as a consequence of reduced food intake. *Pharmacology, Biochemistry, and Behavior, 84,* 353–359.

Thorpe, S. J., and Fabre-Thorpe, M. (2001). Seeking categories in the brain. *Science, 291,* 260–263.

Timmann, D., Drepper, J., Frings, M., Maschke, M., et al. (2010). The human cerebellum contributes to motor, emotional and cognitive associative learning. A review. *Cortex, 46,* 845–857.

Todorov, A., Said, C. P., Engell, A. D., and Oosterhof, N. N. (2008). Understanding evaluation of faces on social dimensions. *Trends in Cognitive Science, 12,* 455–460.

Tolman, E. C. (1949). There is more than one kind of learning. *Psychological Review, 56,* 144–155.

Tolman, E. C., and Honzik, C. H. (1930). Introduction and removal of reward, and maze performance in rats. *University of California Publications in Psychology, 4,* 257–275.

Tom, S. M., Fox, C. R., Trepel, C., and Poldrack, R. A. (2007). The neural basis of loss aversion in decision-making under risk. *Science, 315,* 515–518.

Tootell, R. B. H., Hadjikhani, N. K., Vanduffel, W., Liu, A. K., et al. (1998). Functional analysis of primary visual cortex (V1) in humans. *Proceedings of the National Academy of Sciences, USA, 95,* 811–817.

Tootell, R. B., Silverman, M. S., Hamilton, S. L., DeValois, R. L., et al. (1988). Functional anatomy of macaque striate cortex. III. Color. *Journal of Neuroscience, 8,* 1569–1593.

Tootell, R. B., Silverman, M. S., Switkes, E., and DeValois, R. L. (1982). Deoxyglucose analysis of retinotopic organization in primate striate cortex. *Science, 218,* 902–904.

Tootell, R. B., Tsao, D., and Vanduffel, W. (2003). Neuroimaging weighs in: Humans meet macaques in "primate" visual cortex. *Journal of Neuroscience, 23,* 3981–3989.

Tordoff, M., Rawson, N., and Friedman, M. (1991). 2,5-Anhydro-D-mannitol acts in liver to initiate feeding. *American Journal of Physiology, 261,* R283–R288.

Torrey, E. F., Bowler, A. E., Taylor, E. H., and Gottesman, I. I. (1994). *Schizophrenia and manic depressive disorder.* New York, NY: Basic Books.

Treesukosol, Y., Lyall, V., Heck, G. L., Desimone, J. A., et al. (2007). A psychophysical and electrophysiological analysis of salt taste in *Trpv1* null mice. *American Journal of Physiology, Regulatory, Integrative, and Comparative Physiology, 292,* R1799–R1809.

Treffert, D. A., and Christensen, D. D. (2005). Inside the mind of a savant. *Scientific American, 293*(6), 108–113.

Treisman, A. [M]. (1996). The binding problem. *Current Opinion in Neurobiology, 6,* 171–178.

Treisman, A. M., and Gelade, G. (1980). A feature-integration theory of attention. *Cognitive Psychology, 12,* 97–136.

Treisman, M. (1977). Motion sickness—Evolutionary hypotheses. *Science, 197,* 493–495.

Trimble, M. R. (1991). Interictal psychoses of epilepsy. *Advances in Neurology, 55,* 143–152.

Tronick, R., and Reck, C. (2009). Infants of depressed mothers. *Harvard Review of Psychiatry, 17,* 147–156.

Ts'o, D. Y., Frostig, R. D., Lieke, E. E., and Grinvald, A. (1990). Functional organization of primate visual cortex revealed by high resolution optical imaging. *Science, 249,* 417–420.

Tsuchiya, N., and Adolphs, R. (2007). Emotion and consciousness. *Trends in Cognitive Sciences, 11,* 158–167.

Tuller, D. (2002, January 8). A quiet revolution for those prone to nodding off. *The New York Times* (http://query.nytimes.com/gst/fullpage.html?sec=health&res=980DE5DD1439F93BA35752C0A9649C8B63).

Tulving, E. (1972). Episodic and semantic memory. In E. Tulving and W. Donaldson (Eds.), *Organization of memory* (pp. 381–403). New York, NY: Academic Press.

Tulving, E. (1989). Memory: Performance, knowledge, and experience. *European Journal of Cognitive Psychology, 1,* 3–26.

Tulving, E., Hayman, C. A., and Macdonald, C. A. (1991). Long-lasting perceptual priming and semantic learning in amnesia: A case experiment. *Journal of Experimental Psychology: Learning, Memory, and Cognition, 17,* 595–617.

Turgeon, J. L., McDonnell, D. P., Martin, K. A, and Wise, P. M. (2004). Hormone therapy: Physiological complexity belies therapeutic simplicity. *Science, 304,* 1269–1273.

Turner, E. H., Matthews, A. M., Linardatos, E., Tell, R. A., et al. (2008). Selective publication of antidepressant trials and its influence on apparent efficacy. *New England Journal of Medicine, 358,* 252–260.

Tyack, P. L. (2003). Dolphins communicate about individual-specific social relationships. In F. de Waal and P. L. Tyack (Eds.), *Animal social complexity: Intelligence, culture, and individualized societies* (pp. 342–361). Cambridge, MA: Harvard University Press.

U

Umilta, M. A., Kohler, E., Galiese, V., Fogassi, L., et al. (2001). I know what you are doing: A neurophysiological study. *Neuron, 31,* 155–165.

Ungerleider, L. G., Courtney, S. M., and Haxby, J. V. (1998). A neural system for human visual working memory. *Proceedings of the National Academy of Sciences, USA, 95,* 883–890.

Ursin, H., Baade, E., and Levine, S. (1978). *Psychobiology of stress: A study of coping men.* New York, NY: Academic Press.

V

van Anders, S. M., and Watson, N. V. (2006). Social neuroendocrinology: Effects of social contexts and behaviors on sex steroids in humans. *Human Nature, 17,* 212–237.

Vance, C., Rogelj, B., Hortobágyi, T., DeVos, K. J., et al. (2009). Mutations in FUS, an RNA processing protein, cause familial amyotrophic lateral sclerosis type 6. *Science, 323,* 1208–1211.

Van Dongen, H. P., Maislin, G., Mullington, J. M., and Dinges, D. F. (2003). The cumulative cost of additional wakefulness: Dose-response effects on neurobehavioral functions and sleep physiology from chronic sleep restriction and total sleep deprivation. *Sleep, 26,* 117–126.

Van Essen, D. C., and Drury, H. A. (1997). Structural and functional analyses of human cerebral cortex using a surface-based atlas. *Journal of Neuroscience, 17,* 7079–7102.

Van Gaal, L. F., Rissanen, A. M., Scheen, A. J., Ziegler, O., et al. (2005). Effects of the cannabinoid-1 receptor blocker rimonabant on weight reduction and cardiovascular risk factors in overweight patients: 1-year experience from the RIO-Europe study. *Lancet, 365,* 1389–1397.

Vann, S. D., and Aggleton, J. P. (2004). The mammillary bodies: Two memory systems in one? *Nature Reviews. Neuroscience, 5,* 35–44.

van Os, J., and Kapur, S. (2009). Schizophrenia. *Lancet, 374,* 635–645.

Van Zoeren, J. G., and Stricker, E. M. (1977). Effects of preoptic, lateral hypothalamic, or dopamine-depleting lesions on behavioral thermoregulation in rats exposed to the cold. *Journal of Comparative and Physiological Psychology, 91,* 989–999.

Vargas, C. D., Aballéa, A., Rodrigues, E. C., Reilly, K. T., et al. (2009). Re-emergence of hand-muscle representations in human motor cortex after hand allograft. *Proceedings of the National Academy of Sciences, USA, 106,* 7197–7202.

Vasey, P. L. (1995). Homosexual behaviour in primates: A review of evidence and theory. *International Journal of Primatology, 16,* 173–204.

Vassar, R., Ngai, J., and Axel, R. (1993). Spatial segregation of odorant receptor expression in the mammalian olfactory epithelium. *Cell, 74,* 309–318.

Vaughan, W., and Greene, S. L. (1984). Pigeon visual memory capacity. *Journal of Experimental Psychology: Animal Behavior Processes, 10,* 256–271.

Veraa, R. P., and Grafstein, B. (1981). Cellular mechanisms for recovery from nervous system injury: A conference report. *Experimental Neurology, 71,* 6–75.

Villalobos, M. E., Mizuno, A., Dahl, B. C., Kemmotsu, N., et al. (2005). Reduced functional connectivity between V1 and inferior frontal cortex associated with visuomotor performance in autism. *Neuroimage, 25,* 916–925.

Virkkunen, M., and Linnoila, M. (1993). Brain serotonin, type II alcoholism and impulsive violence. *Journal of Studies on Alcohol. Supplement, 11,* 163–169.

Vita, A., Dieci, M., Silenzi, C., Tenconi, F., et al. (2000). Cerebral ventricular enlargement as a generalized feature of schizophrenia: A distribution analysis on 502 subjects. *Schizophrenia Research, 44,* 25–34.

Vogt, B. A. (2005). Pain and emotion interactions in subregions of the cingulate gyrus. *Nature Reviews. Neuroscience, 6,* 533–544.

Volkow, N. D., Wang, G. J., Kollins, S. H., Wigal, T. L., et al. (2009). Evaluating dopamine reward pathway in ADHD: Clinical implications. *JAMA, 302,* 1084–1091.

Volkow, N. D., and Wise, R.A. (2005). How can drug addiction help us understand obesity? *Nature Neuroscience, 8,* 555–560.

Vythilingam, M., Anderson, E. R., Goddard, A., Woods, S. W., et al. (2000). Temporal lobe volume in panic disorder—A quantitative magnetic resonance imaging study. *Psychiatry Research, 99,* 75–82.

W

Wada, J. A., Clarke, R., and Hamm, A. (1975). Cerebral hemispheric asymmetry in humans. Cortical speech zones in 100 adults and 100 infant brains. *Archives of Neurology, 32,* 239–246.

Wada, J. A., and Rasmussen, T. (1960). Intracarotid injection of sodium amytal for the lateralization of cerebral speech dominance: Experimental and clinical observations. *Journal of Neurosurgery, 17,* 266–282.

Waddell, J., and Shors, T. J. (2008). Neurogenesis, learning and associative strength. *European Journal of Neuroscience, 27,* 3020–3028.

Wager, T. D., Scott, D. J., and Zubieta, J. K. (2007). Placebo effects on human mu-opioid activity during pain. *Proceedings of the National Academy of Sciences, USA, 104,* 11056–11061.

Wagner, A. D., Desmond, J. E., Demb, J. B., Glover, G. H., et al. (1997). Semantic repetition priming for verbal and pictorial knowledge: A functional MRI study of left inferior prefrontal cortex. *Journal of Cognitive Neuroscience, 9,* 714–726.

Wagner, G. C., Beuving, L. J., and Hutchinson, R. R. (1980). The effects of gonadal hormone manipulations on aggressive target-biting in mice. *Aggressive Behavior, 6,* 1–7.

Wagner, U., Gais, S., Haider, H., Verleger, R., et al. (2004). Sleep inspires insight. *Nature, 427,* 352–355.

Wahl, O. F. (1976). Monozygotic twins discordant for schizophrenia: A review. *Psychological Bulletin, 83,* 91–106.

Wahlstrom, J. (2002). Changing times: Findings from the first longitudinal study of later high school start times. *National Association of Secondary School Principals Bulletin, 86,* 3–21.

Walker, E. F. (1991). *Schizophrenia: A life-course developmental perspective.* San Diego, CA: Academic Press.

Wallis, J. D. (2007). Orbitofrontal cortex and its contribution to decision-making. *Annual Review of Neuroscience, 30,* 31–56.

Walters, R. J., Hadley, S. H., Morris, K. D. W., and Amin, J. (2000). Benzodiazepines act on GABA$_A$ receptors via two distinct and separable mechanisms. *Nature Neuroscience, 3,* 1273–1280.

Walther, S., Goya-Maldonado, R., Stippich, C., Weisbrod, M., et al. (2010). A supramodal network for response inhibition. *Neuroreport, 21,* 191–195.

Wang, H., Yu, M., Ochani, M., Amella, C. A., et al. (2003). Nicotinic acetylcholine receptor α7 subunit is an essential regulator of inflammation. *Nature, 421,* 384–388.

Wareing, M., Fisk, J. E., and Murphy, P. N. (2000). Working memory deficits in current and previous users of MDMA ("ecstasy"). *British Journal of Psychology, 91,* 181–188.

Watson, N.V. (2001). Sex differences in throwing: Monkeys having a fling. *Trends in Cognitive Sciences, 5,* 98–99.

Watson, N.V., Freeman, L. M., and Breedlove, S. M. (2001). Neuronal size in the spinal nucleus of the bulbocavernosus: Direct modulation by androgen in rats with mosaic androgen insensitivity. *Journal of Neuroscience, 21,* 1062–1066.

Webb, W. B. (1992). *Sleep, the gentle tyrant* (2nd ed.). Bolton, MA: Anker.

Wehr, T. A., Sack, D. A., Duncan, W. C., Mendelson, W. B., et al. (1985). Sleep and circadian rhythms in affective patients isolated from external time cues. *Psychiatry Research, 15,* 327–339.

Wei, F., Wang G. D., Kerchner, G. A., Kim, S. J., et al. (2001). Genetic enhancement of inflammatory pain by forebrain NR2B overexpression. *Nature Neuroscience, 4,* 164–169.

Weinberger, D. R., Aloia, M. S., Goldberg, T. E., and Berman, K. F. (1994). The frontal lobes and schizophrenia. *Journal of Neuropsychiatry and Clinical Neurosciences, 6,* 419–427.

Weinberger, N. M. (1998). Physiological memory in primary auditory cortex: Characteristics and mechanisms. *Neurobiology of Learning and Memory, 70,* 226–251.

Weiner, R. D. (1994). Treatment optimization with ECT. *Psychopharmacology Bulletin, 30,* 313–320.

Weiss, L. A., Arking, D. E., and The Gene Discovery Project of Johns Hopkins & the Autism Consortium. (2009). A genome-wide linkage and association scan reveals novel loci for autism. *Nature, 461,* 802–808.

Weitzman, E. D. (1981). Sleep and its disorders. *Annual Review of Neurosciences, 4,* 381–417.

Weitzman, E. D., Czeisler, C. A., Zimmerman, J. C., and Moore-Ede, M. C. (1981). Biological rhythms in man: Relationship of sleep-wake, cortisol, growth hormone, and temperature during temporal isolation. In J. B. Martin, S. Reichlin, and K. L. Bick (Eds.), *Neurosecretion and brain peptides* (pp. 475–499). New York, NY: Raven Press.

Wesensten, N. J., Belenky, G., Kautz, M. A., Thorne, D. R., et al. (2002). Maintaining alertness and performance during sleep deprivation: Modafinil versus caffeine. *Psychopharmacology (Berlin), 159,* 238–247.

Wessberg, J., Stambaugh, C. R., Kralik, J. D., Beck, P. D., et al. (2000). Real-time predictions of hand trajectory by ensembles of cortical neurons in primates. *Nature, 408,* 361–365.

Wever, R. A. (1979). Influence of physical workload on freerunning circadian rhythms of man. *Pflügers Archiv European Journal of Physiology, 381,* 119–126.

Wexler, N. S., Rose, E. A., and Housman, D. E. (1991). Molecular approaches to hereditary diseases of the nervous system: Huntington's disease as a paradigm. *Annual Review of Neuroscience, 14,* 503–529.

White, N. M., and Milner, P. M. (1992). The psychobiology of reinforcers. *Annual Review of Psychology, 43,* 443–471.

Whitlock, J. R., Heynen, A. J., Shuler, M. G., and Bear, M. F. (2006). Learning induces long-term potentiation in the hippocampus. *Science, 313,* 1093–1097.

Wible, C. G., Shenton, M. E., Hokama, H., Kikinis, R., et al. (1995). Prefrontal cortex and schizophrenia. A quantitative magnetic resonance imaging study. *Archives of General Psychiatry, 52,* 279–288.

Wiesel, T. N., and Hubel, D. H. (1965). Extent of recovery from the effects of visual deprivation in kittens. *Journal of Neurophysiology, 28,* 1060–1072.

Wilens, T. E., Prince, J. B., Spencer, T. J., and Biederman, J. (2006). Stimulants and sudden death: What is a physician to do? *Pediatrics, 118,* 1215–1219.

Will, B., Galani, R., Kelche, C., and Rosenzweig, M. R. (2004). Recovery from brain injury in animals: Relative efficacy of environmental enrichment, physical exercise or formal training (1990–2002). *Progress in Neurobiology, 72,* 167–182.

Williams, D. (1969). Neural factors related to habitual aggression. *Brain, 92,* 503–520.

Williams, J. H., Waiter, G. D., Gilchrist, A., Perrett, D. I., et al. (2006). Neural mechanisms of imitation and "mirror neuron" functioning in autistic spectrum disorder. *Neuropsychologia, 44*, 610–621.

Williams, T. J., Pepitone, M. E., Christensen, S. E., Cooke, B. M., et al. (2000). Finger-length ratios and sexual orientation. *Nature, 404*, 455–456.

Willis, S. L., Tennstedt, S. L., Marsiske, M., Ball, K., et al. (2006). Long-term effects of cognitive training on everyday functional outcomes in older adults. *JAMA, 296*, 2805–2814.

Wingfield, J. C., Ball, G. F., Dufty, A. M., Hegner, R. E., et al. (1987). Testosterone and aggression in birds. *American Scientist, 75*, 602–608.

Winkowski, D. E., and Knudsen, E. I. (2006). Top-down gain control of the auditory space map by gaze control circuitry in the barn owl. *Nature, 439*, 336–339.

Winocur, G., Wojtowicz, J. M., Sekeres, M., Snyder, J. S., et al. (2006). Inhibition of neurogenesis interferes with hippocampus-dependent memory function. *Hippocampus, 16*, 296–304.

Winslow, J. T., and Insel, T. R. (2002). The social deficits of the oxytocin knockout mouse. *Neuropeptides, 36*, 221–229.

Woldorff, M. G., and Hillyard, S. A. (1991). Modulation of early auditory processing during selective listening to rapidly presented tones. *Electroencephalography and Clinical Neurophysiology, 79*, 170–191.

Wolf, S. S., Jones, D. W., Knable, M. B., Gorey, J. G., et al. (1996). Tourette syndrome: Prediction of phenotypic variation in monozygotic twins by caudate nucleus D2 receptor binding. *Science, 273*, 1225–1227.

Wolfe, J. M. (1994). Guided search 2.0: A revised model of visual search. *Psychonomic Bulletin & Review, 1*, 202–238.

Wolfe, J. M., Horowitz, T. S., and Kenner, N. M. (2005). Cognitive psychology: Rare items often missed in visual searches. *Nature, 435*, 439–440.

Wolk, D. A., Price, J. C., Saxton, J. A., Snitz, B. E., et al. (2009). Amyloid imaging in mild cognitive impairment subtypes. *Annals of Neurology, 65*, 557–568.

Wolkowitz, O. M., Lupien, S. J., Bigler, E., Levin, R. B., et al. (2004). The "steroid dementia syndrome": An unrecognized complication of glucocorticoid treatment. *Annals of the New York Academy of Sciences, 1032*, 191–194.

Womelsdorf, T., Anton-Erxleben, K., and Treue, S. (2008). Receptive field shift and shrinkage in macaque middle temporal area through attentional gain modulation. *Journal of Neuroscience, 28*, 8934–8944.

Wood, J. M., Bootzin, R. R., Kihlstrom, J. F., and Schacter, D. L. (1992). Implicit and explicit memory for verbal information presented during sleep. *Psychological Science, 3*, 236–239.

Wood, N., and Cowan, N. (1995). The cocktail party phenomenon revisited: How frequent are attention shifts to one's name in an irrelevant auditory channel? *Journal of Experimental Psychology. Learning, Memory, and Cognition, 21*, 255–260.

Woolf, C. J., and Salter, M. W. (2000). Neuronal plasticity: Increasing the gain in pain. *Science, 288*, 1765–1769.

World Health Organization. (2001). *The world health report.* Geneva, Switzerland: World Health Organization.

Wren, A. M., Seal, L. J., Cohen, M. A., Brynes, A. E., et al. (2001). Ghrelin enhances appetite and increases food intake in humans. *Journal of Clinical Endocrinology and Metabolism, 86*, 5992–5995.

Wren, A. M., Small, C. J., Ward, H. L., Murphy, K. G., et al. (2000). The novel hypothalamic peptide ghrelin stimulates food intake and growth hormone secretion. *Endocrinology, 141*, 4325–4328.

Wright, A. A., Santiago, H. C., Sands, S. F., Kendrick, D. F., et al. (1985). Memory processing of serial lists by pigeons, monkeys, and people. *Science, 229*, 287–289.

Wright, R. D., and Ward, L. M. (2008). *Orienting of attention.* New York, NY: Oxford University Press.

Wuethrich, B. (2000). Learning the world's languages—before they vanish. *Science, 288*, 1156–1159.

Wurtz, R. H., Goldberg, M. E., and Robinson, D. L. (1982). Brain mechanisms of visual attention. *Scientific American, 246*(6), 124–135.

X

Xerri, C., Stern J. M., and Merzenich, M. M. (1994). Alterations of the cortical representation of the rat ventrum induced by nursing behavior. *Journal of Neuroscience, 14*, 1710–1721.

Y

Yaffe, K., Lui, L. Y., Zmuda, J., and Cauley, J. (2002). Sex hormones and cognitive function in older men. *Journal of the American Geriatrics Society, 50*, 707–712.

Yamazaki, S., Numano, R., Abe, M., Hida, A., et al. (2000). Resetting central and peripheral circadian oscillators in transgenic rats. *Science, 288*, 682–685.

Yang, S. H., Cheng, P. H., Banta, H., Piotrowska-Nitsche, K., et al. (2008). Towards a transgenic model of Hunting-ton's disease in a non-human primate. *Nature, 453*, 921–924.

Yang, T. T., Gallen, C. C., Ramachandran, V. S., Cobb, S., et al. (1994). Noninvasive detection of cerebral plasticity in adult human somatosensory cortex. *Neuroreport, 5*, 701–704.

Yehuda, R. (2002). Post-traumatic stress disorder. *New England Journal of Medicine, 346*, 108–114.

Yin, J. C., DelVecchio, M., Zhou, H., and Tully, T. (1995). CREB as a memory modulator: Induced expression of a dCREB2 activator isoform enhances long-term memory in *Drosophila. Cell, 81*, 107–115.

Yin, L., Wang, J., Klein, P. S., and Lazar, M. A. (2006). Nuclear receptor Rev-erbα is a critical lithium-sensitive component of the circadian clock. *Science, 311*, 1002–1004.

Young, A. B. (1993). Role of excitotoxins in heredito-degenerative neurologic diseases. *Research Publications—Association for Research in Nervous and Mental Disease, 71*, 175–189.

Z

Zaidel, E. (1976). Auditory vocabulary of the right hemisphere following brain bisection or hemidecortication. *Cortex, 12*, 191–211.

Zatorre, R. J., Evans, A. C., and Meyer, E. (1994). Neural mechanisms underlying melodic perception and memory for pitch. *Journal of Neuroscience, 14*, 1908–1919.

Zeki, S., Watson, J. D., Lueck, C. J., Friston, K. J., et al. (1991). A direct demonstration of functional specialization in human visual cortex. *Journal of Neuroscience, 11*, 641–649.

Zeman, A. (2002). *Consciousness: A user's guide.* New Haven, CT: Yale University Press.

Zendel, B. R., and Alain, C. (2009). Concurrent sound segregation is enhanced in musicians. *Journal of Cognitive Neuroscience, 21*, 1488–1498.

Zhang, C. L., Zou, Y., He, W., Gage, F. H., et al. (2008). A role for adult TLX-positive neural stem cells in learning and behaviour. *Nature, 451*, 1004–1007.

Zhang, T. Y., and Meaney, M. J. (2010). Epigenetics and the environmental regulation of the genome and its function. *Annual Review of Psychology, 61*, C1–C3.

Zhang, Y., Proenca, R., Maffei, M., Barone, M., et al. (1994). Positional cloning of the mouse obese gene and its human homologue. *Nature, 372*, 425–432.

Zhao, G. Q., Zhang, Y., Hoon, M. A., Chandrashekar, J., et al. (2003). The receptors for mammalian sweet and umami taste. *Cell, 115,* 255–266.

Zheng, J. L., and Gao, W. Q. (2000). Overexpression of Math1 induces robust production of extra hair cells in postnatal rat inner ears. *Nature Neuroscience, 3,* 580–586.

Zheng, J., Shen, W., He, D. Z., Long, K. B., et al. (2000). Prestin is the motor protein of cochlear outer hair cells. *Nature, 405,* 149–155.

Zhong, Z., Deane, R., Ali, Z., Parisi, M., et al. (2008). ALS-causing SOD1 mutants generate vascular changes prior to motor neuron degeneration. *Nature Neuroscience, 11,* 420–422.

Zihl, J., von Cramon, D., and Mai, N. (1983). Selective disturbance of movement vision after bilateral brain damage. *Brain, 106,* 313–340.

Zimmer, C. (2004). *The soul made flesh: The discovery of the brain—and how it changed the world.* New York, NY: Basic Books.

Zola-Morgan, S., and Squire, L. R. (1986). Memory impairment in monkeys following lesions of the hippocampus. *Behavioral Neuroscience, 100,* 155–160.

Zola-Morgan, S., Squire, L. R., and Ramus, S. J. (1994). Severity of memory impairment in monkeys as a function of locus and extent of damage within the medial temporal lobe memory system. *Hippocampus, 4,* 483–495.

Zonta, M., Angulo, M. C., Gobbo, S., Rosengarten, B., et al. (2003). Neuron-to-astrocyte signalling is central to the dynamic control of brain microcirculation. *Nature Neuroscience, 6,* 43–49.

Zou, Z., and Buck, L. B. (2006). Combinatorial effects of odorant mixes in olfactory cortex. *Science, 311,* 1477–1481.

Zou, Z., Li, F., and Buck, L. B. (2005). Odor maps in the olfactory cortex. *Proceedings of the National Academy of Sciences, USA, 102,* 7724–7729.

Zucker, I. (1976). Light, behavior, and biologic rhythms. *Hospital Practice, 11,* 83–91.

Zucker, I. (1988). Seasonal affective disorders: Animal models non fingo. *Journal of Biological Rhythms, 3,* 209–223.

Zucker, L. M., and Zucker, T. F. (1961). "Fatty," a mutation in the rat. *Journal of Heredity, 52,* 275–278.

Author Index

Subject Index